✓ **W9-ARZ-649**

	DATE DUE	

For Reference

Not to be taken from this room

APA
Concise
Dictionary
Psychology
_of_

Ψ

APA
Concise
Dictionary
of
Psychology

American Psychological Association
Washington, DC

Published by
American Psychological Association
750 First Street, NE
Washington, DC 20002
www.apa.org

To order
APA Order Department
P.O. Box 92984
Washington, DC 20090-2984
Tel: (800) 374-2721; Direct: (202) 336-5510
Fax: (202) 336-5502; TDD/TTY: (202) 336-6123
Online: www.apa.org/books/
E-mail: order@apa.org

In the U.K., Europe, Africa, and the Middle East, copies may be ordered from
American Psychological Association
3 Henrietta Street
Covent Garden, London
WC2E 8LU England

Typeset in Aylesbury, England, by Market House Books, Ltd.
Printer: Edwards Brothers, Ann Arbor, Michigan
Cover Designer: Naylor Design, Washington, DC

Library of Congress Cataloging-in-Publication Data

APA concise dictionary of psychology/American Psychological Association.
    p. cm.
Abridgement of: APA dictionary of psychology.
ISBN-13: 978-1-4338-0391-8
ISBN-10: 1-4338-0391-7
  1. Psychology—Dictionaries. I. American Psychological Association. II. APA dictionary of psychology. III. Title: A.P.A. concise dictionary of psychology. IV. Title: Concise dictionary of psychology.

  BF31.A65 2009
  150.3—dc22

                                        2008007351

British Library Cataloguing-in-Publication Data
A CIP record is available from the British Library.

Printed in the United States of America
First Edition

The citation for this publication is *APA concise dictionary of psychology.* (2009).
Washington, DC: American Psychological Association.

Contents

Preface

The release of the *APA Dictionary of Psychology* in 2006 was a milestone for the American Psychological Association (APA) and its books publishing arm, APA Books. The culmination of some ten years of research and lexicographic activity, the work has received strong critical endorsement from both the publishing and reference library communities. Rapid sales, moreover, resulted in the need for a large-scale second printing within a year of initial release.

In recognition that a more focused version would have additional appeal to the ever-increasing number of thoughtful readers from all walks of life who are interested in the knowledge that the field brings to the problems of everyday living, APA Books is pleased to release this *APA Concise Dictionary of Psychology*.

In the context of shortening the parent dictionary, our editorial process has relied first and foremost on reducing the number of entries: Whereas the parent dictionary contains definitions for some 25,000 terms, the *APA Concise Dictionary* covers some 10,000. This significant reduction was accomplished largely by limiting coverage in several categories that may be thought of as somewhat too technical or too specialized to be of central interest to a general reader. Although we have attempted to maintain reasonable coverage in each, among the more abbreviated categories are the following:

aesthetics	genetics
animal behavior/experimentation	language/linguistics
artificial intelligence	legal psychology
biology	neuroscience
consumer psychology	parapsychology
ergonomics	philosophy
general physical disorders	sport psychology

We may also note that, whereas the parent dictionary included entries on a limited number of historical figures and on organizations and institutions central to the field, this material was omitted in the *APA Concise Dictionary* to save space. However, the biographical appendix in the parent dictionary—a simple listing of those figures described fully in the dictionary's entries—has been retained and expanded, both in terms of the number of individuals listed and the details given for each. Cross-references to entries in the dictionary, moreover, are included for many individuals—a feature that we hope will increase the usefulness of the appendix. It is also appropriate to note in this context that, although considerably expanded, there are still gaps in this biographical appendix and that it represents an interim stage in anticipation of a fully evolved biographical dictionary that APA is currently developing and will publish within the next year or so.

In this vein, moreover, it should be noted that we deleted attributions in many definitions (e.g., to coiners of terms), although we retained attributions in eponymous entries (e.g., *Bayley's Scales of Infant and Toddler Development*) and in entries for important theories, schools of psychology, and the like (e.g., to Harry S. Sullivan in *interpersonal theory* and to John B. Watson in *behaviorism*).

Among secondary strategies for abridging the parent dictionary, three are especially significant: First, in cases where individual entries were densely detailed, some editorial shortening was undertaken, typically by omitting lengthy illustrative information (good examples are found at the headwords *coalition, dream,* and *time sampling*). Second, in some cases, editorial staff amalgamated entries for semantically related terms into a single entry, thus eliminating duplication of information (good examples are the here-composite entries on *aphasia, apraxia,* and *parenting*). Third, in most instances, general (i.e., commonly understood) meanings underlying meanings within psychology were omitted from entries (good examples are *event, homework,* and *repression*).

Additionally—and perhaps most important—it should be noted that the creation of the *APA Concise Dictionary* was not solely the result of such "mechanical" editorial strategies as those noted above, but, in numerous instances, involved a process of active reconsideration and recrafting of the parent definitions (good examples may be found at the headwords *commissure, conscience,* and *criminal profiling*). This process of redefining and updating certain entries was viewed as an early and earnest effort to prepare for a second edition of the full dictionary—an event that we anticipate as a reality within the next several years.

Although almost all of the adaptations noted above were executed by in-house reference staff and by our ever-valued colleagues at Market House Books, Ltd. (a firm with over 30 years of experience in compiling reference works for both British and American audiences), we proudly retain the names of the complete editorial board of the parent *APA Dictionary of Psychology* in this abridgement as continuing recognition of their central role in this ongoing undertaking to define the field of psychology. Their expertise and labor still permeate this book.

As we did with the full dictionary, we invite the users of the *APA Concise Dictionary of Psychology* to assist us in the task of construing the lexicon by contacting us concerning errors of omission and inclusion, inaccuracies, infelicities of phrasing, new terminology, printing errors, and the like. Please contact us by post in care of APA Books, 750 First Street, NE, Washington, DC 20002, Attention: Reference; or by email at apadictionary@apa.org.

Gary R. VandenBos, PhD
APA Publisher

Editorial Staff

Editor in Chief

Gary R. VandenBos, PhD

Senior Editors (American Psychological Association)

Theodore J. Baroody
Julia Frank-McNeil
Patricia D. Knowles
Marion Osmun

Senior Editors (Market House Books, Ltd.)

Alan Isaacs
Jonathan Law
Elizabeth Martin

Editorial Board

Mark Appelbaum, PhD
Elizabeth D. Capaldi, PhD
Debra L. Dunivin, PhD
Alan E. Kazdin, PhD
Joseph D. Matarazzo, PhD
Susan H. McDaniel, PhD
Susan K. Nolen-Hoeksema, PhD
Suparna Rajaram, PhD

Editorial Contributors

John G. Albinson, PhD
Mark Appelbaum, PhD
Bernard J. Baars, PhD
Andrew S. Baum, PhD
Roy F. Baumeister, PhD
Daniel S. Beasley, PhD
Leonard Berkowitz, PhD
David F. Bjorklund, PhD
C. Alan Boneau, PhD
Marc N. Branch, PhD
Laura S. Brown, PhD
Joseph J. Campos, PhD
Daniel Cervone, PhD
Stanley H. Cohen, PhD
Deborah J. Coon, PhD
James C. Coyne, PhD
Robert L. Dipboye, PhD
Maria L. Dittrich, PhD
Gail Donaldson, PhD
Deborah K. Elliott-DeSorbo, PhD
David G. Elmes, PhD
Gary W. Evans, PhD
Leandre R. Fabrigar, PhD

Erica L. Fener, PhD
Donelson R. Forsyth, PhD
Robert G. Frank, PhD
Donald K. Freedheim, PhD
Charles J. Golden, PhD
Maria A. Gomez, DVM, PhD
Kenji Hakuta, PhD
Dennis C. Harper, PhD
Curtis P. Haugtvedt, PhD
Morton A. Heller, PhD
John W. Jacobson, PhD
Robert J. Kastenbaum, PhD
John F. Kihlstrom, PhD
Bruce E. Kline, PsyD
Debra L. Kosch, PhD
Michael J. Lambert, PhD
Joseph LoPiccolo, PhD
George F. Luger, PhD
Raelynn Maloney, PhD
A. David Mangelsdorff, PhD
Colin Martindale, PhD
Kenneth I. Maton, PhD
Randi E. McCabe, PhD, CPsych

Editorial Contributors (continued)

Editorial Consultants

Editorial Assistant (American Psychological Association)

Quick Guide to Format

Headword   **beauty** *n.* the quality of a stimulus that elicits, usually immediately, admiration and pleasure.   **Part-of-speech label**

Beck Anxiety Inventory (BAI) a self-report, 21-item measure used to assess the severity of anxiety in adults and to discriminate anxiety from depression. [Aaron T. **Beck** (1921–), U.S. psychiatrist]   **Abbreviation**

Etymology

behavior hierarchy a ranking of possible responses based on the relative probabilities of their being elicited, with more probable behaviors ranked higher than less probable behaviors. Also called **behavioral hierarchy**.

Alternative name

behaviorism *n.* an approach to psychology, formulated in 1913 by U.S. psychologist John B. Watson (1878–1958), based on the study of objective, observable facts rather than subjective, qualitative processes, such as feelings, motives, and consciousness. To make psychology a naturalistic science, Watson proposed to limit it to quantitative events, such as stimulus–response relationships, effects of conditioning, physiological processes, and a study of human and animal behavior, all of which can best be investigated through laboratory experiments that yield objective measures under controlled conditions. Historically, behaviorists held that mind was not a proper topic for scientific study since mental events are subjective and not independently verifiable. With its emphasis on activity as an adaptive function, behaviorism is seen as an outgrowth of FUNCTIONALISM. See DESCRIPTIVE BEHAVIORISM; METHODOLOGICAL BEHAVIORISM; NEOBEHAVIORISM; RADICAL BEHAVIORISM.   **Cross-references**

Etymology

Hidden entry   **binocular** *adj.* relating to the two eyes. For example, a **binocular cue** is a cue to the perception of depth or distance that requires the use of both eyes, such as BINOCULAR DISPARITY and CONVERGENCE. Compare MONOCULAR.   **Cross-reference**

Sense number   **body** *n.* **1.** the entire physical structure of an organism, such as the human body. See also MIND–BODY PROBLEM. **2.** the main part of a structure or organ, such as the body of the penis. **3.** a discrete anatomical or cytological structure, such as the MAMMILLARY BODY.   **Sense number**

Sense number

Plural form   **brachium** *n.* (*pl.* **brachia**) the upper arm, extending from the shoulder to the elbow, or a structure that resembles an arm. **—brachial** *adj.*   **Derived word**

APA
Concise
Dictionary
Psychology
of

Aa

AA abbreviation for ALCOHOLICS ANONYMOUS.

AAMI abbreviation for AGE-ASSOCIATED MEMORY IMPAIRMENT.

ABA abbreviation for APPLIED BEHAVIOR ANALYSIS.

abandonment *n.* desertion of a dependent by a parent or primary caregiver. Dependents are usually children but may be entire families or individuals who are ill. —**abandon** *vb.*

abasia *n.* severe impairment or complete loss of the ability to walk due to problems in motor coordination. —**abasic** *adj.*

ABCDE technique a procedure used in RATIONAL EMOTIVE BEHAVIOR THERAPY, which suggests that *A*ctivating events (i.e., adversities) are mediated by irrational *B*eliefs in determining inappropriate emotional and behavioral *C*onsequences. ABCDE technique involves *D*isputing these beliefs (i.e., under the guidance of a therapist), which results in several types of *E*ffects (e.g., rational beliefs, appropriate feelings, desirable behaviors).

A-B design the simplest SINGLE-CASE EXPERIMENTAL DESIGN, in which the DEPENDENT VARIABLE is measured throughout the pretreatment or baseline period (the A phase) and then again following the treatment period (the B phase). Numerous variations of this basic design exist, such as the A-B-A design, A-B-A-B design, A-B-B-A design, and A-B-BC-B design. The latter involves two treatment periods (the B phase and the C phase) and is intended to assess the effect of B both in combination with C and apart from C.

abdominal migraine recurrent, severe episodes of abdominal pain that may be accompanied by nausea and vomiting. The episodes last from 1 to 72 hours and occur most frequently in children.

abducens nerve the sixth CRANIAL NERVE, carrying motor fibers for control of the lateral rectus muscle of the eye, which rotates the eyeball outward. Also called **abducent nerve**.

abduction *n.* movement of a limb away from the midline of the body. Any muscle that produces such movement is called an **abductor**. Compare ADDUCTION. —**abduct** *vb.*

abductive reasoning a form of diagnostic reasoning in which conditions are considered in an attempt to determine their causes. It is often described as "reasoning to the best explanation."

aberration *n.* **1.** any deviation, particularly a significant or undesirable one, from the normal or typical. See also MENTAL ABERRATION. **2.** in vision, the failure of light rays to converge at the same point, due either to distortion by a lens (SPHERICAL ABERRATION) or to the formation of colored fringes by a lens (CHROMATIC ABERRATION).

abience *n.* a response or behavior that results in movement away from a stimulus, either by physical withdrawal from the stimulus or by an action designed to avoid the stimulus entirely. Compare ADIENCE. —**abient** *adj.*

ability *n.* existing competence or skill to perform a specific physical or mental act. Although ability may be either innate or developed through experience, it is distinct from capacity to acquire competence (see APTITUDE).

ability test any norm-referenced standardized test designed to measure existing competence to perform a physical or mental act. The index of achievement or performance obtained, reporting the absolute or relative ability of the individual being evaluated, is called an **ability level**.

abiotrophy *n.* loss of function or loss of resistance to a disease through degeneration or failure of body tissues, organs, or systems. Abiotrophy is used particularly to refer to premature degeneration caused by a genetic defect, as in Huntington's disease. —**abiotrophic** *adj.*

ablation *n.* the removal or destruction of part of a biological tissue or structure by a surgical procedure or a toxic substance, usually for treatment or to study its function. When the entire tissue or structure is excised, the process is called **extirpation**. See also BIOPSY.

ableism *n.* discrimination against individuals with disabilities or the tendency to be prejudiced against those with disabilities and to negatively stereotype them as, for example, less intelligent, nonproductive, or dependent on others. —**ableist** *adj.*

abnormal *adj.* relating to any deviation from what is considered typical, usual, or healthy, particularly if the deviation is considered harmful or maladaptive. In statistics, for example, abnormal scores are those that are outside the usual or expected range. The term, however, is most often applied to behavior that differs from a culturally accepted norm, especially when indicative of a mental disorder. —**abnormality** *n.* —**abnormally** *adv.*

abnormal psychology the branch of psychology devoted to the study, prevention, assessment, and treatment of maladaptive behavior. See also PSYCHOPATHOLOGY.

A

abortion *n.* the expulsion from the uterus of an embryo or fetus before it is able to survive independently. An abortion may be either spontaneous, in which case it occurs naturally and is also called a **miscarriage**, or induced, in which case it is produced deliberately by artificial means such as drugs or surgery and done for therapeutic reasons or as an elective decision. The practice is controversial and may involve **abortion counseling**, the provision of guidance, advice, information, and support on issues concerning termination of pregnancy and the alternatives of adoption or raising the child.

abreaction *n.* the therapeutic process of bringing forgotten or inhibited material (i.e., experiences, memories) from the unconscious into consciousness, with concurrent emotional release and discharge of tension and anxiety. See also CATHARSIS.

abscess *n.* a contained but often enlarging area of infection that includes pus and dead tissue. A brain abscess raises INTRACRANIAL PRESSURE and can cause substantial neurological deficits, such as poor coordination, decreased sensation, confusion, and other altered mental states.

abscissa *n.* the horizontal coordinate in a graph or data plot; that is, the *x*-axis. See also ORDINATE.

absence *n.* a brief loss of consciousness or period of mental inattentiveness, with no memory for the event afterward. An **absence seizure** (formerly called **petit mal seizure**) is a type of GENERALIZED SEIZURE during which the individual abruptly ceases activity and is unresponsive and motionless, staring blankly. Seizures of this type typically last from 5 to 15 s each and rarely persist into adulthood.

absence culture an informal organizational NORM that leads employees and managers to believe that they are entitled to take more days off work than the number allowed. In some organizations, for example, employees may have come to regard sick leave as a benefit to be claimed rather than a provision to be utilized only when strictly necessary.

absenteeism *n.* unjustified absence from work or school, especially when regular or persistent. Although absenteeism has been shown to have a relation to job satisfaction, other factors, such as ORGANIZATIONAL CULTURE and the ABSENCE CULTURE in particular, may be more relevant.

absolute *adj.* not conditional on or relative to anything else. In philosophy, the position that there are absolute ethical, aesthetic, or epistemological values is known as **absolutism**. Such a position involves a rejection (in whole or in part) of RELATIVISM. See also CULTURAL UNIVERSALISM. —**absolutist** *adj.*

absolute error the difference between the obtained value and the actual or predicted value of a measured quantity without specification of whether the measurement errs by being too high or too low. See also CONSTANT ERROR; RANDOM ERROR.

absolute-judgment method see METHOD OF ABSOLUTE JUDGMENT.

absolute pitch the ability to identify the pitch of a sound accurately without the use of a reference pitch. Also called **perfect pitch**. Compare RELATIVE PITCH.

absolute rating scale a type of rating instrument in which the targets (e.g., people, objects) are not compared with other targets (as in a **comparative rating scale**) but are judged according to independent criteria.

absolute threshold the lowest or weakest level of stimulation (e.g., the slightest, most indistinct sound) that can be detected consistently and accurately on 50% of trials. Although the name suggests a fixed level at which stimuli effectively elicit sensations, the absolute threshold fluctuates according to alterations in receptors and environmental conditions. Also called **absolute limen (AL)**.

absolute value the numerical value of a figure disregarding its algebraic sign. For example, the absolute value of −1 is 1.

absorption *n.* **1.** an extreme involvement or preoccupation with one object, idea, or pursuit, with inattention to other aspects of the environment. **2.** the uptake of fluid and dissolved substances, such as an administered drug, into a cell across the plasma membrane. Drug absorption into the target organ is dependent on a number of factors, including the method of administration, the properties of the drug, the amount of drug administered, and the characteristics or state of the individual (e.g., body mass, sex, age, presence of disease).

abstinence *n.* the act of refraining from the use of something, particularly alcohol or drugs, or from participation in sexual or other activity. In most instances, abstinence from drugs or alcohol is the primary goal of substance abuse treatment. See also SUBSTANCE WITHDRAWAL. —**abstinent** *adj.*

abstract intelligence the ability to understand and manipulate symbols, ideas, and concepts, particularly those that have no specific material referents (e.g., justice) or that have a meaning apart from any particular (e.g., dog). Compare CONCRETE INTELLIGENCE; SOCIAL INTELLIGENCE.

abstraction *n.* **1.** the formation of general ideas or concepts by extracting similarities from particular instances. The precise cognitive processes by which this occurs remain a subject of investigation. **2.** such a concept, especially a wholly intangible one, such as "goodness" or "truth." **3.** in conditioning, DISCRIMINATION based on a single property of multicomponent stimuli. —**abstract** *vb.*

absurdities test a type of test in which participants identify absurdities, inconsistencies, or incongruities in a picture, story, or other written material. Absurdity tasks are intended to assess reasoning abilities and may be incorporated into intelligence tests and neuropsychological evaluations.

abulia (aboulia) *n.* extreme loss of initiative and willpower, resulting in an inability to make decisions or initiate voluntary actions. —**abulic** *adj.*

abundancy motive the tendency to seek a greater degree of satisfaction than that provided by meeting a particular need, for example, eating more food than the amount actually required to alleviate hunger. Compare DEFICIENCY MOTIVE.

abuse *n.* **1.** interactions in which one person behaves in a cruel, violent, demeaning, or invasive manner toward another person or an animal. The term most commonly implies physical mistreatment but also encompasses sexual and psychological (emotional) mistreatment. **2.** see SUBSTANCE ABUSE. —**abuser** *n.*

abuse potential the ability of a drug to reinforce drug-taking behavior: its propensity for misuse. Factors that determine abuse potential include method of drug administration and the speed of onset, duration, and nature of the drug effect. These factors are themselves determined by complex interactions between the individual, the substance, and the social environment. Also called **abuse liability**.

ABX paradigm a psychophysical procedure in which a pair of auditory stimuli (A and B) are presented, followed by another stimulus (X). In one version of the task, participants are asked to judge whether X is identical to A or B; in another version, they have to judge whether X was included in the A–B pair.

academic achievement in educational psychology, a specific level of proficiency in scholastic work in general or in a specific skill, such as arithmetic or reading.

academic failure any marked insufficiency or inadequacy in the area of scholarship or study, for example, when a learner does not achieve an expected competence. Contributing factors may include home environment and family, peers, economic context, learning environment and attributes of instruction, and individual characteristics.

academic intelligence the intellectual skills that, according to some theories, are particularly important to success in school environments (e.g., analysis, evaluation, judgment, recognition). This term is often used synonymously with ANALYTICAL INTELLIGENCE.

academic intervention the active involvement of school officials and teachers in developing and implementing an effective plan for the prevention or remediation of inappropriate and disruptive student behavior. Successful programs of intervention are most often individualized, child focused, and minimally restrictive.

Academic intervention is the antithesis of reactive strategies, such as loss of privileges and time out.

academic problem a learning problem in a schoolchild who does not acquire the necessary grade-level knowledge or cannot successfully pursue the expected grade-level tasks and scholarly goals. It cannot be attributed to any underlying neurological, psychological, or other disorder and thus is distinct from a LEARNING DISABILITY.

academic self-concept an individual's evaluation of his or her success in scholarship or educational studies. The two aspects of this evaluation are (a) a general academic self-concept in which students assess their overall learning skills and performance; and (b) a specific academic self-concept of their prowess in such specific subjects as mathematics, social science, or language studies.

acalculia *n.* loss of the ability to perform simple arithmetic operations that results from brain injury or disease, usually to the PARIETAL LOBE. It is an acquired condition, whereas DYSCALCULIA is developmental.

acatamathesia (akatamathesia) *n.* loss of the ability to comprehend sensory stimuli in general or speech in particular.

acceleration *n.* **1.** an increase in speed of movement or rate of change. In psychology, the focus is on the range of forces sustained by the human body when it is in a moving vehicle, such as an automobile or aircraft, and the resultant physical, physiological, and psychological consequences (e.g., disturbances of heart rhythm and blood pressure, disorientation and confusion, and loss of consciousness). Compare DECELERATION. **2.** in mathematics and statistics, the rate of change in the SLOPE of a function.

acceleration–deceleration injury see HEAD INJURY.

accent *n.* **1.** in linguistics, phonetic features of an individual's speech that are associated with geographical region, social class, or native language. The standard version of a language (see STANDARD LANGUAGE) is usually considered by native speakers to be unaccented. Compare DIALECT. **2.** a STRESS placed on a syllable of a word, orthographically marked in some languages. **3.** a type of informal fallacy or a persuasive technique in which a speaker or writer gives special emphasis to particular words in a proposition, thereby altering the nature of the argument. An example is emphasizing the word *patriotic* in the sentence *All patriotic Americans support the administration*, so that the statement becomes an example of circular reasoning.

acceptance *n.* **1.** a favorable attitude toward an idea, situation, person, or group. In the context of psychotherapy and counseling, it is the receptive, nonjudgmental attitude of therapists or counselors, which conveys an implicit respect and regard for their clients as individuals. **2.** willing acknowledgment of validity or correctness. In the context of recovery from substance abuse and other addictions, it is essential for a person to accept that he or she has a problem before any interventions can be effective.

acceptance and commitment therapy (**ACT**) a form of COGNITIVE BEHAVIOR THERAPY based on the premise that ineffective strategies to control thoughts and feelings actually lead to problem behaviors. It helps clients to abandon these ineffective control strategies and instead willingly experience difficult thoughts and feelings as a necessary part of a worthy life. Clients then clarify their personal values and life goals, and learn to make life-enhancing behavioral changes accordingly. ACT has been applied to a wide variety of problems, including depression, anxiety, stress, and substance abuse.

acceptance region in SIGNIFICANCE TESTING, the range of values for a test statistic that leads to acceptance of the null hypothesis over the alternative hypothesis. Compare CRITICAL REGION.

acceptance stage the last of the five STAGES OF GRIEF described by Swiss-born U.S. psychiatrist Elisabeth Kübler-Ross (1926–2004). It is characterized by some degree of emotional detachment, objectivity, or resignation on the part of oneself or an important other to the reality of impending or actual death, other great loss, or trauma.

accessible *adj.* **1.** in social psychology and psychotherapy, receptive or responsive to personal interaction and other external stimuli. A client in psychotherapy is thought to be accessible if he or she responds to the therapist in a way that facilitates the development of rapport and, ultimately, fosters the examination of cognitive, emotional, and behavioral issues. **2.** retrievable through memory or other cognitive processes. **3.** of a building and its facilities and fixtures, a site, or the like, easy to approach, enter, or use, particularly by people with disabilities. —**accessibility** *n.*

accessory nerve the 11th CRANIAL NERVE, sometimes so named because one of its functions is that of serving as an accessory to the 10th cranial nerve (the VAGUS NERVE). It innervates the sternomastoid and trapezius muscles in the neck.

accessory symptoms see SECONDARY SYMPTOMS.

accident analysis a systematic process undertaken to determine the causes of an accident with the goal of reducing the likelihood that such an accident will occur again. The most frequently used accident analysis methods include FAILURE MODES AND EFFECTS ANALYSIS and FAULT TREE ANALYSIS.

accident-path model a model used in accident analysis to illustrate the antecedents and causes of an accident using a chronological or otherwise ordered pattern. The goal is to determine the types and extent of interventions necessary to prevent accidents.

accident prevention the use of scientifically tested methods to reduce the number and severity of accidents. These include the systematic study of accidents and the circumstances in which they occur (see ACCIDENT ANALYSIS); the identification and control of workplace hazards (job-safety analysis); the evaluation and redesign of systems and processes (see SAFETY ENGINEERING); and the use of training programs, instruction, and other forms of safety education.

accident proneness a chronic susceptibility to accidents. This concept has been heavily debated since its introduction around 1920, and many question the existence of a fixed accident-prone personality. However, several individual variables and sociological and situational factors have been identified as important predictors of accident involvement, including aggressiveness, impulsiveness, thrill and adventure seeking, workload and cognitive demand, and stress.

acclimatization *n.* adjustment or adaptation to new circumstances or environmental conditions, particularly the physiological changes that improve an individual's ability to tolerate environmental alterations. Also called **acclimation**. —**acclimatize** *vb.*

accommodation *n.* **1.** adjustment or modification. Regarding individuals with disabilities, it refers to REASONABLE ACCOMMODATIONS made to meet their needs. In the context of bargaining and interpersonal negotiations, it refers to modification of the various parties' demands or actions in order to achieve agreement or a mutually beneficial outcome. **2.** the process by which the focus of the eye is changed to allow near or distant objects to form sharp images on the retina. Accommodation is achieved mainly by contraction or relaxation of the CILIARY MUSCLES, which exert tension on the ZONULES attached to the lens, but also involves adjustments in the CONVERGENCE of the eyes and the size of the pupils. **3.** see PIAGETIAN THEORY. —**accommodate** *vb.*

accommodative insufficiency a reduction in the efficiency of the eye's ability to change focus for objects at different distances (visual accommodation), as evidenced primarily by blurring of near vision. It is usually caused by dysfunction of the eye's CILIARY MUSCLES or by midbrain injury.

accountability *n.* **1.** the extent to which a person is answerable to another (e.g., a supervisor or official review body) for his or her behaviors, decisions, or judgments, especially in a professional capacity. **2.** in health care, the responsibility of individual providers, clinics, or hospitals to document their efforts, their resource utilization, and the outcome of their services and to report this information to insurance companies or state or federal agencies. —**accountable** *adj.*

accreditation *n.* the formal process in which an

agency or organization evaluates and approves an institution or program of study as meeting predetermined standards. Accreditation applies to institutions as CERTIFICATION applies to individuals. —**accredited** *adj.*

acculturation *n.* the processes by which groups or individuals integrate the social and cultural values, ideas, beliefs, and behavioral patterns of their culture of origin with those of a different culture. **Psychological acculturation** is an individual's attitudinal and behavioral adjustment to another culture, which typically varies with regard to degree and type. Also called **cultural integration**. Compare DECULTURATION; ENCULTURATION. —**acculturate** *vb.*

accuracy *n.* **1.** in a task or test, a measure of performance, usually based on the proportion of correct responses. **2.** more generally, the degree to which responses or statements are correct. **3.** exactness or freedom from error. See also PRECISION. —**accurate** *adj.*

acetone *n.* a colorless volatile liquid with a sweet, fruity odor that forms in excessive amounts in the blood of people with diabetes or other metabolic disorders in which the body uses fat instead of glucose (sugar) for energy. Also called **dimethyl ketone**.

acetylcholine (**ACh**) *n.* a major, predominantly excitatory but also inhibitory, neurotransmitter in the central nervous system, where it plays an important role in memory formation and learning and is implicated in Alzheimer's disease; and in the peripheral nervous system, where it mediates skeletal, cardiac, and smooth muscle contraction and is implicated in MYASTHENIA GRAVIS and other movement disorders.

acetylcholine receptor (**AChR**) any of certain protein molecules in cell membranes in the central and peripheral nervous systems that are stimulated by acetylcholine or acetylcholine-like substances. There are two main types: MUSCARINIC RECEPTORS and NICOTINIC RECEPTORS.

acetylcholinesterase (**AChE**) *n.* see CHOLINESTERASE.

acheiria (**achiria**) *n.* **1.** the condition of being born with only one or no hands. See also APODIA. **2.** a disorder of sensation in which an individual cannot tell which side of the body is being touched. It is considered a DYSCHEIRIA.

achievement *n.* **1.** the attainment of some goal, or the goal attained. See also NEED FOR ACHIEVEMENT. **2.** acquired knowledge (especially in a particular subject area such as biology), proficiency, or skill. The term is most often used in this sense to mean ACADEMIC ACHIEVEMENT.

achievement goal theory a conceptualization of motivation that identifies two types of achievement goals—task-oriented, involving completing a task well, and ego-oriented, involving obtaining superiority over others—and relates these to differences in individuals'

perceived ability for the task and their behavior. This theory emerged from the work of educational psychologists and subsequently was modified for use in sport psychology as well.

achievement level 1. the degree of proficiency attained in academic work in general or in a specific scholastic skill, such as arithmetic. **2.** an evaluation of individual or group performance on a task or activity (e.g., a chess match or athletic event), particularly following training.

achievement motivation 1. the desire to perform well and be successful. In this sense, the term often is used synonymously with NEED FOR ACHIEVEMENT. **2.** the desire to overcome obstacles and master difficult challenges. High scorers in achievement motivation are likely to set higher standards and work with greater perseverance.

achievement quotient (**AQ**) a measure obtained by dividing an individual's results on an achievement test (i.e., the actual performance) by the results expected based on the person's CAPACITY (i.e., the potential performance, as assessed by an intelligence test). The achievement quotient formerly was called the **accomplishment quotient**.

achievement test any norm-referenced standardized test intended to measure an individual's current level of skill or knowledge in a given subject. Often the distinction is made that achievement tests emphasize ability acquired through formal learning or training, whereas APTITUDE TESTS (usually in the form of intelligence tests) emphasize innate potential.

achromatic *adj.* **1.** without hue; colorless. **Achromatic stimuli** are black, white, or shades of gray. **2.** able to refract light without splitting it into its constituent wavelengths. **Achromatic lenses** do not distort the color of objects viewed through them.

achromatism *n.* total color blindness marked by the inability to perceive any color whatsoever: Everything is seen in different shades of gray. It is a congenital condition stemming from a lack of RETINAL CONES. When acquired as a result of brain injury, it is called **cerebral achromatopsia**. Also called **achromatopsia**. See also DICHROMATISM; MONOCHROMATISM; TRICHROMATISM.

acid *n.* slang for LSD.

acidosis *n.* an abnormally high level of acidity (hydrogen ion concentration) in the blood and tissues, which upsets the body's acid–base balance. The condition has numerous causes and symptoms vary with each, potentially including such neurological abnormalities as confusion, fatigue or lethargy, and irritability. Rapid breathing is often seen as well. Compare ALKALOSIS. —**acidotic** *adj.*

aconuresis *n.* involuntary passage of urine. It is a rare synonym of ENURESIS.

acoustic cue in phonology, one of the physical

properties of a speech sound (e.g., wave frequency, VOICE-ONSET TIME, or intensity) that mark its identity.

acoustic filter a component of some versions of the WORKING MEMORY model that allows only speechlike stimuli to access the model's phonological store.

acoustic nerve see AUDITORY NERVE.

acoustic reflex contraction of the middle ear muscles (the TENSOR TYMPANI and STAPEDIUS MUSCLE), elicited by intense sounds. This reflex restricts movement of the OSSICLES, thus reducing the sound energy transmitted to the inner ear and partially protecting it from damage.

acoustics *n.* the science of sound: a branch of physics concerned with the study of sound, including its physical properties, production, transmission, and reception. See also BIO-ACOUSTICS; PSYCHOACOUSTICS.

acoustic spectrum see SOUND SPECTRUM.

acoustic store a component of short-term memory that retains auditory information based on how items sound. Forgetting occurs when words or letters in acoustic store sound alike. Compare ARTICULATORY STORE.

acoustic trauma physical injury to the inner ear resulting from exposure to intense noise, such as explosions, or continuous prolonged loud music or machinery noise. It is a common cause of sensorineural DEAFNESS.

acquiescent response set the tendency of a respondent to agree with statements of opinion regardless of their content. This often reduces the validity of interviews, questionnaires, and other self-reports.

acquired *adj.* denoting something that has been learned, developed, or obtained on the basis of experience rather than being innate or inborn. For example, an acquired characteristic is a structural, functional, or psychological feature that arises in an organism during its lifespan, and acquired color blindness is defective color vision that develops in a person with previously normal vision as a result of such factors as disease or injury.

acquired dyslexia see DYSLEXIA.

acquired immune deficiency syndrome see AIDS.

acquisition *n.* the attainment by an individual of new behavior, information, or skills or the process by which this occurs. Although often used interchangeably with LEARNING, acquisition tends to be defined somewhat more concretely as the period during which progressive, measurable increases in response strength are seen. —**acquire** *vb.*

acquisitiveness *n.* the tendency or desire to acquire and accumulate objects or possessions. Compare HOARDING. —**acquisitive** *adj.*

acroagnosis *n.* lack of sensory recognition of a limb. Individuals with this condition cannot feel the presence of a limb although they may be able to see it or acknowledge its existence. Also called **acroagnosia**.

acroanesthesia *n.* an absence of sensitivity in the extremities.

acrocinesis *n.* excessive motion or movement. Also called **acrocinesia; acrokinesis**.

acroesthesia *n.* an abnormal sensitivity to stimuli applied to the extremities.

acromegaly *n.* an abnormal enlargement of the bones in the hands, feet, face, and skull due to excessive secretion of growth hormone by the pituitary gland during adulthood. —**acromegalic** *adj.*

acroparesthesia *n.* a feeling of numbness, tingling, or other abnormal sensation in the extremities.

acrophobia *n.* an excessive, irrational fear of heights, resulting in the avoidance of elevations or marked distress when unable to avoid high places. —**acrophobic** *adj.*

ACT abbreviation for ACCEPTANCE AND COMMITMENT THERAPY.

ACTH abbreviation for adrenocorticotropic hormone. See CORTICOTROPIN.

ACTH-releasing factor see CORTICOTROPIN-RELEASING FACTOR.

actin *n.* see MUSCLE FIBER.

acting out 1. the uncontrolled and inappropriate behavioral expression of denied emotions that serves to relieve tension associated with these emotions or to communicate them in a disguised, or indirect, way to others. Such behaviors may include arguing, fighting, stealing, threatening, or throwing tantrums. **2.** in psychoanalytic theory, reenactment of past events as an expression of unconscious emotional conflicts, feelings, or desires—often sexual or aggressive—with no attempt to understand the origin or meaning of these behaviors.

action *n.* **1.** a self-initiated sequence of movements, usually with respect to some goal. It may consist of an integrated set of component behaviors as opposed to a single response. **2.** the occurrence or performance of a process or function (e.g., the action of an enzyme). **3.** the state or process of being active.

action disorganization syndrome a cognitive deficit resulting from damage to the FRONTAL LOBES of the brain and causing individuals to make errors on multistepped but familiar or routine tasks. Types of errors include omissions or additions of steps, disordered sequencing of steps, and object substitutions or misuse.

action-oriented therapy any therapy that emphasizes doing and taking action rather than verbal communication or discussion.

action potential the change in electric potential that propagates along a cell during the transmission of a nerve impulse or the contraction of a muscle. It is marked by a rapid, transient DEPO-

LARIZATION of the cell's plasma membrane, from a RESTING POTENTIAL of about –70 mV (inside negative) to about +30 mV (inside positive), and back again, after a slight HYPERPOLARIZATION, to the resting potential.

action readiness a state of preparedness for action that is elicited as part of an emotional response and associated with such physiological indicators as changes in heart rate, respiratory rate, and muscle tension. The term is often used synonymously with ACTION TENDENCY but also refers to a general readiness for action that does not involve an urge to carry out a specific behavior.

action research socially useful and theoretically meaningful research developed and carried out in response to a social issue or problem, results of which are used to improve the situation.

action-specific energy in classical ethology, a hypothetical supply of motivational energy within an organism that is associated with specific unlearned behavioral responses known as FIXED ACTION PATTERNS. Each response has its own energy supply, which builds up until the organism encounters the appropriate RELEASER.

action tendency an urge to carry out certain expressive or instrumental behaviors that is linked to a specific emotion. For example, the action tendency of fear involves an urge to escape, and that of anger involves an urge to attack. Some theorists argue that the action tendency of an emotional reaction should be regarded as its essential defining characteristic. Compare ACTION READINESS.

action theory all those theories, collectively, that explain behavior in terms of goal-directed human beings acting intentionally with reference to the environment and present situation. Action theory was known originally as **will psychology**, which emphasized and distinguished between motivation and volition.

action tremor trembling of a body part that arises when the individual is engaged in directed voluntary activity and that increases as the movement progresses.

activation *n.* **1.** in many theories of memory, an attribute of the representational units (such as NODES or LOGOGENS) that varies from weaker to stronger, with more strongly activated representations competing to control processing. **2.** the process of alerting an organ or body system for action, particularly arousal of one organ or system by another. —**activate** *vb.* —**activational** *adj.*

activational effect a transient hormonal effect that typically causes a short-term change in behavior or physiological activity in adult animals. For example, increased testosterone in male songbirds in spring leads to increased aggression in territory defense and increased courtship behavior. Compare ORGANIZATIONAL EFFECT.

activation–elaboration a dual-process theory of memory holding that concepts stored in memory vary in their levels both of ACTIVATION and ELABORATION.

activation hypothesis 1. the principle that numerical weightings on the links or nodes of cognitive network models can represent their degree of activity or processing. Consciousness is sometimes attributed to the subset of most highly weighted elements in such models. **2.** the hypothesis that high metabolic activity reflects activation of brain areas subserving mental tasks.

activation–synthesis hypothesis a hypothesis that explains dreams as a product of cortical interpretation of random activation rising from the lower brain structures, including the PONS. See PGO SPIKES.

activation theory of emotion the theory that emotion is measurable as change in the individual's level of neural excitation of the RETICULAR FORMATION and associated degree of cortical and thalamic alertness, as revealed via ELECTROENCEPHALOGRAPHY. It was a refinement of an earlier **activation-arousal theory** equating emotion to change in the difficult-to-measure level of an individual's energy expenditure. Also called **arousal theory**.

active avoidance a type of OPERANT CONDITIONING in which an explicit act prevents or postpones the delivery of an aversive stimulus, such as when pressing a lever blocks the delivery of an electric shock. That is, avoidance is achieved by an overt action. Compare PASSIVE AVOIDANCE.

active deception the process of intentionally misleading research participants, for example, by giving them false information about the purpose of the research or by having them unwittingly interact with CONFEDERATES. Also called **deception by commission**. Compare PASSIVE DECEPTION.

active euthanasia direct action intended to terminate the life of a person (or animal) who is suffering greatly and is considered to have no chance for recovery. Lethal injections and administration of carbon monoxide are the most common types of active euthanasia today. This practice is distinguished from PASSIVE EUTHANASIA, in which treatments are withheld but no direct action to terminate the life is taken. See also ASSISTED DEATH; EUTHANASIA.

active intermodal mapping (**AIM**) the ability of young infants to integrate information from two or more senses and understand the symbolic relationship between the actions of others and the movement of their own body parts. This cognitive ability to translate between "seeing" and "doing" is thought to underlie neonatal imitation.

active learning 1. learning that occurs through the actual performance of behavior or acting out of an idea. Also called **action learn-**

ing. **2.** the active seeking out of new information, rather than simply being a passive recipient of a learning experience. Active learners set goals, select strategies, recognize when they understand, and work with others to further learning.

active listening a psychotherapeutic technique in which the therapist listens to a client closely and attentively, asking questions as needed, in order to fully understand the content of the message and the depth of the client's emotion. The therapist typically restates what has been said to ensure accurate understanding.

active memory a memory that is currently the focus of consciousness or was recently in awareness, as distinct from the vast body of stored memories that are currently inactive. Activation occurs through retrieval, cuing, or prompting.

active placebo an agent used in double-BLIND controlled trials of pharmacological products that has no therapeutic effect but—unlike a completely inert DUMMY placebo—may produce side effects characteristic of the drug under investigation. Active placebos are therefore considered by some to be more likely to reveal true differences in drug–placebo responding.

active therapy any form of psychotherapy in which the therapist departs from classic psychoanalytic practice by assuming an active, directive role. An **active therapist** may express opinions, offer interpretations, make suggestions and recommendations, give advice about the client's actions and decisions, issue injunctions and prohibitions, or urge the client to take a particular action, such as facing an anxiety-provoking situation directly.

active vocabulary see PRODUCTIVE VOCABULARY.

activities of daily living (**ADLs**) activities essential to an individual's personal care, such as getting into and out of bed and chairs, dressing, eating, toileting and bathing, and grooming. A person's ability to perform ADLs is often used as a measure of functional capabilities during the course of a disease or following an injury. See also INSTRUMENTAL ACTIVITIES OF DAILY LIVING.

activity analysis the objective evaluation of activity engaged in by an individual over a specified period, usually by breaking it down into smaller components, such as eating, working, social activities, resting, and so on.

activity cage an enclosed space in which animals move freely while their behavior is observed, recorded, or measured.

activity drive an organism's hypothetical innate desire or urge to be physically active, often expressed as a need to move about, even in the absence of any apparent stimuli motivating movement, such that activity deprivation may cause distress.

activity rhythm the pattern of individual behavior over the course of a day, month, or year

that exhibits a clear cycle of activity more or less in synchrony with temporal cues. For example, rats are generally active for approximately 12 hours a day, during the hours of darkness, but this pattern persists even in the absence of regular changes in light and dark. See BIOLOGICAL RHYTHM.

activity theory 1. a school of thought, developed primarily by Soviet psychologists, that focuses on activity in general—rather than the distinct concepts of behavior or mental states—as the primary unit of analysis. The theory emphasizes a hierarchical structure of activity, object-orientedness, internalization and externalization, mediation (by tools, language, and other cultural artifacts or instruments), and continuous development. Also called **activity psychology**. **2.** a theory proposing that old age is a lively, creative experience characterized by maintaining existing social roles, activities, and relationships or replacing any lost ones with new ones. Compare DISENGAGEMENT THEORY.

activity wheel a revolving drum that turns by the weight of an animal running inside. The activity wheel records the number of revolutions and is often used for various research purposes. Also called **running wheel**.

actomyosin *n.* see MUSCLE FIBER.

actor–observer effect in ATTRIBUTION THEORY, the tendency for individuals acting in a situation to attribute the causes of their behavior to external or situational factors, such as social pressure, but for observers to attribute the same behavior to internal or dispositional factors, such as personality.

act psychology a philosophical and psychological approach based on the proposition that the act and CONTENT of psychological processes are separate functions; for example, the act of seeing color leads to a perception of the visual content, or image. Historically, proponents of act psychology held that acts (mental representation and transformation, judgment, emotion), rather than contents, are the proper subject of psychology, in contrast to the emphasis on introspection and conscious contents in the work of German psychologist and physiologist Wilhelm Wundt (1832–1920). Compare CONTENT PSYCHOLOGY. See also INTENTIONALITY.

actualization *n.* the process of mobilizing one's potentialities and realizing them in concrete form. According to U.S. psychologist Carl Rogers (1902–1987), all humans have an innate **actualizing tendency** to grow and actualize the self fully. See also SELF-ACTUALIZATION. —**actualize** *vb.*

actuarial *adj.* statistical, as opposed to clinical. The use of data about prior instances, in order to estimate the likelihood or risk of a particular outcome, is sometimes cited as an alternative to clinical diagnoses, which are open to human error.

actus reus the illegal act (Latin, "guilty act")

that, combined with a criminal intent in committing it (see MENS REA), constitutes a crime.

acuity *n.* sharpness of perception. Whereas VISUAL ACUITY is sharpness of vision and AUDITORY ACUITY sharpness of hearing, SENSORY ACUITY is the precision with which any sensory stimulation is perceived.

acuity grating a device used to measure an individual's sharpness of visual perception. It consists of alternating black and white lines spaced closely together; the point at which the participant perceives the lines to be homogeneous gives an indication of VISUAL ACUITY. When the contrast of the lines is varied, the acuity grating can be used to test CONTRAST SENSITIVITY.

aculalia *n.* nonsensical speech associated with lack of comprehension of written or spoken language, as occurs in WERNICKE'S APHASIA.

acupressure *n.* a form of COMPLEMENTARY AND ALTERNATIVE MEDICINE in which pressure is applied with the fingers or thumbs to specific points on the body to relieve pain, treat symptoms of disease, or improve overall health.

acupuncture *n.* a form of COMPLEMENTARY AND ALTERNATIVE MEDICINE in which fine needles are inserted into the body at specific points to relieve pain, induce anesthesia (**acupuncture anesthesia**), or treat disease. It is based on the concept in traditional Chinese medicine that "meridians," or pathways, conduct life-force energy known as **chi** between places on the skin and the body's organ systems. Western scientists are unable to explain specifically how acupuncture produces its effects but theorize that the needling sites may be related to trigger points in the GATE-CONTROL THEORY of pain or may stimulate the release of ENDOGENOUS OPIOIDS. —**acupuncturist** *n.*

acute *adj.* **1.** denoting conditions or symptoms of sudden onset, short duration, and often great intensity. Compare CHRONIC. **2.** sharp, keen, or very sensitive (e.g., acute hearing).

acute onset a sudden, rapid, or unanticipated development of a disease or its symptoms.

acute stress disorder a disorder representing the immediate psychological aftermath of exposure to a traumatic stressor. Symptoms are the same as those of POSTTRAUMATIC STRESS DISORDER but do not last longer than 4 weeks. This disorder also includes elements of dissociation, such as DEPERSONALIZATION and DEREALIZATION.

acute tolerance a type of TOLERANCE (physical dependence) that develops rapidly, sometimes in response to a single small dose of a particular drug. See also TACHYPHYLAXIS.

adaptation *n.* **1.** adjustment of a sense organ to the intensity or quality of stimulation, resulting in a temporary change in sensory or perceptual experience, as in VISUAL ADAPTATION when the pupil of the eye adjusts to dim or bright light. **2.** reduced responsiveness in a sensory receptor or sensory system caused by prolonged or repeated stimulation. The adaptation may be specific, for example, to the orientation of a particular stimulus. Also called **sensory adaptation**. **3.** modification to suit different or changing circumstances. In this sense, the term often refers to behavior that enables an individual to adjust to the environment effectively and function optimally in various domains, such as coping with daily stressors. Compare MALADAPTATION. **4.** adjustments to the demands, restrictions, and mores of society, including the ability to live and work harmoniously with others and to engage in satisfying social interactions and relationships. Also called **social adaptation**; **social adjustment**. **5.** the modification of an organism in structure or function that increases its ability to reproduce successfully and its offspring's ability to survive and reproduce successfully. —**adapt** *vb.* —**adaptational** *adj.* —**adaptive** *adj.*

adaptation level (**AL**) the theoretical baseline or zero point, which forms a standard against which new stimuli are evaluated. For example, a person who first lifts a 40 lb weight would then likely judge a 20 lb weight as light, whereas if that person first lifted a 4 lb weight he or she would then likely judge the 20 lb weight as heavy. Although it originated in studies of sensory perception, **adaptation-level theory** has since been applied in other fields, such as aesthetics and attitude change.

adaptive behavior scale 1. any standardized assessment protocol with established psychometric properties used to document and quantify everyday performance of skills necessary for personal independence and social responsibility, consistent with cultural expectations. **2.** any protocol assessing behavioral and social performance that is based on developmental norms, with domains structured in developmental sequence or degree of ascending task complexity or difficulty.

adaptive intelligence the ability to apply knowledge to novel situations, such as solving problems and conversing with others, demonstrating an effective ability to interact with, and learn from, the environment.

adaptive strategy choice model a theoretical model that postulates the existence of multiple strategies of problem solving within a child's cognitive repertoire that compete with one another for use: With time and experience, more efficient strategies are used more frequently, whereas less efficient strategies are used less frequently but never totally disappear. This contrasts with **stage theory of strategy development**, which postulates that more efficient strategies replace less efficient ones.

adaptive testing a testing technique designed to adjust to the response characteristics of individual examinees by presenting items of varying difficulty based on the examinee's responses to previous items. The process continues until a stable estimate of the ability level (see ABILITY TEST) of the examinee can be determined.

ADC abbreviation for AIDS DEMENTIA COMPLEX.

ADD abbreviation for attention-deficit disorder. See ATTENTION-DEFICIT/HYPERACTIVITY DISORDER.

addiction *n.* a state of psychological or physical dependence (or both) on the use of alcohol or other drugs. The equivalent term SUBSTANCE DEPENDENCE is preferred to describe this state because it refers more explicitly to the criteria by which it is diagnosed, which include tolerance, withdrawal, loss of control, and compulsive use of the substance. Chemical substances with significant potential for producing dependence are called **addictive drugs**. They include alcohol, amphetamines and other CNS stimulants, CNS depressants, cocaine and crack, hallucinogens, inhalants, and opioids. —**addictive** *adj.*

additive bilingualism the sociolinguistic situation in which a second language is adopted without threatening the status of the first, or native, language. For example, most English-speaking Canadians learn French in order to gain access to prestige jobs that require bilingualism but continue to use English as their main language. This contrasts with **subtractive bilingualism**, in which the second language comes to replace the functions of the first language. The bilingualism of most immigrant communities is considered subtractive, resulting in LANGUAGE SHIFT within one or two generations.

additive effect the joint effect of two or more independent variables on a dependent variable equal to the sum of their individual effects: The value of either independent variable is unconditional upon the value of the other one. Compare INTERACTION EFFECT.

additive scale a scale with all points distributed equally so that a meaningful result can be obtained by addition (e.g., a metric ruler).

additive task a task or project that a group can complete by aggregating individual members' efforts or contributions (e.g., a five-person group pulling together on a rope to move a heavy object). Groups usually outperform individuals on such tasks, but overall group productivity rarely reaches its maximum potential owing to SOCIAL LOAFING. Compare COMPENSATORY TASK; CONJUNCTIVE TASK; DISJUNCTIVE TASK.

adduction *n.* **1.** movement of a limb toward the midline of the body. Any muscle that produces such movement is called an **adductor**. Compare ABDUCTION. **2.** in CONDITIONING, the production of new behavior by combining the DISCRIMINATIVE STIMULI of separate DISCRIMINATED OPERANTS. —**adduct** *vb.*

adenine (symbol: A) *n.* a purine compound present in the nucleotides of living organisms. It is one of the four bases in DNA and RNA that consti-

tute the GENETIC CODE, the others being cytosine, guanine, and thymine or uracil.

adenoma *n.* a benign (noncancerous) tumor derived from EPITHELIUM that has glandular properties. The most common adenoma in the central nervous system is in the pituitary gland (**pituitary adenoma**). —**adenomatous** *adj.*

adenosine *n.* a compound in living cells consisting of an ADENINE molecule and a ribose sugar molecule. Adenosine functions as a neuromodulator: By binding to special **adenosine receptors**, it influences the release of several neurotransmitters in the central nervous system. Combined with three phosphate units, adenosine becomes ATP (adenosine triphosphate), which functions as an energy source in metabolic activities.

adenosine triphosphate see ATP.

ADH abbreviation for antidiuretic hormone (see VASOPRESSIN).

ADHD abbreviation for ATTENTION-DEFICIT/HYPERACTIVITY DISORDER.

adherence *n.* the ability of an individual to conform to a treatment regimen, especially one involving drug treatment, as outlined by a health care provider. Factors affecting adherence may include familial or cultural value systems influencing the acceptability of the treatment to the individual, the individual's belief in the potency of the treatment, the presence or absence of unpleasant side effects, and the individual's capability to understand or conform to instructions given by the provider. See also NONADHERENCE. Also called **compliance**.

ad hoc for a particular purpose or in response to some particular event or occurrence. For example, an **ad hoc hypothesis** is an explanation of a particular phenomenon, rather than a general theory. [Latin, literally: "to this"]

adience *n.* a response or behavior that results in movement toward a stimulus, either by physical approach or by an action that increases contact with the stimulus. Compare ABIENCE. —**adient** *adj.*

adipose tissue connective tissue consisting largely of fat cells (**adipocytes**), which is found beneath the skin and around major organs. It provides protection and insulation and functions as an energy reserve.

adipsia *n.* an absence of thirst, manifest as a lack of drinking. Adipsia is associated with lesions of the thirst center in the anterior hypothalamus, but may also be caused by head injury, stroke, or other conditions. Compare POLYDIPSIA.

adjective checklist a self-inventory, used in personality assessment, consisting of a list of adjectives (e.g., intelligent, lazy, productive) that the respondent checks off as descriptive of or applicable to him- or herself.

adjudicative competence an umbrella term that encompasses all forms of meaningful participation in proceedings of the criminal justice system, including COMPETENCY TO STAND TRIAL, competency to plead guilty, and competency to waive Miranda rights.

adjunctive behavior relatively unvaried behavior that occurs following, but is otherwise unrelated to, regular delivery of a reinforcer in operant or instrumental conditioning. It differs from simple RESPONDENT BEHAVIOR in that the likelihood of its occurrence is influenced by the time between stimulus presentations. Compare TERMINAL BEHAVIOR.

adjunctive therapy one or more secondary interventions used concurrently with a primary intervention to enhance treatment effectiveness. For example, group psychotherapy may be used secondarily to individual psychodynamic psychotherapy. Adjunctive therapy is typically conducted by a different practitioner than is the primary intervention, which distinguishes it from COMBINATION THERAPY. The term is sometimes used synonymously with ADJUVANT THERAPY. See also COLLABORATIVE CARE.

adjusted mean in the ANALYSIS OF COVARIANCE, the numerical average of a batch of scores on a dependent variable that is obtained after the effects of a covariate are removed.

adjusted R^2 the COEFFICIENT OF MULTIPLE DETERMINATION (R^2) adjusted to take into account the number of independent variables and the sample size so as to provide a truer estimate of the extent to which the independent variables explain the dependent variable.

adjusting schedule of reinforcement in conditioning, any arrangement in which the requirements for reinforcement are varied continuously based on some characteristic of the organism's performance.

adjustment *n.* **1.** a change in attitude, behavior, or both by an individual on the basis of some recognized need or desire to change, particularly to account for the current environment or changing, atypical, or unexpected conditions. It may be assessed via a type of survey called an **adjustment inventory**, which compares a person's emotional and social adjustment with a representative sample of other individuals. A well-adjusted person is one who satisfies his or her needs in a healthy, beneficial manner and demonstrates appropriate social and psychological responses to situations and demands. **2.** modification to match a standard. See METHOD OF ADJUSTMENT. **—adjust** *vb.*

adjustment disorder impairment in social or occupational functioning and unexpectedly severe emotional or behavioral symptoms occurring within three months after an individual experiences a specific identifiable stressful event, such as a divorce, business crisis, or family discord. The event is not as stressful as a traumatic stressor, which can lead to POSTTRAUMATIC STRESS DISORDER. Symptoms may include anxiety, depression, and conduct disturbances and tend to remit following elimination of the stressor.

adjustment process any means through which human beings modify attitudes and behaviors in response to environmental demands. Such attempts to maintain a balance between needs and the circumstances that influence the satisfaction of those needs are influenced by numerous factors that vary widely across situations and individuals and are the subject of much research.

adjustment reaction a temporary, maladjustive psychological response to a situation. Such reactions are now subsumed under the category ADJUSTMENT DISORDER.

adjuvant therapy therapy provided after the initial (primary) form of treatment to enhance effectiveness or to increase the chances of a cure. Adjuvant therapy typically refers to medical rather than psychotherapeutic treatment, particularly any drug therapy used in support of nondrug interventions. The term is sometimes used in psychotherapy as a synonym for the preferred ADJUNCTIVE THERAPY.

Adlerian psychology see INDIVIDUAL PSYCHOLOGY.

ad lib in animal experiments, denoting or relating to a schedule of unlimited access to food, water, or both. The body weight achieved by animals under such conditions is called the **free-feeding weight**. [from Latin *ad libitum*, "as desired"]

ADLs abbreviation for ACTIVITIES OF DAILY LIVING.

administration *n.* **1.** the application of a drug or other agent in the diagnosis or treatment of a disorder. This may be accomplished **enterally** (via the digestive tract) or **parenterally** (via all other means). The former includes oral and sublingual (under the tongue) routes, whereas the latter includes subcutaneous, intramuscular, and intravenous injection; rectal and vaginal suppositories; inhalation; and absorption through skin or mucous membranes. **2.** the giving of a test for the purpose of obtaining information.

administrative controls in SAFETY ENGINEERING, administrative interventions, such as training, rotating work schedules to reduce exposure (e.g., to hazardous chemicals), and clearance requirements (i.e., authorization for only select personnel to have access to certain work areas or equipment), that can help to maintain a safe environment in the workplace. Administrative controls are considered a second resort after ENGINEERING CONTROLS.

admission *n.* the act of registering an individual for treatment or observation in a health care facility. This may be a **first admission** or a **readmission** of a previous patient, as well as voluntary (by the individual's own request) or involuntary (by medical or legal direction). See also INVOLUNTARY HOSPITALIZATION. **—admit** *vb.*

adolescence *n.* the period of human development that starts with puberty (10–12 years of age) and ends with physiological maturity (approximately 19 years of age), although the exact age span varies across individuals. During this period major changes occur at varying rates in physical characteristics, sexual characteristics, and sexual interest, resulting in significant effects on body image, self-concept, and self-esteem. Major cognitive and social developments take place as well: Most young people acquire enhanced abilities to think abstractly, evaluate reality hypothetically, reconsider prior experiences from altered points of view, assess data from multiple dimensions, reflect inwardly, create complex models of understanding, and project complicated future scenarios. Adolescents also increase their peer focus and involvement in peer-related activities, place greater emphasis on social acceptance, and seek more independence and autonomy from parents. —**adolescent** adj., n.

adoption n. the legal process by which an infant or child is permanently placed with a family other than his or her birth family. An adoption may be private, in which a birth parent voluntarily plans for the placement of the child with adoptive parents through intermediaries, or public, in which a child removed from his or her birth parent(s) because of neglect or abuse is placed with adoptive parents through public child welfare agencies. Adoptions may also be closed, allowing no contact between the birth and adoptive parents, or open, permitting varying degrees of pre- and postplacement contact and making possible a relationship between all three parties.

adoption study a research design that investigates the relationships among genetic and environmental factors in the development of personality, behavior, or disorder by comparing the similarities of biological parent–child pairs with those of adoptive parent–child pairs.

ADR abbreviation for ADVERSE DRUG REACTION.

adrenal cortical hyperfunction the excessive production of one or more of the hormones of the adrenal cortex. The manifestations vary with the hormone but potentially include (among others) VIRILISM, hypertension, sudden weight gain, torso obesity, and low blood levels of potassium. Causes may include a tumor or CONGENITAL ADRENAL HYPERPLASIA, a disorder marked by increased adrenal production of cortisol precursors and androgens.

adrenal gland an endocrine gland adjacent to the kidney. Its outer layer, the **adrenal cortex**, secretes a number of hormones, including ANDROGENS, GLUCOCORTICOIDS, and MINERALOCORTICOIDS. Its inner core, the **adrenal medulla**, secretes the hormones EPINEPHRINE and NOREPINEPHRINE, both of which are CATECHOLAMINES and also serve as neurotransmitters. Also called **suprarenal gland**.

adrenaline n. see EPINEPHRINE.

adrenergic adj. responding to, releasing, or otherwise involving EPINEPHRINE (adrenaline). For example, an **adrenergic neuron** is one that employs EPINEPHRINE as a neurotransmitter. The term often is used more broadly to include NOREPINEPHRINE as well.

adrenergic blocking agent any pharmacological substance that inhibits, either partially or completely, the binding of the neurotransmitters norepinephrine or epinephrine to ADRENERGIC RECEPTORS and thus blocks or disrupts the action of these neurotransmitters. Such blocking agents are classed according to which of the two types of receptors they inhibit binding to: **alpha blockers**, used primarily to widen blood vessels in the treatment of hypertension, or **beta blockers**, used to treat hypertension as well but by reducing the rate and force of heart contractions, arrhythmia, tremor, and anxiety-related symptoms. Also called **adrenoceptor blocking agent**; **adrenoreceptor blocking agent**.

adrenergic drug see SYMPATHOMIMETIC DRUG.

adrenergic receptor a molecule in a cell membrane that specifically binds and responds to norepinephrine and, to a lesser extent, epinephrine, which act as neurotransmitters in the sympathetic nervous system. There are two types: **alpha-adrenergic receptors** (or **alpha receptors**) and **beta-adrenergic receptors** (or **beta receptors**). The former are associated with stimulation of smooth muscle, causing (for example) pupil dilation and narrowing of blood vessels. The latter mediate stimulation of heart muscle, causing a faster and stronger heartbeat, and are associated with relaxation of smooth muscle, causing (for example) widening of airways and dilation of blood vessels. Also called **adrenoceptor**; **adrenoreceptor**.

adrenocortical insufficiency a potentially life-threatening condition caused by failure of the adrenal cortex to produce adequate levels of hormones required for normal metabolic functions. Symptoms may include fatigue, muscle weakness, dizziness, anxiety, and depression. Primary adrenocortical insufficiency is caused by abnormal functioning of the adrenal cortex itself and is called **Addison's disease**, whereas secondary adrenocortical insufficiency is caused by failure of the pituitary gland to produce enough CORTICOTROPIN, which stimulates hormone release from the adrenal cortex.

adrenocorticoid n. see CORTICOSTEROID.

adrenocorticotropic hormone (**ACTH**) see CORTICOTROPIN.

adrenogenital syndrome see CONGENITAL ADRENAL HYPERPLASIA.

adrenoreceptor n. see ADRENERGIC RECEPTOR.

Adult Attachment Interview an hour-long PATTERNED INTERVIEW used for classifying a person's subjective evaluation of his or her own attachment experiences with his or her parents, especially centering on hurtful experiences, separations, and discipline. The categories of adult attachment that emerge are **dismissing** (interviewees idealize their early relationships but cannot provide specific supporting examples); **preoccupied** (interviewees describe their early parental relationships as overly involving and angry); and **secure** or **autonomous** (interviewees provide objective, coherent accounts of relationships). A fourth category, **unresolved** or **disorganized**, is used for individuals who have experienced loss of attachment figures and who show lapses in reasoning when discussing such.

adult day care a group program for the nonresidential care and supervision of adults with functional impairments, designed to meet their health, social, and functional needs in a setting other than their homes. See DAY CARE CENTER.

adult foster care the provision of community-based living arrangements to adults who require supervision, personal care, or other services in daily living on a 24-hour basis. Host families open their own homes to, and act as caregivers for, such adults who are unable safely to live independently, which is what distinguishes **adult foster homes** from other RESIDENTIAL CARE facilities.

adult home an ASSISTED-LIVING residence that provides shared rooms, common meals, personal care services, activities, and protective oversight to adults who are unable to live independently. Intensive medical or nursing services are generally not available.

adulthood *n.* the period of human development in which full physical growth and maturity have been achieved and certain biological, cognitive, social, personality, and other changes associated with the aging process occur. Beginning after adolescence, adulthood is sometimes divided into **young adulthood** (roughly 20 to 35 years of age); **middle adulthood** (about 36 to 64 years); and **later adulthood** (age 65 and beyond). The last is sometimes subdivided into **young-old** (65 to 74), **old-old** (75 to 84), and **oldest old** (85 and beyond). The oldest old group is the fastest growing segment of the population in many developed countries.

advance directive a legal mechanism for individuals to specify their wishes and instructions about prospective health care in the event they later become unable to make such decisions. This can be achieved by means of a **durable power of attorney**, a legal document designating someone to make health care decisions on that person's behalf, or a **living will**, a legal document clarifying a person's wishes regarding future medical or, increasingly, mental health treatment.

adventitious *adj.* appearing or occurring unexpectedly or in an unusual place.

adverse drug reaction (**ADR**) any unintended, harmful, and potentially fatal response to a drug. Reactions may be genetically determined (as in the case of HYPERSENSITIVITY), in which case they are highly individual and can be difficult to predict, or they may arise through interactions with other prescribed or nonprescribed drugs or with dietary items (as in the case of MONOAMINE OXIDASE INHIBITORS). This term sometimes is used synonymously with SIDE EFFECT, but an adverse drug reaction more properly denotes an unexpected negative occurrence, whereas side effects may be positive or negative and are usually anticipated. Also called **adverse drug event (ADE)**; **adverse event**; **adverse reaction**.

adverse impact the deleterious effect that certain hiring procedures or selection criteria may have on the employment chances of people belonging to disadvantaged groups, such as women, people with disabilities, or members of ethnic minorities. For example, testing for competence in written English might have an adverse impact on recent immigrants; such testing should therefore be avoided unless this competence is legitimately necessary for successful job performance. Also called **disparate impact**.

advertisement *n.* in animal behavior, a type of signal or display that emphasizes or calls attention to the organism producing it. For example, a male bird defending a territory might use advertisement in the form of bright coloration and conspicuous song both to attract mates and to deter competing males. Compare CAMOUFLAGE.

advertising psychology the study of the psychological impact that various media communications promoting products and services have on prospective buyers and of factors influencing their effectiveness, including presentation techniques and the physical characteristics of advertisements.

advocacy *n.* speaking or acting on behalf of an individual or group to uphold their rights or explain their point of view. For example, health care **advocates** represent consumers to protect their rights to effective treatment, while therapists may act as advocates for clients in court hearings or other situations involving decisions based on the clients' mental health or related issues.

AEP abbreviation for AVERAGE EVOKED POTENTIAL.

aerobic exercise physical activity, typically prolonged and of moderate intensity (e.g., jogging or cycling), that involves the use of oxygen in the muscles to provide the needed energy. Aerobic exercise strengthens the cardiovascular and respiratory systems and is associated with a variety of health benefits including increased endurance, reduction of body fat, and decreased depression and anxiety. Compare ANAEROBIC EXERCISE.

aesthesiometry *n.* see ESTHESIOMETRY.

aesthetics *n.* the philosophical study of beauty and art, concerned particularly with the articula-

A

tion of taste and questions regarding the value of aesthetic experience and the making of aesthetic judgments. See also ENVIRONMENTAL AESTHETICS; PSYCHOLOGICAL AESTHETICS. —**aesthetic** *adj.*

affect *n.* any feeling or emotion, which may be irreflexive or reflexive. **Irreflexive affect** is the direct experience in consciousness of a particular emotional state (as in a person's feeling of elation upon receiving good news). **Reflexive affect** occurs when a person makes his or her feelings objects of scrutiny (as when a person wonders why he or she does not feel particularly elated upon receiving good news). A distinction may also be made between NEGATIVE AFFECT and POSITIVE AFFECT. Along with cognition and conation, affect is one of the three traditionally identified components of mind.

affection *n.* fondness, tenderness, and liking, especially when nonsexual. Feelings of emotional attachment between individuals, particularly human infants and caregivers, are called **affectional bonds.** They are particularly important to ATTACHMENT THEORY, and their presence is evidenced by proximity-seeking behaviors and distress if loss or involuntary separation occurs. —**affectionate** *adj.*

affective *adj.* demonstrating, capable of producing, or otherwise pertaining to emotion or feelings. —**affectivity** *n.*

affective aggression see AGGRESSION.

affective disorder see MOOD DISORDER.

affective education any program in which learning is focused on or derived from emotion rather than reason, for example, a curriculum designed to enhance students' emotional and social growth and encourage positive behavior change. The concept is gaining popularity as a means of reducing conflict and aggression in schools.

affective lability emotional instability; that is, sudden shifts in emotional expression. It is often seen in such disorders as schizophrenia, bipolar disorder, borderline personality disorder, senile dementia, and traumatic brain injury.

affective logic the hypothesis that emotions have their own independent set of mental operations, distinct from those governing other forms of mental life.

affective psychosis originally, a mood alteration so profound as to impair a person's capacity to interact with the environment appropriately and effectively. In essence, it was a synonym for affective disorder, which itself is now a synonym for MOOD DISORDER. In contemporary usage the term refers to a mood disorder accompanied by delusions or hallucinations (i.e., psychotic features). The mood disruption precedes the psychotic symptoms, and the psychotic symptoms only occur during a MAJOR DEPRESSIVE EPISODE or a MANIC EPISODE.

affective theory a framework underlying certain approaches to psychotherapy that emphasizes the importance of feelings and emotions in therapeutic change.

affective tone the mood or feeling associated with a particular experience or stimulus. In psychotherapy, when a client fails to recognize his or her affective tone, the therapist may draw the client's attention to it as a primary element of the therapeutic interaction. Also called **feeling tone.**

afferent *adj.* conducting or conveying from the periphery toward a central point. For example, **afferent nerve fibers** conduct impulses toward the brain or spinal cord. Compare EFFERENT.

affiliation *n.* a social relationship with one or more other individuals, usually based on liking or a personal attachment rather than on perceived material benefits. Affiliation appears to be a basic source of emotional security, given the anxiety, frustration, and loneliness stemming from the absence of such relationships. Some propose that the seeking of cooperative, friendly association with others who resemble or like one or whom one likes is a fundamental human desire, referring to it variously as the **affiliative drive** or **affiliative need.** —**affiliative** *adj.*

affinity *n.* **1.** an inherent attraction to or liking for a particular person, place, or thing, often based on some commonality. See ELECTIVE AFFINITY. **2.** relationship by marriage or adoption rather than blood. This contrasts with **consanguinity,** a biological relationship between individuals who are descended from a common ancestor. **3.** in pharmacology, see BINDING AFFINITY.

affirmative action a U.S. government policy designed to promote equal opportunities by requiring certain employers to develop and implement programs for actively recruiting and promoting people from various disadvantaged groups, including ethnic minorities, women, and people with disabilities. The policy is controversial in some of its aspects and has been subject to legal challenges, particularly on the grounds that it constitutes reverse discrimination.

affirmative therapy a socioculturally informed intervention that empowers clients and their communities, particularly in situations in which ethnic, gender, or sexual orientation diversity has been resisted or in which normal conditions (e.g., gay identity) have been pathologized. Such therapy may be practiced as a distinct intervention or within the context of other psychotherapies.

affordance *n.* in the theory of ECOLOGICAL PERCEPTION, any property of the physical environment that is relevant to motor behavior and thus offers or affords an organism the opportunity for a particular action. An example is the orientation of an object's handle. When the handle is closest to the left hand it affords a left-hand reach and grasp movement. This affordance is provided by an intrinsic property, the physical dimensions necessary for grasping it, as well as an extrinsic property, the distance to the nearest hand.

A fiber a myelinated nerve fiber (axon) of the somatosensory system. A fibers are subdivided by diameter, ranging from largest to smallest: **A-alpha fibers** are 13–20 μm in diameter and transmit information from proprioceptors of skeletal muscles, **A-beta fibers** are 6–12 μm and transmit information from mechanoreceptors of the skin, and **A-delta fibers** are 1–5 μm and transmit temperature and sharp pain information. See also B FIBER; C FIBER.

aftercare *n.* a program of outpatient treatment and support services provided for individuals discharged from an institution, such as a hospital or mental health facility, to help maintain improvement, prevent relapse, and aid adjustment of the individual to the community.

aftereffect *n.* the altered perception of a sensory stimulus that results from prolonged exposure to another stimulus. Aftereffects are often visual and are usually the inverted form of the original stimulus. For example, viewing a pattern of lines tilted to the left will make a pattern of vertical lines appear to be tilted to the right (the **tilt aftereffect**; **TAE**). There are various other types of aftereffects, including the CONTINGENT AFTEREFFECT and the MOTION AFTEREFFECT.

afterimage *n.* the image that remains after a stimulus ends or is removed. A **positive afterimage** occurs rarely, lasts a few seconds, and is caused by a continuation of receptor and neural processes following cessation of the stimulus; it has approximately the color and brightness of the original stimulus. A **negative afterimage** is more common, often more intense, and lasts longer. It is usually complementary to the original stimulus in color and brightness; for example, if the stimulus was bright yellow, the negative afterimage will be dark blue.

age-associated memory impairment (**AAMI**) the minor memory deficits often associated with normal aging, for example, forgetting the name of a recently read book. These changes are not associated with dementias, such as Alzheimer's disease, and affect the ability to acquire and recall new information rather than the recall of established memories (e.g., the name of one's hometown). Also called **benign senescence**; **benign senescent forgetfulness**.

age discrimination differential treatment of individuals on the basis of chronological age, particularly evident in employment, social support, and health care.

age effect 1. in research, any outcome associated with being a certain age. Such effects may be difficult to separate from COHORT EFFECTS and PERIOD EFFECTS. **2.** in the psychology of groups, any of various cognitive and interpersonal consequences that result when group members respond to others on the basis of their age. See also AGEISM.

age equivalent any measure of development or performance expressed in terms of the average chronological age at which the observed score is typically obtained. Also called **age score**.

ageism *n.* the tendency to be prejudiced against older adults and to negatively stereotype them (for example, as unhealthy, helpless, or incompetent) and the resulting discrimination, especially in employment and in health care. —**ageist** *adj.*

agency *n.* the state of being active, usually in the service of a goal, or of having the power and capability to produce an effect or exert influence.

agency theory a theory that describes economic and organizational activity in terms of a series of agreements between principals, who require goods or services, and agents, who supply these goods or services. Central to this theory is the rational economic assumption that both agents (e.g., company managers) and principals (e.g., company shareholders) will attempt to maximize their respective UTILITIES.

agenesis *n.* the failure of a body part to develop fully or to develop at all. —**agenetic** *adj.*

age norm the standard score or range of scores that represent the average achievement level of people of a particular chronological age.

age of onset the chronological age at which symptoms of a disease or disorder first appear in an individual. One of the hallmarks of some genetic syndromes is that the age of onset is earlier in individuals with hereditary susceptibility than in sporadic cases.

age regression a hypnotic technique in which the therapist helps the client recall a crucial experience by inducing amnesia for the present, then suggesting that he or she return, year by year, to the earlier date when a particular experience took place. This technique is also used in forensic contexts to help eyewitnesses and victims recall their experiences. The use of age regression in either context is controversial, given the potential for FALSE MEMORIES and the debatable legitimacy of RECOVERED MEMORIES.

age score see AGE EQUIVALENT.

ageusia (**aguesia**) *n.* loss or absence of the ability to taste. Causes may include a failure of taste receptors to form; a loss of taste receptors due to injury, disease, or advanced age; or damage to the sensory nerves that transport taste sensations to the central nervous system. —**ageusic** *adj.*

aggregation *n.* **1.** a collection of organisms in one location with no obvious social structure or social organization, possessing only a minimum of shared purpose or interdependence. Examples include commuters on a subway platform or a group of butterflies around a puddle of water. Compare GROUP. **2.** in statistics, a structured set of data elements. —**aggregate** *vb.* —**aggregative** *adj.*

aggression *n.* hostile behavior intended to harm others physically or psychologically or to destroy property. It can be distinguished from anger in that anger is oriented at overcoming the target but not necessarily through harm or destruction. Aggression may be instrumentally motivated (proactive) or affectively motivated (reactive). **Instrumental aggression** involves an attack carried out principally to achieve another goal, such as acquiring a desired resource. **Affective aggression** involves an emotional response to an aversive state of affairs, which tends to be targeted toward the perceived source of the distress but may be displaced onto other people or objects if the disturbing agent cannot be attacked (see DISPLACED AGGRESSION). In the classical psychoanalytic theory of Austrian psychiatrist Sigmund Freud (1856–1939), the aggressive impulse is innate and derived from the DEATH INSTINCT, but most nonpsychoanalytically oriented psychologists view it as socially learned or as a reaction to frustration (see FRUSTRATION–AGGRESSION HYPOTHESIS). —**aggressive** *adj.*

aggressive instinct in psychoanalytic theory, a derivative of the DEATH INSTINCT that directs destructive impulses away from the self and toward the outside world.

aggressive mimicry the presence in a predatory species of physical or behavioral traits (or both) that closely resemble those of a nonpredatory species, with the result that potential prey more readily approach the predator. For example, the females of a species of firefly can imitate the sexual flash patterns of a different species, luring males of that species close enough to be eaten.

aggressiveness *n.* a tendency toward social dominance, threatening behavior, and hostility. It may cause a transient change in behavior within an individual or be a characteristic trait of an individual. —**aggressive** *adj.*

aging *n.* the biological and psychological changes associated with chronological age. A distinction is often made between changes that are due to normal biological processes (see PRIMARY AGING) and changes that are caused by age-related pathologies (see SECONDARY AGING).

aging disorder any disruption of the gradual structural and immune changes that occur with the passage of time, leading to increased probability of early death. An example is **progeria** (or **Hutchinson–Gilford syndrome**), a very rare inherited disorder in which children age extremely rapidly and typically die of a heart attack or stroke between the ages of 10 and 15 years. A more common example is Alzheimer's disease.

agitated depression a MAJOR DEPRESSIVE EPISODE in which psychomotor agitation (excessive but purposeless activity), restlessness, and irritability predominate.

agitation *n.* a state of increased but typically purposeless and repetitious activity, as in PSYCHOMOTOR AGITATION.

agnosia *n.* loss or impairment of the ability to recognize or appreciate the nature of sensory stimuli due to brain damage or disorder. Recognition impairment is profound and specific to a particular sensory modality. AUDITORY AGNOSIA, TACTILE AGNOSIA, and VISUAL AGNOSIA are the most common types, and each has a variety of subtypes.

agnosticism *n.* a skeptical position holding that the truth or falsity of certain metaphysical ideas or propositions cannot be known. The word is most often used in regard to theological doctrines, especially to belief in the existence of God. —**agnostic** *adj., n.*

agonadal *adj.* denoting or resulting from absence of the primary sex organs (gonads, i.e., testes or ovaries).

agonist *n.* **1.** a drug or other chemical agent that binds to a particular receptor and produces a physiological effect, typically one similar to that of the body's own neurotransmitter at that receptor. There are **partial agonists**, which stimulate the receptor only somewhat to produce the same physiological effect as the natural neurotransmitter but to a lesser degree, and **inverse agonists**, which act at the receptor to produce a physiological effect opposite to that produced by another agonist at that same receptor. **2.** a contracting muscle whose action generates force in the intended direction. Compare ANTAGONIST. —**agonism** *n.* —**agonistic** *adj.*

agonist–antagonist a substance that simultaneously binds to multiple receptors, mimicking the action of the body's natural neurotransmitter at one type of receptor and inhibiting that action at another, different type of receptor.

agoraphobia *n.* an excessive, irrational fear of being in open or unfamiliar places, resulting in the avoidance of public situations from which escape may be difficult, such as standing in line or being in a crowd. Agoraphobia may accompany PANIC DISORDER, in which an individual experiences unexpected panic attacks, or it may occur in the absence of panic disorder, when an individual experiences paniclike symptoms or limited symptom attacks. —**agoraphobic** *adj.*

agrammatism *n.* a manifestation of APHASIA characterized by loss or impairment of the ability to use speech that conforms to grammatical rules, such as those governing word order, verb tense, and subject–verb agreement. It is distinct from **syntactic aphasia**, which is a more specific manifestation involving loss or impairment only of the ability to adhere to rules governing syntax, that is, to correctly combine or sequence words in sentences. Also called **dysgrammatism**.

agraphia *n.* loss or impairment of the ability to write as a result of neurological damage or disorder. The specific forms of writing difficulties vary considerably, but may include problems with such things as spelling irregular or ambiguous words, writing numbers or particular letters, or performing the motor movements needed for handwriting. Agraphia generally is seen in APHASIA, although there is considerable variability of writing ability within a given aphasia type. Also called **dysgraphia**. —**agraphic** *adj.*

agreeableness *n.* the tendency to act in a cooperative, unselfish manner, construed as a dimension of individual differences in the Big Five and FIVE-FACTOR PERSONALITY MODELS. —**agreeable** *adj.*

agyria *n.* see LISSENCEPHALY.

aha experience the emotional reaction that typically occurs at a moment of sudden insight into a problem or other puzzling issue. For example, in psychotherapy it is a client's sudden insight into his or her motives for cognitions, affects, or behaviors. Also called **aha reaction**.

AI abbreviation for ARTIFICIAL INTELLIGENCE.

aided recall the process of remembering something under circumstances where a prompt is given to assist recall. Aided recall is used, for example, to assist an eyewitness or victim of a crime to retrieve memories relevant to the event or to assist consumers in remembering information contained in a commercial message, as a means of testing the effectiveness of advertising.

AIDS *acquired immune deficiency syndrome*: a clinical condition in which the immune system is so severely damaged from infection with human immunodeficiency virus (see HIV) as to result in certain serious opportunistic infections and diseases. Disclosing one's HIV-positive status can be difficult: The illness is stigmatizing, resulting in social rejection and a diverse array of other psychological processes, including loss, grieving, stress, and coping. Counseling, however, is available, providing guidance, advice, and information to individuals on issues related to HIV infection and AIDS.

AIDS dementia complex (**ADC**) neuropsychological dysfunction directly attributable to HIV infection, found most commonly in those who have developed AIDS. It is marked by impairments such as memory loss and inability to concentrate and by disturbances in behavior, motor coordination, and mood. Also called **HIV dementia**.

AIM abbreviation for ACTIVE INTERMODAL MAPPING.

aim-inhibited *adj.* in psychoanalytic theory, describing a behavior in which the underlying drives are deflected from their original object and obtain reduced gratification through activities or relationships similar to the original aim. Austrian psychiatrist Sigmund Freud (1856–1939) explained affectional relationships within families and platonic friendships as deriving from an aim-inhibited sexual instinct.

aim of the instinct in psychoanalytic theory,

the activity through which an INSTINCT is gratified, resulting in the release of internal tension. For example, kissing may satisfy the oral instinct. Also called **instinctual aim**.

akinesia *n.* loss or reduction of voluntary movement. Also called **akinesis**. —**akinetic** *adj.*

akinesthesia *n.* loss or impairment of the sense that provides information from muscles, tendons, and joints. Also called **akinesthesis**. —**akinesthesic** or **akinesthetic** *adj.*

akinetopsia *n.* inability to see objects in motion as a result of damage to the V5 area of visual cortex. Individuals with akinetopsia perceive moving stimuli as a series of stationary strobelike images and see visual trails behind moving objects. —**akinetopsic** *adj.*

AL 1. abbreviation for absolute limen (see ABSOLUTE THRESHOLD). **2.** abbreviation for ADAPTATION LEVEL.

Al-Anon *n.* an international self-help organization for people who have been affected by the compulsive use of alcohol by a family member or friend. Founded in the United States in 1951, it uses the TWELVE-STEP PROGRAM adapted from ALCOHOLICS ANONYMOUS and includes **Alateen** for younger individuals. Al-Anon members share their experiences with and offer support to one another in order to promote personal recovery and growth.

alarm call a vocalization produced by an animal, often in response to detecting a potential predator, that warns other individuals to either escape or join in mutual attack of the predator. Alarm calls appear to be altruistic acts (placing the caller at increased risk) and are often explained through KIN SELECTION or reciprocal ALTRUISM.

alarm reaction see GENERAL ADAPTATION SYNDROME.

alaryngeal *adj.* without or not involving the larynx, the structure at the top of the trachea (windpipe) that contains the vocal cords.

albinism *n.* any of a group of genetic disorders characterized by defective pigmentation of the eyes, hair, and skin due to inadequate production or distribution of melanin pigment in the body. In addition to pigmentation abnormalities, symptoms may include strabismus (abnormal alignment of the eyes), nystagmus (involuntary rapid eye movement), refractive (focusing) errors, reduced visual acuity, and photophobia (extreme sensitivity to light).

alcohol *n.* short for ethyl alcohol (see ETHANOL).

alcohol abuse a pattern of alcohol consumption that persists despite recurrent significant adverse consequences resulting directly from alcohol use, including neglect of important personal, financial, social, occupational, or recreational activities; absenteeism from work or school; repeated encounters with the police; and the use of alcohol in situations in which drinking is hazardous (e.g., driving while intoxicated).

It is distinct from alcohol dependence in that it does not involve tolerance or withdrawal.

alcohol dependence a pattern of repeated or compulsive use of alcohol despite significant behavioral, physiological, and psychosocial problems, plus indications of physical and psychological dependence—tolerance and characteristic withdrawal symptoms if use is suspended—resulting in impaired control. It is further differentiated from alcohol abuse by the preoccupation with obtaining alcohol or recovering from its effects, and the overwhelming desire for experiencing alcohol's intoxicating result (i.e., craving). Alcohol dependence is known popularly as **alcoholism**.

alcoholic neuropathy any of various neurological disturbances, including weakness and abnormal skin sensations, such as numbness, tingling, and burning, that are secondary to chronic heavy consumption of alcohol. Specific causative factors are not well understood, but appear to include vitamin deficiencies and a directly toxic effect of alcohol on nerves.

Alcoholics Anonymous (**AA**) a worldwide voluntary organization of men and women who, through a TWELVE-STEP PROGRAM, seek to help each other stay sober and learn to live healthy, fulfilling lives. The only requirement for membership is a desire to stop drinking. Two critical components of the AA program are its focus on alcoholics helping alcoholics and its desire to put principles above personalities in conducting its business. Founded in the United States in 1935, AA is the oldest, largest, and best-known self-help organization. Its approach has provided the model for a variety of additional self-help groups addressing drug addiction (e.g., **Cocaine Anonymous** [**CA**], **Narcotics Anonymous** [**NA**]), compulsive gambling (e.g., **Gamblers Anonymous** [**GA**]), and other problems (e.g., **Overeaters Anonymous** [**OA**]).

alcohol intoxication a reversible condition that develops soon after the ingestion of alcohol. It comprises behavioral or psychological changes, such as inappropriate or aggressive behavior, impaired judgment, or impaired social functioning; and physiological changes, such as slurred speech, unsteady gait, and disruption of attention or memory. The effects typically become more marked with increased alcohol intake.

alcoholism *n.* see ALCOHOL DEPENDENCE.

alcohol withdrawal a group of physical symptoms that arise after cessation of repeated and prolonged heavy alcohol consumption. Withdrawal symptoms include autonomic hyperactivity (sweating, pounding heart, dry mouth, etc.), hand tremor, insomnia, nausea or vomiting, PSYCHOMOTOR AGITATION, anxiety, and in some cases hallucinations or illusions, seizures, and DELIRIUM TREMENS.

aldosterone *n.* the principle MINERALOCORTICOID hormone secreted by the adrenal cortex, the outer layer of the ADRENAL GLAND. It helps to regulate mineral and water metabolism by promoting potassium excretion and sodium retention in the kidneys. Excess secretion of aldosterone results in a pathological condition called **aldosteronism** (or **hyperaldosteronism**), marked by headaches, muscle weakness, fatigue, hypertension, and numbness. Primary aldosteronism is caused by abnormal functioning of the adrenal cortex itself and is called **Conn's syndrome**, whereas secondary aldosteronism is the result of a liver, heart, or kidney disease affecting the adrenal glands.

alertness *n.* the state of being awake, aware, attentive, and prepared to act or react. Neurologically, alertness corresponds with high-frequency, low-amplitude brain waves resulting from stimulation of the RETICULAR FORMATION. See also AROUSAL.

alexia *n.* loss or impairment of the ability to comprehend written or printed words as a result of lesions, stroke, or other forms of neurological damage or disorder. It is generally seen in APHASIA but may occur in isolation, in which case it is called **pure alexia** (or **alexia without agraphia**) and characterized by reading impairment with preserved language production and auditory comprehension. Individuals with pure alexia can also write but are frequently unable to read what they have written. See also DYSLEXIA.

alexithymia *n.* an inability to express, describe, or distinguish between one's emotions. It may occur in a variety of disorders (e.g., depression), especially psychosomatic and some substance use disorders, or following repeated exposure to a traumatic stressor.

algesia *n.* the ability to experience the sensation of pain. Compare ANALGESIA. —**algesic** *adj.*

algorithm *n.* a precisely defined procedure for solving a particular problem or for conducting a series of computations that guarantees a correct outcome. Algorithms are essential to computer programming and information processing. Compare HEURISTIC. —**algorithmic** *adj.*

alias *n.* see CONFOUND.

alienation *n.* **1.** estrangement from others, resulting in the absence of close or friendly relationships with people in one's social group (e.g., family, workplace, community). **2.** estrangement from oneself. An individual experiences life as a search for his or her true personal identity, which has been hidden through socialization and nurturing, and a continuous failure to reach an ideal but unattainable level of personal fulfillment. This creates a deep-seated sense of dissatisfaction with one's personal existence and lack of trust in one's social or physical environment or in oneself. **3.** the experience of being separated from reality or isolated from one's thoughts or feelings, as in DEREALIZATION and DEPERSONALIZATION. —**alienated** *adj.*

alien limb syndrome a motor disorder characterized by involuntary hand, arm, or leg movements in place of or in addition to intended movements (e.g., grabbing objects or throwing things) and the person's feeling that he or she has no control over the limb or that it is "foreign," sometimes to the extent that the person does not recognize the limb as his or her own in the absence of visual clues. The syndrome most often affects the left hand (hence its alternative name **alien hand syndrome**) and is typically associated with lesions to the SUPPLEMENTARY MOTOR AREA or CORPUS CALLOSUM.

alkalosis *n.* an abnormally high level of alkalinity (bicarbonate ion concentration) in the blood and tissues, which upsets the body's acid–base balance. The condition is often marked by slow, shallow breathing. It has a variety of causes and additional symptoms vary with each, potentially including neurological abnormalities such as muscle twitching, confusion, tremors or spasms, and numbness. Compare ACIDOSIS. —**alkalotic** *adj.*

allele *n.* an alternate form of a gene that occupies a given position on each of a pair of HOMOLOGOUS chromosomes. Each person typically has two alleles of each gene: One is inherited from the mother and the other from the father. Alleles may be alike (**homozygous**) or different (**heterozygous**), and are responsible for variation in inherited characteristics, such as hair color or blood type. See also DOMINANT ALLELE; RECESSIVE ALLELE. —**allelic** *adj.*

allergy *n.* a condition in which the body produces an abnormal or inappropriate immune response to certain **allergens**, foreign but normally harmless substances, such as house dust or animal dander. In an allergic person the allergens stimulate the release of HISTAMINE, leading to inflammation and other symptoms. See also ANAPHYLAXIS. —**allergic** *adj.*

allesthesia (**allaesthesia; alloesthesia**) *n.* a disturbance of stimulus localization in which individuals experience a given stimulus on the side opposite to the side of stimulation. For example, **visual allesthesia** involves the transposition of images from one position to their opposite in the visual field.

alliance *n.* an association between two or more individuals formed to promote mutual interests. For example, nonhuman animals form alliances that allow members collectively to control resources that one individual could not control alone. See also THERAPEUTIC ALLIANCE.

allocentric *adj.* denoting externality to the self, particularly an orientation toward or focus on groups and connections to others. Compare IDIOCENTRIC. See also SOCIOCENTRISM. —**allocentrism** *n.*

allocheiria (**allochiria**) *n.* a disorder of sensation in which a person experiences pain or touch sensations on the opposite side of the body from the point actually stimulated. It is considered a DYSCHEIRIA.

allocortex *n.* those regions of the cerebral cortex that are phylogenetically older and have fewer than six main layers of cells. The allocortex is involved primarily in olfactory functions and limbic functions related to memory and emotion, and comprises the three-layered **archicortex** (or **archipallium**), found mostly in the hippocampus, and the four- or five-layered **paleocortex** (or **paleopallium**), found mostly in the pyriform area and parahippocampal gyrus. Compare NEOCORTEX.

alloeroticism *n.* the extension of erotic feelings toward and the derivation of sexual satisfaction from others, as opposed to AUTOEROTICISM. Also called **alloerotism**. —**alloerotic** *adj.*

allomone *n.* a chemical signal that is released outside the body by members of one species and affects the behavior of members of another species. Compare PHEROMONE.

allopathy *n.* a system of medicine in which a disease or disorder is treated with agents that produce effects different from or incompatible with those caused by the disease or disorder. Allopathy is often equated with conventional or pharmacological medical practice. Compare HOMEOPATHY. —**allopathic** *adj.*

allopatric *adj.* see SYMPATRIC.

alloplasty *n.* a process of adaptive response that aims to alter the environment, as opposed to altering the self. Compare AUTOPLASTY. —**alloplastic** *adj.*

all-or-none hypothesis the theory that, in any given learning trial, learning occurs either completely and fully or not at all. The all-or-none hypothesis contrasts with a trial-by-trial **incremental hypothesis** of learning.

all-or-none law the principle that the amplitude of the ACTION POTENTIAL in a given neuron is independent of the magnitude of the stimulus. Thus, all stimuli above the neuron's threshold trigger action potentials of identical magnitude. Also called **all-or-none principle**.

allosteric modulation the binding of a substance (called an **allosteric modulator**) to a certain site on a RECEPTOR in a way that alters the conformation of other sites on the receptor, thereby increasing or decreasing the affinity of the receptor for other molecules. Allosteric modulation recently has been recognized as an alternative pharmacological approach to gain selectivity in drug action.

alpha (symbol: α) *n.* the probability of a TYPE I ERROR.

alpha-adrenergic receptor see ADRENERGIC RECEPTOR.

alpha alcoholism one of five types of alcoholism defined by U.S. physician Elvin M. Jellinek (1890–1963), the others being BETA ALCOHOLISM, GAMMA ALCOHOLISM, DELTA ALCOHOLISM, and EPSILON ALCOHOLISM. It is characterized by undisciplined drinking that disturbs interpersonal and family relationships and work life and a reliance on the effects of alcohol for the relief of physical or emotional pain, but it does not involve losing control or inability to abstain.

alpha blocker see ADRENERGIC BLOCKING AGENT.

alpha blocking the suppression of ALPHA WAVES that occurs upon deviation from a wakeful but relaxed state, as, for example, when focusing the eyes on an unexpected stimulus or performing an active mental task. It is sometimes taken as an indicator of orienting or attention. Typically, blocked alpha waves are replaced by faster, low-amplitude, irregular waveforms on the electroencephalogram, a phenomenon called **desynchronization**.

alpha coefficient see CRONBACH'S ALPHA.

alpha error see TYPE I ERROR.

alpha level see SIGNIFICANCE LEVEL.

alpha male the top-ranked or dominant male within a group, with primary access to resources, including food and mates. In many species the alpha male prevents other males from mating or from mating during the peak time of female fertility. There are **alpha females** as well, with primary access to resources within their social groups and who in some species inhibit reproduction among other females.

alpha motor neuron see MOTOR NEURON.

alpha wave in electroencephalography, a type of low-amplitude BRAIN WAVE (frequency 8–12 Hz) that typically occurs when the eyes are unfocused and no active mental processes are taking place, indicating a wakeful but relaxed state. The occurrence of alpha waves may be increased, for example, through meditation or **alpha-wave training**, a type of BIOFEEDBACK training that involves providing a feedback stimulus (typically an auditory tone) when alpha waves appear on the electroencephalogram (EEG). Also called **alpha rhythm**; **Berger rhythm**.

alprazolam n. a BENZODIAZEPINE used for the treatment of generalized anxiety disorder and panic disorder. It is rapidly absorbed and has a relatively brief duration of action. Common side effects include drowsiness, light-headedness, headache, and confusion. U.S. trade name: **Xanax**.

ALS abbreviation for AMYOTROPHIC LATERAL SCLEROSIS.

als ob as if (German). The phrase is associated with the thought of German philosopher Hans Vaihinger (1852–1933), who proposed that certain "fictions," such as free will, immortality, and objective morality, should be supported and lived as if (*als ob*) they were true, because there is biological advantage in doing so. Vaihinger's work influenced that of Austrian psychiatrist Alfred Adler (1870–1937).

alteration hypothesis a theoretical explanation of the MISINFORMATION EFFECT stating that misleading information introduced after a witnessed event replaces, transforms, or impairs the original memory of the event, leading to erroneous reporting of that event. Also called **substitution hypothesis**. Compare COEXISTENCE HYPOTHESIS.

altered state of consciousness (**ASC**) a state of psychological functioning that is significantly different from ordinary states of CONSCIOUSNESS, being characterized by altered levels of self-awareness, affect, reality testing, orientation to time and place, wakefulness, responsiveness to external stimuli, or memorability or by a sense of ecstasy, boundlessness, or unity with the universe. Although in some instances ASCs are symptomatic of mental disorder, in other contexts, such as in certain Eastern philosophies and TRANSPERSONAL PSYCHOLOGY, they are regarded as higher states of consciousness and, often, as indicative of a more profound level of personal and spiritual evolution.

alter ego 1. a second identity or aspect of a person that exists metaphorically as his or her substitute or representative, with different characteristics. **2.** an intimate, supportive friend with whom an individual can share all types of problems and experiences, as if he or she were "another self."

alternate-forms reliability an estimate of the extent to which a test yields consistent reproducible results that is obtained from the correlation of scores on different versions of that test. These **alternate forms** of the test may be of three types: **comparable forms** have items of similar content and difficulty; **equivalent forms** have items of similar content and difficulty but demonstrate differences in certain statistical characteristics (e.g., standard deviations); and **parallel forms** have items of similar content and difficulty and are similar in all statistical characteristics (e.g., means, standard deviations, correlations with other measures). Comparable forms have the least degree of similarity to one another, while parallel forms have the greatest degree of similarity and are essentially interchangeable.

alternative behavior completion a technique in BEHAVIOR THERAPY for extinguishing unwanted habits by substituting an incompatible behavior for the nondesired behavior (e.g., substituting nail care for nail biting). This technique can be practiced in vivo (see IN VIVO DESENSITIZATION) or imaginally in the therapy session or assigned as homework. It is often used as an alternative to mild aversion therapy. See also COMPETING RESPONSE TRAINING.

alternative hypothesis (symbol: H_1) a statement of the position opposite to that of the NULL HYPOTHESIS. It usually outlines the predicted relationship between variables that a researcher is seeking to demonstrate empirically as true. In HYPOTHESIS TESTING, the alternative hypothesis may be considered plausible only when the null hypothesis is rejected at a predetermined SIGNIFICANCE LEVEL.

alternative medicine see COMPLEMENTARY AND ALTERNATIVE MEDICINE.

alternative psychology any approach to understanding psychological issues that ignores or rejects accepted academic, scientific, or mainstream views. These approaches may involve unorthodox metaphysical assumptions and focus on spiritualistic and mystical influences. Emphasis may be on aspects of human thought, feeling, and actions that are ignored by mainstream psychology.

alternative psychotherapy any treatment approach not considered to be within the mainstream of psychotherapy. For example, the use of LSD PSYCHOTHERAPY in the 1960s was considered alternative.

alternative schedule of reinforcement in conditioning, a rule that provides for reinforcement of a response according to either a FIXED-RATIO SCHEDULE or a FIXED-INTERVAL SCHEDULE, whichever is satisfied first.

alternative sentencing the imposition of sanctions other than traditional imprisonment on those convicted of crimes so as to reduce recidivism and help individuals become successful members of society. Examples include diversion programs, the provision of treatment or other services instead of incarceration; electronic monitoring; and community service. Also called **community correction**.

altricial *adj.* describing animals, such as primates (including humans), that are not fully developed at birth and hence require considerable and sustained parental care beyond nursing or feeding in order to survive. Compare PRECOCIAL.

altruism *n.* an apparently unselfish concern for others or behavior that provides benefit to others at some cost to the individual. In humans, it covers a wide range of behaviors, including volunteerism and martyrdom, but the degree to which such behaviors are legitimately without egotistic motivation is subject to much debate. In animal behavior it is difficult to understand how altruism could evolve since NATURAL SELECTION operates on individuals. However, organisms displaying altruism can benefit if they help their relatives (see KIN SELECTION) or if an altruistic act is subsequently reciprocated (**reciprocal altruism**). —**altruistic** *adj.* —**altruist** *n.*

Alzheimer's disease a progressive neurodegenerative disease characterized by cortical atrophy, neuronal death, synapse loss, and accumulation of SENILE PLAQUES and NEUROFIBRILLARY TANGLES, causing DEMENTIA and a significant decline in functioning. Early features include deficits in memory (e.g., rapid forgetting of new information, impaired recall and recognition), executive dysfunction, and subtle personality changes such as decreased energy, social withdrawal, indifference, and impulsivity. As the disease progresses, there is global deterioration of cognitive capacities with intellectual decline, APHASIA, AGNOSIA, and APRAXIA as well as behavioral features including apathy, emotional blunting, mood-dependent delusions, decreased sleep and appetite, and increased motor activity (e.g., restlessness and wandering). Onset of Alzheimer's disease is insidious and typically after age 65, although early-onset cases do occur. Major risk factors for Alzheimer's disease include advanced age, a family history of the disease, and genetic factors, particularly the presence of the ApoE4 allele (see APOLIPOPROTEIN E) on chromosome 19. [first described in 1907 by Alois **Alzheimer** (1864–1915), German neurologist]

amacrine cell any of a diverse class of neurons in the retina that connect RETINAL BIPOLAR CELLS and RETINAL GANGLION CELLS. Amacrine cells have no axons and do not contribute directly to the output of the retina.

amae *n.* an indigenous Japanese concept that describes a behavioral pattern roughly translated as indulgent dependency in which people ask others to perform actions for them that they could actually perform for themselves. Typically found in mother–child relationships, amae is distinguished from true dependency by the inappropriateness of the requests and their presumed acceptance.

Ambien *n.* a trade name for ZOLPIDEM.

ambience (**ambiance**) *n.* an environment or milieu: the context and surroundings of an event or situation, particularly as they influence its emotional effect and the appreciation of it. —**ambient** *adj.*

ambiguity *n.* **1.** the property of a behavior, behavior pattern, or situation that might lead to interpretation in more than one way. **2.** in linguistics, the property of a word, phrase, or sentence that has more than one possible meaning. Ambiguity in a phrase or sentence may be lexical, as in *The students are revolting*, or structural, as in *black cats and dogs*; often there is a combination of both factors. In PSYCHOLINGUISTICS, the main area of interest has been the process used to interpret sentences whose SURFACE STRUCTURE could reflect two quite different DEEP STRUCTURES, as in the instruction *Before opening tin, stand in boiling water for ten minutes*. —**ambiguous** *adj.*

ambiguity tolerance the degree to which one is able to accept, and to function without distress or disorientation in, situations having conflicting or multiple interpretations or outcomes.

ambiguous figure a visual stimulus that can be interpreted in more than one way, such as an EMBEDDED FIGURE or a REVERSIBLE FIGURE. A well-known example is the young girl–old woman image, in which the black-and-white drawing sometimes appears to be of a young girl and sometimes of an old lady. This phenomenon is not restricted to the visual: an **ambiguous stimulus** is one of any sensory modality that can have multiple interpretations.

ambivalence *n.* the simultaneous existence of

contradictory feelings and attitudes, such as friendliness and hostility, toward the same person, object, event, or situation. Swiss psychiatrist Eugen Bleuler (1857–1939), who was the first to use this term in a psychological sense, regarded extreme ambivalence as a major symptom of schizophrenia. **—ambivalent** *adj.*

ambivalent attachment see INSECURE ATTACHMENT.

amblyopia *n.* poor vision caused by abnormal visual experience in early life and not any physical defect of the eye. Common predisposing conditions include misalignment of the eyes (strabismus) and differing refractive powers of the eyes (anisometropia). Also called (colloquially) **lazy eye**. **—amblyopic** *adj.*

ambulation *n.* the act of walking.

ambulatory care medical or psychological services—including observation, diagnosis, treatment, and rehabilitation—provided to individuals on an outpatient, nonemergency basis, often at a doctor's office or clinic.

amelioration *n.* a change for the better in a condition, especially one involving a disease or disorder. **—ameliorative** *adj., n.*

amenorrhea *n.* the absence of menstruation. When menstruation fails to begin after puberty, the condition is called **primary amenorrhea**. If menstrual periods stop, in the absence of pregnancy or menopause, after starting, the condition is known as **secondary amenorrhea**.

American Psychiatric Association (APA) a national medical and professional organization whose physician members specialize in the diagnosis, treatment, and prevention of mental disorders. Founded in 1844, its objectives include the improvement of care for people with mental illnesses, the promotion of research and professional education in psychiatry, and the dissemination of psychological knowledge through nationwide public information, education, and awareness programs and materials. Its extensive publications include the *Diagnostic and Statistical Manual of Mental Disorders* (see DSM–IV–TR), the most widely used psychiatric reference in the world.

American Psychological Association (APA) a scientific and professional organization founded in 1892 that represents psychology in the United States and is the largest association of psychologists worldwide. Its mission is to advance psychology as a science, as a profession, and as a means of promoting health and human welfare. Among its specific goals are the promotion of psychological research and improvement of research methods and conditions; the establishment and maintenance of high standards of professional ethics and conduct of its members; and the increase and diffusion of psychological knowledge through a variety of means, including scholarly journals, the APA *Publication Manual*, books, videotapes, and electronic databases.

American Sign Language (ASL) see SIGN LANGUAGE.

Ames room an irregularly shaped but apparently rectangular room in which cues for DEPTH PERCEPTION are used experimentally to distort the viewer's perception of the relative size of objects within the room. Also called **Ames distorted room**. [Adelbert Ames, Jr. (1880–1955), U.S. psychologist, inventor, and artist]

ametropia *n.* any refractive abnormality of the eye, including MYOPIA (nearsightedness), HYPEROPIA (farsightedness), and ASTIGMATISM. Such an inability of the eye to bend (refract) light into perfect focus on the retina reduces visual acuity and causes blurriness.

amimia *n.* a language or communication disorder characterized by an inability to convey meaning through appropriate gestures (**motor** or **expressive amimia**) or to interpret the gestures of others (**sensory** or **receptive amimia**).

amine *n.* a chemical compound that contains one or more amino groups ($-NH_2$). Several neurotransmitters are amines, including ACETYLCHOLINE, NOREPINEPHRINE, and SEROTONIN. See also BIOGENIC AMINE.

amino acid an organic compound that contains an amino group ($-NH_2$) and a carboxyl group ($-COOH$), 20 of which are constituents of proteins; 9 of these are **essential amino acids**, that is, they cannot be synthesized by the body and must be obtained from foods. Other amino acids (e.g., GLUTAMIC ACID, GLYCINE) are neurotransmitters or precursors to neurotransmitters.

aminoketone *n.* the chemical classification of the antidepressant agent BUPROPION, whose structure and mechanism of action differ from other marketed antidepressants. Although the specific method of action is unknown it is presumed to involve NORADRENERGIC or DOPAMINERGIC mechanisms.

amitriptyline *n.* a TRICYCLIC ANTIDEPRESSANT introduced into clinical use in 1961. It is a potent inhibitor of SEROTONIN reuptake, thereby increasing the availability of serotonin for neurotransmission, but its significant side effects and toxicity in overdose have led to a decline in its use in favor of the SSRIs and other agents. U.S. trade name: **Elavil**.

amnesia *n.* partial or complete loss of memory. Either temporary or permanent, it may be due to physiological factors such as injury, disease, or substance use, or to psychological factors such as a traumatic experience. A disturbance in memory marked by inability to learn new information is called **anterograde amnesia** and one marked by inability to recall previously learned information or past events is called **retrograde amnesia**. When severe enough to interfere markedly with social or occupational functioning or to represent a significant decline from a previous level of functioning, the memory loss is known as **amnestic disorder.** —**amnesiac** *adj.*, *n.* —**amnesic** or **amnestic** *adj.*

amniocentesis *n.* a method of examining fetal chromosomes for any abnormality or for determination of sex. A hollow needle is inserted through the mother's abdominal wall into the uterus, enabling the collection of amniotic fluid, which contains fetal cells. Compare CHORIONIC VILLUS SAMPLING.

amok (**amuck**) *n.* a CULTURE-BOUND SYNDROME observed among males in Malaysia, the Philippines, and other parts of southeast Asia. The individual experiences a period of social withdrawal and apathy, followed by a violent, unprovoked attack on nearby individuals. If not overpowered or killed, the affected male eventually collapses from exhaustion and afterward has no memory of the event. See also MAL DE PELEA.

amorphosynthesis *n.* a disturbance in the ability to synthesize multiple sensory input from a particular side of the body.

AMPA receptor see GLUTAMATE RECEPTOR.

amphetamine abuse a pattern of use of amphetamines or amphetamine-like substances manifested by recurrent significant adverse consequences related to the repeated ingestion of these substances. See also SUBSTANCE ABUSE.

amphetamine dependence a cluster of cognitive, behavioral, and physiological symptoms indicating continued use of an amphetamine or amphetamine-like substance despite significant substance-related problems. See also SUBSTANCE DEPENDENCE.

amphetamine intoxication a reversible syndrome caused by the recent ingestion of amphetamines or amphetamine-like substances. It is characterized by behavioral or psychological changes (e.g., inappropriate aggressive behavior, impaired judgment, suspiciousness, and paranoia), as well as one or more signs of physiological involvement (e.g., unsteady gait, impairment in attention or memory).

amphetamines *pl. n.* a group of drugs that stimulate the RETICULAR FORMATION and cause a release of stored dopamine and norepinephrine. The effect is a prolonged state of arousal and relief from feelings of fatigue (see CNS STIMULANT). Introduced in 1932, amphetamines are prone to abuse and dependence, and tolerance develops progressively with continued use. Although widely used in the past for weight loss, relief of depression, and other indications, modern use of amphetamines is more circumscribed because of their adverse effects. They are now used mainly to manage symptoms of attention deficit/hyperactivity disorder and to treat certain cases of severe depression or narcolepsy.

Amphetamines include **amphetamine** itself (the prototype; U.S. trade name **Benzedrine**), **dextroamphetamine** (or **dexamphetamine**), and **methamphetamine**. Some forms and derivatives (including MDA and MDMA) have been manufactured as recreational hallucinogenic drugs.

amphetamine withdrawal a characteristic withdrawal syndrome that develops after cessation of (or reduction in) prolonged, heavy consumption of an amphetamine or amphetamine-like substance. The essential characteristic is depressed mood, sometimes severe, and there may also be fatigue, disturbed sleep, increased appetite, vivid and unpleasant dreams, or PSYCHO-MOTOR RETARDATION or agitation. See also SUBSTANCE WITHDRAWAL.

amplitude *n.* magnitude or extent (e.g., of a stimulus) or peak value (e.g., of a sinusoid wave).

amusia *n.* loss of musical ability, usually associated with a lesion in the left PARIETAL LOBE. The inability to reproduce melodies is called **motor** (or **expressive**) **amusia**, while the inability to recognize and appreciate various characteristics of musical tones and sequences is called **sensory** (or **receptive**) **amusia**. Although the latter is a type of amusia, it is also considered a type of AUDITORY AGNOSIA.

amygdala *n.* an almond-shaped structure in the TEMPORAL LOBE that is a component of the LIMBIC SYSTEM and considered part of the BASAL GANGLIA. It comprises two main groups of nuclei—the **corticomedial group** and the **basolateral group**—and through widespread connections with other brain areas has numerous viscerosensory and autonomic functions as well as an important role in memory, emotion, perception of threat, and fear learning. Also called **amygdaloid body**; **amygdaloid complex**; **amygdaloid nuclei.** —**amygdaloid** *adj.*

amyloid plaque see SENILE PLAQUE.

amyloid precursor protein (**APP**) see BETA-AMYLOID.

amyotrophic lateral sclerosis (**ALS**) a rapidly progressive adult-onset disease involving degeneration of both lower MOTOR NEURONS, responsible for muscle contraction, and upper motor neurons, responsible for MUSCLE SPINDLE sensitivity, and leading to death within 5 years of diagnosis. Symptoms include muscular atrophy and weakness, partial and complete paralysis, speech impairment, and difficulties swallowing or breathing. Amyotrophic lateral sclerosis is often used interchangeably with MOTOR NEURON DISEASE, especially in the United States. Also called **Lou Gehrig's disease**.

anabolism *n.* see METABOLISM. —**anabolic** *adj.*

anaclitic depression dependent depression: intense sadness and DYSPHORIA stemming from early disruptions in caring relationships, such as deprivation, inconsistency, or overindulgence, that lead to an indefinite fear of loss of love, abandonment, and impoverishment. The individual expresses a child-like dependency; has little capacity for frustration; and desires to be soothed directly and immediately. Compare INTROJECTIVE DEPRESSION.

anaclitic identification in psychoanalytic theory, the first phase of the IDENTIFICATION process, which is rooted in the child's initial total dependence on the mother (as well as others) for basic biological and emotional needs. The child acquires the mother's characteristics in the service of becoming his or her own source of reinforcement and comfort. The child incorporates the mother into his or her superego (see EGO-IDEAL). A weaker version of this is seen with other significant figures in the child's life (e.g., teachers).

anaclitic object choice in psychoanalytic theory, the selection of a mate or other LOVE OBJECT who will provide the same type of assistance, comfort, and support that the individual received from the parents during infancy and early childhood: A woman chooses a man resembling or modeled on her father and a man chooses a woman like his mother. Austrian psychiatrist Sigmund Freud (1856–1939) contrasted this with NARCISSISTIC OBJECT CHOICE, which involves selecting a mate who is similar to oneself. Also called **anaclitic love**.

anaerobic exercise strength-based physical activity, such as weight training and sprinting, that occurs in short, intense bursts with limited oxygen intake. The **anaerobic threshold** is the point at which energy use by the body is so great as to require the muscles to begin producing energy in the absence of adequate oxygen. Compare AEROBIC EXERCISE.

anaesthesia n. see ANESTHESIA.

Anafranil n. a trade name for CLOMIPRAMINE.

anaglyph n. a single picture made from two copies of the same image that differ in color and are slightly displaced from one another in the horizontal plane. When viewed through identically colored glasses, the image appears three dimensional as a result of STEREOPSIS.

anal-aggressive personality in psychoanalytic theory, a personality type characterized by obstinacy, obstructionism, defiance, and passive resistance. Such traits are held to stem from the ANAL STAGE, in which the child asserted himself or herself by withholding feces. Also called **anal-aggressive character**. See also ANAL PERSONALITY.

analgesia n. absence of or reduction in the sensation of pain. Drugs and other substances that alleviate pain are called **analgesics**. The former usually are classed as opioid (narcotic) or nonopioid (nonnarcotic), depending on their chemical composition and potential for physical dependence. Compare ALGESIA. —**analgesic** adj.

analogical thinking thinking characterized by extrapolations from the familiar to the unfamiliar, rather than the use of formal logic or consecutive reasoning. It is particularly important in problem solving and learning, in which known similarities between aspects of certain entities are used to make assumptions about other aspects or entities. Also called **analogical reasoning**.

analogies test a test of the participant's ability to comprehend the relationship between two items and then extend that relationship to a different situation: For example, paintbrush is to paint as pen is to ___.

analogue experiment an experiment in which a phenomenon is produced in the laboratory in order to obtain greater control over the phenomenon. Examples include the use of hypnosis, drugs, and sensory deprivation to produce brief periods of abnormal behavior that simulate those of psychopathological conditions.

analogue study a research design in which the procedures or participants used are similar but not identical to the situation of interest. For example, if researchers are interested in the effects of therapist gender on client perceptions of therapist trustworthiness, they may use undergraduate students who are not clients and provide simulated counseling dialogues that are typed and identified as offered by a male or female therapist. The results of such studies are assumed to offer a high degree of experimental control and to generalize to actual clinical practice. Also called **analogue model**.

analogy n. **1.** in biology, a similarity of function in bodily structures with different evolutionary origins. For example, the hand of a human and the trunk of an elephant are analogous in that both are used for manipulating objects. See also HOMOLOGY. **2.** a method of argument that relies on an inference that a similarity between two or more entities in some attributes justifies a probable assumption that they will be similar in other attributes. —**analogical** adj. —**analogous** adj.

anal personality in psychoanalytic theory, a pattern of personality traits believed to stem from the ANAL STAGE of PSYCHOSEXUAL DEVELOPMENT, when defecation is a primary source of pleasure. Special satisfaction from retention of the feces will result in an adult **anal-retentive personality**, marked by frugality, obstinacy, and orderliness, whereas fixation on expelling feces will produce an aggressive and disorderly **anal-expulsive personality**. Also called **anal character**. See also ANAL-AGGRESSIVE PERSONALITY.

anal stage in psychoanalytic theory, the second stage of PSYCHOSEXUAL DEVELOPMENT, typically occurring during the 2nd year of life, in which the child's interest and sexual pleasure are focused on the expulsion and retention of feces and the sadistic instinct is linked to the desire to both possess and destroy the OBJECT. Fixation during this stage results in an ANAL PERSONALITY. Also called **anal phase**.

analysand n. in psychoanalysis, a patient who is undergoing analysis.

analysis *n.* see PSYCHOANALYSIS. —**analytic** or **analytical** *adj.*

analysis by synthesis any theory of information processing stating that both data-driven processes and conceptually driven processes interact in the recognition and interpretation of sensory input. According to such theories, which are associated particularly with speech perception and language processing, the person analyzes the original physical stimulus input, hypothesizes what it is, based on experience or learning, determines what the input would be like if the hypothesis were correct, and then assesses whether the input is actually like that.

analysis of covariance (**ANCOVA**) an extension of the ANALYSIS OF VARIANCE that adjusts the dependent variable for the influence of a correlated variable (COVARIATE) that is not being investigated but may influence the study results. An analysis of covariance is appropriate in two types of cases: (a) when experimental groups are suspected to differ on a background-correlated variable in addition to the differences attributed to the experimental treatment and (b) where adjustment on a covariate can increase the precision of the experiment.

analysis of variance (**ANOVA**) any of several statistical procedures that isolate the joint and separate effects of independent variables upon a dependent variable and test them for statistical significance (i.e., to determine whether they are greater than they would be if obtained by chance alone). See also GENERAL LINEAR MODEL.

analyst *n.* generally, one who practices psychoanalysis. This is usually a PSYCHOANALYST in the tradition of Austrian psychiatrist Sigmund Freud (1856–1939); however, the term is also applied to therapists adhering to the methods of Swiss psychiatrist Carl Jung (1875–1961) (see ANALYTIC PSYCHOLOGY) or Austrian psychiatrist Alfred Adler (1870–1936) (see INDIVIDUAL PSYCHOLOGY).

analytical intelligence in the TRIARCHIC THEORY OF INTELLIGENCE, the skills measured by conventional tests of intelligence, such as analysis, comparison, evaluation, critique, and judgment. Compare CREATIVE INTELLIGENCE; PRACTICAL INTELLIGENCE.

analytical psychotherapy 1. a short-term method of psychotherapy using psychoanalytic principles but with less depth of analysis, more active intervention on the part of the therapist, and less frequent sessions than are required for a true psychoanalysis. **2.** historically, an alternative method to psychoanalysis proposed by Viennese psychoanalyst Wilhelm Stekel (1868–1940).

analytic psychology the system of psychoanalysis proposed by Swiss psychiatrist Carl Jung (1875–1961), in which the psyche is interpreted primarily in terms of philosophical values, primordial images and symbols, and a drive for self-fulfillment. Jung's basic concepts are (a) the EGO, which maintains a balance between conscious and unconscious activities and gradually develops a unique self through INDIVIDUATION; (b) the PERSONAL UNCONSCIOUS, made up of memories, thoughts, and feelings based on personal experience; (c) the COLLECTIVE UNCONSCIOUS, made up of ancestral images, or ARCHETYPES, that constitute the inherited foundation of an individual's intellectual life and personality; and (d) dynamic polarities, or tension systems, which derive their psychic energy from the LIBIDO and influence the development and expression of the ego: conscious versus unconscious values, introversion versus extraversion, sublimation versus repression, rational versus irrational. Also called **analytical psychology**.

anamnesis *n.* a patient's account of his or her developmental, family, and medical history prior to the onset of a mental or physical disorder. Compare CATAMNESIS.

anaphora *n.* in linguistics, the use of a word (often a pronoun) to refer back to a word used earlier, usually to avoid repetition. In *You take the high road, I'll take the low one*, the use of *one* to mean *road* is an example of anaphora. Ability to form and process such constructions has been a major preoccupation of GENERATIVE GRAMMAR and PSYCHOLINGUISTICS. See also ANTECEDENT. —**anaphoric** *adj.*

anaphylaxis *n.* hypersensitivity to the introduction of a substance (e.g., a food item such as peanuts or a drug such as penicillin) into body tissues, resulting from previous exposure to it. Symptoms, which may include breathing difficulties and wheezing, are sudden and severe, progressing rapidly to **anaphylactic shock**—pulmonary edema, heart arrhythmia, shock, loss of consciousness, and potential respiratory or cardiac arrest—if untreated. —**anaphylactic** *adj.*

anastomosis *n.* (*pl.* **anastomoses**) **1.** the surgical connection of two normally separate structures. **2.** an alternate pathway formed by branching of a main circuit, as found in nerves, blood vessels, and lymphatic vessels.

anatomically detailed doll a doll with anatomically correct genitalia that is used during an interview with a child to help a professional decide whether the child has been sexually abused. Also called **anatomically correct doll**.

anchor *n.* a reference point used when making a series of subjective judgments. For example, in an experiment in which participants gauge distances between objects, the experimenter introduces an anchor by informing the participants that the distance between two of the stimulus objects is a given value. That value then functions as a reference for participants in their subsequent judgments. Also called **anchor point**.

anchoring bias the tendency, in forming perceptions or making quantitative judgments of some entity under conditions of uncertainty, to give excessive weight to the initial starting value (or ANCHOR), based on the first received information or one's initial judgment, and not to modify this anchor sufficiently in light of later information. For example, estimates of the product of $9 \times 8 \times 7 \times 6 \times 5 \times 4 \times 3 \times 2 \times 1$ tend to be higher than estimates of the product of $1 \times 2 \times 3 \times 4 \times 5 \times 6 \times 7 \times 8 \times 9$. Also called **anchoring effect**.

anchor test a specific set of test items used in equating alternate forms of a particular test. One alternate form is administered to one group of participants, another is administered to a different group, and the items comprising the anchor test are administered to both groups. Scores on each alternate form are then compared with scores on the anchor test.

ancillary *adj.* supporting or supplemental but not necessarily critical to some function or event.

ANCOVA acronym for ANALYSIS OF COVARIANCE.

androgen *n.* any of a class of steroid hormones that act as the principal male SEX HORMONES, the major one being TESTOSTERONE. Androgens are produced mainly by the testes and influence the development of masculine primary and secondary SEX CHARACTERISTICS. They are also secreted in small quantities by the cortex of the adrenal gland and can be produced synthetically. —**androgenic** *adj.*

androgen-insensitivity syndrome an inherited condition affecting the development of reproductive and genital organs, caused by varying degrees of insensitivity to androgens. There are two forms: **complete**, in which the insensitivity is total, resulting in external genitalia that are female; and **partial**, in which some sensitivity to the hormones allows for external genitalia that may be structurally ambiguous. In both forms, however, the internal organs are male (i.e., testes). Also called **testicular feminization syndrome**.

androgyny *n.* **1.** the presence of male and female characteristics in one individual. **2.** the state of being neither distinguishably masculine or feminine in appearance, as in dress. See also GYNANDROMORPH; HERMAPHRODITE. —**androgyne** *n.* —**androgynous** *adj.*

anecdotal method an investigational technique in which informal verbal reports of incidents casually observed (e.g., a particular feat of a particular animal) are accepted as useful information. The anecdotal method is scientifically inadequate but can offer clues as to areas of investigation that warrant more systematic, controlled research.

anencephaly *n.* congenital absence of the cranial vault (the bones forming the rear of the skull), with cerebral hemispheres completely missing or reduced to small masses. Infants born with anencephaly are usually blind, deaf, unconscious, and unable to feel pain. —**anencephalic** *adj.*

anesthesia (anaesthesia) *n.* the loss of sensitivity to stimuli, either in a particular area (local) or throughout the body and accompanied by loss of consciousness (general). It may be produced intentionally, for example via the administration of drugs (called **anesthetics**) or the use of techniques such as ACUPUNCTURE or hypnotic suggestion, or it may occur spontaneously as a result of injury or disease. —**anesthetic** *adj.*

aneurysm (aneurism) *n.* an enlargement (widening) at some point in an artery caused by the pressure of blood on weakened tissues, often at junctions where arteries split off from one another. —**aneurysmal** *adj.*

anger *n.* an emotion characterized by tension and hostility arising from frustration, real or imagined injury by another, or perceived injustice. It can manifest itself in behaviors designed to remove the object of the anger (e.g., determined action) or behaviors designed merely to express the emotion (e.g., swearing). Anger is distinct from, but a significant activator of, AGGRESSION, which is behavior intended to harm someone or something. Despite their mutually influential relationship, anger is neither necessary nor sufficient for aggression to occur.

anger control therapy a treatment that makes use of therapist-guided progressive exposure to anger-provoking cues in conjunction with therapist modeling, client rehearsal, assertiveness training, and other forms of coping skills training. Practiced in both individual and group settings, the intervention is used with clients who have general difficulty with anger (e.g., intensity, frequency, or mode of expression) or with clients who have specific disorders.

anger management techniques used by individuals—sometimes in counseling or therapy—to control their inappropriate reactions to anger-provoking stimuli and to express their feelings of anger in appropriate ways that are respectful of others. Such techniques include using relaxation methods to reduce physiological responses to anger, replacing exaggerated or overly dramatic thoughts with more rational ones (see COGNITIVE RESTRUCTURING), communicating more calmly and thoughtfully about one's anger, and removing oneself from situations or circumstances that provoke anger or avoiding them altogether.

anger stage the second of the five STAGES OF GRIEF described by Swiss-born U.S. psychiatrist Elisabeth Kübler-Ross (1926–2004). It is characterized by anger, resentment, or even rage at one's own (or at an important other's) impending or actual death, other great loss, or trauma.

angiography *n.* the visualization of blood vessels by radiological techniques, used as an aid in diagnosing abnormalities or discovering blockages. A dye opaque to X-rays is injected into a vessel and any disruption of blood flow is revealed as a contrasting pattern. When the imaging is of arteries it is also called **arteriography**.

The image produced is called an **angiogram** (or **arteriogram**).

angioma *n.* a tumor of the vascular system: an abnormal mass of blood vessels or lymph vessels.

angiotensin *n.* one of a family of peptides, including angiotensins I, II, and III, that are produced by the enzymatic action of RENIN on a precursor protein (**angiotensinogen**) in the bloodstream. Their effects include narrowing of blood vessels (VASOCONSTRICTION), increased blood pressure, thirst, and stimulation of ALDOSTERONE release from the adrenal glands.

angst *n.* in EXISTENTIALISM, a state of anguish or despair in which a person recognizes the fundamental uncertainty of existence and understands the significance of conscious choice and personal responsibility.

angular gyrus a ridge along the lower surface of the PARIETAL LOBE of the brain, formed by a junction of the superior and middle temporal gyri. This region has been proposed as the key area of reading and writing function. Lesions are associated with ALEXIA and AGRAPHIA, and structural abnormalities with DYSLEXIA.

anhedonia *n.* the inability to enjoy experiences or activities that normally would be pleasurable. It is one of two defining symptoms of a MAJOR DEPRESSIVE EPISODE (the other being a persistent depressed mood), but is also seen in other disorders, including schizophrenia. —**anhedonic** *adj.*

anima *n.* **1.** in the earlier writings of Swiss psychiatrist Carl Jung (1875–1961), a person's innermost being, which is in closest contact with the UNCONSCIOUS and is contrasted with the PERSONA, or the externally directed part of a person. **2.** in Jung's later writings, (a) an ARCHETYPE that represents universal feminine characteristics or (b) the unconscious feminine aspect of the male psyche. Compare ANIMUS.

animal-assisted therapy the therapeutic use of pets to enhance individuals' physical, social, emotional, or cognitive functioning. Animal-assisted therapy may be used, for example, to help people receive and give affection, especially in developing communication and social skills. It may be most effective for people who have suffered losses or separation from loved ones. Also called **pet-assisted therapy**; **pet therapy**.

animal behavior the scientific study of the behavior of animals, typically nonhuman animals. It includes the fields of ETHOLOGY, COMPARATIVE PSYCHOLOGY, and BEHAVIORAL ECOLOGY. Areas of study include aggression, cognition, communication, courtship, defensive behavior, emotionality, grooming behavior, mate selection, play, social behavior, foraging, and parental behavior.

animal care and use the treatment of nonhuman animals used in research and experimentation. Various regulations, standards, and principles have been developed to protect the well-being of such animals and ensure that they are treated in a humane and ethical manner.

animal cognition the inferred processes that are used by animals in solving environmental and social problems but that cannot be observed directly. This includes problem-solving abilities that appear not to depend on rote memory or trial-and-error learning, suggesting that animals may be able to reason about potential solutions and therefore to solve problems with apparent spontaneity. See also ANIMAL INTELLIGENCE; SOCIAL COGNITION; THEORY OF MIND.

animal communication the study of how nonhuman animals communicate with each other either to provide HONEST SIGNALS or to manage or manipulate the behavior of others. Assessment of individuals based on their behavior or signals may be a major function of animal communication.

animal dominance the relationship between animals that allows some individuals to have greater access to resources (e.g., food, shelter, mates) than others in the group. Dominance ranks are often thought to be linear, with a clear ordering from most to least dominant, but may also be dependent (i.e., based on kin or age relationships) or governed by coalitions in which some subordinate individuals can outrank more dominant ones by acting together.

animal–human comparison the use of results from studies of ANIMAL BEHAVIOR to make generalizations about human behavior. Often, studies of animals are specifically designed to provide explicit models for some aspect of human behavior, but studies of the diversity of behavior across different animal species can be used both to understand the origins of certain types of human behavior and to suggest alternative solutions to human problems based on solutions that animals have developed. See COMPARATIVE PSYCHOLOGY.

animal intelligence the various abilities of animals to solve problems in their environment through mechanisms of ANIMAL LEARNING and ANIMAL COGNITION. Psychologists formerly thought that animal intelligence was best measured relative to human skills, with a linear progression of intelligence from simple to complex organisms. Current thinking evaluates skills relative to the particular problems each species faces and argues against simple phylogenetic relationships.

animal learning a field of psychology that studies the learning ability of nonhuman animals. The forms of learning studied are often less complex than those studied in human beings, which enables a degree of precision and control in studies of animal learning that is not always possible with human participants.

animal magnetism a hypothetical physical force that allegedly can have a curative effect when focused on ailing parts of the body, often through the use of a magnetized wand, magnetized rods, or a magnetized bath (baquet). See MESMERISM.

animal model characteristics or conditions of an animal that are similar to those of humans, thus making the animal suitable for studying human behavior, processes, disorders or diseases, and so forth.

animal phobia a persistent and irrational fear of a particular type of animal, such as snakes, cats, dogs, insects, mice, birds, or spiders. The focus of fear is often anticipated harm or danger. Situations in which the phobic animal may be encountered are often avoided or else endured with intense anxiety or distress.

animal psychology see COMPARATIVE PSYCHOLOGY.

animal rights the rights of animals to be treated with respect and to be free from exploitation and abuse by humans. Proponents of animal rights believe that it is morally wrong to harm, kill, or exploit animals for any human uses, including any type of research, and many advocate that all sentient creatures are in some ways the moral equals of humans. Proponents of **animal welfare**, however, typically make a moral distinction between humans and animals and believe that, while individuals have an obligation to treat animals humanely, certain research involving animals is medically and scientifically necessary. See also ANIMAL CARE AND USE.

animism *n.* the belief that natural phenomena or inanimate objects are alive or possess lifelike characteristics, such as intentions, desires, and feelings. A well-known and often cited phenomenon in PRECAUSAL THINKING, animism was considered by Swiss psychologist Jean Piaget (1896–1980) to be characteristic of the thought of children in the PREOPERATIONAL STAGE, later fading out and being replaced by the strong belief in the universal nature of physical causality. —**animistic** *adj.*

animus *n.* in ANALYTIC PSYCHOLOGY, (a) an ARCHETYPE that represents universal masculine characteristics or (b) the unconscious masculine component of the female psyche. Compare ANIMA.

Anna O. the pseudonym of Austrian social worker and feminist Bertha Pappenheim (1859–1936), who was a patient of Austrian physician Josef Breuer (1842–1925), a colleague of Austrian psychiatrist Sigmund Freud (1856–1939). Breuer's treatment of her hysteria was written up in an early case study that was an important precursor to PSYCHOANALYSIS. See also TALKING CURE.

anniversary reaction a strong emotional response on the anniversary of a significant event. It most commonly involves depressive symptoms around the same time of the year that the death of a loved one or a severe disappointment or adverse event occurred.

anoetic *adj.* **1.** not involving or subject to intellectual or cognitive processes. Emotions are sometimes considered anoetic. **2.** describing a level of knowledge or memory in which there is no consciousness of knowing or remembering. Compare AUTONOETIC; NOETIC. —**anoesis** *n.*

anomalous experience any of a variety of conscious states, often categorized as ALTERED STATES OF CONSCIOUSNESS, that are uncommon or that are believed to deviate from the usually accepted explanations of reality. Examples include OUT-OF-BODY EXPERIENCES, mystical experiences, lucid dreaming, and SYNESTHESIA.

anomaly *n.* anything that is irregular or deviates from the norm, often referring to a congenital or developmental defect. —**anomalous** *adj.*

anomia *n.* loss or impairment of the ability to name objects. All individuals with APHASIA exhibit anomia, and the extent of naming difficulty is a good general measure of aphasia severity. —**anomic** *adj.*

anomic aphasia one of eight classically identified types of APHASIA, characterized by impairment in object naming (anomia) in the absence of other significant language deficits. Conversational speech is fluent, with normal utterance length and grammatically well-formed sentences. Auditory comprehension is good for everyday conversation, but there may be some difficulty with complex syntax or in difficult listening situations. Also called **amnestic** (or **amnesic**) **aphasia**; **nominal aphasia**.

anopia *n.* blindness in one or both halves of the visual field as a result of a defect in the peripheral or central visual system. Also called **anopsia**.

anorchism *n.* congenital absence of one or both testes. The etiology is unknown but genetic factors may be involved. Also called **anorchia**.

anorectant *n.* see APPETITE SUPPRESSANT. Also called **anorexiant**.

anorexia *n.* absence or loss of appetite for food or, less commonly, for other desires (e.g., sex), especially when chronic. It may be primarily a psychological disorder, as in ANOREXIA NERVOSA, or it may have physiological causes, such as hypopituitarism. —**anorectic** or **anorexic** *adj., n.*

anorexia nervosa an eating disorder, occurring most frequently in adolescent girls, that involves persistent refusal of food, excessive fear of weight gain, refusal to maintain minimally normal body weight, disturbed perception of body image, and amenorrhea (absence of at least three menstrual periods). See also REVERSE ANOREXIA.

anorgasmia *n.* the inability to achieve orgasm. Also called **anorgasmy**. See also FEMALE ORGASMIC DISORDER; MALE ORGASMIC DISORDER. —**anorgasmic** *adj.*

anorthopia *n.* asymmetrical or distorted vision, sometimes associated with STRABISMUS.

anosmia *n.* absence or loss of the ability to smell, which may be general or limited to certain odors. General or total anosmia implies inability to smell all odorants on both sides of the nose, whereas partial anosmia implies an inability to smell certain odorants. —**anosmic** *adj.*

anosognosia *n.* a neurologically based failure to recognize the existence of a deficit or disorder, such as hearing loss, poor vision, or paralysis. ANTON'S SYNDROME is an example of anosognosia for blindness.

ANOVA acronym for ANALYSIS OF VARIANCE.

anoxemia *n.* the absence of oxygen in the blood, a condition that frequently results in loss of consciousness and brain damage. See also HYPOXEMIA. —**anoxemic** *adj.*

anoxia *n.* total lack of oxygen in the body tissues, including the brain. Consequences depend on the severity of the anoxia and the specific areas of the brain that are affected, but can include generalized cognitive deficits or more focal deficits in memory, perception, or EXECUTIVE FUNCTION. Anoxia sometimes is used as a synonym of HYPOXIA. —**anoxic** *adj.*

ANS abbreviation for AUTONOMIC NERVOUS SYSTEM.

Antabuse *n.* a trade name for DISULFIRAM.

antagonist *n.* **1.** a drug or other chemical agent that inhibits the action of another substance. For example, an antagonist may combine with the substance to alter and thus inactivate it (**chemical antagonism**); an antagonist may reduce the effects of the substance by binding to the same receptor without stimulating it, which decreases the number of available receptors (**pharmacological antagonism**); or an antagonist may bind to a different receptor and produce a physiological effect opposite to that of the substance (**physiological antagonism**). **2.** a contracting muscle whose action generates force opposing the intended direction of movement. This force may serve to slow the movement rapidly as it approaches the target or it may help to define the movement end point. Compare AGONIST. —**antagonism** *n.* —**antagonistic** *adj.*

antecedent *n.* **1.** an event, circumstance, or stimulus that precedes some other event and often elicits, signals, or sets the occasion for a particular behavior or response. See also CONTINGENCY. **2.** in linguistics, the noun or noun phrase to which a pronoun (especially a relative pronoun, such as *who, that,* or *which*) refers back. For example, in *the train that I caught yesterday,* the antecedent of *that* is *train.* See ANAPHORA.

anterior *adj.* in front of or toward the front. In reference to two-legged upright animals, this term is sometimes used interchangeably with VENTRAL to mean toward the top or head. Compare POSTERIOR. —**anteriorly** *adv.*

anterior commissure see COMMISSURE.

anterior horn 1. the frontmost division of each lateral VENTRICLE in the brain. **2.** see VENTRAL HORN.

anterograde amnesia see AMNESIA.

anterograde degeneration a pattern of neu-

ron destruction following axonal injury that spreads forward along the axon, away from the nerve cell body. Also called **Wallerian degeneration**. Compare RETROGRADE DEGENERATION.

anterolateral system a major SOMATOSENSORY SYSTEM consisting of nerve fibers that originate mostly from DORSAL HORN cells and ascend in the white matter of the spinal cord, conveying information about pain, temperature, and touch to higher centers. It includes the SPINOTHALAMIC TRACT; the **spinoreticular tract**, traveling through the spinal cord to the reticular formation of the brainstem; and the **spinomesencephalic tract**, traveling through the spinal cord to the mesencephalon (midbrain).

anthropocentrism *n.* the explicit or implicit assumption that human experience is the central reality and, by extension, the idea that all phenomena can be evaluated in the light of their relationship to humans. —**anthropocentric** *adj.*

anthropoid *adj.* resembling a human being. The term is usually applied to the tailless apes: specifically, gorillas, orangutans, chimpanzees, bonobos, and gibbons.

anthropological linguistics the branch of linguistics that draws connections between the characteristics of a particular language and the cultural practices, social structures, and worldview of the society in which it is spoken (see LINGUISTIC DETERMINISM; LINGUISTIC RELATIVITY).

anthropology *n.* the study of human beings. This typically involves the description and explanation of similarities and differences among human groups in their languages, aesthetic expressions, belief systems, and social structures over the range of human geography and chronology. **Physical anthropology** focuses on the origin, evolution, and environmental adaptation of human groups, while **sociocultural anthropology** is concerned with the development and functioning of customs, beliefs, and institutions. Outside the United States, this latter subdivision is often called ETHNOLOGY. —**anthropological** *adj.* —**anthropologist** *n.*

anthropometry *n.* **1.** the scientific study of how the size and proportions of the human body are affected by such variables as age, sex, and ethnic and cultural groups. **2.** the taking of measurements of the human body for purposes of comparison and study. —**anthropometric** *adj.* —**anthropometrist** *n.*

anthropomorphism *n.* **1.** the attribution of human characteristics to nonhuman entities such as deities, spirits, animals, plants, or inanimate objects. **2.** in COMPARATIVE PSYCHOLOGY, the tendency to interpret the behavior and mental processes of nonhuman animals in terms of human abilities. A variation is anthropocentrism, which uses human behavior as the standard by which the behavior of nonhuman animals, for example, intelligence, is evaluated. Compare ZOOMORPHISM. —**anthropomorphic** *adj.*

antiandrogen *n.* a substance that reduces or blocks the physiological effects of androgens, the male sex hormones, on tissues normally responsive to these hormones. Examples include **bicalutamide** (U.S. trade name: **Casodex**), **finasteride** (U.S. trade name: **Propecia**), **flutamide** (U.S. trade name: **Eulexin**), and **nilutamide** (U.S. trade name: **Nilandron**). They correct the effects of excessive levels of male sex hormones and may be used to control hair loss and prostate cancer in males and to reverse masculine traits (e.g., excessive facial hair) in females. More controversially, antiandrogens have been used in the treatment of repeat sex offenders (see CHEMICAL CASTRATION). Also called **androgen antagonist**.

antianxiety medication see ANXIOLYTIC.

antibody *n.* a modified protein molecule, produced by B LYMPHOCYTES, that interacts with an ANTIGEN and renders it harmless. Each type of antibody is designed to interact with a specific antigen and can be mass-produced following previous exposure to an identical antigen. See IMMUNE SYSTEM.

anticathexis *n.* in psychoanalytic theory, a process in which the EGO withdraws PSYCHIC ENERGY from certain unconscious wishes and ideas and uses it to strengthen other ideas and wishes capable of blocking their entrance into consciousness. The **anticathected** idea may be similar to the original idea or opposite but related to it: for example, philanthropy may neutralize an unconscious wish to hoard. Also called **countercathexis**. See also CATHEXIS.

anticholinergic drug any pharmacological agent that blocks or otherwise interferes with the release of the neurotransmitter acetylcholine and thus disrupts the transmission of impulses along parasympathetic routes. Because they act at MUSCARINIC RECEPTORS (a category of acetylcholine receptors), these agents are also known as **antimuscarinic drugs**. A variety of anticholinergic drugs are used to treat neurological disorders, many as ANTIPARKINSONIAN DRUGS. TRICYCLIC ANTIDEPRESSANTS and some conventional ANTIPSYCHOTICS also have anticholinergic activity. Also called **parasympatholytic drug**.

anticholinergic syndrome a disorder produced by anticholinergic drugs and due to their antagonistic effects at ACETYLCHOLINE RECEPTORS, marked by symptoms involving both the peripheral and central nervous systems. The former include dry mucous membranes, dry mouth, and flushed skin and face, while the latter include ataxia (unsteady gait), drowsiness, slurred speech, confusion and disorientation, hallucinations, and memory deficits, particularly of short-term memory.

anticholinesterase *n.* see CHOLINESTERASE.

anticonformity *n.* a deliberate, self-conscious refusal to comply with accepted social standards, often accompanied by the expression of ideas, beliefs, or judgments that challenge those standards. Anticonformity is motivated by rebelliousness or obstinacy rather than the need to express oneself sincerely. Also called **counterconformity**. Compare CONFORMITY; NONCONFORMITY.

anticonvulsant *n.* any drug used to reduce the frequency or severity of epileptic seizures or to terminate a seizure already underway. Until the advent of the HYDANTOINS in the 1930s, anticonvulsants consisted mainly of BROMIDES and BARBITURATES. Drugs now used include phenytoin, CARBAMAZEPINE, VALPROIC ACID, PHENOBARBITAL, and newer anticonvulsants, such as lamotrigine, gabapentin, tiagabine, topiramate, vigabatrin, and zonisamide. SUCCINIMIDES are also effective antiseizure medications, as are the BENZODIAZEPINES. Also called **antiepileptic**.

antidepressant *n.* any drug administered in the treatment of depression. Most antidepressants work by increasing the availability of monoamine neurotransmitters such as norepinephrine, serotonin, or dopamine, although they do so by different routes. The MONOAMINE OXIDASE INHIBITORS (MAOIs) work by inhibiting monoamine oxidase, one of the principal enzymes that metabolize these neurotransmitters. Most of the other antidepressants, including the TRICYCLIC ANTIDEPRESSANTS (TCAs) and the selective serotonin reuptake inhibitors (see SSRI), inhibit the reuptake of serotonin or norepinephrine (and to a much lesser degree dopamine) into the presynaptic neuron. Either process leaves more of the neurotransmitter free to bind with postsynaptic receptors, initiating a series of events in the postsynaptic neuron that is thought to produce the actual therapeutic effect.

antidiuretic hormone (**ADH**) see VASOPRESSIN.

antiestrogen *n.* a substance that reduces or blocks the physiological effects of estrogens, the female sex hormones, on tissues normally responsive to these hormones. Examples include **tamoxifen** (U.S. trade name: **Nolvadex**), **toremifene** (U.S. trade name: **Fareston**), **fulvestrant** (U.S. trade name: **Faslodex**), and **selective estrogen receptor modulators** (**SERMs**), such as **raloxifene** (U.S. trade name: **Evista**), which have both inhibitory and facilitative effects upon different pathways mediated by estrogen receptors. Antiestrogens are variously used in the treatment or prevention of breast cancer and some estrogenically mediated effects of menopause and also in the treatment of some types of female infertility. Also called **estrogen antagonist**.

antigen *n.* any substance that is treated by the immune system as foreign and is therefore capable of inducing an immune response, particularly the production of ANTIBODIES that render it harmless. The antigen may be a virus, a bacterium, a toxin (e.g., bee venom), or tissue (e.g., blood) of another individual with different genetic characteristics. —**antigenic** *adj.*

antihistamine *n.* any drug or agent that inhibits the effects of HISTAMINE at central or peripheral histamine receptors. They may have sedative effects and are a common component of over-the-counter sleeping aids. Others (e.g., **diphenhydramine**, U.S. trade name: **Benadryl**; and **dimenhydrinate**, U.S. trade name: **Dramamine**) are used in the treatment of allergic reactions or motion sickness. The so-called **nonsedating antihistamines** have less ability to cross the BLOOD–BRAIN BARRIER and are used solely in the management of allergic responses. Also called **histamine antagonist**.

antimuscarinic drug see ANTICHOLINERGIC DRUG.

antiparkinsonian drug any pharmacological agent that reduces the severity of symptoms of Parkinson's disease or drug-induced parkinsonism (common with the use of conventional ANTIPSYCHOTICS), including tremors, movement and gait abnormalities, and muscle rigidity.

antipredator behavior all forms of action by an organism that function to avoid predation, including aggression, camouflage, and MOBBING behavior as well as immobility, rapidly changing, unpredictable confusion behavior (the **confusion effect**), mass movement or activity (the **dilution effect**), flight, or **evasive action** (turning away from the direction of the predator's approach).

antipsychiatry *n.* an international movement that emerged in the 1960s: It contested the scientific and practical validity of psychiatry and radically opposed what its proponents understood as a hospital-centered medical specialty legally empowered to treat and institutionalize individuals with mental disorders. Indeed, many antipsychiatrists argued against the very existence of mental disorders, viewing psychiatry as a form of social repression and a means to control deviance, and treatment as a disguised form of punishment. —**antipsychiatrist** *n.*

antipsychotic *n.* any pharmacological agent used to control the symptoms of schizophrenia and other disorders characterized by impaired reality testing, as evidenced by severely disorganized thought, speech, and behavior. Formerly called **major tranquilizers** and later **neuroleptics**, antipsychotics are commonly divided into two major classes: **conventional** (**first-generation**) **antipsychotics**, including the PHENOTHIAZINES and BUTYROPHENONES, and the newer **atypical** (**novel** or **second-generation**) **antipsychotics**, of which CLOZAPINE is the prototype. The latter class has fewer adverse side effects than the former, particularly the neurologically based

EXTRAPYRAMIDAL SYMPTOMS but also the less serious yet unpleasant autonomic effects, such as dry mouth and blurred vision.

antisocial *adj.* denoting or exhibiting behavior that sharply deviates from social norms and also violates other people's rights. Arson and vandalism are examples of antisocial behavior. Compare PROSOCIAL.

antisocial personality disorder the presence of a chronic and pervasive disposition to disregard and violate the rights of others. Manifestations include repeated violations of the law, exploitation of others, deceitfulness, impulsivity, aggressiveness, reckless disregard for the safety of self and others, and irresponsibility, accompanied by lack of guilt, remorse, and empathy. The disorder has been known by various names, including **dyssocial personality**, **psychopathic personality**, and **sociopathic personality**. It is the most heavily researched of the personality disorders and the most difficult to treat.

antispasmodic drug any pharmacological agent used in the management of spasms of smooth muscle. They are commonly used to treat gastrointestinal conditions such as IRRITABLE BOWEL SYNDROME.

antithesis *n.* **1.** a THESIS, idea, or proposition that is opposite to or contradicts another. **2.** in philosophy, the second stage of a dialectical process based on proposition, contradiction, and the reconciliation of these (thesis, antithesis, and SYNTHESIS). —**antithetical** *adj.*

Anton's syndrome a rare disorder marked by the lack of awareness of blindness. The person genuinely believes he or she can see despite clinical evidence of loss of vision, such as difficulties in getting around, handling objects, and so forth. The condition is a type of visual ANOSOGNOSIA resulting from injury to the occipital lobe of the brain. [first described in 1899 by Gabriel **Anton** (1858–1933), Austrian physician]

anvil *n.* see OSSICLES.

anxiety *n.* an emotion characterized by apprehension and somatic symptoms of tension in which an individual anticipates impending danger, catastrophe, or misfortune. The body often mobilizes itself to meet the perceived threat: Muscles become tense, breathing is faster, and the heart beats more rapidly. Anxiety may be distinguished from FEAR both conceptually and physiologically, although the two terms are often used interchangeably. The former is considered a disproportionate response to a vague, unidentifiable threat whereas the latter is an appropriate response to a clearly identifiable and specific threat. —**anxious** *adj.*

anxiety disorder any of a group of disorders that have as their central organizing theme the emotional state of fear, worry, or anxious apprehension. This category includes OBSESSIVE-COMPULSIVE DISORDER, PANIC DISORDER, various PHOBIAS, POSTTRAUMATIC STRESS DISORDER, and GENERALIZED ANXIETY DISORDER. Anxiety disorders have a chronic course, albeit waxing and waning in intensity, and are among the most common mental health problems in the United States.

anxiety hierarchy a series of graduated anxiety-arousing stimuli centering on a specific source of anxiety in a specific individual. It is used in the treatment of phobias by SYSTEMATIC DESENSITIZATION: Patients proceed along the hierarchy from the least threatening situation toward the most threatening situation.

anxiety scale any of numerous assessment instruments designed to measure the severity of anxiety symptoms. Such scales usually take the form of self-report tests but can also be based on clinician ratings or actual performance.

anxiety sensitivity fear of sensations associated with anxiety because of the belief that they will have harmful consequences. For example, an individual with high anxiety sensitivity is likely to regard feeling lightheaded as a sign of impending illness or fainting, whereas an individual with low anxiety sensitivity would tend to regard this sensation as simply unpleasant. Research indicates that high anxiety sensitivity is a personality risk factor for the development of PANIC ATTACKS and PANIC DISORDER.

anxiolytic n. any of a class of drugs used in the control of anxiety, mild behavioral agitation, and insomnia. Formerly called **minor tranquilizers**, they can also be used as adjunctive agents in the treatment of depression and panic disorder. The most widely used anxiolytics are the BENZODIAZEPINES.

APA 1. abbreviation for AMERICAN PSYCHIATRIC ASSOCIATION. **2.** abbreviation for AMERICAN PSYCHOLOGICAL ASSOCIATION.

apathy n. indifference and lack of response. —**apathetic** adj.

aphagia n. inability to swallow or eat. Compare HYPERPHAGIA. —**aphagic** adj.

aphasia n. an acquired language impairment that results from neurological damage to the language areas of the brain, which are typically located in the left hemisphere. Common causes of damage include stroke, cerebral hemorrhage, brain tumors, and cortical degenerative disorders (e.g., Alzheimer's disease). Traditionally, a distinction has been made between expressive and receptive forms of aphasia, whereby individuals with the former primarily have difficulty producing spoken and written language and those with the latter primarily have difficulty comprehending spoken and written language. A more contemporary distinction, however, is commonly made between **fluent aphasias**, characterized by plentiful verbal output consisting of well-articulated, easily produced utterances of relatively normal length and prosody (rhythm and intonation), and **nonfluent aphasias**, characterized by sparse, effortful utterances of short phrase length and disrupted prosody. Fluent aphasias are associated with posterior lesions

that spare cortical regions critical for motor control of speech, whereas nonfluent aphasias are associated with anterior lesions that compromise motor and premotor cortical regions involved in speech production. Numerous types of aphasia exist, with eight classically identified: ANOMIC APHASIA, BROCA'S APHASIA, CONDUCTION APHASIA, GLOBAL APHASIA, MIXED TRANSCORTICAL APHASIA, and WERNICKE'S APHASIA. Also (but much less preferably) called **dysphasia**. —**aphasic** adj.

aphonia n. loss of the voice resulting from disease of or damage to the larynx or vocal tract.

aphrodisiac n. any agent that is thought to facilitate sexual desire. Substances with such a reputation include perfumes and other odors, foods such as raw oysters, and various drugs, particularly alkaloids such as yohimbine.

aplasia n. the arrested development of a body tissue or organ.

apnea (apnoea) n. temporary suspension of respiration. Apnea can occur during sleep (see SLEEP APNEA) and is also found in many disorders. —**apneic** adj.

apodia n. the condition of being born with only one foot or with no feet. See also ACHEIRIA.

apolipoprotein E (ApoE) a protein that may help break down BETA-AMYLOID. Individuals carrying a particular form of the ApoE gene, the ApoE4 allele, are more likely to develop Alzheimer's disease and other conditions that damage the nervous system.

apoplexy n. hemorrhage into an organ, for example, a **pituitary apoplexy**.

apoptosis n. see PROGRAMMED CELL DEATH. —**apoptotic** adj.

aposematic coloration see WARNING COLORATION.

a posteriori denoting conclusions derived from observations or other manifest occurrences: reasoning causes from facts. When applied to HYPOTHESIS TESTING, this concept of "from what comes after" means an **a posteriori test**, which is a statistical test planned after research data have been examined because certain patterns in the data warrant further study. Compare A PRIORI. [Latin, "from the latter"]

APP abbreviation for amyloid precursor protein. See BETA-AMYLOID.

apparatus n. **1.** any instrument or equipment used during an experiment. **2.** in biology, a group of structures that perform a particular function. It may be microscopic, as in the intracellular GOLGI APPARATUS, or macroscopic, as in the VESTIBULAR APPARATUS.

apparent movement an illusion of motion or change in size of a visual stimulus. Several types have been identified and labeled with Greek letters, among them the familiar **beta movement**, in which successive presentations of stationary stimuli across the visual field produce the perception of a single smoothly moving stimulus, and **gamma movement**, the seeming expansion of an object when it is suddenly presented and contraction when withdrawn. Also called **apparent motion**.

apparition *n.* **1.** the perceived manifestation of a ghost, phantasm, or spirit. **2.** the act of becoming visible.

appearance–reality distinction the knowledge that the appearance of an object does not necessarily correspond to its reality. For example, a sponge shaped like a rock may look like a rock but it is really a sponge. Children younger than 3 may have difficulty making appearance–reality distinctions.

apperception *n.* **1.** the mental process by which a perception or an idea is assimilated into an individual's existing knowledge, thoughts, and emotions (his or her **apperceptive mass**). **2.** the act or process of perceiving something consciously. —**apperceive** *vb.* —**apperceptive** *adj.*

appetite *n.* any desire, but particularly one for food or one relating to the satisfaction of any physiological need. Appetite is influenced by learning and prior experience and thus can be highly flexible. In classical ethology, the active searching behavior leading ultimately to a CONSUMMATORY RESPONSE was termed **appetitive behavior**. —**appetitive** *adj.*

appetite suppressant any agent that reduces desire for food and thus controls body weight, including the amphetamines and other stimulants. Although appetite suppressants may result in short-term weight loss, there is no evidence that they achieve long-term weight reduction unless used in conjunction with a behavioral management program. Also called **anorectant**; **anorexiant**.

applied behavior analysis (**ABA**) the extension of the behavioral principles described by U.S. psychologist B. F. Skinner (1904–1990) to practical settings. Variations of applied behavior analysis may be used clinically (in the form of BEHAVIOR MODIFICATION or BEHAVIOR THERAPY) as treatment for abnormal or problematic behaviors.

applied linguistics the field in which linguistic theories and methods are put to practical use. Contexts in which this occurs include language teaching, the treatment of language disorders, and various aspects of artificial intelligence.

applied psychology the application of the theories, principles, and techniques of psychology to practical concerns, such as problems of living or coping, education, vocational guidance, industry, ergonomics, consumer affairs, advertising, political campaigns, and environmental issues. It may be contrasted with theoretical psychology or academic psychology, in which the emphasis is on understanding for its own sake rather than the utility of the knowledge.

applied relaxation a technique in which clients are taught, in a step-wise fashion, to relax more and more rapidly over a series of sessions in order to master panic, anxiety, phobias, pain, and other symptoms. The goal is for clients to be able to relax in 20–30 seconds in situations in which their symptoms typically occur. See also PROGRESSIVE RELAXATION.

applied research research conducted for the practical purpose of solving a real-world problem rather than developing a theory or obtaining knowledge for its own sake. Compare BASIC RESEARCH.

applied tension a technique in BEHAVIOR THERAPY and EXPOSURE THERAPY that focuses on changing physiological responses (e.g., low blood pressure leading to fainting) by teaching and having the client practice muscle tensing and releasing. The technique was developed and is still primarily used for blood, injury, and injection phobias.

appraisal *n.* the cognitive evaluation of the nature and significance of a phenomenon or event. In **appraisal theories** of emotion, such evaluations are seen as determinants of emotional experience. See COGNITIVE APPRAISAL THEORY. —**appraise** *vb.*

appraisal motive the desire to gain accurate information about the self. It leads people to seek highly diagnostic feedback (see DIAGNOSTICITY) and to reject flattery or other bias. Compare CONSISTENCY MOTIVE; SELF-ENHANCEMENT MOTIVE.

apprehension *n.* **1.** uneasiness or dread about an upcoming event or the future generally. Also called **apprehensiveness**. **2.** the act or capability of grasping something mentally. For example, the **apprehension span** is the maximum number of distinct objects that can be reported from one glance at an array of items (e.g., specific letters from a group of words). Compare COMPREHENSION. —**apprehend** *vb.* —**apprehensible** *adj.* —**apprehensive** *adj.*

approach–approach conflict a situation involving a choice between two equally desirable but incompatible alternatives. Also called **double-approach conflict**. See also APPROACH–AVOIDANCE CONFLICT; AVOIDANCE–AVOIDANCE CONFLICT.

approach–avoidance conflict a situation involving a single goal or option that has both desirable and undesirable aspects or consequences. The closer an individual comes to the goal, the greater the anxiety, but withdrawal from the goal then increases the desire. See also APPROACH–APPROACH CONFLICT; AVOIDANCE–AVOIDANCE CONFLICT.

appropriate death the death a person would choose if given the opportunity. The concept draws attention to the differing needs and values of individuals in the terminal phase of life. PALLIATIVE CARE, especially as given in HOSPICES, attempts to protect individuality and offers a communication process and caring environment providing the maximum possible opportunity for the dying person to make personally meaningful decisions.

appurtenance *n.* in GESTALT PSYCHOLOGY, interaction or mutual influence between parts of a perceptual field so that the parts appear to belong together.

apraxia *n.* loss or impairment of the ability to perform purposeful, skilled movements despite intact motor function and comprehension. The condition may be developmental or induced by neurological dysfunction and is believed to represent an impairment of the ability to plan, select, and sequence the motor execution of movements. There are several major types of apraxia, including **buccofacial (or orofacial) apraxia**, involving difficulty performing skilled facial movements; **ideational apraxia**, involving difficulty carrying out in the proper order a series of acts that comprise a complex task; **ideomotor apraxia**, involving difficulty imitating actions or gesturing to command; **limb kinetic (or melokinetic) apraxia**, involving difficulty making precise, coordinated but individual finger movements; and **speech (or verbal) apraxia**, involving difficulty coordinating the movements necessary for speaking. —**apraxic** *adj.*

a priori denoting conclusions derived from premises or principles: deducing effects from prior assumptions. When applied to HYPOTHESIS TESTING, this concept of "from what comes before" means an **a priori test**, which is a statistical test explicitly planned before research data have been examined and trends observed. Compare A POSTERIORI. [Latin, "prior to"]

aprosexia *n.* inability to focus attention.

aprosody *n.* absence of the normal variations in the rhythm, stress, and pitch of speech, resulting in monotone speech. Unusual or abnormal variations are known as **dysprosody (or dysprosodia)**. Also called **aprosodia**.

aptitude *n.* the capacity to acquire competence or skill through training. **Specific aptitude** is potential in a particular area (e.g., artistic or mathematical aptitude); **general aptitude** is potential in several fields. Both are distinct from ABILITY, which is an existing competence.

aptitude test any assessment instrument designed to measure potential for acquiring knowledge or skill. Aptitude tests are thought of as providing a basis for making predictions for an individual about future success, particularly in either an educational or occupational situation. In contrast, ACHIEVEMENT TESTS are considered to reflect the amount of learning already obtained.

aptitude–treatment interaction a phenomenon in which people with certain attributes (e.g., personality traits, cognitive styles) respond better to one treatment, whereas people with different attributes respond better to another treatment. The influence of personal characteristics upon treatment outcome is of particular interest in educational and psychotherapeutic contexts, given the goal of finding the optimal instructional method or intervention for different types of people.

AQ abbreviation for ACHIEVEMENT QUOTIENT.

aqueous humor see EYE.

arachnoid mater see MENINGES.

arbitrary matching to sample a variation of MATCHING TO SAMPLE in which the correct alternative during the choice phase bears an arbitrary relationship to the stimulus presented as the sample. For example, after presentation of a blue stimulus as a sample, the correct choice may be to select a triangle. Also called **symbolic matching to sample**.

arbitrary symbol a linguistic SIGN (a written or spoken word) that bears no obvious resemblance to the thing or concept signified. Because the vast majority of words in all languages are considered to fall into this category, arbitrariness is often cited as an important characteristic of human languages. Compare ICONIC SYMBOL.

archetype *n.* **1.** a perfect or typical example of something or the original model from which something is held to derive. See also PROTOTYPE. **2.** in ANALYTIC PSYCHOLOGY, a structural component of the mind that derives from the accumulated experience of humankind. These inherited components are stored in the COLLECTIVE UNCONSCIOUS and serve as a frame of reference with which individuals view the world and as one of the major foundations on which the structure of the personality is built. Examples are ANIMA, ANIMUS, PERSONA, SHADOW, supreme being, MAGNA MATER, and hero. —**archetypal** *adj.*

archicortex *n.* see ALLOCORTEX.

architectural constraints the limitations imposed by the structure of the brain on the type of information that it can process and the methods it uses for processing. See also CHRONOTOPIC CONSTRAINTS; REPRESENTATIONAL CONSTRAINTS.

architectural psychology the study of the role of the built environment in human behavior, a major subtopic in ENVIRONMENTAL PSYCHOLOGY.

archival research the use of books, journals, historical documents, and other existing records or data available in storage in scientific research. Archival methods provide unobtrusive observation of human activity in natural settings and permit the study of phenomena that otherwise cannot easily be investigated. A persistent drawback, however, is that causal inferences are always more tentative than those provided by laboratory experiments.

arcuate fasciculus a bundle of nerve fibers linking the parts of the brain involved in the interpretation and control of speech (WERNICKE'S

AREA and BROCA'S AREA, respectively). Lesions of this tract produce CONDUCTION APHASIA.

arcuate nucleus 1. an arc-shaped collection of neurons in the hypothalamus that produce hormones. **2.** any of various small groups of gray matter on the bulge of the medulla oblongata. They are extensions of neurons in the basal PONS and project to the cerebellum.

areflexia *n.* an absence of motor reflexes.

argument *n.* **1.** a sequence of propositions that provides logical reasons for accepting a CONCLUSION as valid or true. A single one of these statements is referred to as a PREMISE. **Argumentation** is the process of making an argument from premise to conclusion. **2.** a parameter on which the value of a mathematical FUNCTION depends.

Aristotelian *adj.* **1.** of or relating to the tradition of formal logic founded by Greek philosopher Aristotle (384–322 BCE) and developed especially by the Scholastic philosophers of the Middle Ages. The term "Aristotelian" is often used to distinguish this tradition of logic from that of modern SYMBOLIC LOGIC. **2.** of or relating to Aristotle, his works, or his thought. In this more general sense, an Aristotelian approach, which gives primacy to particulars over UNIVERSALS and grants a higher value to empirical knowledge, is often contrasted with the approach of PLATONIC IDEALISM or NEOPLATONISM. **—Aristotelianism** *n.*

Aristotle's illusion the tactile perception that a single object is two objects when felt with the crossed index and middle fingers. [**Aristotle** (384–322 BCE), Greek philosopher]

arithmetic mean see MEAN.

armamentarium *n.* the complete equipment of an institution, often a medical institution, necessary or sufficient for instruction, research, or practice. Such equipment includes books, supplies, and instruments.

aromatherapy *n.* a type of therapy purported to improve psychological and physical health through the use of selected essential oils extracted from seeds, herbs, flowers, fruits, and trees. The fragrances of these oils are inhaled or the oils themselves are applied topically, using compresses, baths, or massages, in an effort to induce relaxation, reduce stress and emotional distress, and enhance well-being. So-called evidence supporting the effectiveness of aromatherapy is almost entirely anecdotal. See also COMPLEMENTARY AND ALTERNATIVE MEDICINE.

arousal *n.* **1.** a state of physiological activation or cortical responsiveness, associated with sensory stimulation and activation of fibers from the RETICULAR ACTIVATING SYSTEM. **2.** a state of excitement or energy expenditure linked to an emotion. Usually, arousal is closely related to a person's appraisal of the significance of an event or to the physical intensity of a stimulus. **—arouse** *vb.*

arousal theory 1. the theory that the physical environment can affect arousal levels by stimulation and by stress created when psychological or physical needs are not met. Arousal increases when personal space is diminished or when people are subjected to noise or traffic congestion. **2.** see ACTIVATION THEORY OF EMOTION.

arousal training a technique in BEHAVIOR THERAPY that teaches clients to detect levels of physiological arousal and then to enhance or reduce these levels depending on therapeutic goals. This technique is often used in ANGER CONTROL THERAPY and BEHAVIORAL SEX THERAPY.

arousal transfer an increase in the intensity of one emotion that follows the experience of another emotion. For instance, the intensity of love may increase following an intense experience of fear or anger.

array *n.* any ordered arrangement of data, particularly a two-dimensional grouping of data into rows and columns (i.e., a MATRIX). The concept may be extended to more than two dimensions.

arrhinencephaly (**arhinencephaly**) *n.* a congenital absence of the RHINENCEPHALON, the part of the brain that includes the olfactory bulbs, tracts, and other structures associated with the sense of smell. Also called **arrhinencephalia; arhinencephalia**.

arrhythmia *n.* any variation from the normal rhythm of the heartbeat. Kinds of arrhythmia include (among others) **tachycardia**, any rate above 100 beats per minute; and **bradycardia**, a rate of less than 60 beats per minute. **—arrhythmic** *adj.*

arteriography *n.* see ANGIOGRAPHY.

arteriosclerosis *n.* a group of diseases characterized by hardening and loss of elasticity of the walls of the arteries. A common type is ATHEROSCLEROSIS. **—arteriosclerotic** *adj.*

arteriovenous malformation (**AVM**) an abnormal, congenital tangle of arteries and veins that are directly connected and lack intervening capillaries. When such malformations occur in the brain they can cause mild to severe brain damage and result in a range of neurological symptoms.

arthritis *n.* inflammation of a joint, causing pain, swelling, and stiffness. The most severe and disabling form is **rheumatoid arthritis**, associated with the body attacking its own cells as foreign (see AUTOIMMUNITY). **—arthritic** *adj.*

articulation *n.* **1.** the shaping and production of the sounds required for intelligible speech. It is a complex process involving not only accurate movements of the VOCAL TRACT but also neural integration of numerous other activities. **2.** a joint between bones, which may be fixed or movable. **—articulate** *vb.*

articulator *n.* any of the elements of the vocal tract (e.g., lips, tongue, soft palate) that are involved in articulation, that is, in the shaping and production of speech sounds. Some, but not all, authorities include the cheeks, larynx, uvula, alveolar ridge, nose, and teeth as articulators.

articulatory loop see WORKING MEMORY.

articulatory store a component of short-term memory that retains auditory information based on the motor systems involved in pronouncing items, rather than how they sound. Compare ACOUSTIC STORE.

artifact *n.* an experimental finding that is not a reflection of the true state of nature but rather the consequent of flawed design or analytic error.

artificial intelligence (**AI**) a subdiscipline of computer science that aims to produce programs that simulate human intelligence. There are many branches of AI, including robotics, computer vision, machine learning, game playing, and expert systems. AI has also supported research in other related areas, including COGNITIVE SCIENCE and computational linguistics. See also TURING TEST.

artificial language any language or languagelike system that is not a NATURAL LANGUAGE. The category includes invented languages, such as Esperanto, and the various languages used in computer programming; the **formal languages** of logic and mathematics are also sometimes included. In psycholinguistics, artificial languages are sometimes invented to simulate or to violate certain aspects of natural-language rules.

artificial life a research area of ARTIFICIAL INTELLIGENCE in which computer-based life forms are constructed, often from CELLULAR AUTOMATA. The state of each cell, together with the state of its immediate neighbors, determines its survival. This research area often attempts to simulate the results of communication and other society-based skills on survival.

artificial selection human intervention in animal or plant reproduction to improve the value or utility of succeeding generations. Compare NATURAL SELECTION.

art therapy the use of artistic activities, such as painting and clay modeling, in psychotherapy and rehabilitation. The process of making art is seen as a means of symbolic communication and a vehicle for developing new insights, resolving conflicts, solving problems, and formulating new perceptions.

arugamama *n.* see MORITA THERAPY.

ASC abbreviation for ALTERED STATE OF CONSCIOUSNESS.

ascendance *n.* a personality trait involving a desire to be prominent in group situations, to assert oneself, and to acquire positions of authority over others. Also called **ascendancy**. See also DOMINANCE. —**ascendant** *adj.*

ascending–descending series the two sets of stimuli—one of incrementally increasing magnitude, one of incrementally decreasing magnitude—used in the METHOD OF LIMITS. This procedure controls for HABITUATION and PERSEVERATION errors.

ascending tract a bundle of nerve fibers that carries sensory inputs through the spinal cord toward the brain. Also called **ascending pathway**. Compare DESCENDING TRACT.

asceticism *n.* a character trait or lifestyle characterized by simplicity, renunciation of physical pleasures and worldly goods, social withdrawal, and extreme self-discipline. —**ascetic** *adj.*

Asch situation an experimental paradigm used to study conformity to group opinion. Participants make perceptual judgments as part of a group of confederates who make errors deliberately on certain trials. The extent to which participants publicly agree with the erroneous group judgment or resist the pressure to do so and remain independent provides a measure of conformity. [Solomon **Asch** (1907–1996), Polish-born U.S. psychologist]

ASD abbreviation for AUTISTIC SPECTRUM DISORDER.

asexual *adj.* **1.** lacking sexual characteristics or drive. **2.** capable of reproduction without fertilization. —**asexuality** *n.*

as-if hypothesis an unproven hypothesis that is treated "as if" it were correct, usually because of its value as an explanatory model or its utility as a basis for experiment and research. Many of the hypothetical entities postulated by psychology and psychoanalysis are of this nature.

ASL abbreviation for American Sign Language (see SIGN LANGUAGE).

asocial *adj.* **1.** declining to engage, or incapable of engaging, in social interaction. See also SCHIZOID PERSONALITY DISORDER. **2.** lacking sensitivity or regard for social values or norms. See also ANTISOCIAL PERSONALITY DISORDER. —**asociality** *n.*

asonia *n.* inability to distinguish differences of pitch. Also called **tone deafness**.

aspartate *n.* an amino acid neurotransmitter that is excitatory at many synapses.

Asperger's disorder a pervasive developmental disorder associated with varying degrees of deficits in social and conversational skills, difficulties with transitions from one task to another or with changes in situations or environments, and preference for sameness and predictability of events. Obsessive routines and preoccupation with particular subjects of interest may be present, as may difficulty reading body language and maintaining proper social distance. In contrast to AUTISTIC DISORDER, language skills develop, and there is no clinically significant delay in cognitive or adaptive functioning other than in social interactions. Also called **Asperger's syndrome**. [described in 1944 by Hans **Asperger** (1906–1980), Austrian psychiatrist]

assertiveness training a method of teaching individuals to change verbal and nonverbal signals and behavioral patterns and to enhance interpersonal communication generally through techniques designed to help them express emotions, opinions, and preferences—positive and negative—clearly, directly, and in an appropriate manner. ROLE PLAY or BEHAVIOR REHEARSAL is often used to prepare clients to be appropriately assertive in real-life situations.

assessment *n.* see PSYCHOLOGICAL ASSESSMENT.

assimilation *n.* **1.** the process of absorbing, incorporating, or making similar. In making judgments, for example, it refers to finding similarities between the target being judged and features of the context in which it is judged. Thus, meeting a person at an enjoyable party could lead to a more positive evaluation of that person than would have been the case otherwise. The evaluation of the person has been assimilated toward the positive social context. Compare CONTRAST. **2.** the process by which an immigrant to a new culture adopts the culture's beliefs and practices. This is more properly called SOCIAL ASSIMILATION. **3.** see PIAGETIAN THEORY. —**assimilate** *vb.*

assimilation effect in psychology experiments, an effect in which participants' judgments shift toward an ANCHOR after it is introduced. Compare CONTRAST EFFECT.

assisted death an action taken by one person to end the life of another, at the request of the latter. This action can take the form of either PASSIVE EUTHANASIA or ACTIVE EUTHANASIA. Assisted death differs from MERCY KILLING in that it is generally performed by a physician and is not in response to an acute situation. It is sometimes called **physician-assisted suicide**, which assumes a firm determination of the cause of death. See also EUTHANASIA.

assisted living a form of congregate housing for older adults requiring long-term care services that include meals, personal care, and scheduled nursing care. Typically comprising private rooms or apartments, it encourages a degree of autonomy and independence in residents that is not provided for in NURSING HOMES.

assistive technology (AT) any equipment or system designed to maintain or improve the functional capabilities of individuals with disabilities. **Assistive devices** (or **assistive technology devices**) range from simple low-technology items such as canes, walkers, and reachers to high-technology items such as voice-controlled computers and computerized speech-output devices. These devices are also occasionally referred to as **daily-living aids** or **independent-living aids**. See also BIOENGINEERING.

associate 1. *n.* in learning studies, a word that is paired with another word to be learned with it (see PAIRED-ASSOCIATES LEARNING). **2.** *n.* a word that is suggested by another word by virtue of some implicit connection. **3.** *vb.* to use mental processes to form a connection between ideas, events, objects, and so forth.

association *n.* **1.** a connection or relationship between items, particularly ideas, events, or feelings. Associations are established by experience and are fundamental to LEARNING THEORY and BEHAVIORISM. **2.** the degree of statistical dependence between two or more phenomena. —**associative** *adj.* —**associational** *adj.*

association cortex any of various areas of the CEREBRAL CORTEX that are not involved principally in sensory or motor representations but may be involved in integrative functions. Also called **association area**.

association fiber an axon from any of various neurons that link different parts of the same cerebral hemisphere. Compare COMMISSURAL FIBER.

associationism *n.* the theory that complex mental processes, such as thinking, learning, and memory, can be wholly or mainly explained by the associative links formed between ideas according to specific laws and principles (see ASSOCIATION OF IDEAS). Although Greek philosopher Aristotle (384–322 BCE) cited some of these laws (similarity, difference, contiguity in time or space, etc.), the theory was first stated systematically by English philosopher Thomas Hobbes (1588–1679), who held that all knowledge is compounded from relatively simple sense impressions. The laws and applications of association were later developed by John Locke (1632–1704) and other members of the British empiricist school (see EMPIRICISM). Although the approach taken by such thinkers was relatively static and nonexperimental, there are echoes of associationism in much historical and contemporary psychology. Most importantly, associationism has been invoked to explain the pairing of stimuli and responses. As such, it is a fundamental assumption of modern LEARNING THEORY and all behaviorist approaches (see BEHAVIORISM). Also called **British associationism**.

association of ideas the process by which simple perceptions and ideas are combined into totalities of varying degrees of complexity and abstractness, as, for example, connecting the relatively simple ideas of four legs, furry coat, a certain shape and size, and so on, into the compound concept "cat." The same process is held to explain one's understanding of entirely abstract ideas, such as "power" or "liberalism." The association of ideas was a key concept for the British empiricist school of philosophers (see EMPIRICISM) and remains fundamental in LEARNING THEORY and BEHAVIORISM.

association psychology a psychological approach based on the premise that learning and knowledge are derived from the formation of connections (associations) between ideas. Association psychology developed from British empiricist and associationist philosophy (see ASSOCIATIONISM).

associative-chain theory in LEARNING THEORY and behaviorist psychology (see BEHAVIOR-

A

ISM), a theory of how complex behaviors, including linguistic behaviors, are formed from combinations of simple stimulus–response associations.

associative clustering the tendency for items with preexisting associations to be recalled together during memory recall.

associative learning the process of acquiring new and enduring information via the formation of bonds between elements. In different types of **associationistic learning theories**, these associated elements may be stimulus and response, mental representations of events, or elements in neural networks. Historically, the associationistic theories of U.S. psychologists Clark L. Hull (1884–1952) and Kenneth W. Spence (1907–1967) are contrasted with the nonassociative and cognitive theory of U.S. psychologist Edward C. Tolman (1886–1959).

associative memory retrieval of a memory (e.g., of a stimulus, behavior, place, or past event) that occurs upon recall or presentation of something associated with it.

associative play see SOCIAL PLAY.

associative strength the strength of the link (association) between two or more items (e.g., between stimulus and response or between items in memory), as measured by the capacity of the first item to elicit the second.

associative thinking a relatively uncontrolled cognitive activity in which the mind "wanders" without specific direction among elements based on their connections (associations) with one another, as occurs during reverie, daydreaming, and FREE ASSOCIATION.

assumption *n.* one or more conditions that need to be met in order for a statistical procedure to be fully justified from a theoretical perspective. For example, ANALYSIS OF VARIANCE assumes HOMOGENEITY OF VARIANCE and independence of observations, among other criteria. If the assumptions were to be violated to an extreme extent, the results would be invalid. See ROBUSTNESS.

astasia *n.* severe impairment or complete loss of the ability to stand due to problems in motor coordination. —**astatic** *adj.*

astasia–abasia the ability to walk only with a wobbly, staggering gait, although control is normal while lying down. This is believed to be psychogenic in origin and may be manifested as a symptom of CONVERSION DISORDER. Also called **Blocq's disease.**

astereognosis *n.* inability to identify the form and nature of an object by touch.

asthenia *n.* severe weakness or loss of strength, often associated with general fatigue or certain disorders. —**asthenic** *adj.*

asthenopia *n.* weakness or fatigue of the eyes, usually due to strain and tiring of the eye muscles. —**asthenopic** *adj.*

asthma *n.* a chronic disorder in which intermit-tent inflammation and narrowing of the bronchial passages produces wheezing, gasping, coughing, and chest tightness. Though the precipitating cause is usually an allergen, such as dust or pollen, environmental irritants, respiratory infection, anxiety, stress, and other agents may produce or aggravate symptoms. —**asthmatic** *adj.*

astigmatism *n.* a visual disorder in which the light rays of a visual stimulus do not all focus at a single point on the retina due to uneven curvature of the cornea or lens. The effect is an aberration or distortion of the visual image that makes it difficult to see fine detail. —**astigmatic** *adj.*

astroblastoma *n.* see GLIOMA.

astrocyte *n.* a star-shaped nonneuronal central nervous system cell (GLIA) with numerous extensions that run in all directions. They provide structural support for the brain, are responsible for many homeostatic controls, and may isolate receptive surfaces. Also called **astroglia.**

astrocytoma *n.* see GLIOMA.

astrocytosis *n.* a pathological condition marked by a proliferation of astrocytes into tissues of the central nervous system in which neurons have died due to lack of oxygen or glucose, as during episodes of HYPOXIA or HYPOGLYCEMIA. Also called **astrogliosis.**

asylum *n.* originally, a refuge for criminals (from Greek *asylon*, "sanctuary"). From the 19th century, the terms "asylum" or "insane asylum" were applied to MENTAL INSTITUTIONS. These names are now obsolete, discarded because of their emphasis on refuge rather than treatment.

asymbolia *n.* loss of the ability to understand or use symbols of any kind, including words, gestures, signals, musical notes, chemical formulas, or signs. Also called **asemasia; asemia.**

asymptomatic *adj.* not showing any symptoms. For example, hypertension is considered asymptomatic because usually it does not have any outright physical or behavioral symptoms and can be detected only by measuring the blood pressure.

asymptote *n.* **1.** a straight line that defines the limit of a curve representing a mathematical function: The curve continuously approaches but never reaches the line. **2.** the maximal level of response after many learning trials: The point at which no more incremental increases in performance are seen. —**asymptotic** *adj.*

AT abbreviation for ASSISTIVE TECHNOLOGY.

ataque de nervios a CULTURE-BOUND SYNDROME found among Latinos, characterized by shaking, uncontrollable shouting or crying, a sense of rising heat, loss of control, and verbal or physical aggression, followed by fainting or seizurelike episodes. Symptoms often occur following a stressful event related to the family, and most individuals quickly return to their previous level of functioning.

ataxia *n.* inability to perform coordinated voluntary movements. Ataxia may be seen as a symptom of various disorders, such as multiple sclerosis or cerebral palsy, or it can occur in isolation. It can be heritable, as in FRIEDREICH'S ATAXIA, or acquired from injury or infection affecting the nervous system. When due to damage to the CEREBELLUM it is called **cerebellar ataxia** and when due to loss of sensory feedback from the muscles and joints it is called **sensory ataxia.** —**ataxic** *adj.*

atherosclerosis *n.* a common form of ARTERIOSCLEROSIS resulting from accumulations of lipids such as cholesterol on the inner walls of arteries and their hardening into **atherosclerotic** (or **atheromatous**) **plaques.** —**atherosclerotic** *adj.*

athetosis *n.* slow, involuntary, writhing movements of the body, particularly the extremities such as the fingers and toes. —**athetoid** *adj.* —**athetotic** *adj.*

athletic triad the combination of AMENORRHEA, disordered eating, and osteoporosis observed in some female athletes, particularly those in subjectively evaluated sports (e.g., gymnastics, diving) or endurance sports (e.g., cross-country running).

Ativan *n.* a trade name for LORAZEPAM.

atomism *n.* **1.** the view that psychological phenomena can best be understood by analyzing them into elementary units, such as sensations or conditioned responses, and by showing how these units combine to form thoughts, images, perceptions, and behavior. Also called **atomistic psychology**; **molecularism.** See also ELEMENTARISM; REDUCTIONISM. **2.** in vision, the principle that visual perception of a complex stimulus results from an analysis of its elementary components. —**atomistic** *adj.*

atonia *n.* lack of normal muscle tone. See also DYSTONIA. —**atonic** *adj.*

ATP *adenosine triphosphate:* a nucleotide in living cells that is the source of chemical energy for biological processes. A bond between two of its three component phosphate groups is easily split by a particular enzyme, **ATPase** (**adenosine triphosphatase**), yielding energy when a cell requires it.

at risk vulnerable to a disorder or disease. Risk status for an individual is defined by genetic, physical, and behavioral factors or conditions. For example, children of people with schizophrenia may be considered at risk for schizophrenia, and heavy cigarette smokers are at risk for emphysema and lung cancer.

atrium *n.* (*pl.* **atria**) a body cavity or chamber, such as either of the two upper chambers of the heart. —**atrial** *adj.*

atrophy *n.* a wasting away of the body or a body part, as from lack of nourishment, inactivity, degenerative disease, or normal aging. —**atrophic** *adj.*

attachment *n.* the close emotional bond between a human infant or a young nonhuman animal and its parent figure or caregiver, developed as a step in establishing a feeling of security and demonstrated by calmness while in their presence. Attachment also denotes the tendency to form such strong bonds with certain other individuals in infancy as well as the tendency in adulthood to seek emotionally supportive relationships.

attachment theory a theory that (a) postulates an evolutionarily advantageous need, especially in primates, to form close emotional bonds with significant others: specifically, a need for the young to maintain close proximity to and form bonds with their caregivers; and (b) characterizes the different types of relationships between human infants and caregivers. These relationships have been shown to affect the individual's later emotional development and emotional stability. See also STRANGE SITUATION.

attendant care nonmedical, in-home assistance with dressing, feeding, and other activities of daily living provided to individuals with a physical or developmental disability who otherwise are able to live independently.

attending behavior any behavior engaged in by an individual while attentively listening to and observing a speaker, for example, exhibiting an open, interested posture and maintaining eye contact. Helpful attending behaviors, along with ACTIVE LISTENING, are considered cornerstones of a therapist's or counselor's general ability.

attention *n.* a state of awareness in which the senses are focused selectively on aspects of the environment and the central nervous system is in a state of readiness to respond to stimuli. Because human beings do not have an infinite capacity to attend to everything—focusing on certain items at the expense of others—much of the research in this field is devoted to discerning which factors influence attention and to understanding the neural mechanisms involved in the selective processing of information. See also ATTENUATION THEORY; FILTER THEORY.

attentional blink during the rapid presentation of a stream of visual stimuli (e.g., letters), impairment in the ability to detect the second of two targets that must be identified. Because the impairment only occurs when the targets are presented within 200–500 ms of each other, it is attributed to attentional requirements for processing the target letter and not to perceptual impairment.

attentional narrowing the restricting of attention in high-stress situations to a small set of information sources, with the potential omission of critical, task-relevant information. For example, when driving to the hospital for a medical emergency, the driver may focus attention only on the road ahead and not notice events at the side of the road, such as a pedestrian entering a crosswalk.

attention decrement the tendency for people

to pay less attention to stimuli coming later in a sequential occurrence or presentation and thus to remember them less well. For example, students studying a list of terms and their meanings will have more difficulty focusing on and committing to memory the ones at the end.

attention-deficit/hyperactivity disorder (**ADHD**; **AHD**) a behavioral syndrome characterized by the persistent presence of six or more symptoms involving (a) inattention (e.g., failure to complete tasks or listen carefully, difficulty in concentrating, distractibility) or (b) impulsivity or hyperactivity (e.g., restlessness, fidgeting, difficulty taking turns or staying seated, excessive talking, running about). The symptoms, which impair social, academic, or occupational functioning, appear before the age of 7 and are observed in more than one setting. ADHD has been given a variety of names over the years, including the still commonly used **attention-deficit disorder** (**ADD**).

attention disorder a disturbance characterized by an inability to maintain focus on an activity or by difficulties in taking notice of, responding to, or being aware of the behavior, demands, or requests of other people. Previously, this term was frequently used interchangeably with MINIMAL BRAIN DYSFUNCTION, as impairments of attention are among the most common manifestations of brain damage.

attention overload in resource models of attention, such as the UNITARY-RESOURCE MODEL, a situation in which the demand for attentional resources exceeds the supply.

attention span 1. the length of time an individual can concentrate on one specific task or other item of interest. **2.** the maximum number of distinct factors that can be comprehended from one brief exposure to an array of stimuli.

attenuation *n.* in statistics, a reduction in the estimated size of an effect because of errors of measurement.

attenuation theory a version of the FILTER THEORY of attention proposing that unattended messages are attenuated (i.e., processed weakly) but not entirely blocked from further processing. According to the theory, items in unattended channels of information have different thresholds of recognition depending on their significance to the individual. See also COCKTAIL-PARTY EFFECT.

attitude *n.* a relatively enduring and general evaluation of an object, person, group, issue, or concept on a scale ranging from negative to positive. Attitudes provide summary evaluations of target objects and are often assumed to be derived from specific beliefs, emotions, and past behaviors associated with those objects. **—attitudinal** *adj.*

attitude-congeniality effect the tendency to remember information that is evaluatively consistent with an attitude better than information that is evaluatively inconsistent with an attitude.

attitude measure a procedure in which individuals are assigned quantitative values that reflect systematic variation on some underlying attitude. Several broad categories have been developed, including DIRECT ATTITUDE MEASURES, INDIRECT ATTITUDE MEASURES, EXPLICIT ATTITUDE MEASURES, and IMPLICIT ATTITUDE MEASURES.

attitude object any target of judgment that has an attitude associated with it. Attitude objects may be people, social groups, policy positions, abstract concepts, or physical objects.

attitude system a set of two or more attitudes that are associated with one another in memory. Attitude systems can be characterized in terms of the number of attitudes in the system, the strength, number, and pattern of associations among the attitudes, and the evaluative consistency of the attitudes in the system.

attitudinal types in ANALYTIC PSYCHOLOGY, two personality types defined by habitual EXTRAVERSION on the one hand and habitual INTROVERSION on the other. See INTROVERSION–EXTRAVERSION. See also FUNCTIONAL TYPES.

attraction *n.* **1.** in social psychology, the feeling of being drawn to one or more other individuals and desiring their company, usually but not necessarily always because of a personal liking for them. See also INTERPERSONAL ATTRACTION. **2.** in environmental psychology, a quality affecting proximity relationships between individuals, usually reflecting such factors as their liking for each other. Environmental influences, such as noise, heat, and humidity, decrease attraction between pairs of individuals. See PROXEMICS. **—attractive** *adj.*

attraction–selection–attrition model a model proposing that (a) people are attracted to organizations that are congruent with their values, personalities, and needs; (b) the organization, in turn, employs people with attributes that fit the ORGANIZATIONAL CULTURE; and (c) those employees who do not fit the organizational culture leave. Over time the characteristics of the people who constitute the organization become increasingly homogeneous as the result of this process.

attributable risk in EPIDEMIOLOGY, the incidence rate of a disease or disorder that can be considered to have been caused by exposure to a RISK FACTOR. A large portion of lung cancers can be attributed to tobacco use, constituting a substantial attributable risk for this disease.

attribution *n.* an inference regarding the cause of a person's behavior or an interpersonal event. Three dimensions are often used to evaluate people's **attributional styles**, or characteristic tendencies when inferring such causes: the internal–external dimension (whether they tend to attribute events to the self or to other factors), the stable–unstable dimension (whether they tend to attribute events to enduring or transient causes), and the global–specific dimension (whether they tend to attribute events to causes that affect many events or just a single event).

attribution theory the study of the processes by which people ascribe motives to their own and others' behavior. The motives ascribed may be either internal and personal (DISPOSITIONAL ATTRIBUTION) or external and circumstantial (SITUATIONAL ATTRIBUTION). U.S. social psychologist Harold H. Kelley (1921–2003) identified three general principles of attribution: the **covariation principle**, stating that for a factor to be a cause of behavior it must be present when the behavior occurs and not present when the behavior does not occur; the **discounting principle**, stating that the role of a particular cause in producing a particular effect should be given less weight if other plausible causes are also present; and the **augmentation principle**, stating that if someone performs an action when there are known constraints, costs, or risks, then his or her motive for doing so must be stronger than any of the inhibitory motives. Kelley's work and other prominent attribution theories (e.g., CORRESPONDENT INFERENCE THEORY) emerged from the NAIVE ANALYSIS OF ACTION developed in 1958 by Austrian-born U.S. psychologist Fritz Heider (1896–1988).

attribution theory of leadership a model of leadership emergence and evaluation that assumes that individuals make inferences about leadership ability by observing and interpreting certain environmental and behavioral cues. Like LEADER-CATEGORIZATION THEORY, attribution theory assumes that followers respond more positively to a leader who displays the qualities and behaviors that match their IMPLICIT LEADERSHIP THEORIES.

atypical antipsychotic see ANTIPSYCHOTIC.

atypical features symptoms of a disorder other than the standard diagnostic criteria. For a MAJOR DEPRESSIVE EPISODE or DYSTHYMIC DISORDER, for example, they would include improvement of mood in response to positive events or HYPERSOMNIA.

audibility range the sound frequencies that elicit the sensation of hearing. For humans with average hearing the audibility range is usually specified as 20 Hz to 20 kHz. However, humans are much less sensitive to frequencies at the extremes of this somewhat arbitrary range. Also called **audible range**.

audience effect the influence on behavior of the presence of bystanders. In humans, performance is often improved when the action is simple and well learned (see SOCIAL FACILITATION) but may be inhibited when it is complicated, difficult to perform, or when the person believes the behavior might incur the audience's disapproval (see SOCIAL INHIBITION).

audiogram *n.* a graph relating an individual's PURE-TONE thresholds at selected frequencies to

those of people with average hearing. The *x*-axis is the frequency of the tone; the *y*-axis is **hearing level**, expressed in decibels. The audiogram is a basic clinical measurement for assessing and diagnosing hearing disorders.

audiology *n.* the study of hearing, with an emphasis on the evaluation and treatment of hearing disorders and the rehabilitation of individuals with hearing loss or related disorders (e.g., balance disorders). —**audiological** *adj.* —**audiologist** *n.*

audiometry *n.* the measurement of an individual's hearing ability with electronic devices called **audiometers** to diagnose hearing loss and determine its nature and extent. Also called **diagnostic audiometry**. See also ELECTROPHYSIOLOGIC AUDIOMETRY. —**audiometrician** *n.*

audit *n.* an evaluation or review of the health care services proposed or rendered by a provider. See MEDICAL AUDIT; TREATMENT AUDIT.

audition *n.* see HEARING.

auditory acuity sharpness of hearing: the extent to which one is able to detect and discriminate between sounds that are very similar.

auditory agnosia loss or impairment of the ability to recognize and understand the nature of verbal or nonverbal sounds. Subtypes are distinguished on the basis of the type of auditory stimulus the person has difficulty recognizing, for example, environmental sounds such as a dog barking or keys jingling (**nonverbal auditory agnosia** or **environmental sounds agnosia**), spoken words (PURE WORD DEAFNESS), or music (sensory AMUSIA).

auditory canal see EXTERNAL AUDITORY MEATUS.

auditory cortex the sensory area for hearing, located on the upper side of the TEMPORAL LOBE of the cerebral cortex. It receives and processes input from the medial GENICULATE NUCLEUS in the thalamus, a major structure along the AUDITORY PATHWAY. Also called **auditory projection area**.

auditory discrimination the ability to distinguish between sounds. For example, **pitch discrimination** is the ability to detect changes in sound based upon the subjective attribute of pitch. It is more appropriately called **frequency discrimination**, however, because of uncertainty that the discrimination is based upon pitch (e.g., under certain circumstances a change in frequency produces a change in loudness, and the discrimination could be based on a loudness change rather than a pitch change).

auditory evoked potential a biologically produced electrical response to sound. There are many types of auditory evoked potentials, which differ in their methods of recording and processing sounds.

auditory fatigue a transient form of hearing loss marked by reduced sensitivity to the minimum level of sound that can be detected, due to exposure to loud noises.

auditory feedback the sound of one's own voice heard while one is speaking, which enables adjustments in intensity, pacing, or clarity of speech to be made. Artificial forms of feedback, such as DELAYED AUDITORY FEEDBACK, are used in speech and language therapy.

auditory filter the process responsible for the FREQUENCY SELECTIVITY of the auditory system. The initial stages of auditory processing are often described as consisting of a bank of auditory filters with different center frequencies.

auditory hallucination see HALLUCINATION.

auditory labyrinth see LABYRINTH.

auditory localization the ability to identify the position and changes in position of sound sources based on acoustic information. Also called **sound localization**.

auditory masking a reduction in the ability to detect, discriminate, or recognize one sound (the signal or target) due to the presence of another sound (the masker), measured as an increase in the detection threshold caused by the masker. The ability of one sound to mask another has been used extensively to assess the FREQUENCY SELECTIVITY of the auditory system. See also CRITICAL BAND.

auditory memory the type of memory that retains information obtained by hearing. Auditory memory may be either SHORT-TERM MEMORY or LONG-TERM MEMORY, and the material retained may be linguistic (e.g., words) or nonlinguistic (e.g., music).

auditory nerve the portion of the vestibulo-cochlear nerve concerned with the sense of hearing. It originates in the cochlea, from which nerve fibers pass through several layers of nuclei in the brainstem to terminate predominantly in the AUDITORY CORTEX. Also called **acoustic nerve**; **cochlear nerve**.

auditory pathway the neural route along which auditory information is conveyed from the cochlear HAIR CELLS to the AUDITORY CORTEX. The major structures in the auditory pathway are the COCHLEAR NUCLEUS, SUPERIOR OLIVARY COMPLEX, LATERAL LEMNISCUS, inferior COLLICULUS, and the medial GENICULATE NUCLEUS.

auditory perception the organization and interpretation of sensory information received through the ear. It is a complex process in which pressure changes in the air are funneled into the middle ear, where motion of the TYMPANIC MEMBRANE and the tiny attached bones (see OSSICLES) are transmitted to the inner ear and cause vibrations of membranous structures within the coiled, fluid-filled COCHLEA. Many specialized cells in the cochlea amplify and filter the movements through a variety of electro-mechanical mechanisms. Eventually, HAIR CELLS convert the mechanical motions to neural

stimulation that is transmitted along the AUDITORY PATHWAY to the AUDITORY CORTEX for processing.

auditory processing disorder see CENTRAL AUDITORY PROCESSING DISORDER.

auditory sensory memory see ECHOIC MEMORY.

auditory spectrum a synonym of SOUND SPECTRUM. This term, however, is sometimes used more restrictively to denote the AUDIBILITY RANGE.

auditory system the biological structures and processes responsible for hearing. The **peripheral auditory system**, or **auditory periphery**, includes the external, middle, and inner ears and the AUDITORY NERVE. Auditory structures of the brain, including the AUDITORY CORTEX, constitute the **central auditory system**.

auditory threshold 1. the minimum level of sound that can be detected by an organism. See ABSOLUTE THRESHOLD. **2.** any threshold pertaining to hearing, including DIFFERENCE THRESHOLDS, pain thresholds, acoustic reflex thresholds, and bone-conduction thresholds.

auditory training helping people with hearing loss to better distinguish sounds and understand spoken language by teaching them how to make the most effective use of their residual hearing and to discern contextual clues related to situations and environments.

Aufgabe *n.* a predisposition toward particular mental operations inherent in the nature of a task or conveyed by the instructions for performing it. Introduced by the WÜRZBURG SCHOOL in their introspective experiments on mental processes, the concept became a precursor to the later DETERMINING TENDENCY and the modern MENTAL SET. [German: "assignment"]

augmentation principle see ATTRIBUTION THEORY.

augmentation strategy a mechanism to increase the effectiveness of pharmacological agents by the addition of other agents. Augmentation strategies are most commonly used in the treatment of depression.

aura *n.* **1.** a subjective sensation that precedes an epileptic seizure or migraine headache. It may include such phenomena as strange tastes or odors, flashes of light (a **visual aura**), numbness, and feelings of unreality or DÉJÀ VU. **2.** a subtle halo or emanation that purportedly surrounds every person, animal, plant, or object. Some individuals claim to be able to discern such auras, which can allegedly reveal an individual's personal qualities as well as his or her state of physical health. In SPIRITUALISM and theosophy, a person's aura is sometimes identified with his or her purported supernormal counterpart; in other traditions it may be seen as the manifestation of a life force or energy field.

aural *adj.* pertaining to or perceived by the ear.

auricle *n.* **1.** see PINNA. **2.** a small ear-shaped pouch that extends from the upper anterior portion of each ATRIUM of the heart.

authenticity *n.* **1.** in psychotherapy and counseling, a characteristic of the therapist or counselor who is considered to be genuine and caring. Authenticity is often demonstrated by a professional but down-to-earth attitude that the client senses to be a reflection of the true person and not simply of the therapist acting in his or her professional role. **2.** in EXISTENTIALISM, a mode of being that humans can achieve by accepting the burden of freedom, choice, and responsibility and the need to construct their own values and meanings in a meaningless universe. —**authentic** *adj.*

authoritarian parenting see PARENTING.

authoritarian personality a personality pattern characterized by strict adherence to highly simplified conventional values, an attitude of great deference to authority figures while demanding subservience from those regarded as lower in status, and hostility toward people who deviate from conventional moral prescriptions.

authoritative parenting see PARENTING.

authority *n.* the capacity to influence others. Formal authority enables an individual to exert influence as a result of either high, legally recognized office (**legitimate authority**) or high rank in a long-established but not legally codified hierarchy (**traditional authority**). Informal authority is based on the individual having either attributes that facilitate the achievement of a group's goals (**rational** or **expert authority**) or an attractive and authoritative personality serving to enhance his or her credibility (**charismatic authority**).

authority and social order maintaining orientation see CONVENTIONAL LEVEL.

autism *n.* **1.** abnormal preoccupation with the self and fantasy such that there is lack of interest in or ability to focus on external reality. **2.** a synonym for AUTISTIC DISORDER. —**autistic** *adj.*

autistic disorder a severe neurologically based pervasive developmental disorder characterized by markedly impaired social interactions and verbal and nonverbal communication; narrow interests; and repetitive behavior. Manifestations and features of the disorder appear before age 3 but vary greatly across children according to developmental level, language skills, and chronological age. They may include a lack of awareness of the feelings of others, impaired ability to imitate, absence of social play, abnormal speech, abnormal nonverbal communication, and a preference for maintaining environmental sameness.

autistic savant see SAVANT.

autistic spectrum disorder (**ASD**) any one of a group of disorders with an onset typically occurring during the preschool years and characterized by varying but often marked difficulties in communication and social interaction. The group includes the prototype AUTISTIC DISORDER as well as RETT SYNDROME, ASPERGER'S DISORDER, and CHILDHOOD DISINTEGRATIVE DISORDER. This term is synonymous with PERVASIVE DEVELOPMENTAL DISORDER but is now more commonly used, given its reflection of symptom overlap among the disorders. Also called **autism spectrum disorder**.

autobiographical memory vivid personal memories recalling the time and place of events and factual knowledge about oneself.

autobiography *n.* in therapy or counseling, a technique in which a LIFE HISTORY, written by the client from his or her own point of view, is used to obtain information regarding the client's behavioral patterns and feelings. A **structured autobiography** is based on explicit questions or topic guidelines supplied by the therapist or counselor. An **unstructured autobiography** contains no guidelines.

autocorrelation *n.* the degree of relationship between multiple values of a single attribute obtained during a TIME SERIES or WITHIN-SUBJECTS DESIGN.

autocratic leader see LEADERSHIP STYLE.

autocrine *adj.* describing or relating to a type of cellular signaling in which a chemical messenger is secreted by a cell into its environment and feeds back to elicit a response in the same cell. Compare ENDOCRINE; PARACRINE.

autoeroticism *n.* the creation of sexual excitement and gratification by the self, whether it be through masturbation, other sexual behaviors, or thoughts. Also called **autoerotism**. Compare ALLOEROTICISM. —**autoerotic** *adj.*

autohypnosis *n.* see SELF-HYPNOSIS. —**autohypnotic** *adj.*

autoimmunity *n.* a condition in which the body's immune system fails to recognize its own tissues as "self" and attempts to reject its own cells. It is a primary factor in the development of such diseases as rheumatoid arthritis and systemic lupus erythematosus (called **autoimmune disorders**). —**autoimmune** *adj.*

autokinesis *n.* **1.** any movement that is voluntary. **2.** an illusory perception of movement—often experienced by pilots flying at night—that occurs when fixating on a dim, stationary light source in the dark. Also called **autokinetic effect**; **autokinetic illusion**.

automaintenance *n.* a procedure in which stimulus–reinforcer pairings are used to sustain an already established behavior. It is most commonly used with pigeons. Signals are presented, regardless of behaviors, on a response device (e.g., a pecking disk) and reinforcement (e.g., food) is delivered after a specified time period regardless of the pigeons' pecking activity.

automated desensitization the use of such devices as audiotapes, videotapes, and digitized media to facilitate the presentation of anxiety-provoking and relaxing stimuli during SYSTEM-ATIC DESENSITIZATION.

automatic activation involuntary processing of stimuli and preparation for associated responses. This activation tends to occur more rapidly than that resulting from ATTENTION or INTENTION.

automaticity n. the quality of a mental process that can be carried out rapidly and without effort or intention (an **automatic process**). See also DEAUTOMATIZATION HYPOTHESIS.

automatic reinforcer a physical or sensory consequence of a response that serves to reinforce the response.

automatic thoughts instantaneous, habitual, but unconscious thoughts that affect a person's mood and actions. Helping clients become aware of the presence and impact of negative automatic thoughts and then test their validity is a central task of cognitive therapy.

automatism n. nonpurposeful behavior performed mechanically, without intention, and without conscious awareness (e.g., lipsmacking or sleepwalking).

automatization n. the development of a skill or habit to a point at which it becomes routine and requires little if any conscious effort or direction.

autonoetic adj. describing a level of knowledge or memory in which one is aware not only of the known or remembered thing but also of one's personal experience in relation to that thing. Compare ANOETIC; NOETIC.

autonomic adj. occurring involuntarily, particularly pertaining to the AUTONOMIC NERVOUS SYSTEM or the processes controlled by it. **—autonomically** adv.

autonomic conditioning in PAVLOVIAN CONDITIONING, a procedure in which the unconditioned stimulus is a mildly aversive stimulus such as an electric shock or a loud noise, and the conditioned response measured is an index of physiological arousal, usually an electrodermal measure such as SKIN CONDUCTANCE responses. The conditioned stimulus is usually a simple visual or auditory stimulus presented for 5–10 seconds.

autonomic hyperactivity arousal of the AUTONOMIC NERVOUS SYSTEM resulting in the physiological symptoms associated with anxiety and fear (e.g., sweating, palpitations, dry mouth).

autonomic learning a type of learning in which the responses learned consist of changes in functions involving the AUTONOMIC NERVOUS SYSTEM, such as heart rate or blood pressure. See also CONDITIONED RESPONSE.

autonomic nervous system (**ANS**) the portion of the nervous system innervating smooth muscle and glands, including the circulatory, digestive, respiratory, and reproductive organs. It is divided into the SYMPATHETIC NERVOUS SYS-TEM and PARASYMPATHETIC NERVOUS SYSTEM. **Autonomic responses** typically involve changes in involuntary bodily functions, such as heart rate, salivation, digestion, perspiration, pupil size, hormone secretion, bladder contraction, and engorgement of the penis and clitoris.

autonomous adj. **1.** having an independent existence. **2.** acting or operating under one's own direction. Compare HETERONOMOUS.

autonomous depression a MAJOR DEPRESSIVE EPISODE that does not occur in response to any obvious psychosocial stressor. See also ENDOGENOUS DEPRESSION.

autonomous stage in the theory of moral development proposed by Swiss psychologist Jean Piaget (1896–1980), the stage during which the child, typically 10 years of age or older, eventually understands that rules and laws are not permanent, fixed properties of the world but rather are flexible, modifiable entities created by people. The child gradually relies less on parental authority and more on individual and independent morality and learns that intentions, not consequences or the likelihood of punishment, are important in determining the morality of an act. Also called **autonomous morality**. See MORAL RELATIVISM. Compare HETERONOMOUS STAGE; PREMORAL STAGE.

autonomous syntax the theory that SYNTAX is an autonomous component of language that operates independently of meaning (semantics) and function (pragmatics). Such a view explains how a sentence with no meaningful content or communicative function can nevertheless be recognized as grammatical by native speakers (see GRAMMATICALITY). It also explains why syntactic rules, such as number agreement between subject and verb, operate regardless of the semantic relationship between the sentence elements. For example, in the two sentences *The boy is slamming the doors* and *The doors are being slammed by the boy* the verb takes different forms to agree with the grammatical subject in each case (*boy is*; *doors are*), regardless of the fact that in both cases the boy is the actor and the doors the acted upon. See CASE GRAMMAR.

autonomy n. a state of independence and self-determination. Compare HETERONOMY.

autonomy versus shame and doubt the second of ERIKSON'S EIGHT STAGES OF DEVELOPMENT, between the ages of 1½ and 3 years. During this stage, children acquire a degree of self-reliance and self-confidence if allowed to develop at their own pace but may begin to doubt their ability to control themselves and their world if parents are overcritical, overprotective, or inconsistent.

autoplasty n. adaptation to reality by modifying one's own behavioral patterns, rather than by altering one's environment. Compare ALLOPLASTY. **—autoplastic** adj.

autopsy n. a procedure in which the body of a person is examined after death in an effort to determine the exact cause and time of death. It usually requires a detailed dissection of body tissues, laboratory tests, and other techniques when the death occurs under suspicious circumstances. See also PSYCHOLOGICAL AUTOPSY.

autoreceptor *n.* a molecule in the membrane of a presynaptic neuron that regulates the synthesis and release of a neurotransmitter by that neuron by monitoring how much transmitter has been released and "telling" the neuron.

autoregressive model a model used primarily in the analysis of TIME SERIES, where each successive observation depends, at least in part, on one or more preceding observations.

autoshaping *n.* a method of establishing OPERANT performance that rewards only elicited responses. It is most commonly used with pigeons. Signals are presented, independently of behavior, on a response device (in the case of pigeons, a pecking disk), which records the response and then immediately presents reinforcement.

autosomal dominant see DOMINANT ALLELE.

autosomal recessive see RECESSIVE ALLELE.

autosome *n.* any chromosome that is not a SEX CHROMOSOME. A human normally has a total of 44 autosomes (arranged in 22 HOMOLOGOUS pairs) in the nucleus of each body cell. If a homologous pair of autosomes has an extra chromosome, the condition is called **trisomy**. If one member of a homologous pair is absent, the condition is called **monosomy**. —**autosomal** *adj.*

autosuggestion *n.* the process of making positive suggestions to oneself for such purposes as improving morale, inducing relaxation, or promoting recovery from illness. Also called **self-suggestion**.

autotopagnosia *n.* a type of AGNOSIA involving loss or impairment of the ability to recognize (i.e., point to) parts of one's own or another person's body. Also called **autopagnosia**.

auxiliary inversion in grammar, the reversal of the usual order of subject and auxiliary verb in a declarative sentence to create a question so that, for example, *The poodle is barking* becomes *Is the poodle barking?* Such constructions are of major interest in GENERATIVE GRAMMAR and PSYCHOLINGUISTICS.

availability *n.* the presence of information in memory storage. Availability should be distinguished from **accessibility**, which refers to the ability of a portion of information to be retrieved.

availability heuristic a common strategy for making judgments about likelihood of occurrence in which the individual bases such judgments on the amount of information held in his or her memory about the particular type of event: The more information there is, the more likely the event is judged to be. Compare REPRESENTATIVENESS HEURISTIC.

Aventyl *n.* a trade name for NORTRIPTYLINE.

average error the typical degree to which a se-

ries of observations are inaccurate with respect to an absolute criterion (e.g., a standard weight or length) or a relative criterion (e.g., the mean of the observations within a given condition).

average evoked potential (**AEP**) the summated electrical responses of the brain (see EVOKED POTENTIAL) to repeated presentations of the same stimulus. Since any individual potential typically shows considerable random fluctuations, this technique is used to better distinguish the actual response from background "noise." Also called **average evoked response (AER)**.

aversion *n.* a physiological or emotional response indicating dislike for a stimulus. It is usually accompanied by withdrawal from or avoidance of the objectionable stimulus (an **aversion reaction**). —**aversive** *adj.*

aversive conditioning the process by which a noxious or unpleasant stimulus is paired with an undesired behavior. This technique may be used therapeutically, for example, in the treatment of substance abuse, in which case it is called **aversion** (or **aversive**) **therapy**. Also called **aversion conditioning**.

aversive racism a form of racial PREJUDICE felt by individuals who outwardly endorse egalitarian attitudes and values but nonetheless experience negative emotions in the presence of members of certain racial groups. See also MODERN RACISM.

avian influenza a highly contagious and mortal viral disease among domestic fowl and other birds, colloquially known as **bird flu**. It is brought by migratory birds, which can carry the virus asymptomatically. Cross-transmission to humans has been rare (requiring close contact with infected birds and their feces), but has also been on the rise since 2004. When human infection occurs, typical symptoms range from fever, cough, sore throat, and muscle aches to eye infections, pneumonia, and other severe and potentially mortal complications. As with other influenza viruses, there is potential for mutation, which could lead to humans infecting other humans through person-to-person contact. Because cross-transmission to humans has been infrequent, there is little or no immunity to infection and the development of a vaccine is still in an early stage.

aviation psychology a specialty in APPLIED PSYCHOLOGY that focuses on understanding human psychology as it relates to the operation and control of aviation systems and influences the safety and efficiency of flight.

AVM abbreviation for ARTERIOVENOUS MALFORMATION.

avoidance *n.* the practice or an instance of keeping away from particular situations, environments, individuals, or things because of either (a) the anticipated negative consequences of such an encounter or (b) anxious or painful feelings associated with those things or events. Psychology brings several theoretical perspectives to the study of avoidance: its use as a means of coping; its use as a response to fear or shame; and its existence as a component in ANXIETY DISORDERS.

avoidance–avoidance conflict a situation involving a choice between two equally objectionable alternatives. Also called **double-avoidance conflict**. See also APPROACH–APPROACH CONFLICT; APPROACH–AVOIDANCE CONFLICT.

avoidance conditioning the establishment of behavior that prevents or postpones aversive stimulation. In a typical conditioning experiment a buzzer is sounded, then a shock is applied to the subject (e.g., a dog) until it performs a particular act (e.g., jumping over a fence). After several trials, the dog jumps as soon as the buzzer sounds, avoiding the shock. Also called **avoidance learning; avoidance training**. See also ESCAPE CONDITIONING.

avoidant attachment see INSECURE ATTACHMENT.

avoidant personality disorder a personality disorder characterized by (a) hypersensitivity to rejection and criticism, (b) a desire for uncritical acceptance, (c) social withdrawal in spite of a desire for affection and acceptance, and (d) low self-esteem. This pattern is long-standing and severe enough to cause objective distress and seriously impair the ability to work and maintain relationships.

awareness n. conscious realization, perception, or knowledge. See also SELF-AWARENESS.

axial adj. relating to, along, or otherwise involving an AXIS, particularly the long axis or central part of the body.

axiom n. in logic and philosophy, a universally accepted proposition that is not capable of proof or disproof. An axiom can be used as the starting point for a chain of DEDUCTIVE REASONING. Also called **postulate**. —**axiomatic** adj.

axis n. (pl. **axes**) **1.** in DSM–IV–TR, any of the five dimensions that are helpful for describing individual behavior and thus facilitate clinical assessment. They are clinical disorders (Axis I), personality disorders and mental retardation (Axis II), general medical conditions (Axis III), psychosocial and environmental problems (Axis IV), and global assessment of functioning (Axis V). **2.** an imaginary line that bisects the body or an organ in a particular plane. For example, the **long** or (**cephalocaudal**) **axis** runs in the median plane, dividing the body into right and left halves. **3.** a system made up of interrelated parts, as in the HYPOTHALAMIC–PITUITARY–ADRENOCORTICAL SYSTEM (or axis). **4.** a fixed reference line in a coordinate system. See also ABSCISSA; ORDINATE.

axon n. the long, thin, hollow, cylindrical extension of a NEURON that normally carries a nerve impulse away from the CELL BODY. An axon often branches extensively and may be surrounded by a protective MYELIN SHEATH. Each branch of an axon ends in a **terminal button** (or **synaptic bouton**) from which an impulse is transmitted, through discharge of a NEUROTRANSMITTER, across a SYNAPSE to a neighboring neuron. Also called **nerve fiber**. —**axonal** adj.

axonal transport the transportation of materials along the AXON of a neuron via the flow of the jellylike fluid (**axoplasm**) it contains. Transport may be directed away from the CELL BODY (anterograde) or back toward the cell body (retrograde). Also called **axoplasmic transport**.

axon hillock a cone-shaped part of the CELL BODY of a neuron from which the AXON originates. Depolarization must reach a critical threshold at the axon hillock for the axon to propagate a nerve impulse.

Ayurveda n. a holistic system of healing, originating and practiced primarily in the Indian subcontinent, that has spread to some extent in Western cultures. It includes diet and herbal remedies and emphasizes the use of body, mind, and spirit in disease prevention and treatment.

azaspirone n. any of a class of nonbenzodiazepine ANXIOLYTICS of which the prototype is BUSPIRONE. They produce less sedation than the BENZODIAZEPINES and they lack the abuse potential of these drugs. Other drugs in this class include gepirone, tandospirone, and ipsapirone. Also called **azaspirodecanedione**.

Bb

babbling *n.* prespeech sounds, such as *dadada*, made by infants from around 6 months of age. Also called **babble**.

Babinski reflex the reflex occurring in a healthy infant in which the toes are extended upward when the sole of the foot is gently stimulated. In adults, this response is an indication of neurological disorder and called **Babinski's sign**. [Joseph F. **Babinski** (1857–1932), French neurologist]

baby talk 1. the type of speech used by a young child. **2.** the type of speech used by adults and older children when talking to infants or very young children.

background *n.* in perception, any aspect of the environment that forms a setting for the primary stimulus or stimuli. See also FIGURE–GROUND.

back-translation *n.* see TRANSLATION AND BACK-TRANSLATION.

backward association the formation of an associative link between one item and an item that precedes it in a series or sequence. Compare FORWARD ASSOCIATION.

backward conditioning a procedure in which an UNCONDITIONED STIMULUS is consistently presented before a NEUTRAL STIMULUS. Generally, this arrangement is not thought to produce a change in the effect of a neutral stimulus. Occasionally, however, the neutral stimulus may take on inhibitory functions, presumably because it consistently predicts the absence of the unconditioned stimulus. It may also take on excitatory functions as a result of PSEUDO-CONDITIONING. Also called **backward pairing**. Compare FORWARD CONDITIONING.

backward elimination a technique used in creating MULTIPLE REGRESSION models in which the least important independent (predictor) variables are systematically removed from the REGRESSION EQUATION until a preset criterion is reached. Also called **backward stepwise regression**.

backward masking see MASKING.

Baconian method the inductive method of scientific investigation first set out by English philosopher Francis Bacon (1561–1626). The method involves the inference of general laws or principles from particular instances observed under controlled conditions (i.e., in experiments). To make sure that any such generalization is valid, the observer must seek not only positive instances of an association between things in which one event or state brings about another, but also negative instances in which the event or state fails to occur in the absence of the other. Finally, the observer tries to formulate an explanation for the causal connection so established. See INDUCTIVE REASONING.

bad object in the psychoanalytic theory of Austrian-born British psychoanalyst Melanie Klein (1882–1960), an introjected PART-OBJECT perceived as having negative qualities (see INTROJECTION). It is an early object representation that derives from "splitting" of the object into parts containing negative qualities (i.e., the bad object) and positive qualities (i.e., the GOOD OBJECT).

BAI abbreviation for BECK ANXIETY INVENTORY.

bait shyness an alternative but less common name for CONDITIONED TASTE AVERSION.

balance *n.* **1.** a harmonious relationship or equilibrium of opposing forces or contrasting elements. See BALANCE THEORY; HOMEOSTASIS. **2.** the SENSE OF EQUILIBRIUM mediated by the VESTIBULAR SYSTEM of the inner ear.

balanced design an experimental design in which the number of observations or measurements obtained in each experimental condition is equal.

balanced scale a scale in which, for each alternative, there is another alternative that means the opposite. An example is a rating scale with the four alternatives very poor, poor, good, and very good.

balance theory a particular COGNITIVE CONSISTENCY THEORY specifying that people prefer elements within a cognitive system to be internally consistent with one another (i.e., balanced). Balanced systems are assumed to be more stable and psychologically pleasant than imbalanced ones. These systems are sometimes referred to as **P-O-X triads**, in which P = person (i.e., self), O = other person, and X = some stimulus or event. See also COGNITIVE CONSISTENCY THEORY.

Baldwin effect the influence on intraspecies evolution of behavior change and learning. An individual member of the species acquires a new ability that enables better adaptation to the environment and hence increases probability of survival; the propensity for acquiring this characteristic is conferred in turn on descendants of that species member until a genetic variation occurs and the characteristic itself becomes hereditary. The Baldwin effect was originally called **organic selection**. [described in 1896 by U.S. psychologist James Mark **Baldwin** (1861–1934)]

Bálint's syndrome a spatial and attentional disorder resulting from lesions in the parieto-occipital region of the brain. It consists of inability to visually guide the hand to an object (OPTIC ATAXIA), inability to change visual gaze (**optic apraxia**), and inability to recognize multiple stimuli in a scene and understand their nature as a whole (simultanagnosia; see VISUAL AGNOSIA). [first described in 1909 by Rudolf **Bálint** (1874–1929), Hungarian physician]

ballismus *n.* involuntary throwing or flinging movements of the limbs, caused by severe muscle contractions due to neurological damage. It may involve both sides of the body or, in the case of **hemiballismus**, one side only. Also called **ballism**.

ballistic *adj.* describing a movement (or part of a movement) in which the motion, once initiated, is not altered by feedback-based corrections. Ballistic is sometimes also used, incorrectly, to describe any rapid movement.

banding *n.* an approach to setting cutoff scores in personnel selection. Several ranges of scores known as **score bands** are identified and, rather than being considered individually, all scores falling within the same band are regarded as equivalent.

bandwagon effect the tendency for people in social and sometimes political situations to align themselves with the majority opinion and do or believe things because many other people do or believe the same.

bandwidth *n.* **1.** a range of frequencies, usually expressed in hertz (cycles per second). In INFORMATION THEORY, it is a measure of the amount of information that a communication channel can transmit per unit of time. **2.** the range of information available from measuring instruments. Greater bandwidth is generally associated with lower accuracy (fidelity).

baragnosis *n.* an inability to judge the weights of objects held in the hand. Compare BAROGNOSIS.

barbiturate *n.* any of a family of drugs derived from barbituric acid that depress activity of the central nervous system (see CNS DEPRESSANT). They typically induce profound tolerance and withdrawal symptoms and depress respiration. Use of barbiturates as anxiolytics, sedatives, and hypnotics became common in the 1930s, but they were rapidly supplanted in the 1970s by the BENZODIAZEPINES, which lack the lethality associated with overdose of the barbiturates. The prototype of the group, **barbital**, was introduced into medical practice in 1903.

baresthesia *n.* the sensation of weight or pressure.

bargaining stage the third of the five STAGES OF GRIEF described by Swiss-born U.S. psychiatrist Elisabeth Kübler-Ross (1926–2004). It is characterized by an attempt to negotiate a deal with God or fate that would delay one's own death or that of an important other, or that would mitigate or end other great loss or trauma.

bar graph a way of graphically displaying discrete (nonnumerical) data using bars of varying height with spaces between them. For example, to show the political party affiliation of Americans, bars would represent parties along the *x*-axis, while the heights of the bars would represent numbers of people. Compare HISTOGRAM. Also called **bar chart**.

bariatrics *n.* a field of medicine that focuses on the study of overweight: its causes, prevention, and treatment.

Barnum effect the tendency of individuals to believe that vague predictions or general personality descriptions, such as those offered by astrology, have specific applications to themselves. When first studied in 1949 the effect was termed the **fallacy of personal validation**.

barognosis *n.* the ability to estimate the weights of objects held in the hand. Compare BARAGNOSIS.

Barona equation an equation that uses demographic variables (such as age and education) to estimate IQ prior to brain injury or disease. [Andres **Barona** (1945–), U.S. psychologist]

baroreceptor *n.* a pressure receptor in the heart or a major artery that detects changes in blood pressure and communicates that information to the brain via the autonomic nervous system. Also called **baroceptor**.

barrier-free environment a built space that is free of obstacles to individuals with physical and cognitive disabilities and permits safe, uninhibited movements. See also UNIVERSAL DESIGN.

basal age the highest chronological age at which all items on a given standardized test are consistently answered correctly. This concept is less widely used than in the past because it assumes the use of MENTAL AGES, which are declining in popularity.

basal cell see TYPE IV CELL.

basal forebrain a region of the ventral FOREBRAIN near the corpus callosum containing CHOLINERGIC neurons that project widely to the cerebral cortex and HIPPOCAMPUS and are thought to be important in aspects of memory, learning, and attention. A particular collection of neurons, the **basal nucleus of Meynert** (or **basal magnocellular nucleus**), is implicated in Alzheimer's disease.

basal ganglia a group of nuclei (neuron cell bodies) deep within the cerebral hemispheres of the brain that includes the CAUDATE NUCLEUS, PUTAMEN, GLOBUS PALLIDUS, SUBSTANTIA NIGRA, and SUBTHALAMIC NUCLEUS. The putamen and globus pallidus are together known as the **lenticular** (or **lentiform**) **nucleus**, the lenticular nucleus and caudate nucleus are together known as the **corpus striatum**, and the caudate nucleus and putamen are together called the **striatum**. The basal ganglia are involved in the generation of goal-directed voluntary movement. Also called **basal nuclei**.

basal reader approach a method of reading instruction through the use of a series of books. The vocabulary, content, and sequence of skills to be taught are thus determined by the authors.

baseline *n.* a stable level of performance used as a yardstick to assess the effects of particular manipulations or interventions.

base rate the naturally occurring frequency of a phenomenon in a population. This rate is often contrasted with the rate of the phenomenon under the influence of some changed condition in order to determine the degree to which the change influences the phenomenon.

base-rate fallacy a decision-making error in which information about rate of occurrence of some trait in a population (the base-rate information) is ignored or not given appropriate weight. For example, people might categorize a man as an engineer, rather than a lawyer, if they heard that he enjoyed physics at school, even if they knew that he was drawn from a population consisting of 90% lawyers and 10% engineers. See REPRESENTATIVENESS HEURISTIC.

basic anxiety in EGO PSYCHOLOGY, a feeling of being helpless, abandoned, and endangered in a hostile world. According to German-born U.S. psychoanalyst Karen D. Horney (1885–1952), it arises from the infant's helplessness and dependence on his or her parents or from parental indifference. Defenses against basic anxiety and hostility may produce NEUROTIC NEEDS and NEUROTIC TRENDS, such as a submissive attitude, the need to exert power over others, or withdrawal from relationships.

BASIC ID see MULTIMODAL THERAPY.

basic-level category a category formed at the level that people find most natural and appropriate in their normal, everyday experience of the things so categorized. A basic-level category (e.g., "bird," "table") will be broader than the more specific SUBORDINATE CATEGORIES into which it can be divided (e.g., "hawk," "dining table") but less abstract than the SUPERORDINATE CATEGORY into which it can be subsumed (e.g., "animals," "furniture"). Also called **basic category**; **natural category**.

basic mistrust the unsuccessful resolution of the first stage in ERIKSON'S EIGHT STAGES OF DEVELOPMENT, in which the child in the first 18 months of life comes to experience a fundamental distrust of his or her environment, often due to neglect, lack of love, or inconsistent treatment. The acquisition of BASIC TRUST or hope is considered essential for the development of self-esteem and normal relatedness.

basic need see PHYSIOLOGICAL NEED.

basic reflex any of the infant reflexes of sucking, eye movement, grasping, and sound orientation.

basic research research conducted in order to obtain knowledge or to develop or advance a theory. Also called **pure research**. Compare APPLIED RESEARCH.

basic rest–activity cycle cyclic alternations between activity and nonactivity during waking and sleep, thought typically to involve a 90-minute cycle.

basic rule the fundamental rule of psychoanalysis that the patient must attempt to put all spontaneous thoughts, feelings, and memories into words without censorship, so that they can be analyzed to reveal unconscious wishes and emotions. Also called **fundamental rule**.

basic trust the successful resolution of the first of ERIKSON'S EIGHT STAGES OF DEVELOPMENT, in which the child in the first 18 months of life comes to feel that his or her world is trustworthy. This lays the foundation for self-esteem and positive interpersonal relationships. The growth of basic trust is attributed to a primary caregiver who is responsively attuned to the baby's individual needs while conveying the quality of trustworthiness. Compare BASIC MISTRUST.

basilar membrane a fibrous membrane within the COCHLEA that supports the ORGAN OF CORTI. In response to sound the basilar membrane vibrates; this leads to stimulation of the HAIR CELLS—the auditory receptors within the organ of Corti. The mechanical properties of the basilar membrane vary over its length (34 mm in humans), giving rise to a pattern of movement known as a **traveling wave**, or **Békésy traveling wave**. The location of the maximum movement depends on the frequency of the sound.

basket ending any of the nerve endings that are found around hair follicles and are responsible for sensations of contact and pressure.

Batesian mimicry a form of MIMICRY in which a species that is nontoxic or palatable to predators mimics the physical shape or coloration of a toxic species. For example, some species of flies have black and yellow coloration similar to bees and wasps with stingers. [Henry Walter **Bates** (1825–1892), British naturalist]

battered-child syndrome the effects on a child of intentional and repeated physical abuse by parents or other caregivers. In addition to sustaining physical injuries, the child is at increased risk of experiencing longer term problems, such as depression, POSTTRAUMATIC STRESS DISORDER, substance abuse, decreased self-esteem, and sexual and other behavioral difficulties. See also CHILD ABUSE.

battered-woman syndrome the psychological effects of being physically abused by a spouse or domestic partner. The syndrome includes LEARNED HELPLESSNESS in relation to the abusive spouse, as well as symptoms of posttraumatic stress. See also CYCLE OF VIOLENCE.

Bayesian approach the use of conditional probabilities as an aid in selecting between various options involving a degree of uncertainty, for example, in the delivery of health care services or utilization of limited resources. [Thomas **Bayes** (1702–1761), British mathematician and theologian]

Bayes' theorem a formula derived from probability theory that relates two conditional probabilities: the probability of event *A*, given that event *B* has occurred, *p*(*A*|*B*), and the probability of event *B*, given that event *A* has occurred, *p*(*B*|*A*). It is expressed as

$$p(A|B)p(B) = p(B|A)p(A)$$

[Thomas **Bayes**]

Bayley Scales of Infant and Toddler Development scales for assessing the developmental status of infants and young children aged 1 month to 42 months. Test stimuli, such as form boards, blocks, shapes, household objects (e.g., utensils), and other common items, are used to engage the child in specific tasks of increasing difficulty and elicit particular responses. The Bayley scales were originally published in 1969 and subsequently revised in 1993; the most recent version is the **Bayley–III**, published in 2005. [developed by U.S. psychologist Nancy **Bayley** (1899–1994)]

B-cognition *n.* see BEING COGNITION.

BDD abbreviation for BODY DYSMORPHIC DISORDER.

BDI abbreviation for BECK DEPRESSION INVENTORY.

beat *n.* see ROUGHNESS.

beauty *n.* the quality of a stimulus that elicits, usually immediately, admiration and pleasure.

Beck Anxiety Inventory (**BAI**) a self-report, 21-item measure used to assess the severity of anxiety in adults and to discriminate anxiety from depression. [Aaron T. **Beck** (1921–), U.S. psychiatrist]

Beck Depression Inventory (**BDI**) a self-report questionnaire designed to assess the severity of depressive symptoms in adolescents and adults. Extensively used in both clinical and research settings, it consists of 21 item groups, each of which includes four statements of increasing severity. Participants choose the statement within each group that most accurately reflects how they have felt within the past two weeks. The BDI was originally published in 1961; the most recent version is the **BDI–II**, published in 1996. [Aaron T. **Beck** and colleagues]

Beck Hopelessness Scale (**BHS**) a scale of 20 true–false statements used to measure an individual's attitudes about the future, loss of motivation, and expectations in order to predict suicide risk. [Aaron T. **Beck**]

Beck therapy a COGNITIVE BEHAVIOR THERAPY, with individuals or groups, in which the therapist collaborates with the client to design in-session and homework tasks to test the validity of maladaptive thoughts and perceptions. Clients identify the negative thought or perception,

label it (e.g., overgeneralization, polarized thinking), test its validity, devise alternative explanations, discuss the implications of these alternatives, and complete homework to practice the alternatives. [Aaron T. **Beck**]

Bedlam *n.* the popular name for the Hospital of Saint Mary of Bethlehem in Bishopsgate, London, founded as a monastery in 1247 and converted into an asylum for the insane by Henry VIII in 1547. Many of the inmates were in a state of frenzy, and as they were shackled, starved, beaten, and exhibited to the public for a penny a look, general turmoil prevailed. The word "bedlam" thus became synonymous with wild confusion or frenzy. Sometimes **bedlamism** was used for psychotic behavior, and **bedlamite** for a psychotic individual.

bed-wetting *n.* the involuntary discharge of urine during sleep. Bed-wetting is considered problematic if it occurs in children older than 4 or 5 years of age; it is twice as common in boys. Also called **sleep enuresis**. See also ENURESIS.

before–after design an experimental design in which one or more groups of participants are measured both prior to and following administration of the treatment or manipulation. Also called **pre–post design**; **pretest–posttest design**.

behavior *n.* **1.** an organism's activities in response to external or internal stimuli, including objectively observable activities, introspectively observable activities, and unconscious processes. **2.** more restrictively, any action or function that can be objectively observed or measured in response to controlled stimuli. Historically, objective behavior was contrasted by behaviorists with mental activities, which were considered subjective and thus unsuitable for scientific study. See BEHAVIORISM. —**behavioral** *adj.*

behavioral approach system a brain system theorized to underlie incentive motivation by activating approach behaviors in response to stimuli related to positive reinforcement. It has been suggested that the system is associated as well with the generation of positive affective responses, and that a strong or chronically active behavioral approach system tends to result in extraversion. Also called **behavioral activation system**. Compare BEHAVIORAL INHIBITION SYSTEM.

behavioral approach task an observational assessment technique in which an individual approaches a feared situation until he or she is unable to go further. The task is used to assess levels of avoidance and fear of specific situations associated with phobias. It may also be used to corroborate information obtained in the clinical interview and to measure treatment progress and outcome. Also called **behavioral approach test**; **behavioral avoidance test**.

behavioral assessment the systematic study and evaluation of an individual's behavior using a wide variety of techniques, including direct observation, interviews, and self-monitoring. When used to identify patterns indicative of disorder, the procedure is called **behavioral diagnosis** and is essential in deciding upon the use of specific behavioral or cognitive-behavioral interventions.

behavioral contingency the relationship between a specific response and the frequency, regularity, and level of reinforcement for that response.

behavioral contract an agreement between therapist and client in which the client agrees to carry out certain behaviors, usually between sessions but sometimes during the session as well. Also called **behavior contract**. See also CONTRACT; CONTINGENCY CONTRACT.

behavioral contrast in research, an increased response for a more favorable reward following exposure to a less favorable reinforcer (**positive contrast**), or a decreased response for a less favorable reward following exposure to a more favorable reinforcer (**negative contrast**). The phenomenon illustrates that the effects of reinforcement depend on context.

behavioral counseling a system of counseling in which the primary focus is on changing client behavior through SELF-MANAGEMENT, OPERANT CONDITIONING, and related techniques. Specific behaviors are targeted for modification, and intervention strategies and environmental changes are then established in order to bring about the desired modification.

behavioral couples therapy a COUPLES THERAPY that focuses on interrupting negative interaction patterns through instruction, modeling, rehearsal, feedback, positive behavior exchange, and structured problem solving. This therapy can be conducted with individual couples or in a couples group format. When practiced with legally married partners, it is called **behavioral marital therapy**. See also COMMUNICATION SKILLS TRAINING; INTEGRATIVE BEHAVIORAL COUPLES THERAPY.

behavioral ecology the study of the interaction between the environment and the behavior of organisms within that environment, primarily the adaptive aspects of animal behavior. Initially, many studies focused on the acquisition and use of resources, but more recent studies have focused on the adaptive significance of social interactions, blending behavioral ecology with SOCIOBIOLOGY.

behavioral endocrinology the study of the relationships between behavior and the functioning of the endocrine glands and neuroendocrine cells. For example, gonadal secretion of sex hormones affects sexual behavior, and secretion of corticosteroids by the adrenal glands affects physiological and behavioral responses to stress.

behavioral family therapy a family treatment that is characterized by behavioral analysis of presenting problems and a focus on overt behavior change through application of learning-based behavioral principles and techniques of BEHAVIOR THERAPY. Techniques used to modify targeted behavior patterns include behavioral contracts, instruction, modeling, and rehearsal.

behavioral genetics the study of familial or hereditary behavior patterns and of the genetic mechanisms of behavior traits. Also called **behavior genetics**.

behavioral group therapy a form of GROUP PSYCHOTHERAPY that applies learning-based behavioral principles and techniques, including modeling, rehearsal, social reinforcement, SYSTEMATIC DESENSITIZATION, and other methods of BEHAVIOR THERAPY, in the context of a group. See also COGNITIVE BEHAVIORAL GROUP THERAPY.

behavioral health an interdisciplinary subspecialty of BEHAVIORAL MEDICINE that promotes a philosophy of health emphasizing individual responsibility in the maintenance of one's own health and in the prevention of illness and dysfunction by means of self-initiated activities (jogging, exercising, healthy eating, no smoking, etc.).

behavioral immunogen a behavior or lifestyle associated with a decreased risk of illness and with longer life. Examples of behavioral immunogens are moderate consumption of alcohol, regular exercise, adequate sleep, and a healthy diet. Compare BEHAVIORAL PATHOGEN.

behavioral inhibition a temperamental predisposition characterized by restraint in engaging with the world combined with a tendency to scrutinize the environment for potential threats and to avoid or withdraw from unfamiliar situations or people.

behavioral inhibition system (BIS) a brain system theorized to underlie behavioral inhibition by activating avoidance behaviors in response to perceived threats. It has been suggested that the BIS is associated as well with the generation of negative affective responses, and that a strong or chronically active BIS tends to result in introversion. Compare BEHAVIORAL APPROACH SYSTEM.

behaviorally anchored rating scale (BARS) a behavior-based measure used in evaluating job performance. Employees are evaluated on each performance dimension by comparing their job behaviors with specific behavior examples that anchor each level of performance. Compare MIXED-STANDARD SCALE. See also CRITICAL-INCIDENT TECHNIQUE.

behavioral marital therapy see BEHAVIORAL COUPLES THERAPY.

behavioral medicine a multidisciplinary field that applies behavioral theories and methods to the prevention and treatment of medical and psychological disorders. Areas of application include chronic illness, lifestyle issues (e.g., tobacco, drugs, alcohol, obesity), SOMATOFORM

DISORDERS, and the like. See also BEHAVIORAL HEALTH.

behavioral model a conceptualization of psychological disorders in terms of overt behavior patterns produced by learning and the influence of REINFORCEMENT CONTINGENCIES. Treatment techniques, including SYSTEMATIC DESENSITIZATION and MODELING, focus on modifying ineffective or maladaptive patterns.

behavioral momentum the resistance to change through time of some activity in the face of manipulations intended to disrupt the ongoing activity. The more difficult it is to disrupt an activity, the greater its behavioral momentum.

behavioral neuroscience a branch of NEUROSCIENCE and BIOLOGICAL PSYCHOLOGY that seeks to understand and characterize the specific neural circuitry and mechanisms underlying behavioral propensities or capacities.

behavioral pathogen a behavior or lifestyle that may increase the risk of developing illness or disability and may reduce life expectancy. Examples of behavioral pathogens are smoking, drug abuse, poor diet, unprotected sexual activity, and a sedentary lifestyle. Compare BEHAVIORAL IMMUNOGEN.

behavioral pediatrics a multidisciplinary specialty in psychology that is often part of PEDIATRIC PSYCHOLOGY, clinical child psychology, and HEALTH PSYCHOLOGY. In prevention and intervention, practitioners address such problems as habit disorders, oppositional behavior, sleep and eating disorders, and physical health problems (e.g., traumatic brain injury). In the medical literature, it is also called **developmental-behavioral pediatrics**.

behavioral pharmacology a branch of pharmacology concerned with the physiological and behavioral mechanisms by which drugs operate, encompassing not only the effects of drugs on behavior but also how behavioral factors contribute to the actions of drugs and the ways in which they are used.

behavioral phenotype a pattern of motor, cognitive, linguistic, and social abnormalities that is consistently associated with a biological disorder.

behavioral plasticity the degree to which a person's behavior can be influenced and modified by social experience and learning.

behavioral profile an overall representation of the behavioral characteristics of a participant in a test or experiment, obtained not only from the scores on each individual characteristic but also from the general pattern of these scores.

behavioral psychology an approach to understanding psychological phenomena that focuses on observable aspects of behavior and makes use of BEHAVIOR THEORY for explanation. See also BEHAVIORISM.

behavioral relaxation training a form of relaxation training and BEHAVIOR THERAPY that emphasizes labeling of sensations, modeling, reinforcement, and therapist feedback. See also PROGRESSIVE RELAXATION.

behavioral science any of a number of disciplines, including psychology, psychiatry, sociology, and anthropology, that study the behavior of humans and nonhuman animals from a scientific and research perspective.

behavioral self-control training a technique in BEHAVIOR THERAPY that uses self-monitoring, self-evaluation, self-reinforcement, coaching, behavioral contracts, and relapse prevention techniques to help clients achieve active coping strategies, to increase their sense of mastery, and to decrease undesired habits (e.g., nail biting).

behavioral sex therapy a form of SEX THERAPY that focuses on behavioral analysis of presenting problems and on changes to behavioral sequences that hinder healthy sexual functioning through BEHAVIOR THERAPY methods. Behavioral sequences can include those that are relationship-based (e.g., communication behaviors) or specifically sexually based (e.g., avoidance of sexual stimuli).

behavioral study of obedience the experimental analysis, especially as carried out by U.S. social psychologist Stanley Milgram (1933–1984) in the 1960s, of individuals' willingness to obey the orders of an authority. In Milgram's experiment, each participant played the role of a teacher who was instructed to deliver painful electric shocks to another "participant" for each failure to answer a question correctly. The latter were in fact CONFEDERATES who did not actually receive shocks for their many deliberate errors. Milgram found that a substantial number of participants (65%) were completely obedient, delivering what they believed were shocks of increasing intensity despite the protestations and apparent suffering of the victim. See also DESTRUCTIVE OBEDIENCE.

behavioral toxicology the study of the behavioral impact of toxic exposure. There is increasing evidence that many toxins produce subtle behavioral changes, often in neurosensory functioning, at levels far below thresholds for detectable neurological damage.

behavior analysis the decomposition of behavior into its component parts or processes. This approach to psychology, based on the EXPERIMENTAL ANALYSIS OF BEHAVIOR, emphasizes interactions between behavior and the environment. See APPLIED BEHAVIOR ANALYSIS.

behavior control 1. the use of any type of psychological manipulation, such as threats or promises, to steer individual or group behavior in a desired direction. **2.** the misuse of invasive or intrusive treatments (e.g., drugs or aversive conditioning) to achieve control over the lives of individuals, including patients.

behavior disorder any persistent and repetitive pattern of behavior that violates societal norms or rules or that seriously impairs a person's functioning. The term is used in a very general sense to cover a wide range of disorders or other syndromes. Also called **behavioral disorder**. See also ATTENTION-DEFICIT/HYPERACTIVITY DISORDER; DISRUPTIVE BEHAVIOR DISORDER; PRIMARY BEHAVIOR DISORDER.

behavior hierarchy a ranking of possible responses based on the relative probabilities of their being elicited, with more probable behaviors ranked higher than less probable behaviors. Also called **behavioral hierarchy**.

behaviorism *n.* an approach to psychology, formulated in 1913 by U.S. psychologist John B. Watson (1878–1958), based on the study of objective, observable facts rather than subjective, qualitative processes, such as feelings, motives, and consciousness. To make psychology a naturalistic science, Watson proposed to limit it to quantitative events, such as stimulus–response relationships, effects of conditioning, physiological processes, and a study of human and animal behavior, all of which can best be investigated through laboratory experiments that yield objective measures under controlled conditions. Historically, behaviorists held that mind was not a proper topic for scientific study since mental events are subjective and not independently verifiable. With its emphasis on activity as an adaptive function, behaviorism is seen as an outgrowth of FUNCTIONALISM. See DESCRIPTIVE BEHAVIORISM; METHODOLOGICAL BEHAVIORISM; NEOBEHAVIORISM; RADICAL BEHAVIORISM.

behavior mapping a technique of studying the activities of individuals within a space by noting what happens where. The degree of variability of behavior, as well as its association with certain types of environmental features, is a useful starting point to build or test hypotheses about, for example, architectural design.

behavior modification the use of OPERANT CONDITIONING, BIOFEEDBACK, MODELING, AVERSIVE CONDITIONING, RECIPROCAL INHIBITION, or other learning techniques as a means of changing human behavior. For example, behavioral modification is used in clinical contexts to improve adaptation and alleviate symptoms and in industrial and organizational contexts to encourage employees to adopt safe work practices. The term is often used synonymously with BEHAVIOR THERAPY.

behavior pattern a complex arrangement of two or more responses that occur in a prescribed order. Behavior patterns are also referred to as **chains of behavior**, highlighting their nature as a complex linking of simpler segments of behavior. Also called **behavioral pattern**.

behavior problem a pattern of disruptive behavior that generally falls within social norms and does not seriously impair a person's functioning.

behavior rehearsal a technique used in BEHAVIOR THERAPY or COGNITIVE BEHAVIOR THERAPY for modifying or enhancing social or interpersonal skills. The therapist introduces effective interpersonal strategies or behavior patterns to be practiced and rehearsed by the client until these are ready to be used in a real-life situation. The technique is also commonly used in ASSERTIVENESS TRAINING. Also called **behavioral rehearsal**.

behavior sampling the process of recording a set of observations of a participant's behavior during a designated time frame.

behavior theory the assumption that behavior, including its acquisition, development, and maintenance, can be adequately explained by principles of learning. Behavior theory attempts to describe environmental influences on behavior, often using controlled studies of animals. Also called **general behavior theory**.

behavior therapy a form of psychotherapy that applies the principles of learning, OPERANT CONDITIONING, and PAVLOVIAN CONDITIONING to eliminate symptoms and modify ineffective or maladaptive patterns of behavior. The focus of this therapy is upon the behavior itself and the CONTINGENCIES and environmental factors that reinforce it, rather than exploration of the underlying psychological causes of the behavior. A wide variety of techniques are used in behavior therapy, such as BEHAVIOR REHEARSAL, BIOFEEDBACK, MODELING, and SYSTEMATIC DESENSITIZATION. Also called **behavioral psychotherapy**; **conditioning therapy**.

being-beyond-the-world *n.* in EXISTENTIAL PSYCHOLOGY, the potential for human beings to transcend the limitations of BEING-IN-THE-WORLD, usually through selfless love.

being cognition 1. (B-cognition) in the HUMANISTIC PSYCHOLOGY of U.S. psychologist Abraham Maslow (1908–1970), an exceptional type of cognition that can be distinguished from one's everyday perception of reality (**deficiency cognition** or **D-cognition**). Being cognition takes one of two forms: In the first, a person is aware of the whole universe and the interrelatedness of everything within it, including the perceiver; in the second, a person becomes entirely focused on a single object (e.g., a natural phenomenon, a work of art, or a loved person) to the extent that the rest of the universe, including the perceiver, seems to disappear. See also PEAK EXPERIENCE; TIMELESS MOMENT. **2.** awareness of the inner core of one's existence, that is, one's self or identity.

being-in-the-world *n.* in theories and clinical approaches derived from EXISTENTIALISM, the particular type of being characteristic of humans, in contrast to the type of being of animals, inanimate objects, or abstractions. The word "being" is meant to emphasize that human existence is an activity more than a state or condition. Similarly, "world" is meant to convey a much richer and more meaningful ground for human life than would be conveyed by a more sterile term, such as "environment." Being-in-the-world is by its very nature oriented toward meaning and growth; while it characterizes the type of being of all humans, it is also unique for every person, and can be seen to be offering an explanation of what in other psychological traditions might be called IDENTITY or SELF. Compare BEING-BEYOND-THE-WORLD. See also DASEIN; WORLD DESIGN.

being love (**B-love**) in the HUMANISTIC PSYCHOLOGY of U.S. psychologist Abraham Maslow (1908–1970), a form of love characterized by mutuality, genuine concern for another's welfare and pleasure, and reduced dependency, selfishness, and jealousy. B-love is one of the qualities Maslow ascribes to self-actualizers (see SELF-ACTUALIZATION). Compare DEFICIENCY LOVE.

being motivation see METAMOTIVATION.

being values see METANEEDS.

belief *n.* **1.** acceptance of the truth, reality, or validity of something (e.g., a phenomenon, a person's veracity) particularly in the absence of substantiation. **2.** an association of some characteristic or attribute, usually evaluative in nature, with an attitude object (e.g., this car is reliable).

belief–desire reasoning the process by which one explains and predicts another's behavior on the basis of one's understanding of the other's desires and beliefs. Belief–desire reasoning is the basis for THEORY OF MIND.

belief system a set of two or more beliefs, attitudes, or both that are associated with one another in memory. See also ATTITUDE SYSTEM.

bell curve the characteristic curve obtained by plotting a graph of a NORMAL DISTRIBUTION. With a large rounded peak tapering off on either side, it resembles a cross-sectional representation of a bell. Also called **bell-shaped curve**.

Bell–Magendie law the principle that the VENTRAL ROOTS of the spinal cord are motor in function and DORSAL ROOTS are sensory. [Charles **Bell** (1774–1842), British surgeon and anatomist; François **Magendie** (1783–1855), French physiologist]

Bell's palsy paralysis of the FACIAL NERVE, causing weakness of the muscles on one side of the face and resulting in a distorted expression, inability to close the eye, and often taste loss, and sensitivity to sound. [Charles **Bell**]

belonging *n.* the feeling of being accepted and approved by a group or by society as a whole. Also called **belongingness**.

Bender Visual–Motor Gestalt Test a visuoconstructive test used to assess visual–motor functioning and perceptual ability as well as to diagnose neurological impairment. The participant copies line drawings of geometric figures onto blank pieces of paper, and these reproductions are scored on a 5-point scale, ranging from 0 (no resemblance) to 4 (nearly perfect).

Originally developed in 1938, the test (often shortened to **Bender–Gestalt**) is now in its second edition (published in 2003). [Lauretta **Bender** (1897–1987), U.S. psychiatrist]

beneffectance *n.* a combination of benevolence and effectiveness. According to the U.S. social psychologist who coined the term, Anthony G. Greenwald (1939–), people routinely distort memories of their own prior actions so as to enhance their own sense of beneffectance. That is, they engage in self-deception so as to appear to themselves and others as morally good, well-intentioned, competent, and successful. See POSITIVE ILLUSION.

benign *adj.* **1.** in mental health, denoting a disorder or illness that is not serious and has a favorable prognosis. **2.** denoting a disease condition that is relatively mild, transient, or not associated with serious pathology. See also NEOPLASM. Compare MALIGNANT.

benign senescence (**benign senescent forgetfulness**) see AGE-ASSOCIATED MEMORY IMPAIRMENT.

Benton Visual Retention Test a drawing and recall task in which the participant is briefly shown cards containing two or three geometric designs and then asked to reproduce them from memory. The test assesses visual perception, short-term visual memory, and visuoconstructional ability; it is scored for the number of correct reproductions and for the number and types of errors. [developed in 1946 by Arthur Lester **Benton** (1909–), U.S. psychologist]

Benzedrine *n.* see AMPHETAMINES.

benzodiazepine *n.* any of a family of drugs that depress central nervous system activity (CNS DEPRESSANTS) and also produce sedation and relaxation of skeletal muscles. Benzodiazepines include the prototype CHLORDIAZEPOXIDE and the common sedatives DIAZEPAM and ALPRAZOLAM. They are commonly used in the treatment of generalized anxiety and insomnia and are useful in the management of acute withdrawal from alcohol and in seizure disorders. Clinically introduced in the 1960s, they rapidly supplanted the barbiturates, largely due to their significantly lower toxicity in overdose. Members of the group show considerable variation in ABUSE POTENTIAL: Prolonged use can lead to tolerance and psychological and physical dependence.

bereavement *n.* a feeling of loss, especially over the death of a friend or loved one. The bereaved person may experience emotional pain and distress (see GRIEF; TRAUMATIC GRIEF) and may or may not express this distress to others (see MOURNING; DISENFRANCHISED GRIEF). —**bereaved** *adj.*

bereavement therapy therapy or counseling provided to individuals who are experiencing loss and grief following the death of a loved one. The therapy may include issues of separation, grieving, and carrying on with life. See also GRIEF COUNSELING.

Bernoulli distribution see BINOMIAL DISTRIBUTION. [Jacques **Bernoulli** (1654–1705), Swiss mathematician and scientist]

Bernoulli trial see BINOMIAL DISTRIBUTION. [Jacques **Bernoulli**]

beta (symbol: β) *n.* the probability of a TYPE II ERROR.

beta-adrenergic receptor see ADRENERGIC RECEPTOR.

beta alcoholism one of five types of alcoholism defined by U.S. physician Elvin M. Jellinek (1890–1963), the others being ALPHA ALCOHOLISM, GAMMA ALCOHOLISM, DELTA ALCOHOLISM, and EPSILON ALCOHOLISM. It is characterized by serious medical complications (e.g., liver damage, gastritis, nutritional deficiency) associated with undisciplined drinking but does not involve physical or psychological dependence.

beta-amyloid (β-**amyloid**) *n.* a protein that accumulates—via aberrant processing of **amyloid precursor protein** (**APP**)—in the brains of patients with Alzheimer's disease, forming SENILE PLAQUES and contributing to neuronal impairment and eventual loss. Significant progress has been made recently toward developing therapies that target this processing pathway and several promising pharmacological agents are now in advance-stage clinical trials.

beta blocker see ADRENERGIC BLOCKING AGENT.

beta error see TYPE II ERROR.

beta level the probability of failing to reject the NULL HYPOTHESIS when it is in fact false, that is, making a TYPE II ERROR.

beta movement see APPARENT MOVEMENT.

beta wave in electroencephalography, the type of BRAIN WAVE (frequency 13–30 Hz) associated with alert wakefulness and intense mental activity. Also called **beta rhythm**.

beta weight (symbol: β) in REGRESSION ANALYSIS, the multiplicative constant that reflects a variable's contribution to the prediction of a criterion, given the other variables in the prediction equation (e.g., b in $y = a + bx$). Also called **beta coefficient**.

betrayal trauma theory a conceptual model for explaining why some children are unable to access memories of prior sexual or physical abuse. According to the theory, this sort of REPRESSION occurs when the perpetrator of the abuse is an adult on whom the child is emotionally dependent and it develops out of the child's need to preserve the attachment bond.

between-groups variance the variation in experimental scores that is attributable only to membership in different groups and exposure to different experimental conditions. It is reflected in the ANALYSIS OF VARIANCE by the degree to which the several group means differ from one another and is compared with WITHIN-GROUP VARIANCE to obtain an F RATIO.

between-subjects design any of a large number of experimental designs in which each participant experiences only one experimental condition (treatment). Also called **between-groups design**. Compare WITHIN-SUBJECTS DESIGN.

B fiber a myelinated nerve fiber (axon) of the autonomic nervous system. B fibers are approximately 2 μm or less in diameter and transmit impulses to the SYMPATHETIC CHAIN. See also A FIBER; C FIBER.

BHS abbreviation for BECK HOPELESSNESS SCALE.

bias *n.* **1.** partiality: an inclination or predisposition for or against something. See also PREJUDICE. **2.** a tendency or preference, such as a RESPONSE BIAS or TEST BIAS. **3.** in research, systematic and directional error arising during SAMPLING, data collection, data analysis, or data interpretation. **4.** in statistics, the difference between the expected value of a statistic and the actual value that is obtained. —**biased** *adj.*

biased scanning a hypothetical process in which people alter or maintain a particular SELF-CONCEPT by searching the contents of their memory in a selective manner, focusing especially on memories that fit a predetermined impression.

bibliotherapy *n.* a form of therapy that uses structured reading material. Bibliotherapy is often used as an adjunct to psychotherapy for such purposes as reinforcing specific in-session concepts or strategies or enhancing lifestyle changes. Carefully chosen readings are also used by some individuals as SELF-HELP tools to foster personal growth and development, for example, by facilitating communication and open discussion of problems or enhancing self-concept.

Big Five personality model see FIVE-FACTOR PERSONALITY MODEL.

bilabial *adj.* see LABIAL.

bilateral *adj.* denoting or relating to both sides of the body or an organ. For example, **bilateral symmetry** is the symmetrical arrangement of an organism's body such that the right and left halves are approximately mirror images of one another; **bilateral transfer** is the TRANSFER OF TRAINING or patterns of performance for a skill from one side of the body, where the skill (e.g., handwriting) was originally learned and primarily used, to the other side of the body. —**bilaterally** *adv.*

bilingualism *n.* the regular use of two or more languages by a person or within a group of people See also ADDITIVE BILINGUALISM. —**bilingual** *adj.*

bilis *n.* a CULTURE-BOUND SYNDROME found among Latino groups, who attribute it to extremely strong anger or rage. Symptoms include abrupt tension, headache, screaming, stomach disturbances, vomiting, loss of weight, tremors, chronic tiredness, and—in extreme cases—loss of consciousness or death. Also called **colera**; **muina**.

bill of rights in health care, a document stating the entitlements a patient has with respect to providers, institutions, and THIRD-PARTY PAYERS. See PATIENTS' RIGHTS.

bimodal distribution a set of scores that has two modes (represented by two peaks in their graphical distribution), reflecting a tendency for scores to cluster around two separate values. See also UNIMODAL DISTRIBUTION.

binary feature a feature of the phonemic system of a language that has two mutually exclusive aspects, such as voiced–unvoiced (in English) or aspirated–unaspirated (in Hindi). Such features have a critical contrastive function, working rather like an on–off switch to distinguish one PHONEME from another; in English, for instance, the otherwise very similar sounds [b] and [p] are recognized as distinct phonemes because the former is VOICED and the latter UNVOICED. Binary opposition of this kind is a key concept in the structuralist interpretation of language (see STRUCTURALISM).

binary system a structure or organization composed of two elements or two kinds of elements. In computer science, it is a logical structure composed of two values, commonly called 0 and 1, based on the "off" and "on" modes of electrical circuits and devices. The principle of binary contrast is also of great importance in STRUCTURALISM, particularly structural linguistics. See BINARY FEATURE.

binaural adj. pertaining to or perceived by both ears. Compare MONAURAL.

binaural beat a periodic fluctuation in apparent position or in loudness when two tones differing slightly in frequency are presented to each ear separately but simultaneously. Binaural beats are not present in the stimulus but result from the **binaural interaction** between the tones that occurs within the auditory system.

binaural cue any difference in the sound arriving at the two ears from a given sound source (**interaural difference**) that acts as a cue to permit AUDITORY LOCALIZATION. The common cues are **interaural level differences** (ILD), **interaural time differences** (ITD), and (closely related to ITD) **interaural phase differences** (IPD). Also called **binaural differences**.

binding affinity the tendency of a particular LIGAND (e.g., neurotransmitter or drug) to bind to a particular receptor, measured by the percentage of receptors occupied by the ligand.

binding hypothesis a theory that provides a solution to the BINDING PROBLEM, proposing that the neural mechanism responsible for drawing together disparate information from separate cortical areas and "binding" it into unified percepts is temporal synchrony: that is, the simultaneous firing of action potentials from individual neurons—each coding different properties—is the means by which they are organized into a single representation. Recently, some individuals have emphasized feature binding as essential to consciousness, providing a requisite coherence of mental contents.

binding problem the difficulty of perceiving and representing different features, or conjunctions of properties, as one object or event. This problem arises because different attributes of a stimulus (e.g., hue, form, spatial location, motion) are analyzed by different areas of the cerebral cortex; it is relevant in all areas of knowledge representation, including such complex cognitive representations as THEORY OF MIND.

binge drinking 1. a single occasion of intense, extremely heavy drinking that often results in intoxication. **2.** a pattern of alcohol consumption characterized by the setting aside of repeated periods of time for intense, extremely heavy drinking, with or without sobriety in between.

binge-eating disorder a disorder marked by recurring episodes of binge eating (i.e., discrete periods of uncontrolled consumption of abnormally large quantities of food) and distress associated with this behavior. There is an absence of inappropriate compensatory behaviors (e.g., vomiting, laxative misuse, excessive exercise, fasting). See also EATING DISORDER. Compare BULIMIA NERVOSA.

binocular adj. relating to the two eyes. For example, a **binocular cue** is a cue to the perception of depth or distance that requires the use of both eyes, such as BINOCULAR DISPARITY and CONVERGENCE. Compare MONOCULAR.

binocular cell a cortical cell that responds to a stimulus presented to either the left or the right eye. **Monocular cells**, in contrast, require stimulation through a specific eye to generate a response.

binocular disparity the slight difference between the right and left retinal images. When both eyes focus on an object, the different position of the eyes produces a disparity of visual angle, and a slightly different image is received by each retina. The two images are automatically compared and fused, providing an important cue to depth perception. Also called **retinal disparity**.

binocular rivalry the failure of the eyes to fuse stimuli (see FUSION). For example, if horizontal bars are viewed through the left eye and vertical bars through the right eye, the perception is a patchy and fluctuating alternation of the two patterns, rather than a superimposition of the patterns to form a stable checkerboard. Also called **retinal rivalry**.

binomial distribution the distribution of the outcomes in a sequence of **Bernoulli trials**, experiments of chance that are independent of one another and each have one of two possible outcomes (0 or 1; success or failure), with a fixed probability of each outcome on each trial. Also called **Bernoulli distribution**.

Binswanger's disease a progressive VASCULAR DEMENTIA characterized by DEMYELINATION and multiple INFARCTIONS of subcortical white matter associated with hypertension and subsequent arteriosclerosis. Symptoms include loss of cognitive functioning, memory impairment, and changes in mood and behavior. Also called **subcortical arteriosclerotic encephalopathy**. [Otto Ludvig **Binswanger** (1852–1929), German neurologist]

bioacoustics n. the study of sound production and perception in nonhuman animals and its influence on behavior.

bioavailability n. the quantity of an administered drug that is available for distribution within the body to the target organ or site after absorption into the bloodstream.

biochemical marker a variation in the chemical activity of an organism that accompanies a disorder, irrespective of whether it directly causes the disorder. See also BIOLOGICAL MARKER; CLINICAL MARKER.

biochemistry n. the study of the chemical substances and processes of living organisms. —**biochemical** adj.

biocybernetics n. the study of communication and self-regulatory activities within the body. —**biocybernetic** or **biocybernetical** adj.

bioecological model a paradigm that treats human development as a process that continues both through the life span and across successive generations, thus according importance to historical continuity and change as forces indirectly affecting human development through their impact on proximal processes.

bioecological theory of intelligence a theory postulating that intelligence develops as an interaction between biological dispositions and the environment in which these biological dispositions develop.

bioengineering n. the application of engineering principles and knowledge to living organisms and biological processes, particularly in the design, testing, and manufacture of devices that can substitute for impaired body parts or functions. —**bioengineer** n.

bioequivalence n. a measure comparing the relative BIOAVAILABILITY of two forms or preparations of a drug. In bioequivalent drug preparations, the same proportion of unchanged, active drug reaches the systemic circulation. —**bioequivalent** adj.

bioethics n. the study of ethics and values relevant to the conduct of clinical practice and research in medicine and the life sciences. —**bioethical** adj.

biofeedback n. **1.** information about bodily processes and systems provided by an organism's receptors to enable it to maintain a physiologically desirable internal environment and make adjustments as necessary. **2.** the use of an external monitoring device to provide an individual with information regarding his or her physiological state. When used to help a person obtain voluntary control over autonomic body functions, such as heart rate or blood pressure, the technique is called **biofeedback training**. It may be applied therapeutically to treat various conditions, including chronic pain and hypertension.

biogenic amine any of a group of AMINES that affect bodily processes and nervous system functioning. Biogenic amines are divided into subgroups (e.g., CATECHOLAMINES, INDOLEAMINES) and include the neurotransmitters dopamine, epinephrine, histamine, norepinephrine, and serotonin.

biogenic amine hypothesis any of a variety of hypotheses, such as the CATECHOLAMINE HYPOTHESIS and DOPAMINE HYPOTHESIS, that consider abnormalities in the physiology and metabolism of biogenic amines essential to the etiology of certain mental disorders.

biographical data an individual's personal information and history, typically gathered for use in personnel selection or by therapists and other mental health or medical professionals. Also called **biodata**.

biographical method the systematic use of personal histories—gathered through such means as interviews, focus groups, observations, and individual reflections and other narratives—in psychological research and analysis.

bioinformational theory a general theory of emotional–motivational organization, integrating cognitive and psychophysiological levels of analysis. It holds that information about emotions is contained in associative memory networks that include action information (motor programs) and connections to subcortical motivation circuits. Emotions are viewed as context-specific action or response dispositions activated by input that modifies concepts in the emotion network.

biological clock the mechanism within an organism that controls the periodicity of BIOLOGICAL RHYTHMS, including ACTIVITY RHYTHMS, even in the absence of any external cues. A biological clock in mammals is located in the SUPRACHIASMATIC NUCLEUS of the hypothalamus.

biological determinism the concept that psychological and behavioral characteristics are entirely the result of constitutional and biological factors. Environmental conditions serve only as occasions for the manifestation of such characteristics. Compare ENVIRONMENTAL DETERMINISM. See DETERMINISM; GENETIC DETERMINISM; NATURE–NURTURE.

biological fallacy 1. the questionable assumption that all human phenomena, including rationality, culture, and ethics, can be explained with reference to strictly biological processes. In this sense, the biological fallacy is one of naturalistic REDUCTIONISM. **2.** in the controversial view of some ecological theorists, the "fallacy" of equating life with the life of individual organisms. The term implies that the vital force referred to as "life" is better understood as inherent in, or as a quality of, the totality of the ecosystem.

biological family a person's blood relations as opposed to relations acquired through marriage, adoption, or fostering.

biological intelligence the assertion that intelligence is essentially a genetically determined biological entity.

biologically primary ability an ability, such as language acquisition, that has been selected for in evolution and is acquired universally. Children typically are highly motivated to perform tasks involving these abilities. Compare BIOLOGICALLY SECONDARY ABILITY.

biologically secondary ability an ability, such as reading, that builds upon a BIOLOGICALLY PRIMARY ABILITY but is principally a cultural invention and often requires extensive repetition and external motivation for its mastery.

biological marker a variation in the physiological processes of an organism that accompanies a disorder, irrespective of whether it directly causes the disorder. See also BIOCHEMICAL MARKER; CLINICAL MARKER.

biological motion a display, consisting of about 12 point lights, that is attached to the head and main joints. When the lights move appropriately in relation to each other, they induce a compelling impression of an organism in motion.

biological psychology the science that deals with the area of overlap between psychology and biology and with the reciprocal relations between biological and psychological processes. It includes such fields as BEHAVIORAL NEUROSCIENCE, clinical NEUROSCIENCE, COGNITIVE NEUROSCIENCE, BEHAVIORAL ENDOCRINOLOGY, and PSYCHONEUROIMMUNOLOGY. Also called **biopsychology**.

biological rhythm any periodic variation in a living organism's physiological or psychological function, such as energy level, sexual desire, or menstruation. Such rhythms are usually linked to cyclical changes in environmental cues, such as daylength or passing of the seasons, and tend to be daily (**circadian rhythm**) or annual (**circannual rhythm**). See also INFRADIAN RHYTHM; ULTRADIAN RHYTHM.

biological taxonomy the science of the classification of organisms. Traditional classifications group organisms into a hierarchical system of ranks, in ascending order: species, genus, family, order, class, phylum, and kingdom. Also called **systematics**. See also CLADISTICS.

biological theory of aging any of various explanations of aging based on either programmed biological changes (genetic SENESCENCE) or unpredicted, stochastic changes (DNA damage).

biological therapy any form of treatment for mental disorders that attempts to alter physiological functioning, including various drug therapies, ELECTROCONVULSIVE THERAPY, and PSYCHOSURGERY. Also called **biomedical therapy**.

biology *n.* the study of living organisms and life processes. —**biological** *adj.* —**biologist** *n.*

biomechanics *n.* the application of the principles of mechanics to the study of the structure and function of biological systems, which includes the study of the physical stresses and strains on organisms while at rest and in motion. —**biomechanical** *adj.*

biometrics *n.* see BIOSTATISTICS.

biophysics *n.* the interface of biology and physics, involving the study of biological structures and processes by means of the methods of physics, for example, the application of the principles of physics in the study of vision or hearing.

biopsy *n.* the surgical removal and microscopic study of a small amount of tissue from an organ or body part believed to be diseased or otherwise abnormal. The biopsy specimen is examined for signs of malignancy or other abnormalities that would help determine the proper diagnosis and course of therapy. Compare AUTOPSY.

biopsychology *n.* see BIOLOGICAL PSYCHOLOGY.

biopsychosocial *adj.* denoting a systematic integration of biological, psychological, and social approaches to the study of mental health and specific mental disorders.

biorhythms *pl. n.* according to pseudoscientific belief, three basic cycles (physical, emotional, and intellectual), with which every individual is programmed at birth. It is maintained that these rhythms continue unaltered until death and that good and bad days for various activities can be calculated accordingly. As with astrology, predictions made on this basis do not have a significantly different success rate from those made on a basis of pure chance.

biosocial *adj.* pertaining to the interplay or mingling of biological and social factors, as with human behavior that is influenced simultaneously by complex neurophysiological processes and social interactions.

biostatistics *n.* **1.** data compiled about a population, including the **vital statistics** of rates of birth, disease, and death. See also DEMOGRAPHY. **2.** the application of statistical methods to biological processes, especially in medicine and epidemiology. Also called **biometrics**. —**biostatistical** *adj.* —**biostatistician** *n.*

biosynthesis *n.* the production of chemical compounds by living organisms from nutrients by means of enzyme-catalyzed reactions. —**biosynthetic** *adj.*

biotransformation *n.* the metabolic process by which a substance (e.g., a drug) is changed from one chemical to another by means of a chemical reaction within a living system.

bipolar *adj.* denoting something with two opposites or extremities, such as a BIPOLAR NEURON or the BIPOLAR DISORDERS. —**bipolarity** *n.*

bipolar disorder any of a group of MOOD DISORDERS in which both manic (or hypomanic) and depressive symptoms occur. DSM–IV–TR distinguishes between **bipolar I disorder**, in which the individual has experienced one or more MANIC EPISODES or MIXED EPISODES and usually (but not necessarily) one or more MAJOR DEPRESSIVE EPISODES, and **bipolar II disorder**, characterized by one or more major depressive episodes and at least one HYPOMANIC EPISODE. Also categorized as a bipolar disorder in *DSM–IV–TR* is CYCLOTHYMIC DISORDER. The former official name for bipolar disorders, **manic-depressive illness**, is still in frequent use.

bipolar neuron a neuron with only two processes—an AXON and a DENDRITE—that extend from opposite sides of the CELL BODY. Also called **bipolar cell**. Compare MULTIPOLAR NEURON; UNIPOLAR NEURON.

bipolar rating scale a rating scale anchored at each end by opposite terms (e.g., very fast to very slow). It is distinguished from a **unipolar rating scale** (e.g., very fast to not at all fast, or very slow to not at all slow).

bird flu see AVIAN INFLUENZA.

birth cohort see COHORT.

birth control voluntary regulation of the number and spacing of offspring, including the prevention of conception using intrauterine devices, oral contraceptives, spermicides, the rhythm method, male contraceptive devices, surgical methods of STERILIZATION, and the termination of pregnancy by induced ABORTION.

birth defect see CONGENITAL DEFECT.

birth order the ordinal position of a child in the family (firstborn, second-born, youngest, etc.). There has been much psychological research into how birth order affects personal adjustment and family status, but the notion that it has strong and consistent effects on psychological outcomes is not supported. Current family-structure research sees birth order not so much as a causal factor but rather as an indirect variable that follows more process-oriented variables (e.g., parental discipline, sibling interaction, and genetic and hormonal makeup) in importance.

birth trauma the psychological shock of being born, due to the sudden change from the security of the womb to being bombarded with stimuli from the external world. Austrian psychiatrist Sigmund Freud (1856–1939) viewed birth as the child's first anxiety experience and the prototype of separation anxiety. See also PRIMAL ANXIETY; PRIMAL TRAUMA.

bisection *n.* the act of splitting something into two equal parts. In psychophysics it refers to a scaling method in which a participant adjusts a stimulus until it is perceived as halfway between two other stimuli with respect to a particular dimension.

biserial correlation a measure of the association between continuous and DICHOTOMOUS VARIABLES.

bisexuality *n.* **1.** sexual attraction to or sexual behavior with both men and women. **2.** the existence of both male and female genitals in the same organism. See HERMAPHRODITE. —**bisexual** *adj., n.*

bit *n.* in information theory, the quantity of information that decreases uncertainty or the germane alternatives of a problem by one half. For example, if a dollar bill has been placed in one of 16 identical books standing side by side on a shelf, and one were to ask if the book is to the right (or to the left) of center, the answer would provide one bit of information. [bi(nary) + (digi)t]

bivariate *adj.* characterized by two variables or attributes.

black box a model for a device, system, or other complex entity—humans and nonhuman animals included—whose internal properties and processes must be hypothesized on the basis of observed empirical relationships between external factors (input) and the resulting effects (output).

blackout *n.* **1.** total but temporary loss of consciousness. **2.** amnesia produced by alcoholic intoxication. Also called **alcoholic blackout**.

Blake–Mouton managerial grid a model of leadership in which the behavior of the leader is assessed on two dimensions: concern for people and concern for production. The LEADERSHIP STYLE of a manager is described on nine-point scales on each dimension, giving a total of 81 possible styles. See also GRID ORGANIZATIONAL DEVELOPMENT. [developed in 1964 by Robert R. **Blake** (1918–) and Jane S. **Mouton** (1930–1987), U.S. psychologists]

blaming the victim a social psychological phenomenon in which individuals or groups attempt to cope with the bad things that have happened to others by holding the victim responsible for the trauma or tragedy.

blastocyst *n.* the mammalian EMBRYO at a very early stage of development. It consists of a tiny hollow sphere containing an inner cell mass, enclosed in a thin layer of cells that help implant the blastocyst in the uterine lining.

blended family see STEPFAMILY.

Bleuler's theory a basic underlying symptomatology for SCHIZOPHRENIA, as proposed in 1911 by Swiss psychiatrist Eugen Bleuler (1857–1939). It defined four FUNDAMENTAL SYMPTOMS required for a diagnosis of the condition and regarded manifestations of schizophrenia (e.g., delusions, hallucinations) shared with other disorders as accessory or SECONDARY SYMPTOMS.

blind adj. **1.** denoting a lack of sight. See BLIND-NESS. **2.** denoting a lack of awareness. In research, a blind procedure may be employed deliberately to enhance experimental control: A **single blind** is a procedure in which participants are unaware of the experimental conditions under which they are operating; a **double blind** is a procedure in which both the participants and the experimenters interacting with them are unaware of the particular experimental conditions; and a **triple blind** is a procedure in which the participants, experimenters, and data analysts are all unaware of the particular experimental conditions.

blind analysis a study or interpretation of data or conditions without specific knowledge or previous information about the topic being examined. For example, a clinical psychologist might diagnose a patient without having information concerning any previous psychological diagnoses.

blind judgment an evaluation made without knowledge of information that might influence one's assessment of the situation. Such an approach is used to eliminate conscious or unconscious bias, for example, in clinical experiments and in scholarly peer review of manuscripts.

blindness n. profound, near-total, or total impairment of the ability to perceive visual stimuli, defined in the United States as VISUAL ACUITY of 20/200 or worse in the better eye with best correction or a VISUAL FIELD of 20° or less in the widest meridian of the better eye. Major causes include CATARACT, GLAUCOMA, age-related MACULAR DEGENERATION, and diabetes. See also LOW VISION; VISUAL IMPAIRMENT. **—blind** adj.

blindsight n. the capacity of some individuals with blindness in parts or all of the visual field to detect and localize visual stimuli presented within the blind field region. Discrimination of movement, flicker, wavelength, and orientation may also be present. However, these visual capacities are not accompanied by awareness: They have been demonstrated only in experimental conditions, when participants are forced to guess.

blind spot the area of the monocular visual field in which stimulation cannot be perceived because the image falls on the site of the OPTIC DISK in the eye.

block n. **1.** an abrupt, involuntary interruption in the flow of thought or speech in which the individual is suddenly aware of not being able to perform a particular mental act, such as finding the words to express something he or she wishes to say. Also called **mental block**. See RETRIEVAL BLOCK; TIP-OF-THE-TONGUE PHENOMENON. **2.** in psychotherapy, an obstacle to

progress that is perceived as a barrier that cannot be crossed.

block design an experimental design that divides participants into relatively homogeneous subsets or blocks. The greater the homogeneity of each of the blocks, the greater the statistical power of the analysis. See also RANDOMIZED BLOCK DESIGN.

block-design test an intelligence subtest, found most notably on the Wechsler Intelligence Scales, in which the respondent is asked to use colored blocks to match a specified design.

blocking n. a phenomenon in which previous learning of an A–B association restricts or prevents learning of a C–B association when AC is paired with B.

blood–brain barrier a semipermeable barrier formed by cells lining the blood capillaries that supply the brain and that helps maintain a constant environment in which the brain can function. It prevents large molecules, including many drugs, passing from the blood to the fluid surrounding brain cells and to the cerebrospinal fluid, and thus protects the brain from potentially harmful substances. Ions and small molecules, such as water, oxygen, carbon dioxide, and alcohol, can cross relatively freely.

blood phobia a persistent and irrational fear of blood, specifically of seeing blood. An individual confronting blood experiences a subjective feeling of disgust and fears the consequences of the situation, such as fainting. Blood phobia rarely is called **hematophobia** or **hemophobia**.

blood pressure the pressure exerted by the blood against the walls of the blood vessels, especially the arteries. It varies with the strength of the heartbeat, the elasticity of the artery walls and resistance of the arterioles, and the person's health, age, and state of activity. See also HYPERTENSION.

blood sugar the concentration of GLUCOSE in the blood, which is regulated by the pancreatic hormones INSULIN and GLUCAGON. Abnormally high or low levels (see HYPERGLYCEMIA; HYPOGLYCEMIA) may indicate any of several disease states.

B-love n. see BEING LOVE.

blunted affect a disturbance in which emotional responses to situations and events are dulled.

board certified denoting a physician or other health care professional who has passed an examination set by a specialty board and has been certified as a specialist in that area. A board-certified (or **boarded**) individual is known as a **diplomate**.

bodily-kinesthetic intelligence in the MULTIPLE-INTELLIGENCES THEORY, the skills involved in forming and coordinating bodily movements, such as dancing, playing a violin, or playing basketball.

body n. **1.** the entire physical structure of an organism, such as the human body. See also MIND–BODY PROBLEM. **2.** the main part of a structure or organ, such as the body of the penis. **3.** a discrete anatomical or cytological structure, such as the MAMMILLARY BODY.

body awareness the perception of one's physical self or body at any particular time.

body build a general measure of the body in terms of trunk, limb length, and girth.

body concept see BODY IMAGE.

body dysmorphic disorder (**BDD**) a SOMATOFORM DISORDER characterized by excessive preoccupation with an imagined defect in physical appearance or markedly excessive concern with a slight physical anomaly.

body image the mental picture one forms of one's body as a whole, including both its physical and functional characteristics (**body percept**) and one's attitudes toward these characteristics (**body concept**).

body-image distortion distortion in the subjective image or mental representation of one's own body appearance, size, or movement. The term is usually applied to overestimation of body size or used to define the perceptual experiences of individuals with psychoses. Also called **body-image disturbance**. See also ANOREXIA NERVOSA. Compare BODY DYSMORPHIC DISORDER.

body language the expression of feelings and thoughts, which may or may not be verbalized, through posture, gesture, facial expression, or other movements. Although body language is often called NONVERBAL COMMUNICATION, such movements may be unintentional, and many investigators therefore believe the term "communication" is often inappropriate in this context.

body mass index (**BMI**) a widely used measure of adiposity or obesity based on the following formula: weight (kg) divided by height squared (m^2).

body memory a sensory recollection of trauma in the form of pain, arousal, tension, or discomfort, usually unaccompanied by words or images. See also SENSORIMOTOR MEMORY.

body–mind problem see MIND–BODY PROBLEM.

body percept see BODY IMAGE.

body therapies a group of physical therapies that seek the relief of psychological tensions and other symptoms through body manipulation, relaxation, massage, breathing exercises, and changes in posture and position of body parts. The therapies are based on the theory that the body and its functioning embody an individual's basic personality and way of life. See also BODYWORK.

body type a classification of individuals according to body build or physique. Some have theorized an association between aspects of physique and psychological traits, proposing a variety of CONSTITUTIONAL TYPES and SOMATOTYPES.

bodywork *n.* an adjunctive treatment (see ADJUNCTIVE THERAPY) that may be recommended in addition to psychotherapy. It typically includes massage, movement, and exercises involving touch.

bondage *n.* physical restraint of one person by another to arouse sexual pleasure in one or both partners.

bonding *n.* the process in which ATTACHMENTS or other close relationships are formed between individuals, especially between mother and infant. An early, positive relationship between a mother and a newborn child is considered to be essential in establishing unconditional love on the part of the parent, as well as security and trust on the part of the child. In subsequent development, bonding establishes friendship and trust.

Bonferroni correction a procedure for adjusting the *p*-value (see SIGNIFICANCE LEVEL) of individual related T TESTS. It involves dividing the usual significance level value by the number of comparisons being made, so as to avoid the increased risk of TYPE I ERROR that comes with multiple comparisons. Also called **Bonferroni adjustment**; **Bonferroni test**.

boomerang effect a situation in which a persuasive message produces attitude change in the direction opposite to that intended. Boomerang effects occur when recipients generate counterarguments substantially stronger than the arguments contained in the original message.

booster session in therapy, particularly COGNITIVE BEHAVIOR THERAPY, any occasional periodic session, after the main sessions are officially ended, in order to reinforce progress or troubleshoot obstacles to continuance of positive changes made during the therapy.

bootstrapping *n.* any process or operation in which a system uses its initial resources to develop more powerful and complex processing routines, which are then used in the same fashion, and so on cumulatively. In LANGUAGE ACQUISITION, the term is used of children's ability to learn complex linguistic rules, which can be endlessly reapplied, from extremely limited data. In statistics, it denotes a method for estimating the variability of a parameter associated with a batch of data, such as the standard error. A number of samples of equal size are obtained from the original data by sampling with replacement, the parameter is calculated for each, and the individual parameters are combined to provide an estimate of the overall parameter for the entire sample. —**bootstrap** *vb.*

borderline 1. *adj.* pertaining to any phenomenon difficult to categorize because it straddles two distinct classes, showing characteristics of both. Thus, **borderline intelligence** is supposed to show characteristics of both the average and subaverage categories. **2.** *n.* an inappropriate designation for someone with BORDERLINE PERSONALITY DISORDER or its symptoms.

B

borderline personality disorder a personality disorder characterized by a long-standing pattern of instability in mood, interpersonal relationships, and self-image that is severe enough to cause extreme distress or interfere with social and occupational functioning. Symptoms include impulsive behavior in such areas as gambling, sex, spending, overeating, and substance use; intense but unstable relationships; uncontrollable temper outbursts; self-injurious behavior, such as fights, suicidal gestures, or self-mutilation; and chronic feelings of emptiness.

Boston Naming Test a 60-item fluency test of word retrieval used to evaluate DYSPHASIA. Line drawings of objects—ranging in difficulty from the commonly to the rarely encountered—are presented, and the participant provides the name of each.

bottleneck model any model of attention that assumes the existence of a limited-capacity channel (typically with a capacity of one item) at some specific stage of human information processing.

bottom-up design an inductive approach to the design of a system or product that involves identifying basic user requirements and allowing these to drive the design, as opposed to basing it on existing product designs or abstract models as in a **top-down design**.

bottom-up processing information processing that proceeds from the data in the stimulus input to higher level processes, such as recognition, interpretation, and categorization. Typically, perceptual or cognitive mechanisms use bottom-up processing when information is unfamiliar or highly complex. Also called **bottom-up analysis**; **data-driven processing**. Compare TOP-DOWN PROCESSING. See also SHALLOW PROCESSING.

Boulder model see SCIENTIST-PRACTITIONER MODEL.

boundary n. **1.** a psychological demarcation that protects the integrity of an individual or group or that helps the person or group set realistic limits on participation in a relationship or activity. **2.** in psychotherapy, an important limit that is usually set by the therapist as part of the GROUND RULES in treatment. Boundaries may involve areas of discussion (e.g., the therapist's personal life is off limits) or physical limits (e.g., rules about touching), which are guided by ethical codes and standards. Respect for boundaries by both the therapist and client is an important concept in the therapeutic relationship.

boundary issues ethical issues relating to the proper limits of a professional relationship between a provider of services (e.g., a physician or a psychotherapist) and his or her patient or client, such that the trust and vulnerability of the latter are not abused. A particular area of concern is PROFESSIONAL–CLIENT SEXUAL RELATIONS.

bounded rationality decision making in which the processes used are rational within the constraints imposed by (a) limitations in the individual's knowledge; (b) human cognitive limitations generally; and (c) empirical factors arising from the complex, real-life situations in which decisions have to be made. See also SATISFICE.

bound energy in psychoanalytic theory, PSYCHIC ENERGY that is located within the ego and focused on the individual's external reality. Bound energy is associated with the SECONDARY PROCESSES and is contrasted with the FREE ENERGY of the id.

bowel disorder any disorder of the small or large intestine, which frequently occurs as a response to stress and anxiety, (e.g., chronic constipation, IRRITABLE BOWEL SYNDROME).

Bowen family systems theory see FAMILY SYSTEMS THEORY.

box-and-whisker plot a graphical display of a batch of data involving rectangular boxes with lines or "whiskers" extending outwards from them. The ends of the box indicate the upper and lower HINGES, a dividing line within the box indicates the MEDIAN, and the whiskers extending from both ends indicate the smallest and largest scores. Also called **box plot**.

BPRS abbreviation for BRIEF PSYCHIATRIC RATING SCALE.

brachial plexus a network of nerves that carries signals from the spinal cord to the shoulder, arm, and hand.

brachium n. (pl. **brachia**) the upper arm, extending from the shoulder to the elbow, or a structure that resembles an arm. —**brachial** adj.

bracketed morality a temporary suspension of the usual moral obligation to consider equally the needs and desires of all persons that is due to contextual factors in a particular situation. Such a suspension occurs, for example, when participating in sporting events.

bradycardia n. see ARRHYTHMIA.

bradykinesia n. abnormal slowness in the execution of voluntary movements. Also called **bradykinesis**. Compare HYPOKINESIS. —**bradykinetic** adj.

bradylalia n. abnormal slowness or hesitation in speech.

bradylexia n. abnormal slowness in reading. —**bradylexic** adj.

braille n. a system of letters, numbers, punctuation marks, and scientific and musical symbols adapted as a written language for people with severe visual impairment, using combinations of raised dots that can be touched. [introduced in 1829 by Louis **Braille** (1809–1852), French teacher and inventor]

brain n. the enlarged, anterior part of the CENTRAL NERVOUS SYSTEM within the skull. The brain develops by differentiation of the embryonic NEURAL TUBE along an anterior–posterior axis to form three main regions—the FORE-

BRAIN, MIDBRAIN, and HINDBRAIN—that can be further subdivided on the basis of anatomical and functional criteria. The cortical tissue is concentrated in the forebrain, and the midbrain and hindbrain structures are often considered together as the BRAINSTEM.

brain concussion see CONCUSSION.

brain damage injury to the brain, manifested by impairment of cognitive, motor, or sensory skills mediated by the brain.

brain death the cessation of neurological signs of life. Medical criteria for brain death include absence of reflex response or response to noxious stimuli, fixed pupils, and absence of electroencephalogram (EEG) activity.

brain fag a CULTURE-BOUND SYNDROME originating in west Africa and most often experienced by high school or college students. Symptoms typically include difficulties with concentration, memory, and understanding information; feelings of pain, tightness, and burning around the head and neck; blurred vision; and tiredness associated with excessive thinking.

brain imaging study of the anatomy or activity of the brain through the intact skull by noninvasive computerized techniques, such as MAGNETIC RESONANCE IMAGING, COMPUTED TOMOGRAPHY, and POSITRON EMISSION TOMOGRAPHY. See also NUCLEAR IMAGING.

brain localization theory any of various theories that different areas of the brain serve different functions. Since the early 19th century, opinion has varied between notions of highly precise localization and a belief that the brain, or large portions of it, functions as a whole. For many investigators, however, the concept of extreme parcellation of functions has given way to concepts of distributed control by collective activity of different regions.

brain mapping the creation of a visual representation of the brain in which different functions are assigned to different brain regions.

brain plasticity the capacity of the brain to change as a function of experience, particularly to compensate for losses in brain tissue caused by injury or disease.

brain reserve capacity the ability of remaining brain tissue to take over the function of damaged or destroyed tissue, particularly to attenuate symptoms of neurodegeneration.

brain scan any of a variety of techniques designed either to reveal structural or functional abnormalities of the diseased brain or to measure activity of the healthy brain. See BRAIN IMAGING.

brainstem *n.* the part of the brain that connects the cerebrum with the spinal cord. It includes the MIDBRAIN, PONS, and MEDULLA OBLONGATA and is involved in the autonomic control of visceral activity, such as salivation, respiration, heartbeat, and digestion.

brain stimulation stimulation of specific areas of the brain, for example by ELECTRICAL STIMULATION or TRANSCRANIAL MAGNETIC STIMULATION, as a means of determining their functions and their effects on behavior and as a therapeutic technique. Also called **cerebral stimulation**.

brainstorming *n.* a problem-solving strategy in which ideas are generated spontaneously and uninhibitedly, usually in a group setting, without any immediate critical judgment about their potential value. —**brainstorm** *vb.*

brainwashing *n.* a broad class of intense and often coercive tactics intended to produce profound changes in attitudes, beliefs, and emotions.

brain waves spontaneous, rhythmic electrical impulses emanating from different areas of the brain. According to their frequencies, brain waves are classified as ALPHA WAVES (8–12 Hz), BETA WAVES (13–30 Hz), DELTA WAVES (1–3 Hz), GAMMA WAVES (31–80 Hz), or THETA WAVES (4–7 Hz).

branching *n.* **1.** a form of PROGRAMMED INSTRUCTION that provides additional steps, or branches, to be followed if the standard teaching material has not been adequately mastered to a given level of proficiency. Correct and incorrect answers lead to different branches of new questions so that students complete different sequences depending on how well they perform. Also called **branching program**. **2.** a method of analyzing the formal structure of a sentence in which this is represented diagrammatically as a treelike structure with an organized hierarchy of branches and subbranches. Theories of branching have been used in predicting psycholinguistic phenomena and in creating linguistic typologies.

breathing-related sleep disorder a primary SLEEP DISORDER marked by excessive sleepiness or insomnia arising from sleep disruption due to breathing difficulties during sleep, for example, SLEEP APNEA. See DYSSOMNIA.

breathing retraining a technique used in BEHAVIOR THERAPY and COGNITIVE BEHAVIOR THERAPY, particularly in the treatment of hyperventilation in anxiety and panic disorders. The technique teaches clients slow diaphragmatic breathing through various methods, including therapist modeling and corrective feedback. See also PROGRESSIVE RELAXATION; STRESS MANAGEMENT.

breed *n.* a subtype within a SPECIES sharing certain characteristics that are distinct from other members of the species (e.g., German shepherds and chihuahuas). The term is typically used for variations that have been induced through selective breeding, as distinguished from **subspecies**, which are naturally occurring variations within a species.

brief group therapy group psychotherapy conducted on a short-term (time- or session-limited) or CRISIS-INTERVENTION basis and focused clearly upon a specific treatment goal. See TIME-LIMITED PSYCHOTHERAPY.

brief intensive group cognitive behavior therapy a form of COGNITIVE BEHAVIOR THERAPY conducted in a group setting over a relatively brief period of time but in lengthy sessions (e.g., all day) and often on consecutive days (e.g., weekends). The therapy is typically used to treat anxiety disorders, particularly panic disorder.

Brief Psychiatric Rating Scale (**BPRS**) a system of evaluating the presence and severity of clinical psychiatric signs on the basis of 24 factors, such as bizarre behavior, hostility, emotional withdrawal, and disorientation. Each factor is rated on a 7-point scale ranging from "not present" to "extremely severe," based on the judgments of trained observers.

brief psychodynamic psychotherapy a collection of time-limited PSYCHODYNAMIC PSYCHOTHERAPY approaches that actively address the issue of time to encourage therapeutic change. Therapists are typically active and confronting, focused on present-day client problems particularly as they manifest in the session, and limit the number of sessions in a fixed or flexible way. Also called **short-term dynamic psychotherapy**.

brief psychotherapy see SHORT-TERM THERAPY.

brief psychotic disorder a disturbance involving the sudden onset of incoherence or loosening of associations, delusions, hallucinations, or grossly disorganized or catatonic behavior. The condition lasts no longer than 1 month, with complete remission of all symptoms and a full return to previous levels of functioning.

brief stimulus therapy (**BST**) ELECTROCONVULSIVE THERAPY (ECT) in which the electric current is modified significantly to decrease the duration of stimulus needed to produce a seizure. Also called **brief stimuli therapy**; **brief stimulus technique**.

brightness *n.* the perceptual correlate of light intensity. The brightness of a stimulus depends on its amplitude (energy), wavelength, the ADAPTATION state of the observer, and the nature of any surrounding or intervening stimuli.

brightness constancy the tendency to perceive a familiar object as having the same brightness under different conditions of illumination. Brightness constancy is one of the PERCEPTUAL CONSTANCIES. Also called **lightness constancy**.

brightness contrast the apparent enhanced difference in brightness resulting from simultaneous stimulation by two stimuli of differing brightness. For example, a gray disk looks darker on a white background than on a black background. Also called **lightness contrast**.

Broca's aphasia one of eight classically identified APHASIAS, characterized by nonfluent conversational speech and slow, halting speech production. Auditory comprehension is relatively good for everyday conversation, but there is considerable difficulty with complex syntax or multistep commands. It is associated with injury to BROCA'S AREA of the brain. [Pierre Paul **Broca** (1824–1880), French physician]

Broca's area a region of the posterior portion of the inferior frontal convolution of the left CEREBRAL HEMISPHERE that is associated with the motor control of speech. [discovered in 1861 by Pierre Paul **Broca**]

Brodmann's area any of more than 200 distinctive areas of cerebral cortex characterized by variation in the occurrence and arrangement of cells (see CYTOARCHITECTURE) from that of neighboring areas. These areas are identified by numbers and in many cases have been associated with specific brain functions, such as area 17 (STRIATE CORTEX, or primary visual cortex), areas 18 and 19 (PRESTRIATE CORTEX), area 4 (motor area, or primary MOTOR CORTEX), and area 6 (PREMOTOR AREA). [Korbinian **Brodmann** (1868–1918), German neurologist]

bromide *n.* any of a class of drugs formerly used as anticonvulsants and as sedatives in the treatment of anxiety. Because of their toxicity and the frequency of adverse side effects, bromides were largely supplanted by phenobarbital in the early 20th century.

bronchus *n.* (*pl.* **bronchi**) either one of the two main branches of the windpipe (trachea). —**bronchial** *adj.*

brood parasitism a practice in which female birds of some species lay their eggs in the nest of another species, leaving the other parents to rear the chicks.

Brown–Peterson distractor technique a technique used in memory studies in which participants are allowed a brief period for remembering during which REHEARSAL is minimized. Typically, three items (e.g., words) are presented, after which the participant is asked to count backward for a certain time (as a DISTRACTOR) before attempting to recall the presented items. [John A. **Brown**; Lloyd R. **Peterson** (1922–) and Margaret Jean **Peterson** (1930–), U.S. psychologists]

bruxism *n.* persistent grinding, clenching, or gnashing of teeth, usually during sleep. It can be associated with feelings of tension, anger, frustration, or fear.

BST abbreviation for BRIEF STIMULUS THERAPY.

bubble concept of personal space the theory that an imaginary, private region surrounds a person, serving as a buffer against potential emotional or physical threats and determining the distance to be maintained in communicating with others. The size of the "bubble" varies with different individuals and situations and in different cultures. See also PROXEMICS.

buccofacial apraxia see APRAXIA.

buccolingual masticatory syndrome a

movement disorder associated with the use of conventional ANTIPSYCHOTIC agents and characterized by involuntary movements of the tongue and musculature of the mouth and face. Also called **buccal–lingual masticatory syndrome**; **oral–lingual dyskinesia**. See also TARDIVE DYSKINESIA.

buffer item an irrelevant item interspersed between others in a test or experiment. For example, a buffer item may be a question that is not scored and is introduced only to separate or disguise other items.

bulbar *adj*. pertaining to a bulb or bulblike structure, especially the MEDULLA OBLONGATA.

bulimia *n*. insatiable hunger for food. It may have physiological causes or be primarily a psychological disorder. —**bulimic** *adj., n.*

bulimia nervosa an EATING DISORDER involving recurrent episodes of binge eating (i.e., discrete periods of uncontrolled consumption of abnormally large quantities of food) followed by inappropriate compensatory behaviors (e.g., self-induced vomiting, misuse of laxatives, fasting, excessive exercise). Compare BINGE-EATING DISORDER.

bullying *n*. persistent threatening and aggressive physical behavior or verbal abuse directed toward other people, especially those who are younger, smaller, weaker, or in some other situation of relative disadvantage.

bundle hypothesis the notion that sensory features are "bundled," or bound together, in conscious experience.

bupropion *n*. a stimulant agent commonly used in the treatment of depression. It is also appropriate as an aid to behavioral treatment for smoking cessation and has been used in the treatment of attention-deficit/hyperactivity disorder. U.S. trade names: **Wellbutrin**; **Zyban**.

bureaucratic leader see LEADERSHIP STYLE.

burnout *n*. physical, emotional, or mental exhaustion, especially in one's job or career, accompanied by decreased motivation, lowered performance, and negative attitudes towards oneself and others. It results from performing at a high level until stress and tension, especially from extreme and prolonged physical or mental exertion or an overburdening workload, take their toll. Burnout is most often observed in professionals who work closely with people (e.g., social workers, teachers, correctional officers) in service-oriented vocations and experience chronic high levels of STRESS.

burst *n*. a series of responses elicited at a relatively high rate, for example, in a neuron or at the onset of EXTINCTION, when conditioned responses are no longer rewarded.

burst–pause firing the simultaneous firing and pausing of neurons in the THALAMUS during deep sleep that produces large-amplitude electroencephalogram waves characteristic of SLOW-WAVE SLEEP.

business psychology see INDUSTRIAL AND ORGANIZATIONAL PSYCHOLOGY.

buspirone *n*. an anxiolytic of the AZASPIRONE class that produces relief of subjective symptoms of anxiety without the sedation, behavioral disinhibition, and risk of dependence associated with the benzodiazepines. Its use has been limited due to its relative lack of efficacy compared with benzodiazepines. U.S. trade name: **BuSpar**.

butyrophenone *n*. any of a class of HIGH-POTENCY ANTIPSYCHOTICS used primarily in the treatment of schizophrenia, mania, and severe agitation. They are associated with numerous EXTRAPYRAMIDAL SYMPTOMS, as well as NEUROLEPTIC MALIGNANT SYNDROME and TARDIVE DYSKINESIA. The prototype is HALOPERIDOL.

butyrylcholinesterase *n*. see CHOLINESTERASE.

bystander effect the tendency for people not to offer help when they know that others are present and capable of helping. Research suggests that a number of cognitive and social processes contribute to the effect, including misinterpreting other people's lack of response as an indication that help is not needed, CONFUSION OF RESPONSIBILITY, and DIFFUSION OF RESPONSIBILITY.

Cc

CA 1. abbreviation for Cocaine Anonymous. See ALCOHOLICS ANONYMOUS. **2.** abbreviation for CHRONOLOGICAL AGE.

cachexia *n.* an extreme state of poor health, physical wasting away, and malnutrition, usually associated with chronic illnesses, such as cancer and pulmonary tuberculosis.

cafeteria feeding a technique for studying hunger in children and nonhuman animals by offering a variety of foods and observing the extent to which the participants choose those providing balanced, life-sustaining nutrition.

calcarine fissure a fissure (groove) on the medial surface of each cerebral hemisphere, extending from the most posterior prominence of the OCCIPITAL LOBE to the PARIETO-OCCIPITAL SULCUS. Also called **calcarine sulcus**.

calcium channel an ION CHANNEL in the presynaptic membrane of a neuron that opens in response to the arrival of an ACTION POTENTIAL, resulting in an influx of calcium ions into the neuron that triggers the release of neurotransmitter into the SYNAPTIC CLEFT.

calcium-channel blocker any of a class of drugs, the prototype of which is **verapamil**, used in the treatment of hypertension and abnormal heart rhythms (arrhythmias). Calcium-channel blockers inhibit the flow of calcium ions into the smooth-muscle cells of blood vessels and the cells of heart muscle, which need calcium to contract, thus inducing prolonged relaxation of the muscles.

California Psychological Inventory (**CPI**) a self-report inventory designed to evaluate personality characteristics, interpersonal behavior, and social interaction. It consists of 434 true–false statements and produces scores on 20 scales divided into four measurement classes: (a) poise, ascendancy, self-assurance, and interpersonal adequacy; (b) socialization, responsibility, intrapersonal values, and character; (c) achievement potential and intellectual efficacy; and (d) intellectual and interest modes.

California Verbal Learning Test (**CVLT**) a word-list learning test consisting of 16 items belonging to one of four categories. The test assesses immediate FREE RECALL following each of five learning trials as well as an interference trial. Free recall and CUED RECALL are also assessed following a short-term delay (immediately after the interference trial) and a long-term (20-min) delay. Finally, long-term recognition is assessed using distractors that vary in their likelihood of eliciting false positive errors.

callosal *adj.* referring to the CORPUS CALLOSUM.

calmodulin *n.* a protein that binds calcium ions in many calcium-regulated processes in living cells. For example, calmodulin is involved in muscle contraction and in the cascade of neurochemical events that underlies memory formation.

CAM abbreviation for COMPLEMENTARY AND ALTERNATIVE MEDICINE.

camaraderie *n.* goodwill and light-hearted rapport between friends or members of a social group, especially of a military unit; comradeship.

camouflage *n.* the use of cryptic coloration and vocal signals that are difficult to localize in order to conceal one's location. Many animal species use camouflage, either to escape the notice of predators or to avoid detection by prey. For example, a bird might have plumage that blends in with other features of the environment, making it difficult to detect. Compare ADVERTISEMENT.

camptocormia *n.* a condition in which the back is bent forward at a sharp angle (30–90°). In some cases it may be a rare manifestation of CONVERSION DISORDER and may be accompanied by back pain, tremors, or both.

cancer *n.* any one of a group of diseases characterized by the unregulated, abnormal growth of cells to form malignant tumors (see NEOPLASM), which invade neighboring tissues; the abnormal cells are generally capable of spreading via the bloodstream or lymphatic system to other body areas or organs by the process of **metastasis**. Causes of cancer are numerous but commonly include viruses, environmental toxins, and radiation. Hereditary factors are important in the etiology of many cancers. Cancers are generally classified as **carcinomas** if they involve the EPITHELIUM (e.g., cancers of the lungs, stomach, or skin) and **sarcomas** if the affected tissues are connective (e.g., bone, muscle, or fat). —**cancerous** *adj.*

cannabinoid *n.* any of a class of about 60 substances in the CANNABIS plant that includes those responsible for the psychoactive properties of the plant. The most important cannabinoid is TETRAHYDROCANNABINOL.

cannabis *n.* any of three related plant species (*Cannabis sativa*, *C. indica*, or *C. ruderalis*) whose dried flowering or fruiting tops or leaves are widely used as a recreational drug, known as **marijuana**. When smoked, the principal psychoactive agent in these plants, delta-9-TETRAHYDROCANNABINOL (THC), is rapidly absorbed into the blood and almost immediately distributed to the brain, causing the rapid onset of subjective effects that last 2–3 hours. These effects include a sense of euphoria or well-being, easy laughter, perceptual distortions, impairment of concentration and short-term memory, and craving for food. Adverse effects of anxiety or panic are not uncommon, and hallucinations may occur with high doses. Tolerance to the effects of THC develops with repeated use, but reports of CANNABIS DEPENDENCE are rare.

cannabis abuse a pattern of CANNABIS use manifested by recurrent significant adverse consequences related to its repeated ingestion. See also SUBSTANCE ABUSE.

cannabis dependence a cluster of cognitive, behavioral, and physiological symptoms indicating continued use of cannabis despite significant cannabis-related problems. See also SUBSTANCE DEPENDENCE.

cannabis intoxication a reversible syndrome that occurs during or shortly after the ingestion or smoking of CANNABIS. It consists of clinically significant behavioral or psychological changes (e.g., enhanced sense of well-being, intensification of perceptions, a sense of slowed time), as well as one or more signs of physiological involvement (e.g., increased pulse rate, conjunctivitis, dry mouth and throat).

cannibalism n. **1.** the consumption of human flesh or the ingestion by a nonhuman animal of a member of its own species. **2.** a pathological urge to devour human flesh, occasionally observed in schizophrenia and similar mental disturbances, such as WINDIGO. In classical psychoanalytic theory, cannibalistic impulses are associated with fixation at the oral-biting phase of PSYCHOSEXUAL DEVELOPMENT. —**cannibalistic** adj.

Cannon–Bard theory the theory that emotional states result from the influence of lower brain centers (the hypothalamus and thalamus) on higher ones (the cortex), rather than from sensory feedback to the brain produced by peripheral internal organs and voluntary musculature. According to this theory, the thalamus controls the experience of emotion, and the hypothalamus controls the expression of emotion. [proposed in the 1920s and early 1930s by Walter B. **Cannon** (1871–1945) and Philip **Bard** (1898–1977), U.S. psychologists]

cannula n. a tube that can be inserted into a body cavity to provide a channel for the escape of fluid from the cavity or the introduction of medication.

canon n. a fundamental working principle or rule believed to increase the likelihood of making accurate inferences and meaningful discoveries. —**canonical** adj.

canonical analysis a class of statistical analyses that assess the degree of relationship between two or more sets of measurements. Examples are DISCRIMINANT ANALYSIS and MULTIPLE REGRESSION analysis, among others.

canonical correlation a CORRELATION COEFFICIENT that quantifies the magnitude of linear relationship between a linear combination of one set of variables and a linear combination of a different set of variables.

capability n. an ability, talent, facility, or other characteristic that a person can develop for functional use.

capacity n. the maximum ability of an individual to receive or retain information and hence his or her potential for intellectual or creative development or accomplishment.

capacity model one of a number of models that characterize attention as a finite resource with limited processing power. Attentional deficits occur when the demands on this resource exceed the supply.

capacity sharing in dual-task performance, the dividing of attentional resources between the tasks such that they are processed in parallel (see PARALLEL PROCESSING), although the processing efficiency varies with the amount of resources required.

capitalization on chance the process of basing a conclusion on data wholly or partly biased in a particular direction by chance. A common example of capitalization on chance is the presentation of all the significant results in a study without considering the number of results examined.

capitation n. a method of payment for health care services in which a provider or health care facility is paid a fixed amount for each person served under a risk contract. Capitation is the characteristic payment method of HMOs (health maintenance organizations). —**capitated** adj.

captivity n. in EXPERIMENTAL RESEARCH, the state of an animal that is housed in an environment different from its natural environment and is prevented from returning to its natural environment. Captivity is used to ensure careful control over environmental and social variables.

capture–tag–recapture sampling a type of SAMPLING used to estimate population size. For example, in order to estimate the number of fish in a lake, a random sample of fish (e.g., 100) would be drawn and tagged, then returned to the lake. The lake would be resampled, and the results (i.e., the fraction of tagged fish in the new sample) would be used to estimate the total number of fish in the lake.

carbamate n. any of a class of acetylcholinesterase inhibitors (see CHOLINESTERASE) used in the treatment of dementia. Carbamates can delay the progression of certain dementias, slowing declines in cognitive function and in activities of daily living, and are preferred to earlier generations of acetylcholinesterase inhibitors because of their relatively benign side effects and relative lack of liver toxicity.

carbamazepine *n.* a drug that is related to the TRICYCLIC ANTIDEPRESSANTS, used mainly as an ANTICONVULSANT but also for the relief of symptoms of TRIGEMINAL NEURALGIA and as a MOOD STABILIZER in mania. U.S. trade name (among others): **Tegretol**.

carbohydrate *n.* any of a group of organic compounds that have the general formula $C_x(H_2O)_y$. They range from relatively small molecules, such as simple sugars (e.g., GLUCOSE), to macromolecular substances, such as starch, glycogen, and cellulose, and form a major source of energy in the diet of animals.

carbonic anhydrase inhibitor any of a group of drugs that interfere with the action of the enzyme carbonic anhydrase in the body. Although their primary role was originally as diuretics, **acetazolamide** (the prototype; U.S. trade name: **Diamox**) and other carbonic anhydrase inhibitors are now used primarily for the management of GLAUCOMA and altitude sickness. The drugs are also used as adjunctive agents in the management of epilepsy.

carcinogen *n.* any substance that initiates the development of CANCER (**carcinogenesis**) when exposed to living tissue. Tobacco smoke, which induces lung cancer, is an example. —**carcinogenic** *adj.*

carcinoma *n.* see CANCER.

cardiac muscle the specialized muscle tissue of the heart. It consists of striated fibers that branch and interlock and are in electrical continuity with each other. This arrangement permits ACTION POTENTIALS to spread rapidly from cell to cell, allowing large groups of cells to contract in unison.

cardiac psychology a specialization within HEALTH PSYCHOLOGY that focuses solely on physical and behavioral health and disease related to the cardiovascular system.

cardinal trait a basic and pervasive characteristic or PERSONALITY TRAIT that dominates an individual's total behavior.

cardiogram *n.* a graphic tracing of some aspect of heart activity, usually electrical activity (see ELECTROCARDIOGRAM). The tracing is produced by the stylet of a recording instrument called a **cardiograph**, and the procedure itself is called **cardiography**.

cardiomyopathy *n.* any disease involving the heart muscle, particularly when the specific cause is uncertain.

cardiovascular *adj.* relating to the heart and blood vessels or to blood circulation. For example, **cardiovascular reactivity** is the degree of change in blood pressure, heart rate, and related responses to a psychological or physical challenge or stressor.

cardiovascular disease any disease, congenital or acquired, that affects the heart and blood vessels. Cardiovascular diseases include HYPERTENSION, congestive heart failure, myocardial INFARCTION, ARTERIOSCLEROSIS, and CORONARY HEART DISEASE.

cardiovascular system the heart and blood vessels, which are responsible for the circulation of blood around the body. Also called **circulatory system**.

card-sorting test a test in which the participant is asked to sort randomly mixed cards into specific categories. Such tests may be used to determine frontal lobe functioning, learning ability, discriminatory powers, or clerical aptitude.

CARE acronym for COMMUNICATED AUTHENTICITY, REGARD, EMPATHY.

career counseling consultation, advice, or guidance specifically focused on a person's career opportunities, most often in educational, work, and some community settings. It also may provide consultation with the specific goal of enabling a person to change the direction of his or her career. The counseling will take account of an individual's preferences, intelligence, skill sets, work values, and experience. Also called **career guidance**.

career pattern theory any theory that attempts to describe the stages through which people pass during the course of their working lives. Careers are often depicted as passing through repeated cycles in which individuals grow by acquiring new skills and experience, stabilize their career gains, and then move into a period of transition as they prepare themselves for the next move.

career planning a VOCATIONAL GUIDANCE program designed to assist a client in choosing an occupation. A realistic appraisal of the individual's desires and abilities is formulated in relation to existing occupational opportunities.

caregiver *n.* **1.** a person who attends to the needs of and provides assistance to someone else, such as an infant or an older adult. **2.** in health care, any individual involved in the process of identifying, preventing, or treating an illness or disability. —**caregiving** *adj.*

caregiver burden the stress and other psychological symptoms experienced by family members and other nonprofessional caregivers in response to looking after individuals with mental or physical disabilities, disorders, or diseases. See also BURNOUT; COMPASSION FATIGUE.

carotid artery either of the two major arteries that ascend the right and left sides of the neck to the head and brain. The branch that enters the brain is the **internal carotid artery**, whereas the **external carotid artery** supplies the face and scalp. Both branches arise from the **common carotid artery** on each side of the lower neck.

carotid sinus a small dilation in the common CAROTID ARTERY, at its bifurcation into the external and internal carotids. It contains BARORECEPTORS that, when stimulated, cause slowing of the heart rate, vasodilation, and a fall in blood pressure. It is innervated primarily by the GLOSSOPHARYNGEAL NERVE.

carpal tunnel syndrome (**CTS**) an inflammatory disorder of the hand caused by repetitive stress, physical injury, or other conditions that cause the tissues around the median nerve to become swollen. It occurs either when the protective lining of the tendons within the **carpal tunnel** become inflamed and swell or when the ligament that forms the roof of the tunnel becomes thicker and broader. See REPETITIVE STRAIN INJURY.

carrier *n.* an individual who has a mutation in a gene that conveys either increased susceptibility to a disease or other condition or the certainty that the condition will develop.

carryover effect the effect on the current performance of a research participant of the experimental conditions that preceded the current conditions.

Cartesian dualism the position taken by French philosopher, mathematician, and scientist René Descartes (1596–1650) that the world comprises two distinct and incompatible classes of substance: **res extensa**, or extended substance, which extends through space; and **res cogitans**, or thinking substance, which has no extension in space. The body (including the brain) is composed of extended and divisible substance, whereas the mind is not. For Descartes, this means that the mind would continue to exist even if the material body did not. He accepted that there is interaction between mind and body, holding that in some activities the mind operates independently of bodily influences, whereas in others the body exerts an influence. Similarly, in some bodily activities there is influence from the mind, while in others there is not. Descartes proposed that the locus for the interaction of the mind and body is the point in the pineal gland in the brain termed the **conarium**. However, to the question of how such incompatible substances can interact at all, Descartes had no answer. See DUALISM; MIND–BODY PROBLEM.

Cartesianism *n.* the system of philosophy developed by French philosopher, mathematician, and scientist René Descartes (1596–1650). The three fundamental tenets of the system are (a) that all knowledge forms a unity; (b) that the purpose of knowledge is to provide humankind with the means of mastery over the natural world; and (c) that all knowledge must be built up from a foundation of indubitable first principles, the truth of which can be known intuitively. Many ideas and assumptions influential in psychology can be traced back to Descartes, including the notion of a rational self capable of knowing truth, the contention that the most trustworthy knowledge is of the contents of one's own mind, and the idea that the deductive methods that have been successful in producing certainty in mathematics can be applied to produce equally valid knowledge in other fields of

human endeavor. Of particular importance to the development of psychology are Descartes' understanding of the ego and his attempt to explain the relation of the mind to the body (see CARTESIAN DUALISM). See also RATIONALISM. **—Cartesian** *adj.*

carve out to eliminate coverage for specific health care services (e.g., mental health or substance abuse) from a health care plan and contract for those services from a separate provider. **—carve-out** *n.*

case *n.* **1.** an instance of a disease or disorder, usually at the level of the individual patient. In a **borderline case**, the symptoms resemble those of a disease or disorder but do not fully meet the criteria. See also PROBAND. **2.** a person about whom data are collected or who is the recipient of assistance (e.g., from a health care professional or lawyer). **3.** one of various categories used in CASE GRAMMAR to classify the elements of a sentence in terms of their semantic relations with the main verb.

case-based reasoning 1. an approach in which information about or obtained from previous similar situations (cases) is applied to the current situation, typically to make a decision or prediction or to solve a problem. See also ANALOGICAL THINKING. **2.** in ergonomics, the use of detailed scenarios or cases to elicit users' knowledge, reasoning patterns, motivations, or assumptions regarding a product or system. See KNOWLEDGE ELICITATION.

case grammar in linguistics, an analysis of sentences that gives primacy to the semantic relations between words (e.g., whether they are the actor or the acted-upon of the action described) rather than to their syntactic, grammatical relations (e.g., whether they are the subject or the object of the sentence). In the two sentences *The boy hit the ball* and *The ball was hit by the boy*, a case-grammar analysis would focus on the fact that *boy* is the agent of the action in both sentences, rather than the fact that it is the subject of the first sentence and the object in the second. Psychologists have shown a strong interest in case grammar because of its affinity to psychological categories of meaning.

case load the amount of work required of a psychotherapist, psychiatrist, doctor, social worker, or counselor during a particular period, as computed by the number of clients assigned to him or her and the comparative difficulty of their cases.

case management a system of managing and coordinating the delivery of health care in order to improve the continuity and quality of care as well as reducing costs. Case management is usually a function of a hospital's UTILIZATION REVIEW department.

case study an in-depth investigation of an individual, a family, or other social unit. Multiple types of data (psychological, physiological, biographical, environmental) are assembled in order to understand the subject's background, relationships, and behavior.

casework *n.* the tasks carried out by a professional, usually a social worker known as a **case-worker**, who provides or oversees services being delivered, including counseling or therapy. Casework includes identifying and assessing the needs of the individual and his or her family and providing or coordinating and monitoring the provision of support and services. These services may include private counseling, treatment in a hospital or other institution, or such concrete services as arranging for public assistance, housing, and other aid. Also called **social case-work**.

caste *n.* any system of social stratification regarded as being comparatively rigid, particularly the **Hindu caste system**, involving fixed hereditary classes held to be distinguished by different levels of ritual purity. See also SOCIAL IMMOBILITY.

castration *n.* surgical removal of the testes (see ORCHIDECTOMY); less commonly it can indicate removal of the ovaries (see OVARIECTOMY). Castration eliminates sex hormone production and, in men, may lower sexual drive and function.

castration anxiety fear of injury to or loss of the genitals. In the PREGENITAL PHASE posited by psychoanalytic theory, the various losses and deprivations experienced by the infant boy may give rise to the fear that he will also lose his penis. See also CASTRATION COMPLEX.

castration complex in psychoanalytic theory, the whole combination of the child's unconscious feelings and fantasies associated with being deprived of the PHALLUS, which in boys means the loss of the penis and in girls the belief that it has already been removed. It derives from the discovery that girls have no penis and is closely tied to the OEDIPUS COMPLEX.

CAT 1. abbreviation for COMPUTER ADAPTIVE TESTING. **2.** acronym for computerized axial tomography (see COMPUTED TOMOGRAPHY).

catabolism *n.* see METABOLISM. —**catabolic** *adj.*

catalepsy *n.* a state of sustained unresponsiveness in which a fixed body posture or physical attitude is maintained over a long period of time. It is seen in cases of CATATONIC SCHIZOPHRENIA, EPILEPSY, and other disorders. —**cataleptic** *adj.*

catalyst *n.* a substance that increases the rate of a chemical reaction without itself being used up. An ENZYME is an organic catalyst.

catamnesis *n.* the medical history of a patient following the onset of a mental or physical disorder, either after the initial examination or after discharge from treatment (in the latter case it is also known as **follow-up history**). Compare ANAMNESIS.

cataplexy *n.* a sudden loss of muscle tone that may be localized, causing (for example) loss of grasp or head nodding, or generalized, resulting in collapse of the entire body. It is a temporary condition usually precipitated by an extreme emotional stimulus. —**cataplectic** *adj.*

cataract *n.* a progressive clouding (opacification) of the lens of the eye that eventually results in severe visual impairment if untreated. Central vision in particular is impaired, with symptoms including dim or fuzzy vision, sensitivity to glare, and difficulty seeing at night. Cataract is frequently associated with the degenerative processes of aging, but it may also be congenital or due to disease or injury.

catastrophe cusp theory a theory concerning the interaction of anxiety and physiological arousal. Under conditions of high anxiety, as physiological arousal increases, performance will increase to a certain point, but past this point a catastrophic drop in performance will occur.

catastrophe theory a mathematical theory regarding discontinuous changes in one variable as a function of continuous change in some other variable or variables. It proposes that a small change in one factor may cause an abrupt and large change in another, for example, the dramatic change in the physical properties of water as the temperature reaches 0 °C or 100 °C (32 or 212 °F).

catastrophic reaction highly emotional behavior (extreme anxiety, sudden crying, aggressive or hostile behavior, etc.) sometimes observed in individuals who have suffered brain damage, including those with APHASIA. The origin of this behavior remains unclear, although it has been ascribed to individuals' frustration, embarrassment, or agitation at their struggle to communicate or perform tasks they had previously performed with ease. Also called **catastrophic behavior**.

catastrophize *vb.* to exaggerate the negative consequences of events or decisions. People are said to be catastrophizing when they think that the worst possible outcome will occur from a particular action or in a particular situation. The tendency to catastrophize can unnecessarily increase levels of anxiety and lead to maladaptive behavior.

catatonia *n.* a state of muscular rigidity or other disturbance of motor behavior, such as CATALEPSY. —**catatonic** *adj.*

catatonic schizophrenia a relatively rare subtype of schizophrenia characterized by abnormal motor activity, specifically motor immobility or POSTURING interspersed with excessive motor activity. Other common features include extreme NEGATIVISM (apparently motiveless resistance to all instructions) or MUTISM and ECHOLALIA or ECHOPRAXIA.

catchment area the geographic area served by a health care program (e.g., a community mental health center).

catecholamine *n.* any of a class of BIOGENIC

AMINES formed by a catechol molecule and an amine group. Derived from tyrosine, catecholamines include dopamine, epinephrine and norepinephrine, which are the predominant neurotransmitters in the SYMPATHETIC NERVOUS SYSTEM.

catecholamine hypothesis the hypothesis that deficiencies in the catecholamine neurotransmitters norepinephrine, epinephrine, and dopamine at receptor sites in the brain lead to a state of physiological and psychological depression, and that an excess of such neurotransmitters at these sites is responsible for the production of mania. The catecholamine hypothesis and the related MONOAMINE HYPOTHESIS were prominent in the last half of the 20th century but have largely been abandoned as too simplistic.

catecholaminergic *adj.* responding to, releasing, or otherwise involving CATECHOLAMINES. For example, a **catecholaminergic neuron** is one that releases norepinephrine or another catecholamine as a neurotransmitter.

categorical data data that consist of counts as opposed to measurements. Religion or political party affiliation are examples of categorical data. Also called **nominal data**.

categorical imperative the moral directive articulated by German philosopher Immanuel Kant (1724–1804) that one's behavior should be guided by maxims that one would be comfortable to hold as universal laws governing the actions of all people in the same circumstances. Because it is absolute and unconditional, the categorical imperative contrasts with a HYPOTHETICAL IMPERATIVE of the type "If you would achieve end Y, take action Z." The categorical imperative has been extremely influential in moral philosophy and in theories of moral behavior in psychology. See also UNIVERSALIZABILITY.

categorical perception in speech perception, the phenomenon in which a continuous acoustic dimension, such as VOICE-ONSET TIME, is perceived as having distinct categories with sharp discontinuities at certain points. Whereas discrimination is much more accurate between categories, individuals tested are often unable to discriminate between acoustically different stimuli that fall within the same categorical boundaries. Categorical perception is crucial in the identification of PHONEMES.

categorical scale see NOMINAL SCALE.

categorical variable a variable defined by membership in a group, class, or category, rather than by rank or by scores on more continuous scales of measurement.

categorization *n.* the process by which objects, events, people, or experiences are grouped into classes on the basis of (a) characteristics shared by members of the same class and (b) features distinguishing the members of one class from those of another. Theories of categorization include the PROTOTYPE MODEL, INSTANCE THEORY, and the FAMILY RESEMBLANCE hypothesis. Also called **classification**. —**categorize** *vb.*

categorized list a list used in memory experiments in which the items come from one or more semantic categories (e.g., names, animals, foods). Categorized lists are often used to test FREE RECALL.

category-system method any method of measurement or classification assessment that involves the use of STRUCTURED OBSERVATIONAL MEASURES to sort data elements into categories according to a set of rules. See also INTERACTION-PROCESS ANALYSIS; SYMLOG.

catharsis *n.* in psychoanalytic theory, the discharge of affects connected to traumatic events that had previously been repressed by bringing these events back into consciousness and reexperiencing them. See also ABREACTION. [from Greek, literally: "purgation, purification"] —**cathartic** *adj.*

catheter *n.* any flexible tubular instrument inserted into a body cavity to introduce or remove fluids or to keep a body passage open.

cathexis *n.* in psychoanalytic theory, the investment of PSYCHIC ENERGY in an OBJECT of any kind, such as a wish, fantasy, person, goal, idea, social group, or the self. Such objects are said to be **cathected** when an individual attaches emotional significance (positive or negative affect) to them. See also ANTICATHEXIS; DECATHEXIS.

Cattell–Horn theory of intelligence a theory proposing that there are two main kinds of intellectual abilities nested under general intelligence: *g-c*, or **crystallized intelligence** (or **ability**), which is the sum of one's knowledge and is measured by tests of vocabulary, general information, etc.; and *g-f*, or **fluid intelligence** (or **ability**), which is the set of mental processes that is used in dealing with relatively novel tasks and is used in the acquisition of *g-c*. In later versions of the theory, other abilities have been added, such as *g-v*, or visual intelligence (or ability), which is the set of mental processes used in handling visual-spatial tasks, such as mentally rotating a geometric figure or visualizing what pieces of paper would look like when folded. [Raymond Bernard **Cattell** (1905–1998), British-born U.S. personality psychologist who originally developed the theory in the 1940s; John L. **Horn** (1928–), U.S. psychologist who subsequently contributed to the theory beginning in the 1960s]

Cattell's personality trait theory an approach to personality description based on the identification of traits through FACTOR ANALYSIS and their classification into SURFACE TRAITS and the 16 SOURCE TRAITS that underlie them. [Raymond **Cattell**]

cauda equina the bundle of nerve roots at the base of the spinal cord, so called because of its resemblance to a horse's tail.

caudal *adj.* **1.** pertaining to a tail. **2.** situated at or toward the tail end of an organism. Compare ROSTRAL.

caudate nucleus one of the BASAL GANGLIA, so named because it has a long extension, or tail.

causal analysis an attempt to draw dependable inferences about cause-and-effect relationships from data not obtained from true (randomized) experiments.

causality *n.* in philosophy, the position that all events have causes, that is, that they are consequences of antecedent events. Traditionally, causality has been seen as an essential assumption of NATURALISM and all scientific explanation, although some have questioned whether causality is a necessary assumption of science. Others have suggested that, while causality must be assumed, there are different types of causality, each of which makes different metaphysical assumptions about the nature of the world and adopts different criteria about what types of relationships between phenomena can be considered as legitimately causal. See also CAUSATION; DETERMINISM. **—causal** *adj.*

causal latency 1. the temporal separation of a cause from its effect. Not all causes need have immediate effects; indeed, there may be a lengthy interval between a cause and the effect it produces. Causal latency may be expected to increase when there are other factors in a situation that may influence the cause-and-effect relationship. Some causes studied in psychology and the other social sciences are REMOTE CAUSES, in that they require the presence or activity of other factors or conditions before their effects become manifest. Remote causes may be expected to have large causal latencies. **2.** in the statistical procedure known as PATH ANALYSIS, the quality of a variable that has a measurable statistical effect on prediction only when other predictor variables are also included in the prediction model. Although the statistical relationships identified in such analyses are not, strictly speaking, causal, the language of causality is commonly employed. See CAUSAL PATH.

causal ordering 1. the principle that causes must temporally precede their effects, and never vice versa. See also REVERSE CAUSALITY. **2.** in PATH ANALYSIS and similar statistical procedures, the categorizing of causal variables as either more or less direct. See CAUSAL LATENCY; CAUSAL PATH.

causal path in PATH ANALYSIS and similar statistical procedures, a relatively probable causal sequence among a complex set of potential causes and effects. The analysis is based on first-order and partial correlations among variables indicating possible relations of cause and effect. From the pattern of correlations, conclusions are drawn regarding which set of variables, in which order, represents the most likely path from some presumed cause of interest to some presumed effect of interest.

causation *n.* **1.** the empirical relation between two events, states, or variables such that one (the cause) is held or known to bring about the other (the effect). See also CAUSALITY. **2.** in Aristotelian and rationalist philosophy, the hypothetical relation between two phenomena (entities or events), such that one (the cause) either constitutes the necessary and sufficient grounds for the existence of the other (the effect), or the one possesses the capacity to bring about the other. **—causal** *adj.*

cautious shift a CHOICE SHIFT in which an individual making a decision as part of a group adopts a more cautious approach than the same individual would have adopted had he or she made the decision alone. Studies suggest that such shifts are rarer than the opposite **risky shift**. See also GROUP POLARIZATION.

CBCL abbreviation for CHILD BEHAVIOR CHECKLIST.

CBT abbreviation for COGNITIVE BEHAVIOR THERAPY.

CCRT abbreviation for CORE CONFLICTUAL RELATIONSHIP THEME.

CDI abbreviation for CHILDREN'S DEPRESSION INVENTORY.

ceiling effect a situation in which a large proportion of participants perform as well as, or nearly as well as, possible on a task or other evaluative measure, thus skewing the distribution of scores and making it impossible to discriminate differences among the many individuals at that high level. For example, a test whose items are too easy for those taking it would show a ceiling effect because most people would obtain or be close to the highest possible score of 100. Compare FLOOR EFFECT.

celiac plexus 1. in the nervous system, a network of fibers lying anterior to the aorta at the level of the 12th thoracic vertebra. Most autonomic and visceral afferent nerves pass through this plexus. Also called **celiac nervous plexus**. **2.** in the lymphatic system, a network of afferent and efferent lymphatic vessels in the abdomen. Also called **celiac lymphatic plexus**.

cell *n.* **1.** in biology, the basic unit of organized tissue, consisting of an outer plasma membrane, the NUCLEUS, and various ORGANELLES in a watery fluid together comprising the **cytoplasm**. **2.** in statistics, the space formed at the intersection of a row and a column in a table. For example, a tabular display of a study of handedness in men and women would consist of four cells: left-handed females, left-handed males, right-handed females, and right-handed males.

cell assembly a group of neurons that are repeatedly active at the same time and develop as a single functional unit, which may become active when any of its constituent neurons is stimulated. This enables, for example, a person to form a complete mental image of an object when only a portion is visible or to recall a memory from a partial cue. Cell assembly is influential in biological theories of memory.

cell body the part of a NEURON (nerve cell) that contains the nucleus and most organelles. Also called **soma**.

cell death see PROGRAMMED CELL DEATH.

cell-means model any of a class of linear ANOVA (ANALYSIS OF VARIANCE) models in which the observed score is modeled as a function of the population mean of the CELL in which the score occurs plus a random error.

cellular automata computer programs used in the study of ARTIFICIAL LIFE. Typically, a display is split into an array of cells, with an initial pattern of occupied cells that evolves through a sequence of steps according to certain rules. Programs of this type have been used in investigations of such phenomena as social behavior and evolutionary development.

censor n. in psychoanalytic theory, the mental agency, located in the PRECONSCIOUS, that is responsible for REPRESSION. The censor is posited to determine which of one's wishes, thoughts, and ideas may enter consciousness and which must be kept unconscious because they violate one's conscience or society's standards. The censor is also posited to be responsible for the distortion of wishes that occurs in dreams (see DREAM CENSORSHIP). The idea was introduced in the early writings of Austrian psychiatrist Sigmund Freud (1856–1939), who later developed it into the concept of the SUPEREGO. —**censorship** n.

censored data a set of data in which some values are unobserved, often because the event of interest has not occurred by the end of the study or because the response falls into an unmeasurable portion of the scale.

center n. in neurophysiology, a structure or region that controls a particular function, for example, the respiratory center of the brain.

centered adj. denoting a state of mind characterized by having a firm grip on reality, knowing who one is and what one wants out of life, and being prepared to meet most eventualities in an efficient manner.

Center for Epidemiologic Studies Depression Scale (**CES-D**) a 20-item self-administered rating scale that provides a quantitative measure of different depressive feelings and behaviors during the previous week.

centering n. in sport psychology, a technique used by athletes to assist them in achieving an IDEAL PERFORMANCE STATE that involves focusing on a spot in the center of the body and imagining being in that state.

center–surround antagonism a characteristic of the receptive fields of many visual and somatosensory neurons in which stimulation in the center of the receptive field evokes opposite responses to stimulation in the periphery. Center–surround antagonism greatly increases the sensitivity of the nervous system to CONTRAST.

See also OFF RESPONSE; ON RESPONSE; SIMPLE CELL.

central adj. of or relating to the CENTRAL NERVOUS SYSTEM (CNS), especially to disorders that occur as a result of injury to or dysfunction of the CNS.

central anticholinergic syndrome see ANTICHOLINERGIC SYNDROME.

central auditory processing disorder an impaired ability to decode acoustic messages into meaningful information and to discriminate speech, despite only minor changes in auditory sensitivity to sound. In adults, this disorder is typically associated with brain damage caused by stroke, lesions, and neurodegenerative diseases, such as multiple sclerosis; in children, it is most often associated with microscopic pathology in the brain and maturational delays in language acquisition. Also called **auditory processing disorder**.

central canal the channel in the center of the SPINAL CORD, which contains CEREBROSPINAL FLUID.

central conceptual structure a theoretical integrated repository of mental operations and network of concepts and relationships relevant to a particular domain of experience (e.g., the domain of numbers) and important to task performance. Central conceptual structures are one of two mechanisms proposed by Canadian developmental psychologist Robbie Case (1944–2000) as guiding learning and thinking processes in children, the other being the EXECUTIVE CONTROL STRUCTURE.

central deafness loss or absence of hearing caused by damage to or abnormality of the auditory structures of the brain (i.e., the central AUDITORY SYSTEM), rather than the auditory nerve or the ear itself.

central dyslexia any form of acquired dyslexia characterized by difficulties with the pronunciation and comprehension of written words. Unlike PERIPHERAL DYSLEXIA, the visual analysis system is intact, and the damage is to other, higher level pathways and systems involved in reading (e.g., the semantic system).

central executive see WORKING MEMORY.

central fissure see CENTRAL SULCUS.

central gray see PERIAQUEDUCTAL GRAY.

centrality of an attitude the extent to which an attitude is linked to other attitudes in memory. Increased centrality is associated with enhanced STRENGTH OF AN ATTITUDE.

central limited capacity the observed constraint on processing capacity of the cognitive system associated with consciousness, such that only one conscious or effortful task can be accomplished at any given moment. Simultaneous conscious or effortful tasks will result in degraded performance. See DUAL-TASK COMPETITION.

central limit theorem the statistical principle

that a linear combination of values (including the mean of those values) tends to be normally distributed over repeated samples as the sample sizes increase, whether or not the population from which the observations are drawn is normal in distribution.

central nervous system (**CNS**) the entire complex of NEURONS, AXONS, and supporting tissue that constitute the brain and spinal cord. The CNS is primarily involved in mental activities and in coordinating and integrating incoming sensory messages and outgoing motor messages. Compare PERIPHERAL NERVOUS SYSTEM.

central pattern generator any of the sets of neurons in the spinal cord capable of producing oscillatory behavior and thought to be involved in the control of locomotion and other tasks.

central processing dysfunction impairment in the analysis, storage, synthesis, and symbolic use of information. Because these processes involve memory tasks, the dysfunction is believed to be related to difficulties in learning.

central processor in models of cognition based on analogies to INFORMATION PROCESSING in a computer, that part of the system that carries out operations on stored representations. The idea of a single central processor in the human cognitive system has been challenged by models based on DISTRIBUTED PROCESSING, PARALLEL DISTRIBUTED PROCESSING, and PARALLEL PROCESSING.

central route to persuasion the process by which attitudes are formed or changed as a result of carefully scrutinizing and thinking about the central merits of attitude-relevant information. See also ELABORATION; ELABORATION-LIKELIHOOD MODEL. Compare PERIPHERAL ROUTE TO PERSUASION.

central sulcus a major cleft (see SULCUS) that passes roughly vertically along the lateral surface of each CEREBRAL HEMISPHERE from a point beginning near the top of the cerebrum. It marks the border between the FRONTAL LOBE and the PARIETAL LOBE. Also called **central fissure**; **Rolandic fissure**.

central tendency the middle or center point of a DISTRIBUTION, estimated by a number of different statistics (e.g., MEAN and MEDIAN).

central trait any of a cluster of traits (e.g., compassion, ambition, sociability, helpfulness) that comprise the basic pattern of an individual's personality.

central vision vision provided by the FOVEA CENTRALIS. Compare PARACENTRAL VISION; PERIPHERAL VISION.

centration n. in PIAGETIAN THEORY, the tendency of children in the PREOPERATIONAL STAGE to attend to one aspect of a problem, object, or situation at a time, to the exclusion of others. Compare DECENTRATION.

centrifugal adj. directed away from the center.

For example, a **centrifugal nerve** carries impulses from the central nervous system to a peripheral region of the body. Compare CENTRIPETAL.

centripetal adj. directed toward the center. For example, a **centripetal nerve** carries nerve impulses from the periphery to the central nervous system. Compare CENTRIFUGAL.

cephalic adj. pertaining to or located in the head.

cephalic index the ratio of the maximum breadth of the head to its maximum length, multiplied by 100. The average, or medium, cephalic index for humans is between 75 and 81 (**mesocephalic**). A measure below 75 indicates a narrow head (**dolichocephalic**); a measure above 81 indicates a wide head (**brachycephalic**).

cephalization n. the evolutionary tendency for important structures (brain, major sense organs, etc.) to develop at the anterior (front) end of organisms.

cerebellar adj. of or relating to the CEREBELLUM.

cerebellar cortex the GRAY MATTER, or unmyelinated nerve cells, covering the surface of the CEREBELLUM.

cerebellar peduncle any of the three bundles of nerve fibers that connect each main lobe (hemisphere) of the CEREBELLUM with other parts of the brain. The superior cerebellar peduncle, or **brachium conjunctivum**, connects the cerebellum with the MIDBRAIN; the middle peduncle connects the cerebellum with the PONS; and the inferior peduncle connects the cerebellum with the MEDULLA OBLONGATA.

cerebellum n. (pl. **cerebella**) a portion of the HINDBRAIN dorsal to the rest of the BRAINSTEM, to which it is connected by the CEREBELLAR PEDUNCLES. The cerebellum modulates muscular contractions to produce smooth, accurately timed BALLISTIC movements and it helps maintain equilibrium by predicting body positions ahead of actual body movements.

cerebral adj. referring to the CEREBRUM of the brain.

cerebral aqueduct a passage containing CEREBROSPINAL FLUID that extends through the MIDBRAIN to link the third and fourth cerebral VENTRICLES of the brain. Also called **Sylvian aqueduct**.

cerebral cortex the layer of GRAY MATTER that covers the outside of the CEREBRAL HEMISPHERES in the brain and is associated with higher cognitive functions, such as language, learning, perception, and planning. It consists mostly of NEOCORTEX, which has six main layers of cells (see CORTICAL LAYERS); regions of cerebral cortex that do not have six layers are known as ALLOCORTEX. Differences in the CYTOARCHITECTURE of the layers led to the recognition of distinct areas, called BRODMANN'S AREAS, many of which are known to serve different functions.

cerebral dominance the controlling or disproportionate influence on certain aspects of behavior by one CEREBRAL HEMISPHERE (e.g., language is typically left-lateralized in right-handed people). See DOMINANCE.

cerebral electrotherapy (**CET**) the application of low-voltage pulses of direct electrical current to the brain, occasionally used in the treatment of depression, anxiety, and insomnia.

cerebral hemisphere either half (left or right) of the cerebrum. The hemispheres are separated by a deep LONGITUDINAL FISSURE but they are connected by commissural, projection, and association fibers so that each side of the brain normally is linked to functions of tissues on either side of the body. See also HEMISPHERIC LATERALIZATION.

cerebral palsy (**CP**) a set of nonprogressive movement disorders that results from trauma to the brain occurring prenatally or during the birth process. Symptoms include spasticity, paralysis, unsteady gait, and speech abnormalities. CP is commonly classified into the following types: **spastic**, the most common, resulting from damage to the motor cortex, corticospinal tract, or pyramidal tract; **dyskinetic**, resulting from damage to the basal ganglia; and **ataxic**, resulting from damage to the cerebellum.

cerebrospinal fluid (**CSF**) the fluid within the CENTRAL CANAL of the spinal cord, the four VENTRICLES of the brain, and the SUBARACHNOID SPACE of the brain. It serves as a watery cushion to protect vital tissues of the central nervous system from damage by shock pressure, and it mediates between blood vessels and brain tissue in exchange of materials, including nutrients.

cerebrovascular accident (**CVA**) a disorder of the brain arising from CEREBROVASCULAR DISEASE, such as cerebral HEMORRHAGE, EMBOLISM, or THROMBOSIS, resulting in temporary or permanent alterations in cognition, motor and sensory skills, or levels of consciousness. This term is often used interchangeably with STROKE. Also called **cerebral vascular accident**.

cerebrovascular disease a pathological condition of the blood vessels of the brain. It may manifest itself as symptoms of STROKE or a TRANSIENT ISCHEMIC ATTACK. Also called **cerebral vascular disease**. See also CEREBROVASCULAR ACCIDENT.

cerebrovascular insufficiency failure of the cardiovascular system to supply adequate levels of oxygenated blood to the brain tissues. The condition usually arises when one of the four main arteries supplying the brain, namely the two carotid and two vertebral arteries, is interrupted. Also called **cerebral vascular insufficiency**.

cerebrum *n.* the largest part of the brain, forming most of the FOREBRAIN and lying in front of and above the cerebellum. It consists of two CEREBRAL HEMISPHERES bridged by the CORPUS CALLOSUM. Each hemisphere is divided into four main lobes: the FRONTAL LOBE, OCCIPITAL LOBE, PARIETAL LOBE, and TEMPORAL LOBE. The outer layer of the cerebrum—the CEREBRAL CORTEX—is intricately folded and composed of GRAY MATTER. Also called **telencephalon**.

certainty of paternity the degree to which a putative parent can be certain that he, she, or it is the parent of an offspring. Because of internal fertilization and gestation, all female mammals are certain of maternity, but no male mammal can be 100% certain of paternity.

certifiable *adj.* **1.** describing people who, because of mental illness, may be a danger to themselves or others and are therefore eligible to be institutionalized. **2.** having met the requirements to be formally recognized by the relevant licensing or sanctioning body.

certification *n.* **1.** the formal process by which an external agency affirms that a person has met predetermined standards and has the requisite knowledge and skills to be considered competent in a particular area. Certification applies to individuals and ACCREDITATION applies to institutions. See also CREDENTIALING. **2.** the legal proceedings in which appropriate mental health care professionals formally confirm that a person has a mental disorder, which may result in COMMITMENT of that person. —**certificated** *adj.*

cerveau isolé an animal whose MIDBRAIN has been transected between the inferior and superior colliculi (see COLLICULUS) for experimental purposes. See also ENCÉPHALE ISOLÉ. [French, "isolated brain"]

cervical *adj.* **1.** relating to, occurring in, or affecting the neck, for example, the CERVICAL NERVES. **2.** pertaining to a necklike structure, especially the CERVIX of the uterus.

cervical ganglion any of the collections of neural cell bodies (ganglia) of the SYMPATHETIC NERVOUS SYSTEM that occur in the neck region. They innervate the pupils, sweat glands of the head, salivary glands, and heart.

cervical nerve any of the eight SPINAL NERVES in the neck area. Each has a DORSAL ROOT that is sensory in function and a VENTRAL ROOT that has motor function.

cervix *n.* in anatomy, any necklike part, especially the neck of the UTERUS, which is the portion of the uterus that projects into the vagina.

CES abbreviation for cranial ELECTRICAL STIMULATION.

CES-D abbreviation for CENTER FOR EPIDEMIOLOGIC STUDIES DEPRESSION SCALE.

CET abbreviation for CEREBRAL ELECTROTHERAPY.

C fiber an unmyelinated peripheral nerve fiber (axon) that conducts pain information slowly. C fibers vary from approximately 0.4 to 1.2 µm in diameter. See also A FIBER; B FIBER.

CFS abbreviation for CHRONIC FATIGUE SYNDROME.

chained schedule a SCHEDULE OF REINFORCE-

MENT for a single response in which a sequence of at least two schedules, each accompanied by a distinctive stimulus, must be completed before primary reinforcement occurs. For example, in a chained fixed-ratio 10, fixed-ratio 50 schedule, 10 responses change the stimulus situation and then 50 more result in primary reinforcement. Also called **chained reinforcement**. Compare TANDEM REINFORCEMENT.

chaining *n.* an OPERANT CONDITIONING technique in which a complex behavioral sequence is learned and PRIMARY REINFORCEMENT is contingent on the final response in the series. In **backward chaining**, the final response is taught first. Once established, the stimulus for that response becomes a CONDITIONED REINFORCER that is used to reinforce the next-to-last response in the chain; this stimulus is then used to reinforce another response, and so on. In **forward chaining**, the chain is taught by reinforcing the first step in the sequence, then the second, and so on until the entire sequence is learned.

challenging behavior behavior that is dangerous, or that interferes in participation in preschool, educational, or adult services, and often necessitates the design and use of special interventions. The term is used principally in human services in the United Kingdom and within educational services in the United States and most typically refers to behaviors of people with mental retardation or related conditions.

chance occurrence 1. the occurrence of a phenomenon not resulting from CAUSATION. It is a matter of debate whether there are genuinely chance occurrences. Because CAUSALITY is a dominant assumption in much of philosophy and nearly all science, many would argue that what appear to be chance occurrences are merely occurrences the causes of which are not yet known, or not knowable. **2.** in statistical analysis, the occurrence of a predicted phenomenon under conditions of the NULL HYPOTHESIS. One purpose of statistical hypothesis testing is to assess the probability of chance occurrences.

change agent a specific causative factor or element or an entire process that results in change, particularly in the sense of improvement. In psychotherapy research, a change agent may be a component or process in therapy that results in improvement in the behavior or psychological adaptation of a patient or client.

change blindness an inability to notice changes in the visual array between one scene and another. For example, when a picture of an airplane is shown, followed by a blank screen, participants have surprising difficulty detecting a missing engine in a second picture of the airplane. See also MINDSIGHT.

change effect in parapsychology, a phenomenon in which the physical structure of an object appears to have been altered by paranormal means, as in the alleged structural changes to metal in "spoon-bending" demonstrations. See PSYCHOKINESIS.

change management the process of planning, implementing, and evaluating change within organizations or communities, with the goal of realizing the benefits of change while implementing it as efficiently, smoothly, and cost-effectively as possible. Change management practices include effective communication regarding the change, such as the identification of intended consequences, and the prediction of and preparation for unintended consequences.

change-over delay in CONCURRENT SCHEDULES OF REINFORCEMENT, a delay imposed between an organism's switch between alternative responses and the presentation of REINFORCEMENT.

change score a score based on two or more measurements made on the same person over time. The simplest change score is postscore minus prescore.

channels of communication 1. in the social psychology of groups, the paths available for transmission of information from one person to one or more other people in the group or organization. For example, in a highly centralized communication structure (sometimes termed a **star**) all information must pass through the individual at the center of the structure in order to reach any other member of the organization. **2.** the channels by which information is conveyed in face-to-face communication between people, comprising speech, kinesics (body movement), odor, touch, observation, and proxemics (body placement).

chaos theory an area of mathematics dealing with systems that are profoundly affected by their initial conditions, tiny variations in which can produce complex, unpredictable, and erratic effects. It has been applied by some psychological researchers to the study of human behavior. See NONLINEAR DYNAMICS THEORIES; SENSITIVE DEPENDENCE.

character *n.* **1.** the totality of an individual's attributes and PERSONALITY TRAITS, particularly his or her characteristic moral, social, and religious attitudes. Character is often used synonymously with PERSONALITY. **2.** see CHARACTER TYPE.

character analysis see CHARACTEROLOGY.

character displacement a change in a physical, physiological, or behavioral trait within two or more populations of a species that reduces competition between those populations and, over time, leads to the development of separate species. A classic example is provided by the several types of finches in the Galápagos Islands with different forms of bills for eating seeds of different sizes or capturing insects of different sizes.

characterology *n.* **1.** formerly, the branch of psychology concerned with character and personality. Also called **character analysis**. **2.** a pseudoscience in which character is "read" by external signs, such as hair color or facial type.

character strength a positive trait, such as kindness, teamwork, or hope, that is morally valued in its own right and contributes to the fulfillment of the self and others. Also called **human strength**. See POSITIVE PSYCHOLOGY.

character type 1. see PERSONALITY TYPE. **2.** in psychoanalytic theory, a personality type defined by the kinds of DEFENSE MECHANISM used (e.g., a PHOBIA) or FIXATION at a particular stage in PSYCHOSEXUAL DEVELOPMENT (e.g., an ORAL PERSONALITY).

charisma *n.* the special quality of personality that enables an individual to gain the confidence of large numbers of people. It is exemplified in outstanding political, social, and religious leaders. —**charismatic** *adj.*

charismatic leader see LEADERSHIP STYLE.

Charles Bonnet syndrome complex visual hallucinations without delusions or the loss of insightful cognition, typically occurring in older adults who have severe visual impairment. Such hallucinations are usually nonthreatening and often pleasant and are not indicative of psychological disorder. [Charles **Bonnet** (1720–1793), Swiss naturalist and philosopher]

ChE abbreviation for CHOLINESTERASE.

cheating *n.* in evolutionary psychology, using asocial strategies to gain an evolutionary advantage. For example, males of some species who have formed an exclusive PAIR BOND with a female may nonetheless seek to mate with other females so as to increase their chances of producing offspring. —**cheat** *vb.*, *n.*

checklist *n.* a list of items that are to be observed, recorded, or corrected.

chelation *n.* the formation of chemical bonds between a metal ion and two or more nonmetallic ions. It can be used to remove certain types of ions from biological reactions or from the body, as in the removal of lead or mercury from the body by use of chelating agents.

chemesthesis *n.* the activation of nonolfactory or nongustatory receptors in the eye, nose, mouth, and throat (typically those involved in pain, touch, and thermal awareness) by chemical stimuli. An example is the activation of pain receptors deriving from the burn in the taste of a chili pepper.

chemical antagonism see ANTAGONIST.

chemical castration elimination of the action of testosterone by injection or oral administration of drugs that block the action of the hormone by competing for testosterone receptor sites in the brain. Chemical castration is used for the purposes of managing advanced prostate cancer or, more controversially, to reduce sexual drive in repeat sex offenders.

chemical communication the use of odorants and other substances (see EXTERNAL CHEMICAL MESSENGER) to transmit information between individuals. Chemical signals communicate the identity of species, subspecies, and individuals, reproductive status, dominance status, fear, and territorial boundaries. An advantage of chemical communication is that signals can remain long after the communicator has left.

chemical dependence see SUBSTANCE DEPENDENCE.

chemical senses the senses receptive to chemical stimulation (i.e., through contact with chemical molecules or electrolytes), particularly the senses of SMELL and TASTE. Airborne molecules are inhaled and dissolved in the mucous membrane of the OLFACTORY EPITHELIUM to confer odors. Molecules dissolved in liquids are delivered to the TASTE CELLS on the tongue, soft palate, larynx, and pharynx to confer tastes.

chemoaffinity hypothesis the notion that each neuron has a chemical identity that directs it to synapse on the proper target cell during development.

chemoreceptor *n.* a sensory nerve ending, such as any of those in the TASTE BUDS or OLFACTORY EPITHELIUM, that is capable of reacting to certain chemical stimuli. In humans, there are hundreds of different taste receptor proteins and a total of about 300,000 TASTE CELLS. Humans also have about 1,000 types of OLFACTORY RECEPTORS and about 1,000 receptors of each type, giving a total of one million olfactory receptors; other mammals (e.g., dogs) may have ten times that number.

chemoreceptor trigger zone a cluster of cells in the MEDULLA OBLONGATA that is sensitive to certain toxic chemicals and responds by producing dizziness, nausea, and vomiting, the precise effects depending on the agent and the dosage.

chemosensory event-related potential a specific pattern of electrical activity produced in the brain by a trigeminal event (see TRIGEMINAL CHEMORECEPTION) or gustatory event. This is a more general term than **olfactory-evoked potential** (**OEP**), which refers specifically to electrical potentials produced by olfactory events.

chemotherapy *n.* the use of chemical agents to treat diseases, particularly cancer, in which case it is contrasted with RADIATION therapy. —**chemotherapeutic** *adj.* —**chemotherapist** *n.*

Chicago school a school of psychology that emerged at the University of Chicago in the early 20th century, associated with U.S. psychologists John Dewey (1859–1952), James R. Angell (1869–1949), and Harvey Carr (1873–1954). Their approach, called FUNCTIONALISM, was related to ACT PSYCHOLOGY and was an attempt to modify the subject matter of psychology by introducing the Darwinian idea that mental activities subserve an adaptive biological action function that should be the focus of psychology.

child abuse harm to a child caused by a parent or other caregiver. The harm may be physical (violence), sexual (violation or exploitation), psychological (causing emotional distress), or neglect (failure to provide needed care). See also BATTERED-CHILD SYNDROME.

child advocacy any organized and structured interventions on behalf of children by professionals or institutions, often in relation to such issues as special parenting needs, child abuse, and adoption or foster care.

child analysis the application of psychoanalytic principles (considerably modified from those of CLASSICAL PSYCHOANALYSIS) to the treatment of children. In his first and most famous case, Austrian psychiatrist Sigmund Freud (1856–1939) analyzed 5-year-old LITTLE HANS by having the child answer questions through his father, but Freud never directly analyzed a child patient. Pioneers in the field were Austrian-born British psychoanalysts Melanie Klein (1882–1960), who developed the PSYCHOANALYTIC PLAY TECHNIQUE to achieve a deep analysis of the child's unconscious, and Anna Freud (1895–1982), whose method was more pedagogical and encouraged EGO DEVELOPMENT. See also PLAY THERAPY.

Child Behavior Checklist (**CBCL**) a standardized instrument used to assess the behavioral problems and competencies of children between the ages of 4 and 18 years. The CBCL is administered to parents, who describe their children's behavior by assigning a rating to each of the more than 100 items on the checklist. The items assessed range from "internalizing behaviors" (e.g., fearful, shy, anxious, inhibited) to "externalizing behaviors" (e.g., aggressive, antisocial, undercontrolled).

child care 1. the daytime care of children by a nursery or childminder while parents are at work. **2.** the full-time residential care of children who have no other home or whose home life is seriously troubled.

child custody evaluation a procedure, often conducted by clinical psychologists, that involves evaluating parenting behavior, analyzing parents' capacity to address children's needs, and providing the court with a recommendation regarding child custody arrangements.

child development the sequential changes in the behavior, cognition, and physiology of children as they grow and mature from birth to adolescence. See DEVELOPMENTAL TASK.

child guidance a mental health approach for children that focuses not only on treatment but also on the prevention of possible future disorders by offering instruction, information, and therapeutic aid to the child and his or her family. Child guidance services and treatment are typically provided by specialized **child-guidance clinics**.

childhood *n.* the period between the end of infancy (about 2 years of age) and the onset of puberty, marking the beginning of ADOLESCENCE (10–12 years of age). This period is sometimes divided into (a) early childhood, from 2 years through the preschool age of 5 or 6 years; (b) middle childhood, from 6 to 8–10 years of age; and (c) late childhood or PREADOLESCENCE, which is identified as the 2-year period before the onset of puberty.

childhood amnesia the inability to recall events from early childhood. Childhood amnesia has been attributed to the facts that (a) cognitive abilities necessary for encoding events for the long term have not yet been fully developed and (b) parts of the brain responsible for remembering personal events have not yet matured. Also called **infantile amnesia**.

childhood disintegrative disorder a PERVASIVE DEVELOPMENTAL DISORDER characterized by a significant loss of previously acquired language skills, social skills or adaptive behavior, bowel or bladder control, play, or motor skills. This regression in functioning follows a period of normal development and occurs between the ages of 2 and 10.

child neglect see CHILD ABUSE.

child psychology the branch of psychology concerned with the systematic study of the behavior, adjustment, and growth of individuals from birth to adolescence, as well as with the treatment of their behavioral, mental, and emotional disorders. See also DEVELOPMENTAL PSYCHOLOGY.

child psychotherapy psychotherapy for children up to the age at which they reach puberty. The focus may be on emotions, cognitions, or behavior. The level of parental involvement is typically dependent upon the age of the child, type of problem, or approach used. The child may be treated concurrently in group or family therapy.

child-rearing practice a pattern of raising children that is specific to a particular society, subculture, family, or period in cultural history. Child-rearing practices vary in such areas as methods of discipline, expression of affection, and degree of permissiveness.

Children's Depression Inventory (**CDI**) a self-report questionnaire, based on the BECK DEPRESSION INVENTORY, designed to assess the severity of depression in children aged between 7 and 17 years. Intended primarily as a research tool, the CDI comprises 27 items that each consist of three statements reflecting different levels of severity of a particular symptom. For each item, the participant chooses the statement that best describes himself or herself during the previous two weeks.

child welfare the emotional or physical well-being of children, particularly in the context of legal issues or of social programs designed to enrich or intervene in their lives.

chimera *n.* an organism composed of two or

more kinds of genetically dissimilar cells. For example, a chimera may have received a transplant of genetically different tissue, such as bone marrow, or may have been produced by grafting an embryonic part of one animal onto the embryo of a genetically different animal. —**chimeric** *adj.*

chimeric stimulation a procedure for studying the functions of the two cerebral hemispheres. In a typical experiment participants are shown an image of a **chimeric face**, consisting of the left half of one person's face joined to the right half of another person's face. In participants with a severed corpus callosum (i.e., a SPLIT BRAIN), one hemisphere perceives only one face, while the other hemisphere perceives the other, suggesting that there are two separate spheres of conscious awareness located in the two hemispheres.

Chinese Room argument a philosophical argument that computers or symbol-processing systems can receive only syntactical streams of ordered signs, and not semantic information. The name derives from a thought experiment in which a monolingual English speaker imagines himself or herself in a sealed room attempting to match streams of Chinese characters with Chinese script based only on a set of correspondence rules.

chiropractic *n.* an alternative health care system concerned with the relationship between the structure of the body (particularly the spine) and disease processes. Treatment comprises noninvasive drug-free methods, primarily manipulations and adjustments to the body, theorized to restore proper nerve functioning and to promote health. See also COMPLEMENTARY AND ALTERNATIVE MEDICINE. —**chiropractor** *n.*

chi-square distribution (χ^2 **distribution**) the distribution of the sum of a set of independent squared normal random deviates. If p independent variables are involved, the distribution is said to have p DEGREES OF FREEDOM.

chi-square test a measure of how well a theoretical probability distribution fits a set of data. If values $x_1, x_2, \dots x_p$ are observed $o_1, o_2, \dots o_p$ times and are expected by theory to occur $e_1, e_2, \dots e_p$ times, then chi-square is calculated as

$$(o_1 - e_1)^2/e_1 + (o_2 - e_2)^2/e_2 + \dots$$

Tables of chi-square for different degrees of freedom can be used to indicate the probability that the theory is correct. Also called **chi-square procedure**.

chlordiazepoxide *n.* the first commercially available BENZODIAZEPINE anxiolytic. Developed in 1957, it became one of the most heavily prescribed medications ever developed. Its use in the management of anxiety and insomnia has been largely supplanted by benzodiazepines with less complicated metabolism and more predictable HALF-LIVES, but it remains in common use to protect against the effects of alcohol withdrawal. U.S. trade name: **Librium**.

chloropsia *n.* see CHROMATOPSIA.

chlorpromazine *n.* the first synthesized ANTIPSYCHOTIC agent, initially used to reduce presurgical anxiety and deepen conscious sedation during surgical procedures; its antipsychotic effects were discovered serendipitously. Although effective in managing the acute symptoms of schizophrenia, acute mania, and other psychoses, this low-potency PHENOTHIAZINE causes a number of unwanted adverse effects, including association with TARDIVE DYSKINESIA, and has been largely supplanted by newer antipsychotic agents. It is still used as a referent for dose equivalency of other antipsychotics. It has also been used in lower doses to treat nausea, vomiting, and intractable hiccups. U.S. trade name: **Thorazine**.

choice axiom a mathematical model of decision making that assumes, given several alternatives from which to choose, the probability that a particular alternative will be picked is independent of the sequence of decisions.

choice reaction time the REACTION TIME of a participant in a task that requires him or her to make a simple response (e.g., pressing a key) whenever one stimulus from a predefined set of stimuli is presented. Compare COMPLEX REACTION TIME; SIMPLE REACTION TIME.

choice shift any shift in an individual's choices or decisions that occurs as a result of group discussion, as measured by comparing his or her prediscussion and postdiscussion responses. In many cases the result of such shifts is a **choice-shift effect** within the group as a whole. See also CAUTIOUS SHIFT.

choice stimuli in REACTION-TIME tasks, the array of possible stimuli that may occur in a particular trial. Each stimulus or item in the array is mapped to a different response (e.g., a different key to be pressed). Participants must decide which response to make to a particular stimulus.

choking under pressure a paradoxical effect in which the demands of a situation that calls for good performance, such as a school test or job interview, cause an individual to perform poorly relative to his or her capabilities. "Pressure" denotes the individual's awareness of the need to perform well; "choking" refers to the actual decrement in performance that results.

cholesterol *n.* a steroid derivative abundant in animal tissues, found especially in foods rich in animal fats. Cholesterol is a constituent of plasma membranes, the precursor of other steroids (e.g., the sex hormones), and a component of plasma lipoproteins, especially low-density lipoproteins (LDLs), which are believed to play an important role in forming atherosclerotic plaques (see ATHEROSCLEROSIS).

choline *n.* a BIOGENIC AMINE, often classed as a B vitamin, that is a constituent of many important compounds, such as ACETYLCHOLINE and lecithin (a component of plasma membranes).

C

cholinergic *adj.* responding to, releasing, or otherwise involving ACETYLCHOLINE. For example, a **cholinergic neuron** is one that employs acetylcholine as a neurotransmitter.

cholinergic drug any pharmacological agent that stimulates activity in the PARASYMPA-THETIC NERVOUS SYSTEM because it potentiates the activity of ACETYLCHOLINE or has effects similar to this neurotransmitter. Cholinergic drugs are used for such purposes as treating myasthenia gravis, glaucoma, and urinary retention. Also called **parasympathetic drug**; **parasympathomimetic drug**.

cholinergic receptor another name for an ACETYLCHOLINE RECEPTOR. Also called **cholinoceptor**.

cholinesterase (ChE) *n.* an enzyme that splits ACETYLCHOLINE into choline and acetic acid, thus inactivating the neurotransmitter after its release at a synaptic junction. Cholinesterase occurs in two forms: **acetylcholinesterase (AChE)**, found in nerve tissue and red blood cells; and **butyrylcholinesterase (BuChE,** or **pseudocholin-esterase [PChE])**, found in blood plasma and other tissues. Drugs that block the ability of this enzyme to degrade acetylcholine are called **cholinesterase inhibitors (ChEIs,** or **acetyl-cholinesterase inhibitors [AChEIs],** or **anticholin-esterases)**. Some ChEIs are used clinically as NOOTROPIC DRUGS to slow the progression of dementia in Alzheimer's disease; there is speculation that agents acting on both forms of the enzyme may be beneficial in reducing the formation of the plaques and NEUROFIBRILLARY TANGLES associated with the disease.

chorda tympani a part of the FACIAL NERVE, conveying sensory information from TASTE BUDS on the front of the tongue.

chorea *n.* irregular and involuntary jerky movements of the limbs and facial muscles. Chorea is associated with various disorders, including HUNTINGTON'S DISEASE. —**choreal** *adj.* —**choreic** *adj.*

choreiform *adj.* involving involuntary movement that resembles CHOREA. Also called **choreoid**.

chorionic villus sampling (CVS) a method of diagnosing diseases and genetic and chromosomal abnormalities in a fetus. Samples of cells of the chorionic villi, the microscopic projections in the protective membrane surrounding the fetus, are obtained for analysis of bacteria, metabolites, or DNA. Unlike AMNIOCENTESIS, this procedure can be carried out in the first trimester of pregnancy.

choroid layer the vascular pigmented layer of tissue that covers the back of the eye and is located between the retina and the sclera. The pigment in the choroid layer absorbs stray light, and the blood vessels provide oxygen and sustenance to the photoreceptors. Also called **choroid**; **choroid coat**.

chromatic *adj.* in vision, relating to the attribute of color.

chromatic aberration a defect in the image formed by a lens resulting from the fact that light of short wavelength is refracted to a greater extent than light of long wavelength. It causes different colors to be focused at different distances, so that the image has colored fringes.

chromatic adaptation decreased sensitivity to a particular color as a result of prolonged exposure to a colored stimulus. Also called **color adaptation**.

chromatopsia *n.* an aberration in color vision in which there is excessive visual sensitivity to one color, such that objects appear tinged with that color. There are several forms: **erythropsia** (red vision), **chloropsia** (green vision), **xanthopsia** (yellow vision), and **cyanopsia** (blue vision). Also called **chromopsia**.

chromesthesia *n.* a type of SYNESTHESIA in which perception of nonvisual stimuli (e.g., sounds, tastes, odors) is accompanied by color sensations. For example, the musical note G may be consistently experienced as blue.

chromosomal aberration an abnormal change in the structure of a chromosome.

chromosome *n.* a strand or filament in the cell nucleus composed of nucleic acid (mainly DNA in humans) and proteins that carries the genetic, or hereditary, traits of an individual. The normal human complement of chromosomes totals 46, or 23 pairs (44 AUTOSOMES and 2 SEX CHROMOSOMES), which contain an estimated 20,000–25,000 genes. Each parent contributes one chromosome to each pair, so a child receives half its chromosomes from its mother and half from its father. —**chromosomal** *adj.*

chromosome disorder any disorder caused by a defect or abnormality in the structure or number of one or more chromosomes.

chronesthesia *n.* a hypothetical ability or capacity of the human brain or mind, acquired through evolution, that allows humans to be constantly aware of the past and the future. The key feature of this "mental time travel" is to enable people to anticipate the future—that is, to learn what to avoid and how to behave in the future—by recalling past events.

chronic *adj.* denoting conditions or symptoms that persist or progress over a long period of time and are resistant to cure. Compare ACUTE.

chronically accessible constructs mental contents (e.g., ideas or categories) that are frequently used and therefore come to mind particularly readily.

chronic anxiety a persistent, pervasive state of apprehension that may be associated with aspects of a number of anxiety disorders. These include uncontrollable worries in GENERALIZED ANXIETY DISORDER, fear of a panic attack in PANIC DISORDER, and obsessions in OBSESSIVE-COMPULSIVE DISORDER.

chronic fatigue syndrome (**CFS**) an illness characterized by often disabling fatigue, decrease in physical activity, and flulike symptoms, such as muscle weakness, swelling of the lymph nodes, headache, sore throat, and sometimes depression. The condition is typically not diagnosed until symptoms have been ongoing for several months and it can last for years. The cause is unknown, although certain viral infections can set off the illness.

chronic illness illness that persists for a long period. Chronic illnesses include many major diseases and conditions, such as heart disease, cancer, diabetes, and arthritis. Disease management is important when dealing with chronic illness; this includes ensuring adherence to treatment and maintaining quality of life.

chronic motor or vocal tic disorder a TIC DISORDER characterized by motor or vocal tics (but not both) for a period of more than 1 year, during which any period without tics lasts for no more than 3 months. The disorder has an onset before the age of 18.

chronic obstructive pulmonary disease (**COPD**) a group of lung diseases, most commonly chronic bronchitis and emphysema, that are characterized by limited airflow with varying degrees of lung-tissue damage and alveolar (air-sac) enlargement. Marked by coughing, wheezing, and shortness of breath, COPD is caused by cigarette smoking, exposure to other irritants and pollutants, lung infections, or genetic factors. Also called **chronic obstructive lung disease**.

chronic pain pain that may have been caused by actual tissue damage, disease, or emotional trauma but continues to occur despite all medical and pharmacological efforts at treatment.

chronobiology *n.* the branch of biology concerned with BIOLOGICAL RHYTHMS, such as the sleep–wake cycle.

chronological age (**CA**) the amount of time elapsed since an individual's birth, typically expressed in terms of months and years.

chronometric analysis a method for studying a mental process that involves varying stimulus input conditions and measuring participants' REACTION TIMES to those stimuli. The relations between the stimulus variables and reaction times are then used to make inferences about the underlying mental processes.

chronometry *n.* the measurement of time. —**chronometric** *adj.*

chronotopic constraints the limitations imposed by the development of the brain on the timing of maturational events, such as the acquisition of language-processing ability. See also ARCHITECTURAL CONSTRAINTS; REPRESENTATIONAL CONSTRAINTS.

chunking *n.* the process by which the mind sorts information into small, easily digestible units (**chunks**) that can be retained in SHORT-TERM MEMORY. As a result of this RECODING, one item in memory (e.g., a keyword or key idea) can stand for multiple other items (e.g., a short list of associated points). The capacity of short-term memory is believed to be constant for the number of individual units it can store (see SEVEN PLUS OR MINUS TWO), but the units themselves can range from simple chunks (e.g., individual letters or numbers) to complex chunks (e.g., words or phrases).

ciliary body a part of the eye located behind the iris and consisting of the **ciliary processes** (extensions that project into the posterior of the eye) and the CILIARY MUSCLES.

ciliary muscle smooth muscle in the CILIARY BODY of the eye that changes the shape of the lens to bring objects into focus on the retina. The ciliary muscle regulates the tension of the ZONULES, causing the lens to flatten (which lessens the power of the lens and allows focus of distant objects) or become more curved (which increases the power of the lens and allows focus of near objects). The action of the ciliary muscle is a large component of ACCOMMODATION.

cilium *n.* (*pl.* **cilia**) **1.** an eyelash. **2.** a hairlike extension of a cell, usually occurring in tufts or tracts, as in the stereocilia of HAIR CELLS in the cochlea of the inner ear. —**ciliary** *adj.*

cingulate gyrus a long strip of CEREBRAL CORTEX on the medial surface of each cerebral hemisphere. The cingulate gyrus arches over and generally outlines the location of the CORPUS CALLOSUM, from which it is separated by a groove called the **callosal sulcus**. It is a component of the LIMBIC SYSTEM.

circadian oscillator a neural circuit with an output that repeats about once per day. A circadian oscillator is located in the SUPRACHIASMATIC NUCLEUS of the hypothalamus and is thought to be important in sleep–wake cycles.

circadian rhythm see BIOLOGICAL RHYTHM.

circadian rhythm sleep disorder a sleep disorder that is due to a mismatch between the sleep–wake schedule required by a person's environment and his or her circadian sleep–wake pattern, resulting in excessive sleepiness or insomnia. This disorder was formerly called **sleep–wake schedule disorder**. See DYSSOMNIA. See also DISORDERS OF THE SLEEP–WAKE CYCLE SCHEDULE.

circannual rhythm see BIOLOGICAL RHYTHM.

circle of support a group of people who provide support for an individual. For a person with a developmental disability, for example, the circle often includes family members, friends, acquaintances, coworkers, and sometimes service providers or coordinators, who meet on a regular basis and help the individual accomplish personal goals.

circular behavior any action that stimulates a similar action in others, such as yawning or laughing. Also called **circular response**.

circular reaction in PIAGETIAN THEORY, repetitive behavior observed in children during the SENSORIMOTOR STAGE, characterized as primary, secondary, or tertiary circular reactions. The primary phase involves ineffective repetitive behaviors; the secondary phase involves repetition of actions that are followed by reinforcement, typically without understanding causation; and the tertiary phase involves repetitive object manipulation, typically with slight variations among subsequent behaviors.

circulatory system see CARDIOVASCULAR SYSTEM.

circumcision *n.* the surgical removal of the foreskin of the penis, typically for religious, cultural, or medical reasons.

circumlocution *n.* a mode of speaking characterized by difficulty or inability in finding the right words to identify or explain an object that has been perceived and recognized. It involves the use of a variety of words or phrases that indirectly communicate the individual's meaning. Circumlocution can be a manifestation of damage to the left posterior temporal lobe of the brain, but in some cases it is an indication of disorganized thought processes, as in schizophrenia.

circumplex model of personality and emotion a type of model for determining the degree of similarity between personality traits and emotions by depicting in a circular form the relations and interactions between those traits and emotions. Elements adjacent to one another on the circle are highly similar (positively correlated), while elements opposite each other on the circle are highly dissimilar (negatively correlated) and represent dimensional extremes (e.g., pessimism versus optimism).

circumscribed belief a narrowly defined delusional belief held by some people with paranoia or brain damage who otherwise seem to function entirely normally. For example, such people may believe they are being persecuted by the CIA. The delusional belief system is generally highly consistent and resistant to disproof and appears to function separately from other beliefs held by the same person.

circumstantiality *n.* circuitous, indirect speech in which the individual digresses to give unnecessary and often irrelevant details before arriving at the main point. An extreme form, arising from disorganized associative processes, may occur in schizophrenia, obsessional disorders, and certain types of dementia. Circumstantiality differs from TANGENTIALITY in that the main point is never lost but rather accompanied by a large amount of nonessential information.

cirrhosis *n.* a chronic liver disease marked by widespread formation of fibrous tissue and loss of normal liver function. In most cases, it is a consequence of alcohol abuse, although it may also be due to congenital defects involving meta-bolic deficiencies, exposure to toxic chemicals, or infections (e.g., hepatitis). —**cirrhotic** *adj.*

CISD abbreviation for CRITICAL-INCIDENT STRESS DEBRIEFING.

citation analysis a form of research that traces the history of citations of particular researchers in particular books, articles, or other sources.

civil commitment a legal procedure that permits a person who is not charged with criminal conduct to be certified as mentally ill and to be institutionalized involuntarily.

CJD abbreviation for CREUTZFELDT–JAKOB DISEASE.

cladistics *n.* a method for classifying organisms on the basis of their evolutionary relationships, which are expressed in treelike diagrams called cladograms. —**cladism** *n.* —**cladist** *n.*

claims review an evaluation of the appropriateness of a claim for payment for a medical or mental health service rendered. It will consider whether the claimant is eligible for reimbursement, whether the charges are consistent with customary fees or published institutional rates, and whether the service was necessary.

clairaudience *n.* in parapsychology, the alleged ability to "hear" voices or sounds beyond the normal range of hearing, including supposed messages from spirit guides or the dead. It is the auditory equivalent of CLAIRVOYANCE. See also EXTRASENSORY PERCEPTION. —**clairaudient** *n., adj.*

clairvoyance *n.* in parapsychology, the alleged ability to "see" things beyond the normal range of sight, such as distant or hidden objects or events in the past or future. Compare CLAIRAUDIENCE. Also called **remote viewing**. See also EXTRASENSORY PERCEPTION; SECOND SIGHT. —**clairvoyant** *n., adj.*

clan *n.* in anthropology, a major social division of many traditional societies consisting of a group of families that claim common ancestry. Clans often prohibit marriage between members and are often associated with reverence for a particular TOTEM. See also DESCENT GROUP; SEPT.

clang association an association of words by similarity of sound rather than meaning. Clang association occurs as a pathological disturbance in manic states and schizophrenia. Also called **clanging**.

clarification *n.* a therapist's formulation, in clearer terms and without indicating approval or disapproval, of a client's statement or expression of feelings. Clarification goes further than restatement and REFLECTION OF FEELING but stops short of interpretation.

class *n.* a group, category, or division. For example, in sociology and political theory it denotes a SOCIAL CLASS; in BIOLOGICAL TAXONOMY it refers to a main subdivision of a PHYLUM, consisting of a group of similar, related ORDERS; and in logic and philosophy it is a collection of entities that have a specified property or properties in common: that is, a SET defined by a condition.

classical conditioning see PAVLOVIAN CONDITIONING.

classical psychoanalysis 1. psychoanalytic theory in which major emphasis is placed on the LIBIDO, the stages of PSYCHOSEXUAL DEVELOPMENT, and the ID instincts or drives. The prototypical theory of this kind is that of Austrian psychiatrist Sigmund Freud (1856–1939). Also called **classical theory; drive theory. 2.** psychoanalytic treatment that adheres to Sigmund Freud's basic procedures, using dream interpretation, free association, and analysis of RESISTANCE, and to his basic aim of developing insight into the patient's unconscious life as a way to restructure personality. Also called **orthodox psychoanalysis**.

classical test theory a body of psychometric theory of measurement that partitions observed scores into two components—TRUE SCORES and ERROR SCORES—and estimates error variance by calculating INTERNAL CONSISTENCY reliability, RETEST RELIABILITY, and ALTERNATE-FORMS RELIABILITY. Among the key benefits of this theory—the principal framework for test development prior to the 1970s—are that it is relatively simple to execute and that it can be applied to a broad range of measurement situations. Among its major limitations are that examinee characteristics cannot be separated from test characteristics and that the measurement statistics derived from it are fundamentally concerned with how people perform on a given test as opposed to any single item on that test.

classification *n.* see CATEGORIZATION. —**classify** *vb.*

classification test 1. a test in which participants are required to sort objects, people, events, or stimuli into specific categories. See CATEGORIZATION. **2.** a test in which participants are themselves sorted into categories (e.g., of ability or psychological type) according to the responses given.

classifier system a COGNITIVE ARCHITECTURE consisting of a computational system in which knowledge, in the form of "if → then" classifier rules, is exposed to a reacting environment and as a result undergoes modification over time (learning). The entire system is evaluated over time, with the importance of the individual classifier seen as minimal.

class inclusion the concept that a subordinate class (e.g., dogs) must always be smaller than the superordinate class in which it is contained (e.g., animals). According to PIAGETIAN THEORY, understanding the concept of class inclusion represents an important developmental step.

classroom-behavior modification an instructor's use of basic learning techniques, such as conditioning, to alter the behavior of the students within a learning environment. Specifically, classroom behavior modification may utilize such methods as adjusting classroom seating, providing a flexible time deadline for assignments, or altering the lesson requirements. Such procedures are most useful for students with learning disabilities, attention-deficit/hyperactivity disorder, and other special needs.

class structure the composition, organization, and interrelationship of SOCIAL CLASSES within a society. The term encompasses the makeup of individual classes as well as their economic, political, and other roles within the larger social order.

class theory the notion that conflict between social and economic classes is a fundamental determining force in human affairs, affecting not only systems of government and social organization, but also individual psychology. It is held that one's perceptions, goals, and expectations, and even one's conceptions of psychological health and illness, are heavily influenced by the class of which one is a member. Most modern manifestations of class theory trace their origins to German social theorist Karl Marx (1818–1883).

clause *n.* a linguistic unit smaller than a sentence but larger than a phrase. Clauses are usually divided into two principal types: **main clauses**, which make sense by themselves and can constitute a sentence in their own right, and **subordinate clauses**, which are dependent on a main clause in both these respects. In *I smiled at Jane, who waved back*, for example, the words before the comma constitute a main clause and those after the comma are a subordinate clause. In psycholinguistics, clauses are considered to be an important unit of sentence processing. Sentences that are complex from a syntactic point of view, in that they contain one or more subordinate clauses, are also considered psychologically more complex. —**clausal** *adj.*

claustrophobia *n.* a persistent and irrational fear of enclosed places (e.g., elevators, closets, tunnels) or of being confined (e.g., in an airplane or the backseat of a car). The focus of fear is typically on panic symptoms triggered in these situations, such as feelings of being unable to breathe, choking, sweating, and fears of losing control or going crazy. —**claustrophobic** *adj.*

claustrum *n.* (*pl.* **claustra**) a thin layer of gray matter in the brain that separates the white matter of the lenticular nucleus from the INSULA (from Latin: "barrier"). The claustrum forms part of the BASAL GANGLIA and its function is unknown. —**claustral** *adj.*

clearance (**CL**) *n.* the rate of elimination of a drug from the body in relation to its concentration in a body fluid, as expressed by the equation CL = rate of elimination/C, where C is the concentration of the drug in the body fluid. Clearance is additive, that is, drugs are eliminated by various mechanisms (renal, hepatic, etc.) at differing rates; thus, total clearance is the sum of clearance from each individual organ system.

C

Clever Hans the "thinking horse," reputed to be able to solve mathematical problems, spell words, distinguish colors, and identify coins, that became famous in Berlin around 1900. It signaled its answers by tapping its foot. However, German psychologist Oskar Pfungst (1874–1932), using experimental methods, demonstrated that the horse was responding to minimal cues in the form of involuntary movements on the part of its owner.

client *n.* a person receiving treatment or services, especially in the context of counseling or social work. See PATIENT–CLIENT ISSUE.

client-centered therapy a nondirective form of psychotherapy in which an orderly process of client self-discovery and actualization occurs in response to the therapist's consistent empathic understanding of, acceptance of, and respect for the client's FRAME OF REFERENCE. The therapist reflects and clarifies the ideas of the client, who is able to see himself or herself more clearly and come into closer touch with his or her real self. As therapy progresses, the client resolves conflicts, reorganizes values and approaches to life, and learns how to interpret his or her thoughts and feelings, consequently changing behavior that he or she considers problematic. It was originally known as **nondirective therapy**. Also called **client-centered psychotherapy**; **person-centered psychotherapy**; **Rogerian therapy**.

client–patient issue see PATIENT–CLIENT ISSUE.

client rights the rights of patients or clients to be fully informed of the benefits or risks of treatment procedures and to make informed decisions to accept or reject treatment.

climacteric *n.* the biological stage of life in which reproductive capacity declines and finally ceases. In women this period, which results from changes in the levels of estrogens and progesterone and is known as **menopause** (popularly, **change of life**), occurs between 40 and 55 years of age. During this time, menstrual flow gradually decreases and finally ceases altogether, and hot flashes commonly occur. Men undergo a similar period of hormonal change (**male climacteric**), manifest as reduced energy, sexual drive, and fertility.

clinic *n.* **1.** a health care facility for the diagnosis and treatment of emergency and ambulatory patients. **2.** a brief instructional program or session with diagnostic, therapeutic, or remedial purpose in the areas of mental or physical health or education.

clinical *adj.* **1.** of or relating to the diagnosis and treatment of psychological, medical, or other disorders. Originally involving only direct observation of patients, clinical methods have now broadened to take into account biological and statistical factors in treating patients and diagnosing disorders. **2.** relating to or occurring in a clinic.

clinical assessment the systematic evaluation and measurement of psychological, biological, and social factors in a person presenting with a possible psychological disorder. See also DYNAMIC ASSESSMENT.

clinical counseling counseling that addresses a client's personal or emotional difficulties. The counseling encompasses general goals for the client, for example, greater self-acceptance, better reality orientation, improved decision-making ability, and greater effectiveness in interpersonal relationships. The counselor's responsibilities include gathering and interpretating data, identifying the client's major problems, and formulating and (sometimes) implementing a treatment plan.

clinical diagnosis the process of identifying and determining the nature of a mental disorder through the study of the symptom pattern, review of medical records, investigation of background factors, and, where indicated, administration of psychological tests.

clinical efficacy the effectiveness of clinical interventions based on the evidence of controlled studies. Such studies typically include random assignment to control groups and treatment manuals that guide therapist actions.

clinical evidence information about clients or patients that is relevant to clinical diagnosis and therapy, obtained either directly through questioning or indirectly through observation of their behavior in a clinical setting, their case histories, and the like.

clinical health psychology a specialty field in HEALTH PSYCHOLOGY that applies biopsychosocial theory, research, and practice principles to promote physical health and to help resolve the immediate problems of patients with medical conditions and related family difficulties. Biofeedback, relaxation training, hypnotherapy, and coping skills are among the many methods used by **clinical health psychologists**, who are also active in health policy and in developing and implementing models of preventive intervention.

clinical judgment analysis, evaluation, or prediction of disordered behavior, symptoms, or other aspects of psychological functioning. It includes assessing the appropriateness of particular treatments and the degree or likelihood of clinical improvement. These conclusions are derived from the expert knowledge of mental health professionals, as opposed to conclusions drawn from actuarial tables or statistical methods.

clinical marker an observable sign indicative of disorder or predictive of an upcoming event of special interest. See also BIOCHEMICAL MARKER; BIOLOGICAL MARKER.

clinical method 1. the process by which a clinical psychologist, psychiatrist, or other mental health or medical professional arrives at a conclusion, judgment, or diagnosis about a client or patient in a clinical situation. **2.** the process of collecting data in a natural situation (e.g., home, office, school) rather than in the formal setting of a laboratory.

clinical neurology see NEUROLOGY.

clinical neuropsychology an applied specialty in NEUROPSYCHOLOGY that comprises neuropsychological assessment and rehabilitation, which are critical in cases of neuropsychological injury that results in a range of impairments that disrupt an individual's ability to function.

clinical practice guidelines systematically developed statements to assist providers, as well as clients or patients, in making decisions about appropriate medical or mental health care for specific clinical conditions.

clinical prediction the process of examining such factors as signs, symptoms, and case history to determine the CLINICAL DIAGNOSIS and likely progress of patients. Clinical prediction can be contrasted with statistical prediction, in which formal statistical methods combine numerical information for the same purposes. See CLINICAL JUDGMENT.

clinical psychology the branch of psychology that specializes in the research, assessment, diagnosis, evaluation, prevention, and treatment of emotional and behavioral disorders. The **clinical psychologist** is a doctorate-level professional who has received training in research methods and techniques for the diagnosis and treatment of various psychological disorders (see also PSYCHOLOGIST). Clinical psychologists work primarily in health and mental health clinics, in research, or in group and independent practices. They also serve as consultants to other professionals in the medical, legal, social-work, and community-relations fields. Clinical psychologists comprise approximately one third of the psychologists working in the United States and are governed by the code of practice of the American Psychological Association.

clinical psychopharmacology a branch of pharmacology concerned with how drugs affect the brain and behavior and specifically with the clinical evaluation and management of drugs developed for the treatment of mental disorders. See also PSYCHOPHARMACOTHERAPY.

clinical social work a field devoted to providing individual, family, and group treatment from a psychosocial perspective in such areas as health, mental health, family and child welfare, and correction. Clinical social work additionally involves client-centered advocacy that assists clients with information, referral, and in dealing with local, state, and federal agencies.

clinical sport psychology a specialty within clinical psychology focused on individuals involved in sport. Clinical sport psychologists perform much the same services for athletes as do **educational sport psychologists** (i.e., helping with performance enhancement and consis-

tency), but they also assist athletes with clinical issues that are beyond the training of educational sport psychologists (e.g., depression, eating disorders).

clinical test a test or measurement made in a clinical or research context for the purpose of diagnosis or treatment of a disorder.

clinical trial a research study designed to compare a new treatment or drug with an existing standard of care or other control condition (see CONTROL GROUP). Also called **clinical study**.

clinical type an individual whose pattern of symptoms or behaviors is consistent with a recognizable disorder of clinical psychology and psychiatry.

clinical utility the extent to which clinical interventions can be applied successfully and cost-effectively in real clinical settings. It is one of a proposed set of guidelines for evaluating clinical interventions.

clinical validation the act of acquiring evidence to support the accuracy of a theory by studying multiple cases with specific procedures for diagnosis or treatment.

clinician *n.* a medical or mental health care professional who is directly involved in the care and treatment of patients, as distinguished from one working in other areas, such as research or administration.

clique *n.* a status- or friendship-based subgroup within a larger group or organization. Cliques are particularly common during adolescence, when they are often used to raise social standing, strengthen friendship ties, and reduce feelings of isolation and exclusion.

clitoridectomy *n.* the surgical removal of all or part of the clitoris, usually as an ethnic or religious rite. It is a highly controversial practice and the most common form of FEMALE GENITAL MUTILATION.

clitoris *n.* a small body of erectile tissue situated anterior to the vaginal opening. It is homologous to the penis but usually much smaller. —**clitoral** *adj.*

cloaca *n.* **1.** the common cavity, occurring in early mammalian embryos, into which the intestinal, urinary, and reproductive canals open. The proximity of these functions and the pleasure involved in them are a major factor in the psychosexual theory of Austrian psychoanalyst Sigmund Freud (1856–1939). **2.** in nonmammalian vertebrates, the cavity through which sperm are discharged in the male, and eggs are laid in the female, and through which wastes are eliminated. —**cloacal** *adj.*

clomipramine *n.* a TRICYCLIC ANTIDEPRESSANT drug used for the treatment of obsessive-compulsive disorder (OCD) as well as depression and panic disorder. Although a more potent inhibitor of serotonin reuptake than other tricyclic antidepressants, clomipramine has the same adverse side effects and toxicity and has been largely supplanted by the SSRIs. U.S. trade name: **Anafranil**.

clonazepam *n.* a highly potent BENZODIAZ-EPINE originally developed to treat absence seizures but now used for the treatment of panic disorder and other anxiety disorders and as a MOOD STABILIZER. U.S. trade name: **Klonopin**.

clone *n.* **1.** an organism that is genetically identical to another. This may be because both organisms originate naturally from a single common parent as a result of ASEXUAL reproduction or because one is derived from genetic material taken from the other. **2.** a group of cells derived from a single parent cell. **—clonal** *adj.*

clonic *adj.* of, relating to, or characterized by CLONUS.

clonus *n.* a type of involuntary movement caused by a rapid succession of alternate muscular contractions and relaxations. Although some forms of clonus, such as hiccups, are considered normal, most such movements are abnormal; for example, clonus occurs as part of a TONIC–CLONIC SEIZURE.

closed adoption see ADOPTION.

closed economy an experimental design used in instrumental- or operant-conditioning procedures in which all arranged reinforcement (e.g., food) is obtained within experimental tests, with no supplements occurring outside the experimental context. Compare OPEN ECONOMY.

closed group a counseling or therapy group consisting of only those members who constituted the original group. New members may not join during the course of therapy. Compare OPEN GROUP.

closed skill any motor skill that is performed under the same conditions on every occasion, as in making a free-throw shot in a game of basketball. Compare OPEN SKILL.

closed society see OPEN SOCIETY.

closed system 1. an isolated, self-contained system having no contact with the environment, such as the blood vascular system. **2.** by analogy, a social system that is resistant to new information or change. Compare OPEN SYSTEM.

closure *n.* **1.** the act, achievement, or sense of completing or resolving something. In psychotherapy, for example, a client achieves closure with the recognition that he or she has reached a resolution to a particular psychological issue or relationship problem. **2.** one of the GESTALT PRINCIPLES OF ORGANIZATION. It states that people tend to perceive incomplete forms (e.g., images, sounds) as complete, synthesizing the missing units so as to perceive the image or sound as a whole. Also called **law of closure**; **principle of closure**.

clouding of consciousness a mental state involving a reduced awareness of the environment, inability to concentrate, and confusion. Also called **mental fog**.

clozapine *n.* the first of the atypical ANTI-PSYCHOTICS to be used clinically and released into the U.S. market in 1990. Although regarded by some as the most effective of all antipsychotic drugs, clozapine has problematic side effects that have limited its use, notably agranulocytosis: a decline in the number of certain white blood cells and corresponding suppression of the immune response. Use of clozapine therefore is generally reserved for patients who have responded suboptimally to other antipsychotic agents. U.S. trade name: **Clorazil**.

clumsy automation in ergonomics, any reallocation of system functions from humans to machines that does not lead to the expected gains in safety and efficiency. This is usually because automation alters the human operator's task, resulting in increased workload or UNDERLOAD.

cluster analysis a method of data analysis in which individuals (cases) are grouped together into clusters based on their strong similarity with regard to specific attributes.

cluster evaluation a type of PROGRAM EVALUATION carried out at several sites. Each site has the same evaluation objectives, which are assessed in a coordinated effort by different evaluators in a continuous process. Information so obtained is then shared to enable common program outcomes to be assessed and to identify elements that contributed to the failures or successes of the program.

clustering *n.* the tendency for items to be consistently grouped together in the course of recall. This grouping typically occurs for related items. It is readily apparent in memory tasks in which items from the same category, such as animals, are recalled together. **—cluster** *n., vb.*

cluster sampling a survey sampling method in which the complete population is first subdivided into groups, or clusters, and random samples are then drawn from certain clusters. A common example would be sampling voters in a large jurisdiction (e.g., a state) by identifying clusters on the basis of close geographical proximity (e.g., counties) and then drawing samples from the county clusters (e.g., towns and cities).

cluster suicides a statistically high occurrence of suicides within a circumscribed geographic area, social group, or time period. Such clusters typically occur among adolescents who imitate the suicide of a high-status peer or among dispersed individuals who imitate the suicide of a widely admired role model. Compare MASS SUICIDE.

cluttering *n.* rapid speech that is confused, jumbled, and imprecise, often occurring during a MANIC EPISODE.

CMHC abbreviation for COMMUNITY MENTAL HEALTH CENTER.

CNS abbreviation for CENTRAL NERVOUS SYSTEM.

CNS depressant any of a group of drugs that, at low doses, depress the inhibitory centers of the brain. At somewhat higher doses, they depress other neural functions, slow reaction times, and lower respiration and heart rate. At still higher doses, they can induce unconsciousness, coma, and death. Examples of CNS depressants are AL-COHOL, BARBITURATES, and BENZODIAZEPINES.

CNS stimulant any of a group of drugs that, at low to moderate doses, heighten wakefulness and alertness, diminish fatigue, and provoke feelings of energy and well-being. Caffeine and nicotine are examples. At higher doses, the more powerful stimulants can produce agitation, panic excitement, hallucinations, and paranoia. In general, stimulants exert their effects by enhancing CATECHOLAMINE neurotransmission and increasing activity in the SYMPATHETIC NERVOUS SYSTEM. Some stimulants are used clinically in mental health, and in psychiatric contexts are often referred to as **psychostimulants**. These drugs include the AMPHETAMINES and related or similarly acting compounds, used for the treatment of attention-deficit/hyperactivity disorder, narcolepsy, depression, and organic brain syndromes and as appetite suppressants.

coaching n. specialized instruction and training provided to enable individuals to acquire or enhance particular skills, as in EXECUTIVE COACHING or LIFE COACHING, or to improve performance, as in athletic coaching.

coacting group a group consisting of two or more individuals working in one another's presence on tasks and activities that require little or no interaction or communication (**coaction tasks**), such as clerical staff working at individual desks in an open-design office. Researchers often create coacting groups in laboratory studies to determine the impact of the mere presence of others on performance.

coadaptation n. the interdependence of behavioral adaptations between species. For example, a type of fruit tree that depends on a bird or mammal to disperse seeds away from the parent tree may have fruit coloration and taste that engages the sensory and perceptual systems of these primary dispersers. See also SYMBIOSIS.

coalition n. a temporary alliance formed by two or more individuals in order to gain a better outcome (e.g., power and influence) than can be achieved by each individual alone. Coalitions tend to be adversarial, in that they seek outcomes that will benefit the coalition members at the expense of nonmembers. They also tend to be unstable because (a) they include individuals who would not naturally form an alliance but are obliged or encouraged to do so by circumstances and (b) members frequently abandon one alliance to form a more profitable one. See also MINIMUM POWER THEORY; MINIMUM RESOURCE THEORY.

coarticulation effect a phenomenon in which the performance of one or more actions in a sequence of actions varies according to the other actions in the sequence. The effect is par-

ticularly important in speech, where the formation of certain PHONEMES varies according to the speech sounds that immediately precede or follow: So, for example, the aspirated [p] sound in *pin* differs slightly from the unaspirated [p] in *spin*.

cocaine n. a drug, obtained from leaves of the coca shrub (*Erythroxylum coca*), that stimulates the central nervous system (see CNS STIMULANT), with the effects of reducing fatigue and increasing well-being. These are followed by a period of depression as the initial effects diminish. The drug acts by blocking the reuptake of the neurotransmitters DOPAMINE, SEROTONIN, and NOREPINEPHRINE.

cocaine abuse a pattern of cocaine use manifested by recurrent significant adverse consequences related to the repeated ingestion of the substance. See also SUBSTANCE ABUSE.

Cocaine Anonymous see ALCOHOLICS ANONYMOUS.

cocaine dependence a cluster of cognitive, behavioral, and physiological symptoms indicating continued use of cocaine despite significant cocaine-related problems. See also SUBSTANCE DEPENDENCE.

cocaine intoxication a reversible syndrome due to the recent ingestion of cocaine. It includes clinically significant behavioral or psychological changes (e.g., agitation, aggressive behavior, elation, grandiosity, impaired judgment, talkativeness, hypervigilance), as well as one or more physiological signs (e.g., rapid heartbeat, elevated blood pressure, perspiration or chills, nausea and vomiting).

cocaine withdrawal a characteristic withdrawal syndrome that develops after cessation of (or reduction in) prolonged, heavy consumption of cocaine. The essential characteristic is depressed mood, sometimes severe, and there may also be fatigue, disturbed sleep, increased appetite, vivid and unpleasant dreams, or PSYCHOMOTOR RETARDATION or agitation, or all of these features. See also SUBSTANCE WITHDRAWAL.

coccygeal nerve see SPINAL NERVE.

coccyx n. (*pl.* **coccyges**) the last bone of the SPINAL COLUMN in apes and humans, formed by fusion of the caudal vertebrae. —**coccygeal** adj.

cochlea n. the bony fluid-filled part of the inner ear that is concerned with hearing. Shaped like a snail shell, it forms part of the bony LABYRINTH. Along its length run three canals: the SCALA VESTIBULI, SCALA TYMPANI, and SCALA MEDIA, or cochlear duct. The floor of the scala media is formed by the BASILAR MEMBRANE; the ORGAN OF CORTI, which rests on the basilar membrane, contains the HAIR CELLS that act as auditory receptor organs. —**cochlear** adj.

cochlear implant an electronic device designed to enable individuals with complete deafness to hear and interpret some sounds, particularly those associated with speech. It consists of a microphone to detect sound, a headpiece to transmit sound, a processor to digitize sound, and a receiver to signal electrodes that are surgically implanted in the cochlea to stimulate the auditory nerve.

cochlear microphonic an alternating-current electric potential generated by HAIR CELLS in the inner ear that has a waveform similar to that of the acoustic input.

cochlear nerve see AUDITORY NERVE.

cochlear nucleus a mass of cell bodies of second-order auditory neurons in the brainstem. The principal subdivisions are the ventral, dorsal, and anterior cochlear nuclei.

Cochran Q test a nonparametric statistical test used when each experimental unit is observed under multiple experimental conditions and one wishes to test the hypothesis of equality of the conditions when the case outcomes are binary. [William Gemmell **Cochran** (1909–1980), Scottish-born U.S. statistician]

cocktail-party effect the ability to attend to one of several speech streams while ignoring others, as when one is at a cocktail party. Research in this area in the early 1950s suggested that the unattended messages are not processed, but later findings indicated that meaning is identified in at least some cases. For example, the mention of one's name is processed even if it occurs in an unattended speech stream. See also ATTENUATION THEORY.

codability *n.* the extent to which speakers of a language agree on a name for something. For example, the codability of a color is defined by how much agreement there is about a name for that color. —**codable** *adj.*

codeine *n.* an OPIATE derived from morphine, with which it shares many properties—it is a potent analgesic (used alone or in combination with other analgesics, e.g., aspirin) and it induces euphoria.

code of ethics a set of standards and principles of professional conduct, such as the *Ethical Principles of Psychologists and Code of Conduct* of the American Psychological Association. See ETHICS; PROFESSIONAL ETHICS; STANDARDS OF PRACTICE.

codependency *n.* **1.** the state of being mutually reliant, for example, a relationship between two individuals who are emotionally dependent on one another. **2.** a dysfunctional relationship pattern in which an individual is psychologically dependent on (or controlled by) a person who has a pathological addiction (e.g., alcohol, gambling). —**codependent** *adj.*

code test a test that requires participants to translate one set of symbols into another, for example, by writing *California* in numbers that stand for letters according to the code A = 3, B = 4, C = 5, and so on. Also called **symbol-substitution test**. See also SYMBOL–DIGIT TEST.

codon *n.* a unit of the GENETIC CODE consisting of three consecutive bases in a DNA or messenger RNA sequence. Most codons specify a particular amino acid in protein synthesis, although some act as "start" or "stop" signals.

coefficient *n.* **1.** a number that functions as a measure of some property. For example, the CORRELATION COEFFICIENT is a measure of the degree of linear relatedness. **2.** in algebra, a scalar that multiplies a variable in an equation. For example, in the equation $y = bx$, the scalar quantity b is said to be a coefficient.

coefficient alpha see CRONBACH'S ALPHA.

coefficient of agreement a numerical index that reflects the degree of agreement among a set of raters, judges, or instruments on to which of several categories a case belongs. Coefficients of agreement, such as KAPPA, are often corrected for chance agreement.

coefficient of alienation (symbol: k) a numerical index that reflects the amount of unexplained variance between two variables. It is a measure of the lack of relationship between the two variables.

coefficient of concordance (symbol: W) a numerical index that reflects the degree to which the rankings of k conditions or objects by m raters are in agreement. Also called **Kendall's coefficient of concordance**.

coefficient of determination (symbol: r^2) a numerical index that reflects the degree to which variation in the DEPENDENT VARIABLE is accounted for by one INDEPENDENT VARIABLE.

coefficient of multiple determination (symbol: R^2) a numerical index that reflects the degree to which variation in the DEPENDENT VARIABLE is accounted for by two or more INDEPENDENT VARIABLES.

coefficient of variation a measure of the spread (see DISPERSION) of a set of data. It is determined by dividing the distribution's STANDARD DEVIATION by its MEAN.

coercion *n.* the process of attempting to influence another person through the exercise of physical, psychological, or social power. —**coerce** *vb.* —**coercive** *adj.*

coercive persuasion a controlled program of social influence to bring about substantial changes in behavior and attitude. An example is U.S. Marine Corps basic training, which relies on changing attitudes from civilian perspectives to those of marines. As a countermeasure, military personnel are also trained in methods of **coercive persuasion resistance**, which are designed to enable them to function and survive to the best of their ability under circumstances in which they are subjected to techniques that may produce behavior and attitude changes.

coexistence hypothesis a theoretical explanation of the MISINFORMATION EFFECT stating that when misleading information is introduced after a witnessed event, it exists in competition with the original memory of the event. The false information is more accessible due to the RECENCY EFFECT and is more likely to be retrieved upon questioning, leading to erroneous reporting of the event. Compare ALTERATION HYPOTHESIS.

cofacilitator *n.* a therapist or student in training who assists in leading a therapy group. The cofacilitator may act as an observer or as one who balances the approach of the other group leader.

cofigurative culture a society or culture in which people learn chiefly from other people in the same age group, so that, for example, children learn mostly from children and young adults from young adults. Compare POSTFIGURATIVE CULTURE; PREFIGURATIVE CULTURE.

cognition *n.* **1.** all forms of knowing and awareness, such as perceiving, conceiving, remembering, reasoning, judging, imagining, and problem solving. Along with affect and conation, it is one of the three traditionally identified components of mind. **2.** an individual percept, idea, memory, or the like. —**cognitional** *adj.* —**cognitive** *adj.*

cognitive ability the skills involved in performing the tasks associated with perception, learning, memory, understanding, awareness, reasoning, judgment, intuition, and language.

cognitive–affective personality system a theoretical conception of personality structure in which personality is viewed as a complex system that features a large number of highly interconnected cognitions and emotional tendencies.

cognitive aging nonpathological age-related changes in mental functioning (e.g., attention, memory, decision making) that occur naturally across the adult age span.

cognitive-analytic therapy a time-limited integrative, collaborative psychotherapy that emphasizes SCHEMAS and integrates principles and techniques from PSYCHODYNAMIC PSYCHOTHERAPY and COGNITIVE BEHAVIOR THERAPY.

cognitive appraisal theory the theory that cognitive evaluation is involved in the generation of each and every emotion (see APPRAISAL). This concept is more appropriately expressed in the COGNITIVE–MOTIVATIONAL–RELATIONAL THEORY, as the latter recognizes that cognition is only one of three simultaneously operating processes that contribute to the generation of any emotion. See also CORE RELATIONAL THEMES.

cognitive architecture a hypothesized architecture for human problem solving, usually represented as a component of a computer program. The PRODUCTION SYSTEM is an example. Empirical testing of cognitive phenomena is often used to establish the validity of aspects of this model.

cognitive behavioral couples therapy couples therapy that uses BEHAVIORAL COUPLES THERAPY techniques yet also focuses on the reciprocal influence of the partners' idiosyncratic patterns of ideas about each other and about

couples in general. Interfering ideas are made conscious and explicit, and then modified to improve the couple's relationship using techniques modified from COGNITIVE BEHAVIOR THERAPY. Compare INTEGRATIVE BEHAVIORAL COUPLES THERAPY.

cognitive behavioral group therapy a type of group psychotherapy that uses techniques and methods of COGNITIVE BEHAVIOR THERAPY, such as modeling, restructuring thoughts, relaxation training, and communication skills training, to achieve behaviorally defined goals. Groups can include clients with diverse issues or can be limited to clients with specific problems (e.g., agoraphobia, anger). See also BECK THERAPY.

cognitive behavior theory any theory deriving from general behavioral theory that considers cognitive or thought processes as significant mediators of behavioral change. A central feature in the theoretical formulations of the process is that the human organism responds primarily to cognitive representations of its environments rather than to the environments themselves. The theory has led to popular therapeutic procedures that incorporate cognitive behavior techniques to effect changes in self-image as well as behaviors.

cognitive behavior therapy (CBT) a form of psychotherapy that integrates theories of cognition and learning with treatment techniques derived from COGNITIVE THERAPY and BEHAVIOR THERAPY. CBT assumes that cognitive, emotional, and behavioral variables are functionally interrelated. Treatment is aimed at identifying and modifying the client's maladaptive thought processes and problematic behaviors through COGNITIVE RESTRUCTURING and behavioral techniques to achieve change. Also called **cognitive behavior modification**; **cognitive behavioral therapy**.

cognitive closure 1. the state in which an individual recognizes that he or she has achieved understanding of something. **2.** the final stage in figuratively seeing the total picture and how all pieces of it fit together.

cognitive complexity the state or quality of a thought process that involves numerous constructs, with many interrelationships among them. Such processing is often experienced as difficult or effortful. See also CONCEPTUAL COMPLEXITY.

cognitive complexity and control theory the proposal that the ability to follow rules depends on the development of conscious awareness and self-control and is therefore age related. In general, a 4-year-old child can solve problems requiring the application of more complex rules than he or she could when aged 3.

cognitive conditioning a process in which a stimulus is repeatedly paired with an imagined or anticipated response or behavior. Cognitive conditioning has been used as a therapeutic technique, in which case the stimulus is typically aversive. For example, the client imagines that he or she is smoking a cigarette and gives himself or herself a pinch; the procedure is repeated until the thought produces the effect of discouraging the behavior. See also COGNITIVE REHEARSAL.

cognitive consistency theory any of a broad class of theories postulating that attitude change is a result of the desire to maintain consistency among elements of a cognitive system. See also BALANCE THEORY; COGNITIVE DISSONANCE THEORY; CONGRUITY THEORY.

cognitive coping strategy any COPING STRATEGY in which mental activity is used to counter the problem or situation. Examples include thinking out the cause of the problem, working out how others might handle it, diverting one's attention to something less stressful or anxiety-provoking (e.g., remembering happy times, solving mathematical problems), and meditation or prayer.

cognitive decline reduction in one or more cognitive abilities, such as memory, awareness, judgment, and mental acuity, across the adult life span. Cognitive decline is a part of normal healthy aging and varies with the ability being measured, but a severe decline could be symptomatic of disease, particularly dementia (e.g., ALZHEIMER'S DISEASE).

cognitive deconstruction a mental state characterized by lack of emotion, the absence of any sense of future, a concentration on the here-and-now, and focus on concrete sensation rather than abstract thought. People may cultivate this state to escape from emotional distress or troublesome thoughts.

cognitive defect any impairment in perceptual, learning, memory, linguistic, or thinking abilities. Multiple significant cognitive defects are characteristic of DEMENTIA.

cognitive deficit performance on intellectual and other mentally based tasks (e.g., those involving memory), as measured by individually administered standardized assessments (verbal and nonverbal cognitive measures), that is substantially below that expected given the individual's chronological age and formal educational experience.

cognitive derailment the often abrupt shifting of thoughts or associations so that they do not follow one another in a logical sequence. Cognitive derailment is a symptom of schizophrenia; the term is essentially equivalent to THOUGHT DERAILMENT.

cognitive developmental theory any theory that attempts to explain the mechanisms underlying the growth and maturation of thinking processes. Explanations may be in terms of stages of development in which the changes in thinking are relatively abrupt and discontinuous, or the changes may be viewed as occurring gradually and continuously over time.

cognitive disorder any disorder that involves impairment of the EXECUTIVE FUNCTIONS, affecting performance in many areas, including reasoning, planning, judgment, decision making, emotional engagement, perseveration, awareness, attention, language, learning, memory, and timing.

cognitive dissonance an unpleasant psychological state resulting from inconsistency between two or more elements in a cognitive system. It is presumed to involve a state of heightened arousal and to have characteristics similar to physiological drives (e.g., hunger).

cognitive dissonance theory a theory proposing that people have a fundamental motivation to maintain consistency among elements in their cognitive systems. When inconsistency occurs, people experience an unpleasant psychological state that motivates them to reduce the dissonance in a variety of ways (see DISSONANCE REDUCTION).

cognitive distortion faulty or inaccurate thinking, perception, or belief. An example is OVERGENERALIZATION. Cognitive distortion is a normal psychological process that can occur in all people to a greater or lesser extent.

cognitive ergonomics a specialty area of ERGONOMICS that seeks to understand the cognitive processes and representations involved in human performance. Cognitive ergonomics studies the combined effect of information-processing characteristics, task constraints, and task environment on human performance and applies the results of such studies to the design and evaluation of work systems.

cognitive ethology the study of the cognitive ability of an animal with respect to the problems it faces in its natural environment. A species that might perform poorly on a traditional laboratory task may display apparently complex cognitive skills in the wild. For example, some birds that store seeds over the winter display a high level of SPATIAL MEMORY for large numbers of objects.

cognitive faculty a specific aspect or domain of mental function, such as language, object recognition, or face perception.

cognitive flooding a method used in psychotherapy, mainly to treat phobias, in which the client is encouraged to focus on negative or aversive mental images to generate emotional states similar to those experienced when faced with a feared object or situation. The simulated fear is then seen to be manageable and associated with images that will reduce the original fear. See also IMPLOSIVE THERAPY.

cognitive grammar a theory of grammar in which the constituent units are derived from general cognitive principles, such as associative memory, categorization, and so on, rather than from autonomous linguistic principles. This assumption that language is an integral part of cognition runs counter to the theory of the TASK SPECIFICITY OF LANGUAGE.

cognitive heuristic see HEURISTIC.

cognitive intelligence one's abilities to learn, remember, reason, solve problems, and make sound judgments, particularly as contrasted with EMOTIONAL INTELLIGENCE.

cognitive learning the acquisition and retention of a mental representation of information and the use of this representation as the basis for behavior.

cognitive learning theory any theory postulating that learning requires central constructs and new ways of perceiving events. An example is PURPOSIVE BEHAVIORISM. Cognitive theory is usually contrasted with behavioral learning theories, which suggest that behaviors or responses are acquired through experience.

cognitive load the relative demand imposed by a particular task, in terms of mental resources required. See also COGNITIVE OVERLOAD.

cognitively guided instruction an educational approach in which teachers make decisions about their instruction based on the knowledge and performance level of their students. Students are encouraged to create their own solutions to problems, rather than rely on a set of preconceived, teacher-directed procedures.

cognitive map a mental understanding of an environment, formed through trial and error as well as observation. Human beings and other animals have well-developed cognitive maps that contain spatial information enabling them to orient themselves and find their way in the real world. See also MENTAL MAP.

cognitive–motivational–relational theory an extension of the COGNITIVE APPRAISAL THEORY that puts equal emphasis on three processes involved in the generation of an emotion: (a) appraisal (the cognitive process), (b) the central role of the individual's strivings, intentions, and goals (the motivational process), and (c) the relevance of external events to these strivings (the relational process).

cognitive neuroscience a branch of NEUROSCIENCE and BIOLOGICAL PSYCHOLOGY that focuses on the neural mechanisms of cognition. Although overlapping with the study of the mind in COGNITIVE PSYCHOLOGY, cognitive neuroscience, with its grounding in such areas as experimental psychology, neurobiology, physics, and mathematics, specifically examines how mental processes occur in the brain.

cognitive overload the situation in which the demands placed on a person by mental work (the COGNITIVE LOAD) are greater than the person's mental abilities can cope with.

cognitive penetrability the capacity of a mental process to be influenced by an individual's knowledge, beliefs, or goals. Reflex behavior is said to be **cognitively impenetrable**.

cognitive process 1. any of the mental functions assumed to be involved in cognitive activities, such as attention, perception, language, learning, memory, problem solving, and thinking. This term is often used synonymously with MENTAL PROCESS. **2.** the acquisition, storage, interpretation, manipulation, transformation, and use of knowledge. These processes are commonly understood through several basic theories, including the SERIAL PROCESSING approach, the PARALLEL PROCESSING approach, and a combination theory, which assumes that cognitive processes are both serial and parallel, depending on the demands of the task.

cognitive processing therapy (CPT) a treatment approach, based on INFORMATION PROCESSING theory, that deals with the client's conceptualizations of the self, others, and events. It is often used in the treatment of posttraumatic stress disorder resulting from sexual assault to facilitate the expression of affect and the appropriate accommodation of the traumatic event with more general cognitive schemas regarding one's self and the world.

cognitive psychology the branch of psychology that explores the operation of mental processes related to perceiving, attending, thinking, language, and memory, mainly through inferences from behavior. The cognitive approach, which developed in the 1940s and 1950s, diverged sharply from contemporary BEHAVIORISM in (a) emphasizing unseen knowledge processes instead of directly observable behaviors and (b) arguing that the relationship between stimulus and response was complex and mediated rather than simple and direct. Its concentration on the higher mental processes also contrasted with the focus on the instincts and other unconscious forces typical of psychoanalysis. More recently, cognitive psychology has been influenced by approaches to INFORMATION PROCESSING and INFORMATION THEORY developed in computer science and ARTIFICIAL INTELLIGENCE. See also COGNITIVE SCIENCE.

cognitive rehabilitation specific REHABILITATION interventions designed to address problems in mental processing that are associated with chronic illness, brain injury, or trauma, such as stroke. Rehabilitation may include relearning specific mental abilities, strengthening unaffected abilities, or substituting new abilities to compensate for lost ones.

cognitive rehearsal a therapeutic technique in which a client imagines those situations that tend to produce anxiety or self-defeating behavior and then repeats positive coping statements or mentally rehearses more appropriate behavior.

cognitive response theory a theory postulating that attitude change occurs primarily as a function of people's evaluative responses to attitude-relevant information. This theory holds that it is primarily the number and VALENCE of these responses, rather than memory for the information itself, that determines the magnitude and duration of attitude change.

C

cognitive restructuring a technique used in COGNITIVE THERAPY and COGNITIVE BEHAVIOR THERAPY to help the client identify his or her self-defeating beliefs or cognitive distortions, refute them, and then modify them so that they are adaptive and reasonable.

cognitive schema see SCHEMA.

cognitive science an interdisciplinary approach to understanding the mind and mental processes that combines aspects of cognitive psychology, the philosophy of mind, epistemology, neuroscience, anthropology, psycholinguistics, and computer science.

cognitive slippage a mild form of disconnected thought processes or LOOSENING OF ASSOCIATIONS.

cognitive stage in some theories of cognitive development, especially that of Swiss psychologist Jean Piaget (1896–1980), a plane of cognition that is characterized by a particular, qualitatively different level of thinking than preceding or later stages.

cognitive strategy any predetermined plan to control the process and content of thought. In sport psychology, for example, such strategies involve use of the SELF-TALK dialogue to assist athletes to keep focused, energized, confident, and "in the zone."

cognitive style a person's characteristic mode of perceiving, thinking, remembering, and problem solving. Cognitive styles might differ in preferred elements or activities, such as visual versus verbal ENCODING, and along various dimensions, such as FIELD DEPENDENCE/field independence and REFLECTIVITY–IMPULSIVITY. Many use the term **learning style** interchangeably with cognitive style, whereas others use the former more specifically to mean a person's characteristic cognitive, affective, and psychological behaviors that influence his or her preferred instructional methods and interactions with the learning environment. See also THEORY OF MENTAL SELF-GOVERNMENT.

cognitive task analysis a form of TASK ANALYSIS used to identify the different cognitive processes necessary to perform a task.

cognitive therapy (**CT**) a form of psychotherapy based on the concept that emotional and behavioral problems in an individual are, at least in part, the result of maladaptive or faulty ways of thinking and distorted attitudes toward oneself and others. The objective of the therapy is to identify these faulty cognitions and replace them with more adaptive ones, a process known as COGNITIVE RESTRUCTURING. The therapist takes the role of an active guide who attempts to make the client aware of these distorted thinking patterns and who helps the client correct and revise his or her perceptions and attitudes by citing evidence to the contrary or by eliciting it from the client. See also COGNITIVE BEHAVIOR THERAPY.

cognitive triad a set of three beliefs thought to characterize MAJOR DEPRESSIVE EPISODES. These are negative beliefs about the self, the world, and the future.

cognitive tunneling a psychological state, typical of people concentrating on a demanding task or operating under conditions of stress, in which a single, narrowly defined category of information is attended to and processed. Cognitive tunneling involves the processing of highly critical task-relevant information, with limited or no processing of secondary information that may also be important to the task. Compare SOCIAL TUNNELING.

cognitive unconscious unreportable mental processes, collectively. There are many sources of evidence for a cognitive unconscious, including regularities of behavior due to habit or AUTOMATICITY, inferred grammatical rules, the details of sensorimotor control, and implicit knowledge after brain damage (see TACIT KNOWLEDGE). It is often contrasted with the psychoanalytically derived notion of the dynamic UNCONSCIOUS, which involves material that is kept out of consciousness to avoid anxiety, shame, or guilt.

cognitive vulnerability a set of beliefs or attitudes thought to make a person vulnerable to depression. Examples include PERFECTIONISM, DEPENDENCE, and SOCIOTROPY.

cognitivism *n.* adherence to the principles of COGNITIVE PSYCHOLOGY, especially as opposed to those of BEHAVIORISM.

cohabitation *n.* the state or condition of living together as sexual and domestic partners without being married. —**cohabit** *vb.* —**cohabitee** *n.*

Cohen's kappa (symbol: κ) a numerical index that reflects the degree of agreement between two raters or rating systems classifying data into mutually exclusive categories, corrected for the level of agreement expected by chance alone. [Jacob **Cohen** (1923–1998), U.S. psychologist and statistician]

coherence *n.* **1.** meaningful interconnections between distinct psychological entities. For example, a system of independent beliefs that is logically consistent from one belief to another would be described as **coherent. 2.** a measure of the extent to which energy waves (such as light waves) are correlated between two times (**temporal coherence**) or two points (**spatial coherence**).

cohesion *n.* the unity or solidarity of a group, as indicated by the strength of the bonds that link group members to the group as a whole, the sense of belongingness and community within the group, the feelings of attraction for specific group members and the group itself experienced by individuals, and the degree to which members coordinate their efforts to achieve goals. The higher the cohesion, the stronger the members' motivation to adhere to the group's standards. Group cohesion is frequently considered essential to effective GROUP PSYCHOTHERAPY. Also called **cohesiveness**. See also ESPRIT DE CORPS. —**cohesive** *adj.*

cohort *n.* a group of people who have experienced a significant life event (e.g., marriage) during the same period of time. The term usually refers to a **birth cohort**, or generation.

cohort effect any outcome associated with being a member of a group born at a particular time and therefore influenced by the events and practices at that time. Cohort effects may be difficult to separate from AGE EFFECTS and PERIOD EFFECTS in research.

cohort-sequential design an experimental design in which multiple measures are taken over a period of time from two or more groups of participants of different ages (COHORTS). Such studies essentially are a combination of a LONGITUDINAL DESIGN and a CROSS-SECTIONAL DESIGN.

cold cognition a mental process or activity that does not involve feelings or emotions. For instance, reading a list of nonsense syllables or factoids (brief pieces of invented or inaccurate information) typically involves cold cognition.

coldness *n.* **1.** a thermal sensation produced by a stimulus that is below skin temperature. **2.** a psychological characteristic featuring a relative absence of empathy toward and emotional support of others.

coleadership *n.* **1.** the state of affairs in which the organizational, directive, and motivational duties of LEADERSHIP are shared between two or more individuals. The leadership role may be deliberately divided, or this may occur spontaneously as the various leadership duties become associated with several individuals (see ROLE DIFFERENTIATION). In some cases one leader may have more status than another. **2.** leadership by two equal therapists or counselors, often used in GROUP PSYCHOTHERAPY.

collaboration *n.* the act or process of two or more people working together in order to obtain an outcome desired by all, particularly one in which the parties show sensitivity to the others' needs. —**collaborative** *adj.*

collaborative care 1. collaboration between two or more disciplines or practitioners to assess a client's problem or problems, develop a treatment plan, and monitor progress. **2.** collaboration across agencies to coordinate services to a particular client or client group.

collaborative family health care a form of interdisciplinary practice asserting that health events occur simultaneously on biological, psychological, and social levels and that offers treatment incorporating individual, family, community, and cultural influences. Collaborative clinicians share decision making and responsibility with patients and their families and integrate clinical expertise from relevant disciplines to provide patients with comprehensive and coordinated care.

collaborative learning 1. the interaction between two or more people working on a task that allows greater learning to be achieved, particularly by those who are less skilled, than would occur if the participants worked alone. **2.** the third stage of CULTURAL LEARNING, in which two or more individuals who are equal in expertise or authority work together to solve a common problem. See also IMITATIVE LEARNING; INSTRUCTED LEARNING.

collaborative therapy 1. any form of therapy in which the therapist and client work together as equal partners in addressing issues and fostering change. **2.** MARITAL THERAPY conducted by two therapists, each seeing one spouse but conferring from time to time. Also called **collaborative marriage therapy**; **collaborative marital therapy**.

collateral *adj.* secondary to something else. For example, a **collateral fiber** is a nerve fiber that branches off the main axon of a neuron. —**collaterally** *adv.*

collateral behavior behavior that is not required by a REINFORCEMENT CONTINGENCY but occurs in a regular, temporal relation to behavior directly reinforced by the contingency. Compare MEDIATING BEHAVIOR.

collateral sulcus a fissure that runs along the inferior surface of each cerebral hemisphere from approximately the posterior end of the OCCIPITAL LOBE to the anterior end of the TEMPORAL LOBE.

collective *n.* any aggregate of two or more individuals, but especially a larger, spontaneous, and relatively ephemeral social grouping, such as a crowd or mob. A collective often includes individuals who are dispersed over a wide area and have no direct contact with one another, but who nonetheless display common shifts in opinion or action.

collective conscience the shared values, norms, sentiments, and beliefs that form the basis of moral thinking and action in a cohesive society.

collective consciousness see GROUP MIND.

collective hysteria the spontaneous outbreak of atypical thoughts, feelings, or actions in a group or social aggregate. Manifestations may include psychogenic illness, collective hallucinations, bizarre behavior, and epidemic manias and panics, such as listeners' reactions to the Orson Welles broadcast based on H. G. Wells's *War of the Worlds* in 1938. Also called **mass hysteria**.

collective method any method that relies on groups rather than single individuals to solve problems, perform tasks, make decisions, and so on. In psychological treatment, for example, the collective method is seen in the use of GROUP

PSYCHOTHERAPY, ENCOUNTER GROUPS, and the like.

collective monologue a form of speech in which 2- or 3-year-old children talk among themselves without apparently communicating with each other in a meaningful way, such that the statements of one child seem unrelated to the statements of the others.

collective psychology the scientific study of the mental and emotional states and processes unique to individuals when aggregated in such groups as audiences, crowds, or social movements.

collective representations the institutions, laws, symbols, rituals, and stories that embody a society's key concepts and values and its sense of itself as a distinct community with its own identity and way of life.

collective self the part of the self (or self-concept) that derives from one's relationships with other people and memberships in groups or categories, ranging from family to nationality or race. The collective self is distinguished from the PUBLIC SELF and the PRIVATE SELF. See also SOCIAL SELF.

collective unconscious the part of the UNCONSCIOUS that, according to Swiss psychiatrist Carl Jung (1875–1961), is common to all humankind and contains the inherited accumulation of primitive human experiences in the form of ideas and images called ARCHETYPES. It is the deepest and least accessible part of the unconscious mind. See also PERSONAL UNCONSCIOUS; RACIAL MEMORY.

collectivism *n.* a social or cultural tradition, ideology, or personal outlook that emphasizes the unity of the group or community rather than each person's individuality. Collectivist societies tend to stress cooperation, communalism, constructive interdependence, and conformity to cultural roles and mores. Compare INDIVIDUALISM. —**collectivist** *adj.*

colliculus *n.* (*pl.* **colliculi**) a small elevation. Two pairs of colliculi are found on the dorsal surface of the MIDBRAIN. The rostral pair, the **superior colliculi**, receive and process visual information and help control eye movements. The caudal pair, the **inferior colliculi**, receive and process auditory information.

collinearity *n.* the degree to which a set of variables are so highly interrelated that one of more of the variables in the set can be completely predicted from the remaining variables in the set. —**collinear** *adj.*

colony *n.* a gathering of animals of the same species into a relatively large group that may or may not display SOCIAL ORGANIZATION. A colony may provide the advantage of having many individuals available for locating food and defending against predators, but it has potential costs in terms of increased competition for food or breeding opportunities and increased potential for disease transmission. —**colonial** *adj.* —**colonialism** *n.* —**colonist** *n.* —**colonize** *vb.*

color *n.* the subjective quality of light that corresponds to wavelength as perceived by retinal receptors. Color can be characterized by its HUE, SATURATION, and BRIGHTNESS.

color agnosia see VISUAL AGNOSIA.

color blindness the inability to discriminate between colors and to perceive color hues. Color blindness may be caused by disease, drugs, or brain injury (**acquired color blindness**), but most often is an inherited trait (**congenital color blindness**) that affects about 10% of men (it is rare in women). The most common form of the disorder involves the green or red receptors of the cone cells in the retina, causing a red–green confusion (see DEUTERANOPIA; PROTANOPIA). Total color blindness is called ACHROMATISM and is rare. See also DICHROMATISM; MONOCHROMATISM; TRICHROMATISM.

color constancy the tendency to perceive a familiar object as having the same color under different conditions of illumination. Color constancy is an example of PERCEPTUAL CONSTANCY.

color contrast the effect of one color upon another when they are viewed in close proximity. In **simultaneous contrast**, complementary colors, such as yellow and blue, are enhanced by each other: The yellow appears yellower, and the blue appears bluer. In **successive contrast**, the complement of a color is seen after shifting focus to a neutral surface.

color solid a three-dimensional representation of all aspects of color, including the various degrees and combinations of hue, brightness, and saturation. Various solid shapes can be used to form such a representation; these give rise to different types of color solids, such as the **color cone**, **color pyramid**, and **color spindle**.

color theory any of a variety of theories formulated to explain color phenomena. Examples include the dual process theory of color vision (see OPPONENT PROCESS THEORY OF COLOR VISION), the LADD-FRANKLIN THEORY, and the RETINEX THEORY.

color weakness an impaired ability to perceive hues accurately. The term is often (inaccurately) used interchangeably with COLOR BLINDNESS.

column *n.* in anatomy, a structure that resembles an architectural pillar. Columns range from macroscopic, such as the SPINAL COLUMN, to microscopic, such as CORTICAL COLUMNS. —**columnar** *adj.*

columnar organization see CORTICAL COLUMN.

coma *n.* a profound state of unconsciousness resulting from disease, injury, or poisoning and characterized by little or no response to stimuli, absence of reflexes, and suspension of voluntary activity.

combat stress reactions psychological reactions to traumatic events in military operations, which can range from mild to severe and are normal reactions to the abnormal events. In World War I such reactions were known as SHELL SHOCK, whereas in World War II the terms **battle fatigue**, **combat fatigue**, **combat hysteria**, and **combat neurosis** were widely used. Currently, they are categorized as POSTTRAUMATIC STRESS DISORDERS.

combination *n.* in statistics, the selection of *r* objects from among *n* objects without regard to the order in which the objects are selected. The number of combinations of *n* objects taken *r* at a time is often denoted as $_nC_r$. A combination is similar to a PERMUTATION but distinguished by its irrelevance of order.

combination therapy the application of two or more distinct therapeutic approaches by the same therapist to a client's presenting problem. It is distinct from ADJUNCTIVE THERAPY, which involves multiple practitioners.

combination tone a tone generated in the ear that is produced when two **primary tones** (i.e., two tones differing in frequency) are presented simultaneously. For example, under certain conditions a 1000-Hz tone and a 1200-Hz tone will produce audible combination tones whose frequencies are 200 Hz (a **difference tone**) and 800 Hz (a **cubic difference tone**). Most combination tones are produced by nonlinear distortion that occurs within the cochlea.

combined motor method a technique for measuring and assessing emotional responses to stimuli, in which participants perform a simple movement (e.g., pressing a key) when exposed to a stimulus. The reaction time and characteristics of the movement are recorded and are assumed to indicate the intensity of different emotions. Devised by Russian neuropsychologist Alexander Luria (1902–1977), it is known informally as the **Luria technique**.

combined therapy 1. psychotherapy in which the client is engaged in two or more treatments with the same or different therapists. For example, MARITAL THERAPY may include group therapy with several other couples in addition to individual therapy or CONJOINT THERAPY for each couple. **2.** treatment using a combination of psychotherapy and medication. See also ADJUNCTIVE THERAPY; ADJUVANT THERAPY.

command automatism abnormal responsiveness to instructions such that actions are performed without critical judgment or conscious control. Such behavior is commonly observed in hypnotized individuals.

command style in education, a highly structured, traditional instruction method in which the teacher makes all decisions regarding lesson development and implementation and the students' role is to passively receive the information and perform required tasks. Compare INDIVIDUAL PROGRAM.

commensalism *n.* see INTERSPECIES INTERACTION. —**commensal** *adj.*, *n.*

commissural fiber an axon from any of various neurons that connect the same or equivalent structures in the left and right cerebral hemispheres. Compare ASSOCIATION FIBER.

commissure *n.* a structure that forms a bridge or junction between two anatomical areas, particularly the two cerebral hemispheres or the halves of the spinal cord. Examples include the two key landmarks in brain mapping: the **anterior commissure**, a bundle of myelinated fibers that joins the TEMPORAL LOBES and contains fibers of the OLFACTORY TRACT; and the **posterior commissure**, a bundle of myelinated fibers that connects regions in the midbrain and DIENCEPHALON. See also CORPUS CALLOSUM; GRAY COMMISSURE; WHITE COMMISSURE. —**commissural** *adj.*

commissurotomy *n.* surgical transection or severing of a COMMISSURE, especially surgical separation of the cerebral hemispheres of the brain by severing the CORPUS CALLOSUM (called **callosectomy**, **callosotomy**, or **corpuscallosotomy**) and often the anterior commissure. This procedure is used clinically to treat severe epilepsy and has been used experimentally in animals to study the functions of each hemisphere. See also SPLIT BRAIN.

commitment *n.* confinement to a mental institution by court order following certification by appropriate psychiatric or other mental health authorities. The process may be voluntary but is generally involuntary. See also CIVIL COMMITMENT; CRIMINAL COMMITMENT.

common factors in psychotherapy, variables that are common to various therapies with individuals, such as THERAPEUTIC ALLIANCE and length of treatment, as opposed to factors that are unique to a particular therapy, such as the use of interpretation. THERAPEUTIC FACTORS are similar, but typically apply to therapies with groups.

common fate one of the GESTALT PRINCIPLES OF ORGANIZATION, stating that objects functioning or moving in the same direction appear to belong together, that is, they are perceived as a single unit (e.g., a flock of birds). Also called **law of common fate**; **principle of common fate**.

common-law marriage a relationship between an unmarried but long-term cohabiting couple that is considered legally equivalent to marriage. Most states in the United States do not recognize common-law marriages.

commonsense psychology ideas about psychological issues derived from common experience and not necessarily from empirical laboratory or clinical studies. See FOLK PSYCHOLOGY; POPULAR PSYCHOLOGY.

common trait in the personality theory of U.S. psychologist Gordon W. Allport (1897–1967), any of a number of enduring characteristics that describe or determine an individual's behavior across a variety of situations and that are common to many people and similarly expressed. Common traits, such as assertiveness, thus serve as a basis for comparison of one person to another and are distinct from PERSONAL DISPOSITIONS.

communality *n.* the proportion of the VARIANCE in a variable accounted for by the common factors that make up the variable in FACTOR ANALYSIS. The communality is scaled so that, if the factors completely account for all the variability in the variable, the communality is 1.0.

communal relationship a relationship in which interaction is governed primarily by consideration of the other's needs and wishes. This contrasts with an **exchange relationship**, in which the people involved are concerned mainly with receiving as much as they give.

communicated authenticity, regard, empathy (**CARE**) qualities of a psychotherapist regarded by some theorists as necessary for therapy to be effective and, ultimately, successful. CARE is considered essential to CLIENT-CENTERED THERAPY.

communication *n.* the transmission of information, which may be by verbal (oral or written) or nonverbal means (see NONVERBAL COMMUNICATION). Humans communicate to relate and exchange ideas, knowledge, feelings, experiences and for many other interpersonal and social purposes. Nonhuman animals likewise communicate vocally or nonvocally for a variety of purposes (see ANIMAL COMMUNICATION). Communication is studied by cognitive and experimental psychologists, and COMMUNICATION DISORDERS are treated by mental and behavioral health therapists and by speech and language therapists.

communication deviance lack of clarity in communication, making it hard to follow and difficult for the listener to share a common focus of attention and meaning with the speaker. Communication deviance is thought to be a long-term trait within families that may engender inefficient patterns of thinking and information processing. It is also thought to be associated with schizophrenia and other psychological disorders.

communication disorder any of a group of disorders characterized by difficulties with speech and language. Communication disorders include EXPRESSIVE LANGUAGE DISORDER, MIXED RECEPTIVE-EXPRESSIVE LANGUAGE DISORDER, PHONOLOGICAL DISORDER, and STUTTERING.

communication ergonomics a specialty area of ERGONOMICS that identifies those factors that support or undermine communication in shared tasks. Such factors, including information systems, technical systems, and communication networks and protocols, may be especially important when participants in a task are widely distributed and safety depends on clear, unambiguous communication (as, for example, in air traffic control).

communication skills training an intervention that teaches individuals to express themselves clearly and directly and to listen in an active and empathic way, using such techniques as feedback and modeling, in group, family, or work contexts. Training sessions typically focus on a specific theme (e.g., active listening, problem solving, or conflict resolution) after which homework is assigned. Initially developed for couples and families, the training is now used with such populations as people with developmental impairment and with teams in industry settings.

communicative competence a speaker's knowledge of language and ability to use it appropriately in various communicative settings and with a range of different interlocutors. In contrast to COMPETENCE, which explicitly excludes nonlinguistic factors, the idea of communicative competence stresses the social uses of language and the importance of context.

communicology *n.* an area covering the theory and practice of AUDIOLOGY, speech and language pathology, and improvement in communication.

community *n.* **1.** a socially organized group of people living in a physically defined locality and generally characterized by (a) commonality of interests, attitudes, and values; (b) a general sense of belonging; (c) members' self-identification as community members; and (d) some system of communication, governance, education, and commerce. **2.** in BEHAVIORAL ECOLOGY, a unit comprising all the animal and plant species that coexist and are necessary for each other's survival. Thus a community includes predator and prey species as well as the various plants that animals need for food, shelter, and so forth.

community care comprehensive community-based services and supports for people with developmental or physical disabilities. These facilities or services include sheltered workshops and supported work arrangements, supervised and supportive residences, special education programs for children and young people, in-home treatment and family support, personal-care or home-care assistance, and case management or service coordination.

community correction see ALTERNATIVE SENTENCING.

community inclusion the practice of accepting and encouraging the presence and participation of people with disabilities, in particular developmental disabilities, in the full range of social, educational, work, and community activities.

community integration the practice of assisting people with disabilities, especially developmental disabilities, to participate in community activities. Those with such disabilities are encouraged to attend community functions, engage in social interactions with peers and community members without disabilities, and join formal and informal community groups.

community mental health activities undertaken in the community, rather than in institutional settings, to promote mental health. The community approach focuses primarily on the total population of a single catchment area and involves overall planning and demographic analyses. It emphasizes preventive services as distinguished from therapeutic services (e.g., by identifying sources of stress within the community) and seeks to provide a continuous, comprehensive system of services designed to meet all mental health-related needs in the community.

community mental health center (**CMHC**) a community-based facility or group of facilities providing a full range of prevention, treatment, and rehabilitation services, including full diagnostic evaluation, outpatient individual and group psychotherapy, emergency inpatient treatment, substance abuse treatment, and vocational, educational, and social rehabilitation programs.

community prevention and intervention organized efforts by professionals and others with special competence to deal actively and constructively with community problems and to implement preventive programs as well as systems for intervention. Issues addressed in this way include substance abuse, homelessness, child abuse, juvenile delinquency, and a high suicide rate.

community psychology the branch of psychology that focuses on social issues, social institutions, and other settings that influence individuals, groups, and organizations. Community researchers examine the ways that individuals interact with each other, social groups (e.g., clubs, churches, schools, families), and the larger culture and environment.

community residence a residential setting, usually serving 3 to 15 people and located in a regular house, with live-in or shift staffing. Community residences, some of which provide clinical services in addition to supervision, personal assistance, and training in everyday living skills, represent the most common out-of-home residential setting for people with mental retardation or developmental disabilities.

community services the complex of community-based services and facilities designed to maintain health and welfare, including mental health clinics, public health and adoption services, family services, vocational training facilities, rehabilitation centers, and living facilities (e.g., halfway houses, home care, and foster-family care).

comorbidity *n.* the simultaneous presence in

an individual of two or more mental or physical illnesses, diseases, or disorders. —**comorbid** *adj.*

companionate love a type of love characterized by strong feelings of intimacy and affection for another person but not accompanied by strong passion or emotional arousal in the other's presence. In these respects, companionate love is distinguished from PASSIONATE LOVE. See also TRIANGULAR THEORY OF LOVE.

comparative judgment a psychophysical judgment in which two or more stimuli are compared with one another or with a given standard.

comparative method an experimental research method of analyzing and comparing the behavior of different species of animals, different cultures of humans, and different age groups of humans and other animals.

comparative neuropsychology the study of the relationships between behavior and neural mechanisms in different animal species and human populations in order to understand the neural mechanisms that underlie behavior and the evolution of brain and behavior.

comparative psychology the study of animal behavior with the dual objective of understanding the behavior of nonhuman animals for its own sake as well as furthering the understanding of human behavior. Comparative psychology usually involves laboratory studies (compare ETHOLOGY) and typically refers to any study involving nonhuman species, whether or not the COMPARATIVE METHOD is used. See also ANIMAL–HUMAN COMPARISON.

comparative rating scale see ABSOLUTE RATING SCALE.

comparator hypothesis a theory of PAVLOVIAN CONDITIONING proposing that the strength of conditioning is based on comparing the likelihood that an unconditioned stimulus will occur following a conditioned stimulus with the likelihood that it will occur in the absence of a conditioned stimulus. It predicts that a response will be observed only if the former probability is higher.

compartmentalization *n.* a DEFENSE MECHANISM in which thoughts and feelings that seem to conflict or to be incompatible are isolated from each other in separate and apparently impermeable psychic compartments. In the classical psychoanalytic tradition, compartmentalization produces fragmentation of the EGO, which ideally should be able to tolerate ambiguity and ambivalence. See also ISOLATION. —**compartmentalize** *vb.*

compassion *n.* a strong feeling of SYMPATHY with another person's feelings of sorrow or distress, usually involving a desire to help or comfort that person. —**compassionate** *adj.*

compassion fatigue the BURNOUT and stress-related symptoms experienced by caregivers and other helping professionals in reaction to working with traumatized people over an extended period of time.

compensation *n.* **1.** substitution or development of strength or capability in one area to offset real or imagined lack or deficiency in another. This may be referred to as **overcompensation** when the substitute behavior exceeds what might actually be necessary in terms of level of compensation for the lack or deficiency. Compensation may be a conscious or unconscious process. In his classical psychoanalytic theory, Austrian psychiatrist Sigmund Freud (1856–1939) described compensation as a DEFENSE MECHANISM that protects the individual against the conscious realization of such lacks or deficiencies. The idea of compensation is central to the personality theory of Austrian psychiatrist Alfred Adler (1870–1937), which sees all human striving as a response to feelings of inferiority (see also INFERIORITY COMPLEX). However, many psychologists emphasize the positive aspects of compensation in mitigating the effects of a weakness or deficiency (see COMPENSATORY MECHANISM). **2.** in PIAGETIAN THEORY, a mental process—a form of REVERSIBILITY—in which one realizes that for any operation there exists another operation that compensates for the effects of the first, that is, a change in one dimension can compensate for changes in another. Also called **reciprocity**. —**compensate** *vb.* —**compensatory** *adj.*

compensation effect an increase in group performance that occurs when one or more members work harder to compensate for the real or imagined shortcomings of their fellow members. Compare KÖHLER EFFECT; SUCKER EFFECT.

compensatory education educational programs that are specially designed to enhance the intellectual and social skills of disadvantaged children.

compensatory mechanism a cognitive process that is used to offset a cognitive weakness. For example, someone who is weaker in spatial abilities than in verbal abilities might use compensatory mechanisms to attempt to solve spatial problems, such as mentally rotating a geometric figure by using verbal processes. The underlying theory is that intelligence partly consists of finding ways to compensate for the skills that one has lost over time or in which one was not adept in the first place.

compensatory task a task or project that a group can complete by averaging together individual members' solutions or recommendations. Groups outperform individuals on such tasks when the members are equally proficient at the task and do not share common biases that produce systematic tendencies toward overestimation or underestimation. Compare ADDITIVE TASK; CONJUNCTIVE TASK; DISJUNCTIVE TASK.

competence *n.* **1.** the ability to exert control over one's life, to cope with specific problems effectively, and to make changes to one's behavior and one's environment. Affirming, strengthening, or achieving a client's competence is often a basic goal in psychotherapy. **2.** one's developed repertoire of skills, especially as it is applied to a task or set of tasks. **3.** in linguistics and psycholinguistics, the unconscious knowledge of the underlying rules of a language that enables individuals to speak and understand it. In this sense, competence must be kept distinct from the actual linguistic **performance** of any particular speaker, which may be constrained by such nonlinguistic factors as memory, attention, or fatigue. **4.** in law, the capacity to comprehend the nature of a transaction and to assume legal responsibility for one's actions. See also COMPETENCY TO STAND TRIAL; INCOMPETENCE. Also called **competency**. —**competent** *adj.*

competence knowledge see LEGITIMACY KNOWLEDGE.

competency-based instruction a teaching method in which students work at their own pace toward individual goals in a noncompetitive setting. The teacher works with students in identifying appropriate goals and monitoring their progress toward those goals.

competency to stand trial the capacity to be tried in court as determined by a person's ability, at the time of trial, to understand and appreciate the criminal proceedings against him or her, to consult with an attorney with a reasonable degree of understanding, and to make and express choices among available options. It is a component of ADJUDICATIVE COMPETENCE.

competing response training a technique in BEHAVIOR THERAPY that involves two sequential stages: (a) identification of habit occurrence, including antecedents and warning signs; and (b) creation and practice, in session and through homework, of a competing (i.e., alternative) response to the problem behavior. The competing response should be physically incompatible with the behavioral habit, inconspicuous, and easy to practice. This technique is typically used with habit disorders and is also used in ANGER MANAGEMENT training. See also ALTERNATIVE BEHAVIOR COMPLETION.

competition *n.* any performance situation structured in such a way that success depends on performing better than others. **Interpersonal competition** involves individuals striving to outperform each other; **intergroup competition** involves groups competing against other groups; **intragroup competition** involves individuals within a group trying to best each other. Because competing individuals sometimes increase their chances of success by actively undermining others' performances, such goal structures can create intense rivalries. Compare COOPERATION. —**compete** *vb.* —**competitive** *adj.*

competitiveness *n.* a disposition to compare one's performance against a standard or another person of comparable ability and to seek out situations involving such comparisons. —**competitive** *adj.*

complementarity *n.* see HETEROPHILY.

complementary and alternative medicine (**CAM**) a group of therapies and health care systems that fall outside the realm of conventional Western medical practice. These include but are not limited to ACUPUNCTURE, CHIROPRACTIC, MEDITATION, AROMATHERAPY, HOMEOPATHY, NATUROPATHY, OSTEOPATHY, TOUCH THERAPY, REFLEXOLOGY, REIKI, and the use of certain dietary supplements. Complementary medicine is used as an adjunct to conventional treatment; alternative medicine stands alone and replaces conventional treatment.

completion test a type of test in which the participant is required to supply a missing item, such as a word, number, or symbol.

complex *n.* a group or system of related ideas or impulses that have a common emotional tone and exert a strong but usually unconscious influence on the individual's attitudes and behavior. The term, introduced by Swiss psychoanalyst Carl Jung (1875–1961) to denote the contents of the PERSONAL UNCONSCIOUS, has taken on an almost purely pathological connotation in popular usage, which does not necessarily reflect usage in psychology.

complex cell a neuron in the cerebral cortex that responds to visual stimulation of appropriate contrast, orientation, and direction anywhere in the receptive field. Compare SIMPLE CELL.

complexity hypothesis a hypothesis that conscious events result from neural systems in the DYNAMIC CORE that have high levels of complexity, a mathematical quantity defined as a joint function of neuronal integration and differentiation.

complexity of an attitude the number of distinct dimensions underlying attitude-relevant knowledge. The greater the number of dimensions (i.e., distinct categories of attitude-relevant information), the greater the complexity of an attitude.

complex partial seizure a PARTIAL SEIZURE during which the individual is in an impaired or altered, often trancelike, state of consciousness, typically accompanied by PARAMNESIAS, and may experience such emotions as fear, anxiety, or (less commonly) sadness or pleasure. Stereotyped motor behavior includes grimacing, sucking, chewing, and swallowing, and there may be visual or olfactory hallucinations. Such seizures are commonly associated with abnormal discharges from neurons in the temporal lobe.

complex reaction time the REACTION TIME of a participant in a task that requires him or her to make one of several different responses depending on which one of several different stimuli is presented. Compare CHOICE REACTION TIME; SIMPLE REACTION TIME.

complex tone a sound that consists of two or more components of different frequencies. Compare PURE TONE.

compliance *n.* **1.** submission to the desires of others, often involving a change in a person's behavior in response to a direct request. A variety of techniques have been developed to enhance compliance with requests. Although some techniques may enhance compliance by producing attitude change, behavioral change is the primary goal of these techniques. **2.** in pharmacotherapy, see ADHERENCE. —**compliant** *adj.* —**comply** *vb.*

complicated grief a response to death (or, sometimes, to other significant loss or trauma) that deviates significantly from normal expectations. Three different types of complicated grief are posited: chronic grief, which is more intense, prolonged, or both; delayed grief; and absent grief. The most often observed form of complicated grief is the pattern in which the immediate response to the loss is exceptionally devastating and in which the passage of time does not moderate the emotional pain or restore competent functioning.

complication *n.* an additional disease, disorder, or condition that occurs or develops during the course of another disease or disorder or during a medical procedure. See also COMORBIDITY.

componential analysis 1. any analysis in which a process or system is separated into a series of subprocesses or components. For example, semantics componential analysis involves breaking words down into their separate elements (e.g., man = human + male). **2.** more specifically, a set of information-processing and mathematical techniques that enables an investigator to decompose an individual's performance on a cognitive task into the underlying elementary COGNITIVE PROCESSES. For example, solving an analogy requires encoding of stimuli, inference of the relation between the first two terms of the analogy, and so forth.

componential subtheory see TRIARCHIC THEORY OF INTELLIGENCE.

components-of-variance model an ANOVA (ANALYSIS OF VARIANCE) model in which the parameters of the model are conceived of as RANDOM VARIABLES rather than fixed constants. Also called **random model**.

composite reliability the aggregate reliability of two or more items or judges' ratings. CRONBACH'S ALPHA is an example.

compos mentis in law, mentally competent, that is, neither mentally deficient nor legally insane. See COMPETENCE. Compare NON COMPOS MENTIS.

compound reaction time the total time that elapses between the presentation of a stimulus and the occurrence of a response in a task that requires the participant to make a conscious decision before responding. The time actually required to decide on a response can be calculated using DONDERS'S METHOD.

compound schedule of reinforcement a procedure for studying a single response in which two or more schedules of reinforcement are arranged to alternate, to appear in succession, or to be in effect simultaneously (i.e., concurrently).

comprehension *n.* the act or capability of understanding something, especially the meaning of a communication. Compare APPREHENSION. —**comprehend** *vb.*

comprehensive assessment service a team of professionals, often affiliated with a health care system or hospital, who perform multiple assessments of patients. The team's purposes are to identify specific health conditions and behavioral factors affecting an individual's growth and development and to enhance the value of the individual's referral to subsequent specialized educational or developmental services.

comprehensive functional assessment an assessment that is broad in scope, often implemented by an interdisciplinary team, and most frequently focuses on a person with mental retardation or a related condition. It typically incorporates findings regarding specific developmental strengths and individual preferences, specific functional and adaptive social skills that the individual needs to learn, the nature of any presenting disabilities and their causes, and the need for a wide range of services.

compression *n.* in neurology, pressure on the brain, spinal cord, or a nerve.

compromise formation in psychoanalytic theory, the conscious form of a repressed wish or idea that has been modified or disguised, as in a dream or symptom, so as to be unrecognizable. Thus it represents a compromise between the demands of the ego's defenses and the unconscious wish.

compulsion *n.* a type of behavior (e.g., hand washing, checking) or a mental act (e.g., counting, praying) engaged in to reduce anxiety or distress. Typically the individual feels driven or compelled to perform the compulsion to reduce the distress associated with an OBSESSION or to prevent a dreaded event or situation. Compulsions may also take the form of rigid or stereotyped acts based on idiosyncratic rules that do not have a rational basis (e.g., having to perform a task in a certain way). Compulsions do not provide pleasure or gratification and are disproportionate or irrelevant to the feared situation they are used to neutralize. See OBSESSIVE-COMPULSIVE DISORDER. —**compulsive** *adj.*

compulsive disorder any disorder in which the individual feels forced to perform acts that are against his or her wishes or better judgment. The act may be associated with an experience of pleasure or gratification (e.g., compulsive gambling) or with the reduction of anxiety or distress

(e.g., rituals in OBSESSIVE-COMPULSIVE DISORDER).

compunction *n.* distress or guilt associated with wrongdoing or with an anticipated action or result.

computational linguistics an interdisciplinary field of study in which techniques from computer science and artificial intelligence are used to model theories based on linguistic analysis. Computers have been used experimentally to evaluate a range of hypotheses about phonetic perception and language processing. More practical applications have included the development of automatic translation systems and programs that can simulate or transcribe human speech.

computational model any account of cognitive or psychobiological processes that assumes that the human mind functions like a digital computer, specifically in its ability to form representations of events and objects and to carry out complex sequences of operations on these representations.

computed tomography (**CT**) a radiographic technique for quickly producing detailed, three-dimensional images of the brain or other soft tissues. An X-ray beam is passed through the tissue from many different locations, and the different patterns of radiation absorption are analyzed and synthesized by a computer. Also called **computerized axial tomography** (**CAT**); **computerized tomography**. See also MAGNETIC RESONANCE IMAGING.

computer adaptive testing (**CAT**) a method of computer testing for particular skills or abilities in which the test items are automatically adjusted to match the level of proficiency demonstrated by the participant. The difficulty level of the items is reduced after an incorrect answer and increased after a correct answer. The testing stops once the participant's ability has been estimated to a predetermined level of accuracy.

computer-assisted instruction a sophisticated offshoot of programmed learning, in which a computer is used to provide drill and practice, problem solving, simulation, and gaming forms of instruction. It is also useful for relatively individualized tutorial instruction. Also called **computer-assisted learning**.

computerized assessment evaluation of psychological information about an individual using a computer with access to databases that store previously acquired information from many other individuals in order to make comparisons, diagnoses, and prognoses. Also called **automated assessment**.

computerized diagnosis the use of computer programs for cataloging, storing, comparing, and evaluating psychological and medical data as an aid to CLINICAL DIAGNOSIS. Computerized diagnosis makes use of information based on thousands of similar or related sets of signs and symptoms of previous patients, as well as information on diagnoses and effective treatments stored in databases.

computerized therapy the use of a specially programmed computer to provide therapy, under the auspices of a trained therapist. Computers have been used for assessment, history taking, diagnosis, patient education, and intervention. Computer therapy software operates through a series of if–then statements, which determine how the computer responds to explicit input by the individual.

computer model a computer simulation of an external entity, such as a psychological function, for the purpose of helping to understand its components. Such models are often explicitly designed to investigate specific theories rather than explore general issues. In cognitive psychology, for example, a computer model might be used to enable a scientist to approximate, manipulate, and revise the decision-making processes of a human playing a game of chess.

conation *n.* the proactive (as opposed to habitual) part of motivation that connects knowledge, affect, drives, desires, and instincts to behavior. Along with cognition and affect, conation is one of the three traditionally identified components of mind.

conative *adj.* characterized by volition or self-activation toward a goal.

concentration *n.* **1.** the act of bringing together or focusing, as, for example, bringing one's thought processes to bear on a central problem or subject (see ATTENTION). **2.** the proportion of a dissolved substance in a solution or mixture. **—concentrate** *vb.*

concentrative meditation a type of MEDITATION that focuses on a single stimulus (e.g., breathing); a specific image; a specific sound, syllable, word, or phrase; or a specific thought. It is the opposite of INSIGHT in that thoughts unrelated to the stimulus do not enter the consciousness. See also TRANSCENDENTAL MEDITATION.

concept *n.* **1.** an idea that represents a class of objects or events or their properties, such as "cats," "walking," "honesty," "blue," or "fast." **2.** in conditioning, a class of stimuli to which an organism responds in a similar or identical manner (see STIMULUS GENERALIZATION) and that an organism discriminates from other classes. **—conceptual** *adj.*

concept-discovery task a task in which the participant must try to discern the rule used to define members and nonmembers of a category. Also called **concept-identification task**.

concept-formation test any test used in studying the process of concept formation and in assessing the level of concept acquisition achieved by a specific individual.

concept learning learning the defining features that are characteristic or prototypical of a class (e.g., those describing a bird) or those features that are necessary and sufficient to identify members of a class of objects, relations, or actions (e.g., the concepts triangle, above, or move).

conceptual complexity the degree to which an idea or an argument is difficult to understand, owing to the number of abstract CONCEPTS involved and the intricate ways in which they connect. See also COGNITIVE COMPLEXITY.

conceptual dependency a formalized SEMANTIC NETWORK designed to capture semantic relationships in human language for use in computer programs related to understanding NATURAL LANGUAGE. There are four primitive (or atomic) components of this theory: actions, objects (picture producers), modifiers of actions, and modifiers of objects. See also COMPUTATIONAL LINGUISTICS.

conceptual disorganization irrelevant, rambling, or incoherent verbalizations, frequently including NEOLOGISMS and stereotyped expressions. It is one of the major signs of disorganized thought processes.

conceptually driven processing see TOP-DOWN PROCESSING.

conceptual model a diagram, such as a tree diagram, used to represent in visual form the relations between concepts or between concepts and their attributes.

conceptual nervous system a hypothetical model of the neurological and physiological functions of the nervous system that can be manipulated to provide analogies of behavioral activities. Critics claim that research should be concentrated on the actual nervous system rather than on this type of model, while proponents note that modeling properties of the nervous system has been fruitful in encouraging research.

conclusion *n.* **1.** in logic and philosophy, the proposition to which a line of argument or analysis leads. The conclusion is that which an argument is intended to establish as valid. See INFERENCE. **2.** in science, a general law or principle derived from experimental evidence by a process of INDUCTION.

concomitance *n.* **1.** the co-occurrence of two or more phenomena, especially such that the phenomena are essentially different manifestations of a single underlying reality. For example, a symbol and its meaning may be concomitant. According to Jungian psychology, synchronous events may be concomitant in this way (see SYNCHRONICITY). **2.** in statistics and experimental psychology, unwanted co-occurrence between the dependent variable (i.e., the one under investigation) and a variable other than the independent variable. Certain statistical procedures, such as ANALYSIS OF COVARIANCE, allow the effect to be controlled. **—concomitant** *adj.*

concordance *n.* **1.** the state or condition of being in harmony or agreement. **Affective con-**

cordance is said to exist, for instance, when facial gestures mirror internal states of feeling, such as frowning when perplexed or annoyed, or, in another context, when two or more individuals related through some condition or activity experience the same or similar emotional reactions. **2.** in TWIN STUDIES, the presence of a given trait or disorder in both members of the pair. Evidence for genetic factors in the production of the trait or disorder comes from the comparison of concordance rates between identical and fraternal twins. Compare DISCORDANCE.

concrete intelligence the ability to understand and manipulate objects. It is often contrasted with ABSTRACT INTELLIGENCE and SOCIAL INTELLIGENCE.

concrete operational stage in PIAGETIAN THEORY, the third major stage of cognitive development, occurring approximately from 7 to 12 years of age, in which children can decenter their perception (see DECENTRATION), are less egocentric, and can think logically about physical objects and about specific situations or experiences involving those objects.

concretism *n.* **1.** in ANALYTIC PSYCHOLOGY, a type of thought or feeling that is dependent on immediate physical sensation and displays little or no capacity for abstraction. In some traditional societies, such thinking may manifest itself in fetishism and belief in magic. In the modern world, it may display itself as an inability to think beyond the obvious material facts of a situation. **2.** see CONCRETE OPERATIONAL STAGE.

concurrent schedules of reinforcement a procedure in OPERANT CONDITIONING in which two or more separate reinforcement schedules, each associated with an independent OPERANT (response), are in effect simultaneously.

concurrent therapy 1. the use of two treatments at the same time. **2.** in MARITAL THERAPY and FAMILY THERAPY, the simultaneous treatment of spouses or other family members in individual or group therapy, either by the same therapist or different therapists. See also COMBINED THERAPY.

concurrent validity the extent of correspondence between two measurements at about the same point in time: specifically, the assessment of one test's validity by comparison of its results with a separate but related measurement, such as a standardized test, at the same point in time.

concussion *n.* mild injury to the brain due to trauma or jarring that temporarily disrupts function and usually involves at least brief unconsciousness.

condensation *n.* the fusion of several meanings, concepts, or emotions into one image or symbol. Condensation is particularly common in dreams, in which, for example, one person may exhibit the characteristics of several or one behavior may represent several feelings or reactions.

condition 1. *n.* a logical antecedent on which a conclusion is dependent or an empirical antecedent on which an event or state is dependent. A **necessary condition** is one without which the idea would not logically follow or the event would not occur. A **sufficient condition** is one that directly entails a particular conclusion or that has the power to produce a particular event regardless of other conditions. **2.** *vb.* to inculcate a response or a behavior in an organism by means of PAVLOVIAN CONDITIONING, OPERANT CONDITIONING, or other behaviorist paradigms (see BEHAVIORISM). The term implies that the learning is largely automatic, based on processes more like reflexes than conscious mental activity. **—conditional** *adj.*

conditional discrimination a DISCRIMINATION in which reinforcement of a response in the presence of a stimulus depends on the presence of other stimuli. For example, in a MATCHING-TO-SAMPLE procedure, responding to a comparison stimulus that matches the sample stimulus is reinforced; that is, determining the correctness of a response depends on the sample stimulus.

conditional positive regard an attitude of acceptance and esteem expressed by others that depends on the acceptability of the individual's behavior and the other's personal standards. Conditional regard works against sound psychological development and adjustment in the recipient. Compare UNCONDITIONAL POSITIVE REGARD.

conditional probability the probability that an event will occur given that another event is known to have occurred.

conditional strategy the ability of organisms to develop different behavioral strategies appropriate for current contexts and conditions. An experienced adult male animal, for example, might actively defend a territory and guard females, while a young male does not, instead attempting to copulate with available females. If the resident male dies or disappears, the young male can rapidly change strategies to become a territory-defending male.

conditioned avoidance response an acquired (learned) response that prevents, postpones, or reduces the frequency or intensity of an aversive stimulus. A conditioned response that stops an aversive stimulus is known as a **conditioned escape response**. For example, if a monkey learns to press a lever that turns off a loud noise, the lever press is a conditioned escape response. See AVOIDANCE CONDITIONING.

conditioned emotional response any negative emotional response, typically fear or anxiety, that becomes associated with a neutral stimulus as a result of PAVLOVIAN CONDITIONING. It is the basis for CONDITIONED SUPPRESSION.

conditioned inhibition the diminution of a CONDITIONED RESPONSE that occurs on presentation of a stimulus that has previously been experienced in different circumstances.

conditioned place preference a technique for determining if experience with certain stimuli renders the place where that experience occurred reinforcing. For example, a rat might be injected with cocaine and then restricted to one side of a two-compartment chamber. After a number of trials, a test is conducted in which the rat can freely move between the two compartments. If the rat spends a majority of its time on the side in which it experienced cocaine, an inference is drawn that the dose of cocaine was reinforcing. Also called **place conditioning**.

conditioned reinforcer a neutral stimulus that acquires the ability to act as a reinforcer, usually by being paired with a primary reinforcer (see PRIMARY REINFORCEMENT) or established as a DISCRIMINATIVE STIMULUS. For example, food may be paired with a token, which then becomes the conditioned reinforcer. Also called **secondary reinforcer**.

conditioned response (**CR**) in PAVLOVIAN CONDITIONING, the learned or acquired response to a conditioned stimulus.

conditioned stimulus (**CS**) a neutral stimulus that is repeatedly presented with an UNCONDITIONED STIMULUS until it acquires the ability to elicit a response that it previously did not. In many (but not all) cases, the response elicited by the conditioned stimulus is similar to that elicited by the unconditioned stimulus. A light, for example, by being repeatedly paired with food (the unconditioned stimulus), eventually comes to elicit the same response as food (i.e., salivation) when presented alone.

conditioned suppression a phenomenon that occurs during an OPERANT performance test when a CONDITIONED RESPONSE to a positive stimulus is reduced by another stimulus that is associated with an aversive stimulus. For example, a rat may be trained to press a lever in order to receive food. During this procedure, the rat is occasionally exposed to a series of brief electric shocks that are preceded by a tone (the conditioned stimulus). As a result, when the rat subsequently hears the tone alone, its rate of lever pressing is reduced.

conditioned taste aversion the association of the taste of a food or fluid with an aversive stimulus (usually gastrointestinal discomfort or illness) and subsequent avoidance of that particular taste. Conditioned taste aversion challenges traditional theories of associative learning, since very few PAIRINGS between the food and illness are needed to produce the effect (often one pairing will suffice), the delay between experiencing the taste and then feeling ill can be relatively long, and the aversion is highly resistant to EXTINCTION. Also called **learned taste aversion**; **toxicosis**.

conditioning *n.* the process by which certain kinds of experience make particular actions more or less likely. See INSTRUMENTAL CONDITIONING; OPERANT CONDITIONING; PAVLOVIAN CONDITIONING.

conditions of worth the state in which an individual considers love and respect to be conditional on meeting the approval of others. This belief derives from the child's sense of being worthy of love on the basis of parental approval: As the individual matures, he or she may continue to feel worthy of affection and respect only when expressing desirable behaviors.

conduct *n.* the behavior of an individual, either generally or on a specific occasion, usually as it conforms to or violates social norms.

conduct disorder a persistent pattern of behavior that involves violating the basic rights of others and ignoring age-appropriate social standards. Specific behaviors include lying, theft, arson, running away from home, aggression, truancy, burglary, cruelty to animals, and fighting. This disorder is distinguished from OPPOSITIONAL DEFIANT DISORDER by the increased severity of the behaviors and their occurrence independently of an event occasioning opposition.

conduction *n.* in physiology, the transmission of excitation along a nerve, muscle, or other tissue. In a neuron, subthreshold stimulation results in DECREMENTAL CONDUCTION, whereas suprathreshold stimulation results in a propagated ACTION POTENTIAL, or nerve impulse.

conduction aphasia a form of APHASIA characterized by difficulty in differentiating speech sounds and repeating them accurately, even though spontaneous articulation may be intact. It is associated with lesions in the ARCUATE FASCICULUS, the tract linking the areas of the brain involved in the interpretation and control of speech.

conduction deafness see DEAFNESS.

cone *n.* see RETINAL CONE.

confabulation *n.* the falsification of memory in which gaps in recall are filled by fabrications that the individual accepts as fact. It is not typically considered to be a conscious attempt to deceive others. Confabulation occurs most frequently in KORSAKOFF'S SYNDROME and to a lesser extent in other conditions associated with organically derived amnesia. —**confabulate** *vb.*

confederate *n.* **1.** in an experimental situation, an aide of the experimenter who poses as a participant but whose behavior is rehearsed prior to the experiment. The real participants are sometimes referred to as NAIVE PARTICIPANTS. See also ACTIVE DECEPTION. **2.** in parapsychology, an individual who assists a supposed PSYCHIC by covertly providing him or her with information about a client's concerns, preferences, background, or situation, thus creating or strengthening the illusion of the psychic's paranormal abilities.

confidence interval a range of values (an interval) used for estimating the value of a population parameter from data obtained in a SAMPLE, with a preset, fixed probability that the interval will include the true value of the population parameter being estimated. Most research is done on samples, but it is done in order to draw inferences about the entire relevant population.

confidence limits the upper and lower end points of a CONFIDENCE INTERVAL; that is, the values between which the value of the parameter is anticipated with a known probability to be.

confidentiality *n.* a principle of PROFESSIONAL ETHICS requiring providers of mental health care or medical care to limit the disclosure of a patient's identity, his or her condition or treatment, and any data entrusted to professionals during assessment, diagnosis, and treatment. Similar protection is given to research participants and survey respondents against unauthorized access to information they reveal in confidence. —**confidential** *adj.*

configural learning learning to respond to a combination of two or more stimuli paired with an outcome when none of the stimuli presented alone is paired with that outcome. For example, if neither a tone nor a light presented separately is followed by food, but a tone–light combination is followed by food, configural learning has occurred when a conditioned response is elicited by the tone–light combination.

configural superiority effect in visual perception, a phenomenon in which a configuration of elements or features is easier to identify than a single feature alone. Examples include the WORD-SUPERIORITY EFFECT and the OBJECT-SUPERIORITY EFFECT.

confirmation bias the tendency to gather evidence that confirms preexisting expectations, typically by emphasizing or pursuing supporting evidence while dismissing or failing to seek contradictory evidence.

confirmatory factor analysis one of a set of procedures used in FACTOR ANALYSIS to demonstrate that a group of variables possess a theoretically expected factor structure. In other words, confirmatory factor analysis provides formal statistical tests of a priori hypotheses about the specific underlying (latent) variables thought to explain the data obtained on a set of observed (manifest) variables. Unlike EXPLORATORY FACTOR ANALYSIS, in which all measured variables relate to all latent factors, confirmatory factor analysis imposes explicit restrictions so that the measured variables relate with some (or usually just one) latent factors but do not relate with others.

confirmatory research research conducted with the goal of being able to test certain prespecified hypotheses.

conflict *n.* the occurrence of mutually antagonistic or opposing forces, including events, behaviors, desires, attitudes, and emotions. This general term has more specific meanings within different areas of psychology. For example, in psychoanalytic theory it refers to the opposition between incompatible instinctual impulses or between incompatible aspects of the mental structure (i.e., the ID, EGO, and SUPEREGO) that may be a source of NEUROSIS if it results in the use of defense mechanisms other than SUBLIMATION. In interpersonal relations conflict denotes the disagreement, discord, and friction that occur when the actions or beliefs of one or more individuals are unacceptable to and resisted by others.

conflict-free sphere in EGO PSYCHOLOGY, an area of the ego that develops and functions without giving rise to internal conflict. Functions ordinarily controlled by the conflict-free sphere include speech, motility, and other autonomous ego functions. Also called **conflict-free area**.

conflict theory a sociological approach that stresses the inevitability of conflict in any setting in which resources are unevenly distributed among interactants. See REALISTIC GROUP-CONFLICT THEORY.

confluence model a controversial and probably untenable theory that intelligence of siblings is correlated with family size. According to this model, average intelligence generally declines with BIRTH ORDER.

conformity *n.* the adjustment of one's opinions, judgments, or actions so that they match either (a) the opinions, judgments, or actions of other people or (b) the normative standards of a social group or situation. Conformity includes the temporary COMPLIANCE of individuals, who agree publicly with the group but do not accept its position as their own, as well as the CONVERSION of individuals, who fully adopt the group position. Compare ANTICONFORMITY; NONCONFORMITY. See also MAJORITY INFLUENCE; PEER PRESSURE.

confound *n.* in an experiment using a FACTORIAL DESIGN, a variable that is conceptually distinct but empirically inseparable from one or more other variables. **Confounding** makes it impossible to differentiate that variable's effects in isolation from its effects in conjunction with other variables. These indistinguishable effects are themselves called **aliases**.

confrontation *n.* the act of directly facing, or being encouraged or required to face, a difficult situation, realization, discrepancy, or contradiction involving information, beliefs, attitudes, or behavior. Confrontational techniques may be used therapeutically, for example, to reveal and invite self-examination of inconsistencies in a client's reported and actual behavior, but they have a potential for disruptive as well as constructive effects. —**confrontational** *adj.*

confusion *n.* a disturbance of consciousness

characterized by inability to think clearly or act decisively and DISORIENTATION for time, place, and person.

confusion effect see ANTIPREDATOR BEHAVIOR.

confusion of responsibility the tendency for bystanders to refrain from helping in both emergencies and nonemergencies in order to avoid being blamed by others for causing the problem. This is a contributing factor in the BYSTANDER EFFECT. See also DIFFUSION OF RESPONSIBILITY.

congenital *adj.* denoting a condition or disorder that is present at birth. Also called **connate**.

congenital adrenal hyperplasia an inherited disorder caused by mutations that encode for enzymes involved in one of the various steps of steroid hormone synthesis in the adrenal gland. These defects result in the absence or decreased synthesis of CORTISOL from its cholesterol precursor and a concomitant abnormal increase in the production of androgens. Also called (in older literature especially) **adrenogenital syndrome**.

congenital defect any abnormality present at birth, regardless of the cause. It may be caused by faulty fetal development (e.g., spina bifida, cleft palate), hereditary factors (e.g., Huntington's disease), chromosomal aberration (e.g., Down syndrome), maternal conditions affecting the developing fetus (e.g., fetal alcohol syndrome), metabolic defects (e.g., phenylketonuria), or injury to the brain before or during birth (e.g., some cases of cerebral palsy). A congenital defect may not be apparent until several years after birth or even until after the individual has reached adulthood. Also called **birth defect**; **congenital anomaly**.

congregate living facility a residential complex in which older adults live independently but take meals together as well as share some other social activities.

congruence *n.* in phenomenological personality theory, (a) the need for a therapist to act in accordance with his or her true feelings rather than with a stylized image of a therapist or (b) the conscious integration of an experience into the self. —**congruent** *adj.*

congruity theory a COGNITIVE CONSISTENCY THEORY that focuses on the role of persuasive communications in attitude change. Congruity theory is similar to BALANCE THEORY in that it postulates that people tend to prefer elements within a cognitive system to be internally consistent with one another but differs in taking into account gradations of evaluation of elements and therefore makes more precise predictions regarding the magnitude of change required to restore congruity among elements.

conjoint schedule a type of COMPOUND SCHEDULE OF REINFORCEMENT under which two or more schedules of reinforcement operate simultaneously for a single response.

conjoint therapy therapy in which the partners in a relationship or members of a family are treated together in joint sessions by one or more therapists, instead of being treated separately. The technique is commonly applied in resolving marital disputes, when it is also known as **conjoint marital therapy**. Also called **conjoint counseling**. See also COUPLES THERAPY; FAMILY THERAPY.

conjugate reinforcement a REINFORCEMENT CONTINGENCY in which some aspect of the reinforcer (e.g., its magnitude) varies systematically with some property of behavior (e.g., rate or force).

conjunctive concept a concept that is defined by a set of attributes, every member of which must be present for the concept to apply. For example, the concept "brother" requires the joint presence of the attributes (a) male and (b) sibling, neither of which may be omitted. Compare DISJUNCTIVE CONCEPT.

conjunctive task a group task or project that cannot be completed successfully until all members of the group have completed their portion of the job (e.g., a factory assembly line). This means that the speed and quality of the work are determined by the least skilled member. Compare ADDITIVE TASK; COMPENSATORY TASK; DISJUNCTIVE TASK.

connectionism *n.* **1.** an approach that views human cognitive processes in terms of massively parallel cooperative and competitive interactions among large numbers of simple neuronlike computational units. Although each unit exhibits nonlinear spatial and temporal summation, units and connections are not generally to be taken as corresponding directly to individual neurons and synapses. **2.** as used by U.S. psychologist Edward L. Thorndike (1874–1949), the concept that learning involves the acquisition of neural links, or connections, between stimulus and response. —**connectionist** *adj.*

connectionist model any of a class of theories hypothesizing that knowledge is encoded by the connections among representations stored in the brain rather than in the representations themselves. Connectionist models suggest that knowledge is distributed rather than being localized and that it is retrieved through SPREADING ACTIVATION among connections. The connectionist model concept has been extended to artificial intelligence, particularly to its NEURAL NETWORK models of problem solving.

connotative meaning see DENOTATIVE MEANING.

consanguinity *n.* see AFFINITY.

conscience *n.* an individual's sense of right and wrong or of transgression against moral values. In psychoanalysis, conscience is the SUPEREGO, or ethical component of personality, which acts as judge and critic of one's actions and attitudes. More recent biopsychological approaches suggest that the capacity of conscience may be genetically determined, and research on brain damage connects behavioral inhibitions to specific brain regions (e.g., the PREFRONTAL COR-TEX). Psychosocial approaches emphasize the role of conscience in the formation of groups and societies.

conscientiousness *n.* the tendency to be organized, responsible, and hardworking, construed as a dimension of individual differences in the Big Five and FIVE-FACTOR PERSONALITY MODELS. —**conscientious** *adj.*

conscious 1. (Cs) *n.* in the classical psychoanalytic theory of Austrian psychiatrist Sigmund Freud (1856–1939), the region of the psyche that contains thoughts, feelings, perceptions, and other aspects of mental life currently present in awareness. The content of the conscious is thus inherently transitory and continuously changing. Compare PRECONSCIOUS; UNCONSCIOUS. **2.** *adj.* relating to or marked by awareness or consciousness.

conscious access hypothesis the notion that the primary function of consciousness is to mobilize and integrate brain functions that are otherwise separate and independent.

conscious mentalism any theory that posits the reality of purely mental phenomena, such as thinking, feeling, desiring, preferring, and (particularly) intention, holding that these mental phenomena are the chief causes of behavior and that they are available to the conscious mind. The rise of BEHAVIORISM was largely a reaction against MENTALISM as a causal explanation for behavior. While most forms of conscious mentalism hold that mental phenomena have a nonmaterial existence, some recent mentalistic positions have been materialistic, accepting that mental states and processes have their origin in physical states and processes. Compare ELIMINATIVISM; REDUCTIONISM.

consciousness *n.* **1.** the phenomena that humans report experiencing, including mental contents ranging from sensory and somatic perception to mental images, reportable ideas, inner speech, intentions to act, recalled memories, semantics, dreams, hallucinations, emotional feelings, "fringe" feelings (e.g., a sense of knowing), and aspects of cognitive and motor control. Operationally, these **contents of consciousness** are generally assessed by the ability to report an event accurately (see REPORTABILITY). **2.** any of various subjective states of awareness in which conscious contents can be reported. Consciousness most often refers to the ordinary waking state (see WAKEFULNESS), but it may also refer to the state of sleeping or to an ALTERED STATE OF CONSCIOUSNESS. **Sensory consciousness** of the perceptual world depends on the posterior SENSORY AREA of the brain. **Abstract consciousness** refers to abstract ideas, judgments, specific in-

tentions, expectations, and events of FRINGE CONSCIOUSNESS; it may involve the FRONTAL CORTEX in addition to sensory cortex. See also HIGHER ORDER CONSCIOUSNESS.

consciousness-altering substance any of a large class of psychoactive compounds that affect conscious experience and perception. These substances are related to neurotransmitters (e.g., serotonin) and include LSD, CANNABIS, and alcoholic beverages.

conscious resistance in psychoanalysis, the patient's deliberate withholding of unconscious material that has newly risen into consciousness because of shame, fear of rejection, or distrust of the analyst. See RESISTANCE. Compare ID RESISTANCE; REPRESSION-RESISTANCE.

consensual validation the process by which a therapist helps a client check the accuracy of his or her perception or the results of his or her experience by comparing it with those of others, often in the context of GROUP PSYCHOTHERAPY.

consent *n.* voluntary assent or approval given by an individual: specifically, permission granted by an individual for medical or psychological treatment, participation in research, or both. Individuals should be fully informed about the treatment or study and its risks and potential benefits (see INFORMED CONSENT).

consequate *vb.* to occur as a result of a response. If the response becomes more probable, consequation is said to have resulted in REINFORCEMENT. If the response becomes less probable, consequation has resulted in PUNISHMENT. —**consequation** *n.*

consequent *n.* in a conditional proposition of the *if...then* form, the statement that follows the connective *then*. The consequent is what is expected to be the case given that the ANTECEDENT (the statement following *if*) is true. For example, in the conditional proposition, *If Socrates is a man, then he is mortal*, the statement *he is mortal* is the consequent.

conservation *n.* the awareness that physical quantities do not change in amount when they are altered in appearance, such as when water is poured from a wide, short beaker into a thin, tall one. According to PIAGETIAN THEORY, children become capable of this mental operation in the CONCRETE OPERATIONAL STAGE. See also REVERSIBILITY.

conservatorship *n.* a legal arrangement by which an individual is appointed by a court to protect the interests and property of a person who cannot be declared incompetent (see INCOMPETENCE) but is unable by reason of a physical or mental condition to take full responsibility for managing his or her own affairs.

consilience *n.* the view that the laws of physics and the rules of biological evolution underlie all aspects of human existence. All human endeavor should reflect these influences and exhibit a unity based on a few basic scientific principles arising from them.

consistency motive the desire to get feedback that confirms what one already believes about one's self. This contributes to maintaining a stable, unchanging SELF-CONCEPT, whether positive or negative. Compare APPRAISAL MOTIVE; SELF-ENHANCEMENT MOTIVE. See also SELF-VERIFICATION HYPOTHESIS.

consistency theory see COGNITIVE CONSISTENCY THEORY.

consistent mapping a condition of a SEARCH task in which a given stimulus is either (a) always a target or (b) always one of the DISTRACTOR stimuli among which the target is embedded: It is never a target at one time and a distractor at another. Consistent mapping usually produces a much more efficient search performance. Compare VARIED MAPPING.

consolidation n. the biological processes by which a permanent memory is formed following a learning experience. See PERSEVERATION–CONSOLIDATION HYPOTHESIS.

conspicuity n. the ability of an object to attract attention. In attention studies, when a participant searches for a target among DISTRACTORS in a visual display, a target that has conspicuity will tend to be detected rapidly. See POP-OUT.

constancy n. see PERCEPTUAL CONSTANCY.

constancy of the IQ a tendency for IQ, on average, to remain remarkably constant throughout life, as evidenced by similar results on various administrations of measures of intelligence.

constancy principle the general principle that psychic forces and energies tend to remain in a steady or balanced state or tend to seek a return to a state of balance or of decreased energy. The idea is related to other general conceptions of constancy found in many scientific fields. In the psychology of Austrian psychiatrist Sigmund Freud (1856–1939), constancy refers specifically to the tendency of psychic energy, or LIBIDO, to seek a homeostatic or balanced state. The same principle lies behind Freud's notion of CATHARSIS.

constant error a systematic error in some particular direction. Constant error is computed as the average positive or negative difference between the observed and actual values along a dimension of interest. For example, if a weight of 1 kg is judged on average to be 1.5 kg, the constant error is 500 g. See also ABSOLUTE ERROR; RANDOM ERROR.

constitution n. **1.** the sum of an individual's innate characteristics. **2.** more broadly, the basic psychological and physical makeup of an individual, due partly to heredity and partly to life experience and environmental factors. —**constitutional** adj.

constitutional type a classification of individuals based on physique and other biological characteristics or on a hypothetical relationship between physical and psychological characteristics, such as temperament, personality, and a tendency to develop a specific type of mental disorder. See KRETSCHMER TYPOLOGY; SHELDON'S CONSTITUTIONAL THEORY OF PERSONALITY.

construct n. **1.** a complex idea or concept formed from a synthesis of simpler ideas. **2.** an explanatory model based on empirically verifiable and measurable events or processes—an **empirical construct**—or on processes inferred from data of this kind but not themselves directly observable—a **hypothetical construct**. Many of the models used in psychology are hypothetical constructs.

constructionism n. see CONSTRUCTIVISM.

constructive alternativism in the personality construct theory of U.S. psychologist George A. Kelly (1905–1967), the capacity to view the world from multiple perspectives, that is, to envision a variety of alternative constructs.

constructive hypothesis of consciousness the hypothesis that the function of consciousness is to construct experience in a flexible way depending on the context and available mental contents.

constructive memory a form of remembering marked by the use of general knowledge stored in one's memory to construct a more complete and detailed account of an event or experience.

constructive play a form of play in which children manipulate materials in order to create or build objects, for example, making a sand castle or using blocks to build a house.

constructivism n. the theoretical perspective that people actively build their perception of the world and interpret objects and events that surround them in terms of what they already know. Thus, their current state of knowledge guides processing, substantially influencing how (and what) new information is acquired. Also called **constructionism**. See also SOCIAL CONSTRUCTIVISM.

constructivist psychotherapy 1. a form of individual psychotherapy, derived from CONSTRUCTIVISM, that focuses on meaning-making to help clients reconceptualize their problems in a more life-enhancing way using story, myth, poetry, and other linguistic and nonverbal forms. **2.** a group of psychotherapies all of which rely on a philosophy of interpersonal and social processes of meaning-making. Such therapies are typically derived from constructivism and encompass developments in existential, humanistic, and family therapy. See also NARRATIVE PSYCHOTHERAPY.

constructivist theory of emotion any theory holding that emotions are not INNATE but constructed through social and cultural experience. See SOCIAL CONSTRUCTIVISM.

construct validity the degree to which a test or instrument is capable of measuring a theoretical construct, trait, or ability (e.g., intelligence).

consultant *n.* a mental health care or medical specialist called upon to provide professional advice or services in terms of diagnosis, treatment, or rehabilitation.

consulting psychology the branch of psychology that provides expert psychological guidance to business and industry, federal and state agencies, the armed forces, educational and scientific groups, religious groups, and volunteer and public service organizations. Consulting psychologists offer a wide variety of services, the most common of which are individual assessment, individual and group-process consultation, organizational development, education and training, employee selection and appraisal, research and evaluation test construction, management coaching, and change management.

consumer *n.* an individual who purchases (or otherwise acquires) and uses goods or services. In the context of medical and mental health care, consumers are those who purchase or receive health care services.

consumerism *n.* a movement to protect the rights of the consumer with regard to the quality and safety of available products and services (including psychotherapeutic and medical care). Consumers of mental health care have a number of clearly defined rights, including the right to know, to confidentiality, to choice, to determination of treatment, to nondiscrimination, to treatment review, and to accountability of treating professionals. —**consumerist** *adj.*

consumer psychology the branch of psychology that specializes in the behavior of individuals as consumers and in the techniques of communicating information to influence consumer decisions to purchase a manufacturer's product. **Consumer psychologists** investigate the reasons and psychological processes underlying behavior in for-profit as well as not-for-profit marketing.

consummatory response the final response in a chain of behavior directed toward the satisfaction of a need, resulting in a reduction in a particular DRIVE. Thus eating (to reduce hunger) is the final act of foraging behavior, and copulation (to reduce the sex drive) is the final act of sexual behavior.

contact comfort the positive effects experienced by infants or young animals when in close contact with soft materials. The term originates from experiments in which young rhesus monkeys exposed both to an artificial cloth mother without a bottle for feeding and to an artificial wire mother with a bottle for feeding spent more time on the cloth mother and, when frightened, were more readily soothed by the presence of the cloth mother than the wire mother.

contact desensitization a variation of SYSTEMATIC DESENSITIZATION involving PARTICI-PANT MODELING instead of relaxation training: used especially in the treatment of anxiety. The therapist demonstrates appropriate behaviors, beginning with those in the weakest anxiety-provoking situation for the client, and then assists the client in performing such behaviors. For example, in working with a client who is afraid of spiders, the therapist might first sit near a spider, then touch the spider, and then pick it up while the client observes. The client, with the guidance and assistance of the therapist, would then perform the same activities in the same order.

contact hypothesis the theory that people belonging to one group can become less prejudiced against (and perhaps more favorably disposed toward) members of other groups merely through increased contact with them. It is now thought that greater contact is unlikely to reduce intergroup prejudice unless the people from the different groups are of equal status, are not in competition with each other, and do not readily categorize the others as very different from themselves. Also called **intergroup-contact hypothesis**.

contact language an improvised system of communication, such as a PIDGIN, that emerges in situations of contact between speakers of different languages. Contact languages are usually characterized by a restricted lexicon, simplified sentence structures, and the absence of complex grammatical inflections.

contagion *n.* in social theory, the spread of behaviors, attitudes, and affect through crowds and other types of social aggregation from one member to another. Early analyses of contagion suggested that it resulted from the heightened suggestibility of members, but subsequent studies have argued that contagion is sustained by relatively mundane interpersonal processes, such as comparison, imitation, SOCIAL FACILITATION, CONFORMITY, and UNIVERSALITY. Also called **social contagion**.

containment *n.* in OBJECT RELATIONS THEORY, the notion that either the mother or the analyst aids growth and alleviates anxieties by acting as a "container," or "holding environment," for the projected aspects of the child's or patient's psyche (see PROJECTION). For instance, the infant, overwhelmed by distress and having no context to understand the experience, is held and soothed by the parent, who thus creates a safe context for the child and endows the experience with meaning.

contamination *n.* in testing and experimentation, the process of permitting knowledge, expectations, or other factors about the variable under study to influence the collection and interpretation of data about that variable.

contempt *n.* an emotion characterized by negative regard for anything or anybody considered to be inferior, vile, or worthless. —**contemptuous** *adj.*

content *n.* the thoughts, images, and sensations that occur in conscious experience. Contents are contrasted with the mental processes or the neural structures that underlie them.

content analysis a systematic, quantitative procedure for coding the themes in qualitative material, such as projective-test responses, propaganda, or fiction. For example, content analysis of verbally communicated material (e.g., articles, speeches, films) is done by determining the frequency of specific ideas, concepts, or terms.

content psychology an approach to psychology that is concerned with the role of conscious experience and the CONTENT of that experience. The term is mainly applied to early STRUCTURALISM. Compare ACT PSYCHOLOGY.

content-thought disorder a type of thought disturbance, typically found in schizophrenia and some other mental disorders (e.g., OBSESSIVE-COMPULSIVE DISORDER, MANIA), characterized by multiple fragmented, bizarre delusions.

content validity the extent to which a test measures a representative sample of the subject matter or behavior under investigation. For example, if a test is designed to survey arithmetic skills at a third-grade level, content validity will indicate how well it represents the range of arithmetic operations possible at that level.

content word in linguistics, a word with an independent lexical meaning, that is, one that can be defined with reference to the physical world or abstract concepts and without reference to any sentence in which the word may appear. Nouns, verbs, adjectives, and many adverbs are considered to be content words. Also called **lexical word**. Compare FUNCTION WORD.

context-independent learning the learning of a skill or strategy independently of a specific situation in which the skill will be applied.

context reinstatement a method used to aid the retrieval of memories. In the case of eyewitness recall, the individual is asked to re-create the event to be remembered in its original context and is encouraged to think about a variety of stimuli surrounding the event (e.g., smells, sounds) in the hope of providing additional retrieval cues.

context-specific learning learning that has occurred in a particular place, or context, and is displayed only in that context and not when testing occurs in another context.

contextual interference effect an effect on learning that may occur when training occurs in different contexts or when trials on one task are alternated with those on a different task. Learning is slowed by changing contexts or by intervening tasks, but the knowledge is more enduring and more readily transferable to different tasks or domains.

contextualism *n.* **1.** the theory that memory and learning are not the result only of linkages between events, as in the associationist doctrine, but are due to the meaning given to events by the context surrounding the experiences. **2.** a worldview asserting that the environment in which an event occurs intrinsically informs the event and its interpretation.

contextual subtheory see TRIARCHIC THEORY OF INTELLIGENCE.

contiguity *n.* the co-occurrence of stimuli in time or space. Learning an association between two stimuli is generally thought to depend at least partly on the contiguity of those stimuli. See LAW OF CONTIGUITY. —**contiguous** *adj.*

contiguity learning theory a theory stating that if a pattern of stimulation and a response occur together in time and space, learning occurs by the formation of associations between them, so that the same stimulus pattern will elicit the same response on subsequent occasions.

continence *n.* the ability to control the urge to defecate or urinate. —**continent** *adj.*

contingencies of self-worth particular areas of life in which people invest their SELF-ESTEEM, such that feedback regarding their standing or abilities in these domains has a crucial impact on their SELF-CONCEPT. Research indicates that people choose to stake their self-esteem in different domains, so that for some people material or professional success is vital to their sense of self-worth, whereas for others this is much less important than being well liked or sexually attractive.

contingency *n.* a conditional, probabilistic relation between two events. When the probability of Event B given Event A is 1.0, a perfect **positive contingency** is said to exist. When Event A predicts with certainty the absence of Event B, a perfect **negative contingency** is said to exist. Contingencies may be arranged via dependencies or they may emerge by accident. See also REINFORCEMENT CONTINGENCY.

contingency contract a mutually agreed-upon statement between a teacher and student, a parent and child, or a client and therapist regarding the change or changes desired, typically specifying behaviors and their positive and negative consequences.

contingency-governed behavior behavior that is directly and solely the result of REINFORCEMENT CONTINGENCIES. It occurs without deliberation. Compare RULE-GOVERNED BEHAVIOR.

contingency management in BEHAVIOR THERAPY, a technique in which a reinforcment, or reward, is given each time the desired behavior is performed. This technique is particularly common in substance abuse treatment.

contingency model any theory or model based on the generalization that there is no universal, ideal approach to structuring organizations and managing people. Rather, the most effective approach will depend on factors such as the nature of the task, the culture and environment of the organization, and the characteristics of the people involved.

contingency table a two-dimensional table in which the number of cases that are simultaneously in a given spot in a given row and column of the table are specified. For example, the ages and geographical locations of a sample of individuals applying for a particular job may be displayed in a contingency table, such that there are X number of individuals under 25 from New York City, Y number of individuals under 25 from Los Angeles, Z number of individuals between the ages of 25 and 35 from New York City, and so on. See CROSS-CLASSIFICATION.

contingent aftereffect an altered visual perception in which one stimulus dimension (e.g., color) depends on a separate stimulus dimension (e.g., orientation). The **McCullough effect** is an example in which repeated serial exposure to horizontal red bars followed by vertical green bars induces an aftereffect of horizontal white bars appearing green and vertical white bars appearing red. The color of the aftereffect is contingent on the orientation of the test stimulus.

contingent negative variation a slow EVENT-RELATED POTENTIAL that is recorded from the scalp. Such a potential arises in the interval between a warning signal and a signal that directs action and is indicative of readiness or expectancy.

contingent probability the probability, expressed as a number between 0 and 1, that one specific factor will occur if another one does, for example, the probability that the child of a drug user will become a drug user himself or herself. Unusually high or low contingent probabilities (compared to the general population) may, but do not necessarily, imply a causal relationship between the two factors.

contingent reinforcement the process or circumstances in which the delivery of positive stimulus events (e.g., social or material rewards) and, more rarely, the elimination of negative stimulus events (e.g., penalties) is dependent on the performance of desired behavior. See REINFORCEMENT.

continued-stay review a UTILIZATION REVIEW in which an internal or external auditor determines if continued inpatient care is medically necessary or if the current health care facility is still the most appropriate to provide the level of care required by the patient. See also EXTENDED-STAY REVIEW.

continuing bond the emotional attachment that a bereaved person continues to maintain with the deceased long after the death. The increasingly influential continuing-bond approach focuses on ways in which the emotional and symbolic relationship with the deceased can be reconstructed and integrated into the individ-

ual's life. See also BEREAVEMENT; GRIEF; MOURNING.

continuity-care retirement community a facility that offers a range of services and living arrangements that older adult residents can use as the need arises. A full spectrum of such services and arrangements might include independent living arrangements for the healthy and comparatively healthy; accessibility of on-site nursing care and other medical services for those temporarily ill, recovering from surgery, or returning from an extended stay in a hospital or rehabilitation facility; and terminal care for the dying.

continuity hypothesis the assumption that successful DISCRIMINATION LEARNING or problem solving results from a progressive, incremental, continuous process of trial and error. Responses that prove unproductive are extinguished, whereas every reinforced response results in an increase in ASSOCIATIVE STRENGTH, thus producing the gradual rise of the LEARNING CURVE. Problem solving is conceived as a step-by-step learning process in which the correct response is discovered, practiced, and reinforced. Compare DISCONTINUITY HYPOTHESIS.

continuity theory see DISENGAGEMENT THEORY.

continuity versus discontinuity the scientific debate over whether developmental change is gradual (continuous) or relatively abrupt (discontinuous).

continuous performance test any test that measures sustained attention and concentration, usually by requiring responses to an auditory or verbal target stimulus while ignoring nontarget stimuli.

continuous recognition task a memory task in which a series of items is presented, with some items presented on multiple occasions in the series. The participant responds to each item by indicating whether it is old (seen previously in the series) or new (not seen earlier in the series).

continuous reinforcement in operant and instrumental conditioning, the REINFORCEMENT of every response.

continuous scale a scale in which additional values can always be inserted between any two adjacent scores.

continuous variable a RANDOM VARIABLE that can take on an infinite number of values; that is, a variable measured on a continuous scale, as opposed to a CATEGORICAL VARIABLE.

continuum approach an approach based on the view that behavior ranges over a continuum from effective functioning to severe abnormality. It assumes that differences between people's behavior are a matter of degree rather than kind.

contract *n.* an explicit written agreement between parties or individuals. A contract between a client and therapist may detail (a) both the client's and the therapist's obligations, (b) the provisions for benefits or privileges to be gained through achievements, and (c) the specified consequences of failures (e.g., missing sessions). See also BEHAVIORAL CONTRACT; CONTINGENCY CONTRACT.

contralateral *adj.* situated on or affecting the opposite side of the body. For example, motor paralysis occurs on the side of the body contralateral to the side on which a brain lesion is found. Compare IPSILATERAL. **—contralaterally** *adv.*

contralateral control the arrangement whereby the MOTOR CORTEX of each cerebral hemisphere is mainly responsible for control of movements of the contralateral (opposite) side of the body.

contraprepared *adj.* denoting the state of an organism in relation to responses or associations that are difficult to learn, particularly in reaction to certain stimuli or in the presence of certain reinforcers. In conditioning experiments, for example, rats are contraprepared to associate a tone stimulus with gastric illness but readily learn to associate a distinctive taste with illness.

contrast *n.* **1.** that state in which the differences between one thing, event, or idea and another are emphasized by a comparison of their qualities. This may occur when the stimuli are juxtaposed (simultaneous contrast) or when one immediately follows the other (successive contrast). In making judgments, for example, meeting a person in a social context that includes physically attractive people could lead to a more negative evaluation of the attractiveness of that person than would have been the case otherwise. The evaluation of the person's attractiveness has been contrasted away from the social context. Compare ASSIMILATION. **2.** in the ANALYSIS OF VARIANCE, a comparison among group means using one DEGREE OF FREEDOM.

contrast analysis a focused analysis of data that is designed to determine the specific degree to which obtained data agree with predicted data (i.e., to which they support a hypothesis or theory). Contrast analysis yields an estimate of EFFECT SIZE and an associated level of significance for each contrast computed.

contrast correlation (symbol: $r_{contrast}$) the correlation between scores on the DEPENDENT VARIABLE and the contrast weights (i.e., predicted values) after removing any other sources of variation in the data.

contrast effect in psychology experiments, an effect in which participants' judgments shift away from an ANCHOR after it is introduced. Compare ASSIMILATION EFFECT.

contrast error a type of rating error in which the evaluation of a target person in a group is affected by the level of performance of others in the group. When the others are high in performance, there may be a tendency to rate the target lower than is correct. When the others are

low in performance, there may be a tendency to rate the target higher than is correct.

contrastive rhetoric the theory that different languages have different rhetorical characteristics, as seen, for example, in the different ways they structure and present an argument. The idea of contrastive rhetoric has been much discussed in the field of second-language teaching and is said to explain, for example, why native speakers will often sense something odd or "wrong" about essays, business letters, and so on produced by nonnative speakers, even when the grammar and vocabulary are flawless. Contrastive rhetoric has sometimes been linked to the wider hypothesis that languages embody culture-bound thought patterns (see LINGUISTIC DETERMINISM).

contrast polarity the degree of contrast between two visual elements, particularly figure and background. Contrast can be positive (light objects against dark backgrounds, e.g., a white letter printed upon black paper) or negative (dark objects against light backgrounds, e.g., a black letter printed upon white paper).

contrast sensitivity a measure of spatial RESOLUTION based on an individual's ability to detect subtle differences in light and dark coloring or shading in an object of a fixed size. Detection is affected by the size of contrasting elements and is usually tested using a grating of alternating light and dark bars, being defined by the minimum contrast required to distinguish that there is a bar pattern rather than a uniform screen. See also SPATIAL FREQUENCY.

contributing cause a cause that is not sufficient to bring about an end or event but that helps in some way to bring about that end or event. A contributing cause may be a necessary CONDITION or it may influence events more indirectly by affecting other conditions that make the event more likely.

control *n.* **1.** authority, power, or influence over events, behaviors, situations, or people. **2.** the regulation of all extraneous conditions and variables in an experiment so that any change in the DEPENDENT VARIABLE can be attributed solely to manipulation of the INDEPENDENT VARIABLE. In other words, the results obtained will be due solely to the experimental condition or conditions and not to any other factors.

control analysis psychoanalytic treatment conducted by a trainee under the guidance of a qualified PSYCHOANALYST, who helps the trainee to decide the direction of the treatment and to become aware of his or her COUNTERTRANSFERENCE. Also called **supervised analysis**; **supervisory analysis**.

control condition see CONTROL GROUP.

control experiment an experiment repeated for the purpose of increasing the validity of the original experiment. The experimental conditions may be duplicated exactly either to provide another measure of the DEPENDENT VARIABLE or to assess the impact of a variable that experimenters suspect was not previously controlled.

control group a group of participants in an experiment that are exposed to the **control conditions**, that is, the conditions of the experiment not involving a treatment or exposure to the INDEPENDENT VARIABLE. Compare EXPERIMENTAL GROUP.

controlled association a technique in which the participant's responses must relate to the stimulus in accordance with specific directions. For example, in an experiment involving presentation of stimulus words, the participant may be directed to give a synonym or antonym of each word.

controlled drinking a controversial approach to alcoholism treatment formerly advocated by some behaviorists as a viable alternative to total abstinence. The development of treatment programs based on social learning approaches and training in self-regulation and coping skills did not consistently materialize, and, since the 1980s, research has not supported controlled drinking as an efficacious or ethical primary goal of intervention.

controlled observation an observation made under standard and systematic conditions rather than casual or incidental conditions.

control-mastery theory 1. a perspective, underlying an integrative form of psychotherapy, that focuses on changing a client's unconscious and maladaptive beliefs developed in childhood due to thwarted attempts to achieve attachment and safety in the client's family. The client is seen to have an inherent motivation toward health that results in testing these beliefs through TRANSFERENCE and through passive-into-active behaviors; when such testing is productive, the client is then free to pursue adaptive goals. **2.** an integrative approach to child development that focuses on thoughts, feelings, and behaviors resulting from children's needs for attachment and safety in the family.

control processes those processes that organize the flow of information in an INFORMATION-PROCESSING system. See also EXECUTIVE.

control series replications of experiments or experimental trials, often including checks on procedures, instruments, instructions, and the like.

contusion *n.* a bruise. For example, various kinds of head injury can result in **cerebral contusion**: bruising of the brain in which blood vessels are damaged but not ruptured.

convenience sampling the process of obtaining a sample because it is convenient for the purpose, regardless of whether it is representative of the population being investigated.

conventional antipsychotic see ANTIPSYCHOTIC.

conventional level in KOHLBERG'S THEORY OF MORAL DEVELOPMENT, the intermediate level of moral reasoning, characterized by an individual's identification with and conformity to the expectations and rules of family and society: The individual evaluates actions and determines right and wrong in terms of other people's opinions. This level is divided into two stages: the earlier **interpersonal concordance** (or **good-boy-nice-girl) orientation** (Stage 3), in which moral behavior is that which obtains approval and pleases others; and the later **law-and-order** (or **authority and social order maintaining) orientation** (Stage 4), in which moral behavior is that which respects authority, allows the person to do his or her duty, and maintains the existing social order. Also called **conventional morality**. See also PRECONVENTIONAL LEVEL; POSTCONVENTIONAL LEVEL.

convergence *n.* the rotation of the two eyes inward toward a light source so that the image falls on corresponding points on the foveas. Convergence enables the slightly different images of an object seen by each eye to come together and form a single image.

convergent evolution see DIVERGENT EVOLUTION.

convergent production the capacity to produce the right answer to a question or to choose the best solution to a problem. Compare DIVERGENT PRODUCTION.

convergent thinking critical thinking in which an individual uses linear, logical steps to analyze a number of already formulated solutions to a problem to determine the correct one or the one that is most likely to be successful. Compare DIVERGENT THINKING.

convergent validity a form of CONSTRUCT VALIDITY based on the degree to which the measurement instrument in question exhibits high correlation with conceptually similar instruments. See also DISCRIMINANT VALIDITY.

conversation analysis 1. in ergonomics, a method of evaluating a system or product that involves the examination of conversations occurring between two or more users interacting with it. It is a form of KNOWLEDGE ELICITATION. **2.** in linguistics, see DISCOURSE ANALYSIS.

conversion *n.* **1.** an unconscious process in which anxiety generated by psychological conflicts is transformed into physical symptoms. Traditionally, this process was presumed to be involved in CONVERSION DISORDER, but current diagnostic criteria for the disorder do not make such an implication. **2.** actual change in an individual's beliefs, attitudes, or behaviors that occurs as a result of SOCIAL INFLUENCE. Unlike COMPLIANCE, which is outward and temporary, conversion occurs when the targeted individual is personally convinced by a persuasive message or internalizes and accepts as his or her own the beliefs expressed by other group members. For example, in a therapeutic context, conversion is manifest as the movement of clients away from their initial interpretations to one recommended by their therapists. See also CONFORMITY. —**convert** vb.

conversion disorder a SOMATOFORM DISORDER in which patients present with one or more symptoms or deficits affecting voluntary motor and sensory functioning that suggest a physical disorder but for which there is instead evidence of psychological involvement. These **conversion symptoms** are not intentionally produced or feigned and are not under voluntary control. They include paralysis, loss of voice, blindness, seizures, GLOBUS PHARYNGEUS, disturbance in coordination and balance, and loss of pain and touch sensations.

conversion therapy a highly controversial and generally discredited therapy based on the belief that individuals of same-sex sexual orientation may become heterosexual. Also called **reorientation therapy**; **reparative therapy**.

conviction n. in social psychology, the subjective sense that an ATTITUDE is a valued possession or an important aspect of SELF-CONCEPT. Conviction is related to the STRENGTH OF AN ATTITUDE.

convolution n. a folding or twisting, especially of the surface of the brain.

convulsion n. an involuntary, generalized, violent muscular contraction, in some cases tonic (contractions without relaxation), in others clonic (alternating contractions and relaxations of skeletal muscles).

convulsive therapy any treatment that is based on the induction of a generalized seizure by electrical or chemical means. See ELECTROCONVULSIVE THERAPY.

Cook's D an index used in REGRESSION ANALYSIS to show the influence of a particular case on the complete set of fitted values. [R. Denis **Cook** (1944–), U.S. statistician]

Coolidge effect increased sexual vigor when an animal or human being mates with multiple partners. The phenomenon is named for U.S. President Calvin Coolidge, alluding to a visit that he and his wife made to a farm where Mrs. Coolidge observed a rooster mating frequently. She allegedly asked the farmer to point this out to her husband, who is said to have replied "Same hen each time?"

cooperation n. the process of working together toward the attainment of a goal. This contrasts with COMPETITION, in which an individual's actions in working toward a goal lessen the likelihood of others achieving the same goal. Studies of animals often suggest cooperation, but whether nonhuman animals understand that individuals must act together to reach a common solution or whether they act randomly and occasionally appear to cooperate by chance is still unclear. Often cooperation leads to outcomes, such as increased food, that make it adaptive, but the benefit to each individual is not always obvious. —**cooperate** vb. —**cooperative** adj.

cooperative breeding a type of MATING SYSTEM in which typically only one male and female breed while other group members help in taking care of the offspring.

cooperative learning learning in small groups, to which each student in the group is expected to contribute using interpersonal skills and face-to-face interaction. Students also participate in regular assessment of the group process.

cooperative play see SOCIAL PLAY.

coordination n. the capacity of various parts to function together, particularly body parts (e.g., the two legs while walking or the eyes and hands in visually guided reaching), joints (e.g., the motion at the elbow and shoulder as the arm is swung back and forth), and the muscles producing force at a joint. —**coordinate** vb.

coordination loss in groups, a reduction in productivity caused by the imperfect integration of the efforts, activities, and contributions of each member of the group. See PROCESS LOSS.

coordination of secondary circular reactions in PIAGETIAN THEORY, a type of behavior seen in the SENSORIMOTOR STAGE, in which infants are able to choose and coordinate two or more behavior patterns to achieve a goal. Children become increasingly adept at the purposeful combination of repetitive, secondary CIRCULAR REACTIONS to achieve a desired aim, such as picking up a pillow to get a toy placed underneath.

COPD abbreviation for CHRONIC OBSTRUCTIVE PULMONARY DISEASE.

coping n. the use of cognitive and behavioral strategies to manage the demands of a situation when these are appraised as taxing or exceeding one's resources or to reduce the negative emotions and conflict caused by stress. See also COPING STRATEGY. —**cope** vb.

coping potential an individual's evaluation of the prospects of successfully managing environmental demands or personal commitments. Coping potential differs from COPING in that it deals with prospects of successful management (rather than with actual deployment of resources).

coping-skills training therapy or educational interventions to increase an individual's ability to manage a variety of often uncomfortable or anxiety-provoking situations, ranging from relatively normal or situational problems (e.g., test taking, divorce) to diagnosed disorders (e.g., phobias). The types of skills taught are tailored to the situation and can involve increasing cognitive, behavioral, and affective proficiencies.

coping strategy an action, a series of actions, or a thought process used in meeting a stressful or unpleasant situation or in modifying one's reaction to such a situation. Coping strategies typically involve a conscious and direct approach to problems, in contrast to DEFENSE MECHANISMS.

See also EMOTION-FOCUSED COPING; PROBLEM-FOCUSED COPING.

coping style the characteristic manner in which an individual confronts and deals with stress, anxiety-provoking situations, or emergencies.

coprolalia *n.* spontaneous, unprovoked, and uncontrollable use of obscene or profane words and expressions. It is a symptom that may be observed in individuals with a variety of neurological disorders, particularly TOURETTE'S DISORDER.

coprophagia *n.* the eating of feces.

coprophilia *n.* literally, the love of feces, which is manifested in behavior as an excessive or pathological preoccupation with the bodily product itself or with objects and words that represent it.

copulatory behavior behavior patterns associated with sexual intercourse. Copulatory behavior is distinct from courtship, which refers to behavior preparatory to copulation. Copulatory behavior usually includes mounting, intromission (insertion of the penis into the vagina), and ejaculation.

core area see HOME RANGE.

core conflictual relationship theme (**CCRT**) a method of research, case formulation, and PSYCHODYNAMIC PSYCHOTHERAPY that emphasizes central relationship patterns in clients' stories. Three components are analyzed: the wishes, needs, or intentions of the client with regard to the other person; the other person's expected or actual reaction to these; and the client's emotion, behavior, or symptoms as they relate to the other person's reaction.

core gender identity in psychoanalytic theory, an infant's sense of himself or herself as male or female, typically solidifying in the second year of life. See also GENDER IDENTITY.

core relational themes in the COGNITIVE APPRAISAL THEORY of emotions, a person's judgments of the specific significance of particular events to himself or herself, resulting in the generation of specific emotional states (e.g., anger, joy, envy, or shame) in that person. Any core relational theme has three components: goal relevance, ego involvement, and COPING POTENTIAL.

cornea *n.* the transparent part of the outer covering of the eye, through which light first passes. It is continuous laterally with the SCLERA. The cornea provides the primary refractive power of the eye. —**corneal** *adj.*

corollary discharge a neuronal signal that encodes a copy of an intended motor command, which is sent to a structure in the brain that can compare the intended movement with the sensory feedback (**reafference**) that results from the actual movement. For example, when the eyes move, the world does not appear to move, even though the image of the world moves across the retina. The corollary discharge of the intended movement in effect cancels out the movement

of the world over the retina. Also called **efference copy**.

coronal plane the plane that divides the front (anterior) half of the body or brain from the back (posterior) half. Also called **frontal plane**.

coronary heart disease a cardiovascular disorder characterized by restricted flow of blood through the coronary arteries supplying the heart muscle. The cause is usually ATHEROSCLEROSIS of the coronary arteries and often leads to fatal myocardial INFARCTION. Also called **coronary artery disease**.

coronary-prone behavior a rarely used term for actions or patterns of actions believed to be associated with TYPE A PERSONALITY.

corporal *adj.* of or relating to the body.

corpus *n.* (*pl.* **corpora**) a body or distinct anatomical structure, such as the CORPUS CALLOSUM.

corpus callosum a large tract of nerve fibers running across the LONGITUDINAL FISSURE of the brain and connecting the cerebral hemispheres: It is the principal connection between the two sides of the brain. The largest of the interhemispheric commissures, it is known as the **great commissure**. See also COMMISSURAL FIBER.

corpus luteum a yellowish glandular mass in the ovary that remains after a GRAAFIAN FOLLICLE has ruptured and released an ovum. Its development is stimulated by LUTEINIZING HORMONE secreted by the anterior pituitary gland, and it functions as a transient endocrine gland, secreting PROGESTERONE.

corpus striatum see BASAL GANGLIA.

correct detection in SIGNAL DETECTION TASKS, an accurate perception of a target stimulus (signal) by the participant in trials in which the signal is present, often expressed as a percentage accuracy rate. See also CORRECT REJECTION.

correctional psychology a branch of FORENSIC PSYCHOLOGY concerned with the diagnosis, treatment, and rehabilitation of criminal and juvenile offenders in penal and correctional institutions (e.g., reformatories, training schools, penitentiaries).

correction for attenuation a method for estimating the correlations between the true scores of two measures by adjusting the observed correlation in accordance with the reliabilities of the two measures.

correction for continuity a set of statistical procedures that are applied to correct for the fact that a statistical procedure is based on an assumption that the data have a continuous distribution when, in fact, the distribution is discrete.

correction for guessing a scoring rule for multiple choice items such that the expected value of getting an item correct under the assumption of no knowledge is 0 rather than $1/n$, where n is the number of alternatives.

correction procedure the repetition or continuation of particular stimulus conditions (usually in DISCRIMINATION training) after certain responses (usually errors) or in the absence of certain responses.

correct rejection in SIGNAL DETECTION TASKS, an accurate decision by the participant that a target stimulus (signal) is not present. See also CORRECT DETECTION.

correlation *n.* the degree of a relationship (usually linear) between two attributes.

correlational study a study of the relationship between two or more variables.

correlation coefficient a numerical index reflecting the degree of relationship (usually linear) between two attributes scaled so that the value of +1 indicates a perfect positive relationship, –1 a perfect negative relationship, and 0 no relationship.

correlation ratio a statistical index, often referred to as **eta**, that reflects the magnitude of a nonlinear relationship between two variables.

correspondence problem the requirement that elements in one image must be matched by the visual system with the same elements in another image when the two images differ from one another in some respect. In STEREOPSIS the features seen through the left eye must be matched to the features seen through the right eye before depth information can be inferred. In APPARENT MOVEMENT the elements in one stationary image must be matched with the same elements in the next stationary image if the elements are to be perceived as moving. Theories of object recognition must take into account the ability to recognize objects as the same, even though they may appear from different perspectives in two different scenes.

correspondent inference theory a model describing how people form inferences about other people's stable personality characteristics from observing their behaviors. Correspondence between behaviors and traits is more likely to be inferred if the actor is judged to have acted (a) freely, (b) intentionally, (c) in a way that is unusual for someone in the situation, and (d) in a way that does not usually bring rewards or social approval. See also ATTRIBUTION THEORY.

cortex *n.* (*pl.* **cortices**) the outer or superficial layer or layers of a structure, as distinguished from the central core. In mammals, the cortex of a structure is identified with the name of the gland or organ, for example, the CEREBELLAR CORTEX or CEREBRAL CORTEX. Compare MEDULLA. **—cortical** *adj.*

cortical activation activation of regions of the cerebral cortex or cerebellar cortex. It can be achieved by sensory stimulation or cognitive tasks or by such techniques as TRANSCRANIAL MAGNETIC STIMULATION. The activation can be recorded by noninvasive techniques, such as ELECTROENCEPHALOGRAPHY, FUNCTIONAL MAG-NETIC RESONANCE IMAGING, or POSITRON EMISSION TOMOGRAPHY.

cortical blindness blindness with normal pupillary responses due to complete destruction of the OPTIC RADIATIONS or the STRIATE CORTEX. Because the subcortical structures (white matter) of the visual system are involved, it is also called **cerebral blindness**. Typically caused by a stroke affecting the occipital lobe of the brain, cortical blindness can also result from traumatic injury or HYPOXIA. In children it is often a consequence of hydrocephalus, meningitis, toxic or hypertensive encephalopathy, trauma, or diffuse demyelinating degenerative disease. Complete loss of vision in a portion of the visual field is called **partial cortical blindness**.

cortical column one of the vertical groups of interconnected neurons that span several CORTICAL LAYERS and constitute the basic functional organization of the NEOCORTEX. Columnar organization is most evident in visual cortex (see OCULAR DOMINANCE COLUMN; ORIENTATION COLUMN).

cortical deafness deafness that is caused by damage to auditory centers in the cerebral cortex of the brain. The peripheral auditory system (which includes the retrocochlear neural pathways terminating in the brainstem) can be intact in this condition.

cortical dementia DEMENTIA arising from degeneration of the cortical areas of the brain, rather than the subcortical (deeper) areas. The most common dementia of this type is ALZHEIMER'S DISEASE.

cortical layers the layers of neurons that constitute the structure of the cerebral cortex and cerebellar cortex. In the cerebral cortex the number of layers varies, reaching a maximum of six in the NEOCORTEX. These six layers, identified by Roman numerals and starting from the outer surface, are: I, the **plexiform molecular layer**, a narrow band of myelinated fibers (see MYELIN); II, the **external granular layer**, containing GRANULE CELLS and PYRAMIDAL CELLS; III, the **external pyramidal layer**, with medium-sized pyramidal cells in the outer zone and larger pyramidal cells in the inner zone; IV, the **internal granular layer**, which contains synapses of layer-III cells along with stellate cells categorized as granule cells; V, the **ganglionic** (or **internal pyramidal**) **layer**, which includes large pyramidal cells and the giant Betz cells; and VI, the **polymorphic fusiform** (or **multiform**) **layer**, which contains cells of many shapes but mainly spindle-shaped and pyramidal cells.

cortical map a representation of a sensory modality or motor function in the cerebral cortex. Examples are the representations of the visual field in areas of visual cortex (see RETINOTOPIC MAP) and the tonotopic representations in regions of auditory cortex (see TONOTOPIC ORGANIZATION). The mapping is usually topographic

cortical process any of the mechanisms of the cerebral cortex that are involved in cognition. The early stages of a cognitive process are called **lower cortical processes** or **early cortical processes**; the later, more complex mechanisms are called **higher cortical processes**. See also EXECUTIVE FUNCTIONS.

cortical–subcortical motor loop a loop, made up of projections between the MOTOR CORTEX and structures in the BASAL GANGLIA and the THALAMUS, that monitors and sequences ongoing motor behaviors.

corticobasal ganglionic degeneration a degenerative condition of the BASAL GANGLIA resulting in APRAXIA, rigidity, DYSTONIA, and cognitive deficits. Also called **corticostriatonigral degeneration**.

corticospinal tract see VENTROMEDIAL PATHWAYS.

corticosteroid *n.* any of the steroid hormones produced by the adrenal cortex, the outer layer of the ADRENAL GLAND. They include the GLUCOCORTICOIDS (e.g., CORTISOL), which are involved in carbohydrate metabolism; and the MINERALOCORTICOIDS (e.g., ALDOSTERONE), which have a role in electrolyte balance and sodium retention. Also called **adrenocorticoid**.

corticosterone *n.* a CORTICOSTEROID hormone with GLUCOCORTICOID functions that include regulating the metabolism of proteins, fats, and carbohydrates into energy sources for body cells. The concentration of corticosterone in the plasma is used as an index of stress.

corticotropin *n.* a hormone secreted by the anterior pituitary gland, particularly when a person experiences stress. It stimulates the release of various other hormones (primarily CORTICOSTEROIDS) from the adrenal cortex, the outer layer of the adrenal gland. Also called **adrenocorticotropic hormone** (ACTH); **adrenocorticotropin**.

corticotropin-releasing factor a neuropeptide produced by the hypothalamus that is important in the control of the hypothalamic–pituitary–adrenal response to stress (see HYPOTHALAMIC–PITUITARY–ADRENOCORTICAL SYSTEM). Corticotropin-releasing factor controls the daily rhythm of corticotropin (ACTH) release by the pituitary gland and is also involved in a number of behaviors, such as anxiety, food intake, learning, and memory. Also called **ACTH-releasing factor**; **corticotropin-releasing hormone**).

cortisol *n.* a CORTICOSTEROID hormone whose GLUCOCORTICOID activity increases BLOOD SUGAR levels. Blood levels of cortisol in humans vary according to sleep–wake cycles (being highest around 9:00 a.m. and lowest at midnight) and other factors; for example, they increase with stress and during pregnancy but decrease during diseases of the liver and kidneys. Since 1963, cortisol and its synthetic analogs have been administered in the treatment of chronic inflammatory and autoimmune disorders. Also called **hydrocortisone**.

cortisone *n.* a CORTICOSTEROID that is produced naturally by the adrenal cortex or synthetically. Cortisone is biologically inactive but is converted to the active hormone CORTISOL in the liver and other organs. It is used therapeutically in the management of disorders due to corticosteroid deficiency.

cosmic consciousness a purported sense of awareness of the universe as a whole. This is variously reported to be achieved through PEAK EXPERIENCES, religious ecstasy, the use of hallucinogenic drugs, or metaphysical disciplines, such as meditation, yoga, and Zen Buddhism. See also ALTERED STATE OF CONSCIOUSNESS.

cost analysis a systematic determination of the costs associated with the implementation of a program's services. These include direct personnel, material, and administrative costs, calculated from the perspective of a given purchaser (e.g., government agency, client), budgetary category, and time period. Once determined, these costs are utilized further in cost–benefit or cost-effectiveness analysis.

cost–benefit analysis 1. an analytic procedure that attempts to determine and compare the economic efficiency of different programs. Costs and benefits are reduced to their monetary value and expressed in a **cost–benefit** (or **benefit–cost**) ratio. **2.** in BEHAVIORAL ECOLOGY, a method of predicting which behavioral strategies are likely to be adaptive by comparing the potential costs and potential benefits of each possible behavior. Those behaviors that will lead to greater benefits relative to costs will be those that survive through NATURAL SELECTION.

cost containment a program goal that seeks to control the costs involved in managing and delivering the program outcome. In health administration, a range of fiscal strategies is used to prevent health care costs from increasing. See also COST ANALYSIS.

cost–reward analysis in social psychology, a model that attempts to explain helping behavior in terms of the reinforcements and costs associated with specific helping actions. A helping act that possesses either high reinforcement value or very low cost value is more likely to be performed than a low-reinforcement, high-cost act.

cotherapy *n.* therapy by two therapists working with a client, pair of clients (e.g., a couple), family, or group to enhance understanding and change behavior and relationships during treatment. Also called **dual-leadership therapy**.

couch *n.* in psychoanalysis, the article of furniture on which the patient reclines. The use of the couch is based on the theory that this posture will facilitate FREE ASSOCIATION, encourage the patient to direct attention to his or her inward world of feeling and fantasy, and enable the patient to uncover his or her unconscious mind. The expression "on the couch" is sometimes used popularly to indicate psychoanalytic treatment.

counseling *n.* professional assistance in coping with personal problems, including emotional, behavioral, vocational, marital, educational, rehabilitation, and life-stage (e.g., retirement) problems. The COUNSELOR makes use of such techniques as ACTIVE LISTENING, guidance, advice, discussion, CLARIFICATION, and the administration of tests.

counseling psychology the branch of psychology that specializes in facilitating personal and interpersonal functioning across the life span. Counseling psychology focuses on emotional, social, vocational, educational, health-related, developmental, and organizational concerns—such as improving well-being, alleviating distress and maladjustment, and resolving crises—and addresses issues from individual, family, group, systems, and organizational perspectives. The **counseling psychologist** has received professional education and training in one or more COUNSELING areas, such as educational, vocational, employee, aging, personal, marriage, or rehabilitation counseling. In contrast to a clinical psychologist (see CLINICAL PSYCHOLOGY), who usually emphasizes origins of maladaptations, a counseling psychologist emphasizes adaptation, adjustment, and more efficient use of the individual's available resources.

counseling services professional help provided by a government, social service, or mental health agency to individuals, families, and groups. Services are typically provided by licensed counselors, psychologists, social workers, and nurses. See also COUNSELING.

counselor *n.* an individual professionally trained in counseling, psychology, social work, or nursing who specializes in one or more counseling areas, such as vocational, rehabilitation, educational, substance abuse, marriage, relationship, or family counseling. A counselor provides professional evaluations, information, and suggestions designed to enhance the client's ability to solve problems, make decisions, and effect desired changes in attitude and behavior.

counterbalancing *n.* the process of arranging a series of experimental conditions or treatments in such a way as to minimize the influence of other factors, such as practice or fatigue, on experimental effects. A simple form of counterbalancing would be to administer experimental conditions in the order AB to half the participants and in the order BA to the other half.

countercathexis *n.* see ANTICATHEXIS.

countercompulsion *n.* a COMPULSION that is secondarily developed to resist the original compulsion when the latter cannot be continued. The new compulsion then replaces the original

so that the compulsive behavior can continue. See OBSESSIVE-COMPULSIVE DISORDER.

counterconditioning *n.* an experimental procedure in which an animal, already conditioned to respond to a stimulus in a particular way, is trained to produce a different response to the same stimulus that is incompatible with the original response. This same principle underlies many of the techniques used in BEHAVIOR THERAPY to eliminate unwanted behavior.

counterculture *n.* a social movement that maintains its own alternative mores and values in opposition to prevailing cultural norms. The term is historically associated with the hippie movement and attendant drug culture of the late 1960s and early 1970s, which rejected such societal norms as the work ethic and the traditional family unit. See also SUBCULTURE; YOUTH CULTURE. **—countercultural** *adj.*

counteridentification *n.* in psychoanalysis, a form of COUNTERTRANSFERENCE in which the psychoanalyst identifies with the patient. **—counteridentify** *vb.*

countershock *n.* a mild electric shock administered to a patient undergoing ELECTROCONVULSIVE THERAPY (ECT) for 1 min after the convulsive shock. The countershock is intended to relieve some of the common aftereffects of ECT, such as postconvulsion confusion or amnesia.

countershock phase see GENERAL ADAPTATION SYNDROME.

countertransference *n.* the therapist's unconscious reactions to the patient and to the patient's TRANSFERENCE. These thoughts and feelings are based on the therapist's own psychological needs and conflicts and may be either unexpressed or revealed through conscious responses to patient behavior. The term was originally used to describe this process in psychoanalysis but has since become part of the common lexicon in other forms of psychodynamic psychotherapy and in other therapies. In CLASSICAL PSYCHOANALYSIS, countertransference is viewed as a hindrance to the analyst's understanding of the patient, but to some modern analysts and therapists it may serve as a source of insight into the patient's impact on other people. In either case, the analyst or therapist must be aware of, and analyze, countertransference so that it does not interfere with the therapeutic process. See also CONTROL ANALYSIS.

couples therapy therapy in which both partners in a committed relationship are treated at the same time by the same therapist or therapists. Couples therapy is concerned with problems within and between the individuals that affect the relationship. For example, one partner may have an undiagnosed, physiologically based depression that is affecting the relationship, and both partners may have trouble communicating effectively with one another. Individual sessions may be provided separately to each partner, particularly at the beginning of therapy; most of the course of therapy, however, is provided to both partners together. Couples therapy for married couples is known as **marital therapy**.

course *n.* the length of time a disorder, illness, or treatment typically lasts, its natural progression, and (if applicable) its recurrence over time.

courtship behavior the behavior of different species of animals and of human beings in different societies or social strata during the period prior to reproduction or, in humans, marriage. In animals it involves evaluating a potential mate as well as locating and defending appropriate sites for nests or dens and synchronizing the hormones involved in reproduction. In human courtship, such behavior may take widely different forms in different cultures.

couvade *n.* **1.** a custom in some cultures in which the father takes to bed before or after his child is born, as if he himself suffered the pain of childbirth. **2.** abdominal pain or other somatic symptoms appearing in the male partners of pregnant women, usually presumed to be PSYCHOGENIC in origin. Also called **couvade syndrome**.

covariate *n.* a correlated variable that is often controlled or held constant through the ANALYSIS OF COVARIANCE. Also called **concomitant variable**.

covariation *n.* a relationship between two phenomena (objects or events) such that there is a systematic correlation between variation of the one and variation of the other. So, for example, under stable conditions the volume of a substance will be found to covary with its weight: An increase or decrease to the volume will be found to entail a proportionate increase or decrease to the weight, and vice versa. Unlike mere co-occurrence, covariation carries a strong presumption that there is a causal link between the covarying phenomena. —**covary** *vb.*

covariation principle see ATTRIBUTION THEORY.

covert *adj.* **1.** denoting anything that is not directly observable, open to view, or publicly known, either by happenstance or by deliberate design. **2.** hidden. Compare OVERT.

covert attention attention directed to a location that is different from that on which the eyes are fixated.

covert conditioning a technique of BEHAVIOR THERAPY that relies on the use of imagination and assumes that overt and covert behavior are associated, that each affects the other, and that both forms of behavior depend on the laws of learning. The individual imagines performing a desired behavior in a problematic real-life situation, rewards himself or herself for mentally engaging in the behavior, and finally achieves an actual change in behavior. Also called **covert behavioral reinforcement**.

covert desensitization a form of DESENSITIZATION therapy in which an individual is helped to overcome a fear or anxiety by learning to relax while recollecting the anxiety-producing stimulus in his or her imagination. A hierarchy is devised with a sequence of items that range from the least to the most anxiety-producing aspects of the stimulus. The client then uses relaxation techniques while progressively imagining items on the hierarchy until able to imagine the stimulus without feeling anxious. Compare IN VIVO DESENSITIZATION. See also SYSTEMATIC DESENSITIZATION.

covert extinction a COVERT CONDITIONING procedure in which the client first imagines performing an unwanted behavior and then imagines failing to be rewarded or to receive REINFORCEMENT for the behavior.

covert rehearsal a technique in which either rote or elaborate repetitive rehearsing in one's mind of words or behaviors is used to improve memory or to prepare for overt speech or behavior. See also BEHAVIOR REHEARSAL.

covert response any generally unobservable response, such as a thought, image, emotion, or internal physiological reaction, the existence of which is typically inferred or measured indirectly. For example, covert preparation for physical responses can be observed in an electric brain potential called the LATERALIZED READINESS POTENTIAL and in electromyographic measures of muscle activity. Also called **implicit response**. Compare OVERT RESPONSE.

CP abbreviation for CEREBRAL PALSY.

CPI abbreviation for CALIFORNIA PSYCHOLOGICAL INVENTORY.

CPR fees abbreviation for CUSTOMARY, PREVAILING, AND REASONABLE FEES.

CPT abbreviation for COGNITIVE PROCESSING THERAPY.

CR abbreviation for CONDITIONED RESPONSE.

cranial *adj.* referring or relating to the CRANIUM.

cranial bifida a congenital disorder manifested by a horseshoe-shaped depression of the medial (middle) plane of the forehead. A median-cleft palate, a cleft of the nose ranging from a notch to complete division, and widely spaced eyes are present. Because of a failure of the two sides of the head to fuse normally during prenatal development, the corpus callosum, the nerve tract connecting the two sides of the brain, may be defective. Mental retardation is common.

cranial nerve any of the 12 pairs of nerves that arise directly from the brain and are distributed mainly to structures in the head and neck. Some of the cranial nerves are sensory, some are motor, and some are mixed (i.e., both sensory and motor). Cranial nerves are designated by Roman numerals, as follows: I, OLFACTORY NERVE; II, OPTIC NERVE; III, OCULOMOTOR NERVE; IV, TROCHLEAR NERVE; V, TRIGEMINAL NERVE; VI, ABDUCENS NERVE; VII, FACIAL NERVE;

VIII, VESTIBULOCOCHLEAR NERVE; IX, GLOSSO-PHARYNGEAL NERVE; X, VAGUS NERVE; XI, ACCESSORY NERVE; XII, HYPOGLOSSAL NERVE.

craniotomy *n.* the surgical opening of the skull, a procedure that may be performed, for example, to administer surgical treatment or to release pressure when the brain is expanding due to HYDROCEPHALUS or cerebral EDEMA. Craniotomy is one of the oldest types of surgery: Evidence of it has been found in prehistoric skulls in nearly every part of the world. See also TREPHINATION.

cranium *n.* **1.** the skull. **2.** the portion of the skull that encloses the brain.

creatine kinase an enzyme present in heart muscle, skeletal muscle, and brain tissues. High levels in the blood may be a sign of disease or tissue damage, for example, muscular dystrophy or myocardial infarction. The enzyme consists of two subunits, of which there are two possible alternatives, M and B. The combination of subunits is characteristic of certain tissues and can be identified by electrophoresis techniques as myocardial (MB), skeletal muscle (MM), and brain (BB). The MB form is usually specific for myocardial infarction.

creative genius see EXCEPTIONAL CREATIVITY.

creative intelligence in the TRIARCHIC THEORY OF INTELLIGENCE, the set of skills used to create, invent, discover, explore, imagine, and suppose. This set of skills is alleged to be relatively (although not wholly) distinctive with respect to analytical and practical skills. Compare ANALYTICAL INTELLIGENCE; PRACTICAL INTELLIGENCE.

creative thinking the mental processes leading to a new invention, solution, or synthesis in any area. A creative solution may use preexisting objects or ideas but creates a new relationship between the elements it utilizes. Examples include new machines, social ideas, scientific theories, and artistic creations. Compare CRITICAL THINKING. See also DIVERGENT THINKING.

creativity *n.* the ability to produce or develop original work, theories, techniques, or thoughts. A creative individual typically displays originality, imagination, and expressiveness. Analyses have failed to ascertain why one individual is more creative than another, but creativity does appear to be a very durable trait. See also CREATIVE THINKING; DIVERGENT THINKING. —**creative** *adj.*

creativity test any psychological test designed to identify CREATIVITY or DIVERGENT THINKING. Existing tests focus on a variety of factors, such as an individual's fluency with words and ideas or ability to generate original associations; tasks may involve finding solutions to practical problems, suggesting different endings to stories, or listing unusual uses for objects.

credentialing *n.* the administrative process of reviewing a health care provider's qualifications, practice history, and medical CERTIFICATION or license to determine if criteria for clinical privileges are met. See also PROFESSIONAL LICENSING.

creole *n.* a language that has evolved from profound and prolonged contact between two or more languages and both shares features of the parent languages and evolves altogether novel features. Although typically developing from a PIDGIN, a creole becomes stable over time and will usually have a fully developed grammatical system.

Creutzfeldt–Jakob disease (**CJD**) a rapidly progressive neurological disease caused by abnormal prion proteins and characterized by DEMENTIA, involuntary muscle movements (especially MYOCLONUS), ATAXIA, visual disturbances, and seizures. Vacuoles form in the gray matter of the brain and spinal cord, giving it a spongy appearance; the prion is thought to cause misfolding of other proteins, leading to the cellular pathology. **Classical CJD** occurs sporadically worldwide and typically affects individuals who are middle-aged or older. Early symptoms are muscular incoordination (ataxia), with abnormalities of gait and speech, followed by worsening dementia and myoclonus. Death occurs usually within 1 year of the onset of symptoms. **Variant CJD** (**vCJD**) causes similar symptoms but typically affects younger people, who are believed to have acquired the disease by eating meat or meat products from cattle infected with bovine spongiform encephalopathy (BSE). Also called **Jakob–Creutzfeldt disease**; **subacute spongiform encephalopathy** (**SSE**). See also PRION DISEASE. [Hans Gerhard **Creutzfeldt** (1885–1964) and Alfons **Jakob** (1884–1931), German neuropathologists]

criminal commitment the confinement of people in mental institutions either because they have been found NOT GUILTY BY REASON OF INSANITY or in order to establish their COMPETENCY TO STAND TRIAL as responsible defendants.

criminal intent see MENS REA.

criminal profiling techniques used to narrow a criminal investigation to suspects with certain personality and behavioral traits that might be inferred from the way a crime was committed, where it occurred, and such other information as the background of the victim or victims (i.e., victimology). Psychologists have played a central role in studying and developing these techniques. Although there is some validating research for profiling in helping police to concentrate their investigations in the right directions, there is also controversy regarding such issues as hasty identifications that ignore or foreclose other leads, methodological flaws, and the like.

criminal responsibility a defendant's ability to formulate a criminal intent (see MENS REA) at the time of the crime with which he or she is charged, which must be proved in court before the person can be convicted. Criminal responsibility may be excluded for reason of INSANITY or mitigated for a number of other reasons (see DIMINISHED CAPACITY; DIMINISHED RESPONSIBILITY).

criminology *n.* the scientific study of crime and criminal behavior, including its causes, prevention, and punishment. —**criminologist** *n.*

crisis *n.* (*pl.* **crises**) **1.** a situation (e.g., a traumatic change) that produces significant cognitive or emotional stress in those involved in it. **2.** a turning point for better or worse in the course of an illness. **3.** a state of affairs marked by instability and the possibility of impending change for the worse, for example, in a political or social situation.

crisis center a facility established for emergency therapy or referral, sometimes staffed by medical and mental health professionals and paraprofessionals. See DROP-IN CENTER.

crisis counseling immediate drop-in, phone-in, or on-site professional counseling provided following a trauma or sudden stressful event, often for emergency situations or in the aftermath of a disaster. See DISASTER COUNSELING; HOTLINE.

crisis intervention **1.** the brief ameliorative, rather than specifically curative, use of psychotherapy or counseling to aid individuals, families, and groups who have undergone a highly disruptive experience, such as an unexpected bereavement or a disaster. **2.** psychological intervention provided on a short-term, emergency basis for individuals experiencing mental health crises, such as attempted suicide.

crisis management the organization and mobilization of resources to overcome the difficulties presented by a sudden and unexpected threat. The psychological stress produced by a crisis can reduce the information-processing capacities of those affected, which should be taken into account by crisis managers when considering possible solutions.

crisis team a group of professionals and paraprofessionals trained to help individuals cope with psychological reactions during and following emergencies or mental health crises, for example, natural disasters or suicide threats or attempts.

crista (**crysta**) *n.* the structure within the ampulla at the end of each SEMICIRCULAR CANAL that contains hair cells sensitive to the direction and rate of movements of the head.

criterion *n.* (*pl.* **criteria**) **1.** a standard against which a judgment, evaluation, or comparisons can be made. **2.** a test score or item against which other tests or items can be validated. For example, a well-validated test of creativity might be used as the criterion to select new tests of creativity.

criterion-based content analysis a form of STATEMENT VALIDITY ANALYSIS in which children's statements in instances of alleged abuse

are analyzed in terms of key content criteria, in order to evaluate their truth.

criterion contamination an experimental situation in which the variable to be validated is allowed to influence the criterion (i.e., the variable used for VALIDATION).

criterion cutoff the score on an assessment instrument that serves as a cutoff point separating participants into distinct categories. For example, the criterion cutoff on a particular measure of job performance separates what is considered a successful performance on this dimension from an unsuccessful performance.

criterion group a group tested for traits its members are already known to possess, usually for the purpose of validating a test. For example, a group of children with diagnosed visual disabilities may be given a visual test to assess its VALIDITY as a means of evaluating the presence of visual disabilities.

criterion-referenced testing an approach to testing based on the comparison of a person's performance with an established standard or criterion. The criterion is fixed, that is, each person's score is measured against the same criterion and is not influenced by the performance of others. See NORM-REFERENCED TESTING.

criterion score a predicted score on an attribute or variable that is derived from REGRESSION ANALYSIS.

criterion validity an index of how well a test correlates with a criterion, that is, an established standard of comparison. The criterion can be measured before, after, or at the same time as the test being validated.

criterion variable in statistical analysis, a variable to be predicted; that is, a DEPENDENT VARIABLE.

critical band the band of frequencies in a masking noise that are effective in masking a tone of a given frequency (see AUDITORY MASKING). The width of this band, in hertz (Hz), is the **critical bandwidth**. For example, in detecting a 1-kHz tone in white NOISE, only frequency components in the noise between 920 Hz and 1080 Hz contribute significantly to the masking: The critical band is from 920 to 1080 Hz, and the critical bandwidth is 160 Hz. In psychoacoustics there are many manifestations of critical-band "filtering," including spectral effects in loudness summation and monaural phase effects. See also AUDITORY FILTER; FREQUENCY SELECTIVITY.

critical flicker frequency the rate at which a periodic change, or flicker, in an intense visual stimulus fuses into a smooth, continuous stimulus. A similar phenomenon can occur with rapidly changing auditory stimuli. Also called **flicker fusion frequency**.

critical-incident stress debriefing (**CISD**) a systematic and programmed process designed to help individuals who witness or work at the scene of a critical incident or disaster (e.g., firefighters). The process uses basic stress counseling techniques; formal training in CISD is provided in workshops for personnel in emergency services as well as for mental health professionals.

critical-incident technique a method designed to investigate factors associated with unusually good or unusually poor job performance. Observers record unusual outcomes and specific incidents, behaviors, or system features that may have triggered these outcomes. Data collected in this way are then classified and analyzed to identify key themes. The critical-incident technique is widely used in such areas as ACCIDENT PREVENTION and the creation of behaviorally based rating scales for use in employee evaluation (see BEHAVIORALLY ANCHORED RATING SCALE; MIXED-STANDARD SCALE).

critical life event an event in life that requires major ADJUSTMENT and adaptive behavior. Such events may be regarded in retrospect as unusually formative or pivotal in shaping attitudes and beliefs. Common critical life events include bereavement, divorce, and unemployment. See also LIFE EVENTS.

critical period 1. an early stage in life when an organism is especially open to specific learning, emotional, or socializing experiences that occur as part of normal development and will not recur at a later stage. For example, the first 3 days of life are thought to constitute a critical period for IMPRINTING in ducks, and there may be a critical period for language acquisition in human infants. **2.** in vision, the period of time after birth, varying from weeks (in cats) to months (in humans), in which full, binocular visual stimulation is necessary for the structural and functional maturation of the VISUAL SYSTEM. See also MONOCULAR REARING.

critical region in SIGNIFICANCE TESTING, the range of values for a test statistic that leads to rejection of the null hypothesis in favor of the alternative hypothesis. Also called **rejection region**. Compare ACCEPTANCE REGION.

critical thinking a form of directed, problem-focused thinking in which the individual tests ideas or possible solutions for errors or drawbacks. It is essential to such activities as examining the validity of a hypothesis or interpreting the meaning of research results. Compare CREATIVE THINKING. See CONVERGENT THINKING.

Crocker–Henderson odor system a theory that posits four PRIMARY ODOR qualities: acid, burnt, caprylic, and fragrant. The presence of each primary in an odor is assessed via a 9-point scale (0–8) indicating the relative intensity of each quality. See also HENNING'S ODOR PRISM. [Ernest C. **Crocker** (1888–1964) and Lloyd F. **Henderson**, U.S. chemists]

Cronbach's alpha an index of INTERNAL CONSISTENCY reliability, that is, the degree to which a set of items that comprise a measurement instrument tap a single, unidimensional construct. Also called **alpha coefficient**; **coefficient alpha**. [Lee J. **Cronbach** (1916–2001), U.S. psychologist]

cross-adaptation n. the change in sensitivity to one stimulus caused by adaptation to another. See CROSS-NASAL ADAPTATION.

cross-classification n. classification of items according to more than one characteristic. More specifically, it is a two-way system of classification used in experimentation in which each person or other sampling unit is assigned to the intersection of a row category and a column category. For example, each person may be assigned to a treatment or control (no treatment) row condition and a pass or fail column condition.

cross-cultural psychology a branch of psychology that studies similarities and variances in human behavior across different cultures and identifies the different psychological constructs and explanatory models used by these cultures. It may be contrasted with CULTURAL PSYCHOLOGY, which tends to adopt a systemic, within-culture approach. Also called **ethnopsychology**.

cross-cultural testing testing individuals with diverse cultural backgrounds and experiences using a method and materials that do not favor certain individuals over others. Typically, CULTURE-FAIR TESTS are administered with nonverbal instructions and content, avoid objects indigenous to a particular culture, and do not depend on speed.

cross-cultural treatment treatment in situations in which therapist and client differ in terms of race, ethnicity, gender, language, or lifestyle. Mental health providers should be attentive to cultural differences with clients for the following (among other) reasons: (a) Social and cultural beliefs influence diagnosis and treatment; (b) diagnosis differs across cultures; (c) symptoms are expressed differently across cultures; (d) diagnostic categories reflect majority cultural values; and (e) most providers are from the majority culture.

cross-dressing n. the process or habit of putting on the clothes of the opposite sex. It is done for a variety of reasons, for example, as part of a performance, as social commentary, or as a preliminary stage in sex-reversal procedures (see also TRANSSEXUALISM). Although synonymous with transvestism, cross-dressing is distinct from TRANSVESTIC FETISHISM.

crossed-factor design an experimental design in which each level of one factor occurs together with each level of another (crossed) factor. Thus, if there are four levels of reading ability in a study, and three levels of numbers of hours of tutoring, the factors of reading ability and of amount of tutoring are said to be crossed in a 4 × 3 crossed-factor design. Such a design yields 12 different cells, with each cell containing a set of observations or data obtained from a specific combination of the factor levels.

cross-fostering *n.* **1.** in ANIMAL BEHAVIOR studies, the exchange of offspring between litters as a means of separating the effects of genetics from early experience. Wild rats reared by laboratory rats display less aggressive behavior, and mice from a polygynous species with low levels of territorial aggression that are cross-fostered to monogamous territorial mice display increased aggression and have patterns of brain neuropeptides more similar to their foster parents than to their natural parents. See also SEXUAL IMPRINTING. **2.** a similar technique used for investigating the effect of genetic factors in the development of a disorder. It involves either (a) having the offspring of biological parents who do not show the disorder being studied reared by adoptive parents who do or (b) having offspring of parents who show the disorder reared by parents who do not. Children cross-fostered in this manner are called **index adoptees**, whereas **control adoptees** are children of biological parents who do not show the disorder reared by adoptive parents who also do not show the disorder.

cross-lagged panel design a longitudinal experimental design used to increase the plausibility of causal inference in which two variables, A and B, are measured at time 1 (A_1, B_1) and at time 2 (A_2, B_2). Comparison of **cross-lagged panel correlations** between A_1B_2 and B_1A_2 may suggest a preponderance of causal influence of A over B or of B over A.

cross-linkage theory the concept that biological aging results from functional deterioration of body tissues due to the molecular cross-linkages of and subsequent structural changes in collagen and other proteins.

cross-modal association 1. the coordination of sensory inputs involving different brain regions. It is usually required in tasks that involve matching auditory and visual inputs, tactile and visual inputs, or a similar combination of cognitive functions. Lesions in the temporal, parietal, or occipital lobes may be diagnosed by cross-modal association testing. **2.** a phenomenon in which the input to one sense reliably generates an additional sensory output that is usually generated by the input to a separate sense.

cross-modality matching a DIRECT SCALING method of matching the magnitude of a stimulus (e.g., the brightness of a light) to the magnitude of another stimulus to which a different sense responds (e.g., the loudness of a sound).

cross-modal matching see INTERMODAL MATCHING.

cross-modal perception see INTERSENSORY PERCEPTION.

cross-modal transfer recognition of an object through a sense that differs from the sense through which it was originally encountered.

cross-nasal adaptation OLFACTORY ADAPTA-TION in one side of the nose after presenting a stimulus to the other side of the nose. Typically, cross-nasal adaptation is less pronounced than the adaptation in the side of the nose that receives the stimulus.

crossover design an experimental design in which different treatments are applied to the same sampling units (e.g., individuals) during different periods, as in LATIN SQUARES.

cross-sectional design an experimental design in which individuals of different ages or developmental levels are directly compared, for example, in a **cross-sectional study** comparing 5-year-olds with 10-year-olds. Compare LONGITUDINAL DESIGN.

cross-tabulation *n.* a method of arranging or presenting data (e.g., values, levels) in tabular form to show the mutual influence of one variable or variables on another variable or variables.

cross-tolerance *n.* the potential for a drug, often a CNS DEPRESSANT, to produce the diminished effects of another drug of the same type when tissue tolerance for the effects of the latter substance has developed. Thus, a person with alcohol dependence can substitute a barbiturate or another sedative to prevent withdrawal symptoms, and vice versa. Similarly, cross-tolerance exists among most of the hallucinogens, except marijuana. Also called **cross-addiction**.

cross-validation *n.* a model-evaluation approach in which the VALIDITY of a model is assessed by applying it to new data (i.e., data that were not used in developing the model). For example, a test's validity may be confirmed by administering the same test to a new sample in order to check the correctness of the initial validation. Cross-validation is necessary because chance and other factors may have inflated or biased the original validation.

crowd behavior the characteristic behavior of a group of people who congregate temporarily while their attention is focused on the same object or event. Typically, an audience is relatively passive (smiling, laughing, applauding), a street crowd moves without apparent aim, and a MOB may stampede or act violently.

crowding *n.* **1.** psychological tension produced in environments of high population density, especially when individuals feel that the amount of space available to them is insufficient for their needs. Crowding may have a damaging effect on mental health and may result in poor performance of complex tasks, stressor aftereffects, and increased physiological stress. In animals, crowding can lead to impaired reproduction, decreased life expectancy, and a variety of pathological behaviors. However, crowding per se is often not the main source of pathology, since human beings and animals can live in high densities if appropriate resources are available. Two key mechanisms underlying crowding are lack of control over social interaction (i.e., privacy) and the deterioration of socially supportive relationships. **2.** in learning, a situation in which there are too many items or tasks for the time allowed. Crowding would occur, for example, in an exam requiring the student to respond to 20 in-depth essay questions in 1 hour.

crowd mind a hypothetical explanation for the apparent uniformity of individuals' emotional, cognitive, and behavioral reactions when in large crowds; it supposes that a crowd of people can, in certain instances, become a unified entity that acts as if guided by a single collective mind. This hypothesis is not generally accepted now (see GROUP FALLACY). Also called **crowd consciousness**. Compare GROUP MIND.

crowd psychology 1. the mental and emotional states and processes unique to individuals when they are members of street crowds, MOBS, and other such collectives. **2.** the scientific study of these phenomena.

crypsis *n.* the ability to remain inconspicuous through immobility and other behavior or through the use of CAMOUFLAGE. —**cryptic** *adj.*

cryptic female choice a practice in which females mate with several males but "choose" which one's sperm will fertilize their eggs, concealing these decisions from the males. This practice allows females more choice in MATE SELECTION. In studies demonstrating cryptic female choice, it is the sperm that is genetically most compatible that fertilizes the female's eggs, rather than sperm from the most attractive males.

crystallization *n.* in social psychology, the STRENGTH OF AN ATTITUDE or, more specifically, the level of persistence of an attitude over time and the level of resistance of the attitude to active attempts to change it.

crystallized intelligence (**crystallized ability**) see CATTELL–HORN THEORY OF INTELLIGENCE.

Cs abbreviation for CONSCIOUS.

CS abbreviation for CONDITIONED STIMULUS.

CSF abbreviation for CEREBROSPINAL FLUID.

CT 1. abbreviation for COGNITIVE THERAPY. **2.** abbreviation for COMPUTED TOMOGRAPHY.

CTD abbreviation for cumulative trauma disorder (see REPETITIVE STRAIN INJURY).

CTS abbreviation for CARPAL TUNNEL SYNDROME.

CT scan abbreviation for COMPUTED TOMOGRAPHY scan.

cuckoldry *n.* sexual behavior in which a pair-bonded female mates with a male other than her partner. Only about 10% of bird species that are socially monogamous are genetically monogamous as well (see MONOGAMY). Males whose mates engage in extrapair mating assist in the rearing of resultant unrelated offspring. Females practicing cuckoldry may benefit from having progeny from genetically higher quality males.

cue *n.* **1.** a stimulus that serves to guide behavior. **2.** see RETRIEVAL CUE.

cue-dependent forgetting forgetting caused by the absence at testing of a stimulus (or cue) that was present when the learning occurred. See also CONTEXT-SPECIFIC LEARNING; MOOD-DEPENDENT MEMORY; STATE-DEPENDENT LEARNING.

cued panic attack a PANIC ATTACK that occurs almost invariably upon exposure to, or in anticipation of, a specific situational trigger. For example, an individual with social phobia may have a panic attack as a result of just thinking about an upcoming presentation. Also called **situationally bound panic attack**. Compare UNCUED PANIC ATTACK.

cued recall a type of memory task in which an item to be remembered is presented for study along with a CUE and the participant subsequently attempts to recall the item when given the cue.

cued speech speech that is supplemented with manual gestures for the benefit of people with hearing impairment. Hand positions are used to indicate certain phonemic distinctions that are not visible. For example, the distinction between /p/ and /t/ when spoken is visible, whereas the distinction between /t/ and /d/ is not. Unlike SIGN LANGUAGE and FINGERSPELLING, the hand positions are not adequate to convey communication without the accompanying speech.

cult *n.* **1.** a religious or quasi-religious group characterized by unusual or atypical beliefs, seclusion from the outside world, and an authoritarian structure. Cults tend to be highly cohesive, well-organized, secretive, and hostile to nonmembers. **2.** the system of beliefs and rituals specific to a particular religious group.

cultural competency 1. possession of the skills and knowledge that are appropriate for and specific to a given culture. **2.** the capacity to function effectively in cultural settings other than one's own. This will usually involve a recognition of the diversity both between and within cultures, a capacity for cultural self-assessment, and a willingness to adapt personal behaviors and practices.

cultural deprivation 1. lack of opportunity to participate in the cultural offerings of the larger society due to such factors as economic deprivation, substandard living conditions, or discrimination. **2.** loss of identification with one's cultural heritage as a result of assimilation into a larger or dominant culture. See DECULTURATION. **3.** lack of culturally stimulating phenomena in one's environment.

cultural determinism the theory or premise that individual and group character patterns are produced largely by a given society's economic, social, political, and religious organization. See also DETERMINISM; SOCIAL DETERMINISM.

cultural heritage the customs, language, values, and skills that are handed down from each generation to the next in a particular cultural group and help to maintain its sense of identity.

The cultural heritage also includes specific technological or artistic achievements. See SOCIAL HERITAGE; SOCIAL TRANSMISSION.

cultural learning the transmission of acquired information and behavior both within and across generations with a high degree of fidelity. Cultural learning theory proposes three stagelike levels of cultural learning: IMITATIVE LEARNING, INSTRUCTED LEARNING, and COLLABORATIVE LEARNING.

culturally disadvantaged describing children whose environments hinder their social and intellectual development. See CULTURAL DEPRIVATION.

culturally loaded items test questions that cannot be correctly answered unless the participants are sufficiently familiar with their cultural or subcultural meanings. Culturally loaded items tend to bias a test in favor of the group or social class from whose experience they are drawn. It often is difficult to discern cultural loadings just from looking at test items, as the effects of culture may be subtle. See CULTURE-FAIR TESTS.

cultural monism a view or perspective holding that MULTICULTURALISM operates against social cohesion and that ethnic and other minorities should therefore be encouraged to assimilate with the dominant culture.

cultural pluralism see MULTICULTURALISM.

cultural psychology an interdisciplinary extension of general psychology concerned with those psychological processes that are inherently organized by culture. It is a heterogeneous class of perspectives that focus on explaining how human psychological functions are culturally constituted through various forms of relations between people and their social contexts. As a discipline, cultural psychology relates to cultural anthropology, sociology, semiotics, language philosophy, and culture studies. Within psychology, cultural psychology relates most closely to cross-cultural, social, developmental, and cognitive issues.

cultural relativism the view that attitudes, behaviors, values, concepts, and achievements must be understood in the light of their own cultural milieu and not judged according to the standards of a different culture. In psychology, the relativist position questions the universal application of psychological theory, research, therapeutic techniques, and clinical approaches, since those used or developed in one culture may not be appropriate or applicable to another. See also RELATIVISM. Compare CULTURAL UNIVERSALISM.

cultural test bias bias of a test in favor of those individuals from certain cultures at the expense of those individuals from other cultures. The bias may be in the content of the items, in the format of the items, or in the very act of taking a test itself. See also CULTURALLY LOADED ITEMS.

cultural universalism the view that the values, concepts, and behaviors characteristic of diverse cultures can be viewed, understood, and judged according to universal standards. Such a view involves the rejection, at least in part, of CULTURAL RELATIVISM. Also called **cultural absolutism**.

culture n. **1.** the distinctive customs, values, beliefs, knowledge, art, and language of a society or a community. **2.** the characteristic attitudes and behaviors of a particular group within society, such as a profession, social class, or age group. See also COUNTERCULTURE; SUBCULTURE; YOUTH CULTURE. —**cultural** adj.

culture-bound syndrome a pattern of mental illness and abnormal behavior that is unique to a small ethnic or cultural population and does not conform to Western classifications of psychiatric disorders. Culture-bound syndromes include, among others, AMOK, IMU, KORO, LATAH, MAL DE PELEA, MYRIACHIT, PIBLOKTO, SUSTO, VOODOO DEATH, and WINDIGO. Also called **culture-specific syndrome**.

culture conflict 1. tension or competition between different cultures. It often results in the weakening of a minority group's adherence to cultural practices and beliefs as these are superseded by those of a dominant or adjoining culture. Also called **intergroup culture conflict**. **2.** the conflicting loyalties experienced by individuals who endorse the cultural beliefs of their subgroup but are also drawn to the practices and beliefs of the dominant culture. Also called **internal culture conflict**. See CULTURE SHOCK.

culture-fair tests intelligence tests based on common human experience and alleged to be relatively fair with respect to special cultural influences. Unlike the standard intelligence tests, which reflect predominantly middle-class experience, these tests are designed to apply across social lines and to permit fair comparisons among people from different cultures. Nonverbal, nonacademic items are used, such as matching identical forms, selecting a design that completes a given series, or drawing human figures. Studies have shown, however, that any test reflects certain cultural norms in some degree, and hence may tend to favor members of certain cultures over members of others. See also CROSS-CULTURAL TESTING.

culture-free tests intelligence tests designed completely to eliminate cultural bias by constructing questions that contain either no environmental influences or no environmental influences that reflect any specific culture. However, the creation of such a test is probably impossible. See CULTURE-FAIR TESTS.

culture-relevant tests tests that are designed specifically to be relevant to a given cultural context. These tests typically differ at least somewhat from one culture to another beyond mere differences in language, and they have been carefully screened for appropriateness.

culture shock feelings of inner tension or conflict experienced by an individual or group that has been suddenly thrust into an alien culture or that experiences loyalties to two different cultures.

cumulative record a continuous record to which new data are added. In CONDITIONING, for example, a cumulative record is a graph showing the cumulative number of responses over a continuous period of time. It is often used in such contexts to display performance of FREE-OPERANT behavior under SCHEDULES OF REINFORCEMENT and provides a direct and continuous indicator of the rate of response.

cumulative rehearsal a strategy for retaining information in short-term memory in which a person repeats the most recently presented item (e.g., a word) and then rehearses it (see REHEARSAL) with all the items that have been presented before it, thus reviewing earlier items upon each presentation of a new item. Cumulative rehearsal is associated with higher levels of free-recall performance than is PASSIVE REHEARSAL. Also called **active rehearsal**.

cumulative trauma disorder (CTD) see REPETITIVE STRAIN INJURY.

cuneate fasciculus the lateral portion of either of the DORSAL columns of the spinal cord, which is wedge-shaped in transverse section. It is composed of ascending fibers that terminate in the medulla oblongata. See also GRACILE FASCICULUS.

cupula *n.* a gelatinous cap that forms part of the crista within the ampulla at the end of a SEMICIRCULAR CANAL.

curative factors model a model that seeks to identify those elements present in therapeutic groups that aid and promote personal growth and adjustment. U.S. psychologist Irwin Yalom (1931–) identified 10–15 curative factors, including the installation of hope, UNIVERSALITY, the imparting of information, altruism, and interpersonal learning.

curiosity *n.* the impulse or desire to investigate, observe, or gather information, particularly when the material is novel or interesting. This drive appears spontaneously in animals and in young children, who use sensory exploration and motor manipulation to inspect, bite, handle, taste, or smell practically everything in the immediate environment. —**curious** *adj.*

curriculum-based assessment 1. a complete, broad evaluation profile that reveals the degree of student mastery of a given defined body of content. The evaluation includes teacher-based testing (see CURRICULUM-BASED MEASUREMENT), classroom observation and interactions, standardized tests when relevant, and any other method of evaluation that yields data that can contribute to the overall assessment

profile. **2.** data that help determine specific standards, such as those involved in individualized educational planning, direct performance referrals, and other forms of systematic planning relative to student progress.

curriculum-based measurement a narrow evaluation of student performance based on the material that has actually been taught, as opposed to CURRICULUM-BASED ASSESSMENTS, which are much broader and compare students to state, national, or other standard norms.

curve fitting any of various statistical techniques for obtaining a curve that graphically represents a given set of data.

curvilinear correlation a functional relationship between variables that is not of a straight-line form when depicted graphically.

custodial care 1. care rendered to a patient with prolonged mental or physical disability that includes assisted daily living (e.g., the regular feeding and washing of bedridden patients) but typically not mental health services themselves. **2.** confinement in such institutions as prisons and military correctional facilities that place restrictions on individuals' liberty under the rules of law and that protect and monitor the individual or protect others from the individual's violent and harmful tendencies or potential.

customary, prevailing, and reasonable fees (CPR fees) a criterion invoked in reimbursing health care providers. It is determined by profiling the prevailing fees in a geographic area. Also called **usual, customary, and reasonable** (UCR) **fees**.

customer-relationship management the practice by companies of anticipating the future needs of their customers based on knowledge of past purchasing behaviors. Databases of information about consumers are used for this purpose.

cutaneous receptor a receptor organ that is responsible for sensation through the medium of the skin. Cutaneous receptors include PACINIAN CORPUSCLES, BASKET ENDINGS, MEISSNER'S CORPUSCLES, and MERKEL'S TACTILE DISKS.

cutaneous sense any of the senses that are dependent on receptors in the skin sensitive to contact, pressure, vibration, temperature, or pain. Also called **skin sense**. See PRESSURE SENSE; TEMPERATURE SENSE; TOUCH SENSE.

CVA abbreviation for CEREBROVASCULAR ACCIDENT.

CVLT abbreviation for CALIFORNIA VERBAL LEARNING TEST.

CVS abbreviation for CHORIONIC VILLUS SAMPLING.

cyanopsia *n.* see CHROMATOPSIA.

cybernetic theory the study of how machines or other artificial systems can be made to regulate and guide themselves in the manner of living organisms. Its main application is the design of computer-controlled automated systems in manufacturing, transport, telecommunications, and other fields. The most widely used aspect of cybernetic theory is the self-regulatory model known as the FEEDBACK LOOP.

cycle of violence a conceptual framework for understanding the persistence of battering relationships. The cycle has three phases: (a) a "honeymoon phase," in which the batterer treats the battered partner lovingly; (b) a "tension build-up phase," in which the batterer begins to display irritability and anger toward the battered partner; and (c) the violence phase, in which battering occurs. The phases are then proposed to recycle. As a battering relationship persists over time, the honeymoon phases shorten, and the tension-building and violence phases lengthen. Also called **cycle of abuse**.

cyclic *adj.* characterized by alternating phases. Also called **cyclical**.

cyclic AMP (cyclic adenosine monophosphate) a SECOND MESSENGER that is involved in the activities of DOPAMINE, NOREPINEPHRINE, and SEROTONIN in transmitting signals at nerve synapses. Also called **adenosine 3′,5′-monophosphate**.

cyclic GMP (cyclic guanosine monophosphate) a SECOND MESSENGER that is common in POSTSYNAPTIC neurons.

cyclic nucleotide a substance, such as CYCLIC AMP or CYCLIC GMP, that functions as a SECOND MESSENGER in cells to transduce an incoming signal, such as a hormone or neurotransmitter, into specific activity within the cell.

cyclophoria *n.* an imbalance of the extrinsic eye muscles in which one eye deviates when not focused on an object.

cyclothymic disorder a MOOD DISORDER characterized by periods of hypomanic symptoms and periods of depressive symptoms that occur over the course of at least 2 years (1 year in children and adolescents), during which any symptom-free periods must last no longer than 2 months. The symptoms are those of a MAJOR DEPRESSIVE EPISODE or a HYPOMANIC EPISODE, but the number, duration, and severity of these symptoms do not meet the full criteria for a major depressive episode or a hypomanic episode. Also called **cyclothymia**.

cyclotropia *n.* see STRABISMUS.

cytoarchitecture *n.* the arrangement of cells in organs and tissues, particularly those in the NEOCORTEX. The different types of cortical cells are organized in CORTICAL LAYERS and zones. The number of layers varies in different brain areas, but a typical section of neocortex shows six distinct layers. Differences in cytoarchitecture have been used to divide the neocortex into 50 or more regions, many of which differ in function. The scientific study of the cytoarchitecture of an organ is called **cytoarchitectonics**. Also called **architectonic structure**. See also BRODMANN'S AREA. —**cytoarchitectural** *adj.*

cytochrome P450 a group of proteins located in the liver and elsewhere that, in combination with other oxidative enzymes, is responsible for the metabolism of various chemicals, including many psychotropic drugs. Approximately 50 cytochrome P450 enzymes (so named because their reduced forms show a spectroscopic absorption peak at 450 nm) are currently identified as being active in humans, of which cytochromes belonging to the CYP2D6 subclass, CYP2C variants, and CYP3A4/5 subclass predominate. Cytochromes are mainly active in Phase I DRUG METABOLISM; by donating an atom of oxygen, they tend to make parent drugs more water soluble and therefore more easily excreted. Because numerous drugs are metabolized via the same cytochrome, these enzymes are important in DRUG INTERACTIONS.

cytokine *n.* any of a variety of small proteins or peptides that are released by cells as signals to those or other cells. Each type stimulates a target cell that has a specific receptor for that cytokine. Cytokines mediate many immune responses, including proliferation and differentiation of lymphocytes, inflammation, allergies, and fever.

cytology *n.* the branch of biology that deals with the development, structure, and function of cells. —**cytological** *adj.* —**cytologist** *n.*

cytosine (symbol: C) *n.* a pyrimidine compound present in the nucleotides of living organisms. It is one of the four bases in DNA and RNA constituting the GENETIC CODE, the others being adenine, guanine, and thymine or uracil.

Dd

d′ symbol for D PRIME.

DA 1. abbreviation for DEVELOPMENTAL AGE. **2.** abbreviation for DOPAMINE.

dance therapy the use of various forms of rhythmic movement—classical, modern, folk, or ballroom dancing; exercises to music; and the like—as a therapeutic technique to help individuals achieve greater body awareness and social interaction and enhance their psychological and physical functioning. See also MOVEMENT THERAPY.

dangerousness *n.* the state in which individuals become likely to do harm either to themselves or to others, representing a threat to their own or other people's safety. **—dangerous** *adj.*

dark adaptation the ability of the eye to adjust to conditions of low illumination by means of an increased sensitivity to light. The bulk of the process takes 30 min and involves expansion of the pupils and retinal alterations, specifically the regeneration of RHODOPSIN and IODOPSIN. See also ROD–CONE BREAK. Compare LIGHT ADAPTATION.

dark cell see TYPE I CELL.

Darwinian algorithm in EVOLUTIONARY DEVELOPMENTAL PSYCHOLOGY, an innate domain-specific cognitive program that evolved to accomplish specific adaptive functions. An example is the cognitive mechanism for face recognition. [Charles **Darwin** (1809–1882), British naturalist]

Darwinism *n.* the theory of evolution by NATURAL SELECTION, as originally proposed by British naturalists Charles Darwin (1809–1882) and Alfred Russel Wallace (1823–1913). In the 20th century it was modified, as **neo-Darwinism**, to account for genetic mechanisms of heredity, particularly the sources of genetic variation upon which natural selection works. See also SURVIVAL OF THE FITTEST.

Dasein *n.* in the thought of German philosopher Martin Heidegger (1889–1976), the particular kind of being manifest in humans. It is their being as *Dasein* that allows human beings access to the larger question of being in general, since our access to the world is always through what our own being makes possible. The term is commonly used in EXISTENTIAL PSYCHOLOGY and related therapeutic approaches. See BEING-IN-THE-WORLD. [German, literally: "being there"]

Dasein analysis a method of EXISTENTIAL PSYCHOTHERAPY emphasizing the need to recognize not only one's BEING-IN-THE-WORLD but also what one can become (see DASEIN). Through examination of such concepts as intentionality and intuition, Dasein analysis attempts to help clients to accept themselves and realize their potential.

DAT abbreviation for DEMENTIA OF THE ALZHEIMER'S TYPE.

data *pl. n.* (*sing.* **datum**) observations or measurements, usually quantified and obtained in the course of research.

data analysis the process of applying graphical, statistical, or quantitative techniques to a set of data (observations or measurements) in order to summarize it or to find general patterns.

data-driven processing see BOTTOM-UP PROCESSING.

data pooling combining the data of two or more studies or substudies. This procedure can sometimes lead to misleading conclusions, as in SIMPSON'S PARADOX.

data reduction the process of reducing a set of measurements or variables into a smaller, more manageable, more reliable, or better theoretically justified set or form.

data snooping looking for unpredicted, post hoc effects in a body of data.

date rape sexual assault by an acquaintance, date, or other person known to the victim, often involving alcohol or drugs that may hinder the victim's ability to withhold consent. Also called **acquaintance rape.**

day blindness see HEMERALOPIA.

day camp a facility that provides recreational, educational, or therapeutic services to children on a short-term, day-by-day basis, as opposed to long-term camps that require overnight accommodation.

day care center a nonresidential facility that provides health and social services in a community setting for adults who are unable to perform many ordinary tasks without supervision or assistance. See ADULT DAY CARE.

daydream *n.* a waking FANTASY, or reverie, in which conscious or unconscious wishes, and sometimes fears, are played out in imagination. Part of the stream of thoughts and images that occupy most of a person's waking hours, daydreams may be unbidden and apparently purposeless or simply fanciful thoughts, whether spontaneous or intentional. Researchers have identified at least three ways in which individuals' daydreaming styles differ: positive-constructive daydreaming, guilty and fearful daydreaming, and poor attentional control. These styles are posited to reflect the day-dreamer's overall tendencies toward positive emotion, negative emotion, and other personality traits. See also WISH-FULFILLMENT.

day habilitation a HOME AND COMMUNITY-BASED SERVICE provided for a person with mental retardation or a related condition. This service provides productive daily schedules of activity based on individualized service and support planning, including clinical services, companion services, socialization, recreation, vocational development, and lifestyle enrichment.

day hospital a hospital where patients receive a full range of treatment services during the day and return to their homes at night. Services include individual and group therapy, psychological evaluation, occupational and recreational therapy, and somatic therapy. The concept is now used in rehabilitation as well as mental health care. See PARTIAL HOSPITALIZATION.

daymare *n.* an attack of acute anxiety, distress, or terror, which is similar to a NIGHTMARE but occurs in a period of wakefulness and is precipitated by waking-state fantasies.

day treatment a program of coordinated inter-disciplinary assessment, treatment, and rehabilitation services provided by professionals and paraprofessionals for people with disabilities, mental or physical disorders, or substance abuse problems, usually at a single location for 6 or more hours.

dB symbol for DECIBEL.

deaf-blind *adj.* lacking or having severely compromised vision and hearing concomitantly. **—deaf-blindness** *n.*

deafferentation *n.* the cutting or removal of neurons or axons that conduct impulses toward a particular nervous system structure (e.g., the olfactory bulb).

deafness *n.* the partial or complete loss of the sense of hearing. The condition may be hereditary or acquired by injury or disease. The major kinds are **conduction deafness**, due to a disruption in sound vibrations before they reach the nerve endings of the inner ear; and **sensorineural deafness**, caused by a failure of the nerves or brain centers associated with the sense of hearing to transmit or interpret properly the impulses from the inner ear. **—deaf** *adj.*

death *n.* **1.** the permanent cessation of physical and mental processes in an organism. In the United States in the early 1980s, in the Uniform Determination of Death Act, death was defined as either the irreversible cessation of core physiological functioning (i.e., spontaneous circulatory and respiratory functions) or the irreversible loss of cerebral functioning (i.e., BRAIN DEATH). Given the emergence of sophisticated technologies for cardiopulmonary support, brain death is more often considered the essential determining

factor, particularly within the legal profession. See also ASSISTED DEATH; THANATOLOGY. **2.** the degeneration or disintegration of a biological cell. See NECROSIS.

death anxiety emotional distress and insecurity aroused by reminders of mortality, including one's own memories and thoughts. Classical psychoanalytic theory asserted that the unconscious cannot believe in its own death, therefore THANATOPHOBIA was a disguise for some deeper fear. Existentialists later proposed that death anxiety is at the root of all fears, though often disguised. Research using self-report scales suggests that most people have a low to moderate level of death anxiety.

death education learning activities or programs designed to educate people about death, dying, coping with grief, and the various emotional effects of bereavement. Death education is typically provided by certified thanatologists from a wide array of mental and medical health personnel, educators, clergy, and volunteers. Individual or group sessions provide information, discussion, guided experiences, and exploration of attitudes and feelings.

death instinct in psychoanalytic theory, a drive whose aim is the reduction of psychical tension to the lowest possible point, that is, death. It is first directed inward as a self-destructive tendency and is later turned outward in the form of the AGGRESSIVE INSTINCT. In the DUAL INSTINCT THEORY of Austrian psychiatrist Sigmund Freud (1856–1939), the death instinct, or THANATOS, stands opposed to the LIFE INSTINCT, or EROS, and is believed to be the drive underlying such behaviors as aggressiveness, sadism, and masochism. See also DESTRUDO; MORTIDO.

death system the dynamic patterns through which a society mediates its relationship with mortality in order to remain viable as a culture and meet the needs of the individual. All cultures have a death system whose primary functions are warning and prediction, prevention, care for the dying, disposing of the dead, social consolidation after death, killing, and making sense of death. How these functions are performed is significantly influenced by a number of factors, including economic priorities, religious values, traditions of discrimination and enmity, and level of technological development.

death wish 1. in psychoanalytic theory, a conscious or unconscious wish that another person, particularly a parent, will die. According to Austrian psychiatrist Sigmund Freud (1856–1939), such wishes are a major source of guilt, desire for self-punishment, and depression. **2.** an unconscious desire for one's own death, as manifested in self-destructive or dangerous behaviors. See also DEATH INSTINCT.

deautomatization hypothesis the idea that automatic processes can be brought under conscious, voluntary control. See AUTOMATICITY.

debriefing *n.* the process of giving participants in a completed research project a fuller explanation of the study in which they participated than was possible before or during the research.

debt counseling counseling specifically aimed at helping individuals with financial problems. The help and advice given includes budgeting, credit-card usage, debt consolidation, and awareness of difficulties in managing money. Debt counseling may be part of the counseling or therapy for other problems or it may be carried out by financial planners and accountants.

décalage *n.* in PIAGETIAN THEORY, the invariant order in which cognitive accomplishments develop. See HORIZONTAL DÉCALAGE; VERTICAL DÉCALAGE. [French, "interval," "shift"]

decathexis *n.* in psychoanalytic theory, the withdrawal of LIBIDO from objects (i.e., other people) in the external world. Compare CATHEXIS.

decay theory a theory of FORGETTING stating that learned material leaves in the brain a trace or impression that autonomously recedes and disappears unless the material is practiced and used.

deceleration *n.* a decrease in speed of movement or rate of change. Compare ACCELERATION.

decentralization *n.* the trend to relocate patients with chronic mental illness from long-term institutionalization, usually at government hospitals, to outpatient care in community-based, residential facilities. —**decentralize** *vb.*

decentration *n.* in PIAGETIAN THEORY, the gradual progression of a child away from egocentrism toward a reality shared with others. Decentration includes understanding how others perceive the world, knowing in what ways one's own perceptions differ, and recognizing that people have motivations and feelings different from one's own. It can also be extended to the ability to consider many aspects of a situation, problem, or object, as reflected, for example, in the child's grasp of the concept of CONSERVATION. Also called **decentering**. Compare CENTRATION. —**decenter** *vb.*

deception clue a behavioral indication that an individual is not telling the truth. Deception clues include inconsistencies between voluntary and involuntary behavior and unusual or exaggerated physiological or expressive responses to certain data.

deception research research in which participants are misled or not informed about the nature of the investigation. See ACTIVE DECEPTION; PASSIVE DECEPTION.

decerebrate rigidity bilateral rigid extension, adduction, and hyperpronation of the legs and arms that occur when the brainstem is functionally separated from the cerebral cortex, typically as a result of a brain lesion or vascular disorder.

decerebration *n.* loss of the ability to discriminate, learn, and control movements as a result of transecting the brainstem, surgically removing the CEREBRUM, or cutting off the cerebral blood supply. A **decerebrate** is an animal that has undergone decerebration.

decibel (symbol: dB) *n.* a logarithmic unit used to express the ratio of acoustic or electric power (intensity). An increase of 1 bel is a 10-fold increase in intensity; a decibel is one tenth of a bel and is the more commonly used unit, partly because a 1-dB change in intensity is just detectable (approximately and under laboratory conditions). The **sound intensity** (the numerator of the intensity ratio) or **sound level** is usually specified in **decibels sound-pressure level** (dB SPL). The reference intensity (the denominator of the intensity ratio) for dB SPL is 10^{-12} W/m^2 and corresponds to a SOUND PRESSURE of 20 μPa (micropascal). Often SPL is omitted but is implied from the context: A "60-dB sound" usually means 60 dB SPL.

decile *n.* the tenth part of a statistical distribution. The first 10% of cases comprises the first decile, the second 10% is the second decile, and so on.

decisional balance a method of assessing the positive and negative consequences, for oneself and others, of selecting a new behavior. Decisional balance is frequently used in weighing the consequences of exercise behavior. For example, by beginning a regular early-morning exercise program, an individual would lose weight (a positive consequence) but would incur costs in terms of gym fees and workout clothes (a negative consequence).

decision making the cognitive process of choosing between two or more alternatives. Psychologists have adopted two converging strategies to understand decision making: (a) statistical analysis of multiple decisions involving complex tasks and (b) experimental manipulation of simple decisions, looking at elements that recur within these decisions.

decision-plane model a two-dimensional schema of the risks and benefits of doing research. This permits an informed evaluation of the ethical implications of conducting a particular study.

decision rule in hypothesis testing, the formal statement of the set of values of the test statistic that will lead to rejection of the NULL HYPOTHESIS.

decision theory a broad class of theories in the quantitative, social, and behavioral sciences that aim to explain the decision-making process and identify optimal ways of arriving at decisions (e.g., under conditions of uncertainty) in such a way that prespecified criteria are met.

declarative memory memory that can be consciously recalled in response to a request to remember. In some theories, declarative memory includes EPISODIC MEMORY and SEMANTIC

MEMORY. See also EXPLICIT MEMORY. Compare PROCEDURAL MEMORY.

decompensation *n.* a breakdown in an individual's DEFENSE MECHANISMS, resulting in progressive loss of normal functioning or worsening of psychiatric symptoms.

decomposition *n.* a process in which a complex item is separated into its simpler constituent elements. For example, in problem solving it is a strategy in which a problem is transformed into two or more simpler problems.

deconditioning *n.* a technique in BEHAVIOR THERAPY in which learned responses, such as phobias, are "unlearned" (deconditioned). For example, a person with a phobic reaction to flying might be deconditioned initially by practicing going to the airport when not actually taking a flight and using breathing techniques to control anxiety. See also DESENSITIZATION.

deconstruction *n.* a form of critical analysis of literary texts and philosophical positions based on the twin assumptions that there can be no firm referents for language and no adequate grounding for truth claims. A deconstructive reading of a text will generally use traditional analytical methods to expose the numerous ways in which the text subverts its own claims to meaning and coherence. The term is now taken to be synonymous with the destruction of an idea or of a truth claim. See also POSTSTRUCTURALISM.

decontextualization *n.* the process of examining, considering, or interpreting something separately from the context within which it is embedded. Decontextualization may occur consciously (e.g., with the aim of subjecting a constituent element of some phenomenon or process to closer, individual study) or unconsciously. —**decontextualize** *vb.*

decortication *n.* surgical removal of the outer layer (cortex) of the brain while allowing deeper tissues to remain functional.

decremental conduction the exponential decay in the size of a membrane potential with distance from the site of stimulation when a subthreshold stimulus is applied to an axon. Compare NONDECREMENTAL CONDUCTION.

deculturation *n.* the processes, intentional or unintentional, by which traditional cultural beliefs or practices are suppressed or otherwise eliminated as a result of contact with a different, dominant culture. Compare ACCULTURATION. —**deculturate** *vb.*

decussation *n.* a crossing or intersection in the form of a letter X, as in the decussation of the fibers of the left and right optic nerves in the OPTIC CHIASM.

deduction *n.* **1.** a conclusion derived from formal premises by a valid process of DEDUCTIVE REASONING. **2.** the process of deductive reasoning itself. Compare INDUCTION. —**deductive** *adj.*

deductive reasoning the form of logical reasoning in which a conclusion is shown to follow necessarily from a sequence of premises, the first of which stands for a self-evident truth (see AXIOM) or agreed-upon data. In the empirical sciences, deductive reasoning underlies the process of deriving predictions from general laws or theories. Compare INDUCTIVE REASONING. See also LOGIC.

deep dyslexia a form of acquired dyslexia characterized by semantic errors (e.g., reading *parrot* as *canary*), difficulties in reading abstract words (e.g., *idea*, *usual*) and function words (e.g., *the*, *and*), and an inability to read pronounceable nonwords.

deep processing cognitive processing of a stimulus that focuses on its meaningful properties rather than its perceptual characteristics. It is considered that processing at this semantic level, which usually involves a degree of ELABORATION, produces stronger, longer-lasting memories than SHALLOW PROCESSING.

deep structure in TRANSFORMATIONAL GENERATIVE GRAMMAR, an abstract base form of a sentence in which the logical and grammatical relations between the constituents are made explicit. The deep structure generates the SURFACE STRUCTURE of a sentence through transformations, such as changes in word order or addition or deletion of elements. Also called **base structure**.

Deese paradigm a laboratory memory task used to study false recall. It is based on the report in 1959 that, after presentation of a list of related words (e.g., *snore, rest, dream, awake*), participants mistakenly recalled an unpresented but strongly associated item (e.g., *sleep*). Following renewed research into the technique, it is now generally referred to as the **Deese–Roediger–McDermott paradigm**. [James **Deese** (1921–1999), U.S. psychologist; Henry L. **Roediger** III (1947–) and Kathleen B. **McDermott** (1968–), U.S. cognitive psychologists]

defect *n.* a fault or error in something that prevents it from functioning correctly. —**defective** *adj.*

defect orientation in interdisciplinary team or other individual service-planning processes, an emphasis that focuses on the impairments, limitations, deficits, or defects in functioning of individuals with disabilities, but that excludes corresponding assessment of and emphasis on their skills, abilities, and strengths.

defect theory the proposition that the cognitive processes and behavioral development of people with mental retardation are qualitatively different from those of their peers without mental retardation. Compare DEVELOPMENTAL THEORY.

defense mechanism in classical psychoanalytic theory, an unconscious reaction pattern employed by the EGO to protect itself from the anxiety that arises from psychic conflict. Such mechanisms range from mature to immature, depending on how much they distort reality. In more recent psychological theories, defense mechanisms are seen as normal means of coping with everyday problems, but excessive use of any one, or the use of immature defenses (e.g., DIS-PLACEMENT or REPRESSION), is still considered pathological. Also called **escape mechanism**. See also AVOIDANCE; DENIAL; PROJECTION; REGRESSION; SUBLIMATION; SUBSTITUTION.

defensive behavior aggressive or submissive behavior in response to real or imagined threats of bodily or other harm. A cat, for example, may exhibit defensive aggression by raising the hair along the back of the neck in anticipation of a physical threat, and a person might unconsciously fend off criticism by putting forth self-justifying excuses or by expressing an emotional reaction (e.g., crying) to limit another's disapproval or anger.

defensive conditioning a form of PAVLOVIAN CONDITIONING in which the UNCONDITIONED STIMULUS is noxious.

defensive identification the process by which a victim of abuse psychologically identifies with the perpetrator of abuse, or with the group with which the perpetrator is identified, as a defensive strategy against continuing feelings of vulnerability to further victimization.

defensiveness *n.* a tendency to be sensitive to criticism or comment about one's deficiencies and to counter or deny such criticisms. **—defensive** *adj.*

defensive processing the seeking out, attending to, encoding, interpreting, or elaborating of attitude-relevant information to support or confirm one's initial attitude. For example, defensive processing can involve avoiding attitude-inconsistent information and seeking out attitude-consistent information.

deferred imitation imitation of an act minutes, hours, or days after viewing the behavior. Recent research indicates that deferred imitation of simple tasks can be observed in infants late in their 1st year.

deficiency *n.* a lack or shortage of something. A deficiency may, for example, be a relative or absolute lack of a skill, of a biological substrate or process, or of resources that enable specific functions or actions to be performed.

deficiency cognition see BEING COGNITION.

deficiency love (**D-love**) in the HUMANISTIC PSYCHOLOGY of U.S. psychologist Abraham Maslow (1908–1970), a type of love that is fulfillment-oriented (e.g., based on a need for belonging, self-esteem, security, or power) and characterized by dependency, possessiveness, lack of mutuality, and little concern for the other's true welfare. Compare BEING LOVE.

deficiency motivation in the HUMANISTIC PSYCHOLOGY of U.S. psychologist Abraham Maslow (1908–1970), the type of motivation op-

erating on the lower four levels of his hierarchy of needs (see MASLOW'S MOTIVATIONAL HIERARCHY). Deficiency motivation is characterized by the striving to correct a deficit that may be physiological or psychological in nature. Compare METAMOTIVATION.

deficiency motive the tendency to satisfy a particular need simply in order to counter a deficiency, for example, eating only the amount of food required to alleviate hunger. Compare ABUNDANCY MOTIVE.

deficit *n.* a lack of an essential element in something that prevents it from functioning correctly.

deformity *n.* distortion or malformation of any part of the body.

degeneration *n.* **1.** deterioration or decline of organs or tissues, especially of neural tissue, to a less functional form. **2.** deterioration or decline of moral values. **—degenerate** *vb.*

degradation *n.* in neurophysiology, the process by which neurotransmitter molecules are broken down into inactive metabolites.

degrees of freedom 1. (symbol: *df*; v) the number of elements that are free to vary in a statistical calculation, or the number of scores minus the number of mathematical restrictions. For example, if four individuals have a mean IQ of 100, then there are three degrees of freedom, because knowing three of the IQs determines the fourth IQ. **2.** in motor control, the various joints that can move or the various muscles that can contract to produce a movement.

deindividuation *n.* an experiential state characterized by loss of self-awareness, altered perceptions, and a reduction of inner restraints that results in the performance of unusual, atypical behavior. It can be caused by a number of factors, such as a sense of anonymity or of submersion in a group.

deinstitutionalization *n.* the joint process of moving people with developmental or psychiatric disabilities from structured institutional facilities to their home communities and developing comprehensive community-based residential, day, vocational, clinical, and supportive services to address their needs. See COMMUNITY CARE. **—deinstitutionalize** *vb.*

déjà vu the feeling that a new event has already been experienced or that the same scene has been witnessed before. [French: "already seen"].

delay conditioning in PAVLOVIAN CONDITIONING, a procedure in which the CONDITIONED STIMULUS is presented, and remains present, for a fixed period (the delay) before the UNCONDITIONED STIMULUS is introduced. Compare SIMULTANEOUS CONDITIONING.

delayed alternation task a DELAYED RESPONSE task in which a nonhuman animal must alternate responses between trials. The most common version of this task is one in which a food reward is alternated from side to side with a delay between trials. Also called **delayed response alternation**.

delayed auditory feedback a technique of AUDITORY FEEDBACK in which speakers listen through headphones to their own speech, which is heard a short time after it is spoken. It is one of several techniques that may be used to induce greater fluency and clearer articulation in those with various speech and language disorders, particularly in those who stutter. Paradoxically, however, the delay has also been found to cause DYSFLUENCY in normally fluent speakers.

delayed matching to sample a procedure in which the participant is shown initially one stimulus as a sample (the study phase) and subsequently, after a variable interval, a pair of stimuli (the test phase), the task being to choose the stimulus in the test phase that matches the sample presented in the study phase. Responding to the stimulus that matches the sample is reinforced. In **delayed nonmatching to sample**, the participant must choose the stimulus that was not presented in the study phase.

delayed reinforcement reinforcement that does not occur immediately after a response has been made. The delay may be signaled or unsignaled. If it is signaled, a stimulus change occurs immediately after the response, and this stimulus remains present until the reinforcer is delivered. If the delay is unsignaled, there is no change of stimulus.

delayed response a response that occurs some time after its DISCRIMINATIVE STIMULUS has been removed. The most common **delayed response task** for nonhuman animals is one in which the animal is required to recall the location of a reward after a delay period has elapsed.

delayed speech the failure of speech to develop at the expected age.

deletion *n.* **1.** in genetics, a particular kind of MUTATION characterized by the loss of genetic material from a chromosome. The deletion may involve the loss of one or several base pairs or a much larger segment of a chromosome. **2.** in GENERATIVE GRAMMAR, the process in which a constituent of the DEEP STRUCTURE of a sentence is deleted from the SURFACE STRUCTURE (i.e., the sentence as used). For example, the sentence *I am happy, my mother is too* is derived from the deep structure *I am happy, my mother is happy too*, with the second *happy* deleted. The question of whether deletion can serve as a psychological model of sentence processing has been a subject of much psycholinguistic investigation.

delinquency *n.* behavior violating social rules or conventions. The term is often used to denote the misbehavior of children or adolescents. —**delinquent** *adj., n.*

delirium *n.* a state of disturbed consciousness in which attention cannot be sustained, the environment is misperceived, and the stream of thought is disordered. The individual may experience changes in cognition (which can include disorientation, memory impairment, or disturbance in language), perceptual disturbances, hallucinations, illusions, and misinterpretation of sounds or sights. The episode develops quickly and can fluctuate over a short period. Delirium may be caused by a variety of conditions including, but not limited to, infections, cerebral tumors, substance intoxication and withdrawal, head trauma, and seizures.

delirium tremens (**DTs**) a potentially fatal alcohol withdrawal syndrome involving extreme agitation and anxiety, fearfulness, paranoia, visual and tactile hallucinations, tremors, sweating, and increased heart rate, body temperature, and blood pressure.

Delphi technique a method of developing and improving group consensus by eliminating the effects of personal relationships and dominating personalities. Conflict is managed by circulating a questionnaire, which is edited and summarized based on the last round of comments and then reissued for further response by those participating in the survey.

delta alcoholism one of the five types of alcoholism defined by U.S. physician Elvin M. Jellinek (1890–1963), the others being ALPHA ALCOHOLISM, BETA ALCOHOLISM, GAMMA ALCOHOLISM, and EPSILON ALCOHOLISM. It is characterized by physical and psychological dependence, tolerance, inability to abstain, and withdrawal symptoms if use is suspended. Delta alcoholism is similar to gamma alcoholism but distinguished by the person's inability to abstain, as opposed to his or her complete loss of control over drinking.

delta receptor see OPIOID RECEPTOR.

delta wave the lowest frequency BRAIN WAVE recorded in electroencephalography. Delta waves are large, regular-shaped waves that have a frequency of 1–3 Hz. They are associated with deep, often dreamless, sleep (**delta-wave sleep**). Also called **delta rhythm**.

delusion *n.* an improbable, often highly personal, idea or belief system, not endorsed by one's culture or subculture, that is maintained with conviction in spite of irrationality or evidence to the contrary. Common types include DELUSIONAL JEALOUSY, DELUSIONS OF BEING CONTROLLED, DELUSIONS OF GRANDEUR, DELUSIONS OF PERSECUTION, DELUSIONS OF REFERENCE, nihilistic delusions (see NIHILISM), and SOMATIC DELUSIONS.

delusional disorder any one of a group of psychotic disorders with the essential feature of one or more delusions regarding situations that could conceivably occur in real life (e.g., being followed, poisoned, infected, deceived by one's government, etc.).

delusional jealousy the false but firmly held belief that a spouse or partner is unfaithful.

delusional misidentification syndrome see MISIDENTIFICATION SYNDROME.

delusion of being controlled the false belief that external forces, such as machines or other people, are controlling one's thoughts, feelings, or actions.

delusion of grandeur the false attribution to the self of great ability, knowledge, importance or worth, identity, prestige, power, accomplishment, or the like.

delusion of persecution the false conviction that others are threatening or conspiring against one.

delusion of reference the false conviction of a person that the actions of others and events occurring in the external world have some special meaning or significance (typically negative) to him or her.

demand *n.* a requirement or urgent need, particularly any internal or external condition that arouses a DRIVE in an organism.

demand characteristics in an experiment or research project, cues that may influence or bias participants' behavior, for example, by suggesting the outcome or response that the experimenter expects or desires.

demandment *n.* any self-constructed and often self-defeating and unconscious imperative that converts important desires and goals into absolute demands: "Because I am not performing well, as I *absolutely must,* I am a terrible person."

dementia *n.* a generalized, pervasive deterioration of cognitive functions, such as memory, language, and EXECUTIVE FUNCTIONS, due to any of various causes but commonly including Alzheimer's disease, Pick's disease, and cerebrovascular disease. The loss of intellectual abilities is severe enough to interfere with an individual's daily functioning and social and occupational activity. The age of onset varies with the cause but is usually late in life. When occurring after the age of 65 it is termed **senile dementia** and when appearing before 65 it is called **presenile dementia**. However, dementia should not be confused with AGE-ASSOCIATED MEMORY IMPAIRMENT, which has a much less deleterious impact on day-to-day functioning.

dementia of the Alzheimer's type (DAT) another name for ALZHEIMER'S DISEASE.

dementia praecox the original, now obsolete, name for SCHIZOPHRENIA, first used in 1896 by German psychiatrist Emil Kraepelin (1856–1926) and reflecting the belief that the symptoms of the disorder arose in adolescence or before and involved incurable degeneration. Swiss psychiatrist Eugen Bleuler (1857–1939) questioned both of these views and in 1911 renamed the disorder schizophrenia.

Deming management method an approach to management that emphasizes the strategic role of senior management in meeting customer needs by implementing continuous improvement in the quality of products and services. The method was important in the development of TOTAL QUALITY MANAGEMENT. [W. Edwards **Deming** (1900–1993), U.S. management expert]

democratic leader see LEADERSHIP STYLE.

demography *n.* the statistical study of human populations in regard to various factors and characteristics, including geographical distribution, sex and age distribution, size, structure, and growth trends. See also BIOSTATISTICS. —**demographer** *n.* —**demographic** *adj.*

demonic possession the supposed invasion of the body by an evil spirit or devil that gains control of the mind or soul, producing mental disorder, illness, or criminal behavior. Many forms of physical and psychological illness were formerly attributed to such possession, notably EPILEPSY, SCHIZOPHRENIA, and TOURETTE'S DISORDER.

demoralization hypothesis the idea that effective psychotherapy depends on the therapist overcoming the client's state of demoralization, which can be achieved by encouraging the client to confide, explaining his or her symptoms, and providing a therapeutic ritual through which these may be resolved.

demotivation *n.* negative imagery or negative self-talk that emphasizes why one cannot do well in a task and thus discourages any attempt to perform it.

demyelination *n.* the loss of the MYELIN SHEATH that covers nerve fibers.

dendrite *n.* a branching, threadlike extension of the CELL BODY that increases the receptive surface of a neuron. —**dendritic** *adj.*

dendritic spine a mushroom-shaped outgrowth along the DENDRITE of a neuron, which forms a SYNAPSE with the axon terminals of neighboring neurons.

denervation *n.* removal or interruption of the nerves that supply a part of the body.

denial *n.* a DEFENSE MECHANISM in which unpleasant thoughts, feelings, wishes, or events are ignored or excluded from conscious awareness. It may take such forms as refusal to acknowledge the reality of a terminal illness, a financial problem, an addiction, or a partner's infidelity. Denial is an unconscious process that functions to resolve emotional conflict or reduce anxiety. Also called **disavowal**. —**deny** *vb.*

denial stage the first of the five STAGES OF GRIEF described by Swiss-born U.S. psychiatrist Elisabeth Kübler-Ross (1926–2004). It is characterized by a conscious or unconscious inability to acknowledge or accept one's own or an important other's impending or actual death or some other great loss or trauma.

denotative meaning the objective or literal meaning of a word or phrase as opposed to its **connotative meaning**, which includes the various ideas and emotions that it suggests within a particular culture. So, for example, the word *father* denotes "male parent" but may connote a range of ideas involving protection, authority, and love.

density *n.* **1.** a measure of the amount of physical space per individual. High density can produce crowding, a psychological state of needing more space. Interior indices of density (e.g., people per room) are consistently related to negative psychological consequences, whereas external indices (e.g., people per square mile) are not. **2.** in auditory perception, the quality of a sound representing a TONAL ATTRIBUTE of solidity distinct from PITCH, volume, or TIMBRE. —**dense** *adj.*

density function the mathematical representation of the shape of a probability distribution.

dental *adj.* denoting a speech sound produced with the tongue touching the upper front teeth, as in the French [t] sound.

dental phobia a persistent and irrational fear of dentists or of dental treatment, resulting in the avoidance of dental care or marked distress and anxiety during dental visits. It may be related to a prior negative dental experience, fear of pain, perceived lack of control, or feelings of helplessness or embarrassment.

dentate gyrus a strip of gray matter that connects the HIPPOCAMPUS with the ENTORHINAL CORTEX.

deoxyribonucleic acid see DNA.

Depacon *n.* a trade name for valproate sodium. See VALPROIC ACID.

Depakene *n.* a trade name for VALPROIC ACID.

dependence *n.* **1.** a state in which assistance from others is intuitively expected or actively sought for emotional or financial support, protection, security, or daily care. The dependent person leans on others for guidance, decision making, and nurturance. Whereas some degree of dependence is natural in interpersonal relations, excessive, inappropriate, or misdirected reliance on others is often a focus of psychological treatment. Personality, social, and behavioral psychology, as well as psychoanalytic theory, all contribute different perspectives to the study and treatment of pathological dependence. **2.** see SUBSTANCE DEPENDENCE. **3.** in OPERANT CONDITIONING, a causal relation between a response and a consequence, which results in a CONTINGENCY. Also called **dependency**. —**dependent** *adj.*

dependency need any personal need that must be satisfied by others, including the need for affection, love, shelter, physical care, food, warmth, protection, and security.

dependency-support script a strategy in which caregivers consistently and immediately meet all the needs of an older adult receiving care, which often reduces the autonomy and independence of the person receiving care.

dependent personality disorder a personality disorder manifested in a long-term pattern of passively allowing others to take responsibility for major areas of life and of subordinating personal needs to the needs of others.

dependent variable (**DV**) the "outcome" variable in an experiment that is observed to occur or change after the occurrence or variation of the INDEPENDENT VARIABLE.

depersonalization *n.* a state of mind in which the self appears unreal. Individuals feel estranged from themselves and usually from the external world, and thoughts and experiences have a distant, dreamlike character.

depersonalization disorder a DISSOCIATIVE DISORDER characterized by one or more episodes of DEPERSONALIZATION severe enough to impair social and occupational functioning. Onset of depersonalization is rapid and accompanied by a feeling that one's extremities are changed in size and, in some cases, a feeling that the external world is unreal (DEREALIZATION).

depersonification *n.* **1.** treatment of another person as something other than the unique individual that he or she really is. For example, parents may treat their child as an extension of themselves, which leads to the child having a distorted sense of self. **2.** in psychoanalytic theory, a stage in the maturation of the SUPEREGO that follows INTROJECTION of parental IMAGOES and leads to integration of parental values as abstract ideas. —**depersonify** *vb.*

depolarization *n.* a reduction in the electric potential across the plasma membrane of a cell, especially a neuron, such that the inner surface of the membrane becomes less negative in relation to the outer surface. Depolarization occurs when the membrane is stimulated and sodium ions (Na^+) flow into the cell. If the stimulus intensity exceeds the excitatory threshold of the neuron an ACTION POTENTIAL is created and a nerve impulse propagated. Compare HYPERPOLARIZATION.

depressant *n.* any agent that diminishes or retards any function or activity of a body system or organ, especially a CNS DEPRESSANT.

depression *n.* **1.** a fluctuation in normal mood ranging from unhappiness and discontent to an extreme feeling of sadness, pessimism, and despondency. **2.** in psychiatry, any of the DEPRESSIVE DISORDERS. —**depressed** *adj.*

depression stage the fourth of the five STAGES OF GRIEF described by Swiss-born U.S. psychiatrist Elisabeth Kübler-Ross (1926–2004). It is characterized by feelings of sadness, loss, regret, or uncertainty that typically demonstrate, consciously or unconsciously, some level of acceptance in facing one's own or another's impending or actual death or some other great loss or trauma.

depressive disorder any of the MOOD DISORDERS that typically have sadness as one of their symptoms, such as DYSTHYMIC DISORDER and MAJOR DEPRESSIVE DISORDER.

depressive personality disorder a recently classified and still controversial personality disorder characterized by glumness, pessimism, a lack of joy, the inability to experience pleasure, and a low sense of self-worth and self-esteem.

depressive spectrum the range of severity and disparate symptoms that characterize DEPRESSIVE DISORDERS. The underlying concept is that depression is a range of related disorders, rather than a single diagnostic entity.

deprivation *n.* in CONDITIONING, reduction of access to or intake of a REINFORCER. —**deprive** *vb.*

depth cue any of a variety of means used to inform the visual system about the depth of a target or its distance from the observer. **Monocular depth cues** require only one eye and include signals about the state of the CILIARY MUSCLES and occlusion of distant objects by near objects. **Binocular depth cues** require integration of information from the two eyes and include signals about the CONVERGENCE of the eyes and BINOCULAR DISPARITY.

depth interview an interview designed to reveal deep-seated feelings, attitudes, opinions, and motives by encouraging the individual to express himself or herself freely without fear of disapproval or concern about the interviewer's reactions. Such interviews may be conducted, for example, in counseling and as part of qualitative market research. They tend to be relatively lengthy, unstructured, one-on-one conversations.

depth-of-processing hypothesis the theory that the strength of memory is dependent on the degree of cognitive processing the material receives. Depth has been defined variously as ELABORATION, amount of cognitive effort expended, and the distinctiveness of the MEMORY TRACE formed. This theory is an expanded empirical investigation of the LEVELS-OF-PROCESSING MODEL OF MEMORY.

depth perception awareness of three-dimensionality, solidity, and the distance between the observer and the object. Depth perception is achieved through such cues as visual ACCOMMODATION, BINOCULAR DISPARITY, and CONVERGENCE. See also VISUAL CLIFF.

depth psychology a general approach to psychology and psychotherapy that focuses on unconscious mental processes as the source of emotional disturbance and symptoms, as well as personality, attitudes, creativity, and lifestyle. A typical example is CLASSICAL PSYCHOANALYSIS, but others include the ANALYTIC PSYCHOLOGY of Swiss psychiatrist and psychoanalyst Carl Jung (1875–1961) and the INDIVIDUAL PSYCHOLOGY of Austrian psychiatrist Alfred Adler (1870–1937).

depth therapy any form of psychotherapy, brief or extended, that involves identifying and working through unconscious conflicts and experiences that underlie and interfere with behavior and adjustment. Compare SURFACE THERAPY.

derailment *n.* a symptom of thought disorder

marked by frequent interruptions in thought and jumping from one idea to another unrelated or indirectly related idea. Derailment is essentially equivalent to LOOSENING OF ASSOCIATIONS.

derealization *n.* a state characterized by a sense of unreality; that is, an alteration in the perception of external reality so that it seems strange or unreal ("This can't be happening"), often due to trauma or stress. It may also occur as a feature of SCHIZOPHRENIA or of certain DISSOCIATIVE DISORDERS. See also DEPERSONALIZATION.

derived need a need developed through association with or generalization from a PRIMARY NEED.

derived property in GESTALT PSYCHOLOGY, a property taken on by a part of a whole by virtue of its being in a particular configuration or context. For example, if three noncollinear dots are seen as forming a triangle, each dot then has the derived property of being a vertex of the triangle.

dermatome *n.* an area of skin that is innervated primarily by fibers from the dorsal root of a particular SPINAL NERVE.

dermis *n.* the layer of skin beneath the outermost layer (EPIDERMIS). The dermis contains blood and lymphatic vessels, nerves and nerve endings, and the hair follicles. —**dermal** *adj.*

dermo-optical perception an alleged ability to see or to identify the color of objects by touch alone. It has been suggested that people with this ability detect colors by means of temperature differences due to reflection of hand heat or other heat from the object. Also called **cutaneous perception of color**.

descending tract a bundle of nerve fibers that carries motor impulses from the brain to the spinal cord. There are three major descending tracts: the corticospinal, vestibulospinal, and reticulospinal (see VENTROMEDIAL PATHWAYS). Also called **descending pathway**. Compare ASCENDING TRACT.

descent group any social group, such as a CLAN or SEPT, membership in which depends on real or supposed descent from a common ancestor. See also KINSHIP NETWORK.

descriptive behaviorism an approach to the study of behavior espoused by U.S. psychologist B. F. Skinner (1904–1990), who felt that psychology should limit itself to a description of behaviors of organisms, the conditions under which they occur, and their effects on the environment. It requires that theoretical explanations in terms of underlying biological or hypothetical psychological processes be avoided. See BEHAVIORISM; RADICAL BEHAVIORISM.

descriptive grammar see PRESCRIPTIVE GRAMMAR.

descriptive norm see SOCIAL NORM.

descriptive operant see OPERANT.

descriptive research an empirical investigation designed to provide an overview of existing conditions without aspiring to draw causal inferences.

descriptive statistic a numerical index used to describe (summarize) a particular feature of the data, such as a MEAN or STANDARD DEVIATION.

desensitization *n.* a reduction in emotional or physical reactivity to stimuli that is achieved by such means as gaining insight into its nature or origin or the use of DECONDITIONING techniques.

desexualization *n.* in psychoanalytic theory, the elimination or NEUTRALIZATION of a sexual aim. Also called **delibidinization**. See also SUBLIMATION. **—desexualize** *vb.*

designer drug any of various synthetic opioids, usually with heroinlike effects, designed with chemical structures that circumvent existing legal definitions of controlled substances and hence avoid restrictions on their use.

design matrix a matrix whose elements denote the presence or absence of each participant (row) in a treatment (column) of an experimental design.

desocialization *n.* gradual withdrawal from social contacts and interpersonal communication, with absorption in private thought processes and adoption of idiosyncratic and often bizarre behavior.

despondency *n.* a state characterized by both APATHY and depressed mood. **—despondent** *adj.*

destructive obedience compliance with the direct or indirect orders of a social, military, or moral authority that results in negative outcomes, such as injury inflicted on innocent victims, harm to the community, or the loss of confidence in social institutions. The BEHAVIORAL STUDY OF OBEDIENCE provides an example.

destrudo *n.* the energy associated with THANATOS, the DEATH INSTINCT. Destrudo contrasts with LIBIDO, the energy of EROS, the LIFE INSTINCT. See also MORTIDO.

desymbolization *n.* the process of depriving symbols, especially words, of their accepted meanings and substituting distorted, neologistic, autistic, or concrete ideas for them.

desynchronization *n.* in electroencephalography, the replacement of ALPHA WAVES by fast, low-amplitude, irregular waveforms, often because of an external stimulus, usually one that alerts the individual. See ALPHA BLOCKING.

Desyrel *n.* a trade name for TRAZODONE.

detachment *n.* **1.** a feeling of emotional freedom resulting from a lack of involvement in a problem or with another situation or person. **2.** objectivity: that is, the ability to consider a problem on its merits alone. Also called **intellectual detachment**. **3.** in developmental psychology, the child's desire to have new experiences and

develop new skills, beginning around 2 years of age.

deterioration *n.* progressive impairment or loss of basic functions, such as emotional, judgmental, intellectual, muscular, and memory functions.

determinant *n.* any internal or external condition that is the cause of an event.

determination *n.* **1.** a mental attitude characterized by a strong commitment to achieving a particular goal despite barriers and hardships. **2.** the precise definition or qualification of the attributes of a concept or proposal (e.g., determination of the dependent variable in an experiment).

determining tendency a goal or intended result that directs mental processes. For example, when shown the numbers 6 and 4 and asked to add, a person answers 10, but when asked to subtract, answers 2; the same stimuli lead to different thoughts as intended ends determine what the mind does with the two numbers. The term, introduced by German psychologist Narziss Ach (1871–1946) and derived from the earlier concept of AUFGABE, is essentially equivalent to the modern MENTAL SET.

determinism *n.* **1.** in philosophy, the position that all events, physical or mental, including human behavior, are the necessary results of antecedent causes or other entities or forces. Determinism requires that both the past and the future are fixed. See also CAUSALITY. **2.** in psychology, the position that all human behaviors result from specific efficient causal antecedents, such as biological structures or processes, environmental conditions, or past experience. The relationships between these antecedents and the behaviors they produce can be described by generalizations much like the laws that describe regularities in nature. Determinism contrasts with belief in FREE WILL, which implies that individuals can choose to act in some ways independent of antecedent events and conditions. Those who advocate free-will positions often adopt a position of SOFT DETERMINISM, which holds that free will and responsibility are compatible with determinism. Others hold that free will is illusory, a position known as HARD DETERMINISM. Of contemporary psychological theories, BEHAVIORISM takes most clearly a hard determinist position. Compare INDETERMINISM. **—determinist** *adj., n.* **—deterministic** *adj.*

detoxification *n.* a therapeutic procedure, popularly known as **detox**, that reduces or eliminates toxic substances in the body, particularly as related to intoxication by or withdrawal from drugs or alcohol.

detumescence *n.* the reduction or subsidence of a swelling, especially in the genital organs of either sex following orgasm. Compare TUMESCENCE. **—detumescent** *adj.*

deuteranopia *n.* red–green color blindness in which the deficiency is due to absence of the cone PHOTOPIGMENT sensitive to green light, resulting in loss of green sensitivity and confusion between red and green (see DICHROMATISM). The condition may be unilateral (i.e., color vision may be normal in one eye). See also PROTANOPIA.

devaluation *n.* a DEFENSE MECHANISM that involves denying the importance of something or someone, including the self. —**devalue** *vb.*

development *n.* the progressive series of changes in structure, function, and behavior patterns that occur over the life span of a human being or other organism. —**developmental** *adj.*

developmental age (**DA**) a measure of development expressed in an age unit or AGE EQUIVALENT. For example, a 4-year-old child may have a developmental age of 6 in verbal skills.

developmental cognitive neuroscience the area of study that seeks to understand how the mind and brain jointly develop. See also COGNITIVE NEUROSCIENCE.

developmental coordination disorder a motor skills disorder characterized by performance in activities that require motor coordination substantially below that expected given the child's chronological age and measured intelligence. Significant impairment of academic performance or daily living activities is also observed. However, the difficulties are not due to mental retardation or a physical deficit.

developmental delay delay in the age at which developmental milestones are achieved by a child or delay in the development of communication, social, and daily living skills. It most typically refers to delays in infants, toddlers, and preschool children that are meaningful but do not constitute substantial handicap.

developmental disability a developmental level or status that is attributable to a cognitive or physical impairment, or both, originating before the age of 22. Such an impairment is likely to continue indefinitely and results in substantial functional or adaptive limitations. Examples of developmental disabilities include mental retardation, autistic disorder, and learning disorders. Also called **developmental disorder**.

developmental immaturity the status of a child who exhibits a delay (usually temporary) in reaching developmental landmarks without clinical or historical evidence of damage to the central nervous system. The child may appear younger than his or her chronological age in physical development, gross and fine motor abilities, language development, social awareness, or any combination of these.

developmental invariance a pattern of development in which a skill reaches adult competence early in life and remains stable thereafter. For example, certain sensory and perceptual skills (e.g., vision) function at a high level early in life.

developmental norm the typical skills and expected level of achievement associated with a particular stage of development.

developmental orientation in interdisciplinary team or other individual service-planning processes, an emphasis on the skills, abilities, and strengths of people with disabilities in relation to expected developmental attainments and performance of children or young people without disabilities.

developmental psychology the branch of psychology that studies the changes—physical, mental, and behavioral—that occur from conception to old age.

developmental readiness a student's state of psychological and intellectual preparedness for a given task, subject, or grade level.

developmental retardation abnormally slow growth in any or all areas—intellectual, motor, perceptual, linguistic, or social.

developmental schedule a normative timetable of when certain aspects of physical and behavioral development typically occur. The degree to which an individual has progressed through these **developmental milestones** is assessed with a measurement instrument called a **developmental scale**.

developmental systems approach the view that development is the result of bidirectional interaction between all levels of biological and experiential variables, from the genetic through the cultural.

developmental task any of the fundamental physical, social, intellectual, and emotional achievements and abilities that must be acquired at each stage of life for normal and healthy development.

developmental teaching model a general approach in education in which cognitive, social, and moral development are considered to advance in discrete and distinctive stages.

developmental theory 1. any theory based on the continuity of human development and the importance of early experiences in shaping the personality. Examples are the psychoanalytic theory of PSYCHOSEXUAL DEVELOPMENT, ERIKSON'S EIGHT STAGES OF DEVELOPMENT, learning theories that stress early conditioning, and role theories that focus on the gradual acquisition of different roles in life. **2.** the proposition that mental retardation is due to slower than normal development of cognitive processes and is not qualitatively different from the cognitive processes of other people. Compare DEFECT THEORY.

developmental therapy a method of treatment for children and adolescents with emotional, social, or behavioral problems. A series of graded experiences is used to help clients to function better in various areas, such as interacting with others or managing anger.

developmental toxicology the study of the

effects of toxic (poisonous) substances on the normal development of infants and children: specifically, the study of the adverse effects of certain drugs administered to them or to which they may have been exposed in the uterus.

development cycle in ergonomics, the process of developing a product or system, beginning with a formative idea and continuing through research, design, testing, and improvement, to final release.

deviance *n.* any behavior that deviates significantly from what is considered appropriate or typical for a social group. Also called **deviancy**.

deviation IQ see IQ.

dexterity test a manual test of speed and accuracy.

dextroamphetamine (**dexamphetamine**) *n.* see AMPHETAMINES.

df symbol for DEGREES OF FREEDOM.

dhat a CULTURE-BOUND SYNDROME, specific to India, that involves severe anxiety and hypochondriacal concerns about the discharge of semen, whitish discoloration of the urine, and feelings of weakness and exhaustion. It is similar to SHEN-K'UEI.

diagnosis (**Dx**) *n.* (*pl.* **diagnoses**) **1.** the process of identifying and determining the nature of a disease or disorder by its signs and symptoms, through the use of assessment techniques (e.g., tests and examinations) and other available evidence. **2.** the classification of individuals on the basis of a disease, disorder, abnormality, or set of characteristics. Psychological diagnoses have been codified for professional use, notably in the DSM–IV–TR. —**diagnostic** *adj.*

diagnosis-related groups (**DRGs**) an inpatient or hospital classification used as a financing tool to reimburse health care providers. Each of the DRGs (of which there are currently over 500) has a preset price based on diagnosis, age and sex of patient, therapeutic procedure, and length of stay.

Diagnostic and Statistical Manual of Mental Disorders see DSM–IV–TR.

diagnostic formulation a comprehensive evaluation of a patient, including the most significant features of the patient's total history; the results of psychological and medical examinations; a tentative explanation of the origin and development of his or her disorder; the diagnostic classification of the disorder; a therapeutic plan; and a prognostic evaluation based on carrying out this plan.

diagnostic interview an interview in which a psychologist or other mental health professional explores a patient's presenting problem, current situation, and background, with the aim of formulating a diagnosis and prognosis as well as developing a treatment program.

diagnosticity *n.* the informational value of an interaction, event, or feedback for someone seeking self-knowledge. Information with high diagnosticity has clear implications for the SELF-CONCEPT, whereas information with low diagnosticity may be unclear, ambiguous, or inaccurate.

diagnostic overshadowing the failure, when assessing an individual with multiple disabilities, to discern the presence of one disability because its features are attributed to another, primary disability. In particular, it refers to the failure to recognize a psychiatric condition or mental disorder in a person with mental retardation.

diagnostic prescriptive education the concept that effectiveness of classroom teaching of children with disabilities depends in large part upon the teacher's understanding of the disability.

diagnostic test any examination or assessment measure that may help reveal the nature and source of an individual's physical, mental, or behavioral problem or anomalies.

dialect *n.* a variety of a language that is associated with a particular geographical region, social class, or ethnic group and has its own characteristic words, grammatical forms, and pronunciation. Dialects of a language are generally mutually intelligible. Compare ACCENT; REGISTER. —**dialectal** *adj.*

dialectical behavior therapy a flexible, stage-based therapy that combines principles of BEHAVIOR THERAPY, COGNITIVE BEHAVIOR THERAPY, and MINDFULNESS. Dialectical behavior therapy concurrently promotes acceptance and change, especially with difficult-to-treat patients.

dialectical teaching a method that engages students in a critical examination of their reasoning through repeated questioning of their answers.

dialogue (**dialog**) *n.* in GESTALT THERAPY, a technique in which the client engages in an imaginary conversation (a) with a body part from which he or she feels alienated; (b) with a person, such as his or her mother or father, who is pictured sitting in an empty chair (see EMPTY-CHAIR TECHNIQUE); or (c) with an object associated with a dream. Also called **dialogue technique**.

diary method a technique for compiling detailed data about an individual who is being observed or studied by having the individual record his or her daily behavior and activities.

diaschisis *n.* a loss or deficiency of function in brain regions surrounding or connected to an area of localized damage.

diathesis *n.* a susceptibility to acquiring (not inheriting) certain diseases or disorders (e.g., allergies, arthritic diathesis). Compare GENETIC PREDISPOSITION.

diathesis–stress model the theory that mental and physical disorders develop from a predisposition for that illness (diathesis) combined with stressful conditions that play a precipitating or facilitating role.

diazepam *n.* a long-acting BENZODIAZEPINE that is used for the management of alcohol withdrawal and as an ANTICONVULSANT, ANXIOLYTIC, and MUSCLE RELAXANT. It is broken down in the liver to produce a number of metabolites (metabolic products) of varying HALF-LIVES. U.S. trade name (among others): **Valium**.

dichotic *adj.* affecting or relating to the left and right ears differently, as with the presentation of different sounds to each ear. Compare DIOTIC; MONOTIC.

dichotomous thinking the tendency to think in terms of bipolar opposites, that is, in terms of the best and worst, without accepting the possibilities that lie between these two extremes. This is sometimes thought to be a risk factor for MAJOR DEPRESSIVE DISORDER.

dichotomous variable a variable that can have only two values to designate membership in one of two possible categories, for example, female versus male.

dichromatism *n.* partial color blindness in which the eye contains only two types of cone PHOTOPIGMENT instead of the typical three: Lack of the third pigment leads to confusion between certain colors. Red–green color blindness (see DEUTERANOPIA; PROTANOPIA) is the most common, whereas the blue–green variety (tritanopia) is relatively rare. Another type, yellow–blue (tetartanopia), has been proposed but its existence has yet to be firmly established. Also called **dichromacy** (**dichromasy**); **dichromatopsia**. See also ACHROMATISM; MONOCHROMATISM; TRICHROMATISM. —**dichromatic** *adj.*

didactic teaching 1. a technique in which behavioral and therapeutic concepts and techniques are explained to clients, and instructions are given in both verbal and written form. Such instruction is common in many forms of therapy, with the exception of long-term PSYCHODYNAMIC PSYCHOTHERAPY and PSYCHOANALYSIS. **2.** a component of many undergraduate and graduate psychology courses and multidisciplinary psychotherapy training.

diencephalon *n.* the posterior part of the FOREBRAIN that includes the THALAMUS, EPITHALAMUS, and HYPOTHALAMUS. —**diencephalic** *adj.*

dietary neophobia avoidance of new foods. A nonpathological form is commonly seen in children who display a reluctance to try unfamiliar food.

dieting *n.* the deliberate restriction of the types or amounts of food one eats, usually in an effort to lose weight or to improve one's health. Dieting is viewed by some medical and mental health professionals as a solution to obesity and by others as a primary pathology associated with EATING DISORDERS.

difference judgment the ability to distinguish between two similar stimuli.

difference threshold the smallest difference between two stimuli that can be consistently and accurately detected on 50% of trials. Also called **difference limen** (**DL**); **just noticeable difference** (**JND**; **jnd**). See also WEBER'S LAW.

differential accuracy the ability to determine accurately in what way and to what extent a person's traits differ from a STEREOTYPE associated with his or her age group, ethnic group, professional group, or other relevant group. Compare STEREOTYPE ACCURACY.

differential association the theory that an individual's behavior is influenced by the particular people with whom the individual associates, usually over a prolonged period. This concept was proposed to explain why people living in a neighborhood with a high crime rate were more likely to commit crimes themselves.

differential conditioning a PAVLOVIAN CONDITIONING experiment in which two or more stimuli are used, each paired with different outcomes. Most commonly, one stimulus (the positive conditioned stimulus, e.g., a light) is paired with an unconditioned stimulus (e.g., food), and another (e.g., a tone) is not paired. The usual outcome is that a CONDITIONED RESPONSE is elicited by the positive conditioned stimulus but not by the other stimulus.

differential diagnosis 1. the process of determining which of two or more diseases or disorders with overlapping symptoms a particular patient has. **2.** the distinction between two or more similar conditions by identifying critical symptoms present in one but not the other.

differential emotions theory a theory proposing the existence of a large but limited set of specific emotions that appear without social learning at the age when the emotions can first play an adaptive role in the behavior of the child.

differential psychology the branch of psychology that studies the nature, magnitude, causes, and consequences of psychological differences between individuals and groups, as well as the methods for assessing these differences.

differential reinforcement in conditioning, the REINFORCEMENT of only selected behavior. For example, one might reinforce lever presses that are more than 1 s in duration, but not reinforce those that are less than 1 s in duration.

differential relaxation a technique for exertion of only the amount of muscular tension or energy required to perform an activity successfully. For example, an individual driving an automobile can practice easing and releasing contracted muscles that are not primarily involved in the act of driving (e.g., the shoulders and upper back or the neck and facial muscles) and thus permit more appropriate focus and engagement of those muscles directly involved (e.g., in the hands, arms, legs, and back).

differential validity the accuracy of a battery of tests in differentiating a person's subsequent success in two or more different criterion tasks.

differentiation *n.* **1.** sensory discrimination of differences among stimuli. For example, wines that at first taste identical may, with experience, be readily distinguished. **2.** a conditioning process in which a limited range of behavior types is achieved through selective REINFORCEMENT of only some forms of behavior. **3.** in embryology, the process whereby cells of a developing embryo undergo the changes necessary to become specialized in structure and function.

differentiation theory the theory that perception can be understood as an incremental filtering process enabling environmental noise (i.e., dispensable, incidental information) to be screened out while one learns to distinguish the essential characteristics of sensory patterns.

diffuse axonal injury widespread stretching and tearing of the white matter nerve fibers of the brain caused by any incident resulting in sudden, significant acceleration or deceleration forces to the head. It typically is caused by motor vehicle accidents and is a frequent form of TRAUMATIC BRAIN INJURY.

diffuse-status characteristics general personal qualities, such as age, sex, and ethnicity, that people intentionally and unintentionally consider when estimating the relative competency, ability, and social value of themselves and others. Unlike SPECIFIC-STATUS CHARACTERISTICS, diffuse-status characteristics will have no particular relevance in the given setting and are not indicators of competence, ability, and status.

diffusion of responsibility the lessening of responsibility often experienced by individuals in groups and social collectives. This has been proposed as one reason for the BYSTANDER EFFECT; in groups the obligation to intervene is shared by all onlookers rather than focused on any specific individual. This diffusion process has also been identified as a possible mediator of a number of other group-level phenomena, including CHOICE SHIFTS, DEINDIVIDUATION, SOCIAL LOAFING, and reactions to SOCIAL DILEMMAS. See also CONFUSION OF RESPONSIBILITY.

diffusion process a technique in which the public's general acceptance of a new concept or product depends on acceptance by an initial core of people, whose influence then ripples outward through the surrounding population.

diglossia *n.* the situation in which two varieties of a language coexist and have distinct social functions within a community; these are usually characterized by high (H) and low (L) uses, H being associated with formality and literacy, and L with everyday colloquial usage. See also MULTILINGUALISM; VERNACULAR.

dilator *n.* a muscle or nerve that causes opening or enlargement of a bodily structure.

dilemma *n.* a situation necessitating a choice between two equally desirable or undesirable alternatives. Psychologists, economists, or sociologists may invent dilemmas and present them to individuals or groups in order to study decision making.

dilution effect see ANTIPREDATOR BEHAVIOR.

dimensional theory of emotion any theory postulating that emotions have two or more fundamental dimensions. There is universal agreement among theories on two fundamental dimensions—pleasantness–unpleasantness (hedonic level) and arousal–relaxation (level of activation)—but considerable differences in labeling others.

dimensions of consciousness dimensions along which the overall quality of awareness can vary, including mood, involvement with inner or outer events, changes in immediate memory, sensation and perception, self-awareness, and identification with events outside of oneself.

diminished capacity a legal defense in which a mental or physical condition (e.g., intoxication) is claimed to have limited the defendant's ability to form the requisite criminal intent for the crime with which he or she is charged.

diminished responsibility a legal defense in which evidence of mental abnormality is presented to mitigate or reduce a defendant's accountability for an act. It is distinct from an insanity defense, which takes an all-or-none perspective with regard to CRIMINAL RESPONSIBILITY.

dimorphism *n.* the existence among members of the same species of two distinct forms that differ in one or more characteristics, such as size, shape, or color. **—dimorphic** *adj.*

diotic *adj.* denoting or relating to the presentation of the same sound to both ears. Compare DICHOTIC; MONOTIC.

diplacusis *n.* a condition in which one tone is heard as two.

diplegia *n.* a paralysis that affects corresponding parts on both sides of the body (e.g., both arms). **—diplegic** *adj.*

diploid *adj.* denoting or possessing the normal number of chromosomes, which in humans is 46: 22 HOMOLOGOUS pairs of AUTOSOMES plus the male or female set of XY or XX SEX CHROMOSOMES. Compare HAPLOID.

diplomate *n.* see BOARD CERTIFIED.

diplopia *n.* a visual disorder in which images from the two eyes are seen separately and simultaneously. Diplopia is usually due to weak or paralyzed eye muscles, resulting in a failure of coordination and focus.

direct attitude measure any procedure for assessing attitudes that requires a person to provide a report of his or her attitude. Traditional approaches to attitude measurement, such as LIKERT SCALES, SEMANTIC DIFFERENTIALS, and THURSTONE ATTITUDE SCALES, are examples of direct attitude measures. Compare INDIRECT ATTITUDE MEASURE.

direct coping active, focused confrontation and management or resolution of stressful or otherwise problematic situations.

directional hypothesis a prediction regarding the direction in which one experimental group will differ from another.

directional test see ONE-TAILED TEST.

directive *n.* a command, suggestion, or order specifying the type of action that should be performed. In therapeutic contexts, a directive is a specific statement by the therapist that enjoins the client to act, feel, or think in a particular way when he or she confronts a particular problem or situation.

directive counseling an approach to counseling and psychotherapy in which the therapeutic process is directed along lines considered relevant by the counselor or therapist. Directive counseling is based on the assumption that the professional training and experience of the counselor or therapist equip him or her to manage the therapeutic process and to guide the client's behavior. Therapy is considered to progress along primarily intellectual lines in contrast to the approaches of PSYCHODYNAMIC PSYCHOTHERAPY, which emphasizes unconscious motivation and affective dynamics. Also called **directive psychotherapy**.

directive group psychotherapy a type of group psychotherapy designed to help members adjust to their environment through educational tasks, group guidance, group counseling, and therapeutic recreation.

direct odor effect a change in the nervous system caused by direct stimulation of the OLFACTORY TRACT and related brain structures. In contrast, an **indirect odor effect** is a change in the central nervous system arising from cognitions, such as expectations, associated with the odor.

direct perception the theory that the information required for perception is external to the observer, that is, one can directly perceive an object based on the properties of the DISTAL STIMULUS alone, unaided by inference, memories, the construction of representations, or the influence of other cognitive processes.

direct scaling a procedure for developing numerical scales of magnitude of psychophysical factors in which the observer makes judgments of the magnitude of stimuli. This is in contrast to **indirect scaling**, in which the magnitude scales are derived from PAIRED COMPARISON judgments.

direct selection a form of NATURAL SELECTION in which some behavioral, physical, or physio-

logical trait in an individual improves the likelihood that its offspring will survive to reproduce.

direct suggestion 1. a technique in SUPPORTIVE PSYCHOTHERAPY in which attempts are made to alleviate emotional distress and disturbance in an individual through reassurance, encouragement, and direct instructions. **2.** a technique in HYPNOTHERAPY in which a client under hypnosis is directed to follow instructions of the therapist either in the session or in his or her daily life.

dirt phobia a persistent and irrational fear of dirt, often accompanied by a fear of contamination and a hand-washing compulsion. Fear of dirt is a common obsession associated with OBSESSIVE-COMPULSIVE DISORDER. Also (rarely) called **rupophobia**.

disability *n.* a lasting physical or mental impairment that significantly interferes with an individual's ability to function in one or more central life activities, such as self-care, ambulation, communication, social interaction, sexual expression, or employment. For example, an individual who cannot see has visual disability. See also HANDICAP. —**disabled** *adj.*

disaster counseling counseling offered to victims and their families, emergency workers, and witnesses during or immediately following a traumatic event. Individual therapists and counselors and mental health teams are specially trained (e.g., by the American Red Cross) to respond in disaster situations. Disaster counseling may include defusing, debriefing (e.g., CRITICAL-INCIDENT STRESS DEBRIEFING), and other counseling techniques to help traumatized people cope with stress.

discharge *n.* **1.** the firing or activity of a neuron or group of neurons, resulting in an ACTION POTENTIAL. **2.** the dismissal of a patient from treatment or other services.

dischronation *n.* an aspect of DISORIENTATION in which there is confusion about time.

disconnection syndrome any neurological disorder resulting from a separation or isolation of cortical areas that usually work together. Several neurobehavioral symptoms, including some apraxias and agnosias, are thought to be attributable to disconnection syndrome.

discontinuity effect the markedly greater competitiveness of intergroup interactions relative to the competitiveness of interactions involving individuals.

discontinuity hypothesis the viewpoint that emphasizes the role of sudden insight and perceptual reorganization in successful DISCRIMINATION LEARNING and problem solving. According to this view, a correct answer is only recognized when its relation to the issue as a whole is discovered. Compare CONTINUITY HYPOTHESIS.

discordance *n.* **1.** the state or condition of being

at variance. **Affective discordance** may be observed, for example, during psychotherapy when a client relates a particularly disturbing experience without any facial or vocal indication of distress. **2.** in TWIN STUDIES, dissimilarity between a pair of twins with respect to a particular trait or disease. Compare CONCORDANCE. —**discordant** *adj.*

discounting principle see ATTRIBUTION THEORY.

discourse analysis the study of linguistic structures that extend beyond the single sentence, such as conversations, narratives, or written arguments. Discourse analysis is particularly concerned with the ways in which a sequence of two or more sentences can produce meanings that are different from or additional to any found in the sentences considered separately. An important source of such meanings is the "frame" or format of the discourse (news item, fairytale, joke, etc.), and a recognition of the various norms that this implies. The norms and expectations that govern conversation are a major concern of discourse analysis, as is the structure of conversational language generally.

discovery method a teaching method that seeks to provide students with experience of the processes of science or other disciplines through inductive reasoning and active experimentation, with minimal teacher supervision. Students are encouraged to organize data, develop and test hypotheses, and formulate conclusions or general principles.

discrete data data that are not on a continuous scale but are limited to specific categories or values, which may be ordered or not ordered.

discrete trial a defined, limited occasion to engage in some behavior. For example, each trip through a maze by a rat can be considered a discrete trial.

discrete variable a variable that takes on only a relatively small number of distinct values. Compare CONTINUOUS VARIABLE.

discretionary task a relatively unstructured task that can be solved at the discretion of the group or group leader using a variety of procedures. See ADDITIVE TASK; COMPENSATORY TASK; CONJUNCTIVE TASK; DISJUNCTIVE TASK.

discriminanda *pl. n.* (*sing.* **discriminandum**) stimuli that can be distinguished from one another.

discriminant analysis a MULTIVARIATE statistical method that combines information from a set of predictor variables in order to allow maximal discrimination among a set of predefined groups.

discriminant function any of a range of statistical techniques to situate an item that could belong to any of two or more variables in the correct set, with minimal probability of error.

discriminant validity a form of CONSTRUCT VALIDITY demonstrated by showing that mea-

sures of constructs that are conceptually unrelated do not correlate in the data. See also CONVERGENT VALIDITY.

discriminated operant a conditioned OPERANT that is under stimulus control, that is, a response that is more likely to occur when its DISCRIMINATIVE STIMULUS is present than when it is not present.

discriminating power a measure of the ability of a test to distinguish between two groups being measured.

discrimination *n.* **1.** the ability to distinguish between stimuli or objects that differ quantitatively or qualitatively from one another. **2.** the ability to respond in different ways in the presence of different stimuli. In conditioning, this is usually established in experiments by DIFFERENTIAL REINFORCEMENT or DIFFERENTIAL CONDITIONING techniques. **3.** differential treatment of the members of different ethnic, religious, national, or other groups. Discrimination is usually the behavioral manifestation of PREJUDICE and therefore involves negative, hostile, and injurious treatment of the members of rejected groups. By contrast, **positive discrimination** is the favorable treatment of the oppressed group rather than the typically favored group. —**discriminate** *vb.*

discrimination learning an experience in which an individual must learn to make choices between stimuli in order to reach a goal. For example, a cat may have to learn to find food under a white cup on the left side of an area in which there are white and black cups on both sides.

discrimination reaction time the REACTION TIME of a participant in a task that requires him or her to discriminate between different stimuli, as in a CHOICE REACTION TIME task or a COMPLEX REACTION TIME task.

discrimination training a procedure in which an OPERANT RESPONSE is reinforced in the presence of a particular stimulus but not in the absence of that stimulus. For example, a rat's lever-press response might be reinforced when a stimulus light is on but not when the light is off. This rat will eventually learn to press the lever only when the light is on.

discriminative stimulus (symbol: S^D) in OPERANT CONDITIONING, a stimulus that increases the probability of a response because of a previous history of DIFFERENTIAL REINFORCEMENT in the presence of that stimulus. For example, if a pigeon's key pecks are reinforced when the key is illuminated red, but not when the key is green, the red stimulus will come to serve as an S^D and the pigeon will learn to peck only when the key is red. Compare NEGATIVE DISCRIMINATIVE STIMULUS.

disease *n.* a definite pathological process with organic origins, marked by a characteristic set of symptoms that may affect the entire body or a part of the body and that impairs functioning.

disenfranchised grief grief that society (or some element of it) limits, does not expect, or may not allow a person to express. Examples include the grief of parents for stillborn babies, of teachers for the death of students, and of nurses for the death of patients. Disenfranchised grief may isolate the bereaved individual from others and thus impede recovery. Also called **hidden grief**. See also GRIEF COUNSELING; GRIEFWORK; MOURNING.

disengagement theory a theory proposing that old age involves a gradual withdrawal of the individual from society and of society from the individual. According to this theory, those happiest in old age have turned their attention inward toward the self and away from involvement in the outside world. Empirical research has shown, however, that this mutual withdrawal is not an inevitable component of old age and that a **continuity theory** of aging is most likely, in which older people are happiest when they are able to maintain their preferred level of social involvement. Compare ACTIVITY THEORY.

disequilibrium *n.* **1.** a loss of physical balance. **2.** emotional imbalance, as in individuals with extreme mood swings or AFFECTIVE LABILITY. **3.** in developmental psychology, a state of tension between cognitive processes competing against each other.

disfigurement *n.* a blemish or deformity that mars the appearance of the face or body.

disgust *n.* **1.** a strong aversion, for example, to the taste, smell, or touch of something deemed revolting. **2.** strong distaste for a person or behavior deemed morally repugnant. —**disgusting** *adj.*

dishabituation *n.* the reappearance or enhancement of a habituated response (i.e., one that has been weakened following repeated exposure to the evoking stimulus) due to the presentation of a new stimulus. It is a useful method for investigating perception in nonverbal individuals or animals. Compare HABITUATION.

dishonest signal in animal communication, a signal that provides misleading information about the size, quality, or intention of an individual. Some have argued that dishonest signals are more compatible with the competitive process of NATURAL SELECTION than are HONEST SIGNALS.

disinhibition *n.* **1.** diminution or loss of the normal control exerted by the cerebral cortex, resulting in poorly controlled or poorly restrained emotions or actions. **2.** in conditioning experiments, the reappearance of responding, which has stopped occurring as a result of exposure to EXTINCTION, when a new stimulus is presented.

disintegration *n.* a breakup or severe disorganization of some structure or system of functioning.

disjunctive concept a concept that is based on a set of attributes not all of which are required to be present in every instance. For example, the concept "friend" may involve someone who is male or female. Compare CONJUNCTIVE CONCEPT. See also FAMILY RESEMBLANCE.

disjunctive task a group task or project, such as solving a complex problem, that is completed when a single solution, decision, or group member's recommendation is adopted by the group. This means that the group's performance tends to be determined by the most skilled member. Compare ADDITIVE TASK; COMPENSATORY TASK; CONJUNCTIVE TASK.

dismissive attachment an adult attachment style that combines a positive INTERNAL WORKING MODEL OF ATTACHMENT of oneself, characterized by a view of oneself as competent and worthy of love, and a negative internal working model of attachment of others, characterized by one's view that others are untrustworthy or undependable. Individuals with dismissive attachment are presumed to discount the importance of close relationships and to maintain rigid self-sufficiency. Compare FEARFUL ATTACHMENT; PREOCCUPIED ATTACHMENT; SECURE ATTACHMENT.

disorder *n.* a group of symptoms involving abnormal behaviors or physiological conditions, persistent or intense distress, or a disruption of physiological functioning. See also MENTAL DISORDER.

disorder of written expression a LEARNING DISORDER in which writing skills are substantially below those expected, given the person's chronological age, formal education experience, and measured intelligence. The writing difficulties significantly interfere with academic achievement and activities of daily living that require writing skills.

disorders of excessive somnolence one of four basic types of SLEEP DISORDERS, differentiated from the other types by the presence of excessive sleepiness for at least 1 month. The equivalent psychiatric classification is PRIMARY HYPERSOMNIA. Diagnosis can involve observation in a SLEEP LABORATORY, in which such criteria as nocturnal awakenings; sleep time; sleep continuity; SLEEP LATENCY; and percentage of time in the second, third, and fourth SLEEP STAGES are measured.

disorders of initiating and maintaining sleep one of four basic types of SLEEP DISORDERS, differentiated from the other types by the presence of INSOMNIA, that is, persistent inability to fall asleep or stay asleep. The equivalent psychiatric classification is PRIMARY INSOMNIA. Diagnosis can involve observation in a SLEEP LABORATORY, in which such criteria as nocturnal awakenings; sleep time; sleep efficiency; breathing patterns; percentage of time in the second, third, and fourth SLEEP STAGES; minutes of REM SLEEP; and REM SLEEP LATENCY are measured.

disorders of the sleep–wake cycle schedule one of four basic types of SLEEP DISORDERS, differentiated from the other types in that it results from a mismatch between one's internal circadian rhythm (see BIOLOGICAL RHYTHM) and one's actual sleep schedule. The equivalent psychiatric classification is CIRCADIAN RHYTHM SLEEP DISORDER. Rotating work-shift schedules and jet lag are two common causes of this disorder. Diagnosis can involve observation in a SLEEP LABORATORY, in which such criteria as nocturnal awakening, sleep time, sleep efficiency, breathing patterns, body temperature, minutes of REM SLEEP, and REM SLEEP LATENCY are measured.

disorganization *n.* loss or disruption of orderly or systematic structure or functioning.

disorganized attachment a form of INSECURE ATTACHMENT in which infants show no coherent or consistent behavior during separation from and reunion with their parent.

disorganized behavior behavior that is self-contradictory or inconsistent. It may include childlike silliness, unpurposeful or aimless behavior, unpredictable agitation, or extreme emotional reaction (e.g., laughing after a catastrophe). A typical example is dressing in clothing inappropriate for the weather (e.g., wearing several layers on a warm summer day). Disorganized behavior is commonly seen in individuals with schizophrenia.

disorganized development disruption in the normal course of ATTACHMENT in children in which the child does not learn how to deal with separation from or reunion with a parent. As infants, these children react to their parents with fear or apprehension and do not know how to seek them out when stressed (see DISORGANIZED ATTACHMENT).

disorganized schizophrenia a subtype of schizophrenia characterized primarily by random and fragmented speech and behavior and by flat or inappropriate affect. Also called **hebephrenia**; **hebephrenic schizophrenia**.

disorganized speech speech in which ideas shift from one subject to another or speech that involves responding to questions in an irrelevant way, reaching illogical conclusions, and making up words.

disorientation *n.* a state of impaired ability to identify oneself or to locate oneself in relation to time, place, or other aspects of one's surroundings. Long-term disorientation can be characteristic of disorders; temporary disorientation can be caused by alcohol or drugs or can occur in situations of acute stress. —**disoriented** *adj.*

dispersal *n.* the departure of animals from their natal group to join a different group or find mates elsewhere. Dispersal is thought to be important in reducing inbreeding and avoiding competition with older individuals of the same sex.

dispersion *n.* the degree to which a batch of scores deviate from the mean. Also called **spread**.

displaced aggression the direction of hostility away from the source of frustration or anger and toward either the self or a different person or object.

displacement *n.* the transfer of feelings or behavior from their original object to another person or thing. In psychoanalytic theory, displacement is considered to be a DEFENSE MECHANISM in which the individual discharges tensions associated with, for example, hostility and fear by taking them out on a neutral, nonthreatening or less threatening target. Thus, an angry child might hurt a sibling instead of attacking the father; a frustrated employee might criticize his or her spouse instead of the boss; or a person who fears his or her own hostile impulses might transfer that fear to knives, guns, or other objects that might be used as a weapon. —**displace** *vb.*

display *n.* **1.** the presentation of stimuli to any of the senses. **2.** more or less stereotyped actions (i.e., actions repeated with little variation) that bring about a response in another individual: an integral part of ANIMAL COMMUNICATION. Display behavior may be verbal or nonverbal, usually involving stimulation of the visual or auditory senses. It may include body language that would convey a message of courtship to a member of the opposite sex (e.g., a show of plumage or color) or a suggestion that would be interpreted by an opponent as threatening (e.g., bared teeth or hissing noises).

display rule a socially learned standard that regulates the expression of emotion. Display rules vary from culture to culture; for example, the expression of anger may be considered appropriate in some cultures but not in others.

disposition *n.* a recurrent behavioral or affective tendency that distinguishes an individual from others. See also PERSONAL DISPOSITION.

dispositional attribution the ascription of one's own or another's actions, an event, or an outcome to internal or psychological causes specific to the person concerned, such as moods, attitudes, decisions and judgments, abilities, or effort. Also called **internal attribution**; **personal attribution**. Compare SITUATIONAL ATTRIBUTION.

disruptive behavior disorder a psychiatric disorder in which the primary symptom involves such conduct as the violation of social rules and rights of others, defiance, or hostility and aggression, any of which is severe enough to produce significant impairment in social or occupational functioning. Included in this category are CONDUCT DISORDER and OPPOSITIONAL DEFIANT DISORDER.

dissociated state a reaction to a traumatic event in which the individual splits the components of the event into those that can be faced in the present and those that are too harmful to process. The latter components are repressed and can be recalled later in life if triggered by a similarly traumatic event, introspection, or psychotherapy. See also DISSOCIATIVE DISORDERS.

dissociation *n.* an unconscious defense mechanism in which conflicting impulses are kept apart or threatening ideas and feelings are separated from the rest of the psyche.

dissociative amnesia a DISSOCIATIVE DISORDER characterized by failure to recall important information about one's personal experiences, usually of a traumatic or stressful nature, that is too extensive to be explained by normal forgetfulness. Recovery of memory often occurs spontaneously within a few hours and is usually connected with removal from the traumatic circumstances with which the amnesia was associated.

dissociative disorders a group of disorders characterized by a sudden, gradual, transient, or chronic disruption in the normal integrative functions of consciousness, memory, or perception of the environment. Such disruption may last for minutes or years, depending on the type of disorder. Included in this category are DISSOCIATIVE AMNESIA, DISSOCIATIVE FUGUE, DISSOCIATIVE IDENTITY DISORDER, and DEPERSONALIZATION DISORDER.

dissociative fugue a DISSOCIATIVE DISORDER in which the individual suddenly and unexpectedly travels away from home or a customary place of daily activities and is unable to recall some or all of his or her past. Symptoms also include either confusion about personal identity or assumption of a new identity. No other signs of mental disorder are present, and the fugue state can last from hours to months. Travel can be brief or extended in duration, and there may be no memory of travel once the individual is brought back to the prefugue state.

dissociative identity disorder a DISSOCIATIVE DISORDER characterized by the presence in one individual of two or more distinct identities or personality states that each recurrently take control of the individual's behavior. It is typically associated with severe physical and sexual abuse, especially during childhood. Research suggests that there may be a hereditary component.

dissociative trance disorder a DISSOCIATIVE DISORDER characterized by involuntary alterations in consciousness, identity, awareness or memory, and motor functioning that result in significant distress or impairment. The two subtypes of the disorder are distinguished by the individual's identity state. In **possession trance**, the individual's usual identity is replaced by a new identity perceived to be an external force, and there is loss of memory for the episode of trance. In **trance disorder**, individuals retain their usual identity but have an altered perception of their milieu. These types of dissociative

experiences are common in various cultures and may be part of customary religious practice; they should not be regarded as pathological unless considered abnormal within the context of that cultural or religious group. See also AMOK; ATAQUE DE NERVIOS; LATAH; PIBLOKTO.

dissonance reduction the process by which a person reduces the uncomfortable psychological state that results from inconsistency among elements of a cognitive system (see COGNITIVE DISSONANCE). Dissonance can be reduced by making one or more inconsistent elements consistent with other elements in the system, by decreasing the perceived importance of an inconsistent element, or by adding new consistent elements to the system.

distal *adj.* **1.** situated or directed toward the periphery of the body or toward the end of a limb. **2.** remote from or mostly distantly related to the point of reference or origin. Compare PROXIMAL.

distal stimulus in perception, the actual object in the environment that stimulates or acts on a sense organ. Compare PROXIMAL STIMULUS.

distance cue any of the auditory or visual cues that enable an individual to judge the distance of the source of a stimulus. Auditory distance cues include intensity of familiar sounds (e.g., voices), intensity differences between the ears, and changes in spectral content. In vision, distance cues include the size of familiar objects and ACCOMMODATION.

distance learning the process of acquiring knowledge from a location remote from the teaching source. Typical methods include correspondence coursework, computerized software programmed learning, coursework programmed and accessible on the Internet, live Internet hook-up to an instructor, and live group videoconferencing.

distance therapy any type of psychotherapy in which sessions are not conducted face-to-face because of problems of mobility, geographical isolation, or other limiting factors. Distance therapy includes interventions by telephone, audioconference, or videoconference (known collectively as **telepsychotherapy**) and the Internet (see E-THERAPY).

distance zone in social psychology, the area of physical distance commonly adopted between interacting individuals. Interpersonal distance tends to be relatively small the more familiar the people are to each other and usually increases in proportion to the formality of the relationship, the setting, and the interaction's function.

distorting-photograph procedure a procedure for documenting accuracy of body-size perception by using a photograph distorted to provide an image of an individual that is smaller or larger than actual size. Discrepancy between the size of the selected image and that of an accurate image is used as an index of perceptual accuracy of body size.

distortion *n.* **1.** either the unconscious process of altering emotions and thoughts that are unacceptable in the individual's psyche or the conscious misrepresentation of facts, which often serves the same underlying purpose of disguising that which is unacceptable to or in the self. **2.** in psychoanalytic theory, the outcome of the DREAM-WORK that modifies forbidden thoughts and wishes to make them more acceptable to the EGO. Such distortion of the dream wish through the use of substitutes and symbols means that only an act of INTERPRETATION can uncover the true meaning of the dream.

distractibility *n.* difficulty in maintaining attention or a tendency to be easily diverted from the matter at hand.

distractor *n.* a stimulus or an aspect of a stimulus that is irrelevant to the task or activity being performed. For instance, in a memory study the participant might be given some arithmetic problems to solve as a distractor task between the study and recall phases of an experiment.

distress *n.* **1.** the negative stress response, involving excessive levels of stimulation: a type of stress that results from being overwhelmed by demands, losses, or perceived threats. It has a detrimental effect by generating physical and psychological maladaptation and posing serious health risks for individuals. This generally is the intended meaning of the word STRESS. Compare EUSTRESS. **2.** a negative emotional state in which the specific quality of the emotion is unspecified or unidentifiable. For example, STRANGER ANXIETY in infants is more properly designated **stranger distress** because the infant's negative behavior, typically crying, allows no more specific identification of the emotion. **—distressing** *adj.*

distributed cognition a model for intelligent problem solving in which either the input information comes from separated and independent sources or the processing of this input information takes place across autonomous computational devices.

distributed practice a learning procedure in which practice periods for a particular activity or to improve recall of specific material are separated by regular, lengthy rest periods or periods of practicing different activities or studying other material. In many learning situations, distributed practice is found to be more effective than MASSED PRACTICE.

distributed processing information processing in which computations are made across a series of processors or units, rather than being handled in a single, dedicated CENTRAL PROCESSOR.

distribution *n.* the relation between the values that a variable may take and the relative number of cases taking on each value. A distribution may be simply an empirical description of that relationship or a mathematical (probabilistic) specification of the relationship.

distribution-free test a test of statistical significance that makes relatively few, if any, assumptions about the underlying distribution of scores. See NONPARAMETRIC STATISTICS.

distributive justice the belief that rules can be changed and punishments and rewards distributed according to relative standards, specifically according to equality and equity. In the **equality stage** (ages 8 to 10), children demand that everyone be treated in the same way. In the **equity stage** (ages 11 and older), children make allowances for subjective considerations, personal circumstances, and motive. Compare IMMANENT JUSTICE.

disturbance of association interruption of a logical chain of culturally accepted thought, leading to apparently confused and haphazard thinking that is difficult for others to comprehend. It is one of the FUNDAMENTAL SYMPTOMS of schizophrenia described by Swiss psychiatrist Eugen Bleuler (1857–1939).

disturbance term see ERROR TERM.

disulfiram *n.* a drug used as an aversive agent in managing alcohol abuse or dependence. Disulfiram inhibits the activity of acetaldehyde dehydrogenase, an enzyme responsible for the metabolism of alcohol (ethanol) in the liver. Consumption of alcohol following administration of disulfiram results in accumulation of acetaldehyde, a toxic metabolic product of ethanol, with such unpleasant effects as nausea, vomiting, sweating, headache, a fast heart rate, and palpitations. U.S. trade name: **Antabuse**.

disuse theory of aging the theory that some decline in psychological abilities with aging may be due to the lack of use of those abilities. According to this theory, as adults grow older, they engage their minds less and less with the types of tasks that are found on most psychological tests.

diurnal *adj.* **1.** daily; that is, recurring every 24 hours. **2.** occurring or active during daylight hours. Compare NOCTURNAL. **—diurnality** *n.*

divergence *n.* the tendency for the eyes to turn outward when shifting from near to far fixation. **—divergent** *adj.*

divergent evolution the process by which populations become increasingly different from each other through different SELECTION PRESSURES acting in different habitats. Divergent evolution is a major way in which new species are formed. It contrasts with **convergent evolution**, in which different species become more similar to each other through adaptation to similar habitats.

divergent production the capacity to produce novel solutions to a problem. Compare CONVERGENT PRODUCTION.

divergent thinking creative thinking in which an individual solves a problem or reaches a decision using strategies that deviate from commonly used or previously taught strategies. This term is often used synonymously with LAT-

ERAL THINKING. Compare CONVERGENT THINKING.

divided consciousness a state in which two or more mental activities appear to be carried out at the same time, for example, listening, planning questions, and taking notes during an interview.

divination n. the purported art or practice of discerning future events or hidden knowledge by supernatural means. Among the numerous forms of divination are astrology, augury, crystal gazing, numerology, and palmistry. **—divinatory** adj. **—divine** vb.

divorce n. the legal dissolution of marriage, leaving the partners free to remarry. **—divorcee** n.

dizygotic twins (**DZ twins**) twins, of the same or different sexes, that have developed from two separate ova fertilized by two separate sperm. DZ twins are genetically as much alike as ordinary full siblings born separately. On average, DZ twins are approximately half as genetically similar to one another as MONOZYGOTIC TWINS. Also called **fraternal twins**.

DNA *deoxyribonucleic acid*: one of the two types of NUCLEIC ACID found in living organisms, which is the principal carrier of genetic information in chromosomes. Certain segments of the DNA molecules constitute the organism's genes, with each gene specifying the manufacture of a particular protein or ribosome. Structurally, DNA consists of two intertwined, helically coiled strands of nucleotides—the **double helix**. The nucleotides each contain one of four bases: adenine, guanine, cytosine, or thymine. Each base forms hydrogen bonds with the adjacent base on the other, sister strand, producing consecutive **base pairs** arranged rather like the "rungs" on a helical ladder. Because of DNA's ability to conserve its base sequence when replicating, the genetic instructions it carries are also conserved, both during cell division within a single organism and for that organism's offspring following reproduction. See also RNA.

dogmatism n. a personality trait characterized by the development of BELIEF SYSTEMS containing elements that are isolated from one another and thus may contradict one another. These belief systems are presumed to be resistant to change. **—dogmatic** adj.

dol n. a unit of pain sensation. One dol equals twice the threshold value.

domain n. **1.** the class of entities or events that constitutes the subject matter of a science or other discipline. **2.** in BIOLOGICAL TAXONOMY, the highest category used in some classification systems, comprising one or more kingdoms. Three domains are recognized: Archaea (archaebacteria), Bacteria, and Eukarya (including animals, plants, fungi, and protists).

domain-general ability a cognitive ability, such as general intelligence or speed of information processing, that influences performance over a wide range of situations and tasks.

domain-specific ability a cognitive ability, such as face recognition, that is specific to a task and under control of a specific function of the mind, brain, or both.

domestic partnership two people who live together in a stable, intimate relationship and share the responsibilities of a household in the same way that a married couple would.

domestic violence any action by a person that causes physical harm to one or more members of his or her family unit. For example, it can involve battering of one partner by another, violence against children by a parent, or violence against elders by younger family members.

domiciliary care inpatient institutional care provided because care in the individual's home is not available or not suitable. See also RESIDENTIAL CARE.

dominance n. **1.** the exercise of major influence or control over others. See also ANIMAL DOMINANCE. **2.** the tendency for one hemisphere of the brain to exert greater influence than the other over certain functions, such as language or handedness. The two hemispheres contribute differently to many functions; researchers therefore use the term HEMISPHERIC LATERALIZATION in preference to dominance. **3.** in genetics, the ability of one allele to determine the PHENOTYPE of a HETEROZYGOUS individual. See DOMINANT ALLELE. ~**dominant** adj.

dominance hierarchy 1. in social psychology, a system of stable linear variations in prestige, status, and authority among group members. It defines who gives orders and who carries them out. **2.** any ordering of motives, needs, or other psychological or physical responses based on priority or importance. An example is MASLOW'S MOTIVATIONAL HIERARCHY.

dominance–submission a key dimension of interpersonal behavior in which behavior is differentiated along a continuum ranging from extreme dominance (active, talkative, extraverted, assertive, controlling, powerful) to extreme subordination (passive, quiet, introverted, submissive, weak).

dominance–subordination a form of social relationship within groups with a leader or dominant member who has priority of access to resources over other, subordinate members of the community. Dominance–subordination relationships are highly organized in troops of baboons and in hyena groups, for example.

dominant allele the version of a gene (see ALLELE) whose effects are manifest in preference to another version of the same gene (the RECESSIVE ALLELE) when both are present in the same cell. Hence, the trait determined by a dominant allele (the **dominant trait**) is apparent even when the allele is carried on only one of a pair of HOMOLOGOUS chromosomes. The term **autosomal dominant** is used to describe such patterns of inheritance in which characteristics are conveyed by dominant alleles. For example, Huntington's disease is an autosomal dominant disorder.

Donders's method a method of separating out hypothetical stages of mental processing by requiring participants to perform a set of REACTION TIME tasks in which each successive task differs from its predecessor by the addition of a single mental stage. The time required to complete a particular stage of processing can be inferred by subtracting from the reaction time in one task the reaction time in the preceding task. Also called **subtraction method**. [Franciscus **Donders** (1818–1889), Dutch physician and physiologist]

don't-hold functions cognitive abilities, such as those involved in digit–symbol association, that often deteriorate with adult aging as observed on intellectual or cognitive tests.

door-in-the-face technique a two-step procedure for enhancing COMPLIANCE in which an extreme initial request is presented immediately before the more moderate target request. Rejection of the initial request makes people more likely to accept the target request than would have been the case if the latter had been presented on its own. See also FOOT-IN-THE-DOOR TECHNIQUE; LOW-BALL TECHNIQUE; THAT'S-NOT-ALL TECHNIQUE.

dopa (DOPA) *n.* 3,4-dihydroxyphenylalanine, an amino acid that is a precursor to DOPAMINE and other catecholamines. See also LEVODOPA.

dopamine (DA) *n.* a CATECHOLAMINE neurotransmitter that has an important role in motor behavior and is implicated in numerous mental conditions. For example, destruction of the DOPAMINERGIC neurons in the SUBSTANTIA NIGRA is responsible for the symptoms of Parkinson's disease (e.g., rigidity, tremor), and blockade of the actions of dopamine in other brain regions accounts for the therapeutic activities of antischizophrenic drugs. Dopamine is synthesized from the dietary amino acid tyrosine and may be further metabolized to form norepinephrine and epinephrine, respectively.

dopamine hypothesis the theory that schizophrenia is caused by an excess of dopamine in the brain, due either to an overproduction of dopamine or a deficiency of the enzyme needed to convert dopamine to norepinephrine (adrenaline). Although this hypothesis is still widely discussed and promoted, it has not been empirically supported. See also GLUTAMATE HYPOTHESIS.

dopamine receptor a receptor molecule that is sensitive to dopamine and chemically related compounds. Dopamine receptors are located in parts of the nervous system and also in blood vessels of the kidneys and mesentery. There are several subtypes of dopamine receptors, designated D1, D2, and so on. Substances that bind to and directly activate dopamine receptors, producing physiological effects that mimic those of the neurotransmitter dopamine, are called **dopa-**mine-receptor agonists, whereas substances that reduce the effects of dopamine by competitively binding to, and thus blocking, dopamine receptors are called **dopamine-receptor antagonists**.

dopaminergic *adj.* responding to, releasing, or otherwise involving dopamine. For example, a **dopaminergic neuron** is any neuron in the brain or other parts of the central nervous system for which dopamine serves as the principal neurotransmitter. Three major tracts of dopamine-containing neurons are classically described: the mesolimbic–mesocortical tract (see MESOCORTICAL SYSTEM; MESOLIMBIC SYSTEM), in which excess dopamine activity is hypothesized to be associated with positive and negative symptoms of schizophrenia; the NIGROSTRIATAL TRACT, which is involved in motor functions and Parkinson's disease; and the tuberoinfundibular pathway, a local circuit in the hypothalamus that is involved in the regulation of the pituitary hormone prolactin.

Doppler effect the apparent increase or decrease in wavelength or frequency observed when a source of electromagnetic radiation or sound approaches or recedes from the observer or listener, producing a change in hue or pitch. The **total Doppler effect** may result from motion of both the observer or listener and the source. [Christian Andreas **Doppler** (1803–1853), Austrian mathematician]

Dora case an early and celebrated case of Austrian psychiatrist Sigmund Freud (1856–1939), reported in *Fragment of an Analysis of a Case of Hysteria* (1905). The study of this woman's multiple symptoms (headaches, loss of speech, suicidal thoughts, amnesic episodes) contributed to his theory of REPRESSION and the use of dream analysis as an analytic tool.

dorsal *adj.* pertaining to the back (posterior side) of the body or to the upper (superior) surface of the brain. For example, a **dorsal column** is any of various tracts of sensory nerve fibres that run through the white matter of the spinal cord on its dorsal side. Compare VENTRAL. —**dorsally** *adv.*

dorsal column system a SOMATOSENSORY SYSTEM that transmits most touch information via the DORSAL columns of the spinal cord to the brain.

dorsal horn either of the upper regions of the H-shaped pattern formed by the PERIAQUEDUCTAL GRAY in the spinal cord. The dorsal horns extend toward the dorsal roots and mainly serve sensory mechanisms. Also called **posterior horn**. Compare ANTERIOR HORN.

dorsal root any of the SPINAL ROOTS that convey sensory nerve fibers and enter the spinal cord dorsally on each side. Also called **posterior horn**. Compare VENTRAL ROOT.

dorsal stream a neural system that projects dorsally from the primary visual cortex (VISUAL AREA 1) into the parietal lobe (visual area MT) and is involved in processing object motion and location in space. It is known informally as the "where" or "how" pathway. Compare VENTRAL STREAM.

dorsolateral *adj.* located both dorsally (toward the back) and laterally (toward the side). **—dorsolaterally** *adv.*

dorsolateral prefrontal cortex a region of the PREFRONTAL CORTEX involved in WORKING MEMORY and attentional control. Damage to this region in humans results in an inability to select task-relevant information and to shift attention based on external cues.

dose–response relationship a principle relating the potency of a drug to the efficacy of that drug in affecting a target symptom or organ system. **Potency** refers to the amount of a drug necessary to produce the desired effect; **efficacy** refers to the drug's ability to act at a target receptor or organ to produce the desired effect. Dose–response curves may be graded, suggesting a continuous relationship between dose and effect, or quantal, where the desired effect is an either–or phenomenon, such as prevention of arrhythmias.

dotage *n.* the state of DEMENTIA in old age.

double-agentry *n.* the situation in which the therapist's allegiance to the patient is in conflict with demands from the institution or from other professionals.

double alternation in experimental research, a pattern in which two consecutive events of one kind alternate with two consecutive events of another kind. For example, in an OPERANT CONDITIONING experiment, two consecutive reinforced (R) trials may alternate with two consecutive nonreinforced (N) trials, yielding the pattern RRNNRRNN…. See also SINGLE ALTERNATION.

double-aspect theory the position that mind and body are two attributes of a single substance (see MIND–BODY PROBLEM). This view is particularly associated with Dutch philosopher Baruch Spinoza (1632–1677), who held that there is one (and only one) infinite substance, which he identified as God.

double bind a situation in which an individual receives contradictory messages from another person or from two different people. For example, a parent may respond negatively when his or her child approaches or attempts to engage in affectionate behavior, but then, when the child turns away or tries to leave, reaches out to encourage the child to return. Double-binding communication was once considered a causative factor in schizophrenia.

double blind see BLIND.

double consciousness a condition in which two distinct, unrelated mental states coexist within the same person. This may occur, for example, in an individual with a DISSOCIATIVE IDENTITY DISORDER. Also called **dual consciousness**.

double dissociation a research process for demonstrating the action of two separable psychological or biological systems, such as differentiating between types of memory or the function of brain areas. One experimental variable is found to affect one of the systems, whereas a second variable affects the other. The differentiating variables may be task-related, pharmacological, neurological, or individual differences.

double-simultaneous tactile sensation the ability of a person to perceive that he or she has received two tactile sensations in different areas at the same time, for example, when touched simultaneously on the left and right hands or the right hand and left side of the face. An inability to perceive one or both of the simultaneous tactile sensations is referred to as **tactile extinction**.

double standard the hypocritical belief that a code of behavior is permissible for one group or individual but not for another.

double vision the perception of a single object as a separate image by each eye. Double vision is referred to medically as DIPLOPIA.

doubt *n.* lack of confidence or uncertainty about something or someone, including the self. Doubt may center on everyday concerns (Can I accomplish this task?), issues of daily living (Can I change this ingrained habit?), or the very meaning of life itself (see EXISTENTIAL ANXIETY; EXISTENTIAL CRISIS). It is a perception, typically with a strong affective component, that is frequently a focus during psychotherapeutic intervention.

doubting mania extreme and obsessive feelings of uncertainty about even the most obvious matters. Doubting mania is a common obsession associated with OBSESSIVE-COMPULSIVE DISORDER and often results in checking rituals (e.g., repeatedly looking to see if the door is locked).

Down syndrome a chromosomal disorder characterized by an extra chromosome 21 and manifested by a round flat face and eyes that seem to slant (the disorder was formerly known as **mongolism**). Brain size and weight are below average; affected individuals usually have mild to severe mental retardation, and muscular movements tend to be slow, clumsy, and uncoordinated. Lifespan is reduced compared to the general population, and affected individuals typically show early onset of ALZHEIMER'S DISEASE. Down syndrome is one of the most common organic causes of mental retardation. [described in 1866 by John Langdon Haydon **Down** (1828–1896), British physician]

downward communication the transmission of information from individuals who occupy relatively high-status positions within a group or organization to those who occupy subordinate positions. Such communications tend to be informational and directive, whereas UPWARD COMMUNICATIONS request information, provide factual information, or express grievances.

downward mobility the movement of a person or group to a lower social class. See also SOCIAL MOBILITY. Compare UPWARD MOBILITY.

d prime (symbol: d′) a measure of an individual's ability to detect signals; more specifically, a measure of sensitivity or discriminability derived from SIGNAL DETECTION THEORY that is unaffected by response biases. It is the difference (in standard deviation units) between the means of the NOISE and signal+noise distributions. A value of d′ = 3 is close to perfect performance; a value of d′ = 0 is chance ("guessing") performance.

drama therapy in GROUP PSYCHOTHERAPY, the use of theater techniques to gain self-awareness and increase self-expression. See also PSYCHODRAMA.

dramatization n. 1. the use of attention-getting behavior as a defense against anxiety or insecurity. An example of dramatization is the exaggeration of the symptoms of an illness to make it appear more important than the occurrence of the same illness in another person. 2. in psychoanalytic theory, the expression of repressed wishes or impulses in dreams. —**dramatize** vb.

dread n. 1. intense fear or fearful anticipation. Existential dread (see EXISTENTIALISM) refers to a profound, deep-seated psychic or spiritual condition of insecurity and despair in relation to the human condition and the meaning of life. See also ANGST. 2. in psychoanalysis, anxiety elicited by a specific threat, such as going out on a dark night, as contrasted with anxiety that does not have a specific object.

dream n. a mental state that occurs in sleep and is characterized by a rich array of sensory, motor, emotional, and cognitive experiences. Dreams occur most often, but not exclusively, during periods of REM SLEEP. They are characterized by (a) vivid imagery, especially visual imagery, and a strong sense of movement; (b) intense emotion, especially fear, elation, or anger; (c) delusional acceptance of the dream as a waking reality; and (d) discontinuity in time and space and incongruity of character and plot. Despite the vivid intensity of dreams, it can be difficult to remember them to any extent unless promptly awakened from REM sleep, but even then much content cannot be accurately retrieved.

Diverse theories about the significance of dreams and the process of dream production have arisen from varied sources throughout history. These range from the suggestion of Greek physician Hippocrates (c. 460–c. 377 BCE) that dreams provide early evidence of disease, to the interpretation by Austrian psychiatrist Sigmund Freud (1856–1939) of dreams as a struggle in which the part of the mind representing social strictures (the SUPEREGO) plays out a conflict with the sexual impulses (the LI-BIDO) while the rational part of the mind (the EGO) is at rest, and scientific study of dreaming as a neurocognitive process, a recent product of which is the ACTIVATION–SYNTHESIS HYPOTHESIS. See also DAYDREAM; DREAM STATE; NIGHTMARE. —**dreamlike** adj. —**dreamy** adj.

dream analysis a technique in which the content of dreams is interpreted to reveal underlying motivations or symbolic meanings and representations (i.e., LATENT CONTENT). Also called **dream interpretation**.

dream censorship in psychoanalytic theory, the disguising in dreams of unconscious wishes that would be disturbing to the EGO if allowed conscious expression. According to the classic psychoanalytic theory of Austrian psychiatrist Sigmund Freud (1856–1939), the thoroughness of dream disguise varies directly with the strictness of the censorship. See CENSOR.

dream deprivation a technique used in research in which participants are awakened frequently to minimize the amount of REM SLEEP—and hence time for dreaming—they have during the night. Participants will spontaneously compensate by having longer periods of REM sleep on subsequent nights, a finding often taken to be evidence for the homeostatic nature of dream regulation.

dream interpretation see DREAM ANALYSIS.

dream state (D-state) the state of sleep during which dreaming takes place most often, characterized by rapid eye movements (see REM SLEEP) and patterns on the electroencephalogram that most closely resemble those of wakefulness. It usually occurs four or five times during the night. The lower brainstem appears to be the area most involved in originating the dream state, under the control of genetically and light-regulated diurnal rhythms.

dream-work n. in psychoanalytic theory, the transformation of the LATENT CONTENT of a dream into the MANIFEST CONTENT experienced by the dreamer. This transformation is effected by such processes as CONDENSATION, SYMBOLISM, DISPLACEMENT, and DRAMATIZATION.

DRGs abbreviation for DIAGNOSIS-RELATED GROUPS.

drift hypothesis a sociological concept purporting to explain the higher incidence of schizophrenia in urban poverty centers, suggesting that during the preclinical phase people tend to drift into poverty and social isolation. Also called **downward drift hypothesis**.

drive n. 1. a generalized state of READINESS precipitating or motivating an activity or course of action. Drive is hypothetical in nature, usually created by deprivation of a needed substance (e.g., food), the presence of negative stimuli (e.g., pain, cold), or the occurrence of negative events. 2. in the psychoanalytic theory of Austrian psychiatrist Sigmund Freud (1856–1939), a concept used to understand the relationship between the psyche and the soma (mind and body); drive is conceived as a having a somatic source but creating a psychic effect. Freud identified two separate drives as emerging from somatic sources: LIBIDO and AGGRESSION. See also MOTIVATION.

drive-induction theory the theory that REINFORCEMENT is the degree of drive induced by a given reinforcer. According to this theory, it is the arousal or excitement produced by consummating a reinforcer (e.g., eating, drinking, mating) that produces reinforcement of behavior, and not the reduction of the drive state that the reinforcer may produce.

drive-reduction theory a theory of learning in which the goal of motivated behavior is a reduction of a drive state. It is assumed that all motivated behavior arises from drives, stemming from a disruption in homeostasis, and that responses that lead to reduction of those drives tend to be reinforced or strengthened.

drive theory see CLASSICAL PSYCHOANALYSIS.

drop-in center a facility, often associated with a substance-abuse program, where professional support and advice can be obtained without an advance appointment. A drop-in center also serves as a gathering place providing social, educational, and recreational activities.

drug *n.* **1.** any substance, other than food, that is administered for experimental, diagnostic, or treatment purposes. **2.** any substance that is used recreationally for its effects on motor, sensory, or cognitive activities.

drug abuse see SUBSTANCE ABUSE.

drug abuse treatment see SUBSTANCE ABUSE TREATMENT.

drug addiction see SUBSTANCE DEPENDENCE.

drug dependence see SUBSTANCE DEPENDENCE.

drug discrimination the ability of an organism to distinguish between the internal states produced by different drugs (or by a particular drug and saline). In a typical experimental procedure, an animal is injected with one drug, and a certain response (e.g., pressing the left-hand lever in a two-lever apparatus) is reinforced. When injected with a different drug (or with saline), a different response (e.g., pressing the right-hand lever) is reinforced. Thus, the animal must discriminate between the internal cues produced by the drugs in order to make the correct response.

drug holiday discontinuance of a therapeutic drug for a limited period in order to control dosage and side effects and to evaluate the patient's behavior with and without it. Drug holidays are infrequent in modern clinical practice.

drug interactions the effects of administering two or more drugs concurrently, which alters the pharmacological action of one or more of them. Pharmacokinetic interactions alter the absorption, distribution, metabolism, and excretion of the drugs; they may induce or inhibit the elimination of drugs, leading to unexpected increases or decreases in their concentrations in the body. Pharmacodynamic interactions affect the drugs' activities at target organs or receptor sites; they may be synergistic, enhancing the effectiveness of a drug at a target receptor or organ, or antagonistic, in which the presence of one drug reduces the effectiveness of another.

drug metabolism the process by which a drug is transformed in the body (in the liver and other organs), usually from a more lipid-soluble form, which makes it more readily absorbed into the body, to a more water-soluble form, which facilitates its excretion. Two phases of drug metabolism are recognized. In **Phase I metabolism**, the drug is oxidized, reduced, or hydrolyzed—that is, oxygen is added, oxygen is removed, or hydrogen is added, respectively (see CYTOCHROME P450). In **Phase II metabolism**, functional groups (specific clusters of atoms) are added to drug molecules (e.g., by GLUCURONIDATION).

drug screening instrument a brief interview or a brief self-report instrument that is designed to identify individuals who should be assessed thoroughly for the possibility of substance abuse.

drug synergism an enhancement of efficacy occurring when two or more drugs are administered concurrently, so that their combined pharmacological or clinical effects are greater than those occurring when the drugs are administered individually. Drug synergism can be metabolic, when the administration of one agent interferes with the metabolism of another, or it can be pharmacological, when the administration of two or more agents results in enhanced receptor binding or other activity at target sites.

drug therapy see PHARMACOTHERAPY.

drug withdrawal see SUBSTANCE WITHDRAWAL.

DSM–IV–TR the text revision of the fourth edition of the *Diagnostic and Statistical Manual of Mental Disorders*, prepared by the American Psychiatric Association and published in 2000. The classification presents descriptions of diagnostic categories without favoring any particular theory of etiology. It is largely modeled on the INTERNATIONAL CLASSIFICATION OF DISEASES (9th edition, 1978), developed by the World Health Organization, but contains greater detail and recent changes, as well as a method of coding on different axes (see MULTIAXIAL CLASSIFICATION).

D-state abbreviation for DREAM STATE, as opposed to the S-state (sleeping state) and the W-state (waking state).

DTs abbreviation for DELIRIUM TREMENS.

dual coding theory 1. the theory that linguistic input can be represented in memory in both verbal and visual formats. Concrete words that readily call to mind a picture, such as *table* or *horse*, are remembered better than abstract words, such as *honesty* or *conscience*, which do not readily call to mind a picture, because the concrete words are stored in two codes rather than one. **2.** a theory for explaining the relationship between IMAGERY and performance that suggests there are two ways of gaining information about a skill: the motor channel for encoding human actions and the verbal channel for encoding speech. Using auditory imagery linked with visual imagery is suggested to be the most effective in performance enhancement.

dual diagnosis the identification of two distinct disorders that are present in the same person at the same time, for example, the coexistence of depression or anxiety disorder and a substance-abuse disorder (e.g., alcohol or drug dependence). See also COMORBIDITY.

dual instinct theory in psychoanalytic theory, the view that human life is governed by two antagonistic forces: the LIFE INSTINCT, or EROS, and the DEATH INSTINCT, or THANATOS. This was a late theoretical formulation by Austrian psychiatrist Sigmund Freud (1856–1939), who held that "the interaction of the two basic instincts with or against each other gives rise to the whole variegation of the phenomena of life" (*Beyond the Pleasure Principle*, 1920).

dualism *n.* the position that reality consists of two separate substances, defined by French philosopher René Descartes (1596–1650) as thinking substance (mind) and extended substance (matter). In the context of the MIND–BODY PROBLEM, dualism is the position that the mind and the body constitute two separate realms or substances. Dualistic positions raise the question of how mind and body interact in thought and behavior. Compare MONISM. See also CARTESIAN DUALISM. —**dualist** *adj., n.* —**dualistic** *adj.*

duality of language the concept that language can be represented at two levels: (a) PHONOLOGY, which is the sound that a speaker produces; and (b) meaning, which is a function of SYNTAX and SEMANTICS.

dual process model of persuasion any of various persuasion theories postulating that attitude change can occur as a result of strategies for processing attitude-relevant information that involve either a very high degree of effort or very little effort. The most prominent theories of this type are the ELABORATION-LIKELIHOOD MODEL and the HEURISTIC-SYSTEMATIC MODEL.

dual process theory of color vision see OPPONENT PROCESS THEORY OF COLOR VISION.

dual relationship see MULTIPLE RELATIONSHIP.

dual representation the ability to comprehend an object simultaneously as the object itself and as a representation of something else. For example, a photograph of a person can be represented both as the print itself and as the person it depicts.

dual-store model of memory the concept

that memory is a two-stage process, comprising SHORT-TERM MEMORY, in which information is retained for a few seconds, and LONG-TERM MEMORY, which permits the retention of information for hours to many years. U.S. psychologist and philosopher William James (1842–1910) called these stages PRIMARY MEMORY and SECONDARY MEMORY, respectively. Also called **dual memory theory**.

dual-task competition a phenomenon observed in experimental techniques in which participants are asked to perform two tasks (e.g., speeded reaction time and mental arithmetic) simultaneously. Such tasks require effort (see EFFORTFULNESS) and tend to compete against each other (see RESOURCE COMPETITION), so that their performances degrade.

dual trace hypothesis a restatement of the PERSEVERATION–CONSOLIDATION HYPOTHESIS of memory formation specifying that short-term memory is represented neurally by activity in reverberating circuits and that stabilization of these circuits leads to permanent synaptic change, reflecting the formation of long-term memory. See HEBBIAN SYNAPSE.

duct *n.* in anatomy, a tubular canal or passage, especially one that transports a secretion, such as a bile duct or tear duct. Glands with ducts are called EXOCRINE GLANDS. —**ductal** *adj.*

dummy *n.* in double-blind drug trials (see BLIND), an inert substance that appears identical in all aspects (e.g., dosage form, method of administration) to the active drug under investigation, thereby helping to preserve experimental blinds for both patients and clinical investigators. Since a dummy is completely inert it has no pharmacological activity, unlike an ACTIVE PLACEBO, which may produce side effects.

dummy variable coding a method of assigning numerical values (often 0 and 1) to a CATEGORICAL VARIABLE in such a way that the variable reflects class membership.

Duncan multiple-range test a post hoc MULTIPLE COMPARISONS procedure used to determine which mean, among a set of means, can be said to be significantly different, while controlling the Type I comparison-wise error rate (see TYPE I ERROR) at α (the criterion value: see SIGNIFICANCE LEVEL). [David Beattie **Duncan** (1916–), Australian-born U.S. statistician]

Dunnett's multiple comparison test a MULTIPLE COMPARISON method for comparing all groups with a single control group mean in such a way that the SIGNIFICANCE LEVEL for the set of comparisons is controlled at α (the criterion value). [Charles W. **Dunnett** (1921–), Canadian statistician]

Dunn's multiple comparison test a MULTIPLE COMPARISON method that is based on the BONFERRONI CORRECTION.

durable power of attorney see ADVANCE DIRECTIVE.

dura mater see MENINGES.

duress *n.* acts or threats (e.g., the threat of confinement) that compel people to act or speak against their will (e.g., to make a coerced confession).

duty to protect the obligation of mental health professionals to protect third parties from harm or violence that may result from the actions of their clients. This obligation may involve, but is not necessarily restricted to, a DUTY TO WARN. See TARASOFF DECISION.

duty to warn the obligation of mental health professionals to warn third parties whom their clients intend to harm. See also DUTY TO PROTECT; TARASOFF DECISION.

DV abbreviation for DEPENDENT VARIABLE.

dwarfism *n.* a condition of underdeveloped body structure due to a developmental defect, hormonal or nutritional deficiencies, or diseases. Some forms of dwarfism, such as that due to thyroid-hormone deficiency, are associated with mental retardation.

Dx abbreviation for DIAGNOSIS.

dyad (**diad**) *n.* a pair of individuals in an interpersonal situation. —**dyadic** *adj.*

dyadic therapy see INDIVIDUAL THERAPY.

dynamic *adj.* describing systems of psychology that emphasize motivation, mental processes, and the complexities of force and interaction.

dynamic assessment an approach to CLINICAL ASSESSMENT that follows the same basic principles as DYNAMIC TESTING.

dynamic core a theoretical construct involving a subset of neurons in the THALAMOCORTICAL SYSTEM of the brain that support conscious experience. The specific subset of neurons involved may vary dynamically from moment to moment, but the dynamic core always maximizes high integration and differentiation of information. See COMPLEXITY HYPOTHESIS.

dynamic formulation the ongoing attempt to organize the clinical material elicited about a client's behavior, traits, attitudes, and symptoms into a structure that helps the therapist understand the client and plan his or her treatment more effectively.

dynamic model in psychoanalytic theory, the view that the psyche can be explained in terms of underlying, unconscious drives and instincts that mold the personality, motivate behavior, and produce emotional disorder. Compare ECONOMIC MODEL; TOPOGRAPHIC MODEL.

dynamic psychology a theory of psychology emphasizing causation and motivation in relation to behavior, specifically the stimulus–organism–response chain in which the stimulus–response relationship is regarded as the mechanism of behavior and the drives of the organism are the mediating variable.

dynamic psychotherapy any form or technique of psychotherapy that focuses on the underlying motivational or defensive factors (e.g., unconscious conflicts, interpersonal patterns) that determine a person's behavior and adjustment. See also DEPTH THERAPY.

dynamic social impact theory an extension of SOCIAL IMPACT THEORY that seeks to explain the changes in physiological states, subjective feelings, emotions, cognitions, and behavior that occur as a result of SOCIAL INFLUENCE. The model assumes that influence is a function of the strength, immediacy, and number of people (or, more precisely, sources) present, and that this influence results in consolidation (growth of the majority), clustering (the emergence of small groups whose members hold similar opinions), correlation (the convergence of group members' opinions on a variety of issues), and continuing diversity (the maintenance of the beliefs of the members of the minority) in groups that are spatially distributed and interacting repeatedly over time.

dynamic systems theory a theory that attempts to explain behavior and personality in terms of constantly changing, self-organizing interactions among multiple organismic and environmental factors that operate on multiple timescales and multiple levels of analysis.

dynamic testing a psychometric approach that attempts to measure not only the products or processes of learning but also the potential to learn. It attempts to quantify the process of learning rather than the products of that process. This is done by presenting progressively more challenging tasks and providing continuous feedback on performance.

dynamometry *n.* the measurement of force expended or power, especially muscular effort or strength of humans or animals. A **dynamometer** usually consists of a spring that can be compressed by the force applied. —**dynamometric** *adj.*

dynorphin *n.* see ENDOGENOUS OPIOID.

dysarthria *n.* any of a group of MOTOR SPEECH DISORDERS caused by impairment originating in the central or peripheral nervous system. Respiration, articulation, phonation, resonance, and prosody may be affected. There are four main types: dyskinetic, spastic, peripheral, and mixed. —**dysarthric** *adj.*

dysautonomia *n.* dysfunction of the autonomic nervous system, including impairment, failure, or overactivity of sympathetic or parasympathetic functioning.

dyscalculia *n.* an impaired ability to perform simple arithmetic operations that results from a congenital deficit. It is a developmental condition, whereas ACALCULIA is acquired.

dyscheiria (**dyschiria**) *n.* disordered representation of one side of the body. Types include ACHEIRIA, ALLOCHEIRIA, and SYNCHEIRIA.

dyschromatopsia *n.* a congenital or acquired defect in the discrimination of colors.

D

dyscontrol *n.* an impaired ability to direct or regulate one's functioning in volition, emotion, behavior, cognition, or some other area, which often entails inability to resist impulses and leads to abnormal behaviors without significant provocation.

dysesthesia (**disesthesia; dysaesthesia**) *n.* abnormalities of any sense but particularly that of touch.

dysexecutive syndrome a collection of symptoms that involve impaired executive control of actions, caused by damage to the frontal lobes of the brain. Individuals have difficulty in initiating and switching actions and organizing behavior.

dysfluency *n.* any disturbance in the normal flow or patterning of speech, marked by repetitions, prolongations, and hesitations.

dysfunction *n.* any impairment, disturbance, or deficiency in behavior or operation. —**dysfunctional** *adj.*

dysfunctional family a family in which relationships or communication are impaired and members are unable to attain closeness and self-expression.

dysfunctions associated with sleep, sleep stages, or partial arousals one of four basic types of SLEEP DISORDERS, differentiated from the other types by the presence of physiological activations at inappropriate times during sleep rather than abnormalities in the mechanisms involved in the timing of sleep and wakefulness. This type of sleep disorder includes NIGHTMARE DISORDER, SLEEP TERROR DISORDER, and SLEEP-WALKING DISORDER; these are classified as PARASOMNIAS in psychiatry.

dysgenic *adj.* describing a factor or influence that may be detrimental to heredity. Compare EUGENIC.

dysgeusia *n.* abnormalities of the sense of taste. These gustatory distortions may occur during pregnancy, prior to an epileptic seizure, or as a symptom of psychosis or an eating disorder. See also HYPOGEUSIA.

dysgrammatism *n.* see AGRAMMATISM.

dysgraphia *n.* see AGRAPHIA. —**dysgraphic** *adj.*

dyskinesia *n.* any involuntary (unintended) movement, such as a tic or spasm. The term also is used more imprecisely to denote distorted or impaired voluntary movement. Also called **dyskinesis**. —**dyskinetic** *adj.*

dyslalia *n.* an obsolescent name for impaired articulation for which no physiological cause can be determined.

dyslexia *n.* a neurologically based disorder manifested as severe difficulties in reading, resulting from impairment in the ability to make connections between written letters and their sounds. It can be either acquired (in which case it often is referred to as ALEXIA) or developmental, is independent of intellectual ability, and is unrelated to disorders of speech and vision that may also be present. Investigators have proposed various subtypes of dyslexia but there is no universally accepted system of classification. —**dyslexic** *adj.*

dysmenorrhea *n.* difficult or painful menstruation. —**dysmenorrheic** *adj.*

dysmetria *n.* an impaired ability to control the distance, speed, or power of one's body movements. It is a key sign of cerebellar damage.

dysmetropsia *n.* impairment in the ability to judge the size or shape of objects, although the objects may be recognized for what they are.

dysmnesia *n.* an impairment of memory.

dysnomia–auditory retrieval disorder a speech and language disorder marked by problems in object naming and word retrieval and deficits in AUDITORY MEMORY. Affected children may have difficulty remembering meaningful information (expressed, for example, as sentences or stories) in a sequential fashion, even though they may have good language skills and normal or high verbal output.

dysorexia *n.* any distortion of normal appetite or disturbance in normal eating behavior. See also EATING DISORDER.

dysosmia *n.* any disorder or disability in the sense of smell.

dyspareunia *n.* painful sexual intercourse.

dysphagia *n.* an impaired ability to swallow.

dysphasia *n.* see APHASIA. —**dysphasic** *adj.*

dysphonia *n.* any dysfunction in the production of sounds, especially speech sounds, which may affect pitch, intensity, or resonance.

dysphoria *n.* a mood characterized by sadness, discontent, and sometimes restlessness. —**dysphoric** *adj.*

dyspraxia *n.* an impaired ability to perform skilled, coordinated movements that is neurologically based and not due to any muscular or sensory defect. —**dyspraxic** *adj.*

dysprosody (**dysprosodia**) *n.* see APROSODY.

dysrhythmia *n.* any rhythmic abnormality, as might be detected in speech or in brain waves.

dyssomnia *n.* any of various SLEEP DISORDERS marked by abnormalities in the amount, quality, or timing of sleep. Included in this category are PRIMARY INSOMNIA, PRIMARY HYPERSOMNIA, NARCOLEPSY, CIRCADIAN RHYTHM SLEEP DISORDER, and BREATHING-RELATED SLEEP DISORDER.

dystaxia *n.* a mild degree of ATAXIA, marked by difficulty in performing coordinated muscular movements.

dysthymia *n.* any depressed mood that is mild or moderate in severity. —**dysthymic** *adj.*

dysthymic disorder a DEPRESSIVE DISORDER characterized by a depressed mood for most of the day, occurring more days than not, that persists for at least 2 years. It is distinguished from

MAJOR DEPRESSIVE DISORDER in that the symptoms are less severe but more enduring.

dystonia *n.* impairment of normal muscle tone, causing prolonged muscle contraction that results in abnormal posture, twisting, or repetitive movements. See also ATONIA. —**dystonic** *adj.*

dystrophy *n.* **1.** any degenerative disorder arising from faulty or defective nutrition. **2.** any disorder involving ATROPHY (wasting) and weakening of the muscles. See MUSCULAR DYSTROPHY.

DZ twins abbreviation for DIZYGOTIC TWINS.

D

Ee

EA abbreviation for EDUCATIONAL AGE.

EAP abbreviation for EMPLOYEE ASSISTANCE PROGRAM.

ear *n.* the organ of hearing and balance. In humans and other mammals the ear is divided into external, middle, and inner sections. The PINNA of the EXTERNAL EAR collects sounds that are then funneled through the EXTERNAL AUDITORY MEATUS to the TYMPANIC MEMBRANE. The sounds are vibrations of air molecules that cause the tympanic membrane to vibrate, which in turn vibrates the OSSICLES, three tiny bones in the MIDDLE EAR. The motion of the last of these bones produces pressure waves in the fluid-filled COCHLEA of the INNER EAR. The motion of the fluid in the cochlea is converted by specialized receptors called HAIR CELLS into neural signals that are sent to the brain by the AUDITORY NERVE.

ear canal see EXTERNAL AUDITORY MEATUS.

eardrum *n.* see TYMPANIC MEMBRANE.

early intervention a collection of specialized services provided to children from birth to 3 years of age with identified conditions placing them at risk of developmental disability or with evident signs of developmental delay. Services are designed to minimize the impact of the infant's or toddler's condition, and in addition to stimulatory, social, therapeutic, and treatment programs may include family training, screening, assessment, or health care.

early-selection theory any theory of attention proposing that selection of stimuli for in-depth analysis occurs early in the processing stream, prior to stimulus identification. According to early-selection theory, unattended stimuli receive only a slight degree of processing that does not encompass meaning, whereas attended stimuli proceed through a significant degree of deep, meaningful analysis. Compare LATE-SELECTION THEORY.

Easterbrook hypothesis the hypothesis that the range of cues attended to is inversely related to the degree of arousal, that is, in a state of increased arousal, attention narrows and fewer environmental stimuli are focused on. The hypothesis was proposed as an explanation of YERKES–DODSON LAW, which describes the relationship between arousal and performance. [proposed in 1959 by J. A. **Easterbrook**, 20th-century Canadian psychologist]

eating disorder any disorder characterized primarily by pathological eating behavior, such as ANOREXIA NERVOSA, BULIMIA NERVOSA, and BINGE-EATING DISORDER. Other eating-related disorders include PICA and RUMINATION DISORDER, which are usually diagnosed in infancy or early childhood.

Ebbinghaus curve a graphic depiction of the amount of forgetting over time after learning has taken place, showing a sudden drop in retention shortly following learning, but a more gradual decline thereafter. [Hermann **Ebbinghaus** (1850–1909), German psychologist]

EBV abbreviation for EPSTEIN–BARR VIRUS.

eccentric projection the phenomenon of experiencing a stimulus as being in the external world (as in vision and hearing), rather than at the receptor stimulated (as in touch).

ECG abbreviation for ELECTROCARDIOGRAM.

echocardiography *n.* the production of a graphic record or image (**echocardiogram**) of the internal structures and beating of an individual's heart with an ultrasound device that uses sonarlike reflections. Echocardiography enables the visualization and measurement of all the chambers and valves of the heart as well as the pumping efficiency of the organ.

echoencephalography *n.* a method of mapping brain anatomy for diagnostic purposes by using ultrasonic waves. The waves are transmitted through the skull using an instrument called an **echoencephalograph**, and echoes of the waves from intracranial structures are recorded to produce a visual image called an **echo-encephalogram**.

echoic memory the retention of auditory information for a brief period (2–3 s) after the end of the stimulus. Also called **auditory sensory memory**.

echolalia *n.* mechanical repetition of words and phrases uttered by another individual. It is often a symptom of a neurological or developmental disorder, particular catatonic schizophrenia or autism.

echolocation *n.* the ability to judge the direction and distance of objects from reflected echoes made by acoustic signals. People with visual impairment can learn to develop this ability to find their way and avoid obstacles. Among animals, both bats and marine mammals (e.g., dolphins) can locate objects by emitting high-pitched sounds that are reflected from features of the physical environment and prey objects. See also ULTRASONIC COMMUNICATION.

echopraxia *n.* mechanical repetition of another person's movements or gestures. It is often a symptom of a neurological disorder, particularly catatonic schizophrenia.

eclectic behaviorism an approach to BEHAVIOR THERAPY that does not adhere to one theoretical model but applies, as needed, any of several techniques, including PAVLOVIAN CONDITIONING, MODELING, OPERANT CONDITIONING, self-control mechanisms, and COGNITIVE RESTRUCTURING.

eclectic psychotherapy any PSYCHOTHERAPY that is based on a combination of theories or approaches or uses concepts and techniques from a number of different sources, including the integrated professional experiences of the therapist. The more formalized **prescriptive eclectic psychotherapy** involves the use of a combination of psychotherapy approaches that is specifically sequenced in terms of formats, methods, and processes in order to improve outcome.

ecobehavioral assessment an observational research method used in APPLIED BEHAVIOR ANALYSIS to measure moment-to-moment effects of multiple environmental events on an individual's specific behaviors. These events include the behavior of others, task demands, time of day, and situational changes.

ECoG abbreviation for ELECTROCORTICOGRAM.

ecological niche the function or position of an organism or a population within a physical and biological environment.

ecological perception an organism's detection of the AFFORDANCES and INVARIANCES within its natural, real-world environment, as mediated and guided by the organism's immersion in and movement through that environment. See DIRECT PERCEPTION.

ecological psychology 1. the analysis of **behavior settings** (natural situations) to predict from their physical and social elements the patterns of behavior that will occur. According to this approach, the behavior that will occur in a particular setting is largely prescribed by the roles that exist in that setting and the actions of those in such roles, irrespective of the personalities, age, gender, and other characteristics of the individuals present. **2.** a less common name for the theoretical orientation embodied by the concepts of ecological perception and DIRECT PERCEPTION propounded by U.S. psychologist James J. Gibson (1904–1979).

ecological systems theory an evolving body of theory and research concerned with the processes and conditions that govern the course of human development in the actual environments in which human beings live. Generally, ecological systems theory accords equal importance to the concept of environment as a context for development (in terms of nested systems ranging from micro- to macro-) and to the role of biopsychological characteristics of the individual person.

ecological validity 1. the degree to which research results are representative of conditions in the wider world. For example, psychological research carried out exclusively among university students might have a low ecological validity when applied to the population as a whole. **2.** the degree to which a PROXIMAL STIMULUS (i.e., the stimulus as it impinges on the receptor) covaries with the DISTAL STIMULUS (i.e., the actual stimulus in the physical environment).

ecology *n.* the study of relationships between organisms and their physical and social environments. —**ecological** *adj.* —**ecologist** *n.*

economic model in psychoanalytic theory, the view that the psyche can be explained in terms of the amounts and distributions of PSYCHIC ENERGY associated with particular mental states and processes. Compare DYNAMIC MODEL; TOPOGRAPHIC MODEL.

ecosystem *n.* a self-contained unit comprising a community of individuals of different species and the environment they inhabit. There is an interdependent balance of predators, prey, food resources, and substrates such that a change in any one component is often followed by commensurate changes in the other components.

ecosystemic approach an approach to therapy that emphasizes the interaction between the individual or family and larger social contexts, such as schools, workplaces, and social agencies. The approach emphasizes interrelatedness and interdependency and derives from diverse fields, including psychology, sociology, anthropology, economics, and political science. FAMILY THERAPY, in particular, has made use of this approach in designing interventions for complex families and systems.

ecphoria *n.* the activation of a memory, which involves the RETRIEVAL of a memory by a CUE. Cues or conditions that were present when the memory was formed are stored with the memory, therefore those same conditions need to be reinstated at retrieval to provoke ecphoria. —**ecphoric** *adj.*

ECS abbreviation for electroconvulsive shock. See ELECTROCONVULSIVE THERAPY.

ecstasy *n.* a state of intense pleasure and elation: extreme euphoria. —**ecstatic** *adj.*

Ecstasy *n.* the popular name for MDMA.

ECT 1. abbreviation for ELECTROCONVULSIVE THERAPY. **2.** abbreviation for ELEMENTARY COGNITIVE TASK.

ECT-induced amnesia amnesia that is a by-product of ELECTROCONVULSIVE THERAPY (ECT). Memory can be severely compromised in the hours or days following treatment, but new learning typically returns to normal by 6 months after treatment. Some impairment in the retrieval of events that occurred close to the time of treatment may remain.

ectoderm *n.* see GERM LAYER. —**ectodermal** *adj.*

ectopia *n.* displacement or abnormal positioning

of part of the body. For example, neurons are seen in unusual positions in the cerebral cortex of people with dyslexia. —**ectopic** *adj.*

ED₅₀ (**ED-50**) abbreviation for EFFECTIVE DOSE 50. See also THERAPEUTIC RATIO.

edema *n.* an excess accumulation of fluid in body cells, organs, or cavities. —**edematous** *adj.*

edge detector any of various cells in the visual system or hypothetical processors in models of vision that respond best to a dark–light border or edge.

edge theory a theory proposing that DEATH ANXIETY has a survival function that emerges when individuals perceive themselves to be in life-threatening situations. Edge theory attempts to resolve the apparent discrepancy between other theoretical claims that DEATH ANXIETY is a major motivational force and empirical studies that reveal only low to moderate levels of death anxiety in the general population. It suggests that death anxiety is the subjective or experiential side of a holistic preparation to deal with danger (symbolic of standing at the edge of the void). Heightened arousal is turned on by anxiety surges in emergency situations; psychological difficulties arise when the emergency response has permeated the individual's everyday functioning. See also TERROR MANAGEMENT THEORY.

educational acceleration educational progress at a rate faster than usual through a variety of measures, such as strengthening or compacting the curriculum, accelerating instruction in particular subject areas, or grade skipping. These measures are designed to provide students who are gifted with work more ideally suited to their abilities.

educational age (**EA**) the age at which a particular level of scholastic performance typically is obtained, which may be higher or lower than the student's chronological age.

educational counseling the COUNSELING specialty concerned with providing advice and assistance to students in the development of their educational plans, choice of appropriate courses, and choice of college or technical school. Counseling may also be applied to improve study skills or provide assistance with school-related problems that interfere with performance, for example, learning disabilities. Educational counseling is closely associated with VOCATIONAL COUNSELING because of the relationship between educational training and occupational choice. Also called **educational guidance**; **student counseling**. See also COUNSELING PSYCHOLOGY.

educational diagnosis the process of analytically examining a learning problem, which may involve identification of cognitive, perceptual, emotional, and other factors that influence academic performance or school adjustment.

educational placement the act of matching students with the appropriate educational program or environment for their age, abilities, and needs. Standardized tests, classroom test data, interviews, and past student performance may all be taken into account in arriving at this decision.

educational psychology a branch of psychology dealing with the application of psychological principles and theories to a broad spectrum of teaching, training, and learning issues in educational settings.

educational quotient (**EQ**) a ratio of EDUCATIONAL AGE to CHRONOLOGICAL AGE times 100.

educational sport psychology see CLINICAL SPORT PSYCHOLOGY.

educational therapy individualized treatment interventions for people with learning disabilities or emotional or behavioral problems that significantly interfere with learning. Educational therapy integrates educational techniques and therapeutic practices to promote academic achievement and the attainment of basic skills.

EE abbreviation for EXPRESSED EMOTION.

EEG abbreviation for ELECTROENCEPHALOGRAPHY or electroencephalogram.

effectance *n.* the state of having a causal effect on objects and events in the environment, commonly used in the term **effectance motivation**.

effective dose (**ED**) the minimum amount of a drug that is required to produce a specified effect. It is usually expressed in terms of **median effective dose**, or **effective dose 50** (**ED₅₀, ED-50**), the dose at which 50% of the nonhuman animal test population has a positive response. See also THERAPEUTIC RATIO.

effective stimulus see FUNCTIONAL STIMULUS.

effector *n.* an organ, such as a muscle or a gland, that responds to neural stimulation by producing a particular physical response or initiating a specific physiological event.

effect size the magnitude of an effect (influence of independent variables) in a study. It is often an indicator of the strength of a relationship, the magnitude of mean differences among several groups, or the like.

efferent *adj.* conducting or conveying away from a central point. For example, **efferent nerve fibers** conduct impulses away from the brain or spinal cord. Compare AFFERENT.

efficacy *n.* in pharmacology, see DOSE–RESPONSE RELATIONSHIP.

efficiency *n.* in statistics, the degree to which an ESTIMATOR uses all the information in a sample to estimate a particular parameter. —**efficient** *adj.*

effortfulness *n.* a sense of effort, or consciousness of effort: a feature of many psychological tasks. Effortful tasks compete against each other under dual-task conditions, indicating that effortfulness correlates with demands on mental resources. Because the sense of effort lacks conscious sensory qualities, it can be considered an experience of FRINGE CONSCIOUSNESS. —**effortful** *adj.*

effort justification a phenomenon whereby people come to evaluate a particular task or activity more favorably when it involves something that is difficult or unpleasant. Because expending effort to perform a useless or unenjoyable task, or experiencing unpleasant consequences in doing this, is cognitively inconsistent (see COGNITIVE DISSONANCE), people are assumed to shift their evaluations of the task in a positive direction to restore consistency.

ego *n.* **1.** the SELF, particularly the conscious sense of self (Latin, "I"). In its popular and quasi-technical sense, ego refers to all the psychological phenomena and processes that are related to the self and that comprise the individual's attitudes, values, and concerns. **2.** in psychoanalytic theory, the component of the personality that deals with the external world and its practical demands. More specifically, the ego enables the individual to perceive, reason, solve problems, test reality, and adjust the instinctual impulses of the ID to the behests of the SUPEREGO.

ego analysis psychoanalytic techniques directed toward discovering the strengths and weaknesses of the EGO and uncovering its defenses against unacceptable impulses. Ego analysis is a short form of psychoanalysis: It does not attempt to penetrate to the ultimate origin of impulses and repressions. See also EGO STRENGTH; EGO WEAKNESS.

ego anxiety in psychoanalytic theory, anxiety caused by the conflicting demands of the EGO, ID, and SUPEREGO. Thus, ego anxiety refers to internal, rather than external demands. Compare ID ANXIETY. See also SIGNAL ANXIETY.

ego boundary 1. the concept that individuals are able to distinguish between self and not-self. Someone who is said to lack clear ego boundaries blurs the distinction between himself or herself and others by identifying with them too easily and too much. **2.** in psychoanalysis, the boundary between the EGO and the ID (the **internal boundary**) or between the ego and external reality (the **external boundary**).

egocentric predicament a problematic condition arising from the assumption that each person's experience is essentially private. The problem is commonly expressed in terms of one or more of the following propositions: (a) It is difficult to explain how any person could know anything about another person's experience; (b) it is likewise difficult to understand how general knowledge of the external world is possible apart from one's individual experience; and (c) given that experience is essentially private, it is difficult to understand how genuine communication between two people might be possible, since both the content and symbols of any communication will be similarly private. See also SOLIPSISM.

egocentric speech speech in which there is no attempt to exchange thoughts or take into account another person's point of view.

egocentrism *n.* **1.** the tendency to emphasize one's personal needs and focus on one's individual concerns. Also called **egocentricity**. See also IDIOCENTRIC. Compare SOCIOCENTRISM. **2.** in PIAGETIAN THEORY, the tendency to perceive the situation from one's own perspective, believing that others see things from the same point of view as oneself. —**egocentric** *adj.*

ego-defensive function of an attitude the role an attitude can play in enhancing or maintaining the self-esteem of the person holding that attitude. For example, people may hold very positive attitudes toward social groups to which they belong as a means of maintaining their positive self-regard. See also FUNCTIONAL APPROACH TO ATTITUDES.

ego depletion a state marked by reduction in the self's capacity for VOLITION (initiative, choice, and self-regulation), especially in the context of SELF-REGULATORY RESOURCES THEORY. Ego depletion is typically temporary and is restored by rest, positive emotions, or other means.

ego development 1. the infant's emerging consciousness of being a separate individual distinct from others, particularly the parents. **2.** in classical psychoanalytic theory, the process in which a part of the ID is gradually transformed into the EGO as a result of environmental demands. It involves a preconscious stage, in which the ego is partly developed, and a subsequent conscious stage, in which such ego functions as reasoning, judging, and reality testing come to fruition and help to protect the individual from internal and external threats. Also called **ego formation**.

ego-dystonic *adj.* in psychoanalytic theory, describing impulses, wishes, or thoughts that are unacceptable or repugnant to the EGO or self. Also called **ego-alien**. Compare EGO-SYNTONIC.

ego functions in psychoanalytic theory, the various activities of the EGO, including perception of the external world, self-awareness, problem solving, control of motor functions, adaptation to reality, memory, and reconciliation of conflicting impulses and ideas. The ego is frequently described as the executive agency of the personality, working in the interest of the REALITY PRINCIPLE. See also SECONDARY PROCESS.

ego-ideal *n.* in psychoanalytic theory, the part of the EGO that is the repository of positive identifications with parental goals and values that the individual genuinely admires and wishes to emulate, such as integrity and loyalty, and which acts as a model of how he or she wishes to be. As new identifications are incorporated in later life, the ego-ideal may develop and change. In his later theorizing, Austrian psychoanalyst Sigmund Freud (1856–1939) incorporated the ego-ideal into the concept of the SUPEREGO. Also called **self-ideal**.

ego instinct in psychoanalytic theory, any of the instincts, such as hunger, that are directed toward self-preservation. In the early theory of Austrian psychoanalyst Sigmund Freud (1856–1939), the energy of the ego instincts is used by the EGO to defend against the SEXUAL INSTINCTS.

ego involvement the extent to which a task or other target of judgment is perceived as psychologically significant or important to one's self-esteem. It is presumed to be a determinant of the STRENGTH OF AN ATTITUDE.

egomania n. extreme, pathological preoccupation with oneself, often characterized by an exaggerated sense of one's abilities and worth. This includes the tendency to be totally self-centered, callous with regard to the needs of others, and interested only in the gratification of one's own impulses and desires. —**egomaniac** n.

ego psychology in psychoanalysis, an approach that emphasizes the functions of the EGO in controlling impulses and dealing with the external environment. This is in contrast to ID PSYCHOLOGY, which focuses on the primitive instincts of sex and hostility. Ego psychology differs from CLASSICAL PSYCHOANALYSIS in proposing that the ego contains a CONFLICT-FREE SPHERE of functioning and that it has its own store of energy with which to pursue goals that are independent of instinctual wishes.

ego-splitting n. **1.** in psychoanalytic theory, the EGO's development of opposed but coexisting attitudes toward a phenomenon, whether in the normal, neurotic, or psychotic person. In the normal context, ego-splitting can be seen in the critical attitude of the self toward the self; in neuroses, contrary attitudes toward particular behaviors are fundamental; and in psychoses, ego-splitting may produce an "observing" part of the individual that sees and can report on delusional phenomena. **2.** in the OBJECT RELATIONS THEORY of Austrian-born British psychoanalyst Melanie Klein (1882–1960), fragmentation of the ego in which parts that are perceived as bad are split off from the main ego.

ego strength in psychoanalytic theory, the ability of the EGO to maintain an effective balance between the inner impulses of the ID, the SUPEREGO, and outer reality. An individual with a **strong ego** is thus one who is able to tolerate frustration and stress, postpone gratification, modify selfish desires when necessary, and resolve internal conflicts and emotional problems before they lead to NEUROSIS. Compare EGO WEAKNESS.

ego-syntonic adj. compatible with the ego or conscious SELF-CONCEPT. Thoughts, wishes, impulses, and behavior are said to be ego-syntonic when they form no threat to the ego and can be acted upon without interference from the SUPEREGO. Compare EGO-DYSTONIC.

ego weakness in psychoanalytic theory, the inability of the EGO to control impulses and tolerate frustration, disappointment, or stress. The individual with a **weak ego** is thus one who suffers from anxiety and conflicts, makes excessive use of DEFENSE MECHANISMS or uses immature defense mechanisms, and is likely to develop neurotic symptoms. Compare EGO STRENGTH.

eidetic image a clear, specific, high-quality mental image of a visual scene that is retained for a period (seconds to minutes) after the event. As with a real-time image, an eidetic image can be reviewed to report on its details and their relation to one another. Essentially, people with eidetic imagery continue to see the stimulus even though they know it is no longer there. This type of imagery is more common in children than in adults.

eigenvalue (symbol: λ) n. a numerical index, commonly used in FACTOR ANALYSIS and PRINCIPAL COMPONENT ANALYSIS, that indicates the portion of the total variance among several correlated variables that is accounted for by a more basic, underlying variable. Eigenvalues are of central importance in linear algebra (i.e., matrix algebra). Also called **characteristic value**.

Eigenwelt n. in the thought of German philosopher Martin Heidegger (1889–1976), that aspect of DASEIN (being-in-the-world) that is constituted by a person's relationship to the self. The term was introduced into the vocabulary of psychology chiefly through the work of Swiss existential psychologist Ludwig Binswanger (1881–1966). Compare MITWELT; UMWELT. [German, literally: "own world"]

Einstellung n. an expectation or readiness associated with particular stimuli. It may foster a degree of mental inflexibility by instilling a tendency to respond to a situation in a certain way. For example, a person who successfully solves a series of problems using one formula may apply that same formula to a new problem solvable by a simpler method. The contemporary term for this concept is MENTAL SET. [German: "attitude"]

ejaculation n. see ORGASM. —**ejaculatory** adj.

EKG abbreviation for ELECTROCARDIOGRAM. [from German *Elektrokardiogram*]

elaborated code a linguistic REGISTER typically used in formal situations (e.g., academic discourse), characterized by a wide vocabulary, complex constructions, and unpredictable collocations of word and idea. This contrasts with the **restricted code** used in much informal conversation, which is characterized by a narrow vocabulary, simple constructions, and predictable ritualized forms, with much reliance on context and nonverbal communication to convey meaning.

elaboration n. **1.** the process of interpreting or embellishing information to be remembered or of relating it to other material already known and in memory. The LEVELS-OF-PROCESSING MODEL OF MEMORY holds that the level of elaboration applied to information as it is processed affects both the length of time that it can be retained in memory and the ease with which it can be retrieved. See also DEEP PROCESSING. **2.** the process of scrutinizing and thinking about the central merits of attitude-relevant information. This process includes generating inferences about the information, assessing its validity, and considering the implications of evaluative responses to the information. **—elaborate** *vb.*

elaboration-likelihood model a theory of persuasion postulating that attitude change occurs on a continuum of elaboration and thus, under certain conditions, may be a result of relatively extensive (see CENTRAL ROUTE TO PERSUASION) or relatively little (see PERIPHERAL ROUTE TO PERSUASION) scrutiny of attitude-relevant information. The theory postulates that the STRENGTH OF AN ATTITUDE depends on the amount of elaboration on which the attitude is based.

elaborative rehearsal an ENCODING strategy to facilitate the formation of memory by repeatedly reviewing new information and linking it to what one already knows. See DEPTH-OF-PROCESSING HYPOTHESIS.

elation *n.* a state of extreme joy, exaggerated optimism, and restless excitement. In extreme or prolonged forms, it is a symptom of a number of disorders; in particular, it may be drug-induced or a symptom of acute MANIA, but it is also found in schizophrenia and psychosis with brain tumor. **—elated** *adj.*

Elavil *n.* a trade name for AMITRIPTYLINE.

elder abuse harm to an older adult caused by another individual. The harm can be physical (violence), sexual (nonconsensual sex), psychological (causing emotional distress), material (improper use of belongings or finances), or neglect (failure to provide needed care).

elder care the provision of health-related services, supportive personal care, supervision, and social services to an older adult requiring assistance with daily living because of physical disabilities, cognitive impairments, or other conditions. Elder care may be home based (via specialized programs) or community based (via ASSISTED LIVING, RESIDENTIAL CARE, or a skilled nursing facility).

elder neglect see ELDER ABUSE.

elderspeak *n.* adjustments to speech patterns, such as speaking more slowly, shortening sentences, or using limited or less complex vocabulary, that are sometimes made by younger people when communicating with older adults.

elective affinity a feeling of sympathy, attraction, or connection to a particular person, thing, or idea. The term is often used to mean those preferences and common feelings that constitute a cultural or national identity or that distinguish groups and subgroups from one another.

Electra complex in the writings of Swiss psy-choanalyst Carl Jung (1875–1961), the female counterpart of Sigmund Freud's OEDIPUS COMPLEX, involving the daughter's love for her father, jealousy toward the mother, and blame of the mother for depriving her of a penis. Although Freud rejected the phrase, using the term Oedipus complex to refer to both boys and girls, many modern textbooks of psychology propagate the mistaken belief that Electra complex is a Freudian term. The name derives from the Greek myth of Electra, daughter of Agamemnon and Clytemnestra, who seeks to avenge her father's murder by persuading her brother Orestes to help her kill Clytemnestra and her lover Aegisthus.

electrical stimulation the stimulation of brain cells or sensory or motor neurons by electrical or electronic devices.

electrical synapse a type of connection in which neurons are not separated by a cleft but instead are joined by a GAP JUNCTION so that the nerve impulse is transmitted across without first being translated into a chemical message.

electrocardiogram (**ECG; EKG**) *n.* a wavelike tracing, either printed or displayed on a monitor, that represents the electrical impulses of the conduction system of the heart muscle as it passes through a typical cycle of contraction and relaxation. The electrical currents are detected by electrodes attached to specific sites on the patient's chest, legs, and arms and recorded by an instrument, the **electrocardiograph**. In the procedure, which is called **electrocardiography**, the wave patterns of the electrocardiogram reveal the condition of the heart chambers and valves to provide an indication of cardiac problems.

electrocardiographic effect a change in the electrical activity of the heart as recorded by an electrocardiogram, especially one associated with administration of a drug. Prolongation of segments of the cardiac cycle, particularly the Q-T interval (the period of ventricular contraction), may be observed with excess doses of numerous antipsychotics and tricyclic antidepressants. A malignant form of electrocardiographic change is an arrhythmia known as **torsades de pointes**.

electroconvulsive therapy (**ECT**) a controversial treatment in which a seizure is induced by passing a controlled, low-dose electric current (an **electroconvulsive shock; ECS**) through one or both temples. The patient is prepared by administration of an anesthetic and injection of a muscle relaxant. Now a somewhat rare procedure, it is sometimes used with patients with severe endogenous depression who fail to respond to antidepressant drugs. Benefits are temporary, and the mechanisms of therapeutic action are unknown. Also called **electroconvulsive shock therapy** (**EST**); **electroshock therapy** (**EST**). See also BRIEF STIMULUS THERAPY; ECT-INDUCED AMNESIA.

electrocorticography (**ECoG**) *n.* a method of

studing the electrical activity of the brain using electrodes placed directly on the cerebral cortex, rather than on the scalp as in ELECTROENCEPHA-LOGRAPHY. The resulting record of brain-wave patterns is called an **electrocorticogram**.

electrode *n.* an instrument with a positive-pole cathode and a negative-pole anode used to electrically stimulate biological tissues or record electrical activity in these tissues. See also MICROELECTRODE.

electrodermal response (**EDR**) see GALVANIC SKIN RESPONSE.

electrodiagnosis *n.* the application of an electric current to nerves and muscles for diagnostic purposes. See ELECTROENCEPHALOGRAPHY; ELECTROMYOGRAPHY.

electroencephalography (**EEG**) *n.* a method of studying BRAIN WAVES using an instrument (**electroencephalograph**) that amplifies and records the electrical activity of the brain through electrodes placed at various points on the scalp. The resulting record (**electroencephalogram** [EEG]) of the brain-wave patterns is primarily used in diagnosing epilepsy and other neurological disorders.

electromyography (**EMG**) *n.* the recording (via an instrument called an **electromyograph**) of the electrical activity of muscles through electrodes placed in or on different muscle groups. This procedure is used in the diagnosis of neuromuscular diseases, such as myasthenia gravis or amyotrophic lateral sclerosis. A record of the electric potentials is called an **electromyogram** (EMG).

electronystagmography *n.* a neurological test that measures movements of the eye muscles, used to confirm the presence of NYSTAGMUS. A graphical recording of eye movements is generated and is used to evaluate dizziness, vertigo, and the function of the AUDITORY NERVE and the SEMICIRCULAR CANALS.

electrophysiologic audiometry a large class of procedures for measuring auditory function that use electrical responses evoked by sound stimulation. Included in this class of procedures are averaged **electroencephalographic audiometry**, which measures hearing sensitivity via ELECTROENCEPHALOGRAPHY, and **electrocochleography** (ECochG), which measures electrical activity in the inner ear.

electrophysiology *n.* the study of the electrical properties and processes of tissues. This includes such specialized subfields as electrocardiography, ELECTROENCEPHALOGRAPHY, and ELECTROMYOGRAPHY. —**electrophysiologic** or **electrophysiological** *adj.*

electroretinography *n.* a recording (via an instrument called an **electroretinograph**) of the electrical activity of the retina during visual stimulation using electrodes placed on the anesthetized surface of the eye. Different segments of the recorded waveform (called an **electroretino-**

gram [**ERG**]) correspond to activity in the different cells and layers of the retina.

electroshock therapy (**EST**) see ELECTROCONVULSIVE THERAPY.

electrotherapy *n.* any therapeutic measure that involves the application of an electric current to the body.

electrotonic conduction the passive flow of a change in electric potential along a nerve or muscle membrane. It occurs in response to stimulation that is inadequate to trigger an actively propagated ACTION POTENTIAL (i.e., subthreshold stimulation) but instead generates DEPOLARIZATION in a small area of membrane. This localized depolarization travels to neighboring areas via the drifting fluid within the cell, rapidly attenuating as it spreads.

electrotonus *n.* the change in the excitability, conductivity, or electrical status of a nerve or muscle following application of an electric current.

elegant solution a solution to a question or a problem that achieves the maximally satisfactory effect with minimal effort, materials, or steps. In terms of theories or models of behavior, an elegant solution would be one that satisfies the requirements of the LAW OF PARSIMONY. See also OCCAM'S RAZOR.

elementarism *n.* **1.** in scientific theory, the procedure of explaining a complex phenomenon by reducing it to simple, elemental units. **2.** the belief that such a procedure is appropriate to a science dealing with psychological phenomena, which are explained by reduction to simple elements, such as basic sensations or elementary reflexes. Both psychological STRUCTURALISM and BEHAVIORISM have been described as elementarist approaches. Also called **elementalism**; **elementism**. See also ATOMISM. —**elementarist** *adj.*

elementary cognitive task (**ECT**) a simple laboratory test designed to measure participants' response times as they perform very easy tasks and make what are presumed by the researchers to be simple decisions. Examples of elementary cognitive tasks include selecting the "odd man out" among three or more alternatives and indicating whether or not a statement agrees with a pictorial representation.

eliminativism *n.* the view that mental states, such as beliefs, feelings, and intentions, are not necessary to a scientific account of human behavior. These are regarded as the stuff of FOLK PSYCHOLOGY, informal and intuitive concepts by which human beings offer accounts of their behaviors. According to the eliminativist view, when truly scientific psychology progresses far enough to replace folk psychology, the explanatory language of mental states will probably be replaced by a language of biological states. Also called **eliminative materialism**. See also IDENTITY THEORY; REDUCTIONISM. Compare

CONSCIOUS MENTALISM; MENTALISM. —**eliminativist** *adj.*

embarrassment *n.* a SELF-CONSCIOUS EMOTION in which a person feels awkward or flustered in other people's company or because of the attention of others, as, for example, when being observed engaging in actions that are subject to mild disapproval from others. —**embarrassed** *adj.*

embedded figure a type of AMBIGUOUS FIGURE in which one or more images blend into a larger pattern and so are not immediately obvious.

embeddedness of an attitude the extent to which an attitude is linked to or associated with other cognitive structures in memory. Such structures could include other attitudes, values, and beliefs.

embodied cognition the position that human thinking occurs in the context of a physical body and is dynamically influenced by it. This approach contrasts with the viewpoint of cognition as an abstract power.

embolic stroke see STROKE.

embolism *n.* the interruption of blood flow due to blockage of a vessel by an **embolus**, material formed elsewhere and carried by the bloodstream to become lodged at the site of obstruction. The embolus may be a blood clot, air bubble, fat globule, or other substance.

embryo *n.* an animal in the stages of development between cleavage of the fertilized egg and birth or hatching. In human prenatal development, the embryo comprises the products of conception during the first 8 weeks of pregnancy; thereafter it is called a FETUS. —**embryonic** *adj.*

embryonic stem cell see STEM CELL.

EMDR abbreviation for eye-movement desensitization and reprocessing (see EYE-MOVEMENT DESENSITIZATION THERAPY).

emergence *n.* the idea that complex phenomena (e.g., conscious experience) are derived from arrangements of or interactions among component phenomena (e.g., brain processes) but exhibit characteristics not predictable from those component phenomena.

emergency psychotherapy psychological treatment of individuals who have undergone a traumatic experience (e.g., a road accident) and are in a state of acute anxiety, panic, or shock or are suicidal. Therapists may call on a very broad range of techniques depending on the immediate needs of the client. See also CRISIS INTERVENTION.

emergent feature in ergonomics, an attribute of a graphical display such that the display configurations yield an overall image (e.g., a rectangle or pentagon). When a component of the system is not in the appropriate or normal state, the image will be distorted, alerting the operator to potential problems.

emergent-norm theory an explanation suggesting that the uniformity in behavior often observed in such collectives as crowds and cults is caused by members' conformity to unique standards of behavior (norms) that develop spontaneously in those groups. See UNIVERSALITY.

emergent property a characteristic of a complex system that is not implicit in or predictable from an analysis of the components or elements that make it up and that, thus, often arises unexpectedly. For example, it has been said that conscious experience is not predictable by analysis of the neurophysiological and biochemical complexity of the brain.

emetic therapy the use of drugs that produce aversive states when combined with problem behaviors or stimuli. Side effects of the drugs used and other issues with regard to this form of treatment limit its application. See also AVERSIVE CONDITIONING.

EMG abbreviation for ELECTROMYOGRAPHY.

emic *adj.* **1.** denoting an approach to the study of human cultures that interprets behaviors and practices in terms of the system of meanings created by and operative within a particular cultural context. Such an approach would generally be of the kind associated with ETHNOGRAPHY rather than ETHNOLOGY. Compare ETIC. **2.** in linguistics, see EMIC–ETIC DISTINCTION.

emic–etic distinction **1.** a distinction between two fundamentally different approaches to language analysis, one characteristic of PHONEMICS and the other of PHONETICS. An **emic analysis** puts primacy on the characterization of a particular language through close attention to those features that have a meaningful structural significance within it (e.g., in English the difference between the sounds /r/ and /l/ because this serves to differentiate such words as *rash* and *lash*). By contrast, an **etic analysis** concentrates on universal features of language, particularly the acoustic properties of speech sounds and the physiological processes involved in making them. **2.** the distinction between EMIC and ETIC approaches in anthropology and related disciplines.

emitted behavior a natural response that is not influenced by, or dependent on, any external stimuli. Compare RESPONDENT BEHAVIOR.

Emmert's law the principle that the perceived size of an afterimage is proportional to the distance of the surface on which it is projected: the larger the afterimage, the farther away it is. [Emil **Emmert** (1844–1913), German physiologist]

emmetropia *n.* the state of the eye's normal optical system, in which distant objects are sharply focused on the retina by the curvature of the cornea and the lens. Compare HYPEROPIA; MYOPIA.

emotion *n.* a complex reaction pattern, involving experiential, behavioral, and physiological elements, by which the individual attempts to deal with a personally significant matter or event. The specific quality of the emotion (e.g.,

FEAR, SHAME) is determined by the specific significance of the event. For example, if the significance involves threat, fear is likely to be generated; if the significance involves disapproval from another, shame is likely to be generated. Emotion typically involves FEELING but differs from feeling in having an overt or implicit engagement with the world. —**emotional** *adj.*

emotional abuse nonphysical abuse: a pattern of behavior in which one person deliberately and repeatedly subjects another to acts that are detrimental to behavioral and affective functioning and overall mental well-being. Researchers have yet to formulate a universally agreed upon definition of the concept, but have identified a variety of forms emotional abuse may take, including verbal abuse, intimidation and terrorization, humiliation and degradation, exploitation, harassment, rejection and withholding of affection, isolation, and excessive control. Also called **psychological abuse**.

emotional adjustment the condition or process of personal acceptance of and adaptation to one's circumstances, which may require modification of attitudes and the expression of emotions that are appropriate to a given situation.

emotional cognition the ability to recognize and interpret the emotions of others, notably from such cues as facial expression and voice tone, and to interpret one's own feelings correctly. Impairment of emotional cognition is associated with a range of psychological conditions, notably ASPERGER'S DISORDER.

emotional deprivation lack of adequate interpersonal attachments that provide affirmation, love, affection, and interest, especially on the part of the primary caregiver during a child's developmental years.

emotional development a gradual increase in the capacity to experience, express, and interpret the full range of emotions and in the ability to cope with them appropriately. For example, infants begin to smile and frown around 8 weeks of age and to laugh around 3 or 4 months, and older children begin to learn that hitting others is not an acceptable way of dealing with anger. Also called **affective development**.

emotional disorder 1. any psychological disorder characterized primarily by maladjustive emotional reactions that are inappropriate or disproportionate to reality. Also called **emotional illness**. See also MOOD DISORDER. **2.** loosely, any mental disorder.

emotional expression any verbal or nonverbal communication by an individual of information about his or her intrapsychic state. For example, a high-pitched voice is a sign of arousal, blushing is a sign of embarrassment, and so forth.

emotional handicap a fear-, anxiety-, or other emotionally based condition that results in maladaptive behavior—ranging from withdrawal and isolation to acting out and aggression—and adversely affects a student's academic and social functioning. For example, the inability to form or sustain satisfactory relationships with peers or teachers would constitute an emotional handicap.

emotional insight 1. an awareness of one's own emotional reactions or those of others. **2.** in PSYCHOTHERAPY, the client's awareness of the emotional forces, such as internal conflicts or traumatic experiences, that underlie his or her symptoms. This form of insight is considered a prerequisite to change in many therapeutic approaches.

emotional insulation a defense mechanism characterized by seeming indifference and detachment in response to frustrating situations or disappointing events. In lesser forms it appears as **emotional isolation**.

emotional intelligence the ability to process emotional information and use it in reasoning and other cognitive activities. It comprises four abilities: to perceive and appraise emotions accurately; to access and evoke emotions when they facilitate cognition; to comprehend emotional language and make use of emotional information; and to regulate one's own and others' emotions to promote growth and well-being.

emotional reeducation PSYCHOTHERAPY focused on modifying the client's attitudes, feelings, and reactions by helping the client gain greater insight into emotional conflicts and self-defeating behavior arising from affective disturbance or disorder. Typical objectives are an increase in self-confidence, sociability, and self-reliance. The methods used include group discussions, personal counseling, relationship therapy, and self-exploration.

emotional regulation the ability of an individual to modulate an emotion or set of emotions. Techniques of conscious emotional regulation can include learning to construe situations differently in order to manage them better and recognizing how different behaviors can be used in the service of a given emotional state.

emotional support the verbal and nonverbal processes by which one communicates care and concern for another, offering reassurance, empathy, comfort, and acceptance. It may be a major factor contributing to the effectiveness of SELF-HELP GROUPS, within which members both provide and receive emotional support.

emotion-focused coping a type of COPING STRATEGY that focuses on regulating negative emotional reactions to a stressor, as opposed to taking actions to change the stressor. Emotion-focused coping may include social withdrawal, disengagement, and acceptance of the situation. Also called **passive coping**. See also SECONDARY COPING. Compare PROBLEM-FOCUSED COPING.

emotion-focused couples therapy a form of COUPLES THERAPY that is based on the premise that relationship problems are most often due to thwarted fulfillment of emotional needs, particularly the need for attachment. This intervention involves isolating the conflict regarding thwarted needs, interrupting the negative interaction cycle, reframing the conflict, and accepting the emotional experience of one's partner as valid.

emotion-focused therapy an integrative IN-DIVIDUAL THERAPY that focuses on emotion as the key determinant of personality development and of psychotherapeutic change. In sessions, the therapist helps the client to become aware of, accept, make sense of, and regulate emotions as a way of resolving problems and promoting growth. Techniques are drawn from CLIENT-CENTERED THERAPY, GESTALT THERAPY, and COGNITIVE BEHAVIOR THERAPY.

emotive *adj.* related to or arousing emotion.

emotive technique any of various therapeutic techniques designed to encourage clients to express their thoughts and feelings in an intense and animated manner so as to make these more obvious and available for discussion in therapy. Emotive techniques are used, for example, in attempts to dispute irrational beliefs in order to move from intellectual to emotional insight.

empathy *n.* understanding a person from his or her frame of reference rather than one's own, so that one vicariously experiences the person's feelings, perceptions, and thoughts. In psychotherapy, therapist empathy for the client can be a path to comprehension of the client's cognitions, affects, or behaviors. —**empathic** or **empathetic** *adj.* —**empathize** *vb.*

empathy training 1. a systematic procedure to increase empathetic feeling and communications in an individual. **2.** help given to convicted abusers to enable them to envision their victims' feelings and become sensitive to the pain they have caused, with the aim of decreasing the likelihood that they will commit similar crimes in the future.

empirical *adj.* derived from or denoting experimentation or systematic observation.

empirical-criterion keying a method for developing personality inventories, in which the items (presumed to measure one or more traits) are created and then administered to a criterion group of people known to possess a certain characteristic (e.g., antisocial behavior, significant anxiety, exaggerated concern about physical health) and to a control group of people without the characteristic. Only those items that demonstrate an ability to distinguish between the two groups are chosen for inclusion in the final inventory.

empirical method any method of conducting an investigation that relies upon experimentation and systematic observation rather than theoretical speculation.

empirical psychology an approach to the study and explanation of psychological phenomena that emphasizes objective observation and the EXPERIMENTAL METHOD as the source of information about the phenomena under consideration. Compare RATIONAL PSYCHOLOGY. See also EXPERIMENTAL PSYCHOLOGY.

empirical self the SELF that is known by the self, rather than the self as knower. In the writings of U.S. psychologist William James (1842–1910), the empirical self is held to consist of the **material self** (everything material that can be seen as belonging to the self), the SOCIAL SELF (the self as perceived by others), and the **spiritual self** (the self that is closest to one's core subjective experience of oneself). The empirical self (or "me") is contrasted with the NOMINATIVE SELF (or "I").

empirical validity the degree to which the accuracy of a test, model, or other construct can be demonstrated through experimentation and systematic observation rather than theory alone.

empiricism *n.* **1.** an approach to EPISTEMOLOGY holding that all knowledge of matters of fact either arises from experience or requires experience for its validation. In particular, empiricism denies the possibility of ideas present in the mind prior to any experience, arguing that the mind at birth is like a blank sheet of paper. During the 17th and 18th centuries, empiricism was developed as a systematic approach to philosophy in the work of such British philosophers as John Locke (1632–1704), George Berkeley (1685–1753), and David Hume (1711–1776). These thinkers also developed theories of ASSOCIATIONISM to explain how even the most complex mental concepts can be derived from simple sense experiences. Although there is a strong emphasis on empiricism in psychology, this can take different forms. Some approaches to psychology hold that sensory experience is the origin of all knowledge and thus, ultimately, of personality, character, beliefs, emotions, and behavior. BEHAVIORISM is the purest example of empiricism in this sense. Advocates of other theoretical approaches to psychology, such as PHE-NOMENOLOGY, argue that the definition of experience as only sensory experience is too narrow; this enables them to reject the position that all knowledge arises from the senses, while also claiming to adhere to a type of empiricism. **2.** the view that experimentation is the most important, if not the only, foundation of scientific knowledge and the means by which individuals evaluate truth claims or the adequacy of theories and models. —**empiricist** *adj., n.*

employee assistance program (**EAP**) a designated formal function within an organization that is responsible for helping individual employees with personal problems that affect their job performance (e.g., substance abuse, family difficulties, or emotional problems). EAP services range from screening, assessment, and referral of employees to community resources, through direct clinical treatment by psychologists or other mental health professionals.

employment counseling counseling designed to help an individual with issues related to work, such as job seeking, work compatibility, outside pressures interfering with job performance, termination of employment, and work efficiency. Within an organization, employment counseling is often provided through an EMPLOYEE ASSISTANCE PROGRAM.

employment psychology see INDUSTRIAL AND ORGANIZATIONAL PSYCHOLOGY.

employment test an instrument used to assess the knowledge, skills, abilities, and other characteristics of applicants so as to predict their performance in a job. See also PERSONNEL TEST.

empowerment n. the promotion of the skills, knowledge, and confidence necessary to take greater control of one's life, as in certain educational or social schemes. In psychotherapy, the process involves helping clients become more active in meeting their needs and fulfilling their desires. **—empower** vb.

empty-chair technique a technique originating in GESTALT THERAPY in which the client conducts an emotional dialogue with some aspect of himself or herself or some significant person in his or her life (e.g., a parent), who is imagined to be sitting in an empty chair during the session. The client then exchanges chairs and takes the role of that aspect or of that other person. This technique is now sometimes also referred to as the **two-chair technique**.

emulation n. the ability to comprehend the goal of a model and engage in similar behavior to achieve that goal, without necessarily replicating the specific actions of the model. Emulation facilitates SOCIAL LEARNING.

enabling n. **1.** a process whereby someone unwittingly or knowingly contributes to continued maladaptive or pathological behavior in another person, such as one with substance dependence. **2.** the process of encouraging or allowing individuals to meet their own needs and achieve desired ends. A therapist attempts to enable clients to believe in themselves, have the confidence to act on their desires, and affirm their ability to achieve. See also EMPOWERMENT.

enaction n. the process of putting something into action. The word is preferred to terms such as execution, which have computing or machine-based connotations.

enactive mode the way in which a child first comes to know his or her environment through physical interaction (e.g., touching and manipulating objects, crawling). The enactive mode is knowing through doing, whereas the **iconic mode** is knowing through mental images, and the **symbolic mode** is knowing through language and logic.

encapsulation n. **1.** the process of separating or keeping separate, particularly the ability of some people experiencing delusions to maintain high levels of functioning and prevent their delusions from pervading everyday behavior and cognitive states. **2.** enclosure, as in a sheath or other covering.

encéphale isolé an animal whose brainstem has been surgically severed at the point where the spinal cord and MEDULLA OBLONGATA meet. Such an animal is alert but paralyzed, with a normal sleep–wake cycle on an electroencephalogram. See also CERVEAU ISOLÉ. [French, "isolated brain"]

encephalitis n. inflammation of the brain, typically caused by viral infection. The symptoms, which may be potentially fatal, include fever, vomiting, confusion or disorientation, drowsiness, seizures, and loss of consciousness or coma. **—encephalitic** adj.

encephalization n. a larger than expected brain size for a species, given its body size. For example, an average person weighing 140 lb has an actual brain weight of 2.9 lb instead of the predicted 0.6 lb. This enlargement is the result of evolutionary advancement, with the brains of higher species increasing in anatomical complexity as cognitive functions are transferred from more primitive brain areas to the cerebral cortex.

encephalon n. the anatomical name for the BRAIN.

encephalopathy n. any of various diffuse disorders or diseases of the brain that alter brain function or structure.

encoding n. the conversion of a sensory input into a form capable of being processed and deposited in memory. Encoding is the first stage of memory processing, followed by RETENTION and then RETRIEVAL.

encoding specificity the principle that RETRIEVAL of memory is optimal when the retrieval conditions (such as context or cues present at the time of retrieval) duplicate the conditions that were present when the memory was formed.

encopresis n. repeated voluntary or involuntary defecation in inappropriate places (clothing, floor, etc.) that occurs after the age of 4 (or the equivalent MENTAL AGE) and is not due to a substance (e.g., a laxative) or to a general medical condition. Encopresis may or may not be accompanied by constipation and is often associated with poor toilet training and stressful situations. Also called **functional encopresis**.

encounter group a group of individuals in which constructive insight, sensitivity to others, and personal growth are promoted through direct interactions on an emotional and social level. The leader functions as a catalyst and facilitator rather than as a therapist and focuses on here-and-now feelings and interaction, rather than on theory or individual motivation.

enculturation n. the processes, beginning in

early childhood, by which particular cultural values, ideas, beliefs, and behavioral patterns are instilled in the members of a society. Compare ACCULTURATION. **—enculturate** *vb.*

endemic *adj.* occuring in a specific region or population, particularly with reference to a disease or disorder. Compare EPIDEMIC; PANDEMIC.

endocarditis *n.* inflammation of the **endocardium**, the inner lining of the heart, and often the heart valves. It is typically caused by bacterial or fungal infections. Primary diagnostic symptoms include fever, new or changing heart murmur, and minute hemorrhages (particularly in the extremities and conjunctiva of the eye).

endocrine *adj.* describing or relating to a type of chemical signaling in which a chemical messenger is released by a cell and is carried (e.g., via the bloodstream) to a distant target cell, on which it exerts its effect. Compare AUTOCRINE; PARACRINE.

endocrine gland any ductless gland that secretes hormones directly into the bloodstream to act on distant targets. Such glands include the PITUITARY GLAND, ADRENAL GLAND, THYROID GLAND, gonads (TESTIS and OVARY), and ISLETS OF LANGERHANS. Compare EXOCRINE GLAND.

endocrinology *n.* the study of the morphology, physiology, biochemistry, and pathology of the ENDOCRINE GLANDS. See also NEUROENDOCRINOLOGY. **—endocrinological** *adj.* **—endocrinologist** *n.*

endoderm *n.* see GERM LAYER. **—endodermal** *adj.*

end of life the variable period during which individuals and their families, friends, and caregivers face issues and decisions related to the imminent prospect of death. The end-of-life concept is a way of considering the total context of an approaching death, rather than medical factors only. End-of-life issues include decisions relating to the nature of terminal care (hospice or traditional), whether to resuscitate, the distribution of property and assets, funeral and memorial arrangements, and leave taking and possible reconciliations with family and friends.

endogamy *n.* the custom or practice of marrying within one's KINSHIP NETWORK, CASTE, or other religious or social group. Compare EXOGAMY. **—endogamous** *adj.*

endogenous *adj.* originating within the body as a result of normal biochemical or physiological processes (e.g., ENDOGENOUS OPIOIDS) or of predisposing biological or genetic influences (e.g., ENDOGENOUS DEPRESSION). Compare EXOGENOUS. **—endogenously** *adv.*

endogenous depression depression that occurs in the absence of an obvious psychological stressor and in which a biological or genetic cause is implied. Compare REACTIVE DEPRESSION.

endogenous opioid a substance produced in the body that has the analgesic and euphoric effects of morphine. Three families of endogenous opioids are well known: the **enkephalins**, ENDORPHINS, and **dynorphins**. All are NEUROPEPTIDES that bind to OPIOID RECEPTORS in the central nervous system. Recently, three other endogenous opioid peptides have been identified: **orphanin (nociceptin)** and **endomorphins 1** and **2**.

endolymph *n.* the fluid contained in the membranous labyrinth of the inner ear, that is, within the SCALA MEDIA, SEMICIRCULAR CANALS, SACCULE, and UTRICLE. **—endolymphatic** *adj.*

endometrium *n.* the layer of cells lining the UTERUS. It varies in thickness during the MENSTRUAL CYCLE, reaching a peak of cellular proliferation approximately 1 week after ovulation, in preparation for implantation of a fertilized ovum, and sloughing off as menstrual flow 2 weeks after ovulation if the ovum is not fertilized. **—endometrial** *adj.*

endophenotype *n.* BIOLOGICAL MARKERS that are simpler to detect than genetic sequences and that may be useful in researching vulnerability to a wide range of psychological and neurological disorders. They may be a useful link between genetic sequences and their external emotional, cognitive, or behavioral manifestations.

end organ the structure associated with a motor or sensory nerve ending, such as a muscle END PLATE or a sensory receptor. The latter may be **encapsulated end organs**, which are enclosed in a membranous end sheath and usually located in peripheral tissue, such as the skin. Kinds of encapsulated end organs include MEISSNER'S CORPUSCLES (sensitive to touch) and PACINIAN CORPUSCLES (sensitive to pressure).

endorphin *n.* any of a class of NEUROPEPTIDES, found mainly in the pituitary gland, that function as ENDOGENOUS OPIOIDS. The best known is **beta-endorphin**; the others are **alpha-endorphin** and **gamma-endorphin**. The production of endorphins during intense physical activity is one explanation for the runner's high or exercise high, as well as for an athlete's ability to feel little or no pain during a competition.

end plate a specialized region of a muscle-cell membrane that faces the terminus of a motor neuron within a **neuromuscular junction**. The depolarization that is induced in this muscular region when stimulated by neurotransmitter released from the adjacent motor neuron terminus is called the **end-plate potential (EPP)**. Also called **motor end plate**.

end-stopped cell a neuron in any VISUAL AREA of the cerebral cortex that is maximally responsive to a line of a certain length or to a corner of a larger stimulus. Such neurons have a reduced or absent response when the line or corner is extended beyond a certain point.

enervate *vb.* **1.** to weaken or deprive of energy. **2.** to surgically remove a nerve or a part of a nerve. **—enervation** *n.*

engineering anthropometry measurement of the static and dynamic features of the human body, including dimensions, movements, and center of gravity, and the application of these data to the design and evaluation of equipment for human use.

engineering controls the avoidance of hazards through redesign of machinery or equipment (e.g., by using guards, ventilation systems, and radiation shields) and the replacement or removal of unsafe systems or practices. Engineering controls are considered the first resort in the creation of a safe working environment, followed by ADMINISTRATIVE CONTROLS.

engineering model a belief or hypothesis that living organisms, including humans, can be viewed mechanistically, that is, as machines. See MEDICAL MODEL.

engineering psychology see HUMAN FACTORS PSYCHOLOGY.

engram *n.* the hypothetical MEMORY TRACE that is stored in the brain. The nature of the engram, in terms of the exact physiological changes that occur to encode a memory, is as yet unknown.

engulfment *n.* fear of close interpersonal relationships because of a perceived loss of independence and selfhood and an experience of relationships as overwhelming threats to personal identity. It may be associated with BORDERLINE PERSONALITY DISORDER.

enkephalin *n.* see ENDOGENOUS OPIOID.

enmeshed family a family in which the members are involved in each other's lives to an excessive degree, thus limiting or precluding healthy functioning of the family as a unit and compromising individual autonomy.

enrichment *n.* **1.** enhancement or improvement by the addition or augmentation of some desirable property, quality, or component. For example, **job enrichment** policies are designed to enhance QUALITY OF WORKLIFE and thus employees' interest in and attitude toward work tasks and **marriage-enrichment groups** are intended to enhance the interpersonal relationships of married couples. **2.** the provision of opportunities to increase levels of behavioral or intellectual activity in an otherwise unstimulating (i.e., impoverished) environment. For example, the provision of play materials and opportunities for social contacts has been shown to enhance the development of young children. In laboratory studies of animal behavior, the addition of physical features or task requirements to an environment elicits a more natural behavioral repertoire from the animals. Also called **environmental enrichment**.

enrichment program 1. an educational program designed to supplement the academic curriculum and facilitate the intellectual stimulation of children at risk of educational difficulties or failure, particularly those from culturally or economically disadvantaged homes. Activities, such as arts and music instruction, theater, and science experiments, are typically provided through special preschool or kindergarten classes and intended to facilitate the acquisition of a variety of oral, written, motor, and interpersonal skills. **2.** an educational program designed to provide gifted children with an expanded curriculum. Enrichment programs most often focus on expanding the horizons of learning for gifted students with auxiliary instruction, rather than by providing accelerated instruction in the regular curriculum.

entitativity *n.* the extent to which a group or collective is considered by others to be a real entity rather than a set of independent individuals. In general, groups whose members share a common fate, are similar to one another, and are located close together are more likely to be considered a group rather than a mere AGGREGATION. Also called **entitivity**.

entity theory the belief that psychological attributes, such as level of intelligence, are fixed, essential qualities rather than attributes that develop gradually.

entoptic *adj.* originating within the eyeball itself. The term is used particularly to denote visual sensations caused by stimulation within the eye (**entoptic phenomena**), the classic example of which is seeing faint dark specks moving through the visual field when gazing at a clear, blue sky. These are shadows caused by blood cells moving through the vasculature on the surface of the retina.

entorhinal cortex a region of cerebral cortex in the ventromedial portion of the temporal lobe. It has reciprocal connections with the HIPPOCAMPAL FORMATION and various other cortical and subcortical structures and is an integral component of the medial temporal lobe memory system.

entrainment *n.* in CHRONOBIOLOGY, the process of activating or providing a timing cue for a BIOLOGICAL RHYTHM. For example, the production of gonadal hormones in seasonally breeding animals can be a result of entrainment to increasing day length.

enucleation *n.* **1.** the removal of an entire organic structure, such as a tumor or a bodily organ, without damaging the surrounding structure. Enucleation often refers to the removal of an eyeball in which the optic nerve and connective eye muscles have been severed so that the eye can be removed wholly and cleanly. **2.** the destruction or removal of the nucleus of a cell.

enuresis *n.* repeated involuntary urination in inappropriate places (clothing, floor, etc.) that occurs after the chronological age or equivalent MENTAL AGE when continence is expected and is not due to a substance (e.g., a diuretic) or to a general medical condition. Enuresis is frequently associated with delayed bladder development, poor toilet training, and stressful situations. Also called **functional enuresis**. See also BED-WETTING.

envelope *n.* in acoustics, a slowly varying or "smoothed" change in amplitude. Usually it refers to temporal changes, such as those produced by amplitude MODULATION or beats (see ROUGHNESS), but it can also refer to the shape of a spectrum, as in a **spectral envelope**, or to spatial changes, as in the envelope of the traveling wave (see BASILAR MEMBRANE). Temporal and spectral envelopes are important in auditory perception.

environment *n.* the aggregate of external agents or conditions—physical, biological, social, and cultural—that influence the functions of an organism. See also ECOLOGY. —**environmental** *adj.*

environmental aesthetics analysis of the role of natural objects and environmental characteristics in judgments of beauty, scenic quality, or visual preference. Aesthetic judgments may be heightened by moderate levels of complexity as conveyed, for example, by moving water or views from a height.

environmental approach a therapeutic approach in which efforts are directed either toward reducing external pressures (e.g., employment or financial problems) that contribute to emotional difficulties or toward modifying aspects of the individual's living or working space to improve functioning.

environmental assessment the evaluation of situational and environmental variables that have an influence on behavior. In an organizational context, for example, measures of manager support and availability of resources to accomplish a job would likely be used in the environmental assessment of employee job satisfaction.

environmental constraint any circumstance of a person's situation or environment that discourages the development of skills and abilities, independence, social competence, or adaptive behavior or inhibits the display of skills previously acquired. For example, living in a COMMUNITY RESIDENCE where staff prepare all the meals would act as an environmental constraint for someone who has learned how to make sandwiches, since it would provide no opportunity to display this ability.

environmental deprivation an absence of conditions that stimulate intellectual and behavioral growth and development, such as educational, recreational, and social opportunities.

environmental determinism a philosophical position that attributes INDIVIDUAL DIFFERENCES largely or completely to environmental factors, that is, to nurture as opposed to nature. Compare BIOLOGICAL DETERMINISM; GENETIC DETERMINISM. See DETERMINISM; NATURE–NURTURE.

environmentalism *n.* **1.** the concept that the environment and learning are the chief determinants of behavior. They are, therefore, the major cause of interpersonal variations in ability and adjustment; accordingly, behavior is largely modifiable. Compare HEREDITARIANISM. See also NATURE–NURTURE. **2.** a social movement and position that emphasizes the ecological relationship between humans and the natural environment and strives to protect the environment as an essential resource. —**environmentalist** *n.*

environmental press–competence model a model of stress and adaptation in which adaptive functioning in the environment depends on the interaction between stimuli in a person's physical and social environment that interact with needs and place demands on that individual (**environmental press**) and the individual's competence in meeting these demands, which is shaped by such personal characteristics as physical health and cognitive and perceptual abilities.

environmental psychology a multidisciplinary field that emphasizes the reciprocal effects of the physical environment on human behavior and welfare. Influences may include environmental stressors (e.g., noise, crowding, air pollution, temperature), design variables (e.g., lighting and illumination), the design of technology (see ERGONOMICS), and larger, more ambient qualities of the physical environment, such as floorplan layouts, symbolic elements, the size and location of buildings, and proximity to nature.

environmental stress theory the concept that autonomic and cognitive factors combine to form an individual's appraisal of stressors in the environment as threatening or nonthreatening.

envy *n.* a NEGATIVE EMOTION of discontent and resentment generated by desire for the possessions, attributes, qualities, or achievements of another. Unlike JEALOUSY, with which it shares certain similarities and with which it is often confused, envy need involve only two individuals: the envious person and the person envied. —**envious** *adj.*

enzyme *n.* a protein that acts as a biological catalyst, accelerating the rate of a biochemical reaction without itself becoming permanently altered. Many enzymes require other organic molecules (coenzymes) or inorganic ions (cofactors) to function normally.

enzyme induction the ability of drugs or other substances to increase the activity of enzymes, especially hepatic (liver) enzymes, that are responsible for the metabolism of those drugs or other substances.

enzyme inhibition the ability of drugs or other substances to impair or arrest the ability of enzymes, especially liver (hepatic) enzymes, to metabolize those drugs or other substances. Enyzme inhibition can be competitive, when a drug partially inhibits an enzyme by competing for the same binding site as the substrate (the compound on which the enzyme acts), or irreversible, when a drug binds so completely to an enzyme that it fundamentally alters the enzyme and even partial metabolism of other substances cannot take place.

EP abbreviation for EVOKED POTENTIAL.

ependyma *n.* the membrane lining the brain VENTRICLES and the CENTRAL CANAL of the spinal cord. —**ependymal** *adj.*

ependymal cell a type of nonneuronal central nervous system cell (GLIA) that comprises the ependyma and helps circulate cerebrospinal fluid.

ependymoma *n.* see GLIOMA.

EPI abbreviation for EYSENCK PERSONALITY INVENTORY.

epicritic *adj.* denoting or relating to cutaneous nerve fibers involved in minute sensory discriminations, particularly those involving very small or near-threshold variations in temperature and touch sensations. Compare PROTOPATHIC.

epidemic *adj.* generally prevalent: affecting a significant number of people, particularly with reference to a disease or disorder not ordinarily present in a specific population or present at a much higher rate than is typical. Compare ENDEMIC; PANDEMIC.

epidemiology *n.* the study of the incidence and distribution of specific diseases and disorders. The **epidemiologist** also seeks to establish relationships to such factors as heredity, environment, nutrition, or age at onset. Results of epidemiological studies are intended to find clues and associations rather than necessarily to show causal relationships. See also INCIDENCE; PREVALENCE; RELATIVE RISK. —**epidemiologic** or **epidemiological** *adj.*

epidermis *n.* the outer, protective, nonvascular layer of the skin of vertebrates.

epigenesis *n.* **1.** the theory that characteristics of an organism, both physical and behavioral, arise from an interaction between genetic and environmental influences rather than from one or the other. See also NATURE–NURTURE. **2.** in genetics, the occurrence of a heritable change in gene function that is not the result of a change in the base sequence of the organism's DNA. —**epigenetic** *adj.*

epilepsy *n.* a common neurological disorder associated with disturbances in the electrical discharges of brain cells and characterized by recurrent seizures that may be manifested as alterations in sensation, motor functions, and consciousness. Many forms of epilepsy have been linked to viral, fungal, or parasitic infections of the central nervous system; known metabolic disturbances; the ingestion of toxic agents; brain lesions; tumors or congenital defects; or cerebral trauma. Types of seizure vary depending on the nature of the abnormal electrical discharge and the area of the brain affected. Also called **seizure disorder**. —**epileptic** *adj.*

epileptiform *adj.* resembling epilepsy. Also called **epileptoid**.

epileptogenic *adj.* describing any factor or agent that causes or potentially may induce epileptic seizures.

epileptogenic focus a discrete area of the brain in which originate the electrical discharges that give rise to seizure activity.

epinephrine *n.* a CATECHOLAMINE neurotransmitter and adrenal hormone that is the end product of the metabolism of the dietary amino acid tyrosine. It is synthesized primarily in the adrenal medulla by methylation of norepinephrine, which itself is formed from dopamine. As a hormone, it is secreted in large amounts when an individual is stimulated by fear, anxiety, or a similar stressful situation. As a neurotransmitter, it increases the heart rate and force of heart contractions, relaxes bronchial and intestinal smooth muscle, and produces varying effects on blood pressure as it acts both as a vasodilator and vasoconstrictor. Also called **adrenaline**.

epiphany *n.* a sudden perception of the essential nature of oneself, others, or reality.

epiphenomenon *n.* (*pl.* **epiphenomena**) a mere by-product of a process that has no effect on the process itself. The term is used most frequently to refer to mental events considered as products of brain processes. Thus, while mental events are real in some sense, they are not real in the same way that biological states and events are real, and not necessary to the explanation of mental events themselves. Epiphenomena are conceived of as having no causal power. —**epiphenomenal** *adj.*

episodic memory memory for specific, personally experienced events that happened at a particular time or place. Episodic memory supplements SEMANTIC MEMORY and may decline with normal aging. See also AUTONOETIC; DECLARATIVE MEMORY.

epistemic value the extent to which a theory, model, or cognitive process (e.g. a sense perception or memory) is capable of providing accurate knowledge: also, any specific attribute of a theory or process that is considered to be a sign of its ability to convey such knowledge. For example, FALSIFIABILITY is an important epistemic value in science; consistency and clarity might be considered epistemic values in relation to memory.

epistemology *n.* the branch of philosophy concerned with the nature, origin, and limitations of knowledge. It is also concerned with the justification of truth claims. Mainly owing to the work of French philosopher and mathematician René Descartes (1596–1650), epistemology has been the dominant question in philosophy since the 17th century (see CARTESIANISM). In psychology, interest in epistemology arises from two principal sources. First, as the study of the behavior of human beings, psychology has long had interest in the processes of knowledge acquisition and learning of all sorts. Second, as a science, psychology has an interest in the justification of its knowledge claims. In connection with this concern, most work on epistemology in psychology has concentrated on scientific method and on the justification of scientifically derived knowledge claims. In general, the guiding epistemology of psychology has been EMPIRICISM, although some approaches to the subject, such as PSYCHOANALYSIS, the developmental psychology of Swiss epistemologist and psychologist Jean Piaget (1896–1980), and the HUMANISTIC PSYCHOLOGY of U.S. psychologist Carl Rogers (1902–1987), are heavily influenced by RATIONALISM. **—epistemological** *adj.*

epithalamus *n.* a portion of the DIENCEPHALON that is immediately above and behind the THALAMUS. It includes the PINEAL GLAND and the posterior COMMISSURE.

epithelium *n.* (*pl.* **epithelia**) the cellular layer covering the outer surface of the body and lining body cavities, such as the lungs and gastrointestinal tract. **—epithelial** *adj.*

EPP abbreviation for END-PLATE potential.

EPS abbreviation for EXTRAPYRAMIDAL SYMPTOMS.

epsilon alcoholism the least common of the five types of alcoholism defined by U.S. physician Elvin M. Jellinek (1890–1963), the others being ALPHA ALCOHOLISM, BETA ALCOHOLISM, GAMMA ALCOHOLISM, and DELTA ALCOHOLISM. It is characterized by periodic drinking bouts or binges interspersed with dry periods lasting weeks or months.

EPSP abbreviation for EXCITATORY POSTSYNAPTIC POTENTIAL.

Epstein–Barr virus (**EBV**) a herpes virus that is the cause of infectious mononucleosis. [Michael Anthony **Epstein** (1921–) and Yvonne M. **Barr** (1932–), British pathologists]

EQ abbreviation for EDUCATIONAL QUOTIENT.

equated score the score distribution from measure B transformed to match the distribution of measure A in one or more features. See TRANSFORMATION.

equilibration *n.* in PIAGETIAN THEORY, the process by which an individual uses assimilation and accommodation to restore or maintain a psychological equilibrium, that is, a cognitive state devoid of conflicting SCHEMAS.

equilibrium *n.* balance, particularly in reference to posture (see SENSE OF EQUILIBRIUM) or physiological processes (see HOMEOSTASIS).

equilibrium model of group development in general, any conceptual analysis that assumes that the processes contributing to GROUP DEVELOPMENT fluctuate around, but regularly return to, a resting point where opposing forces (e.g., the accomplishment of group tasks relative to the improvement of interpersonal relationships among group members) are balanced or held in check.

equilibrium potential the state in which the tendency of ions (electrically charged particles) to flow across a cell membrane from regions of high concentration is exactly balanced by the opposing potential difference (electric charge) across the membrane.

equipercentile method a method of equating two measures such that a shared value of X on the two measurements implies that the probability of a subject drawn at random will have a score greater than X is the same for both measures.

equipotentiality *n.* the generalization by U.S. psychologist Karl S. Lashley (1890–1958) that large areas of cerebral cortex have equal potential to perform particular functions, being equally involved in learning and certain other complex processes, such that intact cortical areas can assume to some extent the functions of damaged or destroyed areas. Proposed in 1929 following experimental observations of the effects of different brain lesions on rats' ability to learn a complex maze, the concept has been challenged by subsequent research showing that areas of cortex have relatively specific functions. See also MASS ACTION.

equity theory a theory of justice regarding what individuals are likely to view as a fair return from activities involving themselves and a number of other people. The theory posits that people compare the ratio of the outcome of the activity (i.e., the benefits they receive from it) to their input with the outcome-to-input ratios of those engaged in a comparable activity.

equivalence *n.* a relationship between two or more items (e.g., stimuli or variables) that permits one to replace another.

equivalence class a stimulus group whose members exhibit reflexivity, symmetry, and transitivity in the context of CONDITIONAL DISCRIMINATIONS. That is, the members demonstrate STIMULUS EQUIVALENCE and hence may substitute for one another.

ER abbreviation for evoked response (see EVOKED POTENTIAL).

erectile dysfunction see IMPOTENCE.

ERF abbreviation for EVENT-RELATED MAGNETIC FIELD.

erg *n.* a term used by British-born U.S. psychologist Raymond B. Cattell (1905–1998), in preference to drive or instinct, to denote a type of innate trait that directs an individual toward a goal and provides the motivational energy to obtain it. Examples include curiosity, self-assertion, gregariousness, protectiveness, and hunger.

ERG abbreviation for electroretinogram. See ELECTRORETINOGRAPHY.

ergomania *n.* a compulsion to work and keep busy. Also called **workaholism**. See WORKAHOLIC.

ergometry *n.* the measurement of physical work

performed by the muscles under various task demands. —**ergometric** *adj.*

ergonomics *n.* the discipline that applies a knowledge of human abilities and limitations drawn from physiology, BIOMECHANICS, ANTHROPOMETRY, and other areas to the design of systems, equipment, and processes for safe and efficient performance. This term is often used synonymously with HUMAN FACTORS ENGINEERING. —**ergonomic** *adj.*

ERG theory abbreviation for EXISTENCE, RELATEDNESS, AND GROWTH THEORY.

Ericksonian psychotherapy a form of psychotherapy in which the therapist works with the client to create, through hypnosis (specifically through indirect suggestion) and suggestive metaphors, real-life experiences intended to activate previously dormant, intrapsychic resources. Also called **Ericksonian hypnotherapy**. [Milton H. **Erickson** (1902–1980), U.S. psychiatrist and psychologist]

Eriksen flankers task a task in which stimuli are assigned one of two responses and the participant is required to respond to the target stimulus when this is flanked by other stimuli. Reaction time is slower if the stimuli flanking the target are assigned an alternative response than if they are assigned the same response as the target. This is known as the **flanker compatibility effect**. [Charles **Eriksen**]

Erikson's eight stages of development the theory of psychosocial development proposed by German-born U.S psychologist Erik Erikson (1902–1994), in which **ego identity** (a sense of continuity, worth, and integration) is gradually achieved by facing positive goals and negative risks during eight stages of development across the lifespan. The stages are: (a) infancy: TRUST VERSUS MISTRUST; (b) toddler: AUTONOMY VERSUS SHAME AND DOUBT; (c) preschool age: INITIATIVE VERSUS GUILT; (d) school age: INDUSTRY VERSUS INFERIORITY; (e) adolescence: IDENTITY VERSUS ROLE CONFUSION; (f) young adulthood: INTIMACY VERSUS ISOLATION; (g) middle age: GENERATIVITY VERSUS STAGNATION; and (h) older adulthood: INTEGRITY VERSUS DESPAIR.

erogenous zone an area or part of the body sensitive to stimulation that is a source of erotic or sexual feeling or pleasure. Among the primary zones are the genitals and adjacent areas, the breasts (especially the nipples), the buttocks and anus, and the mouth. Also called **erotogenic zone**.

Eros *n.* the god of love in Greek mythology (equivalent to the Roman Cupid), whose name was chosen by Austrian psychoanalyst Sigmund Freud (1856–1939) to designate a theoretical set of strivings oriented toward sexuality, development, and increased life activity (see LIFE INSTINCT). In Freud's DUAL INSTINCT THEORY, Eros is seen as involved in a dialectic process with THANATOS, the striving toward reduced psychi-

cal tension and life activity (see DEATH INSTINCT). See also LIBIDO.

eroticism *n.* **1.** the quality of being sexually arousing or pleasurable or the condition of being sexually aroused. **2.** in psychoanalytic theory, the pleasurable sensations associated not only with stimulation of the genitals but also with nongenital parts of the body, such as the mouth (oral eroticism) or anus (anal eroticism). Also called **erotism**. See also AUTOEROTICISM; EROTIZATION. —**erotic** *adj.*

erotic love a type of LOVE, identified in certain classifications of love, that is characterized by strong sexual arousal. See also PASSIONATE LOVE.

erotization *n.* the investment of bodily organs and biological functions or other not specifically sensual or sexual activities with sexual pleasure and gratification. Common examples are the erotization of certain areas of the body, such as the oral or anal EROGENOUS ZONES; organs, such as the nipple or skin; functions, such as sucking, defecation, urination, or scopophilic activities (looking at nudity or sexual activity); and olfactory sensations associated with sex. Theoretically, almost any interest or activity can be erotized by the individual; for example, activities such as dancing and eating are not infrequently seen as erotic or as having erotic components. Also called **eroticization**; **sexualization**. —**erotize** *vb.*

ERP abbreviation for EVENT-RELATED POTENTIAL.

error *n.* **1.** in experimentation, any change in a DEPENDENT VARIABLE not attributable to the manipulation of an INDEPENDENT VARIABLE. **2.** in statistics, a deviation of an observed score from a true score, where true score is often defined by the mean (average) of the particular group or condition in which the score being assessed for error occurs, or from the score predicted by a model.

errorless learning a method that prevents the production of incorrect answers during the learning period. Specifically, learning occurs across several sessions, but memory is not tested until the last session. It is thought to be more efficient than standard trial-and-error learning because it eliminates interference.

error of anticipation in the METHOD OF LIMITS, an error in which the participant responds "target present" before it is actually detected, based on the knowledge that the stimuli are being presented in an ascending order.

error of expectation an error arising because of a preconceived idea of the nature of the stimulus to be presented or the timing of the presentation.

error of habituation in the METHOD OF LIMITS, a tendency to continue with the previous response (either "target present" or "target absent") beyond the point at which a transition in judgments should occur.

error score in CLASSICAL TEST THEORY, the

difference between a person's observed measurement or score and his or her expected measurement or score.

error term the element of a statistical equation that indicates what is unexplained by the INDEPENDENT VARIABLES. Also called **disturbance term; residual term**.

error variance unexplained variability in a score that is produced by extraneous factors, such as measurement imprecision, and is not attributable to the INDEPENDENT VARIABLE or other controlled experimental manipulations.

erythropsia *n*. see CHROMATOPSIA.

escalation of commitment continued commitment and increased allocation of resources to a failing course of action, often in the hope of recouping past losses associated with that course of action. Also called **creeping commitment**.

escape conditioning the process in which a subject acquires a response that results in the termination of an aversive stimulus. For example, if a monkey learns that pulling a string frequently results in the elimination of a loud noise, escape conditioning has occurred. Also called **escape learning; escape training**. See also AVOIDANCE CONDITIONING.

escape titration a procedure in which an animal, presented with an aversive stimulus that increases in intensity over time, can by responding decrease the stimulus intensity by some fixed (usually small) amount. Also called **fractional escape**.

ESP abbreviation for EXTRASENSORY PERCEPTION.

esprit de corps a feeling of unity, commitment, purpose, and collective efficacy shared by most or all of the members of a cohesive group or organization. Members of groups with esprit de corps feel close to one another, are committed to the group and its goals, and are in some cases willing to sacrifice their own individual desires for the good of the group. See also COHESION.

essentialism *n*. in philosophy, the position that things (or some things) have "essences"; that is, they have certain necessary properties without which they could not be the things they are. In Marxism, POSTMODERNISM, POSTSTRUCTURALISM, and certain feminist perspectives, essentialism is the rejected position that human beings have an essential nature that transcends such factors as social class, gender, and ethnicity. See also UNIVERSALISM.

essential tremor trembling of the hands, head, or voice that appears to be hereditary. It is the most common type of movement disorder and is thought to be a benign condition, although its etiology and neurological substrates remain unclear. Also called **familial tremor**.

EST abbreviation for electroshock therapy or electroconvulsive shock therapy. See ELECTROCONVULSIVE THERAPY.

establishing operation any event or procedure that changes the efficacy of a stimulus as a reinforcer or punisher. For example, in an operant-conditioning study where food is used to positively reinforce behavior, the establishing operation may be food deprivation, which sets up food as a rewarding and reinforcing stimulus.

esteem needs in MASLOW'S MOTIVATIONAL HIERARCHY, the fourth level in his hierarchy of needs, characterized by striving for a sense of personal value derived from achievement, reputation, or prestige. In this level of development, the admiration and approval of others leads to the development of SELF-ESTEEM.

Estes–Skinner procedure another name for CONDITIONED SUPPRESSION. [after U.S. psychologists William K. **Estes** (1919–) and B. F. **Skinner** (1904–1990), who developed the technique in 1941]

esthesiometry (aesthesiometry) *n*. the measurement of sensitivity to touch. Classically, two different versions of an instrument called an **esthesiometer** have been used. One consists of bristles of different lengths and thicknesses that are applied to determine the minimum pressure intensity required to produce a sensation. The other is a compasslike device to determine the smallest separation distance at which two points of stimulation on the skin are perceived as one. More sophisticated techniques have now been developed, such as those involving electrodes.

estimator *n*. a quantity calculated from the values in a sample according to some rule and used to give an estimate of the value in a population. For example, the sample mean is an estimator for the population mean; the value of the sample mean is the estimate.

estrangement *n*. **1.** a state of increased distance or separation from oneself or others. See ALIENATION. **2.** a significant decrease or discontinuation of contact with individuals with whom one formerly had close relationships, such as a spouse or family member, due to apathy or antagonism. —**estranged** *adj*.

estrogen *n*. any of a class of STEROID HORMONES that are produced mainly by the ovaries and act as the principal female SEX HORMONES, inducing estrus in female mammals and secondary female sexual characteristics in humans. The estrogens occurring naturally in humans are **estradiol** (the most potent), **estrone**, and **estriol**, secreted by the ovarian follicle, corpus luteum, placenta, testes, and adrenal cortex. —**estrogenic** *adj*.

estrous cycle the cyclical sequence of reproductive activity shown by most female mammals (except humans and other primates; see MENSTRUAL CYCLE). Animals that experience one estrous cycle per year are called **monestrous**; those that have multiple estrous cycles annually are **polyestrous**.

eta (symbol: η) *n*. see CORRELATION RATIO.

ethanol *n*. a substance formed naturally or synthetically by the fermentation of glucose and found in beverages such as beers, wines, and dis-

E

tilled liquors. It is the most frequently used and abused CNS DEPRESSANT in many cultures. When consumed its primary effects are on the central nervous system, mood, and cognitive functions. In small doses, it can produce feelings of warmth, well-being, and confidence. As more is consumed, there is a gradual loss of self-control, and speech and control of limbs become difficult; at high consumption levels, nausea and vomiting, loss of consciousness, and even fatal respiratory arrest may occur. Ethanol has been mistakenly identified as a stimulant, since its stimulating effect derives from an associated loss of cortical inhibition. Also called **alcohol**; **ethyl alcohol**. See also ALCOHOL ABUSE; ALCOHOL DEPENDENCE; ALCOHOL INTOXICATION; ALCOHOL WITHDRAWAL.

e-therapy *n.* an Internet-based form of DISTANCE THERAPY used to expand access to clinical services typically offered face-to-face. This therapy can be conducted in real-time messaging, in chat rooms, and in e-mail messages. Also called **online therapy**.

ethical dilemma a situation in which two moral principles conflict with one another. Fictional or hypothetical dilemmas of this kind are often used to assess the moral beliefs or moral reasoning skills of individuals.

ethical judgment a moral decision made by an individual, especially a difficult one made in the context of a real or hypothetical ethical dilemma. Such judgments often reveal the beliefs that an individual applies in discriminating between right and wrong and the attitudes that comprise his or her basic moral orientation. Also called **moral judgment**.

ethical principle orientation see POSTCONVENTIONAL LEVEL.

ethics *n.* **1.** the branch of philosophy that investigates both the content of moral judgments (i.e., what is right and what is wrong) and their nature (i.e., whether such judgments should be considered objective or subjective). The study of the first type of question is sometimes termed **normative ethics** and that of the second **metaethics**. Also called **moral philosophy**. **2.** the principles of morally right conduct accepted by a person or a group or considered appropriate to a specific field (e.g., medical ethics, ethics of animal research). See CODE OF ETHICS; PROFESSIONAL ETHICS. **—ethical** *adj.*

ethnic *adj.* denoting or referring to a group of people having a shared social, cultural, linguistic, religious, and usually racial background.

ethnic group any major social group that possesses a common ethnic identity based on history, culture, language, and, often, religion. Members are likely to be biologically related, but an ethnic group is not equivalent to a RACE.

ethnic identity an individual's sense of being a person who is defined, in part, by membership in a specific ethnic group. This sense is usually considered to be a complex construct involving shared social, cultural, linguistic, religious, and often racial factors but identical with none of them.

ethnocentrism *n.* the tendency to reject and malign other ethnic groups and their members while glorifying one's own group and its members. Just as EGOCENTRISM is the tendency to judge oneself as superior to others, so ethnocentrism is the parallel tendency to judge one's group as superior to other groups. **—ethnocentric** *adj.*

ethnography *n.* the descriptive study of cultures or societies based on direct observation and (ideally) some degree of participation. Compare ETHNOLOGY. See also EMIC. **—ethnographer** *n.* **—ethnographic** *adj.*

ethnolinguistics *n.* the investigation of language within the context of human cultures or societies, paying attention to cultural influences and incorporating the principles of anthropology and ethnography. See also ANTHROPOLOGICAL LINGUISTICS.

ethnology *n.* the comparative, analytical, or historical study of human cultures or societies. Compare ETHNOGRAPHY. See also ETIC. **—ethnological** *adj.* **—ethnologist** *n.*

ethnopsychopharmacology *n.* the branch of pharmacology that deals with issues related to ethnic and cultural variations in the use of and response to psychoactive agents across divergent groups, as well as the mechanisms responsible for such differences. **—ethnopsychopharmacological** *adj.*

ethnotherapy *n.* therapy sensitive to the distinct cultural features of a client from an ethnic minority and the various ways in which the client relates to others, expresses himself or herself, and deals with problems. See also MULTICULTURAL COUNSELING.

ethogram *n.* a detailed listing and description of the behavior patterns of an animal in its natural habitat. The description is objective rather than interpretative. For example, a vocalization given in response to a predator would be described in terms of its acoustic properties rather than its apparent function of alarm call.

ethology *n.* the comparative study of the behavior of animals, typically in their natural habitat but also involving experiments both in the field and in captivity. Ethology is often associated with connotations of innate or species-specific behavior patterns, in contrast with COMPARATIVE PSYCHOLOGY. The theory and methods from both areas are now closely interrelated, and ANIMAL BEHAVIOR is a more neutral and more broadly encompassing term. **—ethological** *adj.* **—ethologist** *n.*

ethos *n.* the distinctive character or spirit of an individual, group, culture, nation, or period, as revealed particularly in its attitudes and values.

etic *adj.* **1.** denoting an approach to the study of human cultures based on concepts or constructs

E

that are held to be universal and applicable cross-culturally. Such an approach would generally be of the kind associated with ETHNOLOGY rather than ETHNOGRAPHY. Compare EMIC. **2.** in linguistics, see EMIC–ETIC DISTINCTION.

etiology *n.* **1.** the causes and progress of a disease or disorder. **2.** the branch of medical and psychological science concerned with the systematic study of the causes of physical and mental disorders. —**etiological** *adj.*

etymology *n.* the study of the origins and historical development of words and MORPHEMES. —**etymological** *adj.*

eudemonism (**eudaemonism**) *n.* **1.** the position that happiness, or **eudemonia**, is the ultimate ground of morality, so that what is good is what brings happiness. Debate then centers on whose happiness is achieved and whether certain means of achieving happiness are immoral. UTILITARIANISM is a eudemonism. **2.** the position that humans will naturally act in ways that bring them happiness. Psychoanalytic, behavioristic, and modern humanistic psychologies can all be seen as modern eudemonisms. Debate centers on whether humans are compelled to act so as to maximize their happiness, as HEDONISM would suggest, or whether the association between happiness and behavior is more subtle. Older versions of eudemonism suggested that the motives for human action included some altruistic impulses, such that the achievement of the happiness of others or a greater good could also be the cause or source of behaviors.

eugenic *adj.* describing a factor or influence that is favorable to heredity. Compare DYSGENIC.

eugenics *n.* a social and political philosophy that seeks to eradicate genetic defects and improve the genetic makeup of populations through selective human breeding. **Positive eugenics** is directed toward promoting reproduction by individuals with superior traits, whereas **negative eugenics** is directed toward preventing reproduction by individuals with undesirable traits. The eugenic position is groundless and scientifically naive, in that many conditions associated with disability or disorder are inherited recessively and occur unpredictably.

euphenics *n.* interventions that aim to improve the outcome of a genetic disease by altering the environment to minimize expression of the disease. For example, people with phenylketonuria can reduce its expression by eliminating major sources of phenylalanine (e.g., soft drinks sweetened with aspartame) from their diet.

euphoria *n.* an elevated mood of well-being and happiness. An exaggerated degree of euphoria that does not reflect the reality of one's situation is a frequent symptom of MANIC EPISODES and HYPOMANIC EPISODES. —**euphoric** *adj.*

eusociality *n.* a social structure among animals, particularly SOCIAL INSECTS, in which there is a marked division of labor, with only a few individuals that reproduce and many more non-

reproductive individuals that guard the nest, gather food and nest materials, or help to care for the young. —**eusocial** *adj.*

eustachian tube a slender tube extending from the middle ear to the PHARYNX, with the primary function of equalizing air pressure on both sides of the tympanic membrane (eardrum). [Bartolommeo **Eustachio** (1524–1574), Italian anatomist]

eustress *n.* the positive stress response, involving optimal levels of stimulation: a type of stress that results from challenging but attainable and enjoyable or worthwhile tasks (e.g., participating in an athletic event, giving a speech). It has a beneficial effect by generating a sense of fulfillment or achievement and facilitating growth, development, mastery, and high levels of performance. Compare DISTRESS.

euthanasia *n.* the act or process of terminating a life to prevent further suffering. Voluntary euthanasia requires the consent of a competent person who has established a valid ADVANCE DIRECTIVE or made his or her wishes otherwise clearly known. Euthanasia is distinguished from the much more widely accepted practice of forgoing invasive treatments, as permitted under natural-death laws throughout the United States. See also ACTIVE EUTHANASIA; ASSISTED DEATH; INFORMED CONSENT; PASSIVE EUTHANASIA.

euthymia *n.* a mood of well-being and tranquillity. The term often is used to refer to a state in patients with a bipolar disorder that is neither manic nor depressive but in between, associated with adaptive behavior and enhanced functioning. —**euthymic** *adj.*

evaluation apprehension uneasiness or worry about being judged by others, especially feelings of worry experienced by participants in an experiment as a result of their desire to be evaluated favorably by the experimenter.

evaluation research the use of scientific principles and methods to assess the effectiveness of social interventions and programs, including those related to mental health, education, and safety (e.g., crime prevention, automobile accident prevention). Evaluation research is thus a type of APPLIED RESEARCH.

evaluative semantic priming measure an IMPLICIT ATTITUDE MEASURE based on the phenomenon that the speed of evaluating some target object is facilitated by a prime (i.e., the prior presentation of another object) that is evaluatively consistent with the target and inhibited by a prime that is evaluatively inconsistent with the target. For example, if the name of a product is presented as a prime immediately prior to a target word likely to be negative to most people (e.g., cockroach), evaluation of the target should be faster if the attitude toward the product is negative and slower if the attitude toward the product is positive. Also called **bona fide pipeline measure**.

event *n.* in probability theory, any of the namable things that can be said to result from a single trial of an experiment of chance. For example, in the roll of a single die, the events could include (among others) any of the six individual numbers, any even number, and any odd number.

event history analysis see SURVIVAL ANALYSIS.

event-related magnetic field (**ERF**) a change in the magnetic field of the brain that is elicited by a cognitive event, such as determining whether a specific word was part of a recently presented list. ERFs allow more accurate localization of function than do event-related potentials because they are less influenced by the surrounding brain structures.

event-related potential (**ERP**) a specific pattern of electrical activity produced in the brain when a person is engaged in a cognitive act, such as discriminating one stimulus from another. There are a number of different ERP components, including the highly researched P3 COMPONENT, and different cognitive operations have been associated with the amplitude and latency of each. Because ERPs provide specific information about the precise timing and (given appropriate caveats) location of mental events, they can yield data about cognitive operations not readily derived from behavioral measures and also serve as an important bridge between psychological function and neural structures. Although the terms are sometimes used synonymously, ERPs are distinct from EVOKED POTENTIALS, which are associated with more elementary sensory stimulation.

event-related-potential measure of attitudes a physiological measure of attitudes based on electrocortical activity. The procedure makes use of the phenomenon that one component of event-related potentials, the late positive potential (or P300), varies as a function of categorization of stimuli. The target attitude object is evaluated as part of a series of objects that are either positive or negative in nature. If a large late positive potential is produced when the attitude object is evaluated in the negative context and a small positive potential is produced when it is evaluated in the positive context, this indicates a positive attitude. The reverse pattern indicates a negative attitude.

event sampling a strategy commonly used in direct observation that involves noting and recording the occurrence of a carefully specified behavior whenever it is seen. For example, a researcher may record each episode of apnea that occurs within a 9-hour period overnight while a person sleeps.

everyday creativity the ability to think divergently and demonstrate flexibility and originality in one's daily work and leisure activities. Examples include redecorating a room at home or devising a novel solution to a business problem. Also called **ordinary creativity**. Compare EXCEPTIONAL CREATIVITY.

everyday intelligence the intellectual skills used in everyday living (e.g., activities such as price comparison shopping and using a map to travel unfamiliar streets). Everyday intelligence refers not to a psychometrically validated construct but to a loosely conceptualized kind of intelligence relevant to the problems people face on a daily basis.

everyday racism differential treatment of individuals on the basis of their racial group that occurs in common, routine social situations (e.g., a White store clerk watching African American shoppers more closely than White shoppers).

evoked potential (**EP**) a specific pattern of electrical activity produced in a particular part of the nervous system, especially the brain, in response to external stimulation, such as a flash of light or a brief tone. Different modalities and types of stimuli produce different types of sensory potentials, and these are labeled according to their electrical polarity (positive- or negative-going) and timing (by serial order or in milliseconds). Although the terms are sometimes used synonymously, EPs are distinct from EVENT-RELATED POTENTIALS, which are associated with higher level cognitive processes. Also called **evoked response** (**ER**).

evolution *n.* the process of gradual change in the appearance of populations of organisms that has taken place over generations. Such changes are widely held to account for the present diversity of living organisms originating from relatively few ancestors since the emergence of life on Earth. —**evolutionary** *adj.*

evolutionary developmental psychology the application of the basic principles of Darwinian evolution, particularly NATURAL SELECTION, to explain contemporary human development. Evolutionary developmental psychology involves the study of the genetic and environmental mechanisms that underlie the universal development of social and cognitive competencies and the evolved epigenetic processes (gene–environment interactions) that adapt these competencies to local conditions.

evolutionary psychology an approach to psychological inquiry that views human cognition and behavior in a broadly Darwinian context of adaptation to evolving physical and social environments and new intellectual challenges. It differs from SOCIOBIOLOGY mainly in its emphasis on the effects of NATURAL SELECTION on INFORMATION PROCESSING and the structure of the human mind.

evolved mechanism a subsystem of the brain (or mind) that is generally seen as having evolved as a result of its success in solving a problem related to survival or reproduction of a species. For example, the elements of the brain's visual system that enable three-dimensional perception (despite the projection of light onto a two-dimensional surface, the retina) would be seen as an evolved mechanism that solved the problem of determining the distance between oneself and objects in the environment.

exceptional creativity the capability of individuals to make unique and important contributions to society through their work and the products of their work. Also called **creative genius**. Compare EVERYDAY CREATIVITY.

exchange relationship see COMMUNAL RELATIONSHIP.

excitability *n.* in neurophysiology, the capacity of neurons and some muscle cells to respond electrically to external stimulation with a sudden, transient increase in their ionic permeability and a change in the electric potential across their cell membrane. —**excitable** *adj.*

excitation *n.* the electrical activity elicited in a neuron or muscle cell in response to an external stimulus, specifically the propagation of an ACTION POTENTIAL.

excitatory conditioning direct PAVLOVIAN CONDITIONING, that is, conditioning in which a conditioned stimulus acts as a signal that a particular unconditioned stimulus will follow.

excitatory–inhibitory processes 1. processes in which the transmission of neuronal signals is activated or inhibited by the effects of neurotransmitters on the postsynaptic membrane. **2.** the stimulation of the cortex and the subsequent facilitation of the processes of learning, memory, and action (excitatory processes) and central nervous system processes that inhibit or interfere with perceptual, cognitive, and motor activities (inhibitory processes). Individuals with predominant inhibitory processes are theorized to be predisposed to a higher degree of INTROVERSION, whereas individuals with predominant excitatory processes are theorized to be predisposed to a higher degree of EXTRAVERSION.

excitatory postsynaptic potential (**EPSP**) a brief decrease in the difference in electrical charge across the membrane of a neuron that is caused by the transmission of a signal from a neighboring neuron across the synapse (specialized junction) separating them. EPSPs increase the probability that the postsynaptic neuron will initiate an ACTION POTENTIAL and hence fire a nerve impulse. Compare INHIBITORY POSTSYNAPTIC POTENTIAL.

excitatory synapse a specialized type of junction at which activity from one neuron (in the form of an ACTION POTENTIAL) facilitates activity in an adjacent neuron by initiating an EXCITATORY POSTSYNAPTIC POTENTIAL. Compare INHIBITORY SYNAPSE.

excitotoxicity *n.* the property that causes neurons to die when overstimulated, for example by large amounts of the excitatory neurotransmitter GLUTAMATE.

executive *n.* a theoretical superordinate mechanism in some models of cognition—particularly those in cognitive science, cognitive neuropsychology, and artificial intelligence—that organizes, initiates, monitors, and otherwise controls information-processing activities and other mental operations. A similar concept specific to WORKING MEMORY is that of the central executive.

executive coaching one-on-one personal counseling and feedback provided to managers in an organization to develop their interpersonal and other managerial skills as a means of enhancing their capability of achieving short- and long-term organizational goals. Executive coaching may be provided by the manager's boss, a peer, a human resources professional within the organization, or an external consultant. See MANAGEMENT DEVELOPMENT.

executive control structure a theoretical mental system governing the use of different cognitive strategies: an internal blueprint. Particularly relevant to problem solving, executive control structures contain representations of situations, their objectives, and the various procedures available for obtaining them. They are one of two mechanisms proposed by Canadian developmental psychologist Robbie Case (1944–2000) as guiding learning and thinking processes in children, the other being the CENTRAL CONCEPTUAL STRUCTURE.

executive functions higher level cognitive processes that organize and order behavior, such as judgment, abstraction and concept formation, logic and reasoning, problem solving, planning, and sequencing of actions. Deficits in executive functioning are seen in various disorders, including Alzheimer's disease and schizophrenia. In the latter, for example, major deficits in such cognitive abilities as selecting goals or task-relevant information and eliminating extraneous information are apparent and are a focus of neurorehabilitative treatment. Also called **central processes**; **higher order processes**.

executive self the agent to which regulation and implementation of voluntary actions is ordinarily attributed. The concept of an executive self has acquired considerable scientific plausibility, being associated with well-studied functions of the PREFRONTAL CORTEX.

exemplar theory see INSTANCE THEORY.

exercise–behavior model an adaptation of the HEALTH–BELIEF MODEL that identifies the relationships of the following to likelihood of exercising: (a) personal predispositions, (b) sociodemographic variables, (c) perceived cost and benefits of exercising, and (d) perceived self-efficacy and locus of control.

exercise play play that involves gross, vigorous movement in various directions, such as running or jumping. It usually begins around 2 years of age and peaks between 5 and 6 years. Exercise play is a form of LOCOMOTOR PLAY and may or may not be social.

exercise psychology see SPORT AND EXERCISE PSYCHOLOGY.

exercise therapy the prevention or treatment of disorders and chronic disease using regular, repetitive physical activity that enhances fitness and mobility. This type of therapy is designed to improve the functional capacity of body structures and has been demonstrated to have beneficial effects for a wide variety of conditions, for example the alleviation of symptoms of depression and multiple sclerosis and the reduction in risk of developing cardiovascular disease and osteoporosis. More generally, there is widespread research evidence for a positive relationship between regular exercise and several indices of mental health and physical well-being.

exhaustion delirium a state of DELIRIUM occurring under conditions of extreme fatigue resulting from prolonged and intense overexertion, particularly when coupled with other forms of stress, such as prolonged insomnia, starvation, excessive heat or cold, or toxic states. It is typically associated with the extreme physical effort required of those who engage in prolonged duration sports or of others facing extreme environmental conditions, as well as with debilitating diseases.

exhaustion stage see GENERAL ADAPTATION SYNDROME.

exhaustive search any SEARCH process in which every item of a set is checked before a decision is made about the presence or absence of a target item. Compare SELF-TERMINATING SEARCH.

exhibitionism n. a PARAPHILIA in which a person repeatedly exposes his or her genitals to unsuspecting strangers as a means of achieving sexual satisfaction. —**exhibitionist** n.

existence, relatedness, and growth theory (ERG theory) a variation of MASLOW'S MOTIVATIONAL HIERARCHY that recognizes three main categories of work motivation: **existence needs**, relating to physical needs such as food and shelter; **relatedness needs**, involving interpersonal relations with others; and **growth needs**, in the form of personal development and improvement.

existential anxiety a general sense of anguish or despair associated with an individual's recognition of the inevitability of death and associated search for purpose and meaning in life, in light of the finitude of past choices and the unknowns inherent to future choices.

existential crisis 1. in EXISTENTIALISM, a crucial stage or turning point at which an individual is faced with finding meaning and purpose in life and taking responsibility for his or her choices. See EXISTENTIAL NEUROSIS; EXISTENTIAL VACUUM. **2.** more generally, any psychological or moral crisis that causes an individual to ask fundamental questions about human existence.

existential–humanistic therapy a form of psychotherapy that focuses on the entire person, rather than just behavior, cognition, or underlying motivations. Emphasis is placed on the client's subjective experiences, free will, and ability to decide the course of his or her own life. Also called **humanistic–existential therapy**.

existential intelligence a kind of intelligence proposed as a "candidate" for inclusion in the MULTIPLE-INTELLIGENCES THEORY. It is involved in understanding larger fundamental questions of existence and the role and place of humans in the universe.

existentialism n. a philosophical and literary movement that emerged in Europe in the period between the two World Wars and became the dominant trend in Continental thought during the 1940s and 1950s. Existentialism is notoriously difficult to sum up in a single definition—partly because many who might be identified with the movement reject the label, and partly because the movement is itself, in many ways, a rejection of systematization and classification. Although there are several important precursors, the first fully developed philosophy of existentialism is usually taken to be the EXISTENTIAL PHENOMENOLOGY elaborated by German philosopher Martin Heidegger (1889–1976) in the 1910s and 1920s. Heidegger's concept of DASEIN strongly influenced the work of the French philosopher and author Jean-Paul Sartre (1905–1980), who is usually seen as the existentialist thinker *par excellence*. In the immediate postwar years Sartre popularized both the term "existentialism" and most of the ideas now associated with it. Existentialism represents a turning away from systematic philosophy, with its emphasis on metaphysical absolutes and principles of rational certainty, and toward an emphasis on the concrete existence of a human being "thrown" into a world that is merely "given" and contingent. Such a being encounters the world as a subjective consciousness, "condemned" to create its own meanings and values in an "absurd" and purposeless universe. The human being must perform this task in the absence of any possibility of rational certainty. However, by accepting the burden of this responsibility, and refusing the "bad faith" of religion and other spurious rationalizations, he or she can achieve AUTHENTICITY. Various forms of EXISTENTIAL PSYCHOLOGY have taken up the task of providing explanations, understandings of human behavior, and therapies based on existentialist assumptions about human existence. —**existential** adj. —**existentialist** n., adj.

existential living the capacity to live fully in the present and respond freely and flexibly to new experience without fear.

existential neurosis NEUROSIS characterized by feelings of despair and anxiety that arise from living inauthentically, that is, from failing to take responsibility for one's own life and to make choices and find meaning in living. See AUTHEN-

TICITY; EXISTENTIAL CRISIS; EXISTENTIAL VACUUM.

existential psychology a general approach to psychological theory and practice that derives from EXISTENTIALISM. It emphasizes the subjective meaning of human experience, the uniqueness of the individual, and personal responsibility reflected in choice. See BEING-IN-THE-WORLD; WORLD DESIGN. See also HUMANISTIC PSYCHOLOGY.

existential psychotherapy a form of psychotherapy that deals with the HERE AND NOW of the client's total situation rather than with the client's past or underlying dynamics. It emphasizes the exploration and development of meaning in life, focuses on emotional experiences and decision making, and stresses a person's responsibility for his or her own existence. See also LOGOTHERAPY.

existential vacuum the inability to find or create meaning in life, leading to feelings of emptiness, alienation, futility, and aimlessness. Most existentialists have considered meaninglessness to be the quintessential symptom or ailment of the modern age. See EXISTENTIAL CRISIS; EXISTENTIAL NEUROSIS. See also LOGOTHERAPY.

exocrine gland any gland that secretes a product onto the outer body surface or into body cavities through a duct, for example, the tear-producing **lacrimal gland** or the salivary gland. Compare ENDOCRINE GLAND.

exogamy *n.* the custom or practice of marrying outside one's KINSHIP NETWORK (such as a CLAN) or other religious or social group. Compare ENDOGAMY. **—exogamous** *adj.*

exogenous *adj.* originating outside the body: referring, for example, to drugs (exogenous chemicals) or to phenomena, conditions, or disorders resulting from the influence of external factors (e.g., exogenous stress). Compare ENDOGENOUS. **—exogenously** *adv.*

exon *n.* a sequence of DNA within a gene that encodes a part or all of the gene's product or function. Exons are separated by noncoding sequences (see INTRON).

expanded consciousness a purported sense that one's mind has been opened to a new kind of awareness or to new concepts, associated particularly with meditation or drug use. See also ALTERED STATE OF CONSCIOUSNESS.

expectancy *n.* the internal state resulting from experience with predictable relationships between stimuli or between responses and stimuli. This basic meaning becomes slightly more specific in some fields. For example, in cognitive psychology it refers to an attitude or MENTAL SET that determines the way in which a person approaches a situation, and in motivation theory it refers to an individual's belief that his or her actions can produce a particular outcome (e.g., attainment of a goal). **—expectant** *adj.*

expectancy effect the effect of one person's expectation about the behavior of another person on the actual behavior of that other person (**interpersonal expectancy effect**) or the effect of a person's expectation about his or her own behavior on that person's actual subsequent behavior (**intrapersonal expectancy effect**). See also EXPERIMENTER EXPECTANCY EFFECT.

expectancy theory 1. a theory that cognitive learning involves acquired expectancies and a tendency to react to certain objects as signs of other objects previously associated with them. PURPOSIVE BEHAVIORISM is a specific form of expectancy theory. **2.** See VALENCE–INSTRUMENTALITY–EXPECTANCY THEORY.

expectant analysis the orthodox technique of psychoanalysis, in which the analyst awaits the gradual, free-floating unfolding of the patient's psyche. Compare FOCUSED ANALYSIS.

expectation-states theory an explanation of status differentiation in groups proposing that group members allocate status not only to those who possess qualities suggesting competence at the task in question but also to those who have qualities that the members (mistakenly) think are indicators of competence and potential, such as sex, age, wealth, and ethnicity.

expected value the mean value of a random variable or one of its functions as derived by mathematical calculation.

experience-dependent synaptogenesis a process whereby SYNAPSES are formed and maintained as a result of the unique experiences of an individual.

experience-expectant synaptogenesis a process whereby SYNAPSES are formed and maintained when an organism has species-typical experiences. As a result, such functions as vision will develop for all members of a species, given species-typical environmental stimulation (e.g., light).

experiential family therapy a type of therapy that emphasizes intuition, feelings, and underlying processes in treating families and that deemphasizes theoretical frameworks. The work is often characterized by the use of the therapist's own feelings and self-disclosures in interactions with clients.

experiential learning learning that occurs by actively performing and participating in an activity.

experiential psychotherapy a broad family of psychotherapies falling under the umbrella of existential–humanistic psychology. A core belief of the approach is that true client change occurs through direct, active "experiencing" of what the client is undergoing and feeling at any given point in therapy, both on the surface and at a deeper level. Experiential therapists typically engage clients very directly with regard to accessing and expressing their inner feelings and experiencing both present and past life scenes, and they offer clients perspectives for integrating

E

such experiences into realistic and healthy self-concepts.

experiential subtheory see TRIARCHIC THEORY OF INTELLIGENCE.

experiment *n.* a series of observations conducted under controlled conditions to study a relationship with the purpose of drawing causal inferences about that relationship. Experiments involve the manipulation of an INDEPENDENT VARIABLE, the measurement of a DEPENDENT VARIABLE, and the exposure of various participants to one or more of the conditions being studied. —**experimental** *adj.*

experimental analysis of behavior an approach to experimental psychology that explores the relationships between particular experiences and changes in behavior, emphasizing the behavior of individuals rather than group averages. It is concerned especially with describing how contingencies of reinforcement control the rate of an instrumental response.

experimental design an outline or plan of the procedures to be followed in scientific experimentation in order to reach valid conclusions, with consideration of such factors as participant selection, variable manipulation, data collection and analysis, and minimization of external influences.

experimental epilepsy induction of repeated episodes of abnormal neural activity (seizures) in a nonhuman animal through electrical or chemical brain stimulation or through repeated sensory stimulation.

experimental group a group of participants in an experiment who are exposed to a particular manipulation of the INDEPENDENT VARIABLE (i.e., a particular TREATMENT LEVEL or, more briefly, a particular treatment). Compare CONTROL GROUP.

experimental method a system of scientific investigation, usually based on a design to be carried out under controlled conditions, that is intended to test a hypothesis and establish a causal relationship between independent and dependent variables.

experimental neurosis a pathological condition induced in an animal during conditioning experiments requiring discriminations between nearly indistinguishable stimuli or involving punishment for necessary activities (e.g., eating). Experimental neurosis may be characterized by any of a range of behavioral abnormalities, including agitation, irritability, aggression, regressive behavior, escape and avoidance, and disturbances in physiological activity, such as pulse, heart, and respiration rates.

experimental philosophy 1. in the late 17th and 18th centuries, a name for the new discipline of experimental science then emerging. Use of the term often went with an optimism about the ability of experimental science to answer the questions that had been posed but unsolved by "natural philosophy." The systematic work of British physicist Isaac Newton (1642–1727) is often given as a defining example of the experimental philosophy. **2.** a late 20th-century movement holding that modern experimental science, particularly neuroscience, will ultimately uncover the biological foundations of thought and thereby provide a material answer to the questions of EPISTEMOLOGY. In other words, experimental philosophy holds that answers to philosophical questions regarding the mind and its activities can, and likely will be, reduced to questions of how the brain functions. See REDUCTIONISM.

experimental psychology the scientific study of behavior, motives, or cognition in a laboratory or other experimental setting in order to predict, explain, or control behavior or other psychological phenomena. Experimental psychology aims at establishing quantified relationships and explanatory theory through the analysis of responses under various controlled conditions and the synthesis of adequate theoretical accounts from the results of these observations. See also EMPIRICAL PSYCHOLOGY.

experimental realism the extent to which an experimental situation is meaningful and engaging to participants, eliciting responses that are spontaneous and natural. See also MUNDANE REALISM.

experimental research research utilizing randomized assignment of participants to conditions and systematic manipulation of variables with the objective of drawing causal inference. It is generally conducted within a laboratory or other controlled environment, which in reducing the potential influence of extraneous factors increases INTERNAL VALIDITY but decreases EXTERNAL VALIDITY.

experimental treatment an intervention or regimen that has shown some promise as a cure or ameliorative for a disease or condition but is still being evaluated for efficacy, safety, and acceptability.

experimental variable an INDEPENDENT VARIABLE: a variable under investigation that is manipulated by the experimenter to determine its relationship to or influence upon some DEPENDENT VARIABLE.

experimenter bias any unintended errors in the experimental process or the interpretation of its results that are attributable to an experimenter's preconceived beliefs about results.

experimenter effect any influence an experimenter may have on the results of his or her research, derived from either interaction with participants or unintentional errors of observation, measurement, analysis, or interpretation. In the former, the experimenter's personal characteristics (e.g., age, sex, race), attitudes, and expectations directly affect the behavior of participants. In the latter, the experimenter's procedural errors (arising from his or her predictions about results) have no effect on participant responses but indirectly distort the experimental findings.

experimenter expectancy effect a type of EXPERIMENTER EFFECT in which the expectations of an experimenter about research findings inadvertently are conveyed to participants and influence their responses in the predicted manner. This distortion of results arises from participants' reactions to subtle cues (DEMAND CHARACTERISTICS) unintentionally given by the experimenter—for example, through body movements, gestures, or facial expressions—and may threaten the ECOLOGICAL VALIDITY of the research. The term is often used synonymously with ROSENTHAL EFFECT.

expert witness an individual who is qualified to testify regarding scientific, technical, or professional matters and provide an opinion concerning the evidence or facts presented in a court of law. Mental health professionals often serve as expert witnesses in such complex issues as insanity pleas and child custody cases.

explant *n.* a small piece of tissue that is isolated from the body and grown in an artificial medium, often for experimental purposes.

explicit attitude measure any procedure for evaluating attitudes in which a person is consciously aware of the fact that his or her attitude toward something or someone is being assessed. Measures of this type are generally DIRECT ATTITUDE MEASURES. Compare IMPLICIT ATTITUDE MEASURE.

explicit memory long-term memory that can be consciously recalled: general knowledge or information about personal experiences that an individual retrieves in response to a specific need or request to do so. This term, proposed in 1985 by Canadian psychologist Peter Graf and U.S. psychologist Daniel Schacter, is used interchangeably with DECLARATIVE MEMORY but typically with a performance-based orientation—that is, a person is aware that he or she possesses certain knowledge and specifically retrieves it to complete successfully a task overtly eliciting that knowledge (e.g., a multiple-choice exam). Compare IMPLICIT MEMORY.

explicit prejudice an unjust negative attitude against a specific social group that is consciously held, even if not expressed publicly. The person is thus aware of and can report on this type of prejudice, typically via questionnaires that require participants to indicate whether they agree or disagree with the statements presented. Compare IMPLICIT PREJUDICE.

explicit process a cognitive event that can be described accurately and that is available to introspection, especially one that involves a defined meaning. Compare IMPLICIT PROCESS.

exploratory behavior the movements made by human beings or other animals in orienting to new environments. A lack of such behavior in a new environment is often used as a measure of fearfulness or emotionality.

exploratory factor analysis one of a set of techniques used in FACTOR ANALYSIS when strong theory is lacking and the observed data are freely explored in search of meaningful patterns among the observations. That is, the data are examined in order to discover the underlying (latent) variables that explain the interrelationships among a larger set of observable (manifest) variables. Compare CONFIRMATORY FACTOR ANALYSIS.

exponential distribution a theoretical distribution of survival times, used in parametric SURVIVAL ANALYSIS when the hazard rate is thought to be constant over time. It is one of the basic distributions useful in psychological research.

exponential function a mathematical expression of the type $y = a^x$, where a is a constant. A particular type has the form $y = e^x$, where e is a fundamental mathematical constant that is the base of natural logarithms (with the value 2.718…).

ex post facto research research that uses existing data collected previously for another purpose or that is conducted following the occurrence of an event of interest. Ex post facto research does not permit the systematic manipulation of variables (i.e, is nonexperimental) but nonetheless is used to identify potential causal relationships. [from Latin *ex post facto*, "after the event"]

exposure therapy a form of BEHAVIOR THERAPY that is effective in treating anxiety disorders. Exposure therapy involves systematic confrontation with a feared stimulus, either in vivo (live) or in the imagination, and may encompass any of a number of behavioral interventions, including DESENSITIZATION, FLOODING, IMPLOSIVE THERAPY, and extinction-based techniques. It works by (a) HABITUATION, in which repeated exposure reduces anxiety over time by a process of EXTINCTION; (b) disconfirming fearful predictions; (c) deeper processing of the feared stimulus; and (d) increasing feelings of SELF-EFFICACY and mastery.

expressed emotion (**EE**) negative attitudes, in the form of criticism, hostility, and emotional overinvolvement, demonstrated by family members toward a person with a mental disorder. High levels of expressed emotion have been shown to be associated with poorer outcomes in mood, anxiety, and schizophrenic disorders and increased likelihood of relapse.

expression *n.* an external manifestation of an internal condition or characteristic. For example, **gene expression** is the process by which the instructions encoded in DNA are used to create observable products, such as proteins (and by extension demonstrable physical attributes, such as hair or eye color). The term, however, is most often used in reference to the communication of a thought, behavior, or emotion, as in EMOTIONAL EXPRESSION or FACIAL EXPRESSION.

expressive aphasia see APHASIA.

expressive language disorder a developmental disorder characterized by impairment in acquiring the ability to use language effectively for communicating with others despite normal language comprehension. Manifestations include below-average vocabulary skills, difficulty producing complete sentences, and problems recalling words.

expressive therapy 1. a form of PSYCHOTHERAPY in which the client is encouraged to talk through his or her problems and to express feelings openly and without restraint. **2.** any of a variety of therapies that rely on nonverbal methods (e.g., art, dance, movement) to facilitate change.

extended care a health care service provided at a residential facility where 24-hour nursing care and rehabilitation therapy are available, usually following an acute hospitalization. A facility that provides such a service is known as an **extended care facility (ECF)**.

extended family 1. a family unit consisting of parents and children living in one household with certain other individuals united by kinship (e.g., grandparents, cousins). **2.** in modern Western societies, the NUCLEAR FAMILY together with various other relatives who live nearby and keep in regular touch.

extended-release preparation see SLOW-RELEASE PREPARATION.

extended-stay review a review of a continuous hospital stay that has equaled or exceeded the period defined by a hospital or third-party UTILIZATION REVIEW. See also CONTINUED-STAY REVIEW.

extended suicide MURDER–SUICIDE in which both the murder and the suicide reflect the suicidal process. The individual first kills those perceived as being a part of his or her identity or extended self and then commits suicide.

extension *n.* the straightening of a joint in a limb (e.g., the elbow joint) so that two parts of the limb (e.g., the forearm and upper arm) are drawn away from each other.

extensional meaning the meaning of a word or phrase as established by a list of the individual instances to which it applies. So, for example, the extensional meaning of *cardinal points of the compass* is "north, south, east, and west." Compare INTENSIONAL MEANING.

extensor a muscle whose contraction extends a part of the body; for example, the triceps muscle group extends, or straightens, the arm. Compare FLEXOR.

external aim see OBJECT OF INSTINCT.

external auditory meatus the canal that conducts sound through the external ear, from the pinna to the tympanic membrane (eardrum). Also called **auditory canal**; **ear canal**.

external capsule a thin layer of myelinated nerve fibers separating the CLAUSTRUM from the PUTAMEN. See also INTERNAL CAPSULE.

external chemical messenger an odorant or other substance that is secreted or released by an organism and influences other organisms. PHEROMONES are examples.

external control see LOCUS OF CONTROL.

external ear the part of the ear consisting of the PINNA, the EXTERNAL AUDITORY MEATUS, and the outer surface of the eardrum (see TYMPANIC MEMBRANE). Also called **outer ear**.

externality effect the tendency of very young infants to direct their attention primarily to the outside of a figure and to spend little time inspecting internal features.

externalization *n.* **1.** a DEFENSE MECHANISM in which one's thoughts, feelings, or perceptions are attributed to the external world and perceived as independent of oneself or one's own experiences. A common expression of this is PROJECTION. **2.** the process of learning to distinguish between the self and the environment during childhood. **3.** the process by which a drive, such as hunger, is aroused by external stimuli, such as food, rather than by internal stimuli.

externalizing–internalizing 1. a broad classification of children's behaviors and disorders based on their reactions to stressors. Externalizing behaviors and disorders are characterized primarily by actions in the external world, such as acting out, antisocial behavior, hostility, and aggression. Internalizing behaviors and disorders are characterized primarily by processes within the self, such as anxiety, SOMATIZATION, and depression. **2.** see EXTERNALIZATION; INTERNALIZATION.

external validity the extent to which the results of research or testing can be generalized beyond the sample that generated the results to other individuals or situations. The more specialized the sample, the less likely it will be that the results are highly generalizable.

exteroception *n.* sensitivity to stimuli that are outside the body, resulting from the response of specialized sensory cells called **exteroceptors** to objects and occurrences in the external environment. Exteroception includes the five senses of sight, smell, hearing, touch, and taste, and exteroceptors thus take a variety of forms (e.g., photoreceptors—retinal rods and cones—for sight; cutaneous receptors—Pacinian corpuscles, Meissner's corpuscles, Merkel's tactile disks—for touch). Compare INTEROCEPTION.

extinction *n.* **1.** in PAVLOVIAN CONDITIONING: (a) a procedure in which pairing of stimulus events is discontinued, either by presenting the CONDITIONED STIMULUS alone or by presenting the conditioned stimulus and the UNCONDITIONED STIMULUS independently of one another; or (b) the result of this procedure, which is a gradual decline in the probability and magni-

tude of the CONDITIONED RESPONSE. **2.** in OPER-
ANT CONDITIONING: (a) a procedure in which
reinforcement is discontinued, that is, the reinforcing stimulus is no longer presented; or (b)
the result of this procedure, which is a decline
in the rate of the formerly reinforced response.
—**extinguish** *vb.*

extirpation *n.* see ABLATION.

extraneous variable a variable that is not
under investigation in an experiment but may
potentially affect the DEPENDENT VARIABLE and
thus influence results.

extrapsychic *adj.* pertaining to that which originates outside the mind or that which occurs between the mind and the environment. Compare
INTRAPSYCHIC.

extrapunitive *adj.* referring to the punishment
of others: tending to direct anger, blame, or hostility away from the self toward the external factors, such as situations and other people,
perceived to be the source of one's frustrations.
Compare INTROPUNITIVE.

extrapyramidal symptoms (**EPS**) a group of
adverse drug reactions attributable to dysfunction of the EXTRAPYRAMIDAL TRACT of the central nervous system, such as rigidity of the limbs,
tremor, and other Parkinson-like signs; dystonia
(abnormal facial and body movements); and
akathisia (restlessness). Extrapyramidal symptoms are among the most common side effects of
the HIGH-POTENCY ANTIPSYCHOTICS.

extrapyramidal tract a motor portion of the
central nervous system that includes the BASAL
GANGLIA and some closely related structures
(e.g., the SUBTHALAMIC NUCLEI) and descending
pathways to the midbrain. It regulates muscle
tone and body posture and coordinates opposing sets of skeletal muscles and movement of
their associated skeletal parts. Also called
extrapyramidal motor system; **extrapyramidal system**.

extrasensory perception (**ESP**) alleged
awareness of external events by other means
than the known sensory channels. It includes
TELEPATHY, CLAIRVOYANCE, PRECOGNITION,
and, more loosely, PSYCHOKINESIS. Despite considerable research, the existence of any of these
modalities remains highly controversial. Also
called **paranormal cognition**. See PARAPSY-
CHOLOGY.

extrastriate cortex see PRESTRIATE CORTEX.

extra sum of squares principle a basic approach for model comparison in the GENERAL
LINEAR MODEL in which the value of an additional parameter in the model is assessed in
terms of the reduction in the SUM OF SQUARES
error that its addition accomplishes.

extraversion (**extroversion**) *n.* one of the elements of the Big Five and FIVE-FACTOR PERSON-
ALITY MODELS, characterized by an orientation
of one's interests and energies toward the outer
world of people and things rather than the inner

world of subjective experience. Extraversion is a
broad personality trait and, like INTROVERSION,
exists on a continuum of attitudes and behaviors. Extroverts are relatively more outgoing,
gregarious, sociable, and openly expressive.
—**extraversive** *adj.* —**extraverted** *adj.* —**extravert** *n.*

extremity of an attitude the extent to which
a person's evaluation of an item deviates from
neutrality. Extremity is related to the STRENGTH
OF AN ATTITUDE.

extrinsic motivation an external incentive to
engage in a specific activity, especially motivation arising from the expectation of punishment
or reward. (e.g., studying to avoid failing an examination). Compare INTRINSIC MOTIVATION.

extrinsic reinforcement provision of a reward for performing an action, such as giving a
child candy for reading. The reward itself is
called an **extrinsic reinforcer**. Some evidence
suggests that extrinsic reinforcement decreases
later involvement in the action unless the reward is given only to induce interest. Compare
INTRINSIC REINFORCEMENT.

extrinsic religion a religious orientation in
which religious practice is largely a means to
other ends, such as social morality or individual
well-being, rather than an end in itself. Compare
INTRINSIC RELIGION.

extroversion *n.* see EXTRAVERSION.

eye *n.* the organ of sight. The human eye has three
layers: (a) the outer **corneoscleral coat**, which includes the transparent CORNEA and the fibrous
SCLERA; (b) the middle layer, called the **uveal
tract**, which includes the IRIS, the CILIARY BODY,
and the CHOROID LAYER; and (c) the innermost
layer, the RETINA, which is sensitive to light. RET-
INAL GANGLION CELLS within the retina communicate with the central nervous system through
the OPTIC NERVE, which leaves the retina at the
OPTIC DISK. The eye also has three chambers.
The **anterior chamber**, between the cornea and
the iris, and the **posterior chamber**, between the
ciliary body, LENS, and posterior aspect of the
iris, are filled with a clear, watery fluid, the **aqueous humor**, and connected by the PUPIL. The
third chamber, the **vitreous body**, is the large
cavity between the lens and the retina filled with
thick, transparent fluid called **vitreous humor**.

eye contact a direct look exchanged between
two people who are interacting. Social-
psychological studies of eye contact generally
find that people typically look more at the other
person when listening to that person than when
they themselves are talking, that they tend to
avoid eye contact when they are embarrassed,
that women are apt to maintain more eye contact than are men, and that the more intimate
the relationship, the greater is the eye contact.
Also called **mutual gaze**.

eye dominance a preference for using one eye
rather than the other, caused mainly by the differential acuity of the two eyes.

eye–hand coordination the integration of visual information-processing skills and appropriate motor responses of the hands in grasping and exploring objects and performing specific tasks.

eyelid conditioning a procedure for studying PAVLOVIAN CONDITIONING in which the UNCONDITIONED STIMULUS (usually an electrical stimulus or a puff of air) elicits an eyeblink.

eye-movement desensitization therapy a treatment methodology used to reduce the emotional impact of trauma-based symptomatology associated with anxiety, nightmares, flashbacks, or intrusive thought processes. The therapy incorporates simultaneous visualization of the traumatic event while concentrating, for example, on the rapid lateral movements of a therapist's finger. Also called **eye-movement desensitization and reprocessing (EMDR)**.

eye movements movements of the eyes caused by contraction of the extrinsic EYE MUSCLES. These include movements that allow or maintain the FIXATION of stationary targets; SMOOTH-PURSUIT MOVEMENTS; VERGENCE movements; and reflexive movements of the eyes, such as the OPTOKINETIC REFLEX and VESTIBULO-OCULAR REFLEX.

eye muscles 1. (extrinsic eye muscles) the muscles that move the eye within the eye socket. There are three pairs: (a) the **superior rectus** and **inferior rectus**, (b) the **lateral rectus** and **medial rectus**, and (c) the **superior oblique** and **inferior oblique. 2. (intrinsic eye muscles)** the muscles that move structures within the eye itself. They include the CILIARY MUSCLES, which alter the shape of the lens during ACCOMMODATION, and the muscles of the IRIS, which change the size of the PUPIL.

eyewitness memory an individual's recollection of an event, often a crime or accident of some kind, that he or she personally saw or experienced. The reliability of eyewitness testimony is a major issue in FORENSIC PSYCHOLOGY, given the existence of such phenomena as the MISINFORMATION EFFECT.

Eysenck Personality Inventory (EPI) a self-report test comprising 57 yes–no questions designed to measure two major personality dimensions: introversion–extraversion and neuroticism. The EPI has been revised and expanded since its initial publication in 1963 to become the **Eysenck Personality Questionnaire (EPQ)**, the most recent version of which (the **EPQ–R**) includes 90 questions and measures the additional personality dimension of psychoticism. [Hans **Eysenck** (1916–1997), German-born British psychologist; Sybil B. G. **Eysenck**, British psychologist]

Ff

fabrication *n.* **1.** the act of concocting or inventing a whole or part of a story, often with the intention to deceive. **2.** a story concocted in this way.

fabulation *n.* random speech that includes the recounting of imaginary incidents by a person who believes these incidents are real. See also DELUSION.

face perception the sum of the sensory, neurological, and cognitive processes involved in the interpretation of FACIAL EXPRESSION and in face recognition. There is much research in this area as faces are extensively represented in different areas of the brain.

face validity apparent validity: the extent to which the items or content of a test or other assessment instrument appear to be appropriate for measuring something, regardless of whether they really are.

facial affect program a hypothetical set of central nervous system structures that accounts for the patterning of universal, basic facial expressions of emotion in humans. Such a program could provide the link between a specific emotion and a given pattern of facial muscular activity.

facial expression a form of nonverbal signaling using the movement of facial muscles. As well as being an integral part of communication, facial expression also reflects an individual's emotional state. Cross-cultural research and studies of blind children indicate that certain facial expressions are spontaneous and universally correlated with such primary emotions as surprise, fear, anger, sadness, and happiness; DISPLAY RULES, however, can modify or even inhibit these expressions.

facial feedback hypothesis the hypothesis that sensory information provided to the brain from facial muscle movements is a major determinant of intrapsychic feeling states, such as fear, anger, joy, contempt, and so on.

facial nerve the seventh CRANIAL NERVE, which innervates facial musculature and some sensory receptors, including those of the external ear and the tongue.

facilitated communication a controversial method of communication in which a person with a severe developmental disability (e.g., AUTISM) is assisted in typing letters, words, phrases, or sentences using a typewriter, computer keyboard, or alphabet facsimile. Facilitated communication involves a graduated manual prompting procedure, with the intent of supporting a person's hand sufficiently to make it more feasible to strike the keys he or she wishes to strike, without influencing the key selection.

facilitation *n.* in neuroscience, the phenomenon in which the threshold for propagation of the action potential of a neuron is lowered due to repeated signals at a SYNAPSE or the SUMMATION of subthreshold impulses. **—facilitate** *vb.*

facilitator *n.* a professionally trained or lay member of a group who fulfills some or all of the functions of a group leader. The facilitator encourages discussion among all group members, without necessarily entering into the discussion.

factitious disorder any of a group of disorders in which the patient intentionally produces or feigns symptoms solely so that he or she may assume the SICK ROLE. It is distinct from MALINGERING, which involves a specific external factor as motivation. See also MUNCHAUSEN SYNDROME.

factor analysis a broad family of mathematical procedures for reducing a set of intercorrelations among MANIFEST VARIABLES to a smaller set of unobserved LATENT VARIABLES (factors). For example, a number of tests of mechanical ability might be intercorrelated to enable factor analysis to reduce them to a few factors, such as fine motor coordination, speed, and attention. This technique is often used to examine the common influences believed to give rise to a set of observed measures (measurement structure) or to reduce a larger set of measures to a smaller set of linear composites for use in subsequent analysis (data reduction).

factorial design an experimental design in which two or more independent variables are simultaneously manipulated or observed in order to study their joint and separate influences on a dependent variable.

factor loading the correlation between a manifest variable and a latent variable (factor) in FACTOR ANALYSIS. The factor loading reflects the degree to which a manifest variable is said to be "made up of" the factor whose loading is being examined.

factor rotation in FACTOR ANALYSIS, the repositioning of factors (latent variables) to a new, more interpretable configuration by a set of mathematically specifiable TRANSFORMATIONS. Rotations can be orthogonal (e.g., varimax, quarimax), in which the rotated factors are uncorrelated, or oblique, in which the rotated factors are correlated.

factor score an estimate of the score that an individual would have on a factor (latent variable) were it possible to measure these directly; the factor is determined through FACTOR ANALYSIS.

factor theory of intelligence any of various theories postulating that intelligence consists of a number of latent variables (factors) that cannot be measured directly but whose existence is proposed as the basis of a mathematical technique called FACTOR ANALYSIS; it is the individual's ability in these factors that underpins his or her test scores. For example, a factor theory of intelligence might hold that underlying scores on the many different tests of intelligence are verbal and nonverbal factors. A variety of **factor theories of personality** also exist, among them CATTELL'S PERSONALITY TRAIT THEORY and the Big Five personality model (see FIVE-FACTOR PERSONALITY MODEL).

factual knowledge knowledge of specific factual items of information. Such knowledge is technically referred to as SEMANTIC KNOWLEDGE.

faculty *n.* see COGNITIVE FACULTY.

fad *n.* an abrupt but short-lived change in the opinions, behaviors, or lifestyles of a large number of widely dispersed individuals. Fads often pertain to relatively trivial matters (e.g., television programs, fashions), and so disappear without leaving any lasting impact on society. Extremely irrational, expensive, or widespread fads are termed **crazes**.

fading *n.* in conditioning, the gradual changing of one stimulus to another, which is often used to transfer STIMULUS CONTROL. Stimuli can be faded out (gradually removed) or faded in (gradually introduced).

failure modes and effects analysis a method of qualitative safety or ACCIDENT ANALYSIS in which the components of a system are listed along with the possible safety consequences that may occur should each of them fail or should the system as a whole go into failure mode.

failure-to-inhibit hypothesis a theory of COGNITIVE AGING that attributes attention and memory problems of older adults to their increasing inability to select relevant information and suppress irrelevant information when performing a cognitive task.

failure to thrive (**FTT**) significantly inadequate gain in weight and height by an infant. It reflects a degree of growth failure due to inadequate release of GROWTH HORMONE and, despite an initial focus on parental neglect and emotional deprivation, is currently believed to have multifactorial etiology, including biological, nutritional, and environmental contributors. The condition is associated with poor long-term developmental, growth, health, and socioemotional outcomes.

fainting *n.* see SYNCOPE.

Fairbairnian theory the psychoanalytic approach of British psychoanalyst W. Ronald D. Fairbairn (1889–1964), which forms a part of OBJECT RELATIONS THEORY. Fairbairn saw personality structure developing in terms of object relationships, rather than in terms of the ID, EGO, and SUPEREGO postulated by Austrian psychoanalyst Sigmund Freud (1856–1939). Fairbairn proposed the existence of an ego at birth, which then splits apart to form the structures of personality. In response to frustrations and excitement experienced in the relationship with the mother, the ego is split into (a) the central ego, which corresponds to Freud's concept of the ego; (b) the libidinal ego, which corresponds to the id; and (c) the antilibidinal ego, which corresponds to the superego.

fairness *n.* the removal from test scores of systematic variance attributable to experiences of racial or cultural socialization. Fundamentally a sociocultural (rather than a technical) issue, fairness is a broad area encompassing quality management in test design, administration, and scoring; adequate coverage of relevant content; sufficient construct validation work; equal learning opportunities and access to testing; and items measuring only the skill or ability under investigation without being unduly influenced by construct-irrelevant variance introduced through test-taker background factors.

faith *n.* unwavering loyalty, belief, and trust. For example, religious faith is belief and trust in a deity or other spiritual force, which usually involves the believer in adherence to a particular religious body and an organized system of ceremonies and doctrines. **—faithful** *adj.*

faith healing 1. the treatment of physical or psychological illness by means of religious practices, such as PRAYER or "laying on of hands." Believers hold that this may be effective even when those being prayed for have no knowledge of the fact and no faith themselves. Also called **faith cure; religious healing; spiritual healing. 2.** any form of unorthodox medical treatment whose efficacy is said to depend upon the patient's faith in the healer or the healing process (see PLACEBO EFFECT). In such cases any beneficial effects may be attributed to a psychosomatic process rather than a paranormal or supernatural one. See also MENTAL HEALING.

faking *n.* the practice of some participants in an evaluation or psychological test who either "fake good" by choosing answers that create a favorable impression or "fake bad" by choosing answers that make them appear disturbed or incompetent. **—fake** *vb.*

falling out a CULTURE-BOUND SYNDROME found in the United States and the Caribbean. Symptoms include sudden collapse, sometimes preceded by feelings of dizziness or "swimming" in the head, and an inability to see, speak, or move.

fallopian tube either of the slender fleshy tubes in mammals that convey ova (egg cells) from each ovary to the uterus and where fertilization may occur. [Gabriele **Fallopius** (1523–1562), Italian anatomist]

false alarm in signal detection tasks, an incorrect observation by the participant that a signal is present in a trial when in fact it is absent. Compare MISS.

false-belief task a type of task used in THEORY-OF-MIND studies in which children must infer that another person does not possess knowledge that they possess. For example, children shown that a candy box contains pennies rather than candy are asked what someone else would expect to find in the box. Children of about 3 or younger would say pennies, whereas older children would correctly reply candy.

false-consensus effect the tendency to assume that one's own opinions, beliefs, attributes, or behaviors are more widely shared than is actually the case. A robustly demonstrated phenomenon, the false-consensus effect is often attributed to a desire to view one's thoughts and actions as appropriate, normal, and correct. Compare FALSE-UNIQUENESS EFFECT.

false dementia a condition that mimics the symptoms of DEMENTIA but is a normal response to certain environmental conditions, such as sensory deprivation, restricted movement, or institutionalization with prolonged medication.

false memory a distorted recollection of an event or, most severely, recollection of an event that never happened at all. False memories are errors of commission, because details, facts, or events come to mind, often vividly, but the remembrances fail to correspond to prior events. Even when people are highly confident that they are remembering "the truth" of the original situation, experimental evidence shows that they can be wrong. For example, one quarter of adults in a particular experiment who were told an untrue story about being lost in a mall as a child—ostensibly obtained from their family members—adopted the belief, sometimes embellishing the reports with vivid sensory detail (e.g., the clothes that the rescuer was wearing). The phenomenon is of particular interest in legal cases, specifically those involving eyewitness memories and **false memory syndrome** (**FMS**), in which adults seem to recover memories of having been physically or sexually abused as children, with such recoveries often occurring during therapy. The label is controversial, as is the evidence for and against recovery of abuse memories; false memory syndrome is not an accepted diagnostic term, and some have suggested using the more neutral phrase RECOVERED MEMORY. Also called **illusory memory**; **paramnesia**; **pseudomemory**.

false negative a case that is incorrectly excluded from a group by the test used to determine inclusion. In diagnostics, for example, a false negative is an individual who, in reality, has a particular condition but whom the diagnostic instrument indicates does not have the condition.

false positive a case that is incorrectly included in a group by the test used to determine inclusion. In diagnostics, for example, a false positive is an individual who, in reality, does not have a particular condition but whom the diagnostic instrument indicates does have the condition.

false pregnancy see PSEUDOCYESIS.

false-uniqueness effect the tendency to underestimate the extent to which others possess the same beliefs and attributes as oneself or engage in the same behaviors, particularly when these characteristics or behaviors are positive or socially desirable. It is often attributed to a desire to view one's thoughts and actions as unusual, arising from personal, internal causes. Compare FALSE-CONSENSUS EFFECT.

falsifiability *n.* the condition of admitting falsification: the logical possibility that an assertion, hypothesis, or theory can be shown to be false by an observation or experiment. The most important properties that make a statement falsifiable in this way are (a) that it makes a prediction about an outcome or a universal claim of the type "All Xs have property Y" and (b) that what is predicted or claimed is observable. Austrian-born British philosopher Karl Popper (1902–1994) argued that falsifiability is an essential characteristic of any genuinely scientific hypothesis. Also called **disconfirmability**; **refutability**. —**falsifiable** *adj.*

familial factor an element or condition in a family, inherited or not, that accounts for a certain disease, disorder, or trait.

familial study a study in which some measure or measures of an attribute or condition (e.g., a disorder, intelligence, suicidal behavior) among people of a known genetic relationship are correlated. The extent to which performance on a given measure varies as a function of genetic similarity is used as an indication of the HERITABILITY of that measure.

familiarity *n.* a form of remembering in which a situation, event, place, person, or the like provokes a subjective feeling of recognition and is therefore believed to be in memory, although it is not specifically recalled. Also called **feeling of familiarity**.

familism *n.* a cultural value common in collectivist or traditional societies that emphasizes strong interpersonal relationships within the EXTENDED FAMILY together with interdependence, collaboration, and the placing of group interests ahead of individual interests. —**familistic** *adj.*

family *n.* **1.** a kinship unit consisting of a group of individuals united by blood or by marital, adoptive, or other intimate ties. Although the family is the fundamental social unit of most human societies, its form and structure vary widely. See EXTENDED FAMILY; NUCLEAR FAMILY; PERMEABLE FAMILY; STEPFAMILY. **2.** in BIOLOGI-

F

CAL TAXONOMY, a main subdivision of an ORDER, consisting of a group of similar, related genera (see GENUS). —**familial** *adj.*

family group psychotherapy therapeutic methods that treat a family as a system rather than concentrating on individual family members. The various approaches include psychodynamic, behavioral, systemic, and structural, but all regard the interpersonal dynamics within the family as more important than individual intrapsychic factors. See also FAMILY THERAPY.

family of origin the family in which an individual was raised, which may or may not be his or her BIOLOGICAL FAMILY.

family pattern a characteristic quality of the relationship between the members of a particular family (e.g., between parents and children). Family patterns vary widely in emotional tone and in the attitudes of the members toward each other. For example, some families are extremely close and symbiotic, whereas in others the members keep each other at a distance; some are open to friends and relatives, others are not. See also PATHOGENIC FAMILY PATTERN.

family psychology a basic and applied specialty in psychology that focuses on interactions within the family and developmentally influential contexts (neighborhood, schools, etc.). Research and clinical intervention in this specialty are taught in doctoral psychology programs, either within a specified family curriculum or more often within broader programs, such as clinical research and applied clinical and counseling programs.

family resemblance in studies of categorization, the idea that a set of instances may form a category or give rise to a concept even though there is no single attribute common to all the instances: It is sufficient that each instance should have one or more attributes in common with one or more other instances. The members of the category that have the most attributes in common with other members are said to have the highest family resemblance. See also DISJUNCTIVE CONCEPT.

family support services partial, periodic, or intermittent services provided to one or more family members of a person with a developmental disability for the purpose of enhancing their ability to care for the person or alleviating stress associated with family living. Examples include day and overnight respite (see RESPITE SERVICES), parent training, behavioral consultation, parent education, transportation to appointments, and sibling services (e.g., counseling).

family systems theory a broad conceptual model underlying various family therapies. Family systems theory focuses on the relationships between and among interacting individuals in the family and combines core concepts from GENERAL SYSTEMS THEORY, CYBERNETIC THEORY, family development theory, OBJECT RELATIONS THEORY, and SOCIAL LEARNING THEORY. Family

systems theory stresses that therapists cannot work only with individual family members to create constructive family changes but must see the whole family to effect systemic and lasting changes. Also called **Bowen family systems theory; family systems model**.

family therapy a form of PSYCHOTHERAPY that focuses on the improvement of interfamilial relationships and behavioral patterns of the family unit as a whole, as well as among individual members and groupings, or subsystems, within the family. Family therapy includes a large number of treatment forms with diverse conceptual principles, processes and structures, and clinical foci. Some family therapy approaches (e.g., OBJECT RELATIONS THEORY) reflect extensions of models of psychotherapy with individuals in the interpersonal realm, whereas others (e.g., STRUCTURAL FAMILY THERAPY) evolved in less traditional contexts. Family therapy potentially allows clinical attention to all levels of the organization of behavior, for example from individual unconscious and conscious dynamics, to the family, and to the community. Family therapy models vary enormously in terms of length, past versus present orientation, techniques used, and treatment goals. See also CONJOINT THERAPY; COUPLES THERAPY; FAMILY GROUP PSYCHOTHERAPY; FAMILY SYSTEMS THEORY.

fan effect the finding that as the number of relations between one concept and others increases, the time required to make a decision about one of those relations increases. For example, if John has one brother and Bill has six, it would take longer to verify that Joe is Bill's brother than it would to verify that Ted is John's brother.

fantasy *n.* **1.** any of a range of mental experiences and processes marked by vivid imagery, intensity of emotion, and relaxation or absence of logic. These experiences may be conscious (thus, under the control of the fantasizing individual) or unconscious to varying degrees. Fantasizing is normal and common and often serves a healthy purpose of releasing tension, giving pleasure and amusement, or stimulating creativity. It can also be indicative of pathology, as in delusional thinking or significant disconnection from reality. **2.** in psychoanalytic theories, a figment of the imagination: a mental image, night DREAM, or DAYDREAM in which a person's conscious or unconscious wishes and impulses are fulfilled (see WISH-FULFILLMENT). —**fantasize** *vb.*

fantasy play pretend or make-believe play that includes an as-if orientation to actions, objects, and peers. It involves taking a stance that is different from reality and using a mental representation of a situation as part of an enactment.

FAP abbreviation for FIXED ACTION PATTERN.

far point the farthest point at which an object can be seen clearly under conditions of relaxed ACCOMMODATION. Compare NEAR POINT.

farsightedness *n.* see HYPEROPIA.

FAS abbreviation for FETAL ALCOHOL SYNDROME.

fascia *n.* (*pl.* **fasciae**) a sheet or band of fibrous tissue covering, separating, or binding together muscles, organs, and other soft-tissue structures of the body. —**fascial** *adj.*

fast mapping the ability of young children to learn new words quickly on the basis of only one or two exposures to these words.

fast muscle fiber a type of muscle fiber found in SKELETAL MUSCLE that contracts rapidly but fatigues readily. Compare SLOW MUSCLE FIBER.

fat *n.* a mixture of lipids, mainly triglycerides, which is typically solid at room temperature. In mammals (including humans) it serves as the most concentrated store of food energy and is deposited primarily beneath the skin and around certain organs.

father surrogate a substitute for a person's biological father, who performs typical paternal functions and serves as an object of identification and attachment. Father surrogates may include such individuals as adoptive fathers, stepfathers, older brothers, teachers, and others. Also called **father figure**; **surrogate father**.

fatigue *n.* **1.** a state of tiredness and diminished functioning. Fatigue is typically a normal, transient response to exertion, stress, boredom, or inadequate sleep but also may be unusually prolonged and indicative of disorder (e.g., chronic fatigue syndrome, anemia, hypothyroidism). **2.** reduced response of a receptor cell or sense organ resulting from excessive stimulation.

fatigue effect a decline in performance on a prolonged or physically demanding research task that is generally attributed to the participant becoming tired or bored with the task.

fatty acid an organic acid with a long, usually unbranched hydrocarbon chain and an even number of carbon atoms. Fatty acids are the fundamental constituents of many important lipids, including triglycerides. Some fatty acids can be synthesized by the body, but others—the **essential fatty acids**, such as linoleic acid—must be obtained from the diet.

fault tree analysis a method of qualitative or quantitative safety or ACCIDENT ANALYSIS in which logic symbols are used to analyze the possible factors contributing to an accident or hazardous system state. The accident or hazardous state forms the "root" of the tree, and the logic symbols representing the possible contributing factors form the "branches."

F distribution a theoretical PROBABILITY DISTRIBUTION widely used in the ANALYSIS OF VARIANCE and other statistical tests of hypotheses about population variances. It is the ratio of the variances of two independent random variables each divided by its DEGREES OF FREEDOM.

fear *n.* an intense emotion aroused by the detection of imminent threat, involving an immediate alarm reaction that mobilizes the organism by triggering a set of physiological changes. These include rapid heartbeat, redirection of blood flow away from the periphery toward the gut, tensing of the muscles, and a general mobilization of the organism to take action (see FEAR RESPONSE; FIGHT OR FLIGHT RESPONSE). According to some theorists, fear differs from ANXIETY in that it has an object (e.g., a predator, financial ruin) and is a proportionate response to the objective threat, whereas anxiety typically lacks an object or is a more intense response than is warranted by the perceived threat. See also FRIGHT.

feared self in analyses of self-concept, a mental representation of psychological attributes that one might possess in the future, in which thoughts about the acquisition of these attributes elicits a sense of anxiety or dread.

fearful attachment an adult attachment style characterized by a negative INTERNAL WORKING MODEL OF ATTACHMENT of oneself and of others. Individuals with fearful attachment doubt both their own and others' competence and efficacy and are presumed not to seek help from others when distressed. Compare DISMISSIVE ATTACHMENT; PREOCCUPIED ATTACHMENT; SECURE ATTACHMENT.

fear of commitment feelings of anxiety and uncertainty related to the decision to become bound to a course of action. Such feelings are commonly aroused by the decision to become emotionally or legally committed to a longstanding relationship with another person and often stem from problems with intimacy and attachment; in an extreme form, fear of commitment may lead to social maladjustment.

fear of failure persistent and irrational anxiety about failing to measure up to the standards and goals set by oneself or others. Fear of failure may be associated with perfectionism and is implicated in a number of psychological disorders, including some ANXIETY DISORDERS and EATING DISORDERS.

fear response a response to a threat in which the threatened organism attempts to guard vulnerable vital organs and to protect the integrity of the self. In addition to these protective functions, the fear response is aimed at removing the person or animal from the threatening situation, either by overt withdrawal or by coping behaviors, such as shutting the eyes to avoid seeing the fear stimulus. Physiological responses vary depending on the situation and the proximity of the threat.

feature *n.* **1.** an attribute of an object or event that plays an important role in distinguishing it from other objects or events and in the formation of category judgments. For example, a particular nose is a feature of one person's face, wings are a feature of the category "bird," line segments of various types are features of letters, and so on. **2.** in phonemics, an attribute of a speech sound that plays a critical role in distinguishing one PHONEME from another. See BINARY FEATURE.

feature abstraction a hypothetical process by

which people learn from their experience with exemplars of different categories which features might be used to define membership in these categories.

feature detector any of various hypothetical or actual mechanisms within the human information-processing system that respond selectively to specific distinguishing features. For example, the visual system has feature detectors for lines and angles of different orientations or even for more complex stimuli, such as faces. Feature detectors are also thought to play an important role in speech perception, where their function would be to detect those BINARY FEATURES that distinguish one PHONEME from another.

feature-integration theory a two-stage theory of visual attention. In the first (preattentive) stage, basic features (e.g., color, shape) are processed automatically, independently, and in parallel. In the second (attentive) stage, other properties, including relations between features of an object, are processed in series, one object (or group) at a time, and "bound" together to create a single object that is perceived.

febrile seizure a seizure arising from a high fever. It is the most common type of seizure in childhood and 20–30% of them have recurrence. Febrile seizure is a benign condition for most children, but experiments with nonhuman animals and neuroimaging studies in humans suggest some febrile seizures may damage the hippocampus.

Fechner's colors illusory sensations of color that arise when a disk with black and white sectors is spun about its axis. The appearance of these subjective colors is widely believed to be governed by local interactions in early, and likely retinal, processing mechanisms. [Gustav Theodor **Fechner** (1801–1887), German physician and philosopher]

Fechner's law a mathematical formula relating subjective experience to changes in physical stimulus intensity: specifically, the sensation experienced is proportional to the logarithm of the stimulus magnitude. It is derived from WEBER'S LAW and expressed as $\Psi = k \log S$, where Ψ is the sensation, k is a constant, and S is the physical intensity of the stimulus. See also STEVENS LAW. [Gustav Theodor **Fechner**]

feeblemindedness *n.* an obsolete name for MENTAL RETARDATION or LEARNING DISABILITY.

feedback *n.* information about a process or interaction provided to the governing system or agent and used to make adjustments that eliminate problems or otherwise optimize functioning. It may be stabilizing NEGATIVE FEEDBACK or amplifying POSITIVE FEEDBACK. The term's origins in engineering and cybernetics lend it a distinct connotation of input–output models that is not as strictly applicable to the wide variety of usages found in psychology, including BIOFEEDBACK. Compare FEEDFORWARD.

feedback loop in CYBERNETIC THEORY, a self-regulatory model that determines whether the current operation of a system is acceptable and, if not, attempts to make the necessary changes. Its operation is summarized by the acronym TOTE (*t*est, *o*perate, *t*est, *e*xit). The two test phases compare the current reality against the goal or standard. Operate refers to any processes or interventions designed to resolve unacceptable discrepancies between the reality and the standard. Exit refers to the closing down of the supervisory feedback loop because the circumstances have been brought into agreement with the standard. Also called **TOTE model**.

feedback system an arrangement in which output information (e.g., biological or mechanical) from a circuit is used to modulate the input to the same circuit. For example, a sensory feedback system is a process in which some output of neuronal circuits returns to the input receptors via the efferent path to modulate its activity and control the system. Although the terms are sometimes used synonymously, feedback system properly denotes the process and FEEDBACK the information involved.

feedforward *n.* **1.** information or control signals sent to a part of the body or other system in order to prepare it for future motor activity or expected sensory input. **2.** information that can be used to forecast the performance of a person, group, product, or system so that adjustments can be made to avoid problems before they occur. Compare FEEDBACK.

feeding and eating disorders of infancy or early childhood a category of disorders characterized by pathological feeding or eating behaviors that are usually first diagnosed in infancy, childhood, or adolescence. They include PICA, RUMINATION DISORDER, and FEEDING DISORDER OF INFANCY OR EARLY CHILDHOOD.

feeding disorder of infancy or early childhood a disorder with an onset before the age of 6 (but typically within the 1st year following birth) characterized by persistent failure to eat adequately that results in significant failure to gain weight or significant loss of weight over a period of 1 month or more. There is no apparent cause.

fee-for-service *adj.* denoting the traditional method of payment for health care services, in which physicians or other providers set their own fees for services, and patients or insurance companies pay all or a percentage of these charges.

feeling *n.* **1.** a self-contained phenomenal experience. Feelings are subjective, evaluative, and independent of the sensory modality of the sensations, thoughts, or images evoking them. They are inevitably evaluated as pleasant or unpleasant but they can have more specific intrapsychic qualities, so that, for example, the AFFECTIVE TONE of fear is experienced as different from that of anger. The core characteristic that differentiates feelings from cognitive, sensory, or perceptual intrapsychic experiences is the link of AFFECT to APPRAISAL. Feelings differ from EMOTIONS in being purely mental, whereas emotions are designed to engage with the world. **2.** any experienced sensation, particularly a tactile or temperature sensation (e.g., pain or coldness).

feeling of knowing a sense of conviction that one possesses certain information despite being unable to retrieve it from memory at a given time. It is a classic experience of FRINGE CONSCIOUSNESS and distinct from the TIP-OF-THE-TONGUE PHENOMENON in that retrieval is not perceived as imminent.

feeling of reality a sense that the world is tangible, which may be lost in mild dissociative conditions (e.g., derealization) and in more serious disorders (e.g., posttraumatic stress disorder, psychosis).

female circumcision see FEMALE GENITAL MUTILATION.

female genital mutilation (**FGM**) any nontherapeutic procedure performed to modify or remove any part of the external genitalia of prepubertal or adolescent girls. It is a traditional practice in certain countries, with the highest prevalence in Africa, and variously associated with cultural norms of femininity, chastity, and religious observance. Female genital mutilation takes one of four forms: excision of the clitoral hood only; excision of the entire clitoris (CLITORIDECTOMY) and often the labia minora; excision of the clitoris, labia minora, and most of the labia majora, and the sewing together of the remaining tissue, leaving only a small vaginal opening (INFIBULATION); and any other injurious procedure, such as incising or burning of the clitoris, cutting of the vagina, and insertion of substances to cause vaginal bleeding. Female genital mutilation is sometimes called **female** (or **clitoral**) **circumcision** and—more recently—**female genital cutting** (**FGC**), terms that downplay its potential adverse medical, psychological, and sexual consequences. These may include (but are not limited to) severe pain, excessive bleeding, infection, gynecological and obstetrical complications, disordered sleeping and eating habits, mood changes, impaired cognition (e.g., poor concentration and difficulty learning), reduced sexual sensitivity, less frequent orgasm, and decreased enjoyment of sexual intercourse.

femaleness *n.* the quality of being female in the anatomical and physiological sense by virtue of possessing the female complement of a pair of X CHROMOSOMES. Compare FEMININITY.

female orgasmic disorder a condition in which a woman recurrently or persistently has difficulty obtaining orgasm or is unable to reach orgasm at all following sexual stimulation and excitement, causing marked distress or interpersonal difficulty. Female orgasmic disorder is the second most frequently reported women's sexual problem. Cognitive behavior therapy has been shown to be an effective treatment and involves promoting attitude and sexually relevant thought changes and anxiety reduction using such exercises as directed masturbation, sensate focus, and systematic desensitization.

female sexual arousal disorder a condition in which a woman recurrently or persistently is unable to attain or maintain adequate vaginal lubrication and swelling during sexual excitement, causing marked distress or interpersonal difficulty. It is a prevalent sexual problem for women and has a complex etiology involving a variety of physiological and psychological factors.

femininity *n.* possession of social-role behaviors that are presumed to be characteristic of a girl or woman, as contrasted with FEMALENESS, which is genetically determined. **—feminine** *adj.*

femininity complex in psychoanalytic theory, a man's envy of women's procreative powers that has its roots in the young boy's envy of the mother's body. Some psychoanalysts see the femininity complex as the male counterpart to the female CASTRATION COMPLEX and PENIS ENVY.

feminist family therapy an intervention model, informed by FEMINIST THERAPY, used by therapists to reorganize the family so that no one is entrapped in dysfunctional roles or patterns of interaction that are based on the politics of power, particularly with regard to patriarchal roles.

feminist psychology an approach to psychological issues that emphasizes the role of the female perspective in thought, action, and emotion in the life of the individual and in society. It is seen by its proponents as an attempt to counterbalance traditional male-oriented and male-dominated psychology, as well as a model for similar approaches for other less represented groups. See also WOMAN-CENTERED PSYCHOLOGY.

feminist therapy an eclectic approach to psychotherapy based conceptually in feminist political analyses and feminist scholarship on the psychology of women and gender. In this orientation, the ways in which gender and gendered experiences inform people's understanding of their lives and the development of the distress that serves as a catalyst for seeking therapy are central. Race, class, sexual orientation, age cohort, and ability, as they interact with gender, are explored. Feminist therapy attempts to empower the client and define the client as an authority equal in value to the therapist. Feminist therapy can be indicated for both female and male clients.

feminization *n.* the process of acquiring FEMININITY, regardless of the sex of the individual. **—feminize** *vb.*

fertility *n.* the potential of an individual to have offspring. Although most frequently applied to females, it may also refer to reproductive capacity in males.

fertilization *n.* the fusion of a sperm and an egg cell to produce a ZYGOTE. In humans, fertilization occurs in a FALLOPIAN TUBE.

fetal age see GESTATIONAL AGE.

fetal alcohol syndrome (FAS) a group of adverse fetal and infant health effects associated with heavy maternal alcohol intake during pregnancy. It is characterized by low birth weight and retarded growth, craniofacial anomalies (e.g., microcephaly), neurobehavioral problems (e.g., hyperactivity), and cognitive abnormalities (e.g., language acquisition deficits); mental retardation may be present. Children showing some (but not all) features of this syndrome are described as having **fetal alcohol effects (FAE)**.

fetal distress the condition of a fetus during late pregnancy or labor whose life or health is threatened, most commonly by an inadequate supply of oxygen via the placenta. Signs of fetal distress include abnormal heart rate, elevated blood acidity, and absence of movement. This term has been criticized as imprecise and nonspecific, and the alternative **nonreassuring fetal status (NRFS)** is recommended by many instead.

fetal tobacco syndrome (FTS) a group of adverse fetal and infant health effects associated with maternal smoking during pregnancy. These include low birth weight, retarded growth, premature labor and preterm delivery, miscarriage, increased risk of sudden infant death syndrome, and neurological damage manifested as developmental delay, intellectual deficits, and behavioral problems.

fetish *n.* **1.** a material object (e.g., a shoe, an undergarment) or nonsexual part of the body (e.g., a foot, lock of hair) that arouses sexual interest or excitement. **2.** any object, idea, or behavior that is the focus of irrational devotion or abnormally excessive attention, for example, punctuality or the pursuit of wealth.

fetishism *n.* a type of PARAPHILIA in which inanimate objects—commonly undergarments, stockings, rubber items, shoes, or boots—are repeatedly or exclusively used in achieving sexual excitement. Fetishism occurs primarily among males and may compete or interfere with sexual contact with a partner. **—fetishistic** *adj.*

fetus *n.* an animal EMBRYO in the later stages of development. In humans, the fetal period is from the end of the eighth week after fertilization until birth. **—fetal** *adj.*

fetus at risk a fetus that has a significant risk of being born with a mental or physical disorder because of known influences from the parents or other family members (e.g., a mother with diabetes or hypertension). The risk of a mental disorder in a child born into a family with no history of mental disorder is relatively small, but the risk may be as much as 50% in certain cases, for example, if the disorder is a SEX-LINKED recessive

trait inherited from the mother's side of the family and the parents are related. See also FETAL DISTRESS.

FFM abbreviation for FIVE-FACTOR PERSONALITY MODEL.

FGM abbreviation for FEMALE GENITAL MUTILATION.

FI abbreviation for fixed interval (see FIXED-INTERVAL SCHEDULE).

fibrillation *n.* a small, local, involuntary muscular contraction due to spontaneous activation of single muscle cells or fibers, especially the rapid, abnormal contraction of individual muscle fibers of the heart.

fibromyalgia syndrome a syndrome of uncertain origin that is characterized by widespread musculoskeletal pain and chronic fatigue. Pain may be triggered by pressure on numerous tender points on the body. Other commonly associated symptoms are muscle stiffness, headaches, sleep disturbance, and depression. Symptoms overlap with those of CHRONIC FATIGUE SYNDROME, and fibromyalgia syndrome often occurs simultaneously with other disorders, such as IRRITABLE BOWEL SYNDROME and migraine.

fiction *n.* **1.** in psychology, an unproven or imaginary concept that may be accepted by an individual as if it were true for pragmatic reasons. See ALS OB; AS-IF HYPOTHESIS. **2.** see GUIDING FICTION. **—fictional** *adj.*

fiduciary *adj.* describing a relationship in which one person holds a position of trust in relation to another and is required to apply his or her skill and effort in the best interests of that other. A psychologist and client have a fiduciary relationship in that the psychologist is assumed to place the welfare and best interests of the client above all else.

field *n.* **1.** a defined area or region of space, such as the VISUAL FIELD. **2.** a complex of personal, physical, and social factors within which a psychological event takes place. See FIELD THEORY. **3.** an area of human activity or knowledge or a division of such an area. **4.** somewhere other than a laboratory, library, or academic setting in which experimental work is carried out or data collected.

field dependence a COGNITIVE STYLE in which the individual consistently relies more on external referents (environmental cues) than on internal referents (bodily sensation cues). The opposite tendency, relying more on internal than external referents, is called **field independence**. Discovered during experiments conducted in the 1950s to understand the factors that determine perception of the upright in space, field dependence–independence typically is measured using the ROD-AND-FRAME TEST.

field research research conducted outside the laboratory, in a natural, real-world setting. Field research has the advantages of ECOLOGICAL VA-

LIDITY and the opportunity to understand how and why behavior occurs in a natural social environment; it has the disadvantages of loss of environmental control and ability to do experimental manipulations.

field theory in psychology, a systematic approach describing behavior in terms of patterns of dynamic interrelationships between individuals and the psychological, social, and physical situation in which they exist. This situation is known as the **field space** or LIFE SPACE, and the dynamic interactions are conceived as forces with positive or negative VALENCES.

field work a less common name for FIELD RESEARCH.

fight-or-flight response a pattern of physiological changes elicited by activity of the SYMPATHETIC NERVOUS SYSTEM in response to threatening or otherwise stressful situations that leads to mobilization of energy for physical activity (e.g., attacking or avoiding the offending stimulus), either directly or by inhibiting physiological activity that does not contribute to energy mobilization. Specific sympathetic responses involved in the reaction include increased heart rate, respiratory rate, and sweat gland activity; elevated blood pressure; decreased digestive activity; pupil dilation; and a routing of blood flow to skeletal muscles.

figural cohesion the tendency for parts of a figure to be perceived as a whole figure even if the parts are disjointed.

figurative knowledge knowledge about static things, acquired by attending to and remembering specific factual information or perceptual details (e.g., vocabulary words, dates, colors, shapes). Compare OPERATIVE KNOWLEDGE.

figure–ground *adj.* relating to the principle that perceptions have two parts: a figure that stands out in good contour and an indistinct, homogeneous background.

file-drawer problem the fact that a large proportion of all studies actually conducted are not available for review because they remain unpublished in "file drawers," having failed to obtain positive results.

filopodium *n.* (*pl.* **filopodia**) a very fine, tubular outgrowth from a cell.

filter *n.* **1.** a device or material that allows some elements of a mixture (e.g., of light, a liquid, or a gas) to pass through but not others. In acoustics, for example, a **low-pass filter** passes low frequencies but not high, thus altering the spectral composition of its input, while a **high-pass filter** does the opposite. A **bandpass filter** is even more restrictive, only passing the small range of frequencies within its **passband. 2.** a hypothetical construct applied to cognitive channels of information that allow only certain aspects of a stimulus to pass into sensory consciousness. Filters are often used in discussions of attention to ex-

plain the ability to focus selectively on aspects of the environment (e.g., a conversation in a noisy room).

filter theory an early theory of attention proposing that unattended channels of information are filtered prior to identification. This theory continues to be influential in the form of its successor, the ATTENUATION THEORY.

fine motor describing activities or skills that require coordination of small muscles to control small, precise movements, particularly in the hands and face. Examples of **fine motor skills** include handwriting, drawing, cutting, and manipulating small objects. Compare GROSS MOTOR.

fingerspelling *n.* the representation of the letters of the alphabet by shapes formed with the hand. Fingerspelling is used in conjunction with SIGN LANGUAGE to spell names and other words for which conventional signs do not exist. Many different manual alphabets exist, including the **American Manual Alphabet** and the **International Manual Alphabet**, each specifying distinct shapes for the different letters.

finite-state grammar a simple model of GENERATIVE GRAMMAR in which it is supposed that the grammar generates sentences one unit at a time in strict linear sequence (i.e., working from left to right); once the first unit has been selected, the choice of subsequent units will be circumscribed at each stage by the sum of the previous choices. U.S. linguist Noam Chomsky (1928–) presented this model, with its obvious inadequacy as an account of sentence generation, to demonstrate the need for the more complex explanations provided by PHRASE-STRUCTURE GRAMMAR and (especially) by TRANSFORMATIONAL GENERATIVE GRAMMAR. Psychological interest in finite-state grammar stems largely from its similarity to certain principles of BEHAVIORISM and OPERATIONALISM.

first-generation antipsychotic see ANTI-PSYCHOTIC.

first impression one's initial perception of another person, typically involving a positive or negative evaluation as well as a sense of physical and psychological characteristics. Such impressions are based on the earliest information received about a person and tend to persist, even in the face of later information that outside observers would consider inconsistent with the initial perception. That is, there is a PRIMACY EFFECT in the impression formation.

first-line medication a drug that is the first choice for treating a particular condition, because it is considered a very effective treatment for that condition with the least likelihood of causing side effects.

first-rank symptoms symptoms originally proposed by German psychiatrist Kurt Schneider (1887–1967) for the differential diagnosis of schizophrenia. They are audible thoughts; hearing voices arguing or commenting on one's ac-

F

tions; thought withdrawal, diffusion, and other disturbances; delusional perceptions; somatic passivity (experiencing external forces as influencing or controlling one's body); and other external impositions on feelings, inputs, and actions. It is now known that these symptoms can also occur in other psychotic disorders, in mood disorders, and in neurological disorders.

Fisher's exact test a statistical test giving the exact probability of departure from chance for data in a fourfold (2 × 2) CONTINGENCY TABLE. [Sir Ronald Aylmer **Fisher** (1890–1962), British statistician and geneticist]

Fisher's r to Z transformation a mathematical transformation of the PRODUCT–MOMENT CORRELATION coefficient (r) to a new statistic (Z) whose sampling distribution is the normal distribution. It is used for testing hypotheses about correlations and constructing CONFIDENCE INTERVALS on correlations. [Sir Ronald Aylmer **Fisher**]

fissure *n.* a cleft, groove, or indentation in a surface, especially any of the deep grooves in the cerebral cortex. See also SULCUS.

fistula *n.* an abnormal passageway between two internal organs or between an internal organ and the outside of the body. A fistula may develop as a result of an injury or infection, as a congenital defect, or as a result of a surgical procedure.

fit *n.* the degree to which values predicted by a model correspond with empirically observed values.

fitness *n.* **1.** a set of attributes that people have or are able to achieve relating to their ability to perform physical work and to carry out daily tasks with vigor and alertness, without undue fatigue, and with ample energy to enjoy leisure pursuits. **2.** in biology, the extent to which an organism or population is able to produce viable offspring in a given environment, which is a measure of that organism's or population's adaptation to that environment. See also INCLUSIVE FITNESS. —**fit** *adj.*

Fitts law the principle of motor control that activities that are performed more quickly tend to be done less accurately (see SPEED–ACCURACY TRADEOFF). It is formulated as MT = $a + b$ f(DW), observed under a wide array of conditions to relate movement time (MT) linearly to a function f(DW) of the ratio of movement distance (D) and target size (W). [Paul Morris **Fitts** (1912–1965), U.S. psychologist]

five-factor personality model (FFM) a model of personality in which five dimensions of individual difference—EXTRAVERSION, NEUROTICISM, CONSCIENTIOUSNESS, AGREEABLENESS, and OPENNESS TO EXPERIENCE—are viewed as core personality structures. Unlike the **Big Five personality model**, which views the five personality dimensions as descriptions of behavior and treats the five-dimensional structure as a taxonomy of individual differences, the FFM also

views the factors as psychological entities with causal force. The two models are frequently and incorrectly conflated in the scientific literature, without regard for their distinctly different emphases.

five-to-seven shift the striking progress in children's cognitive development between the ages of 5 and 7, when very significant advances in such areas as reasoning and logic, linguistic ability, memory, and problem solving occur.

fixation *n.* **1.** an obsessive preoccupation with a single idea, impulse, or aim, as in an IDÉE FIXE. **2.** in psychoanalytic theory, the persistence of an early psychosexual stage (see PSYCHOSEXUAL DEVELOPMENT) or inappropriate attachment to an early psychosexual object or mode of gratification, such as anal or oral activity. **3.** a shortened name for VISUAL FIXATION. —**fixate** *vb.*

fixed action pattern (FAP) in classical ethology, a stereotyped, genetically preprogrammed, species-specific behavioral sequence that is evoked by a RELEASER stimulus and is carried out without sensory feedback. In contemporary ethology the term MODAL ACTION PATTERN is more often used.

fixed-effects model a statistical procedure for analyzing data from experimental designs that use **fixed factors**, independent variables whose levels are specifically selected by the researcher for study rather than randomly chosen from a wide range of possible values. For example, a researcher may wish to investigate the effects of the available dosages of a certain drug on symptom alleviation. Fixed-effects models generally are intended to make inferences solely about the specific levels of the independent variables actually used in the experiment. See also MIXED-EFFECTS MODEL; RANDOM-EFFECTS MODEL.

fixed idea see IDÉE FIXE.

fixed-interval schedule (FI schedule) in conditioning, an arrangement in which the first response after a set interval has elapsed is reinforced. "FI 3 min" means that reinforcement is given to the first response occurring at least 3 min after a previous reinforcement. Often, experience with FI schedules results in a temporal pattern of responding, characterized by little or no responding at the beginning of the interval, followed by an increased rate later on as reinforcement becomes more imminent. This pattern is often referred to as the **fixed-interval scallop**.

fixed-ratio schedule (FR schedule) in conditioning, an arrangement in which reinforcement is given after a specified number of responses. "FR 1" means that reinforcement is given after each response; "FR 50" means that reinforcement is given after 50 responses.

fixed-time schedule (FT schedule) in conditioning, an arrangement in which each reinforcer is delivered at fixed time intervals independent of the organism's behavior.

flaccid paralysis a condition resulting from damage to lower MOTOR NEURONS and marked by loss of muscle tone and absence of TENDON REFLEXES. Compare SPASTIC PARALYSIS.

flashback *n.* **1.** the reliving of a traumatic event after the initial adjustment to the trauma appears to have been made. Flashbacks are part of POSTTRAUMATIC STRESS DISORDER: Forgotten memories are reawakened by words, sounds, smells, or scenes that are reminiscent of the original trauma (e.g., when a backfiring car elicits the kind of anxiety that a combat veteran experienced when he or she was the target of enemy fire). **2.** the spontaneous recurrence of the perceptual distortions and disorientation to time and place experienced during a previous period of hallucinogen intoxication. Flashbacks may occur months or even years after the last use of the drug and are associated particularly with LSD.

flashbulb memory a vivid, enduring memory associated with a personally significant and emotional event. Such memories have the quality of a photograph taken the moment the individual experienced the emotion, including such details as where the individual was or what he or she was doing.

flat affect total or near absence of appropriate emotional responses to situations and events. See also SHALLOW AFFECT.

flavor *n.* a sensation produced by a combination of aroma, taste, texture, and temperature and involving olfactory, gustatory, and tactile sense organs.

flexion *n.* the bending of a joint in a limb (e.g., the elbow joint) so that two parts of the limb (e.g., the forearm and upper arm) are brought toward each other.

flexor *n.* a muscle whose contraction bends a part of the body, such as the biceps muscle of the upper arm. Compare EXTENSOR.

flicker fusion frequency see CRITICAL FLICKER FREQUENCY.

flight from reality a defensive reaction involving withdrawal into inactivity, detachment, or fantasy as an unconscious defense against anxiety-provoking situations. This may be expressed as a number of defensive behaviors, such as RATIONALIZATION, daydreaming, or substance abuse. It may include a retreat into psychotic behavior as a means of avoiding real or imagined problems.

flight into fantasy a defensive reaction in which individuals experiencing disturbing thoughts and impulses retreat into fantasy (e.g., through DAYDREAMS) as a means of avoiding harming themselves or others by acting on these impulses. In this way they can maintain control over their impulses.

flight into health in psychotherapy, an abrupt "recuperation" by a prospective client after or during intake interviews and before entry into therapy proper or, more commonly, by a client in ongoing therapy in order to avoid further confrontation with cognitive, emotional, or behavioral problems. Psychoanalytic theory interprets the flight into health as an unconscious DEFENSE MECHANISM. Also called **transference cure**; **transference remission**.

flight into illness 1. a tendency to focus on or exaggerate minor physical complaints as an unconscious means of avoiding stressful situations and feelings. **2.** in psychotherapy, the sudden development of neurotic or physical symptoms by a client or prospective client. Psychoanalytic theory interprets this as an unconscious DEFENSE MECHANISM that is used to avoid examination of a deeper underlying conflict. Also called **flight into disease**.

flight into reality a defensive reaction in which an individual becomes overinvolved in activity and work as an unconscious means of avoiding threatening situations or painful thoughts and feelings.

flight of colors a succession of colored AFTERIMAGES seen following exposure to a brief intense flash of light in a dark environment.

flight of ideas a rapid, continuous succession of superficially related thoughts and ideas, manifest as hurried speech with frequent abrupt shifts in topic. A common symptom of a MANIC EPISODE, such disturbed thinking occasionally is seen in other disorders as well, including schizophrenia.

flooding *n.* a BEHAVIOR-THERAPY technique in which the individual is exposed directly to a maximum-intensity anxiety-producing situation or stimulus, either in the imagination (see IMAGINAL FLOODING) or in reality (see IN VIVO DESENSITIZATION). Flooding techniques aim to diminish or extinguish the undesired behavior and are used, for example, in the treatment of individuals with phobias. See also IMPLOSIVE THERAPY. Compare SYSTEMATIC DESENSITIZATION.

floor effect a situation in which a large proportion of participants perform as poorly as, or nearly as poorly as, possible on a task or other evaluative measure, this skewing the distribution of scores and making it impossible to discriminate differences among the many individuals at that low level. For example, a test whose items are too difficult for those taking it would show a floor effect because most people would obtain or be close to the lowest possible score of 0. Compare CEILING EFFECT.

flourishing *n.* a condition denoting good mental and physical health: the state of being free from illness and distress but, more important, of being filled with vitality and functioning well in one's personal and social life. Compare LANGUISHING. **—flourish** *vb.*

flow *n.* a state of optimal experience arising from intense involvement in an activity that is enjoyable, such as playing a sport, performing a musical passage, or writing a creative piece. Flow arises when one's skills are fully utilized yet equal to the demands of the task, intrinsic motivation is at a peak, one loses self-consciousness and temporal awareness, and one has a sense of total control, effortlessness, and complete concentration on the immediate situation (the here and now).

fluctuating asymmetry the degree to which the symmetry of body parts of individuals varies from the norm for a given species. This provides information to others about the relative health or well-being of an individual and thus is an important cue in mate-selection decisions.

fluent aphasia see APHASIA.

fluid–crystallized intelligence theory an occasional synonym of CATTELL–HORN THEORY OF INTELLIGENCE.

fluid intelligence (**fluid ability**) see CATTELL–HORN THEORY OF INTELLIGENCE.

fluoxetine *n.* an antidepressant that is the prototype of the SSRIS (selective serotonin reuptake inhibitors). Fluoxetine differs from other SSRIs in that it and its biologically active metabolic product, norfluoxetine, have a prolonged HALF-LIFE of 5–7 days after a single dose. U.S. trade name: **Prozac**.

flutter *n.* see ROUGHNESS.

Flynn effect the gradual cross-cultural rise in raw scores obtained on measures of general intelligence. These increases have been roughly 9 points per generation (i.e., 30 years). [James **Flynn** (1934–   ), New Zealand philosopher who first documented its occurrence]

fMRI abbreviation for FUNCTIONAL MAGNETIC RESONANCE IMAGING.

focal attention consciously directed attention: active concentration on particular stimuli to the exclusion of others, especially for the purpose of comprehension or memorization. Information that is within one's ATTENTION SPAN is said to be in focal attention.

focal psychotherapy SHORT-TERM THERAPY aimed at the relief of a single symptom, such as a phobic anxiety or feelings of guilt, and not involving a DEPTH THERAPY approach.

focal seizure see PARTIAL SEIZURE.

focused analysis a modification of orthodox psychoanalysis in which interpretations are focused on a specific area of the patient's problem or pathology (e.g., a particular symptom, a particular aspect of the TRANSFERENCE). Also called **directed analysis**; **focal therapy**. Compare EXPECTANT ANALYSIS.

focus group a small group of people who share common characteristics and are selected to discuss a topic of which they have personal experience. Originally used in marketing to determine consumer response to particular products, focus groups are now used for determining typical re-actions, adaptations, and solutions to any number of issues, events, or topics.

focusing *n.* in EXPERIENTIAL PSYCHOTHERAPY, a process in which the therapist guides a client to focus silently on his or her body-centered experience of a problem or symptom in a relaxed and nonjudgmental way, often with eyes closed. The client then invites his or her mind to explore intuitively what the issue is about, without attempting to analyze or control thought processes. The method is believed to lead the client to deeper feelings and greater insight about and peace with the problem or symptom.

folie à deux see SHARED PSYCHOTIC DISORDER. [French, "double insanity"]

folklore *n.* the body of beliefs, legends, tales, songs, and other traditions transmitted orally from generation to generation in a specific culture.

folk psychology 1. the everyday, commonsense, implicit knowledge that enables the prediction or explanation of the behavior of others (and of oneself) by reference to the mental states involved. Although such an understanding is accepted in much of social and personality psychology, there are those who view it as illusory or mythological and hold its tenets unworthy of scientific consideration. See also COMMONSENSE PSYCHOLOGY; POPULAR PSYCHOLOGY. **2.** an obsolete name for a branch of psychology that deals with the influence of specific cultural experiences (e.g., legends, religious rituals, indigenous healing practices, etc.) on human behavior and psychological constructs. It is essentially equivalent to modern CROSS-CULTURAL PSYCHOLOGY. **3.** a branch of the psychological system of German psychologist and physiologist Wilhelm Wundt (1832–1920), who believed that an understanding of higher mental processes could be deduced from the study of such cultural products as language, history, myths, art, government, and customs. As such, it is the historical predecessor to modern CULTURAL PSYCHOLOGY.

follicle *n.* a cluster of cells enclosing, protecting, and nourishing a cell or structure within. **—follicular** *adj.*

follicle-stimulating hormone (**FSH**) a GONADOTROPIN released by the anterior pituitary gland that, in females, stimulates the development in the ovary of GRAAFIAN FOLLICLES (see MENSTRUAL CYCLE). The same hormone in males stimulates Sertoli cells in the testis to produce spermatozoa. Also called **follitropin**.

follow-up study a long-term study designed to examine the degree to which effects seen shortly after the imposition of a therapeutic intervention persist over time.

fontanel (**fontanelle**) *n.* a soft, membrane-covered area in the incompletely ossified skull of a newborn infant. Fontanels typically close before the 2nd year of life, as the skull bones gradually fuse. Also called **soft spot**.

food faddism any dietary practice based on exaggerated and often incorrect beliefs about the effects of food or nutrition on health, particularly for the prevention or cure of illness. This is often expressed as strange or inappropriate eating habits and the adoption of cult diets; it may lead to unhealthy weight loss or side effects arising from poor nutrition. It is sometimes associated with eating disorders, such as ANOREXIA NERVOSA.

foot-in-the-door technique a two-step procedure for enhancing compliance in which a minor initial request is presented immediately before the more substantial target request. Agreement to the initial request makes people more likely to agree to the target request than would have been the case if the latter had been presented on its own. See also DOOR-IN-THE-FACE TECHNIQUE; LOW-BALL TECHNIQUE; THAT'S-NOT-ALL TECHNIQUE.

foramen *n.* (*pl.* **foramina**) an anatomical opening or hole, particularly in a bone. For example, the **foramen magnum** is a large opening at the base of the skull through which the spinal cord passes.

forced-choice *adj.* describing any procedural format or assessment instrument in which participants are provided with a predetermined set of alternatives from which they must choose a response. For example, a forced-choice test in signal detection tasks is a test in which two or more intervals are presented, one of which contains the signal. The observer must choose the interval in which the signal was presented. Compare FREE-RESPONSE.

forced compliance effect the tendency of a person who has behaved in a way that contradicts his or her attitude to subsequently alter the attitude to be consistent with the behavior. It is one way of reducing COGNITIVE DISSONANCE. Also called **induced compliance effect**.

forced distribution a rating system in which raters must use a prescribed number of entries for each level of the rating scale used. For example, in employee evaluation it might be required that 5% of employees are categorized as poor, 15% as below average, 60% as average, 15% as above average, and 5% as excellent.

forced treatment therapy administered to an individual with a mental disorder without his or her INFORMED CONSENT, for example, court-ordered administration of psychotropic drugs to a person to restore his or her competency to stand trial or the INVOLUNTARY HOSPITALIZATION of a person considered dangerous to him or herself or others. Many question the ethical acceptability of the practice, citing its infringement of autonomy and the RIGHT TO REFUSE TREATMENT and its lack of scientifically demonstrated effectiveness, with such controversy intensifying in recent decades. Also called **coercive treatment**.

forebrain *n.* the part of the brain that develops from the anterior section of the NEURAL TUBE in the embryo, containing the TELENCEPHALON and the DIENCEPHALON. The former comprises the cerebral hemispheres with their various regions (e.g., BASAL GANGLIA, AMYGDALA, HIPPOCAMPUS); the latter comprises the THALAMUS and HYPOTHALAMUS. Also called **prosencephalon**.

foreclosure *n.* in development, commitment to an IDENTITY, which typically occurs during adolescence. See IDENTITY FORECLOSURE.

foreground–background in perception, the distinction between the object of attention, which is foreground, and details in the background, which are less likely to receive individual attention.

foregrounding *n.* the process or technique of highlighting certain aspects of a complex stimulus to make them the focus of attention. Foregrounding occurs, for example, when a speaker or writer gives prominence to some elements in a communication rather than others, usually by a combination of word order, sentence construction, and more explicit pointers. DISCOURSE ANALYSIS is much concerned with the ways in which speakers and writers tend unconsciously to foreground certain categories of information (see GIVEN–NEW DISTINCTION).

forensic assessment systematic evaluation by a mental health practitioner of a defendant, witness, or offender for the purpose of informing the court about such issues as COMPETENCY TO STAND TRIAL, CRIMINAL RESPONSIBILITY, and RISK ASSESSMENT.

forensic neuropsychology the application of CLINICAL NEUROPSYCHOLOGY to issues of both civil and criminal law, particularly those relating to claims of brain injury.

forensic psychiatry the branch of psychiatry concerned with abnormal behavior and mental disorders as they relate to legal issues. Major areas of concern include insanity pleas, procedures to commit individuals to mental hospitals, and questions of CRIMINAL RESPONSIBILITY, COMPETENCY TO STAND TRIAL, and GUARDIANSHIP.

forensic psychology the application of psychological principles and techniques to situations involving the civil and criminal legal systems. Its functions include assessment and treatment services, provision of ADVOCACY and expert testimony, and research and policy analysis.

foreperiod *n.* in reaction-time experiments, the pause between the ready signal and the presentation of the stimulus.

forethought *n.* the ability of an individual to anticipate the consequences of his or her actions and the actions of others. In SOCIAL-COGNITIVE THEORY, forethought is a key element in learning behavior.

forgetting *n.* the failure to remember material

previously learned. Numerous processes and theories have been proposed throughout its long history of study to account for forgetting, including DECAY THEORY and INTERFERENCE THEORY. Forgetting typically is a normal phenomenon that plays an important adaptive role in restricting access to information that is likely to be needed in current interactions with the environment, but may also be pathological, as, for example, in amnesia.

forgiveness *n.* willfully putting aside feelings of resentment toward an individual who has committed a wrong, been unfair or hurtful, or otherwise harmed one in some way. Forgiveness is not equated with reconciliation or excusing another, and it is not merely accepting what happened or ceasing to be angry. Rather, it involves a voluntary transformation of one's feelings, attitudes, and behavior toward the individual, so that one is no longer dominated by resentment and can express compassion, generosity, or the like toward the individual. Forgiveness is often considered an important process in psychotherapy or counseling.

formal grammar a description of language in terms of its form and structure as opposed to its function and meaning. Compare FUNCTIONAL GRAMMAR.

formal operational stage the fourth and final stage in the PIAGETIAN THEORY of cognitive development, beginning around age 12, during which complex intellectual functions, such as abstract thinking, logical processes, conceptualization, and judgment, develop.

formal thought disorder disruptions in the form or structure of thinking. Examples include DERAILMENT and TANGENTIALITY. It is distinct from THOUGHT DISORDER, in which the disturbance relates to thought content.

formative tendency the general drive toward self-improvement, growth, and SELF-ACTUALIZATION hypothesized in CLIENT-CENTERED THERAPY.

formboard test a type of performance test in which the individual fits blocks or cut-outs of various shapes into depressions in a board.

form perception the process by which the component elements of an object are bound together into a coherent entity that stands apart from the background and from other objects.

form quality the emergent character of a GESTALT, or whole, that makes it recognizable even after transformations. For example, a musical chord remains recognizable even after being transposed to a different key.

fornix *n.* (*pl.* **fornices**) any arch-shaped structure, especially the long tract of white matter in the brain arching between the HIPPOCAMPUS and the HYPOTHALAMUS, projecting chiefly to the MAMMILLARY BODIES.

forward association the formation of an associative link between one item and an item that follows it in a series or sequence. Compare BACKWARD ASSOCIATION.

forward conditioning in PAVLOVIAN CONDITIONING, the PAIRING of two stimuli such that the conditioned stimulus is presented before the unconditioned stimulus. Also called **forward pairing**. Compare BACKWARD CONDITIONING.

forward masking see MASKING.

forward selection a technique used in creating MULTIPLE REGRESSION models in which independent variables are added to the REGRESSION EQUATION in the order of their predictive power until a preset criterion is reached. Also called **forward stepwise regression**.

fossa *n.* (*pl.* **fossae**) a hollow or depressed area, for example, the **anterior cranial fossa**, **middle cranial fossa**, and **posterior cranial fossa** in the base of the cranium for the lobes of the brain.

foster care temporary care provided to children in settings outside their family of origin and by individuals other than their natural or adoptive parents, under the supervision of a public child welfare agency. Foster care is intended to keep children whose parents are unavailable or incapable of proper care safe from harm, with the ultimate goal being to find a secure and permanent home. Typically, a child is placed with a family approved for foster care and paid a fee for such by a public child welfare agency. Although these **foster home** arrangements are most common, children may also be placed in group homes or other institutions. See also ADULT FOSTER CARE.

four-card problem see WASON SELECTION TASK.

Fourier analysis the mathematical analysis of complex waveforms using the fact that they can be expressed as an infinite sum of sine and cosine functions (a **Fourier series**). It is accomplished via a **Fourier transform**, a mathematical operation that analyzes any waveform into a set of simple waveforms with different frequencies and amplitudes. Fourier analysis is particularly important in the study of sound and the theoretical understanding of visual analysis. [Jean Baptiste Joseph **Fourier** (1768–1830), French mathematician and physicist]

fovea centralis a small depression in the central portion of the retina in which RETINAL CONE cells are most concentrated and an image is focused most clearly. Also called **fovea**. —**foveal** *adj.*

FR abbreviation for fixed ratio (see FIXED-RATIO SCHEDULE).

fractionation *n.* a psychophysical procedure to scale the magnitude of sensations in which an observer adjusts a variable stimulus to be half that of a standard stimulus.

fragile X syndrome a genetic condition that differentially affects males and causes a range of developmental problems including learning disabilities and mental retardation. The disorder is so named because of alterations in the *FMR1* gene, on the arm of the X chromosome, that abnormally expand and destabilize it. Males with fragile X syndrome have characteristic physical features that become more apparent with age, such as large ears, prominent jaw and forehead, a long and narrow face, and enlarged testicles. Both males and females with fragile X may exhibit hyperactivity and attention deficits, while some males also show autistic behavior.

fragmentary delusion a disorganized, undeveloped DELUSION or a series of disconnected delusions that is inconsistent and illogical. Also called **unsystematized delusion**. Compare SYSTEMATIZED DELUSION.

fragmentation *n.* division or separation into pieces or fragments. For example, fragmentation of thinking (typically termed LOOSENING OF ASSOCIATIONS) is a disturbance in which thoughts become disjointed to such an extent as to no longer be unified, complete, or coherent; fragmentation of personality (typically termed **personality disintegration**) occurs when an individual no longer presents a unified, predictable set of beliefs, attitudes, traits, and behavioral responses.

frame of reference in social psychology, the set of assumptions or criteria by which a person judges ideas, actions, and experiences. A frame of reference can often limit or distort perception, as in the case of prejudice and stereotypes.

framing *n.* the process of defining the context or issues surrounding a question, problem, or event in a way that serves to influence how the context or issues are perceived and evaluated. Also called **framing effect**. See also REFRAMING.

fraternal twins see DIZYGOTIC TWINS.

F ratio (symbol: *F*) in an ANALYSIS OF VARIANCE or a MULTIVARIATE ANALYSIS OF VARIANCE, the ratio of explained to unexplained variance; that is, the ratio of BETWEEN-GROUPS VARIANCE to WITHIN-GROUP VARIANCE. Also called **F statistic**; **F value**.

free association a basic process in PSYCHOANALYSIS and other forms of PSYCHODYNAMIC PSYCHOTHERAPY, in which the patient is encouraged to verbalize freely whatever thoughts come to mind, no matter how embarrassing, illogical, or irrelevant, without censorship or selection by the therapist. The object is to allow unconscious material, such as traumatic experiences or threatening impulses, and otherwise inhibited thoughts and emotions to come to the surface where they can be interpreted. See BASIC RULE; VERBALIZATION.

freedom to withdraw the right of a research participant to drop out of an experiment at any time.

free energy in psychoanalytic theory, PSYCHIC ENERGY that is located in the ID, is mobile, and is associated with PRIMARY PROCESSES. Compare BOUND ENERGY.

free-floating anxiety a diffuse, chronic sense

of uneasiness and apprehension not directed toward any specific situation or object. It may be a characteristic of a number of anxiety disorders, in particular GENERALIZED ANXIETY DISORDER.

free-floating attention in psychoanalysis and in other forms of psychodynamic psychotherapy, the analyst's or therapist's state of evenly suspended attention during the therapeutic session. This attention does not focus on any one thing the client says, but allows the analyst or therapist to listen to all the material being presented and tune into the client's affects and unconscious ideas. Also called **evenly hovering attention**.

free-floating emotion a diffuse, generalized emotional state that does not appear to be associated with any specific cause. A common example is FREE-FLOATING ANXIETY.

free nerve ending a highly branched terminal portion of a sensory neuron. Found particularly in the different layers of skin, free nerve endings are the most common type of nerve ending and act as pain and temperature receptors.

free operant a response to a situation that may occur freely at any time. See OPERANT CONDITIONING.

free play spontaneous, unstructured play that is not controlled or directed by an adult. The various activities of a child at a playground provide an example. Compare STRUCTURED PLAY.

free recall a type of memory task in which a list of items is presented one at a time and participants attempt to remember them in any order.

free-response *adj.* describing any procedural format or assessment instrument in which participants construct their own responses to items rather than choosing from a list of alternatives as in FORCED-CHOICE techniques. An essay test is an example of a free-response method.

free-running rhythm a cycle of behavior or physiological activity that occurs if external stimuli do not provide ENTRAINMENT.

free will the power or capacity of a human being for self-direction. The function of the WILL is to be inclined or disposed toward an idea or action. The concept of free will thus suggests that inclinations, dispositions, thoughts, and actions are not determined entirely by forces over which people have no independent directing influence. Free will is generally seen as necessary for moral action and responsibility and is implied by much of our everyday experience, in which we are conscious of having the power to do or forbear (see PARADOX OF FREEDOM). However, it has often been dismissed as illusory by advocates of DETERMINISM, who hold that all occurrences, including human actions, are predetermined. See also AGENCY; VOLITION.

frenzy *n.* a temporary state of wild excitement and mental agitation, at times including violent behavior. It has been associated with MANIA and is sometimes considered synonymous with this term.

frequency *n.* the number of repetitions of a periodic waveform in a given unit of time. The standard measure of frequency is the hertz (Hz); this replaces, and is equivalent to, cycles per second (cps).

frequency discrimination see AUDITORY DISCRIMINATION.

frequency distribution a plot of the frequency of occurrence of scores of various sizes, arranged from lowest to highest score.

frequency judgment a participant's judgment of how many times a particular stimulus was presented during a test. Such judgments are used in research on memory and sensory thresholds. See also WORD-FREQUENCY STUDY.

frequency selectivity the property of a system that enables it to be "tuned" to respond better to certain frequencies than to others. The frequency selectivity of the auditory system is a fundamental aspect of hearing and has been a major research theme for many decades. See AUDITORY FILTER; TUNING CURVE.

Freudian slip in the popular understanding of psychoanalytic theory, an unconscious error or oversight in writing, speech, or action that is held to be caused by unacceptable impulses breaking through the EGO's defenses and exposing the individual's true wishes or feelings. See PARAPRAXIS; SLIP OF THE TONGUE; SYMPTOMATIC ACT. [Sigmund **Freud** (1856–1939), Austrian psychiatrist]

fricative *adj.* denoting a speech sound made by forcing a stream of air through a narrow opening of the vocal tract against one or more surfaces. It may be VOICED (e.g., [v], [z], [th]) or UNVOICED (e.g., [f], [s], [sh]).

Friedreich's ataxia a hereditary, progressive form of ATAXIA (muscular incoordination) that results from the degeneration of nerves in the spinal cord and nerves that connect the spinal cord to the arms and legs. Symptoms typically appear in childhood or early adolescence and may include clumsiness, balance problems, difficulty walking, unsteady gait, slurred speech, hearing and vision loss, and rapid involuntary eye movements. [Nikolaus **Friedreich** (1825–1882), German neurologist]

friendship *n.* a voluntary relationship between two or more people that is relatively long-lasting and in which those involved tend to be concerned with meeting the others' needs and interests as well as satisfying their own desires.

fright *n.* the emotional reaction that arises in the face of a dangerous or potentially dangerous situation or encounter. Fright differs from FEAR in that the danger is usually immediate, physical, concrete, and overwhelming. Physiological changes in the body associated with fright include trembling, widening of the eyes, and drawing away from the fear-producing stimulus.

frigidity *n.* a woman's impairment of sexual desire or inability to achieve orgasm. This politically incorrect term has largely been abandoned in favor of female SEXUAL DYSFUNCTION. —**frigid** *adj.*

fringe consciousness aspects of experience that lack focal perceptual qualities (e.g., color, texture, taste) but are nevertheless reported with a high degree of confidence and accuracy. Fringe experiences vary widely, from feelings of EFFORTFULNESS, TIP-OF-THE-TONGUE PHENOMENA, and FEELINGS OF KNOWING to mystical feelings.

frontal *adj.* **1.** pertaining to the front, or anterior, portion of the body or of an organ. **2.** pertaining to the frontal bone of the skull, or forehead.

frontal cortex the CEREBRAL CORTEX of the frontal lobe. See also PREFRONTAL CORTEX.

frontal lobe one of the four main lobes of each cerebral hemisphere of the brain, lying in front of the CENTRAL SULCUS. It is concerned with motor and higher order EXECUTIVE FUNCTIONS. See also PREFRONTAL LOBE.

frontal lobe syndrome deterioration in personality and behavior resulting from lesions in the frontal lobe. Typical symptoms include loss of initiative, inability to plan activities, difficulty with abstract thinking, perseveration, impairments in social judgment and impulse control, and mood disturbances such as apathy or mania.

frontal lobotomy see LOBOTOMY.

frotteurism *n.* a PARAPHILIA in which an individual deliberately and persistently seeks sexual excitement by rubbing against other people. This may occur as apparently accidental contact in crowded public settings, such as elevators or lines.

frustration *n.* **1.** the thwarting of impulses or actions that prevents individuals from obtaining something they have been led to expect based on past experience, as when a hungry animal is prevented from obtaining food that it can see or smell or when a child is prevented from playing with a visible toy. **2.** the emotional state an individual experiences when such thwarting occurs. —**frustrate** *vb.*

frustration–aggression hypothesis the theory that (a) frustration always produces an aggressive urge and (b) aggression is always the result of prior frustrations.

frustration tolerance the ability of an individual to endure tension, to preserve relative equanimity on encountering obstacles, and to delay gratification. The growth of adequate frustration tolerance is a feature of normal cognitive and affective development; poor frustration tolerance typically indicates developmental weaknesses or deteriorations and losses in more adaptive levels that may be strengthened or revived through therapeutic intervention.

F statistic see F RATIO.

FT abbreviation for fixed time (see FIXED-TIME SCHEDULE).

F test any of a class of statistical tests, notably including the widely used ANALYSIS OF VARIANCE, that rely on the assumption that the test statistic—the F RATIO—follows the F DISTRIBUTION when the null hypothesis is true. F tests are tests of hypotheses about population variances.

FTS abbreviation for FETAL TOBACCO SYNDROME.

FTT abbreviation for FAILURE TO THRIVE.

fugitive literature see GRAY LITERATURE.

fugue *n*. **1.** see DISSOCIATIVE FUGUE. **2.** a brief period in which an individual appears to be in a semiconscious state, sometimes engaging in routine activity, and subsequently has no memory for events during that period. This condition is typically associated with epilepsy but may occur in other conditions, such as alcohol intoxication and catatonic excitement.

fulfillment *n*. the actual or felt satisfaction of needs and desires, or the attainment of aspirations. See also WISH-FULFILLMENT. —**fulfill** *vb*.

fulfillment model a basic type of personality theory based on the assumption that the primary motivation for behavior is self-fulfillment, as manifest in a drive to fulfill one's innate potential. Humanistic approaches to psychology, as exemplified by the work of U.S. psychologists Abraham Maslow (1908–1970) and Carl Rogers (1902–1987), are prominent examples of the fulfillment model.

Fullerton–Cattell law a psychophysical generalization regarding the DIFFERENCE THRESHOLD, stating that errors of observation are proportional to the square root of the magnitude of the stimulus. The Fullerton–Cattell law was proposed in 1892 as a replacement for WEBER'S LAW. [George S. **Fullerton** (1859–1925), U.S. philosopher; James McKeen **Cattell** (1860–1944), U.S. psychologist]

full inclusion the practice of providing children with disabilities with services in their home school and of educating them in a regular classroom on a permanent, full-time basis. See also LEAST RESTRICTIVE ENVIRONMENT; MAINSTREAMING.

fully functioning person in CLIENT-CENTERED THERAPY, a person with a healthy personality, who experiences freedom of choice and action, is creative, and exhibits the qualities of EXISTENTIAL LIVING.

function *n*. **1.** in biology, an activity of an organ or an organism that contributes to the organism's FITNESS, such as the secretion of a sex hormone by a gonad to prepare for reproduction or the defensive behavior of a female with young toward an intruder. **2.** (symbol: f) a mathematical procedure that relates one number, quantity, or entity to another according to a defined rule. For example, if $y = 2x + 1$, y is said to be a function of x. This is often written $y = f(x)$.

functional *adj*. **1.** denoting or referring to a dis-

order for which there is no known organic or structural basis. In psychology and psychiatry, functional disorders are improperly considered equivalent to PSYCHOGENIC disorders. **2.** based on or relating to use rather than structure.

functional activities actions associated with basic daily home and work requirements: an umbrella term encompassing both ACTIVITIES OF DAILY LIVING and INSTRUMENTAL ACTIVITIES OF DAILY LIVING.

functional age an individual's age as determined by measures of functional capability indexed by age-normed standards. Functional age is distinct from CHRONOLOGICAL AGE and represents a combination of physiological, psychological, and social age. In adults it is calculated by measuring a range of variables, such as eyesight, hearing, mobility, cardiopulmonary function, concentration, and memory. The functional age of a child is measured in terms of the developmental level he or she has reached.

functional analysis 1. the detailed analysis of a behavior to identify contingencies that sustain the behavior. **2.** a synthesis of a client's behavior problems and the variables that are associated with or hypothesized to cause them.

functional analytic causal model a vector diagram of a functional analysis of an individual client that visually presents a clinician's conjectures or theories about the client's maladaptive behaviors, the objectives of those behaviors, and the variables affecting them.

functional approach to attitudes a theoretical perspective postulating that attitudes are formed to serve one or more different functions and that these functions can influence such processes as attitude change and attitude–behavior consistency.

functional asymmetry activity-related differences between the two cerebral hemispheres, as demonstrated by disparities in various behavioral competencies such as task performance. For example, studies have shown a right-ear advantage for word stimuli, indicating left-hemisphere superiority for language processing.

functional autonomy the ability of a person to perform independently the various tasks required in daily life, a core concept in such areas as rehabilitation and successful aging. For example, decline in functional autonomy is a major component of symptoms in severe dementia. Very few INSTRUMENTAL ACTIVITIES OF DAILY LIVING remain, and there is a gradual loss of self-care, or basic ACTIVITIES OF DAILY LIVING.

functional behavioral assessment an assessment approach that identifies the functions fulfilled by a particular maladaptive or problematic behavior by examining the circumstances and consequences associated with its occurrence. Results of these assessments provide information of immediate utility in designing interventions or treatments to address the behavior.

functional communication training a BE-HAVIOR THERAPY technique used with children and adults diagnosed with developmental impairments, such as autism or mental retardation, who are exhibiting aggressive, self-injurious, or highly disruptive behavior. The technique assesses the function that the negative behavior serves and uses positive reinforcement to replace it with more appropriately adaptive communication or behavior that meets the same need.

functional electric stimulation the application of electric current to peripheral nerves through the use of electrodes in order to generate muscle contractions, which can create functional movements in the extremities of an individual. For example, it has been used to enable individuals with PARAPLEGIA to pedal adapted exercise bicycles or, in combination with custom leg braces, to walk.

functional family therapy a type of FAMILY THERAPY that focuses on both family interaction patterns and on the benefits family members may derive from problem behavior. Using reframing and COGNITIVE BEHAVIOR THERAPY methods, functional family therapy focuses primarily on at-risk and behaviorally troubled youth and their families.

functional fixedness the tendency to perceive an object only in terms of its most common use. For example, people generally perceive cardboard boxes as containers, thus hindering them from potentially flipping the boxes over for use as platforms upon which to place objects (e.g., books).

functional grammar an approach to GRAMMAR using categories that reflect nonlinguistic factors, such as intention and social context, rather than categories based solely on a formal linguistic analysis. Compare FORMAL GRAMMAR. See also PRAGMATICS.

functional invariant in the PIAGETIAN THEORY of cognitive development, either of the processes of ACCOMMODATION and ASSIMILATION, which are conceptualized as characterizing all biological systems and operating throughout the life span.

functionalism *n.* a general psychological approach that views mental life and behavior in terms of active adaptation to environmental challenges and opportunities. Functionalism was developed at the University of Chicago by U.S. psychologists John Dewey (1859–1952), James R. Angell (1869–1949), and Harvey A. Carr (1878–1954) at the beginning of the 20th century as a revolt against the atomistic point of view of STRUCTURALISM, which limited psychology to the dissection of states of consciousness and the study of mental content rather than mental activities. Functionalism emphasized the causes and consequences of human behavior; the union of the physiological with the psychological; the need for objective testing of theories; and the applications of psychological knowledge

to the solution of practical problems, the evolutionary continuity between animals and humans, and the improvement of human life. Also called **functional psychology**. See also CHICAGO SCHOOL.

functional level see OPTIMAL LEVEL.

functional limitation restriction or lack of ability in performing an action or activity that arises as a result of a disability. For example, a person who is unable to move safely about his or her home or community or is otherwise unable to travel independently has a functional limitation with regard to mobility.

functional magnetic resonance imaging (**fMRI**; **functional MRI**) a form of MAGNETIC RESONANCE IMAGING that detects changes in blood flow and therefore identifies regions of the brain that are particularly active during a given task.

functional measurement a procedure that measures the subjective experience of stimuli as that experience changes across different contexts. Two or more stimuli are presented in various combinations to an observer who assigns ratings to each. These ratings are then integrated according to a simple arithmetical law discovered by examining the way in which the observer's ratings change when the combination of stimuli is changed.

functional operant see OPERANT.

functional plasticity the ability of the brain to adapt to loss of or damage to tissue by transferring all or part of the functions previously performed by those injured areas to other regions. The degree to which the brain is able to do this successfully is called **functional reserve** and is thought to depend on several factors, including age and the physical status of the brain.

functional psychology see FUNCTIONALISM.

functional status a measure of an individual's ability to perform ACTIVITIES OF DAILY LIVING and INSTRUMENTAL ACTIVITIES OF DAILY LIVING independently, used as an assessment of the severity of that individual's disability.

functional stimulus in stimulus–response experiments, the characteristic of the stimulus that actually produces a particular effect on the organism and governs its behavior. This may be different from the NOMINAL STIMULUS as defined by the experimenter. For example, if an experimenter presents a blue square to a pigeon as a nominal stimulus, the functional stimulus may simply be the color blue. Also called **effective stimulus**.

functional types in ANALYTIC PSYCHOLOGY, four personality types based on functions of the ego, one of which typically dominates the conscious ego while the others remain unconscious. The individuated person (see INDIVIDUATION) will have integrated all the functions into his or her conscious personality. The functional types are: (a) the **feeling type**, who evaluates experiences in terms of how they make one feel; (b) the **thinking type**, who evaluates logically and rationally; (c) the **sensation type**, who is dominated by sense perception; and (d) the **intuitive type**, who adapts to life by unconscious indications and sharpened interpretation of faintly conscious stimuli.

function word in linguistics, a word that has little or no meaning of its own but plays an important grammatical role: Examples include the articles (*a*, *the*, etc.), prepositions (*in*, *of*, etc.), and conjunctions (*and*, *but*, etc.). Function words are of high frequency and are typically short. The distinction between function words and CONTENT WORDS is of great interest to the study of language disorders, LANGUAGE ACQUISITION, and psycholinguistic processing.

fundamental attribution error in ATTRIBUTION THEORY, the tendency to overestimate the degree to which an individual's behavior is determined by his or her abiding personal characteristics, attitudes, or beliefs and, correspondingly, to minimize the influence of the surrounding situation on that behavior (e.g., financial or social pressures). There is evidence that this tendency is more common in some societies than in others. Also called **correspondence bias**; **overattribution bias**.

fundamental need see PHYSIOLOGICAL NEED.

fundamental rule see BASIC RULE.

fundamental symptoms according to Swiss psychiatrist Eugen Bleuler (1857–1939), the four primary symptoms of schizophrenia: abnormal *a*ssociations in thinking, *a*utistic behavior and thinking, abnormal *a*ffect (including flat and inappropriate affect), and *a*mbivalence. These symptoms are also known as the **Four As**. Compare SECONDARY SYMPTOMS.

furor *n.* a sudden outburst of rage or excitement during which an irrational act of violence may be committed. In rare cases of epilepsy, the occurrence of furor takes the place of a tonic–clonic or complex partial seizure; this is known as **epileptic furor**. See also INTERMITTENT EXPLOSIVE DISORDER; ISOLATED EXPLOSIVE DISORDER.

fusiform gyrus a spindle-shaped ridge on the inferior (lower) surface of each TEMPORAL LOBE in the brain. It lies between the inferior temporal gyrus and the PARAHIPPOCAMPAL GYRUS and is involved in high-level visual processing, including color perception and face recognition.

fusion *n.* the blending into one unified whole of two or more components or elements. This general meaning is applied in a variety of different psychological contexts. In perception, for example, it may denote a blending of sounds received by the two ears (**binaural fusion**) or of images falling on the two retinas (**binocular fusion**), while in psychoanalytic theory it denotes instinctual fusion, the merging of different INSTINCTS, as in the union of sexual and aggressive drives in SADISM. —**fuse** *vb.*

fuzzy trace theory a theory proposing that information is encoded on a continuum from precise, literal memory representations (**verbatim traces**) to gistlike, imprecise representations (**fuzzy traces**). It also proposes that developmental differences in many aspects of cognition can be attributed to age differences in encoding and to differences in sensitivity to output INTERFERENCE.

F value see F RATIO.

Gg

g symbol for GENERAL FACTOR.

GABA abbreviation for GAMMA-AMINOBUTYRIC ACID.

GABA$_A$ receptor one of the two main types of receptor protein that bind the neurotransmitter GAMMA-AMINOBUTYRIC ACID (GABA), the other being the GABA$_B$ RECEPTOR. It is located at most synapses of most neurons that use GABA as a neurotransmitter. The predominant inhibitory receptor in the central nervous system (CNS), it functions as a chloride channel (see ION CHANNEL).

GABA$_B$ receptor one of the two main types of receptor protein that bind the neurotransmitter GAMMA-AMINOBUTYRIC ACID (GABA), the other being the GABA$_A$ RECEPTOR. GABA$_B$ receptors, which are G PROTEIN-coupled receptors, are less plentiful in the brain than GABA$_A$ receptors and their activation results in relatively long-lasting neuronal inhibition.

GAD abbreviation for GENERALIZED ANXIETY DISORDER.

GAI abbreviation for GUIDED AFFECTIVE IMAGERY.

galanin *n.* a NEUROPEPTIDE that is implicated in a variety of functions, including normal growth of the nervous system, recovery of function after nerve injury, and regulation of appetite.

galvanic skin response (GSR) a change in the electrical properties (conductance or resistance) of the skin in reaction to stimuli, owing to the activity of sweat glands located in the fingers and palms. Though strictly an indication of physiological arousal, the galvanic skin response is widely considered a reflection of emotional arousal and stress as well. Also called **electrodermal response** (EDR); **psychogalvanic reflex** or **response** (PGR).

Gamblers Anonymous (GA) see ALCOHOLICS ANONYMOUS.

gambler's fallacy a failure to recognize the independence of chance events, leading to the mistaken belief that one can predict the outcome of a chance event on the basis of the outcomes of past chance events.

gambling *n.* see PATHOLOGICAL GAMBLING.

game *n.* **1.** a social interaction, organized play, or transaction with formal rules. See ZERO-SUM GAME. **2.** in psychotherapy, a situation in which members of a group take part in some activity designed to elicit emotions or stimulate revealing interactions and interrelationships. In PLAY THERAPY games are often used as a projective or observational technique. **3.** in TRANSACTIONAL ANALYSIS, a recurrent and often deceitful ploy adopted by an individual in his or her dealings with others. **4.** in GESTALT THERAPY, an exercise or experiment designed to increase self-awareness, for example, acting out frightening situations or participating in the HOT-SEAT TECHNIQUE.

gamete *n.* either of the female or male reproductive cells that take part in fertilization to produce a zygote. In humans and other animals, the female gamete is the OVUM and the male gamete is the SPERMATOZOON. Gametes contain the HAPLOID number of chromosomes rather than the DIPLOID number found in body (somatic) cells. See also GERM CELL.

gamete intrafallopian transfer an alternative to IN VITRO FERTILIZATION in which ova and sperm are introduced directly into the fallopian tubes, where fertilization takes place. Compare ZYGOTE INTRAFALLOPIAN TRANSFER.

game theory a branch of mathematics concerned with the analysis of the behavior of decision makers (called players) whose choices affect one another. Game theory is often used in both theoretical modeling and empirical studies of conflict, cooperation, and competition, and has helped to structure interactive decision-making situations in numerous disciplines, including economics, political science, social psychology, and ethics.

gametogenesis *n.* the process resulting in the formation of GAMETES from GERM CELLS, which normally involves MEIOSIS. In mammals, gametogenesis in the female is known as OOGENESIS and occurs in the ovaries; in males it is called SPERMATOGENESIS and occurs in the testes.

gamma (symbol: γ) *n.* the distance of a stimulus from the threshold in a psychophysical procedure.

gamma alcoholism one of the five types of alcoholism defined by U.S. physician Elvin M. Jellinek (1890–1963), the others being ALPHA ALCOHOLISM, BETA ALCOHOLISM, DELTA ALCOHOLISM, and EPSILON ALCOHOLISM. It is characterized by physical and psychological dependence, tolerance, loss of control over drinking, and withdrawal symptoms if use is suspended. Jellinek considered gamma alcoholism the predominant form of alcoholism in the United States. Although similar to delta alcoholism, gamma alcoholism is distinguished by the person's complete loss of control, as opposed to his or her inability to abstain.

gamma-aminobutyric acid (GABA) a major inhibitory NEUROTRANSMITTER in the mammalian nervous system that is synthesized from the amino acid GLUTAMIC ACID.

gamma-hydroxybutyrate *n.* see GHB.

gamma motor neuron see MOTOR NEURON.

gamma movement see APPARENT MOVEMENT.

gamma synchrony the coordinated production of GAMMA WAVES across disparate brain areas, such that the waves match each other in amplitude with zero phase lag. This pattern of electrical activity, as recorded via ELECTROENCEPHALOGRAPHY, is predominant during periods of intense concentration and other highly focused mental activities. Growing evidence suggests gamma synchrony as a mechanism for the integration of cognitive processes and even as the neural correlate of consciousness. **Gamma coherence** is a similar pattern but distinguished by a brief phase lag.

gamma wave in electroencephalography, a type of low-amplitude BRAIN WAVE ranging from 31 to 80 Hz (with power peaking near 40 Hz) and associated with higher-level cognitive activities, such as memory storage. Also called **gamma rhythm**.

ganglion *n.* (*pl.* **ganglia**) a collection of CELL BODIES of neurons that lies outside the central nervous system (the BASAL GANGLIA, however, are an exception). Many invertebrates have only distributed ganglia and no centralized nervous system. Compare NUCLEUS. —**ganglionic** *adj.*

ganglion cell see RETINAL GANGLION CELL.

Ganser syndrome a condition characterized most prominently by the giving of approximate answers to simple or familiar questions (e.g., "3 + 3 = 7"; "a horse has five legs"). Often associated with prison environments, this rare and controversial syndrome has been variously categorized as a MALINGERING process, a FACTITIOUS DISORDER, a DISSOCIATIVE DISORDER, a PSYCHOTIC DISORDER, a HISTRIONIC PERSONALITY DISORDER, and an organic illness. [first described in 1898 by Sigbert **Ganser** (1853–1931), German psychiatrist]

Ganzfeld *n.* a homogeneous visual field, resulting from stimulation of both retinas by diffuse, uniform illumination. This is typically accomplished by looking through white spheres (or the halves of a ping-pong ball) in a dimly red-lit room. [German, "whole field"]

gap detection the detection of a temporal interruption in a quasi-continuous sound. For individuals with typical hearing in laboratory situations, a gap of approximately 3 ms is just detectable.

gap junction a type of intercellular junction consisting of a gap of about 2–4 nm between the plasma membranes of two cells, spanned by protein channels that allow passage of electrical signals. See ELECTRICAL SYNAPSE.

Garcia effect an alternative but less common name for CONDITIONED TASTE AVERSION. [John **Garcia** (1917–), U.S. psychologist]

GAS abbreviation for GENERAL ADAPTATION SYNDROME.

gastrula *n.* an early embryo showing differentiation of cells into the three GERM LAYERS that will give rise to all of the major tissue systems in the adult animal.

gate-control theory the hypothesis that the subjective experience of pain is modulated by large nerve fibers in the spinal cord that act as gates, such that pain is not the product of a simple transmission of stimulation from the skin or some internal organ to the brain. Rather, sensations from noxious stimulation impinging on pain receptors have to pass through these SPINAL GATES to the brain in order to emerge as pain perceptions. The status of the gates, however, is subject to a variety of influences (e.g., drugs, injury, emotions, possibly even instructions coming down from the brain itself), which can operate to shut them, thus inhibiting pain transmission, or cause them to be fully open, thus facilitating transmission.

gatekeeper *n.* a health care professional, usually a PRIMARY CARE provider associated with a MANAGED CARE organization, who determines a patient's access to health care services and whose approval is required for referrals to specialists.

gating *n.* the inhibition or exclusion from attention of certain sensory stimuli when attention is focused on other stimuli. That is, while attending to specific information in the environment, other information does not reach awareness. Also called **sensory gating**.

Gaussian distribution see NORMAL DISTRIBUTION. [Karl Friedrich **Gauss** (1777–1855), German mathematician]

Gauss–Markov theorem a fundamental theorem of mathematical statistics that deals with the generation of linear unbiased ESTIMATORS with minimum variance in the GENERAL LINEAR MODEL. It is one of the basic theorems in the ANALYSIS OF VARIANCE. [Karl Friedrich **Gauss**; Andrei **Markov** (1856–1922), Russian mathematician]

gay *adj.* denoting individuals, especially males, who are sexually attracted to and aroused by members of their own sex. See also HOMOSEXUALITY.

gaze *n.* the orientation of the eyes within the face, which can be used by others to interpret where an individual is looking. Gaze direction is an effective way of communicating the location of hidden objects and is functionally similar to pointing. There is some controversy over whether nonhuman animals can understand the function of gaze direction. See also EYE CONTACT.

gaze palsy an inability to move the eyes past mid-position in a particular direction, although the eye muscles are capable of contraction. Typical forms are vertical gaze palsy (affecting up–down movements) and horizontal gaze palsy (affecting left–right movements); in complete gaze palsy, gaze shifts are restricted in all directions.

gelasmus *n.* spasmodic laughter in individuals with certain psychogenic disorders, schizophrenia, and some diseases of the brain (especially of the medulla oblongata). When occurring as an aspect of a psychomotor seizure, this type of spasmodic laughter is termed **gelastic epilepsy.**

gender *n.* the condition of being male, female, or neuter. In a human context, the distinction between gender and sex reflects usage of these terms: Sex usually refers to the biological aspects of maleness or femaleness, whereas gender implies the psychological, behavioral, social, and cultural aspects of being male or female (i.e., masculinity or femininity).

gender bias any one of a variety of stereotypical beliefs about individuals on the basis of their sex, particularly as related to the differential treatment of females and males. These biases often are expressed linguistically, as in use of the phrase *physicians and their wives* (instead of *physicians and their spouses*, which avoids the implication that physicians must be male) or of the term *he* when people of both sexes are under discussion.

gender concept an understanding of the socially constructed distinction between male and female, based on biological sex but also including the roles and expectations for males and females of a culture. Children begin to acquire concepts of gender, including knowledge of the activities, toys, and other objects associated with each gender and of how they view themselves as male or female in their culture, possibly from as early as 18 months of age.

gender consistency the understanding that one's own and other people's sex is fixed across situations, regardless of superficial changes in appearance or activities. See GENDER CONSTANCY.

gender constancy a child's emerging sense of the permanence of being a boy or a girl, an understanding that occurs in a series of stages: GENDER IDENTITY, GENDER STABILITY, and GENDER CONSISTENCY.

gender dysphoria discontent with the physical or social aspects of one's own sex. See also DYSPHORIA.

gender identity a recognition that one is male or female and the internalization of this knowledge into one's self-concept. Although the dominant approach in psychology for many years had been to regard gender identity as residing in individuals, the importance of societal structures, cultural expectations, and personal interactions in its development is now recognized as well. Indeed, significant evidence now exists to support the conceptualization of gender identity as influenced by both environmental and biological factors. See GENDER CONSTANCY. See also GENDER ROLE.

gender identity disorder a disorder characterized by clinically significant distress or impairment of functioning due to cross-gender identification (i.e., a desire to be or actual insistence that one is of the opposite sex) and persistent discomfort arising from the belief that one's sex or gender is inappropriate to one's true self (see TRANSSEXUALISM). The disorder is distinguished from simple dissatisfaction or nonconformity with gender roles. In children, the disorder is manifested as aversion to physical aspects of their sex and rejection of traditional gender roles. In adolescents and adults, it is manifested as the persistent belief that one was born the wrong sex and preoccupation with altering primary and secondary sex characteristics. Disorders such as GENDER DYSPHORIA related to congenital INTERSEXUALITY, stress-related cross-dressing behavior (see TRANSVESTISM), or preoccupation with castration or penectomy (removal of the penis) are considered distinct from gender identity disorder.

gender nonconformity behavior that differs from that of others of the same sex or from cultural expectations of male and female behavior. It sometimes is a developmental marker of adult sexual orientation.

gender reassignment see SEX REASSIGNMENT.

gender role the pattern of behavior, personality traits, and attitudes that define masculinity or femininity in a particular culture. It frequently is considered the external manifestation of the internalized GENDER IDENTITY, although the two are not necessarily consistent with one another.

gender schema the organized set of beliefs and expectations that guides one's understanding of maleness and femaleness.

gender stability the understanding that one's own or other people's sex does not change over time. See GENDER CONSTANCY.

gender stereotype a relatively fixed, overly simplified concept of the attitudes and behaviors considered normal and appropriate for a person in a particular culture, based on his or her biological sex. Research indicates that these STEREOTYPES are prescriptive as well as descriptive. Gender stereotypes often support the social conditioning of gender roles.

gene *n.* the basic unit of heredity, responsible for storing genetic information and transmitting it to subsequent generations. The observable characteristics of an organism (i.e., its PHENOTYPE) are determined by numerous genes, which contain the instructions necessary for the functioning of the organism's constituent cells. Each gene consists of a section of DNA, a large and complex molecule that, in higher organisms, is arranged to form the CHROMOSOMES of the cell nucleus. Instructions are embodied in the chemical composition of the DNA, according to the GENETIC CODE. In classical genetics, a gene is described in terms of the trait that it determines and is investigated largely by virtue of the variations brought about by its different forms, or ALLELES. At the molecular level, most genes encode proteins, which carry out the functions of the cell or act to regulate the expression of other genes.

gene linkage the tendency for genes or GENETIC MARKERS that are located physically close to each other on a chromosome to be inherited together.

gene mapping the creation of a schematic representation of the arrangement of genes, genetic markers, or both as they occur in the genetic material of an organism. In humans and other higher organisms, three different types of map are made. A **genetic map** (or linkage map) shows the relative positions of genes along each chromosome. A **physical map** shows the absolute physical distances between genes along the DNA molecule. A **cytogenetic map** depicts the banded appearance of stained chromosomes; the bands can be correlated with the location of particular genes.

genera *pl. n.* see GENUS.

general adaptation syndrome (**GAS**) the physiological consequences of severe stress. The syndrome has three stages: alarm, resistance, and exhaustion. The first stage, the **alarm reaction** (or **alarm stage**), comprises two substages: the **shock phase**, marked by a decrease in body temperature, blood pressure, and muscle tone and loss of fluid from body tissues; and the **countershock phase**, during which the sympathetic nervous system is aroused and there is an increase in adrenocortical hormones, triggering a defensive reaction, such as the FIGHT-OR-FLIGHT RESPONSE. The **resistance stage** consists of stabilization at the increased physiological levels. Resources may be depleted, and permanent organ changes produced. The **exhaustion stage** is characterized by breakdown of acquired adaptations to a prolonged stressful situation; it is evidenced by such signs as sleep disturbances, irritability, severe loss of concentration, restlessness, trembling that disturbs motor coordination, fatigue, and depressed mood.

general factor (symbol: *g*) a basic ability that underlies the performance of different varieties of intellectual tasks, in contrast to SPECIFIC FACTORS, which are alleged each to be unique to a single task. The general factor represents individuals' abilities to perceive relationships and to derive conclusions from them. See TWO-FACTOR THEORY.

generalizability *n.* the accuracy with which results or findings can be transferred to situations or people other than those originally studied.

generalization *n.* **1.** the process of deriving a concept, judgment, principle, or theory from a limited number of specific cases and applying it more widely, often to an entire class of objects, events, or people. **2.** in conditioning, see STIMULUS GENERALIZATION. —**generalize** *vb.*

generalized anxiety disorder (**GAD**) excessive anxiety and worry about a range of events and activities (e.g., finances, health, work) accompanied by such symptoms as restlessness, fatigue, impaired concentration, irritability, muscle tension, and disturbed sleep.

generalized other in SYMBOLIC INTERACTIONISM, the aggregation of other people's viewpoints. It is distinguished from specific other people and their individual views.

generalized seizure a seizure in which abnormal electrical activity involves the entire brain rather than a specific focal area. The two most common forms are ABSENCE and some TONIC-CLONIC SEIZURES.

general language disability see LANGUAGE DISABILITY.

general linear model a large class of statistical techniques, including REGRESSION ANALYSIS, ANALYSIS OF VARIANCE, and correlational analysis, that describe the relationship between a DEPENDENT VARIABLE and one or more INDEPENDENT VARIABLES. Most statistical techniques employed in the behavioral sciences can be subsumed under the general linear model.

general medical condition a disorder that has known physical causes and observable physical psychopathology. Examples include hypertension and diabetes.

general psychology the study of the basic principles, problems, and methods underlying the science of psychology, including such areas as the physiological basis of behavior, human growth and development, emotions, motivation, learning, the senses, perception, thinking processes, memory, intelligence, personality theory, psychological testing, behavior disorders, social behavior, and mental health. The study is viewed from various perspectives, including physiological, historical, theoretical, philosophical, and practical.

general systems theory an interdisciplinary conceptual framework focusing on wholeness, pattern, relationship, hierarchical order, integration, and organization. It was designed to move beyond the reductionistic and mechanistic tradition in science (see REDUCTIONISM) and integrate the fragmented approaches and different classes of phenomena studied by contemporary science into an organized whole. An entity or phenomenon should be viewed holistically as a set of elements interacting with one another (i.e., as a system), and the goal of general systems theory is to identify and understand the principles applicable to all systems. The impact of each element in a system depends on the role played by other elements in the system and order arises from interaction among these elements. Also called **systems theory**.

general transfer the transfer of general skills or principles acquired in one task or situation to problems in a totally different field: for example, applying the capacity for logical thought acquired in a philosophy course to problems arising in business. Compare SPECIFIC TRANSFER.

generation *n.* **1.** the act or process of reproduction or creation. **2.** all of the offspring that are at the same stage of descent from a common ancestor. **3.** the average time interval between the birth of parents and the birth of their offspring.

generation effect the fact that memory for items to be remembered in an experiment is enhanced if the participants help to generate the items. For example, the word *hot* will be better remembered if the studied item is "Opposite of COLD: H__" than if the word *hot* is simply read.

generative grammar an approach to linguistics whose goal is to account for the infinite set of possible grammatical sentences in a language using a finite set of generative rules. Unlike earlier inductive approaches that set out to describe and draw inferences about grammar on the basis of a corpus of natural language, the theories of generative grammar developed by U.S. linguist Noam Chomsky (1928–) in the 1950s and 1960s took for their basic data the intuitions of native speakers about what is and is not grammatical (see COMPETENCE; GRAMMATICALITY). In taking this approach, Chomsky revolutionized the whole field of linguistics, effectively redefining it as a branch of COGNITIVE PSYCHOLOGY. Much research in PSYCHOLINGUISTICS has since focused on whether the various models suggested by generative grammar have psychological reality in the production and reception of language. See also FINITE-STATE GRAMMAR; GOVERNMENT AND BINDING THEORY; PHRASE-STRUCTURE GRAMMAR; TRANSFORMATIONAL GENERATIVE GRAMMAR.

generativity versus stagnation the seventh stage of ERIKSON'S EIGHT STAGES OF DEVELOPMENT. Generativity is the positive goal of middle adulthood, interpreted in terms not only of procreation but also of creativity and fulfilling one's full parental and social responsibilities toward the next generation, in contrast to a narrow interest in the self, or self-absorption. Also called **generativity versus self-absorption**.

generic knowledge see SEMANTIC KNOWLEDGE.

generic name the nonproprietary name for a pharmaceutical compound.

genetic *adj.* relating to GENES or GENETICS.

genetic algorithm a search procedure from ARTIFICIAL INTELLIGENCE in which populations of solutions of a problem (usually encoded in strings of BITS) are combined to make new possible solutions for the problem. A fitness measure is used to determine which solutions are suitable for making the new populations of solutions. This approach to creating problem solutions is intended to be an analogue of the survival of the fittest in actual evolutionary processes.

genetic code the instructions in genes that "tell" the cell how to make specific proteins. The code resides in the sequence of bases occurring as constituents of DNA or RNA. These bases are represented by the letters A, T, G, and C (which stand for ADENINE, THYMINE, GUANINE, and CYTOSINE, respectively). In messenger RNA, uracil (U) replaces thymine. Each unit, or CODON, of the code consists of three consecutive bases.

genetic counseling an interactive method of educating a prospective parent about genetic risks, benefits and limitations of genetic testing, reproductive risks, and options for surveillance and screening related to diseases with potentially inherited causes.

genetic defect any abnormality (MUTATION) in a gene or a chromosome. These genetic changes may result in a variety of different diseases and conditions (**genetic disorders**).

genetic determinism the doctrine that human and nonhuman animal behavior and mental activity are largely (or completely) controlled by the genetic constitution of the individual and that responses to environmental influences are for the most part innately determined. See BIOLOGICAL DETERMINISM; DETERMINISM; NATURE–NURTURE.

genetic engineering techniques by which the genetic contents of living cells or viruses can be deliberately altered, either by modifying the existing genes or by introducing novel material (e.g., a gene from another species). This is undertaken for many different reasons; for example, there have been attempts to modify defective human body cells in the hope of treating certain genetic diseases. However, considerable public concern focuses on the effects and limits of genetic engineering.

genetic epistemology a term used by Swiss child psychologist Jean Piaget (1896–1980) to denote his theoretical approach to and experimental study of the development of knowledge.

genetic marker a gene or segment of DNA with an identifiable location on a chromosome and whose inheritance can be readily tracked through different generations. Because DNA segments that lie near each other on a chromosome tend to be inherited together, markers are often used to determine the inheritance of a gene that has not yet been identified but whose approximate location is known.

genetic predisposition a tendency for certain physical or mental traits to be inherited, including physical and mental conditions and disorders. Schizophrenia, for example, is a mental disorder with a genetic predisposition that affects less than 1% of the general population but increasingly larger percentages of distant relatives, siblings, and identical twins of individuals affected. Also called **hereditary predisposition**.

genetic psychology the study of the development of mental functions in children and their transformation across the life span. In the 19th and early 20th centuries, the term was preferred over the synonymous DEVELOPMENTAL PSYCHOLOGY, although currently the reverse is true.

genetics *n.* the branch of biology that is concerned with the mechanisms and phenomena of heredity.

genetics of intelligence a controversial research area concerned with the influence of one's genetic makeup on intelligence. Some investigators currently are seeking to identify the precise genes involved in generating individual differences in intelligence.

genetic variation differences in the observable characteristics (PHENOTYPE) of the members of a population or species due to spontaneously occurring genetic alterations or rearrangements. Genetic variation is the basis for NATURAL SELECTION. In some conditions those with certain features will be favored and have higher REPRODUCTIVE SUCCESS, but if conditions change, then individuals with other features might be favored.

geniculate nucleus any of four small oval clusters of nerve cell bodies on the underside of the THALAMUS in the brain. There are two pairs—the **lateral geniculate nuclei (LGN)** and the **medial geniculate nuclei (MGN)**—with one of each pair on either lobe of the thalamus; these relay, respectively, visual impulses and auditory impulses to the cerebral cortex. Also called **geniculate body**.

genitalia *pl. n.* the reproductive organs of the male or female. The **male genitalia** include the penis, testes and related structures, prostate gland, seminal vesicles, and bulbourethral glands. The **female genitalia** consist of the vagina, uterus, ovaries, fallopian tubes, and related structures. The **external genitalia** comprise the VULVA in females and the penis and testicles in males. Also called **genitals**.

genitalization *n.* **1.** in psychoanalytic theory, the focusing of the genital libido on nonsexual objects that resemble or symbolize the sex organs, such as knives, shoes, or locks of hair. See also FETISH. **2.** in psychoanalytic theory, the achievement of a GENITAL PERSONALITY. —**genitalize** *vb.*

genital mutilation the destruction or physical modification of the external genitalia, especially when done for cultural reasons (as in CIRCUMCISION or FEMALE GENITAL MUTILATION) or as a form of self-punishment.

genital personality in psychoanalytic theory, the sexually mature, adult personality that ideally develops during the last stage (the GENITAL STAGE) of PSYCHOSEXUAL DEVELOPMENT. Individuals who have reached this stage of development are posited to have fully resolved their OEDIPUS COMPLEX and to exhibit a mature sexuality that involves true intimacy and expresses

equal concern for their own and their partner's satisfaction. Also called **genital character**.

genital stage in psychoanalytic theory, the final stage of PSYCHOSEXUAL DEVELOPMENT, ideally reached in puberty, when the OEDIPUS COMPLEX has been fully resolved and erotic interest and activity are focused on intercourse with a sexual partner. Also called **genital phase**.

genius *n.* an extreme degree of intellectual or creative ability, or any person who possesses such ability. Genius may be demonstrated by exceptional achievement, particularly the creation of literary, artistic, or scientific masterpieces of extraordinary power or inventiveness, or the production of insights or ideas of great originality. Although a frustratingly vague definition, it is virtually impossible to provide a more precise one, or even a definitive list of attributes, given that the term essentially is an acknowledgment of what a person has done rather than a description of what a person is like. Additionally, genius is seen to emerge as a joint product of heredity and environment and to require a great deal of very hard and dedicated work to achieve.

genocide *n.* the intentional and systematic annihilation of a racial, ethnic, national, or religious group. —**genocidal** *adj.*

genogram *n.* a diagrammatic representation of a family that includes not only PEDIGREE information, that is, individual histories of illness and death, but also incorporates aspects of the interpersonal relationships between the family members.

genome *n.* all of the genetic material contained in an organism or cell. Mapping of the estimated 20,000–25,000 genes in human DNA was one of several goals of the HUMAN GENOME PROJECT.

genotype *n.* the genetic composition of an individual organism as a whole or at one or more specific positions on a chromosome. Compare PHENOTYPE. —**genotypic** *adj.*

genotype–environment effects the proposal that an individual's GENOTYPE influences which environments he or she encounters and the type of experiences he or she has.

genotype–phenotype correlation a correlation between the location or nature of a mutation in a gene and the expression of that mutation in the individual. Attempts at such correlations are made to elucidate which characteristics of a mutation affect the age of onset or severity of diseases with a genetic etiology.

genu *n.* (*pl.* **genua**) **1.** the knee, or an anatomical structure that resembles a knee. **2.** the anterior portion of the CORPUS CALLOSUM as it bends forward and downward.

genus *n.* (*pl.* **genera**) in BIOLOGICAL TAXONOMY, a main subdivision of a FAMILY, containing a group of similar, related SPECIES.

geometric illusion any misinterpretation by the visual system of a figure made of straight or curved lines. Examples of such illusions are the

G

MÜLLER-LYER ILLUSION and the ZÖLLNER ILLUSION.

geometric mean a measure of CENTRAL TENDENCY. The geometric mean of k numbers $x_1...x_k$ is $(x_1x_2x_3...x_k)^{1/k}$.

geon n. see RECOGNITION BY COMPONENTS THEORY.

geophagy n. the eating of dirt or clay. It is most commonly seen in individuals with mental retardation, young children, and occasionally in pregnant women. It is usually a symptom of PICA but in some cultures it is an accepted practice.

geriatric disorder any disease or chronic condition that occurs commonly, but not exclusively, among older people. Examples of geriatric disorders include glaucoma, arthritis, and Alzheimer's disease and other dementias.

geriatric psychology see GEROPSYCHOLOGY.

geriatric psychopharmacology the branch of pharmacology that deals with issues related to the use of and response to psychoactive agents in older adults, as well as the mechanisms responsible. Metabolic changes associated with aging can affect a drug's biological activity and may increase the sensitivity of the patient's central nervous system to drugs.

geriatric rehabilitation the process of restoring, to the fullest extent possible, the functional abilities of older adults following an illness or injury that resulted in loss of the ability to live independently.

geriatrics n. the branch of medicine that deals with the diagnosis and treatment of disorders in older adults. —**geriatric** adj.

germ cell any of the cells in the gonads that give rise to the GAMETES by a process involving growth and MEIOSIS. See OOGENESIS; SPERMATOGENESIS.

germ layer any of the three layers of cells in an animal embryo at the GASTRULA stage, from which the various organs and tissues develop. The outermost layer is the **ectoderm**, the middle layer is the **mesoderm**, and the inner layer is the **endoderm**.

gerontology n. the scientific interdisciplinary study of old age and the aging process. —**gerontological** adj. —**gerontologist** n.

geropsychology n. a branch of psychology dealing with enhancing the welfare and mental health of older adults via the provision of various psychological services. Also called **geriatric psychology**. —**geropsychological** adj. —**geropsychologist** n.

Gerstmann's syndrome a set of four symptoms associated with lesions of a specific area of the (usually left) PARIETAL LOBE. They are inability to recognize one's individual fingers (finger agnosia; see TACTILE AGNOSIA), inability to distinguish between the right and left sides of one's body (RIGHT–LEFT DISORIENTATION), inability to perform mathematical calculations (ACALCU-

LIA), and inability to write (AGRAPHIA). The existence of Gerstmann's syndrome as a true independent entity is subject to debate. [Josef G. **Gerstmann** (1887–1969), Austrian neurologist]

gestalt n. an entire perceptual configuration (from German: "shape," "form"), made up of elements that are integrated and interactive in such a way as to confer properties on the whole configuration that are not possessed by the individual elements.

gestalt principles of organization principles of perception, derived by the Gestalt psychologists, that describe the tendency to perceive and interpret certain configurations at the level of the whole, rather than in terms of their component features. Examples include GOOD CONTINUATION, CLOSURE, and PRÄGNANZ. Also called **gestalt laws of organization**.

Gestalt psychology a psychological approach that focuses on the dynamic organization of experience into patterns or configurations (from German *Gestalt* [pl. *Gestalten*]: "shape," "form," "configuration," "totality"). This view was espoused by German psychologists Wolfgang Köhler (1887–1967), Kurt Koffka (1886–1941), and Max Wertheimer (1880–1943) in the early 20th century as a revolt against STRUCTURALISM, which analyzed experience into static, atomistic sensations, and also against the equally atomistic approach of BEHAVIORISM, which attempted to dissect complex behavior into elementary conditioned reflexes. Gestalt psychology holds, instead, that experience is an organized whole of which the pieces are an integral part. Later experimentation in this approach gave rise to principles of perceptual organization (including CLOSURE, PRÄGNANZ, and PROXIMITY), which were then applied to the study of learning, insight, memory, social psychology, and art.

gestalt therapy a form of PSYCHOTHERAPY in which the central focus is on the totality of the client's functioning and relationships in the HERE AND NOW, rather than on investigation of past experiences and developmental history. One of the themes is that growth occurs by assimilation of what is needed from the environment and that psychopathology arises as a disturbance of contact with the environment. Gestalt techniques, which can be applied in either a group or an individual setting, are designed to bring out spontaneous feelings and self-awareness and promote personality growth. Examples of such techniques are ROLE PLAY, the EMPTY-CHAIR TECHNIQUE, and the HOT-SEAT TECHNIQUE.

gestation n. the development of the embryo and fetus in the uterus until birth. See PREGNANCY. —**gestational** adj.

gestational age the age of a fetus calculated from the date of conception. Also called **fetal age**. See also MENSTRUAL AGE.

gesture *n.* **1.** a movement, such as the waving of a hand, that communicates a particular meaning or indicates the individual's emotional state or attitude. See also NONVERBAL BEHAVIOR. **2.** a statement or act, usually symbolic, that is intended to influence the attitudes of others (as in a *gesture of goodwill*). —**gestural** *adj.*

GH abbreviation for GROWTH HORMONE.

GHB *gamma-hydroxybutyrate:* a potent CNS DEPRESSANT that is a metabolic product of the inhibitory neurotransmitter GAMMA-AMINOBUTYRIC ACID (GABA). It is commonly encountered as a drug of abuse that produces euphoria and sedation and purportedly enhances sexual arousal. Its ability to induce amnesia or unconsciousness has led it to be characterized as a DATE-RAPE drug.

ghost sickness a CULTURE-BOUND SYNDROME found in Native American communities and attributed to ghosts or sometimes witchcraft. Symptoms include recurring nightmares, weakness, loss of appetite, fear, anxiety, hallucinations, confusion, and a sense of suffocation.

giftedness *n.* the state of possessing a great amount of natural ability, talent, or intelligence, which usually becomes evident at a very young age. Giftedness in intelligence is often categorized as an IQ of two standard deviations above the mean or higher (130 for most IQ tests). Many schools and service organizations now use a combination of attributes as the basis for assessing giftedness, including one or more of the following: high intellectual capacity, academic achievement, demonstrable real-world achievement, creativity, task commitment, proven talent, leadership skills, and physical or athletic prowess. —**gifted** *adj.*

gigantism *n.* an abnormally large body size due to excessive secretion of growth hormone by the pituitary gland during childhood.

given–new distinction in a sentence or other linguistic structure, the distinction made between information that is probably new to the recipient and that which is probably already known (or can be regarded as given by the context). A speaker's or writer's assumptions about which information falls into which category will usually affect word order, stress, and other observable features of language. The distinction is important in PRAGMATICS and DISCOURSE ANALYSIS. See FOREGROUNDING.

gland *n.* an organ that secretes a substance for use by or discharge from the body. EXOCRINE GLANDS release their products through a duct onto internal or external bodily surfaces, whereas ENDOCRINE GLANDS are ductless and secrete their products directly into the bloodstream.

glass ceiling an unofficial, intangible barrier that prevents able and ambitious individuals, particularly women and members of minority groups, from rising to positions of authority in many organizations.

glaucoma *n.* a common eye disease marked by raised INTRAOCULAR PRESSURE in one or both eyes, causing progressive peripheral visual field loss. If untreated, glaucoma results in severe visual impairment and ultimately blindness.

glia *n.* nonneuronal tissue in the nervous system that provides structural, nutritional, and other kinds of support to neurons. It may consist of very small cells (MICROGLIA) or relatively large ones (MACROGLIA). The latter include ASTROCYTES, EPENDYMAL CELLS, and the two types of cells that form the MYELIN SHEATH around axons: OLIGODENDROCYTES in the central nervous system and SCHWANN CELLS in the peripheral nervous system. Also called **neuroglia**. —**glial** *adj.*

glioblastoma *n.* see GLIOMA.

glioma *n.* a form of brain tumor that develops from support cells (glia) of the central nervous system. There are three main types, grouped according to the form of support cell involved: **astrocytoma** (from ASTROCYTES), **ependymoma** (from EPENDYMAL CELLS), and **oligodendroglioma** (from OLIGODENDROCYTES). Astrocytomas are classified from Grade I to Grade IV by severity and rate of growth: Grade I tumors (also called **pilocytic astrocytomas**), Grade II **astroblastomas**, Grade III **anaplastic astrocytomas**, and Grade IV **glioblastomas**. Glioma is the most common type of brain cancer and accounts for about a quarter of spinal cord tumors. Also called **neuroglioma**.

gliosis *n.* an excess of nonneuronal cells (glia) in a damaged area of the central nervous system. A particular type involving the proliferation of astrocytes is called ASTROCYTOSIS, although the two terms sometimes are used interchangeably. Gliosis is a prominent feature of some neurological diseases, including stroke.

global amnesia loss of memory for recent events (retrograde amnesia) combined with an inability to remember new information (anterograde amnesia). It is a very rare condition of unknown etiology. See also TRANSIENT GLOBAL AMNESIA.

global aphasia a severe, nonfluent form of APHASIA characterized by a complete loss of or drastic reduction in both expressive language skills—one's ability to use speech and writing to communicate—and receptive language skills—one's ability to comprehend the speech and writing of others. Neurological lesions in global aphasia are extensive and typically involve the entire left perisylvian language zone.

globalization *n.* the process by which many commercial organizations have moved from a local model of production and distribution to an international or global model, largely owing to technological advances and the internationalization of trade, finance, media, and travel. The globalization of a company's activities requires attention to organizational and cultural differences that may impact efficiency and safety. —**globalize** *vb.*

global rating a rating based upon the rater's integration of many attributes into a single unified rating. Global ratings are, as a rule, vague in their definitions.

global workspace theory a theory suggesting that consciousness involves the global distribution of focal information to many parts of the brain.

globus pallidus one of the BASAL GANGLIA. It is the main output region of the basal ganglia: Its output neurons terminate on thalamic neurons, which in turn project to the cerebral cortex.

globus pharyngeus a sensation of having a lump in the throat for which no medical cause can be identified. It can be a symptom of CONVERSION DISORDER and was formerly called **globus hystericus.**

glossolalia *n.* unintelligible utterances that simulate coherent speech, which may have meaning to the utterer but do not to the listener. Glossolalia is found in religious ecstasy ("speaking in tongues"), hypnotic or mediumistic trances, and occasionally in schizophrenia. See also NEOLOGISM.

glossopharyngeal nerve the ninth CRANIAL NERVE, which supplies the pharynx, soft palate, and posterior third of the tongue, including the taste buds of that portion. It contains both motor and sensory fibers and is involved in swallowing and conveying taste information.

glottis *n.* see VOCAL CORDS.

glucagon *n.* a polypeptide hormone, secreted by the A cells of the ISLETS OF LANGERHANS, that increases the concentration of glucose in the blood. It opposes the effects of INSULIN by promoting the breakdown of glycogen and fat reserves to yield glucose.

glucocorticoid *n.* any CORTICOSTEROID hormone that acts chiefly on carbohydrate metabolism. Glucocorticoids include CORTISOL, CORTICOSTERONE, and CORTISONE.

glucoreceptor *n.* any of certain cells in the HYPOTHALAMUS that bind glucose. Glucoreceptors are a putative mechanism for detecting levels of circulating glucose and conveying this information to brain areas.

glucose *n.* a soluble sugar, abundant in nature, that is a major source of energy for body tissues. The brain relies almost exclusively on glucose for its energy needs. Glucose is derived from the breakdown of carbohydrates, proteins, and—to a much lesser extent—fats. Its concentration in the bloodstream is tightly controlled by the opposing actions of the hormones INSULIN and GLUCAGON.

glucostatic theory the theory that short-term regulation of food intake is governed by the rate of glucose metabolism (i.e., utilization), rather than by overall blood levels of glucose. See also LIPOSTATIC HYPOTHESIS.

glucuronidation *n.* a metabolic process by which drugs or other substances are combined with glucuronic acid to form more water-soluble compounds, which are more readily excreted by the kidneys or in bile. Glucuronidation is the most prevalent of the Phase II reactions of DRUG METABOLISM.

glutamate *n.* a salt or ester of the amino acid GLUTAMIC ACID that serves as the predominant excitatory NEUROTRANSMITTER in the brain. Glutamate exerts its effects by binding to GLUTAMATE RECEPTORS on neurons and plays a critical role in cognitive, motor, and sensory functions.

glutamate hypothesis the theory that decreased activity of the excitatory neurotransmitter glutamate is responsible for the clinical expression of schizophrenia. The hypothesis developed from observations that administration of NMDA receptor antagonists, such as PCP (phencyclidine) and KETAMINE, produce psychotic symptoms in humans and is supported by a number of recent studies. See also DOPAMINE HYPOTHESIS.

glutamate receptor any of various receptors that bind and respond to the excitatory neurotransmitter glutamate. There are two main divisions of glutamate receptors: the IONOTROPIC RECEPTORS and the METABOTROPIC RECEPTORS. Ionotropic glutamate receptors are further divided into three classes: **NMDA receptors** (binding NMDA as well as glutamate), **AMPA receptors** (binding AMPA as well as glutamate), and **kainate receptors** (binding kainic acid as well as glutamate). Metabotropic glutamate receptors (mGlu or mGluR) are subdivided into several classes denoted by subscript numbers (i.e., $mGlu_1$, $mGlu_2$, etc.).

glutamic acid an AMINO ACID that is regarded as nonessential in diets but is important for normal brain function. It is converted into GAMMA-AMINOBUTYRIC ACID in a reaction catalyzed by the enzyme glutamic acid decarboxylase and requiring pyridoxal phosphate, formed from vitamin B_6 (pyridoxine), as a coenzyme.

glutaminergic *adj.* responding to, releasing, or otherwise involving GLUTAMATE. For example, a **glutaminergic neuron** is one that uses glutamate as a neurotransmitter.

glycine *n.* an AMINO ACID that serves as one of the two major inhibitory neurotransmitters in the central nervous system (particularly the spinal cord), the other being GAMMA-AMINOBUTYRIC ACID (GABA).

glycogen *n.* a polysaccharide stored in the liver and other body tissues as a primary source of chemical energy. It is easily broken down into glucose molecules as needed for energy.

GnRH abbreviation for GONADOTROPIN-RELEASING HORMONE.

goal setting a process that establishes specific, time-based behavior targets that are measurable, achievable, and realistic. In work-related settings, for example, this practice usually provides employees with both (a) a basis for motivation, in terms of effort expended, and (b) guidelines or cues to behavior that will be required if the goal is to be met. See also LOCKE'S THEORY OF GOAL SETTING.

Golgi apparatus an irregular network of membranes and vesicles within a cell that is responsible for modifying, sorting, and packaging proteins produced within the cell. [Camillo **Golgi** (1843–1926), Italian histologist]

Golgi tendon organ a receptor in muscle tendons that sends impulses to the central nervous system when a muscle contracts. [Camillo **Golgi**]

gonad *n.* either of the primary male and female sex organs, that is, the TESTIS or the OVARY. —**gonadal** *adj.*

gonadopause *n.* the cessation of endocrine-related reproductive function that occurs with age in either sex.

gonadotropin *n.* any of several hormones produced primarily by the anterior pituitary gland that stimulate functions of the gonads, particularly FOLLICLE-STIMULATING HORMONE and LUTEINIZING HORMONE. —**gonadotropic** *adj.*

gonadotropin-releasing hormone (**GnRH**) a HYPOTHALAMIC HORMONE that controls the release of LUTEINIZING HORMONE and FOLLICLE-STIMULATING HORMONE from the anterior pituitary gland.

go/no-go *adj.* in conditioning, denoting a procedure in which a particular action is reinforced in the presence of one stimulus (the go stimulus) and not reinforced in the presence of the other (the no-go stimulus). In neurological assessment, a **go/no-go task** assesses the ability to inhibit a simple motor response after it has been established. A common go/no-go task requires the participant to display two fingers when the examiner presents one finger (go) and to display no fingers when the examiner presents two fingers (no-go).

good-boy-nice-girl orientation see CONVENTIONAL LEVEL.

good continuation one of the GESTALT PRINCIPLES OF ORGANIZATION. It states that people tend to perceive objects in alignment as forming smooth, unbroken contours. For example, when two lines meet in a figure the preferred interpretation is of two continuous lines: a cross is interpreted as a vertical line and a horizontal line, rather than two right angles meeting at their vertices. Also called **law of continuity**; **law of good continuation**; **principle of continuity**; **principle of good continuation**.

good genes hypothesis a hypothesis of female mate selection arguing (a) that GENETIC VARIATION in males is correlated with reproductive success, (b) that there are features of male behavior and body structure that provide information about this variation, and (c) that females respond to this variation by choosing males with good genes as mates. Compare RUNAWAY SELECTION.

good gestalt the quality possessed by an arrangement of stimuli that is complete, orderly, and clear.

goodness of fit any index that reflects the degree to which values predicted by a model agree with empirically observed values.

good object in the OBJECT RELATIONS THEORY of Austrian-born British psychoanalyst Melanie Klein (1882–1960), an introjected PART-OBJECT that is perceived as benevolent and satisfying (see INTROJECTION). It is an early object representation that derives from "splitting" of the object into parts containing positive and negative qualities. The good object forms the core of the infant's immature ego. Compare BAD OBJECT.

good shape one of the GESTALT PRINCIPLES OF ORGANIZATION. Identified in 1923 by German psychologist Max Wertheimer (1880–1943), it states that people tend to perceive figures as the most uniform and stable forms possible. Also called **law of good shape**; **principle of good shape**.

government and binding theory an enhanced version of GENERATIVE GRAMMAR involving multiple levels of abstraction that seeks to explain, among other things, the relation between universals and particulars that accounts for the generativity of all human languages.

G protein any of a class of proteins that are coupled to the intracellular portion of a type of membrane RECEPTOR (**G-protein-coupled receptors**) and are activated when the receptor binds an appropriate ligand (e.g., a neurotransmitter) on the extracellular surface. G proteins thus have a role in signal transduction, serving to transmit the signal from the receptor to other cell components (e.g., ion channels) in various ways, for example by controlling the synthesis of SECOND MESSENGERS within the cell.

graafian follicle a small pouchlike cavity in an ovary in which an ovum develops (see OOGENESIS). At ovulation, one of the follicles ruptures and releases a mature ovum into a FALLOPIAN TUBE, where it may be fertilized. The ruptured follicle becomes the site of the CORPUS LUTEUM. Also called **ovarian follicle**. [Reijner de **Graaf** (1641–1673), Dutch histologist]

graceful degradation a property of cognitive networks in which damage to a portion of the network produces relatively little damage to overall performance, because performance is distributed across the units in the network and no one unit is solely responsible for any aspect of processing.

gracile fasciculus the medial portion of either of the DORSAL columns of the spinal cord, composed of ascending fibers that terminate in the medulla oblongata. See also CUNEATE FASCICULUS.

graded potential any change in electric potential of a neuron that is not propagated along the cell (as is an ACTION POTENTIAL) but declines with distance from the source. Kinds of graded potential include RECEPTOR POTENTIALS, POSTSYNAPTIC POTENTIALS, and SUBTHRESHOLD POTENTIALS.

grade equivalent a measure of achievement or performance expressed in terms of the average grade level at which the observed score is typically obtained by a student. For example, if a third-grader's score conforms to fifth-grade norms, the grade equivalent is expressed as five. Also called **grade score**.

grade norm the standard score or range of scores that represent the average achievement level of students of a particular grade.

gradient *n.* **1.** the slope of a line or surface. **2.** a measure of the change of a physical quantity (e.g., temperature) or other property (e.g., strength of a DRIVE).

graduated and reciprocated initiatives in tension reduction (**GRIT**) an approach to intergroup conflict reduction that encourages the parties to communicate cooperative intentions, engage in behaviors that are consistent with these intentions, and initiate cooperative responses even in the face of competition. GRIT is usually recommended when disputants have a prolonged history of conflict, misunderstanding, misperception, and hostility.

grammar *n.* in linguistics, an abstract system of rules that describes how a language works. Although it is traditionally held to consist of SYNTAX (rules for arranging words in sentences) and MORPHOLOGY (rules affecting the form taken by individual words), PHONOLOGY and SEMANTICS are also included in some modern systems of grammar. —**grammatical** *adj.*

grammaticality *n.* the quality of adhering to the rules of grammar. In the linguistics of U.S. linguist Noam Chomsky (1928–), the grammaticality (or otherwise) of a sentence can be intuited by native speakers and explained by the rules of FORMAL GRAMMAR. A sentence can be recognized as grammatical even when it is otherwise meaningless, as in the case of Chomsky's famous example *Colorless green ideas sleep furiously.*

grandiosity *n.* an exaggerated sense of one's greatness, importance, or ability. In extreme form, it may be regarded as a DELUSION of grandeur.

grand mal see TONIC–CLONIC SEIZURE.

grand mean a mean (numerical average) of a group of means.

grandmother cell any hypothetical neuron in the VISUAL ASSOCIATION CORTEX that is stimulated only by a single highly complex and meaningful stimulus, such as a particular individual (e.g., one's grandmother) or a particular well-known object (e.g., the Sydney Opera House). It is an extension of the FEATURE DETECTOR concept to a degree that has been dismissed by many

as overly simplistic and untenable. However, recent research on the activity patterns of single neurons in memory-linked areas of the brain has provided support for the concept by revealing a much higher degree of neuronal specificity than previously believed.

granule cell a type of small, grainlike neuron found in certain layers of the cerebral cortex and cerebellar cortex.

graph *n.* a visual representation of the relationship between numbers or quantities, which are plotted on a drawing with reference to axes at right angles (the horizontal x-axis and the vertical y-axis) and linked by lines, dots, or the like.

grapheme *n.* a minimal meaningful unit in the writing system of a particular language. It is usually a letter or fixed combination of letters corresponding to a PHONEME in that language. —**graphemic** *adj.*

graphesthesia *n.* the recognition of numbers or letters that are spelled out on the skin, for example with finger movements or a dull pointed object. This form of passive touch has been used as a diagnostic tool for brain damage.

graphology *n.* the study of the physical characteristics of handwriting, particularly as a means of inferring the writer's psychological state or personality characteristics. For example, it is sometimes used in personnel selection as a predictor of job performance. Graphology is based on the premise that writing is a form of expressive behavior, although there is little empirical evidence for its validity. Also called **handwriting analysis**. —**graphological** *adj.* —**graphologist** *n.*

graphomania *n.* a pathological impulse to write, which may degenerate into **graphorrhea**—the compulsive writing of incoherent and meaningless words.

graph theory the study of the use of visual representations (graphs) to describe relationships, structures, and dynamics. Applications in psychology include BALANCE THEORY, SOCIOMETRY, and analyses of SOCIAL NETWORKS and LIFE SPACE.

grasp reflex an involuntary grasping by an individual of anything that touches the palm. This reflex is typical of infants but in older individuals it may be a sign of FRONTAL LOBE damage.

gratification *n.* the state of satisfaction following the fulfillment of a desire or the meeting of a need.

gratification of instincts see SATISFACTION OF INSTINCTS.

grating *n.* in vision, a stimulus that consists of parallel light and dark bars.

gravireceptor (**graviceptor**) *n.* any of various specialized nerve endings and receptors located in the inner ear, joints, muscles, and tendons that provide the brain with information regarding body position, equilibrium, and gravitational forces.

gray commissure a bundle of nerve fibers that surrounds the central canal of the spinal cord and connects the anterior and dorsal horns of GRAY MATTER in each half of the cord.

gray literature research findings that are not readily available because they have not been published in archival sources. Examples of gray literature include dissertations, papers presented at meetings, papers either not submitted or rejected for publication, and technical reports. Also called **fugitive literature**.

gray matter any area of neural tissue that is dominated by CELL BODIES and is devoid of myelin, such as the CEREBRAL CORTEX and the H-shaped PERIAQUEDUCTAL GRAY of the spinal cord. Compare WHITE MATTER.

gray-out *n.* an increasing loss of peripheral vision to the point at which one seems to be looking through a small tube (see TUNNEL VISION). It results from reduced blood flow to the head, as may be experienced, for example, by pilots performing high-speed turning maneuvers in an aircraft.

greater superficial petrosal nerve the sensory nerve that carries taste information from the soft palate. It merges with the **chorda tympani** (the nerve that innervates TASTE BUDS on the front of the tongue) to form the **intermediate nerve** (or **nerve of Wrisberg**), the sensory component of the predominantly motor FACIAL NERVE (seventh cranial nerve).

great man theory a view of political leadership and historical causation that assumes that history is driven by a small number of exceptional individuals with certain innate characteristics that predispose them for greatness. A ZEITGEIST (spirit of the times) view of history, in contrast, supposes that history is largely determined by economics, technological development, and a broad spectrum of social influences.

gregariousness *n.* the tendency for human beings to enjoy the company of others and associate with them in groups, organizations, and activities. In nonhuman animals, gregariousness is seen in the tendency to congregate in herds or flocks. See SOCIAL INSTINCT. —**gregarious** *adj.*

grid organizational development (**grid OD**) a comprehensive intervention designed to increase managers' concerns for both production and people, thereby improving ORGANIZATIONAL EFFECTIVENESS. It consists of six phases: (a) a seminar on the BLAKE–MOUTON MANAGERIAL GRID, (b) teamwork development, (c) intergroup development, (d) development of an ideal strategic corporate model, (e) implementation of the ideal strategic model, and (f) systematic critique.

grief *n.* the anguish experienced after significant loss, usually the death of a beloved person. Grief is distinguished from, but a common component of, the process of BEREAVEMENT and MOURNING. Not all bereavements result in a strong grief response; nor is all grief given public expression (see DISENFRANCHISED GRIEF). Grief often includes physiological distress, SEPARATION ANXIETY, confusion, yearning, obsessive dwelling on the past, and apprehension about the future. See also TRAUMATIC GRIEF.

grief counseling the provision of advice, information, and psychological support to help individuals whose ability to function has been impaired by someone's death, particularly that of a loved one or friend. It includes counseling for the grieving process and practical advice concerning arrangements for the funeral and burial of the loved one. Grief counseling is sometimes offered by staff in specialized agencies (e.g., hospices) or it may be carried out in the context of other counseling. See also BEREAVEMENT THERAPY.

grief cycle model see STAGES OF GRIEF.

griefwork *n.* the theoretical process through which bereaved people gradually reduce or transform their emotional connection to the person who has died and thereby refocus appropriately on their own ongoing lives. It is not necessary to sever all emotional connections with the dead person. Instead, adaptive griefwork will help transform the relationship symbolically, as a CONTINUING BOND that provides a sense of meaning and value conducive to forming new relationships.

grisi siknis a CULTURE-BOUND SYNDROME found in Nicaragua and characterized by headache, anxiety, anger, and the sudden onset of an episode of hyperactivity and potentially dangerous behavior in the form of running or fleeing.

GRIT acronym for GRADUATED AND RECIPROCATED INITIATIVES IN TENSION REDUCTION.

gross motor describing activities or skills that use large muscles to move the trunk or limbs and to control posture to maintain balance. Examples of **gross motor skills** include waving an arm, walking, hopping, and running. Compare FINE MOTOR.

ground *n.* the relatively homogeneous and indistinct background of FIGURE–GROUND perceptions.

ground rules in psychotherapy, the elements of the contract for therapy, including but not limited to the fee; the time, location, and frequency of the sessions; and therapist confidentiality.

group *n.* any collection or assemblage, particularly of items or individuals. For example, in social psychology the term refers to two or more interdependent individuals who influence one another through social interactions that commonly include structures involving roles and norms, a degree of cohesiveness, and shared goals; in animal behavior it refers to an organized collection of individuals that moves together or otherwise acts to achieve some common goal (e.g., protection against predators) that would be less effectively achieved by individual action and is distinguished from an AG-GREGATION; and in research it denotes a collection of participants who all experience the same experimental conditions and whose responses are to be compared to the responses of one or more other collections of research participants.

group-analytic psychotherapy a type of group psychotherapy that focuses on the communication and interaction processes taking place in the group as a whole. Interventions make use of group rather than individual forces as the principal therapeutic agent. Also called **therapeutic group analysis**.

group attribution error the tendency for perceivers to assume that a specific group member's personal characteristics and preferences are similar to the preferences of the group to which he or she belongs. For example, observers may assume that an individual who is a member of a group that publicly announces its opposition to an issue also opposes the issue.

group climate the relative degree of acceptance, tolerance, and freedom of expression that characterizes the relationships within a counseling or therapy group. Interpersonal behavioral boundaries are generally freer and broader than in social contexts, and the meaning of interpersonal behavior is often the specific focus of group discussion.

group consciousness 1. the awareness of the group, its members, and their commonalities exhibited by individual members of the group. Just as SELF-CONSCIOUSNESS pertains to awareness of the self, so group consciousness pertains to awareness of the collective. **2.** a group's total awareness of itself, suggested in some cases to be greater than the sum of individual members' awareness.

group development 1. naturally occurring patterns of growth and change that unfold across the life span of a group. The term usually implies a progressive movement toward a more complete or advanced state. **2.** a strategic intervention designed to alter the processing and functioning of a group; this usually involves assessing the group's current level of development, helping to clarify its mission and goals, and reviewing its operating procedures.

group difference any observed variation between groups of participants in an experiment when considering each group as a single entity.

group dynamics 1. the dynamic rather than static processes, operations, and changes that occur within social groups, which affect patterns of affiliation, communication, conflict, conformity, decision making, influence, leadership, norm formation, and power. **2.** the field of psychology devoted to the study of groups and group processes.

group fallacy 1. the assumption, regarded as erroneous, that groups possess emergent, supervening qualities that cannot be understood com-

pletely through the analysis of the qualities of the individual members. See GROUP MIND. **2.** the mistaken assumption that a group is totally uniform, whereas in fact members differ from one another in many respects. Such a fallacy is involved in many forms of prejudice.

group health plan see INDEMNITY PLAN.

group home a residential facility that offers housing and personal care services, such as meals, supervision, and transportation.

group identification the act or process of associating oneself so strongly with a group and its members that one imitates and internalizes the group's distinctive features (actions, beliefs, standards, objectives, etc.). This process can lead not only to an enhanced sense of group belonging, group pride, and group commitment but also to autostereotyping, in which one accepts as self-descriptive certain stereotypical qualities attributed to the group as a whole, and a reduced sense of individuality.

group interview a conference or meeting in which one or more questioners elicit information from two or more respondents. This method encourages the interviewees to interact with one other in responding to the interviewer.

group mind a hypothetical, transcendent consciousness created by the fusion of the individual minds in a collective, such as a nation or race. This controversial idea, often seen as a prime example of the GROUP FALLACY, assumes that the group mind is greater than the sum of the psychological experiences of the individuals and that it can become so powerful that it can overwhelm the will of the individual. Also called **collective consciousness**.

group network the relatively organized system of connections linking members of a group, unit, or collective, including social or interpersonal evaluations (e.g., friendship, acquaintanceship, dislike), communication, transfer of resources, and formal role relationships (e.g., supervisor–subordinate).

group norm see SOCIAL NORM.

group polarization the tendency for members of a group discussing an issue to move toward a more extreme version of the positions they held before the discussion began. As a result, the group as a whole tends to respond in more extreme ways than one would expect given the sentiments of the individual members prior to deliberation.

group pressure direct or indirect SOCIAL PRESSURE exerted by a group on its individual members to influence their choices. Such pressure may take the form of rational argument and persuasion (informational influence), calls for conformity to group norms (normative influence), or more direct forms of influence, such as demands, threats, personal attacks, and promises of rewards or social approval (interpersonal influence).

group process the interpersonal component of a group session, in contrast to the content (such as decisions or information) generated during the session.

group psychotherapy treatment of psychological problems in which two or more participants interact with each other on both an emotional and a cognitive level, in the presence of one or more psychotherapists who serve as catalysts, facilitators, or interpreters. The approaches of groups vary, but in general they aim to provide an environment in which problems and concerns can be shared in an atmosphere of mutual respect and understanding. Group psychotherapy seeks to enhance self-respect, deepen self-understanding, and improve interpersonal relationships. Also called **group therapy**.

group relations theory the view that behavior is influenced not only by one's unique pattern of traits but also by one's need to conform to social demands and expectations.

group role a coherent set of behaviors expected of a person in a specific position within a group. In addition to the basic roles of leader and follower, groups usually allocate TASK ROLES pertaining to the group's tasks and goals and RELATIONSHIP ROLES that focus on the group members' interpersonal and emotional needs.

group-serving bias any one of a number of cognitive tendencies that contribute to an overvaluing of one's group, particularly the tendency to credit the group for its successes but to blame external factors for its failures (the **ultimate attribution error**). Compare SELF-SERVING BIAS.

group socialization theory a theory of personality development proposing that children are primarily socialized by their peers and that the influences of parents and teachers are filtered through children's peer groups. According to this theory, children seek to be like their peers rather than like their parents.

group structure the complex of processes, forms, and systems that organizes and regulates interpersonal phenomena in a group. Group structure defines the positions and roles in a group and the network of authority, attraction, and communication relations linking members. See also SOCIAL STRUCTURE.

group test a test designed to be administered to several individuals simultaneously. Compare INDIVIDUAL TEST.

group therapy see GROUP PSYCHOTHERAPY.

groupthink *n.* a strong concurrence-seeking tendency that interferes with effective group decision making. Symptoms include apparent unanimity, illusions of invulnerability and moral correctness, biased perceptions of the OUTGROUP, interpersonal pressure, self-censorship, and defective decision-making strategies.

growth function the relationship between a DEPENDENT VARIABLE and several levels of an INDEPENDENT VARIABLE defined in units of time (e.g., days, weeks, months, or years).

growth hormone (**GH**) a hormone, secreted by the anterior PITUITARY GLAND, that promotes the growth of cells and tissues. It stimulates protein synthesis, bone growth in early life, mobilization of fat stores, and carbohydrate storage. Also called **somatotropic hormone**; **somatotropin**.

GSR abbreviation for GALVANIC SKIN RESPONSE.

guanine (symbol: G) *n.* a purine compound in the nucleotides of living organisms. It is one of the four bases in DNA and RNA constituting the GENETIC CODE, the others being adenine, cytosine, and thymine or uracil.

guardianship *n.* a legal arrangement that places the care of a person and his or her property in the hands of another. When people are deemed incompetent by the court, and therefore unable to make decisions about their own care or to manage their own affairs, a **guardian** is appointed to manage their property and ensure their well-being.

guess-who technique a type of personality rating device used chiefly in schools. Students, given short word pictures depicting a variety of personality types, are directed to identify the classmates whose personalities seem to correspond most closely to those descriptions.

guidance program the cumulative resources of staff and techniques used by a school to assist students in resolving scholastic or social problems.

guided affective imagery (**GAI**) in psychotherapy, the drawing out of emotional fantasies, or waking dreams, a technique used to ease CATHARSIS and work on emotions that are present but painful for the client to discuss. The therapist suggests concentration on past images that would bring up the emotional state or, in some cases, images of desired future successes. The technique is often used in SHORT-TERM THERAPY and GROUP PSYCHOTHERAPY. Also called **guided imagery**. See also VISUALIZATION.

guided participation a process in which the influences of social partners and sociocultural practices combine in various ways to provide children and other learners with direction and support, while the learners themselves also shape their learning engagements. It occurs not only during explicit instruction but also during routine activities and communication of everyday life. See SOCIOCULTURAL PERSPECTIVE.

guiding fiction a personal principle that serves as a guideline by which an individual can understand and evaluate his or her experiences and determine his or her lifestyle. In individuals considered to be in good or reasonable mental health, the guiding fiction is assumed to approach reality and be adaptive. In those who are not, it is assumed to be largely unconscious, unrealistic, and nonadaptive.

G

Guilford dimensions of intelligence three dimensions of intelligence postulated by U.S. psychologist Joy Paul Guilford (1897–1987) to underlie individual differences in scores on intelligence tests, namely, contents, operations, and products. Each mental ability represents a combination of these three facets. For example, a verbal-analogies test would represent a combination of cognition (operation) of verbal (content) relations (product). See also STRUCTURE OF INTELLECT MODEL.

Guillain–Barré syndrome an acute, progressive, demyelinating type of PERIPHERAL NEUROPATHY that starts with muscular weakness and loss of normal sensation in the extremities, spreading inward as the disease progresses. The condition often begins in the feet and ascends toward the head. [Georges **Guillain** (1876–1961) and Jean **Barré** (1880–1967), French neurologists]

guilt *n.* a SELF-CONSCIOUS EMOTION characterized by a painful sense of having done (or thought) something that is wrong and often by a readiness to take action designed to undo or mitigate this wrong. —**guilty** *adj.*

guilty but mentally ill a court judgment that may be made in some states when defendants plead INSANITY. Defendants found guilty but mentally ill are treated in a mental hospital until their mental health is restored; they then serve the remainder of their sentence in the appropriate correctional facility.

Gulf War syndrome a collection of unexplained symptoms experienced by some veterans of the 1991 Gulf War. Symptoms may include headaches, fatigue, joint pain, skin rashes, and memory loss.

gustation *n.* the sense of taste. —**gustatory** *adj.*

gustatory neuron types categories into which taste neurons of the peripheral and central nervous system can be grouped according to their sensitivities to PRIMARY TASTE qualities. About 40% of the taste neurons in primates are most responsive to sweet stimuli, 35% to those that are salty, 20% to bitter chemicals, and 5% to acids.

gustatory system the primary structures and processes involved in an organism's detection of and responses to taste stimuli. The gustatory system includes lingual PAPILLAE, TASTE BUDS and TASTE CELLS, TASTE TRANSDUCTION, neural impulses and pathways, and associated brain areas and their functions (see PRIMARY TASTE CORTEX; SECONDARY TASTE CORTEX; SOLITARY NUCLEUS; THALAMIC TASTE AREA). Also called **taste system**.

gustatory transduction see TASTE TRANSDUCTION.

Guttman scale a type of attitude measure consisting of multiple verbal statements that can be ordered to reflect increasing levels of positive evaluation. Endorsement of a particular statement implies endorsement of all statements less extreme than that statement. Although generally used to measure attitudes, this type of scale can also be used to assess other properties of a target of judgment. [first described in 1944 by U.S. experimental psychologist Louis **Guttman** (1916–1987)]

gynandromorph *n.* an organism with both male and female physical characteristics. —**gynandromorphism** *n.*

gyrus *n.* (*pl.* **gyri**) a ridged or raised portion of the cerebral cortex, bounded on either side by a SULCUS.

Hh

H_0 symbol for NULL HYPOTHESIS.

H_1 symbol for ALTERNATIVE HYPOTHESIS.

habilitation *n.* the process of enhancing the independence, well-being, and level of functioning of an individual with a disability or disorder by providing appropriate resources, such as treatment or training, to enable that person to develop skills and abilities he or she had not had the opportunity to acquire previously. Compare REHABILITATION.

habit *n.* a well-learned behavior that is relatively situation-specific and over time has become motorically reflexive and independent of motivational or cognitive influence, that is, it is performed with little or no conscious intent. —**habitual** *adj.*

habitat *n.* the external environment in which an organism lives. An organism's habitat includes other animal and plant species that are important to it, as well as the physical aspects of the environment, including soil, substrate, and climate.

habit reversal a technique of BEHAVIOR THERAPY in which the client must learn a new correct response to a stimulus and stop responding to a previously learned cue. Habit reversal is used in behavioral conditioning, for example, to control such unwanted habits as overeating, smoking, hair pulling (trichotillomania), and nail biting.

habit strength a hypothetical construct said to reflect learning strength, which varies with the number of reinforcements, the amount of reinforcement, the interval between stimulus and response, and the interval between response and reinforcement.

habituation *n.* **1.** the weakening of a response to a stimulus, or the diminished effectiveness of a stimulus, following repeated exposure to the stimulus. Compare DISHABITUATION. **2.** the process of becoming psychologically dependent on the use of a particular drug, such as cocaine, but without the increasing tolerance and physiological dependence that are characteristic of addiction.

hair cell 1. any of the sensory receptors for hearing, located in the ORGAN OF CORTI within the cochlea of the inner ear. They respond to vibrations of the BASILAR MEMBRANE via movement of fine hairlike processes (**stereocilia**) that protrude from the cells. **2.** any of the sensory receptors for balance, similar in structure to the cochlear hair cells. They are located in the inner ear within the ampullae of the SEMICIRCULAR CANALS (forming part of the CRISTA) and within the SACCULE and UTRICLE (forming part of the MACULA).

Halcion *n.* a trade name for TRIAZOLAM.

Haldol *n.* a trade name for HALOPERIDOL.

half-life (symbol: $t_{1/2}$) *n.* in pharmacokinetics, the time necessary for the concentration in the blood of an administered drug to fall by 50%. Half-life is a function of the rate of CLEARANCE of a drug and its VOLUME OF DISTRIBUTION in various body systems; it is expressed by the equation $t_{1/2} = (0.7 \times \text{volume of distribution})/\text{clearance}$. Clinically, half-life varies among individuals as a result of age, disease states, or concurrent administration of other drugs.

halfway house a transitional living arrangement for people, such as individuals recovering from alcohol or substance abuse, who have completed treatment at a hospital or rehabilitation center but still require support to assist them in restructuring their lives.

hallucination *n.* a false sensory perception that has a compelling sense of reality despite the absence of an external stimulus. It may affect any of the senses, but **auditory hallucinations** and **visual hallucinations** are most common. Hallucination is typically a symptom of PSYCHOSIS, although it may also result from substance use or a medical condition, such as epilepsy, brain tumor, or syphilis. Compare DELUSION; ILLUSION.

hallucinogen *n.* a substance capable of producing a sensory effect (visual, auditory, olfactory, gustatory, or tactile) in the absence of an actual stimulus. Because they produce alterations in perception, cognition, and mood, hallucinogens are also called **psychedelic drugs** (from the Greek, meaning "mind-manifesting"). —**hallucinogenic** *adj.*

hallucinogen abuse a pattern of hallucinogen use manifested by recurrent significant adverse consequences related to the repeated ingestion of hallucinogens. See also SUBSTANCE ABUSE.

hallucinogen dependence a cluster of cognitive, behavioral, and physiological symptoms indicating continued use of hallucinogens despite significant hallucinogen-related problems. See also SUBSTANCE DEPENDENCE.

hallucinogen intoxication a reversible syndrome due to the recent ingestion of a specific hallucinogen. Clinically significant behavioral or psychological changes include marked anxiety or depression, DELUSIONS OF REFERENCE, difficulty focusing attention, paranoia, and impaired judgment. These are accompanied by one or more signs of physiological involvement, for example, altered perceptions, pupillary dilation, increased heart rate, sweating, tremors, or incoordination.

hallucinosis *n.* prominent hallucinations due to the direct physiological effects of a substance.

halo effect the tendency for a general evaluation of a person, or an evaluation of a person on a specific dimension, to be used as a basis for judgments of that person on other specific dimensions. For example, a person who is generally liked might be judged as more intelligent, competent, and honest than a person who is generally disliked.

haloperidol *n.* a HIGH-POTENCY ANTIPSYCHOTIC of the BUTYROPHENONE class. The increased safety profile of the second-generation atypical ANTIPSYCHOTICS has led to a significant decline in use of haloperidol. U.S. trade name: **Haldol.**

Halstead–Reitan Neuropsychological Battery (HRNB) a set of tests designed to diagnose and localize brain damage by providing a comprehensive assessment of cognitive functioning. The battery includes five core subtests (Category Test, Tactual Performance Test, Seashore Rhythm Test, Speech-Sounds Perception Test, Finger Tapping Test) and five optional subtests (Trail Making Test, Reitan Indiana Aphasia Screening Test, Reitan–Klove Sensory Perceptual Examination, Grip Strength Test, Lateral Dominance Examination) purportedly measuring elements of language, attention, motor dexterity, sensory–motor integration, abstract thinking, and memory. [Ward C. **Halstead** (1908–1969) and Ralph M. **Reitan** (1922–), U.S. psychologists]

Hamilton Rating Scale for Depression (HAM-D; HRSD) an interview-based, clinician-administered measure of the severity of depressive symptoms, such as DYSPHORIA, insomnia, and weight loss. It is the most widely used measure of the effectiveness of antidepressant medication in clinical trials, and its use is most appropriately restricted to individuals in whom depression has been diagnosed, rather than as a general measure of depressive symptoms. A 38-item self-report version, the **Hamilton Depression Inventory (HDI)**, was developed in 1995. Also called **Hamilton Depression Scale.** [originally published in 1960 by Max **Hamilton** (1912–1988), British psychiatrist]

hammer *n.* see OSSICLES.

handedness *n.* the consistent use of one hand rather than the other in performing certain tasks. Also called **hand dominance.**

handicap 1. *n.* an inability to perform one or more educational, physical, or social tasks, or consistent underperformance in such tasks, as a result of a physical or nonphysical obstacle or hindrance. For example, a nonaccessible entry or exit for a person in a wheelchair would be a physical obstacle, whereas discrimination with regard to employment would be a nonphysical hindrance. See also DISABILITY; EMOTIONAL HANDICAP. **2.** *vb.* to place an individual or group of individuals at a disadvantage, or to hinder or impede progress. —**handicapped** *adj.*

handwriting analysis see GRAPHOLOGY.

haploid *adj.* describing a nucleus, cell, or organism that possesses only one representative of each chromosome, as in a sperm or egg cell. In most organisms, including humans, fusion of the haploid sex cells following fertilization restores the normal DIPLOID condition of body cells, in which the chromosomes occur in pairs. Hence for humans, the **haploid number** is 23 chromosomes, that is, half the full complement of 46 chromosomes.

happiness *n.* an emotion of joy, gladness, satisfaction, and well-being. —**happy** *adj.*

haptic *adj.* relating to the sense of touch or contact and the cutaneous sensory system in general. It typically refers to active touch, in which the individual intentionally seeks sensory stimulation, moving the limbs to gain information about an object or surface.

haptic illusion an illusion in touch perceived by voluntary, directed contact with the object or objects. Compare TACTILE ILLUSION.

haptics *n.* the study of touch, particularly as a means of actively exploring and gaining information about the environment, and the applications of this study in communication systems.

hard determinism the doctrine that human actions and choices are causally determined by forces and influences over which a person exercises no meaningful influence. The term can also be applied to nonhuman events, implying that all things must be as they are and could not possibly be otherwise. Compare SOFT DETERMINISM. See DETERMINISM.

hardiness *n.* an ability to adapt easily to unexpected changes combined with a sense of purpose in daily life and of personal control over what occurs in one's life. Hardiness dampens the effects of a stressful situation through information gathering, decisive actions, and learning from the experience. —**hardy** *adj.*

hard palate see PALATE.

hard-wired *adj.* in neurophysiology, referring to fixed, inflexible NEURAL NETWORKS or NEURAL CIRCUITS.

harmonic *n.* a PURE-TONE component whose frequency is an integer multiple of the fundamental FREQUENCY. For example, the third harmonic of 500 Hz is 1500 Hz. An **overtone** is a harmonic, but the numbering is different: 1500 Hz is the second overtone of 500 Hz. Harmonic is the preferred term.

harmonic mean a measure of CENTRAL TENDENCY. It is computed for n scores as $n/\Sigma(1/x_i)$, that is, n divided by $1/x_1 + 1/x_2 + ...1/x_n$.

harm reduction a theoretical approach in programs designed to reduce the adverse effects of risky behaviors (e.g., alcohol use, drug use, indiscriminate sexual activity), rather than to eliminate the behaviors altogether. Programs focused on alcohol use, for example, do not advocate abstinence but attempt instead to teach people to anticipate the hazards of heavy drinking and learn to drink safely.

hashish *n.* the most potent CANNABIS preparation. It contains the highest concentration of delta-9-TETRAHYDROCANNABINOL (THC) because it consists largely of pure resin from one of the species of the *Cannabis* plant from which it is derived.

hate *n.* a hostile emotion combining intense feelings of detestation, anger, and often a desire to do harm. Also called **hatred**.

hate crime a crime of violence that is motivated by bias or hatred against the group to which the victims of the crimes belong. Examples of hate crimes are killing a man because he is (or is thought to be) gay and bombing a place of worship of a religious minority.

Hawthorne effect the effect on the behavior of individuals of knowing that they are being observed or are taking part in research. The Hawthorne effect is typically positive and is named after the Western Electric Company's Hawthorne Works plant in Cicero, Illinois, where the phenomenon was first observed during a series of studies on worker productivity conducted from 1924 to 1932. These **Hawthorne Studies** began as an investigation of the effects of illumination conditions, monetary incentives, and rest breaks on productivity, but evolved into a much wider consideration of the role of worker attitudes, supervisory style, and GROUP DYNAMICS.

hazard control the process of identifying, evaluating, and eliminating hazards from an environment, system, or product (ENGINEERING CONTROLS) or of protecting users and workers from exposure to hazards where these cannot be completely eliminated (ADMINISTRATIVE CONTROLS). See also SAFETY ENGINEERING.

hazard function a mathematical function that describes the relationship between the risk of a particular event occurring and time. It is one element of SURVIVAL ANALYSIS.

HD abbreviation for HUNTINGTON'S DISEASE.

head injury any physical injury to the scalp or skull or any brain damage that may result. Head injuries are usually caused by blunt force, such as a blow to the head, but may result from significant acceleration or deceleration in the absence of physical contact (an **acceleration–deceleration injury**). They are commonly classified as either closed, in which the head strikes an object (e.g., a concussion), or open (penetrating), in which a foreign object passes through the skull and enters the brain (e.g., a gunshot wound). A variety of transient or permanent neuropsychological consequences may result, including emo-tional, behavior, and personality changes; disturbances of EXECUTIVE FUNCTIONS; memory and attention difficulties; and sensory and motor deficits. Also called **head trauma**.

head-related transfer function a function that describes the spectral characteristics of sound measured at the TYMPANIC MEMBRANE when the source of the sound is in three-dimensional space. It is used to simulate externally presented sounds when the sounds are presented through headphones. It is a function of frequency, azimuth, and elevation and is determined primarily by the acoustical properties of the external ear, the head, and the torso.

health activities questionnaire any questionnaire designed to measure an individual's current repertoire of health-related behaviors. There is an increased emphasis on prevention in health care, and many inventories exist to measure an individual's compliance with physical activity, dietary control, preventive inoculations, and screening for potential health problems, such as mammography and prostate or colon cancer testing.

health–belief model a model that identifies the relationships of the following to the likelihood of taking preventive health action: (a) individual perceptions about susceptibility to and seriousness of a disease, (b) sociodemographic variables, (c) environmental cues, and (d) perceptions of the benefits and costs. See also EXERCISE–BEHAVIOR MODEL.

health care services and delivery related to the health and well-being of individuals and communities, including preventive, diagnostic, therapeutic, rehabilitative, maintenance, monitoring, and counseling services. In its broadest sense, health care relates to both physical and mental health and is provided by medical and mental health professionals. See also MENTAL HEALTH CARE; MENTAL HEALTH SERVICES.

health education any type of education regarding physical, mental, and emotional health. Conducted in school, institutional, and community settings, this education may cover stress management, smoking cessation, nutrition and fitness, reproductive health, self-esteem, relationship issues, health risks, personal safety (e.g., self-defense and rape prevention), and minority health issues.

health locus of control the perceived source of control over health, that is, either personal behaviors or external forces.

health psychology the subfield of psychology that focuses on (a) the examination of the relations between behavioral, cognitive, psychophysiological, and social and environmental factors and the establishment, maintenance, and detriment of health; (b) the integration of psychological and biological research findings in the design of empirically based interventions for the prevention and treatment of illness; and (c) the evaluation of physical and psychological status before, during, and after medical and psychological treatment.

hearing *n.* the ability of an organism to sense sound and to process and interpret the sensations to gain information about the source and nature of the sound. In humans hearing refers to the perception of sound. Also called **audition**.

hearing disorder any disease, injury, or congenital condition resulting in HEARING LOSS or DEAFNESS.

hearing loss the inability to hear a normal range of tone frequencies, a normally perceived level of sound intensity, or both.

hearing theories theories related to the sensation and perception of sound. Until the 1960s such theories related almost exclusively to sound processing in the inner ear. Contemporary theories and models relate to various aspects of hearing, including pitch perception, intensity coding, and BINAURAL hearing.

heart attack sudden, severe chest pain that occurs when one of the coronary arteries becomes blocked. The condition may result in a myocardial infarction (i.e., death of a section of heart muscle), depending upon the extent of damage to the surrounding muscle.

heart rate in emotion changes in heart rate associated with particular emotional states. It is usually held that heart rate increases in states of fear, anger, and scorn and decreases in states of attentiveness, positive emotional reaction, and interest. However, the actual relation between heart rate and emotion is complex and largely mediated by the energy demands of the bodily musculature of the organism in an emotional state.

heat exhaustion a condition resulting from exposure to excessive heat. Dehydration and salt depletion in the body cause such symptoms as headaches, weakness, dizziness, and blurred vision. Heat exhaustion typically is temporary and not life threatening because it does not involve elevation of body temperature, as occurs in HEATSTROKE.

heatstroke *n.* a serious condition caused by a breakdown of the body's temperature-regulation ability following exposure to excessive heat. Since the body is no longer able to cool itself by sweating, the skin feels hot and dry and the person may experience convulsions or seizures and potentially lose consciousness. The elevated body temperature may cause brain damage or death. Emergency treatment involving cooling the patient must be started immediately.

Hebbian synapse a junction between neurons that is strengthened when it successfully fires the POSTSYNAPTIC cell. See DUAL TRACE HYPOTHESIS. [Donald O. **Hebb** (1904–1985), Canadian psychologist]

hebephrenia *n.* see DISORGANIZED SCHIZOPHRENIA.

hebetude *n.* a state of severe emotional dullness, lethargy, and lack of interest.

hedonic contingency hypothesis a theory of affect and information processing postulating that people consider the hedonic implications of information when determining whether to elaborate information. When people are in positive mood states, they will engage in extensive ELABORATION to maintain their positive mood if the information is seen as uplifting, but if it is seen as unpleasant, they will engage in little elaboration. When people are in negative mood states, they tend to elaborate information with little attention to its hedonic consequences because such information is unlikely to make their mood more negative and might make it more positive.

hedonic contrast the concept that preference for a "good" stimulus is enhanced if it is preceded or accompanied by a less pleasing stimulus.

hedonic psychology a psychological perspective that focuses on the spectrum of experiences ranging from pleasure to pain and includes biological, social, and phenomenological aspects and their relationship to motivation and action. See HEDONISM.

hedonics *n.* the branch of psychology concerned with the study of pleasant and unpleasant sensations and thoughts, especially in terms of their role in human motivation.

hedonic theory the view that a fundamental motivational principle in human beings and nonhuman animals is the level of pleasantness or unpleasantness aroused by an interaction or thought.

hedonism *n.* **1.** in philosophy, the doctrine that pleasure is an intrinsic good and the proper goal of all human action. One of the fundamental questions of ethics has been whether pleasure can or should be equated with the good in this way. **2.** in psychology, any theory that suggests that pleasure and the avoidance of pain are the only or the major motivating forces in human behavior. Hedonism is a foundational principle in psychoanalysis, in behaviorism, and even in theories that stress self-actualization and need-fulfillment. To the extent that human beings are hedonistic, it is difficult to admit the possibility of genuine ALTRUISM. Also called **hedonistic psychology**. See EUDEMONISM. —**hedonistic** *adj.*

hegemony *n.* the dominance of one individual, group, or state over others. —**hegemonic** *adj.*

Helmert contrast a procedure in the ANALYSIS OF VARIANCE of longitudinal data in which each level of a repeated measure is compared with the mean of the remaining levels. [Friedrich Robert **Helmert** (1843–1917), German mathematician]

Helmholtz theory in audition, the still-controversial theory that pitch is determined by the place of stimulation along the BASILAR MEMBRANE. The theory is clearly flawed in certain aspects, but the essential notion remains viable. See PLACE THEORY. [Hermann von **Helmholtz** (1821–1894), German physiologist and physicist]

helping a type of PROSOCIAL behavior that involves one or more individuals acting to improve the status or well-being of another or others. Although typically in response to a small request that involves little individual risk, all helping incurs some cost to the individual providing it.

helping model a broadly based educational approach emphasizing the development of the complete individual and the realization of the student's full potential. The helping model is concerned with motor development, perceptual skills, cognitive development, emotional maturity, interpersonal skills, expression, creativity, and ethical values.

helping professions those professions that provide health and education services to individuals and groups, including occupations in the fields of psychology, psychiatry, counseling, medicine, nursing, social work, physical and occupational therapy, teaching, and education.

helplessness *n.* a state of incapacity, vulnerability, or powerlessness defined by low problem-focused COPING POTENTIAL and low future expectancy. See also LEARNED HELPLESSNESS. **—helpless** *adj.*

helplessness theory the theory that LEARNED HELPLESSNESS explains the development of or vulnerability to depression. According to this theory, people repeatedly exposed to stressful situations beyond their control develop an inability to make decisions or engage effectively in purposeful behavior.

hematoma *n.* an abnormal accumulation of blood as a result of vessel leakage or rupture.

hemeralopia *n.* day blindness: a condition in which a person has difficulty seeing in bright light but has good vision in dim light.

hemianopia *n.* loss of vision in half of the visual field. Also called **hemianopsia; hemiopia**. **—hemianopic** *adj.* **—hemianoptic** *adj.*

hemidecortication *n.* surgical removal of the CEREBRAL CORTEX on one side of the brain.

hemineglect *n.* see UNILATERAL NEGLECT.

hemiparesis *n.* weakness or partial paralysis affecting one side of the body.

hemiplegia *n.* complete paralysis that affects one side of the body. **—hemiplegic** *adj.*

hemisphere *n.* either of the symmetrical halves of the cerebrum (see CEREBRAL HEMISPHERE) or the CEREBELLUM. **—hemispheric** or **hemispherical** *adj.*

hemispherectomy *n.* surgical removal of either one of the cerebral hemispheres of the brain.

hemispheric asymmetry the idea that the two cerebral hemispheres of the brain are not identical but differ in size, shape, and function. The functions that display the most pronounced asymmetry are language processing in the left hemisphere and visuospatial processing in the right hemisphere.

hemispheric dominance see HEMISPHERIC LATERALIZATION.

hemispheric encoding–retrieval asymmetry the hypothesis that the left cerebral hemisphere is especially active during the encoding of a memory, whereas the right hemisphere is especially active during the retrieval of the memory.

hemispheric lateralization the processes whereby some functions, such as HANDEDNESS or language, are controlled or influenced more by one cerebral hemisphere than the other and each hemisphere is specialized for particular ways of working. Researchers now prefer to speak of hemispheric lateralization or **hemispheric specialization** for particular functions, rather than **hemispheric dominance** or **lateral dominance** (see DOMINANCE).

hemoglobin *n.* an iron-rich pigment of red blood cells that transports oxygen molecules and is responsible for the color of blood. When saturated with oxygen, the pigment becomes bright red.

hemorrhage *n.* bleeding; any loss of blood from an artery or vein. A hemorrhage may be external, internal, or within a tissue, such as the skin. **—hemorrhagic** *adj.*

hemorrhagic stroke see STROKE.

Henle fiber the cytoplasmic extension that allows a RETINAL CONE in the region of the FOVEA CENTRALIS to reach one of the RETINAL BIPOLAR CELLS. [Friedrich Gustav Jakob **Henle** (1809–1885), German anatomist]

Henning's odor prism a prism-shaped graphic representation of six PRIMARY ODORS and their relationships. Burnt, spicy, resinous, foul, fruity, and flowery are the primaries that occupy the corners of the prism, and each surface represents the positions of odors that are similar to the primaries at the corners of that surface. Also called **Henning's smell prism**. [Hans **Henning** (1885–1946), German psychologist]

hepatitis *n.* inflammation of the liver, marked by diffuse or patchy areas of dead liver cells in the liver lobules. Symptoms range from mild, flulike symptoms to liver failure, which can be fatal. The causes include alcohol and drug abuse, viruses, and other infectious agents.

here and now the immediate situation. In psychotherapy, it comprises the cognitive, affective, and behavioral material arising at any given point in a session, as well as the relationship between the therapist and client at the corresponding point in time. When the **here-and-now approach** is used in psychotherapy, the emphasis is placed on understanding present feelings and interpersonal reactions as they occur in an ongoing treatment session, with little or no emphasis on or exploration of past experience or underlying reasons for the client's thoughts, emotions, or behavior. The approach is often used in PSYCHODYNAMIC PSYCHOTHERAPY with regard to the therapeutic relationship, GESTALT THERAPY, and many forms of FAMILY THERAPY to heighten the client's awareness.

hereditarianism *n.* the view that genetic inheritance is the major influence on behavior. Opposed to this view is the belief that environment and learning account for the major differences between people. The question of heredity versus environment or "nature versus nurture" continues to be controversial, especially as it applies to human intelligence. See GENETIC DETERMINISM; NATURE–NURTURE. **—hereditarian** *adj.*

heredity *n.* the transmission of traits from parents to their offspring. Study of the mechanisms and laws of heredity is the basis of the science of GENETICS. Heredity depends upon the character of the genes contained in the parents' CHROMOSOMES, which in turn depends on the particular GENETIC CODE carried by the DNA of which the chromosomes are composed.

Hering illusion a misperception that occurs when two parallel straight lines are superimposed on a pattern of lines that radiate from a central point. When the two lines are placed equidistant from one another, on opposite sides of the center point, they appear to be bowed outward from the center, rather than straight. [Ewald **Hering** (1834–1918), German physiologist and psychologist]

Hering theory of color vision a theory of color vision postulating that there are three sets of receptors, one of which is sensitive to white and black, another to red and green, and the third to yellow and blue. The breaking down (catabolism) of these substances is supposed to yield one member of these pairs (white, red, or yellow), while the building up (anabolism) of the same substances yields the other (black, green, or blue). See OPPONENT PROCESS THEORY OF COLOR VISION. [proposed in 1875 by Ewald **Hering**]

heritability *n.* an estimate of the contribution of inheritance to a given trait or function. Heritabilities can range from 0, indicating no contribution of heritable factors, to 1, indicating total contribution of heritable factors. The heritability of intelligence is believed to be roughly .5, for example. Heritability is not the same as genetic contribution, because heritability is sensitive only to sources of individual differences. Moreover, a trait can be heritable and yet modifiable.

hermaphrodite *n.* an organism possessing both male and female sex organs (in the human species, for example, possessing both ovarian and testicular tissue). True hermaphroditism oc-

curs more rarely than PSEUDOHERMAPHRODITISM. **—hermaphroditism** *n.*

hermeneutics *n.* the theory or science of interpretation. Hermeneutics is concerned with the ways in which humans derive meaning from language or other symbolic expression. Originally, the term was confined to the interpretation of Scripture. Subsequently, two main strains of hermeneutic thought developed. In the first, which expanded the task of interpretation to include all forms of cultural expression, including artworks, institutions, and historical events, a key concept is the so-called **hermeneutic circle**— the notion that interpretation is always circular, in that particulars will necessarily be interpreted in the light of one's understanding of the whole, and the understanding of the whole will be altered by the understanding of the particulars. Another key assumption is the need to gain insight into the mind of the person or people whose expression is the subject of interpretation. This approach has been criticized on the grounds that such insight is impossible; thus, the methods of hermeneutics will always be imprecise and their results relativistic.

In the second, more radical, strain of hermeneutics, which derives from PHENOMENOLOGY, the project of interpretation was expanded to include DASEIN (human being) itself. This suggests that all human behavior can be understood as meaningful expression, much as one would understand a written text. It also turns the process of interpretation back on the interpreter, as the understanding of the being of human beings entails interpretations of interpretive acts. This move has given rise to a broad movement within philosophy, psychology, and literary criticism in which richness of interpretation is considered more valuable than consistent methodology or arriving at the "correct" interpretation. Such an approach is a clear alternative to a natural scientific psychology. This type of hermeneutics has informed other contemporary movements, notably EXISTENTIALISM, POSTMODERNISM, and POSTSTRUCTURALISM. **—hermeneutic** *adj.*

herniation *n.* the abnormal protrusion of an organ or other bodily structure through an opening in a membrane, muscle, or bone.

heroin *n.* a highly addictive OPIOID that is a synthetic analog of MORPHINE and three times more potent. Its rapid onset of action leads to an intense initial high, followed by a period of euphoria and a sense of well-being.

heroin abuse a pattern of heroin use manifested by recurrent significant adverse consequences related to the repeated ingestion of the substance. See also SUBSTANCE ABUSE.

heroin dependence a cluster of cognitive, behavioral, and physiological symptoms indicating continued use of heroin despite significant heroin-related problems. See also SUBSTANCE DEPENDENCE.

heroin intoxication a reversible syndrome that develops following recent ingestion of heroin, characterized by euphoria, PSYCHOMOTOR RETARDATION, drowsiness, and impaired attention or memory.

heroin withdrawal see OPIOID WITHDRAWAL.

hertz (symbol: Hz) *n.* the unit of FREQUENCY equal to one cycle per second. [Heinrich Rudolf **Hertz** (1857–1894), German physicist]

Heschl's gyrus one of several transverse ridges on the upper side of the TEMPORAL LOBE of the brain that are associated with the sense of hearing. [Richard **Heschl** (1824–1881), Austrian pathologist who first traced the auditory pathways of humans to this convolution]

heterogametic *adj.* referring to the sex that has two dissimilar SEX CHROMOSOMES, such as the male sex in mammals and the female sex in birds. Compare HOMOGAMETIC.

heterogeneity of variance the situation in which populations or CELLS in a experimental design have unequal variances. Compare HOMOGENEITY OF VARIANCE.

heterogeneous *adj.* composed of diverse elements. Compare HOMOGENEOUS.

heteronomous *adj.* under the control of or influenced by various external factors. Compare AUTONOMOUS.

heteronomous stage in the theory of moral development expounded by Swiss psychologist Jean Piaget (1896–1980), the stage at which the child, approximately 6 to 10 years of age, equates morality with the rules and principles of his or her parents and other authority figures. That is, the child evaluates the rightness or wrongness of an act only in terms of adult sanctions for or against it and of the consequences or possible punishment it may bring. Also called **heteronomous morality**. See also IMMANENT JUSTICE; MORAL ABSOLUTISM; MORAL REALISM. Compare AUTONOMOUS STAGE; PREMORAL STAGE.

heteronomy *n.* a state of dependence on others and lack of self-determination. Compare AUTONOMY.

heterophily *n.* any tendency for individuals who differ from one another in some way to make social connections. It is less common than HOMOPHILY. **Complementarity**, which occurs when people with different but complementary characteristics form a relationship, is an example of heterophily.

heteroscedasticity *n.* the situation in which Var($Y|X$) is not the same for all values of X, that is, the variance in Y is a function of the variable X. Compare HOMOSCEDASTICITY. **heteroscedastic** *adj.*

heterosexism *n.* prejudice against any nonheterosexual form of behavior, relationship, or community, in particular the denigration of gay men and lesbians. Whereas HOMOPHOBIA generally refers to an individual's fear or dread of gay men or lesbians, heterosexism denotes a wider system of beliefs, attitudes, and institutional structures that attach value to heterosexuality and denigrate same-sex behavior and orientation.

heterosexuality *n.* sexual attraction to or activity between members of the opposite sex. **heterosexual** *adj.*

heterotopia *n.* the congenital development of gray matter in the area of the brain and spinal cord normally consisting of white matter.

heterozygous *adj.* see ALLELE. **heterozygote** *n.*

heuristic *n.* **1.** a strategy for solving a problem or making a decision that provides an efficient means of finding an answer but cannot guarantee a correct outcome. By contrast, an ALGORITHM guarantees a solution to a problem (if there is one) but may be much less efficient. Also called **cognitive heuristic**. See also AVAILABILITY HEURISTIC; REPRESENTATIVENESS HEURISTIC. **2.** in ergonomics, a procedure in which several experts, working independently, evaluate a product or system according to established usability guidelines and produce structured reports noting any failings. The advantage of this type of evaluation is that it is relatively simple and cheap. The chief disadvantage is that it does not involve testing among target users and so may not identify problems experienced by particular groups (e.g., those with a different cultural background). Compare TASK ANALYSIS.

heuristic search a search through the set of all possible paths to the solution of a given problem that is optimized by the use of strategies that reduce the number of possible paths that need to be attempted.

heuristic-systematic model a theory of persuasion postulating that the validity of a persuasive message can be assessed in two different ways. **Systematic processing** involves the careful scrutiny of the merits of attitude-relevant information in the message. **Heuristic processing** involves the use of a subset of information in the message as a basis for implementing a simple decision rule to determine if the message should be accepted (e.g., judging a message to be valid because its source is highly credible). See also DUAL PROCESS MODEL OF PERSUASION.

Hick's law in experiments or tasks involving CHOICE REACTION TIME, the finding that the time required to classify a stimulus as being from a particular set increases proportionally with the number of stimuli in the set. Also called **Hick–Hyman law**. [William Edmund **Hick** (1912–1974), British psychologist; Ray **Hyman** (1928–), U.S. cognitive psychologist]

hidden observer the phenomenon whereby highly hypnotizable people (see HYPNOTIC SUSCEPTIBILITY) who are asked to block certain stimuli (e.g., pain) can sometimes register the blocked pain or other sensation via hand signals, as if a dissociated observer is simultaneously taking in events that are disavowed by the dominant observer. Such individuals can later recall auditory, visual, or tactile stimuli to which they appeared oblivious at the time.

hierarchically nested design a research design in which two or more levels of sampling units are nested within higher order sampling units, for example, students (A), nested within classrooms (B), nested within schools (C), nested within school systems (D). Analysis of the data of such designs depends on whether the different levels are regarded as fixed or random factors.

hierarchical theory of intelligence any theory of intelligence postulating that the abilities constituting intelligence are arranged in a series of levels (of a hierarchy) ranging from general to specific. Many of these theories are based on recognizing three levels of factors: (a) the general factor, applying to all intellectual tasks; (b) group factors, which apply to some but not all intellectual tasks; and (c) specific factors, applying to individual tasks. Examples of such theories are the THREE-STRATUM MODEL OF INTELLIGENCE and the CATTELL–HORN THEORY OF INTELLIGENCE.

hierarchy *n.* a clear ordering of phenomena on some dimension, such as a DOMINANCE HIERARCHY.

hierarchy of motives (**hierarchy of needs**) see MASLOW'S MOTIVATIONAL HIERARCHY.

higher mental process any of the more complex types of cognition, such as thinking, judgment, imagination, memory, and language.

higher order conditioning in PAVLOVIAN CONDITIONING, a procedure in which the CONDITIONED STIMULUS of one experiment acts as the UNCONDITIONED STIMULUS of another, for the purpose of conditioning a NEUTRAL STIMULUS. For example, after pairing a tone with food, and establishing the tone as a conditioned stimulus that elicits salivation, a light could be paired with the tone. If the light alone comes to elicit salivation, then higher order conditioning has occurred.

higher order consciousness a type of CONSCIOUSNESS that goes beyond sensory contents (see SENSORY CONSCIOUSNESS) to include abstract ideas, language-dependent thinking, and self-consciousness.

higher order interaction in the ANALYSIS OF VARIANCE, the joint effect of three or more independent variables on the dependent variable.

high-involvement management an approach to managing organizations that attempts to tap the potential of employees by obtaining input from them on decisions, sharing information about the business with them, providing training to enhance their skills, and providing incentives for becoming skilled and committed.

high-potency antipsychotic any of various conventional ANTIPSYCHOTICS that have either a relatively high degree of affinity for the dopa-

mine D2 receptor or significant EXTRAPYRAMIDAL SYMPTOMS. HALOPERIDOL is an example.

high-risk participant study research on vulnerable, or "high-risk," participants, who may be predisposed to social, physical, or psychiatric pathology by reason of genetic, constitutional, or environmental factors. The object of these studies is both to identify specific factors that differentiate between those who ultimately develop disorders and those who do not and to establish the statistical probability of different types of pathology.

high threshold a threshold that is never exceeded unless a signal is present. Classical psychophysics assumes a high threshold, although some psychophysical models combine high thresholds with **low thresholds**, which can be exceeded by random NOISE.

hindbrain *n.* the posterior of three bulges that appear in the embryonic brain as it develops from the NEURAL TUBE. The bulge eventually becomes the MEDULLA OBLONGATA, PONS, and CEREBELLUM. Also called **rhombencephalon**.

hindsight bias the tendency, after an event has occurred, to overestimate the extent to which the outcome could have been foreseen.

hinge *n.* either of the scores in a batch of data that divide the lower 25% of cases (the lower hinge) and the upper 25% of cases (the upper hinge) from the remainder of the cases.

hippocampal formation a region of the brain located in the medial temporal lobe and concerned with the consolidation of long-term memory. It comprises the DENTATE GYRUS, HIPPOCAMPUS, and SUBICULUM and communicates with areas of neocortex via the ENTORHINAL CORTEX.

hippocampus *n.* (*pl.* **hippocampi**) a seahorse-shaped part of the forebrain, in the basal medial region of the TEMPORAL LOBE, that is important for DECLARATIVE MEMORY and learning. Because of its resemblance to a ram's horn, 19th-century neuroanatomists named it **Ammon's horn** (**cornu ammonis**; CA) for the horn of the ram that represented the Egyptian deity Ammon. Parts of the hippocampus were then labeled **CA1**, **CA2**, **CA3**, and **CA4**; these designations are still used for the different regions of the hippocampus. —**hippocampal** *adj.*

histamine *n.* a compound that is synthesized from the amino acid histidine and mostly localized in peripheral tissues, where it is involved in allergic reactions or the inflammatory response to injury, causing dilation of blood vessels. In the brain, histamine acts as a neurotransmitter to modulate such functions as arousal, appetite, and regulation of autonomic functions. **Histamine receptors** can be divided into three categories, designated H_1, H_2, and H_3 receptors.

histamine antagonist see ANTIHISTAMINE.

histogenesis *n.* the formation of body tissues.

histogram *n.* a graphical depiction of continuous data using bars of varying height, similar to a BAR GRAPH but with blocks on the *x*-axis adjoining one another so as to denote their continuous nature. For example, to show the average credit card debt of individuals by age, bars along the *x*-axis would represent age and would be connected to one another, while the heights of the bars would represent the dollar amount of debt.

histology *n.* the scientific study of the structure and function of tissues. **—histological** *adj.* **—histologist** *n.*

historical control group a comparison group in which the participants are selected to be similar to those in the treatment group but for whom the data for comparison with the treatment group were collected some time in the past.

historical method the technique of analyzing, counseling, or otherwise offering therapy by focusing on a client's personal history.

history taking the process of compiling the history of a patient or research participant from the individual directly and from others who have direct knowledge of the individual.

histrionic personality disorder a personality disorder characterized by a pattern of long-term (rather than episodic) self-dramatization in which individuals draw attention to themselves, crave activity and excitement, overreact to minor events, experience angry outbursts, and are prone to manipulative suicide threats and gestures.

hit *n.* the accurate identification of a signal in a signal detection task. Compare MISS.

HIV *h*uman *i*mmunodeficiency *v*irus: a parasitic agent in blood, semen, and vaginal fluid that destroys a class of lymphocytes with a crucial role in the immune response. HIV infection can occur by various routes—unprotected sexual intercourse, administration of contaminated blood products, sharing of contaminated needles and syringes by intravenous drug users, or transmission from an infected mother to her child *in utero* or through breast feeding—and is characterized by a gradual deterioration of immune function that can progress to AIDS. Because the diagnosis of HIV infection is stigmatizing and can result in considerable emotional stress and social ostracism, counseling is available in which guidance, advice, and information are provided to individuals on topics related to HIV infection and AIDS, including managing the myriad associated psychological and social issues.

Hi-Wa itck a CULTURE-BOUND SYNDROME found in Mohave American Indian populations that includes symptoms such as depression, insomnia, loss of appetite, and sometimes suicide associated with unwanted separation from a loved one; it generally affects the young wife of an older Mohave male.

hoarding *n.* a COMPULSION, characteristic of OB-

SESSIVE-COMPULSIVE DISORDER, that involves the persistent collection of useless or trivial items (e.g., old newspapers, garbage, magazines) and an inability to organize or discard these. The accumulation of items (usually in piles) leads to the obstruction of living space, causing distress or impairing function. Any attempt or encouragement by others to discard hoards causes extreme anxiety. **—hoard** *vb., n.*

hold functions cognitive abilities—such as those involved in vocabulary and verbal knowledge, object assembly, and picture completion—that typically remain stable or improve with adult aging as observed on intellectual or cognitive tests.

holding environment in the OBJECT RELATIONS THEORY of British psychoanalyst Donald Winnicott (1896–1971), that aspect of the mother experienced by the infant as the environment that literally—and figuratively, by demonstrating highly focused attention and concern—holds him or her comfortingly during calm states. This is in contrast to the mother who is experienced as the object of the infant's excited states.

holiday syndrome sadness, anxiety, and pessimism that tend to occur during major holiday periods.

holism *n.* any approach or theory holding that a system or organism is a coherent, unified whole that cannot be fully explained in terms of individual parts or characteristics. The system or organism may have properties, as a complete entity or phenomenon, in addition to those of its parts. Thus, an analysis or understanding of the parts does not provide an understanding of the whole. **—holistic** *adj.*

holistic education a form of psychotherapy, derived from the approach of HOLISTIC MEDICINE, in which the therapist serves as a teacher and the client as student. The therapist aims to create conditions within which the student may choose to learn. For maximum growth, all aspects of the client's physical, spiritual, emotional, and intellectual life should be explored and developed.

holistic medicine a branch of medicine that, in the prevention and treatment of disease, focuses on the whole person—including physical, mental, spiritual, social, and environmental aspects—rather than on disease symptoms alone. Major features of holistic medicine include patient education about behavioral and attitudinal changes that promote and maintain good health and well-being, and patient self-help and participation in the healing process through diet, exercise, and other measures.

holistic psychology an approach to psychology based on the view that psychological phenomena must be studied as wholes, or that individuals are biological, psychological, and sociocultural totalities that cannot be fully explained in terms of individual components or characteristics. Holistic psychology is not a specific school but a perspective that informs the theories, methodologies, and practice of certain approaches, such as HUMANISTIC PSYCHOLOGY and CLIENT-CENTERED THERAPY.

holographic brain theory a brain theory suggesting that neuronal processes operate by means of fieldlike states of wave interference similar to holograms. Also called **holonomic brain theory.**

holophrase *n.* one of the single-word utterances characteristic of children in the early stages of LANGUAGE ACQUISITION, such as *dada* or *yes.* These are considered to involve a SPEECH ACT going beyond the literal meaning of the single word so that, for example, *biscuit* means *I want a biscuit now.* See RICH INTERPRETATION. —**holophrastic** *adj.*

home and community-based services care or services provided in a patient's place of residence or in a noninstitutional setting located in the community. The aim is to help individuals of all ages with disabilities to live in the community, thereby avoiding more costly residential placements.

home care patient care in the home for people with physical or mental disabilities, including older adults with dementia or physical infirmity. Home care is an alternative to institutionalization, enabling the patient to live in familiar surroundings and preserve family ties. Also called **home health care.**

homeopathy *n.* a system of medicine based on the belief that "like cures like." Small, highly diluted quantities of substances are given to cure symptoms when the same substances given at higher or more concentrated doses would actually cause those symptoms. Homeopathy is considered a form of COMPLEMENTARY AND ALTERNATIVE MEDICINE. Compare ALLOPATHY. —**homeopathic** *adj.*

homeostasis *n.* the regulation by an organism of all aspects of its internal environment, including body temperature, salt–water balance, acid–base balance, and blood sugar level. This involves monitoring changes in the external and internal environments by means of RECEPTORS and adjusting bodily processes accordingly. —**homeostatic** *adj.*

home range the entire space through which an animal moves during its normal activities. The part of the home range in which the greatest activity occurs is known as the **core area.**

home schooling formal instruction of a student in his or her home or other private setting, often by one or both parents or by a tutor. Home schooling is often used for gifted students or for students with special needs, chronic illness, atypical learning styles, or behavior problems.

home-service agency a group, which may be a public health, social service, or voluntary organization, that provides **home health aides** (who as-

sist with personal care) or **homemaker home health aides** (who assist with homemaking tasks, personal care, and rehabilitation) for people with mental or physical disabilities.

homework *n.* tasks assigned to a client to be performed between sessions of therapy. Assignments may require reading, research, or practicing new behaviors (e.g., attending a lecture, speaking to a specific person).

homicidomania *n.* a mental or emotional disturbance characterized by a desire to kill others, often including actual attempts to do so.

homing *n.* the ability of organisms to return to an original home after traveling or being transported to a point that is a considerable distance from the home and that lacks most visual clues as to its location.

hominid *n.* a primate of the family Hominidae, of which humans (*Homo sapiens*) are the only living species.

homogametic *adj.* referring to the sex that has two similar SEX CHROMOSOMES, such as the female sex in mammals and the male sex in birds. Compare HETEROGAMETIC.

homogeneity of variance the condition in which multiple populations, or CELLS in an experimental design, have the same variance: a basic assumption of many statistical procedures. Compare HETEROGENEITY OF VARIANCE.

homogeneous *adj.* having the same, or relatively similar, composition throughout. Compare HETEROGENEOUS.

homolateral *adj.* on the same side of the body. —**homolaterally** *adv.*

homologous *adj.* exhibiting resemblance in terms of structure, location, or origin. For example, DIPLOID organisms, such as humans, possess homologous pairs of chromosomes in the nuclei of their body cells.

homology *n.* a similarity of form in bodily structures of species that are descended from a common ancestor, such as the resemblance in forelimbs of vertebrates. See also ANALOGY. Compare HOMOPLASY. —**homologous** *adj.*

homophily *n.* the tendency for individuals who are socially connected in some way to display certain affinities, such as similarities in demographic background, attitudes, values, and so on. Compare HETEROPHILY.

homophobia *n.* dread or fear of gay men and lesbians.

homoplasy *n.* a similarity of form in bodily structures of species that are not descended from a common ancestor (e.g., the body forms of a tuna and a dolphin). This superficial resemblance often arises through the process of convergent evolution (see DIVERGENT EVOLUTION) because the species live in the same environment. Compare HOMOLOGY. —**homoplastic** *adj.*

homoscedasticity *n.* the situation in which

Var($Y|X$) = Var(Y), that is, the variance of variable Y is unrelated to the value of another variable X. Homoscedasticity is a basic assumption in some forms of REGRESSION ANALYSIS. Compare HETEROSCEDASTICITY. —**homoscedastic** *adj.*

homosexuality *n.* sexual attraction or activity between members of the same sex. Although the term can refer to such sexual orientation in both men and women, current practice distinguishes between gay men and lesbians, and homosexuality itself is now commonly referred to as same-sex sexual orientation or activity. —**homosexual** *adj., n.*

homozygous *adj.* see ALLELE. —**homozygote** *n.*

homunculus *n.* (*pl.* **homunculi**) **1.** a putative process or entity in the mind or the nervous system whose operations are invoked to explain some aspect of human behavior or experience. The problem with such theories is that the behavior or experience of the homunculus usually requires explanation in exactly the same way as that of the person as a whole. As a result, homunculus theories tend to end in circular reasoning or to involve an infinite regression of homunculi. For example, to explain its theory that certain ideas are kept from conscious awareness because they are threatening to the person, psychoanalysis must posit some specialized part of the person that is aware of the ideas, and knows that they are threatening. Similarly, some information-processing theories invoke a "decision-making process" to explain the making of decisions. Both theories invoke a sophisticated level of inner awareness or processing in an attempt to explain another outward level of awareness or processing. For this reason critics would say that they require homunculi, or that they commit the **homunculus fallacy**. **2.** in neuroanatomy, a figurative representation, in distorted human form, of the relative sizes of motor and sensory areas in the brain that correspond to particular parts of the body. For example, the brain area devoted to the tongue is much larger than the area for the forearm, so the homunculus has a correspondingly larger tongue. See MOTOR HOMUNCULUS; SENSORY HOMUNCULUS. —**homuncular** *adj.*

honestly significant difference (**HSD**) see TUKEY'S HONESTLY SIGNIFICANT DIFFERENCE TEST.

honest signal in animal communication, a signal that provides accurate information about an individual's internal state or its intentions. Honest signals have value if they are highly correlated with a physical trait (e.g., body size) that might, for example, provide important information for mate selection or if they are used within a stable social group where DISHONEST SIGNALS can be detected and "cheaters" punished.

honesty *n.* **1.** in general, truthfulness, uprightness, and integrity. **2.** in psychotherapy, the

ability of an individual to express true feelings and communicate immediate experiences, including conflicting, ambivalent, or guilt-ridden attitudes. —**honest** *adj.*

hope *n.* an emotion characterized by the expectation that one will have positive experiences (or that a potentially threatening or negative situation will not materialize or will ultimately result in a favorable state of affairs) and by the belief that one can influence one's experiences in a positive way.

hopelessness *n.* the feeling that one will not experience positive emotions or an improvement in one's condition. Hopelessness is common in DEPRESSIVE DISORDERS and is often implicated in attempted and completed suicides. —**hopeless** *adj.*

Hopkins Symptom Checklist (**HSCL**) a 58-item self-report inventory developed at Johns Hopkins University in the 1970s to identify symptom patterns along five dimensions that yield a total distress score: obsessive-compulsive behavior, anxiety, depression, somatization, and interpersonal sensitivity.

horizontal communication the exchange of messages, written or spoken, among employees occupying positions at the same level of authority in the organization. Compare DOWNWARD COMMUNICATION; UPWARD COMMUNICATION.

horizontal décalage in PIAGETIAN THEORY, the invariant order in which accomplishments occur within a particular stage of development. For example, an understanding of CONSERVATION of quantity is always achieved before understanding conservation of weight. Compare VERTICAL DÉCALAGE.

horizontal mobility the movement of individuals or groups from one position or role to another within the same social class. Compare VERTICAL MOBILITY. See also SOCIAL MOBILITY.

horizontal plane the plane that divides the body or brain into upper and lower parts. Also called **transverse plane**.

horizontal–vertical illusion the misperception that vertical lines are longer than horizontal lines when both are actually the same length. The vertical element of an upper case letter T looks longer than the cross bar, even when the lengths are identical.

hormone *n.* a substance secreted into the bloodstream by an ENDOCRINE GLAND or other tissue or organ to regulate processes in distant target organs and tissues. —**hormonal** *adj.*

hormone replacement therapy (**HRT**) the administration of female sex hormones to postmenopausal women to relieve menopausal symptoms. Long-term use, however, may increase the risk of breast cancer, cardiovascular disease, stroke, and other conditions associated with the aging process.

horopter *n.* the location in space occupied by

points that fall on corresponding locations on the two retinas.

hospice *n.* a place or form of care for terminally ill individuals, often those with life expectancies of less than a year as determined by medical personnel. Instead of curing disease and prolonging life, the emphases of the hospice concept are patient comfort, psychological well-being, and pain management. See also TERMINAL CARE.

hostility displacement the direction of hostility or aggression to a target other than the agent responsible for provoking this behavior. The causes are complex, but conventional accounts typically state that the target is selected because there is no anticipation of punishment for the attack.

Hotelling's T^2 a statistical technique used in MULTIVARIATE analysis for testing the equality of two populations with regard to their mean VECTORS. It is the multivariate generalization of the two-group T TEST. [Harold **Hotelling** (1895–1973), U.S. economist and statistician]

hothousing *n.* the acceleration of young children's academic skills through instruction designed to increase academic achievement. Some theorists believe that hothousing is equivalent to hurrying children and that it is therefore maladaptive to normal development.

hotline *n.* a telephone line maintained by trained personnel for the purpose of providing a crisis intervention service. See TELEPHONE COUNSELING.

hot-seat technique a technique of GESTALT THERAPY in which a client sits in a chair next to the therapist, who encourages the client through direct prompting and questioning to relive stressful experiences and openly express feelings of discomfort, guilt, or resentment. The technique aims to generate a new, more vivid awareness, which leads the client to find his or her own solutions to problems or emotional difficulties. In a GROUP PSYCHOTHERAPY variation of the hot-seat technique, an individual member expresses to the therapist his or her interest in dealing with a particular issue, and the focus moves away from the group into an extended interaction between the group member and group leader for a limited period of time. During the one-on-one interaction, the other group members remain silent; afterward, they give feedback on how they were affected, what they observed, and how their own experiences are similar to those on which the individual member worked. Compare EMPTY-CHAIR TECHNIQUE.

HRNB abbreviation for HALSTEAD–REITAN NEUROPSYCHOLOGICAL BATTERY.

HRSD abbreviation for HAMILTON RATING SCALE FOR DEPRESSION.

HRT abbreviation for HORMONE REPLACEMENT THERAPY.

HSCL abbreviation for HOPKINS SYMPTOM CHECKLIST.

HSD abbreviation for honestly significant difference. See TUKEY'S HONESTLY SIGNIFICANT DIFFERENCE TEST.

hue *n.* the subjective quality of color, which is determined primarily by wavelength and secondarily by amplitude.

Hull's mathematico-deductive theory of learning a mathematical system of learning based on Pavlovian and instrumental conditioning with numerous postulates and corollaries to explain various behaviors. There is major emphasis on NEED REDUCTION as a condition of learning, the building up of HABIT STRENGTH by contiguous reinforcement, EXTINCTION brought about by nonreinforced repetition of responses, and forgetting as a process of decay with the passage of time. [Clark L. **Hull** (1884–1952), U.S. psychologist]

human channel capacity the limit on the amount of information that may be processed simultaneously by the human information-processing system.

human ecology the study of the relationship between human beings and their physical and social environments.

human engineering the design of environments and equipment that promote optimum use of human capabilities and optimum safety, efficiency, and comfort.

human factors 1. in ERGONOMICS, the impact of human beings, with their characteristic needs, abilities, and limitations, on system function and the considerations to be made when designing, evaluating, or optimizing systems for human use, especially with regard to safety, efficiency, and comfort. **2.** the field of ERGONOMICS itself.

human factors engineering an interdisciplinary field concerned with the design, maintenance, operation, and improvement of operating systems in which human beings are components, such as health care systems and transportation systems. This term is often used synonymously with ERGONOMICS.

human factors psychology a branch of psychology that studies the role of HUMAN FACTORS in operating systems, with the aim of redesigning environments, equipment, and processes to fit human abilities and characteristics. Also called **engineering psychology**.

Human Genome Project an international project to map each human gene and determine the complete sequence of base pairs in human DNA. The project began in 1990 and was completed in 2003. It has yielded vast amounts of valuable information about the genes responsible for various diseases.

human immunodeficiency virus see HIV.

humanism *n.* **1.** a perspective that begins with a presumption of the inherent dignity and worth of humankind and, as a scholarly or artistic discipline, focuses attention on the study and representation of human beings and human experiences. The roots of Western humanism lie in the Renaissance period, when those who studied the classical Greek and Roman languages and writings became known as humanists. **2.** any position taken in opposition to religious belief or other forms of supernaturalism. See SECULAR HUMANISM. **3.** in psychology, any perspective that seeks to uphold human values and to resist the reduction of human beings and behaviors to merely natural objects and events. In this spirit, HUMANISTIC PSYCHOLOGIES have resisted not only natural scientific psychology, but also theories that emphasize the negative and pathological aspects of human nature. In contemporary psychology, the term humanism is often applied to theories and perspectives in the tradition of U.S. psychologists Carl Rogers (1902–1987) and Abraham Maslow (1908–1970) or to those inspired by PHENOMENOLOGY and EXISTENTIALISM. —**humanist** *adj.*, *n.* —**humanistic** *adj.*

humanistic–existential therapy see EXISTENTIAL–HUMANISTIC THERAPY.

humanistic psychology an approach to psychology that flourished particularly in academia between the 1940s and the early 1970s and that is most visible today as a family of widely used approaches to psychotherapy and counseling. It derives largely from ideas associated with EXISTENTIALISM and PHENOMENOLOGY and focuses on individuals' capacity to make their own choices, create their own style of life, and actualize themselves in their own way. Its approach is holistic, and its emphasis is on the development of human potential through experiential means rather than analysis of the unconscious or behavior modification. Leading figures associated with this approach include U.S. psychologists Abraham Maslow (1908–1970), Carl Rogers (1902–1987), and Rollo May (1909–1994). Also called **humanistic theory**. See FULFILLMENT MODEL; HUMAN-POTENTIAL MOVEMENT.

humanistic therapy any of a variety of psychotherapeutic approaches that reject psychoanalytic and behavioral approaches; seek to foster personal growth through direct experience; and focus on the development of human potential, the HERE AND NOW, concrete personality change, responsibility for oneself, and trust in natural processes and spontaneous feeling. Some examples of humanistic therapy are CLIENT-CENTERED THERAPY, GESTALT THERAPY, EXISTENTIAL PSYCHOTHERAPY, and EXPERIENTIAL PSYCHOTHERAPY.

human operator modeling the practice of using qualitative or quantitative tools to illustrate the behavior, mental processes, or both of human operators when performing tasks. The use of physical or computer models for this purpose is known as **human operator simulation**. Human operator modeling is used to describe, explain, or predict behavior under a variety of task and environmental conditions.

human-potential model an approach to education that emphasizes the importance of helping learners to achieve the maximum development of their potential in all aspects of their functioning. It is derived from the basic tenets of HUMANISTIC PSYCHOLOGY.

human-potential movement an approach to psychotherapy and psychology based on the quest for personal growth, development, interpersonal sensitivity, and greater freedom and spontaneity in living. The ideas of German-born U.S. psychiatrist Frederick (Fritz) S. Perls (1893–1970) were an influential force in the development of the human-potential movement, which derives its general perspective from HUMANISTIC PSYCHOLOGY. GESTALT THERAPY, SENSITIVITY TRAINING, and ENCOUNTER GROUPS are representative of this approach. Also called **human-growth movement**.

human relations theory a general approach to management that emphasizes the importance of employee attitudes, interpersonal relationships, GROUP DYNAMICS, and LEADERSHIP STYLES in achieving ORGANIZATIONAL EFFECTIVENESS.

human strength see CHARACTER STRENGTH.

humiliation *n.* a feeling of shame due to being disgraced or deprecated.

humor *n.* **1.** the capacity to perceive or express the amusing aspects of a situation. There is little agreement about the essence of humor and the reasons one laughs or smiles at jokes or anecdotes. Among philosophers, both Plato (c. 427–c. 347 BCE) and Thomas Hobbes (1588–1679) claimed that individuals laugh at people and situations that make them feel superior, whereas Immanuel Kant (1724–1804) emphasized surprise and anticlimax. Some writers have seen humor as "playful pain," a way of taking serious things lightly and thereby triumphing over them. Austrian psychiatrist Sigmund Freud (1856–1939) called attention to the many jokes that enable individuals to give free expression to forbidden impulses and explained laughter in terms of a release of the energy normally employed in keeping them out of consciousness. See also INCONGRUITY THEORY OF HUMOR; RELEASE THEORY OF HUMOR. **2.** the semifluid substance that occupies the spaces in the eyeball. **3.** anciently, one of four bodily fluids (blood, black bile, yellow bile, and phlegm) that were thought to be responsible for a person's physical and psychological characteristics (see HUMORAL THEORY). —**humoral** *adj.* —**humorous** *adj.*

humoral theory an ancient theory that explained physical and psychological health or illness in terms of the state of balance or imbalance of various bodily fluids. According to Greek physician Hippocrates (5th century BCE), health was a function of the proper balance of four humors: blood, black bile, yellow bile, and phlegm (the **classical humors** or **cardinal humors**). This idea was also used to explain temperament: A pre-

H

dominance of blood was associated with a **sanguine** type; black bile with a **melancholic** type; yellow bile or choler with a **choleric** type; and phlegm with a **phlegmatic** type. Roman physician Galen (129–199) did much to preserve and promulgate this explanatory approach, which survived well into the 17th century. Humoral theory provides psychology with its earliest personality typology, as well as an early model of the relation between bodily and psychological states.

Hunter's syndrome see MUCOPOLYSACCHARIDOSIS. [Charles **Hunter** (1872–1955), U.S. physician]

Huntington's disease (**HD**) a progressive hereditary disease characterized by degeneration of nerve cells in the brain, marked personality changes, affective disorders, DEMENTIA, involuntary jerking motions (see CHOREA), motor incoordination, and disorders of gait and posture. The age of onset is usually between 30 and 50, but there is a juvenile form of the disease in which symptoms first appear before the age of 20. Also called **Huntington's chorea**. [George **Huntington** (1850–1916), U.S. physician]

Hurler's syndrome see MUCOPOLYSACCHARIDOSIS. [Gertrud **Hurler** (1889–1965), Austrian pediatrician]

hwa-byung *n.* a CULTURE-BOUND SYNDROME specific to Korea and characterized by a range of symptoms that are attributed to the suppression of anger (Korean, literally "anger disease"). Symptoms include a feeling of a mass in the throat, chest, or abdomen, a sensation of heat in the body, headaches, palpitations, indigestion, insomnia, fatigue, panic, dysphoria, fear of impending death, anorexia, generalized aches and pains, and poor concentration.

hybridization *n.* the interbreeding of individuals with different genetic traits. Depending on the nature of the genes involved, **hybrids** might display traits of one or the other parent or some combination of parental traits. Hybridization is used in animal behavior studies as a method to evaluate genetic transmission of behavior. —**hybridize** *vb.*

hydantoin *n.* any of a group of drugs developed primarily to control epileptic seizures. Hydantoin molecules are similar in structure to barbiturates but have the advantage of not altering the threshold for minimal seizures. The prototype of the hydantoins is **phenytoin** (previously called diphenylhydantoin).

hydraulic model any physiological or psychological model based on the analogy of fluid flowing through a system under pressure, such that pressure may build up in the system and seek release. Sigmund Freud's model of the LIBIDO as an energy that can build pressure and seek release (CATHARSIS) is a notable example.

hydrocephalus *n.* a condition caused by excessive accumulation of cerebrospinal fluid in the ventricles of the brain, resulting in raised

INTRACRANIAL PRESSURE, with such symptoms as headache, vomiting, nausea, poor coordination, lethargy, drowsiness, or irritability or other changes in personality or cognition, including memory loss. Also called **hydrocephaly**. —**hydrocephalic** *adj.*

hydrocodone *n.* see OPIOID ANALGESIC.

hydrophobia *n.* **1.** a persistent and irrational fear of water, resulting in avoidance of activities involving water, such as swimming, drinking, or washing one's hands. **2.** a former name for RABIES. —**hydrophobic** *adj.*

hydrotherapy *n.* the use of water, internally or externally, to treat illness, injury, or some other condition or to promote a sense of well-being. Hydrotherapy includes such treatments as bath therapy, hygienic douches, and aquatic sports or exercise for auxiliary therapy and physical rehabilitation.

hygiene factors in the two-factor theory of WORK MOTIVATION, certain aspects of the working situation that can produce discontent if they are poor or lacking but that cannot by themselves motivate employees to improve their job performance. These include pay, relations with peers and supervisors, working conditions, and benefits. Compare MOTIVATORS.

hyperactivity *n.* spontaneous, excessive motor or other activity. —**hyperactive** *adj.*

hyperacusis *n.* unusually acute hearing and a lowered tolerance for loud sounds. Also called **hyperacusia**.

hyperaggressivity *n.* an increased tendency to express anger and hostility in action, as in violent and assaultive behavior.

hyperalgesia *n.* an abnormal sensitivity to pain. Also called **hyperalgia**.

hypercalcemia *n.* high concentrations of calcium in the blood. Hypercalcemia caused by deletion of a segment of chromosome 7 is called **Williams syndrome** and is marked by failure to thrive, an elfin facial appearance, mental retardation, and often aortic stenosis (narrowing of the aorta, restricting blood flow from the heart). Most children with Williams syndrome, however, are sociable and have superior verbal (compared to nonverbal) skills.

hypercathexis *n.* in psychoanalytic theory, an excess of PSYCHIC ENERGY invested in an OBJECT. Compare HYPOCATHEXIS. See CATHEXIS.

hypercolumn *n.* a repeating subdivision of STRIATE CORTEX (primary visual cortex) that contains a full set of ORIENTATION COLUMNS and a pair of OCULAR DOMINANCE COLUMNS. Thus the population of neurons in one hypercolumn includes those responsive to all orientations, as viewed through either eye.

hypercomplex cell a neuron in the visual cortex for which the optimal stimulus is a moving line of specific length or a moving corner.

hyperesthesia *n.* extreme sensitivity in any of

the senses, especially abnormal sensitivity to touch. **—hyperesthetic** *adj.*

hyperfunction *n.* excessive activity of a body function, part, or organ.

hypergeusia *n.* a heightened sensitivity to taste. See SUPERTASTER. **—hypergeusic** *adj.*

hyperglycemia *n.* an excess of glucose in the blood. **—hyperglycemic** *adj.*

hyperkinesis *n.* **1.** excessive involuntary movement. **2.** restlessness or HYPERACTIVITY. Also called **hyperkinesia.** **—hyperkinetic** *adj.*

hyperkinesthesia *n.* a high level of sensitivity to motion and position of the body. Compare HYPOKINESTHESIA.

hyperlexia *n.* the development of extremely good reading skills at a very early age, well ahead of word comprehension or cognitive ability. Children with hyperlexia often start to recognize words without instruction and before any expressive language develops. **—hyperlexic** *adj.*

hypermania *n.* an extreme manic state marked by constant activity, erratic behavior, DISORIENTATION, and incoherent speech. **—hypermanic** *adj.*

hypermetamorphosis *n.* a strong tendency to react excessively or devote an inordinate amount of attention to any visual stimulus.

hypermetria *n.* overreaching an object during voluntary motor activity. Compare HYPOMETRIA.

hypermnesia *n.* **1.** an extreme degree of retentiveness and recall, with unusual clarity of memory images. **2.** remembering more over time rather than less, in contrast to forgetting.

hypermotility *n.* abnormally increased or excessive activity or movement, particularly in the digestive tract.

hyperopia *n.* farsightedness. Hyperopia is a REFRACTIVE ERROR due to an abnormally short eyeball, in which the image is blurred because the focal point of one or both eyes lies behind, rather than on, the retina. Compare EMMETROPIA; MYOPIA.

hyperorexia *n.* a pathologically increased appetite. See also BULIMIA. Compare HYPOPHAGIA.

hyperosmia *n.* abnormally acute sensitivity to odors. Compare HYPOSMIA.

hyperphagia *n.* pathological overeating, particularly when due to a metabolic disorder or to a brain lesion. Compare APHAGIA. **—hyperphagic** *adj.*

hyperphoria *n.* deviation of one eye in an upward direction.

hyperplasia *n.* an abnormal increase in the size of an organ or tissue caused by the growth of an excessive number of new, normal cells. **—hyperplastic** *adj.*

hyperpolarization *n.* an increase in the electric potential across the plasma membrane of a cell, especially a neuron, such that the inner surface of the membrane becomes more negative in relation to the outer surface. It occurs during the final portion of an ACTION POTENTIAL or in response to inhibitory neural messages. Compare DEPOLARIZATION.

hypersensitivity *n.* an excessive responsiveness of the immune system to certain foreign substances, including various drugs. Hypersensitivity reactions may be immediate, involving an acute allergic reaction leading to ANAPHYLAXIS, or more delayed, involving dangerous and sometimes fatal reductions in the number of certain white blood cells (**agranulocytosis**).

hypersomnia *n.* excessive sleepiness during daytime hours or abnormally prolonged episodes of nighttime sleep. This can be a feature of certain DYSSOMNIAS (e.g., NARCOLEPSY) or other sleep or mental disorders, or it can be associated with neurological dysfunction or damage, with a general medical condition, or with substance use. Hypersomnia may, however, occur in the absence of any known cause or of an association with another condition (see PRIMARY HYPERSOMNIA). Compare HYPOSOMNIA.

hypertension *n.* high blood pressure: a circulatory disorder characterized by persistent arterial blood pressure that exceeds readings higher than an arbitrary standard, which usually is 140/90. If there is no obvious cause it is called **essential hypertension**. If a cause is identified, such as tumors of the adrenal gland or chronic kidney disease, it is called **secondary hypertension** and usually cured if its cause is removed or is corrected. **—hypertensive** *adj.*

hyperthyroidism *n.* overactivity of the thyroid gland, resulting in excessive production of thyroid hormones and such symptoms as increased metabolic rate and hyperactivity. See also THYROTOXICOSIS.

hypertonia *n.* a state of increased muscle tension or tonicity. Also called **hypertonicity**. Compare HYPOTONIA. **—hypertonic** *adj.*

hypertrophy *n.* overgrowth of an organ or part due to an increase in the size of its constituent cells. **—hypertrophic** *adj.*

hypertropia *n.* see STRABISMUS.

hyperventilation *n.* abnormally rapid and deep breathing, usually due to anxiety or emotional stress. This lowers the carbon dioxide level of the blood and produces such symptoms as light-headedness and numbness and tingling in the extremities.

hypervigilance *n.* a state of abnormally heightened alertness, particularly to threatening or potentially dangerous stimuli.

hypesthesia *n.* severely diminished sensitivity in any of the senses, especially the touch sense. Also called **hypoesthesia**.

hypnagogic *adj.* describing or relating to a state of drowsiness or light sleep that occurs just before falling fully asleep.

H

hypnalgia *n.* literally, dream pain: pain experienced during sleep.

hypnoanalysis *n.* a modified and shortened form of psychoanalytic treatment, or a technique incorporated into full analysis, in which hypnosis is used (a) to help patients overcome RESISTANCES, (b) to enhance the TRANSFERENCE process, and (c) to recover memories and release repressed material. The material so brought forth is meant to be incorporated into the patient's consciousness for exploration and, ultimately, for interpretation by the therapist. However, this form of therapy is controversial because many psychologists and psychoanalysts question the veracity of repressed memories recovered during a hypnotic state.

hypnogenic *adj.* **1.** sleep-producing. **2.** hypnosis-inducing.

hypnoid state a state resembling hypnosis.

hypnopompic *adj.* relating to the drowsy, semiconscious state between deep sleep and waking.

hypnosis *n.* (*pl.* **hypnoses**) the procedure, or the state induced by that procedure, whereby a hypnotist suggests that a subject experience various changes in sensation, perception, cognition, emotion, or control over motor behavior. Subjects appear to be receptive, to varying degrees, to suggestions to act, feel, and behave differently than in a normal waking state. As a specifically psychotherapeutic intervention, hypnosis is referred to as HYPNOTHERAPY.

hypnosuggestion *n.* the application of direct hypnotic suggestion in therapy. It is used to relieve such problems as insomnia, intractable pain, cigarette smoking, anorexia nervosa, and various types of crises (e.g., combat situations, panic, and dissociative amnesia).

hypnotherapy *n.* the use of hypnosis in psychological treatment, either in SHORT-TERM THERAPY directed toward alleviation of symptoms and modification of behavior patterns or in long-term RECONSTRUCTIVE PSYCHOTHERAPY aimed at personality adaptation or change. Hypnotherapy may use one or a combination of techniques, typically involving the administration by a properly trained professional of therapeutic suggestions to patients or clients who have been previously exposed to a HYPNOTIC INDUCTION procedure. Although discussions of its clinical applications engender controversy, there has been scientific evidence that hypnotherapy can be applied with some success to a wide range of clinical problems (e.g., hypertension, asthma, insomnia, bruxism); chronic and acute pain management; habit modification (e.g., anorexia nervosa, overeating, smoking); mood and anxiety disorders (e.g., some phobias); and personality disorders. There is also some positive evidence demonstrating the effectiveness of hypnosis as an ADJUNCTIVE THERAPY.

hypnotic 1. *n.* a drug that helps induce and sustain sleep by increasing drowsiness and reducing motor activity. In general, hypnotics differ from SEDATIVES only in terms of the dose administered, with higher doses used to produce sleep or anesthesia and lower doses to produce sedation or relieve anxiety. BENZODIAZEPINES are among the most widely prescribed hypnotics, but newer, nonbenzodiazepine hypnotics, such as ZOPICLONE, ZOLPIDEM, and ZALEPLON, are achieving clinical currency because of their relative infrequency of adverse side effects. **2.** *adj.* pertaining to hypnosis or sleep.

hypnotic induction a process by which an individual comes under the influence of verbal suggestions or other stimuli during hypnosis.

hypnotic regression a therapeutic technique in which an individual under hypnosis is induced to relive a previous experience that may be contributing to current emotional difficulties. An example is AGE REGRESSION.

hypnotic susceptibility the degree to which an individual is able to enter into hypnosis. Although many individuals can enter at least a light trance, people vary greatly in their ability to achieve a moderate or deep trance. Also called **hypnotizability**.

hypoactive sexual desire disorder persistent deficiency or absence of sexual interest and desire to engage in sexual activity. This may be global, involving all forms of sexual activity, or situational, limited to one partner or one type of sexual activity.

hypoactivity *n.* abnormally slowed or deficient motor or other activity.

hypocathexis *n.* in psychoanalytic theory, an abnormally low investment of PSYCHIC ENERGY in an OBJECT. Compare HYPERCATHEXIS. See CATHEXIS.

hypochondria *n.* morbid concern with the state of one's health, including unfounded beliefs of ill health. —**hypochondriac** or **hypochondriacal** *adj.* —**hypochondriac** *n.*

hypochondriasis *n.* a SOMATOFORM DISORDER characterized by a preoccupation with the fear or belief that one has a serious physical disease based on the incorrect and unrealistic interpretation of bodily symptoms. This fear or belief persists for at least 6 months and interferes with social and occupational functioning in spite of medical reassurance that no physical disorder exists.

hypofunction *n.* reduced function or activity, especially of an organ, such as a gland.

hypogastric nerve either of a pair of single large nerves, or sets of smaller parallel nerves, that extend into the pelvic region and carry postganglionic fibers that innervate the bladder, rectum, and genitalia.

hypogeusia *n.* diminished sensitivity to taste. See also DYSGEUSIA. —**hypogeusic** *adj.*

hypoglossal nerve the 12th cranial nerve, a sensory nerve that innervates the tongue, lower jaw, and areas of the neck and chest.

hypoglycemia *n.* the condition of having a low

blood-sugar level, due to interference with the formation of sugar in the blood or excessive utilization of sugar. **—hypoglycemic** *adj.*

hypokinesis *n.* abnormal slowness in the initiation of voluntary movement. Compare BRADY-KINESIA. Also called **hypokinesia. —hypokinetic** *adj.*

hypokinesthesia *n.* a diminished level of sensitivity to motion and position of the body. Compare HYPERKINESTHESIA.

hypomanic episode a period of elevated, expansive, or irritable mood lasting at least 4 days and accompanied by at least three of the following (four if the mood is irritable): inflated self-esteem, a decreased need for sleep, increased speech, racing thoughts, distractibility, increase in activity or PSYCHOMOTOR AGITATION, and increased involvement in risky activities (e.g., foolish investments, sexual indiscretions), all of which affect functioning and are noticeable by others but do not cause marked impairment. Also called **hypomania**.

hypometria *n.* underreaching an object during voluntary motor activity. Compare HYPERMETRIA.

hypomotility *n.* abnormally decreased or deficient activity or movement.

hypophagia *n.* pathologically reduced food intake. Compare HYPERPHAGIA.

hypophoria *n.* deviation of one eye in a downward direction.

hypoplasia *n.* underdevelopment of an organ or tissue, usually due to an inadequate number of cells or diminished size of cells forming the structure. **—hypoplastic** *adj.*

hyposmia *n.* decreased sensitivity to some or all ODORS. Compare HYPEROSMIA.

hyposomnia *n.* a reduction in a person's sleep time, often as a result of INSOMNIA or some other sleep disturbance. See also SLEEP DISORDER. Compare HYPERSOMNIA.

hypotaxia *n.* poor motor coordination. **—hypotaxic** *adj.*

hypotension *n.* abnormally low blood pressure, causing dizziness and fainting. See also ORTHOSTATIC HYPOTENSION. **—hypotensive** *adj.*

hypothalamic hormone any hormone secreted by neurons of the hypothalamus. Neuroendocrine cells in the hypothalamus produce the hormones OXYTOCIN and VASO-PRESSIN. Other neuroendocrine cells in the hypothalamus produce either RELEASING HORMONES, which stimulate secretion of anterior pituitary hormones, or inhibiting hormones, which prevent secretion of anterior pituitary hormones.

hypothalamic–pituitary–adrenocortical system a neuroendocrine system that is involved in the physiological response to stress. Outputs from the amygdala to the hypothalamus stimulate the release of CORTICOTROPIN-

RELEASING FACTOR (CRF) into the HYPOTHA-LAMIC–PITUITARY PORTAL SYSTEM. CRF elicits the release from the anterior pituitary of CORTICOTROPIN, which in turn regulates the production and release of stress hormones (e.g., cortisol) from the adrenal cortex into the bloodstream.

hypothalamic–pituitary portal system a system of blood capillaries that transports RELEASING HORMONES from the hypothalamus to the anterior pituitary. Also called **hypothalamic–hypophyseal portal system**.

hypothalamus *n.* (*pl.* **hypothalami**) part of the DIENCEPHALON of the brain, lying ventral to the THALAMUS, that contains nuclei with primary control of the autonomic (involuntary) functions of the body. It also helps integrate autonomic activity into appropriate responses to internal and external stimuli. **—hypothalamic** *adj.*

hypothesis *n.* (*pl.* **hypotheses**) an empirically testable proposition about some fact, behavior, relationship, or the like, usually based on theory, that states an expected outcome resulting from specific conditions or assumptions.

hypothesis testing the process of using any of a collection of statistical tests to assess the likelihood that an experimental result might have been the result of a chance or random process.

hypothetical imperative in the moral teaching of German philosopher Immanuel Kant (1724–1804), a maxim of the type "If you would achieve end X, take action Y." Such maxims of skill or prudence differ from the CATEGORICAL IMPERATIVE of morality in that (a) they are aimed at particular material ends rather than absolute and unconditional ends and (b) they cannot be defended as a universal and transitational law. See also UNIVERSALIZABILITY.

hypothetico-deductive method a method of examining the accuracy of predictions made on the basis of some theory, in which the theory gains credibility as more predictions are found to be accurate.

hypothetico-deductive reasoning the abstract logical reasoning that, according to the PIAGETIAN THEORY of cognitive development, emerges in early adolescence and marks the FORMAL OPERATIONAL STAGE. Hypothetico-deductive reasoning is distinguished by the capacity for abstract thinking and hypothesis testing.

hypothyroidism *n.* underactivity of the thyroid gland. In adults, it is marked by decreased metabolic rate, tiredness, and lethargy.

hypotonia *n.* decreased muscle tone or strength. Compare HYPERTONIA. **—hypotonic** *adj.*

hypotropia *n.* see STRABISMUS.

hypoxemia *n.* a deficiency of oxygen in the blood. See also ANOXEMIA. **—hypoxemic** *adj.*

hypoxia *n.* reduced oxygen in the body tissues, including the brain. This can result in wide-

H

spread brain injury depending on the degree of oxygen deficiency and its duration. Signs and symptoms of hypoxia vary according to its cause, but generally include shortness of breath, rapid pulse, fainting, and mental disturbances (e.g., delirium, euphoria). See also AN-OXIA. —**hypoxic** *adj.*

hysterectomy *n.* the surgical removal of the uterus. It may be **total hysterectomy**, including excision of the cervix; **subtotal hysterectomy**, in which only the uterus above the cervix is removed; or **radical hysterectomy**, with excision of a part of the vagina with the uterus and cervix.

hysteresis *n.* the tendency for a perceptual state to persist under gradually changing conditions. For example, stereoscopic fusion can persist, producing the appearance of depth even when BIN-OCULAR DISPARITY between the two images becomes so great that they would normally not be able to be fused. —**hysteretic** *adj.*

hysteria *n.* the historical name for the condition now classified as SOMATIZATION DISORDER. Although technically outdated, it is often used as a lay term for any psychogenic disorder characterized by such symptoms as paralysis, blindness, loss of sensation, and hallucinations and often accompanied by suggestibility, emotional outbursts, and histrionic behavior. Austrian psychiatrist Sigmund Freud (1856–1939) interpreted hysterical symptoms as defenses against guilty sexual impulses (e.g., a paralyzed hand cannot masturbate), but other conflicts are now recognized. Freud also included dissociative conditions in his concept of hysteria, but these are now regarded as separate disorders. —**hysterical** *adj.*

Hz symbol for HERTZ.

H

Ii

IADLs abbreviation for INSTRUMENTAL ACTIVITIES OF DAILY LIVING.

iatrogenic *adj.* denoting or relating to a disease or pathological condition that is caused inadvertently by treatment. For example, an **iatrogenic addiction** is a dependence on a substance, most often a painkiller, originally prescribed by a physician to treat a physical or psychological disorder.

IBS abbreviation for IRRITABLE BOWEL SYNDROME.

ICD abbreviation for INTERNATIONAL CLASSIFICATION OF DISEASES.

iconic memory the brief retention of an image of a visual stimulus beyond cessation of the stimulus. This iconic image usually lasts less than a second. In a MULTISTORE MODEL OF MEMORY, iconic memory precedes SHORT-TERM MEMORY. Also called **visual sensory memory**.

iconic mode see ENACTIVE MODE.

iconic symbol a linguistic SIGN (written or spoken word) that has a physical resemblance, rather than an arbitrary relation, to its referent. Examples include onomatopoeic coinages, such as *choo-choo* (train), and the signs used in pictographic languages. Compare ARBITRARY SYMBOL.

ICP abbreviation for INTRACRANIAL PRESSURE.

ictus *n.* a sudden event, particularly a seizure.

id *n.* in psychoanalytic theory, the component of the personality that contains the instinctual, biological drives that supply the psyche with its basic energy or LIBIDO. Austrian psychiatrist Sigmund Freud (1856–1939) conceived of the id as the most primitive component of the personality, located in the deepest level of the unconscious; it has no inner organization and operates in obedience to the PLEASURE PRINCIPLE. Thus the infant's life is dominated by the desire for immediate gratification of instincts, such as hunger and sex, until the EGO begins to develop and operate in accordance with reality. See also PRIMARY PROCESS; STRUCTURAL MODEL.

id anxiety in psychoanalytic theory, anxiety deriving from instinctual drives. This is the main cause of PRIMARY ANXIETY. Compare EGO ANXIETY.

idea *n.* in cognitive psychology, a mental image or cognition that is ultimately derived from experience but that may occur without direct reference to perception or sensory processes.

idealism *n.* **1.** in philosophy, the position that reality, including the natural world, is not independent of mind. Positions range from strong forms, holding that mind constitutes the things of reality, to weaker forms holding that reality is correlated with the workings of the mind. There is also a range of positions as to the nature of mind, from those holding that mind must be conceived of as absolute, universal, and apart from nature itself to those holding that mind may be conceived of as individual minds. See also MIND–BODY PROBLEM. **2.** commitment to moral, political, or religious ideals. **3.** see PLATONIC IDEALISM. Compare MATERIALISM. —**idealist** *n.* —**idealistic** *adj.*

idealization *n.* **1.** the exaggeration of the positive attributes and minimization of the imperfections or failings associated with a person, place, thing, or situation, so that it is viewed as perfect or nearly perfect. **2.** in psychoanalytic theory, a DEFENSE MECHANISM that protects the individual from conscious feelings of ambivalence toward the idealized OBJECT. Idealization of the parents and other important figures plays a role in the development of the EGO-IDEAL. —**idealize** *vb.*

ideal observer a hypothetical person whose sensory and perceptual systems operate without error or bias. The concept of the ideal observer is used most commonly within the context of psychophysical testing, particularly SIGNAL DETECTION THEORY. Performance of the ideal observer can be simulated and compared with actual human performance.

ideal performance state the state of cognitive and physiological activation that permits optimal performance for an individual. See ZONE OF OPTIMAL FUNCTIONING.

ideal self in models of self-concept, a mental representation of an exemplary set of psychological attributes that may or may not be part of one's actual self.

ideational apraxia see APRAXIA.

idée fixe 1. a firmly held, irrational idea or belief that is maintained despite evidence to the contrary. It may take the form of a delusion and become an obsession. Also called **fixed belief**; **fixed idea**. **2.** a subconscious unit of mental processing (see AUTOMATISM) that has become split off or dissociated from consciousness and, as a result, interferes with the normal processing of information. In some theories, this is considered a primary mechanism for the symptoms of HYSTERIA.

identical twins see MONOZYGOTIC TWINS.

identification *n.* **1.** the process of associating

the self closely with other individuals and their characteristics or views. Identification operates largely on an unconscious or semiconscious level. **2.** in psychoanalytic theory, a DEFENSE MECHANISM in which the individual incorporates aspects of his or her OBJECTS inside the EGO in order to alleviate the anxiety associated with OBJECT LOSS or to reduce hostility between himself or herself and the object.

identification transference in GROUP PSYCHOTHERAPY, the client's identification with other members of the group and desire to emulate them.

identified patient a member of a structured group (especially a family) who exhibits the symptoms of a mental disorder and for whom treatment may be sought by the other group members. Clinical investigation may reveal that there is a complex and seriously maladaptive behavioral pattern among members of the group as a whole but that the psychological stigma has fallen primarily on one person, the identified patient.

identity *n.* **1.** an individual's sense of self defined by (a) a set of physical and psychological characteristics that is not wholly shared with any other person and (b) a range of social and interpersonal affiliations (e.g., ethnicity) and social roles. Identity involves a sense of continuity: the feeling that one is the same person today that one was yesterday or last year (despite physical or other changes). Such a sense is derived from one's body sensations, one's body image, and the feeling that one's memories, purposes, values, and experiences belong to the self. Also called **personal identity**. **2.** in cognitive development, awareness that an object remains the same even though it may undergo many transformations. For example, a piece of clay may be made to assume various forms but is still the same piece of clay.

identity crisis a phase of life marked by role experimentation, changing, conflicting, or newly emerging values, and a lack of commitment to one's usual roles in society (especially in work and family relationships).

identity diffusion 1. lack of stability or focus in the view of the self or in any of the elements of an individual's IDENTITY. **2.** in the EGO PSYCHOLOGY of German-born U.S. psychologist Erik Erikson (1902–1994), a possible outcome of the IDENTITY VERSUS ROLE CONFUSION stage in which the individual emerges with an uncertain sense of identity and confusion about his or her wishes, attitudes, and goals.

identity foreclosure in the development of identity, the unquestioning acceptance by individuals (usually adolescents) of the role, values, and goals that others (e.g., parents, close friends, teachers, athletic coaches) have chosen for them.

identity theory the theory that mental states are identical with brain states. In **token identity**

theory, identical mental and brain states occur within the individual. **Type identity theory** extends this to theorize that when two or more people share a mental state (e.g., the belief that ice is cold) they also have the same brain state. See also MIND–BODY PROBLEM.

identity versus role confusion the fifth of ERIKSON'S EIGHT STAGES OF DEVELOPMENT, marked by an identity crisis that occurs during adolescence. During this stage the individual may experience a psychosocial MORATORIUM, a period of time that permits experimentation with social roles. The individual may "try on" different roles and identify with different groups before forming a cohesive, positive identity that allows him or her to contribute to society; alternatively, the individual may identify with outgroups to form a negative identity, or may remain confused about his or her sense of identity, a state Erikson calls IDENTITY DIFFUSION.

ideomotor activity movement related to ongoing thoughts but produced without volition. Ideomotor activity explains a variety of phenomena, including nonverbal gestures during conversations and various spiritualist phenomena, such as may be experienced with the Ouija board.

ideomotor apraxia see APRAXIA.

ideomotor compatibility the extent to which stimuli resemble the sensory feedback from their assigned responses. For example, if the stimulus is the speech sound [a] and the response is to say the letter aloud, stimulus and response have high ideomotor compatibility.

ideomotor theory the hypothesis that actions are evoked impulsively by mental images and are carried out spontaneously in the absence of inhibitory events. Hence, it claims that images have motivational power.

idiocentric *adj.* denoting internality to the self, particularly an orientation toward or focus on personal needs and interests. See also EGOCENTRISM. Compare ALLOCENTRIC. —**idiocentrism** *n.*

idiogenesis *n.* origin without evident cause, particularly the origin of an IDIOPATHIC disease.

idiographic *adj.* relating to the description and understanding of an individual case, as opposed to the formulation of NOMOTHETIC general laws describing the average case. U.S. psychologists Kenneth MacCorquadale (1919–1986) and Paul Meehl (1920–2003) identified these as two contrasting traditions in explaining psychological phenomena. An **idiographic approach** involves the thorough, intensive study of a single person or case in order to obtain an in-depth understanding of that person or case, as contrasted with a study of the universal aspects of groups of people or cases.

idiolect *n.* a DIALECT spoken at the level of an individual. The term is typically reserved for the most idiosyncratic forms of personal language use, especially those involving eccentricities of construction or vocabulary. An idiolect of this kind may be developed by a person who acquires a second language unsystematically, especially if this occurs in an unusual or isolated learning environment. Some poets and writers also develop distinctive idiolects in their writings. **—idiolectal** *adj.*

idiopathic *adj.* without known cause or of spontaneous origin: usually denoting diseases, such as some forms of epilepsy, whose ETIOLOGY is obscure.

idiophrenic *adj.* denoting a mental disorder that is caused by a disease of the brain.

idiosyncrasy *n.* a peculiarity of an individual, such as a habit or abnormal susceptibility to something (e.g., a drug). **—idiosyncratic** *adj.*

idiosyncrasy-credit model an explanation of the leniency that groups sometimes display when high-status members violate group norms. This model assumes that such individuals, by contributing to the group in significant ways and expressing loyalty to it, build up **idiosyncrasy credits**, which they "spend" whenever they make errors or deviate from the group's norms.

idiosyncratic intoxication a condition characterized by sudden and extreme changes in personality, mood, and behavior following the ingestion of an amount of alcohol usually considered to be too little to account for the degree of the changes. It may include extreme excitement, impulsive and aggressive behavior, persecutory ideas, disorientation, and hallucinations. The episode ends when the individual falls into a deep sleep, after which there is often complete loss of memory for it. Some researchers believe that the condition may be related to stress or may be due in part to a psychomotor seizure triggered by alcohol. See also FUROR.

idiosyncratic reaction an unexpected reaction to a drug resulting in effects that may be contrary to the anticipated results. Idiosyncratic reactions can result in various symptoms, but generally refer to an extreme sensitivity or an extreme insensitivity to a particular agent.

idiot savant (*pl.* **idiot savants** or **idiots savants**) see SAVANT. [French, "learned idiot"]

id psychology in psychoanalysis, an approach that focuses on the unorganized, instinctual impulses contained in the ID that seek immediate pleasurable gratification of primitive needs. The id is believed to dominate the lives of infants and is frequently described as blind and irrational until it is disciplined by the other two major components of the personality: the EGO and the SUPEREGO. Compare EGO PSYCHOLOGY.

id resistance in psychoanalysis, a form of RESISTANCE to therapy that is motivated by unconscious ID impulses, whose underlying motive is the REPETITION COMPULSION. Compare REPRESSION-RESISTANCE; SUPEREGO RESISTANCE.

IEP abbreviation for INDIVIDUALIZED EDUCATION PROGRAM.

if...then profiles a methodology for describing personal dispositions in which within-person variations across social contexts are charted in terms of the behaviors evoked by particular situations.

iich'aa *n.* a CULTURE-BOUND SYNDROME found in Navaho communities, with symptoms similar to those of AMOK.

I–It *adj.* describing a relationship in which a subject ("I") treats something or someone else exclusively as an impersonal object ("It") to be used or controlled. German Jewish philosopher Martin Buber (1878–1965), who originated the term, maintained that this type of relationship between people stands in the way of human warmth, mutuality, trust, and group cohesiveness. Compare I–THOU.

illegitimacy *n.* the status of a child whose parents were unmarried at the time of birth. In Western societies, the term has fallen into virtual disuse with changing family structures (e.g., the large numbers of children now born to cohabiting but unmarried parents), the fading of the stigma formerly attached to illegitimacy, and the disappearance of most legal distinctions between legitimate and illegitimate children. **—illegitimate** *adj.*

illicit *adj.* illegal: often referring to widely abused psychoactive drugs for which there are few or no legitimate medical uses.

illocutionary act in the theory of SPEECH ACTS, the act that is performed by saying something (such as asking, ordering, or threatening), as opposed to the act of speaking itself (the **locutionary act**) or the act of causing a particular effect on others (such as persuading, amusing, or inspiring) as a result of speech (the **perlocutionary act**). In practice, most utterances involve the performance of all three acts simultaneously.

illuminance *n.* (symbol: *E*) the light (luminous flux) falling on a unit area of a surface. The standard unit of illuminance is the **lux**.

illusion *n.* a false perception. Illusions result from the misinterpretation of sensory stimuli and are normal occurrences. Visual (or optical) illusions are particularly common and include the well-known MÜLLER-LYER ILLUSION. **—illusory** *adj.*

illusion of agency the illusion of controlling an action that is not actually under one's control. Also called **illusion of will**.

illusion of control see POSITIVE ILLUSION.

illusion of unique invulnerability the false belief that the self is somehow safeguarded from the dangers and misfortunes that afflict other people.

illusory conjunction the attribution of a characteristic of one stimulus to another stimulus when the stimuli are presented only briefly. Illusory conjunctions are most common with visual stimuli when, for example, the color of one form can be attributed to a different form.

illusory correlation the appearance of a relationship that in reality does not exist or an overestimation of the degree of relationship (i.e., correlation) between two variables.

image *n.* **1.** in cognitive psychology, a likeness or representation of an earlier sensory experience recalled without external stimulation. For example, imagining the shape of a horse or the sound of a jet airplane brings to mind an image derived from earlier experiences with these stimuli. **2.** a representation of an object produced by an optical system. See also RETINAL IMAGE.

imagery *n.* **1.** the generation of mental images. **2.** such images considered collectively.

imagery code the ENCODING of an object, idea, or impression in terms of its visual imagery. For example, the item "typewriter" might be remembered as a mental picture of a typewriter, rather than as the word *typewriter*. Compare SEMANTIC CODE.

imagery cue a cognitively created signal used to direct behavior. Examples are mental images of a stop sign when one has negative thoughts or of a butterfly when one wants to exhibit delicate, free-flowing motion in a skating routine.

imagery technique the use of imagined scenes as a therapeutic technique, often in HYPNOTHERAPY but also in therapies that use breathing and relaxation techniques to reduce anxiety. For example, an anxious client may be directed to imagine a placid scene recalled from memory, such as sitting, relaxed and calm, on a beach. The technique may be used by an individual in stressful situations, for example, by a nervous passenger in an aircraft. See also GUIDED AFFECTIVE IMAGERY.

imaginal flooding a type of EXPOSURE THERAPY used for treating individuals with obsessive, hypochondriacal, or phobic conditions or posttraumatic stress disorder. Vivid imagery evoked through speech is used by the therapist to expose the client mentally to an anxiety-evoking stimulus. See also FLOODING.

Imaginary *n.* the realm of images: one of three aspects of the psychoanalytic field defined by French psychoanalyst Jacques Lacan (1901–1981). The Imaginary is that state of being in which the infant has no sense of being a subject distinct from other people or the external world and no sense of his or her place in human culture. After the infant's entry into the SYMBOLIC (the world of language, culture, and morality), he or she can return to the wholeness of the Imaginary only in fantasy. See also REAL.

imaginary companion a fictitious person, animal, or object created by a child or adolescent. The individual gives the imaginary companion a name, talks, shares feelings, and pretends to play with it. The phenomenon is considered an elaborate but common form of SYMBOLIC PLAY.

imagination *n.* the faculty that produces ideas and images in the absence of direct sensory data, often by combining fragments of previous sensory experiences into new syntheses. **—imaginary** *adj.* **—imagine** *vb.*

imagination inflation the increased likelihood of a person judging that an event has actually occurred (e.g., during that person's childhood) when the person imagines the event before making such a judgment.

imaging *n.* **1.** the process of scanning the brain or other organs or tissues to obtain an optical image. Techniques used include COMPUTED TOMOGRAPHY, POSITRON EMISSION TOMOGRAPHY (PET), anatomical MAGNETIC RESONANCE IMAGING (aMRI), and FUNCTIONAL MAGNETIC RESONANCE IMAGING (fMRI). **2.** in therapy, the use of suggested mental images to control body function, including the easing of pain. See also IMAGERY TECHNIQUE; VISUALIZATION.

imago *n.* an unconscious mental image of another person, especially the mother or father, that influences the way in which an individual relates to others. The imago is typically formed in infancy and childhood and is generally an idealized or otherwise not completely accurate representation. The term was originally used by Austrian psychiatrist Sigmund Freud (1856–1939) and the early psychoanalysts, and its meaning has carried over into other schools of psychology and psychotherapy.

imago therapy a type of therapy for relationship problems based on the theory that people carry unconscious composite images (see IMAGO) of the character traits and behaviors of their primary childhood caretakers that impel them to select certain partners and to behave in ways that are meant to heal earlier emotional wounds but that actually create relationship problems. Structured exercises, either in groups (for individuals or couples) or in COUPLES THERAPY, reveal the imago and help individuals learn to become less defensive and more compassionate toward partners as well as themselves.

imipramine *n.* a TRICYCLIC ANTIDEPRESSANT (TCA) with a tertiary amine molecular structure. It is considered the prototype TCA and, like all tricyclic agents, its use as an antidepressant has been largely supplanted by less toxic drugs. It continues, however, to have a therapeutic role as a sedative and adjunct in the management of neuromuscular or musculoskeletal pain. U.S. trade name: **Tofranil**.

imitation *n.* the process of copying the behavior of another person, group, or object, intentionally or unintentionally. Some theorists propose that true imitation requires that an observer be able to take the perspective of the model. This contrasts with other forms of SOCIAL LEARNING, such as EMULATION, LOCAL ENHANCEMENT, and MIMICRY. There is controversy concerning whether true imitation occurs in nonhuman animals or whether they either merely emulate the actions of others or are attracted to the location of others and by chance appear to show imitation. **—imitate** *vb.*

imitative learning the first stage of CULTURAL LEARNING, which occurs when the learner internalizes aspects of the model's behavioral strategies and intentions for executing the behavior. According to cultural learning theory, imitative learning is followed by INSTRUCTED LEARNING and COLLABORATIVE LEARNING.

immanent justice the belief that rules are fixed and immutable and that punishment automatically follows misdeeds regardless of extenuating circumstances. Children up to the age of 8 equate the morality of an act only with its consequences; not until later do they develop the capacity to judge motive and subjective considerations. See MORAL ABSOLUTISM; MORAL REALISM. Compare DISTRIBUTIVE JUSTICE.

immaterialism *n.* the philosophical position that denies the independent existence of matter as a substance in which qualities (see PRIMARY QUALITY; SECONDARY QUALITY) might inhere. Sensible objects are held to exist as the sum of the qualities they produce in the perceiving mind, with no material substratum. The best known philosophy of this kind is that of Anglo-Irish philosopher George Berkeley (1685–1753). It is difficult to distinguish such a position from IDEALISM, which holds that mind is essential to all reality and that things and qualities exist only as perceived.

immediate experience current experience and impressions of that experience without any analysis (see MEDIATE EXPERIENCE).

immediate memory another name for SHORT-TERM MEMORY.

immune system a complex system in vertebrates that helps protect the body against pathological effects of foreign substances (ANTIGENS), such as viruses and bacteria. The organs involved include the bone marrow and THYMUS, in which LYMPHOCYTES—the principal agents responsible for specific **immune responses**—are produced, together with the spleen, lymph nodes, and other lymphoid tissues and various chemicals (e.g., CYTOKINES) that mediate the immune response.

immunology *n.* the branch of medicine that specializes in the study of immunity and immune reactions. **—immunological** *adj.* **—immunologist** *n.*

impact analysis a quantitative analytic procedure used to assess the net success or failure of a program, appropriate when the program's objectives are specifiable and measurable and the outcome measures are reliable and valid.

impaired judgment difficulty in forming evaluative opinions or reaching conclusions concerning available evidence, often about people and courses of action. Impaired judgment may lead to seemingly irrational actions and risk-taking behaviors.

impairment *n.* any departure from the body's typical physiological or psychological functioning.

impairment index a measure of impairment on a series of cognitive tests. The best known such index is the **Halstead–Reitan Impairment Index**, which reflects the percentage of tests in the impaired range; the higher the percentage, the greater the likelihood of brain damage.

impenetrability *n.* the state of certain cognitive capacities, such as syntax, that are claimed to be inherently walled off from conscious access and not available to introspective analysis.

imperative *n.* in psychoanalytic theory, a demand of the SUPEREGO that represents the commanding voice of parental or social rule, and operates on an unconscious level to direct the behavior of the individual.

imperceptible *adj.* below THRESHOLD. For example, an **imperceptible difference** is a physical difference between two stimulus events that is below an observer's DIFFERENCE THRESHOLD. This results in the two events being judged as the same psychologically when they are not the same physically.

implanted memory the apparent recollection of an event that never occurred because someone has convinced the person that it did occur. There have been allegations that some psychotherapists have implanted memories in their clients by leading questioning.

implicit association test an IMPLICIT ATTITUDE MEASURE in which participants perform a series of categorization tasks on computer for a set of words representing an attitude object (e.g., words such as *ant*, *fly*, and *grasshopper* representing the attitude object of insects) and for a second set of intermixed words, selected to be highly evaluative in nature. In one phase of the test, the computer response key used to indicate membership in the specified category is the same as that used to indicate a positive word. In a different phase, the key used to indicate membership in the specified category is the same as that used to indicate a negative word. If attitudes are positive, judging the target words should be faster when the same response key is used for category membership and positive words than when the same response key is used for category membership and negative words. Negative attitudes produce the opposite pattern.

implicit attitude measure an ATTITUDE MEASURE in which a person is not consciously aware of the fact that his or her attitude is being assessed. Measures of this type are generally INDIRECT ATTITUDE MEASURES. Compare EXPLICIT ATTITUDE MEASURE.

implicit leadership theories perceivers' general assumptions about the traits, character-

I

241

istics, and qualities that distinguish leaders from the people they lead. Unlike the LEADERSHIP THEORIES developed by psychologists, these cognitive frameworks are based on intuition and personal experience and are usually not stated explicitly. See also ATTRIBUTION THEORY OF LEADERSHIP; LEADER-CATEGORIZATION THEORY.

implicit learning learning of a cognitive or behavioral task that occurs without intention to learn or awareness of what has been learned. Implicit learning is evidenced by improved task performance rather than as a response to an explicit request to remember.

implicit measure of personality any measure that does not ask people to report explicitly on their psychological characteristics but instead employs subtle indices capable of tapping mental content that individuals may not wish to express or perhaps are not even aware they possess because the mental content is not explicitly represented in consciousness. Measures of the time it takes individuals to answer questions, irrespective of the content of their answers, are one commonly employed implicit measure.

implicit memory memory for a previous event or experience that is produced indirectly, without an explicit request to recall the event and without awareness that memory is involved. For instance, after seeing the word *store* in one context, a person would complete the word fragment *st_r_* as *store* rather than *stare*, even without remembering that *store* had been recently encountered. This term, proposed in 1985 by Canadian psychologist Peter Graf and U.S. psychologist Daniel Schacter, is used interchangeably with NONDECLARATIVE MEMORY. Compare EXPLICIT MEMORY.

implicit prejudice a prejudice against a specific social group that is not consciously held. Compare EXPLICIT PREJUDICE.

implicit process a cognitive event that cannot be described accurately, even under optimal conditions. Compare EXPLICIT PROCESS.

implosive therapy a technique in BEHAVIOR THERAPY in which the client is repeatedly encouraged to imagine an anxiety-arousing situation, or to recall the incident that led to trauma, and to experience anxiety as intensely as possible while doing so. Since there is no actual danger in the situation, the anxiety response is not reinforced and therefore is gradually extinguished. Also called **implosion therapy**. See also FLOODING; PARADOXICAL INTENTION.

importance of an attitude the extent to which an individual personally cares about an attitude object or attaches psychological significance to it. Importance is related to the STRENGTH OF AN ATTITUDE.

impostor syndrome 1. the tendency to attribute achievements and success to external factors rather than internal factors, associated with a persistent belief in one's lack of ability despite consistent objective evidence to the contrary. As a result, the individual may feel like a fraud and have low self-esteem and identity problems. **2.** a personality pattern characterized by pathological lying, which takes the form of fabricating an identity or a series of identities in an effort to gain recognition and status.

impotence *n.* the inability of a man to complete the sex act due to partial or complete failure to achieve or maintain erection. This condition is called **male erectile disorder** in DSM–IV–TR and **erectile dysfunction** in clinical contexts. If the man has never been able to achieve penile erection sufficient for sexual intercourse the condition is considered primary, and if the man was previously able to achieve and maintain erection but no longer is the condition is considered secondary. —**impotent** *adj.*

impression formation the process in which an individual develops a PERCEPTUAL SCHEMA of some object, person, or group. Early research on impression formation demonstrated that the accuracy of impressions was frequently poor; more recent studies have focused on the roles played in the process by such factors as the perceiver's cognitive processes (e.g., how readily some types of ideas come to mind) and feelings (e.g., anger can predispose the perceiver to stereotype an individual).

impression management behaviors that are designed to control how others perceive one's self, especially by guiding them to attribute desirable traits to the self. Impression management has been offered as an alternative explanation for some phenomena that have traditionally been interpreted in terms of COGNITIVE DISSONANCE theory. Some psychologists distinguish impression management from SELF-PRESENTATION by proposing that impression management involves only deliberate, conscious strategies.

imprinting *n.* a simple yet profound and highly effective learning process that occurs during a CRITICAL PERIOD in the life of some animals. A well-known example is that of newly hatched chicks following the first moving object, human or animal, they see. Some investigators believe that such processes are instinctual; others regard them as a form of PREPARED LEARNING.

impuberism *n.* a state of not having reached puberty. Also called **impuberty**.

impulse *n.* **1.** a sudden and compelling urge to act immediately, often resulting in action without deliberation for a purpose that cannot be recalled. Also called **impulsion**. **2.** see NERVE IMPULSE. **3.** in psychoanalytic theory, the movement of PSYCHIC ENERGY associated with instinctual drives, such as sex and hunger.

impulse-control disorder a disorder characterized by a failure to resist impulses, drives, or temptations to commit acts that are harmful to oneself or to others. Other disorders that may involve problems of impulse control include substance-use disorders, paraphilias, conduct disorders, and mood disorders.

impulsive *adj.* describing or displaying behavior characterized by little or no forethought, reflection, or consideration of the consequences. Compare REFLECTIVE. **—impulsiveness** or **impulsivity** *n.*

imu *n.* a CULTURE-BOUND SYNDROME resembling LATAH, observed among the Ainu and Sakhalin women of Japan. It is characterized by an extreme STARTLE RESPONSE involving automatic movements, imitative behavior, infantile reactions, and obedience to command. See also MYRIACHIT.

inaccessibility *n.* **1.** the state of being impossible to reach, approach, or use. **2.** unresponsiveness to external stimuli, most commonly associated with the state of withdrawal sometimes seen in autism and schizophrenia. **—inaccessible** *adj.*

inappetence *n.* impaired appetite or desire.

inappropriate affect emotional responses that are not in keeping with the situation or are incompatible with expressed thoughts or wishes, for example, smiling when told about the death of a friend.

inattention *n.* a state in which there is a lack of concentrated or focused attention or in which attention drifts back and forth.

inattentional blindness failure to notice and remember otherwise perceptible stimuli in the visual background while the focus of attention is elsewhere. Research into inattentional blindness has led some to conclude that there is no conscious perception of the world without attention.

inbreeding *n.* the mating of individuals that are closely related, usually for the purpose of preserving certain preferred traits while preventing the acquisition of unwanted traits in the offspring.

incentive motivation in HULL'S MATHEMATICO-DEDUCTIVE THEORY OF LEARNING, an inducement, such as the expectation of a reward or punishment, that serves as an intervening variable to influence response strength.

incentive theory the theory that motivation arousal depends on the interaction between environmental incentives (i.e., stimulus objects)—both positive and negative—and an organism's psychological and physiological states (e.g., drive states).

incest *n.* sexual activity between people of close blood relationship (e.g., brother and sister) that is prohibited by law or custom. Incest taboos of some kind are found in practically every society. **—incestuous** *adj.*

incidence *n.* the rate of occurrence of new cases of a given event or condition, such as a disorder, disease, symptom, or injury, in a particular population in a given period. An **incidence rate** is normally expressed as the number of cases per some standard proportion (1,000 or 100,000 are commonly used) of the entire population at risk per year. See also PREVALENCE.

incidental learning learning that is not premeditated, deliberate, or intentional and that is acquired as a result of some other, possibly unrelated, mental activity. Some theorists believe that much learning takes place without any intention to learn, occurring incidentally to other cognitive processing of information. See also LATENT LEARNING. Compare INTENTIONAL LEARNING.

incident process a system in which learners begin with inadequate data and ask questions to gain additional information. The instructor has all the data and reveals a limited amount at the beginning, then reveals more in response to specific questions, so that the group can reach decisions. The system is designed to teach the skills of analysis, synthesis, and interrogation that are relevant to problem solving and investigative techniques.

inclusion *n.* the practice of teaching students with disabilities in the same classroom as other students to the fullest extent possible, via the provision of appropriate supportive services. See also FULL INCLUSION.

inclusion–exclusion criteria in clinical research, criteria used for determining which individuals are eligible to participate in a particular study. Inclusion criteria might specify, for example, age range, whereas exclusion criteria might specify, for example, the existence of more than one illness or psychological disorder.

inclusive fitness the REPRODUCTIVE SUCCESS not only of an individual but of all that individual's relatives in proportion to their coefficient of relatedness (mean number of genes shared). In calculating estimates of reproductive success, it is assumed that parents, offspring, and siblings have an average of 50% of their genes in common, grandparents and grand-offspring, and uncles and nieces, share 25% of genes, and so forth.

inclusiveness *n.* one of the GESTALT PRINCIPLES OF ORGANIZATION. It states that there is a tendency to perceive only the larger figure when a smaller figure is completely encompassed within it. Also called **law of inclusiveness**; **principle of inclusiveness**.

incoherence *n.* inability to express oneself in a clear and orderly manner, most commonly manifested as disjointed and unintelligible speech. This may be an expression of disorganized and impaired thinking. **—incoherent** *adj.*

incompatible response method a technique used to break bad habits in which an undesirable response is replaced by a more acceptable one that cannot coexist with the undesirable response.

incompetence *n.* **1.** the inability to carry out a required task or activity adequately. **2.** in law, the inability to make sound judgments regarding one's transactions or personal affairs. With regard to the criminal justice system, incompetence is the inability of a defendant to participate meaningfully in criminal proceedings. See also COMPETENCE; COMPETENCY TO STAND TRIAL. —**incompetent** *adj.*

incomplete factorial design a FACTORIAL DESIGN in which every level of every factor (IN-DEPENDENT VARIABLE) does not occur together with every level of every other factor, as it would in a complete factorial design. An example is the LATIN SQUARE.

incomplete-pictures test a test of visual recognition and interpretation in which drawings in varying degrees of completion are presented, and the participant attempts to identify the object as early in the series as possible.

incongruence *n.* lack of consistency or appropriateness, as in INAPPROPRIATE AFFECT or as when one's subjective evaluation of a situation is at odds with reality. —**incongruent** *adj.*

incongruity theory of humor an explanation of the ability of HUMOR to elicit laughter that emphasizes the juxtaposition of incompatible or contradictory elements. For example, British-born U.S. comedian Bob Hope (1903–2003) once quipped in regard to a place he was visiting: "The mosquitoes here are huge. Last night I shot one in my pajamas. They were tight on him too." Such theories have roots in the work of German philosophers Immanuel Kant (1724–1804) and Arthur Schopenhauer (1788–1860), British philosopher Herbert Spencer (1820–1903), and Austrian psychiatrist Sigmund Freud (1856–1939). See also RELEASE THEORY OF HUMOR.

incontinence *n.* an inability to control basic body functions, particularly urination (**urinary incontinence**) and defecation (**fecal incontinence**). —**incontinent** *adj.*

incoordination *n.* a lack of harmony or coordination of movement.

incorporation *n.* in psychoanalytic theory, the fantasy that one has ingested an external OBJECT, which is felt to be physically present inside the body. According to the theory, it first occurs in the ORAL STAGE, when the infant fantasizes that he or she has ingested the mother's breast. Incorporation is often confused with IDENTIFICATION and INTROJECTION. —**incorporate** *vb.*

incremental *adj.* describing or relating to changes that take place in small, cumulative steps rather than in large jumps.

incremental hypothesis see ALL-OR-NONE HYPOTHESIS.

incremental validity an increase in the accuracy level of decisions made on the basis of a test over the level of accuracy obtained had the test not been employed.

incus *n.* see OSSICLES.

indemnity plan a system of health insurance in which the insurer pays for the costs of covered services after care has been given. Such plans typically offer participants considerable freedom to choose their own health care providers and are contrasted with **group health plans**, which provide service benefits through groups of associated physicians.

independence *n.* **1.** freedom from the influence or control of other individuals or groups. **2.** complete lack of relationship between two or more events, sampling units, or variables such that none is influenced by any other and that changes in any one have no implication for changes in any other. **3.** in probability theory, the condition in which the probability of an event does not depend on the probability of some other event. If A and B are independent events, then $\Pr(A/B) = \Pr(A)$. —**independent** *adj., n.*

independent living 1. the ability of an individual to perform—without assistance from others—all or most of the daily functions typically required to be self-sufficient, including those tasks essential to personal care (see ACTIVITIES OF DAILY LIVING) and to maintaining a home and job. **2.** a philosophy and civil reform movement promoting the rights of people with disabilities to determine the course of their lives and be full, productive members of society with access to the same social and political freedoms and opportunities as individuals without disabilities. Central to the philosophy are the concepts of self-determination and self-worth, peer support, consumer-controlled assistance and support services, and political and social reform.

independent self-construal a view of the self that emphasizes one's unique traits and accomplishments and downplays one's embeddedness in a network of social relationships. Compare INTERDEPENDENT SELF-CONSTRUAL.

independent variable (**IV**) the variable in an experiment that is specifically manipulated. Independent variables may or may not be causally related to the DEPENDENT VARIABLE. In statistical analysis, an independent variable is likely to be referred to as a **predictor variable**.

indeterminacy *n.* the inability to uniquely determine the form or magnitude of a mathematical relationship or other entity.

indeterminism *n.* **1.** in psychology, the doctrine that humans have FREE WILL and are able to act independently of antecedent or current situations, as in making choices. Compare DETERMINISM. See also HARD DETERMINISM; SOFT DETERMINISM. **2.** in philosophy, the position that events do not have necessary and sufficient causes. —**indeterminist** *adj.*

index *n.* **1.** a reference point, standard, or indicator. **2.** a variable that is employed to indicate the presence of another phenomenon or event.

index case see PROBAND.

indicator variable a variable used with the

GENERAL LINEAR MODEL for quantitatively indicating the class of a qualitative attribute.

indirect attitude measure any procedure for assessing attitudes that does not require a person to provide a report of his or her attitude. Nontraditional approaches to attitude measurement, such as the LOST LETTER PROCEDURE and the IN-FORMATION-ERROR TECHNIQUE, are examples of indirect attitude measures. Compare DIRECT ATTITUDE MEASURE.

indirect odor effect see DIRECT ODOR EFFECT.

indirect scaling see DIRECT SCALING.

indirect speech act a SPEECH ACT whose purpose does not appear explicitly from the form or content of the utterance but must be inferred. For example, the apparent observation *It's so cold in here!* may well be intended as a request that someone close the window.

individual differences traits or other characteristics by which individuals may be distinguished from one another. This is the focus of DIFFERENTIAL PSYCHOLOGY, for which the term **individual differences psychology** increasingly is used.

individualism *n.* **1.** a social or cultural tradition, ideology, or personal outlook that emphasizes the individual and his or her rights, independence, and relationships with other individuals. Compare COLLECTIVISM. **2.** in ethical and political theory, the view that individuals have intrinsic value. Once granted, this implies that the unique values, desires, and perspectives of individuals should also be valued in their own right. Thus, individualism often manifests itself as an approach to life that emphasizes the essential right to be oneself and to seek fulfillment of one's own needs and desires. **—individualist** *n.* **—individualistic** *adj.*

individualization *n.* any process in which an individual becomes distinguishable from one or more other members of the same species, sex, or other category. **—individualize** *vb.*

individualized education program (**IEP**) a plan for providing specialized educational services and procedures that meet the unique needs of a child with a disability. Each IEP must be documented in writing, tailored to a particular child, and implemented in accordance with the requirements of U.S. federal law.

individual program an instructional method in which the student is responsible for developing and carrying out his or her own program. This method is most often used for children who possess a high level of motivation and cognitive development. Compare COMMAND STYLE.

individual psychology 1. the psychological theory of Austrian psychologist Alfred Adler (1870–1937), which is based on the idea that throughout life individuals strive for a sense of mastery, completeness, and belonging and are governed by a conscious drive to overcome their sense of inferiority by developing to their fullest potential, obtaining their life goals, and creating their own styles of life, as opposed to the view that human beings are dominated by "blind," irrational instincts operating on an unconscious level. Also called **Adlerian psychology**. **2.** historically, a synonym for DIFFERENTIAL PSYCHOLOGY.

individual test a test administered to a single examinee at a time. Compare GROUP TEST.

individual therapy psychotherapy conducted on a one-to-one basis (i.e., one therapist to one client). Also called **dyadic therapy**; **individual psychotherapy**. Compare GROUP PSYCHOTHERAPY.

individuation *n.* **1.** the physiological, psychological, and sociocultural processes by which a person attains status as an individual human being and exerts himself or herself as such in the world. **2.** in the psychoanalytic theory of Swiss psychiatrist Carl Jung (1875–1961), the gradual development of a unified, integrated personality that incorporates greater and greater amounts of the UNCONSCIOUS, both personal and collective, and resolves any conflicts that exist, such as those between introverted and extraverted tendencies. Also called **self-realization**.

indoctrination *n.* the social inculcation of beliefs, especially by those in positions of power or authority. Such beliefs are characterized by their inflexibility. **—indoctrinate** *vb.*

indoleamine *n.* any of a class of BIOGENIC AMINES formed by an indole molecule, which is produced as a breakdown metabolite of tryptophan, and an amine group. Indoleamines include the neurotransmitter serotonin and the hormone melatonin.

induced color a color change in a visual field resulting from stimulation of a neighboring area, rather than from stimulation of the part of the field in which the change appears.

induced movement an illusion of movement that occurs when a small stationary stimulus is surrounded by a large moving stimulus. The small object appears to move, while the large object appears to be still.

induction *n.* **1.** a general conclusion, principle, or explanation derived by reasoning from particular instances or observations. See INDUCTIVE REASONING. Compare DEDUCTION. **2.** the process of inductive reasoning itself. **3.** in conditioning, the phenomenon in which REINFORCEMENT of some forms of behavior results in an increased probability not only of these forms but also of similar but nonreinforced forms. For example, if lever presses with forces between 0.2 and 0.3 N are reinforced, presses with forces less than 0.2 N or greater than 0.3 N will increase in frequency although they are never explicitly reinforced. Also called **response generalization**. **4.** in developmental biology, the process by which one set of cells influences the fate of neighboring cells, usually by secreting a chemical factor that changes gene expression in the target cells. **—inductive** *adj.*

induction test a series of test items in which the participant must apply INDUCTIVE REASONING to derive or formulate a general law, rule, or principle based on several relevant facts or cases.

inductive reasoning the form of reasoning in which inferences and general principles are drawn from specific observations and cases. Inductive reasoning is a cornerstone of the scientific method (see BACONIAN METHOD) in that it underlies the process of developing hypotheses from particular facts and observations. Compare DEDUCTIVE REASONING.

industrial and organizational psychology (**I/O psychology**) the branch of psychology that studies human behavior in the work environment and applies general psychological principles to work-related issues and problems, notably in such areas as personnel selection and training, employee evaluation, working conditions, accident prevention, job analysis, job satisfaction, leadership, team effectiveness, organizational effectiveness, work motivation, and the welfare of employees. Also called **business psychology**; **employment psychology**; **occupational psychology**; **work psychology**.

industrial democracy a system of managing an organization in which employees participate in important decisions. An example would be the use of autonomous work groups in which employees determine their work procedures and assignments and are responsible for evaluating and rewarding performance.

industrial ergonomics a specialty area of ERGONOMICS that applies knowledge of human physical capabilities and limitations to the design of industrial WORK SYSTEMS, including work processes.

industry versus inferiority the fourth of ERIKSON'S EIGHT STAGES OF DEVELOPMENT, covering the Freudian LATENCY STAGE of ages 6 to 11 years, during which the child learns to be productive and to accept evaluation of his or her efforts. If the child is not encouraged to be industrious, the risk is that he or she will feel inferior or incompetent.

ineffability *n.* the quality of certain kinds of feelings or experiences that are difficult to describe explicitly. The sense of something being ineffable is often attributed to spiritual, aesthetic, or affective states. **—ineffable** *adj.*

infancy *n.* the earliest period of postnatal life, in humans generally denoting the time from birth through the first year. **—infant** *n.*

infant development program a coordinated program of stimulatory, social, therapeutic, and treatment services provided to children from birth to 3 years of age with identified conditions placing them at risk of developmental disability or with evident developmental delays. Services can include assessment, stimulation, parent or family training, and assistance to families in identifying and accessing appropriate community services. Also called **early intervention program**.

infanticide *n.* the killing of an infant or child. Infanticide has been observed in many animal species and in the past was an accepted practice in some societies, often as a response to scarcity or overpopulation or as a means of eliminating offspring deemed unfit. **—infanticidal** *adj.*

infantile amnesia the inability to remember clearly or accurately the first years of life (from infancy through about 5 years of age).

infantile sexuality in psychoanalytic theory, the concept that PSYCHIC ENERGY or LIBIDO concentrated in various organs of the body throughout infancy gives rise to erotic pleasure. This is manifested in sucking the mother's breast during the ORAL STAGE of development, in defecating during the ANAL STAGE, and in self-stimulating activities during the early GENITAL STAGE. The term and concept, first enunciated by Austrian psychiatrist Sigmund Freud (1856–1939), proved highly controversial from the start, and it is more in line with subsequent thought to emphasize the sensual nature of breast feeding, defecation, and discovery of the body in childhood and the role of the pleasurable feelings so obtained in the origin and development of sexual feelings.

infantile speech speech or verbalizations using the sounds and forms characteristic of infants or very young children beyond the stage when such speech is normal.

infantilism *n.* behavior, physical characteristics, or mental functioning in older children or adults that is characteristic of that of infants or young children. See REGRESSION.

infarction *n.* an area of dead tissue resulting from obstruction of a supplying artery. For example, a **myocardial infarction** involves death of a segment of the heart muscle, usually due to obstruction of a coronary artery, and is a common cause of death. Also called **infarct**. See STROKE.

inference *n.* **1.** a conclusion deduced from an earlier premise or premises according to valid rules of inference, or the process of drawing such a conclusion. Some hold that an inference, as contrasted with a mere conclusion, requires that the person making it actually believe that the inference and the premises from which it is drawn are true. Also called **logical inference. 2.** in statistical analysis, the process of drawing conclusions about a population based on a sample. The most common example of this type of inference is statistical hypothesis testing. **—inferential** *adj.*

inferential statistics a broad class of statistical techniques that allows inferences about characteristics of a population to be drawn from a sample of data from that population while controlling (at least partially) the extent to which errors of inference may be made. These techniques include approaches for testing hypotheses and estimating the value of parameters.

inferential validity the extent to which causal inferences made in a laboratory setting are applicable to the real-life experiences they are meant to represent.

inferior *adj.* in anatomy, lower, below, or toward the feet. Compare SUPERIOR.

inferior colliculus see COLLICULUS.

inferiority complex a basic feeling of inadequacy and insecurity, deriving from actual or imagined physical or psychological deficiency, that may result in behavioral expression ranging from the "withdrawal" of immobilizing timidity to the overcompensation of excessive competition and aggression. See also SUPERIORITY COMPLEX.

inferotemporal cortex a region of the brain on the inferior portion of the temporal lobe that is particularly involved in the perception of form.

infertility *n.* inability to produce offspring. —**infertile** *adj.*

infibulation *n.* the removal of the entire clitoris and most of the LABIA and sewing together of the remaining tissue, leaving a small opening for menstruation and urination. It is practiced in some cultures as the most severe form of FEMALE GENITAL MUTILATION, usually being done in early childhood or in the prepubertal years.

influence analysis a set of statistical techniques that allows one to determine the degree to which one or a small number of cases affect the overall result of an analysis, particularly in the GENERAL LINEAR MODEL.

informal communications in organizational settings, communications among employees that do not occur through the formally prescribed CHANNELS OF COMMUNICATION. Even informal communications, such as gossip and rumors, often serve important functions that are instrumental to achieving organizational objectives.

informant *n.* an expert who is consulted in ethnographic and related research for information about particular individual, group, and cultural characteristics and behaviors.

information *n.* **1.** in communication theory, the reduction in uncertainty provided in a message; that is, information tells us something we do not already know. The BIT is the common unit of information in INFORMATION THEORY. **2.** knowledge about facts or ideas gained through investigation, experience, or practice.

informational influence 1. see SOCIAL PRESSURE. **2.** the degree to which a person's judgments or opinions about an unclear situation are accepted by others as correct, that is, as reflecting the reality of that situation.

information-error technique an INDIRECT ATTITUDE MEASURE that consists of a series of objective-knowledge multiple-choice questions

about an attitude object. These questions are constructed so that people are unlikely to know the true answers, but with response options that imply positive or negative evaluations of the attitude object. The procedure is based on the assumption that participants will use their attitudes as a basis for guessing, that is, they will tend to select answers that support their attitudes.

information hypothesis the theoretical claim that conscious sensory processes may be modeled and explained by reference to the formal concepts of INFORMATION THEORY.

information overload the state that occurs when the amount or intensity of environmental stimuli exceeds the individual's processing capacity, thus leading to an unconscious or subliminal disregard for some environmental information.

information processing (**IP**) in cognitive psychology, the flow of INFORMATION through the human nervous system, involving the operation of perceptual systems, memory stores, decision processes, and response mechanisms. **Information processing psychology** is the approach that concentrates on understanding these operations.

information theory the principles relating to the communication or transmission of INFORMATION, which is defined as any message that reduces uncertainty. These principles deal with such areas as the encoding and decoding of messages, types of CHANNELS OF COMMUNICATION and their capacity to throughput information, the application of mathematical methods to the process, the problem of noise (distortion), and the relative effectiveness of various kinds of FEEDBACK.

informed consent voluntary agreement to participate in a research or therapeutic procedure on the basis of the participant's or patient's understanding of its nature, its potential benefits and possible risks, and available alternatives.

infradian rhythm any periodic variation in physiological or psychological function recurring in a cycle of less than 24 hours. See also BIOLOGICAL RHYTHM.

infrared theory of smell a theory that the olfactory sense organ functions as an infrared spectrometer. It assumes that odorants each have a unique infrared absorption spectrum, which produces transient cooling of the cilia in the OLFACTORY EPITHELIUM. The theory is called into question by the fact that isomers of some odorants have identical infrared absorption spectrums but produce different odors.

infrasonic communication the use of sound frequencies below the range of human hearing (i.e., below 20 Hz) for ANIMAL COMMUNICATION. Both elephants and whales use infrasonic communication extensively. The low frequencies have very long wavelengths that are transmitted for very long distances: They have been shown

I

to coordinate activity between individuals over distances of several kilometers. Compare ULTRASONIC COMMUNICATION.

infundibulum *n.* (*pl.* **infundibula**) a funnel-shaped anatomical structure, in particular the stalk of the PITUITARY GLAND, situated just below the THIRD VENTRICLE of the brain and above the sphenoid sinus at the base of the skull.

ingenuity *n.* cleverness at solving routine problems of daily life: everyday creativity. —**ingenious** *adj.*

ingratiation *n.* efforts to win the liking and approval of other people, especially by deliberate IMPRESSION MANAGEMENT. Ingratiation is usually regarded as consisting of illicit or objectionable strategies, especially for manipulative purposes, which distinguish it from sincere efforts to be likable. —**ingratiate** *vb.*

ingroup *n.* any group to which one belongs or with which one identifies, but particularly a group judged to be different from, and often superior to, other groups (OUTGROUPs).

ingroup bias the tendency to favor one's own group, its members, its characteristics, and its products, particularly in reference to other groups. The favoring of the ingroup tends to be more pronounced than the rejection of the OUTGROUP, but both tendencies become more pronounced during periods of intergroup contact. At the regional, cultural, or national level, this bias is often termed ETHNOCENTRISM.

ingroup extremity effect the tendency to describe and evaluate INGROUP members, their actions, and their products in exaggeratedly positive ways. Compare OUTGROUP EXTREMITY EFFECT.

inhalant *n.* any of a variety of volatile substances that can be inhaled to produce intoxicating effects. Anesthetic gases (e.g., ether, chloroform, nitrous oxide), industrial solvents (e.g., toluene, gasoline, trichloroethylene, various aerosol propellants), and organic nitrites (e.g., amyl nitrite) are common inhalants.

inhalant abuse a pattern of inhalant use manifested by recurrent significant adverse consequences related to the repeated ingestion of these substances. See also SUBSTANCE ABUSE.

inhalant dependence a cluster of cognitive, behavioral, and physiological symptoms indicating continued use of inhalants despite significant inhalant-related problems. See also SUBSTANCE ABUSE.

inhalant intoxication a reversible syndrome resulting from the recent ingestion of inhalants. It includes clinically significant behavioral or psychological changes (e.g., confusion, belligerence, assaultiveness, apathy, impaired judgment, and impaired social or occupational functioning), as well as one or more signs of physiological involvement (e.g., dizziness, visual disturbances, involuntary eye movements, incoordination, slurred speech, unsteady gait,

tremor). At higher doses, lethargy, PSYCHOMOTOR RETARDATION, generalized muscle weakness, depressed reflexes, stupor, or coma may develop. See also SUBSTANCE INTOXICATION.

inheritance *n.* the transmission of physical or psychological traits from parents to their offspring.

inhibition *n.* **1.** the process of restraining or prohibiting, particularly one's impulses or behavior. The term is also applied to a variety of other contexts and occurrences: For example, in RESPONSE SELECTION inhibition is the suppression of COVERT RESPONSES in order to prevent incorrect responses, whereas in conditioning it is the active blocking or delay of a response to a stimulus. **2.** in psychoanalysis, an unconscious mechanism in which the SUPEREGO controls instinctive impulses that would threaten the EGO if allowed conscious expression. For example, inhibited sexual desire may result from unconscious feelings of guilt implanted by parents. —**inhibit** *vb.* —**inhibited** *adj.*

inhibition of delay in DELAY CONDITIONING, a reduction in the magnitude of the conditioned response (CR) during the early part of the conditioned stimulus (CS). For example, if a 15-s tone (the CS) precedes delivery of food (the unconditioned stimulus) to a dog, salivation (the CR) will eventually occur only after the tone has been on for a few seconds, not when it first comes on.

inhibition of return (**IOR**) difficulty in returning attention to a previously attended location. When attention has been directed to a location for a period of time, it is more difficult to redirect attention to that location than to direct it to another location.

inhibitory postsynaptic potential (**IPSP**) a brief increase in the difference in electrical charge across the membrane of a neuron that is caused by the transmission of a signal from a neighboring neuron across the synapse (specialized junction) separating them. IPSPs decrease the probability that the postsynaptic neuron will initiate an ACTION POTENTIAL and hence fire a nerve impulse. Compare EXCITATORY POSTSYNAPTIC POTENTIAL.

inhibitory synapse a specialized type of junction at which activity from one neuron (in the form of an ACTION POTENTIAL) reduces the probability of activity in an adjacent neuron by initiating an INHIBITORY POSTSYNAPTIC POTENTIAL. Compare EXCITATORY SYNAPSE.

initial insomnia difficulty in falling asleep, usually due to tension, anxiety, or depression. Some people with INSOMNIA due to anxiety become so worried about being unable to fall asleep or about the effects of loss of sleep that they cannot relax sufficiently to induce sleep. Initial insomnia may be a symptom of a MAJOR DEPRESSIVE EPISODE. Compare MIDDLE INSOMNIA; TERMINAL INSOMNIA.

initial interview in psychotherapy, the first interview with a client, which has some or all of the following goals: to establish a positive relationship; to listen to the client's problem described in his or her own words; to make a tentative diagnosis; and to formulate a plan for diagnostic tests, possible treatment, or referral.

initiative versus guilt the third of ERIKSON'S EIGHT STAGES OF DEVELOPMENT, which occurs during the child's 3rd through 5th years. Central to this stage is the child's feeling of freedom in planning, launching, and initiating all forms of fantasy, play, and other activity. If resolution of the two earlier stages was unsuccessful, or if the child is consistently criticized or humiliated, guilt and a feeling of not belonging will develop in place of initiative.

injunctive norm see SOCIAL NORM.

inkblot test see RORSCHACH INKBLOT TEST.

innate *adj.* inborn, native, or natural: denoting a capability or characteristic existing in an organism from birth, that is, belonging to the original or essential constitution of the body or mind. Innate processes should be distinguished from those that develop later under maturational control or through experience.

innate releasing mechanism (IRM) in ethology, the hypothesized neurological means by which organisms exhibit a FIXED ACTION PATTERN given a particular RELEASER, suggesting that there is a direct correspondence between a specific elicitor and a specific behavioral event.

inner conflict see INTRAPSYCHIC.

inner ear the part of the ear that comprises the bony and membranous LABYRINTHS and contains the sense organs responsible for hearing and balance. For hearing the major structure is the COCHLEA. For the sense of balance, the major structures are the SEMICIRCULAR CANALS, SACCULE, and UTRICLE.

inner nuclear layer the layer of retinal cell bodies interposed between the photoreceptors and the RETINAL GANGLION CELLS. The inner nuclear layer contains AMACRINE CELLS, RETINAL HORIZONTAL CELLS, RETINAL BIPOLAR CELLS, and MÜLLER FIBERS.

inner plexiform layer the synaptic layer in the retina in which contacts are made between the dendrites of RETINAL GANGLION CELLS, BIPOLAR NEURONS, and AMACRINE CELLS.

inner psychophysics a systematic attempt to relate experience in the mind to states of excitation in the sensory apparatus. Compare OUTER PSYCHOPHYSICS. See PSYCHOPHYSICAL LAW.

innervation *n.* the supply of nerves to an organ (e.g., muscle or gland) or a body region. —**innervate** *vb.*

innervation ratio the ratio expressing the number of muscle fibers innervated by a single motor axon. It may vary from 3 muscle fibers per axon for small muscles in the fingers to 150 muscle fibers per axon for large muscle bundles of the arms and legs. The lower the ratio, the finer is the control of movements.

innovation *n.* in the psychology of groups, a change in some aspect of the group, such as its operating procedures or general orientation, away from a long-held or unquestioned position to a novel, and in many cases previously unpopular, position.

inoculation theory a theory postulating that resistance to persuasion can be created by exposing people to weak persuasive attacks that are easily refuted. This helps people to practice defending their attitudes, as well as making them aware that their attitudes can be challenged, and thereby creates resistance to subsequent stronger messages.

inositol *n.* a compound (similar to glucose) that occurs in many foods and is sometimes classed as a vitamin. It is a component of cell-membrane phospholipids and plasma lipoproteins; phosphorylated derivatives (**inositol phosphates**) function as SECOND MESSENGERS in cells.

inpatient *n.* a person who has been formally admitted to a hospital for a period of at least 24 hours for observation, care, diagnosis, or treatment, as distinguished from an OUTPATIENT or an emergency-room patient.

insanity *n.* in law, a condition of the mind that renders a person incapable of being responsible for his or her criminal acts. Defendants who are found to be NOT GUILTY BY REASON OF INSANITY therefore lack CRIMINAL RESPONSIBILITY for their conduct. Whether a person is insane, in this legal sense, is determined by judges and juries, not psychologists or psychiatrists. Numerous legal standards for determining criminal responsibility have been used at various times in many jurisdictions. —**insane** *adj.*

insecure attachment in the STRANGE SITUATION, one of several patterns of generally negative parent–child relationship in which the child fails to display confidence when the parent is present, sometimes shows distress when the parent leaves, and reacts to the returning parent by not seeking close contact (**avoidant attachment**) or by simultaneously seeking and avoiding close contact (**ambivalent attachment**). See also DISORGANIZED ATTACHMENT.

insecurity *n.* a feeling of inadequacy, lack of self-confidence, and inability to cope, accompanied by general uncertainty and anxiety about one's goals, abilities, or relationships with others. —**insecure** *adj.*

insight *n.* **1.** the clear and often sudden discernment of a solution to a problem by means that are not obvious and may never become so, even after one has tried hard to work out how one has arrived at the solution. There are many different theories of how insights are formed and of the kinds of insights that exist. For example, one theory posits three main kinds of insights: (a) selective encoding insights, used to distinguish relevant from irrelevant information; (b) selective comparison insights, used to distinguish what information already stored in long-term mem-

I

ory is relevant for one's purposes; and (c) selective combination insights, used to put together the information available so as to formulate a solution to a given problem. **2.** in psychotherapy, an awareness of underlying sources of emotional, cognitive, or behavioral difficulty in oneself or another person. See also EPIPHANY.

insightful learning a form of learning involving the mental rearrangement or restructuring of the elements in a problem to achieve an understanding of the problem and arrive at a solution. Originally described in the 1920s, based on observations of apes stacking boxes or using sticks to retrieve food, insightful learning was offered as an alternative to learning based on conditioning.

insight therapy any form of psychotherapy based on the theory that deep and lasting personality changes cannot be brought about unless the client understands the origin of his or her distorted attitudes and defensive measures. This approach (characteristic, for example, of PSYCHOANALYSIS and PSYCHODYNAMIC PSYCHOTHERAPY) contrasts with therapies directed toward removal of symptoms or behavior modification.

insomnia *n.* difficulty in initiating or maintaining a restorative sleep that results in fatigue, the severity or persistence of which causes clinically significant distress or impairment in functioning. Such sleeplessness may be caused by a transient or chronic physical condition or psychological disturbance. See INITIAL INSOMNIA; MIDDLE INSOMNIA; PRIMARY INSOMNIA; TERMINAL INSOMNIA. —**insomniac** *n.*

inspection time in DISCRIMINATION LEARNING, the amount of time it takes an individual to make simple visual discriminations, such as which of two lines is longer, under specific experimental conditions. Inspection time is found to be correlated with IQ.

inspiration–expiration ratio the ratio of the duration of the inspiration phase of the respiratory cycle to the duration of the exhalation phase, that is, the time taken to breathe in divided by the time taken to breathe out. This ratio is typically used in studies of emotion: Fearful states have high I/E ratios, whereas nonfearful attentive states have low I/E ratios.

instance theory the hypothesis that categorization depends on specific remembered instances of the category, as opposed to an abstract PROTOTYPE or a feature-based rule that defines category membership. Instance theory has also been applied to questions of attention, skill acquisition, and social decision making, among other problems. Also called **exemplar theory**.

instinct *n.* **1.** an innate, species-specific biological force that impels an organism to do something, particularly to perform a certain act or respond in a certain manner to specific stimuli. **2.** in psychoanalytic theory, a basic biological drive (e.g., hunger, thirst, sex, or aggression) that

must be fulfilled in order to maintain physical and psychological equilibrium. Austrian psychiatrist Sigmund Freud (1856–1939) classified instincts into two types: those derived from the LIFE INSTINCT and those derived from the DEATH INSTINCT. See also SEXUAL INSTINCT. **3.** in popular usage, any inherent or unlearned predisposition (behavioral or otherwise) or motivational force. —**instinctive** or **instinctual** *adj.*

institution *n.* **1.** an established practice, tradition, behavior, or system of roles and relationships, such as marriage, that is considered normative within a society. Sociologists usually distinguish between four main types of institution: political institutions (e.g., monarchy), economic institutions (e.g., capitalism), cultural institutions (e.g., religion and accepted forms of artistic expression), and kinship institutions (e.g., the extended family). **2.** a building or building complex in which individuals are cared for or confined for extended periods of time, especially a psychiatric hospital or a prison. —**institutional** *adj.*

institutionalism *n.* see SOCIAL BREAKDOWN SYNDROME.

institutionalization *n.* **1.** placement of an individual in an institution for therapeutic or correctional purposes. **2.** an individual's gradual adaptation to institutional life over a long period, especially when this is seen as rendering him or her passive, dependent, and generally unsuited to life outside the institution. —**institutionalize** *vb.*

institutionalized racism differential treatment of individuals on the basis of their racial group by social institutions, including religious organizations, governments, businesses, the media, and educational institutions. Examples include DISCRIMINATION in hiring, promotion, and advancement at work, restrictive housing regulations that promote segregation, unfair portrayal of minority members in newspapers and magazines, and legal statutes that restrict the civil liberties of the members of specific racial categories.

institutional review board (**IRB**) a committee named by an agency or institution to review research proposals originating within that agency for ethical acceptability.

instructed learning the second stage of CULTURAL LEARNING, in which a more accomplished person instructs a less accomplished person. The process requires that learners grasp the instructor's understanding of the task and then compare it with their own understanding. See also COLLABORATIVE LEARNING; IMITATIVE LEARNING.

instructional set the attitude toward a task or test that is communicated (intentionally or unintentionally) by the experimenter to the participants. It conveys information on how they should approach the task or test, for example, that speed is more (or less) important than accuracy.

instrument *n.* any tool or device used in performing specific operations, particularly in psychology those of measuring, recording, or testing.

instrumental activities of daily living (**IADLs**) activities essential to an individual's ability to function autonomously, including cooking, doing laundry, using the telephone, managing money, shopping, getting to places beyond walking distance, and the like. See also ACTIVITIES OF DAILY LIVING.

instrumental aggression see AGGRESSION.

instrumental behavior 1. behavior that is learned and elicited via positive or negative reinforcement of target (rather than instinctive) responses. The term is used synonymously with OPERANT BEHAVIOR, usually for describing behavior during CONDITIONING procedures that involves long sequences of activity, such as solving a puzzle box. **2.** actions that directly affect or manage the behavior of others, such as a subordinate animal engaging in infantile behavior to inhibit threatening or aggressive actions.

instrumental conditioning any form of CONDITIONING in which the correct response is essential for REINFORCEMENT. Instrumental conditioning is similar to OPERANT CONDITIONING and usually involves complex activities in order to reach a goal, such as when a rat is trained to navigate a maze to obtain food. It contrasts with PAVLOVIAN CONDITIONING, in which reinforcement is given regardless of the response.

instrumentalism *n.* **1.** in the philosophy of science, the position that theories are not to be considered as either true or false but as instruments of explanation that allow observations of the world to be meaningfully ordered. **2.** a theory of knowledge that emphasizes the pragmatic value, rather than the truth value, of ideas. In this view, the value of an idea, concept, or judgment lies in its ability to explain, predict, and control one's concrete functional interactions with the experienced world. This view is related to PRAGMATISM. **3.** the view or attitude that the primary motivation for social interaction is the attaining of some positive advantage or good for the self, such that others are regarded and used as instruments in attaining such advantage. —**instrumentalist** *adj., n.*

instrumentality theory the theory that a person's attitude toward an event will depend on his or her perception of its function as an instrument in bringing about desirable or undesirable consequences.

instrumental relativist orientation see PRECONVENTIONAL LEVEL.

instrumental response any response that achieves a goal or contributes to its achievement, such as a response that is effective in gaining a reward or avoiding pain (e.g., a rat's bar pressing to obtain food).

insula *n.* (*pl.* **insulae**) a region of the cerebral cortex of primate brains that is buried in a cleft near the lower end of the LATERAL SULCUS. Also called **island of Reil**.

insulin *n.* a hormone, secreted by the B cells of the ISLETS OF LANGERHANS in the pancreas, that facilitates the transfer of glucose molecules through cell membranes. Together with GLUCAGON, it plays a key role in regulating BLOOD SUGAR and carbohydrate metabolism. In the absence of sufficient concentrations of insulin, glucose accumulates in the blood and is excreted, as in diabetes mellitus.

intake interview 1. the initial interview with a client by a therapist or counselor to obtain both information regarding the issues or problems that have brought the client into therapy or counseling and preliminary information regarding personal and family history. **2.** the initial interview with a patient who is being admitted into a psychiatric hospital, day treatment, or inpatient substance abuse facility. Intake interviews are also common in government-funded mental health services, such as those provided at community mental health centers, in determining eligibility and appropriateness of the client for services offered. An intake interview may be carried out by a specialist who may not necessarily treat the patient, but the information obtained is used to determine the best course of treatment and the appropriate therapist to provide it.

integrated delivery system a type of MANAGED CARE organization that is completely integrated operationally and clinically and that offers a full range of health care services, including physician, hospital, and adjunct services. It comes in varying formats, one of the more typical being an alliance between hospitals and individual physicians or groups of associated physicians.

integration *n.* the coordination or unification of parts into a totality. This general meaning has been incorporated into a wide variety of psychological contexts and topics. For example, the integration of personality denotes the gradual bringing together of constituent traits, behavioral patterns, motives, and so forth to form an organized whole that functions effectively and with minimal effort or without conflict.

integrative behavioral couples therapy couples therapy that uses techniques of BEHAVIORAL COUPLES THERAPY but also focuses on each person's emotional acceptance of his or her partner's genuine incompatibilities, which may or may not be amenable to change. It is based on the conviction that focusing on changing incompatibilities leads to a resistance to change when change is possible or that this focus results in unnecessary frustration for both partners when change is not possible.

integrative complexity the extent to which an attitude object is seen as having both positive and negative features and the extent to which these features are seen as related to one another.

integrative medicine the combination of conventional medical treatments and complementary therapies that have demonstrated scientific merit with regard to safety and efficacy. See also COMPLEMENTARY AND ALTERNATIVE MEDICINE.

integrative psychotherapy psychotherapy that selects models or techniques from various therapeutic schools to suit the client's particular problems. For example, PSYCHODYNAMIC PSYCHOTHERAPY and GESTALT THERAPY may be combined through the practice of INTERPRETATION of material in the HERE AND NOW. There is growing interest in and use of such combined therapeutic techniques. Also called **integrated therapy**; **psychotherapy integration**. See also ECLECTIC PSYCHOTHERAPY.

integrity group psychotherapy a type of GROUP PSYCHOTHERAPY in which openness and honesty are expected from all participants, and experienced members of the group serve as models of sincerity and involvement.

integrity versus despair the eighth and final stage of ERIKSON'S EIGHT STAGES OF DEVELOPMENT, which occurs during old age. In this stage the individual reflects on the life he or she has lived and may develop either integrity—a sense of satisfaction in having lived a good life and the ability to approach death with equanimity—or despair—a feeling of bitterness about opportunities missed and time wasted, and a dread of approaching death. Also called **ego integrity versus despair**.

intellect *n.* an individual's capacity for abstract, objective reasoning, especially as contrasted with his or her capacity for feeling, imagining, or acting. —**intellectual** *adj.*

intellectual disability see MENTAL RETARDATION.

intellectual impoverishment diminished intellectual capacity, such as problem-solving ability and concentration. This condition is observed in many people with chronic schizophrenia, senility, or depression and in individuals living in a deprived, unstimulating environment.

intellectual insight in psychotherapy, an objective, rational awareness of experiences or relationships. Some theorists posit that intellectual insight by itself does not advance the therapeutic process and may even impede it because little or no feeling (i.e., emotional content) is involved.

intellectualism *n.* **1.** in philosophy, a position consistent with IDEALISM or RATIONALISM that emphasizes the preeminence of mind or idea. **2.** in psychology, the doctrine that cognitive functions are preeminent, such that emotive and mo-

tivational experiential states can be explained by, or originate from, more fundamental cognitive states. —**intellectualist** *adj.*

intellectual plasticity the extent to which an individual's intellectual abilities are modifiable and thus subject to various kinds of change.

intelligence *n.* the ability to derive information, learn from experience, adapt to the environment, understand, and correctly utilize thought and reason. There are many different definitions of intelligence, and there is currently much debate, as there has been in the past, over the exact nature of intelligence. —**intelligent** *adj.*

intelligence quotient see IQ.

intelligence test an individually administered test measuring a person's ability to solve problems, form concepts, reason, acquire detail, and perform other intellectual tasks. It comprises mental, verbal, and performance tasks of graded difficulty that have been standardized by use on a representative sample of the population.

intensional meaning the meaning of a word or phrase as defined by listing the essential or salient properties of the thing or concept referred to. For example, the intensional meaning of *sister* is "female sibling." Compare EXTENSIONAL MEANING.

intensive psychotherapy broad, thorough, and prolonged psychological treatment of an individual's concerns and problems. The qualifier "intensive" indicates both the nature of the discussions, which typically involve extensive examination of the individual's life history and conflicts, and the duration of the therapy. Compare COUNSELING; SHORT-TERM THERAPY.

intention *n.* a conscious decision to perform a behavior. In experiments, intention is often equated with the goals defined by the task instructions. —**intentional** *adj.*

intentional forgetting inaccessibility of a memory that is due to REPRESSION or to an unconscious wish to forget. See also FORGETTING.

intentionality *n.* a characteristic of an individual's acts that requires the individual (a) to have goals, desires, and standards; (b) to select behaviors that are in the service of attaining the goal (e.g., means to an end); and (c) to call into conscious awareness a desired future state. Investigators differ as to whether (a) alone, (a) and (b) but not (c), or (a), (b), and (c) are required for intentionality to be attributable to an individual. The concept of intentionality, as developed by German philosopher and psychologist Franz Brentano (1838–1917), has been very influential in ACT PSYCHOLOGY, PHENOMENOLOGY, and related approaches in HERMENEUTICS.

intentional learning learning that is planned or deliberate and therefore consciously employs MNEMONICS or other strategies. Compare INCIDENTAL LEARNING.

intentional stance a strategy for interpreting

and predicting behavior that views organisms as rational beings acting in a reasonable manner according to their beliefs and desires (i.e., their intentions).

intention movement a physical behavior that precipitates another physical response, such that the first behavior may signal the second. For example, when two people are talking, one may exhibit certain postural behaviors (e.g., changing stance, shifting weight) predictive of terminating the interaction, before actually ending the conversation and walking away.

intention tremor trembling of a body part that arises near the conclusion of a directed, voluntary movement, such as attempting to touch something.

interactional model of anxiety a model of anxiety proposing that STATE ANXIETY is determined by the interaction of factors relating to the situation (**situational factors**) and factors relating to the individual (**person factors**).

interaction analysis a variety of methods used to describe, categorize, and evaluate instances of person–person interaction, person–system interaction, or team and group interaction. Interaction analysis is used in specialties such as HUMAN FACTORS ENGINEERING, human-computer interaction, cultural studies, and communication studies.

interaction effect the joint effect of two or more independent variables on a dependent variable above and beyond the sum of their individual effects: The independent variables combine to have a different (and multiplicative) effect, such that the value of one is contingent upon the value of another. This indicates that the relationship between the independent variables changes as their values change. Interaction effects contrast with—and may obscure—MAIN EFFECTS. Compare ADDITIVE EFFECT.

interactionism *n.* **1.** the position that mind and body are distinct, incompatible substances that nevertheless interact, so that each has a causal influence on the other. This position is particularly associated with French philosopher René Descartes (1596–1650). See CARTESIAN DUALISM; MIND–BODY PROBLEM. **2.** a set of approaches, particularly in personality psychology, in which behavior is explained not in terms of personality attributes or situational influences but by references to interactions that typify the behavior of a certain type of person in a certain type of setting. —**interactionist** *adj.*

interactionist view of intelligence the view that intelligence always develops as an interaction between biological dispositions and environmental conditions and that it is difficult or impossible to separate the contributions of these two factors. Interactionists point out that genes always express themselves (manifest their effects in an individual) through a given set of environments and that the expression of the genes may be different as a function of the environment(s) in which they are expressed.

interaction-process analysis a technique used to study the emotional, intellectual, and behavioral interactions among members of a group, for example, during GROUP PSYCHOTHERAPY. It requires observers to classify every behavior displayed by a member of a group into one of 12 mutually exclusive categories, such as "asks for information" or "shows tension." See also CATEGORY-SYSTEM METHOD; STRUCTURED OBSERVATIONAL MEASURES.

interactive group psychotherapy see INTERPERSONAL GROUP PSYCHOTHERAPY.

interaural difference see BINAURAL CUE.

interbehavioral psychology a system of psychology concerned with interactions between an organism and its environment. The focus is on the interaction of stimulus functions (the use or role of a stimulus) and response functions (the purpose served by a response) and how context and experience shape those interactions. Also called **interbehaviorism**.

intercorrelation *n.* the correlation between each variable and every other variable in a group of variables.

interdependence *n.* a state in which factors rely on or react with one another such that one cannot change without affecting the other. Also called **interdependency**. —**interdependent** *adj., n.*

interdependence theory an approach to analyzing social interactions and relationships that focuses on how each person's outcomes depend on the actions of others.

interdependent self-construal a view of the self that emphasizes one's embeddedness in a network of social relationships and downplays one's unique traits or accomplishments. Compare INDEPENDENT SELF-CONSTRUAL.

interdisciplinary approach a manner of dealing with psychological, medical, or other scientific questions in which individuals from different disciplines or professions collaborate to obtain a more thorough, detailed understanding of the nature of the questions and consequently develop more comprehensive answers. Also called **multidisciplinary approach**.

interest test a SELF-REPORT INVENTORY in which the participant is required to express likes or dislikes for a range of activities and attitudes, particularly as a means of assessing the participant's suitability for different types of work. Also called **interest inventory**.

interference *n.* **1.** the blocking of learning or recall by the learning or remembering of other, conflicting material. Interference has many sources, including prior learning (**proactive interference**), subsequent learning (**retroactive interference**), competition during recall (**output interference**), and presentation of other material. **2.** the mutual effect on meeting of two or more light, sound, or any other waves, the overlap of which produces a new pattern of waves. In constructive interference, the waves are in phase and the wave motions are reinforced, which results in alternating areas of increased and decreased wave amplitude (e.g., as light and dark lines or louder and softer sound); in destructive interference, the waves are out of phase and the wave motions are decreased or cancelled. **3.** the distortion of a signal due to the presence of NOISE. **4.** see LANGUAGE TRANSFER.

interference theory the hypothesis that forgetting is due to competition from other learning or other memories.

interhemispheric transfer the transfer of MEMORY TRACES or learning experiences from one cerebral hemisphere to the other. Interhemispheric transfer can be demonstrated in humans when information presented to one visual field (and therefore one hemisphere) is known by the other hemisphere.

interitem reliability INTERNAL CONSISTENCY reliability of a set of items. It is indexed in two ways: (a) the average INTERCORRELATION (r) of each item with every other item and (b) the reliability of the sum or mean of all the items taken together.

intermarriage n. **1.** marriage between two individuals belonging to different racial, ethnic, or religious groups. **2.** marriage between two closely related individuals, as in a consanguineous marriage. **—intermarry** vb.

intermediate care facility a facility providing an appropriate level of nursing and other medical care to individuals who do not require the degree of care and treatment provided by a hospital or skilled nursing facility but need more than room and board.

intermediate cell see TYPE III CELL.

intermittent explosive disorder an impulse-control disorder consisting of multiple episodes in which the individual fails to resist aggressive impulses and commits assaultive acts or destroys property. These aggressive acts are significantly out of proportion to any precipitating factors, are not caused by any other mental disorder or a general medical condition, and are not substance-induced. Compare ISOLATED EXPLOSIVE DISORDER.

intermittent reinforcement in operant or instrumental conditioning, any pattern of REINFORCEMENT in which only some responses are reinforced. Also called **partial reinforcement**.

intermodal matching the ability to recognize an object initially inspected with one modality (e.g., touch) via another modality (e.g., vision). Also called **cross-modal matching**.

internal aim see OBJECT OF INSTINCT.

internal capsule a large band of nerve fibers in the corpus striatum (see BASAL GANGLIA) that extends between the CAUDATE NUCLEUS on its me-

dial side and the GLOBUS PALLIDUS and PUTAMEN on its lateral side. It contains afferent and efferent fibers from all parts of the cerebral cortex as they converge near the brainstem. See also EXTERNAL CAPSULE.

internal consistency the degree to which all the items on a test measure the same thing.

internal control see LOCUS OF CONTROL.

internalization n. **1.** the unconscious mental process by which the characteristics, beliefs, feelings, or attitudes of other individuals or groups are assimilated into the self and adopted as one's own. **2.** in psychoanalytic theory, the process of incorporating an OBJECT relationship inside the psyche, which reproduces the external relationship as an intrapsychic phenomenon. For example, through internalization the relationship between father and child is reproduced in the relationship between SUPEREGO and EGO. Internalization is often mistakenly used as a synonym for INTROJECTION. **—internalize** vb.

internal object an image or representation of a person (particularly someone significant to the individual, such as a parent) that is experienced as an internalized "presence" within the mind. In her development of OBJECT RELATIONS THEORY, Austrian-born British psychoanalyst Melanie Klein (1882–1960) saw the psyche as being made up of internal objects whose relations to each other and to the individual determine his or her personality and symptoms. See also PART-OBJECT.

internal validity the degree to which a study or experiment is free from flaws in its internal structure and its results can therefore be taken to represent the true nature of the phenomenon.

internal working model of attachment a cognitive construction or set of assumptions about the workings of relationships, such as expectations of support or affection. The earliest relationships may form the template for this internal model, which may be positive or negative.

International Classification of Diseases (ICD) a system of categories of disease conditions compiled by the World Health Organization (WHO) in conjunction with 10 WHO collaborating centers worldwide. The **ICD-10** (10th revision), published in 1992 as the *International Statistical Classification of Diseases and Related Health Problems*, uses a four-character alphanumeric coding system to classify diseases and disorders and their subtypes. Such standardization permits international statistical analyses and comparisons of mortality data, although the ICD is often used in epidemiological studies and by systems of payment for health care. See also DSM–IV–TR.

interneuron n. any neuron that is neither sensory nor motor but connects other neurons within the central nervous system. Also called **internuncial neuron**.

interoception n. sensitivity to stimuli that are

inside the body, resulting from the response of specialized sensory cells called **interoceptors** to occurrences within the body (e.g., from the viscera). Compare EXTEROCEPTION.

interoceptive conditioning PAVLOVIAN CONDITIONING that requires direct access to internal organs, through fistulas, balloons inserted into the digestive tract, or implanted electrical devices, to present the conditioned stimulus.

interocular transfer the ability of an aftereffect to be produced by stimulation through only one eye but to be experienced by looking only through the other eye. The presence of interocular transfer implies that the afterimage is mediated by a postretinal structure, such as the cerebral cortex, since the two eyes have no direct communication prior to the activation of BINOCULAR CELLS in the striate cortex.

interpersonal *adj.* pertaining to actions, events, and feelings between two or more individuals. For example, **interpersonal skill** is an aptitude enabling a person to carry on effective relationships with others, such as an ability to communicate thought and feeling or to assume appropriate social responsibilities.

interpersonal concordance orientation see CONVENTIONAL LEVEL.

interpersonal group psychotherapy a group approach to the treatment of psychological, behavioral, and emotional problems that emphasizes the curative influence of interpersonal learning, including the analysis of group events, experiences, and relationships, rather than the review of issues that are external to the group. Also called **interactive group psychotherapy**.

interpersonal influence see SOCIAL PRESSURE.

interpersonal intelligence in the MULTIPLE-INTELLIGENCES THEORY, the intelligence involved in understanding and relating to other people. Interpersonal intelligence is alleged to be relatively independent of other intelligences posited by the theory.

interpersonal learning group any group formed to help individuals extend their self-understanding and improve their relationships with others, such as an experiential group or T-GROUP.

interpersonal process recall a method used for understanding the processes of psychotherapy and for the training of counselors and therapists. It involves videotaping or audiotaping counseling or psychotherapy sessions, which are later reexperienced and analyzed by the counselor or therapist in the presence of a supervisor, who questions and discusses the thoughts and feelings of the counselor or therapist and client.

interpersonal psychotherapy (**IPT**) a form of psychotherapy, originally based on the INTERPERSONAL THEORY of U.S. psychiatrist Harry Stack Sullivan (1892–1949), positing that rela-

tions with others constitute the primary force motivating human behavior. A central feature of IPT is the clarification of the client's interpersonal interactions with significant others, including the therapist. The therapist helps the client explore current and past experiences in detail, relating not only to interpersonal reaction but also to environmental influences generally on personal adaptive and maladaptive thinking and behavior.

interpersonal reconstructive psychotherapy an INTEGRATIVE PSYCHOTHERAPY and method of symptom analysis that blends psychodynamic and cognitive behavior techniques and focuses on presenting problems and symptoms as they relate to long-term interpersonal difficulties. Interventions are active and focused on attachment-based factors that maintain current problems.

interpersonal theory the theory of personality developed by U.S. psychoanalyst Harry Stack Sullivan (1892–1949), which is based on the belief that people's interactions with other people, especially SIGNIFICANT OTHERS, determine their sense of security, sense of self, and the dynamisms that motivate their behavior. For Sullivan, personality is the product of a long series of stages in which the individual gradually develops "good feeling" toward others and a sense of a "good me" toward himself or herself. The individual also learns how to ward off anxiety and correct distorted perceptions of other people; learns to verify his or her ideas through CONSENSUAL VALIDATION; and above all seeks to achieve effective interpersonal relationships on a mature level.

interpersonal trust the confidence a person has in the honesty and reliability of others.

interpretation *n.* in psychotherapy, explanation by the therapist in terms that are meaningful to the client of the client's issues, behaviors, or feelings. Interpretation typically is made along the lines of the particular conceptual framework or dynamic model of the form of therapy. In psychoanalysis, for example, the analyst uses the constructs of psychoanalytic theory to interpret the patient's early experiences, dreams, character defenses, and resistance. Although interpretation exists to some extent in almost any form of therapy, it is a critical procedural step in psychoanalysis and in other forms of PSYCHODYNAMIC PSYCHOTHERAPY.

interquartile range an index of the dispersion within a batch of scores: the difference between the 75th and 25th percentile scores within a distribution.

interrater reliability the consistency with which different examiners produce similar ratings in judging the same abilities or characteristics in the same target person or object. It usually refers to continuous measurement assignments.

interresponse time (**IRT**) the time between

successive responses, especially between successive responses of the same type.

interrole conflict the form of ROLE CONFLICT that occurs when individuals have more than one role within a group and the expectations and behaviors associated with one role are not consistent with the expectations and behaviors associated with another. Compare INTRAROLE CONFLICT. See GROUP ROLE.

interrupted-time-series design an experimental design in which the effects of an intervention are evaluated by comparing outcome measures obtained at several time intervals before, and several time intervals after, the intervention was introduced.

intersensory perception the coordination of information presented through separate modalities into an integrated experience. Information from one sensory source is transmitted to the ASSOCIATION CORTEX, where it can be integrated with information from another sensory source. Also called **cross-modal perception**.

intersexuality *n.* the condition of possessing the sexual characteristics of both sexes, particularly secondary characteristics and in some cases partial development of the internal or external sex organs. —**intersexual** *adj.*

interspecies interaction all forms of interaction between species. Long-term interactions include **parasitism**, in which one species lives on or in another at a cost to the host; **mutualism**, in which both species benefit from the interaction; and **commensalism**, in which the species coexist with neither cost nor benefit. Shorter term interspecies interactions include predator–prey relationships and the mixed flocking of birds to feed and give ALARM CALLS together.

interstimulus interval (**ISI**) the time between stimulus presentations, usually timed from the end of one stimulus presentation to the beginning of the next.

interstitial cell any of the cells that fill the spaces between other tissues and structures. The interstitial cells of the TESTIS surround the seminiferous tubules and secrete testosterone when stimulated by LUTEINIZING HORMONE.

intersubjectivity *n.* the property of being accessible in some way to more than one mind, implying a communication and understanding among different minds and the possibility of converting subjective, private experiences into objective, public ones. —**intersubjective** *adj.*

intertrial interval (**ITI**) the time between successive presentations of the stimulus in a series of experimental trials.

interval of uncertainty the interval between the upper threshold (the stimulus just noticeably greater than the standard) and the lower threshold (the stimulus just noticeably less than the standard) when finding a DIFFERENCE THRESHOLD.

interval reinforcement the REINFORCEMENT of the first response to a stimulus after a predetermined interval has lapsed. Reinforcement may be given at uniform or variable intervals; the number of responses during the interval is irrelevant. Compare RATIO REINFORCEMENT.

interval scale a scale marked in equal intervals so that the difference between any two consecutive values on the scale is equivalent regardless of the two values selected. Interval scales lack a true, meaningful zero point, which is what distinguishes them from RATIO SCALES.

intervention *n.* **1.** action on the part of a therapist to deal with the issues and problems of a client. The selection of the intervention is guided by the nature of the problem, the orientation of the therapist, the setting, and the willingness and ability of the client to proceed with the treatment. **2.** a technique in addictions counseling in which significant individuals in a client's life meet with him or her, in the presence of a trained counselor, to express their observations and feelings about the client's addiction and related problems. The session, typically a surprise to the client, may last several hours, after which the client has a choice of seeking a recommended treatment immediately (e.g., as an inpatient) or ignoring the intervention. If the client chooses not to seek treatment, participants state the interpersonal consequences. **3.** a similar confrontation between an individual and family and friends, but outside of the formal structure of counseling or therapy, usually over similar issues and with the goal of urging the confronted individual to seek help with an attitudinal or behavioral problem.

interview *n.* a directed conversation intended to elicit specific information from an individual for purposes of research, diagnosis, treatment, or employment. Interviews may be either highly structured, including set questions, or unstructured, varying with material introduced by the interviewee.

interviewer effects the influence of an interviewer's attributes and behaviors on a respondent's answers. The interviewer's appearance, demeanor, training, age, sex, and ethnicity may all produce effects of this kind. The term **interviewer bias** refers more specifically to an interviewer's expectations, beliefs, and prejudices as they influence the interview process and the interpretation of the data it provides.

interview group psychotherapy a type of GROUP PSYCHOTHERAPY for adolescents and adults. A balanced therapeutic group is selected on the basis of common problems and personal characteristics, and participants are encouraged to reveal their attitudes, symptoms, and feelings.

intimacy *n.* an interpersonal state of extreme emotional closeness such that each party's PERSONAL SPACE can be entered by any of the other parties without causing discomfort to that person. Intimacy characterizes close, familiar, and usually affectionate or loving personal relationships and requires the parties to have a detailed knowledge or deep understanding of each other. —**intimate** *adj.*

intimacy problem difficulty in forming close relationships and becoming intimate with others, whether physically or psychologically, which might involve difficulties with sexual contact, self-disclosure, trust, or commitment to a lasting relationship. See also FEAR OF COMMITMENT.

intimacy versus isolation the sixth of ERIKSON'S EIGHT STAGES OF DEVELOPMENT, which extends from late adolescence through courtship and early family life to early middle age. During this period, individuals must learn to share and care without losing themselves; if they fail, they will feel alone and isolated. The development of a cohesive identity in the previous stage provides the opportunity to achieve true intimacy.

intoxicant *n.* a substance capable of producing transient alterations in mental function, ranging from minor perceptual changes or a sense of euphoria or well-being to behavioral disinhibition, hallucinations, or delirium and potentially loss of motor control and cognitive and autonomic function, resulting in coma or death.

intoxication *n.* see SUBSTANCE INTOXICATION.

intraclass correlation 1. an index of the homogeneity of members (people, items, etc.) within a group. **2.** the average intercorrelation among randomly formed pairs of cases within a group.

intraconscious personality a phenomenon of DISSOCIATIVE IDENTITY DISORDER in which one personality functioning on a subconscious level is aware of the thoughts and outer world of another personality functioning on a conscious level.

intracranial pressure (**ICP**) the pressure within the skull. Excessive intracranial pressure can cause brain damage and impede blood flow within the brain, with a range of effects that may include memory loss, balance problems, dementia, coma, and death. Causes of raised ICP include hydrocephalus, hemorrhage, hematomas, brain tumors, and head injuries.

intracranial stimulation stimulation of a brain region by direct application of an electric current through implanted electrodes. When this stimulation is controlled by the individual being stimulated it is called **intracranial self-stimulation**. In animal experiments, this is achieved by the animal performing an OPERANT RESPONSE, such as lever pressing. When the electrodes are placed in certain areas of the brain, animals will press the lever quite frequently, indicating that stimulation of these brain areas is rewarding.

intransitivity *n.* the quality of a relationship among elements such that relationships do not transfer across elements (i.e., that relationships

do not exhibit TRANSITIVITY). For example, a transitive relationship would be: Given that a > b, and b > c, it must be the case that a > c. An intransitive relationship would be one in which such a conclusion did not necessarily follow. Such relationships appear to be illogical and inconsistent but are often found in matters of personal preference or other subjective judgments. For example, a person might prefer the color blue over red, and red over green, but when given a choice prefer green over blue. —**intransitive** *adj.*

intraocular pressure (**IOP**) the pressure inside the eye. Intraocular pressure is determined by **tonometry**, in which the resistance of the surface of the eye to a puff of air is measured. Increased pressure may indicate GLAUCOMA, a disease in which the pressure inside the eye increases to the point at which it causes impaired vision and eventually blindness if untreated.

intrapersonal *adj.* describing factors operating or constructs occurring within the person, such as attitudes, decisions, self-concept, self-esteem, or self-regulation.

intrapersonal intelligence in the MULTIPLE-INTELLIGENCES THEORY, the intelligence involved in self-understanding and in reflecting upon oneself, one's skills, one's motives, etc. Intrapersonal intelligence is alleged to be relatively independent of other intelligences posited by the theory.

intrapsychic *adj.* pertaining to impulses, ideas, conflicts, or other psychological phenomena that arise or occur within the psyche or mind. An **intrapsychic** (or **inner**) **conflict**, for example, is the clash of opposing forces within the psyche, such as conflicting drives, wishes, or agencies. Compare EXTRAPSYCHIC.

intrarole conflict the form of ROLE CONFLICT caused by incompatibility among the behaviors and expectations associated with a single role. These inconsistencies may result from the inherent complexity of the role itself, the ambiguity of the role, or a superordinate group's lack of consensus in defining the role and its demands. Compare INTERROLE CONFLICT. See GROUP ROLE.

intrinsic activity a measure of the efficacy of a drug-receptor complex in producing a pharmacological effect.

intrinsic motivation an incentive to engage in a specific activity that derives from the activity itself (e.g., a genuine interest in a subject studied), rather than because of any external benefits that might be obtained (e.g., course credits). Compare EXTRINSIC MOTIVATION.

intrinsic reinforcement the obtainment of a positively valued outcome from the performance of an action. The outcome itself is inherent to the activity and called an **intrinsic reinforcer**. For example, blowing on a harmonica naturally produces sounds. If the sounds serve to reinforce blowing on the harmonica, then the sounds provide intrinsic reinforcement. Compare EXTRINSIC REINFORCEMENT.

intrinsic religion a religious orientation in which religious practice is an end itself, rather than a means to other ends. Compare EXTRINSIC RELIGION.

introjection *n.* **1.** a process in which an individual unconsciously incorporates aspects of reality external to himself or herself into the self, particularly the attitudes, values, and qualities of another person or a part of another person's personality. Introjection may occur, for example, in the mourning process for a loved one. **2.** in psychoanalytic theory, the process of internalizing the qualities of an external OBJECT into the psyche in the form of an internal object or mental REPRESENTATION, which then has an influence on behavior. This process is posited to be a normal part of development, as when introjection of parental values and attitudes forms the SUPEREGO, but may also be used as a DEFENSE MECHANISM in situations that arouse anxiety. Compare IDENTIFICATION; INCORPORATION. **—introject** *vb.* **—introjective** *adj.*

introjective depression self-critical depression: intense sadness and DYSPHORIA stemming from punitive, relentless feelings of self-doubt, self-criticism, and self-loathing that often are related to the internalization of the attitudes and values of harsh and critical parental figures. The individual with introjective depression becomes involved in numerous activities in an attempt to compensate for his or her excessively high standards, constant drive to perform and achieve, and feelings of guilt and shame over not having lived up to expectations.

intron *n.* a sequence of DNA within a gene that does not encode any part of the gene's ultimate product. Such sequences are transcribed into messenger RNA (mRNA) but then removed during formation of the mature mRNA, which instructs the cell to synthesize a protein. Compare EXON.

intropunitive *adj.* referring to the punishment of oneself: tending to turn anger, blame, or hostility internally, against the self, in response to frustration. Compare EXTRAPUNITIVE. **—intropunitiveness** *n.*

introspection *n.* the process of attempting to access directly one's own internal psychological processes, judgments, perceptions, or states. **—introspective** *adj.*

introspectionism *n.* the doctrine that the basic method of psychological investigation is or should be INTROSPECTION. Historically, such an approach is associated with the school of psychological STRUCTURALISM. **—introspectionist** *adj.*

introversion *n.* orientation toward the internal private world of one's self and one's inner thoughts and feelings, rather than toward the outer world of people and things. Introversion is a broad personality trait and, like EXTRAVER-

SION, exists on a continuum of attitudes and behaviors. Introverts are relatively more withdrawn, retiring, reserved, quiet, and deliberate; they may tend to mute or guard expression of positive affect, adopt more skeptical views or positions, and prefer to work independently. See also INTROVERSION–EXTRAVERSION. **—introversive** *adj.* **—introvert** *n.* **—introverted** *adj.*

introversion–extraversion the range, or continuum, of self-orientation from INTROVERSION, characterized by inward and self-directed concerns and behaviors, to EXTRAVERSION, characterized by outward and social-directed concerns and behaviors. See also FIVE-FACTOR PERSONALITY MODEL.

intrusion error in a memory test, the recall of an item that was not among the material presented for remembering. Intrusion errors can be informative about the nature of forgetting, for instance, if the intrusion is a synonym, rhyme, or associate of a correct item.

intrusive thoughts mental events that interrupt the flow of ongoing and task-related thoughts in spite of persistent efforts to avoid them. They are a common aspect of such disorders as posttraumatic stress and obsessive-compulsive disorder.

intuition *n.* immediate insight or perception as contrasted with conscious reasoning or reflection. Intuitions have been characterized alternatively as quasi-mystical experiences or as the products of instinct, feeling, minimal sense impressions, or unconscious forces. **—intuit** *vb.* **—intuitive** *adj.*

intuitionism *n.* the tendency of people to prefer to think, reason, and remember by processing inexact memory representations rather than working logically from exact representations. See FUZZY TRACE THEORY.

in utero in the uterus, that is, before birth.

invalid *adj.* lacking VALIDITY.

invariance *n.* **1.** in the theory of ECOLOGICAL PERCEPTION, any property of an object that remains constant although the point of observation or surrounding conditions may change. **2.** in statistics, the property of being unchanged by a TRANSFORMATION. **—invariant** *adj.*

invariant sequence in stage theories of development, such as PIAGETIAN THEORY, the unchanging order in which the stages of development occur. Children must progress sequentially through these stages, none of which can be skipped.

invasive *adj.* **1.** denoting procedures or tests that require puncture or incision of the skin or insertion of an instrument or foreign material into the body. **2.** able to spread from one tissue to another, or having the capacity to spread, as in the case of an infection or a malignant tumor. Compare NONINVASIVE.

inventory *n.* a list of items, often in question

form, used in describing and studying behavior, interests, and attitudes.

inverse agonist see AGONIST.

inverted-U hypothesis a proposed correlation between motivation (or AROUSAL) and performance such that performance is poorest when motivation or arousal is at very low or very high states. This function is typically referred to as the YERKES–DODSON LAW. Emotional intensity (motivation) increases from a zero point to an optimal point, increasing the quality of performance; increase in intensity after this optimal point leads to performance deterioration and disorganization, forming an inverted U-shaped curve. The optimal point is reached sooner (i.e., at lower intensities) the less well learned or more complex the performance; increases in emotional intensity supposedly affect finer skills, finer discriminations, complex reasoning tasks, and recently acquired skills more readily than routine activities. However, the correlation is considered weak; at best, the inverted U-function represents an entire family of curves in which the peak of performance takes place at different levels of arousal.

in vitro referring to biological conditions or processes that occur or are made to occur outside the living body, usually in a laboratory dish (Latin, literally: "in glass"). Compare IN VIVO.

in vitro fertilization (**IVF**) a procedure in which an ovum (egg) is removed from a woman's body, fertilized externally with sperm, and then returned to the uterus. It is used to treat the most difficult cases of INFERTILITY, but success rates for the procedure are not high.

in vivo referring to biological conditions or processes that occur or are observed within the living organism. Compare IN VITRO. [Latin, literally: "in life"]

in vivo desensitization a technique used in BEHAVIOR THERAPY, usually to reduce or eliminate phobias, in which the client is exposed to the stimuli that induce anxiety. The therapist, in discussion with the client, produces a hierarchy of anxiety-invoking events or items relating to the anxiety-producing stimulus or phobia. The client is then exposed to the actual stimuli in the hierarchy, rather than being asked to imagine them. Success depends on the client overcoming anxiety as the events or items are encountered. Compare COVERT DESENSITIZATION. See also SYSTEMATIC DESENSITIZATION.

in vivo exposure therapy BEHAVIOR THERAPY in which the client is exposed to anxiety-provoking situations or stimuli in real-world conditions in order to master anxiety and be able to function adequately in the presence of these situations or stimuli. For example, a client who fears flying could be accompanied by a therapist to the airport to simulate boarding a plane while practicing anxiety-decreasing techniques, such as deep breathing. See also EXPOSURE THERAPY. Compare IN VIVO DESENSITIZATION.

involuntary *adj.* describing activity, movement, behavior, or other processes (e.g., REFLEXES) that occur without intention or volition, as opposed to those that are consciously (deliberately) initiated.

involuntary attention attention that is captured by a prominent stimulus, for example in the peripheral visual field, rather than deliberately applied or focused by the individual.

involuntary hospitalization the confinement of a person with a serious mental disorder or illness to a mental hospital by medical authorization and legal direction. Individuals so hospitalized may be considered dangerous to themselves or others, may fail to recognize the severity of their illness and the need for treatment, or may be unable to have their daily living and treatment needs otherwise met in the community or survive without medical attention. Compare VOLUNTARY ADMISSION.

iodopsin *n.* see PHOTOPIGMENT.

ion *n.* an atom or molecule that has acquired an electrical charge by gaining or losing one or more electrons. —**ionic** *adj.*

ion channel a group of proteins forming a channel that spans a cell membrane, allowing the passage of ions between the extracellular environment and the cytoplasm of the cell. Ion channels are selective, allow passage of ions of a particular chemical nature, size, or electrostatic charge, and may be ungated (i.e., always open) or gated, opening and closing in response to chemical, electrical, or mechanical signals. Ion channels are important in the transmission of neural signals between neurons at a SYNAPSE. See also CALCIUM CHANNEL.

ionotropic receptor a RECEPTOR protein that includes an ION CHANNEL that is opened when the receptor is activated. Compare METABOTROPIC RECEPTOR.

IOP abbreviation for INTRAOCULAR PRESSURE.

I/O psychology abbreviation for INDUSTRIAL AND ORGANIZATIONAL PSYCHOLOGY.

IOR abbreviation for INHIBITION OF RETURN.

IP abbreviation for INFORMATION PROCESSING.

ipsative *adj.* referring back to the self. For example, ipsative analyses of personal characteristics involve assessing multiple psychological attributes and conducting within-person analyses of the degree to which an individual possesses one attribute versus another.

ipsative scale a scale in which the points distributed to all of the items in that scale must sum to a specific total. In such a scale, all participants will have the same total score but the distribution of the "points" among the various items within the scale will differ for each individual.

ipsilateral *adj.* situated on or affecting the same side of the body. Compare CONTRALATERAL. —**ipsilaterally** *adv.*

I

IPSP abbreviation for INHIBITORY POSTSYNAPTIC POTENTIAL.

IPT abbreviation for INTERPERSONAL PSYCHOTHERAPY.

IQ intelligence quotient: a standard measure of an individual's intelligence level based on psychological tests. In the early years of intelligence testing, IQ was calculated by dividing the MENTAL AGE by the CHRONOLOGICAL AGE and multiplying by 100 to produce a **ratio IQ**. This concept has now mostly been replaced by the **deviation IQ**, computed as a function of the discrepancy of an individual score from the mean (or average) score. The mean IQ is customarily 100, with slightly more than two thirds of all scores falling within plus or minus 15 points of the mean (usually one standard deviation).

Some tests yield more specific IQ scores, such as a **verbal IQ**, which measures VERBAL INTELLIGENCE, and **performance IQ**, which measures NONVERBAL INTELLIGENCE. Discrepancies between the two can be used diagnostically to detect learning disabilities or specific cognitive deficiencies.

There are critics who consider the concept of IQ (and other intelligence scales) to be flawed. They point out that the IQ test is more a measure of previously learned skills and knowledge and also refer to cases of misrepresentation of facts in the history of IQ research.

IRB abbreviation for INSTITUTIONAL REVIEW BOARD.

iris *n.* a muscular disk that surrounds the pupil of the eye and controls the amount of light entering the eye by contraction or relaxation. The stroma of the iris, which faces the cornea, contains a pigment that gives the eye its coloration; the back of the iris is lined with a dark pigment that restricts light entry to the pupil, regardless of the apparent color of the iris.

IRM abbreviation for INNATE RELEASING MECHANISM.

ironic mental control the phenomenon whereby the attempt to suppress some mental content from consciousness results in an unexpectedly high level of awareness of that very content.

irrationality *n.* the state, condition, or quality of lacking rational thought. The term is typically used in relation to cognitive behavior (e.g., thinking, decision making) that is illogical.

irrational type in ANALYTIC PSYCHOLOGY, one of the two major categories of FUNCTIONAL TYPE: It comprises the intuitive type and the sensation type. Compare RATIONAL TYPE.

irreversible decrement model the view that physical and psychological changes associated with aging are caused by biological deterioration and thus are not amenable to training or intervention.

irritability *n.* **1.** a state of excessive, easily provoked anger, annoyance, or impatience. **2.** in physiology, the ability of a cell or tissue to respond to stimuli (e.g., NEURAL IRRITABILITY). —**irritable** *adj.*

irritable bowel syndrome (IBS) a common functional disorder of the intestines characterized by abdominal pain or discomfort (e.g., bloating) and changes in bowel habits, with some people experiencing increased constipation, others increased diarrhea, and others alternating between the two. As yet there is no known cause, though stress and emotional factors are currently thought to play a role.

IRT 1. abbreviation for INTERRESPONSE TIME. **2.** abbreviation for ITEM RESPONSE THEORY.

ischemia *n.* deficiency of blood in an organ or tissue, due to functional constriction or actual obstruction of a blood vessel. —**ischemic** *adj.*

ISI abbreviation for INTERSTIMULUS INTERVAL.

island of Reil see INSULA. [Johann Reil (1759–1813), German physician]

islets of Langerhans clusters of ENDOCRINE cells within the PANCREAS. The A (or alpha) cells secrete GLUCAGON, the B (or beta) cells secrete INSULIN, and the D (or delta) cells secrete SOMATOSTATIN. Together these hormones play a key role in regulating BLOOD SUGAR and carbohydrate metabolism. [Paul **Langerhans** (1847–1888), German anatomist]

isocortex *n.* see NEOCORTEX.

isolated explosive disorder an IMPULSE-CONTROL DISORDER characterized by a single, discrete episode in which the individual commits a violent, catastrophic act, such as shooting strangers during a sudden fit of rage. The episode is out of all proportion to any precipitating stress, is not due to any other mental disorder or to a general medical condition, and is not substance-induced. Compare INTERMITTENT EXPLOSIVE DISORDER.

isolation *n.* **1.** the condition of being separated from other individuals. See LONELINESS. **2.** in psychoanalytic theory, a DEFENSE MECHANISM that relies on keeping unwelcome thoughts and feelings from forming associative links with other thoughts and feelings, with the result that the unwelcome thought is rarely activated. See also COMPARTMENTALIZATION. —**isolate** *vb.*

isolation experiment the removal of an animal from social or other contact with other members of its species in order to observe behavioral or other effects.

isomorphism *n.* **1.** a one-to-one structural correspondence between two or more different entities or their constituent parts. **2.** the concept, especially in GESTALT PSYCHOLOGY, that there is a structural correspondence between perceptual experience and psychoneural activity in the brain. —**isomorph** *n.* —**isomorphic** *adj.*

I statement a communication tool in which the first person pronoun is used in talking about relationship issues. Therapists may coach clients to use "I" instead of "you" in statements, for example, "I am bothered by your habit" rather than "You have a bad habit" (which is a **you statement**). I statements tend to reduce the negativity and blame directed toward the other person and put the ownership of the issue with the speaker, not the listener.

item analysis a set of procedures used to evaluate the statistical merits of individual items comprising a psychological measure or test. These procedures may be used to select items for a test from a larger pool of initial items or to evaluate items on an established test.

item response theory (**IRT**) a psychometric theory of measurement based on the concept that the probability that an item will be correctly answered is a function of an underlying trait or ability that is not directly observable, that is, a latent trait (see LATENT TRAIT THEORY). Item response theory models differ in terms of the number of parameters contained in the model (as in the RASCH MODEL).

item-to-item reliability (symbol: r_{ii}) the correlation of responses to one particular item in a test or subtest with responses to another particular item in that test or subtest.

item validity the extent to which an individual item in a test or experiment measures what it purports to measure.

iteration *n.* the repetition of a certain computational step until further repetition no longer changes the outcome or until the repetition meets some other predefined criterion.

I–Thou *adj.* denoting a relationship in which a subject ("I") treats someone or something else as another unique subject ("Thou") and in which there is complete personal involvement. German Jewish philosopher Martin Buber (1878–1965), who introduced the term, held that this type of relationship between individuals is characterized by mutual openness to, and recognition of, the unique personhood of the other. The I–Thou relationship is transformative for both people. In forms of EXISTENTIAL–HUMANISTIC THERAPY especially, I–Thou moments are prized and denote a significant contact and understanding between client and therapist. Compare I–IT.

ITI abbreviation for INTERTRIAL INTERVAL.

IV abbreviation for INDEPENDENT VARIABLE.

IVF abbreviation for IN VITRO FERTILIZATION.

Jj

jackknife *n.* a procedure estimating the variability of a parameter associated with a batch of data, such as the standard error. A number of samples are obtained from the original data by eliminating one observation at a time, the parameter calculated for each, and the individual parameters combined to provide an estimate of the overall parameter for the entire sample.

Jackson's law the principle that when mental deterioration results from brain disease, the higher and more recently developed functions are lost first. [John **Jackson** (1835–1911), British neurologist]

James–Lange theory the theory that different feeling states stem from the feedback from the viscera and voluntary musculature to the brain: that is, the physiological response precedes rather than follows the feeling. [William **James** (1842–1910), U.S. psychologist and philosopher; Carl Georg **Lange** (1834–1900), Danish physiologist]

jargon *n.* the specialized words and forms of language used within a particular profession or field of activity. Although jargon is often unavoidable in dealing with technical or specialist subjects, inappropriate or unnecessary use can alienate outsiders, who find it unintelligible.

jealousy *n.* a NEGATIVE EMOTION in which an individual resents a third party for appearing to take away (or likely to take away) the affections of a loved one. Jealousy requires a triangle of social relationships between three individuals: the one who is jealous, the partner with whom the jealous individual has or desires a relationship, and the rival who represents a preemptive threat to that relationship. Romantic relationships are the prototypic source of jealousy, but any significant relationship (with parents, friends, and so on) is capable of producing it. It differs from ENVY in that three people are always involved. —**jealous** *adj.*

Jensenism *n.* the controversial theory that racial differences in IQ are at least partly heritable. [Arthur **Jensen** (1923–), U.S. psychologist]

jigsaw classroom a team-learning technique used to foster a cooperative learning environment, to reduce social isolation, and to improve academic achievement. Students work in groups on a content unit. The teacher assigns specific topics in the unit to each group member and allows students with the same topics to leave their group to study the topic with others who have that same assignment. The students then return to their original groups and teach their topics to the other members.

jiryan *n.* a CULTURE-BOUND SYNDROME found in India, with symptoms similar to those of SHEN-K'UEI.

JND (**jnd**) abbreviation for just noticeable difference (see DIFFERENCE THRESHOLD).

job analysis the collection and study of information about the behaviors, tools, working conditions, skills, and other characteristics of a specific job. Job analysis is the first step in developing effective personnel selection, employee evaluation, job evaluation, and personnel training programs.

job-characteristics model a model that attempts to characterize the basic parameters of a job as they affect the psychological state of the employee, especially with regard to motivation. The five core **job dimensions** are identified as skill variety, TASK IDENTITY, TASK SIGNIFICANCE, autonomy, and feedback.

job involvement the degree to which a person psychologically identifies with his or her job. A person who has a high level of job involvement usually obtains major life satisfaction from the job.

job-placement stage a level of rehabilitation and work-preparedness training at which a person with a disability is presumed to be ready to move into the competitive job market.

job redesign systematic efforts to improve work methods, equipment, and the working environment. Major approaches to job redesign include **methods analysis**, which focuses on the development of efficient work methods; HUMAN FACTORS ENGINEERING, which is primarily concerned with the design of equipment, facilities, and environments; and **job enlargement** or **job enrichment**, which aim to expand the variety, complexity, and responsibility of jobs.

joint attention attention overtly focused by two or more people on the same object, person, or action at the same time, with each being aware of the others' interest. Joint attention is an important developmental tool; by focusing attention on an object as well as on the adult's reaction to it, children can learn about the world. This technique is also used in primate studies. Also called **shared attention**.

jouissance *n.* in the theory of French psychoanalyst Jacques Lacan (1901–1981), enjoyment or pleasure that goes beyond mere satisfaction of an INSTINCT. Such pleasure is seen as a subversive and destabilizing force. The term was later adopted by literary and philosophical critics in the traditions of DECONSTRUCTION and POSTSTRUCTURALISM. [French, literally: "enjoyment," "pleasure"]

joy *n.* a feeling of extreme gladness, delight, or exultation of the spirit arising from a sense of wellbeing or satisfaction. Joy promotes confidence and an increase in energy, which in turn tend to promote positive feelings about the self.

judgment *n.* **1.** the capacity to recognize relationships, draw conclusions from evidence, and make critical evaluations of events and people. **2.** in psychophysics, the ability to determine the presence or relative magnitude of stimuli.

Jungian psychology the psychoanalytical theory and approach to psychotherapy of Swiss psychiatrist and psychoanalyst Carl Jung (1875–1961). See ANALYTIC PSYCHOLOGY.

Jungian typology a theory of personality that classifies individuals into types according to (a) attitudes of INTROVERSION and EXTRAVERSION (see ATTITUDINAL TYPES) and (b) the dominant functions of the psyche (see FUNCTIONAL TYPES). [Carl **Jung** (1875–1961), Swiss psychiatrist and psychoanalyst]

jurisprudential teaching model a teaching model that emphasizes the role of social interaction and uses case studies as a paradigm for information processing and evaluating social issues.

justification *n.* **1.** in ethics, the process of determining right actions and appropriate beliefs. **2.** in clinical psychology, the defensive intellectualization of behavior.

just noticeable difference (JND; jnd) see DIFFERENCE THRESHOLD.

just-world hypothesis the need to believe that the environment is a just and orderly place where what happens to people generally is what they deserve. This belief in a just world enables an individual to confront his or her physical and social environment as though they were stable and orderly but may, for example, result in the belief that the innocent victim of an accident must somehow be responsible for, or deserve, it. Also called **just-world bias**; **just-world phenomenon**.

juvenile period the period when an animal is no longer dependent on its parents for survival but is not yet sexually active. In nonhuman mammals, this constitutes the time between the cessation of weaning (the end of infancy) and the onset of sexual activity.

Kk

k symbol for COEFFICIENT OF ALIENATION.

kainate receptor see GLUTAMATE RECEPTOR.

Kanizsa figure any one of several figures that induce the perception of illusory contours defining a shape that appears to be brighter than the background. The most common example is the **Kanizsa triangle**, which is induced by three black circles—each with a wedge removed—placed as the apexes of a triangle. Even though nothing connects the circles, a strong impression of a triangle that is brighter than the background is perceived. [Gaetano **Kanizsa** (1913–1993), Italian psychologist]

kansei engineering an engineering and design practice that elicits and analyzes users' subjective feelings about aspects of a product or range of products and incorporates these findings into subsequent designs. [Japanese: "psychological feeling"]

kappa *n.* an index of the degree to which a group of judges, tests, or instruments rate an attribute in the same way, corrected for chance association. See COHEN'S KAPPA.

kappa effect the interaction between the perceived duration of a stimulus and the spatial extent of the stimulus. When a small visual stimulus and a large visual stimulus are both flashed for the same length of time, the duration of the large stimulus is perceived as longer than that of the small stimulus.

kappa receptor see OPIOID RECEPTOR.

kappa wave a type of BRAIN WAVE with a frequency similar to that of an ALPHA WAVE (8–12 Hz) but with a much weaker amplitude. Kappa waves are associated with thinking, particularly such activities as problem solving or recall of a partly learned task.

karyotype *n.* **1.** the chromosomal constitution of a cell, including the number of chromosomes, their structural features, and any abnormalities. **2.** a photograph of an individual's chromosomes, which shows them in an ordered, numbered array.

K complex a characteristic brief, high-amplitude pattern of electrical activity recorded from the brain during the early stages of sleep.

Keller plan a personalized system of education in which material to be learned is divided into units and students work at their own pace, using textbooks and other written materials as primary resources. Fundamental understanding of each unit's content must be demonstrated before a student may advance to the next one. [Fred S. **Keller** (1899–1996), U.S. psychologist]

Kendall's coefficient of concordance see COEFFICIENT OF CONCORDANCE. [Maurice George **Kendall** (1907–1983), British statistician]

Kendall's tau (symbol: τ) a nonparametric measure of the degree of association between two ordinal variables (i.e., rank-ordered data). [Maurice **Kendall**]

kernel-of-truth hypothesis the idea that STEREOTYPES, despite being exaggerated generalizations about a group of diverse individuals, sometimes contain elements that accurately describe the qualities of the stereotyped group.

ketamine *n.* a drug that is closely related to PCP (phencyclidine) and formerly used as a dissociative anesthetic (producing analgesia, amnesia, and sedation without loss of consciousness). Disorientation and perceptual distortions may result from its use, which have limited its utility in surgical anesthesia but have made it a sought-after and common drug of abuse. U.S. trade name: **Ketalar**.

kindling *n.* an alteration in brain functioning that results from repeated minor electrical or chemical stimulation, culminating in the appearance of electrographic abnormalities and often generalized seizures.

kindness *n.* benevolent and helpful action intentionally directed toward another person. Kindness is motivated by the desire to help another, not to gain explicit reward or to avoid explicit punishment. See ALTRUISM. —**kind** *adj.*

kindred *n.* an extended family.

kinematics *n.* the study of the motion of objects and their patterns of movement. —**kinematic** *adj.*

kinesics *n.* the study of the part played by body movements, such as hand gestures, eye movements, and so on, in communicating meaning. See BODY LANGUAGE.

kinesiology *n.* the study of the mechanics of body movement, especially their relationship to anatomical characteristics and physiological functions. —**kinesiological** *adj.* —**kinesiologist** *n.*

kinesiotherapy *n.* the application of progressive physical exercise and activities to treat individuals with FUNCTIONAL LIMITATION or to aid those interested in improving or maintaining general physical and emotional health, formerly called **corrective therapy**. A **kinesiotherapist** (formerly a **corrective therapist**) is a certified professional who develops a specific treatment plan for each individual, determining appropriate therapeutic exercises and physical-education activities and directing their implementation.

kinesis *n.* a type of movement in which an organism's response is related to the intensity of the stimulation but is not oriented in any spatial direction. Compare TAXIS; TROPISM.

kinesthesis *n.* the sense that provides information about the position, movement, tension, and so forth of body parts via specialized **kinesthetic receptors** in the muscles, tendons, and joints. This information, called **kinesthetic feedback**, enables humans and other animals to control and coordinate their movements. Also called **kinesthesia**. See PROPRIOCEPTION. —**kinesthetic** *adj.*

kinesthetic aftereffect any perceptual distortion of movement. For example, in a baseball game swinging two bats during warm-up may create the perception that one then swings a single bat faster at the plate.

kinesthetics *n.* awareness of the position and movement of body parts.

kinetic depth effect the impression that a visual figure has three dimensions when in motion. For example, a stationary pattern of apparently random elements will organize into a coherent three-dimensional structure when set in motion.

kinetic information in clinical assessment and therapy, the observed gestures, postures, and other body-language clues used in making an evaluation of a client or patient.

kingdom *n.* traditionally, the highest category used in BIOLOGICAL TAXONOMY, which contains related PHYLA. Modern classifications recognize five kingdoms—Bacteria, Protista (or Protoctista), Animalia, Fungi, and Plantae—which in some systems are grouped into DOMAINS.

kin selection a variation of natural selection that favors behavior by an individual that increases the chances of its relatives surviving and reproducing successfully (see ALTRUISM). If an individual risks its own ability to reproduce or survive but helps its parents or more than two siblings to survive or reproduce, the sacrificing individual will benefit indirectly by gaining INCLUSIVE FITNESS.

kinship *n.* the state of being related by birth, common ancestry, marriage, or adoption. Notions of who is and who is not kin may vary considerably from one culture to another.

kinship network the system of formal and informal relationships that make up an EXTENDED FAMILY in a given culture or society, typically based on blood ties, marriage, or adoption. The analysis of kinship networks and DESCENT GROUPS in preindustrial societies has been a major concern of cultural anthropology. Also called **kinship system**.

Kleinian *adj.* denoting or in accordance with the theories and methods of the school of psychoanalysis founded by Austrian-born British psychoanalyst Melanie Klein (1882–1960), including such concepts as INTERNALIZATION and IDEALIZATION.

kleptomania *n.* an IMPULSE-CONTROL DISORDER characterized by a repeated failure to resist impulses to steal objects that have no immediate use or intrinsic value to the individual, accompanied by feelings of increased tension before committing the theft and either pleasure or relief during the act. The stealing is not done out of anger or in response to a delusion or hallucination and is not better accounted for by another disorder, such as conduct disorder or a manic episode. —**kleptomaniac** *n.*

Klinefelter's syndrome a disorder in which males are born with an extra X chromosome, resulting in small testes, absence of sperm, enlarged breasts, mental retardation, and abnormal behavior. Also called **XXY syndrome**. [Harry F. **Klinefelter** (1912–), U.S. physician]

Klonopin *n.* a trade name for CLONAZEPAM.

Klüver–Bucy syndrome a condition resulting from damage to both medial temporal lobes and marked by hypersexuality, a tendency to examine all objects by placing them in the mouth, visual AGNOSIA, and decreased emotional responsivity (including loss of normal fear and anger responses). [Heinrich **Klüver** (1897–1975), German-born U.S. neurologist; Paul **Bucy** (1904–1992), U.S. neurosurgeon]

knee-jerk reflex see PATELLAR REFLEX.

knockdown *n.* the alteration of a particular gene in an individual organism, or a line of organisms, by an experimenter so that it is present but its effects are not manifested.

knockout *n.* the elimination or inactivation of a particular gene in an individual organism, or a line of organisms, by an experimenter.

knowledge *n.* **1.** the state of being familiar with something or aware of its existence, usually resulting from experience or study. **2.** the range of one's understanding or information. In some contexts the words knowledge and memory are used synonymously.

knowledge base an individual's general background knowledge, which influences his or her performance on most cognitive tasks.

knowledge elicitation in ergonomics, a variety of methods used to educe the content and structure of users' knowledge or reasoning regarding a product or system. Methods used include CASE-BASED REASONING, CONVERSATION ANALYSIS, and TASK ANALYSIS.

knowledge function of an attitude the role an attitude can play in helping to interpret ambiguous information or to organize information. For example, a positive attitude toward a friend may assist in attributing that person's negative behavior to situational factors rather than personal characteristics. See also FUNC-TIONAL APPROACH TO ATTITUDES.

Kohlberg's theory of moral development as proposed by U.S. psychologist Lawrence Kohlberg (1927–1987), the theory that the cognitive processes associated with moral judgment develop through a number of universal, invariant stages. According to the theory, there are three main levels: the PRECONVENTIONAL LEVEL, the CONVENTIONAL LEVEL, and the POSTCONVENTIONAL LEVEL.

Köhler effect an increase in motivation that sometimes occurs among individuals working in groups on CONJUNCTIVE TASKS that require persistence but little coordination of effort. The effect is likely due to the increased effort expended by the less capable group members. Compare COMPENSATION EFFECT. [O. **Köhler**, early German researcher who confirmed the effect empirically]

Kolmogorov–Smirnov test a nonparametric test of the distributional equivalence of two samples or of the fit of a sample to a theoretical distribution. [Andrei Nikolaevich **Kolmogorov** and Nikolai Vasilevich **Smirnov**, 20th-century Soviet mathematicians]

koro *n.* a CULTURE-BOUND SYNDROME observed primarily in males in China and southeast Asia. It is an acute anxiety reaction in which the male suddenly fears that his penis is shrinking and will disappear into his abdomen, bringing death. (In females, the fear is focused on the vulva and nipples.) Individuals may also experience shame if they associate the fear with immoral sexual behavior. Also called **jinjinia bemar; rok-joo; shook yong; shuk yang; suk-yeong; suo yang**.

Korsakoff's syndrome amnesia caused by thiamine (vitamin B$_1$) deficiency. Individuals have a severe, enduring difficulty in learning new information and often cannot recall memories of events from recent years, although general intellectual functioning and SEMANTIC MEMORY are unimpaired. Korsakoff's syndrome frequently is associated with alcoholism and often follows an episode of WERNICKE'S ENCEPHALOPATHY (see WERNICKE–KORSAKOFF SYNDROME). [first described in 1887 by Sergei **Korsakoff** (1853–1900), Russian neurologist]

Kraepelin's theory the concept of DEMENTIA PRAECOX, the disorder now known as SCHIZOPHRENIA. Kraepelin's theory emphasized the progressive intellectual deterioration (dementia) and the early onset (praecox) of the disorder. [first presented in 1898 by Emil **Kraepelin** (1856–1926), German psychiatrist]

Krause end bulb a specialized sensory nerve ending enclosed in a capsule in the skin. It is associated with temperature sensations. [Wilhelm **Krause** (1833–1910), German anatomist]

Kretschmer typology a controversial classification of individuals by German psychiatrist Ernst Kretschmer (1888–1964) based on a hypothetical relationship between body build and personality characteristics. According to this classification, the short, stocky **pyknic type** is jovial and subject to mood swings; the tall, thin **asthenic type** is introversive and sensitive; the muscular **athletic type** is energetic and aggressive; and the mixed **dysplastic type** presents a combination of traits.

Kruskal–Shepard scaling MULTIDIMENSIONAL SCALING applied to judgments of similarity or dissimilarity for pairs of items (e.g., cities). The dissimilarities are represented by distances between items, with larger distances indicating greater dissimilarity. [William Henry **Kruskal** (1919–2005), U.S. statistician; Roger N. **Shepard** (1929–), U.S. experimental and cognitive psychologist]

Kruskal–Wallis test a nonparametric method for determining statistical significance of the equality of centrality with ranked data. It is analogous to ONE-WAY ANALYSIS OF VARIANCE. [William **Kruskal** and Wilson Allen **Wallis** (1912–1998), U.S. statisticians]

K-strategy *n.* a reproductive strategy that involves a high degree of parental investment in a relatively small number of offspring over the individual's reproductive life, as in human beings and other primates. Compare R-STRATEGY.

kurtosis *n.* the fourth central MOMENT of a probability distribution. It is a statistical description of the degree of peakedness of that distribution.

kyphosis *n.* an abnormal outward curvature of the spine at the cervical level, producing a rounded back. See also LORDOSIS; SCOLIOSIS.

Ll

LAAM L-alpha-acetyl-methadol: a long-acting OPIOID AGONIST that is used in the management of opioid dependence. Its possible adverse effects on heart rate and interactions with other drugs have limited its clinical use.

labeled-line theory of taste coding a theory postulating that each GUSTATORY NEURON TYPE comprises a private circuit (labeled line) through which is signaled the presence of its associated PRIMARY TASTE quality. The taste is perceived exclusively as a product of activity in that labeled line; activity in neurons outside the labeled line contributes only noise. Compare PATTERNING THEORY OF TASTE CODING.

labeling theory the sociological hypothesis that describing an individual in terms of particular behavioral characteristics (i.e., labeling) may have a significant effect on his or her behavior, as a form of SELF-FULFILLING PROPHECY.

la belle indifférence inappropriate lack of concern about the seriousness or implications of one's physical symptoms, often seen in CONVERSION DISORDER.

labia *pl. n.* (*sing.* **labium**) four lip-shaped folds of tissue forming part of the female external genitalia (see VULVA). The labia—comprising a larger, outer pair, the **labia majora** (*sing.* **labium majus**), and a thinner, inner pair, the **labia minora** (*sing.* **labium minus**)—enclose the clitoris and the openings of the urethra and vagina.

labial *adj.* **1.** of or relating to the lips. **2.** denoting a speech sound made with the lips, for example, [b], [p], [m], [w], [f], or [v]. If the sound is made with both lips, it is described as **bilabial**; if the sound is made with the lower lip and the upper teeth, it is termed **labiodental** (or **labial dental**).

labile affect highly variable, suddenly shifting emotional expression.

labiodental *adj.* see LABIAL.

laboratory-method model an approach to education in which the role of social interaction is emphasized. The development of personal awareness and interpersonal skills is a major area of concern.

labyrinth *n.* in anatomy, the complex system of cavities, ducts, and canals within the temporal bone of the skull that comprises the inner ear. The **bony** (or **osseous**) **labyrinth** is a system of bony cavities that houses the **membranous labyrinth**, a membrane-lined system of ducts containing the receptors for hearing and balance.

laceration *n.* a jagged tear or cut: a wound with rough, irregular edges.

lack of fit the degree to which the predicted values that are generated from a model diverge from the corresponding empirical values.

lacunar stroke see STROKE.

Ladd-Franklin theory a formerly influential but now superseded theory of color vision. It is based on the notion that light of certain wavelengths causes substances to be released from a highly developed photosensitive molecule in the retina and that these substances stimulate the retina, causing the perception of red, green, or blue. [introduced in 1929 by Christine **Ladd-Franklin** (1847–1930), U.S. psychologist and mathematician]

laissez-faire leader see LEADERSHIP STYLE.

lalling *n.* speech characterized by the omission or substitution of sounds, particularly the substitution of the [l] sound for other sounds that are more difficult for the speaker to produce, for example, saying "lellow" for *yellow*.

Lamarckism *n.* the theory that changes acquired by an organism during its lifetime, for example, through use or disuse of particular parts, can be inherited by its offspring. Evidence for such **inheritance of acquired characteristics**, however, is lacking. [Jean-Baptiste **Lamarck** (1744–1829), French natural historian] —**Lamarckian** *adj.*

Lamaze method a variation of the method of NATURAL CHILDBIRTH in which the mother learns about childbirth anatomy and physiology and practices pain management through relaxation, massage, and breathing exercises. See also LEBOYER TECHNIQUE. [Ferdinand **Lamaze** (1890–1957), French obstetrician]

laminar organization the horizontal layering of cells found in some brain regions. See CORTICAL LAYERS.

Land effect a demonstration in which a multicolored scene is photographed with black and white film, once through a red filter and once through a blue–green filter. When the resulting images are projected simultaneously onto a screen through the opposite filter used to photograph the image, the original multicolored scene is perceived. [Edwin Herbert **Land** (1909–1991), U.S. inventor]

Land theory of color vision see RETINEX THEORY. [Edwin Herbert **Land**]

language *n.* **1.** a system for expressing or communicating thoughts and feelings through speech sounds or written symbols. See NATURAL LANGUAGE. **2.** the specific communicative system used by a particular group of speakers, with its distinctive vocabulary, grammar, and phonological system. **3.** any comparable nonverbal means of communication, such as SIGN LANGUAGE or the languages used in computer programming (see ARTIFICIAL LANGUAGE).

language acquisition the process by which children learn language. Although often used interchangeably with LANGUAGE DEVELOPMENT, this term is preferred by those who emphasize the active role of the child as a learner with considerable innate linguistic knowledge.

language acquisition device a hypothetical faculty used to explain a child's ability to acquire language. In the early model proposed by U.S. linguist Benjamin Lee Whorf (1897–1941), it is an inherited mechanism that enables children to develop a language structure from linguistic data supplied by parents and others. As reinterpreted by U.S. linguist Noam Chomsky (1928–), however, the language acquisition device contains significant innate knowledge that actively interprets the input: Only this can explain how a highly abstract COMPETENCE in language results from a relatively deprived input. See NATIVISTIC THEORY.

language acquisition support system the adults and older children who help a young child to acquire language. Children learn language in and from conversation: Family members talk to them, tailoring their language to the children's level of comprehension and often using higher pitch and exaggerated intonation. The language acquisition support system is conceptualized as essential to language learning and may interact with the LANGUAGE ACQUISITION DEVICE of the younger child.

language deficit an absence, loss, or delay in the normal speech and language development of a child.

language development the process by which children learn to use language. Although this term is often used interchangeably with LANGUAGE ACQUISITION, it is preferred by those who wish to emphasize the continuity of language development with cognitive and social development.

language disability any significant difficulty with or impairment of language development or function. When the difficulty or impairment is restricted to a specific aspect of language development or a specific language function, it is termed **specific language disability**. When the difficulty or impairment is more pervasive and not restricted to a particular aspect or function, the term **general language disability** is used.

language disorder see SPEECH AND LANGUAGE DISORDER.

language-experience approach a method of reading instruction that uses the child's spoken language to supply the words and stories for teaching reading. In this approach, the child is encouraged to describe personal experiences, which are recorded by the teacher. They then read these written stories together until the child can associate written and spoken forms of words and read independently.

language localization the processing of various functions of spoken and written words in particular areas of the brain. Research has identified numerous cortical centers associated with visual and auditory language processing (including the oft-cited BROCA'S AREA and WERNICKE'S AREA), as well as neural pathways linking these areas.

language-origin theory speculation about the origin and early development of language in the human species. The numerous early theories on this subject tend to fall into three main categories: (a) those that see language developing from conscious imitation by early humans of animal noises and other natural sounds; (b) those that see it emerging from the involuntary sounds produced by rage, pleasure, hunger, and so on; and (c) NATIVISTIC THEORIES that see the language faculty as innate to human beings and postulate an inherent relation between sound and meaning (phonetic symbolism).

language pathology see SPEECH AND LANGUAGE PATHOLOGY.

language retardation delayed acquisition of language skills, manifested, for example, by single word utterances or unintelligible sounds, due to neurological causes.

language shift a movement in the language preference of an immigrant or minority community from its ethnic language to the majority language, eventually resulting in monolingualism in the majority language.

language transfer in second-language acquisition, the tendency to transfer the phonology, syntax, and semantics of the native language into the learning of the second language. **Negative transfer** (or **interference**) occurs when differences between the two languages' structures lead to systematic errors in the learning of the second language or to an intermediate state short of full proficiency. **Positive transfer** occurs when areas of similarity between the two languages facilitate learning.

languishing *n.* the condition of absence of mental health, characterized by ennui, apathy, listlessness, and loss of interest in life. Compare FLOURISHING. **—languish** *vb.*

laryngopharynx *n.* the portion of the PHARYNX that lies below the hyoid bone (a small, U-shaped bone below and supporting the tongue). **—laryngopharyngeal** *adj.*

Lasthenie de Ferjol syndrome a type of PATHOMIMICRY consisting of life-threatening hemorrhages caused by secretly self-inflicted wounds.

latah (lattah) *n.* a CULTURE-BOUND SYNDROME first observed in Malaysia and Indonesia, although similar syndromes have been found in many other parts of the world. The condition primarily affects middle-aged women and is characterized by an exaggerated startle reaction. Its major symptoms, besides fearfulness, are imitative behavior in speech (see ECHOLALIA) and body movements (see ECHOPRAXIA), a compulsion to utter profanities and obscenities (see COPROLALIA), command obedience, and disorganization. See also IMU; MYRIACHIT.

latency stage in psychoanalytic theory, the stage of PSYCHOSEXUAL DEVELOPMENT in which overt sexual interest is sublimated and the child's attention is focused on skills and peer activities with members of his or her own sex. This stage is posited to last from about the resolution of the OEDIPUS COMPLEX, at about age 6, to the onset of puberty during the 11th or 12th year. Also called **latency**; **latency phase**.

latent content 1. the hidden or disguised meanings, wishes, and ideas beneath the MANIFEST CONTENT of any utterance or other form of communication. **2.** in psychoanalytic theory, the unconscious wishes seeking expression in dreams or fantasies. This unconscious material is posited to encounter censorship (see CENSOR) and to be distorted by the DREAM-WORK into symbolic representations in order to protect the EGO. Through DREAM ANALYSIS, the latent content may be uncovered. See also DREAM CENSORSHIP.

latent inhibition retardation of PAVLOVIAN CONDITIONING as a result of prior exposures to the CONDITIONED STIMULUS before it is paired with an UNCONDITIONED STIMULUS. Also called **conditioned stimulus preexposure effect**.

latent learning learning that is not manifested as a change in performance until a specific need for it arises. For example, a rat allowed to explore a maze without reward will later learn to find the goal more rapidly than a rat without prior exposure to the maze. See also INCIDENTAL LEARNING.

latent trait theory a general psychometric theory contending that observed traits, such as intelligence, are reflections of more basic unobservable traits (i.e., latent traits). Several quantitative models (e.g., ITEM RESPONSE THEORY and FACTOR ANALYSIS) have been developed to allow for the identification and estimation of these latent traits from manifest observations.

latent variable a hypothetical, unobservable characteristic that is thought to underlie and explain observed, manifest attributes that are directly measurable. The values of latent variables are inferred from patterns of interrelationships among the MANIFEST VARIABLES.

lateral *adj.* toward the side of the body or of an organ. Compare MEDIAL. —**laterally** *adv.*

lateral geniculate nucleus (**LGN**) see GENICULATE NUCLEUS.

lateral hypothalamic syndrome a four-stage pattern of recovery from lesions of the **lateral hypothalamus** (**LH**) induced in nonhuman animals. The stages are marked by: (a) an initial inability to eat and drink (aphagia and adipsia); (b) continued inability to drink and poor appetite for food (adipsia-anorexia); (c) improving appetite but continued avoidance of water; and (d) the establishment of new, altered feeding and drinking habits and a stable, albeit lower, body weight. Compare VENTROMEDIAL HYPOTHALAMIC SYNDROME.

lateral inhibition in perception, a mechanism for detecting contrast in which a sensory neuron is excited by one particular receptor but inhibited by neighboring (lateral) receptors. In vision, for example, lateral inhibition is seen in neurons that respond to light at one position but are inhibited by light at surrounding positions.

lateralized readiness potential (**LRP**) an EVENT-RELATED POTENTIAL that is a measure of the difference in activation between the left and right motor areas of the brain. This potential is taken to indicate preparation to respond with one hand or the other, since each hand is controlled by the contralateral hemisphere.

lateral lemniscus a bundle of nerve fibers running from auditory nuclei in the brainstem upward through the PONS and terminating in the inferior COLLICULUS and medial GENICULATE NUCLEUS. It is part of the LEMNISCAL SYSTEM.

lateral sulcus a prominent groove that runs along the lateral surface of each CEREBRAL HEMISPHERE, separating the TEMPORAL LOBE from the FRONTAL LOBE and PARIETAL LOBE. Also called **fissure of Sylvius**; **lateral fissure**; **Sylvian fissure**.

lateral thinking creative thinking that deliberately attempts to reexamine basic assumptions and change perspective or direction in order to provide a fresh approach to solving a problem. This term is often used synonymously with DIVERGENT THINKING.

lateral ventricle see VENTRICLE.

late-selection theory any theory of attention proposing that selection occurs after stimulus identification. According to late-selection theory, within sensory limits, all stimuli—both attended and unattended—are processed to the same deep level of analysis until stimulus identification occurs; subsequently, only the most important stimuli are selected for further processing. Compare EARLY-SELECTION THEORY.

Latin square an experimental design in which treatments, denoted by Latin letters, are administered in sequences that are systematically varied such that each treatment occurs equally often in each position of the sequence (e.g., first, second, third, etc.). The number of treatments administered must be the same as the number of groups or individual participants receiving them. For example, one group might receive treatments A, then B, and then C, while a second group receives them in sequence B, C, A, and a third group in sequence C, A, B.

laughter *n.* vocal expression of the emotions of amusement, enjoyment, or derision, characterized by inspiratory and expiratory movements occurring in rapid succession. Laughter is pleasurable because it serves to release tension built up when people listen to an amusing story or watch an amusing event (see RELEASE THEORY OF HUMOR). Laughter may also result when states of threat occur in a safe context or from an abrupt resolution of a cognitive incongruity. Unrestrained or paroxysmal **laughing spells** have been found to precipitate cataplectic attacks, to be a common manifestation in manias, and to be an occasional symptom of psychomotor seizure among children, termed gelastic epilepsy. Spasmodic laughter, or GELASMUS, is also found in schizophrenia, hysteria, and organic (especially bulbar and pseudobulbar) diseases of the brain. See also HUMOR. —**laugh** *vb.*

law *n.* **1.** a formal statement describing a regularity (e.g., of nature) to which no exceptions are known or anticipated. **2.** in science, mathematics, philosophy, and the social sciences, a theory that is widely accepted as correct and that has no significant rivals in accounting for the facts within its domain.

law-and-order orientation see CONVENTIONAL LEVEL.

law of closure see CLOSURE.

law of common fate see COMMON FATE.

law of constancy in psychoanalytic theory, see PRINCIPLE OF CONSTANCY.

law of contiguity a principle of association stating that forming connections between ideas, events (e.g., stimuli and responses), or other items depends on their proximity in space or time. The law of contiguity is fundamental to ASSOCIATIONISM and is considered a keystone of most contemporary theories of learning, memory, and knowledge.

law of continuity see GOOD CONTINUATION.

law of contrast a principle of association stating that opposites are reminders of one another: encountering or thinking about the one (e.g., a snow-covered field) tends to bring to mind the other (e.g., a sunny beach). Initially proposed as a distinct, essential concept in ASSOCIATIONISM, the law of contrast later came to be viewed as a special case of the LAW OF CONTIGUITY.

law of effect broadly, the principle that consequences of behavior act to modify the future probability of occurrence of that behavior. As originally postulated by U.S. psychologist Edward L. Thorndike (1874–1949), the law of effect stated that responses followed by a satisfying state of affairs are strengthened and responses followed by an unpleasant or annoying state of affairs are weakened. Thorndike later revised the law to include only the response-strengthening effect of reinforcement.

law of frequency a principle of association stating that the more often ideas, events (e.g., stimuli and responses), or other items co-occur, the stronger the connections between them. The law of frequency is a concept of ASSOCIATIONISM.

law of good continuation see GOOD CONTINUATION.

law of good shape see GOOD SHAPE.

law of inclusiveness see INCLUSIVENESS.

law of initial values the principle that the initial level of a physiological response is a major determinant of a later response in that system. Thus, if an individual's pulse rate is high, his or her cardiovascular response to an emotion-provoking stimulus will be weaker than if the initial pulse rate had been low.

law of parsimony the principle that the simplest explanation of an event or observation is the preferred explanation. Simplicity is understood in various ways, including the requirement that an explanation should (a) make the smallest number of unsupported assumptions, (b) postulate the existence of the fewest entities, and (c) invoke the fewest unobservable constructs. Also called **economy principle**; **principle of economy**. See ELEGANT SOLUTION; OCCAM'S RAZOR.

law of Prägnanz see PRÄGNANZ.

law of proximity see PROXIMITY.

law of similarity 1. a principle of association stating that like produces like: Encountering or thinking about something (e.g., one's birthday month) tends to bring to mind other similar things (e.g., other people one knows with the same birthday month). The law of similarity is fundamental to ASSOCIATIONISM. **2.** see SIMILARITY.

law of symmetry see SYMMETRY.

laws of learning statements describing the circumstances under which learning is generally known to occur. Originally formulated in 1911 by U.S. psychologist Edward L. Thorndike (1874–1949) to include the laws of readiness (individuals learn when ready to), exercise (repetition is key), and effect, they have been modified numerous times since. Currently, the LAW OF EFFECT is still considered a major tenet of learning, along with the LAW OF CONTIGUITY, the LAW OF FREQUENCY, the PRIMACY EFFECT, and the RECENCY EFFECT.

lay analysis psychoanalytic therapy performed by a person who has been trained in psychoanalytic theory and practice but is not a physician (i.e., a layperson). This is to be distinguished from psychoanalysis performed by a fully accredited psychiatrist.

lazy eye see AMBLYOPIA.

LD 1. abbreviation for LEARNING DISABILITY. **2.** abbreviation for LEARNING DISORDER. **3.** abbreviation for LETHAL DOSE.

L data life data: information about an individual

270

gathered from his or her *l*ife record or life history. See also O DATA; Q DATA; T DATA.

leader-categorization theory an information-processing model that assumes that perceivers automatically and spontaneously appraise the extent to which people, including themselves, can be classified as leaders. Such judgments are determined by IMPLICIT LEADERSHIP THEORIES that organize perceivers' general beliefs about the characteristics that most leaders possess.

leaderless group therapy a form of GROUP PSYCHOTHERAPY in which leaderless meetings are held either (a) on an occasional or regularly scheduled basis as an adjunct to the traditional therapist-led process or (b) on an entirely self-directed basis in which a group always meets without a designated leader.

leader–member exchange theory (LMX theory) a dyadic, relational approach to leadership that assumes that (a) leaders develop exchange relationships with each one of their subordinates and (b) the quality of these leader–member exchange (LMX) relationships influences subordinates' responsibility, influence over decisions, access to resources, and performance.

leadership *n.* **1.** the processes involved in leading others, including organizing, directing, coordinating, and motivating their efforts toward achievement of certain group or organizational goals. **2.** the traits or behaviors characteristic of an effective leader. See LEADERSHIP THEORIES.

leadership style the stable behavioral tendencies and methods displayed by a particular leader when guiding a group. Some common leadership styles are **autocratic**, in which the leader exercises unrestricted authority by setting all goals, making all decisions, and solving all problems; **bureaucratic**, in which the leader rigidly adheres to prescribed routine and makes no allowance for extenuating circumstances; **charismatic**, in which the leader articulates distal goals and visions and generates high levels of dedication, enthusiasm, and commitment from his or her followers; **democratic**, in which the leader establishes and maintains an egalitarian group climate in which members themselves plan activities, resolve issues, and make choices; and **laissez-faire**, in which the leader provides little guidance for activities, interacts minimally with group members, and provides input only when directly asked.

leadership substitute any aspect of the social setting, including the nature of the work task, the characteristics of the group members, or the qualities of the group or organization itself, that reduces or eliminates the need for a specific individual who performs such typical leadership behaviors as organizing, directing, coordinating, supporting, and motivating the group members.

leadership theories theories advanced to explain the effectiveness or ineffectiveness of leaders. The main types include **trait theories of leadership**, which focus on such characteristics as supervisory ability, intelligence, self-assurance, and decisiveness; **behavioral** (or **style**) **theories of leadership**, which focus on the task-based and relationship-based activities of the leader; **contingency theories of leadership**, which attempt to describe what type of leadership style is most effective in different situations; and **cognitive theories of leadership**, such as LEADER-CATEGORIZATION THEORY or the ATTRIBUTION THEORY OF LEADERSHIP, which describe the way subordinates' perceptions of their leaders influence leadership effectiveness. See also IMPLICIT LEADERSHIP THEORIES.

learned helplessness a phenomenon in which repeated exposure to uncontrollable stressors results in individuals failing to use any control options that may later become available. Essentially, individuals learn that they lack behavioral control over environmental events, which, in turn, undermines the motivation to make changes or attempt to alter situations. Learned helplessness was first described in 1967 by U.S. psychologists J. Bruce Overmier (1938–) and Martin E. P. Seligman (1942–) following experiments in which animals exposed to a series of unavoidable electric shocks later failed to learn to escape these shocks when tested in a different apparatus, whereas animals exposed to shocks that could be terminated by a response did not show interference with escape learning in another apparatus. In the 1970s, Seligman extended the concept from nonhuman animal research to clinical depression in humans (see HELPLESSNESS THEORY). Subsequent researchers have noted a robust fit between the concept and POSTTRAUMATIC STRESS DISORDER.

learned optimism an acquired explanatory style that attributes causes for negative events to factors that are more external, unstable, and specific: that is, problems are believed to be caused by other people or situational factors, the causes are seen as fleeting in nature, and are localized to one or a few situations in one's life. According to LEARNED HELPLESSNESS theory, the manner in which individuals routinely explain the events in their lives can drain or enhance motivation, reduce or increase persistence, and enhance vulnerability to depression or protect against it, making learned optimism a putative mechanism by which therapy ameliorates depression.

learning *n.* the process of acquiring new and relatively enduring information, behavior patterns, or abilities, characterized by modification of behavior as a result of practice, study, or experience.

learning curve a graphic representation of the course of learning of an individual or a group. A measure of performance (e.g., gains, errors) is plotted along the vertical axis; the horizontal axis plots trials or time.

learning disability (LD) any of various conditions with a neurological basis that are marked by substantial deficits in acquiring certain scholastic or academic skills, particularly those associated with written or expressive language. Learning disabilities include learning problems that result from perceptual disabilities, brain injury, and MINIMAL BRAIN DYSFUNCTION but exclude those that result from visual impairment or hearing loss, mental retardation, emotional disturbance, or environmental, cultural, or economic factors.

learning disorder (**LD**) any neurologically based information-processing disorder characterized by achievement that is substantially below that expected for the age, education, and intelligence of the individual, as measured by standardized tests in reading, mathematics, and written material. Major types of learning disorders are DISORDER OF WRITTEN EXPRESSION, MATHEMATICS DISORDER, NONVERBAL LEARNING DISORDER, and READING DISORDER. This term essentially is synonymous with LEARNING DISABILITY.

learning model a general perspective on human development in which children are viewed as passively absorbing the relevant features of the environment in a continuous line of development. This emphasis on environmental conditions is less influential within developmental psychology than previously, rapidly being eclipsed by the LIFE-SPAN PERSPECTIVE and other approaches.

learning set a phenomenon observed when a participant is given a succession of discriminations to learn, such as learning that one object contains a food reward and a different object does not. After a large number of such problems the participant acquires a rule or MENTAL SET for solving them, and successive discriminations are learned faster.

learning style see COGNITIVE STYLE.

learning theory a body of concepts and principles that seeks to explain the learning process. Learning theory encompasses a number of specific theories whose common interest is the description of the basic LAWS OF LEARNING.

learning trial a single presentation of the information to be learned in a learning experiment. Examples include a single pairing of the conditioned stimulus and the unconditioned stimulus in Pavlovian conditioning and a single presentation of a word to be remembered in a memory experiment. Also called **acquisition trial**.

learning without awareness a phenomenon said to occur when an individual's behavior has been affected without that individual being aware of the conditions affecting the behavior, or of the relationship between those conditions and the behavior, or of the fact that the behavior has changed. The existence of such learning is controversial, but evidence has been found in PAVLOVIAN CONDITIONING, PROCEDURAL LEARNING, IMPLICIT LEARNING, and SUBLIMINAL LEARNING.

least effort principle the basic behavioral hypothesis that an organism will choose a course of action that appears to require the smallest amount of effort or expenditure of energy.

least restrictive alternative the U.S. legal directive that less treatment rather than more (e.g., community care versus hospitalization) is the most desirable objective in treating people with chronic mental disorder. The principal consideration is combining safety concerns with the minimum level of restrictions on personal liberty.

least restrictive environment (**LRE**) in the United States, an educational setting that gives a student with disabilities the opportunity to receive instruction within a classroom that meets his or her learning needs and physical requirements. See also FULL INCLUSION; MAINSTREAMING.

least significant difference (**LSD**) a value representing the point at which a difference between the means of experimental groups being compared can be considered not to have been caused by chance. It is a method of controlling for TYPE I ERROR and must be calculated for each experiment according to specific criteria. The least significant difference concept currently is one of several different approaches to making MULTIPLE COMPARISONS.

least squares regression see STEPWISE REGRESSION.

Leboyer technique an approach to childbirth that focuses on the feelings and sensations of the baby. It advocates quiet, dim lights, delay in severing the umbilical cord, body contact between newborn and parents, and an immediate warm bath that approximates the conditions within the womb. See also LAMAZE METHOD. [Frédéric **Leboyer** (1918–), French obstetrician]

lecture method the formal, verbal presentation of information or other material by an instructor to a group of students or other learners. The lecture method is used mainly when groups are large or time is limited (e.g., in personnel training).

Lee–Boot effect a prolonged period of sexual inactivity between two estrous cycles in polyestrous mammals, induced by pheromones, that occurs when a female animal is housed with other females. [first reported in 1955 by S. van der **Lee** and L. M. **Boot**, Dutch biologists]

left hemisphere the left half of the cerebrum, the part of the brain concerned with sensation and perception, motor control, and higher level cognitive processes. The two CEREBRAL HEMISPHERES differ somewhat in function; for example, in most people the left hemisphere has greater responsibility for speech. Some have proposed that, given this involvement in speech, the left hemisphere is the seat of consciousness,

L

an idea known as **left-hemisphere conscious-ness**. See HEMISPHERIC LATERALIZATION. Compare RIGHT HEMISPHERE.

legitimacy knowledge in social psychology, the role played by an individual's major GROUP IDENTIFICATIONS in contributing to SELF-IMAGE and estimates of personal value. It is often contrasted with **competence knowledge**, which is the component of self-image that derives from individual talents and accomplishments.

lek mating a mating system in which several males congregate at one location during the mating season, forming small individual territories and competing with each other for mates by giving complex, elaborate visual and vocal displays.

lemniscal system a major SOMATOSENSORY SYSTEM consisting of long, ascending neural pathways projecting to the thalamus. It includes the MEDIAL LEMNISCUS, LATERAL LEMNISCUS, and secondary trigeminal projections.

length of stay (**LOS**) the duration of an inpatient's continuous stay in a hospital. A UTILIZATION REVIEW will normally compare the LOS under review with regional norms.

leniency error a type of rating error in which the ratings are consistently overly positive, particularly as regards the performance or ability of the participants. Also called **leniency bias**. Compare SEVERITY ERROR.

lens *n.* in vision, a transparent, biconvex structure in the anterior portion of the eyeball (just behind the IRIS) that provides the fine, adjustable focus of the optical system. It is composed of tiny hexagonal prism-shaped cells, called lens fibers, fitted together in concentric layers. See ACCOMMODATION.

lenticular nucleus see BASAL GANGLIA.

leptin *n.* a protein, manufactured and secreted by fat cells, that may communicate to the brain the amount of body fat stored and may help to regulate food intake. Leptin receptors have been found in the hypothalamus, and when they are stimulated food intake is reduced.

lesbianism *n.* female–female sexual orientation or behavior. See also HOMOSEXUALITY. —**lesbian** *adj., n.*

Lesch–Nyhan syndrome an X-linked recessive disorder associated with deficiency of the enzyme hypoxanthine–guanine phosphoribosyltransferase (essential to purine metabolism) and consequent overproduction of uric acid. It is characterized by significant mental retardation, self-mutilation by biting the lips and fingers, and abnormal motor development. [described in 1964 by Michael **Lesch** (1939–) and William L. **Nyhan** (1926–), U.S. pediatricians]

lesion *n.* any disruption of or damage to the normal structure or function of a tissue or organ.

less-is-more hypothesis the proposition that the cognitive limitations of infants and young children may serve to simplify the body of lan-

guage they process, thus making it easier for them to learn the complicated syntactical system of any human language.

lethal dose (**LD**) the minimum amount of a drug that is required to cause death. It is generally expressed in terms of the **median lethal dose** (**LD$_{50}$**; **LD-50**), the amount required to cause death (within a specified time frame) in 50% of nonhuman animals to which the drug is administered. See also THERAPEUTIC RATIO.

lethality scale a set of criteria used to predict the probability of a suicide or attempted suicide occurring. A variety of such scales exist, most including gender, prior suicide attempts, and psychiatric diagnosis and history.

letter cancellation test any of a variety of tests that measure attentional skills, visuomotor abilities, and other functions by requiring the participant to cross out a specific letter repeatedly interspersed among long lines of random letters.

leukocyte (**leucocyte**) *n.* a type of blood cell that plays a key role in the body's defense against infection. Leukocytes include **granulocytes**, which ingest foreign particles; and LYMPHOCYTES, which are involved in the production of antibodies and other specific immune responses. Also called **white blood cell**.

leukotomy (**leucotomy**) *n.* see LOBOTOMY.

level *n.* in experimental design, the quantity, magnitude, or category of the independent variable (or variables).

Level I–Level II theory the theory that cognitive abilities can be viewed as being arranged hierarchically at two different levels. The first level is of associative processing (exemplified by rote learning and short-term memory), the second of more conceptual processing (exemplified by categorization, abstraction, and reasoning).

level-of-aspiration theory a conceptual approach to group and individual performance that assumes that the emotional, motivational, and behavioral consequences of any particular performance will be determined not only by the absolute degree of success attained but also by the ideal outcome or goal envisioned prior to undertaking the task.

levels of consciousness levels of awareness ranging from alert wakefulness, through relaxed wakefulness, drowsiness, sleep, and deep sleep to coma.

levels-of-processing model of memory the theory that ENCODING into memory, and therefore subsequent retention, depends on the depth of cognitive ELABORATION that the information receives and that deeper encoding improves memory.

Levinson's adult development theory a model of human development in which adulthood is divided into early, middle, and late segments, each consisting of transitional stages, which are often times of uncertainty, self-examination, and exploration, and intervening periods of relative stability. [proposed by Daniel Levinson (1920–1994), U.S. psychologist]

levodopa (**L-dopa**) *n.* the naturally occurring form of dihydroxyphenylalanine, a precursor of the neurotransmitter dopamine. Synthetic levodopa is a DOPAMINE-RECEPTOR agonist used in the treatment of Parkinson's disease.

Lewy body dementia a specific type of DEMENTIA associated with the presence of abnormal proteins called **Lewy bodies** in the brain. It is characterized by hallucinations and delusions occurring early in the disease process, marked day-to-day fluctuations in cognition, and spontaneous PARKINSONISM. [Frederich Heinrich Lewy (1885–1950), German neurologist]

lexical access in psycholinguistics, the process by which an individual produces a specific word from his or her MENTAL LEXICON or recognizes it when used by others. See PRODUCTIVE VOCABULARY; RECEPTIVE VOCABULARY.

lexical decision a task in which the participant is presented with strings of letters, such as HOUSE or HOUPE, and is required to determine whether each string spells a word.

lexical hypothesis the supposition that any significant individual difference, such as a central personality trait, will be encoded into the natural-language lexicon; that is, there will be a term to describe it in any or all of the languages of the world. Also called **fundamental lexical hypothesis**.

lexical word see CONTENT WORD.

lexicon *n.* the vocabulary of a language and, in psychology, the lexical knowledge of an individual. See MENTAL LEXICON. See also PRODUCTIVE VOCABULARY; RECEPTIVE VOCABULARY.

LH abbreviation for LUTEINIZING HORMONE.

libido *n.* **1.** in psychoanalytic theory, either the PSYCHIC ENERGY of the LIFE INSTINCT in general, or the energy of the SEXUAL INSTINCT in particular. In his first formulation, Austrian psychiatrist Sigmund Freud (1856–1939) conceived of this energy as narrowly sexual, but subsequently he broadened the concept to include all expressions of love, pleasure, and self-preservation. See also EROS. **2.** in ANALYTIC PSYCHOLOGY, the general life force that provides energy for all types of activities: biological, sexual, social, cultural, and creative. **3.** more generally, sexual energy or desire. —**libidinal** *adj.* —**libidinize** *vb.* —**libidinous** *adj.*

Librium *n.* a trade name for CHLORDIAZEPOXIDE.

lie scale a group of items on a test (e.g., the MINNESOTA MULTIPHASIC PERSONALITY INVENTORY) used to help evaluate the general truthfulness of a person's responses on the test.

life coaching a form of teaching and encouragement (one-to-one or coach-to-group) based on counseling principles of sensitivity to needs and personality differences.

life crisis a period of distress and major adjustment associated with a significant life experience, such as divorce or death of a family member.

life events important occasions throughout the life span that are either age-related and thus expected (e.g., marriage, retirement) or unrelated to age and unexpected (e.g., accidents, relocation).

life history in therapy and counseling, a systematic account of the client's development from birth to the present, including the meaningful aspects of the client's emotional, social, and intellectual development. The account is taken by the therapist or counselor directly from the client and may additionally be derived from autobiographical material.

life instinct in psychoanalytic theory, the drive comprising the SELF-PRESERVATION INSTINCT, which is aimed at individual survival, and the SEXUAL INSTINCT, which is aimed at the survival of the species. In the DUAL INSTINCT THEORY of Austrian psychiatrist Sigmund Freud (1856–1939), the life instinct, or EROS, stands opposed to the DEATH INSTINCT, or THANATOS. Also called **erotic instinct**.

lifeline *n.* a therapeutic technique used in group or individual therapy in which each individual draws lines representing his or her life, marking past and future expected events with angles indicating even, upward, or downward progression of functioning, as well as specific dates and the affect surrounding these events. Discussion of this diagram with the therapist can enhance awareness and understanding of the individual's life patterns.

life review the tendency of individuals, especially older adults, to reflect upon and analyze past life experiences. Life review, or analytical REMINISCENCE, is often made use of in counseling older adults showing symptoms of mild depression or people with terminal illness, sometimes as an adjunct to psychotherapy.

life satisfaction the extent to which a person finds life rich, meaningful, full, or of high quality. Improved life satisfaction is often a goal of treatment, especially with older people. See also QUALITY OF LIFE.

life space in the FIELD THEORY of German-born U.S. psychologist Kurt Lewin (1890–1947), the "totality of possible events" for one person at a particular time, that is, a person's possible options together with the environment that contains them. The life space is a representation of the environmental, biological, social, and psychological influences that define one person's unique reality at a given moment in time. Contained within the life space are positive and negative valences, that is, forces or pressures on the individual to approach a goal or move away from a perceived danger.

life-span developmental psychology the study of psychological and behavioral change across and within individuals from birth through death using a LIFE-SPAN PERSPECTIVE. Such an approach assumes that human developmental processes are complex, interactive, and fully understood only in the context of influencing events. It also assumes that there is no end state of maturity, that no specific period of the life course is more important or influential than another in subsequent development, and that not all developmental change is related to chronological age.

life-span perspective a general perspective emphasizing (a) that human development is a lifelong process of change; (b) that developmental change is multidimensional and multidirectional, involving both growth and decline in one's performance (e.g., of cognitive tasks); and (c) that there is plasticity in human behavior throughout the entire life span.

lifestyle *n.* the typical way of life or manner of living that is characteristic of an individual or group, as expressed by behaviors, attitudes, interests, and other factors.

lifetime risk the odds of a person being diagnosed with a disease or condition during his or her lifetime (usually stated in terms of 70 to 85 years).

ligand *n.* a molecule that binds to a specific site on another molecule, for example, a hormone binding to its receptor molecule at the surface of a cell.

light adaptation the process by which the eye adjusts to conditions of high illumination, such as occurs when exiting a dark theater into a sunny parking lot. It takes less than 10 min and involves constriction of the pupil and a shift in the sensitivity of the retina so that the RETINAL CONES become active in place of the RETINAL RODS. Compare DARK ADAPTATION.

light cell see TYPE II CELL.

light reflex see PUPILLARY REFLEX.

light therapy see PHOTOTHERAPY.

likelihood *n.* in statistics, the probability of obtaining a particular set of results given a set of assumptions about the distribution of the phenomena in the population and the parameters of that distribution.

likelihood principle in visual perception, the generality that the visual system prefers the most likely interpretation of a stimulus (i.e., the one with the highest probability of being correct). This is in contrast to the **simplicity principle**, which states that the visual system prefers the simplest interpretation (i.e., the one with the shortest description).

likelihood ratio the ratio of two probabilities, *a*/*b*, where *a* is the probability of obtaining the data observed if a particular research hypothesis (A) is true and *b* is the probability of obtaining the data observed when a different hypothesis (B) is true.

Likert scale a type of DIRECT ATTITUDE MEA-SURE that consists of statements reflecting strong positive or negative evaluations of an attitude object. Respondents indicate their reaction to each statement on a response scale ranging from "strongly agree" to "strongly disagree," and these ratings are summed to provide a total attitude score. [Rensis **Likert** (1903–1981), U.S. psychologist]

limbic system a loosely defined, widespread group of brain nuclei that innervate each other to form a network that is involved in autonomic and visceral processes and mechanisms of emotion, memory, and learning. It includes portions of the cerebral cortex, THALAMUS, and certain subcortical structures, such as the AMYGDALA, HIPPOCAMPUS, and SEPTAL AREA.

limb kinetic apraxia see APRAXIA.

limen *n.* see THRESHOLD.

liminal *adj.* relating to the THRESHOLD of a sensation.

limited competency a determination by a court that a person has the capacity to manage some but not all of his or her activities. A limited guardian is appointed to assist the individual in exercising certain legal rights, such as the right to enter into contracts, get married, provide consent (e.g., for medical treatment), or vote.

linear causation the simplest type of causal relationship between events, usually involving a single cause that produces a single effect or a straightforward sequence of events producing a single effect. Linear causation is often contrasted with more complex models of causation involving multiple causes and effects, FEEDBACK LOOPS, and indirect or REMOTE CAUSES.

linearity *n.* a relationship in which one variable is expressed as a linear function of another variable, that is, all COEFFICIENTS are to the first power. Linear relationships are often, but not necessarily, straight-line relationships.

linear model any model for empirical data that attempts to relate the values of the dependent variable to linear functions of the independent variables. Most commonly used statistical techniques (analysis of variance, regression analysis, etc.) can be represented as linear models.

linear perspective one of the monocular DEPTH CUES, arising from the principle that the size of an object's visual image is a function of its distance from the eye. Thus, two objects appear closer together as the distance from them increases, as seen in the tracks of a railroad that appear to converge on the horizon.

linear program a form of PROGRAMMED IN-STRUCTION in which the learner independently studies information presented (e.g., via a booklet) in small, discrete, step-by-step frames that usually become progressively more complex. Correct answers to review questions are given after each frame so as to provide immediate feedback and continuous reinforcement.

linear regression a REGRESSION ANALYSIS that

assumes that the predictor (independent) variable is related to the criterion (dependent) variable through a linear function.

linear transformation a transformation of X to Y by means of the equation $Y = a + bX$, where a and b are numerical constants.

lingual *adj.* of or relating to the tongue or to speech and languages.

lingual gyrus a relatively short convolution of the inferior (lower) brain surface extending from the occipital to temporal lobes, medial to the FUSIFORM GYRUS. It is important in recognizing faces and landmarks and has been implicated in the generation and recall of dreams.

lingual nerve a branch of the TRIGEMINAL NERVE that supplies fibers to the mucous membranes of the mouth and the anterior (front) two thirds of the tongue, including the taste-bud papillae. Also called **gustatory nerve**.

linguistic approach a method of reading instruction that applies what the child already knows about language from having learned to speak it. Letters and sound equivalents are taught by being embedded in meaningful words with regular spelling patterns in order to maximize the similarities between the familiar spoken language and the unfamiliar written language.

linguistic determinism the hypothesis that the semantic structure of a particular language determines the structure of mental categories among its speakers. Because languages differ in how they refer to basic categories and dimensions, such as time, space, and duration, native speakers of these languages are assumed to show corresponding differences in their ways of thinking. Also called **Sapir–Whorf hypothesis**; **Whorfian hypothesis**. Compare LINGUISTIC RELATIVITY.

linguistic intergroup bias the tendency to describe and evaluate positive behaviors by INGROUP members and negative behaviors by OUTGROUP members more abstractly than negative ingroup and positive outgroup behaviors. See also INGROUP BIAS.

linguistic relativity the observation that languages differ in the ways in which semantic space is identified and categorized. For example, the Native American language Hopi uses a completely different word for water in a natural setting and water in a vessel but has only one word for flying objects, which is applied to birds, insects, airplanes, and the like. Linguistic relativity is not to be equated with LINGUISTIC DETERMINISM, which is a theoretical commitment to the idea that these differences have cognitive consequences. See ANTHROPOLOGICAL LINGUISTICS.

linguistics *n.* the scientific study of the physical, structural, functional, psychological, and social characteristics of human language. See also PSYCHOLINGUISTICS; SOCIOLINGUISTICS.

link analysis in ergonomics, the analysis of operational sequences and the movements of workers or objects that these entail in order to determine the design of tools, equipment, jobs, and facilities that will best serve worker efficiency and safety.

lipostatic hypothesis a hypothesis stating that the long-term regulation of food intake is governed by the concentration in the blood of free fatty acids, which result from the metabolism of fat. See also GLUCOSTATIC THEORY.

lipreading *n.* a method used by some people with hearing loss to understand spoken words in which the listener interprets the speaker's lip movements. Also called **speechreading**.

lisp *n.* incorrect production of SIBILANT sounds caused by faulty tongue placement or abnormalities of the articulatory mechanism. —**lisping** *n.*

lissencephaly *n.* severe malformation of the convolutions (GYRI) in the cerebral cortex due to abnormal neuronal migration during development. It is an umbrella term encompassing several conditions: **agyria**, the complete absence of convolutions; **pachygyria** (or **macrogyria**), unusually thick convolutions; and **polymicrogyria** (or **micropolygyria**), unusually small but numerous convolutions. Lissencephaly results in severe developmental delay, severe to profound mental retardation, motor impairment, and epilepsy.

literalism *n.* verbal or nonverbal answers of "yes" or "no," without cognitive elaboration, to questions during HYPNOSIS, asserted by some but strongly refuted by others to be a marker of hypnotic trance.

lithium *n.* an element of the alkali metal group whose salts are used in psychopharmacotherapy as MOOD STABILIZERS, particularly in managing acute manic phases of bipolar disorder. Its mechanism of action remains unclear and it has a narrow therapeutic margin of safety, making close monitoring of blood levels necessary. U.S. trade names (among others): **Eskalith**; **Lithobid**.

Little Hans a landmark case of Austrian psychiatrist Sigmund Freud (1856–1939), illustrating the OEDIPUS COMPLEX. Freud traced a child's phobia for horses to CASTRATION ANXIETY stemming from masturbation, to repressed death wishes toward the father, and to fear of retaliation owing to rivalry with the mother, with DISPLACEMENT of these emotions onto horses. Freud never actually met the boy but analyzed him through written communication with the father. The case was reported in "Analysis of a Phobia in a Five-Year-Old Boy" (1909).

living will see ADVANCE DIRECTIVE.

Lloyd Morgan's canon the principle that the behavior of an animal should not be interpreted in complex psychological terms if it can instead be interpreted with simpler concepts. Some recent authors have argued that its application oversimplifies the abilities of animals. [Conway **Lloyd Morgan** (1852–1936), British comparative psychologist]

LMX theory abbreviation for LEADER–MEMBER EXCHANGE THEORY.

LNNB abbreviation for LURIA–NEBRASKA NEUROPSYCHOLOGICAL BATTERY.

lobe *n.* a subdivision of an organ, such as the brain or the lungs, particularly when rounded and surrounded by distinct structural boundaries, such as fissures. —**lobar** *adj.* —**lobate** *adj.*

lobectomy *n.* complete or partial surgical removal of a lobe, particularly in the brain.

lobotomy *n.* incision into various nerve tracts in the FRONTAL LOBE of the brain. The original surgical procedure, called **prefrontal** (or **frontal**) **lobotomy**, was introduced in 1936 by Portuguese neurologist Antonio Egas Moniz (1874–1955): Connections between the frontal lobe and other brain structures—notably the thalamus—were severed by manipulating a narrow blade known as a leukotome inserted into brain tissue through several small holes drilled in the skull. A second procedure, called **transorbital lobotomy**, was devised in 1945 and involved the manipulation of a pointed instrument resembling an ice pick driven with a mallet through the thin bony wall of the eye socket and into the prefrontal brain. Both procedures were widely used to relieve the symtoms of severe mental disorder (including depression and schizophrenia) until the advent of ANTIPSYCHOTIC drugs in the 1950s. These operations have been replaced by more sophisticated, stereotactic forms of neurosurgery that are less invasive and whose effects are more certain and less damaging. Also called **leukotomy**.

LOC abbreviation for LOSS OF CONSCIOUSNESS.

local enhancement a form of SOCIAL LEARNING in which one or more individuals engaging in some behavior with an object in a particular location draw the attention of another to that location, which facilitates the acquisition of similar behavior by that observer. The attraction of attention to a particular place in the environment, and not any specific social interactions among the demonstrators and observer, is what leads to learning. For example, ducks in a pen may ignore an escape hole unless they are near another duck who escapes through the hole, thus drawing their attention to it.

local excitatory state the localized increase in negative potential on the surface of a neuron in response to stimulation below threshold level, which results in temporarily increased NEURAL IRRITABILITY. Also called **local excitatory potential**.

local–global distinction the difference between perceiving a whole form and perceiving the subunits that make up that form. For example, if a large letter S is formed from an arrangement of small letter *p*s, perception is at the local level if it focuses on the *p*s, and at the global level if it focuses on the *S*.

localization *n.* **1.** the ability to determine the physical position or spatial location of a stimulus in any sensory modality. **2.** see LOCALIZATION OF FUNCTION.

localization of function the concept that specific parts of the cerebral cortex are relatively specialized for particular types of cognitive and behavioral processes. Also called **cortical localization**; **localization**.

location-invariant neuron any of various neurons located in the PRESTRIATE CORTEX, particularly those in the INFEROTEMPORAL CORTEX, that respond regardless of the location of a stimulus in the receptive field. Many of these cells are also **size-invariant neurons**, which respond when presented with a particular object, regardless of its size.

lock-and-key theory in olfaction, see STEREOCHEMICAL SMELL THEORY.

locked-in syndrome a neurological condition in which the individual is conscious and cognizant but completely paralyzed, unable to speak or move.

locked ward a secured hospital unit in which patients with severe mental disorders reside. The present trend is toward elimination of locked wards.

Locke's theory of goal setting a theory suggesting that (a) specific goals direct activity more effectively than do vague or general goals, (b) difficult or challenging goals produce better performance than do moderate or easy goals, and (c) short-term goals can be used to attain long-range goals. [Edwin A. **Locke** (1938–), U.S. industrial psychologist]

locomotion *n.* movement of an organism from one place to another. Different species may have different typical modes of locomotion, such as crawling, swimming, flying, quadrupedal walking, and bipedal walking. —**locomotor** *adj.*

locomotor play play that involves exaggerated, repetitive movement and is physically vigorous, such as chasing, climbing, and wrestling. There are three distinctive forms: RHYTHMIC STEREOTYPY, EXERCISE PLAY, and ROUGH-AND-TUMBLE PLAY. Locomotor play is one of three traditionally identified basic types of play, the others being OBJECT PLAY and SOCIAL PLAY.

locura *n.* a CULTURE-BOUND SYNDROME found among Latino groups in the United States and Latin America. Symptoms include incoherence, agitation, auditory and visual hallucinations, social dysfunction, erratic behavior, and possibly violence.

locus *n.* (*pl.* **loci**) **1.** the place or position of an anatomical entity. **2.** the position of a gene on a chromosome.

locus ceruleus (**locus coeruleus; locus caeruleus**) a small bluish-tinted NUCLEUS in the brainstem whose neurons produce NOREPINEPHRINE and modulate large areas of the forebrain.

locus of control a construct that is used to categorize people's basic motivational orientations and perceptions of how much control they have over the conditions of their lives. People with an **external locus of control** tend to behave in response to external circumstances and to perceive their life outcomes as arising from factors out of their control. People with an **internal locus of control** tend to behave in response to internal states and intentions and to perceive their life outcomes as arising from the exercise of their own agency and abilities.

locutionary act see ILLOCUTIONARY ACT.

logic *n.* **1.** the branch of EPISTEMOLOGY that is concerned with the forms of argument by which a valid conclusion may be drawn from accepted premises. As such it is also concerned with distinguishing correct from fallacious reasoning. See also DEDUCTIVE REASONING; INFERENCE. **2.** a particular rule-governed form of symbolic expression used to analyze the relations between propositions. See SYMBOLIC LOGIC. —**logical** *adj.*

logical-mathematical intelligence in the MULTIPLE-INTELLIGENCES THEORY, the set of skills used in reasoning, abstraction, and numerical analysis and computation. These abilities are alleged to be relatively independent of the abilities involved in other types of intelligences.

logical positivism a philosophical perspective that is committed to the principle of VERIFICATION, which holds that the meaning and truth of all nontautological statements is dependent on empirical observation. In the early 20th century, the school of positivists based in Vienna sought to establish the essential unity of logic, philosophy, and science and to distinguish these disciplines from such others as metaphysics, ethics, and religion, which were dismissed for their speculative character. The positivist view of science was influential during the period in which psychology emerged as a science and has had a recognizable influence on the discipline. This is most pronounced in BEHAVIORISM and in psychology's commitment to empirical scientific methods. Logical positivism had waned by the middle of the century. See POSITIVISM. See also PHYSICALISM; POSTPOSITIVISM; REDUCTIONISM.

logistic regression a statistical technique for the prediction of a binary DEPENDENT VARIABLE from one or more continuous variables.

log–linear model a class of statistical techniques used to study the relationship among several CATEGORICAL VARIABLES. As compared with CHI-SQUARE TESTS, log–linear models use odds, rather than proportions, and they can be used to examine the relationship among several nominal variables in the manner of ANALYSES OF COVARIANCE.

logogen *n.* a theoretical memory unit corresponding to a word, letter, or digit, which when excited results in the output (recognition) of the unit and recall of characteristics and information associated with that unit. For example, the logogen for *table* is activated by hearing the component sounds or seeing the typographical features of the word, bringing to mind such knowledge as the typical structure and shape of a table and its general function.

logotherapy *n.* an approach to psychotherapy that focuses on the "human predicament," helping the client to overcome crises in meaning. The therapeutic process typically consists of examining three types of values: (a) creative (e.g., work, achievement); (b) experiential (e.g., art, science, philosophy, understanding, loving); and (c) attitudinal (e.g., facing pain and suffering). Each client is encouraged to arrive at his or her own solution, which should incorporate social responsibility and constructive relationships. Also called **meaning-centered therapy**. See also EXISTENTIAL PSYCHOTHERAPY; EXISTENTIALISM.

loneliness *n.* affective and cognitive discomfort or uneasiness from being or perceiving oneself to be alone or otherwise solitary. Psychological theory and research offer multiple perspectives: For example, social psychology emphasizes the emotional distress that results when inherent needs for intimacy and companionship are not met, while cognitive psychology emphasizes the unpleasant and unsettling experience that results from a perceived discrepancy between an individual's desired and actual social relationships.

longitudinal *adj.* **1.** in anatomy, referring to the long AXIS of the body. **2.** in research, referring to the time dimension, that is, running over an extended period.

longitudinal design the study of a variable or group of variables in the same cases or participants over a period of time, sometimes of several years. Compare CROSS-SECTIONAL DESIGN.

longitudinal fissure a deep groove that marks the division between the left and right cerebral hemispheres of the brain. At the bottom of the groove the hemispheres are connected by the CORPUS CALLOSUM. Also called **interhemispheric fissure**; **sagittal fissure**.

long-term care facility an EXTENDED CARE institution, such as a NURSING HOME, that provides medical and personal services for patients who are unable to live independently but do not require the inpatient services of a hospital.

long-term depression a long-lasting decrease in the amplitude of neuronal response due to persistent weak synaptic stimulation (in the case of the hippocampus) or strong synaptic stimulation (in the case of the cerebellum). Compare LONG-TERM POTENTIATION.

long-term memory (LTM) a relatively permanent information storage system, enabling one to retain, retrieve, and make use of skills and knowledge hours, weeks, or even years after they were originally learned. Various theories have been proposed to explain the biological processes by which this occurs (e.g., the PERSEVERATION–CONSOLIDATION HYPOTHESIS) and a major distinction is made between LTM and SHORT-TERM MEMORY. Additionally, LTM is divided into several categories, including DECLARATIVE MEMORY and PROCEDURAL MEMORY. See also SECONDARY MEMORY.

long-term potentiation (**LTP**) a long-lasting enhancement of synaptic efficiency caused by repeated brief stimulations of one nerve cell that trigger stimulation of a succeeding cell. The capacity for potentiation has been best shown in hippocampal tissue. LTP is studied as a model of the neural changes that underlie memory formation and it may be a mechanism involved in some kinds of learning. Compare LONG-TERM DEPRESSION.

long-term therapy psychotherapy over a period of many months or years. Classic PSYCHO-ANALYSIS, which may last 2–5 years or longer, is a primary example.

looking-glass self a SELF-CONCEPT formed by learning how other people perceive and evaluate one. The term suggests a self that is a reflection of other people's impressions, reactions, and opinions. See REFLECTED APPRAISALS; SYMBOLIC INTERACTIONISM.

loose culture a heterogeneous social group whose diverse members tend to value originality, risk-taking, and a flexible adherence to the collective norms of their culture or group. Compare TIGHT CULTURE.

loosening of associations a thought disturbance demonstrated by speech that is disconnected and fragmented, with the individual jumping from one idea to another unrelated or indirectly related idea. It is essentially equivalent to DERAILMENT.

lorazepam *n.* a highly potent BENZODIAZEPINE approved for the treatment of anxiety and as premedication in surgical anesthesia. Unlike many other benzodiazepines, it has no active metabolic products. U.S. trade name (among others): **Ativan**.

lordosis *n.* **1.** an abnormal inward curvature of the spine in the lumbar and cervical regions. See also KYPHOSIS; SCOLIOSIS. **2.** in many rodents, a similar but normal posture that is assumed by females during periods of sexual receptivity and serves to facilitate copulation with a male. See PRESENTING.

LOS abbreviation for LENGTH OF STAY.

loser effect in many species, the reduced likelihood that an individual will win future contests over resources after repeated experiences of losing in such contests. Often physiological changes, such as increased glucocorticoids (e.g., cortisone, cortisol) or decreased testosterone, occur with the loser effect. Compare WINNER EFFECT.

loss of affect loss of the ability to respond emotionally, which results in FLAT AFFECT.

loss of consciousness (**LOC**) a state in which an organism capable of consciousness can no longer experience events or exert voluntary control. Examples of conditions associated with loss of consciousness include fainting (syncope), deep sleep, coma, general anesthesia, narcolepsy, and epileptic absence.

lost letter procedure an INDIRECT ATTITUDE MEASURE used at an aggregate group level. Two sets of stamped envelopes are created, one addressed to a group likely to adopt a particular attitudinal position on the target issue and the other addressed to a group likely to adopt the opposite position. Equal numbers of each version of the envelope are randomly distributed in a particular community. The procedure is based on the logic that a person finding a letter that has apparently been inadvertently dropped is more likely to place the letter in a mailbox if it is addressed to a group that shares his or her position.

loudness *n.* the subjective magnitude of sound. It is determined primarily by intensity but is also affected by other physical properties, such as frequency, spectral configuration, and duration. The unit of loudness is the **sone**: One sone is the loudness of a 1-kHz tone presented at 40 dB SPL (sound-pressure level). The **loudness level** is the level in decibels SPL of a 1-kHz tone that is judged equally loud to the test sound. The unit is the **phon**.

Lou Gehrig's disease see AMYOTROPHIC LATERAL SCLEROSIS. [Henry (**Lou**) Gehrig (1903–1941), U.S. baseball player who died of the disease]

love *n.* a complex emotion involving strong feelings of affection and tenderness for a person, pleasurable sensations in his or her presence, devotion to his or her well-being, and sensitivity to his or her reactions to oneself. Although love takes many forms, the TRIANGULAR THEORY OF LOVE proposes three essential components: passion, intimacy, and commitment. Social psychological research in this area has focused largely on PASSIONATE LOVE, in which passion (sexual desire and excitement) is predominant, and COMPANIONATE LOVE, in which passion is relatively weak and commitment is strong.

love needs in MASLOW'S MOTIVATIONAL HIERARCHY, the third level of the hierarchy of needs, characterized by the striving for affiliation and acceptance. Also called **belongingness and love needs**.

love object 1. the person in whom an individual invests the emotions of affection, devotion, and, usually, sexual interest. **2.** in psychoanalytic theory, the person who is loved by the individual's EGO, as opposed to the OBJECT that satisfies an INSTINCT.

low-ball technique a procedure for enhancing compliance by first obtaining agreement to a request and then revealing the hidden costs of this request. Compliance to the target request is greater than would have been the case if these costs had been made clear at the time of the initial request. See also DOOR-IN-THE-FACE TECH-NIQUE; FOOT-IN-THE-DOOR TECHNIQUE; THAT'S-NOT-ALL TECHNIQUE.

lower motor neuron see MOTOR NEURON.

low threshold see HIGH THRESHOLD.

low vision reduction of visual capacity (especially visual acuity and visual field) that cannot be corrected with glasses, contact lenses, or medical or surgical treatment. Low vision interferes with the performance of everyday tasks and is often associated with a decline in quality of life, an increased risk of depression, and decreased functional status. See also BLINDNESS; VISUAL IMPAIRMENT.

LRE abbreviation for LEAST RESTRICTIVE ENVIRONMENT.

LRP abbreviation for LATERALIZED READINESS POTENTIAL.

LSD 1. *ly*sergic acid *d*iethylamide: a highly potent HALLUCINOGEN that structurally resembles the neurotransmitter SEROTONIN and is capable of producing visual distortions or frank hallucinations, together with feelings of euphoria or arousal; it became a widely used and controversial recreational drug during the mid-1960s and early 1970s. The effects of LSD were the subject of research during the 1950s as a possible model for psychosis, and various attempts were made to use LSD as an aid to psychotherapy although they did not prove effective. **2.** abbreviation for LEAST SIGNIFICANT DIFFERENCE.

LSD psychotherapy an experimental technique, used in the 1960s, in which the drug LSD (lysergic acid diethylamide) was administered to patients with chronic alcoholism and serious mental disorders (e.g., schizophrenia) as a means of facilitating the process of uncovering and reliving memories and increasing the patients' ability to communicate their thoughts and feelings. Subsequent research not only failed to confirm therapeutic value but also revealed significant physiological, behavioral, and mental health risks in the therapeutic use of LSD, resulting in the abandonment of the technique. See HALLUCINOGEN; PSYCHEDELIC THERAPY.

LTM abbreviation for LONG-TERM MEMORY.

lucid dream a dream in which the sleeper is aware that he or she is dreaming.

lumbar *adj.* referring to the lower part of the back or spinal cord.

lumbar nerve see SPINAL NERVE.

lumbar puncture a procedure used to obtain a sample of cerebrospinal fluid for diagnostic purposes by inserting a needle into the SUBARACHNOID SPACE of the spinal cord at a point between two lumbar vertebrae. Also called **spinal tap**.

luminance *n.* the amount of light reflected or emitted from an object as measured in candelas per square meter.

luminosity *n.* the visual sensation of the brightness of a light source. It depends on the power emitted by the source and on the sensitivity of the eye to different wavelengths of light.

luminous flux (symbol: Φ_v) the rate at which light is emitted from a source or reflected from a surface. It is measured in **lumens** by reference to a standard source.

lupus erythematosus an autoimmune disorder causing chronic inflammation of connective tissue and characterized by joint pains, a butterfly-shaped rash on the nose and cheeks, and scaly red patches on the skin. The condition may be limited to the skin (**discoid lupus erythematosus; DLE**) or it may also affect internal organs, such as the heart, lungs, and central nervous system (**systemic lupus erythematosus; SLE**) and involve neurological abnormalities, such as seizures and psychosis.

lure *n.* an incorrect item presented among correct items in testing memory, to serve as a DISTRACTOR.

Luria–Nebraska Neuropsychological Battery (**LNNB**) a set of tests to assess the cognitive functioning of individuals aged 15 years and older that is used to diagnose general and specific cerebral dysfunction and to localize impaired brain areas. It includes 11 clinical scales, each representing different aspects of relevant skills: motor functions, tactile functions, visual functions, rhythm, receptive speech, expressive speech, writing, reading, arithmetic, memory, and intellectual processess. [Alexander **Luria** (1902–1977), Russian neuropsychologist]

luteinizing hormone (**LH**) a GONADOTROPIN secreted by the anterior pituitary gland that, in females, stimulates the rapid growth of a graafian follicle (small, pouchlike cavity) in the ovary until it ruptures and releases an ovum (see MENSTRUAL CYCLE). In males it stimulates the interstitial cells of the TESTIS to secrete androgens. Also called **interstitial cell-stimulating hormone** (**ICSH**).

lymphocyte *n.* a type of blood cell (see LEUKOCYTE) that plays a key role in specific immune responses. **B lymphocytes** (or **B cells**), which develop and mature in the bone marrow, are responsible for humoral immunity: They produce circulating antibodies when they bind to an appropriate antigen and are costimulated by certain T cells. **T lymphocytes** (or **T cells**), which mature in the thymus, are responsible for cell-mediated immunity: They are characterized by the presence of particular cell-surface molecules and are capable of antigen recognition. —**lymphocytic** *adj.*

lymphokine *n.* any of a group of proteins, secreted by lymphocytes, that have a role in cell-mediated immunity by inducing other cells of the immune system to divide. See CYTOKINE.

lysergic acid diethylamide see LSD.

lysine *n.* an essential AMINO ACID that cannot be synthesized by the body and must be supplied in the diet.

Mm

M 1. abbreviation for memory. **2.** symbol for MEAN.

MA abbreviation for MENTAL AGE.

Mach bands an illusion produced by two or more adjacent rectangular gray stimuli or bands that differ in lightness. The part of the light band that borders the dark band appears to be lighter than the rest of the light band, while the part of the dark band along the border between the two bands appears to be darker than the rest of the dark band. [Ernst **Mach** (1838–1916), Czechborn Austrian physicist]

Machiavellian hypothesis the hypothesis that the evolution of intelligence, especially in its social aspects, was largely dependent on behavior characterized by a desire and striving for power. Individuals who were more Machiavellian in their behavior were more likely to be successful in adaptation and thus more likely to spread their genes to future generations. [Niccolò **Machiavelli** (1469–1527), Italian political theorist]

Machiavellianism *n.* a personality trait marked by a calculating attitude toward human relationships and the viewing of other people more or less as objects to be manipulated in pursuit of one's goals, if necessary through deliberate deception. [Niccolò **Machiavelli**, who argued that an effective ruler must be prepared to act in this way]

mAChR abbreviation for MUSCARINIC RECEPTOR.

MacLean's theory of emotion an extension of PAPEZ'S THEORY OF EMOTION emphasizing the importance of all parts of the LIMBIC SYSTEM, especially the hippocampus and amygdala, in the control of emotional experience. [Paul D. **MacLean** (1913–), U.S. neurologist]

macrocephaly *n.* a condition in which the head is abnormally large in relation to the rest of the body. Compare MICROCEPHALY. **—macrocephalic** *adj.*

macroergonomics *n.* an approach to ERGONOMICS that examines any given WORK SYSTEM from a broad perspective in which all of its various elements—physical, organizational, environmental, and cognitive—are given due consideration. Compare MICROERGONOMICS.

macroglia *n.* a relatively large type of non-neuronal central nervous system cell (GLIA), including ASTROCYTES, EPENDYMAL CELLS, and OLIGODENDROCYTES. **—macroglial** *adj.*

macrogyria *n.* see LISSENCEPHALY.

macropsia *n.* a VISUAL ILLUSION in which an object appears to be larger than it is in reality. See also METAMORPHOPSIA. Compare MICROPSIA.

macula *n.* (*pl.* **maculae**) **1.** in hearing, a patch of sensory tissue in the UTRICLE and SACCULE of the inner ear that provides information about the position of the body in relation to gravity. The macula contains sensory HAIR CELLS whose processes (stereocilia) are embedded in a gelatinous matrix (**cupula**) containing calcareous particles (**otoliths**). When the orientation of the head changes, the relatively dense otoliths respond to gravity, causing the gelatinous mass to shift and the stereocilia to flex. This triggers nerve impulses in the hair-cell fibers, which act as signals to the brain. **2.** in vision, see MACULA LUTEA.

macula lutea a small spot in the retina that is in direct alignment with the optics of the eye. It contains a yellow pigment and a central depression, the FOVEA CENTRALIS. Also called **macula**.

macular degeneration dystrophy of the MACULA LUTEA, which affects both eyes and causes progressive loss of central vision. There are two types: **exudative** (or **wet**) **macular degeneration**, in which blood vessels grow under the retina and hemorrhage in the area of the macula; and **atrophic** (or **dry**) **macular degeneration**, in which one of the retinal layers degenerates or atrophies.

maculopathy *n.* any abnormal condition of the MACULA LUTEA, resulting in deterioration of visual acuity.

magazine training in OPERANT CONDITIONING, the training needed to familiarize an experimental animal with the mechanism (usually a feeder) that delivers the REINFORCER.

magical thinking the belief that events or the behavior of others can be influenced by one's thoughts, wishes, or rituals. Magical thinking is normal in children up to 4 or 5 years of age, after which reality thinking begins to predominate.

Magna Mater in the writings of Swiss psychoanalyst Carl Jung (1875–1961), an ARCHETYPE of the primordial mother image, based on the Great Mother of the Roman gods, Cybele. She represents that which is loving, sustaining, and fostering of growth and creativity. See also MOTHER ARCHETYPE. [Latin: "great mother"]

magnetic resonance imaging (**MRI**) a noninvasive diagnostic technique that uses the responses of hydrogen in tissue molecules to strong magnetic impulses to form a three-dimensional picture of body organs and tissues (e.g., the brain) with more accuracy than COM-PUTED TOMOGRAPHY. See also FUNCTIONAL MAGNETIC RESONANCE IMAGING.

magnetoencephalography (**MEG**) *n.* the measurement of the magnetic signals arising from the electrical activity of the brain, using a device called a **magnetoencephalograph** (MEG).

magnitude estimation a psychophysical procedure in which the participant makes subjective judgments of the magnitude of stimuli by assigning them numerical values along a scale.

magnitude production a DIRECT SCALING procedure in which the observer is provided with a number representing the magnitude of a stimulus and is required to adjust the stimulus to produce a sensation that corresponds to this number, with reference to a standard stimulus to which a magnitude number has also been assigned.

magnitude scaling of attitudes a procedure for measuring attitudes and other constructs by representing them as physical stimuli. Participants indicate their attitudes by regulating some perceptual property of a stimulus, such as the brightness of a light, the length of a line, or the pitch of a tone. For example, they might indicate their evaluation of an object by turning a brightness dial on a light, with no light representing an extremely negative attitude and maximum brightness representing an extremely positive attitude.

magnocellular system the part of the visual system that projects to or originates from large neurons in the two most ventral layers (the **magnocellular layers**) of the lateral GENICULATE NUCLEUS. It allows the rapid perception of movement, form, and changes in brightness but is relatively insensitive to stimulus location and color. See also M-CELL. Compare PARVO-CELLULAR SYSTEM.

main effect the consistent total effect of a particular independent variable on a dependent variable over all other independent variables in an experimental design. It is separate from, but may be obscured by, an INTERACTION EFFECT.

mainstreaming *n.* the placement of children with disabilities into regular classroom environments on a part-time basis, such that they attend only some regular education classes during the school day and spend the remaining time in special education classes. The aim is to offer each child the opportunity to learn in an environment that has the highest probability of facilitating rehabilitation efforts and supporting academic growth, although some critics have denounced the practice as requiring that children with disabilities "earn" their opportunity to participate in a regular classroom. See also FULL INCLUSION; LEAST RESTRICTIVE ENVIRONMENT.

maintenance rehearsal repeating items over and over to maintain them in SHORT-TERM MEMORY, as in repeating a telephone number until it has been dialed (see REHEARSAL). According to the LEVELS-OF-PROCESSING MODEL OF MEMORY, maintenance rehearsal does not effectively promote long-term retention because it involves little ELABORATION of the information to be remembered.

maintenance therapy treatment or therapy designed to maintain patients in a stable condition and to promote gradual healing or prevent relapse. It usually (but not always) refers to **maintenance drug therapy** (**maintenance pharmacotherapy** or **prophylactic maintenance**). Drug therapy is generally divided into three phases—acute, continuation, and maintenance—roughly corresponding to intervals of 1 month, 6 months, and a year or longer. Patients who respond in the acute and continuation phases may be placed on maintenance pharmacotherapy in the hopes of preventing relapse.

major depressive disorder a DEPRESSIVE DISORDER in which the individual has experienced at least one MAJOR DEPRESSIVE EPISODE but has never experienced a MANIC EPISODE, MIXED EPISODE, or HYPOMANIC EPISODE. Also called **major depression**.

major depressive episode an episode of a MOOD DISORDER in which, for at least 2 weeks, the individual has either persistent depressed mood or ANHEDONIA as well as at least four other symptoms. These other symptoms include: poor or increased appetite with significant weight loss or gain; insomnia or excessive sleep; PSYCHOMOTOR AGITATION or PSYCHOMOTOR RETARDATION; loss of energy with fatigue; feelings of worthlessness or inappropriate guilt; reduced ability to concentrate or make decisions; and recurrent thoughts of death, SUICIDAL IDEATION, or attempted suicide. All of these symptoms cause significant distress or impair normal functioning (social, occupational, etc.).

majority influence social pressure exerted by the larger portion of a group on individual members and smaller factions within the group. The majority tends to push for CONFORMITY and stability, and members usually respond to this either by accepting the majority's position as their own (CONVERSION) or by conforming publicly but retaining their own position privately (COMPLIANCE). Compare MINORITY INFLUENCE.

major tranquilizers a name formerly applied to ANTIPSYCHOTICS to distinguish them from anxiolytic, sedative, and hypnotic drugs (which were called minor tranquilizers).

maladaptation *n.* a condition in which biological traits or behavior patterns are detrimental, counterproductive, or otherwise interfere with optimal functioning in various domains, such as successful interaction with the environment and effectual coping with the challenges and stresses of daily life. Compare ADAPTATION. **—maladaptive** *adj.*

maladjustment *n.* **1.** inability to maintain effective relationships, function successfully in various domains, or cope with difficulties and stresses. **2.** any emotional disturbance of a relatively minor nature. **—maladjusted** *adj.*

malaise *n.* a vague feeling of general illness, discomfort, or uneasiness.

malapropism *n.* a linguistic error in which one word is mistakenly used for another having a similar sound, often to ludicrous effect, as in *She was wearing a cream casserole* (for *camisole*).

mal de ojo a CULTURE-BOUND SYNDROME, reported in many Mediterranean regions and most commonly affecting children, that is characterized by fever, sleep disturbances, and gastrointestinal problems.

mal de pelea a CULTURE-BOUND SYNDROME found in Puerto Rico that is similar to AMOK.

maldevelopment *n.* the abnormal development of an individual because of genetic, dietary, or external factors that interfere with growth of tissues and bodily functions.

male erectile disorder see IMPOTENCE.

maleness *n.* the quality of being male in the anatomical and physiological sense by virtue of possessing the XY combination of SEX CHROMOSOMES. Compare MASCULINITY.

male orgasmic disorder persistent or recurrent delay in, or absence of, male orgasm during sexual stimulation that produces arousal. This diagnosis does not apply if the condition is due to the effects of drugs or medical conditions.

malevolent transformation a term used by U.S. psychiatrist Harry Stack Sullivan (1892–1949) to describe the feeling that one lives among enemies and can trust no one.

malformation *n.* any abnormality of structure: a DEFORMITY.

malfunction *n.* failure to work properly.

malignant *adj.* **1.** describing a disorder that gets progressively worse or is resistant to treatment, eventually causing death. **2.** describing a tumor that invades and destroys tissues and may also spread to other sites (i.e., undergo metastasis). See CANCER; NEOPLASM. Compare BENIGN.

malingering *n.* the deliberate feigning of an illness or disability to achieve a particular desired outcome. For example, it may take the form of faking mental illness as a defense in a trial or faking physical illness to win compensation. Malingering is distinguished from FACTITIOUS DISORDER in that it involves a specific external factor as the motivating force. **—malingerer** *n.*

malleus *n.* see OSSICLES.

malpractice *n.* professional misconduct or negligent behavior on the part of a practitioner (e.g., a psychotherapist, psychiatrist, doctor, lawyer, or financial adviser) that may lead to legal action.

maltreatment *n.* ABUSE or NEGLECT of another person, which may involve emotional, sexual, or physical action or inaction, the severity or chronicity of which can result in significant harm or injury. Maltreatment also includes such

actions as exploitation and denial of basic needs (e.g., food, shelter, medical attention).

mammillary body either of a pair of small, spherical NUCLEI at the base of the brain, slightly posterior to the infundibulum (pituitary stalk), that are components of the LIMBIC SYSTEM.

managed care any system of health care delivery that regulates the use of member benefits to contain expenses. The term originally referred to prepaid health plans (e.g., HMOs) but is now applied to many different kinds of reimbursement and UTILIZATION REVIEW mechanisms. It is also used to denote the organization of health care services and facilities into groups to increase cost-effectiveness. **Managed care organizations** (**MCOs**) include HMOs (health maintenance organizations), PPOs (preferred provider organizations), point of service plans (POSs), exclusive provider organizations (EPOs), physician–hospital organizations (PHOs), INTEGRATED DELIVERY SYSTEMS (IDSs), and inde-pendent practice associations (IPAs).

management development programs used to improve the effectiveness with which people in managerial or executive positions perform their roles, including classroom training, counseling, mentoring, EXECUTIVE COACHING, plus business games and other role play techniques.

managerial psychology the application of a knowledge of human behavior to issues that arise in the management of organizations, especially with regard to decision making, problem solving, leadership, and human relations. Although often used synonymously with INDUSTRIAL AND ORGANIZATIONAL PSYCHOLOGY, the term suggests an approach that adopts the perspective of the employer.

mand *n.* in linguistics, a category of UTTERANCES in which the speaker makes demands on the hearer, as in *Listen to me* or *Pass the salt, please*. According to the behaviorist analysis of language, this form of verbal behavior is reinforced by the compliance of the listener. See BEHAVIORISM.

mandated reporting the legal requirement in the United States that psychologists and other human services personnel (e.g., social workers and nurses) report any suspected or known cases of child abuse or neglect.

mania *n.* excitement, overactivity, and PSYCHOMOTOR AGITATION, often accompanied by impaired judgment.

manic episode a period lasting at least 1 week characterized by elevated, expansive, or irritable mood with three or more of the following symptoms: an increase in activity or PSYCHOMOTOR AGITATION; talkativeness or PRESSURED SPEECH; FLIGHT OF IDEAS or racing thoughts; inflated self-esteem or grandiosity; a decreased need for sleep; extreme distractibility; and involvement in pleasurable activities that are likely to have unfortunate consequences, such as buying sprees or sexual indiscretions. All of these symptoms impair normal functioning and relationships with others.

manifest anxiety in psychoanalysis, anxiety with overt symptoms that indicate underlying emotional conflict or repression.

manifest content 1. the matter that is overtly expressed and consciously intended in any utterance or other form of communication. **2.** in psychoanalytic theory, the images and events of a DREAM or FANTASY as experienced and recalled by the dreamer or fantasist, as opposed to the LATENT CONTENT, which is posited to contain the hidden meaning. See also DREAM ANALYSIS; DREAM CENSORSHIP; DREAM-WORK.

manifest variable a variable that is directly observed or measured, as opposed to one whose value is inferred (see LATENT VARIABLE).

manipulandum *n.* (*pl.* **manipulanda**) an object designed to be manipulated in a psychological test or experiment.

manipulation *n.* conscious behavior designed to exploit, control, or otherwise influence others to one's advantage.

manipulation check any means by which an experimenter evaluates the efficacy of the experimental manipulation, that is, verifies that the manipulation affected the participants as intended.

Mann–Whitney U test a nonparametric statistical test of centrality for ranked data that contrasts scores from two independent samples in terms of the probabilities of obtaining the ranking distributions. [Henry Berthold **Mann** (1905–2000), Austrian-born U.S. mathematician; Donald Ransom **Whitney** (1915–), U.S. statistician]

MANOVA acronym for MULTIVARIATE ANALYSIS OF VARIANCE.

manual communication communication with the hands rather than by speech. Manual communication encompasses SIGN LANGUAGE and FINGERSPELLING and is used primarily with or between people who are deaf or have severe hearing loss.

manualized therapy interventions that are performed according to specific guidelines for administration, maximizing the probability of therapy being conducted consistently across settings, therapists, and clients. Also called **manual-assisted therapy**; **manual-based therapy**.

MAOI (**MAO inhibitor**) abbreviation for MONOAMINE OXIDASE INHIBITOR.

MAP abbreviation for MODAL ACTION PATTERN.

marathon group an ENCOUNTER GROUP that meets in seclusion for a long period, usually varying from 6 hours to several days. Marathon groups are based on the theory that a single, extended session will elicit more intense interactions, foster a greater sense of intimacy and sharing, and encourage a freer expression of feelings as the time elapses than a series of shorter, interrupted sessions. They are often organized around addressing a single issue or related set of issues.

marginal 1. *adj.* borderline or on the periphery. **2.** *n.* in statistics, see MARGINAL FREQUENCY.

marginal consciousness the background contents of CONSCIOUSNESS that, although above the threshold of awareness, are not the center of attention. Marginal stimuli are not equivalent to subliminal stimuli (see SUBLIMINAL PERCEPTION).

marginal frequency the sum of any one of the rows or columns in a data matrix, such as a table of students classified by sex and area of study. In this example, the number of female students, regardless of area of study, would be one marginal frequency, and the number of students enrolled in a specific area of study, regardless of sex, would be another. Also called **marginal**.

marginalization *n.* a reciprocal process through which an individual or group with relatively distinctive qualities, such as idiosyncratic values or customs, becomes identified as one that is not accepted fully into the larger group. —**marginalize** *vb.*

marijuana (**marihuana**) *n.* see CANNABIS.

marital adjustment the process by which married couples attain mutual gratification and achieve common goals while simultaneously maintaining an appropriate degree of individuality. A variety of related factors have been identified, such as affection, sharing of activities, communication, cooperation and agreement, and cohesion.

marital conflict open or latent antagonism between marriage partners. The nature and intensity of conflicts varies greatly, but studies indicate that the prime sources are often sexual disagreement, child-rearing differences, temperamental differences, and, to a lesser extent, religious differences, differences in values and interests, and disagreements over money management.

marital therapy COUPLES THERAPY when the couples are married. Also called **marriage therapy**.

market research research undertaken to understand the competitive challenges in a particular market by assessing the relative positions of various suppliers in the mind of consumers. For example, a comparison may be made between restaurants that are perceived to offer good service and high-quality food at a low price with those perceived to provide good service and high-quality food at a high price.

Marlowe–Crowne Social Desirability Scale (**M–C SDS**) a widely used research scale that attempts to assess the degree to which participants answer questions in such a manner as to present themselves in a favorable light. Test scores are often used in research where people might be inclined to bias their behavior in a socially desirable direction, rather than being perfectly frank. [David **Marlowe** (1931–) and Douglas P. **Crowne** (1928–), U.S. psychologists]

marriage *n.* the social institution in which two (or, less frequently, more) people commit themselves to a socially sanctioned relationship in which sexual intercourse is legitimated and there is legally recognized responsibility for any offspring as well as for each other. Although there are exceptions, the marital partners typically live together in the same residence. **—marital** *adj.*

marriage counseling couples COUNSELING when the couples are married. Also called **marital counseling**.

masculinity *n.* possession of social-role behaviors that are presumed to be characteristic of a man, as contrasted with MALENESS, which is genetically determined. **—masculine** *adj.*

masculinization *n.* see VIRILISM.

masking *n.* in perception, the partial or complete obscuring of one stimulus (the target) by another (the masker). The stimuli may be sounds (AUDITORY MASKING), visual images (**visual masking**), tastes, odorants, or tactile stimuli. **Forward masking** occurs when the masker is presented a short time before the target stimulus, **backward masking** occurs when it is presented shortly afterward, and **simultaneous masking** occurs when the two stimuli are presented at the same instant. **—mask** *vb.*

masking level difference a change in detection threshold for auditory stimuli produced by changes in the interaural characteristics of the masker or the signal (see AUDITORY MASKING). The masking level difference and related phenomena have provided valuable insights into the mechanisms involved in BINAURAL hearing and sound localization (see AUDITORY LOCALIZATION). Also called **binaural masking level difference**.

Maslach Burnout Inventory a method for the evaluation of BURNOUT on three dimensions: emotional exhaustion, DEPERSONALIZATION, and reduced personal accomplishment. It consists of 22 statements about feelings and attitudes to which participants respond in terms of frequency on a 7-point scale ranging from "never" to "every day." [Christina **Maslach** (1946–), U.S. psychologist]

Maslow's motivational hierarchy the hierarchy of human motives, or needs, as described by U.S. psychologist Abraham Maslow (1908–1970). Maslow's hierarchy represents a reaction against the determinism of the theories of Austrian psychiatrist Sigmund Freud (1856–1939) and U.S. psychologist B. F. Skinner (1904–1990). PHYSIOLOGICAL NEEDS (air, water, food, sleep, sex, etc.) are at the base; followed by safety and security (the SAFETY NEEDS); then love, affection, and gregariousness (the LOVE NEEDS); then prestige, competence, and power (the ESTEEM

NEEDS); and, at the highest level, aesthetic needs, the need for knowing, and SELF-ACTUALIZATION (the METANEEDS).

Maslow's theory of human motivation the humanistic view of motivation proposed by U.S. psychologist Abraham Maslow (1908–1970), in which the higher human needs for understanding, aesthetic values, self-realization, and PEAK EXPERIENCES are emphasized. Maslow contrasted the METAMOTIVATION arising from such METANEEDS with the DEFICIENCY MOTIVATION arising from physical needs, insecurity, and alienation.

masochism *n.* **1.** a condition in which the individual derives pleasure from experiencing pain and humiliation inflicted by others or, in some cases, by himself or herself. Masochistic sexual gratification might be associated with being whipped or other forms of domination, for example. However, the term is also applied to experiences that do not obviously involve sex, such as martyrdom, religious flagellation, or asceticism. **2.** in psychoanalytic theory, the tendency to bring suffering and humiliation upon oneself. It is interpreted as resulting from the DEATH INSTINCT or from aggression turned inward because of excessive guilt feelings. See also MORAL MASOCHISM. [Leopold Sacher **Masoch** (1835–1895), Austrian writer] **—masochist** *n.* **—masochistic** *adj.*

masochistic personality disorder a self-defeating personality disorder in which individuals persistently and characteristically obtain gratification or freedom from guilt feelings as a consequence of humiliation, self-derogation, and self-sacrifice.

mass action the generalization of U.S. psychologist Karl S. Lashley (1890–1958) that the size of a cortical lesion, rather than its specific location, determines the extent of any resulting performance decrement. Proposed in 1929 following experimental observations of the effects of different brain lesions on rats' ability to learn a complex maze, the concept reflects Lashley's belief that large areas of the cortex function together in learning and other complex processes. See also EQUIPOTENTIALITY.

massage *n.* the structured stroking or kneading of a body area or of the entire body by hand or by a mechanical or electrical device. Among the benefits of massage are improved circulation, the promotion of relaxation and healing from injury, and release from tension and psychological stress.

massed practice a learning procedure in which material is studied either in a single lengthy session or in sessions separated by short intervals. Massed practice is often found to be less effective than DISTRIBUTED PRACTICE.

mass hysteria see COLLECTIVE HYSTERIA.

mass psychology 1. the mental and emotional states and processes that occur in a large body of individuals who, although they may not share

M

285

any common characteristics, are considered as a whole. **2.** the scientific study of these phenomena, including the study of mass movements, mass hysteria, and the effects of the mass media.

mass suicide the deliberate ending of the lives of all or most of the members of an intact social group or aggregate by the members themselves, either directly through self-injurious behavior or indirectly by choosing a course of action that will very likely be fatal (e.g., the suicides of the 39 Heaven's Gate followers of Marshall Appelwhite in San Diego in 1997). Mass suicide often occurs at the command of a charismatic leader and may be provoked not by despair but by the desire to seek a "higher state of existence" promised by the leader. Also called **collective suicide**. Compare CLUSTER SUICIDES.

MAST acronym for MICHIGAN ALCOHOLISM SCREENING TEST.

master status a culturally defined aspect of one's identity, such as "mother" or "athlete," that serves to shape self-concept and to dominate others' perceptions of one's traits and behaviors, thereby possibly affecting one's life opportunities.

mastery learning a theory of education in which students learn material in several different ways over a series of study sessions, until they understand the material well enough to teach it to others.

mastery orientation an adaptive pattern of achievement behavior in which individuals enjoy and seek challenge, persist in the face of obstacles, and tend to view their failings as due to lack of effort or poor use of strategy rather than to lack of ability.

mastoid *n.* a projection from the anterior part of the temporal bone containing air spaces that communicate with the cavity of the middle ear. Also called **mastoid process**.

masturbation *n.* manipulation of one's own genital organs for purposes of sexual gratification. —**masturbate** *vb.*

matched-group design an experimental design in which experimental and control groups are matched on one or more background variables before being exposed to the experimental or control conditions. Compare RANDOMIZED-GROUP DESIGN.

matching hypothesis the proposition that people tend to form relationships with individuals who have a similar level of physical attractiveness to their own. Research indicates that this similarity tends to be greater for couples having a romantic relationship than for friends.

matching law in OPERANT CONDITIONING, a law that describes the distribution of responses when numerous task options are available. It states that the proportion of responses allocated to an alternative will match the proportion of reinforcement obtained from that alternative. For example, if a pigeon receives two thirds of its

food allocation from alternative A and one third from alternative B, it will make two thirds of its responses (and give two thirds of its time) to alternative A.

matching patients the process of prescribing specific interventions or choosing specific therapists for particular patients or diagnostic groups of patients to improve compliance with or effectiveness of treatment. The process is based on the diagnoses, needs, problems, and characteristics of particular patients; on therapist variables, such as race, ethnicity, and experience levels; and on setting variables, such as inpatient or outpatient clinics. Also called **psychotherapy matching**.

matching test a test in which items (e.g., words) selected from one list are matched with the appropriate items (e.g., definitions) on another list.

matching to sample a CONDITIONAL-DISCRIMINATION procedure in which each trial begins with presentation of a sample stimulus. Once the organism responds to that stimulus, two or more additional stimuli (called comparison stimuli) appear, only one of which matches the first stimulus. Reinforcement is contingent on responding to the stimulus that matches.

mate guarding a method of preventing a mate from reproducing with others. Immediately after copulation a male stays close to its mate and prevents other males from approaching or mating with the female until such time as additional mating will not result in fertilization. In some cases a **copulatory lock** literally keeps mates connected for several minutes or hours. See also SPERM COMPETITION.

materialism *n.* **1.** the philosophical position that everything, including mental events, is composed of physical matter and is thus subject to the laws of physics. From this perspective, the mind is considered to exist solely as a set of brain processes (see MIND–BODY PROBLEM). Such philosophies can be traced back to ancient times but gained a new impetus from advances in the physical sciences beginning in the 17th century. **2.** a value system that emphasizes the pursuit and acquisition of material goods and luxuries, typically perceived by the individual as a measure of personal worth and achievement, often at the expense of moral, psychological, and social considerations. **3.** the position that the causes of behavior are to be found in the material of the body, particularly the nervous system. It is nearly always associated with strict determinism. See also IDENTITY THEORY; PHYSICALISM. Compare IDEALISM; IMMATERIALISM. —**materialist** *adj., n.* —**materialistic** *adj.*

maternal behavior the actions of female animals associated with caring for their young. These can range from nursing in mammals and feeding in other species to protection, thermoregulation, and teaching skills to the young.

maternal deprivation lack of adequate nurturing for a young animal or child due to the absence or premature loss of, or neglect by, its mother or primary caregiver.

mate selection the choice of an appropriate partner for reproduction. In species where female parental investment is high, females are thought to be more careful in their choice of mates than males. However, in species where parental contribution to survival of offspring is more nearly equal, mate selection is shown by both sexes. Mate selection may be based on (a) behavioral traits, such as ability to defend a territory or to be dominant over others; (b) exaggerated signals of quality, such as bright tail plumage in the peacock; or (c) evaluations made during animal courtship. See also SEXUAL SELECTION.

mathematical learning theory a statistical learning model that makes assumptions about how an organism's probability of a correct response changes from trial to trial as a result of the outcome experienced on each trial. An important example is the STIMULUS SAMPLING THEORY.

mathematical model the representation of a psychological or physiological function, or other process, in mathematical terms, such as formulas or equations (e.g., FECHNER'S LAW).

mathematical psychology an approach to psychological phenomena that uses mathematical techniques to model the underlying processes and to make predictions of the outcomes of these processes. Closely related to PSYCHOMETRICS and STATISTICS, it is used across several major subdisciplines, especially cognitive psychology, psychophysics, and perception.

mathematics disorder a LEARNING DISORDER in which mathematical ability is substantially below what is expected given the person's chronological age, formal education experience, and measured intelligence. It may involve (among other problems) difficulties in counting, learning multiplication tables, understanding mathematical problems and performing mathematical operations, reading numerical symbols, and copying numbers.

mating behavior the activities that are involved in reproduction, including animal courtship, MATE SELECTION, and COPULATORY BEHAVIOR. Different species exhibit different MATING SYSTEMS, and mating behavior may have several functions in addition to successful conception: preparing both mates physiologically, providing cues for mate selection, and coordinating behavior of mates for nest building and subsequent care of young.

mating system the organization of typical mating patterns within a species. Mating systems include MONOGAMY, in which two individuals mate exclusively with each other; POLYGYNY, in which a male mates with multiple females; POLYANDRY, in which a female mates with multiple males; and polygynandry, in which both sexes mate with multiple partners.

matriarchy *n.* **1.** a society in which descent and inheritance is **matrilineal**, that is, traced through the female only. **2.** more loosely, a family, group, or society in which women are dominant. Compare PATRIARCHY. —**matriarchal** *adj.*

matricide *n.* **1.** the killing of one's own mother. **2.** a person who kills his or her own mother. Compare PATRICIDE. —**matricidal** *adj.*

matrilocal *adj.* denoting a living arrangement in which a married couple resides with or in close proximity to the wife's mother or relatives, or a culture in which this is the norm. Compare NEOLOCAL; PATRILOCAL.

matrix *n.* **1.** a context or environment within which something else is enclosed, embedded, originates, or develops. **2.** a rectangular ordered arrangement (ARRAY) of numbers in rows and columns.

matrix organization a complex type of organizational structure in which employees are grouped not only by the function they perform (e.g., marketing, research and development) but also by the product or project on which they are working. Employees working within a matrix organization report to both a functional boss and a product or project boss.

maturation *n.* the process of becoming functional or fully developed.

maturational crisis a life-changing event, such as marriage or retirement, that often is encountered during the typical course of development and that requires significant psychological, behavioral, or other adjustments.

maturational lag slowness or delay in some aspects of neurological development that may affect cognition, perception, and behavior.

maturation hypothesis a generalization that some behaviors and processes, such as language acquisition, are innate but do not appear until appropriate organs and neural systems have matured.

maximum likelihood an estimation technique in which estimates of the values of parameters of a distribution are based on the most likely sample of observations that one might have obtained from that population.

maze *n.* a complex system of intersecting paths and blind alleys that must be navigated from an entrance to an exit. Various types of mazes are used in learning experiments for animals and humans.

MBD abbreviation for MINIMAL BRAIN DYSFUNCTION.

MBTI abbreviation for MYERS–BRIGGS TYPE INDICATOR.

M-cell *n.* any of various large neurons in the two most ventral layers of the lateral GENICULATE NUCLEUS. M-cells are the origin of the MAGNOCELLULAR SYSTEM. The large RETINAL GANGLION

M

CELLS that provide input to the M-cells of the lateral geniculate nucleus are called **M-ganglion cells**.

MCI abbreviation for MILD COGNITIVE IMPAIRMENT.

MCMI abbreviation for MILLON CLINICAL MULTIAXIAL INVENTORY.

McNemar test a test of equality of proportions in samples in which the observations are correlated, such as the proportion of cases exceeding a criterion in a BEFORE–AFTER DESIGN. [Quinn McNemar (1900–1986), U.S. psychologist]

MCO abbreviation for managed care organization (see MANAGED CARE).

M–C SDS abbreviation for MARLOWE–CROWNE SOCIAL DESIRABILITY SCALE.

MD abbreviation for MUSCULAR DYSTROPHY.

MDA n. 3,4-methylenedioxyamphetamine: a synthetic HALLUCINOGEN that at low doses acts as a CNS STIMULANT and euphoriant. It is thought that MDA's psychostimulant properties occur through enhanced neurotransmission of norepinephrine and its hallucinogenic action through augmentation of serotonin transmission. MDA is a metabolite of MDMA and may be responsible for much of MDMA's action.

MDMA n. 3,4-methylenedioxymethamphetamine: a catecholamine-like HALLUCINOGEN with amphetamine-like stimulant properties that is among the most commonly used illicit drugs, generally sold under the name **Ecstasy**. Taken orally, onset of effects is rapid; the high lasts several hours, and residual effects can be experienced for several days. Intoxication is characterized by euphoria, feelings of closeness and spirituality, and diverse symptoms of autonomic arousal.

mean (symbol: $\bar{X}$; M) n. the numerical average of a batch of scores (X_i): the most widely used statistic for describing CENTRAL TENDENCY. It is computed as:

$$\bar{X} = (\Sigma X_i)/n,$$

where n is the number of scores; that is, the scores are added up, and the total is divided by the number of scores. Also called **arithmetic mean**.

mean deviation for a set of numbers, a measure of dispersion or spread equal to the average of the differences between each number and the mean value. It is given by $(\Sigma |x_i - \mu|)/n$, where μ is the mean value and n the number of values.

meaning n. cognitive or emotional significance. This may include a range of implied or associated ideas (connotative meaning) as well as a literal significance (DENOTATIVE MEANING). The study of meaning in language is SEMANTICS, and that of meaning in symbolic systems generally is SEMIOTICS. —**mean** vb. —**meaningful** adj.

meaninglessness n. a pervasive sense of the absence of significance, direction, or purpose. A sense of meaninglessness regarding one's life or life in general is sometimes a focal issue in psychotherapy.

mean length of utterance a measure of language development in young children based on the mean length of UTTERANCES in their spontaneous speech. It is usually calculated by counting MORPHEMES rather than words, and is based on at least 100 successive utterances.

means–ends analysis a technique to solve problems that sets up subgoals as means to achieve the goals (ends) and compares subgoals and goals using a recursive goal-reduction search procedure. Means–ends analysis originated in artificial intelligence and expanded into human cognition as a general problem-solving strategy.

mean square a SUM OF SQUARES divided by its DEGREES OF FREEDOM. The mean square is a variance ESTIMATOR.

measurement error a difference between an observed measurement and the true value of the parameter being measured that is attributable to flaws or biases in the measurement process.

measurement level the degree of specificity, accuracy, and precision reflected in a particular set of observations or measurements. Examples of common levels of measurement include NOMINAL SCALES, ORDINAL SCALES, INTERVAL SCALES, and RATIO SCALES.

measure of association any of various indices of the degree to which two or more variables are related.

measure of location any of a class of descriptive statistics that reflect the central point of a DISTRIBUTION (e.g., the mean or median).

mechanical intelligence the ability to understand and manage concrete objects.

mechanism n. **1.** in general, a device or physical property by which something is accomplished, or an explanation that relies on such a device or property. **2.** a philosophical position, similar to that of MATERIALISM, that provides explanations in terms of underlying physical properties. See MECHANISTIC THEORY. **3.** in psychodynamics, see MENTAL MECHANISM.

mechanistic interactionism a theory that considers both individual (dispositional) and situational variables in the determination of behavior. The relative weight assigned to dispositional and situational factors may be affected by certain moderating variables, for example, the nature of a situation: A highly structured situation may influence behavior more than will dispositional factors, and a highly ambiguous situation may allow dispositional factors to play a larger role in determining behavior.

mechanistic theory the assumption that psychological processes and behaviors can ultimately be understood in the same way that mechanical or physiological processes are understood. Its explanations of human behavior are based on the model or metaphor of a machine, reducing complex psychological phenomena to

M

simpler physical phenomena. Also called **mechanistic approach**. See REDUCTIONISM.

mechanoreceptor *n.* a receptor that is sensitive to mechanical forms of stimuli. Examples of mechanoreceptors are the receptors in the ear that translate sound waves into nerve impulses, the touch receptors in the skin, and the receptors in the joints and muscles.

medial *adj.* toward or at the middle of the body or of an organ. Compare LATERAL. —**medially** *adv.*

medial forebrain bundle a collection of nerve fibers passing through the midline of the forebrain to the hypothalamus. It includes tracts originating in the LOCUS CERULEUS, SUBSTANTIA NIGRA, and VENTRAL TEGMENTAL AREA and provides the chief pathway for reciprocal connections between the hypothalamus and the BIOGENIC AMINE systems of the brainstem.

medial geniculate nucleus (MGN) see GENICULATE NUCLEUS.

medial lemniscus either of a pair of somatosensory tracts in the midbrain carrying fibers from the spinal cord that communicate with the thalamus. They form part of the LEMNISCAL SYSTEM.

medial temporal amnesia memory loss caused by damage to the medial TEMPORAL LOBE.

median *n.* the score that divides a DISTRIBUTION into two equal-sized halves.

median nerve a nerve that supplies sensory and motor fibers to the arm and hand. Its fibers run through the BRACHIAL PLEXUS.

median test a nonparametric statistical procedure that tests the equality of the medians in two or more samples.

media richness the relative intensity and complexity of a communication channel. Face-to-face communication is a good example of a **rich medium**, as it involves a complex interaction of verbal and nonverbal cues; by contrast, communication exclusively via written messages is a **lean medium**.

mediated generalization a type of STIMULUS GENERALIZATION in which a CONDITIONED RESPONSE is elicited by a new stimulus that is notably different from, but in some way associated with, the original CONDITIONED STIMULUS. For example, a person conditioned to feel anxious on hearing a bell may also become anxious on hearing the word "bell."

mediate experience conscious awareness and interpretation of external events and stimuli. Mediate experience provides meaning and additional information not contained in the event or stimulus itself. It is contrasted with **immediate experience**: the elements or characteristics of the event or stimuli as perceived directly and without interpretation. INTROSPECTION makes use of immediate experience in analyzing the contents of mediate experience.

mediating behavior behavior that improves either the rate or probability of reinforcement of a target behavior for which reinforcement is arranged. Compare ADJUNCTIVE BEHAVIOR; COLLATERAL BEHAVIOR.

mediation *n.* in dispute resolution, use of a neutral outside person—the **mediator**—to help the contending parties communicate and reach a compromise. The process of mediation has gained popularity, for example for couples involved in separation or divorce proceedings.

mediational deficiency in problem solving, inability to make use of a particular strategy to benefit task performance even if it is taught to a person. Compare PRODUCTION DEFICIENCY; UTILIZATION DEFICIENCY.

mediational learning a concept of learning that assumes the presence of mediators to bridge the association between two or more events that are not directly contiguous in space or time. The mediators are events or processes that serve as CUES.

mediation process any of the COGNITIVE PROCESSES that are presumed to occur in the mind between reception of a stimulus and initiation of a response. These may include interpretation of sense data, retrieval of stored information, judgments and evaluations, computations, reasoning, and other mental operations.

mediation theory the hypothesis that stimuli affect behavior indirectly through an intervening process, as opposed to a simpler stimulus–response model. For example, cognitive therapists maintain that the effect an external event has on an individual is influenced by the individual's thoughts and perceptions of that event.

medical audit a systematic evaluation of the effectiveness of diagnostic and treatment procedures. A **retrospective medical audit** is based on a review of a patient's charts after he or she has been discharged; a **concurrent medical audit** is conducted while the patient is still under treatment.

medical care evaluation a health care review in which an assessment of the quality of care and its utilization is made. It will include an investigation of any suspected problems, analysis of the problems identified, and a plan for corrective action.

medical family therapy a form of psychotherapy that combines a BIOPSYCHOSOCIAL systems approach with FAMILY SYSTEMS THEORY to help individuals and their families deal with the health problems of the individual. This therapy emphasizes collaboration with others—physicians, nurses, occupational therapists, nutritionists, and the like—in the individual's health care team.

medical model 1. the concept that mental and emotional problems are analogous to biological problems, that is, they have detectable, specific, physiological causes (e.g., an abnormal gene or

M

damaged cell) and are amenable to cure or improvement by specific treatment. **2.** in evaluation research, a systems-analysis approach to evaluation that considers the interrelatedness of all the factors that may affect performance and monitors possible side effects of treatment. The medical model is in contrast to the **engineering model**, which is a simple comparison of gains for different groups, some of which have been exposed to the program of interest.

medical psychology an area of applied psychology devoted to psychological questions arising in the practice of medicine, including emotional reactions to illness; attitudes toward terminal illness and impending death; psychological means of relieving pain (e.g., hypnotic suggestion); and reactions to disability.

medical rehabilitation the process of restoring to the fullest possible degree the physical functioning of an individual who has a physiological or anatomical impairment.

medication *n.* PSYCHOACTIVE DRUGS that aid in the treatment of affective and behavioral disorders. Until recently, in the United States only medical physicians could legally prescribe psychoactive drugs, but prescription privileges have now been extended to psychologists in the military and to those in New Mexico and Louisiana. **Overmedication**—the taking of more than the prescribed dose of a drug or drugs—may occur when medication is not properly monitored. **Self-medication** is usually associated with individuals who use drugs or alcohol inappropriately to alleviate emotional problems.

meditation *n.* profound and extended contemplation or reflection, sometimes in order to attain an ALTERED STATE OF CONSCIOUSNESS. Traditionally associated with spiritual and religious exercises, it is now increasingly also used to provide relaxation and relief from stress. See also CONCENTRATIVE MEDITATION; TRANSCENDENTAL MEDITATION.

medulla *n.* **1.** the central or innermost region of an organ, such as the adrenal medulla. Compare CORTEX. **2.** see MEDULLA OBLONGATA. —**medullary** *adj.*

medulla oblongata the most inferior (lowest), or caudal (tailward), part of the HINDBRAIN. It contains many nerve tracts that conduct impulses between the spinal cord and higher brain centers, as well as autonomic nuclei involved in the control of breathing, heartbeat, and blood pressure. Also called **myelencephalon**.

MEG abbreviation for MAGNETOENCEPHALOGRAPHY or magnetoencephalograph.

megadose pharmacotherapy a dosing strategy popular in the 1970s and 1980s, generally involving the rapid administration of very high doses of an antipsychotic drug in the hopes that this would hasten an antipsychotic response. This strategy was largely ineffective and had numerous adverse effects, such as severe movement disorders and death due to NEUROLEPTIC MALIG-

NANT SYNDROME. Because of the lack of clinical benefit and the high incidence of adverse side effects associated with megadose pharmacotherapy, it has fallen into disuse. Also called **rapid neuroleptization**.

megalomania *n.* a highly inflated conception of one's importance, power, or capabilities.

megavitamin therapy the use of very high doses of vitamins and mineral supplements, particularly vitamin C (ascorbic acid), nicotinic acid (niacin), vitamin B_6 (pyridoxine), and magnesium, to treat certain mental disorders. Such an approach is not widely adopted, and effectiveness is uncertain.

meiosis *n.* a special type of division of the cell nucleus that occurs during the formation of the sex cells—ova and spermatozoa. During meiosis, a parental cell in the gonad produces four daughter cells that are all HAPLOID, that is, they possess only one of each chromosome, instead of the normal DIPLOID complement of homologous pairs of chromosomes. During the process of fertilization, the ova and spermatozoa undergo fusion, which restores the double set of chromosomes within the nucleus of the zygote thus formed.

Meissner's corpuscle a type of small, oval sensory-nerve ending that is sensitive to touch. Meissner's corpuscles are abundant in the fingertips, nipples, lips, and the tip of the tongue. [Georg **Meissner** (1829–1905), German anatomist and physiologist]

mel *n.* a unit for measuring PITCH. By definition the pitch of a 1000-Hz tone presented at 40 dB SPL (40 phons) is 1000 mels. A sound whose pitch is twice that of a 1000-mel tone has a pitch of 2000 mels, and so on.

melanocyte-stimulating hormone (**MSH**) a hormone secreted by the anterior pituitary gland that stimulates dispersal of melanin granules within pigment cells (melanophores) of the skin of certain vertebrates (e.g., amphibians) thereby darkening the skin. In mammals it may play a role in regulating eating behavior.

melatonin *n.* an AMINE hormone, produced mainly by the PINEAL GLAND as a metabolic product of the neurotransmitter SEROTONIN, that helps to regulate seasonal changes in physiology and may also influence puberty. It is implicated in the initiation of sleep and in the regulation of the sleep–wake cycle.

Mellaril *n.* a trade name for THIORIDAZINE.

melodic intonation therapy speech therapy that uses melody to regain or improve speech in individuals with certain kinds of APHASIA, MOTOR SPEECH DISORDER, or EXPRESSIVE LANGUAGE DISORDER. Based on the theory of right-hemisphere dominance for music, melodic intonation therapy trains the speaker to intone, or "sing," text in pitches and rhythms that parallel natural spoken prosody. It is primarily an auxiliary to other forms of speech therapy.

M

membrane potential a difference in electric potential across a membrane, especially the plasma membrane of a cell. See also RESTING POTENTIAL.

memory *n.* **1.** the ability to retain information or a representation of past experience, based on the mental processes of learning or ENCODING, RETENTION across some interval of time, and RETRIEVAL or reactivation of the memory. **2.** specific information or a specific past experience that is recalled. **3.** the hypothesized part of the brain where traces of information and past experiences are stored (see MEMORY STORAGE; MEMORY SYSTEM).

memory disorder any impairment in the ability to encode, retain, or retrieve information or representations of experiences. A notable example is AMNESIA. Memory disorders may be partial or global, mild or severe, permanent or transitory, anterograde (pertaining to difficulty with new information) or retrograde (pertaining to difficulty with previously known information).

memory distortion any inaccurate or illusory recall or recognition, such as DÉJÀ VU, a FALSE MEMORY, or a MEMORY ILLUSION.

memory hardening an increased conviction, with the passage of time, that FALSE MEMORIES or PSEUDOMEMORIES are accurate. The phenomenon is of particular concern in the context of eyewitness testimony and hypnosis.

memory illusion a distortion in remembering, analogous to a perceptual illusion, in which one remembers inaccurately or remembers something that in fact did not occur. The DEESE PARADIGM is a memory illusion.

memory retraining strategies to help individuals with neurological deficits improve their ability to process information in WORKING MEMORY. These strategies are typically applied with patients with brain injury or Alzheimer's disease and those with HIV/AIDS who are experiencing memory problems.

memory span the number of items that can be recalled immediately after one presentation. Usually, the items consist of letters, words, numbers, or syllables that the participant must reproduce in order. A distinction may be drawn between **visual memory span** and **auditory memory span**, depending on the nature of the presentation.

memory storage the retention of memories in an organism. Historically, explanations of this process have included the continuous operation or "reverberation" of loops of neurons in cell assemblies (see CELL ASSEMBLY; REVERBERATORY CIRCUIT), the growth of new nerve endings grouped in synaptic knobs, and the encoding of information in complex molecules, such as RNA. Contemporary biological research suggests changes in synaptic efficiency as the basis of memory storage.

memory system any of several different kinds of memory that are hypothesized to be located in separate brain areas and primarily employed in different sorts of memory tasks. Examples of hypothesized systems include WORKING MEMORY (a temporary store used in manipulating information), SEMANTIC MEMORY (general knowledge), EPISODIC MEMORY (memories of one's personal past), and PROCEDURAL MEMORY (habits and skills).

memory trace a hypothetical modification of the nervous system that encodes a representation of information or experience. See ENGRAM.

menarche *n.* the first incidence of MENSTRUATION in a female, marking the onset of puberty. The age at which menarche occurs varies among individuals and cultures. —**menarcheal** *adj.*

Mendelian inheritance a type of inheritance that conforms to the basic principles developed around 1865 by Austrian monk Gregor Mendel (1822–1884), regarded as the founder of genetics. Mendelian inheritance is essentially determined by genes located on chromosomes, which are transmitted from both parents to their offspring. It includes autosomal dominant (see DOMINANT ALLELE), autosomal recessive (see RECESSIVE ALLELE), and SEX-LINKED inheritance.

Ménière's disease a disorder of balance and hearing due to excessive fluid in the inner ear, resulting in dizziness, nausea, TINNITUS, and deafness. [Prosper **Ménière** (1799–1862), French physician]

meninges *pl. n.* (*sing.* **meninx**) the three membranous layers that provide a protective cover for the brain and spinal cord. They consist of a tough outer **dura mater**, a middle **arachnoid mater**, and a thin, transparent **pia mater**, which fits over the various contours and fissures of the cerebral cortex.

meningioma *n.* a benign brain tumor that develops in the arachnoid layer of the MENINGES. Meningiomas are typically slow growing and cause damage mainly by pressure against the brain.

meningitis *n.* inflammation of the meninges, the three membranous layers that cover the brain and spinal cord, usually due to infection by bacteria, viruses, or fungi. Symptoms include high fever, nausea, vomiting, stiff neck, and headache. If untreated or not treated promptly, many types of meningitis can result in confusion, lethargy, coma, and eventually death.

meningocele *n.* a congenital herniation (protrusion) of the meninges (the three membranous layers that cover the brain and spinal cord) through an abnormal opening in the skull or spinal cord, with seepage of cerebrospinal fluid into the protrusion. If the herniation contains neural tissue, the condition is identified as an **encephalocele**.

meningoencephalitis *n.* inflammation of the brain and the meninges covering it.

meningomyelocele *n.* protrusion of the spinal

cord and its covering meninges through a defect in the spinal column. This results in an external sac containing cerebrospinal fluid, poorly formed meninges, and a malformed spinal cord. Also called **myelomeningocele**. See SPINA BIFIDA.

menopausal depression severe DYSPHORIA occurring during the female CLIMACTERIC (menopause), particularly among women who have had a prior tendency to depression.

menopause *n.* see CLIMACTERIC. —**menopausal** *adj.*

menses *pl. n.* see MENSTRUATION.

mens rea the malicious or blameworthy state of mind (Latin, "guilty mind") that must be proved in addition to the ACTUS REUS in order to establish CRIMINAL RESPONSIBILITY and secure a conviction. It involves a conscious disregard for the law, which is presumed to be known by the defendant.

menstrual age the age of a fetus calculated from the beginning of the mother's last MENSTRUATION. At full term it is normally 280 days or 40 weeks, that is, usually 2 weeks longer than the GESTATIONAL AGE.

menstrual cycle a modified ESTROUS CYCLE that occurs in most primates, including humans (in which it averages about 28 days). The events of the cycle are dependent on cyclical changes in the concentrations of GONADOTROPINS secreted by the anterior pituitary gland, under the control of GONADOTROPIN-RELEASING HORMONE, and can be divided into two phases. In the follicular phase, FOLLICLE-STIMULATING HORMONE (FSH) and LUTEINIZING HORMONE (LH) stimulate development of an ovum and secretion of estrogen within the ovary, in a GRAAFIAN FOLLICLE, culminating in OVULATION, which occurs half way through the cycle. The estrogen stimulates thickening of the ENDOMETRIUM of the uterus in preparation to receive a fertilized ovum. The luteal phase begins immediately after ovulation, when the ruptured follicle becomes the CORPUS LUTEUM and secretes progesterone, which inhibits further secretion of releasing hormone (and hence of FSH and LH). If fertilization does not occur, this phase ends with menstruation and a repeat of the follicular phase.

menstrual taboo any culture-bound tradition associated with menstruating women, typically involving physical separation from men, abstention from sexual intercourse, or the exclusion of women from certain daily activities (e.g., the preparation of food).

menstruation *n.* a periodic discharge of blood and endometrial tissue from the uterus through the vagina that occurs in fertile women as part of the MENSTRUAL CYCLE. Also called **menses**; **menstrual** (or **monthly**) **period**.

mental *adj.* **1.** of or referring to the MIND or to processes of the mind, such as thinking, feeling, sensing, and the like. **2.** phenomenal or consciously experienced. In contrast to physiological or physical, which refer to objective events or processes, mental denotes events known only privately and subjectively; it may refer to the COGNITIVE PROCESSES involved in these events, to differentiate them from physiological processes.

mental aberration 1. a pathological deviation from normal thinking. **2.** any mental or emotional disorder or an individual symptom of such a disorder.

mental abilities abilities as measured by tests of an individual in areas of spatial visualization, perceptual speed, number facility, verbal comprehension, word fluency, memory, inductive reasoning, and so forth.

mental age (**MA**) a numerical scale unit derived by dividing an individual's results in an intelligence test by the average score for other people of the same age. Thus, a 4-year-old child who scored 150 on an IQ test would have a mental age of 6 (the age-appropriate average score is 100; therefore, $MA = (150/100) \times 4 = 6$). The MA measure of performance is not effective beyond the age of 14.

mental coaching a field of teaching expertise, used mainly for counseling, business, and sports, that is focused on the direct cognitive features of behavior. It is used for such purposes as improving overall performance, restoring confidence, enhancing motivation, enhancing concentration, focusing better under pressure, and performing more consistently.

mental combination in PIAGETIAN THEORY, a type of cognitive processing typical of the final subphase of the SENSORIMOTOR STAGE, in which children of 18 to 24 months of age begin to use mental images to represent objects and to engage in mental problem solving.

mental deficiency another (and now seldom used) name for mental retardation, sometimes referring to severe or profound mental retardation with known organic causes.

mental disorder a disorder characterized by psychological symptoms, abnormal behaviors, impaired functioning, or any combination of these. Such disorders may cause clinically significant distress and impairment in a variety of domains of functioning and may be due to organic, social, genetic, chemical, or psychological factors. Specific classifications of mental disorders are elaborated in the American Psychiatric Association's *Diagnostic and Statistical Manual of Mental Disorders* (see DSM–IV–TR) and the World Health Organization's INTERNATIONAL CLASSIFICATION OF DISEASES. Also called **mental illness**; **psychiatric disorder**; **psychiatric illness**.

mentalese *n.* a hypothetical language of thought that combines cognitive and semantic systems and operates on concepts and propositions.

M

mental function any cognitive process or activity, such as thinking, sensing, or reasoning.

mental handicap the condition of being unable to function independently in the community because of arrested or delayed cognitive development. Also called **mental disability**.

mental healing the process of alleviating or attempting to alleviate mental or physical illness through the power of the mind, typically utilizing such methods as visualization, suggestion, and the conscious manipulation of energy flow. See also FAITH HEALING.

mental health a state characterized by emotional well-being, good behavioral adjustment, and a capacity to establish constructive relationships and cope with the ordinary demands and stresses of life.

mental health care a category of health care service and delivery involving scientific and professional disciplines across several fields of knowledge and technology involved in psychological assessment and intervention (psychology, psychiatry, neurology, social work, etc.). This type of care includes but is not limited to psychological screening and testing, psychotherapy and family therapy, and neuropsychological rehabilitation. See also MENTAL HEALTH SERVICES.

mental health clinic an outpatient facility for the diagnosis and treatment of psychological and behavioral problems.

mental health services any interventions—assessment, diagnosis, treatment, or counseling—offered in private, public, inpatient, or outpatient settings that are aimed at the maintenance or enhancement of mental health or the treatment of mental or behavioral disorders in individual and group contexts.

mental hospital see PSYCHIATRIC HOSPITAL.

mental hygiene a general approach aimed at maintaining mental health and preventing mental disorder through such means as educational programs, promotion of a stable emotional and family life, prophylactic and early treatment services (see PRIMARY PREVENTION), and public health measures. The term itself is now less widely used than formerly.

mental illness see MENTAL DISORDER.

mental institution a treatment-oriented facility in which patients with mental retardation or severe psychological disorder are provided with supervised general care and therapy by trained psychologists and psychiatrists as well as auxiliary staff. The patients of a mental institution will generally be those who are unable to function independently as outpatients when supported by psychoactive drugs. See also PSYCHIATRIC HOSPITAL.

mentalism *n.* a position that insists on the reality of explicitly mental phenomena, such as thinking and feeling. It holds that mental phenomena cannot be reduced to physical or physiological phenomena (see REDUCTIONISM). The term is often used as a synonym for IDEALISM, although some forms of mentalism may hold that mental events, while not reducible to physical substances, are nonetheless grounded in physical processes. Most modern cognitive theories are examples of this latter type of mentalism. Compare ELIMINATIVISM; IDENTITY THEORY. See also CONSCIOUS MENTALISM. —**mentalist** *adj.*

mental lexicon the set of words that a person uses regularly (see PRODUCTIVE VOCABULARY) or recognizes when used by others (see RECEPTIVE VOCABULARY). Psycholinguistics has proposed various models for such a lexicon, in which words are mentally organized with respect to such features as meaning, lexical category (e.g., noun, verb, etc.), frequency, length, and sound. Also called **lexical memory**.

mental map a mental representation of the world or some part of it based on subjective perceptions rather than objective geographical knowledge. Such a map will normally prioritize the individual's neighborhood, city, and nation and give prominence to more distant places according to personal experience (e.g., vacations), cultural connections (e.g., family history or language links), and the level of coverage in the mass media. The map will also incorporate the individual's negative or positive feelings about these places. See COGNITIVE MAP.

mental measurement the use of quantitative scales and methods in measuring psychological processes. See PSYCHOMETRICS.

mental mechanism in psychoanalytic and psychodynamic theory, the psychological functions, collectively, that help individuals meet environmental demands, protect the ego, satisfy inner needs, and alleviate internal and external conflicts and tensions. Among them are (a) language, which enables expression of thoughts; (b) memory, which stores information needed in solving problems; and (c) perception, which involves recognition and interpretation of phenomena.

mental model any internal representation of the relations between a set of elements, as, for example, between workers in an office or department, the elements of a mathematics or physics problem, the terms of a syllogism, or the configuration of objects in a space. Such models may contain perceptual qualities and may be abstract in nature. They can be manipulated to provide dynamic simulations of possible scenarios and are thought to be key components in decision making.

mental process any process that takes place in the mind. This term is often used synonymously with COGNITIVE PROCESS. See also HIGHER MENTAL PROCESS.

mental rehearsal the use of IMAGERY to practice behavioral patterns or skills, for example, reacting without impatience to a request that seems unnecessary or performing a defensive play in basketball.

mental representation a hypothetical entity that is presumed to stand for a perception, thought, memory, or the like in the mind during cognitive operations. For example, when doing mental arithmetic, one presumably operates on mental representations that correspond to the digits and numerical operators; when one imagines looking at the reverse side of an object, one presumably operates on a mental representation of that object.

mental retardation (**MR**) a disorder characterized by intellectual function that is significantly below average: specifically that of an individual with a measured IQ of 70 or below, whose level of performance of tasks required to fulfill typical roles in society—including maintaining independence and meeting cultural expectations of personal and social responsibility—is impaired, and in whom the condition is manifested during the developmental period, defined variously as below the ages of 18 or 22. Mental retardation may be the result of brain injury, disease, or genetic causes. Also called **intellectual disability**.

mental rotation the ability to mentally manipulate stimuli some degree clockwise or counterclockwise from their normal orientations.

mental set a temporary readiness to perform certain psychological functions that influences response to a situation or stimulus, such as the tendency to apply a previously successful technique in solving a new problem. It is often determined by instructions but need not be. Essentially synonymous with the earlier term EINSTELLUNG, mental set is the embodiment of the prior concepts of AUFGABE and DETERMINING TENDENCY.

mental status the global assessment of an individual's cognitive, affective, and behavioral state as revealed by examination that covers such factors as general health, appearance, level of alertness, affect, speech, motor activity, thought, sensory awareness, orientation, memory, general intelligence level, abstraction and interpretation ability, and judgment.

mental status examination (**MSE**) a comprehensive evaluation of a patient, based on interviews, tests, and other sources of information and including details of mental status, personality characteristics, diagnosis, prognosis, and treatment options.

mental synthesis the process by which ideas and images are combined and formed into objects of thought, or by which objects of consciousness are brought together into meaningful wholes.

mental test 1. any test that measures one or more cognitive abilities. **2.** an intelligence test.

mentation *n.* thinking or mental activity in general.

mentoring *n.* the provision of instruction, encouragement, and other support to an individual (e.g., a student, youth, or colleague) to aid his or her overall growth and development or the pursuit of greater learning skills, a career, or other educational or work-related goals. Numerous **mentoring programs** exist today within occupational, educational, and other settings; they use frequent communication and contact between **mentors** and their respective protégés as well as a variety of other techniques and procedures to develop positive productive relationships.

mercy killing a direct action intended to end what would otherwise be the prolonged agony of a dying person or animal. The concept has been known since ancient times: Warriors often were expected to kill a desperately wounded comrade or enemy. Severely injured animals are also put out of their misery by mercy killing. See also ASSISTED DEATH; EUTHANASIA.

mere-exposure effect the finding that individuals show an increased preference (or liking) for a stimulus (e.g., a name, sound, or picture) as a consequence of repeated exposure to that stimulus. Research indicates that this effect is most likely to occur when there is no preexisting negative attitude toward the stimulus object, and that it tends to be strongest when the person is not consciously aware of the stimulus presentations.

mere-thought polarization the finding that merely thinking about an attitude can result in polarization in the direction of that attitude. For example, thinking about a moderately positive attitude can result in that attitude becoming extremely positive.

Merkel's tactile disk a type of sensory-nerve ending in the tough, thick skin on the palms of the hands and soles of the feet and in the hairy skin. Also called **Merkel's corpuscle**. [Friedrich Siegmund **Merkel** (1845–1919), German anatomist]

mescaline *n.* a HALLUCINOGEN derived from the peyote cactus. Its effects often include nausea and vomiting as well as visual hallucinations involving lights and colors; they have a slower onset than those of LSD and usually last 1–2 hours.

mesencephalon *n.* see MIDBRAIN. —**mesencephalic** *adj.*

mesmerism *n.* an old name, used in the mid-18th through the mid-19th centuries, for HYPNOSIS. See ANIMAL MAGNETISM. [Franz Anton **Mesmer** (1733–1815), Austrian physician and an early proponent of hypnosis] —**mesmerist** *n.* —**mesmeric** *adj.*

mesocortical system a network of DOPAMINERGIC neurons in the brain that consists of the medial PREFRONTAL CORTEX and the anterior CINGULATE GYRUS. It has connections to other parts of the limbic system, including the NUCLEUS ACCUMBENS and AMYGDALA. It receives input from the VENTRAL TEGMENTAL AREA, and its activity is related to emotion, reward, and substance abuse.

mesoderm *n.* see GERM LAYER. —**mesodermal** *adj.*

mesolimbic system a network of DOPAMIN-ERGIC neurons in the brain consisting of the NU-CLEUS ACCUMBENS, AMYGDALA, and OLFACTORY TUBERCLE. It receives input from the VENTRAL TEGMENTAL AREA and its activity is related to emotion, reward, and substance abuse.

mesopic vision vision that involves aspects of both PHOTOPIC VISION and SCOTOPIC VISION, thus being mediated by both rods and cones.

mesostriatal system a set of DOPAMINERGIC neurons whose axons arise from the midbrain and innervate the BASAL GANGLIA. It includes neurons connecting the substantia nigra to the striatum.

message-learning approach a theory that conceptualizes attitude change as a type of learning process in which the extent of attitude change is determined by how well the arguments in a persuasive message are learned. This process is seen as having five steps: exposure, attention, comprehension, yielding, and retention.

meta-analysis *n.* a quantitative technique for synthesizing the results of multiple studies of a phenomenon into a single result by combining the EFFECT SIZE estimates from each study into a single estimate of the combined effect size or into a distribution of effect sizes.

meta-attention *n.* awareness of the factors that influence one's attention.

metabolic defect any deficiency in the structure or enzymatic function of protein molecules or in the transport of substances across cell membranes.

metabolism *n.* the physical and chemical processes within a living cell or organism that are necessary to maintain life. It includes **catabolism**, the breaking down of complex molecules into simpler ones, often with the release of energy; and **anabolism**, the synthesis of complex molecules from simple ones. —**metabolic** *adj.*

metabotropic receptor a neurotransmitter RECEPTOR that does not itself contain an ION CHANNEL but may use a G PROTEIN to open a nearby ion channel. Compare IONOTROPIC RECEPTOR.

metacognition *n.* awareness of one's own cognitive processes, often involving a conscious attempt to control them. The so-called TIP-OF-THE-TONGUE PHENOMENON, in which one struggles to "know" something that one knows one knows, provides an interesting example of metacognition. —**metacognitional** *adj.*

metacommunication *n.* auxiliary or covert messages, usually conveyed in the form of subtle gestures, movements, and facial expressions, about the procedural aspects or the dynamics

(rather than the actual content) of communication between two or more parties. For example, the metacommunication of a manager in response to a request for help from an employee may be an unspoken yet noticeable displeasure related to a belief that the employee should have been able to handle the situation alone.

metacontrast *n.* a form of backward MASKING in which the perception of a visible stimulus (the target) is altered by the subsequent presentation of a second visual stimulus (the mask) in a different spatial location. The target is often a small dot, while the mask is a ring that surrounds it. Each stimulus is presented very briefly (10–100 ms), at intervals that are varied systematically, and the quality of the target's percept is measured. Compare PARACONTRAST.

metaemotion *n.* one's awareness of and attitude toward one's own and others' emotions. For example, some people have negative attitudes toward anger in themselves or anyone else; others like to encourage anger. Some are ashamed of being too happy; others strive for such a state.

metaesthetic range the range of weak pain sensations just below the level of obvious, unmistakable pain.

metalanguage *n.* **1.** a language or set of symbols that is used to describe another language or set of symbols. Examples are English words used in teaching a foreign language, the instructions that accompany a computer program, and the use of mathematical symbols to analyze the logic of an argument (see SYMBOLIC LOGIC). Also called **second-order language**. **2.** any use of language to discuss or analyze language, as in formal linguistic study, literary criticism, or the attempts of speakers to make sure that they understand one another correctly.

metalinguistic awareness a conscious awareness of the formal properties of language as well as its functional and semantic properties. It is associated with a mature stage in language and metacognitive development (see METACOGNITION) and does not usually develop until around age 8. The arrival of metalinguistic awareness often signaled by an interest in PUNS and word games. Also called **linguistic awareness**.

metamemory *n.* awareness of one's own memory processes, often involving a conscious attempt to direct or control them. It is an aspect of METACOGNITION.

metamorphopsia *n.* a visual disorder in which objects appear to be distorted in size (see MICROPSIA; MACROPSIA), contour (e.g., irregular wavy edges), position (e.g., tilted), distance (see TELEOPSIA), and color (e.g., fading of colors). Metamorphopsia can result from a variety of causes, but frequently is due to displacement of the retina.

metamorphosis *n.* a change in form or structure, typically from one developmental stage to another. —**metamorphose** *vb.*

M

metamotivation *n.* in the HUMANISTIC PSY-CHOLOGY of U.S. psychologist Abraham Maslow (1908–1970), those motives that impel an individual to "character growth, character expression, maturation, and development": that is, the motivation that operates on the level of SELF-ACTUALIZATION and transcendence in MAS-LOW'S MOTIVATIONAL HIERARCHY. In Maslow's view, metamotivation is distinct from the motivation operating in the lower level needs, which he calls DEFICIENCY MOTIVATION, and it emerges after the lower needs are satisfied. Also called **being motivation**; **B-motivation**; **growth motivation**. See METANEEDS. See also MAS-LOW'S THEORY OF HUMAN MOTIVATION.

metaneeds *pl. n.* in the HUMANISTIC PSYCHOL-OGY of U.S. psychologist Abraham Maslow (1908–1970), the highest level of needs that come into play primarily after the lower level needs have been met. Metaneeds constitute the goals of self-actualizers and include the needs for knowledge, beauty, and creativity. In Maslow's view, the inability to fulfill them results in **metapathology**. Also called **being values**; **B-values**. See METAMOTIVATION. See also MAS-LOW'S THEORY OF HUMAN MOTIVATION.

metaphor therapy a system that focuses on the symbolic meaning of language and the use of metaphors in therapy. It is theorized that metaphors may provide means for restructuring thinking and approaches to problem solving in treatment.

metapsychology *n.* the study of, or a concern for, the fundamental underlying principles of any psychology. The term was used by Austrian psychiatrist Sigmund Freud (1856–1939) to denote his own psychological theory, emphasizing its ability to offer comprehensive explanations of psychological phenomena on a fundamental level. Freud's criteria for a metapsychology were that it should explain a psychical phenomenon in terms of (a) its dynamics, (b) its topology, and (c) its economic aspects. Although these specific criteria apply most clearly to Freud's own theory, the notion of metapsychology as explanation at a fundamental and comprehensive level continues to be a useful construct. —**metapsychological** *adj.*

metatheory *n.* a higher order theory about theories, allowing one to analyze, compare, and evaluate competing theories. The concept of a metatheory suggests that theories derive from other theories such that there are always prior theoretical assumptions and commitments behind any theoretical formulation. These prior assumptions and commitments are worthy of study in their own right, and an understanding of them is essential to a full understanding of derivative theories. —**metatheoretical** *adj.*

metathetic *adj.* **1.** denoting a stimulus dimension in which a change of magnitude can cause a qualitative change in the psychological sensation produced. For example, a faint smell may be quite pleasing, whereas an increase in intensity may cause revulsion. Compare PROTHETIC. **2.** relating to a change in place or condition, particularly the transposition of two PHONEMES in a word or the exchange of elements between chemical compounds to create different kinds of compounds. —**metathesis** *n.*

metempirical *adj.* describing or pertaining to knowledge that is not subject to verification by experience, and thus cannot be established by the methods of science. As described by British writer George Henry Lewes (1817–1878), the metempirical is roughly equivalent to the notion of the transcendent (see TRANSCENDENCE) developed by German philosopher Immanuel Kant (1724–1804).

metencephalon *n.* the portion of the BRAIN-STEM that includes the PONS and CEREBELLUM. With the medulla oblongata, the metencephalon forms the HINDBRAIN. —**metencephalic** *adj.*

methadone *n.* a synthetic OPIOID ANALGESIC that is used for pain relief and as a substitute for heroin in METHADONE MAINTENANCE THERAPY. It is quite effective when orally ingested and has a long duration of action. U.S. trade name (among others): **Dolophine**.

methadone maintenance therapy a drug-rehabilitation therapy in which those with HER-OIN DEPENDENCE are prescribed a daily oral dose of METHADONE to blunt craving for opioid drugs. A controversial treatment, it is nonetheless widely considered the most effective approach to heroin addiction.

methamphetamine *n.* see AMPHETAMINES.

method *n.* the procedures and system of analysis used in scientific investigation in general or in a particular research project.

method of absolute judgment a psychophysical procedure in which stimuli are presented in random order to a participant, whose task is to place each stimulus in a particular category. The stimuli usually vary along one or two dimensions, such as brightness or loudness. Also called **absolute-judgment method**.

method of adjustment a psychophysical technique in which the participant adjusts a variable stimulus to match a constant or standard. For example, the observer is shown a standard visual stimulus of a specific intensity and is asked to adjust a comparison stimulus to match the brightness of the standard. Also called **adjustment method**; **error method**; **method of average error**; **method of equivalents**.

method of choice a psychophysical procedure in which the participant is presented with several arrays of stimuli, one of which contains the target stimulus. The participant's task is to choose the array that contains the target stimulus.

method of constant adjustment see METHOD OF LIMITS.

method of constant stimuli a psychophysical procedure for determining the sensory threshold by randomly presenting several stimuli known to be close to the threshold. The threshold is the stimulus value that was detected 50% of the time. Also called **constant stimulus method**.

method of equal-appearing intervals in psychophysics, a procedure in which magnitudes between pairs of stimuli are adjusted so that the differences between stimuli within each pair are perceived as equal.

method of just noticeable differences a psychophysical procedure to determine the smallest difference between stimuli that can be perceived. A standard stimulus is presented together with a variable stimulus whose magnitude is increased in some trials and decreased in others until a just perceptible difference between the stimuli is reported. The average of the two series is taken, and the threshold is calculated at the point where the difference can be recognized 50% of the time.

method of limits a psychophysical procedure for determining the sensory threshold by gradually increasing or decreasing the magnitude of the stimulus presented in discrete steps. That is, a stimulus of a given intensity is presented to a participant; if it is perceived, a stimulus of lower intensity is presented on the next trial, until the stimulus can no longer be detected. If it is not perceived, a stimulus of higher intensity is presented, until the stimulus is detected. The threshold is the average of the stimulus values at which there is a detection-response transition (from "yes" to "no," or vice versa). An alternative procedure, the **method of constant adjustment**, allows the participant to adjust a stimulus continuously until it can no longer be perceived.

method of loci a MNEMONIC in which the items to be remembered are converted into mental images and associated with specific positions or locations. For instance, to remember a shopping list, each product could be imagined at a different location along a familiar street.

method of ratio estimation a psychophysical procedure in which two stimuli of different intensity are presented, and the observer estimates the ratio of the perceived intensities.

method of successive approximations a method of shaping OPERANT BEHAVIOR by reinforcing responses similar to the desired behavior. Initially, responses roughly approximating the desired behavior are reinforced. Later, only responses closely approximating the desired behavior are reinforced. The process gradually leads to the desired behavior. Also called **successive-approximations method**.

methodological behaviorism a form of BEHAVIORISM that concedes the existence and reality of conscious events but contends that the only suitable means of studying them scientifically is via their expression in behavior.

Compare RADICAL BEHAVIORISM. See NEO-BEHAVIORISM.

methodological pluralism the acceptance of the value of using more than one METHODOLOGY in approaching research.

methodology n. **1.** the science of method or orderly arrangement; specifically, the branch of logic concerned with the application of the principles of reasoning to scientific and philosophical inquiry. **2.** the system of methods, principles, and rules of procedure used within a particular discipline.

methylphenidate n. a stimulant related to the AMPHETAMINES and with a similar mechanism of action. It blocks the reuptake of catecholamines from the synaptic cleft and stimulates presynaptic release of catecholamines. Methylphenidate is used for the treatment of attention-deficit/hyperactivity disorder (ADHD) and narcolepsy and as an adjunct to antidepressant therapy and to increase concentration and alertness in patients with brain injuries, brain cancer, or dementia. U.S. trade names (among others): **Concerta**; **Metadate**; **Ritalin**.

methylxanthines pl. n. methylated derivatives of **xanthines** (stimulant plant alkaloids) with similar pharmacological actions. The most common are **caffeine**, the active ingredient in coffee; **theobromine**, the active ingredient in cocoa; and **theophylline**, the active ingredient in tea. At low doses, methylxanthines cause CNS stimulation and arousal; at high doses, anxiety, agitation, and coma may result.

metonymy n. **1.** a figure of speech in which not the literal word but one associated with it is used, as *the sword* for *war*. **Synecdoche** is the form of metonymy in which a whole is represented by a part or vice versa, as in referring to a laborer as a *hand* or a police officer as *the police*. **2.** in speech pathology, a disturbance in which imprecise or inappropriate words and expressions are used. —**metonymic** adj.

Michigan Alcoholism Screening Test (**MAST**) a widely used measure designed to provide a rapid screening for problematic alcohol consumption, alcohol abuse, and alcoholism. It comprises 25 yes–no questions, such as "Do you ever feel guilty about your drinking?" or "Are you able to stop drinking when you want to?"

microcephaly n. a condition in which the head is abnormally small in relation to the rest of the body. Compare MACROCEPHALY. —**microcephalic** adj.

microelectrode n. an electrode with a tip no larger than a few micrometers in diameter, sometimes less than 1 μm, that can be inserted into a single cell. In the **microelectrode technique**, used in studies of neurophysiology and disorders of the nervous system, intracellular microelectrodes with tips less than 1 μm in diameter are able to stimulate and record activity within a single neuron (**single-cell** or **single-unit recording**).

M

microergonomics *n.* an approach to ERGO-NOMICS that focuses on the detailed examination of individual operator–machine interfaces or combinations. Compare MACROERGONOMICS.

microgenetic method a research methodology that looks at developmental change within a single set of individuals over relatively brief periods of time, usually days or weeks.

microglia *n.* an extremely small type of non-neuronal central nervous system cell (GLIA) that removes cellular debris from injured or dead cells. —**microglial** *adj.*

micrographia *n.* a disorder characterized by very small, often unreadable, writing and associated most often with PARKINSON'S DISEASE.

micropolygyria *n.* see LISSENCEPHALY.

micropsia *n.* a VISUAL ILLUSION in which an object appears to be smaller than it is in reality. See also METAMORPHOPSIA. Compare MACROPSIA.

microscopic level an investigative approach that focuses on the smallest recognizable units of analysis. Microscopic psychology is sometimes associated with physiological psychology at the cellular level. See MOLECULAR ANALYSIS.

microsleep *n.* a brief interval of dozing or loss of awareness that occurs during periods when a person is fatigued and trying to stay awake while doing monotonous tasks, such as driving a car, looking at a computer screen, or monitoring controls. Such periods of "nodding off" typically last for 2–30 s and are more likely to occur in the predawn and mid-afternoon hours.

microtome *n.* a device for cutting thin sections (slices) of tissue, used, for example, in preparing brain sections for microscopic examination.

microtubule *n.* a small, hollow, cylindrical structure (typically 20–26 nm in diameter), numbers of which occur in various types of cell. Microtubules are part of the cell's internal scaffolding (cytoskeleton) and form the spindle during cell division. In neurons, microtubules are involved in AXONAL TRANSPORT.

microvillus *n.* (*pl.* **microvilli**) a slender, minute structure projecting from the surface of a cell. For example, in taste perception, a microvillus is the hairlike extension of each TASTE CELL that projects through the pore of a TASTE BUD to sample the environment. Although a microvillus accounts for only 3% of the surface area of a taste cell, it is studded with receptor proteins that recognize specific molecules and is the site of TASTE TRANSDUCTION.

midbrain *n.* a relatively small region of the upper brainstem that connects the FOREBRAIN and HINDBRAIN. It contains the TECTUM (and associated inferior and superior COLLICULI), TEGMENTUM, and SUBSTANTIA NIGRA. Also called **mesencephalon**.

middle class a general socioeconomic class between the working class and the upper class. It is sometimes held to consist of an **upper middle class** of professionals and managers and a **lower middle class** of skilled and semiskilled white-collar workers. Also called **bourgeoisie**. See SOCIAL CLASS; SOCIOECONOMIC STATUS.

middle ear a membrane-lined cavity in the temporal bone of the skull. It is filled with air and communicates with the nasopharynx through the EUSTACHIAN TUBE. It contains the OSSICLES, which transmit sound vibrations from the outer ear and the tympanic membrane (eardrum) to the OVAL WINDOW of the inner ear. Also called **tympanic cavity**.

middle insomnia a period of sleeplessness that occurs after falling asleep normally, with difficulty in falling asleep again. It is a common symptom of a MAJOR DEPRESSIVE DISORDER. Compare INITIAL INSOMNIA; TERMINAL INSOMNIA.

middle knowledge a floating cognitive state in which terminally ill people allow themselves to realize their mortal danger to a greater or lesser degree. Selective attention, denial, resistance, or some other protective strategy tends to be used more or less intensively depending on many factors, including physical condition, security within close relationships, and the ability to integrate the prospect of death into the overall evaluation of one's life.

midlife crisis a period of psychological distress occurring in some individuals during the middle years of adulthood, roughly from ages 35 to 65. Causes may include significant life events and health or occupational problems and concerns.

midpoint *n.* the point or value halfway between the highest and lowest values in a FREQUENCY DISTRIBUTION.

migraine *n.* a headache that is recurrent, usually severe, usually limited to one side of the head, and likely to be accompanied by nausea, vomiting, and PHOTOPHOBIA. Migraine headaches may be preceded by an AURA of flickering or flashing light, blacking out of part of the visual field, or illusions of colors or patterns.

migration *n.* **1.** in animal behavior, travel over relatively long distances to or from breeding areas. Migration is observed in birds, fish, and some mammals and insects (among others). In some species it is seasonal, involving movement from a breeding area to an overwintering area; in others, particularly the salmon, it is observed only once in the lifetime of an individual. **2.** in the development of the nervous system, the movement of nerve cells from their origin in the ventricular zone to establish distinctive cell populations, such as brain nuclei and layers of the cerebral cortex.

MIH abbreviation for MÜLLERIAN-INHIBITING HORMONE.

mild cognitive impairment (**MCI**) a transitional condition between normal healthy aging and early DEMENTIA, characterized by a memory impairment greater than would be expected for age and education. Other cognitive functions are intact, and activities of daily living are normal. Individuals with MCI are at increased risk for developing ALZHEIMER'S DISEASE.

mild depression a MINOR DEPRESSIVE DISORDER or a MAJOR DEPRESSIVE EPISODE with mild or few symptoms.

mild mental retardation a diagnostic and classification category applying to those with IQs of 50 to 69, comprising 80% of people with MENTAL RETARDATION. These individuals usually develop good communication skills and reach a sixth-grade level of academic performance in their late teens, but may not develop beyond the social skill levels typical of adolescents. Usually they are able to learn life and vocational skills adequate for basic self-support and independent living.

milieu *n.* (*pl.* **milieux**) the environment in general or, more typically, the social environment.

milieu therapy psychotherapeutic treatment based on modification or manipulation of the client's life circumstances or immediate environment. Milieu therapy attempts to organize the social and physical setting in which the client lives or is being treated in such a way as to promote healthier, more adaptive cognitions, emotions, and behavior. See also THERAPEUTIC COMMUNITY.

military psychology the application of psychological principles, theories, and methods to the evaluation, selection, assignment, and training of military personnel, as well as to the design of military equipment. This field of applied psychology also includes the application of clinical and counseling techniques to the maintenance of morale and mental health in military settings and covers human functioning in a variety of environments during times of peace and war.

Millon Clinical Multiaxial Inventory (**MCMI**) a true–false questionnaire, consisting of 175 items, that is widely used to assess clinical conditions and personality disorders in psychiatric patients in the United States. It includes 24 scales arranged into four groups: clinical personality patterns, severe personality pathology, clinical syndromes, and severe clinical syndromes. [Theodore **Millon** (1929–), U.S. psychologist]

mimicry *n.* **1.** the presence of physical or behavioral traits in one species that so closely resemble those of another species that they confuse observers. This serves either to evade predators (see BATESIAN MIMICRY; MÜLLERIAN MIMICRY) or to attract prey (see AGGRESSIVE MIMICRY). **2.** a form of SOCIAL LEARNING that involves duplication of a behavior without any understanding of the goal of that behavior.

mind *n.* **1.** most broadly, all intellectual and psychological phenomena of an organism, encompassing motivational, affective, behavioral, perceptual, and cognitive systems; in other words, the organized totality of the MENTAL and PSYCHIC processes of an organism and the struc-

tural and functional cognitive components on which they depend. The term, however, is often used more narrowly to denote only cognitive activities and functions, such as perceiving, attending, thinking, problem solving, language, learning, and memory. The nature of the relationship between the mind and the body, including the brain and its mechanisms or activities, has been, and continues to be, the subject of much debate. See MIND–BODY PROBLEM; PHILOSOPHY OF MIND. **2.** a set of EMERGENT PROPERTIES automatically derived from a brain that has achieved sufficient biological sophistication. In this sense, the mind is considered more the province of humans and of human consciousness than of organisms in general. **3.** human consciousness regarded as an immaterial entity distinct from the brain. See CARTESIAN DUALISM. **4.** the brain itself and its activities: in this view, the mind essentially is both the anatomical organ and what it does. **5.** intention or volition.

mind–body intervention therapeutic approaches that focus on harnessing the power of the mind to bring about change in the body or achieve reduction of symptoms of disease or disorder. The various techniques used include relaxation training (e.g., PROGRESSIVE RELAXATION) and MEDITATION. See also COMPLEMENTARY AND ALTERNATIVE MEDICINE.

mind–body problem the problem of accounting for and describing the relationship between mental and physical processes (psyche and soma). Solutions to this problem fall into six broad categories: (a) **interactionism**, in which mind and body are separate processes that nevertheless exert mutual influence (see CARTESIAN DUALISM); (b) **parallelism**, in which mind and body are separate processes with a point-to-point correspondence but no causal connection (see OCCASIONALISM); (c) IDEALISM, in which only mind exists and the soma is a function of the psyche; (d) DOUBLE-ASPECT THEORY, in which body and mind are both functions of a common entity; (e) epiphenomenalism, in which mind is a by-product of bodily processes; and (f) MATERIALISM, in which body is the only reality and the psyche is nonexistent. Categories (a) and (b) are varieties of DUALISM; the remainder are varieties of MONISM. In the context of psychopathology, two central questions arising from the mind–body problem are which sphere takes precedence in the genesis and development of illness and how does each sphere affect the other. Also called **body–mind problem**.

mind control 1. an extreme form of social influence used to indoctrinate an individual in the attitudes and beliefs of a group, usually one that is religious or political in nature. See BRAINWASHING; COERCIVE PERSUASION. **2.** the control of physical activities of the body, particularly autonomic functions, by mental processes. See BIOFEEDBACK; TRANSCENDENTAL MEDITATION. See also MIND–BODY INTERVENTION.

M

mindfulness *n.* full awareness of one's internal states and surroundings: the opposite of absent-mindedness. The concept has been applied to various therapeutic interventions—for example, mindfulness-based COGNITIVE BEHAVIOR THERAPY, mindfulness-based stress reduction, mindfulness for addictions, and mindfulness MEDITATION—to help people avoid destructive or automatic habits and responses by learning to observe their thoughts, emotions, and other present-moment experiences without judging or reacting to them. —**mindful** *adj.*

mind reading a form of alleged EXTRASENSORY PERCEPTION in which an individual claims to have access to the thoughts in the mind of another person. With THOUGHT TRANSFERENCE it is one of the two main forms of TELEPATHY.

mindsight *n.* a proposed mode of visual perception, hypothesized to work in parallel with everyday vision, in which a person registers a nonvisual sense of change in visual information before conscious awareness of the change through actually "seeing" it. Research on mindsight arises out of work on CHANGE BLINDNESS.

mineralocorticoid *n.* any CORTICOSTEROID hormone that affects ion concentrations in body tissues and helps to regulate the excretion of salt and water. In humans the principal mineralocorticoid is ALDOSTERONE.

minimal brain dysfunction (**MBD**) a relatively mild impairment of brain function that is presumed to account for a variety of SOFT SIGNS seen in certain learning or behavioral disabilities. These signs include hyperactivity, impulsivity, emotional lability, and distractibility.

minimal group a temporary group of anonymous people lacking interdependence, COHESION, structure, and other characteristics typically found in social groups. An example is a group of people disembarking from a bus. Minimal groups are an essential component of a particular research procedure, used mainly in studies of intergroup conflict, called the **minimal intergroup situation** or the **minimal group paradigm**. It has been found that individuals in such groups respond in biased ways when allocating resources to INGROUP and OUTGROUP members, even though the groups are not psychologically or interpersonally meaningful.

minimization *n.* COGNITIVE DISTORTION consisting of a tendency to present events to oneself or others as insignificant or unimportant. Minimization often involves being unclear or nonspecific, so the listener does not have a complete picture of all the details and may be led to draw inaccurate or incomplete conclusions.

minimum power theory an analysis of COALITION formation processes that assumes that (a) all members who control sufficient resources to turn a winning coalition into a losing one or a losing coalition into a winning one are equal in terms of power; and (b) individuals' expectations

concerning the division of the coalition's payoff will conform to an equity norm (see EQUITY THEORY), but one based on power rather than resources. This theory predicts that the most likely coalition to form in a group will be one that wins but comprises the individuals with the smallest amounts of power consistent with this outcome. Compare MINIMUM RESOURCE THEORY.

minimum resource theory an analysis of COALITION formation processes that assumes that (a) people in group situations will behave hedonistically and will thus be motivated to maximize their power, outcomes, and payoffs by forming coalitions; and (b) individuals' expectations concerning the division of the coalition's payoff will conform to an equity norm (see EQUITY THEORY). The minimum resource theory predicts that the most likely coalition to form in a group will be the one that contains those individuals whose total, combined resources are the fewest needed to control the outcome of the entire group. Compare MINIMUM POWER THEORY.

Minnesota Multiphasic Personality Inventory (**MMPI**) a PERSONALITY INVENTORY first published in 1940 and now one of the most widely used SELF-REPORT INVENTORIES for assessing personality and psychological maladjustment across a range of mental health, medical, substance abuse, forensic, and personnel screening settings. It features 567 true–false questions that assess symptoms, attitudes, and beliefs that relate to emotional and behavioral problems.

minor depressive disorder a mood disorder in which symptoms do not meet the criteria for DYSTHYMIC DISORDER and, according to proposed formal diagnostic criteria, occur in an individual who has never had a MAJOR DEPRESSIVE EPISODE. However, in clinical practice, a diagnosis of minor depressive disorder is widely applied to people who have significant symptoms of, but fail to meet the full criteria for, MAJOR DEPRESSIVE DISORDER, regardless of their history of depression.

minority group a population subgroup with social, religious, ethnic, racial, or other characteristics that differ from those of the majority of the population. The term is sometimes extended to cover any group that is the subject of oppression and discrimination, whether or not it literally comprises a minority of the population. See also ETHNIC GROUP; SUBCULTURE.

minority influence social pressure exerted on the majority faction of a group by a smaller faction of the group. Studies suggest that minorities who argue consistently for change prompt the group to reconsider even long-held or previously unquestioned assumptions and procedures.

minor tranquilizers see ANXIOLYTIC.

mirror cell a type of cell in the brains of primates that responds in the same way to a given action (e.g., reaching out to grasp an object) whether it is performed by the primate itself or whether the primate has merely observed another primate perform the same action.

mirroring *n.* **1.** reflecting or emulating speech, affect, behavior, or other qualities in psychotherapeutic contexts. A therapist may adopt the movements, speech style, or locutions of a client, and vice versa, to indicate comprehension of what is being said or to reflect bonding, either unconsciously or with the intent of empathizing. **2.** the positive responses of parents to a child that are intended to instill internal self-respect. **3.** see MIRROR TECHNIQUE.

mirror phase the stage in development occurring around 6–18 months of age when the infant becomes able to imagine himself or herself as an autonomous ego in the image of the parent and also starts to recognize his or her reflection in a mirror. In sum, the child begins to acquire a self-image. French psychoanalyst Jacques Lacan (1901–1981), who introduced the phrase, saw this as marking the start of the infant's transition from the realm of the IMAGINARY to that of the SYMBOLIC.

mirror technique 1. the conscious use of ACTIVE LISTENING by the therapist in psychotherapy, accompanied by reflection of the client's affect and body language in order to stimulate a sense of empathy and to further the development of the THERAPEUTIC ALLIANCE. **2.** in PSYCHODRAMA, a technique in which one group member imitates another group member's behavior patterns to show that person how others perceive and react to him or her. Also called **mirroring**.

misandry *n.* hatred or contempt for men. Compare MISOGYNY. **—misandrist** *n., adj.*

misanthropy *n.* a hatred, aversion, or distrust of human beings and human nature. **—misanthrope** *n.* **—misanthropic** *adj.*

misidentification syndrome a disorder characterized by the delusional failure to correctly identify oneself, other people, places, or objects. The misidentification may be expressed as the mistaken belief that a person has altered his or her identity in some way, either physically or psychologically, or that some place or object has undergone some aspect of transformation. Also called **delusional misidentification syndrome**.

misinformation effect a phenomenon in which a person mistakenly recalls misleading information that an experimenter has provided, instead of accurately recalling the correct information that had been presented earlier. The misinformation effect is studied in the context of EYEWITNESS MEMORY.

misogamy *n.* hatred of or aversion to marriage. **—misogamist** *n.*

misogyny *n.* hatred or contempt for women. Compare MISANDRY. **—misogynist** *n.* **—misogynistic** *adj.*

misorientation effect difficulty recognizing

an object when it appears in an orientation different from that in which it was initially learned. The effect is critical when navigating using visual images or maps that may be presented in different orientations, and usually results in slower recognition and lower accuracy.

miss *n.* in signal detection tasks, an incorrect indication by the participant that a signal is absent in a trial when it is actually present. Compare FALSE ALARM; MISS.

mitochondrion *n.* (*pl.* **mitochondria**) an ORGANELLE that is the main site of energy production in cells. Mitochondria are most numerous in cells with a high level of metabolism. They also have their own DNA (mitochondrial DNA). **—mitochondrial** *adj.*

mitosis *n.* (*pl.* **mitoses**) the type of division of a cell nucleus that produces two identical daughter nuclei, each possessing the same number and type of chromosomes as the parent nucleus. It is usually accompanied by division of the cytoplasm, leading to the formation of two identical daughter cells. Compare MEIOSIS. **—mitotic** *adj.*

Mitwelt *n.* in the thought of German philosopher Martin Heidegger (1889–1976), that aspect of DASEIN (being-in-the-world) that is constituted by a person's relationships and interactions with other people. It was introduced into psychology by Swiss existentialist psychologist Ludwig Binswanger (1881–1966). Compare EIGENWELT; UMWELT. [German, literally: "with world"]

mixed-effects model a statistical procedure for analyzing data from experimental designs that use one or more independent variables whose levels are specifically selected by the researcher (fixed factors; e.g., male and female) and one or more additional independent variables whose levels are chosen randomly from a wide range of possible values (random factors; e.g., age). See also FIXED-EFFECTS MODEL; RANDOM-EFFECTS MODEL.

mixed episode an episode of a MOOD DISORDER lasting at least 1 week in which symptoms meeting criteria for both a MAJOR DEPRESSIVE EPISODE and a MANIC EPISODE are prominent over the course of the disturbance.

mixed-motive game a simulation of social interaction that is structured so that players can reach their goals either by competing against others or by cooperating with others. Players in the PRISONER'S DILEMMA game, for example, will earn greater rewards in the short term if they compete against others, but if all players compete, rewards will be lower overall. See also SOCIAL DILEMMA; SOCIAL TRAP.

mixed receptive-expressive language disorder a communication disorder characterized by levels of language comprehension and production substantially below those expected for intellectual ability and developmental level.

mixed reinforcement schedule a COM-POUND SCHEDULE OF REINFORCEMENT in which two or more schedules alternate. The same stimulus is used for all schedules, therefore no discriminative cues are available (see DISCRIMINATIVE STIMULUS).

mixed schizophrenia a form of schizophrenia in which either both negative and positive symptoms are prominent or neither is prominent.

mixed-standard scale a behavior-based rating procedure used in employee evaluation. Raters are presented with examples of good, average, and bad behaviors for a job and told to evaluate the performance of the employee in terms of whether it is better than, the same as, or poorer than each of the three behaviors. Compare BEHAVIORALLY ANCHORED RATING SCALE. See also CRITICAL-INCIDENT TECHNIQUE.

mixed transcortical aphasia a form of APHASIA resulting from lesions in both the anterior speech areas (**transcortical motor aphasia; TMA**) and the posterior speech areas (**transcortical sensory aphasia; TSA**) of the brain. Individuals have poor word comprehension but relatively preserved word repetition, sometimes to the point of ECHOLALIA. Also called **isolation syndrome**.

MMPI abbreviation for MINNESOTA MULTIPHASIC PERSONALITY INVENTORY.

MMT abbreviation for MULTIMODAL THERAPY.

mnemonic n. any device or technique used to assist memory, usually by forging a link or association between the new information to be remembered and information previously encoded. For instance, one might remember the numbers in a password by associating them with familiar birth dates, addresses, or room numbers. See also METHOD OF LOCI; PEG-WORD MNEMONIC SYSTEM.

mnestic adj. related to memory.

mob n. a disorderly, unruly, and emotionally charged crowd. Early mob psychology argued that individuals in mobs were so overwhelmed by their emotions and the CROWD MIND that they could no longer control their actions. Contemporary studies suggest that members of mobs may respond impulsively but rarely lose cognitive control, that mysterious social or psychological processes do not force them to behave abnormally in such situations, and that mobs tend to be organized and goal-directed rather than irrational and frenzied.

mobbing n. a response to a predator in which a group of animals join together to chase the predator away. Mobbing, which is usually accompanied by loud, distinctive vocalizations, can be observed in many small birds and mammals.

mobility n. the capacity to move or be moved, for example, the ability of an infant to creep, crawl, walk, or otherwise move through space or the extent to which individuals are able to move between localities, occupations, or social classes (see SOCIAL MOBILITY). —**mobile** adj.

mob psychology CROWD PSYCHOLOGY, as applied to mobs.

modal action pattern (**MAP**) the typical or most common behavioral pattern expressed in response to a RELEASER. In classical ethology the term FIXED ACTION PATTERN was used to describe behavioral responses, but this term obscures the variation in behavior typically seen within and between individuals.

modality n. **1.** a particular therapeutic technique or process. **2.** a medium of sensation, such as vision or hearing. See SENSE.

modality effect the tendency for the final items of a list to be better recalled if the items are presented auditorily rather than visually.

modal model of memory a generic theory of memory incorporating assumptions common to most models. The modal model includes a SHORT-TERM MEMORY and a LONG-TERM MEMORY and provides details on how information is encoded and later retrieved from memory.

mode n. the most frequently occurring score in a batch of data, which is sometimes used as a measure of CENTRAL TENDENCY.

model n. **1.** a graphic, theoretical, or other type of representation of a concept (e.g., a disorder) or of basic behavioral or bodily processes that can be used for various investigative and demonstrative purposes, such as enhancing understanding of the concept, proposing hypotheses, showing relationships, or identifying epidemiological patterns. **2.** see MODELING.

modeling n. **1.** a technique used in COGNITIVE BEHAVIOR THERAPY and BEHAVIOR THERAPY in which learning occurs through observation and imitation alone, without comment or reinforcement by the therapist. **2.** in DEVELOPMENTAL PSYCHOLOGY, the process in which one or more individuals or other entities serve as examples (**models**) that a child will emulate. Models are often parents, other adults, or other children, but may also be symbolic, for example, a book or television character. See also SOCIAL LEARNING THEORY.

modeling effect a type of EXPERIMENTER EFFECT in which a participant is unwittingly influenced to give responses similar to the responses the experimenter would give if the experimenter were a participant.

modeling theory the idea that changes in behavior, cognition, or emotional state result from observing someone else's behavior or the consequences of that behavior. See OBSERVATIONAL LEARNING; SOCIAL LEARNING THEORY.

moderate mental retardation a diagnostic and classification category applying to those with IQs of 35 to 49, comprising about 12% of people with MENTAL RETARDATION. These individuals rarely progress beyond the second grade in academic subjects, but can learn to take care of themselves and to develop sufficient social and occupational skills to be able to perform unskilled or semiskilled work under supervision in appropriate work environments.

moderator variable in statistics, a variable that alters the relationship between other variables. In REGRESSION ANALYSIS, for example, it is a variable that is unrelated to a criterion variable but is retained in the REGRESSION EQUATION because of its significant relationship to other predictor variables.

modernism *n.* a philosophical position generally agreed as having its onset in the 17th century in the work of French philosopher René Descartes (1596–1650), with its attempt to establish a systematic account of reality on a radically new basis (see CARTESIANISM; CARTESIAN DUALISM). The defining characteristics of modernism include a sense that religious dogma and classical metaphysics can no longer provide a sure foundation in intellectual matters and a quest for certain knowledge from other sources; the latter is sustained by confidence in absolutes in EPISTEMOLOGY and ETHICS and confidence in the new methods of EXPERIMENTAL PHILOSOPHY, or natural science. Traditional psychology can be seen to be the product of modernism to the extent that it is characterized by faith in scientific method, pursuit of control and prediction of behavior, explanation in terms of laws and principles, and the assumption that human behavior is ultimately rational as opposed to irrational. Some thinkers argue that modernism was superseded by POSTMODERNISM in the late 20th century, although others would dispute such a claim. **—modernist** *adj., n.*

modernization *n.* the complex set of processes by which a largely rural and traditional society becomes a developed industrial society. Modernization is often contrasted with the TRADITIONALISM of undeveloped or underdeveloped societies, which are often identified as religious and rural, with limited technology, low social mobility, weak political structures, and so forth. Conceptualizations of this dichotomy are currently in debate, however, pointing to the highly variable social and psychological adjustments that occur in different societies as they respond to development. **—modernize** *vb.*

modern racism a contemporary form of PREJUDICE against members of other racial groups that is expressed indirectly and covertly, typically by condemning the cultural values of the OUTGROUP or by experiencing aversive emotions when interacting with its members but not acting on those negative emotions (see AVERSIVE RACISM). Changed social attitudes have brought about a decline in the direct expression of racial discrimination and hostility toward minority groups (**old-fashioned racism**), with a corresponding increase in the less blatant modern racism.

MODE theory Motivation and Opportunity as *De*terminants theory: a theory of attitude–behavior consistency postulating that the process by which attitudes influence behavior differs according to the amount of deliberation involved. When people are motivated and able to deliberate about their actions, attitudes influence behavior in a manner similar to that postulated by the THEORY OF REASONED ACTION. When people are not motivated or able to deliberate, attitudes toward the target of the behavior can be activated in memory and affect the way the target is perceived. These perceptions in turn influence how people define the behavioral event, which in turn determines behavior.

modularity *n.* a theory of the human mind in which the various components of cognition are characterized as independent MODULES, each with its own specific domain and particular properties. An earlier, related notion, the TASK SPECIFICITY OF LANGUAGE, characterized the human language faculty as a unique "mental organ" differing qualitatively from other aspects of cognition. More recently, evolutionary psychologists have shown interest in the idea that the various modules may be adaptive specializations. Compare COGNITIVE GRAMMAR.

modulation *n.* changes in some parameter of a waveform so that the information contained by the variations of this parameter can be transmitted by the wave, which is known as the **carrier wave**. **Amplitude modulation** (AM) refers to changes in amplitude that are relatively slow compared to the usually sinusoidal variations in the carrier. In **frequency modulation** (FM) the frequency of the carrier is varied but its amplitude remains constant. In **phase modulation** the relative phase of the carrier wave is varied in accordance with the amplitude of the signal variations.

modulatory site a site on a RECEPTOR molecule that, when bound by a ligand (e.g., a drug), alters the receptor's response on binding of its agonist (e.g., a neurotransmitter) to the usual site.

module *n.* **1.** in cognitive theory, a hypothetical center of information processing that is presumed to be relatively independent and highly specialized in its operations, such as a language module or face-processing module. **2.** in neuroscience, a unit of a region of the central nervous system. For example, regions of the NEOCORTEX in the brain are divided into CORTICAL COLUMNS of basically similar structure. **—modular** *adj.*

molar analysis the analysis of behavioral processes as holistic units, extended through time. Molar analyses consider overall relations between measures, such as average response rates to rates of reinforcement (e.g., food), of a large number of responses spread across a period of time. Also called **global analysis**. Compare MOLECULAR ANALYSIS.

molecular analysis the analysis of behavioral processes that breaks them down into their component parts and examines them on a moment-by-moment basis and at the level of individual response-reinforcement sequences. Compare MOLAR ANALYSIS.

molestation *n.* the act of making sexual advances toward a person who does not want them. Molestation generally implies sexual fondling or touching an individual without his or her consent. See also SEX OFFENSE. —**molest** *vb.*

Molyneux's question the question posed by William Molyneux (1656–1698), a member of the Irish parliament, to English philosopher John Locke (1632–1704), who later discussed it in his *Essay Concerning Human Understanding* (1690). Molyneux's question was whether a man born blind but able to distinguish two distinct shapes by feeling them with his hands would be able to distinguish them by sight alone, without also touching them, if he were suddenly able to see. Locke's answer—and Molyneux's as well—was that the person would not be able to distinguish them by sight immediately because the sense modalities act independently and can be integrated only by experience.

moment *n.* the power to which the expected value of a RANDOM VARIABLE is raised. Thus, $E(x^k)$ is the *k*th moment of *x*. Moments are used for computing distribution measures, such as the MEAN, VARIANCE, SKEWNESS, and KURTOSIS.

monad *n.* in the thought of German philosopher Gottfried Wilhelm Leibniz (1646–1716), one of the ultimate indivisible units of existence. Monads are independent of one another and innately have the power of action and direction toward some end. Although no monad in reality acts on any other, they work in a divinely "preestablished harmony" so that an appearance of causal connection is maintained. The concept of the monad was intended, in part, to address the MIND–BODY PROBLEM arising from CARTESIAN DUALISM.

monaural *adj.* relating to or perceived by one ear only. Compare BINAURAL.

monism *n.* the position that reality consists of a single SUBSTANCE, whether this is identified as mind, matter, or God. In the context of the MIND–BODY PROBLEM, monism is any position that avoids DUALISM. —**monist** *adj., n.* —**monistic** *adj.*

monoamine *n.* an AMINE that contains only one amine group, $-NH_2$. Monoamines include neurotransmitters, such as the CATECHOLAMINES norepinephrine and dopamine and the INDOLEAMINE serotonin.

monoamine hypothesis the theory that depression is caused by a deficit in the production or uptake of monoamines (serotonin, norepinephrine, and dopamine). This theory has been used to explain the effects of MONOAMINE OXIDASE INHIBITORS, but is now regarded as too simplistic.

monoamine oxidase inhibitor (**MAOI**; **MAO inhibitor**) any of a group of antidepres-

sant drugs that function by inhibiting the activity of the enzyme **monoamine oxidase** in presynaptic neurons, thereby increasing the amounts of monoamine neurotransmitters (serotonin, norepinephrine, and dopamine) available for release at the presynaptic terminal. There are two categories of MAOIs: irreversible and reversible inhibitors. **Irreversible MAOIs** bind tightly to the enzyme and permanently inhibit its ability to metabolize any monoamine. This may lead to dangerous interactions with foods and beverages containing the amino acid tryptophan or the amine tyramine, which are present in many foods. **Reversible inhibitors of monoamine oxidase** (RIMAs) do not bind irreversibly to the enzyme, thereby freeing it to take part in the metabolism of amino acids and other amines. The availability of other effective antidepressants lacking the drug–food interactions of the MAOIs has led to a precipitous decline in their use, particularly of the irreversible agents.

monochromatism *n.* a partial color blindness in which the eye contains only one type of cone PHOTOPIGMENT instead of the typical three: Everything appears in various shades of a single color. Also called **monochromacy**; **monochromasy**; **monochromatopsia**. See also ACHROMATISM; DICHROMATISM; TRICHROMATISM.

monocular *adj.* referring to one eye. For example, a **monocular cue** is a cue to the perception of distance or depth that involves only one eye, such as LINEAR PERSPECTIVE, relative position, relative movement, and ACCOMMODATION. Also called **uniocular**. Compare BINOCULAR.

monocular cell see BINOCULAR CELL.

monocular rearing an experimental paradigm in which an animal is raised from birth with vision restricted to one eye by suturing the eyelids closed or by inserting an opaque contact lens in one eye. Monocular rearing during the CRITICAL PERIOD has profound structural and functional consequences for the developing visual system, including a shift in the OCULAR DOMINANCE of cortical neurons to favor the nonoccluded eye and a broadening of the OCULAR DOMINANCE COLUMNS corresponding to the open eye.

monogamy *n.* **1.** a MATING SYSTEM in which two individuals mate exclusively with each other. Many species display **serial monogamy**, in which there is an exclusive social bond with each of a series of sexual partners at different times during the individual's life. Compare POLYANDRY; POLYGYNY. **2.** traditionally, marriage to only one spouse at a time. Compare POLYGAMY. —**monogamous** *adj.*

monomania *n.* **1.** extreme enthusiasm or zeal for a single subject or idea, often manifested as a rigid, irrational idea. See also IDÉE FIXE. **2.** an obsolete name for a pattern of abnormal behavior with reference to a single subject in an otherwise apparently normally functioning individual. **—monomaniac** *n.*

monomorphism *adj.* describing or relating to a species in which both sexes are similar in body size, coloration, or other features.

monophagism *n.* a pathological eating behavior in which the individual habitually eats only one type of food or only one meal a day.

monophasic sleep a sleep pattern in which sleeping occurs in one long period once a day, typically at night. Both it and biphasic sleep (see POLYPHASIC SLEEP) contribute to physical and emotional health and greater alertness. See also SLEEP–WAKE CYCLE.

monosomy *n.* see AUTOSOME. **—monosomic** *adj.*

monosymptomatic *adj.* denoting a disorder that is characterized by a single marked symptom.

monosynaptic arc a simple NEURAL ARC that involves just two neurons with a synapse between them. Compare POLYSYNAPTIC ARC.

monotic *adj.* denoting or relating to the presentation of sound to one ear only. Compare DICHOTIC; DIOTIC.

monotonic *adj.* denoting a variable that progressively either increases or decreases as a second variable increases or decreases but that does not change its direction. For example, a monotonically increasing variable is one that rises as a second variable increases.

monozygotic twins (MZ twins) twins, always of the same sex, that develop from a single fertilized ovum (zygote) that splits in the early stages of MITOSIS to produce two individuals who carry exactly the same complement of genes; that is, they are clones, with identical DNA. Also called **identical twins**. Compare DIZYGOTIC TWINS.

Montessori method an educational system that focuses on the development of young children's initiative and emphasizes self-directed learning. The method is characterized by multi-age classrooms, a special set of educational materials, student-chosen work in long time blocks, collaboration, the absence of grades and tests, and individual and small group instruction in both academic and social skills. [Maria **Montessori** (1870–1952), Italian educational reformer]

mood *n.* **1.** any short-lived emotional state, usually of low intensity (e.g., a cheerful mood, an irritable mood). **2.** a disposition to respond emotionally in a particular way that may last for hours, days, or even weeks, perhaps at a low level and without the person knowing what prompted the state. Moods differ from EMOTIONS in lacking an object; for example, the emotion of anger can be aroused by an insult, but an angry mood may arise when one does not know what one is angry about or what elicited the anger. Disturbances in mood are characteristic of MOOD DISORDERS.

mood-as-information theory a theory of affect and information processing postulating that a person often uses his or her current emotional state or mood as a piece of information when making social judgments. The theory also proposes that current affective states can influence the processing strategy (careful and deliberative or less effortful) that people adopt when making decisions.

mood-as-resource model a theory stating that positive moods are useful to individuals, making them better able to process goal-related information, better at coping with negative stimuli, and more flexible and constructive in dealing with situational demands.

mood-dependent memory a condition in which memory for some event can be recalled more readily when one is in the same emotional mood (e.g., happy or sad) as when the memory was initially formed. See also STATE-DEPENDENT MEMORY.

mood disorder a psychiatric disorder in which the principal feature is a prolonged, pervasive mood disturbance, such as a DEPRESSIVE DISORDER (e.g., MAJOR DEPRESSIVE DISORDER, DYSTHYMIC DISORDER) or BIPOLAR DISORDER. A mood disorder is less commonly called an **affective disorder**.

mood induction any method for producing a negative or positive change in mood, often by selectively reminding individuals of pleasant or unpleasant aspects of their lives.

moodiness *n.* an affective state characterized by irritability or DYSPHORIA combined with sensitivity to negative interpersonal cues. **—moody** *adj.*

mood stabilizer any of various drugs used in the treatment of cyclic mood disorders (BIPOLAR DISORDERS and CYCLOTHYMIC DISORDER). Because they reduce the symptoms of mania or manic episodes, mood stabilizers are sometimes known as **antimanics**. LITHIUM is usually the FIRST-LINE MEDICATION for bipolar I disorder, but ANTICONVULSANTS, such as VALPROIC ACID, CARBAMAZEPINE, and oxcarbazine, are becoming more commonly used for this condition and are now preferred for other cyclic disorders.

moon illusion see SIZE–DISTANCE PARADOX.

moral *adj.* relating to the distinction between right and wrong or to behavior that is considered ethical or proper.

moral absolutism the belief that the morality or immorality of an action can be judged according to fixed standards of right and wrong. According to Swiss psychologist Jean Piaget (1896–1980), moral absolutism is characteristic of young children in the HETERONOMOUS STAGE of moral development, who interpret laws and rules as absolute. See MORAL REALISM. Compare MORAL RELATIVISM; SITUATION ETHICS.

moral development the gradual formation of an individual's concepts of right and wrong, conscience, ethical and religious values, social attitudes, and behavior. Some of the major theorists in the area of moral development are Austrian psychiatrist Sigmund Freud (1856–1939), Swiss psychologist Jean Piaget (1896–1980), German-born U.S. psychologist Erik Erikson (1902–1994), and U.S. psychologist Lawrence Kohlberg (1927–1987).

morality *n.* a system of beliefs or set of values relating to right conduct, against which behavior is judged to be acceptable or unacceptable.

moral masochism in psychoanalytic theory, the unconscious need for punishment by authority figures caused by unconscious guilt arising from the repressed OEDIPUS COMPLEX. It is a nonsexual form of MASOCHISM.

moral realism the type of thinking characteristic of younger children, who equate good behavior with obedience just as they equate the morality of an act only with its consequences. For example, 15 cups broken accidentally would be judged to be a far worse transgression than 1 cup broken mischievously, because more cups are broken. Moral realism shapes the child's thinking until the age of about 8, when the concepts of intention, motive, and extenuating circumstances begin to modify the child's early MORAL ABSOLUTISM. Compare MORAL RELATIVISM.

moral relativism the belief that the morality or immorality of an action is determined by social custom rather than by universal or fixed standards of right and wrong. According to Swiss psychologist Jean Piaget (1896–1980), moral relativism is characteristic of children in the AUTONOMOUS STAGE of moral development, who consider the intention behind an act along with possible extenuating circumstances when judging its rightness or wrongness. Compare MORAL ABSOLUTISM; MORAL REALISM; SITUATION ETHICS.

moratorium *n.* in ERIKSON'S EIGHT STAGES OF DEVELOPMENT, the experimental period of adolescence in which, during the task of discovering who one is as an individual separate from family of origin and as part of the broader social context, young people try out alternative roles before making permanent commitments to an IDENTITY. Adolescents who are unsuccessful at negotiating this stage risk confusion over their role in life. See also IDENTITY VERSUS ROLE CONFUSION.

morbid *adj.* **1.** unhealthy or diseased. **2.** in psychology, abnormal or deviating from the norm.

morbidity *n.* a pathological (diseased) condition or state, either organic or functional.

morbidity risk in EPIDEMIOLOGY, the statistical chance that an individual will develop a certain disease or disorder. The probability is often expressed in terms of risk factors, using 1.0 as a base: The larger the number, the greater the morbidity risk.

morbid obesity excess body weight that causes disease. People who are obese gradually develop HYPOXEMIA (decreased blood oxygen) and SLEEP APNEA (periodic cessation of breathing while asleep), which may result in chronic fatigue and SOMNOLENCE and, eventually, high blood pressure, pulmonary hypertension, myocarditis, right-sided heart failure, and ultimately death.

mores *pl. n.* social customs and usages that are accepted by members of a culture or population.

Morgan's canon see LLOYD MORGAN'S CANON.

Morita therapy a therapy for SHINKEISHITSU consisting of an initial 7-day period of strict and isolated bed rest followed by step-by-step OCCUPATIONAL THERAPY and final reintegration into job and family. A central concept is the attainment of **arugamama**, an attitude of acceptance toward one's self and one's feelings. [Shoma **Morita** (1874–1938), Japanese psychiatrist]

morpheme *n.* in linguistic analysis, a unit of meaning that cannot be analyzed into smaller such units. For example, the word *books* is composed of two morphemes, *book* and the suffix *-s* signifying a plural noun. —**morphemic** *adj.*

morphine *n.* the primary active ingredient in OPIUM, first synthesized in 1806 and widely used as an analgesic and sedative, especially in terminally ill cancer patients (see OPIATE; OPIOID ANALGESIC). Prolonged administration or abuse can lead to dependence and to withdrawal symptoms on cessation.

morphogenesis *n.* the development of the form and structure of an organism. —**morphogenetic** or **morphogenic** *adj.*

morphology *n.* **1.** the branch of biology concerned with the forms and structures of organisms. **2.** the branch of linguistics that investigates the form and structure of words. It is particularly concerned with the regular patterns of word formation in a language. With SYNTAX, morphology is one of the two traditional divisions of GRAMMAR. —**morphological** *adj.*

Morris water maze a device used to test animal spatial learning, consisting of a water-filled tank with a platform hidden underwater. An animal is placed in the water and can escape only by finding and climbing on the hidden platform. Typically a variety of external cues are provided for spatial reference. [devised in 1981 by Richard G. M. **Morris**, British neuroscientist]

mortality salience the cognitive accessibility of thoughts about the inevitability of one's death. Such thoughts are believed by some theorists to be a motivating force behind a diverse set of actions designed to defend oneself or one's social group.

mortido *n.* in psychoanalytic theory, the energy of the DEATH INSTINCT and counterpart to the LIBIDO. See also DESTRUDO.

morula *n.* an early stage of embryological development, extending from the first cleavage of the zygote until the BLASTOCYST is formed by further divisions of daughter cells.

mosaicism *n.* a condition of genetic abnormality in which an individual is made up of two or more different cell lines derived from a single zygote. In a typical case, a mosaic individual will have some cells with the usual number of chromosomes and others with an extra chromosome.

mother archetype in ANALYTIC PSYCHOLOGY, the primordial image of the generative and sustaining mother figure that has occurred repeatedly in various cultural concepts and myths since ancient times and is located within the COLLECTIVE UNCONSCIOUS. See also ARCHETYPE; MAGNA MATER.

motherese *n.* the distinctive form of speech used by parents and other caregivers when speaking to infants and young children. It is characterized by grammatically simple and phonologically clear utterances, often delivered in a high-pitched sing-song intonation.

mother figure 1. a person who occupies the mothering role in relation to a child: a MOTHER SURROGATE. **2.** in psychoanalytic theory, a person onto whom the patient transfers feelings and attitudes that he or she had toward the real mother. Also called **mother substitute**.

mother surrogate a substitute for an individual's biological mother (e.g., a sister, grandmother, stepmother, or adoptive mother), who assumes the responsibilities of that person and may function as a role model and significant attachment figure. Also called **mother figure**; **surrogate mother**.

motility *n.* the capacity for spontaneous, independent movement. —**motile** *adj.*

motion aftereffect the perception that a stationary object or scene moves following prolonged fixation of a moving stimulus. The illusory movement is in the opposite direction to the movement of the stimulus that induced the effect. The best known example is the **waterfall illusion**, produced by watching a waterfall for a period and then shifting one's gaze to the stationary surrounding scenery; the stationary objects appear to move upward.

motion economy a set of principles for the efficient performance of vocational tasks. Its recommendations, such as use of continuous, curved movements rather than straight-line motions and arrangement of work to avoid long reaches, are intended to eliminate unnecessary work and permit an easy, natural rhythm that uses the fewest movements possible.

motivated forgetting a memory lapse motivated by a desire to avoid a disagreeable recollection. It is one of the cognitive mechanisms that has been suggested as a cause of delayed memories of childhood trauma.

motivation *n.* **1.** the impetus that gives purpose or direction to human or animal behavior and operates at a conscious or unconscious level. Motives are frequently divided into (a) physiological, primary, or organic motives, such as hunger, thirst, and need for sleep, and (b) personal, social, or secondary motives, such as affiliation, competition, and individual interests and goals. An important distinction must also be drawn between internal motivating forces and external factors, such as rewards or punishments, that can encourage or discourage certain behaviors. See EXTRINSIC MOTIVATION; INTRINSIC MOTIVATION. **2.** a person's willingness to exert physical or mental effort in pursuit of a goal or outcome, as for example in WORK MOTIVATION. The ability to encourage followers to exert themselves in pursuit of a group or organizational goal is an important function of LEADERSHIP. —**motivate** *vb.* —**motivated** *adj.* —**motivational** *adj.*

motivational enhancement therapy a transtheoretical treatment, based on the STAGES OF CHANGE, that matches clients to interventions on the basis of individual differences in readiness to change. This treatment was initially applied to substance abuse but has now generalized to other problem behaviors.

motivational hierarchy see MASLOW'S MOTIVATIONAL HIERARCHY.

motivators *pl. n.* in the two-factor theory of WORK MOTIVATION, those aspects of the working situation that can increase satisfaction and motivation. Motivators involve the work itself rather than the work context and are increased by means of job ENRICHMENT and expansion of responsibilities. Compare HYGIENE FACTORS.

motor *adj.* involving, producing, or referring to muscular movements.

motor aphasia another name for BROCA'S APHASIA.

motor cortex the region of the frontal lobe of the brain responsible for the control of voluntary movement. It is divided into two parts. The **primary motor cortex**, or **motor area**, is the main source of neurons in the corticospinal tract (see VENTROMEDIAL PATHWAYS). The **secondary** (or **nonprimary**) **motor cortex**, made up of the PREMOTOR AREA and the SUPPLEMENTARY MOTOR AREA, is specialized for planning upcoming movements and learning new movements. Lesions in the primary motor cortex due to stroke or traumatic injury usually cause initial paralysis that may improve to a condition involving weakness and poor muscle tone. Lesions in the secondary motor cortex usually cause complex disruptions in motor planning for complex movements (see APRAXIA). Also called **motor strip**.

motor equivalence the ability to use different movements, produced by either the same or different parts of the body, to perform a task under different conditions. For example, the task of writing one's name may be performed (a) on paper, with a pen held in the hand, by moving the fingers and wrist; (b) on a blackboard, with

M

chalk held in the hand, by moving the arm; or (c) in the sand, using a toe, by moving the leg.

motor evoked potential a type of EVOKED POTENTIAL associated with motor neurons and motor cortex. For example, activity in spinal motor neurons may be studied by directly stimulating motor areas in the brain (see TRANSCRANIAL MAGNETIC STIMULATION) and observing the evoked potential in the spinal cord. Compare SENSORY EVOKED POTENTIAL.

motor homunculus a figurative representation, in distorted human form, of the SOMATOTOPIC ORGANIZATION of the MOTOR CORTEX. Within this mapping, the size of the brain region associated with a body part reflects the complexity of the activities carried out with that part of the body rather than its size. Compare SENSORY HOMUNCULUS.

motor impersistence a neurologically based inability to sustain a simple act or posture, such as keeping the mouth open or turning the head, for longer than a few seconds.

motor learning the process of acquiring and perfecting motor skills and movements, either simple acts or complex sequences of movements, which comes about through varying types of practice, experience, or other situations.

motor memory knowledge of motor skills: the capacity to remember previously executed movements, such as the steps of a dance or the actions involved in tying one's shoes.

motor neglect underutilization of or failure to use motor functions on one side of the body despite the presence of normal strength, reflexes, and sensibility. It results from damage to various cerebral structures, including the thalamus and frontal and parietal lobes.

motor nerve any nerve that terminates in a muscle or gland, conveying impulses from the brain or spinal cord.

motor neuron a neuron whose axon connects directly to muscle fibers. Because motor neurons are the final stage of output from the nervous system and are the only means of stimulating muscle fibers, they are known as the **final common path**. There are two types: **lower motor neurons** (or **alpha motor neurons**), found in the cranial nerves and the ANTERIOR HORN of the spinal cord and which are responsible for muscle contraction; and **upper motor neurons** (or **gamma motor neurons**), found in the corticospinal tract (see VENTROMEDIAL PATHWAYS) and which modulate the sensitivity of MUSCLE SPINDLES, thus influencing activity of the lower motor neurons. Also called **motoneuron**.

motor neuron disease any one of a group of degenerative disorders of the lower MOTOR NEURONS or both the lower and upper motor neurons, marked by progressive weakness and wasting of skeletal muscles and paralysis. This group of disorders includes several forms, but—

especially in the United States—the term often is applied specifically to AMYOTROPHIC LATERAL SCLEROSIS.

motor overflow a condition in which intentional motor behavior in one muscle group is accompanied by unintentional movement in another muscle group as a result of neurological dysfunction. For instance, while performing a fine motor task with the right hand, the left hand may move as well.

motor pathway a NEURAL PATHWAY that originates in the brain or brainstem and descends down the spinal cord to control the motor neurons. The motor pathways can control posture, reflexes, and muscle tone, as well as the conscious voluntary movements associated with the MOTOR SYSTEM.

motor program a stored representation, resulting from motor planning and refined through practice, that is used to produce a coordinated movement. Motor programs store the accumulated experience underlying skill at a task.

motor set see SET.

motor speech disorder any of several communication disorders arising from inaccurate production of speech sounds because of lack of strength or coordination of the muscles involved in speaking.

motor strip see MOTOR CORTEX.

motor system the complex of skeletal muscles, neural connections with muscle tissues, and structures of the central nervous system associated with motor functions. Also called **neuromuscular system**.

motor theory of speech perception the view that speech perception relies on the processes that are used in speech production, such that listeners interpret a spoken message by unconsciously computing what motor operations would be required to produce that sequence of sounds. The theory was advanced as an explanation of CATEGORICAL PERCEPTION in the processing of speech sounds.

motor tract any bundle of nerve fibers that convey signals from the higher centers of the brain to the spinal cord.

motor unit a group of muscle fibers that respond collectively and simultaneously because they are connected by nerve endings to a single motor neuron.

mourning *n.* the process of feeling or expressing grief following the death of a loved one, or the period during which this occurs. It typically involves feelings of apathy and dejection, loss of interest in the outside world, and diminution in activity and initiative. These reactions are similar to depression, but are less persistent and are not considered pathological. See also BEREAVEMENT.

movement disorder any abnormality in motor processes, relating primarily to posture, coordination, or locomotion. **Medication-**

induced movement disorders, such as TARDIVE DYSKINESIA, occur as an adverse effect of medication and are particularly common with antipsychotic drugs.

movement therapy a therapeutic technique in which individuals use rhythmic exercises and bodily movements to achieve greater body awareness and social interaction and enhance their psychological and physical functioning. See also DANCE THERAPY.

moving-edge detector any of the cells in the visual system that respond best to a dark–light border moved through the receptive field. A particular speed and direction of movement may be required to elicit the optimum response from a moving-edge detector. See also FEATURE DETECTOR.

MR abbreviation for MENTAL RETARDATION.

MRI abbreviation for MAGNETIC RESONANCE IMAGING.

MS abbreviation for MULTIPLE SCLEROSIS.

MSE abbreviation for MENTAL STATUS EXAMINATION.

MSH abbreviation for MELANOCYTE-STIMULATING HORMONE.

MSP abbreviation for MUNCHAUSEN SYNDROME BY PROXY.

mucopolysaccharidosis (MPS) *n.* any of various metabolic disorders, classified into six groups (I–VI), that are marked by excess mucopolysaccharide—glycosaminoglycan (GAG), a complex carbohydrate—in the tissues. Certain forms of the disease are associated with mental retardation, such as **Hunter's syndrome, Hurler's syndrome**, and **Sanfilippo's syndrome**.

Müller fibers elongated glial cells that traverse and support all the layers of the retina. Also called **Müller cells**. [Heinrich **Müller** (1820–1864), German anatomist]

Müllerian ducts paired ducts that occur in a mammalian embryo and develop into female reproductive structures (fallopian tubes, uterus, and upper vagina) if testes are not present in the embryo. Compare WOLFFIAN DUCT. [Johannes **Müller** (1801–1858), German anatomist]

Müllerian-inhibiting hormone (MIH) a hormone produced by the testes early in prenatal development that inhibits feminization of the fetus by preventing the Müllerian ducts from differentiating into the female sex organs. Also called **anti-Müllerian hormone (AMH)**; **Müllerian-inhibiting substance (MIS)**; **Müllerian regression hormone (MRH)**.

Müllerian mimicry a form of MIMICRY in which two or more species, each of which is toxic or potentially harmful, have similar body shape or coloration. For predators, a single experience with a member of one of these species can lead to learned avoidance of all similar-looking animals, conferring protection on all the mi-

metic species. [Johann Friedrich Theodor **Müller** (1822–1897), German zoologist]

Müller-Lyer illusion a GEOMETRIC ILLUSION in which a difference is perceived in the length of a line depending upon whether arrowheads at either end are pointing toward each other or away from each other. [first described in 1889 by Franz **Müller-Lyer** (1857–1916), German psychiatrist]

Müller–Urban method a psychophysical procedure for estimating the DIFFERENCE THRESHOLD for data obtained using the METHOD OF CONSTANT STIMULI. It is based on the assumption that the best measure of the threshold is the median of the best fitting ogive (S-shaped function) for the distribution. [Georg Elias **Müller** (1850–1934), German experimental psychologist and philosopher; Frank M. **Urban**, 20th-century U.S. psychologist]

multiaxial classification a system of classifying mental disorders according to several categories of factors, for example, social and cultural influences, as well as clinical symptoms. DSM–IV–TR uses multiaxial classification, which takes account of the many factors involved in the etiology of these disorders and enables a more comprehensive clinical assessment to be made. See AXIS.

multicollinearity *n.* in MULTIPLE REGRESSION, a state that occurs when the INDEPENDENT (PREDICTOR) VARIABLES are extremely highly interrelated, making it difficult to determine separate effects on the DEPENDENT VARIABLE.

multicultural counseling 1. psychotherapies that take into account not only the increasing racial and ethnic diversity of clients in many countries but also diversity in spirituality, sexual orientation, ability and disability, and social class and economics; the potential cultural bias (e.g., racism, sexism) of the practitioner; the history of oppressed and marginalized groups; diversity within diversity; acculturation and issues involving living in two worlds; and the politics of power as they affect clients. Also called **cross-cultural counseling**; **multicultural therapy**. Compare TRANSCULTURAL PSYCHOTHERAPY. **2.** any form of therapy that assesses, understands, and evaluates a client's behavior in the multiplicity of cultural contexts (e.g., ethnic, national, demographic, social, and economic) in which that behavior was learned and is displayed.

multicultural education a progressive approach to education that emphasizes social justice, equality in education, and understanding and awareness of the traditions and language of other cultures and nationalities. Multicultural programs involve two or more ethnic or cultural groups and are designed to help participants define their own ethnic or cultural identity and to appreciate that of others. The purpose is to promote inclusiveness and cultural pluralism in society.

multiculturalism *n.* **1.** the quality or condition of a society in which different ethnic and cultural groups have equal status but each maintains its own identity, characteristics, and mores. **2.** the promotion or celebration of cultural diversity within a society. Also called **cultural pluralism**. Compare CULTURAL MONISM. —**multicultural** *adj.*

multicultural therapy see MULTICULTURAL COUNSELING.

multidimensional *adj.* **1.** describing any form of analysis in which factors or variables are represented on more than one dimension. **2.** of scales or measures, having a number of different dimensions. **3.** having many aspects that may engender many points of view. **4.** complex. Compare UNIDIMENSIONAL.

multidimensional scaling a scaling method that represents perceived similarities among stimuli by arranging similar stimuli in spatial proximity to one another, while disparate stimuli are represented far apart from one another. Multidimensional scaling is an alternative to FACTOR ANALYSIS for dealing with large multidimensional matrices of data or stimuli.

multidisciplinary approach see INTERDISCIPLINARY APPROACH.

multifactorial inheritance inheritance of a trait, such as height or predisposition to a certain disease, that is determined not by a single gene but by many different genes acting cumulatively. Such traits show continuous, rather than discrete, variation among the members of a given population and are often significantly influenced by environmental factors, such as nutritional status.

multi-infarct dementia see VASCULAR DEMENTIA.

multilingualism *n.* the sociolinguistic situation in which several languages are used within the same community, usually resulting from geographical, economic, or militaristic interactions. Typically, the various languages serve different social functions and have different status. See DIGLOSSIA.

multimodal therapy (**MMT**) a form of psychotherapy in which the therapist assesses the client's significant *Behaviors, Affective* responses, *Sensations, Imagery, Cognitions, Interpersonal* relationships, and the need for *Drugs* and other biological interventions. The first letters yield the acronym **BASIC ID**, which summarizes the seven basic interactive modalities of the approach. MMT posits that these modalities exist in a state of reciprocal transaction and flux, connected by complex chains of behavior and other psychophysiological processes. The therapist, usually in concert with the client, determines which specific problems across the BASIC ID are most salient. MMT uses an eclectic approach drawing mainly from a broad-based social and cognitive learning theory. Also called **multimodal behavior therapy**.

multimodal treatment a manner of treating a disease, disorder, or syndrome by simultaneously applying several different methods, often from different disciplines or traditions.

multinomial distribution a theoretical probability distribution that describes the distribution of *n* objects sampled at random from a population of *k* kinds of things with regard to the number of each of the kinds that appears in the sample.

multiple baseline design a type of SINGLE-CASE EXPERIMENTAL DESIGN in which two or more behaviors are assessed before and after an experimental manipulation.

multiple classification the ability to classify items in terms of more than one dimension simultaneously, such as shape and color. According to PIAGETIAN THEORY, this ability is not achieved until the CONCRETE OPERATIONAL STAGE.

multiple comparisons a set of comparisons (differences) among the means of samples from *k* populations that are generally tested in a post hoc manner in order to keep the TYPE I ERROR rate controlled at a prespecified level.

multiple correlation (symbol: *R*) a numerical index of the degree of relationship between a particular variable (e.g., a dependent variable) and two or more other variables (e.g., independent variables).

multiple drafts hypothesis the theory that conscious perception occurs not in a specific location in the brain, but rather through many copies (drafts) of sensory input that are widely distributed over the sensory cortex.

multiple family therapy a form of GROUP PSYCHOTHERAPY in which a group of two or more family members meets with two or more therapists at once. See also FAMILY THERAPY; COTHERAPY.

multiple-intelligences theory the idea that intelligence is made up of eight distinct categories: linguistic, musical, bodily-kinesthetic, logical-mathematical, spatial, naturalist, intrapersonal, and interpersonal.

multiple marital therapy a form of therapy in which each marital partner is treated independently by individual therapists. The two therapists may meet privately to discuss their clients, and sessions involving all four parties or a combination of the parties may be held. See also CONJOINT THERAPY.

multiple mating a strategy used by females to prevent CERTAINTY OF PATERNITY in males and as a MATE-SELECTION mechanism. A female mammal might mate with most males in its group, thus giving each male a potential stake in helping to protect the female and its young.

multiple regression a statistical technique for examining the linear relationship between a continuous DEPENDENT VARIABLE and a set of two or more INDEPENDENT VARIABLES. It is often used to predict the score of individuals on a criterion variable from multiple predictor variables.

multiple reinforcement schedule a COMPOUND SCHEDULE OF REINFORCEMENT in which two or more schedules alternate and each schedule is associated with a different stimulus. For example, under a multiple fixed-interval extinction schedule, a tone could be present while the fixed-interval schedule is in effect and absent when extinction is in effect.

multiple relationship in a therapeutic context, a situation in which a psychologist has more than one type of relationship with a client. A multiple relationship occurs when a psychologist is in a professional role with a person and (a) concurrently is in another role with the same person, (b) concurrently is in a relationship with a person closely associated with or related to the client, or (c) promises to enter into another relationship in the future with the client or a person closely associated with or related to the client. Psychologists are ethically expected to refrain from entering into a multiple relationship because it might impair their objectivity, competence, or effectiveness in performing their functions as a psychologist or exploit or harm the client with whom the professional relationship exists. Also called **dual relationship**.

multiple-resource model a model that views attention as comprising many pools of resources, each pool being specific to one stimulus modality or type of response. Different tasks place varying demands on different resources, and performance suffers less if two tasks draw on different resource pools than if they draw on the same pool. For example, talking while riding a bicycle presents fewer problems than trying to have two conversations at once. Compare UNITARY-RESOURCE MODEL.

multiple sclerosis (**MS**) a chronic disease of the central nervous system characterized by inflammation and multifocal scarring of the protective MYELIN SHEATH of nerves, which damages and destroys the sheath and the underlying nerve, disrupting neural transmission. Symptoms include visual disturbances, fatigue, weakness, numbness, tremors, difficulties with coordination and balance, and difficulties with speaking. The cause of MS is unknown, but the destruction of myelin may be due to an autoimmune response (see AUTOIMMUNITY).

multiple trace hypothesis the hypothesis that when a stimulus is presented on multiple occasions, each occasion creates an entirely new record in memory rather than strengthening or otherwise updating an already existing record.

multiplex *n.* a method of coding information enabling two or more messages or data streams to be transmitted simultaneously over the same communication channel.

multipolar neuron a neuron that has many dendrites and a single axon extending from the CELL BODY. Also called **multipolar cell**. Compare BIPOLAR NEURON; UNIPOLAR NEURON.

multistage sampling a sampling technique in which samples are drawn first from higher order groupings (e.g., states) and in later stages of the process from successively lower level groupings (e.g., counties within states, towns within counties) in order to avoid the necessity of having a SAMPLING FRAME for the entire population.

multistore model of memory any theory hypothesizing that information can move through and be retained in any of several memory storage systems, usually of a short-term and a long-term variety.

multitrait–multimethod matrix an integrative multivariable framework for systematically gathering information about CONVERGENT VALIDITY and DISCRIMINANT VALIDITY in a single study. With this approach, one assesses two or more constructs (or traits) using two or more measurement techniques (or methods) and then intercorrelates these various measurements.

multivariate *adj.* consisting of or otherwise involving two or more variables. For example, a **multivariate analysis** is any statistical technique that simultaneously assesses multiple dependent variables; examples include the MULTIVARIATE ANALYSIS OF VARIANCE and FACTOR ANALYSIS.

multivariate analysis of variance (**MANOVA**) an extension of the ANALYSIS OF VARIANCE (ANOVA) model that identifies the simultaneous effects of the independent variables upon a set of dependent variables.

Munchausen syndrome a severe and chronic form of FACTITIOUS DISORDER characterized by repeated and elaborate fabrication of clinically convincing physical symptoms and a false medical and social history. Other features are recurrent hospitalization and PEREGRINATION, and there may be multiple scars from previous (unnecessary) investigative surgery. [Baron Karl Friedrich Hieronymus von **Münchhausen** (1720–1797), German soldier-adventurer famous for his tall tales]

Munchausen syndrome by proxy (**MSP**) a psychological disorder in which caregivers fabricate or intentionally cause symptoms in those they are caring for in order to seek and obtain medical investigation or treatment. Typically, the caregiver is a parent, who behaves as if distressed about the child's illness and denies knowing what caused it. Also called **factitious disorder by proxy**.

mundane realism the extent to which an experimental situation resembles a real-life situation or event. This is related to EXPERIMENTAL REALISM, the degree to which experimental procedures elicit valid responses even if the events of the experiment do not resemble ordinary occurrences.

murder–suicide the intentional killing of an-

M

other person followed by the suicide of the killer. See also EXTENDED SUICIDE.

mu receptor see OPIOID RECEPTOR.

muscarinic receptor (**mAChR**) a type of ACETYLCHOLINE RECEPTOR that responds to the alkaloid muscarine as well as to acetylcholine. Muscarinic receptors are found in smooth muscle, cardiac muscle, endocrine glands, and the central nervous system and mediate chiefly the inhibitory activities of acetylcholine. Compare NICOTINIC RECEPTOR.

muscle *n.* contractile tissue that generates force and moves parts of the body. The main types of muscle are SMOOTH MUSCLE, SKELETAL MUSCLE, and CARDIAC MUSCLE.

muscle contraction a shortening of the MUSCLE FIBERS in response to electrical stimulation from a MOTOR NEURON by which a muscle exerts force on the tissues to which it is attached. This stimulation initiates an electrochemical sequence in which myosin filaments, powered by ATP (adenosine triphosphate), detach from a nearby actin filament, swing forward to reattach further along the actin filament, and then swing back causing the actin and myosin filaments to slide in opposite directions.

muscle dysmorphia a form of body dysmorphia characterized by chronic dissatisfaction with one's muscularity and the perception that one's body is inadequate and undesirable, although objective observers would disagree with such an assessment. This condition often leads to excessive exercising, steroid abuse, and eating disorders. See also REVERSE ANOREXIA.

muscle fiber a microscopic strand of muscle tissue that functions as a molecular machine converting chemical energy into force. Thousands of muscle fibers are linked by connective tissue into a muscle. Each fiber is, in turn, composed of millions of longitudinally aligned protein filaments. It is the interaction of **actin** and **myosin** protein molecules (sometimes together referred to as **actomyosin**) in these filaments that creates MUSCLE CONTRACTION.

muscle relaxant any of various drugs used in the management of spasms of skeletal muscle. Most act on the central nervous system or its associated structures to reduce muscle tone and spontaneous activity. Common muscle relaxants include BENZODIAZEPINES, baclofen, dantrolene, and botulinum toxin.

muscle spindle a receptor that lies within skeletal muscle, parallel to the main contractile MUSCLE FIBERS, and sends impulses to the central nervous system when the muscle is stretched.

muscular dystrophy (**MD**) any of a group of inherited disorders marked by degeneration of the muscles, which gradually weaken and waste away due to abnormalities in the muscle structural protein dystrophin and in a series of glycoproteins that are critical to maintaining the structural integrity of muscle fibers. There are various kinds of muscular dystrophy, each differentiated by pattern of inheritance, age of onset, rate of progression, and distribution of weakness. One of the most common and severe types is **Duchenne muscular dystrophy**. Individuals with this disorder usually are unable to walk by the age of 12 and frequently die from complications before the age of 20.

musculoskeletal system the system of SKELETAL MUSCLES and bones that generally function together to move parts of the body and maintain its general form.

musical intelligence in the MULTIPLE-INTELLIGENCES THEORY, the skills used in writing, playing, remembering, and understanding music.

music therapy the use of music as an adjunct to the treatment or rehabilitation of individuals to enhance their psychological, physical, cognitive, or social functioning. Also called **musical therapy**.

mutation *n.* a permanent change in the genetic material of an organism. It may consist of an alteration to the number or arrangement of chromosomes (a **chromosomal mutation**) or a change in the composition of DNA, generally affecting only one or a few bases in a particular gene (a **point mutation**). Mutations can occur spontaneously, but many are due to exposure to agents (**mutagens**) that significantly increase the rate of mutation; these include X-rays and other forms of radiation and certain chemicals. A mutation occurring in a body cell (i.e., a **somatic mutation**) cannot be inherited, whereas a mutation in a reproductive cell producing ova or spermatozoa (i.e., a **germ-line mutation**) can be transmitted to that individual's offspring.

mutilation *n.* **1.** the destruction or removal of a limb or an essential part of the body. **2.** a destructive act causing a disfiguring injury to the body.

mutism *n.* lack or absence of speaking due to physical or PSYCHOGENIC factors. The condition may result from neurological damage or disorder, a structural defect in the organs necessary for speech, congenital or early deafness in which an individual's failure to hear spoken words inhibits the development of speech, psychological disorders (e.g., CONVERSION DISORDER, CATATONIC SCHIZOPHRENIA), or severe emotional disturbance (e.g., extreme anger). The condition may also be voluntary, as in monastic vows of silence or the decision to speak only to selected individuals. See also SELECTIVE MUTISM; STUPOR.

mutual help a form of SELF-HELP that is not professionally guided and that involves joining with others similar to oneself to explore ways to cope with life situations and problems. Mutual help can occur in person, by telephone, or through the Internet.

mutualism *n.* see INTERSPECIES INTERACTION.

mutual pretense an interaction pattern in

which all participants try to act as if they are unaware of the most crucial facts in a situation (e.g., a situation in which one of the participants is terminally ill). This pattern is often regarded by therapists and researchers as an anxiety-driven strategy that inhibits communication, increases tension, and leads to missed opportunities for meaningful mutual support.

mutual support group a group composed of individuals who meet on a regular basis to help one another cope with a shared life problem. This term is sometimes used by researchers and practitioners instead of the traditional term SELF-HELP GROUP, as it emphasizes the mutual, interdependent nature of self-help group processes.

myasthenia *n.* muscular weakness or lack of muscular endurance.

myasthenia gravis an autoimmune disorder (see AUTOIMMUNITY) in which the body produces antibodies against ACETYLCHOLINE RECEPTORS, causing faulty transmission of nerve impulses at neuromuscular junctions. Affected muscles—initially those of the face and neck—are easily fatigued and may become paralyzed temporarily (e.g., muscles involved in eating may fail to function normally toward the end of a meal, or speech may become slurred after a period of talking). The disease is progressive, eventually affecting muscles throughout the body.

myelencephalon *n.* see MEDULLA OBLONGATA.

myelin *n.* the substance that forms the insulating MYELIN SHEATH around the axons of many neurons. It consists mainly of phospholipids, with additional **myelin proteins**, and accounts for the whitish color of WHITE MATTER. **Myelinated fibers** conduct nerve impulses much faster than nonmyelinated fibers (see SALTATION).

myelin sheath the insulating layer around many axons that increases the speed of conduction of nerve impulses. It consists of MYELIN and is laid down by GLIA, which wrap themselves around adjacent axons in a process called **myelination**. The myelin sheath is interrupted by small gaps, called NODES OF RANVIER, which are spaced about every millimeter along the axon.

myelitis *n.* inflammation of the spinal cord.

myelocele *n.* protrusion of the spinal cord through an abnormal opening in the vertebral column, as found in SPINA BIFIDA.

myelomeningocele *n.* see MENINGOMYELOCELE.

Myers–Briggs Type Indicator (**MBTI**) a personality test designed to classify individuals according to their expressed choices between contrasting alternatives in certain categories of traits. The categories, based on JUNGIAN TYPOLOGY, are (a) Extraversion–Introversion, (b) Sensing–Intuition, (c) Thinking–Feeling, and (d) Judging–Perceiving. The participant is assigned a type (e.g., INTJ or ESFP) according to the pattern of choices made. The test has little credibility among research psychologists but is widely used in educational counseling and human resource management to help improve work and personal relationships, increase productivity, and identify interpersonal communication preferences and skills. [Isabel Briggs **Myers** (1897–1980), U.S. personologist, and her mother Katharine Cook **Briggs** (1875–1968)]

myoclonus *n.* rapid, involuntary contraction of a muscle or group of muscles. This may occur normally, as when a limb or other part of the body suddenly jerks while falling asleep (**nocturnal myoclonus**), or abnormally, as in CREUTZFELDT–JAKOB DISEASE and other neurological disorders.

myopathy *n.* any disease or disorder of the muscles, hereditary or acquired.

myopia *n.* nearsightedness, a REFRACTIVE ERROR due to an abnormally long eye: The retinal image is blurred because the focal point of one or both eyes lies in front of, rather than on, the retina. Compare EMMETROPIA; HYPEROPIA.

myosin *n.* see MUSCLE FIBER.

myriachit *n.* a CULTURE-BOUND SYNDROME found in Siberian populations. Similar to LATAH, it is characterized by indiscriminate, apparently uncontrolled imitations of the actions of other people encountered by the individual. Also called **ikota**; **irkunii**; **menkeiti**; **olan**. See also IMU.

mysticism *n.* **1.** the view that there are real sources of knowledge and truth other than sensory experience and rational deduction, such as inspiration, revelation, or mysterious private experiences. A common implication is that such knowledge cannot readily be shared with or conveyed to others but must be individually achieved. **2.** the belief that an immediate knowledge of, or union with, the divine can be achieved through personal religious experience. Accounts of mystical experiences typically describe a state of intense, trancelike contemplation in which a sense of profound insight is accompanied by feelings of ecstatic self-surrender. —**mystic** *n., adj.* —**mystical** *adj.*

mythology *n.* **1.** a body of traditional stories (myths) associated with the early history of a particular culture. Such stories generally involve supernatural beings and events and often seek to explain particular natural or cultural phenomena (e.g., the cycle of the seasons or a specific custom) in terms of their supposed origins. **2.** the study of myths. Austrian psychiatrist Sigmund Freud (1856–1939) compared myths to DREAMS, which contain hidden meanings, and believed they throw unique light on the cultures from which they stem, and in some instances, as in the myth of Oedipus, on human nature in general. **3.** in ANALYTIC PSYCHOLOGY, primordial images, or ARCHETYPES, that are stored in the COLLECTIVE UNCONSCIOUS. —**mythological** *adj.*

MZ twins abbreviation for MONOZYGOTIC TWINS.

Nn

n symbol for the number of scores or observations obtained from a particular experimental condition or subgroup.

N **1.** symbol for the total number of cases (participants) in an experiment or study. **2.** abbreviation for NUMERICAL ABILITY.

NA abbreviation for Narcotics Anonymous. See ALCOHOLICS ANONYMOUS.

n-Ach abbreviation for NEED FOR ACHIEVEMENT.

nAchR abbreviation for NICOTINIC RECEPTOR.

n-Aff abbreviation for NEED FOR AFFILIATION.

naive analysis of action in ATTRIBUTION THEORY, a set of rules by which laypersons determine whether another person (an "actor") caused a certain action. See CORRESPONDENT INFERENCE THEORY.

naive hedonism see PRECONVENTIONAL LEVEL.

naive observer an observer who has little or no prior information about the events that he or she is observing or the people involved in them. The reactions of a naive observer may be highly revealing when contrasted with those of other observers who have been given selected pieces of information (or misinformation) about an observed situation or the actors in it (e.g., that a particular individual has a criminal conviction).

naive participant a participant who has not previously participated in a particular research study and has not been made aware of the experimenter's hypothesis. Compare CONFEDERATE.

naive personality theories a set of ideas that laypeople tend to hold about how specific personality traits cluster together within a person. Such theories, which are often held implicitly rather than explicitly, are a major concern of ATTRIBUTION THEORY. See NAIVE ANALYSIS OF ACTION.

naive realism 1. the belief or assumption that one's sense perceptions provide direct knowledge of external reality, unconditioned by one's perceptual apparatus or individual perspective. Since the advent of CARTESIANISM, most philosophy has assumed that such a position is untenable. The cognitive development theory of Swiss psychologist Jean Piaget (1896–1980) stressed the child's progress away from naive realism and toward conceptualization and logical reasoning. As conceptualization and reasoning develop, naive realism is presumed to diminish. Also called **direct realism**. **2.** in social psychology, the tendency to assume that one's perspective of events is a natural, unbiased reflection of objective reality and to infer bias on the part of any-

one who disagrees with one's views. See FALSE-CONSENSUS EFFECT.

naltrexone *n.* an OPIOID ANTAGONIST that, like the shorter acting naloxone, prevents the binding of opioid agonists to opioid receptors. Accordingly, both drugs may precipitate a rapid withdrawal syndrome. If naltrexone is taken prior to use of opiate drugs, it will prevent their reinforcing effects, and can therefore be used for the management of opioid dependence in individuals desiring abstinence. Naltrexone is also appropriate as an adjunctive treatment in the management of alcoholism. U.S. trade name: **ReVia**.

narcissism *n.* **1.** excessive self-love or egocentrism. See NARCISSISTIC PERSONALITY DISORDER. **2.** in psychoanalytic theory, the taking of one's own EGO or body as a sexual object or focus of the LIBIDO or the seeking or choice of another for relational purposes on the basis of his or her similarity to the self. See PRIMARY NARCISSISM. **—narcissist** *n.* **—narcissistic** *adj.*

narcissistic object choice in psychoanalytic theory, selection of a mate or other LOVE OBJECT similar to oneself. Compare ANACLITIC OBJECT CHOICE.

narcissistic personality disorder a personality disorder with the following characteristics: (a) a long-standing pattern of grandiose self-importance and exaggerated sense of talent and achievements; (b) fantasies of unlimited sex, power, brilliance, or beauty; (c) an exhibitionistic need for attention and admiration; (d) either cool indifference or feelings of rage, humiliation, or emptiness as a response to criticism, indifference, or defeat; and (e) various interpersonal disturbances, such as feeling entitled to special favors, taking advantage of others, and inability to empathize with the feelings of others.

narcoanalysis *n.* a form of psychoanalysis in which injections of drugs (often opioids) are used to induce a semihypnotic state in order to facilitate exploration and ventilation of feelings, uncover repressed traumatic memories, and, through the analyst's review and interpretation with the patient afterward, promote the patient's insight into the unconscious forces that underlie his or her symptoms. The technique was developed initially to treat COMBAT STRESS REACTIONS in the 1940s and is rarely if ever used now.

narcolepsy *n.* a disorder consisting of excessive daytime sleepiness accompanied by brief "attacks" of sleep during waking hours. These sleep attacks may occur at any time or during any activity, including in potentially dangerous situations, such as driving an automobile. The attacks are marked by immediate entry into REM SLEEP without going through the usual initial stages of sleep. Also called **paroxysmal sleep**. —**narcoleptic** *adj.*

narcotic 1. *n.* originally, any drug that induces a state of stupor or insensibility (narcosis). More recently, the term referred to strong OPIOIDS used clinically for pain relief but this usage is now considered imprecise and pejorative; the term is still sometimes used in legal contexts to refer to a wide variety of abused substances. **2.** *adj.* of or relating to narcotics or narcosis.

narcotic agonist see OPIOID AGONIST.

narcotic analgesic see OPIOID ANALGESIC.

narcotic antagonist see OPIOID ANTAGONIST.

Narcotics Anonymous (**NA**) see ALCOHOLICS ANONYMOUS.

narrative psychotherapy treatment for individuals, couples, or families that helps clients reinterpret and rewrite their life events into true but more life-enhancing narratives or stories. Narrative therapy posits that individuals are primarily meaning-making beings who are the linguistic authors of their lives and who can reauthor these stories by learning to deconstruct them, by seeing patterns in their ways of interpreting life events or problems, and by reconstruing problems or events in a more helpful light. See also CONSTRUCTIVISM; CONSTRUCTIVIST PSYCHOTHERAPY; DECONSTRUCTION.

narrative theory any theory of consciousness stating that beliefs arise as part of an explanatory narrative about oneself and society.

nasal 1. *adj.* of or relating to the nose. **2.** *adj.* denoting a speech sound produced by letting all or most of the airstream pass through the nasal (rather than the oral) cavity, for example, [ng] in *sing*, or the sound of -*on* in the French word *bon*.

nasopharynx *n.* the portion of the PHARYNX that lies above the level of the soft PALATE. The nasopharynx is closed off from other parts of the pharynx during swallowing and speaking by reflex raising of the soft palate.

National Institute of Mental Health (**NIMH**) an agency of the federal government established in 1949 to understand the mind, the brain, and behavior and thereby reduce the burden of mental illness through research. It is committed to scientific programs to educate and train future mental health researchers, including scientists trained in molecular science, cognitive and affective neuroscience, and other disciplines required for the study of mental illness and the brain.

nationalism *n.* **1.** strong, often excessive, feelings of pride in and allegiance to one's nation and its culture or belief in its superiority. **2.** a goal or policy of national independence, es-

pecially in relation to a dominant colonial or occupying power. —**nationalist** *n.*, *adj.* —**nationalistic** *adj.*

Native American a member of any of various indigenous peoples of the western hemisphere who populated that territory prior to European colonization. When referring to the indigenous peoples of North America, the term **American Indian** is also used.

nativism *n.* **1.** the doctrine that the mind has certain innate structures and that experience plays a limited role in the creation of knowledge. See also NATIVISTIC THEORY. Compare CONSTRUCTIVISM; EMPIRICISM. **2.** the doctrine that mental and behavioral traits are largely determined by hereditary, rather than environmental, factors. See NATURE–NURTURE. **3.** the theory that individuals are born with all perceptual capabilities intact, although some capabilities may depend on the biological maturation of perceptual systems to reach adult levels. —**nativist** *adj.*, *n.* —**nativistic** *adj.*

nativistic theory in linguistics, the theory that human beings are born with an innate knowledge of language that enables them to structure and interpret the data they encounter as language learners. Although certain theories about the origins of human language in prehistory have been termed nativistic (see LANGUAGE-ORIGIN THEORY), the term is now mainly associated with the theory of language acquisition in young children put forward by U.S. linguist Noam Chomsky (1928–). See LANGUAGE ACQUISITION DEVICE.

natural category see BASIC-LEVEL CATEGORY.

natural childbirth a method of labor and child delivery that does not include (or is designed to eliminate) the need for medical interventions, such as anesthetics. The mother receives preparatory education in such areas as breathing and relaxation coordination, exercise of the muscles involved in labor and delivery, and postural positions that make labor more comfortable and allow for conscious participation in delivery. See also LAMAZE METHOD.

natural experiment a natural event, often a natural disaster (e.g., a flood, tornado, or volcanic eruption), that is treated as an experimental condition to be compared to some control condition. Since natural events cannot be manipulated or prearranged, natural experiments are "quasi experiments" rather than true experiments. See QUASI-EXPERIMENTAL RESEARCH.

natural group 1. any group formed through natural social processes, particularly when compared to ad hoc laboratory groups created by researchers in their studies of group processes. Examples include an audience, board of directors, clique, club, committee, crowd, dance troupe, family, gang, jury, orchestra, sorority, and support group. **2.** a group whose members are united through common descent or custom, such as a family or tribe.

N

naturalism *n.* in philosophy, the doctrine that reality consists solely of natural objects and that therefore the methods of natural science offer the only reliable means to knowledge and understanding of reality. Naturalism is closely related to PHYSICALISM and MATERIALISM and explicitly opposes any form of supernaturalism or MYSTI-CISM positing the existence of realities beyond the natural and material world. See also POSITIV-ISM. **—naturalistic** *adj.*

naturalistic environment a type of laboratory environment that attempts to include many of the features found in natural environments. Examples are underground burrows for fossorial animals, flight cages for birds, and trees or other climbing structures for arboreal animals. Naturalistic environments allow the study of more species-typical behavior in captive animals while maintaining control over many other variables.

naturalistic observation data collection in a field setting, usually without laboratory controls or manipulation of variables. These procedures are usually carried out by a trained observer, who watches and records the everyday behavior of participants in their natural environments. Examples of naturalistic observation include an ethologist's study of the behavior of chimpanzees and an anthropologist's observation of playing children. See OBSERVATIONAL STUDY.

naturalist intelligence in the MULTIPLE-INTELLIGENCES THEORY, the intelligence involved in detecting patterns and regularities in natural phenomena, used, for example, in identifying varieties of plants or birds.

natural language a language that has evolved naturally for use among humans, as opposed to an ARTIFICIAL LANGUAGE, such as that used in computer programming.

natural language category a class of things, people, or the like that is defined as a category distinct from other categories by the semantic structure of a particular NATURAL LANGUAGE, rather than by an extralinguistic (scientific or logical) system of classification. Some researchers believe that each natural language category is defined by a cognitive prototype and that membership in the category is determined by an entity's degree of resemblance to this prototype. For example, the category "birds" is defined by a prototype consisting of a set of features (has a beak, has feathers, can fly, etc.) representing the ideal or typical bird: An entity that has all or most of these features will be accepted as belonging to this category.

natural law theory in ethics and political philosophy, the position that there are certain ethical principles that are true and universal, originating in the very nature of reality itself or in the decrees of a divine law giver. In the dominant strain of natural law theory, it is assumed that these principles can be discerned by reason and apply only to beings capable of rational thought. Natural law theory can be traced back to the ancient Greek Stoic philosophers; it strongly influenced Roman law and was subsequently developed by Christian philosophers of the Middle Ages and later periods. Compare REL-ATIVISM.

natural selection the process by which such forces as competition, disease, and climate tend to eliminate individuals who are less well adapted to a particular environment and favor the survival and reproduction of better adapted individuals. Hence, over successive generations, the nature of the population changes. This is the fundamental mechanism driving the evolution of living organisms and the emergence of new species, as originally proposed independently by British naturalists Charles Darwin (1809–1882) and Alfred Russel Wallace (1823–1913). See DAR-WINISM; EVOLUTION; SELECTION; SURVIVAL OF THE FITTEST. Compare ARTIFICIAL SELECTION.

nature *n.* **1.** the entirety of physical reality. **2.** the phenomena of the natural world, including plants, animals, and physical features, as opposed to human beings and their creations. **3.** the fundamental or inherent qualities of something: its essence. **4.** the innate, presumably genetically determined, characteristics and behaviors of an individual. In psychology, those characteristics most often and traditionally associated with nature are temperament, body type, and personality. Compare NURTURE. **—natural** *adj.*

nature–nurture the dispute over the relative contributions of hereditary and constitutional factors (NATURE) and environmental factors (NURTURE) to the development of the individual. Nativists emphasize the role of heredity, whereas environmentalists emphasize sociocultural and ecological factors, including family attitudes, child-rearing practices, and economic status. Most scientists now accept that there is a close interaction between hereditary and environmental factors in the ontogeny of behavior (see EPIGENESIS). Also called **heredity–environment** or **nature–nurture issue**.

naturopathy *n.* an alternative health care system that aims to prevent disease and promote physical and mental health by using natural and physiologically based therapies (e.g., dietary measures, acupuncture, and massage) to address underlying disease processes. See also COMPLE-MENTARY AND ALTERNATIVE MEDICINE.

navigation *n.* the mechanisms used by an organism to find its way through the environment, for example, to a migration site or to its home site. A variety of cues have been documented in nonhuman animals, including using the sun or stars as a compass (see SUN COMPASS), magnetic lines, olfactory cues, visual cues (e.g., rivers or coastlines), and wind-sheer effects from air masses crossing mountain ranges. See also HOMING; MIGRATION.

nay-saying *n.* answering questions negatively regardless of their content, which can distort the results of surveys, questionnaires, and similar instruments. Compare YEA-SAYING.

N1 component the first negative component of an EVENT-RELATED POTENTIAL, occurring approximately 100 ms after stimulus onset. The N1 component is usually larger for attended stimuli than for unattended stimuli, a phenomenon known as the **N1 attention effect**. Hence, it is thought to reflect the initial sensory and attentional processing of a stimulus by specific areas of the cerebral cortex.

near-death experience (**NDE**) an image, perception, event, interaction, or feeling (or a combination of any of these) reported by some people after a life-threatening episode. Typical features include a sense of separation from the body, often accompanied by the ability to look down on the situation; a peaceful and pleasant state of mind; and an entering into the light, sometimes following an interaction with a spiritual being. There is continuing controversy regarding the existence, cause, and nature of NDEs. Spiritual, biomedical, and contextual lines of explanation are still in play, and there is no solid evidence to support the proposition that NDEs prove survival of death.

near point the shortest distance at which an object is in focus for a single eye. Also called **near point of accommodation**. Compare FAR POINT.

near point of convergence the shortest distance at which an object is in focus when viewed with both eyes, without appearing as a double image.

nearsightedness *n.* see MYOPIA.

Necker cube a line drawing of a cube in which all angles and sides can be seen, as if it were transparent. It is an AMBIGUOUS FIGURE whose three-dimensionality fluctuates when viewed for a prolonged period of time. [Louis Albert **Necker** (1730–1804), Swiss crystallographer]

necrosis *n.* the death of cells (e.g., neurons, muscle cells) from any of a variety of causes, including obstruction of blood supply to the affected part, disease, injury, or toxins. **—necrotic** *adj.*

need *n.* **1.** a condition of tension in an organism resulting from deprivation of something required for survival, well-being, or personal fulfillment. **2.** a substance, state, or any other thing (e.g., food, water, security) whose absence generates this condition.

need–fear dilemma 1. a simultaneous need for and fear of close relationships with others. **2.** a conflicting set of conditions facing those who need structured control but have an aversion to external control or influence. In marked form, it is a characteristic condition in schizophrenia, particularly in terms of both greatly needing and greatly fearing other people.

need for achievement (**n-Ach**) a strong desire to accomplish goals and attain a high standard of performance and personal fulfillment.

People with a high need for achievement often undertake tasks in which there is a reasonable probability of success and avoid tasks that are either too easy (because of lack of challenge) or too difficult (because of fear of failure).

need for affection the degree to which a person wants to be close or distant in a relationship with another. In intimate relationships, need for affection is often expressed concretely as a desire to be touched or held or to be commended verbally. An exaggerated need for affection and approval is considered by many to be a NEUROSIS and is often seen as resulting from early deprivation, especially of physical affection.

need for affiliation (**n-Aff**) a strong desire to socialize and be part of a group. People with a high need for affiliation often seek the approval and acceptance of others.

need for closure 1. the motivation to achieve finality and absoluteness in decisions, judgments, and choices. A person with a high need for closure will often have a low tolerance of ambiguity and uncertainty and may be attracted to dogmatic political or religious views. **2.** the need to achieve a sense of finality at the close of a painful or difficult episode in one's life. Some estranged couples, for example, feel a need to obtain a formal divorce for emotional as well as practical reasons. See CLOSURE.

need for cognition a personality trait reflecting a person's tendency to enjoy engaging in extensive cognitive activity. This trait primarily reflects a person's motivation to engage in cognitive activity rather than his or her actual ability to do so. Individuals high in need for cognition tend to develop attitudes or take action based on thoughtful evaluation of information.

need reduction the decrease of a need, often achieved through a CONSUMMATORY RESPONSE. Also called **need gratification**. See DRIVE-REDUCTION THEORY.

needs assessment 1. the identification of currently unmet service needs in a community or other group, done prior to implementing a new service program or modifying an existing service program. The perceived needs are generally assessed from multiple perspectives, including those of community or group leaders and those of each individual in the community or group. **2.** the identification of those areas that should be the focus of a PERSONNEL TRAINING program. Needs assessment involves analyses in three key areas: (a) the knowledge, skills, abilities, and other characteristics of employees; (b) the requirements of the tasks that are performed by employees; and (c) the requirements of the organization.

need to belong the motivation to be a part of relationships, belong to groups, and to be viewed positively by others.

need to evaluate a personality trait reflecting a person's tendency to engage in extensive evaluative thinking when encountering people,

N

issues, or objects. People who are high in need to evaluate tend to form attitudes and categorize objects spontaneously along a positive–negative scale. People who are low in need to evaluate tend to think of objects in evaluative terms only when the context encourages such categorization.

negation *n.* in PIAGETIAN THEORY, a mental process—a form of REVERSIBILITY—in which one realizes that any operation can always be negated, or inverted. Also called **inversion**. —**negate** *vb.*

negative affect the internal feeling state (AFFECT) that occurs when one has failed to achieve a goal or to avoid a threat or when one is not satisfied with the current state of affairs. The tendency to experience such states is known as **negative affectivity**.

negative attitude in psychotherapy and counseling, the client's feeling of rejection or disapproval of the therapist or counselor or of the therapeutic or counseling process, of another person, or of himself or herself. Compare POSITIVE ATTITUDE.

negative discriminative stimulus (symbol: S^Δ or S–) in OPERANT CONDITIONING, a stimulus signifying that a given response will not be reinforced, implying that there is at least one other stimulus circumstance in which the response will be reinforced. Compare DISCRIMINATIVE STIMULUS.

negative emotion an unpleasant, often disruptive, emotional reaction designed to express a NEGATIVE AFFECT. Negative emotion is not conducive to progress toward obtaining one's goals. Examples are anger, envy, sadness, and fear. Compare POSITIVE EMOTION.

negative feedback 1. an arrangement whereby some of the output of a system, whether mechanical or biological, is fed back to reduce the effect of input signals. Such systems, which measure the deviation from a desired state and apply a correction, are important in achieving HOMEOSTASIS, whereas systems employing POSITIVE FEEDBACK tend to amplify small deviations and become highly unstable. See FEEDBACK SYSTEM. **2.** in social psychology, nonconstructive criticism, disapproval, and other negative information received by a person in response to his or her performance.

negative Oedipus complex in psychoanalytic theory, the opposite or reverse aspect of the OEDIPUS COMPLEX, in which the son desires the father and regards the mother as rival, or the daughter is attached to the mother and regards the father as rival. The more familiar attachment is the heterosexual form (the positive Oedipus complex). Austrian psychiatrist Sigmund Freud (1856–1939) held that both aspects are part of the normal Oedipus complex in boys and girls. Also called **inverted Oedipus complex**.

negative priming the ability of a preceding stimulus to inhibit the response to a subsequent stimulus. This is measured by the detectability of the second stimulus or the time taken to make a response to the second stimulus. The most striking examples occur when the participant is instructed to ignore a feature of the first stimulus (e.g., its color) and then to attend to that same feature in the second stimulus. PRIMING effects are usually facilitative.

negative punishment punishment that results because some stimulus or circumstance is removed as a consequence of a response. For example, if a response results in a subtraction of money from an accumulating account, and the response becomes less likely as a result of this experience, then negative punishment has occurred. Compare POSITIVE PUNISHMENT.

negative recency in recalling a list of items, the tendency to recall fewer of the final items of the list than the middle and early items. Negative recency contrasts with the enhanced recall of final items seen in the RECENCY EFFECT. Also called **negative recency effect**.

negative reinforcement the removal, prevention, or postponement of an aversive stimulus as a consequence of a response, which, in turn, increases the probability of that response. Compare POSITIVE REINFORCEMENT.

negative schizophrenia a form of schizophrenia characterized by a predomination of NEGATIVE SYMPTOMS, suggesting deficiency or absence of behavior normally present in a person's repertoire, as shown in apathy, blunted affect, emotional withdrawal, poor rapport, and lack of spontaneity. Compare POSITIVE SCHIZOPHRENIA.

negative stereotype a STEREOTYPE that purports to describe the undesirable, objectionable, or unacceptable qualities and characteristics of the members of a particular group or social category. Compare POSITIVE STEREOTYPE.

negative symptom a deficit in the ability to perform the normal functions of living—logical thinking, self-care, social interaction, planning, initiating, and carrying through constructive actions, and so forth—as shown in apathy, blunted affect, emotional withdrawal, poor rapport, and lack of spontaneity. In schizophrenia, a predominance of negative symptoms is often associated with a poor prognosis. Compare POSITIVE SYMPTOM. See NEGATIVE SCHIZOPHRENIA.

negative transfer 1. a process in which previous learning obstructs or interferes with present learning. For instance, tennis players who learn racquetball must often unlearn their tendency to take huge, muscular swings with the shoulder and upper arm. See also TRANSFER OF TRAINING. Compare POSITIVE TRANSFER. **2.** see LANGUAGE TRANSFER.

negative transference in psychoanalysis, transfer of anger or hostility felt toward the parents, or other individuals significant during childhood, onto the therapist. Compare POSITIVE TRANSFERENCE.

negativism *n.* **1.** an attitude characterized by persistent resistance to the suggestions of others (**passive negativism**) or the tendency to act in ways that are contrary to the expectations, requests, or commands of others (**active negativism**), typically without any identifiable reason for opposition. In young children and adolescents, such reactions may be considered a healthy expression of self-assertion. Negativism may also be associated with a number of disorders (extreme negativism is a feature of CATATONIC SCHIZOPHRENIA) and it can be an expression of opposition, withdrawal, or anger or a method of gaining attention. See also OPPOSITIONAL DEFIANT DISORDER; PASSIVE-AGGRESSIVE PERSONALITY DISORDER. **2.** any philosophy or doctrine based on negation, such as nihilism or skepticism. —**negativistic** *adj.*

negativistic personality disorder see PASSIVE-AGGRESSIVE PERSONALITY DISORDER.

neglect *n.* **1.** failure to provide for the basic needs of a person in one's care. The neglect may be emotional (e.g., rejection or apathy), material (e.g., withholding food or clothing), or service-oriented (e.g., depriving of education or medical attention). See CHILD ABUSE; ELDER ABUSE. See also MALTREATMENT. **2.** a syndrome characterized by lack of awareness of a specific area or side of the body caused by a brain injury. It may involve failure to recognize the area as belonging to oneself or ignoring the existence of one side of the body or one side of the visual field (see UNILATERAL NEGLECT; VISUAL NEGLECT). This is most often associated with an injury to the right cerebral hemisphere with corresponding left-sided neglect. Neglect has also been found in auditory, tactile, and proprioceptive tasks. Also called **perceptual neglect**. See also MOTOR NEGLECT; SENSORY NEGLECT; SPATIAL NEGLECT.

neglect dyslexia a form of acquired DYSLEXIA associated with VISUAL NEGLECT, a condition in which a person is unaware of half of the visual field as a result of neurological damage. Either the initial parts of words are misread (left neglect) or the terminal parts of words are misread (right neglect), and the errors are not simple deletions but typically guesses of real though incorrect words with approximately the right number of letters.

negligence *n.* failure to fulfill a duty or to provide some response, action, or level of care that it is appropriate or reasonable to expect. In ergonomics, for example, negligence involves failure to take reasonable care to protect human safety or equipment in the design, development, or evaluation of a system. A variety of different types of negligence exist in law. See also MALPRACTICE. —**negligent** *adj.*

neoassociationism *n.* theories of association formation developed subsequently to traditional philosophical ASSOCIATIONISM. Neoassociationism typically encompasses learning and conditioning theories, such as that of U.S. psychologist Clark L. Hull (1884–1952).

neoassociationist theory in general, any modern theory that accounts for behavior as a conditioned or unconditioned response to an antecedent event. Specifically, the term was applied by U.S. psychologist Leonard Berkowitz (1926–) to his theory explaining aggression as a response to triggering conditions that activate an associative network of responses. See also FRUSTRATION–AGGRESSION HYPOTHESIS; WEAPONS EFFECT.

neobehaviorism *n.* an approach to psychology, influenced by LOGICAL POSITIVISM, that emphasized the development of comprehensive theories and frameworks of behavior, such as those of U.S. psychologists Clark L. Hull (1884–1952) and Edward C. Tolman (1886–1959), through empirical observation of behavior and the use of consciousness and mental events as explanatory devices. It thus contrasts with classical BEHAVIORISM, which was concerned with freeing psychology of mentalistic concepts and explanations. According to some authorities, neobehaviorism replaced classical behaviorism as the dominant 20th-century program for experimental psychology in about 1930; its influence began to wane in the 1950s. See also RADICAL BEHAVIORISM. —**neobehaviorist** *adj.*, *n.*

neocortex *n.* regions of the CEREBRAL CORTEX that are the most recently evolved and contain six main layers of cells. Neocortex, which comprises the majority of human cerebral cortex, includes the primary sensory and motor cortex and association cortex. Also called **isocortex**; **neopallium**. Compare ALLOCORTEX; ARCHICORTEX. —**neocortical** *adj.*

neodissociative theory a theory that explains the paradoxical phenomena of hypnosis as a result of DIVIDED CONSCIOUSNESS. For example, hypnotic analgesia can produce subjectively reported relief from pain while physiological measures indicate that pain is still being registered.

neo-Freudian 1. *adj.* denoting an approach that derives from the CLASSICAL PSYCHOANALYSIS of Austrian psychiatrist Sigmund Freud (1856–1939), but with modifications and revisions that typically emphasize social and interpersonal elements over biological instincts. The term is not usually applied to the approaches of Freud's contemporaries, such as Austrian psychiatrist Alfred Adler (1870–1937) and Swiss psychiatrist Carl Jung (1875–1961), who broke away from his school quite early. German-born U.S. psychologist Erik Erikson (1902–1994), German-born U.S. psychoanalyst Erich Fromm (1900–1980), German-born U.S. psychoanalyst Karen Horney (1885–1952), and U.S. psychiatrist Harry Stack Sullivan (1892–1949) are considered to be among the most influential neo-Freudian theorists and practitioners. **2.** *n.* an analyst or theoretician who adopts such an approach.

neolocal *adj.* denoting a living arrangement in which a newly married couple begins a new household separate from their kin, or a culture in which this is the norm. Compare MATRILOCAL; PATRILOCAL.

neologism *n.* a recently coined word or expression. In a psychopathological context neologisms, whose origins and meanings are usually nonsensical and unrecognizable (e.g., "klipno" for watch), are typically associated with APHASIA or SCHIZOPHRENIA. —**neologistic** *adj.*

neonatal drug dependency syndrome a syndrome in which a baby is born with drug dependence due to the mother's drug abuse (most often opioid abuse) during the latter part of pregnancy. Such babies are often of low birth weight. Other severe problems that accompany drug abuse by pregnant women include increased risk of intrauterine death, premature delivery, and increased neonatal mortality.

neonatal period in human development, the period from birth to approximately 1 month of age for infants born after a full-term pregnancy (for infants born prematurely, the period is longer). Among nonhuman species, the neonatal period varies depending on the species. For example, in dogs the period extends from birth to approximately 12 to 14 days of age; for some rats it lasts approximately 21 days from birth.

neonate *n.* a newborn human or nonhuman animal. Human infants born after the normal gestational period of 36 weeks are known as **full-term neonates**; infants born prematurely before the end of this period are known as **preterm neonates** (or, colloquially, as "preemies").

neonativism *n.* the belief that much cognitive knowledge, such as OBJECT PERMANENCE and certain aspects of language, is innate, requiring little in the way of specific experiences to be expressed. Neonativists hold that cognitive development is influenced by biological constraints and that individuals are predisposed to process certain types of information. Also called **structural constraint theory**. —**neonativist** *adj., n.*

NEO Personality Inventory (**NEO-PI**) a personality questionnaire designed to assess the factors of the FIVE-FACTOR PERSONALITY MODEL. Revised in 1992 (**NEO-PI-R**), the inventory takes its name from three factors of the model: *n*euroticism, *e*xtraversion, and *o*penness to experience. It is available in two versions (Form S for self-reports and Form R for observer ratings), each comprising 240 statements to which participants respond using a 5-point LIKERT SCALE format, ranging from "strongly disagree" to "strongly agree."

neophenomenology *n.* an approach to psychology that emphasizes the role of the individual's phenomenological (immediate and conscious) experience in the determination of action. See PERSONALISTIC PSYCHOLOGY; PHENOMENOLOGY.

neophobia *n.* **1.** a persistent and irrational fear of change or of anything new, unfamiliar, or strange. **2.** the avoidance of new stimuli, especially foods. —**neophobic** *adj.*

neoplasm *n.* a new, abnormal growth, that is, a benign or malignant tumor. The term is generally used to specify a malignant tumor (see CANCER). A neoplasm usually grows rapidly by cellular proliferation but generally lacks structural organization. A malignant neoplasm is usually invasive, destroying or damaging neighboring normal tissues, and can spread to distant sites by the process of metastasis; benign neoplasms are usually encapsulated and do not spread, but may damage neighboring tissues by compression. —**neoplastic** *adj.*

Neoplatonism *n.* a school of philosophy based on a particular understanding of the teachings of Greek philosopher Plato (c. 427–c. 347 BCE), especially as interpreted by Alexandrian philosopher Plotinus (204–270). Neoplatonism retains Plato's view that there is another perfect and eternal world that accounts for the things of the physical world (see PLATONIC IDEALISM). In the strain developed by Plotinus, however, there is greater emphasis on an ultimate unity of the universe, and a new sense that MYSTICISM, as opposed to reason, is the way through which the other world is experienced. Neoplatonism was influential in the reconciliation of Christianity with classical philosophy in the Middle Ages and the Renaissance. —**Neoplatonist** *n., adj.*

neostriatum *n.* a portion of the BASAL GANGLIA that has evolved relatively recently. It includes the PUTAMEN and the CAUDATE NUCLEUS. It is contrasted with the phylogenetically older **paleostriatum**, which is represented by the GLOBUS PALLIDUS. —**neostriatal** *adj.*

nerve *n.* a bundle of nerve fibers (see AXON) outside the central nervous system (CNS), enclosed in a sheath of connective tissue to form a cordlike structure. Nerves serve to connect the CNS with the tissues and organs of the body. They may be motor, sensory, or mixed (containing axons of both motor and sensory neurons). See CRANIAL NERVE; SPINAL NERVE. Compare TRACT.

nerve ending the terminus of an AXON. There are various types of nerve ending, among them, for example, MEISSNER'S CORPUSCLES and FREE NERVE ENDINGS.

nerve fiber 1. the AXON of a neuron, extending from the cell body. **2.** loosely, the neuron itself.

nerve growth factor an endogenous polypeptide that stimulates the growth and development of neurons in SPINAL GANGLIA and in the ganglia of the SYMPATHETIC NERVOUS SYSTEM.

nerve impulse a wave of DEPOLARIZATION, in the form of an ACTION POTENTIAL, that is propagated along a neuron or chain of neurons as the means of transmitting signals in the nervous sys-

N

tem. Also called **nervous impulse**; **neural impulse**. See also SYNAPSE.

nerve root the part of a nerve that connects directly to the brain or spinal cord. Spinal nerves arise from the spinal cord via a DORSAL ROOT and a VENTRAL ROOT, which then combine to form the spinal nerve. Certain CRANIAL NERVES also are formed by the combination of two nerve roots.

nervios *n.* a wide range of symptoms affecting Latino groups in the United States and Latin America (the word literally means "nerves") and attributed to stressful and difficult life experiences and circumstances. Symptoms include headache, dizziness, concentration difficulties, sleep disturbance, stomach upsets, and tingling sensations; mental disorder may or may not be present. See also ATAQUE DE NERVIOS.

nervous *adj.* **1.** in a transient emotional state of anxious apprehension. **2.** of an excitable, highly strung, or easily agitated disposition. **3.** referring to the structures or functions of the nervous system. See also NEURAL.

nervous breakdown a lay term for an emotional illness or other mental disorder that has a sudden onset, produces acute distress, and significantly interferes with one's functioning. Also called **nervous prostration**.

nervousness *n.* a state of restless tension and emotionality in which people tend to tremble, feel apprehensive, or show other signs of anxiety or fear.

nervous system the system of NEURONS, NERVES, TRACTS, and associated tissues that, together with the endocrine system, coordinates activities of the organism in response to signals received from the internal and external environments. The nervous system of higher vertebrates is often considered in terms of its divisions, principally the CENTRAL NERVOUS SYSTEM, the PERIPHERAL NERVOUS SYSTEM, and the AUTONOMIC NERVOUS SYSTEM. See also CONCEPTUAL NERVOUS SYSTEM.

nervus terminalis a collection of nerve fibers that originates near the OLFACTORY EPITHELIUM. Its origin suggests that it is part of the VOMERONASAL SYSTEM and is involved in the perception of PHEROMONES, although its true function is the subject of debate.

nesting *n.* in an experimental design, the appearance of the levels of one factor (the **nested factor**) only within a single level of another factor. For example, classrooms are nested within a school because each specific classroom is found only within a single school; similarly, schools are nested within school districts. See HIERARCHICALLY NESTED DESIGN.

network *n.* **1.** the system of interpersonal interactions and relationships in an individual's environment that play an important part in the production of mental health or psychological disorder. The specific impact that these interactions and relationships have on the development of psychopathology is called the **network effect**. **2.** in SOCIOMETRY, a complex chain of interrelations that shape social tradition and public opinion, either spontaneously or through propaganda. See SOCIAL NETWORK. See also GROUP NETWORK; KINSHIP NETWORK; SEMANTIC NETWORK.

network analysis the study of the relations among sampling units (e.g., individuals) within a specific NETWORK (e.g., a friendship network) and the implications of these networks for the system in which they occur. In industrial and organizational psychology, it involves the identification of patterns of communication, influence, liking, and other interpersonal behaviors and attitudes among a collection of people. Properties of systems are assumed to be emergent, that is, not immediately predictable from a knowledge of networks among individuals. See also SOCIOMETRY.

network-memory model the concept that LONG-TERM MEMORY is made up of a series of knowledge representations that are connected or linked together. The strength of the connections is determined by experience factors, such as repetition and associations. See also CONNECTIONIST MODEL; SPREADING ACTIVATION.

neural *adj.* pertaining to the nervous system, its parts, and its functions.

neural arc the pathway followed by nerve impulses from a RECEPTOR to an EFFECTOR. In a REFLEX ARC a sensory neuron (or bundle of neurons) is connected either directly or via one or more INTERNEURONS to one or more MOTOR NEURONS; in more complex behaviors the pathways are longer and the connections are more complicated.

neural axis 1. the CENTRAL NERVOUS SYSTEM as a whole. **2.** the structures of the central nervous system that lie along the midline, including the spinal cord and brainstem but excluding the cerebral hemispheres and the cerebellar hemispheres. Also called **neuraxis**.

neural circuit an arrangement of NEURONS and their interconnections. Neural circuits often perform particular limited functions, such as NEGATIVE FEEDBACK circuits or POSITIVE FEEDBACK circuits. In a **local circuit** the neurons are all contained within a level of brain organization of a particular region.

neural constructivism the theory that brain development, and thus cognitive development, proceeds as a dynamic interaction between the development of the NEURAL SUBSTRATE and the environment.

neural Darwinism a biological theory of mind that attempts to explain specific cognitive functions, such as learning or memory, in terms of the selection of particular groups of neuronal structures inside individual brains. This selection of the best adapted structures is placed within the general framework of the Darwinian theory of NATURAL SELECTION. Critics of the theory argue that natural selection cannot apply without reproduction. Also called **neuronal group selection; selectionist brain theory**.

neuralgia *n.* pain, typically recurrent, sharp, and spasmodic, that occurs along the course of a nerve or a group of nerves. See TRIGEMINAL NEURALGIA. —**neuralgic** *adj.*

neural impulse see NERVE IMPULSE.

neural integration the algebraic summation of excitatory and inhibitory POSTSYNAPTIC POTENTIALS, which governs the excitability and firing of the postsynaptic neuron.

neural irritability a property of nerve tissue that makes it sensitive to stimulation and capable of responding by transmitting ACTION POTENTIALS. It is dependent on rapid, transient movement of ions through ion channels in the plasma membrane, causing a reversible DEPOLARIZATION of the membrane.

neural network 1. a technique for modeling the neural changes in the brain that underlie cognition and perception in which a large number of simple hypothetical neural units are connected to one another. **2.** a form of ARTIFICIAL INTELLIGENCE system used for learning and classifying data. Neural networks are usually abstract structures modeled on a computer and consist of a number of interconnected processing elements (**nodes**), each with a finite number of inputs and outputs. The elements in the network can have a "weight" determining how they process data, which can be adjusted according to experience. In this way, the network can be "trained" to recognize patterns in input data by optimizing the output of the network. The analogy is with the supposed action of neurons in the brain. Neural networks are used in research in such areas as pattern recognition, speech recognition, and machine translation of languages. They also have applications in other fields, such as financial prediction.

neural pathway any route followed by a nerve impulse through central or peripheral nerve fibers of the nervous system. A neural pathway may consist of a simple REFLEX ARC or a complex but specific routing, such as that followed by impulses transmitting a specific wavelength of sound from the COCHLEA to the auditory cortex. Also called **nerve pathway**.

neural plasticity 1. the ability of the nervous system to change in response to experience or environmental stimulation. **2.** the change in reactivity of the nervous system and its components as a result of constant, successive activations. Also called **neuroplasticity**.

neural quantum theory a theory to explain linear psychophysical functions, which are sometimes obtained instead of the ogival (S-shaped) form, whereby changes in sensation are assumed to occur in discrete steps and not along a continuum, based on the all-or-none law of neural activity. In this context, quantum refers

to a functionally distinct unit in the neural mechanisms that mediate sensory experience—that is, a perceptual rather than a physical unit. Also called **quantal hypothesis; quantal theory**.

neural regeneration regrowth of injured neurons, which occurs at a very slow rate. Complete replacement of injured neurons is rare in mammals but common in some fish and amphibians. Even in mammals, severed axons in the peripheral nervous system regrow readily.

neural reinforcement the strengthening of a neuron's response by the simultaneous or contingent activity of a second neuronal response.

neural substrate the part of the nervous system that mediates a particular behavior.

neural tube a structure formed during early development of an embryo, when folds of the neural plate curl over and fuse. Cells of the neural tube differentiate along its length on the anterior–posterior axis to form swellings that correspond to the future FOREBRAIN, MIDBRAIN, and HINDBRAIN; the posterior part of the tube develops into the spinal cord. The cavity of the tube ultimately becomes the interconnected cerebral VENTRICLES and the central canal of the spinal cord. Many congenital defects of the nervous system originate at this stage of development. See also NEURULATION.

neuritic plaque see SENILE PLAQUE.

neuritis *n.* inflammation of a nerve, especially resulting from infection or autoimmune factors. See also NEUROPATHY.

neuroanatomy *n.* the study of the structures and relationships among the various parts of the nervous system. —**neuroanatomist** *n.*

neurobiology *n.* a branch of biology that studies the structures and processes of the nervous system. —**neurobiological** *adj.*

neurobiotaxis *n.* the growth of a nerve fiber toward the tissue it will innervate, which occurs during embryological development. Those factors that influence neurobiotaxis are currently the subject of research on nerve growth in adult organisms, suggesting the possibility of nerve regeneration or replacement after injury or disease.

neuroblast *n.* an undifferentiated cell that is capable of developing into a neuron.

neuroblastoma *n.* a type of tumor that develops from nerve cells that resemble the primitive neural cells of the embryo. The cells of a neuroblastoma are very small with very large nuclei, often arranged in sheets, clumps, or cords. Most such tumors develop in the adrenal medulla or autonomic nervous system.

neurochemistry *n.* the branch of NEUROSCIENCE that deals with the roles of atoms, molecules, and ions in the functioning of nervous systems. Because chemical substances in a physiological system obey the laws of nature that apply in other environments, the activities of neurotransmitters, drugs, and other molecules in the nervous system can be explained in terms of basic chemical concepts.

neuroendocrinology *n.* the study of the relationships between the nervous system, especially the brain, and the endocrine system. Some cells within the nervous system release hormones into the local or systemic circulation; these are called **neuroendocrine** (or **neurosecretory**) **cells**. The HYPOTHALAMUS, for example, produces RELEASING HORMONES that regulate secretion of pituitary hormones. Certain substances, such as NOREPINEPHRINE, act both as hormones and as neurotransmitters. —**neuroendocrinological** *adj.* —**neuroendocrinologist** *n.*

neuroethology *n.* a branch of biology that studies animal behavior in relation to neural processes and structures. See ETHOLOGY.

neurofeedback *n.* a learning strategy that enables people to alter their own brain waves using information about their brain-wave characteristics that is made available through electroencephalograph recordings that may be presented to them as a video display or an auditory signal. Also called **neurobiofeedback**. See BIOFEEDBACK.

neurofibrillary tangles twisted strands of abnormal filaments within neurons that are associated with Alzheimer's disease. The filaments form microscopically visible knots or tangles consisting of tau protein, which normally is associated with MICROTUBULES. If the structure of tau is rendered abnormal, the microtubule structure collapses, and the tau protein collects in neurofibrillary tangles.

neurofibroma *n.* a tumor of peripheral nerves caused by abnormal proliferation of SCHWANN CELLS. A neurofibroma is very similar to a SCHWANNOMA but is distinguished by its lack of a capsule.

neurogenic *adj.* pertaining to a condition or event caused or produced by a component of the nervous system.

neurogenic communication disorder any speech or language problem due to nervous system impairment that causes some level of difficulty or inability in exchanging information with others.

neuroglia *n.* see GLIA. —**neuroglial** *adj.*

neuroglioma *n.* see GLIOMA.

neurogram *n.* **1.** a wavelike tracing, either printed or displayed on a monitor, that represents the electrical impulses of neurons. **2.** a three-dimensional image of nerves in the brain provided by a specialized MAGNETIC RESONANCE IMAGING technique.

neurohormone *n.* a hormone produced by neural tissue and released into the general circulation. See NEUROENDOCRINOLOGY.

neuroleptic *n.* see ANTIPSYCHOTIC.

neuroleptic malignant syndrome a rare complication of therapy with conventional (typical or first-generation) ANTIPSYCHOTICS, characterized by fever, inability to regulate blood pressure, difficulty in breathing, and changes in consciousness (including coma); mortality rates approaching 25% have been observed. It occurs primarily at the start of treatment or with a sudden increase in dose. The incidence of the syndrome, never high, has declined further with the abandonment of MEGADOSE PHARMACOTHERAPY with conventional antipsychotics and the advent of second-generation atypical antipsychotics.

neuroleptic syndrome the series of effects observed in individuals who have taken ANTIPSYCHOTICS. It is characterized by reduced motor activity and emotionality, an indifference to external stimuli, and a decreased ability to perform tasks that require good motor coordination. With high doses, patients may become cataleptic.

neurolinguistic programming (**NLP**) a set of techniques and strategies designed to improve interpersonal communications and relations by modifying the "mental programs," or MENTAL MODELS of the world, that individuals develop and use to respond to and interact with the environment and other people. This approach uses principles derived from NEUROLINGUISTICS and presumes that these programs, as well as the behaviors they influence, result from the interaction among the brain, language, and the body. In order to achieve desired change, one must first understand subjective experience and the structures of thought (i.e., mental programs) underlying that experience, and then learn to modify these programs as needed, for example, to enhance adaptive behavior across a variety of situations or to attain excellence in personal performance. Although originally applied to psychotherapy and counseling, neurolinguistic programming has developed applications in other fields, such as business management, artificial intelligence, and education.

neurolinguistics *n.* the branch of linguistics that investigates how language organization and language processing are encoded in the brain.

neurological evaluation analysis of the data gathered by an examining physician of an individual's mental status and sensory and motor functioning. The examination typically includes assessment of cognition, speech and behavior, orientation and level of alertness, muscular strength and tone, muscle coordination and movement, tendon reflexes, cranial nerves, pain and temperature sensitivity, and discriminative senses.

neurology *n.* a branch of medicine that deals with the nervous system in both healthy and diseased states. The diagnosis and treatment of diseases of the nervous system is called **clinical neurology**; **neurologists** diagnose and treat patients with stroke, dementia, headaches, and back pain, among other disorders. —**neurological** *adj.*

neuromodulator *n.* a substance that modulates the effectiveness of neurotransmitters by influencing the release of the transmitters or the RECEPTOR response to the transmitter.

neuromuscular disorder any pathological condition that involves the nerves and muscles. Common symptoms include weakness, cramps, and paralysis. Examples of such disorders include MUSCULAR DYSTROPHY, MYASTHENIA GRAVIS, and the MYOPATHIES.

neuromuscular system see MOTOR SYSTEM.

neuron (**neurone**) *n.* the basic cellular unit of the nervous system. Each neuron is composed of a CELL BODY; fine, branching extensions (DENDRITES) that receive incoming nerve signals; and a single, long extension (AXON) that conducts nerve impulses to its branching terminal. The axon terminal transmits impulses to other neurons, or to effector organs (e.g., muscles and glands), via junctions called SYNAPSES or neuromuscular junctions. Neurons can be classified according to their function as MOTOR NEURONS, SENSORY NEURONS, or INTERNEURONS. There are various structural types, including UNIPOLAR NEURONS, BIPOLAR NEURONS, and MULTIPOLAR NEURONS. The axons of vertebrate neurons are often surrounded by a MYELIN SHEATH. Also called **nerve cell**. —**neuronal** *adj.*

neuropathology *n.* the study of diseases of the nervous system. —**neuropathological** *adj.* —**neuropathologist** *n.*

neuropathy *n.* disease of the nervous system, particularly the peripheral nerves. See PERIPHERAL NEUROPATHY. —**neuropathic** *adj.*

neuropeptide *n.* any of several peptides that are released by neurons as NEUROTRANSMITTERS or NEUROHORMONES. They include the ENDOGENOUS OPIOIDS (e.g., enkephalin and endorphin); peptides found in both the brain and the peripheral nervous system (e.g., SUBSTANCE P and neurotensin); hypothalamic RELEASING HORMONES (e.g., thyrotropin-releasing hormone); pituitary hormones (e.g., GROWTH HORMONE and prolactin); and other circulating peptides (e.g., atrial natriuretic peptide and bradykinin).

neuropharmacology *n.* the scientific study of the effects of drugs on the nervous system. —**neuropharmacological** *adj.* —**neuropharmacologist** *n.*

neurophysiology *n.* a branch of NEUROSCIENCE that is concerned with the normal and abnormal functioning of the nervous system, including the chemical and electrical activities of individual neurons. —**neurophysiological** *adj.* —**neurophysiologist** *n.*

neuroprotective *adj.* denoting agents, such as drugs and hormones, that are believed to prevent damage to the brain or spinal cord.

neuropsychological assessment an evaluation of the presence, nature, and extent of brain damage or dysfunction derived from the results of various NEUROPSYCHOLOGICAL TESTS.

neuropsychological rehabilitation the use of psychological techniques to treat and manage cognitive, emotional, and behavioral problems that arise from brain damage or dysfunction.

neuropsychological test any of various clinical instruments for assessing cognitive impairment, including those measuring memory, language, learning, attention, and visuospatial and visuoconstructive functioning. Examples of batteries of such tests are the HALSTEAD–REITAN NEUROPSYCHOLOGICAL BATTERY and the LURIA–NEBRASKA NEUROPSYCHOLOGICAL BATTERY.

neuropsychology *n.* the branch of science that combines neuroscience and psychology. See also CLINICAL NEUROPSYCHOLOGY. —**neuropsychological** *adj.* —**neuropsychologist** *n.*

neuroreceptor *n.* a RECEPTOR molecule located in a neuron cell membrane that binds molecules of a particular neurotransmitter, hormone, drug, or the like and initiates a particular response within the neuron. Also called **neurotransmitter receptor**.

neuroscience *n.* the scientific study of the nervous system, including NEUROANATOMY, NEUROCHEMISTRY, NEUROLOGY, NEUROPHYSIOLOGY, and NEUROPHARMACOLOGY, and its applications in psychology and psychiatry. See also BEHAVIORAL NEUROSCIENCE; COGNITIVE NEUROSCIENCE.

neurosecretion *n.* **1.** the secretion of substances, such as hormones or neurotransmitters, by neural tissue. **2.** a substance secreted in this way.

neurosis *n.* any one of a variety of mental disorders characterized by significant anxiety or other distressing emotional symptoms, such as persistent and irrational fears, obsessive thoughts, compulsive acts, dissociative states, and somatic and depressive reactions. The symptoms do not involve gross personality disorganization, total lack of insight, or loss of contact with reality (compare PSYCHOSIS). In psychoanalysis, neuroses are generally viewed as exaggerated, unconscious methods of coping with internal conflicts and the anxiety they produce. In DSM-IV-TR, most of what used to be called neuroses are now classified as ANXIETY DISORDERS. Also called **psychoneurosis**. —**neurotic** *adj., n.*

neurosurgery *n.* surgical procedures performed on the brain, spinal cord, or peripheral nerves for the purpose of restoring functioning or preventing further impairment. See also PSYCHOSURGERY. —**neurosurgeon** *n.* —**neurosurgical** *adj.*

neurotic anxiety in psychoanalytic theory, anxiety that originates in unconscious conflict and is maladaptive in nature: It has a disturbing effect on emotion and behavior and also intensifies resistance to treatment. Neurotic anxiety contrasts with realistic anxiety, about an external danger or threat, and with moral anxiety, which is guilt posited to originate in the superego.

neurotic conflict 1. in psychoanalytic theory, an INTRAPSYCHIC conflict that leads to persistent maladjustment and emotional disturbance. **2.** in the approach of German-born U.S. psychoanalyst Karen D. Horney (1885–1952), the clash that occurs between opposing NEUROTIC NEEDS, such as an excessive need for power and independence and the need for love and dependence. See also NEUROTIC TREND.

neuroticism *n.* **1.** the state of being neurotic or a proneness to NEUROSIS. **2.** a mild condition of neurosis. **3.** one of the dimensions of the FIVE-FACTOR PERSONALITY MODEL and the Big Five personality model, characterized by a chronic level of emotional instability and proneness to psychological distress.

neurotic needs in psychoanalytic theory, excessive drives and demands that may arise out of the strategies individuals use to defend themselves against BASIC ANXIETY. German-born U.S. psychoanalyst Karen D. Horney (1885–1952) enumerated ten neurotic needs: for affection and approval, for a partner to take over one's life, for restriction of one's life, for power, for exploitation of others, for prestige, for admiration, for achievement, for self-sufficiency and independence, and for perfection. When an individual's personality is dominated by a few neurotic needs he or she may exhibit a NEUROTIC TREND.

neurotic trend in the theory of German-born U.S. psychoanalyst Karen D. Horney (1885–1952), one of three basic tendencies stemming from an individual's choice of strategies to counteract BASIC ANXIETY. These strategies generate insatiable NEUROTIC NEEDS, which group themselves into three trends: (a) moving toward people, or clinging to others (the **compliant character**); (b) moving away from people, or insisting on independence and self-dependence (the **detached character**); and (c) moving against people, or seeking power, prestige, and possessions (the **aggressive character**).

neurotoxic *n.* any substance that is destructive to the central or peripheral nervous system, causing temporary or permanent damage.

neurotoxicology *n.* the study of the effects of toxins and poisons on the nervous system. **—neurotoxicological** *adj.*

neurotransmission *n.* the process by which a signal or other activity in a neuron is transferred to an adjacent neuron or other cell. Synaptic transmission, which occurs between two neurons via a SYNAPSE, is largely chemical, by the release and binding of NEUROTRANSMITTER, but it may also be electrical (see ELECTRICAL SYNAPSE). Neurotransmission also occurs between a neuron and an effector organ or gland and between a neuron and a skeletal muscle cell. Also called **neural transmission**; **neuronal transmission**.

neurotransmitter *n.* any of a large number of chemicals that can be released by neurons to mediate transmission or inhibition of nerve signals across the junctions (SYNAPSES) between neurons. When triggered by a nerve impulse, the neurotransmitter is released from the terminal button of the AXON, travels across the SYNAPTIC CLEFT, and binds to and reacts with RECEPTOR molecules in the postsynaptic membrane. Neurotransmitters include amines, such as ACETYLCHOLINE, NOREPINEPHRINE, DOPAMINE, and SEROTONIN; and amino acids, such as GAMMA-AMINOBUTYRIC ACID, GLUTAMATE, and GLYCINE. Also called **chemical transmitter**; **synaptic transmitter**.

neurotrophic factor a polypeptide that is synthesized by and released from neurons and helps certain neurons to grow and survive.

neurulation *n.* the process of development of the rudimentary nervous system in early embryonic life, including formation of the NEURAL TUBE from the neural plate.

neutrality *n.* a role or a manner of behavior adopted by the therapist, who not only remains passive and permissive but also does not express judgments of right and wrong or suggest what is proper behavior on the part of the client.

neutralization *n.* in psychoanalytic theory, the use of sexual or aggressive energy in the service of the EGO rather than for gratification of the INSTINCTS, that is, in functions such as problem solving, creative imagination, scientific inquiry, and decision making. SUBLIMATION uses neutralized energy. Also called **taming of the instinct**. See also DESEXUALIZATION. **—neutralize** *vb.*

neutral stimulus in PAVLOVIAN CONDITIONING, a stimulus that does not elicit a response of the sort to be measured as an index of conditioning. For example, the sound of a bell has no effect on salivation, therefore it is a neutral stimulus with respect to salivation and a good candidate for conditioning of that response.

new-age therapy any of a number of popular treatments that lack a sound scientific basis and are generally not accepted by mental health professionals as valid, effective therapeutic practice. Support for such therapies does not come from independent scientific studies, but rather is derived primarily from the "insights" and observations of their founders or the analysis and evaluation of participant feedback. An example of a new-age therapy is REBIRTHING.

new-look theory of cognitive dissonance a theory postulating that COGNITIVE DISSONANCE is a result of behavior that causes unpleasant consequences. If a person assumes responsibility for these consequences (i.e., if the person freely chose to perform the behavior and the consequences were foreseeable), this results

N

in physiological arousal. In order for cognitive dissonance to occur, people must then perceive this arousal state as negative and due to the consequences.

Newman–Keuls test a MULTIPLE COMPARISON testing procedure used for making post hoc pairwise comparisons among a set of means.

nicotine *n.* an alkaloid obtained primarily from the TOBACCO plant (*Nicotiana tabacum*). One of the most widely used psychoactive drugs, nicotine is the primary active ingredient in tobacco and accounts for both the acute pharmacological effects of smoking or chewing tobacco (e.g., a discharge of EPINEPHRINE, a sudden release of glucose, an increase in blood pressure, respiration, heart rate, and cutaneous vasoconstriction) and the dependence that develops (see NICOTINE DEPENDENCE; NICOTINE WITHDRAWAL). The behavioral effects of the drug include enhanced alertness and feelings of calm. Nicotine produces multiple pharmacological effects on the central nervous system by activating NICOTINIC RECEPTORS, facilitating the release of several neurotransmitters, particularly dopamine (a reaction similar to that seen with such drugs as cocaine and heroin), along with other actions in the periphery. In large doses it is highly poisonous, producing such symptoms as dizziness, diarrhea, vomiting, tremors, spasms, unconsciousness, heart attack, and potentially death via paralysis of the muscles of respiration. **—nicotinic** *adj.*

nicotine dependence a cluster of cognitive, behavioral, and physiological symptoms indicating continued use of nicotine despite significant nicotine-related problems. There is a pattern of repeated nicotine ingestion resulting in tolerance, characteristic withdrawal symptoms if use is suspended (see NICOTINE WITHDRAWAL), and an uncontrollable drive to continue use. See also SUBSTANCE DEPENDENCE.

nicotine withdrawal a characteristic withdrawal syndrome that develops after cessation of (or reduction in) prolonged, heavy nicotine consumption. Some of the following are typically required for a diagnosis of nicotine withdrawal: DYSPHORIA or depressed mood; insomnia; irritability, frustration, or anger; anxiety; difficulty in concentrating; restlessness; decreased heart rate; and increased appetite or weight gain.

nicotinic receptor (nAchR) a type of ACETYLCHOLINE RECEPTOR that responds to NICOTINE as well as to acetylcholine. Nicotinic receptors mediate chiefly the excitatory activities of acetylcholine, including those at neuromuscular junctions. Compare MUSCARINIC RECEPTOR.

night blindness a visual impairment marked by partial or complete inability to see objects in a dimly lighted environment. Night blindness can be inherited or due to defective DARK ADAPTATION or dietary deficiency of vitamin A. Also called **nyctalopia**.

night-eating syndrome an eating disorder characterized by INSOMNIA, nocturnal HYPER-

PHAGIA, and morning ANOREXIA that persist for at least 3 months. Recent research suggests night-eating syndrome is related to hormonal irregularities and a disturbed circadian rhythm of food intake, although chronic stress may also be a contributing factor.

nightmare *n.* a frightening or otherwise disturbing dream, in which fear, sadness, despair, disgust, or some combination of these forms the emotional content. Nightmares contain visual imagery and some degree of narrative structure and typically occur during REM SLEEP. The dreamer tends to waken suddenly from a nightmare and is immediately alert and aware of his or her surroundings. The occurrence of frequent nightmares is classified as NIGHTMARE DISORDER. Nightmares are also a symptom of POSTTRAUMATIC STRESS DISORDER. **—nightmarish** *adj.*

nightmare disorder a SLEEP DISORDER characterized by the repeated occurrence of frightening dreams that lead to awakenings from sleep. It was formerly known as **dream anxiety disorder**. See PARASOMNIA.

night terror see SLEEP TERROR DISORDER.

nihilism *n.* **1.** the delusion of nonexistence: a fixed belief that the mind, body, or the world at large—or parts thereof—no longer exists. Also called **delusion of negation**; **nihilistic delusion**. **2.** the belief that existence is without meaning. **—nihilistic** *adj.*

NIMH abbreviation for NATIONAL INSTITUTE OF MENTAL HEALTH.

nitric oxide a compound present in numerous body tissues, where it has a variety of functions. In the body it is synthesized by the enzyme nitric oxide synthase from arginine, NADPH, and oxygen. Nitric oxide functions as a neurotransmitter, or an agent that influences neurotransmitters, in the brain and other parts of the central nervous system. In peripheral tissues it is involved in the relaxation of smooth muscle, and thus acts as a vasodilator, a bronchodilator, and as a relaxant of smooth muscle in the penis and clitoris, being involved in erection and other components of the sexual response.

NLP abbreviation for NEUROLINGUISTIC PROGRAMMING.

NMDA N-methyl-D-aspartate: an AGONIST that binds to a class of GLUTAMATE RECEPTORS that are both ligand-gated and voltage-sensitive.

NMDA hypothesis of consciousness a speculative hypothesis proposing that because the NMDA receptor complex is centrally involved in working memory, and working memory is intimately involved in consciousness, NMDA may be a component in the neural underpinnings of consciousness.

NMDA receptor see GLUTAMATE RECEPTOR.

NMR abbreviation for NUCLEAR MAGNETIC RESONANCE.

nocebo *n.* an adverse or otherwise unwanted

physical or emotional symptom caused by the administration of a PLACEBO.

nociception *n.* see PAIN PERCEPTION. —**nociceptive** *adj.*

nociceptor *n.* a sensory RECEPTOR that responds to stimuli that are generally painful or detrimental to the organism. Also called **pain receptor**.

nocturnal *adj.* active or occurring during the dark period of the daily cycle. Compare DIURNAL.

node *n.* **1.** a point in a graph, tree diagram, or the like at which lines intersect or branch. **2.** a single point or unit in an associative model of memory. Nodes typically represent a single concept or feature, are connected to other nodes (usually representing semantically related concepts and features) by links in an associative network, and may be activated or inhibited to varying degrees, depending on the conditions. **3.** in communications, a point in a network at which two or more pathways are interconnected. **4.** in artificial intelligence, see NEURAL NETWORK. —**nodal** *adj.*

node of Ranvier any of successive regularly spaced gaps in the MYELIN SHEATH surrounding an axon. The gaps permit the exchange of ions across the plasma membrane at those points, allowing the nerve impulse to leap from one node to the next in so-called SALTATION along the axon. [Louis A. **Ranvier** (1835–1922), French pathologist]

noëgenesis *n.* the production of new knowledge from sensory or cognitive experience. There are three laws of noëgenesis: (a) the apprehension of experience (by which new stimuli are encoded), (b) the eduction—or apprehension— of relations (by which the nature of relations between stimuli is inferred), and (c) the eduction of correlates (by which a relation previously inferred is applied in a new context). —**noëgenetic** *adj.*

noetic *adj.* describing a level of knowledge or memory in which there is awareness of the known or remembered thing but not of one's personal experience in relation to that thing. Compare ANOETIC; AUTONOETIC.

noise *n.* **1.** any unwanted sound or, more generally, any unwanted disturbance (e.g., electrical noise). **2.** a random or aperiodic waveform whose properties are described statistically. There are many types of noise, which are distinguished by their spectral or statistical properties. **White noise** (or **background noise**) has equal energy at all frequencies; **broadband noise** has energy over a relatively wide frequency range (e.g., 50 Hz to 10 kHz for audition); **pink noise** has energy that is inversely proportional to frequency. **3.** anything that interferes with, obscures, reduces, or otherwise adversely affects the clarity or precision of an ongoing process, such as the communication of a message or signal.

nomenclature *n.* a systematic classification of technical terms used in an art or science.

nominal data see CATEGORICAL DATA.

nominal group technique a structured technique of group problem solving that aims to improve the quality of group decisions by reducing the pressures on group members to conform. Individuals first state their ideas privately and anonymously, and these ideas are posted for discussion and clarification. The group votes anonymously on the ideas and then goes through another round of discussion and clarification, followed by another round of voting. The intent is to reach a consensus on the relative merits of the ideas generated by the group.

nominalism *n.* in medieval philosophy, the position that only concrete particulars have real substantial existence, UNIVERSALS (i.e., general qualities, such as "redness" or "beauty") being mere names with, at most, a mental existence. Compare PLATONIC IDEALISM; REALISM. —**nominalist** *n.*, *adj.*

nominal scale a scale of measurement in which data are simply classified into mutually exclusive categories, without indicating order, magnitude, a true zero point, or the like. Also called **categorical scale**.

nominal stimulus in stimulus–response experiments, the stimulus as defined and presented by the experimenter. This may be different from the FUNCTIONAL STIMULUS experienced by the organism.

nominative self the self as knower of the self, rather than the self so known. In the psychology of U.S. psychologist William James (1842–1910) the nominative self, or "I," is contrasted with the EMPIRICAL SELF, or "me."

nomological net a conceptual network, often comprising inferences about a variable. The CONSTRUCT VALIDITY of a test is ascertained through a nomological network reflecting research and other experience with the test.

nomology *n.* **1.** the science or study of law and lawfulness. **2.** the branch of science concerned with the formulation of natural laws, especially causal laws. A nomological approach is one that strives for causal explanations of phenomena, rather than merely classifying them. See CAUSALITY; NATURAL LAW THEORY. —**nomological** *adj.*

nomothetic *adj.* relating to the formulation of general laws as opposed to the study of the individual case. A **nomothetic approach** involves the study of groups of people or cases for the purpose of discovering those general and universally valid laws or principles that characterize the average person or case. Compare IDIOGRAPHIC.

nonadaptive trait a trait that has no specific value with respect to NATURAL SELECTION, being neither useful nor harmful for REPRODUCTIVE SUCCESS. In human beings eye color, earlobe size, and being able to curl one's tongue are nonadaptive traits.

nonadditive *adj.* describing values or measurements that cannot be meaningfully summarized through addition because the resulting overall value does not correctly reflect the underlying properties of and associations between the component values.

nonadherence *n.* failure of an individual to follow a prescribed therapeutic regimen. Although nonadherence has traditionally been ascribed to oppositional behavior, it is more likely due to inadequate communication between the practitioner and the individual, physical or cognitive limitations that prevent the patient from following therapeutic recommendations (e.g., language differences between patient and practitioner, physical disabilities), or adverse effects that are not being adequately addressed. A primary aspect of health psychology involves methods of reducing nonadherence and increasing adherence. Also called **noncompliance**.

nonattitude *n.* an extremely weak attitude that has little persistence over time and minimal resistance to persuasion. Such attitudes have little impact on information processing and behavior. In extreme cases, nonattitudes may be reports of attitudes that reflect no meaningful evaluation of the ATTITUDE OBJECT. See also STRENGTH OF AN ATTITUDE.

noncentrality parameter a parameter in many probability distributions used in hypothesis testing that has a value different from zero when a sample is obtained from a population whose parameters have values different from those specified by the NULL HYPOTHESIS under test. This parameter is important in determining the POWER of a statistical procedure.

non compos mentis in law, mentally deficient or legally insane and therefore not responsible for one's conduct. See INCOMPETENCE; INSANITY. Compare COMPOS MENTIS.

nonconformity *n.* expressing opinions, making judgments, or performing actions that are inconsistent with the opinions, judgments, or actions of other people or the normative standards of a social group or situation. Nonconformity can reflect individuals' ignorance of the group's standards, an inability to reach those standards, independence (as when individuals retain their own personally preferred position despite group pressure to change it), and the ANTICONFORMITY of individuals who deliberately disagree with others or act in atypical ways. Compare CONFORMITY.

nonconscious *adj.* describing anything that is not available to conscious report. See UNCONSCIOUS.

noncontingent reinforcement the process or circumstances in which a stimulus known to be effective as a REINFORCER is presented independently of any particular behavior. Because contingencies may arise by accident, behavior-independent presentation of stimuli cannot guarantee that no contingency exists between a response and the stimuli. See REINFORCEMENT.

nondeclarative memory a collection of various forms of memory that operate automatically and accumulate information that is not accessible to conscious recollection. For instance, one can do something faster if one has done it before, even if one cannot recall the earlier performance. Nondeclarative memory includes PROCEDURAL LEARNING and PRIMING. Nondeclarative memory does not depend on the medial temporal lobes and is preserved in individuals with amnestic disorder. Compare DECLARATIVE MEMORY.

nondecremental conduction the propagation of a nerve impulse along an axon in which the amplitude of the impulse is maintained as it progresses. Compare DECREMENTAL CONDUCTION.

nondirectional test see TWO-TAILED TEST.

nondirective approach an approach to psychotherapy and counseling in which the client leads the way by expressing his or her own feelings, defining his or her own problems, and interpreting his or her own behavior, while the therapist or counselor establishes an encouraging atmosphere and clarifies the client's ideas rather than directing the process. This approach is a cornerstone of CLIENT-CENTERED THERAPY.

nondirective play therapy a form of PLAY THERAPY based on the principle that a child has the capacity to revise his or her own attitudes and behavior. The therapist provides a variety of play materials and either assumes a friendly, interested role without giving direct suggestions or interpretations or engages the child in conversation that focuses on the child's present feelings and present life situations. The therapist's accepting attitude encourages the child to try new and more appropriate ways of dealing with problems.

nondirective teaching model a person-oriented teaching model, associated with the therapeutic approach of U.S. psychologist Carl Rogers (1902–1987), that is primarily concerned with developing the capacity for self-instruction while emphasizing self-discovery, self-understanding, and the realization of one's innate potential.

nondirective therapy see CLIENT-CENTERED THERAPY.

nonepileptic seizure an episode that resembles an epileptic seizure but is not produced by an abnormal electrical discharge in the brain. Such seizures may be classified as **physiologic nonepileptic seizures**, which are associated with metabolic disturbances (e.g., changes in heart rhythm or sudden drops in blood pressure) and include SYNCOPE and TRANSIENT ISCHEMIC ATTACKS, or as PSYCHOGENIC NONEPILEPTIC SEIZURES. Nonepileptic seizures are also called **nonepileptic events** (or **attacks**).

nonequivalent-groups design a NONRANDOMIZED DESIGN in which the responses of a treatment group and a control group are compared on measures collected at the beginning and end of the research.

nonfluency *n.* a type of speech that involves such disturbances as dysprosody (altered speech rhythms or intonation), dysarthria (impaired articulation), and agrammatism (deviation from grammatical rules).

nonfluent aphasia see APHASIA.

nongenetic inheritance the transmission of behavioral or physiological functions between generations without any direct genetic basis. For example, because dominant female macaques intervene more frequently and successfully on behalf of their offspring than do subordinate females, the offspring inherit the status of their female parents. The type of maternal care a young rodent or monkey receives can lead to permanent physiological and neurological changes that affect its subsequent adult parental behavior.

noninvasive *adj.* **1.** denoting procedures or tests that do not require puncture or incision of the skin or insertion of an instrument or device into the body for diagnosis or treatment. **2.** of a tumor, not capable of spreading from one tissue to another (see NEOPLASM). Compare INVASIVE.

nonjudgmental approach in psychotherapy, the presentation or display of a neutral, noncritical attitude on the part of the therapist in order to encourage the client to give free expression to ideas and feelings. See also NEUTRALITY.

nonlinear *adj.* describing any relationship between two variables (X and Y) that cannot be expressed in the form $Y = a + bX$, where a and b are numerical constants. The relationship therefore does not appear to be a straight line when depicted graphically.

nonlinear dynamics theories a family of theories, including CHAOS THEORY, concerning the behavior of neurons and neural assemblies in stochastic processes. Nonlinear theories may be able to account for behavior of complex systems that would appear random in deterministic models.

nonlinear regression model any regression model that is not linear in its parameters. Such models cannot be solved by the methods of ordinary least squares regression techniques. Also called **curvilinear regression model**.

nonmanipulated variable a variable observed in research but not experimentally manipulated.

nonorthogonal design a FACTORIAL DESIGN in which the number of subjects or observations in each CELL differs or in which the cell sizes do not have a certain constant of PROPORTIONALITY. Compare ORTHOGONAL DESIGN.

nonparametric statistics statistical tests that do not make assumptions about the distribution of the attribute (or attributes) in the population being tested, such as normality and homo-

geneity of variance. Compare PARAMETRIC STATISTICS.

nonrandomized design any of a large number of research designs in which sampling units are not assigned to experimental conditions at random.

nonrapid-eye-movement sleep see NREM SLEEP.

nonregulatory drive a DRIVE that serves functions that are unrelated to preserving physiological HOMEOSTASIS and thus not necessary for the physical survival of the individual organism, for example, sex or achievement. Also called **general drive**. Compare REGULATORY DRIVE.

non-REM sleep see NREM SLEEP.

nonreversal shift in DISCRIMINATIONS involving two alternatives, a change in contingencies such that stimuli that were irrelevant in the initial phase of training become the relevant stimuli in a later phase. For example, in initial training involving the presentation of different shapes, white shapes might be designated correct and black ones incorrect. In a following condition, squares (which were one of the shapes in the original task) might be designated correct and circles (also present in the earlier phase) incorrect. Compare REVERSAL SHIFT.

nonsense syllable any three-letter nonword used in learning and memory studies to study learning of items that do not already have meaning or associations with other information in memory.

nonshared environment in behavior genetic analyses, those aspects of an environment that individuals living together (e.g., in a family household) do not share and that therefore cause them to become dissimilar to each other. Examples of nonshared environmental factors include the different friends or teachers that siblings in the same household might have outside of the home. Also called **unshared environment**. Compare SHARED ENVIRONMENT.

nonspecific effect a result or consequence whose specific cause or precipitating factors are unknown, for example, the effect on a patient of the belief that he or she has received medication or some other intervention when no true treatment has been given. See also PLACEBO EFFECT.

nonstate theories of hypnosis explanations of the hypnotic state simply as variations of the psychological, physiological, and behavioral aspects of waking consciousness, rather than as a unique altered state of consciousness. Compare STATE THEORIES OF HYPNOSIS.

nonsteroidal anti-inflammatory drugs see NSAIDS.

nonstriate visual cortex the many regions of cortex that surround the STRIATE CORTEX and participate in the processing of visual stimuli beyond the simple analysis of features that occurs in striate cortex. The nonstriate visual cortex includes parietal regions associated with visuospatial functions, temporal regions important for object recognition, and cortical areas that contribute to eye movements. It is thus somewhat more extensive than PRESTRIATE CORTEX.

nontraditional marriage a marriage that deviates from the traditional patterns of marriage in a society. In the United States and western Europe, such marriages may include marriages without the intent of having children or that permit the partners to have sexual relations with other people. Compare TRADITIONAL MARRIAGE.

nonverbal behavior actions that can indicate an individual's attitudes or feelings without the need for speech. Nonverbal behavior can be apparent in FACIAL EXPRESSION, gaze direction, interpersonal distance, posture and postural changes, and gestures. It serves a number of functions, including providing information to other people (if they can detect and understand the signals), regulating interactions among people, and revealing the degree of intimacy between those present. Nonverbal behavior is often used synonymously with NONVERBAL COMMUNICATION, despite the fact that nonverbal actions are not always intended for, or understood by, other people.

nonverbal communication the act of conveying information without the use of words. Nonverbal communication occurs through facial expressions, gestures, body language, tone of voice, and other physical indications of mood, attitude, approbation, and so forth, some of which may require knowledge of the culture or subculture to understand. In psychotherapy, clients' nonverbal communication can be as important to note as their verbal communication. See also NONVERBAL BEHAVIOR.

nonverbal intelligence an expression of intelligence that does not require language. Nonverbal intelligence can be measured with PERFORMANCE TESTS.

nonverbal learning disorder a LEARNING DISABILITY that is characterized by limited skills in critical thinking and deficits in processing nonverbal information. This affects a child's academic progress as well as other areas of functioning, which may include social competencies, visual-spatial abilities, motor coordination, and emotional functioning. Also called **nonverbal learning disability**.

nonverbal reinforcement any form of NONVERBAL COMMUNICATION, such as a gesture, facial expression, or body movement, that increases the frequency of the behavior that immediately precedes it. For example, a parent's smile following a desired response from a child, such as saying "thank you," reinforces the child's behavior. See also REINFORCEMENT.

non-Western therapies alternatives or complements to traditional Western forms of and approaches to psychotherapy and counseling that emphasize the body (e.g., ACUPUNCTURE, yoga)

and the interdependency of all beings and deemphasize individualism and rigid autonomy. These therapies have typically developed outside of Europe and North America. See also COMPLEMENTARY AND ALTERNATIVE MEDICINE.

nonzero-sum game in GAME THEORY, a situation in which the rewards and costs experienced by all players do not balance (i.e., they add up to less than or more than zero). In such a situation, unlike a ZERO-SUM GAME, one player's gain is not necessarily another player's loss.

nootropic drugs drugs that are used to enhance cognitive function, usually in the treatment of progressive dementias, such as Alzheimer's disease, but also of cognitive dysfunction due to traumatic brain injury. They do not reverse the course of the dementia, but are reported to slow its progress in mild to moderate forms of the disease. Many of these drugs work by inhibiting the activity of acetylcholinesterase in the central nervous system, thereby counteracting the disruption of cholinergic neurotransmission observed in patients with Alzheimer's disease. Other drugs use different mechanisms for improving cognitive performance in patients with Alzheimer's disease, including NMDA receptor (see GLUTAMATE RECEPTOR) antagonism and potentially the prevention of BETA-AMYLOID plaque formation in the brain. Current nootropics include tacrine, donepezil, rivastigmine, and galantamine. Also called **cognitive enhancers**; **memory-enhancing drugs**.

noradrenergic *adj.* responding to, releasing, or otherwise involving norepinephrine (noradrenaline). For example, a **noradrenergic neuron** is one that employs norepinephrine as a neurotransmitter.

noradrenergic receptor any of certain receptors in the central nervous system and sympathetic nervous system that bind and respond to NOREPINEPHRINE (noradrenaline) or substances that mimic its action. See ADRENERGIC RECEPTOR.

norepinephrine *n.* a catecholamine NEUROTRANSMITTER and hormone produced mainly by brainstem nuclei and in the adrenal medulla. Also called **noradrenaline**.

norm *n.* **1.** a standard or range of values that represents the typical performance of a group or of an individual (of a certain age, for example) against which comparisons can be made. **2.** a conversion of a raw score into a scaled score that is more easily interpretable, such as percentiles or IQ scores. —**normative** *adj.*

normal distribution a theoretical continuous PROBABILITY DISTRIBUTION that is a function of two parameters: the EXPECTED VALUE, μ, and the VARIANCE, σ^2. It is given by

$$(x) = [\exp(-(x-\mu)^2/2\sigma^2)]/\sigma\sqrt{(2\pi)}$$

The normal distribution is the type of distribution expected when the same measurement is taken several times and the variation about the mean value is random. It has certain convenient properties in statistics, and unknown distributions are often assumed to be normal distributions. Also called **Gaussian distribution**.

normality *n.* a broad concept that is roughly the equivalent of MENTAL HEALTH. Although there are no absolutes and there is considerable cultural variation, some flexible psychological and behavioral criteria can be suggested: (a) freedom from incapacitating internal conflicts; (b) the capacity to think and act in an organized and reasonably effective manner; (c) the ability to cope with the ordinary demands and problems of life; (d) freedom from extreme emotional distress, such as anxiety, despondency, and persistent upset; and (e) the absence of clear-cut symptoms of mental disorder, such as obsessions, phobias, confusion, and disorientation.

normalization principle the concept that people with mental or physical disability should not be denied social and sexual relationships and participation in community life merely because of their disability. Social and sexual relationships can include a wide range of emotional and physical contacts, from simple friendship to sexual stimulation and satisfaction. Participation in community life includes engaging in typical life activities, such as work and recreation. See also SOCIAL ROLE VALORIZATION.

normative influence see SOCIAL PRESSURE.

norm-referenced testing an approach to testing based on a comparison of one person's performance with that of a specifically selected norm group on the same test. Norm-referenced testing differentiates among individuals and ranks them on the basis of their performance. For example, a nationally standardized norm-referenced test will indicate how a given person performs compared to the performance of a national sample. See CRITERION-REFERENCED TESTING.

nortriptyline *n.* a TRICYCLIC ANTIDEPRESSANT, a so-called secondary tricyclic, that is the principal metabolic product of AMITRIPTYLINE. Although its clinical efficacy is the same as other tricyclics, nortriptyline and the other secondary tricyclic agent, desipramine, were often preferred because they were less sedating and had fewer adverse side effects. A THERAPEUTIC WINDOW is thought to exist for nortriptyline: Although plasma levels do not always correlate with clinical effectiveness, optimum responses are thought to occur when serum levels of the drug are between 50 and 150 ng/ml. Plasma levels over 500 ng/ml are toxic. The availability of newer antidepressants that do not require therapeutic monitoring has led to a decline in its use. U.S. trade names: **Aventyl**; **Pamelor**.

NOS abbreviation for NOT OTHERWISE SPECIFIED.

nose *n.* the organ that contains the sensory tissue (about 600 mm^2) that underlies olfactory sensitivity (see OLFACTORY EPITHELIUM). The major functions of the nose are to modulate the temperature and adjust the humidity of inspired air and to direct that air toward the sensory tissue in the nasal cavity.

nosocomial *adj.* denoting or relating to a hospital-acquired infection that is unrelated to the patient's primary illness.

nosological approach a method or procedure that focuses on the naming and classifying of disorders together with the identification of PATHOGNOMONIC signs and symptoms and their grouping into syndromes for diagnostic purposes. The nosological approach contrasts with the psychodynamic approach, which emphasizes causal factors.

nosology *n.* the scientific study and classification of diseases and disorders, both mental and physical. —**nosological** *adj.*

nostalgia *n.* **1.** a longing to return to an earlier period or condition of life recalled as being better than the present in some way. **2.** a longing to return to a place to which one feels emotionally bound (e.g., home or a native land). —**nostalgic** *adj.*

no-suicide contract a specific agreement, used when the potential for suicide is at issue, made between the client and the therapist that the client will not take his or her own life. It is often used as an intermediary measure for an agreed-upon period of time (e.g., until the next therapy session). See also CONTRACT.

not guilty by reason of insanity a final judgment made in a court of law if the defendant has been found to lack the mental capacity to be held criminally responsible for his or her actions. See CRIMINAL RESPONSIBILITY; INSANITY.

not otherwise specified (**NOS**) in DSM-IV-TR, denoting a broad-based diagnostic category. The NOS diagnosis is chosen when the patient's problems seem to fall into a particular family of disorders (e.g., depressive disorders, anxiety disorders), but the syndrome is not typical or there is not enough information available at the time of diagnosis to specify more accurately the type of disorder that is present.

novel antipsychotic see ANTIPSYCHOTIC.

novelty *n.* the quality of being new and unusual. It is one of the major determining factors directing attention. The attraction to novelty has been shown to begin as early as 1 year of age; for example, when infants are shown pictures of visual patterns, they will stare longer at a new pattern than at a pattern they have already seen. In consumer behavior, the attraction to novelty is manifested as a desire for a change, even in the absence of dissatisfaction with the present situation.

novelty hypothesis the claim that the contents of CONSCIOUSNESS can be predicted by their novelty, based on the observation that novel or unexpected events frequently intrude in ongoing conscious functioning.

novelty preference task a task in which an infant is shown a new object simultaneously with a familiar one. It is used in studies of infant cognition, based on the fact that infants will visually inspect a new object in preference to looking at a familiar object. The duration of the infant's visual gaze is used to quantify attention, surprise, and novelty versus familiarity.

noxious stimulus an aversive stimulus that can serve as a negative reinforcer of behavior, in severe cases because it causes pain or damage to the experiencing organism and in lesser cases because it is unpleasant.

NREM sleep *n*onrapid-*eye-m*ovement sleep: periods of sleep in which dreaming, as indicated by RAPID EYE MOVEMENTS (REM), usually does not occur. During these periods, which occur most frequently in the first hours of sleep, the electroencephalogram shows only minimal activity, and there is little or no change in pulse, respiration, and blood pressure. Also called **non-REM sleep**. Compare REM SLEEP.

NSAIDs *n*onsteroidal *a*nti-*i*nflammatory *d*rugs: a large class of analgesic and anti-inflammatory agents that includes aspirin, ibuprofen, naproxen, and many others. They achieve their effects by blocking the synthesis of PROSTA-GLANDINS involved in inflammation and the pain response.

nuclear complex as used in some psychoanalytic theories, a central conflict or problem that is rooted in infancy, for example, feelings of inferiority (according to Austrian psychiatrist Alfred Adler [1870–1937]) or the OEDIPUS COMPLEX (according to Austrian psychiatrist Sigmund Freud [1856–1939]).

nuclear family a family unit consisting of two parents and their dependent children (whether biological or adopted). With various modifications, the nuclear family has been and remains the norm in developed Western societies. Compare EXTENDED FAMILY; PERMEABLE FAMILY.

nuclear imaging imaging that involves scanning for emissions from radioactive isotopes injected into the body. Techniques include POSITRON EMISSION TOMOGRAPHY (PET) and SINGLE PHOTON EMISSION COMPUTED TOMOGRAPHY (SPECT). These forms of scanning yield information not only about the anatomy of an organ but also about its functions; they are therefore valuable for medical diagnosis and research. See also BRAIN IMAGING.

nuclear magnetic resonance (**NMR**) the response of atomic nuclei to changes in a strong magnetic field. The atoms give off weak electric signals, which can be recorded by detectors placed around the body and used for imaging parts of the body, including the brain. See BRAIN IMAGING; MAGNETIC RESONANCE IMAGING.

nuclear schizophrenia a type of schizophrenia whose defining features, which include social inadequacy and withdrawal, blunted affect, and feelings of DEPERSONALIZATION and DE-REALIZATION, are highly similar to those described by German psychiatrist Emil Kraepelin (1856–1926) for DEMENTIA PRAECOX. It is of early, insidious onset and is associated with a degenerative, irreversible course and poor prognosis. This term is often used interchangeably with PROCESS SCHIZOPHRENIA. Also called **authentic schizophrenia**; **true schizophrenia**; **typical schizophrenia**.

nucleic acid a large molecule that consists of a chain of NUCLEOTIDES. Nucleic acids are of two types, DNA and RNA, and are important constituents of living cells.

nucleotide *n.* a compound consisting of a nitrogenous base, a sugar, and one or more phosphate groups. Nucleotides such as ATP are important in metabolism. The nucleic acids (DNA and RNA) comprise long chains of nucleotides (i.e., polynucleotides).

nucleus *n.* (*pl.* **nuclei**) **1.** a large membrane-bound compartment, found in the cells of nonbacterial organisms, that contains the bulk of the cell's genetic material in the form of chromosomes. **2.** in the central nervous system, a mass of CELL BODIES belonging to neurons with the same or related functions. Examples are the amygdaloid nuclei (see AMYGDALA), the basal nuclei (see BASAL GANGLIA), the thalamic nuclei (see THALAMUS), and the NUCLEUS ACCUMBENS. Compare GANGLION.

nucleus accumbens one of the largest of the septal nuclei (see SEPTAL AREA), which receives dopaminergic innervation from the VENTRAL TEGMENTAL AREA. Dopamine release in this region may mediate the reinforcing qualities of many activities, including drug abuse.

nuisance variable a variable that has no intrinsic significance to the experiment but may contribute to an increase in experimental error.

null finding the result of an experiment indicating that there is no relationship, or no significant relationship, between variables. Also called **null result**.

null hypothesis (symbol: H_0) the statement that an experiment will find no difference between the experimental and control conditions, that is, no relationship between variables. Statistical tests are applied to experimental results in an attempt to disprove or reject the null hypothesis at a predetermined SIGNIFICANCE LEVEL. See also ALTERNATIVE HYPOTHESIS.

numerical ability (**N**) one of the seven PRIMARY ABILITIES proposed by U.S. psychologist L. L. Thurstone (1887–1955). Thurstone measured this ability with arithmetic computation problems and relatively simple word problems.

numerical competence the ability of some animals to identify the cardinal numbers associated with differing quantities of objects and to arrange these numbers in correct order. Some parrots and chimpanzees can count the number of items presented to them, and some can rank numbers, as in the ascending sequence 1, 5, 8.

numerical scale any scale or measurement instrument that yields a quantitative (numerical) representation of an attribute.

nursing home a LONG-TERM CARE FACILITY that provides 24-hour nursing care in addition to supportive services for people with chronic disability or illness, particularly older people who have mobility, eating, and other self-care problems.

nurture *n.* the totality of environmental factors that influence the development and behavior of a person, particularly sociocultural and ecological factors such as family attributes, child-rearing practices, and economic status. Compare NATURE. See also NATURE–NURTURE.

nutrient *n.* any substance required as part of the diet for growth, maintenance, and repair of the body's tissues or as a source of energy. Nutrients include CARBOHYDRATES, fats (see FATTY ACID), PROTEINS (see also AMINO ACID), VITAMINS, and some minerals (e.g., calcium, sodium, potassium).

nyctalopia *n.* see NIGHT BLINDNESS.

nystagmus *n.* involuntary, rapid movement of the eyeballs. The eyeball motion may be rotatory, horizontal, vertical, or a mixture.

N

Oo

OA abbreviation for Overeaters Anonymous. See ALCOHOLICS ANONYMOUS.

OAEs abbreviation for OTOACOUSTIC EMISSIONS.

obesity *n.* the condition of having excess body fat resulting in overweight, typically defined in terms of weight–height ratio (see BODY MASS INDEX). Although genetic, environmental, and behavioral factors all contribute, overeating may also have a psychological cause (see BINGE-EATING DISORDER; NIGHT-EATING SYNDROME) or be due to an organic disorder (see HYPER-PHAGIA). The consequences of obesity are a matter for concern: It predisposes to heart disease, diabetes, and other serious medical conditions (see MORBID OBESITY), and obese individuals may develop emotional and psychological problems relating to BODY IMAGE. —**obese** *adj.*

object *n.* **1.** the "other," that is, any person or symbolic representation of a person that is not the self and toward whom behavior, cognitions, or affects are directed. The term is sometimes used to refer to nonpersonal phenomena (e.g., an interest might be considered to be an "object") but the other-person connotation is far more typical and central. **2.** in psychoanalytic theory, the person, thing, or part of the body through which an INSTINCT can achieve its aim of gratification. See also OBJECT RELATIONS THEORY. **3.** the person who is loved by an individual's EGO: his or her LOVE OBJECT.

object choice in psychoanalytic theory, the selection of a person toward whom LIBIDO or PSYCHIC ENERGY is directed. See ANACLITIC OBJECT CHOICE; NARCISSISTIC OBJECT CHOICE.

object constancy the tendency for an object to be perceived more or less unchanged despite variations in the conditions of observation, such as changes in orientation or illumination.

objective 1. *adj.* having actual existence in reality, based on observable phenomena. **2.** *adj.* impartial or uninfluenced by personal feelings, interpretations, or prejudices. Compare SUBJEC-TIVE. **3.** *n.* something that is to be obtained or worked toward. **4.** *n.* the lens or lens system in an optical instrument, such as a microscope. Also called **object glass**; **objective lens**; **object lens**.

objective responsibility in the moral judgment typical of children under the age of 10, the idea that the rightness or wrongness of an act is based almost exclusively on its material result, without consideration of the indiviual's motives for doing it. For example, accidentally breaking

five cups is worse than deliberately breaking one. Compare SUBJECTIVE RESPONSIBILITY.

objective self-awareness a reflective state of self-focused attention in which a person acknowledges his or her limitations and the existing disparity between the ideal self and the actual self. Objective self-awareness is often a necessary part of SELF-REGULATION.

objective test a type of assessment instrument consisting of a set of factual items that have specific correct answers, such that no interpretation or personal judgment is required in scoring. A "true or false" test is an example of an objective test. Compare SUBJECTIVE TEST.

objectivism *n.* **1.** the position that judgments about the external world can be established as true or false independent of personal feelings, beliefs, and experiences. **2.** in ethics, the position that the ideals, such as "the good," to which ethical propositions refer are real. Objectivism holds that ethical prescriptions do not reduce to mere statements of personal or cultural preference. Compare SUBJECTIVISM. —**objectivist** *n.*, *adj.*

objectivity *n.* **1.** the tendency to base judgments and interpretations on external data rather than on subjective factors, such as personal feelings, beliefs, and experiences. **2.** a quality of a research study such that its hypotheses, choices of variables studied, measurements, techniques of control, and observations are as free from bias as possible. Compare SUBJECTIV-ITY.

object loss in psychoanalytic theory, the actual loss of a person who has served as a GOOD OB-JECT, which precedes INTROJECTION and is involved in SEPARATION ANXIETY. Anxiety about the possible loss of a good object begins with the infant's panic when separated from its mother. In this perspective adult GRIEF and MOURNING are related to object loss and separation anxiety in infancy and childhood, which often intensifies and complicates the grief reaction.

object love in psychoanalytic theory, love of a person other than the self. It is a function of the EGO and not the instincts. See LOVE OBJECT.

object of instinct in psychoanalytic theory, that which is sought (the **external aim**, e.g., a person, object, or behavior) in order to achieve satisfaction (the **internal aim**). See AIM OF THE IN-STINCT.

object permanence knowledge of the continued existence of objects even when they are not directly perceived. In cognitive development, milestones that indicate the acquisition of object permanence include reaching for and retrieving a covered object (about 8 months), retrieving an object at location B even though it was previously hidden several times at location A (the **A-not-B task**, about 12 months), and removing a series of covers to retrieve an object, even though the infant only witnessed the object being hidden under the outermost cover (**invisible displacement**, about 18 months).

object play play that involves the manipulation of items in the environment, such as banging toys together, throwing them around, or arranging them in specific configurations. It is one of three traditionally identified basic types of play (the others being LOCOMOTOR PLAY and SOCIAL PLAY) and may occur in a solitary or social context.

object relations theory any psychoanalytically based theory that views the need to relate to OBJECTS as more central to personality organization and motivation than the vicissitudes of the INSTINCTS. These theories developed from and in reaction to classic Freudian theories of psychodynamics. Some theories view the personality as organized in terms of a complex world of internal object representations and their relationships with each other, for example, FAIRBAIRNIAN THEORY and the approach of Austrian-born British psychoanalyst Melanie Klein (1882–1960).

object-superiority effect in visual perception tasks, the finding that judgments about a briefly presented line are made more efficiently when the line is part of a drawing of a three-dimensional object than when it is part of a two-dimensional figure. See CONFIGURAL SUPERIORITY EFFECT.

oblique *adj.* not at right angles, which in graphical representations of mathematical computations (such as FACTOR ANALYSIS) and other research indicates correlated (not independent) variables. Compare ORTHOGONAL.

oblique rotation see FACTOR ROTATION.

observation *n.* the careful, close examination of an object, process, or other phenomenon for the purpose of collecting data about it or drawing conclusions. —**observational** *adj.*

observational learning the acquisition of information, skills, or behavior through watching the performance of others. Also called **vicarious learning**. See also MODELING THEORY.

observational study a study in which the experimenter passively observes the behavior of the participants without any attempt at intervention or manipulation of the behaviors being observed. Such studies typically involve observation of cases under naturalistic conditions rather than the random assignment of cases to experimental conditions.

observer bias any expectations, beliefs, or personal preferences of a researcher that unintentionally influence his or her observations during an OBSERVATIONAL STUDY. See EXPERIMENTER EFFECT.

observing response behavior that results in the presentation or clarification (e.g., enhanced view) of DISCRIMINATIVE STIMULI.

obsession *n.* a persistent thought, idea, image, or impulse that is experienced as intrusive and inappropriate and results in marked anxiety, distress, or discomfort. Common obsessions include repeated thoughts about contamination, a need to have things in a particular order or sequence, repeated doubts, aggressive or horrific impulses, and sexual imagery. Obsessions can be distinguished from excessive worries about everyday occurrences in that they are not concerned with real-life problems. The response to an obsession is often an effort to ignore or suppress the thought or impulse or to neutralize it by a COMPULSION. See OBSESSIVE-COMPULSIVE DISORDER. —**obsessional** *adj.* —**obsessive** *adj.*

obsessive-compulsive disorder (**OCD**) an ANXIETY DISORDER characterized by recurrent obsessions, compulsions, or both that are time consuming (more than one hour per day), cause significant distress, or interfere with the individual's functioning. The obsessions and compulsions are recognized as excessive or unreasonable.

obsessive-compulsive personality disorder a personality disorder characterized by an extreme need for perfection, an excessive orderliness, an inability to compromise, and an exaggerated sense of responsibility.

obstruction method an experimental technique in which a nonhuman animal is presented with one or more goals of various drives, for example, food (hunger) versus water (thirst), and is required to overcome an obstacle (e.g., an electrified grid) in order to reach the goal. The delay before attempting to overcome the obstacle, as well as the animal's choice of which goal to pursue, may be used to represent drive strength and drive dominance.

obtrusive measure any method of obtaining measurements or observations in which the participants are aware that a measurement is being made. Compare UNOBTRUSIVE MEASURE.

Occam's razor (**Ockham's razor**) the maxim that, given a choice between two hypotheses, the one involving the fewer assumptions should be preferred. See also ELEGANT SOLUTION; LAW OF PARSIMONY. [William of **Occam** or **Ockham** (c. 1285–1347), English Franciscan monk and Scholastic philosopher]

occasionalism *n.* the philosophical doctrine that events are not directly caused by the antecedent events that appear to produce them, and particularly that material things cannot cause mental phenomena or mental phenomena influence material things. Rather, all things material and mental are caused by God's volitional acts. A change in a mental or material condition provides God with the occasion to produce a change in some other mental or material condition. Thus, the material or mental phenomena that might appear to be real and direct causes are merely **occasional causes**. Extreme forms of occasionalism reject causal influence of any mental or material phenomena on any others. Occasionalism was first formulated by French philosopher Nicolas Malebranche (1638–1715), largely as a response to the MIND–BODY PROBLEM arising from CARTESIAN DUALISM. —**occasionalist** *adj.*

occasion setter in PAVLOVIAN CONDITIONING, a stimulus that is differentially paired with a stimulus–stimulus contingency. For example, after presentation of a light, a tone might be followed by the delivery of food. In the absence of the light, the tone is not followed by food. If the tone is effective in eliciting salivation only after the light is presented, the light is designated as an occasion setter.

occipital cortex the CEREBRAL CORTEX of the occipital lobe of the brain. See VISUAL CORTEX.

occipital lobe the most posterior lobe of each cerebral hemisphere, associated with the visual sense.

occlusion *n.* obstruction or closure, for example of an artery. —**occlusive** *adj.*

occult *adj.* mysterious, incomprehensible, or secret. The term is mainly applied to certain esoteric traditions of magical belief and practice but is sometimes used of other alleged phenomena that cannot be explained in either everyday or scientific terms, such as premonitory dreams, CLAIRVOYANCE, and telepathic communications (see TELEPATHY). See PARAPSYCHOLOGY. —**occultism** *n.* —**occultist** *n.*

occupational adjustment the degree to which an individual's abilities, interests, and personality are compatible with a particular occupation. The term differs from VOCATIONAL ADJUSTMENT in its emphasis on the interaction between an individual's personal characteristics and the objective requirements, conditions, and opportunities associated with the job.

occupational culture a distinctive pattern of thought and behavior shared by members of the same occupation and reflected in their language, values, attitudes, beliefs, and customs. For example, police officers can be regarded as having a distinct culture of this kind. See also ORGANIZATIONAL CULTURE.

occupational ergonomics a specialty area of ERGONOMICS that attempts to make work systems and processes within particular occupations more responsive to the physical, cognitive, and psychosocial characteristics of workers.

occupational health psychology a specialty within psychology devoted to understanding workplace sources of health, illness, and injury and the application of this knowledge to improve the physical and mental well-being of employees.

occupational psychology see INDUSTRIAL AND ORGANIZATIONAL PSYCHOLOGY.

occupational segregation the extent to which people of the same gender or ethnicity are employed in some occupations to the exclusion of others. For example, the fact that a high proportion of nurses are women could suggest that this may be a sex-segregated occupation.

occupational stress a state of physiological and psychological response to events or conditions in the workplace that is detrimental to health and well-being. It is influenced by such factors as autonomy and independence, decision latitude, workload, level of responsibility, job security, physical environment and safety, the nature and pace of work, and relationships with coworkers and supervisors.

occupational therapy (**OT**) a therapeutic, rehabilitative process that uses purposeful tasks and activities to improve health; prevent injury or disability; enhance quality of life; and develop, sustain, or restore the highest possible level of independence of individuals who have been injured or who have an illness, impairment, or other mental or physical disability or disorder. OT involves assessment of an individual's FUNCTIONAL STATUS, the development and implementation of a customized treatment program, and recommendations for adaptive modifications in home and work environments as well as training in the use of appropriate ASSISTIVE TECHNOLOGY devices.

OCD abbreviation for OBSESSIVE-COMPULSIVE DISORDER.

oceanic feeling an expansion of consciousness beyond one's body (limitless extension) and a sense of unlimited power associated with identification with the universe as a whole. According to psychoanalytic theory, this feeling originates in the earliest period of life, before the infant is aware of the outside world or the distinction between the ego and nonego. Oceanic feelings may be revived later in life as a delusion or as part of a religious or spiritual experience.

octave effect in conditioning, the phenomenon in which a nonhuman animal, after experiencing REINFORCEMENT at one sound frequency, will react to a new sound frequency an octave away from the original frequency because it is more similar to the original than it is to a frequency within that octave.

ocular *adj.* relating to the eye.

ocular dominance a response characteristic of neurons in the STRIATE CORTEX. Many neurons respond more vigorously to stimulation through one eye than they do to stimulation through the other eye. See also OCULAR DOMINANCE COLUMN.

ocular dominance column a vertical slab of STRIATE CORTEX in which the neurons are preferentially responsive to stimulation through one of the two eyes. It is important for binocular vision. Ocular dominance columns for each eye alternate in a regular pattern, so that an electrode inserted tangentially to the cortical surface encounters neurons that are responsive to stimulation through first the IPSILATERAL eye, then the CONTRALATERAL eye, then back to the ipsilateral eye. See also MONOCULAR REARING. Compare ORIENTATION COLUMN.

ocular flutter a rapid horizontal oscillation occurring in both eyes when gazing straight ahead. Flutter may also appear following a SACCADE (**flutter dysmetria**). Ocular flutter is typically caused by injury to the cerebellum.

oculogyral illusion the apparent movement of a stationary faint light in a dark room when the observer rotates around it, due to involuntary, rapid movements of the eyeballs (vestibular nystagmus).

oculomotor nerve the third CRANIAL NERVE, which innervates most of the muscles associated with movement and accommodation of the eye and constriction of the pupil (i.e., all the muscles of the eye except the external rectus and superior oblique muscles).

oculomotor palsy paralysis of any of the extrinsic EYE MUSCLES. This may be due to damage to the muscle itself (myogenic), the motor end plate (neuromuscular), or the third, fourth, or sixth cranial nerves (neurogenic). The most common causes are diabetes, hypertension, and multiple sclerosis. Also called **ocular palsy**.

O data other data: information about an individual gathered from the observations, judgments, and evaluations of third parties who know him or her personally, such as family and friends. See also L DATA; Q DATA; T DATA.

oddity from sample a procedure similar to MATCHING TO SAMPLE except that reinforcement is arranged for responding to a stimulus that does not match the sample stimulus.

odor *n.* the property of an airborne volatile substance that is perceptible as a sensory experience produced by stimulation of the olfactory nerve. See SMELL.

oedipal phase in psychoanalytic theory, the later portion of the PHALLIC STAGE of psychosexual development, usually between ages 3 and 5, during which the OEDIPUS COMPLEX manifests itself. Also called **oedipal stage**.

Oedipus complex in psychoanalytic theory, the erotic feelings of the son toward the mother, accompanied by rivalry and hostility toward the father, during the PHALLIC STAGE of development. The corresponding relationship between the daughter and father is referred to as the **female Oedipus complex**. The complete Oedipus complex includes both this heterosexual form, called the **positive Oedipus complex**, and its homosexual counterpart, the NEGATIVE OEDIPUS COMPLEX. Austrian psychiatrist Sigmund Freud

(1856–1939) derived the name from the Greek myth in which Oedipus unknowingly killed his father and married his mother. Freud saw the Oedipus complex as the basis for NEUROSIS when it is not adequately resolved by the boy's fear of castration and gradual IDENTIFICATION with the father. The female Oedipus complex is posited to be resolved by the threat of losing the mother's love and by finding fulfillment in the feminine role. Contemporary psychoanalytic thought has decentralized the importance of the Oedipus complex and has largely modified the classical theory by emphasizing the earlier, primal relationship between child and mother. Also called **oedipal conflict**; **oedipal situation**. See also CASTRATION COMPLEX; NUCLEAR COMPLEX.

OEP abbreviation for olfactory-evoked potential. See CHEMOSENSORY EVENT-RELATED POTENTIAL.

off-center/on-surround referring to a concentric RECEPTIVE FIELD in which stimulation of the center inhibits the neuron of interest, whereas stimulation of the surround excites it. See CENTER–SURROUND ANTAGONISM. Compare ON-CENTER/OFF-SURROUND.

off-label *adj.* denoting or relating to the clinical use of a drug for a purpose that has not been approved by the U.S. Food and Drug Administration. Manufacturers generally do not promote drugs for off-label uses, although medical literature may support such uses.

off response (**OFF response**) the depolarization of a neuron in the visual system that occurs in response to light decrement. Neurons with off responses in the center of their receptive fields are often called **off cells**. See also CENTER–SURROUND ANTAGONISM. Compare ON RESPONSE.

oldest old see ADULTHOOD.

old-old *adj.* see ADULTHOOD.

olfaction *n.* the sense of smell, involving stimulation of receptor cells in the OLFACTORY EPITHELIUM (located in the nasal passages) by airborne volatile substances called odorants. Specifically, OLFACTORY RECEPTORS extend numerous cilia into the OLFACTORY MUCOSA in the roof of the nasal cavity; these cilia, together with villi of supporting tissue cells, form a layer of hairlike projections. Molecules of odorants are absorbed into nasal mucus and carried to the OLFACTORY EPITHELIUM, where they stimulate the receptor sites of the cilia. The olfactory receptors carry impulses in axonal bundles through tiny holes in the cribriform plate, the bony layer separating the base of the skull from the nasal cavity. On the top surface of the cribriform plate rests the OLFACTORY BULB, which receives the impulses and sends them on to the PERIAMYGDALOID CORTEX. —**olfactory** *adj.*

olfactometry *n.* the measurement of the acuity of smell. Also called **odorimetry**.

olfactory adaptation a decrease in olfactory sensitivity subsequent to stimulation of the sense of smell. This temporary phenomenon is measured by increases in odor thresholds and reported declines in odor intensities.

olfactory bulb a bulblike ending on the olfactory nerve in the anterior region of each cerebral hemisphere. This first synapse in the olfactory system picks up excitation from the nose, specifically from the cilia in the OLFACTORY EPITHELIUM. See also TUFTED CELL.

olfactory cortex see PYRIFORM AREA.

olfactory cross-adaptation a reduction in sensitivity to an odor following adaptation to another odor. Unlike other senses, there are usually no changes in the perceived quality of single odorants following adaptation to other single odorants. Cross-adaptation is observed, however, in an odorant mixture that contains the single odorant adapting stimulus.

olfactory dysfunction any alteration in the perception of odor quality or odor sensitivity, such as ANOSMIA, HYPEROSMIA, HYPOSMIA, PAROSMIA, PHANTOSMIA, and TROPOSMIA.

olfactory epithelium an area of OLFACTORY RECEPTORS in the lining of the upper part of the nose. The epithelium is separated from the OLFACTORY BULB by a sievelike layer in the skull called the cribriform plate, through which the receptor cells synapse with cells in the olfactory bulb.

olfactory evoked potential (OEP) see CHEMOSENSORY EVENT-RELATED POTENTIAL.

olfactory mucosa the superior portion of the nasal cavity containing mucus-secreting cells and subsuming the OLFACTORY EPITHELIUM, the OLFACTORY NERVE, and supporting cells.

olfactory nerve the first CRANIAL NERVE, which carries sensory fibers concerned with the sense of smell. It originates in the olfactory lobe and is distributed to the nasal mucous membrane (see OLFACTORY RECEPTOR).

olfactory receptor a spindle-shaped receptor cell in the OLFACTORY EPITHELIUM of the nasal cavity that is sensitive to airborne volatile substances (odorants). Cilia at the base of the olfactory receptors contain receptor sites for odorants. The receptors themselves collectively form the OLFACTORY NERVE, which synapses with cells in the OLFACTORY BULB.

olfactory system the primary structures and processes involved in an organism's detection of and responses to airborne volatile substances. The olfactory system includes several million OLFACTORY RECEPTORS in the nasal cavity, the OLFACTORY EPITHELIUM and VOMERONASAL SYSTEM, OLFACTORY TRANSDUCTION, neural impulses and pathways (see OLFACTORY NERVE), and associated brain areas and their functions.

olfactory tract a band of nerve fibers that originates in the OLFACTORY BULB and extends backward along the bottom side of the frontal lobe of the brain to a point called the **olfactory trigone**, at which point the tract divides into three strands leading to the medial and lateral olfactory gyri and the olfactory tubercle.

olfactory transduction the sequence of events involved in converting chemical molecules into olfactory signals. As in other sense systems, the conjoint activation of many receptors and the modulating effects of SECOND MESSENGERS play important roles in olfactory transduction.

olfactory tubercle a small oval elevation near the base of the OLFACTORY TRACT that contains auxiliary olfactory nerve fibers and cells. The olfactory tubercle is particularly prominent in animals that depend on a sense of smell to survive.

oligodendrocyte n. a type of nonneuronal central nervous system cell (GLIA) that forms MYELIN SHEATHS around axons. Also called **oligodendroglia**.

oligodendroglioma n. see GLIOMA.

olivary nucleus an olive-shaped mass of gray matter in the medulla oblongata.

olivocochlear bundle a tract of centrifugal or efferent fibers extending from the SUPERIOR OLIVARY COMPLEX through the descending neural pathways to the cochlear HAIR CELLS.

olivopontocerebellar atrophy a slowly progressive neurological disorder characterized by degeneration of neurons in the pons, cerebellum, and OLIVARY NUCLEUS. Symptoms are highly variable across individuals but typically include ATAXIA, difficulties with balance and walking, tremors, and DYSARTHRIA.

omega squared (symbol: ω^2) a measure of the STRENGTH OF ASSOCIATION based on the proportion of variance of one measure predictable from variance in other measures.

omnibus test any statistical test of significance in which more than two conditions are compared simultaneously or in which there are two or more INDEPENDENT VARIABLES.

omnipotence n. in psychology, the delusion that one can personally direct, or control, reality outside of the self by thought or wish alone. In psychoanalytic theory, the main emphasis is on the infant's feeling that he or she is all-powerful, which is thought to arise (a) out of the fact that the child's slightest gesture leads to satisfaction of the need for food; (b) out of increasing abilities; and (c) as a REACTION FORMATION to feelings of helplessness and anxiety. Psychology generally considers feelings of omnipotence to fall anywhere between neurosis, in its milder forms, and psychosis, when the delusion is expressed as alienation from or outright denial of reality. See also MEGALOMANIA. —**omnipotent** adj.

on-center/off-surround referring to a concentric RECEPTIVE FIELD in which stimulation of the center excites the neuron of interest, whereas stimulation of the surround inhibits it. See CENTER–SURROUND ANTAGONISM. Compare OFF-CENTER/ON-SURROUND.

oncology *n.* the study and treatment of benign and malignant tumors (see NEOPLASM). This branch of medicine and of behavioral or population sciences deals with CANCER and is subdivided into medical, radiation, surgical, behavioral, and epidemiological subtypes. —**oncologist** *n.*

one-tailed test a statistical test of an experimental hypothesis in which the expected direction of an effect or relationship is specified. Also called **directional test**. Compare TWO-TAILED TEST.

one-way analysis of variance a statistical test of the probability that the means of three or more samples have been drawn from the same population; that is, an ANALYSIS OF VARIANCE with a single independent variable.

one-way design an experimental design in which one independent variable is manipulated to observe its influence on a dependent variable. Also called **single-factor design**.

one-word stage the developmental period, between approximately 10 and 18 months, when children use one word at a time when speaking. For example, depending on the context and how the word is spoken, *milk* may mean *That is milk, I want more milk*, or *I spilled the milk*. Also called **holophrastic stage**. See HOLOPHRASE.

online self-help group a self-help group composed of individuals who communicate via personal computer over the Internet on a regular basis to help one another cope with a shared life problem. Online groups overcome some of the traditional barriers to self-help participation, including lack of local group availability, rarity of problem, and time or transportation constraints. They are a relatively recent form of self-help group.

online therapy see E-THERAPY.

on–off cell a type of neuron in the visual system, particularly the retina, that depolarizes when the retina is stimulated with either light onset or light offset.

on response (**ON response**) the depolarization of a neuron in the visual system that occurs in response to light increment. Neurons with on responses in the center of their receptive fields are often called **on cells**. See also CENTER–SURROUND ANTAGONISM. Compare OFF RESPONSE.

onset of action the point at which the activity of a drug is apparent, generally measured in terms of the time elapsed between administration and the appearance of its pharmacological effects.

ontogenetic fallacy the false assumption that anything that looks like a common pattern of change with age is a basic, normative process of aging. An example is the assumption that because disability is often seen in the elderly it is a natural, universally experienced outcome of the aging process.

ontogeny *n.* the biological origin and development of an individual organism from fertilization of the egg cell until death. Also called **ontogenesis**. Compare PHYLOGENY. —**ontogenetic** *adj.*

ontogeny of conscious experience the developmental origins of conscious sensory experience in an organism. In humans, conscious experience can be demonstrated from the 5th or 6th month of gestation.

ontology *n.* the branch of philosophy that deals with the question of existence itself. From some philosophical perspectives, ontology is synonymous with metaphysics, in that both ask fundamental questions about what reality is. However, from the perspective of contemporary EXISTENTIALISM and HERMENEUTICS, ontology implies a concern with the meaning of existence that is largely lacking in traditional metaphysics. Whereas metaphysics asks "What is there?" or "What is fundamental?," the question of ontology is often posed as "What does it mean to 'be' at all?" Contemporary approaches to ontology often take their analytical point of departure from the work of German philosopher Martin Heidegger (1889–1976). In this tradition, psychology is the pursuit of an adequate understanding of the ontology of human beings. It asks, or ought to ask, "What does it mean to be a human being?" See BEING-IN-THE-WORLD; DASEIN. —**ontological** *adj.*

oogenesis *n.* the process by which germ cells divide and differentiate to produce female gametes (ova). In human females, **primary oocytes** are formed in the ovary during embryonic development by the proliferation and differentiation of precursor cells called **oogonia** (*sing.* **oogonium**). The primary oocytes enter into the first division of MEIOSIS but then remain suspended at this stage of cell division until puberty. Thereafter, roughly once a month until the menopause, one primary oocyte resumes meiosis and completes the first meiotic division to produce two unequally sized daughter cells: The larger one is the **secondary oocyte**, while the smaller is a **polar body**. Following OVULATION, the secondary oocyte undergoes the second meiotic division to produce an ovum and another polar body. The first polar body might also divide to produce two tiny cells, resulting in three polar bodies, which are normally nonfunctional and degenerate.

open adoption see ADOPTION.

open-classroom method an approach to teaching and learning that emphasizes the student's right to make decisions and views the teacher as a facilitator of learning rather than a transmitter of knowledge. The open-classroom method may include grouping of students across grades, independent study, individualized rates of progression, open-plan schools without interior walls, or unstructured time and curricula.

open economy an experimental design used in operant-conditioning experiments in which an organism's intake of food or water includes not only that provided during experimental sessions but also supplemental amounts provided independently of behavior in the home cage. This ensures that a particular level of body weight, or some other measure of deprivation, is maintained. Compare CLOSED ECONOMY.

open-field chamber an enclosed space in which animals can move freely while their ambulatory and defecatory behavior is observed and measured.

open group a psychotherapy or counseling group to which new members may be admitted during the course of therapy. Also called **continuous group**. Compare CLOSED GROUP.

opening technique the means by which a therapist establishes initial rapport and trust at the beginning of a professional relationship with a client in therapy or at the beginning of each session in individual or family therapy. Also called **opening moves**.

openness to experience a dimension of the Big Five personality model and the FIVE-FACTOR PERSONALITY MODEL that refers to individual differences in the tendency to be open to new aesthetic, cultural, or intellectual experiences.

open skill any motor skill that is performed under varying conditions on each occasion, as in making a jump shot in a game of basketball. Compare CLOSED SKILL.

open society a form of social organization characterized by respect for human rights, freedom to voice dissenting opinions, elective government, and the rule of law. Essential to this concept is an awareness of the imperfect nature of government and the need for constant critical evaluation of social policy so that it evolves with changing circumstances or new insights. A **closed society**, by contrast, is one characterized by inflexible social structures and a fixed ideology that cannot accept criticism or tolerate difference.

open system 1. a system with permeable boundaries that permit exchange of information or materials with the environment. **2.** a biological system in which growth can occur without conforming to laws of thermodynamics or a demonstrated constancy of energy relations. Compare CLOSED SYSTEM.

open system theory a theoretical perspective that views the organization as open to influence from the environment. The organization is viewed as transforming human and physical resources from the environment into goods and services, which are then returned to the environment.

open word see PIVOT GRAMMAR.

operandum *n.* in OPERANT CONDITIONING, a device that a nonhuman animal operates or manipulates to produce automatic recording of a response. For example, in a simple conditioning experiment for a rat, a lever that the rat can press

would be the operandum. See also MANIPULANDUM.

operant *n.* a class of responses that produces a common effect on the environment. An operant is defined by its effect rather than by the particular type of behavior producing that effect. A distinction may be made between the behavior required to achieve the effect (**descriptive operant**) and what alternative forms of behavior constitute the class and may also occur (**functional operant**). In the former, the class might include all forms of behavior that result in a lever being moved 4 mm downward. In the latter case, the class includes all forms of behavior that become more probable; for example, a rat's two-handed lever presses might increase in probability, but one-handed presses might not. Compare RESPONDENT.

operant behavior behavior that produces an effect on the environment and whose likelihood of recurrence is influenced by consequences (see OPERANT). Operant behavior is nearly synonymous with VOLUNTARY behavior.

operant chamber see OPERANT CONDITIONING CHAMBER.

operant conditioning the process in which behavioral change (i.e., learning) occurs as a function of the consequences of behavior. Examples are teaching a dog to do tricks and rewarding behavioral change in a misbehaving child (see BEHAVIOR THERAPY). The term is essentially equivalent to INSTRUMENTAL CONDITIONING.

operant conditioning chamber an apparatus used to study FREE-OPERANT behavior. Generally, it provides a relatively small and austere environment that blocks out extraneous stimuli. Included in the environment are devices that can present stimuli (e.g., reinforcers) and measure free-operant responses. For example, the apparatus for a rat might consist of a 25-cm^3 space containing a food tray, which can be filled by an automatic feeder located outside the space, and a small lever that the rat may press to release food from the feeder. Measurement of behavior and presentation of stimuli in the apparatus are usually automatic. The apparatus, initially developed in the 1930s by U.S. psychologist B. F. Skinner (1904–1990), later became known colloquially as the **Skinner box**.

operant conditioning therapy a therapeutic approach that relies on the use of antecedents, behaviors, and consequences. For example, REINFORCEMENT through rewards may be used to improve behaviors in everyday situations.

operant level a baseline probability or frequency of behavior that occurs naturally, before REINFORCEMENT is arranged, for example, the amount of lever pressing by a rat before any food reward or other reinforcer is introduced.

operant paradigm 1. the experimental arrangement of a CONTINGENCY between an operant response and a consequence, such as reinforcement. **2.** more generally, the assumption that much human behavior is controlled by its consequences.

operant response a single instance from an OPERANT class. For example, if lever pressing has been conditioned, each single lever press is an operant response.

operation *n.* a PIAGETIAN THEORY, a type of cognitive SCHEME that requires symbols, derives from action, exists in an organized system in which it is integrated with all other operations (**structures of the whole**), and follows a set of logical rules, most importantly that of REVERSIBILITY.

operational analysis analysis of the decision-making processes involved in the accomplishment of complex tasks. Generally the tasks involve the tracing of inputs through a process and the tracking of outputs. The analysis usually involves mathematical modeling and statistical techniques and aims at maximizing the effectiveness of the process.

operational definition a definition of something in terms of the operations (procedures, actions, or processes) by which it could be observed and measured. For example, the operational definition of anxiety could be in terms of a test score, behavioral withdrawal, or activation of the sympathetic nervous system.

operationalism *n.* the position that the meaning of a scientific concept depends upon the procedures used to establish it, so that each concept can be defined by a single observable and measurable operation. An example is defining an emotional disorder as a particular score on a diagnostic test. This approach was mainly associated with radical BEHAVIORISM. Also called **operationism**.

operational sex ratio the relative number of males and females present at the time when reproduction is possible. In mammals with internal gestation and lactation, there are often fewer females receptive to copulation than available males, creating an operational sex-ratio bias toward males, even though adults of both sexes may be present in equal numbers.

operational thought in PIAGETIAN THEORY thought characteristic of the last two stages of a child's cognitive development, the CONCRETE OPERATIONAL STAGE and FORMAL OPERATIONAL STAGE.

operationist view of consciousness the notion that conscious experiences may be reduced to publicly observable events, such as discriminative responses.

operations research the application of advanced analytical methods, such as mathematical modeling and computer simulation, to the study of complex situations so as to obtain a comprehensive understanding that allows for accurate predictions and enables more rational,

effective decision making. It is used particularly in business contexts.

operative knowledge knowledge acquired in the process of performing OPERATIONS, thought to be more basic and more predictive of later intellectual functioning than FIGURATIVE KNOWLEDGE (e.g., factual knowledge).

ophthalmology *n.* the medical specialty concerned with the study of the eye and the diagnosis and treatment of eye disease. A physician who specializes in ophthalmology is called an **ophthalmologist**. Compare OPTOMETRY.

opiate *n.* any of a variety of natural and semisynthetic compounds derived from OPIUM. They include the alkaloids MORPHINE and CODEINE and their derivatives (e.g., HEROIN [diacetylmorphine]). Opiates, together with synthetic compounds having the pharmacological properties of opiates, are known as OPIOIDS.

opioid *n.* any of a group of compounds that include the naturally occurring OPIATES (e.g., morphine, codeine) and their semisynthetic derivatives (e.g., heroin); synthetic compounds with morphinelike effects (OPIOID AGONISTS, e.g., meperidine, methadone); OPIOID ANTAGONISTS (e.g., naloxone, naltrexone) and mixed agonist–antagonists (e.g., buprenorphine); and ENDOGENOUS OPIOIDS. The effects of opioids include analgesia, drowsiness, euphoria or other mood changes, RESPIRATORY DEPRESSION, and reduced gastrointestinal motility. Opioids are used clinically as pain relievers, anesthetics, cough suppressants, and antidiarrheal drugs, and many are subject to abuse and dependence.

opioid abuse a pattern of opioid use manifested by recurrent significant adverse consequences related to the repeated ingestion of an opioid. See also SUBSTANCE ABUSE.

opioid agonist any drug with enhancing effects at OPIOID RECEPTORS in the central nervous system. Opioid agonists may be complete (pure) or partial agonists. MORPHINE is a pure opioid agonist; other examples include CODEINE, HEROIN, METHADONE, and LAAM. Partial opioid agonists (e.g., buprenorphine, tramadol) have lower levels of activity than complete opioid agonists at the same receptors. Also called **narcotic agonist**.

opioid analgesic any OPIOID used clinically to reduce both the sensation of pain and the emotional response to pain. CODEINE, **dihydrocodeine**, and **hydrocodone** are among opioids used for the relief of mild to moderate pain; severe pain is managed with more potent agents, such as MORPHINE and **oxycodone** (U.S. trade name: **OxyContin**). Side effects associated with opioid analgesics include nausea and vomiting, constipation, sedation, and respiratory depression; many also have the potential for abuse and physical dependence. Also called **narcotic analgesic**.

opioid antagonist an agent that binds to OPIOID RECEPTORS but does not produce the ef-

O

fects of euphoria, respiratory depression, or anal-gesia that are observed with opioid agonists. Opioid antagonists may be complete (pure) or mixed. Complete antagonists, such as **naloxone** (U.S. trade name: **Narcan**), NALTREXONE, **nalmefene** (U.S. trade name: **Revex**), and **nalorphine**, are generally used to reverse the ef-fects of opiate overdose (notably respiratory de-pression). Mixed AGONIST–ANTAGONIST opioids, such as **butorphanol** (U.S. trade name: **Stadol**) and **pentazocine** (U.S. trade name: **Talwin**), were developed in attempts to produce opioid analge-sics that did not possess the abuse potential of opioid agonists. Also called **narcotic antago-nist**.

opioid dependence a cluster of cognitive, be-havioral, and physiological symptoms indicat-ing continued use of opioids despite significant opioid-related problems. Also called **narcotic dependence**. See also SUBSTANCE DEPENDENCE.

opioid intoxication a reversible syndrome due to the recent ingestion of an opioid. It in-cludes clinically significant behavioral or psy-chological changes (e.g., initial euphoria followed by apathy, DYSPHORIA, PSYCHOMOTOR AGITATION or PSYCHOMOTOR RETARDATION, im-paired judgment, and impaired social or occupa-tional functioning), as well as one or more signs of physiological involvement (e.g., pupillary constriction, drowsiness or unconsciousness, slurred speech, RESPIRATORY DEPRESSION).

opioid receptor a RECEPTOR that binds OPIOIDS (including ENDOGENOUS OPIOIDS) and mediates their effects via G PROTEINS. Opioid re-ceptors are widely distributed in the brain, spinal cord, and periphery and each type of receptor is differentially distributed. **Mu receptors** are largely responsible for the analgesic and eu-phoric effects associated with opioid use and also mediate the respiratory depression, sedation, and reduced gastrointestinal motility associated with opioids. Stimulation of **kappa receptors** produces more modest analgesia and dysphoric responses and may also be responsible for some of the perceptual and cognitive effects of opioids. **Delta receptors** may potentiate activity of opioids at the mu receptor site and have a less direct involvement in the production of analge-sia. The more recently discovered **N/OFQ recep-tor** has not been completely characterized.

opioid withdrawal a characteristic with-drawal syndrome that develops after cessation of (or reduction in) prolonged, heavy opioid con-sumption. Features may include DYSPHORIA or anxiety, nausea or vomiting, muscle aches, dila-tion of the pupils, piloerection (goose flesh) or sweating, diarrhea, fever, and insomnia. See also SUBSTANCE WITHDRAWAL.

opium *n.* the dried resin of the unripe seed pods of the opium poppy, *Papaver somniferum*. Opium contains more than 20 alkaloids, the principal one being MORPHINE, which accounts for most of its pharmacological (including addictive)

properties. Natural and synthetic derivatives (see OPIATE; OPIOID) induce analgesia and euphoria and produce a deep, dreamless sleep.

opponent cell a type of neuron in the visual system that depolarizes when a particular stimu-lus (e.g., red light) comes on in the center of the neuron's receptive field and when the "oppo-site" stimulus (e.g., green light) is extinguished in the surrounding zone of the receptive field. **Double-opponent cells** depolarize when the red light comes on or the green light is extinguished in the center of the receptive field, while the same stimuli produce the opposite effects in the receptive field surround.

opponent process theory of acquired motivation a theory that a stimulus or event simultaneously arouses a primary affective state, which may be pleasurable or aversive, and an op-ponent (opposite) affective state, which serves to reduce the intensity of the primary state: These two states together constitute emotional experi-ence. According to this theory, the opponent state has a long latency, a sluggish course of in-crease, and a sluggish course of decay after the initiating stimulus is removed, all of which lead to its domination for a period following removal of the stimulus. In contrast to the primary state, it is also strengthened through use and weak-ened through disuse. This theory sought to ac-count for such diverse acquired motives as drug addiction, love, affection and social attachment, and cravings for sensory and aesthetic experi-ences.

opponent process theory of color vision any one of a class of theories describing color vi-sion on the basis of the activity of mechanisms, which may correspond to cells, that respond to red–green, blue–yellow, or black–white. The HERING THEORY OF COLOR VISION, the most highly developed opponent process theory, con-trasted with the YOUNG–HELMHOLTZ THEORY OF COLOR VISION, which relied on receptors sensitive to specific regions of the spectrum. Although both theories explained many phe-nomena, both had deficiencies. In the 1950s it was suggested that both theories were correct, the Young–Helmholtz model describing a first stage of processing in the visual system, while the outputs of that system were fed into an op-ponent process. This combined theory is known as the **dual process theory of color vision**.

opportune family individuals considered to be family to someone, even though they may not be legally related to that person. These indi-viduals are involved in decision making regard-ing the person's household, responsibilities, and significant relationships.

opportunism *n.* the ability to exploit resources not available to others. For example, kelp gulls introduced in Argentina rapidly expanded in numbers by feeding on refuse from fish factories and subsequently learned to attack and eat flesh from whales calving and nursing young in nearby waters.

opportunistic sampling the selection of participants or other sampling units for an experiment or survey simply because they are readily available.

opportunity class a class in the PULL-OUT PROGRAM for students who do not fit the norm, such as gifted, emotionally challenged, or at-risk students.

opportunity structure a matrix that relates personal characteristics (e.g., age, disability, race, gender, education, financial status) to the cultural and social opportunities and options that are available to an individual throughout his or her life. According to some psychologists, barred or restricted access to legitimate opportunities for success, due to economic or social disadvantage, leads some individuals to seek success by illegitimate means (**illegitimate opportunity structure**), such as delinquency or other criminal activity. Also called **opportunity matrix**.

oppositional defiant disorder a behavior disorder of childhood characterized by recurrent disobedient, negativistic, or hostile behavior toward authority figures that is more pronounced than usually seen in children of similar age and lasts for at least 6 months. It is manifest as temper tantrums, active defiance of rules, dawdling, argumentativeness, stubbornness, or being easily annoyed. The defiant behaviors typically do not involve aggression, destruction, theft, or deceit, which distinguishes this disorder from CONDUCT DISORDER.

opsin *n.* the protein component of visual PHOTOPIGMENTS. The other component is a vitamin A derivative known as **retinal**. There is one opsin for all rods (rod opsin, or scotopsin), which together with retinal forms the rod photopigment rhodopsin. There are three different cone opsins (photopsins), which convey different peak wavelength sensitivities to each of the three different cone photopigments (iodopsins).

optical flow pattern the total field of apparent velocities of visual stimuli that impinge upon a physical or theoretical visual system when objects move relative to the visual system or the visual system moves relative to the objects.

optical projection the localization of objects in space that correspond to the image on the retina.

optic ataxia inability to direct the hand to an object under visual guidance, typically caused by damage to the cortex of the PARIETAL LOBE. It is a feature of BÁLINT'S SYNDROME. Also called **visuomotor ataxia**.

optic chiasm the location at the base of the brain at which the optic nerves from the two eyes meet. In humans, the nerve fibers from the nasal half of each retina cross, so that each hemisphere of the brain receives input from both eyes. This partial crossing is called a **partial decussation**.

optic disk the area of the retina at which the axons of the RETINAL GANGLION CELLS gather before leaving the retina to form the optic nerve. Because this region contains no photoreceptors, it creates a BLIND SPOT in the visual field.

optic nerve the second CRANIAL NERVE, which carries the axons of RETINAL GANGLION CELLS and extends from the retina to the OPTIC CHIASM.

optic radiations nerve fibers that project from the lateral GENICULATE NUCLEUS to the VISUAL CORTEX in the occipital lobe and to the pretectum, a structure in the midbrain important for the reflexive contraction of the pupils in the presence of light. As the optic radiations sweep around the lateral ventricles they are called **Meyer's loop**.

optics *n.* the study of the physics of light, including its relations to the mechanisms of vision.

optic tract the bundle of optic nerve fibers after the partial decussation of the optic nerves at the OPTIC CHIASM. The major targets of the optic tract are the lateral GENICULATE NUCLEUS in the thalamus and the superior COLLICULUS in the midbrain.

optimal design a type of experimental design in which all the participants are assigned to the several CELLS of the design in order to optimize a feature of the design, for example, to obtain equally precise estimates of a parameter from each population.

optimal foraging theory a theory of foraging behavior arguing that NATURAL SELECTION has created optimal strategies for food selection (based on nutritional value and costs of locating, capturing, and processing food) and for deciding when to depart a particular patch to seek resources elsewhere.

optimal level the maximum (highest) level of complexity of a skill that an individual can control. It has been suggested that when acquiring a skill an individual moves from the optimal level, at which the skill can be performed with assistance from others, to the **functional level**, at which a skill can be performed independently but possibly at a lower than optimal level. See SKILL THEORY.

optimism *n.* the attitude that things happen for the best and that people's wishes or aims will ultimately be fulfilled. **Optimists** are people who expect good things to happen to them and to others; they anticipate positive outcomes, whether serendipitously or through perseverance and effort. Optimism can be defined in terms of EXPECTANCY: confidence of attaining desired goals (compare PESSIMISM). Most individuals lie somewhere on the spectrum between the two polar opposites of pure optimism and pure pessimism but tend to demonstrate sometimes strong, relatively stable or situational tendencies in one direction or the other. —**optimistic** *adj.*

optokinetic reflex the compensatory eye movements that allow the eyes to maintain fixation on a visual target during relatively large, slow head movements. The optokinetic reflex is driven by visual signals. Compare VESTIBULO-OCULAR REFLEX.

optometry *n.* the clinical field concerned primarily with the optics of the eye and the devices and procedures that can correct optical defects. **Optometrists** can prescribe corrective lenses and exercises but are generally prohibited from prescribing drugs or performing eye surgery. Optometrists are more clinically oriented than **opticians**, who make spectacle lenses, but have fewer clinical privileges than ophthalmologists (see OPHTHALMOLOGY).

oral personality in psychoanalytic theory, a pattern of personality traits derived from fixation at the ORAL STAGE of PSYCHOSEXUAL DEVELOPMENT. If the individual has experienced sufficient sucking satisfaction and adequate attention from the mother during the oral-sucking phase, he or she is posited to develop an **oral-receptive personality** marked by friendliness, OPTIMISM, generosity, and dependence on others. If the individual does not get enough satisfaction during the sucking and biting phases, he or she is posited to develop an **oral-aggressive personality** marked by tendencies to be hostile, critical, envious, exploitative, and overcompetitive. Also called **oral character**.

oral stage in psychoanalytic theory, the first stage of PSYCHOSEXUAL DEVELOPMENT, occupying the first year of life, in which the LIBIDO is concentrated on the mouth, which is the principal erotic zone. The stage is divided into the early **oral-sucking phase**, during which gratification is achieved by sucking the nipple during feeding, and the later **oral-biting phase**, when gratification is also achieved by biting. FIXATION during the oral stage is posited to cause an oral personality. Also called **oral phase**.

orbitofrontal cortex the CEREBRAL CORTEX of the ventral part of each FRONTAL LOBE, having strong connections to the HYPOTHALAMUS. Lesions of the orbitofrontal cortex can result in loss of inhibitions, forgetfulness, and apathy broken by bouts of euphoria.

orchidectomy *n.* the surgical removal of a testis. An orchidectomy may be performed when a testis is injured or diseased, as when the male reproductive system has been affected by cancer. Also called **orchiectomy**. See also CASTRATION.

order *n.* in BIOLOGICAL TAXONOMY, a main subdivision of a CLASS, containing a group of similar, related FAMILIES.

ordered scale a scale of measurement in which the scaling units can be ranked from smallest to largest.

order effect in WITHIN-SUBJECTS DESIGNS, the effect of the order in which treatments are administered, that is, the effect of being the first administered treatment (rather than the second, third, and so forth). This is often confused with the SEQUENCE EFFECT.

order of magnitude the approximate magnitude of a number or value within a range, usually to the nearest power of 10. For example, 2,500 (2.5×10^3) and 4,300 (4.3×10^3) are of the same order of magnitude, but both are one order of magnitude greater than 240 (2.4×10^2).

order statistic a statistic based only on the position of an observation within a set of observations (e.g., the largest observation).

ordinal scale a measurement system developed in such a manner as to reflect the rank ordering of participants on the attribute being measured.

ordinate *n.* the vertical coordinate in a graph or data plot; that is, the *y*-axis. See also ABSCISSA.

organelle *n.* a specialized, membrane-bound structure within a cell, such as a MITOCHONDRION or the GOLGI APPARATUS.

organic *adj.* denoting a condition or disorder that results from structural alterations of an organ or tissue. In psychology and psychiatry, the term is equivalent to somatic or physical, as contrasted with FUNCTIONAL or PSYCHOGENIC.

organic approach the theory that all mental disorders have a physiological basis, resulting from structural brain changes or alterations in other bodily organs.

organic defect a congenital disorder that is not the result of a genetic anomaly. For example, a mental or physical disability in an individual can result from maternal disorders or other conditions in pregnancy, including preeclampsia, viral infections (e.g., rubella), sexually transmitted infections, protozoan infections (e.g., toxoplasmosis), dietary deficiencies, or drug abuse (e.g., alcoholism).

organ inferiority the sense of being deficient or somehow less than others as a result of negative feelings about any type of real or imagined abnormal organ function or structure.

organism *n.* an individual living entity, such as an animal, plant, or bacterium, that is capable of reproduction, growth, and maintenance.

organismic *adj.* having components (**organs**) serving various functions that interact to produce the integrated, coordinated total functioning that characterizes an organism.

organismic model the theory that development is directed by constraints inherent in the relationship among elements within the organism as they act upon themselves and each other. Not only are biological processes (e.g., maturation) seen as critical in directing development, but so also are the behaviors of the organism.

organismic personality theory an approach to personality theory in which personal functioning is understood in terms of the action of the whole, coherent, integrated organism, rather than in terms of psychological variables representing one versus another isolated aspect of body or mind.

organismic psychology an approach to psychology that emphasizes the total organism, rejecting distinctions between mind and body. It embraces a comprehensive approach and integrated framework that takes account of the interaction between the organism and its environment. See HOLISM; HOLISTIC PSYCHOLOGY.

organismic valuing process in client-centered theory, the presumed healthy and innate internal guidance system that a person can use to "stay on the track" toward self-actualization. One goal of treatment within the client-centered framework is to help the client listen to this inner guide. See CLIENT-CENTERED THERAPY.

organization *n.* **1.** a structured entity consisting of various components that interact to perform one or more functions. Business, industrial, and service entities are constituted in this way. **2.** in GESTALT PSYCHOLOGY, an integrated perception composed of various components that appear together as a single whole, for example, a face. See GESTALT PRINCIPLES OF ORGANIZATION. **3.** in memory research, the structure discovered in or imposed upon a set of items in order to guide memory performance. —**organizational** *adj.*

organizational approach in the study of emotion, a conceptual framework, based on GENERAL SYSTEMS THEORY, emphasizing the role of emotions as regulators and determinants of both intrapersonal and interpersonal behaviors, as well as stressing the adaptive role of emotions. The organizational approach also emphasizes how perception, motivation, cognition, and action come together to produce important emotional changes.

organizational assessment activities involved in evaluating the structure, process, climate, and environmental factors that influence the effectiveness of an organization and the morale and productivity of employees. General or specific evaluations (e.g., readiness to change, job satisfaction, turnover) may be performed by practitioners from a variety of disciplines, including CONSULTING PSYCHOLOGY and INDUSTRIAL AND ORGANIZATIONAL PSYCHOLOGY.

organizational commitment an employee's dedication to an organization and wish to remain part of it. Organizational commitment is often described as having both an emotional or moral element (**affective commitment**) and a more prudential element (**continuance commitment**).

organizational culture a distinctive pattern of thought and behavior shared by members of the same organization and reflected in their language, values, attitudes, beliefs, and customs. The culture of an organization is in many ways analogous to the personality of an individual. See also OCCUPATIONAL CULTURE.

organizational development the application of principles and practices drawn from psychology, sociology, and related fields to the planned improvement of ORGANIZATIONAL EFFECTIVENESS. Although many different types of interventions are included under this umbrella, the role of the organizational development consultant is typically described as helping organizational participants to (a) identify and diagnose their own problems and (b) generate solutions to these problems. The consultant facilitates the creation of an environment in which participants engage in self-renewal and continuous improvement.

organizational effect a long-term effect of hormonal action typically occurring in fetal development or the early postnatal period that leads to permanent changes in behavior and neural functioning. The presence of testosterone in young male rats leads to long-term male-typical behavior, and female rats can be masculinized by neonatal exposure to testosterone. Compare ACTIVATIONAL EFFECT.

organizational effectiveness a multidimensional construct defining the degree of success achieved by an organization. Various factors, such as the extent to which the organization is able to achieve its goals in an efficient manner; the organization's ability to achieve long-term survival, which involves acquiring resources, adapting to changes in the environment, and maintaining the internal health of the system; and the ability of the organization to minimally satisfy the expectations of its strategic constituencies are generally included in an assessment of an organization's effectiveness.

organizational hypothesis the hypothesis that steroids produced by the newly formed testis during development masculinize the developing brain to alter behavior permanently.

organizational psychology see INDUSTRIAL AND ORGANIZATIONAL PSYCHOLOGY.

organizational structure the arrangement and interrelationship of the various parts or elements of an organization. Organizational structures can be described on several dimensions, including simple versus complex, centralized versus decentralized, and hierarchical versus nonhierarchical. A distinction can also be made between the formal organizational structure—the official patterns of coordination and control, workflow, authority, and communication that channel the activity of members—and the informal structure—those patterns that are not officially recognized but that emerge from the daily interactions of employees.

organ of Corti a specialized structure that sits on the BASILAR MEMBRANE within the cochlea in the inner ear. It contains the HAIR CELLS (the sensory receptors for hearing), their nerve endings, and supporting cells (**Deiters cells**). See also

TECTORIAL MEMBRANE. [Alfonso **Corti** (1822–1876), Italian anatomist]

orgasm *n.* the climax of sexual stimulation or activity, when the peak of pleasure is achieved, marked by the release of tension and rhythmic contractions of the perineal muscles, anal sphincter, and pelvic reproductive organs. In men, orgasm is also accompanied by the emission of semen (**ejaculation**); in women, it is accompanied by contractions of the wall of the outer third of the vagina. See also SEXUAL-RESPONSE CYCLE. —**orgasmic** or **orgastic** *adj.*

orgasmic dysfunction inability of a woman to reach orgasm in general or with certain forms of sexual stimulation. It may be primary, in which the woman has never been able to achieve an orgasm with any type of stimulation, with or without a partner; secondary, in which the woman had previously been but is currently unable to attain orgasm through physical contact; or situational, in which the woman is unable to experience orgasm with a particular partner or in a particular situation. Orgasmic dysfunction is a gender-specific term, whereas **orgasmic disorder** is gender neutral and includes FEMALE ORGASMIC DISORDER, MALE ORGASMIC DISORDER, and PREMATURE EJACULATION.

orgone therapy the therapeutic approach of Austrian psychoanalyst Wilhelm Reich (1897–1957), based on the concept that the achievement of "full orgastic potency" is the key to psychological well-being. Reich believed the orgasm to be the emotional-energy regulator of the body, the purpose of which is to dissipate sexual tensions that would otherwise be transformed into neuroses. He further held that the orgasm derives its power from a hypothetical cosmic force—**orgone energy**—which accounts not only for sexual capacity but also for all functions of life and for the prevention of disease. The psychoanalytic community largely rejected and disavowed Reich's highly unorthodox theories and approaches. Also called **vegetotherapy**.

orientation *n.* **1.** awareness of the self and of the external environment, that is, the ability to identify one's self and to know the time, the place, and other aspects of one's surroundings and activities. See also REALITY ORIENTATION. **2.** the act of directing the body or of moving toward an external stimulus, such as light, gravity, or some other aspect of the environment. **3.** relative position or alignment. For example, in vision orientation refers to the degree of tilt of the long axis of a visual stimulus (e.g., a vertical bar is oriented at 0°; a horizontal bar is oriented at 90°). Many neurons in the visual system respond most vigorously to a stimulus of a certain orientation: They are said to be **orientation selective**. **4.** the process of familiarizing oneself with a new setting (e.g., a new home, neighborhood, or city) so that movement and use do not depend upon memory cues, such as maps, and eventually become habitual. —**orient** *vb.*

orientation and mobility training (**O&M training**) guided instruction in the cognitive and motor skills necessary for people with visual impairment to orient themselves in space and to move safely in the environment. O&M training includes instruction in the use of the long cane or the handling of a service animal, as well as in the use of available senses, including any residual vision, to enable the individual to navigate safely. O&M training is a key component of VISION REHABILITATION and is usually provided by professional O&M specialists (formerly called **peripatologists**).

orientation column a vertical slab of STRIATE CORTEX in which all the neurons are maximally responsive to stimuli of the same ORIENTATION. Adjacent columns have slightly different orientation preferences, so that electrode penetration tangential to the cortical surface that passes through many columns would encounter neurons with orientation preferences that shift smoothly around a reference axis. Compare OCULAR DOMINANCE COLUMN.

orienting response 1. a behavioral response to an altered, novel, or sudden stimulus, for example, turning one's head toward an unexpected noise. Various physiological components of the orienting response have subsequently been identified as well, including dilation of pupils and blood vessels and changes in heart rate and electrical resistance of the skin. **2.** any response of an organism in relation to the direction of a specific stimulus. See TAXIS; TROPISM. Also called **orienting reflex**.

originality *n.* see CREATIVITY.

orthogonal *adj.* at right angles, which in graphical representations of mathematical computations (such as FACTOR ANALYSIS) and other research indicates unrelated (independent) variables. Compare OBLIQUE.

orthogonal design a FACTORIAL DESIGN in which all CELLS contain the same number of subjects or observations or in which there is a certain constant of proportionality in cell sizes. Compare NONORTHOGONAL DESIGN.

orthogonal rotation see FACTOR ROTATION.

orthography *n.* **1.** the formal writing system of a language. **2.** the study of the conventions of spelling in such a system. —**orthographic** *adj.*

orthonasal olfaction sensations of smell arising via the introduction of an airborne volatile substance through the nares (nostrils). This is the common route for olfactory sensation. Compare RETRONASAL OLFACTION.

orthopsychiatry *n.* an interdisciplinary approach to mental health in which psychiatrists, psychologists, social workers, pediatricians, sociologists, nurses, and educators collaborate on the early treatment of mental disorders, with an emphasis on their prevention. —**orthopsychiatric** *adj.* —**orthopsychiatrist** *n.*

orthostatic hypotension a drop in blood

pressure when moving from a lying or sitting position to a standing position, causing lightheadedness, tunnel vision, and potentially loss of consciousness. It may result from a variety of causes, including disorders such as diabetes mellitus, amyloidosis, and Parkinson's disease. Also called **postural hypotension**.

orthotics *n.* a medical specialization concerned with the fitting and use of braces and other orthopedic (supportive or corrective) appliances. Compare PROSTHETICS.

oscillopsia *n.* the sensation of perceiving oscillating movement of the environment. This illusory movement can be caused by (bilateral) vestibular cerebellar injury, paralysis of extrinsic eye muscles, or nystagmus, but may also be due to cerebral disorders (e.g., seizures, occipital lobe infarction).

osmoreceptor *n.* a hypothetical receptor in the HYPOTHALAMUS that responds to changes in the concentrations of various substances in the body's extracellular fluid and to cellular dehydration. It also regulates the secretion of VASOPRESSIN and contributes to thirst.

osmosis *n.* the passive movement of solvent molecules through a differentially permeable membrane (e.g., a cell membrane) separating two solutions of different concentrations. The solvent tends to flow from the weaker solution to the stronger solution. —**osmotic** *adj.*

osmotic pressure the pressure required to prevent the passage of water (or other solvent) through a semipermeable membrane (e.g., a cell membrane) from an area of low concentration of solute to an area of higher concentration. It results from the spontaneous movement of molecules occurring when different concentrations are separated by a semipermeable membrane.

ossicles *pl. n.* any small bones, but particularly the auditory ossicles: the chain of three tiny bones in the middle ear that transmit sound vibrations from the tympanic membrane (eardrum) to the OVAL WINDOW of the inner ear. They are the **malleus** (or hammer), which is attached to the tympanic membrane; the **incus** (or anvil); and the **stapes** (or stirrup), whose footplate nearly fills the oval window. The ossicles allow efficient transmission of sound from air to the fluid-filled cochlea.

osteopathy *n.* a health care system based on the belief that many disorders are caused by structural defects in the musculoskeletal system. It focuses on primary care, prevention, a holistic approach to patient health, and—especially—manipulation of the affected joints and muscles (particularly of the spine) in conjunction with traditional medical, surgical, and pharmacological treatment to address underlying disease processes. Also called **osteopathic medicine**. See also COMPLEMENTARY AND ALTERNATIVE MEDICINE. —**osteopath** *n.* —**osteopathic** *adj.*

OT abbreviation for OCCUPATIONAL THERAPY.

OTC abbreviation for OVER-THE-COUNTER.

other-conscious emotion see SELF-CONSCIOUS EMOTION.

otoacoustic emissions (**OAEs**) weak sounds produced by the COCHLEA that are recorded using a microphone placed in the EXTERNAL AUDITORY MEATUS. **Spontaneous otoacoustic emissions** (SOAEs) are recorded in the absence of externally presented sound. **Evoked otoacoustic emissions** (EOAEs) are responses to sounds, typically transients (clicks), sustained PURE TONES, or pairs of tones. EOAEs are not the result of reflections, and thus the alternative term **cochlear echo** is not technically correct. All OAEs appear to require normal cochlear function and provide strong evidence for an active mechanical process occurring within the cochlea, probably mediated by movement of the outer HAIR CELLS.

otolaryngology *n.* the medical discipline concerned with the assessment and treatment of diseases of the ears, nose, and throat and associated structures of the head and neck.

otology *n.* the medical discipline concerned with the study, diagnosis, and treatment of disorders of the ear. —**otological** *adj.* —**otologist** *n.*

otoneurology *n.* the study of neurology as related to audition. —**otoneurological** *adj.* —**otoneurologist** *n.*

otosclerosis *n.* a formation of spongy bone that develops in the middle ear and immobilizes the STAPES at the point of attachment to the oval window facing the inner ear. Otosclerosis is marked by progressive deafness as the OSSICLES fail to transmit vibrations from the tympanic membrane to the inner ear. —**otosclerotic** *adj.*

ototoxic *adj.* damaging to the ears, especially the structures for hearing and balance within the inner ear. —**ototoxicity** *n.*

ought self in analyses of self-concept, a mental representation of a set of attributes that one is obligated to possess according to social norms or one's personal responsibilities.

outcome expectancies cognitive, emotional, and behavioral outcomes that individuals believe are associated with future, or intended, behaviors (e.g., alcohol consumption, exercise) and that are believed to either promote or inhibit these behaviors.

outcome measures assessments of the effectiveness of an intervention on the basis of measurements taken before, during, and after the intervention.

outcome research a systematic investigation of the effectiveness of a single type or technique of psychotherapy, or of the comparative effectiveness of different types or techniques, when applied to one or more disorders. See also PSYCHOTHERAPY RESEARCH.

outer ear see EXTERNAL EAR.

outer psychophysics an attempt to establish the direct relationship between the physical intensity of sensory stimuli and the intensity of the related mental experience. Compare INNER PSYCHOPHYSICS. See PSYCHOPHYSICAL LAW.

outgroup *n.* any group to which one does not belong or with which one does not identify, but particularly a group that is judged to be different from, and inferior to, one's own group (the INGROUP).

outgroup extremity effect the tendency to describe and evaluate OUTGROUP members, their actions, and their products in extremely positive or extremely negative ways. Compare INGROUP EXTREMITY EFFECT.

outgroup homogeneity bias the tendency to assume that the members of other groups are very similar to each other, particularly in contrast to the assumed diversity of the membership of one's own groups. See also GROUP ATTRIBUTION ERROR; GROUP FALLACY.

outlier *n.* an extreme observation or measurement, that is, one that significantly differs from all others obtained. Outliers can have a high degree of influence on summary statistics and estimates of parametric values and their precision and may distort research findings if they are the result of error.

out-of-body experience a dissociative experience in which the individual imagines that his or her mind, soul, or spirit has left the body and is acting or perceiving independently. Such experiences are sometimes reported by those who have recovered from the point of death (see NEAR-DEATH EXPERIENCE); they have also been reported by those using hallucinogens or under hypnosis. Certain occult or spiritualistic practices may also attempt to induce such experiences.

outpatient *n.* a person who obtains diagnosis, treatment, or other service at a hospital, clinic, physician's office, or other health care facility without overnight admission. See also AMBULATORY CARE. Compare INPATIENT.

outpatient commitment a form of court-ordered psychiatric or psychological treatment in which individuals are allowed to remain in the community so long as they are closely monitored and continue to receive treatment.

outplacement counseling practical and psychological assistance given to employees whose employment with an organization has been terminated. It can include VOCATIONAL GUIDANCE and coaching in job-hunting skills as well as psychological help in dealing with the transition. The program is usually conducted by specialty firms outside the organization. See also VOCATIONAL COUNSELING.

output interference see INTERFERENCE.

oval window a membrane-covered opening in the bony wall of the cochlea in the ear (see SCALA VESTIBULI). Vibration of the stapes (see OSSICLES) is transmitted to the oval window and into the cochlear fluids.

ovariectomy *n.* the surgical removal of an ovary. This procedure may be performed when the ovaries are diseased or injured or in some circumstances, such as when a woman is at very high risk for ovarian cancer, as a preventive measure. Also called **oophorectomy**.

ovary *n.* the female reproductive organ, which produces ova (egg cells) and sex hormones (estrogens and progesterone). In humans the two ovaries are almond-shaped organs, normally located in the lower abdomen on either side of the upper end of the uterus, to which they are linked by the FALLOPIAN TUBES. See also GRAAFIAN FOLLICLE; MENSTRUAL CYCLE; OOGENESIS. —**ovarian** *adj.*

overactivity *n.* excessive, restless activity that is usually less extreme than HYPERACTIVITY.

overclassification *n.* a phenomenon in which, at levels ranging from local schools to national patterns of education, children who are members of ethnic minority groups are at heightened risk of being classified as SPECIAL EDUCATION students.

overcompensation *n.* see COMPENSATION. —**overcompensate** *vb.*

overdetermination *n.* in psychoanalytic theory, the concept that several unconscious factors may combine to produce one symptom, dream, disorder, or aspect of behavior. Because drives and defenses operate simultaneously and derive from different layers of the personality, a dream may express more than one meaning, and a single symptom may serve more than one purpose or fulfill more than one unconscious wish. —**overdetermined** *adj.*

overdose *n.* the ingestion of an excessive amount of a drug, with resulting adverse and potentially lethal effects. The precise toxic effects differ according to many factors, including the properties and dosage of the drug, the body weight and health of the individual, and the individual's tolerance for the drug.

Overeaters Anonymous (OA) see ALCOHOLICS ANONYMOUS.

overexpectation *n.* in PAVLOVIAN CONDITIONING, a decrease in responding to two (or presumably more) conditioned stimuli individually after they have been joined into a compound stimulus and then paired with the unconditioned stimulus previously used to establish each part of the compound as an independent conditioned stimulus.

overextension *n.* the tendency of very young children to extend the use of a word beyond the scope of its specific meaning, for example, by referring to all animals as "doggie."

overgeneralization *n.* **1.** a cognitive distortion in which an individual views a single event as an invariable rule, so that, for example, failure at accomplishing one task will predict an endless pattern of defeat in all tasks. **2.** the tendency of young children to generalize standard grammatical rules to apply to irregular words, for exam-

ple, pluralizing *foot* to *foots*. See OVEREXTENSION; OVERREGULARIZATION.

overjustification effect a paradoxical effect in which rewarding (or offering to reward) a person for his or her performance can lead to lower, rather than higher, effort and attainment. It occurs when introduction of the reward weakens the strong INTRINSIC MOTIVATION that was the key to the person's original high performance.

overlearning *n.* practice that is continued beyond the point at which the individual knows or performs well. The benefits of overlearning may be seen in increased persistence of the learning over time. **—overlearned** *adj.*

overload *n.* a psychological condition in which situations and experiences are so cognitively, perceptually, and emotionally stimulating that they tax or even exceed the individual's capacity to process incoming information. See COGNITIVE OVERLOAD; INFORMATION OVERLOAD; SENSORY OVERLOAD; STIMULUS OVERLOAD.

overprotection *n.* the process of coddling, sheltering, and indulging a child to such an extent that he or she fails to become independent and may experience later adjustment and other difficulties, including development of a DEPENDENT PERSONALITY DISORDER.

overregularization *n.* a transient error in linguistic development in which the child attempts to make language more regular than it actually is, for example, by saying *breaked* instead of *broken*. See also OVEREXTENSION; OVERGENERALIZATION.

overshadowing *n.* in PAVLOVIAN CONDITIONING, a decrease in conditioning with one conditioned stimulus because of the presence of another conditioned stimulus. Usually a stronger stimulus will overshadow a weaker stimulus. **—overshadow** *vb.*

overt *adj.* **1.** denoting anything that is directly observable, open to view, or publicly known. **2.** not hidden. Compare COVERT. **3.** deliberate or attracting attention.

over-the-counter (**OTC**) *adj.* able to be pur-

chased without a doctor's prescription. A variety of OTC drugs, including acetaminophen and aspirin, are available.

overtone *n.* see HARMONIC.

overtraining syndrome the unwanted physical and mental effects, collectively, of training beyond the individual's capacities. Characteristic symptoms include decreased performance, easily tiring, loss of motivation, emotional instability, inability to concentrate, and increased susceptibility to injury and infection.

overt response any observable or external reaction, such as pointing to indicate one's preference from among a set of objects or verbally answering "yes" to a question. Compare COVERT RESPONSE.

overvalued idea a false or exaggerated belief that is maintained by an individual, but less rigidly and persistently than a delusion (e.g., the idea that one is indispensable in an organization).

ovulation *n.* the production of a mature secondary oocyte (see OOGENESIS) and its release from a GRAAFIAN FOLLICLE at the surface of the ovary. Rupture of the follicle causes the oocyte to be discharged into a fallopian tube. In humans, the oocyte matures into an OVUM in the strict sense only if it is penetrated by a sperm during its passage along the fallopian tube.

ovum *n.* (*pl.* **ova**) a single female GAMETE that develops from a secondary oocyte following its release from the ovary at OVULATION. Also called **egg cell**. See also OOGENESIS.

own control a WITHIN-SUBJECTS DESIGN in which pre- and post-manipulation measurements are taken on the same group or individual such that the participants serve as their own control.

oxytocin *n.* a hormone produced in the hypothalamus and secreted by the posterior lobe (neurohypophysis) of the PITUITARY GLAND in response to direct neural stimulation. It stimulates smooth muscle, particularly in the mammary glands during lactation and in the wall of the uterus during labor.

Pp

p symbol for PROBABILITY.

P300 see P3 COMPONENT.

pacemaker *n.* a natural or artificial device that helps establish and maintain certain biological rhythms. Unqualified, the term usually refers to a cardiac pacemaker. Natural pacemakers include the sinoatrial node, which regulates heart rhythm, and the thalamic pacemaker.

pachygyria *n.* see LISSENCEPHALY.

Pacinian corpuscle a type of cutaneous receptor organ that is sensitive to contact and vibration. It consists of a nerve-fiber ending surrounded by concentric layers of connective tissue. Pacinian corpuscles are found in the fingers, the hairy skin, the tendons, and the abdominal membrane. Also called **Pacinian body**. [Filippo Pacini (1812–1883), Italian anatomist]

PAG abbreviation for PERIAQUEDUCTAL GRAY.

pain *n.* an unpleasant sensation due to damage to nerve tissue, stimulation of free nerve endings, or excessive stimulation (e.g., extremely loud sounds). Physical pain is elicited by stimulation of pain receptors, which occur in groups of myelinated or unmyelinated fibers throughout the body, but particularly in surface tissues. Pain that is initiated in surface receptors generally is perceived as sharp, sudden, and localized; pain experienced in internal organs tends to be dull, longer lasting, and less localized. Because of psychological factors, as well as previous experience and training in pain response, individual reactions vary widely. Although pain is generally considered a physical phenomenon, it involves various cognitive, affective, and behavioral factors: It is an unpleasant emotional as well as sensory experience. Pain may also be a feeling of severe distress and suffering resulting from acute anxiety, loss of a loved one, or other psychological factors. Psychologists have made important contributions to understanding pain by demonstrating the psychosocial and behavioral factors in the etiology, severity, exacerbation, maintenance, and treatment of both physical and mental pain. See also CHRONIC PAIN; GATE-CONTROL THEORY.

pain disorder a SOMATOFORM DISORDER characterized by severe, prolonged pain that significantly interferes with a person's ability to function. The pain cannot be accounted for solely by a medical condition, and there is evidence of psychological involvement in its onset, severity, exacerbation, or maintenance. Although not feigned or produced intentionally (compare FACTITIOUS DISORDER; MALINGER-ING), the pain may serve such psychological ends as avoidance of distasteful activity or gaining extra attention or support from others.

pain management the prevention, reduction, or elimination of physical or mental suffering or discomfort, which may be achieved by pharmacotherapy (e.g., administration of opioids or other analgesics), behavioral therapies, neurological and anesthesiologic methods (e.g., nerve blocks, self-administered pumps), complementary or alternative methods (e.g., ACUPUNCTURE or ACUPRESSURE), or a combination of these. A wide range of psychological interventions have been used successfully in treatment to help people deal with or control their pain. For example, BIOFEEDBACK and RELAXATION have been used alone and in conjunction with other cognitive techniques to treat chronic headaches and facial pain. HYPNOTHERAPY has also been used successfully to treat acute pain and pain associated with burns and metastatic disease. Cognitive and behavioral COPING-SKILLS TRAINING, along with neutral or positive IMAGERY, problem solving, communication skills, and psychotherapeutic approaches, have been combined with physical modalities in the treatment of CHRONIC PAIN syndromes.

pain mechanisms neural mechanisms that mediate pain. These extend from peripheral nerve endings to the cerebral cortex, especially the CINGULATE GYRUS. Some investigators propose that sharp pain sensations are transmitted by rapidly conducting A FIBERS and dull pain sensations are transmitted by slowly conducting C FIBERS. See also GATE-CONTROL THEORY.

pain pathway any neural pathway that mediates sensations of pain. Afferent pain pathways include rapidly conducting myelinated A FIBERS and slowly conducting unmyelinated C FIBERS, ascending tracts in the ANTEROLATERAL SYSTEM, the PERIAQUIDUCTAL GRAY matter, the RETICULAR FORMATION, and many thalamic and cerebral cortical areas, especially the CINGULATE GYRUS. There are also efferent pathways that inhibit pain signals at various levels down to spinal synapses, including release of ENDOGENOUS OPIOIDS that inhibit pain.

pain perception the perception of physiological pain, usually evoked by stimuli that cause or threaten to cause tissue damage. In some cases, such as PHANTOM LIMB pain, the persistence of pain cannot be explained by stimulation of neural pathways. Pain perception can be measured in terms of its intensity and can be classified according to several categories: These include sharp or dull; focal or general; and chronic or intermittent or transitory. Also called **nociception**.

pain receptor see NOCICEPTOR.

pair bond a relationship between two individuals characterized by close affiliative behavior between partners, emotional reaction to separation or loss, and increased social responsiveness on reunion. Pair bonds are important in species with biparental care, providing the female with increased likelihood of male cooperation in the care of the young and the male with increased CERTAINTY OF PATERNITY.

paired-associates learning a technique used in studying learning in which participants learn syllables, words, or other items in pairs and are later presented with one half of each pair to which they must respond with the matching half. Also called **paired-associates method**.

paired comparison 1. a systematic procedure for comparing a set of stimuli or other items. A pair of stimuli is presented to the participant, who is asked to compare them on a particular dimension, such as size, loudness, or brightness; the process is continued until every item in the set has been compared with every other item. The method is mainly associated with research into psychophysical judgments. **2.** a method of employee evaluation in which each worker in a selected group is compared with every other worker on a series of performance measures. Employees are then rated on the basis of the number of favorable comparisons they receive.

pairing n. in behavioral studies, the juxtaposing of two events in time. For example, if a tone is presented immediately before a puff of air to the eye, the tone and the puff have been paired.

pairwise contrast a contrast that involves only two group means.

palate n. the roof of the mouth, consisting of an anterior bony portion (**hard palate**) and a posterior fibromuscular portion (**soft palate**).

paleocortex n. see ALLOCORTEX.

paleopsychology n. **1.** the study of certain psychological processes in contemporary humans that are believed to have originated in earlier stages of human and, perhaps, nonhuman animal evolution. These include unconscious processes, such as the COLLECTIVE UNCONSCIOUS. **2.** the present-day reconstruction of the psychological reactions of prehistoric human beings. **—paleopsychological** adj.

palinopsia n. the persistence or reappearance of a visual image after the stimulus has been removed. Palinopsia is associated with posterior brain injury, drug effects, and seizures. Also called **palinopia**; **paliopsy**; **visual perseveration**. See also AFTERIMAGE; VISUAL ILLUSION.

palliative care terminal care that focuses on symptom control and comfort instead of aggressive, cure-oriented intervention. This is the basis of the HOSPICE approach. Emphasis is on careful assessment of the patient's condition throughout the end phase of life in order to provide the most effective medications and other procedures to relieve pain.

pallidotomy n. a neurosurgical technique in which electrodes are used to selectively lesion the GLOBUS PALLIDUS. Pallidotomy is used for the management of disorders involving damage to the EXTRAPYRAMIDAL TRACT, such as Parkinson's disease.

palsy n. an obsolete name for paralysis, still used in such compound names as CEREBRAL PALSY, BELL'S PALSY, and PROGRESSIVE SUPRANUCLEAR PALSY.

Pamelor n. a trade name for NORTRIPTYLINE.

pancreas n. a gland, located near the posterior wall of the abdominal cavity, that is stimulated by the hormone secretin to secrete pancreatic juice, which contains various digestive enzymes. In addition, small clusters of cells within the pancreas (see ISLETS OF LANGERHANS) function as an ENDOCRINE GLAND, secreting the hormones INSULIN and GLUCAGON. **—pancreatic** adj.

pandemic adj. widespread or universal: affecting significant proportions of many populations over a large area (e.g., several countries), particularly with reference to a disease or disorder. Compare ENDEMIC; EPIDEMIC.

panel study a longitudinal study (see LONGITUDINAL DESIGN) in which one or more groups (panels) are followed over time.

panic n. a sudden, uncontrollable fear reaction that may involve terror, confusion, and irrational behavior, precipitated by a perceived threat (e.g., earthquake, fire, or being stuck in an elevator).

panic attack a sudden onset of intense apprehension and fearfulness, in the absence of actual danger, accompanied by the presence of such physical symptoms as palpitations, difficulty in breathing, chest pain or discomfort, choking or smothering sensations, excessive perspiration, and dizziness. The attack occurs in a discrete period of time and often involves fears of going crazy, losing control, or dying. Attacks may occur in the context of any of the ANXIETY DISORDERS as well as in other mental disorders (e.g., mood disorders, substance-related disorders) and in some general medical conditions (e.g., hyperthyroidism). See also CUED PANIC ATTACK; UNCUED PANIC ATTACK.

panic control treatment a COGNITIVE BEHAVIOR THERAPY for panic disorder focusing on education about panic, training in slow breathing, and graded in vivo exposures to cues associated with panic.

panic disorder an ANXIETY DISORDER characterized by recurrent, unexpected PANIC ATTACKS that are associated with (a) persistent concern about having another attack, (b) worry about the possible consequences of the attacks, (c) significant change in behavior related to the attacks (e.g., avoiding situations, not going out alone), or (d) a combination of any or all of these (see also AGORAPHOBIA).

panpsychism *n.* the view that all elements of the natural world possess some quality of soul (psyche) or some form of sentience. Some equate this view with **hylozoism**, which holds that all natural objects possess the quality of life, whereas others distinguish between life and soul or sentience. Also called **psychism**. See also ANIMISM.

pansexualism *n.* the view that all human behavior is motivated by the sexual drive. Austrian psychiatrist Sigmund Freud (1856–1939) has been popularly associated with such a view; however, although he emphasized the power of the sexual instinct, Freud also recognized nonsexual interests, such as the self-preservative drives (e.g., hunger and thirst) and the aggressive drive associated with the DEATH INSTINCT. —**pansexual** *adj.*

Panum's fusional area the region in space surrounding a HOROPTER in which images that appear at different points on the two retinas are nonetheless fused by the visual system and so appear as single images. If visual targets appear outside this area (either in front of or behind it) they will appear as double images, and the observer will experience double vision. [Peter Ludwig **Panum** (1820–1885), Danish physiologist]

Papez circuit a circular network of nerve centers and fibers in the brain that is associated with emotion and memory. It includes the hippocampus, FORNIX, MAMMILLARY BODY, anterior thalamus, CINGULATE GYRUS, and PARAHIPPOCAMPAL GYRUS. Damage to any component of this system leads to amnesia. Also called **Papez circle**. See also PAPEZ'S THEORY OF EMOTION. [first described in 1937 by James W. **Papez** (1883–1958), U.S. neuroanatomist]

Papez's theory of emotion a modification of the CANNON–BARD THEORY proposing that the PAPEZ CIRCUIT is the site of integration and control of emotional experience in the higher brain centers. See also MACLEAN'S THEORY OF EMOTION. [James **Papez**]

papilla *n.* (*pl.* **papillae**) any of the four types of swellings on the tongue. In humans, some 200 fungiform papillae are toward the front of the tongue; 10–14 foliate papillae are on the sides; 7–11 circumvallate papillae are on the back; and filiform papillae, with no taste function, cover most of the tongue's surface. Also called **lingual papilla**.

papilledema *n.* a swelling of the OPTIC DISK due to an increase in intracranial pressure. The condition may occur because the meningeal membranes of the brain are continuous with the sheaths of the optic nerve, so that pressure can be transmitted to the eyeball. Also called **choked disk**.

paracentral vision a form of vision that utilizes the retinal area immediately surrounding, but not including, the FOVEA CENTRALIS. Compare CENTRAL VISION; PERIPHERAL VISION.

paracontrast *n.* a form of forward MASKING in which the perception of a visible stimulus (the target) is altered by the prior presentation of another visual stimulus (the mask) in a different spatial location. The target is often a small dot, while the mask is a ring that surrounds it. Each stimulus is presented very briefly (10–100 ms), at intervals that are varied systematically, and the quality of the target's percept is measured. Compare METACONTRAST.

paracrine *adj.* describing or relating to a type of cellular signaling in which a chemical messenger is released from a cell and diffuses to a nearby target cell, on which it exerts its effect, through the intervening extracellular space. Compare AUTOCRINE; ENDOCRINE.

paracusia *n.* **1.** partial deafness, especially to deeper tones. **2.** any abnormality of hearing other than simple deafness, such as **paracusia localis**, impairment in determining the direction from which a sound comes.

paradigm *n.* **1.** a model, pattern, or representative example, as of the functions and interrelationships of a process, a behavior under study, or the like. **2.** an experimental design or plan of the various steps of an experiment. **3.** a grammatical category or a collection of all inflectional forms of a word. **4.** a set of assumptions, attitudes, concepts, values, procedures, and techniques that constitutes a generally accepted theoretical framework within, or a general perspective of, a discipline.

paradoxical directive an instruction by a therapist to the client to do precisely the opposite of what common sense would dictate in order to show the absurdity or self-defeating nature of the client's original intention. See also PARADOXICAL TECHNIQUE.

paradoxical intention a psychotherapeutic technique in which the client is asked to magnify a distressing, unwanted symptom. For example, an individual who is afraid of shaking in a social situation would be instructed to imagine the feared situation and purposely exaggerate the shakiness. The aim is to help clients distance themselves from their symptoms, often by appreciating the humorous aspects of their exaggerated responses. In this way clients can learn that the predicted catastrophic consequences attributed to their symptoms are very unlikely to occur. Paradoxical intention may be used to treat anxiety disorders but is not appropriate for suicidal behavior or schizophrenia.

paradoxical motion the global perception of motion in a MOTION AFTEREFFECT even though the individual elements in the image do not appear to move.

paradoxical reaction in pharmacology, a drug reaction that is contrary to the expected effect, for example, worsening of anxiety after the administration of an anxiolytic agent.

paradoxical sleep see REM SLEEP.

paradoxical technique a therapeutic technique in which a client is directed by the therapist to continue undesired symptomatic behavior, and even increase it, to show that the client has voluntary control over the symptoms. Also called **paradoxical intervention**. See also PARADOXICAL DIRECTIVE.

paradox of freedom a fundamental paradox that arises under assumptions of DETERMINISM in human behavior: namely, that although specific behaviors can be attributed to specific antecedent causes, humans almost universally experience a sense of being free to perform or refrain from performing any given behavior at the point of action. HARD DETERMINISM resolves this paradox by insisting that the sense of free choice is illusory, whereas SOFT DETERMINISM argues that such a sense is not in fact incompatible with causal explanations.

paragrammatism n. a form of APHASIA consisting of substitutions, reversals, or omissions of sounds or syllables within words or reversals of words within sentences. Paragrammatic speech may be unintelligible if the disturbance is severe. —**paragrammatic** adj.

parahippocampal gyrus a ridge (gyrus) on the medial (inner) surface of the TEMPORAL LOBE of cerebral cortex, lying over the HIPPOCAMPUS. It is a component of the LIMBIC SYSTEM thought to be involved in spatial or topographic memory. Also called **parahippocampal cortex**.

parakinesia n. awkwardness or clumsiness of movement.

paralalia n. **1.** a speech disorder or disturbance that involves the substitution of one speech sound for another (e.g., saying "wabbit" for *rabbit* or "lellow" for *yellow*). See also LALLING. **2.** a rarely used term for speech disorders generally.

paralanguage n. the vocal but nonverbal elements of communication by speech. Paralanguage includes not only SUPRASEGMENTAL features of speech, such as tone and stress, but also such factors as volume and speed of delivery, voice quality, hesitations, and nonlinguistic sounds, such as sighs, whistles, or groans. These **paralinguistic cues** (or **paralinguistic features**) can be enormously important in shaping the total meaning of an utterance; they can, for example, convey the fact that a speaker is angry or sarcastic when this would not be apparent from the same words written down. In some uses, the term paralanguage is extended to include gestures, facial expressions, and other aspects of BODY LANGUAGE.

paralexia n. the substitution or transposition of letters, syllables, or words during reading.

parallax n. an illusion of movement of objects in the visual field when the head is moved from side to side. Objects beyond a point of visual fix-

ation appear to move in the same direction as the head movement; those closer seem to move in the opposite direction. Parallax provides a monocular cue for DEPTH PERCEPTION.

parallel distributed processing any model of cognition based on the idea that the representation of information is distributed as patterns of activation over a richly connected set of hypothetical neural units that function interactively and in parallel with one another. See DISTRIBUTED PROCESSING; PARALLEL PROCESSING. See also GRACEFUL DEGRADATION.

parallel fiber any of the axons of the GRANULE CELLS that form the outermost layer of the CEREBELLAR CORTEX.

parallel play see SOCIAL PLAY.

parallel processing INFORMATION PROCESSING in which two or more sequences of operations are carried out simultaneously by independent processors. A capacity for parallel processing in the human mind would account for people's apparent ability to carry on different cognitive functions at the same time, as, for example, when driving a car while also listening to music and having a conversation. However, those who believe that there is no truly parallel processing in the brain explain this ability in terms of very rapid shifts between functions and information sources. The term parallel processing is usually reserved for processing at a higher, symbolic level, as opposed to the level of individual neural units described in models of PARALLEL DISTRIBUTED PROCESSING. Also called **simultaneous processing**. Compare SERIAL PROCESSING.

parallel search in a search task, the process of searching for many items at the same time, with no decrease in efficiency. Compare SERIAL SEARCH.

paralogia n. insistently illogical or delusional thinking and verbal expression, sometimes observed in schizophrenia. Swiss psychiatrist Eugen Bleuler (1857–1939) cited the example of a patient who justified his insistence that he was Switzerland by saying "Switzerland loves freedom. I love freedom. I am Switzerland." Also called **paralogical thinking**; **perverted logic**; **perverted thinking**.

paralysis n. loss of function of voluntary muscles. A common cause is a lesion of the nervous or muscular system due to injury, disease, or congenital factors. The lesion may involve the central nervous system, as in a stroke, or the peripheral nervous system, as in GUILLAIN–BARRÉ SYNDROME. See also FLACCID PARALYSIS; SPASTIC PARALYSIS. —**paralytic** adj.

parameter n. **1.** a numerical constant that characterizes a population with respect to some attribute, for example, the location of its central point. **2.** an ARGUMENT of a function. —**parametric** adj.

parametric statistics statistical procedures

that are based on assumptions about the distribution of the attribute (or attributes) in the population being tested. Compare NONPARAMETRIC STATISTICS.

paramnesia *n.* see FALSE MEMORY.

paranoia *n.* **1.** a PARANOID STATE. **2.** a former diagnosis for a relatively rare disorder, distinct from paranoid schizophrenia, in which the person reasons rightly from a wrong premise and develops a persistent, well-systematized, and logically constructed set of persecutory delusions, such as being conspired against or poisoned or maligned. The current diagnostic equivalent is persecutory-type DELUSIONAL DISORDER. **—paranoiac** *n., adj.*

paranoid delusion loosely, any of a variety of false personal beliefs tenaciously sustained even in the face of incontrovertible evidence to the contrary: delusions of grandeur, delusional jealousy, or, most frequently, delusions of persecution.

paranoid personality disorder a personality disorder characterized by (a) pervasive, unwarranted suspiciousness and mistrust (such as expectation of trickery or harm, guardedness and secretiveness, avoidance of accepting blame, overconcern with hidden motives and meanings, and pathological jealousy); (b) hypersensitivity (such as being easily slighted and quick to take offense, exaggerated concern over insignificant behaviors or events, and readiness to counterattack); and (c) restricted affectivity (such as emotional coldness, no true sense of humor, or absence of tender feelings).

paranoid schizophrenia a subtype of SCHIZOPHRENIA, often with a later onset than other types, characterized by prominent delusions or auditory hallucinations. Delusions are typically persecutory, grandiose, or both; hallucinations are typically related to the content of the delusional theme. Cognitive functioning and mood are affected to a much lesser degree than in other types of schizophrenia.

paranoid state a condition characterized by delusions of persecution or grandiosity that are not as systematized and elaborate as in a DELUSIONAL DISORDER or as disorganized and bizarre as in paranoid schizophrenia. Also called **paranoid condition**.

paranormal *adj.* denoting any purported phenomenon involving the transfer of information or energy that cannot be explained by existing scientific knowledge. The term is particularly applied to those forms of alleged EXTRASENSORY PERCEPTION that are the province of parapsychological investigation (see PARAPSYCHOLOGY).

paraphasia *n.* a speech disturbance characterized by the use of incorrect, distorted, or inappropriate words, which in some cases resemble the correct word in sound or meaning and in other cases are irrelevant or nonsensical. For example, a wheelchair may be called a "spinning wheel," and a hypodermic needle might be called a "tie pin." The disorder is seen most commonly in organic brain disorders and PICK'S DISEASE. **—paraphasic** *adj.*

paraphemia *n.* a speech disorder marked by the habitual introduction of inappropriate words or by the meaningless combination of words.

paraphilia *n.* a sexual disorder in which unusual or bizarre fantasies or behavior are necessary for sexual excitement. The fantasies or acts persist over a period of at least 6 months and may take several forms: preference for a nonhuman object, such as animals or clothes of the opposite sex; repetitive sexual activity involving real or simulated suffering or humiliation, as in whipping or bondage; or repetitive sexual activity with nonconsenting partners. Paraphilias include such specific types as FETISHISM, FROTTEURISM, PEDOPHILIA, EXHIBITIONISM, VOYEURISM, SEXUAL MASOCHISM, and SEXUAL SADISM. **—paraphiliac** *adj.*

paraphrasia *n.* see WORD SALAD. **—paraphrasic** *adj.*

paraplegia *n.* paralysis of the legs and lower part of the trunk. **—paraplegic** *adj.*

parapraxis *n.* an error that is believed to express unconscious wishes, attitudes, or impulses. Examples of such errors include slips of the pen, SLIPS OF THE TONGUE, forgetting significant events, mislaying objects with unpleasant associations, unintentional puns, and motivated accidents. Also called **parapraxia**. See also FREUDIAN SLIP; SYMPTOMATIC ACT.

parapsychology *n.* the systematic study of alleged psychological phenomena involving the transfer of information or energy that cannot be explained in terms of presently known scientific data or laws. Such study has focused largely on the various forms of EXTRASENSORY PERCEPTION, such as TELEPATHY and CLAIRVOYANCE, but also encompasses such phenomena as alleged poltergeist activity and the claims of mediums. Although parapsychology is committed to scientific methods and procedures, it is still regarded with suspicion by most scientists, including most psychologists. **—parapsychological** *adj.* **—parapsychologist** *n.*

parasitism *n.* **1.** see INTERSPECIES INTERACTION. **2.** a social relationship in which one individual habitually benefits from the generosity of others without making any useful return.

parasomnia *n.* a SLEEP DISORDER characterized by abnormal behavior or physiological events occurring during sleep or the transitional state between sleep and waking. Types include NIGHTMARE DISORDER, SLEEP TERROR DISORDER, and SLEEPWALKING DISORDER. The parasomnias form one of two broad groups of primary sleep disorders, the other being DYSSOMNIAS.

parasuicide *n.* a range of behaviors involving deliberate self-harm that falls short of suicide and may or may not be intended to result in

P

death. It includes attempted suicide and passive suicide (i.e., ambiguous self-destructive behavior).

parasympathetic nervous system one of two branches of the AUTONOMIC NERVOUS SYSTEM (ANS, which controls smooth muscle and gland functions), the other being the SYMPATHETIC NERVOUS SYSTEM. Anatomically it comprises the portion of the ANS whose preganglionic fibers leave the central nervous system from the brainstem via the OCULOMOTOR, FACIAL, GLOSSOPHARYNGEAL, and VAGUS NERVES and the spinal cord via three sacral nerves (see SPINAL NERVE). It is defined functionally as the system controlling rest, repair, enjoyment, eating, sleeping, sexual activity, and social dominance, among other functions. The parasympathetic nervous system stimulates salivary secretions and digestive secretions in the stomach and produces pupillary constriction, decreases in heart rate, and increased blood flow to the genitalia during sexual excitement. Also called **parasympathetic division**.

parasympatholytic drug see ANTICHOLINERGIC DRUG.

parasympathomimetic drug see CHOLINERGIC DRUG.

parataxic distortion in psychoanalytic theory, a distorted perception or judgment of others on the basis of past experiences or of the unconscious. Also called **transference distortion**.

parathyroid gland a small, paired endocrine gland found in the area of the thyroid gland. It secretes parathyroid hormone, which takes part in the control of calcium and phosphate metabolism.

paratype n. the totality of environmental influences that act on an organism to produce individual expression of a genetic trait or character.

paraverbal therapy a method of psychotherapy for children who have difficulty communicating verbally and are also affected by such conditions and disorders as hyperactivity, autism, withdrawal, or language disturbances. Assuming that these children would feel more intrigued and less threatened by a nonverbal approach, the therapy uses various expressive media, including the components of music (tempo and pitch), mime, movement, and art to help the children express themselves. The therapist participates on the children's level, and eventually the children feel safe enough to verbalize their real feelings, enabling them to participate in more conventional therapy.

parental investment theory the proposition that many sex differences in sexually reproducing species (including humans) can be understood in terms of the amount of time, energy, and risk to their own survival that males and females put into parenting versus mating (including the seeking, attaining, and maintaining of a mate). Differences in parenting and mating investment between males and females vary among species and as a function of environmental conditions.

parental rejection persistent denial of approval, affection, or care by one or both parents, sometimes concealed beneath a cover of overindulgence or overprotection. The frequent result is corrosion of the child's self-esteem and self-confidence, a poor self-image, inability to form attachments to others, tantrums, generalized hostility, and development of psychophysical and emotional disturbances. See CHILD ABUSE.

parent effectiveness training (**PET**) a set of principles providing guidance for prosocial interactions between children and parents related to discipline, communication, and responsible relationships. Guidelines are also provided for client-centered discussions of principles, practices, and problems of child rearing conducted by a mental health professional on a group basis. A balance is maintained between the child's feelings and needs and those of the parents.

parenting n. all actions related to the raising of offspring. Researchers have described different human **parenting styles**—ways in which parents interact with their children—with most classifications varying on the dimensions of emotional warmth (warm versus cold) and control (high in control versus low in control). One of the most influential of these classifications is that of U.S. developmental psychologist Diana Baumrind (1927–), which involves four types of styles: **authoritarian parenting**, in which the parent or caregiver stresses obedience, deemphasizes collaboration and dialogue, and employs strong forms of punishment; **authoritative parenting**, in which the parent or caregiver encourages a child's autonomy yet still places certain limitations on behavior; **permissive parenting**, in which the parent or caregiver is accepting and affirmative, makes few demands, and avoids exercising control; and **rejecting–neglecting parenting**, in which the parent or caregiver is unsupportive, fails to monitor or limit behavior, and is more attentive to his or her needs than those of the child.

parent management training a treatment approach based on the principles of OPERANT CONDITIONING. Parents use antecedents, behaviors, and consequences to change child and adolescent behavior at home, at school, and in other settings. The goals are to help children develop prosocial behaviors and decrease oppositional, aggressive, and antisocial behaviors.

parent–offspring conflict a conflict that arises when parents cease providing care for current offspring and invest in producing the next set of offspring. The parents will benefit in terms of REPRODUCTIVE SUCCESS by breeding again as soon as the current offspring have a high probability of surviving independently. The offspring, however, will gain more by continued investment from their parents, creating the conflict. Parent–offspring conflict is manifested through

P

regressive behavior, including tantrums, by the older offspring and through SIBLING RIVALRY.

paresis *n.* partial or incomplete paralysis.

paresthesia *n.* an abnormal skin sensation, such as tingling, tickling, burning, itching, or pricking, in the absence of external stimulation. Paresthesia may be temporary, as in the "pins and needles" feeling that many people experience (e.g., after having sat with legs crossed too long), or chronic and due to such factors as neurological disorder or drug side effects. —**paresthetic** *adj.*

parietal cortex the cerebral cortex of the PARIETAL LOBE.

parietal lobe one of the four main lobes of each cerebral hemisphere (see CEREBRUM). It occupies the upper central area of each hemisphere, behind the FRONTAL LOBE, ahead of the OCCIPITAL LOBE, and above the TEMPORAL LOBE. Parts of the parietal lobe participate in somatosensory activities, such as discrimination of size, shape, and texture of objects; visual activities, such as visually guided actions; and auditory activities, such as speech perception.

parieto-occipital sulcus a groove (sulcus) that runs upward along the medial (inner) side of each cerebral hemisphere, extending from a junction with the CALCARINE FISSURE at a point posterior to the SPLENIUM.

parkinsonism *n.* any disorder whose symptoms resemble those of PARKINSON'S DISEASE without the actual presence of the disease entity. Antipsychotic agents with strong dopamine-blocking activity, particularly the HIGH-POTENCY ANTIPSYCHOTICS (e.g., haloperidol), may cause the reversible syndrome known as **drug-induced parkinsonism (pseudoparkinsonism)**.

Parkinson's disease a progressive neurodegenerative disease caused by the death of dopamine-producing neurons in the SUBSTANTIA NIGRA of the brain, which controls balance and coordinates muscle movement. Symptoms typically begin late in life with mild tremors, increasing rigidity of the limbs, and slowness of voluntary movements. Later symptoms include postural instability, impaired balance, and difficulty walking. DEMENTIA occurs in some 20–60% of patients, usually in older patients in whom the disease is far advanced. [first described in 1817 by James **Parkinson** (1755–1824), British physician]

parole *n.* **1.** in psychology and psychiatry, a method of maintaining supervision of a patient whose treatment is mandated by the court and who has not been discharged, but who is away from the confines of a restrictive setting, such as a mental institution or halfway house. A patient on parole may be returned to the hospital at any time without formal action by a court. **2.** supervised release from confinement in a correctional facility.

parosmia *n.* a disorder of the sense of smell in which a person is unable to distinguish odors correctly. For example, when presented with an odor of beer the person might say it smells of bleach. Also called **parosphresia**. See also DYSOSMIA; TROPOSMIA.

paroxetine *n.* an antidepressant of the SSRI class. It is currently one of the most commonly prescribed antidepressants. Like other SSRIs, it is used to treat depression and anxiety disorders, such as panic disorder, social phobia, and obsessive-compulsive disorder. It differs from other SSRIs in that most patients find it to be sedating rather than activating; paroxetine should therefore be taken in the evening rather than on rising. It should not be taken by patients who are already taking MONOAMINE OXIDASE INHIBITORS. Paroxetine is available in immediate- and controlled-release preparations. U.S. trade name: **Paxil**.

paroxysm *n.* **1.** the sudden intensification or recurrence of a disease or an emotional state. **2.** a convulsion, spasm, or seizure. —**paroxysmal** *adj.*

parsimony *n.* see LAW OF PARSIMONY.

part correlation the correlation between two variables with the influence of a third variable removed from one (but only one) of the two variables. Also called **semipartial correlation**. Compare PARTIAL CORRELATION.

parthenogenesis *n.* literally, virgin birth: the production of offspring without fertilization of the egg cells by sperm. It is the usual means of reproduction in some species. —**parthenogenetic** *adj.*

partial agonist see AGONIST.

partial correlation the correlation between two variables with the influence of one or more other variables on their intercorrelation statistically removed or held constant. Compare PART CORRELATION.

partial hospitalization hospital treatment of patients on a part-time basis (i.e., less than 24 hours per day). See DAY HOSPITAL; WEEKEND HOSPITALIZATION.

partial insanity a borderline condition in which mental impairment is present but is not sufficiently severe to render the individual completely irresponsible for his or her criminal acts. In legal proceedings, a conclusion of partial insanity may arise when there is evidence that a mental disorder was probably a contributing cause to a defendant's actions, or that the disorder rendered the individual incapable of deliberation, premeditation, malice, or another mental state usually requisite for first-degree offenses; in such circumstances it may lead to conviction for a lesser offense. See also DIMINISHED RESPONSIBILITY; INSANITY.

partial least squares a variant on MULTIPLE REGRESSION analysis designed for the construction of predictive models when there are many highly interrelated predictor variables.

partially ordered scale a scale of measurement that falls partway between a NOMINAL SCALE and an ORDINAL SCALE, such that the scaling units can, on average (but not always), be ordered or ranked from smallest to largest.

partial reinforcement see INTERMITTENT REINFORCEMENT.

partial reinforcement effect increased resistance to extinction after intermittent reinforcement rather than after continuous reinforcement. Also called **partial reinforcement extinction effect**.

partial report a method of testing memory in which only some of the total information presented is to be recalled. For example, if several rows of letters are shown to the participant, a cue given afterward may prompt recall of only one particular row. Partial report methods are used to minimize output INTERFERENCE in studies of ICONIC MEMORY. Compare WHOLE REPORT.

partial seizure a seizure that begins in a localized area of the brain, although it may subsequently progress to a GENERALIZED SEIZURE. **Simple partial seizures** produce no alteration of consciousness despite clinical manifestations, which may include sensory, motor, or autonomic activity. **Complex partial seizures** may produce similar sensory, motor, or autonomic symptoms but are also characterized by some impairment or alteration of consciousness during the event. Partial seizures of both types are most commonly focused in the temporal lobe. Also called **focal seizure**.

participant *n.* a person who takes part in an investigation, study, or experiment, for example by performing tasks set by the experimenter or by answering questions set by a researcher. The participant may be further identified as an **experimental participant** (see EXPERIMENTAL GROUP) or a **control participant** (see CONTROL GROUP). Participants are also called SUBJECTS, although the former term is now often preferred when referring to humans.

participant modeling a procedure for changing behavior in which effective styles of behavior are modeled (i.e., demonstrated, broken down step by step, and analyzed) by a therapist for an individual. Various aids are introduced to help the individual master the tasks, such as viewing videotaped enactments of effective and ineffective behavioral responses to prototypical situations in a variety of social contexts (e.g., at school or work).

participant observation a type of observational method in which a trained observer enters the group under study as a member, while avoiding a conspicuous role that would alter the group processes and bias the data. Cultural anthropologists become **participant observers** when they enter the life of a given culture to study its structure and processes.

participation *n.* **1.** taking part in an activity, usually one that involves others in a joint endeavor. **2.** the interaction of two or more systems that mutually influence each other. **3.** in PIAGETIAN THEORY, the tendency of children to confuse their wishes, fantasies, or dreams with reality. —**participate** *vb.*

participative decision-making the management practice of allowing employees to participate in the decision-making process. The extent of participation can vary from a relatively low level, in which employees provide input or consult with decision-makers, to the highest level, in which employees are fully involved and actually make the decisions. See INDUSTRIAL DEMOCRACY.

participative leadership a LEADERSHIP STYLE in which followers are allowed to become involved in decision-making and are given autonomy in performing their tasks.

particularism *n.* **1.** in philosophy, a solution to the so-called **criterion problem**, which states that one cannot know whether one has knowledge because to recognize particular bits of knowledge one would need to know the criteria by which they are judged to be knowledge, and in order to know the criteria, one would already have to be able to recognize bits of knowledge. Particularism resolves this problem by stating that no general criteria are necessary to determine particular bits of knowledge. **2.** in ethics, the doctrine that there are no general moral principles and that judgments of moral behavior cannot be made on the basis of such principles. Moral judgments must take account of many particular factors in a person's background and current situation. This position tends toward moral RELATIVISM. See also SUBJECTIVISM. —**particularist** *adj.*

part-list cuing inhibition in a RECALL test, impairment of the capacity to recall individual items if some of the other items in the list studied are provided as retrieval CUES. Also called **part-set cuing effect**.

part method of learning a learning technique in which the material is divided into sections, each to be mastered separately in a successive order. Compare WHOLE METHOD OF LEARNING.

partner abuse see DOMESTIC VIOLENCE.

part-object *n.* **1.** in psychoanalytic theory, an OBJECT toward which a "component instinct" is directed. Such an object is usually a part of the body rather than a whole person. **2.** in the OBJECT RELATIONS THEORY of Austrian-born British psychoanalyst Melanie Klein (1882–1960), an early object representation that derives from SPLITTING the object into parts containing negative and positive qualities. It is held that such objects constitute the infant's first experience of the world, being perceived as a GOOD OBJECT or a BAD OBJECT according to whether they are gratifying or frustrating. INTERNALIZATION of part-objects is further posited to represent the beginning of the inner world of objects whose relationships create the infant's personality.

parvocellular system the part of the visual system that projects to or originates from small neurons in the four dorsal layers (the **parvocellular layers**) of the lateral GENICULATE NUCLEUS. It allows the perception of fine details, colors, and large changes in brightness. The parvocellular system is expanded in primates compared to other animals; it conducts information relatively slowly because of its small cells and slender axons. Compare MAGNOCELLULAR SYSTEM.

pascal *n.* see SOUND PRESSURE.

passion *n.* **1.** an intense, driving, or overwhelming feeling or conviction. Passion is often contrasted with emotion, in that passion affects a person unwillingly. **2.** intense sexual desire. **3.** a strong liking or enthusiasm for or devotion to an activity, object, concept, or the like. —**passionate** *adj.*

passionate love a type of love in which sexual passion and a high level of emotional arousal are prominent features; along with COMPANIONATE LOVE, it is one of the two main types of love identified by social psychologists. Passionate lovers typically are greatly preoccupied with the loved person, want their feelings to be reciprocated, and are usually greatly distressed when the relationship seems awry. See also ROMANTIC LOVE; TRIANGULAR THEORY OF LOVE.

passive-aggressive *adj.* characteristic of behavior that is seemingly innocuous, accidental, or neutral but that indirectly displays an unconscious aggressive motive. For example, a child who appears to be compliant but is routinely late for school, misses the bus, or forgets his or her homework may be expressing unconscious resentment at having to attend school.

passive-aggressive personality disorder a personality disorder of long standing in which AMBIVALENCE toward the self and others is expressed by such means as procrastination, dawdling, stubbornness, intentional inefficiency, "forgetting" appointments, or misplacing important materials. These maneuvers are interpreted as passive expressions of underlying ambivalence and NEGATIVISM. The pattern persists even where more adaptive behavior is clearly possible; it frequently interferes with occupational, domestic, and academic success. This disorder is sometimes given an alternative name, **negativistic personality disorder**.

passive avoidance a type of OPERANT CONDITIONING in which the individual must refrain from an explicit act or response that will produce an aversive stimulus. Compare ACTIVE AVOIDANCE.

passive-avoidance learning a commonly used misnomer for PUNISHMENT. It is usually used in situations in which the behavior that is punished occurs without specific training. For

example, a mouse on a platform might step down onto an electrified grid; subsequently, the mouse no longer steps down.

passive deception the withholding of certain information from research participants, such as not informing them of the full details of the study. Also called **deception by omission**. Compare ACTIVE DECEPTION.

passive euthanasia the intentional withholding of treatment that might prolong the life of a person who is approaching death. It is distinguished from ACTIVE EUTHANASIA, in which direct action (e.g., a lethal injection) is taken to end the life. Courts have ruled that physicians do not have to try every possible intervention to prolong life, but opinions differ on where the line should be drawn. See also EUTHANASIA.

passive listening in psychotherapy and counseling, attentive listening by the therapist or counselor without intruding upon or interrupting the client in any way. See also ACTIVE LISTENING.

passive rehearsal a strategy for retaining information in short-term memory in which a person includes few (usually one) unique items per REHEARSAL set. Compare CUMULATIVE REHEARSAL.

passive touch a form of touch characterized by sensory experiences that occur when the observer does not move. In passive touch, stimulation is imposed on the skin of the individual.

passivity phenomena phenomena in which individuals feel that some aspect of themselves is under the control of others. These aspects can include acts, impulses, movements, emotions, or thoughts; patients typically report feeling that they are being made to do or think things by someone else or that they are experiencing the behaviors or emotions of someone else.

PASS model a model of intelligence based on the theory of Russian neuropsychologist Alexander Luria (1902–1977), according to which intelligence comprises separate abilities for simultaneous and successive processing. The four elements of the model are *p*lanning, *a*ttention, *s*imultaneous processing, and *s*uccessive processing.

pastoral counseling a form of counseling or psychotherapy in which insights and principles derived from the disciplines of theology and the behavioral sciences are used in working with individuals, couples, families, groups, and social systems to achieve healing and growth. Pastoral counseling is centered in theory and research concerning the interaction of religion and science, spirituality and health, and spiritual direction and psychotherapy. A **pastoral counselor** receives advanced training in one or several of the behavioral sciences (often psychology specifically) in addition to religious training, theological training, or both. Also called **pastoral psychotherapy**.

patch-clamp technique the use of very fine-bore pipette MICROELECTRODES, clamped by suction onto tiny patches of the plasma membrane of a neuron, to record the electrical activity of a single square micrometer of the membrane, including single ION CHANNELS.

patellar reflex a reflex in which tapping the tendon beneath the knee causes an upward kick of the leg. Also called **knee-jerk reflex**.

paternal behavior actions by males directed toward care and protection of their young. **Direct paternal behavior** consists of such actions as feeding, carrying, or otherwise nurturing the offspring; **indirect paternal behavior** consists of acquiring resources or defending the group from harm, which indirectly leads to increased survival of the young. Males of species with biparental care undergo some hormonal changes similar to those in females: increased secretion of the hormone prolactin and ESTROGENS. Early experience with young offspring is important for competent paternal behavior in many species.

path analysis a set of quantitative procedures used to verify the existence of causal relationships among several variables, displayed in graph form showing the various hypothesized routes of causal influence. The causal relationships are theoretically determined, and the path analysis determines both the accuracy and the strength of the hypothesized relationships.

path–goal theory of leadership a LEADERSHIP THEORY stating that leaders will be effective in so far as they make it clear to followers how they can achieve goals and obtain rewards. By doing so, leaders enhance their followers' expectancy that hard work will lead to task success and that task success will lead to valued rewards. The four basic LEADERSHIP STYLES proposed in this theory are instrumental (directive), supportive, participative, and achievement-oriented leadership. Each of these styles can be effective or ineffective, depending on the nature of the work environment and the characteristics of subordinates. Also called **path–goal theory**. See also VALENCE–INSTRUMENTALITY–EXPECTANCY THEORY.

pathogenesis n. the origination and development of a mental or physical disease or disorder. Also called **nosogenesis; pathogeny**. —**pathogenetic** adj.

pathogenic family pattern negative or harmful family attitudes, standards, and behavior that lay the groundwork for mental and behavioral disorder. Examples are parental rejection; TRIANGULATION of the child into the marital relationship between the parents; and excessively harsh, excessively lenient, or inconsistent discipline.

pathognomonic adj. describing a sign, symptom, or a group of signs or symptoms that is indicative of a specific physical or mental disorder and not associated with other disorders.

pathological aging changes that occur be-

cause of age-related disease, as distinct from changes associated with normal healthy aging.

pathological gambling an impulse-control disorder characterized by chronic, maladaptive wagering, leading to significant interpersonal, professional, or financial difficulties.

pathology n. **1.** functional changes in an individual or an organ related to or resulting from diseases or disorders. **2.** the scientific study of functional and structural changes involved in physical and mental disorders and diseases. —**pathological** adj. —**pathologist** n.

pathomimicry n. conscious or unconscious mimicking, production, or feigning of symptoms of disease or disorder. Also called **pathomimesis**. See FACTITIOUS DISORDER; LASTHENIE DE FERJOL SYNDROME; MALINGERING.

pathophysiology n. the functional alterations that appear in an individual or organ as a result of disease or disorder, as distinguished from structural alterations. —**pathophysiological** adj.

patient n. a person receiving health care from a licensed health professional (including the services of most psychologists and psychiatrists). See INPATIENT; OUTPATIENT. See also PATIENT–CLIENT ISSUE.

patient–client issue the dilemma of how to identify the recipient of psychological services or intervention (i.e., the nomenclature used for the recipient). Psychiatrists, many clinical psychologists, and some other mental health providers tend to follow the traditional language of the medical model and refer to the people seeking their services as **patients**. Counseling psychologists, some clinical psychologists, social workers, and counselors tend to avoid the word "patient," which is associated with illness and dysfunction, using instead the word **client** to refer to the person seeking their services.

patients' rights any statement, listing, summary, or the like that articulates the rights that health care providers (e.g., physicians, medical facilities) ethically ought to provide to those receiving their services in such basic categories as (a) the provision of adequate information regarding benefits, risks, costs, and alternatives; (b) fair treatment (e.g., respect, responsiveness, timely attention to health issues); (c) autonomy over medical decisions (e.g., obtaining full consent for medical interventions); and (d) CONFIDENTIALITY.

patriarchy n. **1.** a society in which descent and inheritance is **patrilineal**, that is, traced through the male only. See also DESCENT GROUP. **2.** more loosely, a family, group, or society directed and governed by men. Compare MATRIARCHY. —**patriarchal** adj.

patricide n. **1.** the murder of one's own father. **2.** a person who murders his or her own father. Compare MATRICIDE. —**patricidal** adj.

patrilocal adj. denoting a living arrangement in

which a married couple resides with or in close proximity to the husband's father or relatives, or a culture in which this is the norm. Compare MATRILOCAL; NEOLOCAL.

pattern coding the coding of information in sensory systems based on the temporal pattern of action potentials.

patterned interview a type of interview, often used in personnel selection, that is designed to cover certain specific areas (e.g., work history, education, home situation, etc.), but at the same time to give the interviewer the chance to steer the dialogue into side channels and ask questions on points that need to be clarified. Also called **semistructured interview**. Compare STRUCTURED INTERVIEW; UNSTRUCTURED INTERVIEW.

patterning *n.* **1.** establishing a system or pattern of responses to stimuli. **2.** a pattern of stimuli that will evoke a new or different set of responses.

patterning theory of taste coding a theory postulating that each taste stimulus evokes a unique pattern of neural activity from the TASTE-CELL population and that this pattern serves as the neural representation of the evoking stimulus. Taste quality is coded in the shape of the evoked pattern, while intensity is represented by the total discharge rate. Compare LABELED-LINE THEORY OF TASTE CODING.

pattern recognition 1. the ability to recognize and identify a complex whole composed of, or embedded in, many separate elements. Pattern recognition is not only a visual ability; in audition, it refers to (a) the recognition of temporal patterns of sounds or (b) the recognition of patterns of excitation of the BASILAR MEMBRANE, such as that which occurs during the perception of vowels in speech. **2.** the identification and classification of meaningful patterns of data input by computers, based on the extraction and comparison of the characteristic properties or features of the data.

pattern theory a theory maintaining that the nerve impulse pattern for pain is produced by intense stimulation of nonspecific receptors, since there are no specific fibers or endings exclusively for the experience of pain. According to this theory, the nerves involved in detecting and reporting pain are shared with other senses, such as touch, and the most important feature of pain is the amount of stimulation involved. Also called **nonspecificity theory**. Compare GATE-CONTROL THEORY; SPECIFICITY THEORY.

Pavlovian conditioning a type of learning in which an initially neutral stimulus—the CONDITIONED STIMULUS (CS)—when paired with a stimulus that elicits a reflex response—the UNCONDITIONED STIMULUS (US)—results in a learned, or conditioned, response (CR) when the CS is presented. For example, the sound of a tone may be used as a CS, and food in a dog's mouth as a US. After repeated pairings, namely, the tone followed immediately by food, the tone, which initially had no effect on salivation (i.e., was neutral with respect to it), will elicit salivation even if the food is not presented. Also called **classical conditioning**; **respondent conditioning**; **Type I conditioning**; **Type S conditioning**. See CONDITIONING. [discovered in the early 20th century by Ivan **Pavlov** (1849–1936), Russian physiologist]

Paxil *n.* a trade name for PAROXETINE.

payoff matrix a schedule or table that lists the costs and benefits arising from every possible course of action that could be chosen by an individual—for example, by a player in a game or a participant in a signal detection experiment. An ideal participant will show shifts in response or decision criteria that maximize the payoff.

P1 component the first positive component of an EVENT-RELATED POTENTIAL, occurring approximately 100 ms after stimulus onset. The P1 component is usually larger for attended stimuli than for unattended stimuli, a phenomenon known as the **P1 attention effect**. Hence it is thought to reflect the initial sensory and attentional processing of a stimulus by specific areas of the cerebral cortex.

P3 component the third positive component of an EVENT-RELATED POTENTIAL, which appears approximately 300 ms after stimulus onset and is thus sometimes called the **P300**. First reported in 1965, the P3 component is thought to reflect attentional resource allocation and memory-updating operations and has become a major focus of research into event-related potentials.

PCP 1. *n.* 1-(1-*p*henylcyclohexyl)*p*iperidine (phencyclidine): a hallucinogenic drug originally developed for use in surgical anesthesia and later found to produce a psychedelic or dissociative reaction. Its medical use was discontinued because of adverse reactions, including agitation, delirium, disorientation, and hallucinations. PCP has a complex mechanism of action. It binds as an ANTAGONIST to the NMDA receptor (see GLUTAMATE RECEPTOR); it also acts as a DO-PAMINE-RECEPTOR agonist and blocks the re-uptake of dopamine, norepinephrine, and serotonin, among other actions. Because intoxication with PCP can produce symptoms resembling both the positive and negative symptoms of schizophrenia, some consider it to be a useful drug model of schizophrenia. High doses of PCP may induce stupor or coma. PCP became common as an illicit drug in the 1970s. It can be smoked (often in combination with marijuana or tobacco), insufflated (inhaled nasally), or taken orally or intravenously (angel dust). Despite speculation about its potential ability to damage nerve tissue, it remains a popular illicit drug. See also HALLUCINOGEN. **2.** abbreviation for PRIMARY CARE provider.

Pcs abbreviation for PRECONSCIOUS.

PDM abbreviation for PSYCHODYNAMIC DIAGNOSTIC MANUAL.

Peabody Picture Vocabulary Test (PPVT) a norm-referenced screening, diagnostic, and progress-monitoring test in which sets of four full-color drawings are presented to the participant, who selects the one that corresponds to a word uttered by the examiner. There are 228 stimulus words each in two parallel forms (A and B) that are administered individually. The test, now in its fourth edition (**PPVT–4**, 2006), may be used with individuals aged 2 years 6 months to over 90 years to assess receptive vocabulary and verbal ability.

peak experience in the humanistic theory of U.S. psychologist Abraham Maslow (1908–1970), a moment of awe, ecstasy, or transcendence that may at times be experienced by self-actualizers (see SELF-ACTUALIZATION). Peak experiences represent sudden insights into life as a powerful unity transcending space, time, and the self. See also BEING COGNITION; TIMELESS MOMENT; TRANSPERSONAL PSYCHOLOGY.

peak procedure a procedure, used in behavioral studies, in which repetitions of a FIXED-INTERVAL SCHEDULE of reinforcement are interspersed with periods, usually two or three times as long as the fixed interval, in which reinforcement is omitted.

peak shift 1. a phenomenon, seen in STIMULUS GENERALIZATION, that occurs after DISCRIMINATION TRAINING involving two stimuli along a common dimension (e.g., brightness). The peak of the response gradient (i.e., the point at which the organism shows maximum response) is shifted in a direction away from the less favorable stimulus (e.g., a dim light) to a point beyond the value of the stimulus associated with reinforcement (e.g., beyond the value of a bright light to that of a very bright light). **2.** in aesthetics, the phenomenon that an extreme form of a preferred stimulus (a SUPERNORMAL STIMULUS) is preferred over the normal form of that stimulus.

Pearson product–moment correlation see PRODUCT–MOMENT CORRELATION.

pediatric psychology an interdisciplinary field of research and practice that addresses the interaction of physical, behavioral, and emotional development with health and illness issues affecting children, adolescents, and families. Related to the larger field of HEALTH PSYCHOLOGY, pediatric psychology differs not only in its specific focus but also in its emphasis on the child in the contexts of the family, school, and health care settings. The field tends to take a normative developmental view of adaptation based on physical conditions, medical treatment, and psychosocial interactions with family and peers, rather than a psychopathological view of adjustment to disease and disorders.

pediatric psychopharmacology the branch of pharmacology that is involved in the understanding and administration of drugs used in the treatment of mental and behavioral disorders of childhood and adolescence. It helps determine the choice of drug according to the age of the child, the diagnosis, the duration of the disorder, the severity of the illness, and the availability of the patient for behavioral and laboratory monitoring of the drug effects.

pedigree *n.* **1.** in medical genetics, a pictoral representation of the history of an illness in a family. It depicts the relationship of family members and—for each member—current status (alive or not), the date of diagnosis, kind of relevant illness, and age at diagnosis. Geneticists can often estimate a family member's likelihood of developing the disease from reviewing such a pedigree. **2.** family lineage or ancestry, especially when this is regarded as distinguished or notable. **3.** the line of descent of a pure-bred animal, or a record of such descent.

pedophilia *n.* a PARAPHILIA in which sexual acts or fantasies with prepubertal children are the persistently preferred or exclusive method of achieving sexual excitement. The children are usually many years younger than the **pedophile** (or **pedophiliac**). Sexual activity may consist of looking and touching, but sometimes includes intercourse, even with very young children. Pedophilia is rarely seen in women. —**pedophilic** *adj.*

peduncle *n.* a stalklike bundle of nerve fibers, for example, the cerebellar peduncle or the cerebral peduncle. —**peduncular** *adj.*

peduncular hallucinosis recurrent visual hallucinations caused by pathological processes in the upper brainstem, which indirectly affect the central visual system. The hallucinations, which may be long-lasting, vivid, and scenic, are often accompanied by agitation and sleep disturbances. The hallucinations are usually recognized as such by the patient, who may see a panorama of people and events from his or her past life. Peduncular hallucinosis may be mixed with nonhallucinatory perceptions.

peer counseling counseling by an individual who has a status equal to that of the client, such as a college student trained to counsel other students or an employee trained to counsel his or her coworkers.

peer group a group of individuals who share one or more characteristics, such as age, social status, economic status, occupation, or education. Members of a peer group typically interact with each other on a level of equality and exert influence on each other's attitudes, emotions, and behavior (see PEER PRESSURE). Although children begin to interact before the age of 2, genuine peer groups based on shared age typically do not develop until the age of 5 years or later.

peer pressure the influence exerted by a PEER GROUP on its individual members to fit in with or adapt to group expectations by thinking, feeling, and (most importantly) behaving in a simi-

P

lar or acceptable manner (see CONFORMITY). Peer pressure may have positive SOCIALIZATION value but may also have negative consequences for mental or physical health. Also called **peer-group pressure**.

peer review the evaluation of scientific or academic work, such as research or articles submitted to journals for publication, by other qualified professionals practicing in the same field.

pegboard test a test of manual dexterity and fine motor speed in which the participant—first with his or her dominant hand, then with the nondominant hand, and finally with both hands—inserts pegs in a series of holes as rapidly as possible. One of the best known examples is the **Purdue Pegboard Test**.

peg-word mnemonic system a MNEMONIC strategy used to remember lists, in which each item is associated in imagination with a number–word pair (the **peg**). For example, if the pegs are the rhyming pairs "one is a bun, two is a shoe," and so on, the first item to be remembered would be associated with a bun, the second with a shoe, and so on.

penetrance *n.* in genetics, the extent to which the effects of an ALLELE are manifest in the individuals possessing it, expressed as the fraction or percentage of individuals carrying that allele who manifest the trait associated with it. If all persons who possess a particular dominant allele develop the associated trait, the allele is said to show **complete penetrance** (100%). In contrast, **incomplete penetrance** occurs when some individuals with a particular allele do not develop the associated trait.

penis *n.* the male organ for urination and intromission, which enters the female's vagina to deliver semen. The urethra runs through the penis, which is composed largely of erectile tissue and has a mushroom-shaped cap (glans penis). —**penile** *adj.*

penis envy in the classic psychoanalytic theory of Austrian psychiatrist Sigmund Freud (1856–1939), the hypothesized desire of girls and women to possess a male genital organ. Freud held it to originate in the PHALLIC STAGE, between ages 3 and 6, when the girl discovers that she lacks this organ, and further posited that the girl feels "handicapped and ill-treated," blames her mother for the loss, and wants to have her penis back. German-born U.S. psychoanalyst Karen D. Horney (1885–1952), among others, later argued that penis envy is not an envy of the biological organ itself but represents women's envy of men's superior social status. In any sense, the concept has been actively disputed from the beginning and is rarely considered seriously in current psychology. See also CASTRATION COMPLEX.

people-first language language that places a person before his or her disability by describing what a person has rather than equating the person with the disability. Examples of the use of such language include "a child with a learning disability" (rather than "a learning-disabled child"), "a child with Down syndrome" (rather than "a Down child"), and "a person who uses a wheelchair" (rather than "a wheelchair-bound person").

peptide *n.* a short chain of AMINO ACIDS linked by **peptide bonds**. Peptides are usually identified by the number of amino acids in the chain, for example, dipeptides have two, tripeptides three, tetrapeptides four, and so on. See also POLYPEPTIDE; PROTEIN.

peptide hormone any hormone that is classed chemically as a PEPTIDE. Peptide hormones include CORTICOTROPIN, CORTICOTROPIN-RELEASING FACTOR, OXYTOCIN, and VASOPRESSIN.

perceived behavioral control the extent to which a person believes a behavior is under his or her active control. See THEORY OF PLANNED BEHAVIOR.

perceived reality a person's subjective experience of reality, in contrast to objective, external reality. Client-centered, humanistic-existential, and related phenomenological theories propose that individuals behave in accordance with perceived, rather than objective, reality.

perceived risk the extent to which individuals feel they are subject to a health threat. Risk is a joint function of the probability of occurrence of a negative event and the magnitude of its consequence.

perceived self the subjective appraisal of personal qualities that one ascribes to oneself.

perceived self-efficacy an individual's subjective perception of his or her capability for performance in a given setting or ability to attain desired results, often proposed as a primary determinant of emotional and motivational states and behavioral change.

perceived simultaneity the integration of stimuli into a single, conscious percept despite small discrepancies in their actual time of arrival, so that they are perceived as occurring simultaneously.

perceived susceptibility a subjective estimate of the likelihood of personally contracting a disease, without any consideration of severity. Also called **perceived vulnerability**.

percentage reinforcement in operant conditioning, a procedure in which a fixed percentage of scheduled reinforcers is omitted.

percentile *n.* the location of a score in a distribution coded to reflect the percentage of cases in the batch that have scores equal to or below the score in question. Thus, if a score is said to be at the 90th percentile, the implication is that 90% of the scores in the batch are equal to or lower than that score.

percentile reinforcement in operant conditioning, a procedure in which the likelihood that a response will be reinforced depends on the response exceeding (or being less than) a value based on a distribution from previous responses. Usually, the distribution is based on some set of the most recent responses and it is updated with each response. For example, the current response might be eligible for reinforcement if its peak force falls above the 90th PERCENTILE of the distribution of forces from the previous 50 responses. The most recent force then replaces the earliest one in the distribution so that the distribution remains based on 50 entries.

percept *n.* the product of PERCEPTION: the stimulus object or event as experienced by the individual.

perception *n.* the process or result of becoming aware of objects, relationships, and events by means of the senses, which includes such activities as recognizing, observing, and discriminating. These activities enable organisms to organize and interpret the stimuli received into meaningful knowledge.

perceptron *n.* a connected network of input nodes and output nodes that acts as a useful model of associative NEURAL NETWORKS. A simple (single-layer) perceptron might stand for two connected neurons, while more complicated perceptrons have additional hidden layers between input and output. The connections between the inputs and outputs can be weighted to model the desired output. The goal is to develop a theoretical understanding of the way neural connections process signals and form associations (memories). **Back-propagation** (**backprop**) **algorithms** describe the most common process by which the weightings between input and output are adjusted. The output is compared to a desired endpoint and changes needed in the strengths of the connections are transmitted back through the perceptron.

perceptual anchoring 1. the process in which the qualities of a stimulus are perceived relative to another, anchoring, stimulus. **2.** see SYMBOL GROUNDING.

perceptual closure the process by which an incomplete stimulus (e.g., a line drawing of a circle with a segment missing) is perceived to be complete (e.g., an entire circle). See CLOSURE.

perceptual constancy the phenomenon in which a perceived object or its properties (e.g., size, shape, color) appears to remain unchanged despite variations in the stimulus itself or in the external conditions of observation, such as object orientation or level of illumination. Examples of perceptual constancy include BRIGHTNESS CONSTANCY, COLOR CONSTANCY, SHAPE CONSTANCY, and SIZE CONSTANCY.

perceptual cues 1. features of a stimulus that are perceived and used by an organism in a particular situation or setting to identify and make judgments about that stimulus and its properties. **2.** features of a situation that indicate the expected behavior. See DEMAND CHARACTERISTICS.

perceptual cycle hypothesis the theory that cognition affects perceptual exploration but is in turn modified by real-world experience, creating a cycle of cognition, attention, perception, and the real world in which each influences the others. Thus, sensory experience is neither totally internal nor totally external.

perceptual deficit an impaired ability to organize and interpret sensory experience, causing difficulty in observing, recognizing, and understanding people, situations, words, numbers, concepts, or images. Also called **perceptual defect**.

perceptual distortion an inaccurate interpretation of perceptual experience. Examples include the distorted images produced by dreams or hallucinogenic drugs, geometric illusions (e.g., the MÜLLER-LYER ILLUSION), visions occurring in states of sensory deprivation or dehydration, and distortions produced by modifying auditory stimuli. Perceptual distortion may also occur as a consequence of acquired brain injury. See also METAMORPHOPSIA.

perceptual disturbance a disorder of perception, such as (a) recognizing letters but not words, (b) inability to judge size or direction, (c) confusing background with foreground, (d) inability to filter out irrelevant sounds or sights, (e) a body-image distortion, or (f) difficulty with spatial relationships (e.g., perceiving the difference between a straight line and a curved line). Also called **perceptual disorder**.

perceptual extinction an effect of lesions in the parieto-occipital region on one side of the brain in which a stimulus, usually tactual or visual, is not detected. If a single stimulus is presented on either side of the midline, it is detected; however, when two similar stimuli are presented at the same time, one on each side of the midline, the stimulus on the side of the body opposite the location of the lesion is not detected. This phenomenon is utilized in neuropsychological research on attention mechanisms. Also called **sensory extinction**; **sensory inattention**.

perceptual field in GESTALT PSYCHOLOGY, the totality of the environment that an individual perceives at a particular time; that is, all of the aspects of the environment of which the person is aware at a given time.

perceptual filtering the process of focusing attention on a selected subset of the large number of sensory stimuli that are present at any one time. Perceptual filtering is necessary because the cognitive and physical capacity of an individual to process and respond to multiple sources of information is limited. See also BOTTLENECK MODEL.

perceptual fluency the ease with which a visual target is processed. The **perceptual fluency theory** of visual attention holds that the repeated presentations of a given target between presentations of distractors in successive trials increases the perceptual fluency for that target, thus making it easier to distinguish from the distractors.

perceptual learning learning to perceive the relationships between stimuli and objects in the environment or the differences among stimuli.

perceptual organization the process enabling such properties as structure, pattern, and form to be imposed on the senses to provide conceptual organization. Each of the senses establishes (or learns) such organizational schemata. According to traditional GESTALT PSYCHOLOGY, the parts of a group are organized to form whole figures that constitute more than the parts separately (see GESTALT PRINCIPLES OF ORGANIZATION). Recent research has more precisely defined the properties that enable such organized tasks. Artists have traditionally used the principles of perceptual organization to create desired moods or feelings and to challenge viewers' expectations. Also called **perceptualization**.

perceptual representation system a MEMORY SYSTEM whose function is to identify objects and words, allowing quick recognition of previously encountered stimuli. Perceptions are specifically recognized in the form previously experienced, that is, a word as seen versus a word as heard. The system does not recognize the meaning of stimuli, which is handled by SEMANTIC MEMORY.

perceptual rivalry the incompatibility of different perceptions of the same object. When an AMBIGUOUS FIGURE that allows two different perceptual interpretations is viewed, only one perceptual diagnosis can be made at any one time, so that perception alternates between the two rival interpretations. This switching between percepts is primarily involuntary.

perceptual schema a mental model that provides a FRAME OF REFERENCE for interpreting information entering the mind through the senses or for activating an expectation of how a particular perceptual scene may look. See SCHEMA.

perceptual sensitization the lowering of an individual's sensory thresholds for events that are emotionally sensitive or threatening.

perceptual set 1. a temporary readiness to perceive certain objects or events rather than others. For example, a person driving a car has a perceptual set to identify anything that might impact his or her safety. See SELECTIVE PERCEPTION; SET. **2.** a SCHEMA or FRAME OF REFERENCE that influences the way in which a person perceives objects, events, or people. For example, an on-duty police officer and a painter might regard a crowded street scene with very different perceptual sets.

perceptual speed see PRIMARY ABILITIES.

perceptual transformation 1. any modifi-

cation in a PERCEPT produced by (a) an addition to, deletion from, or alteration in a physical stimulus or (b) a novel interpretation of the stimulus, a change in a SET or attitude, or a sudden insight concerning the material. **2.** change in the way a problem, event, or person is perceived by the inclusion of new information or a different perspective.

percipient *adj.* capable of perception.

peregrination *n.* widespread or excessive traveling from place to place. Peregrination is one of the essential features of MUNCHAUSEN SYNDROME: The individual feels impelled to travel from town to town or from hospital to hospital in order to find a new audience every time the false nature of the illness is discovered. Also called **itinerancy**.

perfectionism *n.* the tendency to demand of others or of oneself an extremely high or even flawless level of performance, particularly when this is not required by the situation. It is thought by some to be a risk factor for depression. —**perfectionist** *adj., n.*

perfect pitch see ABSOLUTE PITCH.

performance *n.* **1.** any activity or collection of responses that leads to a result or has an effect upon the environment. **2.** the behavior of an organism (the **performer**) when faced with a specific task. **3.** in linguistics, see COMPETENCE.

performance anxiety anxiety associated with the apprehension and fear of the consequences of being unable to perform a task or of performing the task at a level that will lead to expectations of higher levels of performance achievement. Fear of taking a test, public speaking, participating in classes or meetings, playing a musical instrument in public, or even eating in public are common examples. If the fear associated with performance anxiety is focused on negative evaluation by others, embarrassment, or humiliation, the anxiety may be classified as a SOCIAL PHOBIA.

performance IQ see IQ.

performance-operating characteristic (**POC**) the measure of performance on one task plotted against the measure of performance on a second task that is performed simultaneously. The POC shows how improvements in performance on one of the tasks might trade with performance decrements in the other task.

performance test any test of ability requiring primarily motor, rather than verbal, responses, such as a test requiring manipulation of a variety of different kinds of objects.

periamygdaloid cortex an ill-defined region surrounding the AMYGDALA of the brain that is associated with the sense of smell. The proportion of the brain that it occupies in a particular species seems to depend on the importance of the sense of smell for survival: the greater the importance, the larger the proportion. Dogs, for example, have a larger proportion of olfactory nerve tissue than do human beings.

periaqueductal gray (**PAG**) a region of the brainstem, rich in nerve cell bodies (i.e., gray matter), that surrounds the CEREBRAL AQUEDUCT. A component of the LIMBIC SYSTEM, it plays an important role in organizing defensive behaviors (e.g., freezing). Also called **central gray**.

perilymph *n.* the fluid that fills the space between the membranous LABYRINTH and the walls of the bony labyrinth in the inner ear. —**perilymphatic** *adj.*

perimetry *n.* the measurement of the extent of the visual field.

period effect any outcome associated with living during a particular time period or era, regardless of how old one was at the time. Period effects may be difficult to distinguish from AGE EFFECTS and COHORT EFFECTS in research.

periodicity *n.* the state of recurring more or less regularly, that is, at intervals.

periodicity pitch see VIRTUAL PITCH.

periodicity theory the theory that pitch is encoded in the temporal structure of the neural responses to sounds, specifically in the timing of neural discharges ("spikes"). For periodic sounds, those that elicit strong pitch, the discharges of auditory nerve fibers tend to occur at integer multiples of the period of the sound. See PHASE LOCKING. Compare PLACE THEORY.

peripheral *adj.* **1.** in the nervous system, located or taking place outside the brain and spinal cord. Compare CENTRAL. **2.** in vision, toward the margins of the visual field, rather than close to the center. The onset of a peripheral stimulus tends to draw attention to that location. **3.** situated on the surface of a body. **4.** situated away from a center and toward the outside edge.

peripheral anticholinergic syndrome see ANTICHOLINERGIC SYNDROME.

peripheral cue a factor external to the merits of an argument that can be used to provide a relatively low-effort basis for determining whether an ATTITUDE OBJECT should be positively or negatively evaluated. See also ELABORATION-LIKELIHOOD MODEL; PERIPHERAL ROUTE TO PERSUASION.

peripheral dyslexia a form of acquired DYSLEXIA that is characterized by difficulties in processing the visual aspects of words (e.g., difficulties identifying letter forms) and—unlike CENTRAL DYSLEXIA—results from damage to the visual analysis system.

peripheral nervous system (**PNS**) the portion of the nervous system that lies outside the skull and spinal column, that is, all parts outside the CENTRAL NERVOUS SYSTEM. Afferent fibers of the PNS bring messages from the sense organs to the central nervous system; efferent fibers transmit messages from the central nervous system to the muscles and glands. It includes the CRANIAL NERVES, SPINAL NERVES, and parts of the AUTONOMIC NERVOUS SYSTEM.

peripheral neuropathy a neuromuscular disorder of the extremities caused by damage to the peripheral nervous system and usually characterized by weakness, numbness, clumsiness, and sensory loss. Causes are numerous and include diabetes, nutritional deficiencies, injury or trauma, and exposure to toxic substances. It is seen in 5–15% of chronic alcoholics (see ALCOHOLIC NEUROPATHY).

peripheral route to persuasion the process by which attitudes are formed or changed as a result of using PERIPHERAL CUES rather than carefully scrutinizing and thinking about the central merits of attitude-relevant information. See also ELABORATION; ELABORATION-LIKELIHOOD MODEL. Compare CENTRAL ROUTE TO PERSUASION.

peripheral vision vision provided by retinal stimulation considerably outside the FOVEA CENTRALIS. Compare CENTRAL VISION; PARACENTRAL VISION.

perirhinal cortex a structure in the medial TEMPORAL LOBE adjacent to the hippocampus that plays an important role as an interface between visual perception and memory.

peritraumatic dissociation a transient dissociative experience (see DISSOCIATION) that occurs at or around the time of a traumatic event. Affected individuals may feel as if they are watching the trauma occur to someone else, as if in a movie, or they may feel "spaced out" and disoriented after the trauma. The occurrence of peritraumatic dissociation is a predictor for the later development of POSTTRAUMATIC STRESS DISORDER.

periventricular white matter tissue consisting largely of myelinated nerve fibers (i.e., WHITE MATTER) that surrounds the lateral cerebral VENTRICLES.

Perky effect the tendency for an imagined stimulus to interfere with seeing an actual target stimulus when the imagined form is close to that of the target. For example, a participant is positioned in front of a blank screen and asked to imagine a leaf, while simultaneously, without the participant's knowledge, a blurry picture of a leaf is projected onto the screen, gradually becoming brighter; the intensity of the picture is well above the threshold for detection before the participant reports seeing it. [described in 1910 by Cheves West **Perky** (1874–1940), U.S. psychologist]

perlocutionary act see ILLOCUTIONARY ACT.

permeability *n.* the state of being permeable to gases, liquids, or dissolved substances, for example by having fine pores through which substances can pass. A perfect membrane has no permeability, but most biological membranes are **selectively** (or **partially**) **permeable** (or **semipermeable**), permitting the selective pas-

P

sage of certain substances, such as the flow of nutrients through a cell membrane. See also OSMOTIC PRESSURE. —**permeable** *adj.*

permeable family a more fluid and flexible version of the NUCLEAR FAMILY that some sociologists regard as an emerging norm in contemporary Western society. The permeable family differs from the stereotypical nuclear family in five main areas: (a) the greater variety of family structures produced by divorce, remarriage, and the acceptance of cohabitation and single-parent families; (b) a looser sense of family boundaries, so that the offspring of former relationships may be regarded as part of the family unit for some purposes but not for others; (c) the erosion of traditional sex roles within the family produced by feminism and the greater role played by women in the workforce; (d) the erosion of a sense of hierarchy and deference within the family, so that children and teenagers expect greater freedom and respect for their views and preferences; and (e) the tendency for all members of the family to expect greater autonomy, so that individual activities sometimes take precedence over shared pursuits and rituals (e.g., family meals).

permissiveness *n.* **1.** an interpersonal style or approach that involves giving a wide range of freedom and autonomy to those with whom one has dealings or over whom one has authority. **2.** an approach to child rearing in which the child is given wide latitude in expressing his or her feelings and opinions, even in ACTING OUT, and in which artificial restrictions and punishment are avoided as much as possible. —**permissive** *adj.*

permissive parenting see PARENTING.

permutation *n.* an ordered sequence of elements from a set. A permutation is similar to a COMBINATION but distinguished by its emphasis on order.

permutation test a technique of testing hypotheses based on all possible permutations (ordered sequences) of cases to groups.

perseveration *n.* **1.** in neuropsychology, the inappropriate repetition of behavior that is often associated with damage to the FRONTAL LOBE of the brain. **2.** an inability to interrupt a task or to shift from one strategy or procedure to another. Perseveration may be observed, for example, in workers under extreme task demands or environmental conditions (mainly heat stress). **3.** according to the PERSEVERATION–CONSOLIDATION HYPOTHESIS, the repetition, after a learning experience, of neural processes that are responsible for memory formation, which is necessary for the consolidation of LONG-TERM MEMORY. **4.** in speech and language, the persistence of abnormal or inappropriate repetition of a sound, word, or phrase, as occurs in stuttering. **5.** the persistence or prolongation of a speech mode beyond the particular developmental stage at which it is typical or accepted, such as baby talk continuing into later childhood or adulthood. —**perseverate** *vb.*

perseveration–consolidation hypothesis the hypothesis that information passes through two stages in memory formation. During the first stage the memory is held by perseveration (repetition) of neural activity and is easily disrupted. During the second stage the memory becomes fixed, or consolidated, and is no longer easily disrupted. The perseveration–consolidation hypothesis guides much contemporary research on the biological basis of long-term learning and memory. Also called **consolidation hypothesis**; **consolidation–perseveration hypothesis**. See also DUAL TRACE HYPOTHESIS.

perseveration set a tendency or predisposition that is acquired in a previous situation and is transferred to another situation where it may facilitate or interfere with the task at hand.

perseverative error the continuing recurrence of an error, for example, continuing to call a square a circle even after feedback that the name is wrong, or repeating the same answer to a series of different questions.

persistence *n.* **1.** continuance or repetition of a particular behavior, process, or activity despite cessation of the initiating stimulus. **2.** the quality or state of maintaining a course of action or keeping at a task and finishing it despite the obstacles (such as opposition or discouragement) or the effort involved. Also called **industriousness**; **perseverance**. **3.** continuance of existence, especially for longer than is usual or expected. —**persistent** *adj.*

persistent vegetative state (**PVS**) a prolonged biomedical condition in which rudimentary brain function and, usually, spontaneous respiration continue but there is no awareness of self or environment, no communication, and no voluntary response to stimuli. The condition should be distinguished from BRAIN DEATH. The term **permanent vegetative state** is sometimes used for people who have been in PVS for an extended period.

persona *n.* in the approach of Swiss psychoanalyst Carl Jung (1875–1961), the public face an individual presents to the outside world, in contrast to more deeply rooted and authentic personality characteristics. This sense has now passed into popular usage.

personal attribution see DISPOSITIONAL ATTRIBUTION.

personal-care attendant a person hired by an individual with a disability to provide assistance with ACTIVITIES OF DAILY LIVING (dressing, eating, etc.).

personal construct one of the concepts by which an individual perceives, understands, predicts, and attempts to control the world. Understanding a client's personal constructs is a central way of beginning to help that person change rigid or negative beliefs. See REPERTORY GRID.

personal construct therapy a therapy based on the concept of the PERSONAL CONSTRUCT. The essence of the approach is to help individuals test the usefulness and validity of their constructs and to revise and elaborate them as necessary to enhance their understanding and positive interpretations of and interactions with the world.

personal disjunction an individual's feeling or perception of dissimilarity or discrepancy between what is or might be and the objective reality or likelihood.

personal disposition in the personality theory of U.S. psychologist Gordon W. Allport (1897–1967), any of a number of enduring characteristics that describe or determine an individual's behavior across a variety of situations and that are peculiar to and uniquely expressed by that individual. Personal dispositions are divided into three categories according to their degree of influence on the behavior of the person possessing them. **Cardinal dispositions**, such as a thirst for power, are so pervasive as to influence virtually every behavior of that person; **central dispositions**, such as friendliness, are less pervasive but nonetheless generally influential and easy to identify; and **secondary dispositions**, such as a tendency to keep a neat desk, are much more narrowly expressed and situation specific.

personal distance zone in social psychology, the DISTANCE ZONE adopted by those interacting with friends and personal acquaintances. The personal distance zone is defined as the area from 0.5 to 1.5 m (1½ to 4 ft). Compare PUBLIC DISTANCE ZONE. See also PROXEMICS.

personal equation 1. the difference in performance attributed to INDIVIDUAL DIFFERENCES. **2.** historically, a difference in reaction time between two observers.

personalistic psychology a school of psychology in which the primary emphasis is on personality as the core of psychology, the uniqueness of every human being, and the study of an individual's traits (and organization of traits) as the key to personality and adjustment to the environment. Personalistic psychology originated with German psychologists Eduard Spranger (1882–1963) and William Stern (1871–1938) and was developed by U.S. psychologist Gordon Allport (1897–1967).

personality *n.* the configuration of characteristics and behavior that comprises an individual's unique adjustment to life, including major traits, interests, drives, values, self-concept, abilities, and emotional patterns. Personality is generally viewed as a complex, dynamic integration or totality, shaped by many forces, including: hereditary and constitutional tendencies; physical maturation; early training; identification with significant individuals and groups; cultur-ally conditioned values and roles; and critical experiences and relationships. Various theories explain the structure and development of personality in different ways but all agree that personality helps determine behavior.

personality assessment the evaluation of such factors as intelligence, skills, interests, aptitudes, creative abilities, attitudes, and facets of psychological development by a variety of techniques. These include (a) observational methods that use behavior sampling, interviews, and rating scales; (b) personality inventories, such as the MINNESOTA MULTIPHASIC PERSONALITY INVENTORY; and (c) projective techniques, such as the RORSCHACH INKBLOT TEST and THEMATIC APPERCEPTION TEST. The uses of personality assessment are manifold, for example, in clinical evaluation of children and adults; in educational and vocational counseling; in industry and other organizational settings; and in rehabilitation.

personality correlates 1. personality traits that are associated with a particular illness or disorder. For example, personality correlates of stress sensitivity may include introversion, obsession, and dependency. **2.** variables that correlate with measures of personality. Correlations between personality traits and observed behaviors, for example, provide evidence for the validity of measures of such traits.

personality development the gradual development of personality in terms of characteristic emotional responses or temperament, a recognizable style of life, personal roles and role behaviors, a set of values and goals, typical patterns of adjustment, characteristic interpersonal relations and sexual relationships, characteristic traits, and a relatively fixed self-image.

personality disorders a group of disorders involving pervasive patterns of perceiving, relating to, and thinking about the environment and the self that interfere with long-term functioning of the individual and are not limited to isolated episodes. Among the specific types are paranoid, schizoid, schizotypal, histrionic, narcissistic, antisocial, borderline, avoidant, dependent, and obsessive-compulsive—each of which has its own entry in the dictionary.

personality inventory a personality assessment device that usually consists of a series of statements covering various characteristics and behavioral patterns to which the participant responds by fixed answers, such as True, False, Always, Often, Seldom, or Never, as applied to himself or herself. The scoring of such tests is objective, and the results are interpreted according to standardized norms. An example is the MINNESOTA MULTIPHASIC PERSONALITY INVENTORY.

personality processes the dynamics of personality functioning, that is, personality systems that change over time and across situations as the individual interacts with different people and events in the environment. Personality pro-

P

cesses are usually contrasted with PERSONALITY STRUCTURE, that is, the stable, enduring elements of an individual's personality.

personality psychology the systematic study of the human personality, including (a) the nature and definition of personality; (b) its maturation and development; (c) the structure of the self; (d) key theories (e.g., trait theories, psychoanalytic theories, role theories, learning theories, type theories); (e) personality disorders; (f) individual differences; and (g) personality tests and measurements. Personality psychologists tend to study more-or-less enduring and stable individual differences in adults and have traditionally assigned a central role to human motivation and the internal dynamics of human behavior, including both conscious and unconscious motivational forces, factors, and conflicts. Personality theories aim to synthesize cognitive, emotional, motivational, developmental, and social aspects of human individuality into integrative frameworks for making sense of the individual human life. The major families of personality theories include the psychodynamic, behavioral, and humanistic families.

personality structure the organization of the personality in terms of its basic components and their relationship to each other. Structural theories vary widely according to their key concepts, for example, clusters of PERSONALITY TRAITS in personality trait theories, such as the surface traits and source traits in CATTELL'S PERSONALITY TRAIT THEORY; ID, EGO, and SUPEREGO of Austrian psychiatrist Sigmund Freud (1856–1939); the individual style of life posited by Austrian psychiatrist Alfred Adler (1870–1937); and needs and motivations in MASLOW'S MOTIVATIONAL HIERARCHY.

personality test any instrument used to help evaluate personality or measure PERSONALITY TRAITS. Personality tests may collect self-report data, in which participants answer questions about their personality or select items that describe themselves, or they may take the form of projective tests (see PROJECTIVE TECHNIQUE), which claim to measure unconscious aspects of a participant's personality.

personality trait a relatively stable, consistent, and enduring internal characteristic that is inferred from a pattern of behaviors, attitudes, feelings, and habits in the individual. Personality traits can be useful in summarizing, predicting, and explaining an individual's conduct, and a variety of **personality trait theories** exist. However, because personality trait theories do not explain the proximal causes of behavior nor provide a developmental account, they must be supplemented by dynamic and processing concepts, such as motives, schemas, plans, projects, and life stories.

personality type any of the specific categories into which human beings may be classified on the basis of personality traits, attitudes, behavior

patterns, physique (see CONSTITUTIONAL TYPE), or other outstanding characteristics. Examples are the INTROVERSION–EXTRAVERSION distinction and FUNCTIONAL TYPES of Swiss psychoanalyst Carl Jung (1875–1961) and the character types of German-born U.S psychoanalyst Erich Fromm (1900–1980), such as the so-called exploitative, hoarding, and marketing orientations.

personal space an area of defended space around an individual. Patterns of personal-space use may vary among species as well as among human cultures. Personal space differs from other types of defended space (e.g., territory) by being a surrounding "bubble" that moves with the individual (see BUBBLE CONCEPT OF PERSONAL SPACE). It may have been used by various species throughout evolutionary history to protect the individual organism against intraspecies aggression and threats to personal autonomy. Because human use of personal space varies among cultures, at least part of it must represent a learned behavior. See PROXEMICS.

personal unconscious in the ANALYTIC PSYCHOLOGY of Swiss psychiatrist Carl Jung (1875–1961), the portion of each individual's unconscious that contains the elements of his or her own experience as opposed to the COLLECTIVE UNCONSCIOUS, which contains the ARCHETYPES universal to humankind. The personal unconscious consists of everything subliminal, forgotten, and repressed in an individual's life. Some of these contents may be recalled to consciousness, but others cannot and are truly unconscious. In Jung's view the personal unconscious must be integrated into the conscious EGO for INDIVIDUATION to occur.

person-centered planning an individual planning process that focuses on people's gifts, strengths, preferences, and achievements. In the case of a person with a developmental disability, emphasis is placed on the person, his or her family members, and the supports needed to enable the person to make choices, participate in the community, and achieve dignity. The process requires an extended commitment from participants and the development of an action-oriented plan. Methods of person-centered planning include Essential Lifestyles Planning, Making Action Plans (MAPS), Personal Future Planning, Planning Alternative Tomorrows with Hope (PATH), and Whole Life Planning.

person-centered psychotherapy see CLIENT-CENTERED THERAPY.

person–environment interaction the relationship between a person's psychological and physical capacities and the demands placed on those capacities by the person's social and physical environment (environmental press). Quality of life is strongly influenced by **person–environment congruence**: Too little or too much environmental press can lead to poor quality of life.

personnel psychology the branch of INDUS-

TRIAL AND ORGANIZATIONAL PSYCHOLOGY that deals with the selection, placement, training, promotion, evaluation, and counseling of employees.

personnel test any test used in personnel selection, placement of newly hired or existing employees, or employee evaluation. Such tests include (a) aptitude tests, which measure basic abilities and skills; (b) achievement tests, which measure job-specific abilities such as typing skill; and (c) personality and interest inventories, which are used as predictors of job performance. See EMPLOYMENT TEST.

personnel training in industrial and organizational settings, a program designed to achieve such goals as orientation of new employees, development of knowledge and skills, or modification of supervisor or employee attitudes. The learning procedures used in personnel training may include classes or lectures, use of audiovisual aids or simulator devices, role play, laboratory training, case discussions, behavioral modeling, business games, or programmed instruction. The training may be provided outside or inside the usual work setting. Also called **employee training**. See also EXECUTIVE COACHING.

personology *n.* **1.** the study of personality from the holistic point of view, based on the theory that an individual's actions and reactions, thoughts and feelings, and personal and social functioning can be understood only in terms of the whole person. **2.** the theory of personality as a set of enduring tendencies that enable individuals to adapt to life, proposed by U.S. psychologist Henry Alexander Murray (1893–1988). According to Murray, personality is also a mediator between the individual's fundamental needs (see VISCEROGENIC NEED; PSYCHOGENIC NEED), and the demands of the environment.

person perception the processes by which people think about, appraise, and evaluate other people. An important aspect of person perception is the attribution of motives for action (see ATTRIBUTION THEORY).

person-years *pl. n.* the sum of the number of years that each individual in a population of interest has been affected by an event, occurrence, or condition of interest (e.g., by a particular disorder or disease or by a certain treatment protocol).

perspective *n.* **1.** the ability to view objects, events, and ideas in realistic proportions and relationships. **2.** the ability to interpret relative position, size, and distance of objects in a plane surface as if they were three-dimensional. **3.** the capacity of an individual to take into account and potentially understand the perceptions, attitudes, or behaviors of him- or herself and of other individuals.

perspective theory a theory postulating that self-reports of attitudes on rating scales depend on the content and perspective of a person's atti-

tude. **Content** refers to the evaluative responses that a person actually associates with an ATTITUDE OBJECT. **Perspective** refers to the range of possible evaluative responses that a person considers when rating an attitude object. A self-report of an attitude can change as a result of a change in content or perspective, that is, an actual change in the attitude or a change in what a person defines as an extremely positive or negative attitude.

persuasion *n.* an active attempt by one person to change another person's attitudes, beliefs, or emotions associated with some issue, person, concept, or object. See also DUAL PROCESS MODEL OF PERSUASION. —**persuasive** *adj.*

persuasion therapy a type of SUPPORTIVE PSYCHOTHERAPY in which the therapist attempts to induce the client to modify faulty attitudes and behavior patterns by appealing to the client's powers of reasoning, will, and self-criticism. The technique was advocated as a briefer alternative to earlier Freudian and neo-Freudian reconstructive methods (see RECONSTRUCTIVE PSYCHOTHERAPY).

persuasive arguments theory an analysis of GROUP POLARIZATION that assumes that the opinions of group members discussing an issue or choice will tend to become more extreme when a majority of the members favor a basic position, because the group will generate more arguments favoring the majority position. See also CHOICE SHIFT.

pertinence model **1.** a model of attention in which various stimuli or sources of information are weighted in terms of their relevance. **2.** a model of perception according to which a stimulus that is highly relevant can attract attention even if it is weak.

perturbation *n.* **1.** an anxious or distressed mental state. In the context of a completed or attempted suicide, it is a measure of the extent to which a person is (or was) upset or disturbed. **2.** an influence or activity that causes an interruption or interference in a mental or physical phenomenon or system.

pervasive developmental disorder any one of a class of disorders characterized by severe and widespread impairment in social interaction and verbal or nonverbal communication or the presence of stereotyped behavior, interests, and activities. These disorders are frequently apparent from an early age; they include ASPERGER'S DISORDER, AUTISTIC DISORDER, CHILDHOOD DISINTEGRATIVE DISORDER, and RETT SYNDROME. This term is synonymous with AUTISTIC SPECTRUM DISORDER.

perversion *n.* a culturally unacceptable or prohibited form of behavior, particularly sexual behavior. See SEXUAL PERVERSION.

pessimism *n.* the attitude that things will go wrong and that people's wishes or aims are unlikely to be fulfilled. **Pessimists** are people who expect unpleasant or bad things to happen to them and to others or who are otherwise doubtful or hesitant about positive outcomes of behavior. Pessimism can be defined in terms of expectancy: lack of confidence of attaining desired goals (compare OPTIMISM). Most individuals lie somewhere on the spectrum between the two polar opposites of pure optimism and pure pessimism but tend to demonstrate sometimes strong, relatively stable or situational tendencies in one direction or the other. —**pessimistic** *adj*.

PET 1. abbreviation for PARENT EFFECTIVENESS TRAINING. **2.** acronym for POSITRON EMISSION TOMOGRAPHY.

pet-assisted therapy see ANIMAL-ASSISTED THERAPY.

petit mal see ABSENCE.

P factor analysis FACTOR ANALYSIS that involves statistically analyzing multiple responses provided by a single individual across multiple occasions, rather than studying multiple responses of a large number of individuals, each of whom is studied on only one occasion.

PG abbreviation for PROSTAGLANDIN.

PGO spikes pontine–geniculo–occipital spikes: peaks, recorded on an electroencephalogram, that occur during sleep and indicate neural activity in the pons, lateral geniculate nucleus, and occipital cortex. They are associated with dreaming. See DREAM STATE.

phallic personality in psychoanalytic theory, a pattern of narcissistic behavior exemplified by boastfulness, excessive self-assurance, vanity, compulsive sexual behavior, and in some cases aggressive or exhibitionistic behavior. Also called **phallic character**.

phallic stage in the classic psychoanalytic theory of Austrian psychiatrist Sigmund Freud (1856–1939), the stage of PSYCHOSEXUAL DEVELOPMENT occurring at about age 3, when the LIBIDO is focused on the genital area (penis or clitoris) and discovery and manipulation of the body become a major source of pleasure. During this period boys are posited to experience CASTRATION ANXIETY, girls to experience PENIS ENVY, and both to experience the OEDIPUS COMPLEX. Also called **phallic phase**.

phallocentric *adj*. **1.** denoting a culture or belief system in which the phallus (penis) is regarded as a sacred giver of life, source of power, or symbol of fertility. **2.** more generally, focused or fixated on the penis as a symbol of male potency. —**phallocentrism** *n*.

phallus *n*. (*pl*. **phalli**) the PENIS or an object that resembles the form of the penis (the latter often referred to as a **phallic symbol**). As a symbolic object, it often represents fertility or potency.

phantasy *n*. in the OBJECT RELATIONS THEORY of Austrian-born British psychoanalyst Melanie Klein (1882–1960), one of the unconscious constructions, wishes, or impulses that are presumed to underlie all thought and feeling. The *ph* spelling is used to distinguish this from the everyday form of FANTASY, which can include conscious daydreaming.

phantom limb the feeling that an amputated limb is still present, often manifested as a tingling or, occasionally, painful sensation in the area of the missing limb (**phantom limb pain**). In some cases the individual may even deny that the limb has been removed. It is thought that the brain's representation of the limb remains intact and, in the absence of normal somesthetic stimulation, becomes active spontaneously or as a result of stimulation from other brain tissue.

phantosmia *n*. perception of an odor when no smell stimulus is present (i.e., an olfactory hallucination). See also DYSOSMIA.

pharmacodynamics *n*. the study of the interactions of drugs with the RECEPTORS that are responsible for their actions on the body. It involves studying the effects of drugs on the body and their mechanism of action. Basic studies involve the activity of drugs at the receptor sites to which the drugs attach as well as the changes in cell function and behavior that result. —**pharmacodynamic** *adj*.

pharmacodynamic tolerance a form of drug TOLERANCE in which the chemistry of the brain becomes adjusted to the presence of the drug, which in turn then loses its capacity for modifying brain activity. Neurons adapt to continued drug presence by reducing the number or sensitivity of receptors available to the drug (i.e., down-regulation). This cellular-adaptive tolerance is associated with the use of many drugs, including sedative-hypnotics and psychostimulants, and may be followed by withdrawal symptoms when regular doses of the drug are interrupted. This may be contrasted with **metabolic tolerance**, in which the body reacts to continued presence of the drug by metabolizing it at an increased rate. Both forms of tolerance lead to higher doses of the drug being needed to produce the same effects.

pharmacogenetics *n*. the study of genetic factors that influence the response of individuals to different drugs and to different dosages of drugs. Inherited variations in enzymes or other metabolic components can affect the efficacy of a drug or cause adverse reactions to normal doses. For example, some 40–70% of Caucasians have an enzyme variant that causes them to metabolize the antituberculosis drug, isoniazid, very slowly. They require only a fraction of the standard dose.

pharmacogenomics *n*. the study of the ways in which genetic knowledge can be utilized for the accurate and effective administration of medications and other drugs.

pharmacokinetics *n*. the study of how pharmacological agents are processed within a biological system, in vivo or in vitro, including factors that influence the absorption, distribution, metabolism, and elimination of the substance or its metabolic products.

pharmacological antagonism see ANTAGONIST.

pharmacology *n.* the branch of science that involves the study of substances that interact with living organisms to alter some biological process affecting the HOMEOSTASIS of the organism. Therapeutic (or medical) pharmacology deals with the administration of substances to correct a state of disease or to enhance well-being. —**pharmacological** or **pharmacologic** *adj.*

pharmacotherapy *n.* the treatment of a disorder by the administration of drugs, as opposed to such means as surgery, psychotherapy, or complementary and alternative methods. Also called **drug therapy**. See PSYCHOPHARMACOTHERAPY.

pharynx *n.* the muscular and membranous tube running from the mouth and nostrils to the entrance to the esophagus (gullet) that acts as the passage for food and respiratory gases. It consists of three major sections: the lower laryngopharynx, the middle oropharynx, and the upper nasopharynx. —**pharyngeal** *adj.*

phase locking the tendency for a neural ACTION POTENTIAL to occur at a certain phase of a PURE-TONE stimulus. In general, an action potential will not occur on every cycle, but when it is generated it tends to occur at the same point or phase in the stimulus. More generally, phase locking refers to the ability of a neuron to synchronize or follow the temporal structure of a sound. Phase locking underlies the ability to localize sounds based on interaural phase differences or interaural time differences (see BINAURAL CUE). Its role in monaural hearing is uncertain, but it has been proposed as a mechanism for the coding of pitch.

phase shift 1. a disruption of the normal sleep–wake cycle, with the result that the individual is alert during a usual sleeping period and sleepy when he or she should be alert. See CIRCADIAN RHYTHM SLEEP DISORDER; DISORDERS OF THE SLEEP–WAKE CYCLE SCHEDULE. **2.** a change in the diurnal or circadian rhythm brought about by such things as changes in daylight exposure or changing time zones.

phasic receptor a RECEPTOR cell that shows a rapid fall in the frequency of discharge of nerve impulses as stimulation is maintained. Compare TONIC RECEPTOR.

phencyclidine *n.* see PCP.

phenobarbital *n.* an anticonvulsant BARBITURATE used for treatment of generalized tonic–clonic or partial seizures. Formerly widely used as a sedative and hypnotic, it has been largely supplanted for these purposes by safer medications lacking the toxicity and adverse effects associated with barbiturates. Phenobarbital is also sometimes used in the management of SEDATIVE, HYPNOTIC, OR ANXIOLYTIC WITHDRAWAL. U.S. trade name: **Luminal**.

phenomenalism *n.* the doctrine that access to, and thus knowledge of, the external world is always through sensory experience of phenomena. Propositions about physical objects are therefore to be analyzed in terms of actual or possible sensory experiences. The position is compatible with certain forms of IDEALISM, in that physical entities are defined in terms of mental experience, but also with EMPIRICISM and POSITIVISM. —**phenomenalist** *adj.*

phenomenal self the SELF as experienced by the individual at a given time. Only a small portion of self-knowledge is active in working memory or consciousness at any time, with the remainder lying dormant or inactive. The same person might have a very different phenomenal self at different times, without any change in actual self-knowledge, simply because different views are brought into awareness by events. Also called **working self-concept**.

phenomenal space the environment as experienced by a given individual at a given time. The term refers not to objective reality but to personal and subjective reality, including everything within one's field of awareness. In the phenomenological personality theory of U.S. psychologist Carl Rogers (1902–1987), it is also known as the **phenomenological field**. Also called **phenomenal field**.

phenomenistic causality in the theory of Swiss child psychologist Jean Piaget (1896–1980), an inference of causality between events, drawn only on the basis of spatial or temporal contiguity. Such inferences are typical of much thinking in prescientific cultures and of the thought processes of a child. For example: "It is dark outside because I am sleepy."

phenomenological analysis an approach to psychology in which mental experiences are described and studied without theoretical presuppositions or speculation as to their causes or consequences. In general, such an approach will favor observation and description over analysis and interpretation; it will also attempt to understand a person's experience from the point of view of that person, rather than from some more abstract theoretical perspective. See also PHENOMENOLOGY.

phenomenological death the subjective sense that one has become inert, insensitive, and unresponsive. Phenomenological death occurs in some psychotic conditions. Patients may speak of themselves as dead and behave (although inconsistently) in accord with that belief. Phenomenological death is conceived as the extreme point on a continuum of self-assessment; it is not necessarily a condition that is permanent.

phenomenological theory an approach to personality theory that places questions of individuals' current experiences of themselves and their world at the center of analyses of personality functioning and change. See also PERSONAL CONSTRUCT.

P

phenomenological therapy any form of therapy, perhaps best exemplified by CLIENT-CENTERED THERAPY, in which the emphasis is on the client's process of self-discovery as opposed to an interpretive focus, such as that found in psychoanalysis.

phenomenology *n.* a movement in modern European philosophy initiated by German philosopher Edmund Husserl (1859–1938). Husserl argued for a new approach to human knowledge in which both the traditional concerns of philosophy (such as metaphysics and epistemology) and the modern concern with scientific causation would be set aside in favor of a careful attention to the nature of immediate conscious experience. Mental events should be studied and described in their own terms, rather than in terms of their relationship to events in the body or in the external world. However, phenomenology should be distinguished from introspection as it is concerned with the relationship between acts of consciousness and the objects of such acts (see INTENTIONALITY). Husserl's approach proved widely influential in psychology—especially GESTALT PSYCHOLOGY and EXISTENTIAL PSYCHOLOGY. —**phenomenological** *adj.* —**phenomenologist** *n.*

phenomenon *n.* (*pl.* **phenomena**) **1.** an observable event or physical occurrence. **2.** in philosophy, something perceived by the senses. In Greek philosophy, most notably that of Plato (c. 427–c. 347 BCE), phenomena are the sensible things that constitute the world of experience, as contrasted with the transcendent realities that are known only through reason. German philosopher Immanuel Kant (1724–1804) used the term *phenomena* to refer to things as they appear to the senses and are interpreted by the categories of the human understanding. For Kant, knowledge of phenomena is the kind of knowledge available to human beings, as knowledge of "noumena," or things in themselves, remains beyond human experience or reason. **3.** an occurrence or entity that defies explanation. —**phenomenal** *adj.*

phenothiazines *pl. n.* a group of chemically related compounds most of which are used as ANTIPSYCHOTIC drugs, originally developed as such in the 1950s. The drugs in this class of traditional (or first-generation) antipsychotics were formerly the most widely used agents for the treatment of schizophrenia. It is commonly assumed that their therapeutic effects are produced by blockade of dopamine D2 receptors (see DOPAMINE RECEPTOR); they also block acetylcholine, histamine, and norepinephrine receptors, actions that are associated with many of their adverse effects. Phenothiazines are used for the treatment of acute mania, psychotic agitation, and schizophrenia as well as nausea and vomiting and for preanesthesia sedation. A variety of adverse side effects is associated with their use, including EXTRAPYRAMIDAL SYMPTOMS, TARDIVE DYSKINESIA, and sedation.

phenotype *n.* the observable characteristics of an individual, such as morphological or biochemical features and the presence or absence of a particular disease or condition. Phenotype is determined by the expression of the individual's GENOTYPE coupled with the effects of environmental factors (e.g., nutritional status or climate). —**phenotypic** *adj.*

pheromone *n.* a chemical signal that is released outside the body by members of a species and that influences the behavior of other members of the same species. For example, it may serve to attract the opposite sex or to act as an alarm. In nonhuman animals, sensitivity to pheromones occurs via the VOMERONASAL SYSTEM. The existence of true pheromones in humans is controversial, although scents (e.g., perfumes, body odors) may play a role in sexual attraction and arousal. Also called **ectohormone**. Compare ALLOMONE.

phi coefficient (symbol: ϕ) a measure of association for two dichotomous RANDOM VARIABLES. The phi coefficient is the PRODUCT–MOMENT CORRELATION when both variables are coded (0,1).

philosophical psychology the branch of psychology that studies the philosophical issues relevant to the discipline and the philosophical assumptions that underlie its theories and methods. It approaches psychology from a wide perspective informed by a knowledge of metaphysics, epistemology, ethics, the history of ideas, the philosophy of science, and the tools of formal philosophical analysis. Philosophical psychologists tend to concentrate on the larger issues arising from the field rather than on model building and data gathering. See also RATIONAL PSYCHOLOGY.

philosophical psychotherapy psychotherapy based on philosophical principles of belief and attitude generally, as they relate to cognition, emotion, and behavior, or based on the principles of some particular philosophical perspective (e.g., EXISTENTIAL PSYCHOTHERAPY). Training in philosophy without appropriate training in the mental health field, however, is deemed inadequate for offering psychotherapy or counseling services.

philosophy *n.* the intellectual discipline that uses careful reasoned argument to elucidate fundamental questions, notably those concerning the nature of reality (metaphysics), the nature of knowledge (EPISTEMOLOGY), and the nature of moral judgments (ETHICS). As such, it provides an intellectual foundation for many other disciplines, including psychology. Psychology as a scientific discipline has its roots in the epistemological preoccupations of 18th- and 19th-century philosophy and continues to be influenced by philosophical ideas. See PHILOSOPHICAL PSYCHOLOGY. —**philosopher** *n.* —**philosophical** *adj.*

philosophy of mind the branch of philosophy

concerned with questions about the nature and functioning of mind and consciousness and the relationship of mind and mental activity to brain and body and to the external world (see MIND–BODY PROBLEM). It is deeply concerned with the relationships among language, thought, and action.

phi phenomenon 1. an illusion seen when two lights flash on and off about 150 m apart. The light appears to move from one location to the other. The phi phenomenon is a form of beta movement (see APPARENT MOVEMENT). **2.** a sensation of pure movement independent of any other attributes of the stimulus, such as its form.

phlebotomy *n.* removal of blood from the body for diagnostic or therapeutic purposes. This is ordinarily achieved by inserting a needle or catheter into a vein and then applying negative pressure. Through the early and mid-19th century, this practice was known as **bloodletting** and involved the removal of considerable quantities of blood as a means of curing or preventing disease. Also called **venesection**.

phobia *n.* a persistent and irrational fear of a specific situation, object, or activity (e.g., heights, dogs, water, blood, driving, flying), which is consequently either strenuously avoided or endured with marked distress. The many types of individual phobia are classified as SPECIFIC PHOBIAS. See also SOCIAL PHOBIA. —**phobic** *adj.*

phon *n.* see LOUDNESS.

phone *n.* a single speech sound.

phoneme *n.* a speech sound that plays a meaningful role in a language and cannot be analyzed into smaller meaningful sounds, conventionally indicated by slash symbols: /b/. A speech sound is held to be meaningful in a given language if its contrast with other sounds is used to mark distinctions of meaning: In English, for example, /p/ and /b/ are phonemes because they distinguish between [pan] and [ban] and other such pairs. —**phonemic** *adj.*

phonemic restoration effect a psycholinguistic phenomenon in which a person listening to speech recordings in which PHONEMES have been replaced by white noise or have otherwise been made inaudible does not notice the interruption. It is assumed that the listener's perceptual mechanism must have restored the missing phonemes. This is considered strong evidence for an active process of speech perception.

phonemics *n.* the branch of linguistics concerned with the classification and analysis of the PHONEMES in a language. While PHONETICS tries to characterize all possible sounds represented in human language, phonemics identifies which of the phonetic distinctions are considered meaningful by a given language. See EMIC–ETIC DISTINCTION.

phonetics *n.* the branch of linguistics that studies the physical properties of speech sounds and the physiological means by which these are pro-

duced and perceived (placing the tongue or lip in contact with the teeth, directing the airstream against the hard palate, etc.).

phonics *n.* **1.** a method of teaching reading, popularly known as **sounding out**, that is based on the sounds of the letters in a word rather than on the word as a unit, that is, trying to match GRAPHEMES and PHONEMES. Also called **phonic method**. Compare WHOLE-WORD METHOD. **2.** a former name for ACOUSTICS.

phonogram *n.* a graphic or symbolic representation of a phoneme, syllable, or word.

phonological disorder a communication disorder characterized by failure to develop and consistently use speech sounds that are appropriate for the child's age. It most commonly involves misarticulation of the later acquired speech sounds, such as [l], [r], [s], [z], [ch], [sh], or [th] (see LALLING; LISP), but may also include substitution of sounds (e.g., [t] for [k]) or omission of sounds (e.g., final consonants). These problems are not due to, or are in excess of those normally associated with, hearing loss, structural deficits in the mechanism of speech production (e.g., cleft palate), or a neurological disorder.

phonological dyslexia a form of acquired DYSLEXIA characterized primarily by difficulties in reading pronounceable nonwords. Semantic errors are not seen in this type of dyslexia, a feature that distinguishes it from DEEP DYSLEXIA. See also SURFACE DYSLEXIA.

phonological loop see WORKING MEMORY.

phonology *n.* the branch of linguistics that studies the system of speech sounds in a language or in language generally. The term is less specific than either PHONEMICS or PHONETICS. —**phonological** *adj.*

phonosurgery *n.* surgical intervention to maintain or improve the voice or the ease with which phonation occurs, such as the removal of polyps from the vocal cords or THYROPLASTY.

phosphene *n.* a sensation of a light flash in the absence of actual light stimulation to the eye. It may occur with the eyes closed and can be caused by mechanical stimulation of the retina, by rubbing the eyes, or by direct electrical stimulation of the visual cortex. Also called **visual phosphene**. See also PHOTOPSIA.

phosphoinositide *n.* any of a class of SECOND MESSENGERS that are common in postsynaptic cells.

photobiology *n.* the study of the effects of light on organisms, including the more specific study of the effects of color on mood, cognition, physiology, and behavior and the use of color in treating a variety of disorders (**chromotherapy**). —**photobiological** *adj.* —**photobiologist** *n.*

photographic memory see EIDETIC IMAGE.

photoma *n.* a visual hallucination in which sparks or light flashes are seen in the absence of external stimuli. See also PHOSPHENE; PHOTOPSIA.

photometry *n.* the measurement of the intensity of light.

photoperiodism *n.* the behavioral and physiological reactions of animals and plants to changes in the length of days or in the intensity of light in the environment. Photoperiodism in animals is involved in the timing of seasonal migration behavior, reproductive cycles, changes in plumage or pelage, and hibernation. The shedding of leaves in autumn and winter dormancy are signs of photoperiodism in plants.

photophobia *n.* an extreme and often painful sensitivity to light. It may be associated with migraine headaches or with certain types of brain trauma. —**photophobic** *adj.*

photopic vision the type of vision associated with light levels during daylight. Photopic vision is mediated by RETINAL CONES, while vision at twilight and at night is mediated by RETINAL RODS. Also called **daylight vision**. Compare SCOTOPIC VISION.

photopigment *n.* a substance in a RETINAL ROD or RETINAL CONE that interacts with light to initiate a chemical cascade resulting in the conversion of light energy into an electrical signal. All rods contain the photopigment **rhodopsin**, while cones have one of three different photopigments (**iodopsins**), each with a different wavelength sensitivity. Photopigment is located on disks of membrane in the outer segment of a rod or cone. Also called **visual pigment**.

photopsia *n.* visual sensations in the absence of external visual stimuli, which can be unstructured (see PHOSPHENE) or structured. Structured photopsia consists of regular achromatic or chromatic visual patterns (e.g., circles, squares, diamonds) and is caused by pathological activation of prestriate cortical neurons. See also VISUAL HALLUCINATION. Also called **photopsy**.

photoreceptor *n.* a visual receptor, especially a RETINAL ROD or a RETINAL CONE.

photosensitivity *n.* sensitivity to light, especially sunlight, as occurs in ALBINISM and photogenic epilepsy. Conditions marked by increased sensitivity to the effects of sunlight on the skin include systemic LUPUS ERYTHEMATOSUS and xeroderma pigmentosum. Photosensitivity may occur as an adverse reaction to certain drugs, such as the phenothiazines (e.g., chlorpromazine), carbamazepine, St. John's wort, thiazides, sulfonamides, and tetracyclines. Photosensitivity may also represent an immune reaction in some individuals who manifest allergy symptoms after exposure to intense light. —**photosensitive** *adj.*

phototherapy *n.* therapy involving exposure to ultraviolet or infrared light, which is used for treating not only certain skin conditions or disorders (e.g., jaundice, psoriasis) but also depression, particularly for patients with SEASONAL AFFECTIVE DISORDER (SAD). Also called **bright light therapy**; **light therapy**.

phrase-structure grammar a type of GENERATIVE GRAMMAR in which a system of **phrase-structure rules** (or **rewrite rules**) is used to describe a sentence in terms of the grammatical structures that generate its form and define it as grammatical. The phrase-structure rules are usually set out in the form X → Y + Z, in which the arrow is an instruction to reformulate ("rewrite") X in terms of its immediate constituents (Y + Z). So, for example, the sentence *The dogs chase the cats* can be described by the following set of rules:

sentence (S) → noun phrase (NP) + verb phrase (VP)
NP → determiner (det) + noun (N)
VP → verb (V) + NP
det → *the*
N → *cats*, *dogs*
V → *chase*

Formal phrase-structure analysis of this kind was developed by U.S. linguist Noam Chomsky (1928–), who also, however, pointed out its limitations as a description of how language works. Chomsky's TRANSFORMATIONAL GENERATIVE GRAMMAR added an important new dimension by proposing that sentences have a DEEP STRUCTURE as well as the linear SURFACE STRUCTURE described in phrase-structure grammar, and that the relationship between the two levels can be described through a system of transformational rules.

phrenic nerve a nerve that originates in the cervical plexus of the neck and sends sensory and motor branches to the heart, diaphragm, and other parts of the chest and abdomen.

phrenology *n.* a theory of personality formulated in the 18th and 19th centuries by German physician Franz Josef Gall (1757–1828) and Austrian philosopher and anatomist Johann Kaspar Spurzheim (1776–1832). It stated that specific abilities or personality traits are represented by specific areas of the brain: The size of these brain areas determines the degree of the corresponding skill or trait. Proponents of the theory argued that the size of such locations could be indicated by bumps and hollows on the skull surface, based on the observation that the contours of the brain follow the skull contours. Although wrong in most respects, the theory suggested the idea of LOCALIZATION OF FUNCTION. See also PHYSIOGNOMY. —**phrenological** *adj.* —**phrenologist** *n.*

phylogenetic principle the theory that ONTOGENY recapitulates PHYLOGENY in the development of an organism: In humans, this supposes that human life, across development from embryo to adult, repeats the stages of organic and social evolution.

phylogeny *n.* **1.** the evolutionary origin and development of a particular group of organisms. Also called **phylogenesis**. Compare ONTOG-

P

ENY. **2.** a diagram that shows genetic linkages between ancestors and descendants. Also called **phylogenetic tree**. —**phylogenetic** *adj.*

phylum *n.* (*pl.* **phyla**) in BIOLOGICAL TAXONOMY, a main subdivision of a KINGDOM, containing a group of similar, related CLASSES.

physiatrics (**physiatry**) *n.* see PHYSICAL MEDICINE.

physical dependence the state of an individual who has repeatedly taken a drug and will experience unpleasant physiological symptoms (see SUBSTANCE WITHDRAWAL) if he or she stops taking the drug. SUBSTANCE DEPENDENCE with physical (or physiological) dependence is diagnosed if there is evidence of withdrawal or TOLERANCE. Compare PSYCHOLOGICAL DEPENDENCE.

physical determinism the type of DETERMINISM presumed to operate among physical objects in the natural world. In psychology, physical determinism is the assumption that psychological events and behaviors have physical causes and can be described in terms of models and theories borrowed from the physical sciences. See HARD DETERMINISM.

physicalism *n.* **1.** the doctrine that reality is composed of matter and that mind is therefore reducible to matter. See IDENTITY THEORY; MATERIALISM; MIND–BODY PROBLEM. **2.** the view that all meaningful propositions can be stated in the language of the physical sciences and in operational definitions. See LOGICAL POSITIVISM; POSITIVISM. —**physicalist** *adj.*

physical medicine the branch of medicine that specializes in the diagnosis and treatment of illness and disorders through physical means (e.g., exercise and massage) and mechanical devices. Physical medicine is also concerned with the REHABILITATION of patients with physical disabilities. Also called **physiatrics**; **physiatry**.

physical symbol system hypothesis a hypothesis concerning the necessity and sufficiency of capturing intelligence in computational systems: A necessary and sufficient condition for a physical system to exhibit general intelligent action is that it be a physical symbol system. "Necessary" means that any physical system that exhibits general intelligence will be an instance of a physical symbol system. "Sufficient" means that any physical symbol system can be organized further to exhibit general intelligent action. This hypothesis has been a driving factor for much research in ARTIFICIAL INTELLIGENCE and COGNITIVE SCIENCE.

physical therapy (**PT**) **1.** the treatment of pain, injury, or disease using physical or mechanical methods, such as exercise, heat, water, massage, or electric current (diathermy). The treatment is administered by a trained **physical therapist**. Also called **physiotherapy**. **2.** a branch of medicine and health care that identifies, corrects, alleviates, and prevents temporary,

prolonged, or permanent movement dysfunction or physical disability.

physiognomic perception the tendency to see expressive properties in objects, such that, for example, dark objects may be perceived as gloomy, or bright ones may be perceived as happy.

physiognomy *n.* **1.** the form of a person's physical features, especially the face. **2.** the attempt to read personality from the facial features and expression, assuming, for example, that a person with a receding chin is weak or one with a high forehead is bright. The idea dates back to Greek philosopher Aristotle (383–322 BCE) and was later developed into a pseudoscientific system by Swiss pastor Johann Lavater (1741–1801) and Italian psychiatrist Cesare Lombroso (1835–1909). Also called **physiognomics**. See also CHARACTEROLOGY; PHRENOLOGY.

physiological age a measurement of the level of development or deterioration of an individual in terms of functional norms for various body systems.

physiological antagonism see ANTAGONIST.

physiological arousal aspects of AROUSAL shown by physiological responses, such as increases in blood pressure and rate of respiration and decreased activity of the gastrointestinal system. Such primary arousal responses are largely governed by the SYMPATHETIC NERVOUS SYSTEM, but responses of the PARASYMPATHETIC NERVOUS SYSTEM may compensate or even overcompensate for the sympathetic activity. See also AUTONOMIC NERVOUS SYSTEM.

physiological correlate an association between a physiological measure and a behavioral measure. The existence of a physiological correlate may suggest a causal relation, but it does not establish a cause.

physiological need any of the requirements for survival, such as food, water, oxygen, and sleep. Physiological needs make up the lowest level of MASLOW'S MOTIVATIONAL HIERARCHY. Also called **basic need**; **fundamental need**. See also PRIMARY NEED; VISCEROGENIC NEED.

physiological nystagmus the normal small, rapid movement of the eyes that permits sustained viewing of a scene. See also NYSTAGMUS.

physiological paradigm the concept that mental disorders are caused by abnormalities in neurological structures and processes. This perspective, which underlies the field and practice of psychiatry, holds that mental disorders can be treated with drugs, surgery, or other techniques ordinarily used to correct malfunctioning of the body.

physiology *n.* the science of the functions of living organisms, including the chemical and physical processes involved and the activities of the cells, tissues, and organs, as opposed to static anatomical or structural factors. —**physiological** *adj.* —**physiologist** *n.*

physiopathology *n.* the study of PATHOPHYSI-OLOGY.

PI abbreviation for progressive interval. See PROGRESSIVE-INTERVAL SCHEDULE.

pia-arachnoid *n.* the inner two coverings of the brain and spinal cord—the pia mater and arachnoid mater—considered as a single structure. See MENINGES.

Piagetian theory the theory of cognitive development proposed by Swiss child psychologist Jean Piaget (1896–1980), according to which intelligence develops through four major stages: (a) the sensorimotor stage (roughly 0–2 years), (b) the preoperational stage (roughly 2–7 years), (c) the concrete operational stage (roughly 7–12 years), and (d) the formal operational stage (roughly 12 years and beyond). According to this theory, each stage builds upon the preceding one. Passage through the stages is facilitated by a balance of two processes: **assimilation**, in which new information is incorporated into already existing cognitive structures; and **accommodation**, in which new information that does not fit into already existing cognitive structures is used to create new cognitive structures.

pia mater see MENINGES.

piblokto *n.* a CULTURE-BOUND SYNDROME observed primarily in female Inuit and other arctic populations. Individuals experience a sudden dissociative period of extreme excitement in which they often tear off clothes, run naked through the snow, scream, throw things, and perform other wild behaviors. This typically ends with convulsive seizures, followed by an acute coma and amnesia for the event. Also called **arctic hysteria**; **pibloktoq**.

pica *n.* a rare eating disorder found primarily in young children and marked by a persistent craving for unnatural, nonnutritive substances, such as plaster, paint, hair, starch, or dirt.

Pick's disease a form of DEMENTIA characterized by progressive degeneration of the frontal and temporal areas of the brain with the presence of particles called **Pick bodies** in the cytoplasm of the neurons. The disease is characterized by personality changes and deterioration of social skills and complex thinking; symptoms include problems with new situations and abstractions, difficulty in thinking or concentrating, loss of memory, lack of spontaneity, gradual emotional dullness, loss of moral judgment, and disturbances of speech. [described in 1892 by Arnold **Pick** (1851–1924), Czech psychiatrist and neuroanatomist]

picture-arrangement test a subtest of the Wechsler intelligence scales, in which the participant is required to arrange in proper order a series of sketches that tell a brief story. See also WECHSLER ADULT INTELLIGENCE SCALE.

picture-completion test a type of test consisting of drawings of familiar objects with features missing. The task is to recognize and specify the missing parts. See also INCOMPLETE-PICTURES TEST.

picture-interpretation test a test in which the participant is asked to interpret a visual image (e.g., a drawing, photograph, or painting). This type of test may aid in the assessment of intelligence or personality traits.

pidgin *n.* an improvised CONTACT LANGUAGE incorporating elements of two or more languages, often devised for purposes of trading. Pidgins are characterized by simple rules and limited vocabulary. Compare CREOLE.

pie chart a graphic display in which a circle is cut into pielike wedges, the area of the wedge being proportional to the percentage of cases in the category represented by that wedge.

pigment epithelium the single cuboidal layer of pigmented cells that abuts the tips of the photoreceptors in the RETINA. The pigment in the cells reduces light scatter by absorbing photons that elude the PHOTOPIGMENTS in the photoreceptors. The pigment epithelium is also critical for the health of the photoreceptors because it phagocytoses (engulfs) disks of membrane that are continually shed by the photoreceptors. Also called **retinal pigment epithelium (RPE)**.

pilot study a preliminary research project designed to evaluate and (if required) modify procedures in preparation for a subsequent and more detailed research project. Pilot studies are designed to reveal information about the viability and, to a lesser extent, the potential outcomes of a proposed experiment.

pineal gland a small, cone-shaped gland attached by a stalk to the posterior wall of the THIRD VENTRICLE of the brain. In amphibians and reptiles, the gland appears to function as a part of the visual system. In mammals it secretes the hormone MELATONIN. Also called **pineal body**.

Pinel's system a classification of mental disorders and symptoms outlined in the 18th century. The four major categories in this classification were melancholias, manias with delirium, manias without delirium, and dementia or mental deterioration. [Philippe **Pinel** (1745–1826), French psychiatrist]

pinna *n.* (*pl.* **pinnae**) the part of the external ear that projects beyond the head. Also called **auricle**.

pitch *n.* the subjective attribute that permits sounds to be ordered on a musical scale. The pitch of a PURE TONE is determined primarily by its frequency, the pitch of a complex periodic sound by its fundamental frequency. However, other physical parameters, such as intensity and duration, can affect pitch. The unit of pitch is the MEL.

pitch discrimination see AUDITORY DISCRIMINATION.

pituitarism *n.* disordered functioning of the pituitary gland, which may be overactive (hyper-pituitarism) or underactive (hypopituitarism).

pituitary gland a gland, pea-sized in humans, that lies at the base of the brain, connected by a stalk (the infundibulum) to the HYPOTHALAMUS. The pituitary gland is divided into an anterior and a posterior lobe, which differ in function. The anterior lobe (**adenohypophysis**) produces and secretes seven hormones—thyroid-stimulating hormone, follicle-stimulating hormone, corticotropin, growth hormone, luteinizing hormone, prolactin, and melanocyte-stimulating hormone—in response to RELEASING HORMONES from the hypothalamus. The posterior lobe (**neurohypophysis**) secretes two hormones, vasopressin and oxytocin, which are synthesized in the hypothalamus and transported down axons in the infundibulum to the neuro-hypophysis in response to direct neural stimulation. The pituitary's role of secreting TROPIC HORMONES, which regulate the production of other hormones, has resulted in its designation as the "master gland of the endocrine system." Also called **hypophysis**; **hypophysis cerebri**.

pivot grammar a type of simple grammar displayed in the early stages of language development (especially the TWO-WORD STAGE). Pivot grammar is characterized by two-word utterances in which one word (the **pivot word**) is typically a FUNCTION WORD, such as a determiner or preposition, and the other (the **open word**) is a CONTENT WORD, such as a noun or verb. A small child has relatively few pivot words in his or her vocabulary but uses them often and always in the same position relative to the open word. Open words are used less frequently, but the child learns more of them and can use them anywhere in a phrase. *More juice, light off,* and *all gone* are typical examples of pivot grammar: *More, off,* and *all* are pivot words; *juice, light,* and *gone* are open words.

placebo *n.* (*pl.* **placebos**) **1.** a pharmacologically inert substance, such as a sugar pill, that is often administered as a control in testing new drugs. Placebos used in double-BLIND trials may be DUMMIES or ACTIVE PLACEBOS. Formerly, placebos were occasionally used as diagnostic or psychotherapeutic agents, for example, in relieving pain or inducing sleep by suggestion, but the ethical implications of deceiving patients in such fashion makes this practice problematic. **2.** any medical or psychological intervention or treatment that is believed to be "inert," thus making it valuable as a control condition against which to compare the intervention or treatment of interest. See PLACEBO EFFECT.

placebo effect a clinically significant response to a therapeutically inert substance or nonspecific treatment. It is now recognized that placebo effects accompany the administration of any drug (active or inert) and contribute to the therapeutic effectiveness of a specific treatment. See PLACEBO.

place cells neurons in the HIPPOCAMPUS that fire selectively when an animal is in a particular spatial location or moving toward that location.

place learning 1. the learning of locations or physical positions of goals (e.g., where food can be found). Compare RESPONSE LEARNING. **2.** in conditioning, learning an association between a place and an unconditioned stimulus, such as food or poison. See CONDITIONED PLACE PREFERENCE.

placement counseling 1. services designed to advise and assist individuals to find suitable or optimal employment. Placement counseling may include coaching or training for job interviews, procedures for filling out applications, and assistance with other activities relevant to obtaining a job. **2.** in education, a service that provides guidance to students in deciding upon an appropriate educational program, class, or level of instruction. **3.** in foster care, services provided to help children and their adoptive parents adjust to adoptive placement. **4.** in VOCATIONAL REHABILITATION, a service that advises and prepares people with disabilities for appropriate job opportunities.

placenta *n.* the specialized organ produced by the mammalian embryo that attaches to the wall of the uterus to permit removal of waste products and to provide nutrients, energy, and gas exchange for the fetus via the maternal circulation. —**placental** *adj.*

place theory the theory that (a) different frequencies stimulate different places along the BASILAR MEMBRANE and (b) pitch is coded by the place of maximal stimulation. The first proposition is strongly supported by experimental evidence and stems from the fact that the mammalian auditory system shows TONOTOPIC ORGANIZATION. The second hypothesis remains controversial.

plan *n.* in cognitive psychology, a MENTAL REPRESENTATION of an intended action, such as an utterance or a complex movement, that is presumed to guide the individual in carrying it out. See also COGNITIVE PLAN.

PLAN acronym for PROGRAM FOR LEARNING IN ACCORDANCE WITH NEEDS.

planned behavior behavior that is under the organism's direct control, as opposed to more reactive behavior or REFLEXIVE BEHAVIOR. In social psychology, the THEORY OF PLANNED BEHAVIOR suggests that the intent to engage in a specific behavior is determined by attitudes, norms, and perceived control surrounding the behavior in question.

planned comparison a comparison among two or more means in ANALYSIS OF VARIANCE or REGRESSION ANALYSIS that has been specified prior to the observation of the data. Also called **planned contrast**. Compare POST HOC COMPARISON.

plantar reflex the reflex flexing of the toes when the sole of the foot is stroked.

planum temporale a region of the superior temporal cortex of the brain, adjacent to the primary AUDITORY CORTEX, that includes part of WERNICKE'S AREA. In most people it is larger in the left cerebral hemisphere than in the right hemisphere.

plaque *n.* a small patch or area of abnormal tissue that usually has a different appearance from the surrounding normal tissue. Kinds of plaque include atherosclerotic (or atheromatous) plaques, consisting of lipid deposits on the lining of arterial walls (see ATHEROSCLEROSIS); demyelination plaques, which develop on the protective nerve sheaths of patients with multiple sclerosis; and SENILE PLAQUES, which occur in Alzheimer's disease.

plasticity *n.* flexibility and adaptability. Plasticity of the nervous or hormonal systems makes it possible to learn and register new experiences. Early experiences can also modify and shape gene expression to induce long-lasting changes in neurons or endocrine organs. See also FUNCTIONAL PLASTICITY; NEURAL PLASTICITY. Compare RIGIDITY.

Platonic idealism a general philosophical position deriving both directly and indirectly from the writings of Greek philosopher Plato (c. 427–c. 347 BCE), which holds that the phenomena of our world are to be truly known by contemplating them in their ideal forms or abstract essences. Such knowledge is to be achieved by the rational intellect, rather than the senses or the understanding. In *The Republic,* Plato developed a philosophical system around the central notion that the things of this world are shadows or reflections of their ideal forms existing in a transcendent realm outside time and space (the "analogy of the cave"). This realm is the "real" world because the forms that comprise it are perfect and eternal, not being subject to change, decay, or limitation like the things of our world.

Plato's thought is partly an attempt to solve the logical and other problems involved in relating particulars to UNIVERSALS (e.g., relating blue things to the term "blue" or good things to the concept "goodness"); however, it also had a metaphysical or religious dimension, which was later emphasized and extended by NEOPLATONISM.

Platonic love a type of love in which there is no overt sexual behavior or desire. The term derives from a misunderstanding of the teachings of Greek philosopher Plato (c. 427–c. 347 BCE).

play *n.* activities that appear to be freely sought and pursued solely for the sake of individual or group enjoyment. Although play is typically regarded as serving no immediate purpose beyond enjoyment, studies indicate that it contributes significantly to development. Various types of play have been described, ranging from locomotor play to social play to cognitive play, and numerous theories about play have been proposed. Swiss psychologist Jean Piaget (1895–1980), for example, regarded it as advancing children's cognitive development through mastery play, playing games with defined rules (such as hide-and-seek), and symbolic play. Advocates of the **practice theory of play** propose that play prepares children for activities or roles they will encounter as adults, whereas others suggest that it serves a more immediate function, such as exercise, establishing social relations among peers, or using up excess energy. Although the preponderance of research on play focuses on the activities of children, the play behavior of nonhuman animals is also actively studied.

playacting *n.* dramatic play in which children, adolescents, or adults (including group-therapy participants) take different roles. In the process, the participants test relationships; rehearse different ways of dealing with situations; identify with significant figures; and play out any of a broad range of affective states and behaviors within the safe realm of make-believe. See also PSYCHODRAMA.

playfulness *n.* the tendency to see the light or bright side of life, to joke with others, and not to take matters too seriously. Playfulness is considered to be a foundation of humor. —**playful** *adj.*

play-group psychotherapy a technique used in group therapy for preschool and early elementary school children. Materials of many kinds (e.g., clay, toys, blocks, and figurines) are used to foster the expression of conflicts and fantasies and to give the therapist an opportunity to ask questions and help the children in the group understand their feelings, behavior, and relationships within the context of the group.

play therapy the use of play activities and materials (e.g., clay, water, blocks, dolls, puppets, drawing, and finger paint) in CHILD PSYCHOTHERAPY. Play-therapy techniques are based on the theory that such activities mirror the child's emotional life and fantasies, enabling the child to "play out" his or her feelings and problems and to test out new approaches and understand relationships in action rather than words. This form of psychotherapy, which focuses on a child's internal world and unconscious conflicts in addition to his or her daily life and current relationships, may be nondirective (see NONDIRECTIVE PLAY THERAPY), but may alternatively be conducted on a more directive or a more analytic, interpretive level.

pleasantness *n.* a conscious, hedonic state, typically deemed highly desirable, that is experienced when an event is congruent with one's goals or is associated with pleasure. See also DIMENSIONAL THEORY OF EMOTION. —**pleasant** *adj.*

pleasure center any of various areas of the brain (including areas of the hypothalamus and limbic system) that, upon intracranial self-stimulation (see INTRACRANIAL STIMULATION), have been implicated in producing pleasure. The existence of pure pleasure centers has not been definitively established, particularly because the self-stimulation response rate varies according to such factors as the duration and strength of the electrical stimulation. Also called **reward center**.

pleasure principle the view that human beings are governed by the desire for instinctual gratification, or pleasure, and for the discharge of tension that builds up as pain or "unpleasure" when gratification is lacking. According to psychoanalytic theory, the pleasure principle is the psychic force that motivates people to seek immediate gratification of instinctual, or libidinal, impulses, such as sex, hunger, thirst, and elimination. It dominates the ID and operates most strongly during childhood. Later, in adulthood, it is opposed by the REALITY PRINCIPLE of the EGO. Also called **pleasure–pain principle**.

plethysmography *n.* the process of measuring and recording volume or volume changes in organs or body tissues, such as the blood supply flowing through an organ.

plexus *n.* a network of similar structures (e.g., nerves, blood vessels) that are functionally or anatomically interconnected, for example, the brachial plexus or the cervical plexus.

plosive 1. *adj.* denoting a speech sound in which the airstream is partially or totally obstructed and suddenly released. A plosive sound may be VOICED (e.g., [b], [d], [g]) or UNVOICED (e.g., [p], [t], [k]). **2.** *n.* a plosive speech sound. Also called **obstruent**; **stop**.

pluralistic ignorance the state of affairs in which virtually every member of a group privately rejects what are held to be the prevailing attitudes and beliefs of the group. Each member falsely believes that these standards are accepted by everyone else in the group. It has been suggested that apparently sudden changes in social mores (e.g., with regard to sexual behavior) can be explained by the gradual recognition by many individuals that others in the group think the same as themselves.

PM abbreviation for PRIMARY MEMORY.

PMS abbreviation for PREMENSTRUAL SYNDROME.

PNS abbreviation for PERIPHERAL NERVOUS SYSTEM.

POC abbreviation for PERFORMANCE-OPERATING CHARACTERISTIC.

poetry therapy a form of BIBLIOTHERAPY that employs the reading or writing of poetry to facilitate emotional expression in an individual and foster healing and personal growth. Also (but less frequently) called **psychopoetry**.

point biserial correlation the correlation (association) between two random variables, one continuous and one dichotomous.

point localization the ability to locate a point on the skin that is stimulated. The **point-localization test** is a somatosensory test in which a skin area, usually on the hand, is touched twice with an intervening period of 1 s. The participant is required to determine whether the points touched were in the same place. Also called **tactual localization**.

point of subjective equality the value of a comparison stimulus that, for a given observer, is equally likely to be judged as higher or lower than that of a standard stimulus.

Poisson distribution a theoretical statistical distribution that generates the probability of occurrence of rare events that are randomly distributed in time or space. [Siméon D. **Poisson** (1781–1840), French mathematician]

Poisson regression model a NONLINEAR REGRESSION MODEL used to describe the occurrence of rare events as a function of one or more predictor variables. [Siméon **Poisson**]

polarization *n.* **1.** a difference in electric potential between two surfaces or two sides of one surface because of chemical activity. Polarization occurs normally in living cells, such as neurons and muscle cells, which maintain a positive charge on one side of the plasma membrane and a negative charge on the other. **2.** a condition in which light waves travel in parallel paths along one plane.

police psychology a branch of psychology that provides specialized assistance to law enforcement. Typical duties of a **police psychologist** may involve the screening and selection of recruits, fitness for duty evaluations, and counseling.

poliomyelitis *n.* an inflammatory process due to viral infection. In minor cases it is characterized by fever, headache, sore throat, and vomiting that typically disappear within 72 hours. In major cases, the inflammation affects the gray matter of the spinal cord and may lead to muscular weakness and paralysis, which can affect the muscles controlled by autonomic nerves, as well as skeletal muscles, so that breathing, swallowing, or similar functions are disrupted. Cognitive problems may arise as a secondary result of breathing difficulties. Also called **infantile paralysis**; **polio**.

political psychology 1. the study of political issues, processes, and dynamics, at both the individual and group levels, from the perspective of psychological principles. **2.** the application of psychological principles and knowledge to the formation of public policy, particularly as related to mental health and associated issues. See also PUBLIC SERVICE PSYCHOLOGY.

polyandry *n.* **1.** in animals, a MATING SYSTEM in which a female mates with more than one male but a male mates with only one female. The female mates with and forms a social relationship with multiple males during one reproductive cycle. **2.** marriage of a woman to more than one husband at the same time, which is an accepted custom in certain cultures. Compare MONOG-

AMY; POLYGAMY; POLYGYNY. **—polyandrous** *adj.*

polydipsia *n.* excessive thirst, manifest as an extreme amount of drinking. It commonly results from diabetes, and can be an important diagnostic sign of the condition, or—in the case of **psychogenic polydipsia**—may be related to psychological factors. It may also be induced by conditioning procedures (**schedule-induced polydipsia**). Compare ADIPSIA.

polygamy *n.* marriage to more than one spouse at the same time, which is an accepted custom in certain cultures. See also POLYANDRY; POLYGYNY. Compare MONOGAMY. **—polygamous** *adj.* **—polygamist** *n.*

polygenic trait a trait that is determined by numerous genes rather than only one. An example is average intelligence. Also called **polygenetic trait**. See MULTIFACTORIAL INHERITANCE.

polygyny *n.* **1.** in animals, a MATING SYSTEM in which a male mates with more than one female but a female mates with only one male. **2.** marriage of a man to more than one wife at the same time, which is an accepted custom in certain cultures. Compare MONOGAMY; POLYANDRY; POLYGAMY. **—polygynous** *adj.*

polymerase chain reaction a method for reproducing a particular RNA or DNA sequence manyfold, allowing amplification for sequencing or manipulating the sequence.

polymicrogyria *n.* see LISSENCEPHALY.

polymodal *adj.* involving several sensory modalities.

polymorphism *n.* **1.** in biology, the condition of having multiple behavioral or physical types within a species or population. In some fish species there are two distinct sizes of males: Larger males defend territory and attract females to mate with them; much smaller males, often with the physical appearance of females, stay close to the large male and inseminate some of the eggs. **2.** in genetics, the presence in a population of two or more variants of a gene (i.e., ALLELES) at a given genetic locus. For example, the variety of human blood groups is due to polymorphism of particular genes governing the characteristics of red blood cells. **—polymorphic** *adj.*

polymorphous perversity in the classic psychoanalytic theory of Austrian psychiatrist Sigmund Freud (1856–1939), the response of the human infant to many kinds of normal, daily activities posited to provide sexual excitation, such as touching, smelling, sucking, viewing, exhibiting, rocking, defecating, urinating, hurting, and being hurt.

polynomial regression a class of linear regression models (see LINEAR MODEL) in which one or more of the terms is raised to a power greater than 1 (e.g., $Y_i = \beta_0 + \beta_1 X_i + \beta_2 X_i^2 + \beta_3 X_i^3 + \ldots$).

polyopia *n.* the formation of multiple images of one object on the retina due to a refractive error of the eye, brain injury (see PALINOPSIA), fatigue, or PSYCHOGENIC disorder. See VISUAL ILLUSION.

polypeptide *n.* a molecule consisting of numerous (usually more than 10–20) AMINO ACIDS linked by peptide bonds (see PEPTIDE). The synthesis of polypeptides in living cells takes place at RIBOSOMES according to the genetic instructions encoded in the cell's DNA. Polypeptides are assembled by the cell into PROTEINS.

polypharmacy *n.* the simultaneous use of a variety of drugs of the same or different classes with the intent of producing a more robust therapeutic response. Polypharmacy for mental disorders may, for example, involve the administration of two or more antidepressants in the hope that agents with different mechanisms of action will produce greater clinical improvement than that seen with any one drug alone.

polyphasic sleep a sleep pattern in which sleep occurs in relatively short naps throughout a 24-hour period. A human infant may begin life with a polyphasic sleep rhythm that consists of half a dozen sleep periods. The rhythm becomes monophasic, with one long, daily sleep period, by about school age. **Biphasic sleep** patterns, which include one daytime nap period in addition to the long, typically nocturnal, period of sleep, are seen in a variety of cultures (e.g., as the siesta) and in older adults. See also SLEEP–WAKE CYCLE. Compare MONOPHASIC SLEEP.

polysemy *n.* the condition in which a word has more than one meaning, as in *dear* meaning "loved" or "expensive." Psycholinguistic experiments to probe the structure of the MENTAL LEXICON frequently make use of polysemy. **—polysemic** *adj.*

polysomnography *n.* the recording of various physiological processes (e.g., eye movements, brain waves, heart rate, penile tumescence) throughout the night, for the diagnosis of sleep-related disorders. **—polysomnograph** *n.*

polysynaptic arc a NEURAL ARC involving several SYNAPSES, for example, when one or more sensory neurons are connected to one or more motor neurons via one or several interneurons. Also called **multisynaptic arc**. Compare MONOSYNAPTIC ARC.

POMS acronym for PROFILE OF MOOD STATES.

pons *n.* a part of the brainstem lying between the MIDBRAIN and the MEDULLA OBLONGATA, appearing as a swelling on the ventral surface of the brainstem. It consists of bundles of transverse, ascending, and descending nerve fibers and nuclei, including FACIAL NERVE nuclei. It serves primarily as a bridge, or transmission structure, between different areas of the nervous system. It also works with the CEREBELLUM in controlling equilibrium, and with the CEREBRAL CORTEX in smoothing and coordinating voluntary movements. With the cerebellum it forms the region called the metencephalon. **—pontine** *adj.*

pontine–geniculo–occipital spikes see PGO SPIKES.

pontine sleep dreaming sleep; sleep characterized by the presence of PGO SPIKES. See DREAM STATE.

pooled interdependence a task condition in which the task is split among a number of individuals, units, or groups, each of which performs independently with no flow of work between them and little if any contact or coordination required. The output of each individual, unit, or group is eventually pooled and contributes to the overall goals of the organization as a whole. Pooled interdependence means that the results achieved by each individual or group will depend very little on the accomplishments of the other individuals or groups.

pooling n. a procedure for combining several independent estimates of a parameter into a single estimate. This may be done by calculating the average of the independent estimates, with or without WEIGHTING. However, note that a pooled estimate is not obtained by simply combining all data into a single data set and calculating the estimate of the parameter on the massed data points.

pop-out n. in visual search tasks, a target that is different from the DISTRACTORS. One or more basic features will mark the pop-out as distinct from the other stimuli, hence allowing the target to be easily detected and identified regardless of the number of distractors.

popular psychology 1. psychological knowledge as understood by members of the general public, which may be oversimplified, misinterpreted, and out of date. See also COMMONSENSE PSYCHOLOGY; FOLK PSYCHOLOGY. **2.** psychological knowledge intended specifically for use by the general public, such as self-help books and television and radio advice programs.

population n. **1.** the total number of individuals (humans or other organisms) in a given geographical area. **2.** in statistics, a theoretically defined, complete group of objects (people, animals, institutions) from which a sample is drawn in order to obtain empirical observations and to which results can be generalized. Also called **universe**.

population stereotype in ergonomics, generalizations about the perceptual, cognitive, or physical characteristics of a group of users, such as an ethnic or cultural group, that are relevant to the design of systems or products for that group. For example, in the United States, users have a right bias (i.e., a tendency to move right, select doors on the right, etc.) and the color red carries connotations of "stop," "danger," or "turn off."

population vector the mechanism used in the MOTOR CORTEX to encode the direction of an intended movement. The activity in each neuron increases when the intended movement is close to its preferred direction. The direction of the intended movement is derived from the activity across the population of neurons.

Porter–Lawler model of motivation a model of work motivation that integrates the VALENCE–INSTRUMENTALITY–EXPECTANCY THEORY with other theoretical perspectives, including EXISTENCE, RELATEDNESS, AND GROWTH THEORY, EQUITY THEORY, and theories of INTRINSIC MOTIVATION. [Lyman W. **Porter** (1930–) and Edward E. **Lawler** III (1938–), U.S. management theorists]

position n. **1.** the location in space of an object in relation to a reference point or other objects. **2.** in the social psychology of groups, an individual's situation relative to others in the group, particularly with regard to social standing or rank or to his or her stand on an issue.

positive addiction a concept based on the assumption that some life activities in which a person feels a need or urge to participate, such as meditation or exercising, are positive even though they may possibly attain a level or a form of addiction. Positive addictions are considered healthy therapeutic alternatives relative to negative addictions, such as drug abuse, alcohol dependence, or cigarette smoking.

positive affect the internal feeling state (AFFECT) that occurs when a goal has been attained, a source of threat has been avoided, or the individual is satisfied with the present state of affairs. The tendency to experience such states is called **positive affectivity**.

positive attitude in psychotherapy, the client's feelings of self-approval or of acceptance and approval of the therapist or another person, object, or event. Compare NEGATIVE ATTITUDE.

positive discrimination see DISCRIMINATION.

positive discriminative stimulus (symbol: S+) a stimulus associated with a contingency of POSITIVE REINFORCEMENT.

positive emotion an emotional reaction designed to express a POSITIVE AFFECT, such as happiness when one attains a goal, relief when a danger has been avoided, or contentment when one is satisfied with the present state of affairs. Compare NEGATIVE EMOTION.

positive family history a family history that shows the characteristics sufficient for the family to be considered to have a genetic syndrome or inherited disease. The Amsterdam criteria, for example, are the criteria by which a family history of colon cancer is evaluated to determine whether the family has hereditary nonpolyposis colorectal cancer (HNPCC) or familial adenomatous polyposis (FAP).

positive feedback 1. an arrangement whereby some of the output of a system, whether mechanical or biological, is fed back to increase the effect of input signals. Positive feedback is rare in biological systems. See FEEDBACK SYSTEM. **2.** acceptance, approval, affirmation, or praise received by a person in response to his or her performance. Compare NEGATIVE FEEDBACK.

positive hit rate 1. the number of instances in which the choice of a particular alternative proved correct divided by the total number of instances in which that alternative was chosen. **2.** in personnel selection, the proportion of people hired who actually succeed on the job.

positive illusion a belief about oneself that is pleasant or positive and that is held regardless of its truth. The most common positive illusions involve exaggerating one's good traits (see BENEFFECTANCE), overestimating one's degree of control over personally important events (**illusion of control**), and sustaining unrealistic optimism (see REPRESSIVE COPING STYLE).

positive interdependence a relationship in which the success of one party increases the likelihood of another party's success and one party's failure increases the likelihood that others will fail. This type of interdependence tends to elicit cooperative, conflict-free interactions. Also called **promotive interdependence**.

positive psychology a field of psychological theory and research that focuses on the psychological states (e.g., contentment, joy), individual traits or CHARACTER STRENGTHS (e.g., intimacy, integrity, altruism, wisdom), and social institutions that make life most worth living. A manual, *Character Strengths and Virtues: A Handbook and Classification*, serves this perspective in a manner parallel to the DSM–IV–TR for the categorization of mental illness.

positive punishment punishment that results because some stimulus or circumstance is presented as a consequence of a response. For example, if a response results in presentation of a loud noise and the response becomes less likely as a result of this experience, then positive punishment has occurred. Compare NEGATIVE PUNISHMENT.

positive regard 1. a parent's warm, caring, accepting feelings for a child. Positive regard is considered necessary for the child to develop a consistent sense of self-worth. **2.** the therapist's feelings for the client as a unique individual whom he or she cares for and values. See also CONDITIONAL POSITIVE REGARD; UNCONDITIONAL POSITIVE REGARD.

positive reinforcement 1. an increase in the probability of occurrence of some activity because that activity results in the presentation of a stimulus or of some circumstance. **2.** the procedure of presenting a positive reinforcer after a response. See REINFORCEMENT. Compare NEGATIVE REINFORCEMENT.

positive schizophrenia a form of schizophrenia in which POSITIVE SYMPTOMS predominate, as evidenced in the person's bizarre behavior, illogical speech or writing, or expression of hallucinations and delusions. Although more dramatically evident than NEGATIVE SCHIZO-

PHRENIA, the positive aspect is usually less challenging to treat.

positive stereotype a stereotype that purports to describe the admirable, desirable, or beneficial qualities and characteristics of the members of a particular group or social category. Although stereotypes about other groups are often negative, generalizations about one's own groups tend to be positive. Compare NEGATIVE STEREOTYPE.

positive symptom a symptom of schizophrenia that represents an excess or distortion of normal function, as distinct from a deficiency in or lack of normal function (compare NEGATIVE SYMPTOM). Positive symptoms include delusions or hallucinations, disorganized behavior, and manifest conceptual disorganization. Positive symptoms are more dramatic than negative symptoms and are less distinctive of schizophrenia. See POSITIVE SCHIZOPHRENIA.

positive transfer 1. the improvement or enhancement of present learning by previous learning. For instance, learning to program a videocassette recorder could facilitate learning to program a digital telephone. See also TRANSFER OF TRAINING. Compare NEGATIVE TRANSFER. **2.** see LANGUAGE TRANSFER.

positive transference in psychoanalytic theory, DISPLACEMENT onto the therapist of feelings of attachment, love, idealization, or other positive emotions that were originally experienced toward the parents or other significant individuals. Compare NEGATIVE TRANSFERENCE. See TRANSFERENCE.

positivism *n.* a family of philosophical positions holding that all meaningful propositions must be reducible to sensory experience and observation, and thus that all genuine knowledge is to be built on strict adherence to empirical methods of verification. Positivism first became an explicit position in the work of French thinkers Auguste Comte (1798–1857) and Claude Henri de Rouvroy, Comte de Saint-Simon (1760–1825), although it is implicit to varying degrees in most earlier forms of EMPIRICISM. Its effect is to establish science as the model for all forms of valid inquiry and to dismiss the truth claims of religion, metaphysics, and speculative philosophy. Positivism, particularly LOGICAL POSITIVISM, was extremely influential in the early development of psychology and helped to form its commitment to empirical methods. It continues to be a major force in contemporary psychology. —**positivist** *adj.*

positron emission tomography (**PET**) a technique used to evaluate cerebral metabolism using radiolabeled tracers, such as 2-deoxyglucose labeled with fluorine-18, which emit positrons as they are metabolized. This technique enables documentation of functional changes that occur during the performance of mental activities.

postcentral area a sensory region of the PARIETAL LOBE of the brain, posterior to the CENTRAL

SULCUS, that has neurons involved in the perception of touch, proprioception, kinesthesis, and taste.

postcentral gyrus a ridge in the PARIETAL LOBE of the brain, just behind the CENTRAL SULCUS, that is the site of the PRIMARY SOMATOSENSORY AREA.

postcognition *n.* in parapsychology, the experiencing of a past event as if it were occurring in the present. In a test of postcognition, the participant would be asked to guess the outcome of an earlier set of trials involving ZENER CARDS or similar stimulus materials. Compare PRECOGNITION. —**postcognitive** *adj.*

postconcussion syndrome persistent, pervasive changes in cognitive abilities and emotional functioning that occur as a result of diffuse trauma to the brain during concussion. An individual with this syndrome may appear to be within normal limits neurologically but suffers from persistent depression, fatigue, impulse-control problems, and difficulties with concentration and memory. Postconcussion syndrome is frequently seen in individuals who have been repeatedly beaten on the head and face, such as battered children or women (see BATTERED-CHILD SYNDROME; BATTERED-WOMAN SYNDROME).

postconventional level in KOHLBERG'S THEORY OF MORAL DEVELOPMENT, the third and highest level of moral reasoning, characterized by an individual's commitment to moral principles sustained independently of any identification with family, group, or country. This level is divided into two stages: the earlier **social contract orientation** (Stage 5), in which moral behavior is that which demonstrates an understanding of social mutuality, balancing general individual rights with public welfare and democratically agreed upon societal rights; and the later **ethical principle orientation** (Stage 6), in which moral behavior is based upon self-chosen, abstract ethical standards. Also called **postconventional morality**. See also CONVENTIONAL LEVEL; PRECONVENTIONAL LEVEL.

postemployment services 1. in VOCATIONAL REHABILITATION, follow-up assistance or programs designed to help recently employed individuals with disabilities adjust to their new job situation. Examples include counseling, financial support, and continuing medical treatment and care. **2.** training and services provided to help individuals who are economically disadvantaged (e.g., those receiving public assistance in the form of welfare) obtain employment, develop various work-related skills essential to sustained long-term employment, and enhance their potential for wage increases and career advancement. Such services may include access to and assistance with child care and transportation; flexible work hours; on-the-job training; continuing education classes; and mentoring

programs designed to help newly hired individuals adjust to the workplace.

posterior *adj.* in back of or toward the back. In reference to two-legged upright animals, this term sometimes is used interchangeably with DORSAL to mean toward the bottom or tail. Compare ANTERIOR.

posterior commissure see COMMISSURE.

posterior cortex in neuroanatomy, the OCCIPITAL CORTEX of mammals, including the STRIATE CORTEX (Brodmann area 17) and PRESTRIATE CORTEX (area 18).

posterior distribution in Bayesian analysis, the estimated distribution of the parameters of interest obtained by combining empirical data with one's prior expectation of the probable values of the parameters in question.

posterior horn 1. the backmost division of each lateral VENTRICLE in the brain. **2.** see DORSAL HORN.

posterior root see DORSAL ROOT.

postfigurative culture a society or culture in which the young learn chiefly from their parents, grandparents, and other adults. Compare COFIGURATIVE CULTURE; PREFIGURATIVE CULTURE.

postformal thought the complex ways in which adults structure their thinking based on the complicated nature of adult life. It develops as an extension of the FORMAL OPERATIONAL STAGE, which according to PIAGETIAN THEORY occurs in adolescence, to encompass adult cognition and includes an understanding of the relative, nonabsolute nature of knowledge; an acceptance of contradiction as a basic aspect of reality; the ability to synthesize contradictory thoughts, feelings, and experiences into more coherent, all-encompassing wholes; and the ability to resolve both ill- and well-defined problems.

post hoc comparison a comparison among two or more means in ANALYSIS OF VARIANCE or MULTIPLE REGRESSION analysis that is formulated after the data have been examined. Also called **post hoc contrast**. Compare PLANNED COMPARISON.

post hoc fallacy in statistics and experimental design, the erroneous inference that because B followed A (in a temporal sense), A caused B.

posthypnotic amnesia an individual's incapacity to remember what transpired during a hypnotic trance. Typically, the participant is instructed to forget the hypnotic experience until receiving a prearranged cue from the hypnotist; at that point, memory of the experience returns. However, highly susceptible individuals may show spontaneous posthypnotic amnesia.

posthypnotic suggestion a suggestion made to a person under hypnosis and acted upon after awakening from the hypnotic trance. Usually, the act is carried out in response to a prearranged

P

cue from the hypnotist, and the participant does not know why he or she is performing the act.

postictal *adj.* following a sudden attack, especially a seizure or a stroke. During the **postictal period** following a seizure, the individual may be confused, disoriented, and unable to form new memories. The length of the postictal period may vary from less than a second to many hours and depends on the type of seizure.

postmodernism *n.* a number of related philosophical tendencies that developed in reaction to classical MODERNISM during the late 20th century. Most postmodern positions reject traditional metaphysics for its pursuit of a reality independent of the world of lived experience, traditional epistemology for its pursuit of certain knowledge and objectivity, and traditional ethical theories because of their reliance on metaphysics and epistemology. More specifically, they see the ideal of objective truth that has been a guiding principle in the sciences and most other disciplines since the 17th century as basically flawed: There can be no such truth, only a plurality of "narratives" and "perspectives." Postmodernism emphasizes the construction of knowledge and truth through discourse and lived experience, the similar construction of the self, and RELATIVISM in all questions of value. It is therefore a form of radical skepticism. See also POSTSTRUCTURALISM. —**postmodern** *adj.*

postpartum depression a MAJOR DEPRESSIVE EPISODE or, less commonly, MINOR DEPRESSIVE DISORDER that affects women within 4 weeks after childbirth.

postpositivism *n.* **1.** the general position of U.S. psychology since the mid-20th century, when it ceased to be dominated by LOGICAL POSITIVISM, HYPOTHETICO-DEDUCTIVE METHODS, and OPERATIONISM. Postpositivistic psychology is a broader and more human endeavor, influenced by such developments as SOCIAL CONSTRUCTIONISM and the Continental tradition of PHENOMENOLOGY and EXISTENTIALISM. **2.** more generally, any approach to science and the philosophy of science that has moved away from a position of strict POSITIVISM. See also POSTMODERNISM. —**postpositivist** *adj., n.* —**postpositivistic** *adj.*

postreinforcement pause in operant conditioning, the period of time that elapses from the end of REINFORCEMENT until the next response from the class that is being reinforced.

postschizophrenic depression a depressive episode that may follow an acute schizophrenic episode. Postschizophrenic depression is viewed variously as a routine event in recovery from schizophrenic decompensation, as a mood disturbance that existed previously and was masked by the schizophrenic episode, or as a side effect to drug treatment for schizophrenia.

poststructuralism *n.* a broad intellectual movement that developed from French STRUCTURALISM in the late 1960s and 1970s. It is represented by the work of Jacques Derrida (1930–2004) in philosophy and criticism, Jacques Lacan (1901–1981) in philosophy and psychoanalysis, Michel Foucault (1926–1984) in the history of ideas, and Hélène Cixous (1937–) and Julia Kristeva (1941–) in feminist theory, among others. These thinkers share a starting point in the structuralist account of language given by Swiss linguist Ferdinand de Saussure (1857–1913), which holds that linguistic SIGNS acquire meaning only through structural relationships with other signs in the same language system. Poststructuralism endorses the arbitrariness of the sign, but from this basis proceeds to question the whole idea of fixed and determinate meaning. In the DECONSTRUCTION of Derrida, structures and systems of meaning are found to be unstable, contradictory, and endlessly self-subverting. This skepticism extends to the idea of personal identity itself; according to Derrida, the self is merely another "text" to be deconstructed.

In psychology, poststructuralism is mainly significant because of its influence on the radical psychoanalytical theories of the 1960s and 1970s. Lacan, who trained and practiced as a psychiatrist, rejected the idea of a stable autonomous EGO and reinterpreted the Freudian UNCONSCIOUS in terms of Saussure's structural linguistics. His unconventional ideas and methods led to his exclusion from the International Society of Psychoanalysts in 1963. Both Kristeva (another practicing psychoanalyst) and Cixous were deeply influenced by Lacan's ideas of sexuality, consciousness, and language, which are given a radical feminist twist in their writings. —**poststructuralist** *adj.*

postsynaptic *adj.* **1.** of or relating to the region of a neuron within a SYNAPSE that receives and responds to a neurotransmitter. **2.** of or relating to a neuron that receives a signal via a synapse. Compare PRESYNAPTIC.

postsynaptic potential (**PSP**) the electric potential at a dendrite or other surface of a neuron after an impulse has reached it across a SYNAPSE. Postsynaptic potentials may be either EXCITATORY POSTSYNAPTIC POTENTIALS or INHIBITORY POSTSYNAPTIC POTENTIALS.

postsynaptic receptor any receptor that is located on the cell membrane or in the interior of a postsynaptic neuron. Interaction with an effector substance (e.g., a neurotransmitter), released either by the presynaptic neuron or from another site, initiates a chain of biochemical events contributing, for example, to excitation or inhibition of the postsynaptic neuron.

posttest 1. *n.* a test administered after completion of the principal test or instruction program. It may be given in conjunction with a PRETEST to assess comprehension of the content and nature of the main test as well as its effectiveness as an assessment instrument. **2.** *n.* a test administered after the application of an intervention or control condition. **3.** *vb.* to administer a posttest.

posttest counseling a type of GENETIC COUNSELING that occurs during and after disclosure of genetic test results. Posttest counseling focuses on the individual's understanding of the meaning of the test result and of the options for SCREENING. Considerable attention is given to the psychological status of the individual and to assessing whether the individual needs further genetic or psychological services.

posttraumatic amnesia 1. a period of amnesia following a psychological trauma. The traumatic event may be forgotten (retrograde amnesia), or events following the trauma may be forgotten (anterograde amnesia). The period of forgetting may be continuous, or the person may experience vague, incomplete recollections of the traumatic event. **2.** a disturbance of memory for events that immediately follow a head injury.

posttraumatic disorders emotional or other disturbances whose symptoms appear after a patient has endured a traumatic experience. Common posttraumatic disorders include POSTTRAUMATIC STRESS DISORDER, ACUTE STRESS DISORDER, the DISSOCIATIVE DISORDERS, and some types of PHOBIAS and ANXIETY DISORDERS.

posttraumatic epilepsy epileptic seizures that occur as a complication of traumatic brain injury. The seizures may occur either soon after the injury or, in some cases, months or years later.

posttraumatic personality disorder a personality disorder occasionally observed after a severe head injury. Some patients become indifferent and withdrawn, but most are irritable, impulsive, petulant, extremely selfish, and irresponsible. Older patients and those suffering from frontal-lobe damage may show impaired memory with CONFABULATION. See also POSTCONCUSSION SYNDROME.

posttraumatic stress disorder (**PTSD**) a disorder that results when an individual lives through or witnesses an event in which he or she believes that there is a threat to life or physical integrity and safety and experiences fear, terror, or helplessness. The symptoms are characterized by (a) reexperiencing the trauma in painful recollections, flashbacks, or recurrent dreams or nightmares; (b) diminished responsiveness (emotional anesthesia or numbing), with disinterest in significant activities and with feelings of detachment and estrangement from others; and (c) chronic physiological arousal, leading to such symptoms as exaggerated startle response, disturbed sleep, difficulty in concentrating or remembering, guilt about surviving when others did not (see SURVIVOR GUILT), and avoidance of activities that call the traumatic event to mind. When the symptoms do not last longer than 4 weeks a diagnosis of ACUTE STRESS DISORDER is given instead.

postulate *n.* see AXIOM.

postural aftereffect a change in posture that arises as an aftereffect of prior stimulation. For example, when viewing a moving scene, a person typically leans in the direction of the motion. When viewing ends, body posture returns to a vertical position and then, briefly, leans in the opposite direction.

posturing *n.* the assumption of a bizarre or inappropriate body position or attitude for an extended period of time. It is commonly observed in CATATONIA.

potency *n.* **1.** the ability of a male to perform sexual intercourse, that is, to maintain an erection and achieve ejaculation. Compare IMPOTENCE. **2.** in pharmacology, see DOSE–RESPONSE RELATIONSHIP. —**potent** *adj.*

potential *n.* **1.** the capacity to develop or come into existence. **2.** electric potential, measured in volts: a property of an electric field equal to the energy needed to bring unit electric charge from infinity to a given point. The potential difference between two points is the driving force that causes a current to flow. Because messages in the nervous system are conveyed by electrochemical potentials, many kinds of potential are of importance in neuroscience and biological psychology, including the ACTION POTENTIAL, GRADED POTENTIAL, MEMBRANE POTENTIAL, POSTSYNAPTIC POTENTIAL, and RESTING POTENTIAL.

potentiation *n.* a form of DRUG INTERACTION in which the addition of a second drug intensifies certain properties of the first drug administered. It often refers to the ability of a nontoxic drug to render the effects of a toxic drug more severe than when the toxic agent is administered singly.

Pötzl phenomenon (**Poetzl phenomenon**) the phenomenon whereby words or pictures that are presented subliminally may appear in imagery or dreams a short time later. It is taken as an example of SUBLIMINAL PERCEPTION. [Otto Pötzl (1877–1962), Austrian neurologist and psychiatrist]

poverty of speech excessively brief speech with few elaborations that occurs in schizophrenia or occasionally in the context of a major depressive episode. It is distinct from **poverty of content of speech**, in which the quality of speech is diminished. Also called **laconic speech**.

POW abbreviation for PRISONER OF WAR.

power *n.* **1.** the capacity to influence others, even when they try to resist this influence. Social power derives from a number of sources: control over rewards and punishments; a right to require and demand obedience; others' identification with, attraction to, or respect for the powerholder; others' belief that the powerholder possesses superior skills and abilities; and the powerholder's access to and use of informational resources. **2.** in hypothesis testing, the probability that the NULL HYPOTHESIS will be rejected when the ALTERNATIVE HYPOTHESIS is true. In this case, it is likely that the experiment will be able to yield the results that the researcher expects because the alternative hypothesis typically expresses the belief of the researcher.

power function 1. a relationship in which the values for one variable vary as a function of another variable raised to a power. In mathematics, it is expressed by the equation $Y = aX^b$, where X and Y are the variables and a and b are numerical constants. Power functions have been used to characterize the scales relating perceived and physical intensity, as well as to characterize the relationship between response speed and practice. **2.** in HYPOTHESIS TESTING, a functional relationship between the power of a statistical test and one of the variables that affect power, such as sample size.

power law 1. the law stating that sensory magnitude grows as a POWER FUNCTION of stimulus magnitude. **2.** a generalization demonstrated by a LEARNING CURVE in which each increment in the performance variable (e.g., learning or memory) corresponds with a logarithmic increase in the practice variable. For instance, if the successive units of practice are 1 trial, 10 trials, 100 trials, the resulting learning curve is a straight line.

power test a type of test intended to calculate the participant's level of mastery of a particular topic under conditions of little or no time pressure. The test is designed so that items become progressively more difficult. Compare SPEED TEST.

P-O-X triads see BALANCE THEORY.

PPVT abbreviation for PEABODY PICTURE VOCABULARY TEST.

PR abbreviation for progressive ratio. See PROGRESSIVE-RATIO SCHEDULE.

practical intelligence the ability to apply one's intelligence in practical, everyday situations. In the TRIARCHIC THEORY OF INTELLIGENCE it is the aspect of intelligence that requires adaptation to, shaping of, and selection of new environments. Compare ANALYTICAL INTELLIGENCE; CREATIVE INTELLIGENCE.

practice guidelines criteria and strategies designed to assist mental health clinicians and practitioners and physicians in the recognition and treatment of specific disorders and diseases, as well as for ethical practice. Such guidelines are often based on the latest and best available scientific research or the considered judgment of expert panel committees representing specific professions or subdisciplines. See also CLINICAL PRACTICE GUIDELINES.

practicum supervision a diversified and comprehensive training experience for students planning to become professional practitioners in a given field. Management of the on-site experience is provided by an instructor or other experienced practitioner.

Prader–Willi syndrome a congenital disorder marked by mental retardation, short stature, hypotonia (flaccid muscles), hypogonadism (underdeveloped sex organs), obesity, insensitivity to pain, and short hands and feet. Caused by an abnormality of chromosome 15, it is observed most frequently in males, perhaps because the gonadal abnormality is more easily detected in males. Affected individuals have an excessive appetite and are constantly foraging for food. When diabetes mellitus is associated with the condition, it is called **Royer's syndrome**. [reported in 1956 by Andrea **Prader** (1919–) and Heinrich **Willi** (1900–1971), with Alexis **Labhart** (1916–), Swiss pediatricians]

pragmatics *n.* the analysis of language in terms of its functional communicative properties (rather than its formal and structural properties, as in PHONOLOGY, SEMANTICS, and GRAMMAR) and in terms of the intentions and perspectives of its users. See also FUNCTIONAL GRAMMAR.

pragmatism *n.* a philosophical position holding that the truth value of a proposition or a theory is to be found in its practical consequences: If, for example, the hypothesis of God makes people virtuous and happy, then it may be considered true. Although some forms of pragmatism emphasize only the material consequences of an idea, more sophisticated positions, including that of U.S. psychologist William James (1842–1910), recognize conceptual and moral consequences. Arguably, all forms of pragmatism tend toward RELATIVISM, because they can provide no absolute grounds—only empirical grounds—for determining truth, and no basis for judging whether the consequences in question are to be considered good or bad. See also INSTRUMENTALISM. —**pragmatist** *adj.*, *n.*

Prägnanz *n.* one of the GESTALT PRINCIPLES OF ORGANIZATION. It states that people tend to perceive forms as the simplest and most meaningful, stable, and complete structures that conditions permit. Also called **law of Prägnanz**; **principle of Prägnanz**. [German: "terseness"]

praxis *n.* **1.** a medical name for **motor planning**, or the brain's ability to conceive, organize, and carry out a sequence of actions. Inadequate praxis is APRAXIA. **2.** practice, as opposed to theory. The term is sometimes used to denote knowledge derived from and expressed chiefly in practical or productive activity, as opposed to theoretical or conceptual knowledge.

prayer *n.* communication (voiced or contemplative) with a deity or other such entity, generally for the purposes of praise, thanksgiving, supplication, or self-examination or to seek forgiveness, guidance, or serenity. Psychological study of the behavior has yielded often contradictory results, so that prayer has been seen, on the one hand, as a defense or escape from the exploration of painful issues and as a form of magical thinking, or, on the other hand, as cognitively meaningful and therapeutically beneficial for those with specific religious beliefs or SPIRITUALITY. In appropriate circumstances, prayer may be explicitly used by some therapists as a component of intervention and treatment for such client-oriented goals as personal or interpersonal healing, forgiveness and the ability to forgive, and the ability to examine problems and issues freely and with discernment.

preadolescence *n.* the period of CHILDHOOD that precedes adolescence, comprising approximately the two years preceding the onset of puberty. Also called **prepubertal stage**; **prepuberty**; **prepubescence**. —**preadolescent** *adj., n.*

preattentive processing unconscious mental processing of a stimulus that occurs before attention has focused on this particular stimulus from among the array of those present in a given environment. An example of this is the disambiguation of the meaning of a particular word from among an array of words present in a given visual stimulus before conscious perception of the word. Also called **preattentive analysis**; **unconscious processing**. See also PARALLEL PROCESSING.

preaversive stimulus in conditioning, a stimulus that precedes the presentation of an aversive stimulus. See CONDITIONED SUPPRESSION; ESTES–SKINNER PROCEDURE.

precategorical acoustic storage a SENSORY MEMORY that momentarily retains auditory information before it is interpreted and comprehended: a theoretical explanation of the phenomenon of ECHOIC MEMORY. Precategorical acoustic storage is regarded as a parallel store to the visual system's ICONIC MEMORY.

precausal thinking the tendency of a young child (below the age of 8) to perceive natural events, such as rain, wind, and clouds, in terms of intentions and willful acts, that is, in anthropomorphic rather than mechanical terms. See also ANIMISM.

precedence effect 1. the effect of the brain in locating the source of a sound without being aware of reflected sounds from different locations. For example, if a sound is produced by a particular source and is then reflected off the walls, the listener only perceives the first source, provided that the sound from the second source arrives within a short period of time (less than 70 ms). **2.** the tendency for global features of a stimulus to dominate local features in performance tasks.

precentral gyrus a ridge in the FRONTAL LOBE of the brain, just in front of the CENTRAL SULCUS, that is crucial for motor control, being the site of the primary MOTOR CORTEX.

precipitating cause the particular factor, sometimes a traumatic or stressful experience, that is the immediate cause of a mental or physical disorder. A single precipitating event may turn a latent condition into the manifest form of the disorder. Compare PREDISPOSING CAUSE.

precision *n.* a measure of accuracy. In statistics, an estimate with a small STANDARD ERROR is regarded as having a high degree of precision. —**precise** *adj.*

preclinical psychopharmacology the area of psychopharmacology that precedes the actual clinical application of a new drug on an individual patient or patient population. It usually includes laboratory studies of the pharmacological mechanisms of the drug, extrapolation of research data into human-use terms, and evaluation of possible interactions with current drugs or in patients with various medical conditions.

precocial *adj.* describing animals that show a high degree of behavior development at birth or hatching. For example, young geese can follow their mother and forage for food a day after hatching, whereas other birds must be provisioned for several weeks before they leave the nest. In mammals, ungulates (e.g., cattle and sheep) are much more behaviorally advanced at birth than primates. Compare ALTRICIAL.

precocious puberty abnormally early development of sexual maturity, usually before the age of 8 in a female and 10 in a male. True precocious puberty is marked by mature gonads capable of ovulation or spermatogenesis, adult levels of female or male sex hormones, and secondary sexual characteristics. **Pseudoprecocious puberty** is a condition usually caused by an endocrine tumor that results only in premature development of secondary sex characteristics. Also called **pubertas praecox**.

precocity *n.* very early, often premature, development in a child of physical or mental functions and characteristics. —**precocious** *adj.*

precognition *n.* in parapsychology, the purported ability to see or experience future events through some form of EXTRASENSORY PERCEPTION. In a test of precognition, the participant would be asked to predict the outcome of a future set of trials involving ZENER CARDS or similar stimulus materials. Compare POSTCOGNITION. —**precognitive** *adj.*

preconscious (Pcs) 1. *n.* in the classical psychoanalytic theory of Austrian psychiatrist Sigmund Freud (1856–1939), the level of the psyche that contains thoughts, feelings, and impulses not presently in awareness, but which can be more or less readily called into consciousness. Examples are the face of a friend, a verbal cliché, or the memory of a recent event. Compare CONSCIOUS; UNCONSCIOUS. **2.** *adj.* denoting or relating to thoughts, feelings, and impulses at this level of the psyche. Also called **foreconscious**.

preconventional level in KOHLBERG'S THEORY OF MORAL DEVELOPMENT, the first level of moral reasoning, characterized by the child's evaluation of actions in terms of material consequences. This level is divided into two stages: the earlier **punishment and obedience orientation** (Stage 1), in which moral behavior is that which avoids punishment; and the later **naive hedonism** (or **instrumental relativist**) **orientation**, (Stage 2), in which moral behavior is that which obtains reward or serves one's needs. Also called **preconventional morality**. See also CONVENTIONAL LEVEL; POSTCONVENTIONAL LEVEL.

precue *n.* a piece of advance information available from the environment (in experimental situations, manipulated by the experimenter) giving partial details that can be used to constrain planning for an upcoming movement. Studies of how precues reduce the time necessary for motor planning once the full movement specification is made available have been an important tool in discerning the structure of motor plans.

precursor *n.* in biochemistry, a compound from which another is formed by a chemical reaction. For example, TYROSINE is a precursor of the catecholamine neurotransmitters (e.g., norepinephrine, dopamine).

predation *n.* the act or practice of stalking, capturing, and killing other animals for food. **Prey choice** can be broad or highly specific, and some species store captured prey for future use. Captured prey may be shared with young or other group members and may not be consumed exclusively by the successful predator.

predatory behavior behavior in which one animal stalks, attacks, and kills another. Predatory behavior has been described in terms of foraging and eating, but some animals will hunt and kill others without eating the prey. A cat, for example, may hunt and kill a mouse but refrain from eating it.

prediction *n.* **1.** an attempt to foretell what will happen in a particular case, generally on the basis of past instances or accepted principles. A **theoretical prediction** gives the expected results of an experiment or controlled observation in accordance with the logic of a particular theory. In science, the use of prediction and observation to test hypotheses is a cornerstone of the empirical method (see FALSIFIABILITY). However, by their very nature, the theories, constructs, and explanatory models current in psychology are not always open to direct validation or falsification in this way. In psychological assessment, personality tests and other psychometric instruments can often predict participants' behaviors or other characteristics with an impressive level of accuracy. In psychiatry, it may be possible to predict the general behavior or prognosis of patients whose personality pattern is known but not their specific behavior, since so many factors are involved. See also PROBABILISM. **2.** in parapsychology, see DIVINATION; PRECOGNITION. —**predict** *vb.* —**predictable** *adj.* —**predictive** *adj.*

predictive validity an index of how well a test correlates with a variable that is measured in the future, at some point after the test has been administered. For example, the predictive validity of a test designed to predict the onset of a disease would be calculated by the extent to which it was successful at identifying those individuals who did, in fact, later develop that disease.

predictor variable see INDEPENDENT VARIABLE.

predisposing cause a factor that increases the probability that a mental or physical disorder or hereditary characteristic will develop but is not the immediate cause of it. Compare PRECIPITATING CAUSE.

predisposition *n.* **1.** a susceptibility to developing a disorder or disease, the actual development of which is initiated by the interaction of certain biological, psychological, or environmental factors. **2.** in genetics, any hereditary factor that, given the necessary conditions, will lead to the development of a certain trait or disease. **Predisposition testing** is genetic testing for mutations that are less than 100% penetrant (see PENETRANCE). Thus, a positive test result indicates that the individual has an increased predisposition to develop the disease, but might not necessarily do so. If a mutation is fully penetrant, the testing is referred to as **predictive testing**, since all those who carry the mutated gene will develop the disease.

preexperimental design a research design in which there is no CONTROL GROUP and no random assignment of cases (participants) to experimental conditions (treatments). Such a design therefore is of minimal value in establishing causality.

preference *n.* **1.** in conditioning, the probability of occurrence of one of two or more concurrently available responses, usually expressed as either a relative frequency (compared to the frequency of all the measured responses) or a ratio. **2.** more generally, the act of choosing one alternative over others. —**preferential** *adj.*

preference for consistency a personality trait reflecting the extent to which a person desires to maintain consistency among elements in his or her cognitive system. See also COGNITIVE DISSONANCE.

preferential looking technique a method for assessing the perceptual capabilities of nonverbal human infants and animals. Infants will preferentially fixate a "more interesting" stimulus when it is presented at the same time as a "less interesting" stimulus, but only if the stimuli can be distinguished from one another. To minimize bias, on each trial the investigator is positioned so that he or she can observe the infant and make a judgment about which stimulus the infant fixates, but the stimuli themselves are visible only to the infant.

prefigurative culture a society or culture in which people typically learn from those younger than themselves. Because of the extremely rapid rate of social and technological change in the modern world, it has been proposed that contemporary Western society may be moving toward a prefigurative culture in which the young possess a keener intuition of the present than their elders. Compare COFIGURATIVE CULTURE; POSTFIGURATIVE CULTURE.

prefrontal cortex the most anterior (forward) part of the cerebral cortex of each FRONTAL LOBE in the brain. It functions in attention, planning, and memory and is divided into a dorsolateral region and an orbitofrontal region (see ORBITOFRONTAL CORTEX). Damage to the prefrontal cortex in humans leads to emotional, motor, and cognitive impairments. Also called **frontal association area**.

prefrontal lobe the furthest forward area of each CEREBRAL HEMISPHERE of the brain, which is concerned with such functions as memory and learning, emotion, and social behavior. See also FRONTAL LOBE.

prefrontal lobotomy see LOBOTOMY.

pregenital phase in psychoanalytic theory, the early stages of PSYCHOSEXUAL DEVELOPMENT that precede the organization of the LIBIDO around the genital zone (i.e., the ORAL STAGE and the ANAL STAGE). Some theorists also include the PHALLIC STAGE in the pregenital phase, whereas others use the term synonymously with the PREOEDIPAL phase.

pregnancy *n.* the state of a woman who is carrying a developing embryo, which normally lasts 266 days from conception until the birth of the baby (see PRENATAL PERIOD). Embryonic development normally occurs within the uterus, but occasionally it may be extrauterine. Also called **fetation**; **gravidity**. See also PSEUDOCYESIS.

prejudice *n.* **1.** a negative attitude toward another person or group formed in advance of any experience with that person or group. Prejudices include an affective component (emotions that range from mild nervousness to hatred), a cognitive component (assumptions and beliefs about groups, including STEREOTYPES), and a behavioral component (negative behaviors, including DISCRIMINATION and violence). They tend to be resistant to change because they distort the prejudiced individual's perception of information pertaining to the group. Prejudice based on racial grouping is RACISM; prejudice based on sex is SEXISM. **2.** any preconceived attitude or view, whether favorable or unfavorable.

prelinguistic *adj.* denoting or relating to the period of an infant's life before it has acquired the power of speech. The **prelinguistic period** includes the earliest infant vocalizations as well as the babbling stage typical of the second half of the first year. HOLOPHRASES usually emerge around the time of the child's first birthday.

Premack's principle the view that the opportunity to engage in behavior with a relatively high BASELINE probability will reinforce behavior of lower baseline probability. For example, a hungry rat may have a high probability of eating but a lower probability of pressing a lever. Making the opportunity to eat depend on pressing the lever will result in reinforcement of lever pressing. Also called **Premack's rule**. [David Premack (1925–), U.S. psychologist]

premature ejaculation a sexual dysfunction in which EJACULATION occurs with minimal sexual stimulation, before, on, or shortly after penetration or simply earlier than desired. The diagnosis takes into account such factors as age, novelty of the sexual partner, and the frequency and duration of intercourse. The diagnosis does not apply if the disturbance is due to the direct effect of a substance (e.g., withdrawal from opioids).

prematurity *n.* a state of underdevelopment, as in the birth of an offspring before it has completed the normal fetal processes of development. Premature (preterm) babies have low birth weight and are at risk for such complications as respiratory distress syndrome and jaundice. See also PRENATAL STRESS.

premenstrual dysphoric disorder a MOOD DISORDER in women that begins in the week prior to the onset of menstruation and subsides within the first few days of menstruation. Women experience emotional mood swings, including markedly depressed mood, anxiety, feelings of helplessness, and decreased interest in activities. In contrast to PREMENSTRUAL SYNDROME, the symptoms must be severe enough to impair functioning in social activities, work, and relationships. The symptoms of premenstrual dysphoric disorder are of comparable severity to those experienced in MINOR DEPRESSIVE DISORDER. Also called **premenstrual stress syndrome**.

premenstrual syndrome (**PMS**) a collection of psychological and physical symptoms experienced by women during the week prior to the onset of menstruation and subsiding within the first few days of menstruation. Symptoms can include mood swings, irritability, fatigue, headache, bloating, abdominal discomfort, and breast tenderness. In contrast to the more severe PREMENSTRUAL DYSPHORIC DISORDER, premenstrual syndrome has a less distinctive pattern of symptoms and does not involve major impairment in social and occupational functioning. Also called **premenstrual stress syndrome**.

premise *n.* a proposition forming part of a larger argument: a statement from which a further statement is to be deduced, especially as one of a series of such steps leading to a CONCLUSION.

premoral stage 1. in the theory of moral development proposed by Swiss child psychologist Jean Piaget (1896–1980), the stage at which young children (under the age of 5) are unaware of rules as cooperative agreements, that is, they are unable to distinguish right from wrong. Compare AUTONOMOUS STAGE; HETERONOMOUS STAGE. **2.** the stage that precedes the PRE-

CONVENTIONAL LEVEL in KOHLBERG'S THEORY OF MORAL DEVELOPMENT and corresponds to infancy (birth to roughly 18 months).

premorbid *adj.* characterizing an individual's condition before the onset of a disease or disorder. —**premorbidity** *n.*

premorbid personality 1. personality traits that existed before a physical injury or other traumatic event or before the development of a disease or disorder. **2.** personality strengths and weaknesses that predispose the individual toward mental health and well-being or to a particular mental disorder (e.g., depression or schizophrenia) or that affect the speed or likelihood of recovery from a disorder. Also called **primary personality**.

premotor area an area of the MOTOR CORTEX concerned with motor planning. In contrast to the SUPPLEMENTARY MOTOR AREA, input to the premotor area is primarily visual, and its activity is usually triggered by external events. Also called **Brodmann's area 6**; **intermediate precentral area**; **premotor cortex**.

premotor theory of attention a theory proposing that attention is a consequence of the mechanisms that generate actions or motor responses. It is based on neurophysiological evidence that space is coded in several cortical circuits that have specific motor purposes. Those circuits that represent space for programming eye movements are considered to play the primary role in spatial attention. Preparing to move the eyes to a specific location increases the readiness to act in that region of space and facilitates the processing of stimuli located in that region.

prenatal masculinization the masculinizing effects of ANDROGENS on fetal sexual anatomy and on neural pathways in the brain prior to birth.

prenatal period the developmental period between conception and birth, in humans commonly divided into the germinal stage (approximately the first two weeks), the embryonic stage (the following six weeks), and the fetal stage (from two months to birth).

prenatal stress stress in a pregnant woman, which is marked by elevation of stress hormones and other biological changes, with an increased likelihood of intrauterine infection. Preterm births and low birth weight are among the most widely recognized effects of maternal stress during pregnancy. Women who experience high levels of psychological stress are significantly more likely to deliver preterm. Preterm babies are susceptible to a range of complications, including chronic lung disease. Some recent studies suggest that stress in the womb can also affect a baby's temperament and neurobehavioral development: Infants whose mothers experienced high levels of stress while pregnant, particularly in the first trimester, show signs of increased depression and irritability.

preoccupation *n.* a state of being self-absorbed

and "lost in thought," which ranges from transient absent-mindedness to a symptom of schizophrenia in which the individual withdraws from external reality and turns inward upon the self. Also called **preoccupation with thought**.

preoccupied attachment an adult attachment style that combines a negative INTERNAL WORKING MODEL OF ATTACHMENT of oneself, characterized by doubt in one's own competence and efficacy, and a positive internal working model of attachment of others, characterized by one's trust in the ability and dependability of others. Individuals with preoccupied attachment are presumed to seek others' help when distressed. Compare DISMISSIVE ATTACHMENT; FEARFUL ATTACHMENT; SECURE ATTACHMENT.

preoedipal *adj.* **1.** in psychoanalytic theory, pertaining to the first stages of PSYCHOSEXUAL DEVELOPMENT, before the development of the OEDIPUS COMPLEX during the PHALLIC STAGE. During this phase the mother is the exclusive love object of both sexes and the father is not yet considered either a rival or a love object. **2.** more generally, denoting organization or functions before the onset of the Oedipus complex. See also PREPHALLIC.

preoperational stage in PIAGETIAN THEORY, the second major period of cognitive development, approximately between the ages of 2 and 7, when the child becomes able to record experience in a symbolic fashion and to represent an object, event, or feeling in speech, movement, drawing, and the like. During the later 2 years of the preoperational stage, egocentrism diminishes noticeably with the emerging ability to adopt the point of view of others. Also called **symbolic stage**. See also CONCRETE OPERATIONAL STAGE; FORMAL OPERATIONAL STAGE; SENSORIMOTOR STAGE.

preoptic area a region of the HYPOTHALAMUS lying above and slightly anterior to the OPTIC CHIASM. Nuclei here are involved in temperature regulation and in the release of HYPOTHALAMIC HORMONES.

preparatory set a special alertness or preparedness to respond in a particular manner to an expected stimulus, action, or event. A preparatory set may be manifested physically, as with a tennis player preparing to receive a serve, or experienced mentally, as with a chess player anticipating an opponent's next move. See MENTAL SET; PERCEPTUAL SET; SET.

prepared learning a species-specific and innate tendency to quickly learn a certain type of knowledge. Some associations between stimuli, responses, and reinforcers may be more easily formed than CONTRAPREPARED associations, due to biological PREPAREDNESS. For example, animals may be prepared to associate new foods with illness, and it has been suggested that humans learn certain phobias more readily due to preparedness.

preparedness *n.* a genetically influenced predisposition for certain stimuli to be more effective than others in eliciting particular responses. For example, flavors may be more effective as stimuli in establishing a CONDITIONED TASTE AVERSION than are colors of lights.

prephallic *adj.* in psychoanalytic theory, referring to the stages of PSYCHOSEXUAL DEVELOPMENT preceding the PHALLIC STAGE (i.e., the ORAL STAGE and the ANAL STAGE). See also PREGENITAL PHASE; PREOEDIPAL.

pre–post design see BEFORE–AFTER DESIGN.

prepotent response a response that takes priority over other potential responses (e.g., a pain response).

prepuberty *n.* see PREADOLESCENCE.

prepulse inhibition diminution of a reflex response by presenting a weak stimulus just before the strong stimulus that elicits the response. For example, a loud noise can elicit a startle reaction, but presentation of a tone before the noise will diminish the startle reaction.

prepyriform area the olfactory PROJECTION AREA at the base of the temporal lobe of the brain.

presbycusis *n.* the gradual diminution of hearing acuity associated with aging.

presbyopia *n.* a normal, age-related change in vision due to decreased lens elasticity and accommodative ability, resulting in reduced ability to focus vision on near tasks (e.g., reading). Usually beginning in middle age, presbyopia is correctable with reading glasses or glasses with bifocal or trifocal lenses.

preschool program an educational curriculum for children who are below the required minimum age for participation in regular classroom work. Preschool programs for intellectually or emotionally challenged children are designed to develop social skills and provide stimulation at levels appropriate for each child.

prescription privilege the legal right to prescribe drugs and other medications necessary for the treatment of medical or mental health disorders.

prescriptive grammar an approach to grammar in which a series of rules is used to distinguish proper from improper usage and a standard version of the language is identified and promoted (see STANDARD LANGUAGE). It is often contrasted with **descriptive grammar**, in which the goal is to provide an accurate account of language use without specification as to correctness.

presenile dementia see DEMENTIA.

presenilin *n.* any member of a family of transmembrane proteins, mutations in which are associated with early-onset familial ALZHEIMER'S DISEASE.

presenility *n.* **1.** DEMENTIA that occurs prior to old age (typically, prior to age 65). **2.** the period of life immediately preceding dementia in old age.

presenting *n.* behavior in which a female animal turns its back toward a male and raises its posterior, which allows the male to mate. Presenting is also seen in subordinate animals directed toward dominant animals outside a mating context. LORDOSIS is a specific form of presenting seen in many rodents.

presenting symptom a symptom or problem that is offered by a client or a patient as the reason for seeking treatment. In psychotherapy, a client may present with depression, anxiety, panic, anger, chronic pain, or family or marital problems, for example; such symptoms may become the focus of treatment or may represent a different, underlying problem that is not recognized or regarded by the client as requiring help. Also called **presenting problem**.

prespeech development development of the earliest forms of perceptual experience, learning, and communication, which precedes actual speech and is necessary for its development. For example, babies attend to sound at birth and can differentiate the human voice from other sounds within the 1st month. Cross-cultural studies reveal that mothers routinely use techniques that help their infants acquire language; for example, they shorten their expressions, stress important words, simplify syntax, and speak in a higher register and with exaggerated distinctness. See BABBLING.

pressure *n.* in psychology, excessive or stressful demands, imagined or real, made on an individual by another individual or group to think, feel, or act in particular ways. The experience of pressure is often the source of cognitive and affective discomfort or disorder, as well as of maladaptive coping strategies, the correction of which may be a mediate or end goal in psychotherapy.

pressured speech accelerated and sometimes uncontrolled speech that often occurs in the context of a HYPOMANIC EPISODE or a MANIC EPISODE. Also called **pressure of speech**.

pressure of ideas a characteristic symptom of MANIA in which there is increased spontaneity and productivity of thought: Numerous, widely varied ideas arise quickly and pass through the mind rapidly. It is usually manifested as pressured speech or pressure of activity. Also called **thought pressure**.

pressure sense the sensation of stress or strain, compression, expansion, pull, or shear, usually caused by a force in the environment. Pressure receptors may interlock or overlap with pain receptors so that one sensation is accompanied by the other. The pressure sense is similar to the sensation of contact.

prestige *n.* the degree of respect, regard, and admiration afforded an individual by his or her peers or the whole community. Prestige derives from various sources, including success, achievement, rank, reputation, authority, illustriousness, or position within a social structure. **—prestigious** *adj.*

prestriate cortex visually responsive regions in the cerebral cortex outside the STRIATE COR-TEX. The prestriate cortex includes BRODMANN'S AREAS 18 and 19, as determined by CYTOARCHI-TECTURE, and additional areas in the temporal and parietal lobes. On the basis of function and connectivity, the prestriate cortex has been divided into multiple VISUAL AREAS, including V2, V4, and V5. Also called **extrastriate cortex**; **prestriate area**.

presynaptic *adj.* **1.** referring to the region of a neuron within a SYNAPSE that releases neurotransmitter. **2.** referring to a neuron that is transmitting a signal to one or more other neurons via its synapses. Compare POSTSYNAPTIC.

pretest 1. *n.* a preliminary test or trial run to familiarize the person or group tested with the content and nature of a particular test. It may be given in conjunction with a POSTTEST. **2.** *n.* a trial run administered before the application of an intervention or control condition. **3.** *vb.* to administer a pretest.

pretest counseling a type of GENETIC COUN-SELING undertaken before deciding whether to undergo genetic testing. Pretest counseling includes educating individuals about the contribution of genetics to the etiology of disease, taking a family history and creating a PEDIGREE, estimating risk, and discussing the risks, benefits, and limitations of genetic testing.

pretest–posttest design see BEFORE–AFTER DESIGN.

pretest sensitization the extent to which the administration of a PRETEST affects the subsequent responses of the participant to experimental treatments.

prevalence *n.* the total number of cases (e.g., of a disease or disorder) existing in a given population at a given time (**point prevalence**) or during a specified period (**period prevalence**). See also INCIDENCE.

prevention *n.* behavioral, biological, or social interventions intended to reduce the risk of disorders, diseases, or social problems for both individuals and entire populations. See PRIMARY PREVENTION; SECONDARY PREVENTION; TER-TIARY PREVENTION.

prevention design in ergonomics, the design of tools or systems so as to reduce the possibility of human error. See ENGINEERING CONTROLS.

preventive care care that aims to prevent disease or its consequences, emphasizing early detection and early treatment of conditions and generally including routine physical examination, immunizations, and well-person care. See also PREVENTION; PRIMARY PREVENTION.

preverbal *adj.* before the acquisition of language. Preverbal children communicate using nonword sounds and gestures.

pride *n.* a SELF-CONSCIOUS EMOTION that occurs when a goal has been attained and one's achievement has been recognized and approved by others. It differs from JOY and HAPPINESS in that these emotions do not require the approval of others for their existence. Pride can become antisocial if the sense of accomplishment is not deserved or the reaction is excessive. **—proud** *adj.*

primacy effect the tendency for facts, impressions, or items that are presented first to be better learned or remembered than material presented later in the sequence. This can occur in both formal learning situations and social contexts. For example, it can result in a **first-impression bias**, in which the first information gained about a person has an inordinate influence on later impressions and evaluations of that person. Also called **law of primacy**. Compare RECENCY EFFECT.

primal anxiety in psychoanalytic theory, the most basic form of anxiety, first experienced when the infant is separated from the mother at birth and suddenly has to cope with the flood of new stimuli. See also BIRTH TRAUMA; PRIMAL TRAUMA.

primal scene in psychoanalytic theory, the child's first observation, in reality or fantasy, of parental intercourse or seduction, which is interpreted by the child as an act of violence.

primal trauma in psychoanalytic theory, a painful situation to which an individual was subjected in early life that is presumed to be the basis of a neurosis in later life. The primal trauma is considered by some in psychoanalysis to be the BIRTH TRAUMA. See also PRIMAL ANXIETY.

primary abilities the unitary factors proposed in the early 20th century to be essential components of intelligence. There are seven primary abilities: VERBAL ABILITY (V), WORD FLUENCY (WF), NUMERICAL ABILITY (N), SPATIAL INTELLI-GENCE (S), MEMORY (M), perceptual speed (P), and REASONING (R). These factors are measured by the **Primary Mental Abilities Test**. Also called **primary mental abilities**.

primary aging changes associated with normal aging that are inevitable and caused by intrinsic biological or genetic factors. Examples include the appearance of gray hair and skin wrinkles. However, some age-related diseases have genetic influences, making the distinction between primary aging and SECONDARY AGING imprecise.

primary anxiety in psychoanalytic theory, anxiety experienced as a spontaneous response to trauma or in response to dissolution of the EGO. Also called **automatic anxiety**. Compare SIGNAL ANXIETY.

primary appraisal in the COGNITIVE AP-PRAISAL THEORY of emotions, evaluation of the relevance of an event to one's goals, one's moral norms, and one's personal preferences. It is followed by SECONDARY APPRAISAL. See also CORE RELATIONAL THEMES.

P

primary behavior disorder any of various behavior problems in children and adolescents, including habit disturbances (e.g., nail biting, temper tantrums), bed-wetting, conduct disorders (e.g., vandalism, fire setting, alcohol or drug use, sex offenses, stealing), and school-centered difficulties (e.g., truancy, school phobia, disruptive behavior).

primary care the basic or general health care a patient receives when he or she first seeks assistance from a health care system. General practitioners, family practitioners, internists, obstetricians, and pediatricians are known as **primary care providers (PCPs)**. Also called **primary health care**. Compare SECONDARY CARE; TERTIARY CARE.

primary care psychology a specialty discipline within health, clinical, and counseling psychology that involves providing psychological preventive and treatment services under the auspices of medical professionals in such settings as clinics, hospitals, and private practices, either on site or on a consultation basis.

primary cause a condition or event that predisposes an individual to a particular disorder, which probably would not have occurred in the absence of that condition or event. Sexual contact, for example, is a common primary cause of a sexually transmitted disease.

primary circular reaction in PIAGETIAN THEORY, a type of repetitive action that represents the earliest nonreflexive infantile behavior. For example, in the first months of life, a hungry baby may repeatedly attempt to put a hand in the mouth. This does not result in effective goal-oriented behavior, but it does indicate a primitive link between goal (easing hunger) and action (attempting to suck on the hand). Primary circular reactions develop in the SENSORIMOTOR STAGE, following the activation of such reflexes as sucking, swallowing, crying, and moving the arms and legs. See also SECONDARY CIRCULAR REACTION; TERTIARY CIRCULAR REACTION.

primary coping a type of COPING STRATEGY that enhances one's sense of control over environmental circumstances and oneself. Primary coping includes actions directed toward changing stressors (i.e., objective events or environmental conditions). Also called **primary control coping**. Compare SECONDARY COPING.

primary cortex any of the regions of the CEREBRAL CORTEX that receive the main input from sensory receptors or send the main output to muscles. Examples are primary MOTOR CORTEX, primary visual cortex (see STRIATE CORTEX), PRIMARY TASTE CORTEX, and the PRIMARY SOMATOSENSORY AREA. The primary motor cortex has a lower threshold for elicitation of motor responses than do adjacent motor cortical regions. Most neurons in primary sensory regions have more direct sensory input than do neurons in adjacent sensory cortical regions.

primary drive an innate DRIVE, which may be universal or species-specific, that is created by deprivation of a needed substance (e.g., food) or the need to engage in a specific activity (e.g., nest building in birds). Compare SECONDARY DRIVE.

primary emotion any one of a limited set of emotions that typically are manifested and recognized universally across cultures. They include FEAR, ANGER, JOY, SADNESS, DISGUST, CONTEMPT, and SURPRISE; some theorists also include SHAME, SHYNESS, and GUILT. Also called **basic emotion**. Compare SECONDARY EMOTION.

primary empathy an approach to CLIENT-CENTERED THERAPY in which the therapist actively tries to experience the client's situation as the client has and then tries to restate the client's thoughts, feelings, and experiences from the client's point of view.

primary gains in psychoanalytic theory, the basic psychological benefits derived from possessing neurotic symptoms, essentially relief from anxiety generated by conflicting impulses or threatening experiences. Also called **paranosic gains**. Compare SECONDARY GAINS.

primary group any of the small, long-term groups characterized by face-to-face interaction and high levels of COHESION, solidarity, and GROUP IDENTIFICATION. These groups are primary in the sense that they are the initial socializers of the individual members, providing them with the foundation for attitudes, values, and a social orientation. Families, partnerships, and long-term psychotherapy groups are examples of such groups. Compare SECONDARY GROUP.

primary hypersomnia a sleep disorder characterized by excessive sleepiness (evidenced by prolonged episodes of sleep, daytime episodes of sleep on an almost daily basis, or both), the severity and persistence of which cause clinically significant distress or impairment in functioning. The disorder is not caused by a general medical condition and is not an aspect of another sleep disorder or mental disorder. See DYSSOMNIA. See also DISORDERS OF EXCESSIVE SOMNOLENCE. Compare PRIMARY INSOMNIA.

primary identification in psychoanalytic theory, the first and most basic form of IDENTIFICATION, which occurs during the ORAL STAGE of development when the infant experiences the mother as part of himself or herself. After weaning, the infant begins to differentiate between the self and external reality and then becomes capable of SECONDARY IDENTIFICATION.

primary insomnia a sleep disorder characterized by difficulty in initiating or maintaining a restorative sleep to a degree in which the severity and persistence of the sleep disturbance causes clinically significant distress, impairment in a significant area of functioning, or both. The dis-

P

order is not caused by a general medical condition or the effects of a substance and is not exclusively an aspect of another sleep disorder or mental disorder. See DYSSOMNIA. See also INSOMNIA. Compare PRIMARY HYPERSOMNIA.

primary masochism in psychoanalytic theory, the portion of the DEATH INSTINCT or AGGRESSIVE INSTINCT that is directed toward the self after the LIBIDO has absorbed it emotionally and directed a large portion of it toward the external world.

primary memory (**PM**) memory that retains a few items for only several seconds, in contrast to SECONDARY MEMORY. The term was used in DUAL-STORE MODELS OF MEMORY before being replaced by SHORT-TERM MEMORY.

primary motor cortex see MOTOR CORTEX.

primary narcissism in psychoanalytic theory, the earliest type of NARCISSISM, in which the infant's LIBIDO is directed toward his or her own body and its satisfaction rather than toward the environment or OBJECTS. At this stage the child forms a narcissistic EGO-IDEAL stemming from his or her sense of OMNIPOTENCE.

primary need an innate need that arises out of biological processes and leads to physical satisfaction, for example, the need for water and sleep. See also PHYSIOLOGICAL NEED; VISCEROGENIC NEED.

primary odor in various theories of odor perception, any of a number of posited odor qualities that somehow combine to produce the perception of an odor. See CROCKER–HENDERSON ODOR SYSTEM; HENNING'S ODOR PRISM; ZWAARDEMAKER SMELL SYSTEM.

primary prevention research and programs, designed for and directed to nonclinical populations or populations at risk, that seek to promote and lay a firm foundation for mental, behavioral, or physical health so that psychological disorders, illness, or disease will not develop. Compare SECONDARY PREVENTION; TERTIARY PREVENTION.

primary process in psychoanalytic theory, unconscious mental activity in which there is free, uninhibited flow of PSYCHIC ENERGY from one idea to another. Such thinking operates without regard for logic or reality, is dominated by the PLEASURE PRINCIPLE, and provides hallucinatory fulfillment of wishes. Examples are the dreams, fantasies, and magical thinking of young children. These processes are posited to predominate in the ID.

primary quality in the philosophy of English empiricist philosopher John Locke (1632–1704), a sensible quality of an object that is a physical property, or the result of a physical property, of the object itself, such as weight, size, or motion. Locke contrasted such properties with so-called SECONDARY QUALITIES, such as color, taste, and smell.

primary reinforcement 1. in OPERANT CONDITIONING, the process in which presentation of a stimulus or circumstance following a response increases the future probability of that response, without the need for special experience with the stimulus or circumstance. That is, the stimulus or circumstance, known as an **unconditioned primary reinforcer**, functions as effective REINFORCEMENT without any special experience or training. **2.** the contingent occurrence of such a stimulus or circumstance after a response. Also called **unconditioned reinforcement**. See also CONDITIONED REINFORCER.

primary repression in psychoanalytic theory, the first phase of REPRESSION, in which ideas associated with instinctual wishes are screened out and prevented from becoming conscious. Primary repression contrasts with REPRESSION PROPER, in which the repressed material has already been in the realm of consciousness. Also called **primal repression**.

primary sensory area any area within the NEOCORTEX of the brain that acts to receive sensory input—for most senses, from the thalamus. The primary sensory area for hearing is in the temporal lobe, for vision in the occipital lobe (see STRIATE CORTEX), and for touch and taste in the parietal lobe (see PRIMARY SOMATOSENSORY AREA; PRIMARY TASTE CORTEX). Compare SECONDARY SENSORY AREA.

primary somatosensory area (**S1**) an area of the cerebral cortex, located in a ridge of the anterior PARIETAL LOBE just posterior to the CENTRAL SULCUS, where the first stage of cortical processing of tactile information takes place (see SOMATOSENSORY AREA). It receives input from the ventroposterior nuclear complex of the thalamus and projects to other areas of the parietal cortex. See also SECONDARY SOMATOSENSORY AREA.

primary symptoms 1. see FUNDAMENTAL SYMPTOMS. **2.** symptoms that are a direct result of a disorder and essential for its diagnosis. **3.** symptoms that appear in the initial stage of a disorder. Compare SECONDARY SYMPTOMS.

primary taste any of certain qualities posited as being basic to the entire sense of TASTE, in that all taste sensations are composed of them. The number of proposed primary tastes has ranged historically from 2 to 11, but sweet, salty, sour, and bitter, now joined by umami (the earthy or savory taste associated with meats, fish, mushrooms, etc.), are the most widely accepted. However, the evidence that primary tastes exist is not definitive.

primary taste cortex the area of cerebral cortex that is the first cortical relay for taste. Located along the sharp bend that includes the frontal operculum laterally and the anterior INSULA medially, it receives taste, touch, visceral, and other sensory inputs from the thalamus and permits an integrated evaluation of a chemical. Its output goes to regions that control oral and visceral reflexes in response to foods. See SECONDARY TASTE CORTEX.

primary thought disorder a disturbance of cognition, observed primarily in schizophrenia, characterized by incoherent and irrelevant intellectual functions and peculiar language patterns (including bizarre syntax, NEOLOGISMS, and WORD SALAD). See SCHIZOPHRENIC THINKING.

primary visual cortex see STRIATE CORTEX.

primary visual system the major visual pathway in primates, in which processing of visual information is done by the FOVEA CENTRALIS, enabling careful analysis of stimulus properties. Signals pass from the retina to the OPTIC NERVE, OPTIC TRACT, lateral GENICULATE NUCLEUS, and OPTIC RADIATIONS, terminating in the STRIATE CORTEX. It is the phylogenetically more recent visual system and functions poorly in newborns. Compare SECONDARY VISUAL SYSTEM.

primate *n.* a member of the Primates, an order of mammals that includes the lemurs, monkeys, apes, and humans. Characteristics of the order include an opposable thumb (i.e., a thumb capable of touching other digits), a relatively large brain, and binocular vision. The young are usually born singly and mature over an extended period.

priming *n.* **1.** in cognitive psychology, the effect in which recent experience of a stimulus facilitates or inhibits later processing of the same or a similar stimulus. In REPETITION PRIMING, presentation of a particular sensory stimulus increases the likelihood that participants will identify the same or a similar stimulus later in the test. In SEMANTIC PRIMING, presentation of a word or sign influences the way in which participants interpret a subsequent word or sign. **2.** in animal behavior, the ability of a PHEROMONE to gradually alter the behavior of another member of the same species. —**prime** *vb.*

primitive *adj.* **1.** belonging to the earliest stages of the development of something, such as a language, a species, or a technology. **2.** describing a society or culture that is preliterate, economically and technologically undeveloped, and appears to be characterized by relatively simple forms of social organization. The term is now generally avoided by social scientists, as it implies acceptance of the discredited view that all societies pass through the same stages of development and that certain cultural practices belong to an "earlier" stage of human evolution. Note also that technologically undeveloped societies may be highly developed in other respects, having complex religious and kinship systems. See also MODERNIZATION; TRADITIONALISM.

primitive defense mechanism in psychoanalytic theory, any DEFENSE MECHANISM that protects against anxiety associated with the DEATH INSTINCT. Primitive defense mechanisms include DENIAL, SPLITTING, PROJECTION, and IDEALIZATION.

primitivization *n.* in psychoanalytic theory, the REGRESSION of higher EGO functions, such as objective thinking, reality testing, and purposeful behavior, with a return to primitive stages of development characterized by magical thinking (e.g., wish-fulfilling fantasies and hallucinations), helplessness, and emotional dependence. Primitivization occurs primarily in traumatic neuroses, in which higher functions are blocked by the overwhelming task of meeting the emergency, and in advanced schizophrenia, in which the ego breaks down and PSYCHIC ENERGY is withdrawn from external reality and concentrated on a narcissistic fantasy life.

principal component analysis a statistical technique in which the interrelationship among many correlated variables can be completely reproduced by a smaller number of new variables (called principal components) that are mutually orthogonal and ordered in terms of the percentage of the total system variance for which they account. Often, most of the total variance can be captured in the first few principal components. This technique is similar in its aims to FACTOR ANALYSIS but has different technical features.

principle of closure see CLOSURE.

principle of common fate see COMMON FATE.

principle of constancy in psychoanalytic theory, the idea that all mental processes tend toward a state of equilibrium and the stability of the inorganic state. Also called **constancy law**; **law of constancy**. See also DEATH INSTINCT; PRINCIPLE OF INERTIA.

principle of continuity see GOOD CONTINUATION.

principle of distributed repetitions the concept that better learning occurs when repetitions of the material are spread out or distributed in time rather than being massed together. See DISTRIBUTED PRACTICE.

principle of good continuation see GOOD CONTINUATION.

principle of good shape see GOOD SHAPE.

principle of inclusiveness see INCLUSIVENESS.

principle of inertia in psychoanalytic theory, the tendency of the organism to expend minimum energy by preferring unconscious automatic actions to conscious ones. This principle is posited to be the mechanism that underlies the REPETITION COMPULSION and is one type of ID RESISTANCE. Also called **inertia principle**. See also DEATH INSTINCT.

principle of optimal stimulation the theory that organisms tend to learn those responses that lead to an optimal or preferred level of stimulation or excitation. Also called **optimal stimulation principle**.

principle of Prägnanz see PRÄGNANZ.

principle of similarity see SIMILARITY.

prion disease any of a group of fatal neuro-

P

degenerative diseases (e.g., CREUTZFELDT–JAKOB
DISEASE) caused by self-replicating abnormal
prion proteins (i.e., aberrant counterparts of normal cellular protein) in the brain. Symptoms
include gait disturbance, lack of coordination,
muscle tremors and jerks, and difficulty in swallowing. Prion diseases are also known as **spongiform encephalopathies** because of the post-
mortem appearance of the brain.

prisoner of war (**POW**) a person held captive
by an enemy during a war. Personality disturbances can occur in individuals subjected to the
physical and psychological strains of a POW experience. The reactions vary greatly from individual to individual but can include (a)
depression due to loss of freedom and identity;
(b) personality changes, such as sullen withdrawal and suspiciousness; (c) inertia and loss of
interest due to confinement and debilitating
conditions; (d) the effects of coercive persuasion,
particularly if BRAINWASHING is involved; (e)
loss of ego strength; and (f) occasionally, death.

privacy *n.* **1.** the state in which an individual's or
a group's desired level of social interaction is not
exceeded. **2.** the right to control (psychologically and physically) others' access to one's personal world, for example by regulating others'
input through use of physical or other barriers
(e.g., doors, partitions) and by regulating one's
own output in the form of communication with
others. **3.** the right of patients and others (e.g.,
consumers) to control the amount and disposition of the information they divulge about
themselves. See PRIVILEGED COMMUNICATION.
—**private** *adj.*

private practice **1.** the practice of a medical or
mental health care professional who operates as
a self-employed individual. **2.** in the United
Kingdom, any medical practice outside the National Health Service.

private self the part of the SELF that is known
mainly to oneself, such as one's inner feelings
and SELF-CONCEPT. The private self is distinguished from the PUBLIC SELF and the COLLEC-
TIVE SELF.

privilege *n.* the legal right of an individual to
confidentiality of personal information obtained by a professional in the course of their relationship, as between a patient and a health
care professional during the course of treatment
or diagnosis. See PRIVILEGED COMMUNICATION.

privileged communication confidential information, especially as provided by an individual to a professional in the course of their
relationship, that may not be divulged to a third
party without the knowledge and consent of
that individual. This protection applies to communications not only between patients and
physicians, clinical psychologists, psychiatrists,
or other health care professionals, but also between clients and attorneys, confessors and
priests, and spouses.

proactive aggression see AGGRESSION.

proactive interference see INTERFERENCE.

probabilism *n.* **1.** in psychology and other empirical sciences, the concept that events or sequences of events can be predicted with a high,
though not perfect, degree of probability and validity on the basis of rational and empirical data.
In statistical hypothesis testing associated with
empirical research, probabilism is fundamental
to the practice of attaching a probability to the
truth or falsity of the NULL HYPOTHESIS. See also
STOCHASTIC. **2.** in ethical theory, the notion
that when solutions to ethical questions are unclear, one should follow the course with the
greatest estimated probability of being ethically
correct. Evidence of a high probability of being
correct can be found in agreement among persons of respected moral judgment. —**probabil-
ist** *adj.* —**probabilistic** *adj.*

probabilistic functionalism **1.** a theory of
perception proposing that environmental cues
are at best approximate indices of the objects
they refer to, that organisms select the cues that
are most useful for responding, and that the veracity of perceptions should therefore be considered probabilistic rather than certain. **2.** the view
that behavior is best understood in terms of its
probable success in attaining goals.

probability (symbol: *p*) *n.* the degree to which
an event is likely to occur. —**probabilistic** *adj.*

probability distribution a curve that specifies, by the areas below it, the probability that a
random variable occurs at a particular point. The
best known example is the bell-shaped NORMAL
DISTRIBUTION; others include CHI-SQUARE DIS-
TRIBUTION, Student's T DISTRIBUTION, and F DIS-
TRIBUTION.

probability sample a sample chosen from a
population in such a way that the likelihood of
each unit in the population being selected is
known in advance of the sampling. See RANDOM
SAMPLING.

probabilogical model a theory of attitude
and belief structure postulating that BELIEFS can
be viewed as interlinked networks of syllogisms.
These networks of syllogisms have vertical structure in that a syllogism containing two beliefs
(i.e., the premises) can logically imply a third belief (i.e., the conclusion). They have horizontal
structure in that the conclusion for one syllogism can serve as the conclusion for other syllogisms.

proband *n.* the family member whose possible
genetic disease or disorder forms the center of
the investigation into the extent of the illness in
the family. He or she is the person around whom
a PEDIGREE is drawn and from whom the information about other family members is obtained.
Also called **index case**.

probing *n.* in psychotherapy, the use of direct
questions intended to stimulate additional discussion, in the hope of uncovering relevant information or helping the client come to a

particular realization or achieve a particular insight.

probit analysis a form of REGRESSION ANALYSIS for a dichotomous dependent variable. In this model an observable independent variable is thought to affect a latent continuous variable that determines the probability that a dichotomous event will occur.

problem checklist a type of self-report scale listing various personal, social, educational, or vocational problems. The participant indicates the items that apply to his or her situation.

problem-focused coping a type of COPING STRATEGY that is directed toward decreasing or eliminating stressors, for example, by generating possible solutions to a problem. The coping actions may be directed at the self, the environment, or both. Also called **active coping**. See also PRIMARY COPING. Compare EMOTION-FOCUSED COPING.

problems in living concrete problems with which patients with chronic mental illness (e.g., schizophrenia) frequently struggle (e.g., inability to keep a job or a place of residence), which are believed to be the most useful next focus of treatment after symptoms stabilize with medication. Problems in living are often addressed in day treatment or in aftercare following hospitalization.

problem solving the process by which individuals attempt to overcome difficulties, achieve plans that move them from a starting situation to a desired goal, or reach conclusions through the use of higher mental functions, such as reasoning and CREATIVE THINKING. In laboratory studies, many animals display problem-solving strategies, such as the WIN–STAY, LOSE–SHIFT STRATEGY, which allows an animal to solve a new problem quickly, based on whether the first response was successful or unsuccessful. In terms of CONDITIONING, problem solving involves engaging in behavior that results in the production of DISCRIMINATIVE STIMULI in situations involving new CONTINGENCIES.

procedural learning the process of acquiring skill at a task, particularly a task that eventually can be performed automatically (i.e., without attention), as opposed to acquiring FACTUAL KNOWLEDGE about it.

procedural memory long-term memory for the skills involved in particular tasks. Procedural memory is demonstrated by skilled performance and is often separate from the ability to verbalize this knowledge (see DECLARATIVE MEMORY). Knowing how to type or skate, for example, requires procedural memory. Also called **sensorimotor memory**.

proceptivity *n.* the period during MATING BEHAVIOR when females actively solicit males for copulation. Proceptivity is distinguished from the more passive RECEPTIVITY to indicate the female's active role in mating.

process consultation an ORGANIZATIONAL DEVELOPMENT intervention in which work groups are observed by a consultant, who provides feedback on how to improve the effectiveness with which members work together.

process experiential psychotherapy an approach to psychotherapy that focuses on the client's moment-to-moment experience and guides the client's cognitive and affective processing in the direction of client-defined goals. The THERAPEUTIC ALLIANCE, internal patterns of viewing the self and others, and an emphasis on therapeutic process over content are core elements of this therapy. See also CLIENT-CENTERED THERAPY; GESTALT THERAPY; HUMANISTIC THERAPY.

processing-efficiency theory a theory that attempts to explain the relationship between anxiety and performance. It suggests that (a) anxiety increases worry and takes part of the attentional resources, and (b) the worry created serves a monitoring function by identifying the task as important, so that the individual increases the effort, which overcomes the depleted attentional capacity (see CAPACITY MODEL).

process loss in the social psychology of groups, any action, operation, or dynamic that prevents the group from reaching its full potential, such as reduced effort (SOCIAL LOAFING), inadequate coordination of effort (COORDINATION LOSS), poor communication, or ineffective leadership. See also RINGELMANN EFFECT.

process–reactive *adj.* relating to a disease model of schizophrenia based on the distinction between gradual and acute onset of symptoms. PROCESS SCHIZOPHRENIA is marked by a long-term gradual deterioration before the disease is manifest, whereas REACTIVE SCHIZOPHRENIA is associated with a rapid onset of symptoms after a relatively normal premorbid period.

process research the study of various psychological mechanisms or processes of psychotherapy as they influence the outcome of treatment or the reactions that the therapist or client may have. A basic goal of such research is to identify therapeutic methods and processes that are most effective in bringing about positive change, as well as inadequacies and other limitations. See also PSYCHOTHERAPY RESEARCH.

process schizophrenia a form of schizophrenia that begins early in life, develops gradually, is believed to be due to endogenous (biological or physiological) rather than environmental factors, and has a poor prognosis. Psychosocial development before the onset of the disorder is poor; individuals are withdrawn, socially inadequate, and indulge in excessive fantasies. This term is often used interchangeably with NUCLEAR SCHIZOPHRENIA. Compare REACTIVE SCHIZOPHRENIA.

process study any investigation undertaken to assess the mechanisms and variables that contribute to and influence the outcome of a partic-

P

ular activity. For example, a process study of GROUP PSYCHOTHERAPY sessions may seek to determine characteristics of the therapeutic interaction that are associated with positive, neutral, or negative changes individually and across the group. See also PROCESS RESEARCH.

process variable 1. an interpersonal, affective, cognitive, or behavioral factor that is operative during the course of psychotherapy or counseling and influences the progress or the course of behavior. **2.** any set of PSYCHOLOGICAL FACTORS that has an effect on the development or modification of a process over time.

Procrustes rotation a LINEAR TRANSFORMATION of the points represented in a MATRIX X to best conform, in a least-squares sense, to the points in a target matrix, Y. Usually the points in the target matrix represent some theoretical factor structure or the results of a FACTOR ANALYSIS on a different population. The name derives from the robber in Greek mythology who forced his victims to fit his bed by stretching them or cutting off their limbs.

prodigy *n.* an individual, typically a child, who displays unusual or exceptional talent or intelligence, quite often in a discrete area of expertise, such as mathematics, music, or chess. Even if naturally endowed with such exceptional abilities, prodigies still require the opportunity and dedication to train and develop their gifts. Prodigies do not always develop into accomplished adults: There appears to be an important transition between the two, and only a proportion of prodigies successfully negotiate this transition. See also GIFTEDNESS.

prodromal syndrome a set of traits, symptoms, or neurological deficits that may predispose an individual to developing a psychological or neurological disorder.

prodrome *n.* an early symptom or symptoms of a mental or physical disorder. A prodrome frequently serves as a warning or premonitory sign that may, in some cases, enable preventive measures to be taken. Examples are the AURAS that often precede epileptic seizures or migraine headaches and the headache, fatigue, dizziness, and insidious impairment of ability that often precede a stroke. Also called **prodromic phase**. —**prodromic** *adj.* —**prodromal** *adj.*

prodrug *n.* a drug that is either biologically inert or of limited activity until metabolized to a more active derivative.

production deficiency in problem solving, failure to find the right or best strategy for completing a task (even, sometimes, after successful instruction), as opposed to failure in implementing it. Compare MEDIATIONAL DEFICIENCY; UTILIZATION DEFICIENCY.

production system a rule-based computer program that makes decisions or solves problems. It operates according to a set of "if" (state)–"then" (action) rules, such that when a certain state occurs, an associated action is executed,

thus altering the state, which produces a new action, and so on. A production system consists of three components: (a) the set of "production memory," represented as sets of "if–then" rules; (b) the "working memory," which contains information related to the present state of the problem solving, represented as patterns to be submitted to the production memory; and (c) a control regime that takes the patterns (representing the current state of the problem solving) from working memory to the set of production rules. When a production rule matches this pattern, it "fires" and produces a new pattern (reflecting the new state of the problem solving), which is then placed in working memory. This cycle continues until no patterns in working memory match the production rules. The production system approach is used as a COGNITIVE ARCHITECTURE by many researchers in cognitive science.

productive orientation in psychoanalytic theory, a personality pattern in which the individual is able to develop and apply his or her potentialities without being unduly dependent on outside control. Such an individual is highly active in feeling, thinking, and relating to others, and at the same time retains the separateness and integrity of his or her own self.

productive vocabulary an individual's vocabulary as defined by the words that he or she regularly uses, as opposed to those that he or she can understand when used by others. Also called **active vocabulary**; **working vocabulary**. Compare RECEPTIVE VOCABULARY.

productivity *n.* **1.** the relationship between the quantity or quality of output (goods created or services provided) and the input (time, materials, etc.) required to create it. **2.** the capacity to produce goods and services having exchange value. VOCATIONAL REHABILITATION programs often use the productivity of people with disabilities as a major measure of the effectiveness of the programs. **3.** one of the three formal properties of language, consisting of the ability to combine individual words to produce an unlimited number of sentences. See SEMANTICITY.

product–moment correlation (symbol: r) a statistic that indexes the degree of linear relationship between two variables. Invented by British statistician Karl Pearson (1857–1936), it is often known as the **Pearson product–moment correlation**.

proecological behavior behavior that promotes the quality of the natural environment. Examples include recycling, efficient use of energy, use of mass transportation, and birth control. Among topics examined in the analysis of these behaviors are environmental attitudes, economic and political impediments, and sociodemographic factors. See also SOCIAL TRAP.

professional–client sexual relations a boundary violation (see BOUNDARY ISSUES) in which a health care professional engages in sexual relations with a patient under his or her care. See also PROFESSIONAL ETHICS.

professional development the continuing education or training that is often expected or required of people employed in a profession. Professional organizations often assist the professional development of their members by providing courses, conferences, literature, and other services. See also MANAGEMENT DEVELOPMENT.

professional ethics rules of acceptable conduct that members of a given profession are expected to follow. See BOUNDARY ISSUES; CODE OF ETHICS; ETHICS; PROFESSIONAL STANDARDS; STANDARDS OF PRACTICE.

professional licensing the imposition of state-regulated minimal standards for legal employment as a member of a given profession. Professional licensing usually consists of three parts: provisional certification, full certification, and recertification.

professional standards the levels of performance and conduct required or expected in a particular profession. See also CODE OF ETHICS; PROFESSIONAL ETHICS; STANDARDS OF PRACTICE.

profile analysis a MULTIVARIATE statistical technique that compares groups of individuals with regard both to the shape of their score profiles on several variables and to the values of their scores on those variables.

Profile of Mood States (**POMS**) a brief self-report instrument measuring six dimensions of transient and fluctuating mood states over time: tension or anxiety, depression or dejection, anger or hostility, vigor or activity, fatigue or inertia, and confusion or bewilderment. Participants indicate on a 5-point scale ranging from "not at all" to "extremely" whether each of the 65 adjectives (e.g., confused, spiteful, energetic, good-natured) listed is descriptive of themselves within the specified time frame. A mentally healthy profile on the POMS is known as the **iceberg profile**.

profiling n. **1.** see CRIMINAL PROFILING. **2.** in sport, an exercise in which athletes first identify the most important physical and mental components necessary for optimal performance and then assess the degree to which they possess each of these components at that time.

profound mental retardation a diagnostic category for those with IQs below 20, comprising about 1% of people with MENTAL RETARDATION. It is due to sensorimotor abnormalities as well as intellectual factors; typical developmental attainments include rudimentary speech and limited self-care, and affected individuals require lifelong, highly structured environments with constant aid and supervision.

progesterone n. a hormone, secreted mainly by the CORPUS LUTEUM in the ovary, that stimulates proliferation of the ENDOMETRIUM (lining) of the uterus required for implantation of an embryo. If implantation occurs, progesterone con-

tinues to be secreted—first by the corpus luteum and then by the placenta—maintaining the pregnant uterus and preventing further release of egg cells from the ovary. It also stimulates development of milk-secreting cells in the breasts.

progestogens pl. n. steroids that include the natural hormone PROGESTERONE and synthetic steroids (known as **progestins**) with physiological effects similar to those of progesterone. Progestins may be derived from progesterone or testosterone. While progesterone has an antiestrogenic action, progestins may have different effects, such as proestrogenic activity. They are used in oral contraceptives, HORMONE REPLACEMENT THERAPY, and medications for menstrual disorders.

prognosis n. in general medicine and mental health science, a prediction of the future course, duration, severity, and outcome of a condition, disease, or disorder. Prognosis may be given whether or not treatment is undertaken, in order to give the client an opportunity to weigh the benefits of different treatment options. —**prognostic** adj.

program evaluation a process of applying social research tools that contributes to decisions on installing, continuing, expanding, certifying, or modifying programs, depending on their effectiveness. Program evaluation is also used to obtain evidence to rally support for or opposition to a program and to contribute to basic knowledge in the social and behavioral sciences about social interventions and social experimentation.

Program for Learning in Accordance with Needs (**PLAN**) an individualized instructional system covering language arts, mathematics, science, and social studies in grades 1 through 12. It is based on learning objectives developed by the teacher and the student together. This system illustrated how programmed learning and, ultimately, computers could play an important and integral role in individualizing education.

programmed cell death the orderly death and disposal of surplus tissue cells, which occurs as part of tissue remodeling during development, or of worn-out and infected cells, which occurs throughout life. Also called **apoptosis**.

programmed instruction a learning technique, used for self-instruction and in academic and some applied settings, in which the material is presented in a series of sequential, graduated steps, or **frames**. The learner is required to make a response at each step: If the response is correct, it leads to the next step; if it is incorrect, it leads to further review. Also called **programmed learning**.

program monitoring the use of key indicators to measure program performance. The purposes and regularity of this activity vary widely and include PROCESS EVALUATION, information provided from management information systems, and performance measurement that assesses program outcomes. Typically, these methods do not assess the impact of the program.

progressive education a broad educational approach originally associated with the philosophy of U.S. educator and psychologist John Dewey (1859–1952). It emphasizes experimentalism as opposed to dogmatism in teaching, learning by doing, recognition of individual rates of learning, latitude in selecting areas of study according to interest, and a close relationship between academic learning and experience in the world outside the classroom.

progressive-interval schedule (**PI schedule**) in conditioning, an arrangement in which the presentation of each reinforcer is dependent on the first response that occurs after a fixed interval of time has passed, with this interval increasing after each reinforcement. For example, a progressive-interval schedule might begin with an interval of 30 s, which is then increased by 30 s after each subsequent reinforcement.

progressive-ratio schedule (**PR schedule**) in conditioning, an arrangememt in which each reinforcer is presented on the completion of a particular number of responses and the number of responses required increases after each reinforcement. Progressive-ratio schedules are often used to measure the effectiveness of reinforcers.

progressive relaxation a technique in which the individual is trained to relax the entire body by becoming aware of tensions in various muscle groups and then relaxing one muscle group at a time. In some cases, the individual consciously tenses specific muscles or muscle groups and then releases tension to achieve relaxation throughout the body. Also called **Jacobson relaxation method**. See also RELAXATION.

progressive supranuclear palsy a progressive neurological disorder usually starting in the 6th decade of life and characterized by OCULOMOTOR PALSY, with downward gaze particularly affected. The condition may be accompanied by PARKINSONISM, postural instability, speech and swallowing difficulties, DYSTONIA, personality changes, and typically mild cognitive impairment. Pathology often shows loss of neurons and GLIOSIS in various regions of the brainstem, basal ganglia, and midbrain. Also called **Steele–Richardson–Olszewski syndrome**; **supranuclear palsy**.

projection *n.* the process by which one attributes one's own individual positive or negative characteristics, affects, and impulses to another person or group. This is often a DEFENSE MECHANISM in which unpleasant or unacceptable impulses, stressors, ideas, affects, or responsibilities are attributed to others. For example, the defense mechanism of projection enables a person conflicted over expressing anger to change "I hate him" to "He hates me." Such defensive patterns are often used to justify prejudice or evade responsibility; in more severe cases, they may develop into paranoid delusions. In classical psychoanalytic theory, projection permits the individual to avoid seeing his or her own faults, but modern usage has largely abandoned the requirement that the projected trait remain unknown in the self. —**project** *vb.*

projection area an area of the CEREBRAL CORTEX that receives inputs from a particular sense organ. Each sense sends messages to two or more projection areas.

projection fiber a nerve fiber that carries impulses from the cerebral cortex to subcortical structures (e.g., the thalamus, hypothalamus, or basal ganglia).

projective identification 1. in psychoanalysis, a DEFENSE MECHANISM in which the individual projects qualities that are unacceptable to the self onto another individual and that person—through unconscious or conscious interpersonal pressure—internalizes the projected qualities and believes himself or herself to be characterized by them appropriately and justifiably. See PROJECTION. **2.** in the object relations theory of Austrian-born British psychoanalyst Melanie Klein (1882–1960), a defense mechanism in which a person fantasizes that part of his or her EGO is split off and projected into the OBJECT in order to control or harm it, thus allowing the individual to maintain a belief in his or her omnipotent control.

projective psychotherapy a treatment procedure in psychotherapy in which selected responses on various projective tests are fed back to the client, who associates with them in much the same way that psychoanalytic patients make FREE ASSOCIATIONS to dreams.

projective technique any personality assessment procedure that consists of a fixed series of relatively ambiguous stimuli designed to elicit unique, sometimes highly idiosyncratic, responses. Examples of this type of procedure are the RORSCHACH INKBLOT TEST, the THEMATIC APPERCEPTION TEST, and various sentence completion and word association tests. Projective techniques are quite controversial, with opinions ranging from the belief that personality assessment is incomplete without data from at least one or more of these procedures to the view that such techniques lack reliability and validity and that interpretations of personality organization and functioning derived from them are completely hypothetical and unscientific. Also called **projective method**.

project method a teaching structure in which students work alone or together to initiate, develop, and carry through learning projects with a minimal amount of direct guidance from the teacher.

promiscuity *n.* transient, casual sexual relations with a variety of partners. In humans, this type of behavior is generally regarded unfavorably; however, it has been argued that there can be healthy promiscuity in the simple enjoyment of casual, consensual, nonexploitative relationships. In bonobos (pygmy chimpanzees) sexual activity occurs frequently both between and within sexes in exchange for resources (e.g., food) or to calm tensions. In many species females appear to display promiscuity to prevent CERTAINTY OF PATERNITY but often mate with the most dominant or successful male at the time when conception is most likely. **—promiscuous** *adj.*

prompting *n.* in psychotherapy, suggesting or hinting at topics by the therapist to encourage the client to discuss certain issues. Prompting may include reminding the client of previously discussed material, tying previously discussed topics together, or finishing a sentence or thought for the client to aid in his or her understanding of an issue.

pronoun reversal a speech phenomenon observed in children with AUTISTIC DISORDER, in which the child refers to him- or herself in the second or third person (e.g., *you, him, she*) while identifying others by first-person pronouns (e.g., *me*). Also called **pronominal reversal**.

proof *n.* **1.** the establishment of a proposition or theory as true, or the method by which it is so established. There is much debate as to whether propositions or theories can ever be truly proven. In logic and philosophy, even a valid argument can be untrue if its first premise is false: *All trees are pines: I have a tree in my garden: Therefore my tree is a pine.* In empirical sciences such as psychology, both logical and methodological problems make it impossible to prove a theory or hypothesis true. Disciplines that rely on empirical science must settle for some type of PROBABILISM based on empirical support of its theories and hypotheses. See also FALSIFIABILITY. **2.** in mathematics and logic, a sequence of steps formally establishing the truth of a theorem or the validity of a proposition. **3.** in law, evidence that establishes and supports the truth of claims made by either party in a dispute. Only evidence presented at trial can constitute proof; the judge or jury must then decide whether such evidence constitutes adequate proof. In criminal cases the standard of proof required to obtain a conviction is proof **beyond reasonable doubt**.

propaedeutic *n.* **1.** introductory instruction provided by a teacher to a student before formal instruction of a full concept or idea begins. **2.** an introduction to any art or science.

propaganda *n.* a method of social control that attempts to strengthen or change the beliefs, attitudes, and actions of others by presenting highly biased information or sometimes disinformation (publicly announced or planted misinformation). It usually involves an appeal to emotion that is designed to win support for an idea or course of action or to belittle or disparage the ideas or programs of others.

prophylaxis *n.* the use of methods or procedures designed to avoid or prevent mental or physical disease or disorder. **—prophylactic** *adj., n.*

proportionality *n.* in statistics, a relationship between two variables in which one changes in constant ratio to another. Two variables are directly proportional (written $x \propto y$) if $x = ay$, where a is a constant. They are inversely proportional ($x \propto 1/y$) if $x = a/y$. The constant a is called the **constant of proportionality**.

propositional knowledge the abstract representation of knowledge, words, or images. Propositions are the smallest units of meaningful thought, and knowledge is represented as a series of propositional statements or as a network of interconnected propositions.

proprietary drug any chemical used for medicinal purposes that is formulated or manufactured under a name that is protected from competition by trademark or patent. The ingredients, however, may be components of generic drugs that have the same or similar effects.

propriety standards the legal and ethical requirements of an evaluation research study. These standards include having formal or written agreements between parties in the study, protecting the rights of participants, avoiding conflicts of interest by both program evaluators and participants, conducting complete and fair program assessments, fully reporting all findings, and maintaining fiscal soundness.

proprioception *n.* the sense of body movement and position, resulting from stimulation of specialized receptors called **proprioceptors** located in the muscles, tendons, and joints and of VESTIBULAR RECEPTORS in the labyrinth of the inner ear. Proprioception enables the body to determine its spatial orientation without visual clues and to maintain postural stability. **—proprioceptive** *adj.*

proprium *n.* a concept of the self, or that which is consistent, unique, and central in the individual, that was developed by U.S. psychologist Gordon W. Allport (1897–1967). According to Allport, the proprium incorporates body sense, self-identity, self-esteem, self-extension, rational thinking, self-image, and knowing.

prosencephalon *n.* see FOREBRAIN.

prosocial *adj.* denoting or exhibiting behavior that benefits one or more other people, such as providing assistance to an older adult crossing the street. Compare ANTISOCIAL.

prosody *n.* a phonological feature of speech, such as stress, intonation, intensity, or duration, that pertains to a sequence of PHONEMES rather than to an individual SEGMENT. See PARALANGUAGE; SUPRASEGMENTAL.

prosopagnosia *n.* see VISUAL AGNOSIA.

prospective memory remembering to do something in the future, such as taking one's medicine later. Prospective memory contrasts with **retrospective memory**, or remembering past events.

prospective research research that is planned before the data have been collected; that is, research that starts with the present and follows subjects forward in time, as in randomized experiments and in longitudinal research. Compare RETROSPECTIVE RESEARCH.

prospective sampling a SAMPLING method that selects cases on the basis of their exposure to a risk factor. Participants are then followed in order to see if the condition of interest develops. A study design using this method is referred to as a **prospective study**. See RETROSPECTIVE SAMPLING.

prospect theory a theory of decision making that attempts to explain how people's decisions are influenced by their attitudes toward risk, uncertainty, loss, and gain. In general, it finds that people are motivated more strongly by the fear of loss than the prospect of making the equivalent gain.

prostaglandin (**PG**) *n.* any of a group of chemically related substances that act as local hormones in animal tissue and cause a variety of physiological effects. There are several basic types, designated by capital letters with subscript numbers indicating the degree of saturation of fatty acid side chains (e.g., PGE_2, PGH_2). Among their many activities, they influence blood pressure, cause stimulation of smooth muscle, and promote inflammation.

prostate a gland in male mammals, walnut-sized in humans, that surrounds the urethra immediately beneath the urinary bladder. It secretes a thin, alkaline fluid that increases in volume during sexual stimulation and becomes part of SEMEN during ejaculation. **Prostate cancer**, which develops most frequently after the age of 50, is the second most common malignancy among U.S. males, with only lung cancers responsible for more deaths. It can be detected early by physical examination and blood tests and is treatable by a variety of means, including surgery, radiation, hormonal therapy, or chemotherapy.

prosthetics *n.* a medical specialization concerned with the design and construction of artificial body parts for individuals. Compare ORTHOTICS.

protanomaly *n.* a type of red color blindness in which the red-sensitive retinal cones do not function normally, although there is evidence that some red sensitivity is present.

protanopia *n.* red–green color blindness in which the deficiency is due to the absence of the core PHOTOPIGMENT sensitive to red light, resulting in red stimuli appearing very dim and confusion between red and green (see DICHROMATISM). The condition may be unilateral (i.e., color vision may be normal in one eye). See also DEUTERANOPIA.

protected relationships professional provider–client contacts that are subject to ethical standards regarding confidentiality of records and other information provided by the client, information about sessions, and the existence of the professional relationship itself.

protein *n.* a molecule that consists of a long-chain polymer of AMINO ACIDS. Proteins are involved in virtually every function performed by a cell; they are the principal building blocks of living organisms and, in the form of ENZYMES, the basic tools for construction, repair, and maintenance. Proteins play an essential role in human nutrition, including the provision of all of the essential amino acids that humans cannot produce themselves. See also PEPTIDE.

protein hormone any of a class of hormones that are PROTEINS. Examples are parathyroid hormone, prolactin, GROWTH HORMONE, and INSULIN.

protensity *n.* the temporal attribute (i.e., duration spread) of a mental process or of consciousness.

prothetic *adj.* describing a sensory dimension along which stimuli vary in degrees of magnitude or quantity, but not in quality. Compare METATHETIC.

protocol *n.* **1.** the original notes of a case, study, or experiment recorded during or immediately after a particular session or trial. **2.** a case history and work-up (patient evaluation). **3.** a treatment plan.

protolanguage *n.* a posited common ancestor of the members of a language family. Most protolanguages have been partially reconstructed using the COMPARATIVE METHOD among different members of a language family. The most celebrated protolanguage is Proto-Indo-European, the unrecorded prehistoric language that is presumed to be the ancestor of all Indo-European languages.

protopathic *adj.* denoting or relating to peripheral nerve fibers responsive to gross sensory stimulation, particularly pain, temperature extremes, and strong touch. Compare EPICRITIC.

prototype *n.* **1.** in the formation of concepts, the best or average exemplar of a category. For example, the prototypical bird is some kind of mental average of all the different kinds of birds of which a person has knowledge or with which a person has had experience. Also called **cognitive prototype**. **2.** more generally, an object, event, or person that is held to be typical of a category and comes to represent or stand for that category. **3.** an early model of something that represents or demonstrates its final form. —**prototypal**, **prototypical**, or **prototypic** *adj.*

prototype model a theory of CATEGORIZATION proposing that people form an average of the members of a category and then use the average as a PROTOTYPE for making judgments about category membership.

provider *n.* a health care professional or facility, such as a psychologist, psychiatrist, physician, hospital, or skilled nursing or intensive care facility, that provides health care services to patients.

provocative testing any type of testing in which symptoms of a condition are intentionally caused or reproduced in a patient or other person presenting for evaluation. This can be done in order to test the effectiveness of treatments for the condition, to rule in or rule out the possibility of a similar diagnosis, or, in the case of PSYCHOGENIC disorders, to test the veracity of the condition. For example, provocative testing has been used somewhat controversially in distinguishing NONEPILEPTIC SEIZURES from neurologically based epileptic seizures.

proxemics *n.* the study of interpersonal spatial behavior. Proxemics is concerned with TERRITORIALITY, interpersonal distance, spatial arrangements, CROWDING, and other aspects of the physical environment that affect behavior.

proximal *adj.* **1.** situated near or directed toward the trunk or center of an organism. **2.** near, or mostly closely related, to the point of reference or origin. Compare DISTAL. **—proximally** *adv.*

proximal stimulus the physical energy from a stimulus as it directly stimulates a sense organ or receptor, in contrast to the DISTAL STIMULUS in the actual environment. In reading, for example, the distal stimulus is the print on the page of a book, whereas the proximal stimulus is the light energy reflected by the print that stimulates the photoreceptors of the retina. Also called **proximal variable**.

proximate cause the most direct or immediate cause of an event. In a sequence of occurrences, it is the one that directly produces the effect. For example the proximate cause of Smith's aggression may be an insult, but the REMOTE CAUSE may be Smith's early childhood experiences. In law, proximate cause is important in liability cases where it must be determined whether the actions of the defendant are sufficiently related to the outcome to be considered causal, or if the action set in motion a chain of events that led to an outcome that could have been reasonably foreseen.

proximate explanation an explanation for behavior in terms of physiological mechanisms or developmental experiences, rather than in terms of the adaptive value of the behavior (see ULTIMATE EXPLANATION).

proximity *n.* one of the GESTALT PRINCIPLES OF ORGANIZATION. It states that people tend to organize objects close to each other into a perceptual group and interpret them as a single entity. Also called **law of proximity**; **principle of proximity**.

proximodistal development the progression of physical and motor development from the center of an organism toward the periphery. For example, children learn to control shoulder movements before they learn to control arm and finger movements.

proxy variable a variable, B, used in place of another, A, when B and A are substantially correlated but scores only on variable B are available, often because of the difficulty or costs involved in collecting data for variable A.

Prozac *n.* a trade name for FLUOXETINE.

PRP abbreviation for PSYCHOLOGICAL REFRACTORY PERIOD.

pruning *n.* in neural development, the loss of neurons and neural connections that are not used or are unnecessary, especially in children. Children are born with considerably more neural connections than necessary for adult functioning, which enables the fast rate of cognitive development in children.

pruritus *n.* itching that may result from physiological or psychological conditions. **—pruritic** *adj.*

pseudoangina *n.* **1.** chest pain that resembles the pain (angina pectoris) of a HEART ATTACK but for which there is no clinical evidence of heart disease. **2.** chest pain that resembles angina pectoris but originates from damage to the SPINAL ROOTS in the neck (cervical) region. Compression of the root of the seventh cervical nerve by a prolapsed intervertebral disk (slipped disk) is commonly identified as the cause. Also called **cervical angina**.

pseudocommunity *n.* a group of real or imagined persons believed, in a persecutory delusion, to be organized for the purpose of conspiring against, threatening, harassing, or otherwise negatively focusing upon one. Also called **paranoid pseudocommunity**.

pseudoconditioning *n.* in circumstances of PAVLOVIAN CONDITIONING, elicitation of a response by a previously neutral stimulus when it is presented following a series of occurrences of a conditioned stimulus. For example, after flinching in response to each of several presentations of electric shock, a person is likely to flinch if a loud tone is then presented.

pseudocyesis *n.* a condition in which a woman shows many or all of the usual signs of pregnancy when conception has not taken place. In some cases the condition is psychogenic, whereas in others it is due to a medical condition (e.g., a tumor or an endocrine disorder). Also called **false pregnancy**; **pseudopregnancy**.

pseudodementia *n.* deterioration or impairment of cognitive functions in the absence of neurological disorder or disease (compare DEMENTIA). The condition may occur, reversibly, in a MAJOR DEPRESSIVE EPISODE—particularly among older adults, in which case the preferred term is **dementia syndrome of depression**—or as a psychological symptom of FACTITIOUS DISORDER.

pseudogroup *n.* a group of participants in a research procedure who are led to believe that they are working on tasks as a group, whereas in fact they are working individually. This procedure is used to study the psychological impact of group membership.

pseudohermaphroditism *n.* a congenital abnormality in which the gonads (ovaries or testicles) are of one sex, but one or more contradictions exist in the morphological criteria of sex. In female pseudohermaphroditism, the individual is a genetic and gonadal female with partial masculinization, such as an enlarged clitoris resembling a penis and labia majora resembling a scrotum. In male pseudohermaphroditism, the individual is a genetic and gonadal male with incomplete masculinization, including a small penis, and a scrotum that lacks testes. —**pseudohermaphrodite** *n.*

pseudomemory *n.* a fake memory, such as a spurious recollection of events that never took place, as opposed to a memory that is merely inaccurate (see FALSE MEMORY). Pseudomemory is a cause of particular concern when using hypnosis to help eyewitnesses retrieve memories. See also CONFABULATION; RECOVERED MEMORY.

pseudoneurological *adj.* suggesting a neurological condition. The term is generally used in reference to SOMATIZATION DISORDER: According to DSM-IV-TR, at least one pseudoneurological symptom must be present in order to diagnose this disorder.

pseudopsychology *n.* an approach to understanding or analyzing the mind or behavior that utilizes unscientific or fraudulent methods. Examples include palmistry, PHRENOLOGY, and PHYSIOGNOMY. See also PARAPSYCHOLOGY. —**pseudopsychological** *adj.*

psi *n.* **1.** the Greek letter ψ, often used to symbolize psychology. **2.** the phenomena or alleged phenomena studied by PARAPSYCHOLOGY, including EXTRASENSORY PERCEPTION, PRECOGNITION, and PSYCHOKINESIS.

psi-hitting *n.* in parapsychology experiments, performance on a test that is significantly above chance expectations. Compare PSI-MISSING.

psilocin *n.* an indolealkylamine HALLUCINOGEN that is the principal psychoactive compound in "magic mushrooms" of the genus *Psilocybe*, which were used by the Aztecs for religious and ceremonial purposes. **Psilocybin**, first isolated in 1958, differs from psilocin only in having an additional phosphate group; it is rapidly metabolized in the body and converted to psilocin. Like other indolealkylamine hallucinogens (e.g., LSD), psilocin is active at various SEROTONIN RECEPTORS: Agonism at $5-HT_{1A}$ and $5-HT_{2A}$ receptors in the cerebral cortex of the brain appears to be responsible for the psychoactive effects of these drugs.

psi-missing *n.* in parapsychology experiments, performance on a test that is significantly below chance expectations. Compare PSI-HITTING.

PSP abbreviation for POSTSYNAPTIC POTENTIAL.

psyche *n.* in psychology, the mind in its totality, as distinguished from the physical organism. The term, which earlier had come to refer to the soul or the very essence of life, derives from the character of Psyche in Greek mythology, a beautiful princess who, at the behest of her divine lover, Eros, son of Aphrodite, is made immortal by Zeus.

psychedelic drugs a name for HALLUCINOGENS (from Greek, literally: "mind-manifesting"), proposed in 1956 by Humphry Osmond (1917–2004), friend of British writer Aldous Huxley, in response to Huxley's proposal, "phanerothyme." Also called **psychedelics**.

psychedelic therapy the now-discredited use of HALLUCINOGENS (or psychedelics; so-called mind-expanding or mind-enhancing drugs) in the treatment of some types of mental or physical illness. LSD was used in the 1950s and 1960s in combination with psychotherapy to assist patients in enhancing their awareness of cognitive and psychological processes; it was also used in the management of a number of significant conditions, such as schizophrenia and alcoholism. MDMA was similarly used in the 1980s. However, various studies have revealed no lasting benefit; indeed, some patients claim to have been harmed by such treatments. These findings, coupled with reclassification of these drugs as illegal, ended the use of such agents in psychotherapy.

psychiatric hospital a public or private institution providing a wide range of diagnostic techniques and treatment to individuals with mental disorders on an inpatient basis. Also called **mental hospital**. See also PSYCHIATRIC UNIT.

psychiatric unit a unit of a general hospital organized for treatment of acutely disturbed psychiatric patients on an inpatient basis. Such units usually include provision for emergency coverage and admission; treatment with psychotropic drugs or electroconvulsive therapy; group therapy; psychological examinations; and adjunctive modalities, such as social work services, occupational therapy, art therapy, movement therapy, music therapy, and discussion groups.

psychiatry *n.* the medical specialty concerned with the study, diagnosis, treatment, and prevention of personality, behavioral, and mental disorders. As a medical specialty, psychiatry is based on the premise that biological causes are at the root of mental and emotional problems, although some psychiatrists do not adhere exclusively to the biological model and additionally treat problems as social and behavioral ills. Training for psychiatry includes the study of psychopathology, biochemistry, psychopharmacology, neurology, neuropathology, psychology, psychoanalysis, genetics, social science, and community mental health, as well as the many theories and approaches advanced in the field itself. —**psychiatric** *adj.*

psychic 1. *adj.* denoting phenomena associated with the mind. **2.** *adj.* denoting a class of phenomena, such as TELEPATHY and CLAIRVOYANCE, that appear to defy scientific explanation. The term is also applied to any putative powers, forces, or faculties associated with such phenomena. See PSI. **3.** *n.* a medium, sensitive, or other person with alleged paranormal abilities.

psychic apparatus in psychoanalytic theory, mental structures and mechanisms. Austrian psychiatrist Sigmund Freud (1856–1939) initially (1900) divided these into unconscious, preconscious, and conscious areas or systems and later (1923) into the ID, EGO, and SUPEREGO: The id is described as unconscious, and the ego and superego as partly conscious, partly preconscious, and partly unconscious. Also called **mental apparatus**. See also STRUCTURAL MODEL; TOPOGRAPHIC MODEL.

psychic energy in psychoanalytic theory, the dynamic force behind all mental processes. According to Austrian psychiatrist Sigmund Freud (1856–1939), the basic sources of this energy are the INSTINCTS or drives that are located in the ID and seek immediate gratification according to the PLEASURE PRINCIPLE. Swiss psychoanalyst Carl Jung (1875–1961) also believed that there is a reservoir of psychic energy, but objected to Freud's emphasis on the pleasurable gratification of biological instincts and emphasized the means by which this energy is channeled into the development of the personality and the expression of cultural and spiritual values. Also called **mental energy**. See also LIBIDO.

psychic numbing a posttraumatic symptom pattern in which the individual feels incapable of emotional expression, love, or closeness to others. See ALEXITHYMIA.

psychic seizure a type of complex partial seizure marked by psychological disturbances, such as illusions, hallucinations, affective experiences, or cognitive alterations (e.g., déjà vu).

psychoacoustics *n.* the scientific study of the physical effects of sound on biological systems, including the sensations produced by sounds and problems of communication. A branch of PSYCHOPHYSICS, this interdisciplinary study includes physiology, physics, audiology, psychology, music, engineering, and otolaryngology.

psychoactive drugs a group of drugs that have significant effects on psychological processes, such as thinking, perception, and emotion. Psychoactive drugs include those deliberately taken to produce an altered state of consciousness (e.g., HALLUCINOGENS, OPIOIDS, INHALANTS, CANNABIS) and therapeutic agents designed to ameliorate a mental condition; these include ANTIDEPRESSANTS, MOOD STABILIZERS, SEDATIVES, HYPNOTICS, and ANXIOLYTICS (which are CNS depressants), and ANTIPSYCHOTICS. Psychoactive drugs are often referred to as **psychotropic drugs** (or **psychotropics**) in clinical contexts.

psychoanalytic play technique

psychoanalysis *n.* an approach to the mind, psychological disorders, and psychological treatment originally developed by Austrian psychiatrist Sigmund Freud (1856–1939) at the beginning of the 20th century. The hallmark of psychoanalysis is the assumption that much of mental activity is unconscious and, consequently, that understanding people requires interpreting the unconscious meaning underlying their overt, or manifest, behavior. Psychoanalysis (often shortened to **analysis**) focuses primarily, then, on the influence of such unconscious forces as repressed impulses, internal conflicts, and childhood traumas on the mental life and adjustment of the individual. The foundations on which classic psychoanalysis rests are: (a) the concept of INFANTILE SEXUALITY; (b) the OEDIPUS COMPLEX; (c) the theory of INSTINCTS; (d) the PLEASURE PRINCIPLE and the REALITY PRINCIPLE; (e) the threefold division of the psyche into ID, EGO, and SUPEREGO; and (f) the central importance of anxiety and DEFENSE MECHANISMS in neurotic reactions. Psychoanalysis as a form of therapy is directed primarily to psychoneuroses, which it seeks to eliminate by bringing about basic modifications in the personality. This is done by establishing a constructive therapeutic relationship, or TRANSFERENCE, with the analyst, which enables him or her to elicit and interpret the unconscious conflicts that have produced the neurosis. The specific methods used to achieve this goal are FREE ASSOCIATION, DREAM ANALYSIS, analysis of RESISTANCES and defenses, and WORKING THROUGH the feelings revealed in the transference process. —**psychoanalytic** *adj.*

psychoanalyst *n.* a therapist who has undergone special training in psychoanalytic theory and practice and who applies the techniques developed by Austrian psychiatrist Sigmund Freud (1856–1939) to the treatment of mental disorders. In the United States, psychoanalysts are usually trained first as psychiatrists or clinical psychologists and then undergo extensive training at a psychoanalytic institute; European institutes permit so-called LAY ANALYSIS and accept other interested and qualified professionals for psychoanalytic training. All recognized training centers, however, require a thorough study of the works of Freud and others in the field, supervised clinical training, a TRAINING ANALYSIS, and a personal program of psychoanalysis. See also ANALYST.

psychoanalytic group psychotherapy GROUP PSYCHOTHERAPY in which basic psychoanalytic concepts and methods, such as FREE ASSOCIATION, analysis of RESISTANCES and defenses, and DREAM ANALYSIS, are used in modified form.

psychoanalytic play technique a method of CHILD ANALYSIS developed by Austrian-born British psychoanalyst Melanie Klein (1882–1960) during the 1920s, in which play activity is interpreted as symbolic of underlying fantasies and conflicts and substitutes for FREE ASSOCIA-TION. The therapist provides toys for the child and encourages free, imaginative play in order to reveal the child's unconscious wishes and conflicts.

psychoanalytic psychotherapy therapy conducted in the form of classical PSYCHOANALY-SIS or in one of the generally shorter forms of treatment that evolved from the classical form, such as PSYCHODYNAMIC PSYCHOTHERAPY or DYNAMIC PSYCHOTHERAPY. Generally, it involves a systematic one-on-one interaction between a therapist and a client that emphasizes the importance of unconscious motives and conflicts as determinants of human behavior while helping the client overcome abnormal behavior or adjust to the problems of life. The use of FREE ASSOCIATION and therapist interpretation, as well as the development of a THERAPEU-TIC ALLIANCE, are common techniques.

psychobiography n. a form of biographical literature that offers a psychological profile or analysis of an individual's personality in addition to the usual account of his or her life and experiences. —**psychobiographical** adj.

psychobiology n. **1.** a school of thought in the mental health professions in which the individual is viewed as a holistic unit and both normal and abnormal behavior are explained in terms of the interaction of biological, sociological, and psychological determinants. **2.** a rare synonym for BIOLOGICAL PSYCHOLOGY. —**psychobiological** adj.

psychochemistry n. the study of the relationships between chemicals, behavior (including the genetic or metabolic aspects of behavior), and psychological processes.

psychodiagnosis n. **1.** any procedure designed to discover the underlying factors that account for behavior, especially disordered behavior. **2.** diagnosis of mental disorders through psychological methods and tests.

psychodrama n. a technique of psychotherapy in which clients achieve new insight and alter undesired patterns of behavior through acting out roles or incidents. The process involves: (a) a **protagonist**, or client, who presents and acts out his or her emotional problems and interpersonal relationships; (b) trained **auxiliary egos**, who play supportive roles representing significant individuals in the dramatized situations; and (c) a **director**, or therapist, who guides this process and leads an interpretive session when it is completed. Various special techniques are used to advance the therapy, among them exchanging roles, soliloquy, enactment of dreams, and hypnotic dramatizations.

Psychodynamic Diagnostic Manual (PDM) a handbook for the diagnosis and treatment of mental health disorders that attempts to characterize an individual's personality and the full range of his or her emotional, social, and interpersonal functioning. Published in 2006, by a task force of various major psychoanalytical organizations, the *PDM* is meant to serve as a complement to the *Diagnostic and Statistical Manual of Mental Disorders* (see DSM–IV–TR) and the *ICD* (see INTERNATIONAL CLASSIFICATION OF DISEASES). Based on current neuroscience and treatment OUTCOME RESEARCH and concepts from classical PSYCHOANALYTIC PSYCHOTHER-APY, the diagnostic framework describes (a) healthy and disordered personality functioning; (b) individual profiles of mental functioning, including patterns of relating, comprehending, and expressing emotions, coping with stress and anxiety, self-observation of emotions and behaviors, and forming moral judgments; and (c) symptom patterns, including differences in each individual's experience of his or her symptoms.

psychodynamic psychotherapy those forms of psychotherapy, falling within or deriving from the psychoanalytic tradition, that view individuals as reacting to unconscious forces (e.g., motivation, drive), that focus on processes of change and development, and that place a premium on self-understanding and making meaning of what is unconscious. Most psychodynamic approaches share common features, such as emphasis on dealing with the unconscious in treatment, emphasis on the role of analyzing TRANSFERENCE, and the use of dream analysis and INTERPRETATION.

psychodynamics n. **1.** any system or perspective emphasizing the development, changes, and interaction of mental and emotional processes, motivation, and drives. **2.** the pattern of motivational forces, conscious or unconscious, that gives rise to a particular psychological event or state, such as an attitude, action, symptom, or mental disorder. These forces include drives, wishes, emotions, and defense mechanisms, as well as biological needs (e.g., hunger and sex). See also DYNAMIC PSYCHOLOGY. —**psychodynamic** adj.

psychodynamic theory a constellation of theories of human functioning that are based on the interplay of drives and other forces within the person, especially (and originating in) the psychoanalytic theories developed by Austrian psychiatrist Sigmund Freud (1856–1939) and his colleagues and successors, such as Anna Freud (1895–1982), Carl Jung (1875–1961), and Melanie Klein (1882–1960). Later psychodynamic theories, while retaining concepts of the interworking of drives and motives to varying degrees, moved toward the contemporary approach, which emphasizes the process of change and incorporates interpersonal and transactional perspectives of personality development.

psychoendocrinology n. the study of the hormonal system in order to discover sites and processes that underlie and influence biological, behavioral, and psychological processes. It is often concerned with identifying biochemical abnormalities that may play a significant role in the production of mental disorders.

psychogenesis *n.* **1.** the origin and development of personality, behavior, and mental and psychic processes. **2.** the origin of a particular psychic event in an individual. See PSYCHOGENIC. —**psychogenetic** *adj.*

psychogenetics *n.* the study of the inheritance of psychological attributes. —**psychogenetic** *adj.*

psychogenic *adj.* resulting from mental factors. The term is used particularly to denote or refer to a disorder that cannot be accounted for by any identifiable organic dysfunction and is believed to be due to psychological factors (e.g., a conversion disorder). In psychology and psychiatry, psychogenic disorders are improperly considered equivalent to FUNCTIONAL disorders.

psychogenic need in the PERSONOLOGY of U.S. psychologist Henry Alexander Murray (1893–1988), a need that is concerned with emotional satisfaction as opposed to biological satisfaction. The psychogenic needs defined by Murray include the affiliative, dominance, and seclusion needs. Compare VISCEROGENIC NEED.

psychogenic nonepileptic seizure a behavioral or emotional manifestation of psychological distress, conflict, or trauma that resembles an epileptic SEIZURE but is not produced by abnormal electrical activity in the brain. Most PNESs are **conversion nonepileptic seizures**, resulting from conversion disorder, but they may also be associated with FACTITIOUS DISORDER or MALINGERING. Also called **psychogenic seizure**.

psychographics *n.* in marketing or advertising, an extended form of demographics that surveys the values, activities, interests, and opinions of populations or population segments to predict consumer preferences and behavior. Psychographic profiling is generally carried out with proprietary techniques developed by private research firms. The information is then used in the development of advertising messages, as well as in products designed to appeal to individuals with specific profiles. —**psychographic** *adj.*

psychohistory *n.* the application of psychoanalytic theory to the study of historical figures, events, and movements. Also called **historical psychoanalysis**.

psychokinesis *n.* the alleged ability to control external events and move or change the shape of objects through the power of thought. Examples include the supposed ability of certain psychics to influence the roll of dice or to bend a piece of metal by exerting "mind over matter" (see CHANGE EFFECT). Also called **parakinesis**; **telekinesis**. —**psychokinetic** *adj.*

psycholinguistics *n.* a branch of psychology that employs formal linguistic models to investigate language use and the cognitive processes that accompany it. In particular, the models of GENERATIVE GRAMMAR proposed by U.S. linguist Noam Chomsky (1928–) and others have been used to explain and predict LANGUAGE ACQUISITION in children and the production and comprehension of speech by adults. To this extent psycholinguistics is a specific discipline that can be distinguished from the more general area of psychology of language, which encompasses many other fields and approaches. —**psycholinguistic** *adj.*

psychological abuse see EMOTIONAL ABUSE.

psychological aesthetics a branch of psychology that studies the response to beauty and the underlying factors that contribute to its experience, particularly during the production and observation of works of art, such as paintings, music, sculpture, and photographs.

psychological assessment the gathering and integration of data in order to make a psychological evaluation, decision, or recommendation. Psychologists assess diverse psychiatric problems (e.g., anxiety, substance abuse) and nonpsychiatric concerns (e.g., intelligence, career interests), and assessment can be conducted with individuals, dyads, families, groups, and organizations. Assessment data may be gathered through various methods, such as clinical interviews, behavior observation methods, psychological tests, physiological or psychophysiological measurement devices, or other specialized test apparatuses.

psychological autopsy an analysis that is conducted following a person's death in order to determine his or her mental state prior to death. Psychological autopsies are often performed when a death occurs in a complex or ambiguous manner and are frequently used to determine if a death was the result of natural causes, accident, homicide, or suicide. Attention is given to the total course of the individual's life in order to reconstruct the facts, motivations, and meanings associated with the death.

psychological dependence dependence on a psychoactive substance for the reinforcement it provides. It is signaled by a high rate of drug use, drug craving, and the tendency to relapse after cessation of use. Many believe reinforcement is the driving force behind drug addiction, and that TOLERANCE and PHYSICAL DEPENDENCE are related phenomena that sometimes occur but are probably not central to the development of dependency-inducing patterns of drug use. Compare PHYSICAL DEPENDENCE.

psychological disorder see MENTAL DISORDER; PSYCHOPATHOLOGY.

psychological distress a set of psychological and physical symptoms of both anxiety and depression that occur in individuals who do not meet the criteria for any particular psychological disorder. It is thought to be what is assessed by many putative self-report measures of depression. Psychological distress likely reflects normal fluctuations of mood in most people, but may indicate the beginning of a MAJOR DEPRESSIVE EPISODE in individuals with a history of MAJOR DEPRESSIVE DISORDER.

psychological examination examination of

a patient by means of interviews, observations of behavior, and administration of psychological tests in order to evaluate personality, adjustment, abilities, interests, and functioning in important areas of life. The purpose of the examination may be to assess the patient's needs, difficulties, and problems and contribute to the diagnosis of mental disorder and determination of the type of treatment required.

psychological factors functional factors—as opposed to organic (constitutional, hereditary) factors—that contribute to the development of personality, the maintenance of health and well-being, and the etiology of mental and behavioral disorder. A few examples of psychological factors are the nature of significant childhood and adult relationships, the experience of ease or stress in social environments (e.g., school, work), and the experience of trauma.

psychological field in the social psychology of German-born U.S. psychologist Kurt Lewin (1890–1947), the individual's LIFE SPACE or environment as he or she perceives it at any given moment. See also FIELD THEORY.

psychological model 1. a theory, usually including a mechanism for predicting psychological outcomes, intended to explain specific psychological processes. See also CONSTRUCT. **2.** a representation of human cognitive and response characteristics used to approximate and evaluate the performance of an actual individual in a complex situation, such as a novel aircraft cockpit.

psychological need 1. any need that is essential to mental health or that is otherwise not a biological necessity. It may be generated entirely internally, as in the need for pleasure, or it may be generated by interactions between the individual and the environment, as in the need for social approval, justice, or job satisfaction. See also SOCIAL MOTIVE. **2.** any need from the four higher levels of MASLOW'S MOTIVATIONAL HIERARCHY. Compare PHYSIOLOGICAL NEED.

psychological rapport 1. as defined by Swiss psychiatrist Carl Jung (1875–1961), an intensified tie to the analyst that acts as a compensation for the patient's defective relationship to his or her present reality: that is, TRANSFERENCE. Jung saw this as an inevitable feature of every analysis. **2.** more generally, a kind of agreement or affinity between individuals in their typical ways of thinking, affective responses, and behaviors.

psychological refractory period (PRP) the period after response to a stimulus during which response to a second stimulus, presented shortly after the first, is delayed. Reaction time for the second task is increased when the stimulus for it occurs immediately (i.e., within one fourth of a second) after the stimulus for the first task. This **PRP effect** has been attributed to a response-selection bottleneck.

psychological rehabilitation the development or restoration of an effective, adaptive identity in an individual with a congenital or acquired physical impairment (e.g., through accident, injury, or surgery) through such psychological approaches as individual or group therapy, counseling, ability assessment, and psychopharmacology. The object is to help the individual to improve or regain his or her self-image, ability to cope with emotional problems, competence, and autonomy.

psychological skills training a program of instruction and practice of psychological skills relevant to athletic performance, including RELAXATION, CONCENTRATION, IMAGERY, and GOAL SETTING.

psychological test a standardized instrument (i.e., a test, inventory, or scale) used in measuring intelligence, specific mental abilities (reasoning, comprehension, abstract thinking, etc.), specific aptitudes (mechanical aptitude, manual coordination, dexterity, etc.), achievement (reading, spelling, arithmetic, etc.), attitudes, values, interests, personality or personality disorders, or other attributes of interest to psychologists.

psychological time the subjective estimation or experience of time. This is mainly dependent upon the processing and interpretation by the brain of time-related internal or external stimuli (see TIME SENSE) but can be influenced by other factors. In general, time is experienced as passing more slowly when one is bored or inactive and more rapidly when one is engaged in an absorbing activity. Certain PEAK EXPERIENCES can produce a sense of time dissolving or being suspended (see TIMELESS MOMENT). Drugs and hypnosis can also be used to alter the perception of time.

psychological treatment various forms of treatment and psychoeducation—including psychotherapy, clinical intervention, and behavior modification, among others—aimed at increasing the client's adaptive and independent functioning. Psychological treatment is the specific purview of trained mental health professionals and incorporates a wide array of diverse theories and techniques for producing healthy and adaptive change in a client's actions, thoughts, and feelings. The term is sometimes used in contrast to treatment through the use of medication, although medication is sometimes used as an adjunct to various forms of psychological treatment (see ADJUNCTIVE THERAPY).

psychological universal a psychological feature that occurs and is recognized across diverse cultures, albeit sometimes in different forms. In 1980 U.S. psychologist Walter J. Lonner (1934–) proposed a seven-level structure to categorize ideas and concepts that may qualify as psychological universals: (a) **simple universals** (e.g., the absolute facticity of human aggression); (b) **variform universals** (e.g., aggression takes on various forms in different cultures, but it always occurs); (c) **functional universals** (societal variations that have the same social consequences, but equilibrated for local relevance); (d) **diachronic universals** (universals of behavior that are temporally invariant, but interpreted differently); (e) **ethologically oriented universals** (those with phylogenetic, Darwinian links); (f) **systematic behavioral universals** (various subcategories in psychology); and (g) **cocktail-party universals** (those things that all people feel but can only discuss as phenomena that defy measurement).

psychological warfare a broad class of activities designed to influence the attitudes, beliefs, and behavior of soldiers and civilians with regard to military operations. Such activities include attempts to bolster the attitudes and morale of one's own people as well as to change or undermine the attitudes and morale of an opposing army or civilian population.

psychologist *n.* an individual who is professionally trained in the research, practice, or teaching (or all three) of one or more branches or subfields of PSYCHOLOGY. Training is obtained at a university or a school of professional psychology, leading to a doctoral degree in philosophy (PhD), psychology (PsyD), or education (EdD). Psychologists work in a variety of settings, including laboratories, schools, colleges, universities, social agencies, hospitals, clinics, the military, industry and business, prisons, the government, and private practice. The professional activities of psychologists are also varied but can include psychological counseling, health care services, educational testing and assessment, research, teaching, and business and organizational consulting. Formal CERTIFICATION or PROFESSIONAL LICENSING is required in order to practice independently in many of these settings and activities.

psychology *n.* **1.** the study of the mind and behavior. Historically, psychology was an area of philosophy (see EPISTEMOLOGY). It is now a diverse scientific discipline comprising several major branches of research (e.g., experimental psychology, biological psychology, cognitive psychology, developmental psychology, personality, and social psychology), as well as several subareas of research and applied psychology (e.g., clinical psychology, industrial/organizational psychology, school and educational psychology, human factors, health psychology, neuropsychology, cross-cultural psychology). Research in psychology involves observation, experimentation, testing, and analysis to explore the biological, cognitive, emotional, personal, and social processes or stimuli underlying human and animal behavior. The practice of psychology involves the use of psychological knowledge for any of several purposes: to understand and treat mental, emotional, physical, and social dysfunction; to understand and enhance behavior in various settings of human activity (e.g., school, workplace, courtroom, sports arena, battlefield, etc.); and to improve machine and building design for human use. **2.** the supposed collection of behaviors, traits, attitudes, and so forth that characterize an individual or a group (e.g., the psychology of women). —**psychological** *adj.*

psychology of religion the empirical or academic study of spiritual experience or organized religion from a psychological perspective. This has involved the description and analysis of certain specialized types of experience, such as those associated with mysticism, as well as an investigation of the more ordinary ways in which religious faith affects the behaviors and cognitive processes of believers.

psychometric function see PSYCHOPHYSICAL FUNCTION.

psychometrics *n.* **1.** the psychological theory and technique (e.g., the science and process) of mental measurement. **2.** the branch of psychology dealing with measurable factors. Also called **psychometric psychology**; **psychometry**.

psychometric theories of intelligence theories of intelligence based on or tested by scores on conventional tests of intelligence, such as number-series completions and verbal analogies. These theories are often, but not always, based on FACTOR ANALYSIS, that is, they specify a set of factors alleged to underlie human intelligence. Among the most famous of such theories are the TWO-FACTOR THEORY of British psychologist Charles Spearman (1863–1945) and the theory of PRIMARY ABILITIES of U.S. psychologist Louis Thurstone (1887–1955). See also RADEX THEORY OF INTELLIGENCE; THREE-STRATUM MODEL OF INTELLIGENCE.

psychometry *n.* **1.** see PSYCHOMETRICS. **2.** in parapsychology, the reputed ability of some people to hold an object in their hands and become aware of facts about its history or about people who have been associated with it. There is, however, no verified evidence of such an ability.

psychomimetic *adj., n.* see PSYCHOTOMIMETIC.

psychomotor *adj.* relating to movements or motor effects that result from mental activity.

psychomotor agitation restless physical and mental activity that is inappropriate for its context. It includes pacing, hand wringing, and pulling or rubbing clothing and other objects and is a common symptom of both MAJOR DEPRESSIVE EPISODES and MANIC EPISODES. Also called **psychomotor excitement**.

psychomotor retardation a slowing down or inhibition of mental and physical activity, manifested as slow speech with long pauses before answers, slowness in thinking, and slow body movements. Psychomotor retardation is a common symptom of MAJOR DEPRESSIVE EPISODES.

psychoneuroendocrinology *n.* the study of the relations among psychological factors, the nervous system, and the endocrine system in determining behavior and health. It includes the effects of psychological stress on neuroendocrine systems (see NEUROENDOCRINOLOGY) and how changes in these systems affect behavior in normal and psychopathological states.

psychoneuroimmunology *n.* the study of how the brain and behavior affect immune responses. —**psychoneuroimmunological** *adj.*

psychoneuromuscular theory a theory to explain how IMAGERY can improve performance. It states that, during imagery, the brain sends impulses to the muscles. These impulses are identical to those that cause muscle contraction with movement but are of lower intensity; the neural pathways are thereby strengthened.

psychonomic *adj.* denoting an approach to psychology that emphasizes quantitative measurement, experimental control, and OPERATIONAL DEFINITIONS, especially in the area of experimental, laboratory psychology. See EXPERIMENTAL PSYCHOLOGY.

psychooncology *n.* the study of psychological, behavioral, and psychosocial factors involved in the risk, detection, course, treatment, and outcome (in terms of survival) of cancer. The field examines responses to cancer on the part of patients, families, and caregivers at all stages of the disease. —**psychooncological** *adj.* —**psychooncologist** *n.*

psychopathology *n.* **1.** the scientific study of mental disorders, including theory, etiology, progression, symptomatology, diagnosis, and treatment. This broad field of study may involve psychology, biochemistry, pharmacology, psychiatry, neurology, endocrinology, and other related subjects. The term in this sense is sometimes used synonymously with ABNORMAL PSYCHOLOGY. **2.** the behavioral or cognitive manifestations of such disorders. The term in this sense is sometimes considered synonymous with MENTAL DISORDER itself. —**psychopathological** *adj.* —**psychopathologist** *n.*

psychopathy *n.* a former name for ANTISOCIAL PERSONALITY DISORDER.

psychopharmacology *n.* the study of the influence of drugs on mental, emotional, and behavioral processes. Psychopharmacology is concerned primarily with the mode of action of various substances that affect different areas of the brain and nervous system, including drugs of abuse. See also CLINICAL PSYCHOPHARMACOLOGY; GERIATRIC PSYCHOPHARMACOLOGY; PEDIATRIC PSYCHOPHARMACOLOGY; PRECLINICAL PSYCHOPHARMACOLOGY. —**psychopharmacological** *adj.* —**psychopharmacologist** *n.*

psychopharmacotherapy *n.* the use of pharmacological agents in the treatment of mental disorders. For example, acute or chronic schizophrenia is treated by administration of antipsychotic drugs or other agents. Although such drugs do not cure mental disorders, they may—when used appropriately—produce significant relief from symptoms.

psychophysical *adj.* of or relating to the relationship between physical stimuli and mental events.

psychophysical function a psychometric relationship between a stimulus and judgments about the stimulus, as expressed in a mathematical formula. In the METHOD OF CONSTANT STIMULI, it is the proportion of "yes" responses (i.e., that the stimulus was perceived) as a function of physical magnitude of the stimuli. Also called **psychometric function**.

psychophysical law a mathematical relationship between the strength of a physical stimulus and the intensity of the sensation experienced. Psychophysical laws were first developed from early empirical research aimed at direct scientific investigation of the MIND–BODY PROBLEM, work that established the foundation of psychology as an experimental science. See also INNER PSYCHOPHYSICS; OUTER PSYCHOPHYSICS.

psychophysical scaling method any of the techniques used to construct scales relating physical stimulus properties to perceived magnitude. Methods are often classified as direct or indirect, based on whether the observer directly judges magnitude. See DIRECT SCALING.

psychophysics *n.* a branch of psychology that deals with relationships between stimulus magnitudes, stimulus differences, and corresponding sensory processes.

psychophysiological assessment the use of physiological measures via electroencephalography, electrocardiography, electromyography, and electrooculography to infer psychological processes and emotion. Also called **psychophysiological monitoring**.

psychophysiology *n.* the study of the relation between psychological and physiological functioning as they pertain to processes and behavior. See also PSYCHOSOMATIC MEDICINE. —**psychophysiological** *adj.* —**psychophysiologist** *n.*

psychosexual development in the classic psychoanalytic theory of Austrian psychiatrist Sigmund Freud (1856–1939), the step-by-step growth of sexual life as it affects personality development. Freud posited that the impetus for psychosexual development stems from a single energy source, the LIBIDO, which is concentrated in different organs throughout infancy and produces the various **psychosexual stages**: the ORAL STAGE, ANAL STAGE, PHALLIC STAGE, LATENCY STAGE, and GENITAL STAGE. Each stage gives rise to its own characteristic erotic activities (e.g., sucking and biting in the oral stage) and the early expressions may lead to "perverse" activities later in life, such as SADISM, MASOCHISM, VOYEURISM, and EXHIBITIONISM. Moreover, the different stages leave their mark on the individual's character and personality, especially if sexual development is arrested in a FIXATION at one particular stage. Also called **libidinal development**.

P

psychosis *n.* **1.** an abnormal mental state characterized by serious impairments or disruptions in the most fundamental higher brain functions—perception, cognition and cognitive processing, and emotions or affect—as manifested in behavioral phenomena, such as delusions, hallucinations, and significantly disorganized speech. See PSYCHOTIC DISORDER. **2.** historically, any severe mental disorder that significantly interferes with functioning and ability to perform activities essential to daily living.

psychosocial *adj.* describing the intersection and interaction of social and cultural influences on mental health, personality development, and behavior.

psychosocial development 1. according to the theory of German-born U.S. psychologist Erik Erikson (1902–1994), personality development as a process influenced by social and cultural factors throughout the life span. See ERIKSON'S EIGHT STAGES OF DEVELOPMENT. **2.** the development of normal social behavior, both prosocial behavior (e.g., cooperation) and negative (e.g., aggressive) behavior. Psychosocial development involves changes not only in children's overt behavior but also in their SOCIAL COGNITION. For example, they become able to take the perspective of others and to understand that other people's behavior is based on their knowledge and desires.

psychosocial factors social, cultural, and environmental phenomena and influences that affect the mental health and behavior of the individual and of groups. Such influences include social situations, relationships, and pressures, such as competition for and access to education, health care, and other social resources; rapid technological change; work deadlines; and changes in the roles and status of women and minority groups.

psychosocial rehabilitation the process of restoring normal psychological, behavioral, and social skills to individuals after mental illness, often with assistance from specialized professionals using focused programs and techniques. It aims to help individuals who have been residing in mental institutions or other facilities (e.g., prisons) to reenter the community.

psychosocial therapy psychological treatment with a strong emphasis on interpersonal aspects of problem situations, which is designed to help an individual with emotional or behavioral disturbances adjust to situations that require social interaction with other members of the family, work group, community, or any other social unit.

psychosomatic *adj.* characterizing an approach based on the belief that the mind (psyche) plays a role in all the diseases affecting the various bodily systems (soma).

psychosomatic disorder a type of disorder in which psychological factors are believed to play an important role in the origin or course (or both) of the disease.

psychosomatic medicine a field of study that emphasizes the role of psychological factors in causing and treating disease.

psychostimulant *n.* see CNS STIMULANT.

psychosurgery *n.* the treatment of a mental or neurological disorder by surgical intervention on parts of the brain, for example, destruction of selective brain areas. Examples include TEMPORAL LOBECTOMY for severe temporal lobe epilepsy and, historically, prefrontal LOBOTOMY for severe psychiatric disorders, particularly schizophrenia. Psychosurgery was most popular from 1935 to 1960 and is among the most controversial of all psychiatric treatments ever introduced. Contemporary psychosurgery approaches are far more precisely targeted and confined in extent than the early techniques, employing high-tech imaging and a variety of highly controllable methods of producing minute lesions.

psychotherapeutic process whatever occurs between and within the client and psychotherapist during the course of psychotherapy. This includes the experiences, attitudes, emotions, and behavior of both client and therapist, as well as the dynamic, or interaction, between them. See also PROCESS RESEARCH.

psychotherapy *n.* any psychological service provided by a trained professional that primarily uses forms of communication and interaction to assess, diagnose, and treat dysfunctional emotional reactions, ways of thinking, and behavior patterns of an individual, family (see FAMILY THERAPY), or group (see GROUP PSYCHOTHERAPY). There are many types of psychotherapy, but generally they fall into four major categories: psychodynamic (e.g., PSYCHOANALYSIS; CLIENT-CENTERED THERAPY), cognitive-behavioral (see BEHAVIOR THERAPY; COGNITIVE BEHAVIOR THERAPY; COGNITIVE THERAPY), humanistic (e.g., EXISTENTIAL PSYCHOTHERAPY), and INTEGRATIVE PSYCHOTHERAPY. The **psychotherapist** is an individual who has been professionally trained and licensed (in the United States by a state board) to treat mental, emotional, and behavioral disorders by psychological means. He or she may be a clinical psychologist (see CLINICAL PSYCHOLOGY), PSYCHIATRIST, counselor (see COUNSELING PSYCHOLOGY), social worker, or psychiatric nurse. Also called **therapy**; **talk therapy**. —**psychotherapeutic** *adj.*

psychotherapy research the use of scientific methods to describe, explain, and evaluate psychotherapy techniques, processes, and effectiveness.

psychotic *adj.* of, relating to, or affected by PSYCHOSIS or a PSYCHOTIC DISORDER.

psychotic disorder any one of a number of severe mental disorders, regardless of etiology, characterized by gross impairment in REALITY TESTING. The accuracy of perceptions and thoughts is incorrectly evaluated, and incorrect inferences are made about external reality, even in the face of contrary evidence. Specific symptoms indicative of psychotic disorders are delusions, hallucinations, and markedly disorganized speech, thought, or behavior; individuals may have little or no insight into their symptoms.

psychotomimetic 1. *adj.* tending to induce hallucinations, delusions, or other symptoms of psychosis. **2.** *n.* one of a group of drugs originally used in laboratory experiments to determine if they could induce psychoses, or states mimicking psychoses, on the basis of their effects. The group includes LSD and AMPHETAMINES. Also called **psychomimetic**.

psychotropic drugs see PSYCHOACTIVE DRUGS.

PT abbreviation for PHYSICAL THERAPY.

ptosis *n.* (*pl.* **ptoses**) the sinking or dropping of an organ or part of the body, especially drooping of the eyelid. This may be caused by injury to the third cranial (oculomotor) nerve or the eye muscles. It is also a characteristic sign of MYASTHENIA GRAVIS. —**ptotic** *adj.*

PTSD abbreviation for POSTTRAUMATIC STRESS DISORDER.

ptyalism *n.* **1.** the excessive production of saliva. Normal production of the parotid, submaxillary, and sublingual salivary glands is between 1,000 and 1,500 ml per day for an adult human. Ptyalism may be associated with epilepsy, encephalitis, certain medications, high blood pressure, deep emotion, or high anxiety. Also called **sialorrhea**. **2.** a condition in which saliva production is normal but the patient is unable to swallow the saliva as fast as it is secreted, as in cases of parkinsonism, bulbar or pseudobulbar paralysis, or bilateral facial-nerve palsy.

puberty *n.* the stage of development when the genital organs reach maturity and secondary SEX CHARACTERISTICS begin to appear, signaling the start of ADOLESCENCE. It is marked by ejaculation of sperm in the male, onset of menstruation and development of breasts in the female, and, in both males and females, growth of pubic hair and increasing sexual interest. —**pubertal** *adj.*

puberty rite the initiation into adult life of a pubescent member of a community through ceremonies, cultural-lore indoctrination, and similar customs. For young males in traditional societies this may often involve a physical and psychological ordeal in which they are forced to experience pain, hardship, and fear. See RITE OF PASSAGE.

pubescence *n.* the period or process of reaching puberty. —**pubescent** *adj.*

publication ethics the principles and standards associated with the process of publishing the results of scientific research or scholarly work in general. These include such matters as giving the appropriate credit and authorship status to those who have earned it and not submitting for republication results that have already been published elsewhere without indicating that fact.

public distance zone in social psychology, the DISTANCE ZONE adopted by people in formal, official, or ceremonial interactions. The public distance zone is defined as an area of 3.5–7.5 m (11½–24½ ft). Compare PERSONAL DISTANCE ZONE. See also PROXEMICS.

public health approach a community-based approach to mental and physical health in which agencies and organizations focus on enhancing and maintaining the well-being of individuals by ensuring the existence of the conditions necessary for them to lead healthy lives. The approach involves such activities as monitoring community health status; identifying and investigating health problems and threats to community health; ensuring the competency of health care providers and personnel; disseminating accurate information and educating individuals about health issues; developing, modifying, and enforcing policies and other regulatory measures that support community health and safety; and ensuring the accessibility of quality health services.

public self information about the self, or an integrated view of the self, that is conveyed to others in actions, self-descriptions, appearance, and social interactions. An individual's public self will vary with the people who constitute the target or audience of such impressions. The public self is often contrasted with the PRIVATE SELF. See also COLLECTIVE SELF; SOCIAL SELF.

public service psychology an area of psychology defined by the activities of psychologists employed by public sector agencies (e.g., in community mental health centers, state hospitals, correctional facilities, police and public safety agencies) and the psychological condition of people served by these agencies. Particular interests include advocacy, access to services, education and training, public policy formulation, research and program evaluation, and prevention efforts.

pudendum *n.* (*pl.* **pudenda**) human external genitalia, especially those of the female. See VULVA. —**pudendal** *adj.*

pull-out program an educational plan in which students who spend most of the day in traditional classrooms are, for a portion of the day, taken to a separate class for specialized work, either above or below the standard of instruction in their regular classrooms. See also OPPORTUNITY CLASS.

pulmonary embolism the lodgment of a blood clot or other obstructing material (see EMBOLISM) in a pulmonary artery with consequent obstruction of blood supply to the lung tissue. The clot most commonly derives from deep vein THROMBOSIS.

pulse *n.* **1.** the pressure waves caused by rhythmic contraction and relaxation of the walls of arteries as blood is pumped from the heart. The pulse, which can be detected manually at superficial arteries, provides a measure of the heart rate. The strength of the pulse at various points in the body (e.g., the ankle) gives an indication of the adequacy of circulation. **2.** an increase followed by a decrease in magnitude of a signal.

pun *n.* an expression that makes deliberate use of verbal AMBIGUITY, generally for humorous effect; an example is "That's the psychologist who went for a walk and fell into a depression." Many puns exploit the phenomenon of homophony, in which words sounding the same (or nearly the same) have different meanings. See also POLYSEMY.

punctate *adj.* relating to or marked by small points or spots. **Punctate stimuli** are applied to points on the skin.

punishment *n.* **1.** in OPERANT CONDITIONING, the process in which the relationship, or CONTINGENCY, between a response and some stimulus or circumstance results in the response becoming less probable. For example, a pigeon's pecks on a key may at first occasionally be followed by presentation of food; this will establish some probability of pecking. Next, each peck produces a brief electric shock (while the other conditions remain as before). If pecking declines as a result, then punishment is said to have occurred, and the shock is called a **punisher. 2.** a painful, unwanted, or undesirable event or circumstance imposed as a penalty on a wrongdoer. **—punish** *vb.*

punishment and obedience orientation see PRECONVENTIONAL LEVEL.

pupil *n.* the aperture through which light passes on entering the eye. It is located immediately in front of the LENS. The size of the opening is controlled by a circle of muscle (the IRIS) innervated by fibers of the autonomic nervous system.

pupillary reflex the automatic change in size of the pupil in response to light changes. The pupil constricts in response to bright light and dilates in dim light. Also called **light reflex**. See also ACCOMMODATION.

pupillometry (pupilometrics) *n.* **1.** the scientific measurement of the pupil of the eye. Also called **pupillometry. 2.** a research method in which pupillary responses to stimuli (usually visual images) are measured in order to determine the participant's interest in the stimuli.

pure alexia see ALEXIA.

pure research see BASIC RESEARCH.

pure tone a sound whose instantaneous SOUND PRESSURE is a sinusoidal function of time. A pure tone has only one frequency component. Also called **simple tone; sinusoid**. Compare COMPLEX TONE.

pure word deafness a type of AUDITORY AGNOSIA in which an individual is unable to understand spoken language but can comprehend nonverbal sounds and read, write, and speak in a

relatively normal manner. The syndrome is considered "pure" in the sense that it is relatively free of the language difficulties encountered in the APHASIAS.

purging *n.* the activity of expelling food that has just been ingested, usually by vomiting or the use of laxatives. Purging often occurs in conjunction with an eating binge in ANOREXIA NERVOSA or BULIMIA NERVOSA; its purpose is to eliminate or reduce real or imagined weight gain.

Purkinje cell a type of large, highly branched cell in the CEREBELLAR CORTEX of the brain that receives incoming signals about the position of the body and transmits signals to spinal nerves for coordinated muscle actions. [Johannes Evangelista **Purkinje** (1787–1869), Czech physiologist and physician]

Purkinje shift a visual phenomenon in which colors appear to change with the level of illumination. A rose, for example, may appear bright red and its leaves bright green at the beginning of twilight, then gradually change to a black flower with light gray leaves as the level of daylight declines. The Purkinje shift affects the brilliance of the red end of the spectrum before the blue end. [Johannes Evangelista **Purkinje**]

purpose in life the internal, mental sense of a goal or aim in the process of living or in existence itself. This concept is of special significance in EXISTENTIAL PSYCHOTHERAPY, in which it is considered to be central to the development and treatment of anxiety, depression, and related emotional states. Having a clear purpose in life reduces negative states.

purposive behaviorism a cognitive theory of learning postulating that behavioral acts have a goal or purpose that selects and guides the behavioral sequence until the goal or purpose is attained. Purposive behaviorism incorporates the gestalt concepts of FIELD THEORY and contrasts with behavioral learning theories, which reduce behavior to smaller units of learned stimuli and responses. See also S–S LEARNING MODEL.

purposive psychology an approach to psychology that makes the primary assumption that organisms usually have conscious goals that motivate and organize their behavior. See also PURPOSIVE BEHAVIORISM; TELEOLOGY.

purposive sampling SAMPLING from a subpopulation that is already known to have the same characteristics as the total population.

push-down stack a model of memory that compares its storage procedures to stacks of cafeteria trays in spring-loaded compartments. New items in memory are like trays added to the top of the stack, with other items being pushed down to accommodate them. Access to memory items is only from the "top." The model originated in computing but is now often applied to SHORT-TERM MEMORY in humans.

putamen *n.* a part of the lenticular nucleus in the BASAL GANGLIA of the brain. It receives input from the motor cortex and is involved in control of movements.

puzzle box in experimental research, a box in which an animal must manipulate some type of device, such as a latch, in order to escape from the box or to get a reward. It was originally used in 1898 in the form of the **Thorndike Puzzle Box** (a wooden box with slatted sides and a door that could be opened by the animal inside) by U.S. psychologist Edward L. Thorndike (1874–1949) in studying animal learning and intelligence.

p-value *n.* see SIGNIFICANCE LEVEL.

PVS abbreviation for PERSISTENT VEGETATIVE STATE.

Pygmalion effect a consequence or reaction in which the expectations of a leader or superior lead to behavior on the part of followers or subordinates that is consistent with these expectations: a form of SELF-FULFILLING PROPHECY or EXPECTANCY EFFECT. For example, raising manager expectations regarding the performance of subordinate employees has been found to enhance the performance of those employees. Compare UPWARD PYGMALION EFFECT.

pyramidal cell a type of large neuron that has a roughly pyramid-shaped CELL BODY and is found in the cerebral cortex. See CORTICAL LAYERS.

pyramidal tract the primary pathway followed by motor neurons that originate in the motor area of the cortex, the premotor area, somatosensory area, and the frontal and parietal lobes of the brain. Fibers of the pyramidal tract communicate with fibers supplying the peripheral muscles. Because of the contralateral relationship between left and right hemispheres of the brain and motor activity on the opposite sides of the body, pyramidal-tract fibers cross in the pyramids of the medulla. The pyramidal tract includes the corticospinal tract (see VENTROMEDIAL PATHWAYS), and the two terms are occasionally used synonymously. Also called **pyramidal motor system; pyramidal system**. See also EXTRAPYRAMIDAL TRACT.

pyriform area (piriform area) a pear-shaped region of the RHINENCEPHALON, at the base of the medial temporal lobe of the brain, that receives OLFACTORY TRACTS of the second order and input from the inferior temporal lobe, and relays impulses to the HIPPOCAMPAL FORMATION. Also called **olfactory cortex**.

pyromania *n.* an impulse-control disorder characterized by (a) repeated failure to resist impulses to set fires and watch them burn, without monetary, social, political, or other motivations; (b) an extreme interest in fire and things associated with fire; and (c) a sense of increased tension before starting the fire and intense pleasure, gratification, or release while committing the act.

P

Qq

QALYs acronym for QUALITY ADJUSTED LIFE YEARS.

Q data *q*uestionnaire data: information about an individual gathered from the observations, judgments, and evaluations of that person as provided via subjective self-report inventories—and therefore also known as **S data** (self data)—or questionnaires. See also L DATA; O DATA; T DATA.

Q sort an IPSATIVE data-collection procedure, often used in personality measurement, in which participants sort stimuli (e.g., attitude items, pictures) into various categories, under a restriction that a predetermined number of stimuli must be placed in each category.

Q test see COCHRAN Q TEST.

quadrangular therapy marital therapy involving the married couple and each spouse's individual therapist working together (see COUPLES THERAPY). Each spouse may meet with his or her therapist separately and then come together as a group.

quadrantanopia *n.* loss of vision in one fourth, or one quadrant, of the visual field. Also called **quadranopia; quadrantanopsia**.

quadriparesis *n.* muscle weakness or partial paralysis in all four limbs, associated with neurological injury or disorder.

quadriplegia *n.* paralysis of all four limbs, resulting from damage to the spinal cord or brain. **—quadriplegic** *adj.*

quale *n.* (*pl.* **qualia**) the characteristic or quality that determines the nature of a mental experience (sensation or perception) and makes it distinguishable from other such experiences, so that (for example) the experiencer differentiates between the sensations of heat and cold. Qualia bear some conceptual relationship to the empiricist notion of PRIMARY QUALITIES and SECONDARY QUALITIES; in some systems, however, they take on the quality of basic or fundamental units of experience. Other thinkers, primarily those in the materialist tradition, reject the notion of qualia as an unnecessary construct with little explanatory value.

qualitative research a type of research methodology that produces descriptive (nonnumerical) data, such as observations of behavior or personal accounts of experiences. The goal of gathering this **qualitative data** is to examine how things look from different vantage points. A variety of techniques are subsumed under qualitative research, including interviews, PARTICIPANT OBSERVATION, and CASE STUDIES.

quality *n.* a characteristic of a sensation or other entity that makes it unique. Quality denotes a difference in kind rather than in quantity, as between various sounds of the same note played on different instruments, which produces a different distribution of overtones, as opposed to the quantity or volume of the sound. Also called **sense quality**. See PRIMARY QUALITY; SECONDARY QUALITY. See also QUALE.

quality adjusted life years (**QALYs**) a measure that combines the quantity of life, expressed in terms of survival or life expectancy, with the quality of life. The value of a year of perfect health is taken as 1; a year of ill health is worth less than 1; death is taken as 0. The measure provides a method to assess the benefits to be gained from medical procedures and interventions.

quality assurance in health administration, a systematic process used continuously to improve the quality of health care services; it involves not only evaluating them in terms of effectiveness, appropriateness, and acceptability, but also implementing solutions to correct any identified deficiencies and assessing the results.

quality of care the extent to which health services are consistent with professional standards and increase the likelihood of desired outcomes.

quality of life the extent to which a person obtains satisfaction from life. The following are important for a good quality of life: emotional, material, and physical well-being; engagement in interpersonal relations; opportunities for personal (e.g., skill) development; exercising rights and making self-determining lifestyle choices; and participation in society. Enhancing quality of life is a particular concern for those with chronic disease or developmental and other disabilities and for those undergoing medical or psychological treatment.

quality of worklife the extent to which a person obtains satisfaction from his or her job and feels a sense of ORGANIZATIONAL COMMITMENT. A variety of factors are important for a good quality of worklife, including salary, benefits, safety, and efficiency, as well as variety and challenge, responsibility, contribution, and recognition.

quantal hypothesis (**quantal theory**) see NEURAL QUANTUM THEORY.

quantitative research a type of research methodology that produces numerical data, such as test scores or measurements of reaction time. The goal of gathering this **quantitative data** is to understand the nature of a phenomenon, particularly through the development of models and theories. Quantitative research techniques include experiments and surveys.

quantitative trait loci locations in the GENOME containing a number of genes that contribute to variation in a given quantitative (continuously distributed) trait, such as height.

quantum hypothesis of consciousness an extension of NEURAL QUANTUM THEORY proposing that quantum-level neuronal events are a crucial aspect of consciousness.

quantum theory see NEURAL QUANTUM THEORY.

quartile *n.* one fourth of a statistical distribution. For example, the first quartile of a distribution would be the lowest 25% of scores, the second quartile would range from 26% to 50%, and so on.

quasi-control subject a research participant who is asked to reflect on the context in which an experiment was conducted and to speculate on the ways in which the context may have influenced his or her own and other participants' behaviors.

quasi-experimental research research in which the investigator cannot randomly assign units to conditions, cannot control or manipulate the independent variable, and cannot limit the influence of extraneous variables. Examples of quasi-experimental research are studies that deal with the responses of large groups to natural disasters or widespread changes in social policy.

queer *adj.*, *n.* controversial slang, in the main pejorative, referring (in both the adjectival and noun senses) to gays and lesbians or relating to same-sex sexual orientation. The original and still common use of the word, to describe anything that is unusual in an odd or strange way, was extended to refer to gays in the late 19th and throughout much of the 20th century, when it acquired a predominantly negative, derogatory connotation. During the late 1960s and onward, it was appropriated by some members within the gay community as a term of identification that carried no negative connotation and, indeed, took on the role of a label of pride and self-respect. This usage is not embraced, however, by all members of the gay community.

questionnaire *n.* a set of questions asked to obtain information from a respondent about a topic of interest, such as his or her attitudes, behaviors, or other characteristics.

quid pro quo an advantage given in return for something done or promised (from Latin, literally: "one thing for another"). The phrase has come to be associated with a form of SEXUAL HARASSMENT in which sexual demands are made with the explicit or implicit suggestion that compliance will have positive employment consequences (e.g., promotion), while failure to comply could have the opposite effect (e.g., termination of employment).

quota sampling a method of selecting participants for a study in which a prespecified number of individuals with specific background characteristics, such as a particular age, race, sex, or education, is selected in order to obtain a sample with the same proportional representation of these characteristics as the target population.

Rr

r symbol for PRODUCT–MOMENT CORRELATION.

r^2 symbol for COEFFICIENT OF DETERMINATION.

R symbol for MULTIPLE CORRELATION.

R^2 symbol for COEFFICIENT OF MULTIPLE DETERMINATION.

rabies *n.* an infectious viral disease of the central nervous system that can be transmitted from animals to humans, usually through the bite of an infected animal. It causes pain, fever, excessive salivation, agitation, and paralysis or contractions of muscles, particularly those of the respiratory tract. Aversion to water is a major symptom, especially in later stages of the disease, due to painful spasms associated with swallowing. Unless vaccine is given before symptoms appear, death occurs within 2–10 days.

race *n.* a socially defined concept sometimes used to designate a portion, or "subdivision," of the human population with common physical characteristics, ancestry, or language. The term is also loosely applied to geographic, cultural, religious, or national groups. The significance often accorded to racial categories might suggest that such groups are objectively defined and homogeneous; however, there is much heterogeneity within categories, and the categories themselves differ across cultures. Moreover, self-reported race frequently varies owing to changing social contexts and an individual's identification with more than one race. —**racial** *adj.*

race norming in personnel selection, the use of different cutoff scores for applicants from different ethnic groups. Race norming has been declared illegal in U.S. federal civil-rights legislation. See also BANDING.

rachischisis *n.* a congenital fissure of the spinal column, as in SPINA BIFIDA.

racial discrimination the differential treatment of individuals because of their membership in a racial group. Discrimination is in most cases the behavioral manifestation of PREJUDICE and therefore involves less favorable, negative, hostile, or injurious treatment of the members of rejected groups. See also RACISM.

racial identity an individual's sense of being a person whose identity is defined, in part, by membership of a particular RACE. The strength of this sense will depend on the extent to which an individual has processed and internalized the psychological, sociopolitical, cultural, and other contextual factors related to membership of the group.

racial memory thought patterns, feelings, and traces of experiences held to be transmitted from generation to generation and to have a basic influence on individual minds and behavior. Psychoanalysts Carl Jung (1875–1961) and Sigmund Freud (1856–1939) both embraced the concept of a phylogenetic heritage (see PHYLOGENY), but focused on different examples. Freud cited religious rituals designed to relieve feelings of anxiety and guilt, which he explained in terms of the OEDIPUS COMPLEX. Jung cited images, symbols, and personifications that spontaneously appear in different cultures, which he explained in terms of the ARCHETYPES of the COLLECTIVE UNCONSCIOUS. Also called **racial unconscious**.

racism *n.* a form of PREJUDICE that assumes that the members of racial categories have distinctive characteristics and that these differences result in some racial groups being inferior to others. Racism generally includes negative emotional reactions to members of the group, acceptance of NEGATIVE STEREOTYPES, and RACIAL DISCRIMINATION against individuals; in some cases it leads to violence. —**racist** *adj., n.*

radex theory of intelligence a PSYCHOMETRIC THEORY OF INTELLIGENCE postulating that the organization of mental abilities forms a radial order of complexity (or **radex**). The radex comprises two parts: (a) a simplex, which is the relative distance from the center of a circle, with abilities that are closer to the center of the circle therefore being closer to the construct of general intelligence; and (b) a circumplex, which is the relative distance around the circle, with abilities that are more highly correlated therefore being located closer to each other.

radial glia a type of nonneuronal cell (GLIA) that forms early in development, spanning the width of the emerging cerebral hemispheres to guide migrating neurons.

radial nerve the combined sensory and motor nerve that innervates the medial (inner) side of the forearm and hand, including the thumb. Its fibers are derived from the fifth through eighth cervical SPINAL NERVES and the first thoracic spinal nerve and they pass through the BRACHIAL PLEXUS.

radiation *n.* **1.** energy transmitted in the form of waves, such as electromagnetic radiation (e.g., heat, light, microwaves, short radio waves, ultraviolet rays, or X-rays), or in the form of a stream of nuclear particles (e.g., alpha particles, beta particles, gamma rays, electrons, neutrons, or protons). The use of such waves or particles for diagnostic, therapeutic, or experimental purposes, particularly the destruction of cancer cells, is called **radiation therapy**. Side effects commonly include fatigue, hair loss, nausea and vomiting, and loss of appetite. **2.** in neuroscience, the spread of excitation to adjacent neurons.

radical behaviorism the view that behavior, rather than consciousness and its contents, should be the proper topic for study in psychological science. This term is often used to distinguish classical BEHAVIORISM, as originally formulated in 1913 by U.S. psychologist John B. Watson (1878–1958), from more moderate forms of NEOBEHAVIORISM. However, it has evolved to denote as well the DESCRIPTIVE BEHAVIORISM later proposed by U.S. psychologist B. F. Skinner (1904–1990), which emphasized the importance of reinforcement and its relationship to behavior (i.e., the environmental determinants of behavior).

radical empiricism 1. a metaphysical position propounded by U.S. psychologist William James (1842–1910) in 1904: It holds that reality consists not of subject and object (mind and matter) but of pure experience. The position is therefore one of neutral MONISM. **2.** the associated position, also propounded by William James, that the whole of human experience is the legitimate domain for psychological investigation. This was in contrast to the tendency of certain schools of psychology, such as STRUCTURALISM, to define the subject much more narrowly. The methodological implication of radical empiricism is that psychology should not be restricted to a single method, but that it should employ methods appropriate to the study of any phenomenon that forms part of human experience. **3.** the general position that (a) empirical methods provide the only reliable sources of knowledge and (b) that only propositions that can be tested by such methods have real meaning. See EMPIRICISM; LOGICAL POSITIVISM; POSITIVISM.

radical psychiatry a variant of RADICAL THERAPY proposing that the psychological problems of individuals are the result of their victimization by the social, economic, and political system in which they live. As such, it is the system, not the individual, that should be the target of intervention and change. This view was most seriously considered during the 1970s and 1980s.

radical therapy any clinical intervention that focuses on the harmful psychological effects of social problems on individuals and that encourages individuals to help themselves by changing society. This approach was actively advanced by some psychologists in the 1970s and 1980s.

radiculopathy *n.* any disorder of a SPINAL ROOT. Radiculopathies are often due to vertebrae compressing the nerve roots, as in the condition popularly known as **slipped disk**.

radiography *n.* the technique of producing negative-image film records (**radiographs**, or

radiograms) using radiation, usually X-rays or gamma rays, which is widely used as a diagnostic aid. See also RADIOLOGY. —**radiographer** *n.* —**radiographic** *adj.*

radioimmunoassay (**RIA**) *n.* an immunological technique to measure the concentration of a substance of interest (e.g., a hormone) in a sample of blood or a tissue. A mixture of the substance to be assayed and a form of the substance tagged with a radioactive isotope is allowed to react with an antibody specific to that substance. The amount of radioactivity that is bound by the antibody reflects the amount of substance in the sample: The greater the concentration of the substance in the sample, the less radioactivity will be bound.

radiology *n.* the medical discipline or specialty in which radiographic imaging techniques (see RADIOGRAPHY) are used to diagnose disease (**diagnostic radiology**) and radioactive substances and other forms of radiation are used to treat disease (**therapeutic radiology**). The latter is more commonly referred to as radiation therapy. —**radiological** *adj.* —**radiologist** *n.*

rage *n.* intense, typically uncontrolled anger. It is usually differentiated from hostility in that it is not necessarily accompanied by destructive actions but rather by excessive expressions. In animals, rage appears to be a late stage of AGGRESSION when normal deterrents to physical attack, such as submissive signals, are no longer effective.

rage disorder any disturbance characterized by one or more episodes of extreme anger and aggression, such as incidents of ROAD RAGE, or any clinical disorder in which episodes of rage are a primary symptom, such as INTERMITTENT EXPLOSIVE DISORDER.

ramp movement a slow, sustained movement that is thought to be generated in the BASAL GANGLIA. Also called **smooth movement**.

random assignment see RANDOMIZE.

random control a control condition for PAVLOVIAN CONDITIONING in which the conditioned stimulus and the unconditioned stimulus are presented with equal probability but independently of each other. Such an arrangement results in a zero CONTINGENCY.

random-effects model a statistical procedure for analyzing data from experimental designs that use **random factors**, independent variables whose levels have been chosen randomly from a wide or even unlimited range of possible values. For example, a researcher wishing to investigate the effects of temperature on frequency of aggressive behavior could not easily examine each temperature value and so instead examines a random sample of such values. Although random-effects models tend to be less powerful than FIXED-EFFECTS MODELS, they enable generalization to be made to levels of the independent variable not actually employed in the study. See also MIXED-EFFECTS MODEL.

R

random error an error due to chance alone. Random errors are nonsystematic (occurring arbitrarily) and generally assumed to form a NORMAL DISTRIBUTION around a true score. Also called **variable error**. See also ABSOLUTE ERROR; CONSTANT ERROR.

random-interval schedule (RI schedule) in conditioning, an arrangement in which the first response after an interval has elapsed is reinforced, the duration of the interval varies randomly from reinforcement to reinforcement, and a fixed probability of reinforcement over time is used to reinforce a response. For example, if every second the probability that reinforcement would be arranged for the next response was .1, then the random-interval schedule value would be 10 s (i.e., RI 10 s).

randomization test an approach to HYPOTHESIS TESTING in which the observed data from all participants and experimental conditions is combined and randomly sorted into new samples (groups), a test of statistical significance performed, and the value obtained compared with the value obtained for the data as arranged originally. This process is repeated many times, theoretically for all possible rearrangements (permutations) of the data, although the sheer number of possible permutations generally precludes this and a subset of permutations (10,000 often is recommended) is used instead. A randomization test is a distribution-free approach, that is, it does not make assumptions about the distribution of the data.

randomize *vb.* to assign participants or other sampling units to the conditions of an experiment at random, that is, in such a way that each participant or sampling unit has an equal chance of being assigned to any particular condition. —**randomization** *n.*

randomized block design a research design in which participants are first classified into groups (blocks), on the basis of a variable for which the experimenter wishes to control. Individuals within each block are then randomly assigned to one of several treatment groups.

randomized-group design an experimental design in which the participants are assigned at random to either experimental or control groups without matching one or more background variables. Compare MATCHED-GROUP DESIGN.

randomized-response technique a procedure for reducing SOCIAL DESIRABILITY bias when measuring attitudes or other constructs at an aggregate group level. Participants are presented with a pair of questions that have dichotomous response options (e.g., agree or disagree, yes or no), one question being the target question and the other an innocuous filler question. They roll a die (or use a similar randomization procedure) to determine which question they should answer but do not tell the interviewer which one it is. The ambiguity regarding which question has been answered is assumed to reduce participants' concerns about the social desirability of their answers.

random-ratio schedule (RR schedule) in conditioning, an arrangement in which the number of responses required for each reinforcement varies randomly from reinforcement to reinforcement. It is usually arranged by having the same probability of reinforcement for each response regardless of the history of reinforcement for prior responses. For example, a random-ratio 100 schedule would result from a reinforcement probability of .01 for any given response.

random sampling a process for selecting individuals for a study from a larger potential group of individuals in such a way that each is selected with a fixed probability of inclusion. This selected group of individuals is called a **random sample**.

random variable a variable whose value depends upon the outcome of chance. Also called **stochastic variable**.

range *n.* in statistics, a measure of DISPERSION, obtained by subtracting the lowest score from the highest score in a distribution.

range fractionation a hypothesis of perception of stimulus intensity, stating that a wide range of intensity values can be encoded by a group of cells, each of which is a specialist for a particular range of stimulus intensities.

range of motion the degree of movement of a joint that can be achieved without tissue damage, such as how far a person can turn his or her neck. It is determined by the contour of the joint, the restraining bones, and the ligaments of the capsule surrounding the joint.

range restriction see RESTRICTION OF RANGE.

rank *n.* a particular position along an ordered continuum.

rank correlation a measure of the degree of relationship between two variables that have each been arranged in ascending or descending order of magnitude (i.e., ranked). It is an assessment not of the association between the actual values of the variables but rather of the association between their rankings. Also called **rank order correlation**; **Spearman rank correlation**.

rape *n.* the nonconsensual oral, anal, or vaginal penetration of an individual by another person with a part of the body or an object, using force or threats of bodily harm, or by taking advantage of someone incapable of giving consent. U.S. laws defining rape vary by state, but in contrast to older definitions the crime of rape is no longer limited to female victims, to vaginal penetration alone, or to forcible situations only, and the exclusion of spouses as possible perpetrators of rape has been dropped.

rape counseling provision of guidance and support for victims of rape and sexual assault. **Rape crisis centers** offer expert counseling for the psychological trauma that individuals typically experience following a sexual attack; both the affected individuals and their families are counseled. Community education and prevention outreach programs are increasingly part of the purview of this area of counseling.

rape-trauma syndrome the symptoms of POSTTRAUMATIC STRESS DISORDER (PTSD) experienced by an individual who has been sexually assaulted. The term was coined prior to the wide acceptance and use of the more inclusive concept of PTSD.

raphe nucleus a group of SEROTONERGIC neurons in the midline of the brainstem that project widely to the spinal cord, thalamus, basal ganglia, and cerebral cortex.

rapid cycling mood disturbance that fluctuates over a short period, most commonly between manic and depressive symptoms. A rapid-cycling BIPOLAR DISORDER is characterized by four or more mood episodes over a 12-month period; the episodes must be separated by symptom-free periods of at least 2 months or must be delimited by switching to an episode of opposite polarity (e.g., a major depressive episode switches to a manic, mixed, or hypomanic episode).

rapid eye movement (**REM**) the rapid, jerky, but coordinated movement of the eyes behind closed lids, observed during dreaming sleep. See REM SLEEP.

rapid neuroleptization see MEGADOSE PHARMACOTHERAPY.

rapport *n.* a warm, relaxed relationship of mutual understanding, acceptance, and sympathetic compatibility between or among individuals. The establishment of rapport with the client in psychotherapy is frequently a significant mediate goal for the therapist in order to facilitate and deepen the therapeutic experience and promote optimal progress and improvement in the client.

rapprochement *n.* **1.** generally, a state of cordial relations between individuals or groups. **2.** in the theory of SEPARATION–INDIVIDUATION of Austrian child psychoanalyst Margaret Mahler (1897–1985), the phase, after about 18 months of age, in which the child makes active approaches to the mother. This contrasts with the preceding stage in which the child was relatively oblivious to the mother.

RAS abbreviation for RETICULAR ACTIVATING SYSTEM.

Rasch model the simplest model for ITEM RESPONSE THEORY, in which only a single parameter, item difficulty, is specified. [proposed in 1960 by Georg **Rasch** (1901–1980), Danish statistician]

rate 1. *n.* relative frequency. **2.** *vb.* to evaluate or judge subjectively, especially by assigning a numerical value. For example, a supervisor could assess an employee's quality of work by choosing a number from 1 (excellent) to 10 (poor). Any in-

strument used in this process is called a **rating scale**.

rating scale judgment task a signal detection task in which participants assign confidence ratings to their "yes" or "no" responses. Each rating category defines a different response criterion relative to which the evidence is judged, allowing a RECEIVER-OPERATING CHARACTERISTIC CURVE to be constructed efficiently.

ratio IQ see IQ.

rational *adj.* **1.** pertaining to REASONING or, more broadly, to higher thought processes. **2.** influenced by thought rather than by emotion. —**rationally** *adv.*

rational emotive behavior therapy (**REBT**) a form of COGNITIVE BEHAVIOR THERAPY based on the concept that an individual's irrational or self-defeating beliefs and feelings influence and cause his or her undesirable behaviors and damaging self-concept. Originally called **rational emotive therapy** (RET), it teaches the individual, through a variety of cognitive, emotive, and behavioral techniques, to modify and replace self-defeating thoughts to achieve new and more effective ways of feeling and behaving. In the process of the therapy, the irrational beliefs and feelings are first unmasked then altered by (a) showing how the beliefs and feelings produce the individual's problems and (b) indicating how they can be changed through behavior therapy. Also called **rational psychotherapy**. See also ABCDE TECHNIQUE.

rationalism *n.* **1.** any philosophical position holding that (a) it is possible to obtain knowledge of reality by reason alone, unsupported by experience, and (b) all human knowledge can be brought within a single deductive system. This confidence in reason is central to classical Greek philosophy, notably in its mistrust of sensory experience as a source of truth and the preeminent role it gives to reason in epistemology. However, the term "rationalist" is chiefly applied to thinkers in the Continental philosophical tradition initiated by French philosopher René Descartes (1596–1650), most notably Dutch Jewish philosopher Baruch Spinoza (1632–1677) and German philosopher Gottfried Wilhelm Leibniz (1646–1716). Rationalism is usually contrasted with EMPIRICISM, which holds that knowledge comes from or must be validated by sensory experience. In psychology, psychoanalytical approaches, humanistic psychology, and some strains of cognitive theory are heavily influenced by rationalism. **2.** in religion, a perspective that rejects the possibility or the viability of divine revelation as a source of knowledge. **3.** in general language, any position that relies on reason and evidence rather than on faith, intuition, custom, prejudice, or other sources of conviction. —**rationalist** *adj., n.*

rationality of emotions the proposition that emotions show an implacable logic, in that they follow from APPRAISALS made by the individual as inevitably as logical conclusions follow from axioms and premises. This view counters the traditional idea that emotions and reason are in opposition to one another.

rationalization *n.* in psychotherapy, an explanation, or presentation, in which apparently logical reasons are given to justify unacceptable behavior that is motivated by unconscious instinctual impulses. In psychoanalytic theory, such behavior is considered to be a DEFENSE MECHANISM. Rationalizations are used to defend against feelings of guilt, to maintain self-respect, and to protect from criticism. In psychotherapy, rationalization is considered counterproductive to deep exploration and confrontation of the client's thoughts and feelings and of how they affect behavior. —**rationalize** *vb.*

rational psychology an approach to the study and explanation of psychological phenomena that emphasizes philosophy, logic, and deductive reason as sources of insight into the principles that underlie the mind and that make experience possible. This approach is in sharp contrast to that of EMPIRICAL PSYCHOLOGY. See also PHILOSOPHICAL PSYCHOLOGY.

rational psychotherapy see RATIONAL EMOTIVE BEHAVIOR THERAPY.

rational type in ANALYTIC PSYCHOLOGY, one of the two major categories of FUNCTIONAL TYPE: It comprises the thinking type and the feeling type. Compare IRRATIONAL TYPE.

ratio reinforcement in OPERANT CONDITIONING, reinforcement presented after a prearranged number of responses, in contrast to reinforcement delivered on the basis of a time schedule only. In such schedules (e.g., FIXED-RATIO SCHEDULE, PROGRESSIVE-RATIO SCHEDULE), the rate of reinforcement is a direct function of the rate of responding. Compare INTERVAL REINFORCEMENT.

ratio scale a measurement scale having a true zero (i.e., zero on the scale indicates an absence of the measured attribute) and a constant ratio of values. Thus, on a ratio scale an increase from 3 to 4 (for example) is the same as an increase from 7 to 8. The existence of a true zero point is what distinguishes a ratio scale from an INTERVAL SCALE.

Rat Man a landmark case of Austrian psychiatrist Sigmund Freud (1856–1939), which he described in "Notes upon a Case of Obsessional Neurosis" (1909). The name was applied to a patient of Freud's, a 30-year-old lawyer whose obsessional fear of rats was traced to repressed death wishes toward his father generated by oedipal conflicts. One example of the patient's obsession was his belief that a rat that appeared to come out of his father's grave had eaten the corpse; another was a fantasy that a rat had been placed in his father's anus and had eaten through his intestines. Freud's analysis of these reactions laid the groundwork for the psychoanalytic interpreta-

tion of obsessional neurosis. See also OEDIPUS COMPLEX.

Raven's Progressive Matrices a nonverbal test of mental ability consisting of abstract designs, each of which is missing one part. The participant chooses the missing component from several alternatives in order to complete the design. The test comprises 60 designs arranged in five groups of 12; the items within each group become progressively more difficult. The test, introduced in 1938, is often viewed as the prototypical measure of general intelligence. [John C. **Raven** (1902–1970), British psychologist]

reactance theory a model stating that in response to a perceived threat to or loss of a behavioral freedom a person will experience **psychological reactance** (or, more simply, **reactance**), a motivational state characterized by distress, anxiety, resistance, and the desire to restore that freedom. According to this model, when people feel coerced or forced into a certain behavior, they will react against the coercion, often by demonstrating an increased preference for the behavior that is restrained, and may perform the opposite behavior to that desired.

reaction formation in psychoanalytic theory, a DEFENSE MECHANISM in which unacceptable or threatening unconscious impulses are denied and are replaced in consciousness with their opposite. For example, to conceal an unconscious prejudice an individual may preach tolerance; to deny feelings of rejection, a mother may be overindulgent toward her child. Through the symbolic relationship between the unconscious wish and its opposite, the outward behavior provides a disguised outlet for the tendencies it seems to oppose.

reaction time (**RT**) the time that elapses between onset or presentation of a stimulus and occurrence of a response to that stimulus. There are several specific types, including SIMPLE REACTION TIME and COMPOUND REACTION TIME.

reactive *adj.* **1.** in general, responsive to a given stimulus or situation. **2.** describing or relating to an episode, such as a depressive or psychotic episode, that is secondary to a traumatic event, stress, or emotional upheaval in the life of the individual. A reactive episode generally has a more favorable prognosis than a similar episode that is ENDOGENOUS in origin and unrelated to a specific happening.

reactive aggression see AGGRESSION.

reactive attachment disorder a disorder of infancy and early childhood characterized by disturbed and developmentally inappropriate patterns of social relating not resulting from mental retardation or pervasive developmental disorder. It is evidenced either by persistent failure to initiate or respond appropriately in social interactions (inhibited type) or by indiscriminate sociability without appropriate selective attachments (disinhibited type). There must also

R

be evidence of inadequate care (e.g., ignoring the child's basic physical or emotional needs, frequent changes of primary caregiver), which is assumed to be responsible for the disturbed social relating.

reactive depression a MAJOR DEPRESSIVE EPISODE that is apparently precipitated by a distressing event or situation, such as a career or relationship setback. Also called **exogenous depression**. Compare ENDOGENOUS DEPRESSION.

reactive measure a measure that alters the response under investigation. For example, if participants are aware of being observed, their reactions may be influenced more by the observer and the fact of being observed than by the stimulus object or situation to which they are ostensibly responding. See also UNOBTRUSIVE MEASURE.

reactive schizophrenia an acute form of schizophrenia that clearly develops in response to predisposing or precipitating environmental factors, such as extreme stress. The prognosis is generally more favorable than for PROCESS SCHIZOPHRENIA.

readiness n. **1.** a state of preparedness to act or to respond to a stimulus. **2.** a state of receptivity to an experience or activity, such as school readiness or readiness to change substance-use behaviors.

reading disability a reading ability that is below that expected for a child of a given age and stage of development. It is associated with neurological damage or impairment, typically in language processing and visual reasoning areas of the brain, that results in difficulty understanding the associations between letters and sounds.

reading disorder a LEARNING DISORDER that is characterized by a level of reading ability substantially below that expected for a child of a given age, intellectual ability, and educational experience. The reading difficulty, which involves faulty oral reading, slow oral and silent reading, and often reduced comprehension, interferes with achievement or everyday life and is not attributable to neurological impairment, sensory impairment, mental retardation, or environmental deprivation.

reading span 1. the amount of written or printed material that a person can apprehend during a single FIXATION of the eye during reading. The greater the reading span, the fewer times the eye needs to stop along a line of text. A span of 7–10 characters is considered typical. **2.** in memory tests, the number of words a person can remember on being asked to recall the last word of each sentence in a passage that he or she has just read.

reafference principle a concept developed to explain the regulation and interaction of internal signals and sensory signals in directing and coordinating bodily movements. It requires storage of a copy of each spontaneous activation of a motor unit by the processing unit (see COROLLARY DISCHARGE). This copy fixes the reference value of the parameters required to execute the movement, which guides the response until the reafference (feedback) from a sensory unit to the processing unit indicates an accordance with the reference value or set point. The reafference principle has also been used to explain some perceptual phenomena (e.g., the role of internal signals in determining the motion of objects in the world).

Real n. the realm of nature or reality: one of three aspects of the psychoanalytic field defined by French psychoanalyst Jacques Lacan (1901–1981). The Real is posited to be unknown and unknowable—in effect, unreal—because all individuals ultimately possess are images and symbols. The other realms are the IMAGINARY and the SYMBOLIC.

real–ideal self congruence the degree to which the characteristics of a person's ideal self match his or her actual characteristics. The discrepancy between the two, when large enough, creates psychological pain; it is theorized to be a motivating force for entering treatment and is the focus of treatment in CLIENT-CENTERED THERAPY.

realism n. **1.** the philosophical doctrine that objects have an existence independent of the observer. Compare IDEALISM. See also NAIVE REALISM. **2.** the older philosophical doctrine that UNIVERSALS, such as general terms and abstract ideas, have a greater genuine reality than the physical particulars to which they refer, as in so-called PLATONIC IDEALISM. Compare NOMINALISM. —**realist** adj., n.

realistic group-conflict theory a conceptual framework predicated on the assumption that intergroup tensions will occur whenever social groups must compete for scarce resources (e.g., food, territory, jobs, wealth, power, and natural resources) and that this competition fuels prejudice and other antagonistic attitudes that lead to conflicts such as rivalries and warfare. Also called **realistic conflict theory**. See CONFLICT THEORY.

reality confrontation an activity in which the therapist raises the possibility that the patient has misconstrued events or the intentions of others. The confrontation is thought to be helpful in reducing maladaptive behaviors that result from distorted thinking.

reality monitoring see SOURCE MONITORING.

reality orientation in psychotherapy, a form of REMOTIVATION that aims to reduce a client's confusion about time, place, or person. The therapist continually reminds the client who he or she is, what day it is, where he or she is, and what is happening or is about to take place.

reality principle in psychoanalytic theory, the regulatory mechanism that represents the demands of the external world and requires the individual to forgo or modify instinctual gratification or to postpone it to a more appropriate time. In contrast to the PLEASURE PRINCIPLE, which is posited to dominate the life of the infant and child and govern the ID, or instinctual impulses, the reality principle is posited to govern the EGO, which controls impulses and enables people to deal rationally and effectively with the situations of life.

reality testing 1. in general, any means by which an individual determines and assesses his or her limitations in the face of biological, physiological, social, or environmental actualities or exigencies. **2.** the objective evaluation of sense impressions, which enables the individual to distinguish between the internal and external worlds, and between fantasy and reality. Defective reality testing is the major criterion of PSYCHOSIS.

reality therapy treatment that focuses on present ineffective or maladaptive behavior and the development of the client's ability to cope with the stresses of reality and take greater responsibility for the fulfillment of his or her needs (i.e., discover what he or she really wants and the optimal way of achieving it). To these ends, the therapist plays an active role in examining the client's daily activities, suggesting healthier, more adaptive ways for the client to behave. Reality therapy tends to be of shorter duration than many other traditional psychotherapies (see SHORT-TERM THERAPY).

real–simulator model an experimental design in which some participants are instructed to simulate hypnosis, or some other psychological state, while other participants are genuinely experiencing it. The experimenter is usually unaware which participants are experiencing the state and which are simulators.

reasonable accommodations adjustments made within an environment or setting that allow an individual with a physical, cognitive, or psychiatric disability to perform required tasks and essential functions. This might include installing ramps in an office cafeteria for wheelchair accessibility, altering the format of a test for a person with learning disabilities, or providing a sign language interpreter for a person with hearing loss. Provisions for reasonable accommodations must be made by employers and educators according to the 1990 Americans With Disabilities Act and the 1973 Rehabilitation Act.

reasoned action model see THEORY OF REASONED ACTION.

reasoning *n.* thinking in which logical processes of an inductive or deductive character are used to draw conclusions from facts or premises. —**reason** *vb.*

reassurance *n.* in psychotherapy and counseling, a supportive approach that encourages clients to believe in themselves and in the possibilities of improvement. The technique is common and has widespread use across many forms of psychotherapy. It is used frequently in SUPPORTIVE PSYCHOTHERAPY and occasionally in RECONSTRUCTIVE PSYCHOTHERAPY to encourage a client in the process of exploring new relationships and feelings. Reassurance is also used to diminish anxiety, for example, by explaining to a client that a period of heightened depression or tension is temporary and not unexpected. Also called **assurance**.

rebirthing *n.* **1.** the therapeutic use of continuous, focused breathing and reflection, initially under the guidance of a rebirthing practitioner (a **rebirther**), to release tension, stress, and intense emotions and attain a state of deep peace and total relaxation that leads to personal growth and positive changes in health, consciousness, and self-esteem (i.e., a personal and spiritual "rebirth"). This type of therapy is increasingly being termed **breathwork** or **rebirthing breathwork**. **2.** a highly controversial form of therapy, now largely discredited (both scientifically and ethically), in which an individual attempts to reexperience being born (e.g., through hypnotic age regression) in order to resolve supposed pre- and perinatal conflicts and emotions and to develop new and different outlooks on life.

rebound phenomenon an effect in which an activity or occurrence previously suppressed or prevented temporarily increases once the restrictions imposed on it are removed. The term is used particularly to denote the temporary reappearance of symptoms following abrupt discontinuation of a medication used for treatment. An example is **rebound insomnia**, in which the discontinuation of the use of hypnotic agents, particularly short-acting BENZODIAZEPINES, results in a transitory return of insomnia, possibly of increased severity.

reboxetine *n.* a drug that inhibits the reuptake of norepinephrine but has little or no effect on neurotransmission of serotonin, dopamine, acetylcholine, or histamine. It was the first selective norepinephrine reuptake inhibitor developed for clinical use as an antidepressant. U.S. trade name (among others): **Vestra**.

REBT abbreviation for RATIONAL EMOTIVE BEHAVIOR THERAPY.

recall 1. *vb.* to transfer prior learning or past experience to current consciousness: that is, to retrieve and reproduce information. **2.** *n.* the process by which this occurs.

recall method a technique of evaluating memory in terms of the amount of learned material that can be correctly reproduced, as in an essay exam or in reproducing a list of words. Recall can be tested immediately after learning or after various delay intervals. Also called **recall test**. Compare RECOGNITION METHOD.

receiver-operating characteristic curve (**ROC curve**) in a detection, discrimination, or recognition task, the relationship between the HIT rate (the proportion of correct "yes" responses) and the FALSE-ALARM rate (the proportion of incorrect "yes" responses). This is plotted as a curve to determine what effect the observer's response criterion is having on the results.

recency effect a memory phenomenon in which the most recently presented facts, impressions, or items are learned or remembered better than material presented earlier. This can occur in both formal learning situations and social contexts. For example, it can result in inaccurate ratings or impressions of a person's abilities or other characteristics due to the inordinate influence of the most recent information received about that person. Compare NEGATIVE RECENCY; PRIMACY EFFECT.

receptive aphasia see APHASIA.

receptive field the spatially discrete region and the features associated with it that can be stimulated to cause the maximal response of a sensory cell. In vision, for example, the receptive field of a retinal ganglion cell is the area on the retina (containing a particular number of photoreceptors) that evokes a neural response.

receptive vocabulary an individual's vocabulary as defined by the words that he or she can understand, rather than the words that he or she normally uses. Also called **passive vocabulary**; **recognition vocabulary**. Compare PRODUCTIVE VOCABULARY.

receptivity *n.* the period of time when a female is responsive to sexual overtures from a male, typically (but not exclusively) around the time of ovulation. Receptivity has a connotation of passive female acceptance or tolerance of male sexual overtures. In contrast, PROCEPTIVITY conveys active solicitation of males by females. —**receptive** *adj.*

receptor *n.* **1.** the cell in a sensory system that is responsible for stimulus TRANSDUCTION. Receptor cells are specialized to detect and respond to specific stimuli in the external or internal environment. Examples include the RETINAL RODS and RETINAL CONES in the eye and the HAIR CELLS in the cochlea of the ear. **2.** a molecule in a cell membrane that specifically binds a particular molecular messenger (e.g., a neurotransmitter, hormone, or drug) and elicits a response in the cell.

receptor potential the electric potential produced by stimulation of a receptor cell, which is roughly proportional to the intensity of the sensory stimulus and may be sufficient to trigger an ACTION POTENTIAL in a neuron that is postsynaptic to the receptor. Also called **generator potential**.

receptor site a region of specialized membrane on the surface of a cell (e.g., a neuron) that contains RECEPTOR molecules, which receive and react with particular messenger molecules (e.g., neurotransmitters).

recessive allele the version of a gene (see ALLELE) whose effects are manifest only if it is carried on both members of a HOMOLOGOUS pair of chromosomes. Hence, the trait determined by a recessive allele (the **recessive trait**) is apparent only in the absence of another version of that same gene (the DOMINANT ALLELE). The term **autosomal recessive** is used to describe such patterns of inheritance in which characteristics are conveyed by recessive alleles. For example, Tay–Sachs disease is an autosomal recessive disorder.

recidivism *n.* relapse. The term typically denotes the repetition of delinquent or criminal behavior, especially in the case of a habitual criminal, or **repeat offender**, who has been convicted several times. —**recidivist** *n.*, *adj.* —**recidivistic** *adj.*

reciprocal altruism see ALTRUISM.

reciprocal determinism a concept that opposes the radical or exclusive emphasis on environmental determination of responses and instead maintains that the environment influences behavior, behavior influences the environment, and both influence the individual, who also influences them. This concept is associated with SOCIAL LEARNING THEORY.

reciprocal inhibition a technique in BEHAVIOR THERAPY that aims to replace an undesired response with a desired one by COUNTERCONDITIONING. It relies on the gradual substitution of a response that is incompatible with the original one and is potent enough to neutralize the anxiety-evoking power of the stimulus. See also SYSTEMATIC DESENSITIZATION.

reciprocal innervation the principle of MOTOR NEURON activity stating that when one set of muscles receives a signal for a reflex action, the antagonistic set of muscles receives a simultaneous signal that inhibits reaction.

reciprocity *n.* the quality of an act, process, or relation in which one person receives benefits from another and, in return, provides the giver with an equivalent benefit. —**reciprocal** *adj.*

reciprocity law a general principle that the magnitude of sensation is the product of the duration of the stimulus multiplied by its intensity.

reciprocity norm the social standard (NORM) that people who help others will receive equivalent benefits from these others in return. Compare SOCIAL JUSTICE NORM; SOCIAL RESPONSIBILITY NORM.

recoding *n.* the translation of material held in memory from one form into another. For example, a series of random digits (e.g., 239812389712) could be recoded as a series of four-digit prices ($23.98, $12.38, $97.12), thereby making the series much easier to recall. See CHUNKING; ELABORATION. —**recode** *vb.*

recognition *n.* a sense of awareness and familiarity experienced when one encounters people, events, or objects that have been encountered before or when one comes upon material that has been learned in the past.

recognition by components theory the theory that perception of objects entails their decomposition into a set of simple three-dimensional elements called **geons**, together with the skeletal structure connecting them.

recognition method a technique of measuring the amount of material learned or remembered by testing a person's capacity to later identify the content as having been experienced before. Previously studied items are presented along with new items, or LURES, and the participant attempts to identify those items that were studied before and those items that were not. Compare RECALL METHOD.

recollection *n.* remembrance, particularly vivid and detailed memory for past events or information pertaining to a specific time or place.

recombination *n.* the exchange of genetic material between paired chromosomes during the formation of sperm and egg cells. It involves the breaking and rejoining of chromatids (filament-like subunits) of homologous chromosomes in a process called **crossing over**. It results in offspring having combinations of genes that are different from those of either parent.

reconstituted family see STEPFAMILY.

reconstitution *n.* **1.** revision of one's attitudes or goals. **2.** a mental or attitudinal outcome of the grieving process experienced by some patients with catastrophic illnesses resulting in disability.

reconstruction *n.* **1.** in psychoanalysis, the revival and analytic interpretation of past experiences that have been instrumental in producing present emotional disturbance. **2.** the logical recreation of an experience or event that has been only partially stored in memory. **—reconstruct** *vb.*

reconstructive memory a form of remembering marked by the logical recreation of an experience or event that has been only partially stored in memory. It draws on general knowledge and SCHEMAS or on memory for what typically happens in order to reconstruct the experience or event.

reconstructive psychotherapy psychotherapy directed toward basic and extensive modification of an individual's character structure, by enhancing his or her insight into personality development, unconscious conflicts, and adaptive responses. Examples are Freudian PSYCHOANALYSIS, Adlerian INDIVIDUAL PSYCHOLOGY, Jungian ANALYTIC PSYCHOLOGY, and the approaches of German-born U.S. psychoanalyst Karen D. Horney (1885–1952) and U.S. psychiatrist Harry Stack Sullivan (1892–1949).

recovered memory the subjective experience of recalling details of a prior traumatic event, such as sexual or physical abuse, that has previously been unavailable to conscious recollection. Before recovering the memory, the person may be unaware that the traumatic event has occurred. The phenomenon is controversial: Because such recoveries often occur while the

person is undergoing therapy, there is debate about their veracity vis-à-vis the role that the therapist may have played in suggesting or otherwise arousing them. Also called **repressed memory**.

recovery *n.* the period during which an individual exhibits consistent progress in terms of measurable return of abilities, skills, and functions following illness or injury.

recreational drug see DRUG.

recreational therapy the use of individualized recreational activities (arts and crafts, sports, games, group outings, etc.) as an integral part of the rehabilitation or therapeutic process for individuals with physical or psychological disabilities or illness. Also called **therapeutic recreation**.

recuperative theory a theory that the function of sleep is to allow the body to recuperate from the rigors of waking, to regather resources, and to reestablish internal HOMEOSTASIS.

recurrent *adj.* occurring repeatedly or reappearing after an interval of time or a period of remission: often applied to disorders marked by chronicity, relapse, or repeated episodes (e.g., depressive symptoms).

redintegration *n.* restoration to completeness, particularly the process of recollecting memories from partial cues or reminders, as in recalling an entire song when a few notes are played. Also called **reintegration**. **—redintegrative** *adj.*

red nucleus see RUBROSPINAL TRACT.

reduced model in the GENERAL LINEAR MODEL, a model with fewer parameters than the most highly parameterized model in a set of models to be compared.

reductionism *n.* the strategy of explaining or accounting for some phenomenon or construct A by claiming that, when properly understood, it can be shown to be some other phenomenon or construct B, where B is seen to be simpler, more basic, or more fundamental. The term is mainly applied to those positions that attempt to understand human culture, society, or psychology in terms of animal behavior or physical laws. In psychology, a common form of reductionism is that in which psychological phenomena are reduced to biological phenomena, so that mental life is shown to be merely a function of biological processes. See also EPIPHENOMENON; IDENTITY THEORY; MATERIALISM.

redundancy *n.* in linguistics and information theory, the condition of those parts of a communication that could be deleted without loss of essential content. Redundancy includes not only repetitions, tautologies, and polite formulas, but also the multiple markings of a given meaning required by conventions of grammar and syntax. For example, in the sentence *All three men were running*, the plurality of the subject is signaled four times: by *all*, *three*, and the plural forms *men* and *were*. It is largely owing to redundancies of this kind that one can so often guess the correct content of messages that have been only partially heard or misprinted. **—redundant** *adj.*

reduplicative paramnesia a disturbance of memory characterized by the subjective certainty that a familiar person or place has been duplicated, such as the belief that the hospital where one is treated is duplicated and relocated to another site. It can be caused by a variety of neurological disorders, but brain lesions commonly involve the frontal lobes, the right hemisphere, or both.

reeducation *n.* **1.** learning or training that focuses on replacing maladaptive cognitions, affects, or behaviors with healthier more adaptive ones or on learning forgotten or otherwise lost skills anew. **2.** a form of psychological treatment in which the client learns effective ways of handling and coping with problems and relationships through a form of nonreconstructive therapy, such as RELATIONSHIP THERAPY, BEHAVIOR THERAPY, hypnotic suggestion (see HYPNOSUGGESTION), COUNSELING, PERSUASION THERAPY, nonanalytic group therapy, or REALITY THERAPY. Also called **reeducative therapy**.

reenactment *n.* in some forms of psychotherapy, the process of reliving traumatic events and past experiences and relationships while reviving the original emotions associated with them. See also ABREACTION.

reentrant *adj.* in neuropsychology, involving the mutual exchange of signals between neural areas along massively parallel connections, enabling the association of activity in different regions of the brain.

reference group a group or social aggregate that individuals use as a standard or frame of reference when selecting and appraising their own abilities, attitudes, or beliefs. Reference groups include formal and informal groups that the individual identifies with and admires, statistical aggregations of noninteracting individuals, imaginary groups, and even groups that deny the individual membership (**nonmembership reference groups**). According to the general conceptual framework known as **reference-group theory**, individuals' attitudes, values, and self-appraisals are shaped, in part, by their identification with, and comparison to, reference groups. For example, a reference-group theory of values suggests that individuals adopt, as their own, the values expressed by the majority of the members of their reference group.

referral *n.* **1.** the act of directing a patient to a therapist, physician, agency, or institution for evaluation, consultation, or treatment. **2.** the individual who is so referred. **—refer** *vb.*

referred sensation a sensation that is localized (i.e., experienced) at a point different from the area stimulated. For example, when struck on the elbow, the mechanical stimulation of the nerve may cause one to feel tingling of the fingers.

reflected appraisals the evaluative feedback that a person receives from others. Some theories of self have treated reflected appraisals as the most important basis for the SELF-CONCEPT, claiming that people learn about themselves chiefly from others. See LOOKING-GLASS SELF; SYMBOLIC INTERACTIONISM.

reflection *n.* **1.** see MEDITATION. **2.** in philosophy, the process by which simple unorganized sensations are converted through mental processes into complex ideas and abstractions. **3.** see MIRRORING. **—reflect** *vb.*

reflection of feeling a statement made by a therapist or counselor that is intended to highlight the feelings or attitudes implicitly expressed in a client's communication. The statement reflects and communicates the essence of the client's experience from the client's point of view so that hidden or obscured feelings can be exposed for clarification. Also called **reflection response**.

reflective *adj.* describing or displaying behavior characterized by significant forethought and slow, deliberate examination of available options. Compare IMPULSIVE. **—reflectivity** *n.*

reflective consciousness aspects of consciousness that allow it to refer to its own activities.

reflectivity–impulsivity *n.* a dimension of COGNITIVE STYLE based on the observation that some people approach tasks impulsively, preferring to act immediately on their first thoughts or impressions, whereas others are more reflective, preferring to make a careful consideration of a range of alternatives before acting. Also called **reflection–impulsivity**.

reflex *n.* any of a number of automatic, unlearned, relatively fixed responses to stimuli that do not require conscious effort and that often involve a faster response than might be possible if a conscious evaluation of the input was required. Reflexes are innate in that they do not arise as a result of any special experience. An example is the PUPILLARY REFLEX.

reflex arc a NEURAL CIRCUIT that is involved in a reflex. In its simplest form it consists of an afferent, or sensory, neuron that conducts nerve impulses from a receptor to the spinal cord, where it connects directly or via an INTERNEURON to an efferent, or motor, neuron that carries the impulses to a muscle or gland.

reflex epilepsy a type of epilepsy marked by seizures that are triggered by specific sensory input, such as a flashing light.

reflexive behavior responses to stimuli that are involuntary or free from conscious control (e.g., the salivation that occurs with the presentation of food) and therefore serve as the basis for PAVLOVIAN CONDITIONING. Compare PLANNED BEHAVIOR; VOLUNTARY.

reflexology *n.* **1.** a late 19th-century and early 20th-century school of psychology based on research dealing solely with the outwardly observed and fixed manifestations and reactions of the human being. The simple reflex was seen as the elementary unit or building block of behavior. **2.** a form of COMPLEMENTARY AND ALTERNATIVE MEDICINE based on the principle that there are reflex points or zones in the feet and hands that correspond to every part of the body and that manipulating and pressing on these points has beneficial health effects. **—reflexologist** *n.*

reflex sympathetic dystrophy overactivity of the SYMPATHETIC NERVOUS SYSTEM, which may occur following local injury, usually to an upper or lower limb, associated with damage to nerves and blood vessels, resulting in pain; limb disuse; shiny, thin skin; loss of hair; and bone demineralization.

refraction *n.* in vision, the bending of light as it passes through the cornea and lens of the eye so that it is focused on the retina.

refractive error (**refractive disorder**) a defect in the eye such that it does not refract, or bend, incident light into perfect focus on the retina, so that visual acuity is reduced. Examples include ASTIGMATISM, HYPEROPIA, and MYOPIA.

refractory period a period of inactivity after a neuron or muscle cell has undergone excitation. As the cell is being repolarized, it will not respond to any stimulus during the early part of the refractory period, called the **absolute refractory period**. In the subsequent **relative refractory period**, it responds only to a stronger than normal stimulus.

reframing *n.* a process of reconceptualizing an idea for the purpose of changing an attitude by seeing it from a different perspective. In changing the conceptual or emotional context of a problem, and placing it in a different frame that fits the given facts equally well but changes its entire meaning, perceptions of weakness or difficulty in handling the problem may be changed to strength and opportunity. In psychotherapy, the manner in which a client frames behavior may be part of the problem. Part of the therapist's response might be to reframe thoughts or feelings so as to provide alternative ways to evaluate the situation or respond to others. Compare RESTATEMENT.

regenerative medicine a branch of research and applied medicine that studies the body's capacities for and processes of self-healing, as well as the ability to create new tissues for transplant. See also STEM CELL.

regimen *n.* in medicine, a detailed treatment program for the regulation of diet, exercise, rest, medication, and other therapeutic measures. Various forms of psychotherapy, such as COGNITIVE BEHAVIOR THERAPY, may also make use of regimens during the course of treatment. Such programs typically include a schedule and specify the components, methods, and duration of the program.

regional cerebral blood flow the rate of flow of blood through a particular area of the brain, measured by BRAIN IMAGING techniques such as positron emission tomography and single photon emission computed tomography. It is used to assess the differential involvement of brain regions in various cognitive functions.

register *n.* a form of a language associated with specific social functions and situations or with particular subject matter. Examples include the different types of language considered appropriate for a scientific meeting, a kindergarten class, or a barroom story. Register differs from DIALECT in that it varies with social context rather than with the sociological characteristics of the user. See ELABORATED CODE.

regression *n.* **1.** generally, a turning or going backward. In psychology, this typically indicates a return to a prior, lower state of cognitive, emotional, or behavioral functioning. **2.** in psychoanalytic theory, a DEFENSE MECHANISM in which the individual reverts to immature behavior or to an earlier stage of PSYCHOSEXUAL DEVELOPMENT when threatened with anxiety caused by overwhelming external problems or internal conflicts. **—regress** *vb.* **—regressive** *adj.*

regression analysis any of several statistical techniques that are designed to allow the prediction of the score on one variable, the DEPENDENT VARIABLE, from the scores on one or more other variables, the INDEPENDENT VARIABLES. Regression analysis is a subset of the GENERAL LINEAR MODEL.

regression equation the mathematical expression of the relationship between the dependent variable and one or more independent variables that results from conducting a REGRESSION ANALYSIS. It usually takes the form $y = a + bx + e$, in which y is the dependent variable, x is the independent variable, a is the intercept, b is the **regression coefficient** (a specific WEIGHT associated with x), and e is the error term.

regression toward the mean a phenomenon in which earlier measurements that were extremely deviant from a sample mean will tend, on retesting, to result in a value closer to the sample mean than the original value.

regressive reconstructive approach a technique in psychotherapy in which the client is encouraged to reexperience with emotional intensity traumatic situations from an earlier stage of life. Through such concurrent or subsequent mechanisms as TRANSFERENCE and INTERPRETATION, the approach is posited to help bring about personality change and development of greater emotional adaptation and maturity in the client.

regret *n.* an emotional response to remembrance of a past state, condition, or experience that one wishes had been different.

regulation of consciousness any activity aimed at managing or changing the state and content of CONSCIOUSNESS, including pain avoidance, pleasure seeking, and variety seeking.

Self-destructive activities, such as self-mutilation and chemical intoxication, may also be efforts to regulate states of consciousness.

regulatory drive any drive that helps preserve physiological HOMEOSTASIS and thus is necessary for the survival of the individual organism, such as hunger and thirst. Compare NONREGU-LATORY DRIVE.

rehabilitation *n.* the process of bringing an individual to a condition of health or useful and constructive activity, restoring to the fullest possible degree their independence, well-being, and level of functioning following injury, disability, or disorder. It involves providing appropriate resources, such as treatment or training, to enable such a person (e.g., one who has had a stroke) to redevelop skills and abilities he or she had acquired previously or to compensate for their loss. Compare HABILITATION.

rehabilitation medicine the branch of medicine that specializes in the development of individuals to the fullest physical, psychological, cognitive, social, vocational, or educational potential that is consistent with their physiological or anatomical impairment and environmental limitations.

rehabilitation psychology a specialty branch of psychology devoted to the application of psychological knowledge and understanding to the study, prevention, and treatment of disabling and chronic health conditions. **Rehabilitation psychologists** consider the entire network of factors (biological, psychological, social, environmental, and political) that affect functioning to help individuals attain optimal physical, psychological, and interpersonal functioning.

rehearsal *n.* **1.** preparation for a forthcoming event or confrontation that is anticipated to induce some level of discomfort or anxiety. By practicing what is to be said or done in a future encounter, the event itself may be less stressful. Rehearsal may be carried out in psychotherapy with the therapist coaching or role-playing to help the client practice the coming event. See also BEHAVIOR REHEARSAL; MENTAL REHEARSAL; ROLE PLAY. **2.** the repetition of information in an attempt to maintain it longer in memory. According to the DUAL-STORE MODEL OF MEMORY, rehearsal occurs in SHORT-TERM MEMORY and may allow a stronger trace to be then stored in LONG-TERM MEMORY. Although rehearsal implies a verbal process, it is hypothesized to occur also in other modalities.

reification *n.* treating an abstraction, concept, or formulation as though it were a real object or static structure.

reiki *n.* a complementary therapy that aims to promote physical, emotional, and spiritual healing through the use of energy and the laying on of hands, which is believed to improve the flow of life energy in the patient. See also COMPLEMENTARY AND ALTERNATIVE MEDICINE.

reinforcement *n.* **1.** in OPERANT CONDITION-ING, a process in which the frequency or probability of a response is increased by a dependent relationship, or contingency, with a stimulus or circumstance (the REINFORCER). **2.** the procedure that results in the frequency or probability of a response being increased in such a way. **3.** in PAVLOVIAN CONDITIONING, the presentation of an unconditioned stimulus after a conditioned stimulus.

reinforcement contingency the contingency (relationship) between a response and a REINFORCER. The contingency may be positive (if the occurrence of the reinforcer is more probable after the response) or negative (if it is less probable given the response). Reinforcement contingencies can be arranged by establishing dependencies between a particular type of response and a reinforcer (as when an experimenter arranges that a rat's lever presses are followed by presentation of food), or they can occur as natural consequences of a response (as when a door opens when pushed), or they can occur by accident.

reinforcement schedule see SCHEDULE OF RE-INFORCEMENT.

reinforcement therapy a therapeutic process based on OPERANT CONDITIONING and the use of positive reinforcement to initiate and maintain behavioral change.

reinforcer *n.* a stimulus or circumstance that acts effectively to produce REINFORCEMENT when it occurs in a dependent relationship, or contingency, with a response. See CONDITIONED REINFORCER.

reintegration *n.* see REDINTEGRATION.

Reissner's membrane a membrane of the auditory LABYRINTH that separates the SCALA VESTIBULI from the SCALA MEDIA inside the cochlea. [Ernst **Reissner** (1824–1878), German anatomist]

rejecting–neglecting parenting see PAR-ENTING.

rejection region see CRITICAL REGION.

relapse *n.* the recurrence of symptoms of a disorder or disease after a period of improvement or apparent cure.

relapse prevention procedures that are used after successful treatment of a condition, disease, or disorder in order to reduce relapse rates. These often include a combination of cognitive and behavioral skills that are taught to clients before therapy is terminated. Such procedures are often used with disorders (e.g., addictions and depression) that have unusually high relapse rates. See also TERTIARY PREVENTION.

relation *n.* **1.** any kind of meaningful connection between two or more events or entities. The specific nature of this connection varies with the context and discipline. In science, for example, a relation is primarily a causal relation. See CAU-SALITY; RELATIONSHIP. **2.** an individual connected to another by blood, marriage, or adoptive ties. See also KINSHIP.

relational discrimination in conditioning, a DISCRIMINATION based on the relationship between or among stimuli rather than on absolute features of the stimuli. For example, an animal can be trained to respond to the larger of two stimuli, regardless of the absolute size of the two stimuli.

relational frame a hypothesized unit that permits one to describe the relationships between new entities based on previous experience. Through experience with many such relationships, frames are learned into which new entities can be placed. For example, after many experiences with conditions in which one thing is larger than another, and having learned in those situations to say, for example, "The cow is bigger than the dog," one is then in position to say "My cat is bigger than yours" when comparing the two cats for the first time.

relational shift the developmental change in ANALOGICAL THINKING that occurs when the child moves from focusing on perceptual similarity to focusing on relational similarity when solving problems.

relationship *n.* **1.** a connection between objects, events, variables, or other phenomena. Research often involves the study of the relationship between variables. **2.** a continuing and usually binding association between two or more people, as in a family, friendship, marriage, partnership, or other interpersonal link in which the participants have some degree of influence on each other's thoughts, feelings, and even actions. In psychotherapy, the THERAPIST–PATIENT RELATIONSHIP is thought to be an essential aspect of patient improvement.

relationship role one of several identifiable roles adopted by members of a group who perform particular behaviors to maintain or enhance interpersonal relationships within the group. Some commonly cited relationship roles include the **gatekeeper**, who controls the CHANNELS OF COMMUNICATION in such a way that everyone has a chance to contribute; the **harmonizer**, who facilitates group unity by mediating between opposing views; the **compromiser**, who accedes partly or wholly to an opposing viewpoint to facilitate group progress; the **encourager**, who offers praise and support; and the **comedian**, who relieves tension and raises morale through humor. Compare TASK ROLE. See also GROUP ROLE.

relationship therapy any form of psychotherapy, from direct guidance to psychoanalysis, in which the relationship between client and therapist is a key factor. Relationship therapy provides emotional support, creating an accepting atmosphere that fosters personality growth and elicits attitudes and past experiences for examination and analysis during sessions.

relative deprivation the perception by an individual that the amount of a desired resource (e.g., money, social status) he or she has is less than some comparison standard. This standard can be the amount that was expected or the amount possessed by others with whom the person compares him- or herself. A distinction has been made between **egoistic relative deprivation**, the perceived discrepancy between an individual's own current position and the comparison standard; and **fraternalistic relative deprivation**, the perceived discrepancy between the position that the person's ingroup actually has and the position the person thinks it ought to have.

relative efficiency for two tests (A and B) of the same hypothesis operating at the same SIGNIFICANCE LEVEL, the ratio of the number of cases needed by test A to the number of cases needed by test B in order for the two tests to have the same POWER.

relative pitch the ability to identify the pitch of a sound accurately by mentally comparing it to a known reference pitch. Compare ABSOLUTE PITCH.

relative risk the ratio of the incidence of a certain disorder or condition in groups exposed to (or possessed of) a specific risk factor and groups not exposed to (or possessed of) that factor.

relative sensitivity the capacity to discriminate differences in stimuli (e.g., in terms of intensity or quality) when one stimulus is judged relative to another. When only one stimulus is presented at a time, sensitivity to stimulus differences is reduced.

relativism *n.* any position that challenges the reality of absolute standards of truth or value. In EPISTEMOLOGY, relativism is the assertion that there exist no absolute grounds for truth or knowledge claims. Thus, what is considered true will depend on individual judgments and local conditions of culture, reflecting individual and collective experience. Such relativism challenges the validity of science except as a catalog of experience and a basis for ad hoc empirical prediction. In ethics, relativism is the claim that no moral absolutes exist. Thus, judgments of right and wrong are based on local culture and tradition, on personal preferences, or on artificial principles. Standards of conduct vary enormously across individuals, cultures, and historical periods, and it is impossible to arbitrate among them or to produce universal ethical principles because there can be no means of knowing that these are true. See also PARTICULARISM; POSTMODERNISM. **—relativist** *adj.*

relaxation *n.* **1.** abatement of intensity, vigor, energy, or tension, resulting in calmness of mind, body, or both. **2.** the return of a muscle to its resting condition after a period of contraction. **—relax** *vb.*

relaxation therapy the use of muscle-relaxation techniques as an aid in the treatment of emotional tension. Also called **therapeutic relaxation**. See also DIFFERENTIAL RELAXATION; PROGRESSIVE RELAXATION.

relaxation training see PROGRESSIVE RELAXATION.

relearning method the learning again of material that was once known but is now forgotten, a technique for measuring knowledge that may be present even if unrecallable. Savings in time or trials over the original learning indicate the amount of retention. Also called **savings method**.

release from proactive interference restoration of the capacity to readily remember items of one type after switching categories of materials to be recalled. For instance, successively trying to memorize dates leads to the buildup of proactive INTERFERENCE, causing a decline in immediate recall of dates; switching to remembering names releases proactive interference, and retention improves (i.e., names are remembered more easily than dates were).

releaser n. in ethology, a stimulus that, when presented under the proper conditions, initiates a FIXED ACTION PATTERN (see also MODAL ACTION PATTERN). For example, a red belly on a male stickleback fish elicits aggressive behavior from other male sticklebacks but is attractive to gravid female sticklebacks. Also called **sign stimulus**. See also INNATE RELEASING MECHANISM; VACUUM ACTIVITY.

release theory of humor the theory that people laugh out of a need to release pent-up psychic energy. According to Austrian psychiatrist Sigmund Freud (1856–1939), humor permits the expression of normally taboo impulses and the energy it releases is that normally used in keeping such impulses out of consciousness. Compare INCONGRUITY THEORY OF HUMOR.

release therapy any therapy whose ultimate value is in the release of deep-seated, forgotten, or inhibited emotional and psychic pain through open expression and direct experience of anger, sorrow, or hostility in the therapy context. The technique is used, for example, in PLAY THERAPY and in PSYCHODRAMA.

releasing hormone any of a class of HYPOTHALAMIC HORMONES that travel via the HYPOTHALAMIC–PITUITARY PORTAL SYSTEM to control the release of hormones by the anterior pituitary gland. Examples are CORTICOTROPIN-RELEASING FACTOR and GONADOTROPIN-RELEASING HORMONE.

reliability n. the ability of a measurement instrument (e.g., a test) to measure an attribute consistently, yielding the same results across multiple applications to the same sample. The basic index of reliability is the CORRELATION COEFFICIENT. —**reliable** adj.

religion n. a system of spiritual beliefs, practices, or both, typically organized around the worship of an all-powerful deity (or deities) and involving such behaviors as prayer, meditation, and participation in public rituals. Other common features of organized religions are the belief that certain moral teachings have divine authority and the recognition of certain people, places, texts, or objects as being holy or sacred. See also PSYCHOLOGY OF RELIGION. —**religious** adj.

REM abbreviation for RAPID EYE MOVEMENT.

REM behavior disorder a SLEEP DISORDER involving motor activity during REM SLEEP, which typically includes an actual physical enactment of dream sequences. Because the dreams that are acted out are generally unpleasant or combative, this behavior is usually disruptive and can result in violence.

remedial therapy intervention aimed at assisting a person to achieve a normal or increased level of functioning when functioning is below expectation in a particular area (e.g., reading).

remembering n. the process of consciously reviving or bringing to awareness previous events, experiences, or information, or the process of retaining such material. Methods of assessing remembering include the RECALL METHOD, RECOGNITION METHOD, and RELEARNING METHOD.

remember–know procedure a procedure used to measure two different ways of accessing events from one's past and as an assessment of EPISODIC MEMORY and SEMANTIC MEMORY, respectively. In this context, remembering is the conscious and vivid recollection of a prior event such that a person can mentally travel to the specific time and place of the original event and retrieve the details; he or she is able to bring back to mind a particular association, image, or something more personal from the time of the event. Knowing refers to the experience in which a person is certain that an event has occurred but fails to recollect anything about its actual occurrence or what was experienced at the time of its occurrence.

remembrance n. the act of remembering or the state of being remembered.

reminiscence n. **1.** the recalling of previous experiences, especially those of a pleasant nature. Events that occurred in adolescence and early adulthood (often called the **reminiscence bump**) are most often remembered. Unlike RECOLLECTION, reminiscence does not necessarily involve vivid and detailed memory. **2.** an increase in the amount remembered, or in performance, that occurs after a delay interval following the initial exposure to the information, instead of the more usual forgetting after a delay.

reminiscence therapy the use of LIFE HISTORIES—written, oral, or both—to improve psychological well-being. The therapy is often used with older people.

remission n. a reduction or significant abatement in symptoms of a disease or disorder, or the period during which this occurs. Remission of symptoms does not necessarily indicate that a disease or disorder is fully cured. See also SPON-TANEOUS REMISSION.

REM latency the time between onset of sleep and the first occurrence of RAPID EYE MOVEMENT (REM).

remorse *n.* a strong sense of guilt and regret for a past action.

remote association an association between one item in a list or series and another item that does not adjoin it.

remote cause a cause that is removed from its effect in time or space but is nevertheless the ultimate or overriding cause. In a sequence of occurrences, it may be considered to be the precipitating event without which the chain would not have begun (the original cause). For example, the PROXIMATE CAUSE of Smith's aggression may be a trivial snub, but the remote cause may be Smith's early childhood experiences. See also CAUSAL LATENCY.

remotivation *n.* intervention aimed at increasing the likelihood that a person will cooperate with and benefit from treatments.

REM rebound the increased recurrence of REM SLEEP, the stage of sleep in which dreaming is associated with mild involuntary eye movements, following a period in which it was inhibited. It is an example of a REBOUND PHENOMENON.

REM sleep rapid-*eye*-*m*ovement sleep: the stage of sleep in which dreaming occurs and the electroencephalogram shows activity characteristic of wakefulness (hence it is also known as **paradoxical sleep**) except for inhibition of motor expression other than coordinated movements of the eyes. It accounts for one quarter to one fifth of total sleep time. Compare NREM SLEEP.

renal system the kidneys and related structures, including the ureters, bladder, urethra, blood supply, and nerve supply, which are involved with the excretion of waste materials from the body.

renin *n.* an enzyme that is released by the kidneys when blood pressure falls. It specifically cleaves the plasma globulin protein angiotensinogen to form ANGIOTENSIN.

reorganization principle the principle that new learning or perception disrupts old cognitive structures, requiring a reorganized structure. This is in opposition to the associationist principle that new learning is essentially added on to existing structures (see ASSOCIATIONISM).

reorientation therapy see CONVERSION THERAPY.

reparameterization *n.* the process of recasting the parameters of a model in different terms, usually for the purpose of removing technical difficulties in the solution of the GENERAL LINEAR MODEL from the original parameterization.

reparation *n.* amelioration of or expiation for harm previously done.

reparative therapy 1. therapy given to people who have experienced a sexual assault, including childhood sexual abuse and adult rape. Procedures generally involve working through the emotional trauma that was experienced and cognitive therapy on such issues as self-blame. The aim is to enable a return to normal functioning emotionally, interpersonally, and sexually. **2.** see CONVERSION THERAPY.

reparenting *n.* **1.** a controversial therapeutic procedure used to provide a client with missed childhood experiences. The client, who typically has severe problems, is treated as a child or infant; for example, he or she may be fed with a spoon or bottle, hugged, sung to, and provided with what the client or therapist feels the client missed in childhood. Reparenting has been unethically used to justify recreation of the birth process by wrapping a client in a blanket and having him or her struggle to get out. **2.** in self-help and some forms of counseling, a therapeutic technique in which individuals are urged to provide for themselves the kind of parenting attitudes or actions that their own parents were unable to provide.

repeatability *n.* the degree to which specific research studies obtain similar results when they are conducted again and again.

repeated acquisition a procedure in which sequences of responses are learned but the sequence changes from observation period to observation period. For example, a person might be asked to press a sequence of keys in the presence of seven different stimuli presented in sequence. Having learned to do so, the person would be required to learn a different sequence of key presses in response to the same seven stimuli in the next test period.

repeated measures design see WITHIN-SUBJECTS DESIGN.

repertoire *n.* the sum total of potential behavior or responses that a person or nonhuman animal is capable of performing. It usually refers to behavior that has been learned and is generally quantified through the study of past behavior.

repertory grid a technique used to analyze an individual's PERSONAL CONSTRUCTS. A number of significant concepts are selected, each of which is rated by the participant on a number of dimensions using a numerical scale. The findings are displayed in matrix form and can be subjected to statistical analysis to reveal correlations.

repetition compulsion in psychoanalytic theory, an unconscious need to reenact early traumas in the attempt to overcome or master them. In repetition compulsion the early painful experience is repeated in a new situation symbolic of the repressed prototype. Repetition compulsion acts as a RESISTANCE to therapeutic change, since the goal of therapy is not to repeat but to remember the trauma and to see its relation to present behavior.

repetition effect the fact that repeated presentation of information or items typically leads to better memory for the material. The repetition effect is a general principle of learning, although there are exceptions and modifiers. For instance, **spaced repetitions** are usually more effective than **massed repetitions**.

repetition priming a change in the processing of a stimulus (e.g., speed of response, number of errors) due to previous exposure to the same or a related stimulus.

repetitive strain injury (RSI) a group of musculoskeletal disorders involving chronic inflammation of the muscles, tendons, or nerves and caused by overuse or misuse of a specific body part. An example is CARPAL TUNNEL SYNDROME. Repetitive strain injuries result in pain and fatigue of the affected areas and are often associated with occupational situations; their prevention is an important issue in ERGONOMICS and HUMAN FACTORS. Also called **cumulative trauma disorder (CTD)**; **repetitive motion disorder** or **injury (RMD; RMI)**; **repetitive stress injury**.

replacement sampling see SAMPLING WITH REPLACEMENT.

replacement therapy 1. treatment in which a natural or synthetic substance is substituted for one that is deficient or lacking in an individual. See HORMONE REPLACEMENT THERAPY. **2.** the process of replacing abnormal thoughts or behavior with healthier ones through the use of therapy focused on constructive activities and interests.

replication *n.* the repetition of an original experiment to bolster confidence in its results, based on the assumption that correct hypotheses and procedures consistently will be supported. In **exact replication**, procedures are identical to the original experiment or duplicated as closely as possible. In **modified replication**, alternative procedures and additional conditions may be incorporated. In **conceptual replication**, different techniques and manipulations are introduced to gain theoretical information.

reportability *n.* the quality of psychological events that enables them to be described by the experiencing individual. It is the standard behavioral index of conscious experience.

representation *n.* that which stands for or signifies something else. For example, in cognitive psychology the term denotes a MENTAL REPRESENTATION whereas in psychoanalytic theory it refers to the use of a SYMBOL to stand for a threatening object or a repressed impulse. —**represent** *vb.* —**representational** *adj.* —**representative** *adj.*

representational change a young child's false memory for an initial belief as demonstrated by performance in a FALSE-BELIEF TASK. For example, children shown a box marked as containing pencils and asked what it contains are likely to reply that it contains pencils; the box is then opened to reveal that it actually contains pennies. When later asked what they originally thought was in the box, most children of 3 years and younger say pennies, whereas older children remember their original belief.

representational constraints the limitations imposed by the brain on the form and content of mental constructions, as reflected in the innateness of some types of knowledge (e.g., simple concepts of addition and subtraction). See also ARCHITECTURAL CONSTRAINTS; CHRONOTOPIC CONSTRAINTS.

representational insight the knowledge that an entity (e.g., a word, photograph) can stand for something other than itself.

representationalism *n.* the view that in perception the mind is not directly aware of the perceived object but of a mental representation of it. See PHENOMENALISM. —**representationalist** *adj.*

representational redescription the mental processes by which a child produces a new description of his or her existing representations. This recoding of information enables the child to think more flexibly and use knowledge in a more sophisticated way.

representational stage in PIAGETIAN THEORY, another name for the PREOPERATIONAL STAGE.

representative design an experimental design in which background variables are intentionally not controlled so that research results will apply more realistically to the real world.

representativeness *n.* the correspondence between a sample and the population from which it is drawn such that the sample accurately symbolizes its population, reproducing the essential characteristics and constitution in correct proportions.

representativeness heuristic a strategy for making categorical judgments about a given person or target based on how closely the exemplar matches the typical or average member of the category. For example, given a choice of the two categories "poet" and "accountant," judges are likely to assign a person in unconventional clothes reading a poetry book to the former category; however, the much greater frequency of accountants in the population means that such a person is more likely to be an accountant. The representativeness heuristic is thus a form of the BASE-RATE FALLACY. Compare AVAILABILITY HEURISTIC.

representative sampling the selection of individuals for a study from a larger group (population) in such a way that the sample obtained accurately reflects the total population.

repressed memory see RECOVERED MEMORY.

repression *n.* **1.** in classic psychoanalytic theory and other forms of DEPTH PSYCHOLOGY, the basic DEFENSE MECHANISM that consists of excluding painful experiences and unacceptable impulses from consciousness. Repression operates on an unconscious level as a protection against anxiety produced by objectionable sexual wishes, feelings of hostility, and ego-threatening experiences of all kinds. It also comes into play in most other forms of defense, as in denial, in which individuals avoid unpleasant realities by first repressing them and then negating them. See PRIMARY REPRESSION; REPRESSION PROPER. **2.** the suppression or exclusion of individuals or groups within the social context, through limitations on personal rights and liberties. Compare SUPPRESSION. —**repress** *vb.*

repression proper in psychoanalytic theory, a form of REPRESSION that acts upon experiences and wishes that have been conscious to make them unconscious. This is in contrast to PRIMARY REPRESSION, which operates on material that has never been conscious. Austrian psychiatrist Sigmund Freud (1856–1939) also called this form of repression **afterexpulsion** because material is expelled from consciousness after it has become conscious. Also called **secondary repression**.

repression-resistance *n.* in psychoanalysis, the RESISTANCE deployed by the patient in order to maintain REPRESSION of unacceptable impulses. This may manifest itself in the patient's forgetting of events, an impeded flow of FREE ASSOCIATIONS, or in the patient's application of interpretations offered by the analyst to others but not to himself or herself. Also called **ego resistance**. Compare ID RESISTANCE.

repression–sensitization defense mechanisms involving approach and avoidance responses to threatening stimuli. The sensitizing process involves intellectualization in approaching or controlling the stimulus, whereas repression involves unconscious denial in avoiding the stimulus.

repressive coping style a pattern of dealing with life characterized by downplaying problems or misfortunes and maintaining an artificially positive view. Repressive coping is diagnosed by a combination of high scores on SOCIAL DESIRABILITY bias and low scores on reported anxiety. See also POSITIVE ILLUSION.

reproductive behavior activity that leads to propagation of individuals. The mechanisms range from simple cell division in a unicellular organism or budding of new offspring in simple multicellular organisms to a merger of chromosomes contributed by the male and female parents in sexual reproduction, often followed by supervision of the offspring until they can survive independently. Courtship behavior, mate selection, copulatory behavior, and parental behavior are components of reproductive behavior.

reproductive memory accurate recall of information. This type of memory is subject to errors of CONSTRUCTIVE MEMORY or RECON-

STRUCTIVE MEMORY, especially when material consists of stories or prose passages.

reproductive success the degree to which an individual is successful in producing progeny that in turn are able to produce progeny of their own. Individuals vary in their success in finding mates and reproducing successfully. NATURAL SELECTION is based on this differential reproductive success. The genetic and behavioral traits that lead to greatest reproductive success survive in a population over generations, while traits producing low reproductive success eventually become extinct within a population. See also INCLUSIVE FITNESS.

reproductive suppression the inability of one or several individuals within a group to reproduce, despite having reached reproductive maturity. In many COOPERATIVE-BREEDING species, dominant, breeding individuals suppress reproduction in subordinates. It can be temporary, as in wolves, marmosets, or meerkats, in which an individual can quickly become a breeder in the absence of cues from the dominant animal, or it can be permanent, as in SOCIAL INSECTS.

Rescorla–Wagner theory an influential theory of PAVLOVIAN CONDITIONING that posits that conditioning proceeds from pairing to pairing as a fixed proportion of the maximum amount of conditioning that can be achieved with the UNCONDITIONED STIMULUS (US). For example, if food (the US) produces 100 ml of salivation (the unconditioned response [UR]), and after one pairing of a tone with food, the tone elicits a CONDITIONED RESPONSE (CR) of 40 ml of salivation (i.e., 0.4 of the maximum amount achievable), a second trial will increase the magnitude of the CR by 24 ml (i.e., $0.4 \times [100-40]$), so that the response will be 64 ml. After a third trial, the magnitude will be 78.4 ml—that is, $40 + 24 + (0.4 \times [100-64])$—and so on until the CR is 100 ml (the maximum achievable). Also called **Rescorla–Wagner model**. [proposed in 1972 by Robert **Rescorla** (1940–   ) and Alan **Wagner** (1934–   ), U.S. experimental psychologists]

research *n.* the systematic effort to discover or confirm facts or to investigate a problem or topic, most often by scientific methods of observation and experiment.

research design an outline or plan of the procedures to be followed during a study in order to reach valid conclusions, with particular consideration given to data collection and analysis. Research designs may take a variety of forms, including not only experiments but also quasi-experiments (see QUASI-EXPERIMENTAL RESEARCH), OBSERVATIONAL STUDIES, surveys, focus groups, and other nonexperimental methods.

research ethics the values, principles, and standards by which are judged the conduct of individual researchers and the moral status of the research procedures they employ.

research method a system for the formulation

and evaluation of hypotheses that is intended to reveal relationships between variables and provide an understanding of the phenomenon under investigation. Generally in psychology this involves empirical testing and takes the form of the SCIENTIFIC METHOD.

reserve capacity the difference between performance on a psychological task and the individual's maximum capability to perform that task. Training, intervention, and practice can be used to minimize reserve capacity on a given task.

residential care long-term care for older adults, patients with chronic illness, or individuals undergoing rehabilitation that provides housing and meals and may also provide medical, nursing, and social services. See also DOMICILIARY CARE.

residential treatment treatment that takes place in a hospital, special center, or other facility that offers a treatment program and residential accommodation. Some programs require residence for a specific time (e.g., a one-month treatment for addictions), and some may include provision for the client to learn or work in the community during the day.

residual 1. *n.* in statistics, the difference between the value of an empirical observation and the value of that observation predicted by a model. **2.** *adj.* denoting a condition in which acute symptoms have subsided but chronic or less severe symptoms remain. **3.** *adj.* denoting remaining ability (e.g., residual hearing) or a remaining disability (e.g., residual loss of vision) after a trauma or surgery.

residual schizophrenia a subtype of schizophrenia diagnosed when there has been at least one schizophrenic episode but positive symptoms (e.g., delusions, hallucinations, disorganized speech or behavior) are no longer present and only negative symptoms (e.g., flat affect, poverty of speech, or avolition) or mild behavioral and cognitive disturbances (e.g., eccentricities, odd beliefs) occur.

residual term see ERROR TERM.

residue pitch see VIRTUAL PITCH.

resilience *n.* the process and outcome of successfully adapting to difficult or challenging life experiences, especially through mental, emotional, and behavioral flexibility and adjustment to external and internal demands. A number of factors contribute to how well people adapt to adversities, predominant among them (a) the ways in which individuals view and engage with the world, (b) the availability and quality of social resources, and (c) specific COPING STRATEGIES. Psychological research demonstrates that resources and skills in each of these domains associated with more positive adaptation (i.e., greater resilience) can be cultivated and practiced. See also COPING-SKILLS TRAINING. **—resilient** *adj.*

resistance *n.* **1.** in psychotherapy and analysis, unconscious obstruction, through the client's words or behavior, of the therapist's or analyst's methods of eliciting or interpreting psychic material brought forth in therapy. Psychoanalytic theory classically interprets resistance as a form of defense and distinguishes three types: CONSCIOUS RESISTANCE, ID RESISTANCE, and REPRESSION-RESISTANCE. **2.** the degree to which an organism can defend itself against disease-causing microorganisms. See IMMUNE SYSTEM. **3.** the degree to which disease-causing microorganisms withstand the action of drugs. **—resist** *vb.* **—resistant** *adj.*

resocialization *n.* the process of enabling individuals with mental disorders to resume appropriate interpersonal activities and behaviors and, generally, to participate in community life through more adaptive attitudes and skills.

resolution *n.* in optics, a measure of the ability of the eye to detect two distinct objects when these are close together.

resource competition in consciousness, the process in which concurrent attentional or conscious processes compete for limited brain resources. See DUAL-TASK COMPETITION.

resource theory a theory of interpersonal relationships holding that the amount of resources (e.g., information, love, status, money, goods, services) possessed by each of the participants greatly affects the nature of their relationship. Those having more resources than they require for themselves can withhold their excess from the other party and thus heighten conflict, whereas the relationship is harmonious when each party is equally powerful and cooperative in the exchange of resources.

respiration *n.* **1.** the series of chemical reactions that enables organisms to convert the chemical energy stored in food into energy that can be used by cells. Also called **cellular respiration**; **internal respiration**. **2.** the process by which an animal takes up oxygen from its environment and discharges carbon dioxide into it. Also called **external respiration**.

respiratory depression slow and shallow breathing that can be induced by opioids and CNS DEPRESSANTS. These drugs raise the threshold level of respiratory centers in the medulla oblongata of the brain that normally would react to increased carbon dioxide in the tissues by increasing the rate and depth of breathing.

respiratory sinus arrhythmia the normal tendency for the heart rate to increase and decrease in synchrony but slightly out of phase with inhalation and exhalation. When observed, respiratory sinus arrhythmia can be taken as a sign of vagal function.

respite services assistance, supervision, and recreational or social activities provided for a person who is unable to care for him- or herself (e.g., because of a disability or chronic illness) for a limited period in order to temporarily relieve family members from caregiving responsibilities or enable them to conduct necessary personal or household affairs. These services may be provided either in the home or at another location. Also called **respite care**.

respondent *n.* in conditioning, any REFLEX that can be conditioned by PAVLOVIAN CONDITIONING procedures. Compare OPERANT.

respondent behavior behavior that is evoked by a specific stimulus and will consistently and predictably occur if the stimulus is presented. Also called **elicited behavior**. Compare EMITTED BEHAVIOR.

respondent conditioning see PAVLOVIAN CONDITIONING.

response *n.* any glandular, muscular, neural, or other reaction to a stimulus. A response is a clearly defined, measurable unit of behavior discussed in terms of its result (e.g., pressing a lever) or its physical characteristics (e.g., raising an arm).

response acquiescence see YEA-SAYING.

response amplitude the magnitude of a response, especially in conditioning.

response bias a tendency to give one response more than others, regardless of the stimulus condition. In SIGNAL DETECTION THEORY, response bias is the overall willingness to say "yes" (signal present) or "no" (signal not present), regardless of the actual presence or absence of the signal.

response competition in choice reaction tasks, the interference of an irrelevant stimulus or stimulus feature in producing a response such that CHOICE REACTION TIME to produce the correct response is slowed. For example, in the STROOP COLOR–WORD INTERFERENCE TEST, in which participants are asked to name the color of letters that themselves spell the name of another color, reaction time is slowed because response activation from the irrelevant information (what the letters spell) competes with that from the relevant information (the color of the letters).

response cost a procedure in OPERANT CONDITIONING in which certain responses result in loss of a valued commodity. The intent of such procedures is to produce punishment. See NEGATIVE PUNISHMENT.

response deprivation in operant conditioning, an approach to identifying reinforcers before their effectiveness has been demonstrated. It holds that if the opportunity to engage in some activity is restricted below its normal level, then opportunity to engage in that activity can serve as reinforcement for some other behavior.

response generalization see INDUCTION.

response hierarchy the arrangement of a group of responses or response sequences in the order in which they are likely to be evoked by a specific stimulus or to occur in a particular stimulus situation.

response latency the time that elapses be-

tween the onset of a stimulus and the onset of a response, which may be used as an indicator of the strength of CONDITIONING.

response learning learning to perform a specific series of movements or responses. In a maze, for example, one could learn a sequence of left–right responses as contrasted with learning a cognitive map of the maze (PLACE LEARNING).

response magnitude the amplitude, duration, or intensity of a response.

response maintenance the extent to which changes are maintained for a period of time after an intervention has been completed.

response prevention a type of behavior therapy used to treat OBSESSIVE-COMPULSIVE DISORDER, involving exposure to situations or cues that trigger OBSESSIONS or provoke COMPULSIONS, followed by the prevention of the compulsive behavior. Also called **exposure and response prevention**.

response selection an intermediate stage of human information processing in which a response to an identified stimulus is chosen. Response selection is typically studied by varying relationships between the stimuli and their assigned responses.

response set a tendency to answer questions in a systematic manner that is unrelated to their content. Examples include the ACQUIESCENT RESPONSE SET and SOCIAL DESIRABILITY RESPONSE SET.

response–shock interval see SIDMAN AVOIDANCE SCHEDULE.

response strength a hypothetical entity that summarizes the likelihood of occurrence, magnitude, and resistance to disruption of a class of responses, often measured by response rate or RESPONSE LATENCY.

response suppression a decrease in the rate or probability of a response due to some experimental operation. For example, PUNISHMENT results in response suppression.

response variable the DEPENDENT VARIABLE in a study.

restatement *n.* in psychotherapy and counseling, the verbatim repetition or rephrasing by the therapist or counselor of a client's statement. The purpose is not only to confirm that the client's remarks have been understood, but also to provide a "mirror" in which the client can see his or her feelings and ideas more clearly (see MIRRORING). Compare CLARIFICATION; INTERPRETATION; REFRAMING.

resting potential the electric potential across the plasma membrane of a neuron when it is in the nonexcited, or resting, state. It is usually in the range –50 to –100 mV for vertebrate neurons, representing an excess of negatively charged ions on the inside of the membrane. See also ACTION POTENTIAL.

resting tremor a trembling that occurs when the individual's affected body part is at rest. It is a characteristic symptom of Parkinson's disease, in which case it sometimes is referred to as a **parkinsonian tremor**. The term parkinsonian tremor, however, more properly is used to denote any tremor associated with Parkinson's disease, whether a resting tremor or an ACTION TREMOR.

restoration effect a phenomenon in which the mind unconsciously restores information missing from a stimulus. The best known example is the so-called PHONEMIC RESTORATION EFFECT, in which the perceiver fails to notice that certain PHONEMES have been masked out in speech recordings. The restoration effect is considered evidence of TOP-DOWN PROCESSING.

restoration therapy 1. treatment that is directed toward the reestablishment of structure and function in a body part or system following disease or injury. For example, vision restoration therapy for individuals following postgeniculate visual system lesions is intended to enlarge the size of the visual field and facilitate recovery of more complex visual function. **2.** a form of COMPLEMENTARY AND ALTERNATIVE MEDICINE that uses techniques and concepts from massage, chiropractic, osteopathy, shiatsu, acupressure, and herbal formulas to treat specific ailments and enhance overall health by balancing the body's life-force energy (chi) and breaking down soft tissues, which then rebuild themselves.

restorative environment an environment, often a natural setting, that rejuvenates and can help restore depleted attention resources or reduce emotional and psychophysiological stress. Characteristic features of restorative environments include legibility (the ease with which they can be represented cognitively) and elements that give rise to contemplation and provide a break from one's normal routine. There is growing interest in the incorporation of restorative elements into health care settings because of evidence that they speed recovery.

restricted code see ELABORATED CODE.

restriction of range the limitation by a researcher—via sampling, measurement procedures, or other aspects of experimental design—of the full range of total possible scores that may be obtained to only a narrow, limited portion of that total. For example, in a study of the grade-point averages of university students, restriction of range would occur if only students from the dean's list were included. Range restriction on a particular variable may lead to a failure to observe, or the improper characterization of, a relationship between the variables of interest.

resurgence *n.* in conditioning, the reappearance of previously reinforced and then extinguished responses during a period of EXTINCTION for a subsequently learned response. For example, a rat might be presented with two levers. First, presses on lever A are reinforced; next, presses on lever A are subjected to extinction and presses on lever B are reinforced. Pressing lever A will cease, and pressing lever B will occur. Finally, extinction is arranged for presses on lever B, so that no reinforcement is available in the situation. As responding on lever B declines, pressing on lever A will increase temporarily.

RET abbreviation for rational emotive therapy. See RATIONAL EMOTIVE BEHAVIOR THERAPY.

retardation *n.* a slowing down of or delay in an activity or process, as in PSYCHOMOTOR RETARDATION or MENTAL RETARDATION.

retention *n.* **1.** the storage and maintenance of a memory. Retention is the second stage of memory, after ENCODING and before RETRIEVAL. **2.** the inability or refusal of an individual to defecate or urinate. —**retentive** *adj.*

retention curve a graphic representation of a person's remembrance of material over a period of time.

retest reliability an estimate of the ability of an assessment instrument (e.g., a test) to measure an attribute consistently: It is obtained as the correlation between scores on two administrations of the test to the same individual. Also called **test–retest reliability**.

reticular activating system (**RAS**) a part of the RETICULAR FORMATION thought to be particularly involved in the regulation of arousal, alertness, and sleep–wake cycles.

reticular formation an extensive network of nerve cell bodies and fibers within the brainstem, extending from the medulla oblongata to the upper part of the midbrain, that is widely connected to the spinal cord, cerebellum, thalamus, and cerebral cortex. It is most prominently involved in arousal, alertness, and sleep–wake cycles, but also functions to control some aspects of action and posture.

reticulospinal tract see VENTROMEDIAL PATHWAYS.

retina *n.* the innermost, light-sensitive layer of the eye. A layer of neurons lines the inner surface of the back of the eye and provides the sensory signals required for vision. The retina contains the photoreceptors, that is, the RETINAL RODS and RETINAL CONES, as well as additional neurons that process the signals of the photoreceptors and convey an output signal to the brain by way of the OPTIC NERVE. This inner layer of the retina is sometimes called the **neural retina**, to distinguish it from the retinal PIGMENT EPITHELIUM, which abuts the tips of the photoreceptors.

retinal 1. *adj.* of or relating to the retina. **2.** *n.* an aldehyde of vitamin A that is a component of the PHOTOPIGMENT rhodopsin. Also called **retinene**.

retinal bipolar cell any of various neurons in the INNER NUCLEAR LAYER of the retina that receive input from the photoreceptors (RETINAL RODS and RETINAL CONES) and transmit signals to RETINAL GANGLION CELLS and AMACRINE

CELLS. Rods and cones are served by different populations of retinal bipolar cells, called **rod bipolars** and **cone bipolars**, respectively.

retinal cone any of various photoreceptors in the retina that require moderate to bright light for activation, as opposed to RETINAL RODS, which require very little light for activation. In primates retinal cones are concentrated in the FOVEA CENTRALIS of the retina, where their high spatial density and the pattern of connections within the cone pathway are critical for high-acuity vision. The cone pathways also provide information about the color of stimuli. This is achieved by the presence of three different populations of cones, each having their maximum sensitivity to light in the short, middle, or long wavelengths of the spectrum, respectively. Other animals may have additional populations of cones; for example, some fish have cones that are sensitive to ultraviolet wavelengths. See also PHOTOPIC VISION; PHOTOPIGMENT.

retinal disparity see BINOCULAR DISPARITY.

retinal ganglion cell the only type of neuron in the retina that sends signals to the brain resulting from visual stimulation. Retinal ganglion cells receive input from RETINAL BIPOLAR CELLS and AMACRINE CELLS, the axons of retinal ganglion cells forming the OPTIC NERVE.

retinal horizontal cell any of various neurons in the retina that make lateral connections between photoreceptors, RETINAL BIPOLAR CELLS, and one another. Their cell bodies are located in the INNER NUCLEAR LAYER of the retina.

retinal image the inverted picture of an external object formed on the retina of the eye.

retinal pigment epithelium see PIGMENT EPITHELIUM.

retinal rivalry see BINOCULAR RIVALRY.

retinal rod any of various photoreceptors in the retina that respond to low light levels, as opposed to RETINAL CONES, which require moderate to bright light for activation. In primates, which have both rods and cones, the rods are excluded from the center of the retina, the FOVEA CENTRALIS. All rods contain the same PHOTOPIGMENT, rhodopsin; therefore the rod pathways do not provide color information to the visual system. The connections of the rod pathway enhance retinal sensitivity to light, while acuity is relatively poor. See also SCOTOPIC VISION.

retinex theory a theory based on the idea that color registration is carried out in the brain. Demonstrations, such as the LAND EFFECT, suggest that various wavelengths register on the color-sensitive components of the retina as a large number of color-separated "photos." The visual mechanisms in the brain then average together and compare long-wave photos with the average of the shorter-wave photos, assigning different colors to them according to the ratios between them. Also called **Land theory of color vision**.

retinitis pigmentosa a hereditary disorder of the retina marked by progressive atrophy of the photoreceptors (affecting rods more than cones) and disturbances in the retinal PIGMENT EPITHELIUM. Retinitis pigmentosa causes NIGHT BLINDNESS and visual field loss (see TUNNEL VISION).

retinotopic map the point-by-point representation of the retinal surface in another structure in the visual system, such as the STRIATE CORTEX. **Visuotopic map** is sometimes used synonymously for retinotopic map but more properly refers to the representation of the visual field in any neural structure.

retirement counseling individual or group counseling of employees to help them prepare for retirement. Discussions usually include such topics as norms for this transition, mental and physical health, recreational activities, part-time or consultant work, finances, insurance, government programs, and issues related to change of residence.

retrieval n. the process of recovering or locating information stored in memory. Retrieval is the final stage of memory, after ENCODING and RETENTION.

retrieval block a brief inability to recall a specific piece of information, accompanied by the feeling that there is an impediment or block to its recollection, as in the well-known TIP-OF-THE-TONGUE PHENOMENON.

retrieval cue a prompt or stimulus used to guide memory recall.

retroactive interference see INTERFERENCE.

retrocochlear hearing loss any auditory disorder related to the neural pathways of the eighth cranial nerve (see AUDITORY NERVE) and the higher centers of the central nervous system (that is, beyond the cochlea).

retrograde amnesia see AMNESIA.

retrograde degeneration a pattern of neuron destruction following axonal injury that spreads backward along the axon, toward and then encompassing the nerve cell body. Compare ANTEROGRADE DEGENERATION.

retrogression n. the return to a previous inappropriate behavior or to a behavior appropriate to an earlier stage of maturation when more adult techniques fail to solve a conflict. It is approximately equivalent to REGRESSION, but without the full psychoanalytic connotations.

retronasal olfaction sensations of smell arising via the nasopharynx, from an odorant in the mouth (compare ORTHONASAL OLFACTION). Retronasal olfaction is easily confused with gustatory (taste) sensations.

retrospection n. an observation or review of an experience from the past, typically not the distant past. Compare INTROSPECTION.

retrospective memory see PROSPECTIVE MEMORY.

retrospective research observational, non-experimental research that tries to explain the present in terms of past events; that is, research that starts with the present and follows subjects backward in time. For example, a **retrospective study** may be undertaken in which individuals are selected on the basis of whether they exhibit a particular problematic symptom and are then studied to determine if they had been exposed to a risk factor of interest. Compare PROSPECTIVE RESEARCH.

retrospective sampling a SAMPLING technique that selects cases on the basis of their previous exposure to a risk factor or the completion of some particular process. Participants are then examined in the present to see if a particular condition or state exists, often in comparison to others who were not exposed to the risk or did not complete the particular process. See also PROSPECTIVE SAMPLING.

Rett syndrome a degenerative condition that occurs in children (typically girls) who develop normally early in life but then, between 6 and 18 months, undergo rapid regression in motor, cognitive, and social skills; these skills subsequently stabilize at a level that leaves the child with mental retardation. Affected children exhibit autistic features and stereotyped hand movements (e.g., hand wringing); in some, seizures and scoliosis (sideways spinal curvature) occur, and deceleration of head growth is pronounced. Also called **Rett disorder**. [Andreas **Rett** (1924–1997), Austrian pediatrician]

reuptake *n.* the process by which neurotransmitter molecules that have been released at a SYNAPSE are taken up by the presynaptic neuron that released them. Reuptake is performed by TRANSPORTER proteins in the presynaptic membrane.

reverberatory circuit a CELL ASSEMBLY that is more or less continuously active, recirculating nerve impulses that were initially activated in response to stimuli. A theory of reverberatory circuits has been proposed to explain learning and memory processes. Also called **reverberating circuit**.

reversal design an experimental design that attempts to counteract the confounding effects (see CONFOUND) of sequence, order, and treatment in LATIN SQUARES by alternating baseline conditions (A) with treatment conditions (B), for example by employing two sets of three observations (A then B then A; B then A then B) to yield counterbalanced estimates of A versus B.

reversal error a mistake in which a letter or word is read or written backward (e.g. *tip* for *pit* or *b* as *d*). When reversal errors are marked and developmentally inappropriate, they are indicative of DYSLEXIA.

reversal learning in DISCRIMINATIONS involving two alternatives, the effects of reversing the contingencies associated with the two alternatives. For example, a monkey could be trained under conditions in which lever presses when a red light is present result in food presentation and lever presses when a green light is on are without effect. The contingencies are then reversed, so that presses when the red light is on are ineffective and presses when the green light is on result in food presentation. If the monkey's behavior adapts to the new contingencies (i.e., it presses the lever only when the green light is present), reversal learning has occurred.

reversal of affect in psychoanalytic theory, a change in the AIM OF THE INSTINCT into its opposite, as when a masochistic impulse to hurt the self is transformed into a sadistic impulse to hurt others, or vice versa. Also called **affect inversion**; **inversion of affect**.

reversal shift in DISCRIMINATIONS involving two alternatives, a reversal of contingencies as compared with an immediately preceding set of conditions. For example, in initial training a white stimulus might be designated as correct and black as incorrect. A reversal shift would mean that, in a later phase of the training, black becomes correct and white incorrect. Compare NONREVERSAL SHIFT.

reversal theory a theory of motivation, emotion, and personality that attempts to explain the relationship between AROUSAL and performance. It suggests that the way an individual interprets the arousal, rather than the amount of arousal, affects performance and that he or she can reverse the positive–negative interpretation from moment to moment.

reverse anorexia a condition characterized by an individual's desire to increase body size, particularly muscularity. As with ANOREXIA NERVOSA, in which the desire is to lose weight or reduce body size, the drive to alter body size is not diminished by achieving extensive body modification. The individual's unhappiness with self-image, despite excessive gains in muscle mass and definition, is still present. See also MUSCLE DYSMORPHIA.

reverse causality in seeking to understand causal relationships, the common error of mistaking cause for effect and vice versa. Asking if an event or condition commonly considered to be the cause of a phenomenon might in reality be its effect can be a useful check against preconceptions and generate fresh, challenging ideas. For example, the poverty of Mr. X is usually thought to be an effect of his financial irresponsibility, but what if this acknowledged irresponsibility is in fact an effect of his poverty? Considering a reversed causality is also a useful strategy for dealing with questions of causality based on correlational data.

reverse tolerance an effect of certain drugs, particularly CNS stimulants, in which repeated use alters the body's sensitivity so that repeated administration of a drug will enhance the effects of that drug. Also called **sensitization**.

reversibility *n.* in PIAGETIAN THEORY, a mental operation that reverses a sequence of events or restores a changed state of affairs to the original condition. It is exemplified by the ability to realize that a glass of milk poured into a bottle will remain the same in amount when poured back into the glass. Reversibility can be expressed in terms of NEGATION or COMPENSATION. See also CONSERVATION.

reversible figure an AMBIGUOUS FIGURE in which the perspective is easily reversed. Examples include the NECKER CUBE and RUBIN'S FIGURE.

revolving-door phenomenon the repeated readmission of patients to hospitals or other institutions, often because they were discharged before they had adequately recovered.

reward *n.* a lay word that is nearly synonymous with REINFORCEMENT. Sometimes it is used to describe the intent of someone providing consequences for behavior, rather than the effectiveness of a consequence (as is required in the definition of reinforcement) in influencing the frequency or probability of occurrence of a particular behavior.

RHC abbreviation for RURAL HEALTH CLINIC.

rhinencephalon *n.* the portion of the brain that includes the limbic system; olfactory nerves, bulbs, and tracts; and related structures.

rhizomelic *adj.* relating to or affecting the hip, shoulder, or both.

rhizotomy *n.* a surgical procedure in which a spinal nerve root is severed within the spinal canal. A rhizotomy may be performed for the relief of pain or to control muscle spasms. The different types of rhizotomy include **anterior rhizotomy**, in which an anterior (motor) spinal nerve is cut; **posterior rhizotomy**, in which a posterior (sensory) spinal nerve is cut; and **trigeminal rhizotomy**, in which the sensory root fibers of the trigeminal nerve are transected.

rhodopsin *n.* see PHOTOPIGMENT.

rhombencephalon *n.* see HINDBRAIN.

rhythmic stereotypy a gross motor movement, such as body rocking or foot kicking, that has no apparent function. It is a form of LOCOMOTOR PLAY that occurs in the 1st year of life.

RI abbreviation for random interval. See RANDOM-INTERVAL SCHEDULE.

RIA abbreviation for RADIOIMMUNOASSAY.

ribonucleic acid see RNA.

ribosome *n.* an organelle, consisting of RNA and proteins, found in large numbers in all cells and responsible for the translation of genetic information (in the form of messenger RNA) and the assembly of proteins. **—ribosomal** *adj.*

Ricco's law the principle that VISUAL THRESHOLD is a function of the intensity of a visual image and its area on the fovea. [Annibale **Ricco** (1844–1919), Italian astrophysicist]

rich interpretation an approach to analyzing the language of young children that goes beyond the literal sense of the word or words used and takes into account the surrounding verbal and nonverbal contexts to infer the full meaning of the utterance and draw conclusions about the child's linguistic COMPETENCE. See HOLOPHRASE.

Riddoch's phenomenon the ability of patients with injury to the visual system beyond the optic chiasm to see moving, but not stationary, light stimuli (**statokinetic dissociation**). Riddoch's phenomenon can also be associated with damage to the optic nerve. [first described in 1917 by George **Riddoch** (1888–1947), British neurologist]

right hemisphere the right half of the CEREBRUM, the part of the brain concerned with sensation and perception, motor control, and higher level cognitive processes. The two CEREBRAL HEMISPHERES differ somewhat in function; for example, in most people the right hemisphere has greater responsibility for spatial attention. Some have proposed the hypothesis of **right-hemisphere consciousness**, specifying that the right hemisphere is conscious, like the LEFT HEMISPHERE, even though it has no control of spoken communication. The right hemisphere is postulated to function in a holistic, nonlinear manner, specialized for spatial and SUPRASEGMENTAL (prosodic) perception. See HEMISPHERIC LATERALIZATION.

right–left disorientation a disorder characterized by general difficulty in distinguishing between the right and left sides or right and left directions. Although thought to be related to disorders of the left parietal lobe of the cerebral cortex, it also occurs to a mild degree in otherwise healthy adults.

right to die the right to physician-assisted suicide that some consider should be available for terminally ill patients (see ASSISTED DEATH). This is distinguished from the RIGHT TO REFUSE TREATMENT in cases in which the patient is on life support.

right to refuse treatment 1. the right of patients with mental illness to refuse treatment that may be potentially hazardous or intrusive (e.g., ELECTROCONVULSIVE THERAPY or PSYCHOACTIVE DRUGS), particularly when such treatment does not appear to be in the best interests of the patient. In the United States, various state laws and court rulings support the rights of patients to receive or reject certain treatments, but there is a lack of uniformity in such regulations. See also FORCED TREATMENT. **2.** the right of terminally ill patients (e.g., those on life-support systems) to refuse treatment intended to prolong their lives. See also RIGHT TO DIE.

right to treatment a statutory right, established at varying governmental levels, stipulating that people with disabilities or disorders, usually persistent or chronic in nature, have the right to receive care and treatment suited to their needs. Such statutory rights may apply nationally or to certain state or provincial areas, or they may be limited to certain conditions and disabilities.

rigidity *n.* **1.** stiffness or inflexibility, particularly muscular rigidity. **2.** a personality trait characterized by strong resistance to changing one's behavior, opinions, or attitudes or inability to do this. —**rigid** *adj.*

Ringelmann effect the tendency for groups to become less productive in terms of output per member as they increase in size. The effect is named for Max Ringelmann (1861–1931), a French agricultural engineer who studied the productivity of horses, oxen, men, and machines in various agricultural applications. He found that groups often outperform individuals, but that the addition of each new member to the group yields less of a gain in productivity. Subsequent studies suggest that this loss of productivity is caused by the reduction of motivation experienced in groups (SOCIAL LOAFING) and the inefficiency of larger groups.

risk *n.* **1.** the probability or likelihood that an event will occur, such as the risk that a disease or disorder will develop. **2.** the probability of experiencing loss or harm that is associated with an action or behavior. See also AT RISK; MORBIDITY RISK; RISK FACTOR. —**risky** *adj.*

risk-as-feelings theory a model stating that decision making in situations involving a degree of risk is often driven by emotional reactions, such as worry, fear, or anxiety, rather than by a rational assessment of (a) the desirability and (b) the likelihood of the various possible outcomes (see SUBJECTIVE–EXPECTED UTILITY).

risk assessment the process of determining the threat an individual would be likely to pose if released from the confinement in which he or she is held as a result of mental illness or criminal acts. It may be a clinician-based prediction of dangerous or violent behavior (**clinical risk assessment**) or it may be based on a specific formula or weighting system using empirically derived predictors (**actuarial risk assessment**).

risk aversion the tendency, when choosing between alternatives, to avoid options that entail a risk of loss, even if that risk is relatively small.

risk factor a clearly defined behavior or constitutional (e.g., genetic), environmental, or other characteristic that is associated with an increased possibility or likelihood that a disease or disorder will subsequently develop in an individual.

risk level the amount of risk of making a TYPE I ERROR that one is willing to accept in null hypothesis SIGNIFICANCE TESTING.

risk perception an individual's subjective assessment of the level of risk associated with a particular hazard. Risk perceptions will vary ac-

cording to such factors as past experiences, age, gender, and culture. For example, women tend to overestimate their risk of developing breast cancer.

risk taking 1. a pattern of unnecessarily engaging in activities or behaviors that are highly subject to chance or dangerous. This pattern of behavior is often associated with substance abuse, gambling, and high-risk sexual behaviors. **2.** accepting a challenging task that simultaneously involves potential for failure as well as for accomplishment or personal benefit. It is often associated with creativity and taking calculated risks in the workplace or in educational settings.

risk tolerance the level of risk to which an individual is willing to be exposed while performing an action or pursuing a goal. Tolerance of risk is usually based upon an assumption (justified or not) that the risk is slight, the consequences are minor, and that both are outweighed by immediate benefits.

risky shift see CAUTIOUS SHIFT.

Ritalin *n.* a trade name for METHYLPHENIDATE.

rite of passage a ritual that marks a specific life transition, such as birth, marriage, or death, or a developmental milestone, such as a bar mitzvah, graduation, or PUBERTY RITE. In many prescientific societies such rites are considered essential if the individual is to make a successful transition from one status to another.

ritual *n.* **1.** a form of COMPULSION involving a rigid or stereotyped act that is carried out repeatedly and is based on idiosyncratic rules that do not have a rational basis (e.g., having to perform a task in a certain way). Rituals may be performed in order to reduce distress and anxiety caused by an OBSESSION. **2.** a ceremonial act or rite, usually involving a fixed order of actions or gestures and the saying of certain prescribed words. Anthropologists distinguish between several major categories of ritual: magic rituals, which involve an attempt to manipulate natural forces (e.g., pouring water on the ground to make rain); calendrical rituals, which mark the changing of the seasons and the passing of time; liturgical rituals, which involve the reenactment of a sacred story or myth; RITES OF PASSAGE; and formal procedures that have the effect of emphasizing both the importance and the impersonal quality of certain social behaviors, as in a court of law. —**ritualism** *n.* —**ritualistic** *adj.*

ritual abuse organized, repetitive, and highly sadistic abuse of a physical, sexual, or emotional nature, perpetrated principally on children. The abuse is reported as using rituals and symbols from religion (e.g., upside-down crosses), the occult, or secret societies. Victims may be forced to engage in heinous acts, such as the killing of animals, as a means of coercing their participation and silence.

ritualization *n.* the process by which a normal behavioral or physiological action becomes a communication signal representing the behavior or its physiological consequence. For example, the flushed face associated with anger and the pale face associated with fear initially derive from actions of the sympathetic nervous system related to vasodilation and vasoconstriction, respectively.

RNA *ribonucleic acid*: a nucleic acid that directs the synthesis of protein molecules in living cells. There are three main types of RNA. **Messenger RNA** carries the GENETIC CODE from the cell nucleus to the cytoplasm. **Ribosomal RNA** is found in ribosomes, small particles where proteins are assembled from amino acids. **Transfer RNA** carries specific amino acids for protein synthesis. RNA is similar to DNA in structure except that it consists of a single strand of nucleotides (compared with the double strands of DNA), the base uracil (U) occurs instead of thymine (T), and the sugar unit is ribose, rather than deoxyribose.

road rage aggressive or confrontational behavior while driving, typically triggered by an actual or imagined transgression by another driver. Often associated with traffic congestion, road rage varies in severity and can involve hostile verbal expression, hazardous driving, and interpersonal violence.

robustness *n.* the ability of a hypothesis-testing or estimation procedure to produce valid results in spite of violations of the assumptions upon which the methodology is based.

ROC curve abbreviation for RECEIVER-OPERATING CHARACTERISTIC CURVE.

rod *n.* see RETINAL ROD.

Rod-and-Frame Test a widely used measure of FIELD DEPENDENCE and field independence in which the participant adjusts a movable rod inside a frame to a true vertical position as the position of the frame is changed. The larger the degree of error, the more field dependent the participant is; the smaller the degree of error, the more field independent he or she is.

rod–cone break the shift in visual sensitivity that occurs during DARK ADAPTATION when the sensitivity of the RETINAL RODS first exceeds that of the RETINAL CONES. When visual sensitivity is measured in the dark following a very bright flash of light, the cones reach maximum sensitivity after about 7 minutes. However, overall visual sensitivity continues to improve for about 20 more minutes as RHODOPSIN regenerates and the rods reach their maximum sensitivity.

Rogerian therapy see CLIENT-CENTERED THERAPY.

Rolandic fissure see CENTRAL SULCUS. [Luigi Rolando (1773–1831), Italian anatomist]

role *n.* a coherent set of behaviors expected of an individual in a specific position within a group or social setting. Since the term is derived from the dramaturgical concept of role (the dialogue and actions assigned to each performer in a play), there is a suggestion that individuals' actions are regulated by the part they play in the social setting rather than by their personal predilections or inclinations. See also GROUP ROLE; RELATIONSHIP ROLE; SOCIAL ROLE; TASK ROLE.

role ambiguity indefinite expectations about the behaviors to be performed by individuals who occupy particular positions within a group. Role ambiguity is often caused by lack of clarity in the role itself, lack of consensus within the group regarding the behaviors associated with the role, or the individual role taker's uncertainty with regard to the types of behaviors expected.

role conflict a state of tension or distress caused by inconsistent or discordant expectations associated with one's social or group role, as when a role's demands are inconsistent with each other (INTRAROLE CONFLICT) or individuals occupy more than one role and the behaviors required by these roles are incompatible with one another (INTERROLE CONFLICT).

role confusion 1. a state of uncertainty about a given social or group role. **2.** GENDER ROLE behavior in a male or female that is traditionally associated with the opposite sex. See also GENDER IDENTITY DISORDER; TRANSGENDER. **3.** see IDENTITY VERSUS ROLE CONFUSION.

role deprivation the denial of culturally and psychologically significant statuses and roles to certain individuals or groups. Individuals can be unfairly deprived of social roles, as when they are required to retire at a specific age, or unfairly denied group roles, as when they are excluded from leadership positions for no valid reason.

role differentiation in groups and other social systems, the gradual increase in the number of roles and decrease in the scope of these roles that tends to occur over time as each role becomes more narrowly defined and specialized. For example, in many cases the all-inclusive leadership role divides, over time, into two: the task leader role and the relationship leader role. See COLEADERSHIP.

role-enactment theory a social psychological explanation of hypnosis according to which the person under hypnosis takes on a role assigned by the hypnotist and behaves in accordance with this role while in the hypnotic condition.

role overload a situation in which one is asked to do more than one is capable of doing in a specific period of time (**quantitative overload**) or in which one is taxed beyond one's knowledge, skills, and abilities (**qualitative overload**).

role play a technique used in human relations training and psychotherapy in which participants act out various social roles in dramatic situations. Originally developed in PSYCHODRAMA, role play is now widely used in industrial, educational, and clinical settings for such purposes as training employees to handle sales problems, testing out different attitudes and relationships in group and family psychotherapy, and rehearsing different ways of coping with stresses and conflicts.

role reversal a technique used for therapeutic and educational purposes in which an individual exchanges roles with another individual in order to experience alternative cognitive styles (e.g., in problem solving), feelings, and behavioral approaches. Role reversal is used in management development programs, for example, an exchange of roles between a supervisor and an employee.

role set the group of people (and their associated ROLES) who are related to and interact meaningfully with the occupant of a particular role, communicating the attitudes and behaviors appropriate to that role.

role therapy in psychotherapy, a system that uses real-life PSYCHODRAMA. The client selects a role model, works out the aspects of the model with the therapist, and then role-plays the model both in the therapeutic session and in real life.

rolfing *n.* a deep-massage technique developed in the 1930s. It aims to relieve muscular tension, improve posture and balance, and enhance personal functioning through realignment of body structure. The technique is based on a theory that muscle massage will relieve both physical and psychological pain. Also called **structural integration**. [devised by Ida P. **Rolf** (1896–1979), U.S. physical therapist]

romantic love a type of love in which intimacy and passion are prominent features (see TRIANGULAR THEORY OF LOVE). In some taxonomies of love, romantic love is identified with PASSIONATE LOVE and distinguished from COMPANIONATE LOVE; in others, it is seen as involving elements of both.

Romberg's sign a diagnostic sign of certain neurological disorders, including locomotor ATAXIA, that consists of a swaying motion and unsteadiness when the individual stands with the eyes closed, feet together, and arms outstretched. [Moritz **Romberg** (1795–1873), German physician]

rootedness *n.* the need to establish bonds or ties with others that provide emotional security and serve to reduce a sense of isolation and insignificance.

Rorschach Inkblot Test a projective test in which the participant is presented with ten unstructured inkblots (mostly in black and gray but sometimes in color) and is asked "What might this be?" or "What do you see in this?" The examiner classifies the responses according to such structural and thematic (content) factors as color (C), movement (M), detail (D), whole (W), popular or common (P), animal (A), form (F), and human (H). Various scoring systems, either qualitative or quantitative, are used. The object is to interpret the participant's personality structure in terms of such factors as emotionality, cognitive style, creativity, impulse control, and various defensive patterns. Perhaps the best known, and certainly one of the most controversial, assessment instruments in all of psychology—it is almost considered "representative" by the general public—the Rorschach is widely used and has been extensively researched, with results ranging from those that claim strong support for its clinical utility (e.g., for selecting treatment modalities or monitoring patient change or improvement over time) to those that demonstrate little evidence of robust or consistent validity and that criticize the instrument as invalid and useless. [Hermann **Rorschach** (1884–1922), Swiss psychiatrist]

Rosenthal effect an effect in which the expectancy an experimenter has about the outcome of an experiment unwittingly affects the outcome of the experiment in the direction of the expectancy. The term is often used synonymously with EXPERIMENTER EXPECTANCY EFFECT. [Robert **Rosenthal** (1933–), U.S. psychologist]

rostral *adj.* situated or occurring toward the nose, or beak, of an organism, or toward the front or anterior portion of an organ. Compare CAUDAL. **—rostrally** *adv.*

rotation *n.* in statistics, movement around the origin in a multidimensional space. See FACTOR ROTATION; PROCRUSTES ROTATION. **—rotational** *adj.*

rote learning the type of learning in which acquisition occurs through drill and repetition, sometimes in the absence of comprehension. Rote learning may lead to the production of correct answers, but without awareness of the reasoning behind or the logical implications of the response.

rote recall precise recollection of information that has been stored in its entirety (e.g., an address, chemical formula, color pattern, or piece of music).

rough-and-tumble play (R & T play) play that involves vigorous contact with others, such as wrestling and mock fighting. R & T play is a form of LOCOMOTOR PLAY and is necessarily social as it involves another person, usually a peer. Observed in animals and children, R & T play tends to be more frequent in males than females.

roughness *n.* **1.** the tactile quality of an object that is coarse, as in sandpaper. **2.** a subjective quality used as part of a continuum to describe the percepts produced by amplitude-modulated sounds. Slow, regular amplitude fluctuations that can be perceived as loudness changes are described as **beats**. Higher fluctuation rates, above approximately 15 Hz, are described as **flutter**, whereas those above approximately 40 Hz are described as being **rough**.

round window a membrane-covered opening in the cochlea where it borders the middle ear (see SCALA TYMPANI). Pressure changes in the cochlea produced by vibration of the OVAL WINDOW are ultimately transmitted to the round window. This permits displacement of the BASI-

LAR MEMBRANE and stimulation of the sensory receptors.

route learning learning to navigate within a spatial environment through the acquisition of specific directions, distances, and landmarks. Route knowledge is represented as a series of directions to follow to get from one place to another (compare SURVEY KNOWLEDGE). Also called **way finding**.

RR abbreviation for random ratio. See RANDOM-RATIO SCHEDULE.

RSI abbreviation for REPETITIVE STRAIN INJURY.

r-strategy *n.* a reproductive strategy that involves a high rate of reproduction with low parental investment. Compare K-STRATEGY.

RT abbreviation for REACTION TIME.

Rubin's figure an ambiguous figure that may be perceived either as one goblet or as two facing profiles. [Edgar **Rubin** (1886–1951), Danish philosopher]

rubrospinal tract a MOTOR PATHWAY that arises from the **red nucleus** (a collection of cell bodies that receives input from the cerebellum) in the brainstem and descends laterally in the spinal cord, where it stimulates flexor motor neurons and inhibits extensor motor neurons.

Ruffini's corpuscle a type of sensory-nerve ending in the subcutaneous tissues of human fingers. Ruffini's corpuscles are believed to mediate sensations of skin stretch, motion detection, and hand and finger position. Also called **Ruffini's ending**. [Angelo **Ruffini** (1864–1929), Italian anatomist]

rule-assessment approach a theory that explains cognitive development in terms of the rules and the increasingly powerful strategies children use to solve problems. See also ADAPTIVE STRATEGY CHOICE MODEL.

rule-governed behavior any behavior that is influenced by verbal antecedents, such as following instructions (as when a child cleans his or her room because told to do so) or reacting to one's own private thinking (as when an adult begins an exercise program after thinking "I need to lose weight"). Compare CONTINGENCY-GOVERNED BEHAVIOR.

rule learning in psychology experiments, the process in which a participant gradually acquires knowledge about a fixed but unstated standard that defines, for example, the acceptability of a response or membership of a category.

rumination *n.* **1.** obsessional thinking involving excessive, repetitive thoughts or themes that interfere with other forms of mental activity. It is a common feature of OBSESSIVE-COMPULSIVE DISORDER. **2.** the voluntary regurgitation of food from the stomach to the mouth, where it is masticated and tasted a second time. **—ruminate** *vb.*

rumination disorder a disorder characterized by the repeated voluntary regurgitation of ingested food involving ejection or reswallowing, but without nausea. It lasts for a period of at least 1 month and generally occurs during infancy (age 3 to 12 months), following a period of normal feeding.

runaway selection a theory of female MATE SELECTION proposing that certain traits in males are sexually attractive to females, which choose mates with these traits and thereby ensure that any male offspring will also be attractive to females, independent of genetic quality. Compare GOOD GENES HYPOTHESIS.

rural health clinic (**RHC**) a clinic, physician practice, or country health department that is located in a medically underserved area and uses a physician, physician assistant, nurse practitioner, or some combination of these to deliver primary outpatient health care.

R

Ss

s symbol for SPECIFIC FACTOR.

S– symbol for NEGATIVE DISCRIMINATIVE STIMU-LUS.

S+ symbol for POSITIVE DISCRIMINATIVE STIMU-LUS.

SA abbreviation for SOCIAL AGE.

saccade *n.* a rapid movement of the eyes that allows visual fixation to jump from one location to another in the visual field. Once initiated, a saccade cannot change course. Compare SMOOTH-PURSUIT MOVEMENT. —saccadic *adj.*

saccule *n.* the smaller of the two VESTIBULAR SACS of the inner ear, the other being the UTRICLE. Like the utricle, it contains a sensory structure called a MACULA. Movements of the head relative to gravity exert a momentum pressure on hair cells within the macula, which then fire impulses indicating a change in body position in space. —saccular *adj.*

sacral nerve see SPINAL NERVE.

SAD abbreviation for SEASONAL AFFECTIVE DISORDER.

S-adenosylmethionine (SAM) *n.* a nonprotein chemical compound that mediates numerous metabolic reactions, including those involving certain proteins, phospholipids, neurotransmitters, and nucleic acids. It is commonly used as a dietary supplement in the treatment of depression as it may increase levels of serotonin in the brain. It also has been implicated in Alzheimer's disease: Low S-adenosylmethionine levels often are observed in those with the disorder, which may be a sign of alteration of SAM metabolism.

sadism *n.* the derivation of pleasure through cruelty and inflicting pain, humiliation, and other forms of suffering on individuals. The term generally denotes SEXUAL SADISM. Compare MASOCHISM. [Donatien Alphonse François, Comte (Marquis) de Sade (1740–1814), French soldier and writer] —sadist *n.* —sadistic *adj.*

sadness *n.* an emotional state of unhappiness, ranging in intensity from mild to extreme and usually aroused by the loss of something that is highly valued, for example, by the rupture or loss of a relationship. Persistent sadness is one of the two defining symptoms of a MAJOR DEPRESSIVE EPISODE, the other being ANHEDONIA. —sad *adj.*

sadomasochism *n.* 1. sexual activity between consenting partners in which one partner enjoys inflicting pain (see SEXUAL SADISM) and the other enjoys experiencing pain (see SEXUAL MASOCHISM). 2. a PARAPHILIA in which a person is both sadistic and masochistic, deriving sexual arousal from both giving and receiving pain. —sadomasochist *n.* —sadomasochistic *adj.*

safe sex sexual activity in which the exchange of bodily fluids is inhibited as much as possible to help reduce the risk of unwanted pregnancy or contracting sexually transmitted diseases. Precautions may include avoidance of high-risk behaviors, careful selection of one's partners, and the use of preventive barriers (e.g., condoms, dental dams).

safety engineering a discipline that applies multiple approaches to the design and evaluation of work systems and processes with the aim of eliminating or reducing hazard. See also HAZARD CONTROL.

safety needs the second level in MASLOW'S MOTIVATIONAL HIERARCHY of needs after basic PHYSIOLOGICAL NEEDS: It consists of the needs for freedom from illness or danger and the need for a secure, familiar, predictable environment.

safety psychology a subdiscipline of applied psychology that studies behavioral aspects of hazardous situations in human–environment systems, paticularly within occupational contexts. Safe and unsafe behavior of employees is studied systematically to derive guidelines that can be transmitted into practical actions.

sagittal *adj.* describing or relating to a plane that divides the body or an organ into left and right portions. A **midsagittal** (or **medial sagittal**) **plane** divides the body centrally into halves, whereas a **parasagittal plane** lies parallel but to one side of the center. —sagittally *adv.*

sagittal fissure see LONGITUDINAL FISSURE.

salience hypothesis a general theory of perception according to which highly salient stimuli (objects, people, meanings, etc.) will be perceived more readily than those of low salience. It has applications in social perception, advertising, and linguistics.

salient *adj.* distinctive or prominent. A salient stimulus in a multielement array will tend to be easily detected and identified. See POP-OUT. —salience *n.*

salivary gland any of several glands located in the wall of the mouth that secrete a fluid (saliva) containing the enzyme α-amylase (ptyalin). The major salivary glands are the paired parotid, submaxillary, and sublingual glands; smaller glands are scattered over the cheeks and tongue.

salpingectomy *n.* the surgical removal of one

or both fallopian tubes, typically performed as a STERILIZATION measure.

saltation *n.* **1.** a type of conduction of nerve impulses that occurs in myelinated fibers (see MYELIN), in which the impulses skip from one NODE OF RANVIER to the next. This permits much faster conduction velocities compared with unmyelinated fibers. Also called **saltatory conduction**. **2.** the phenomenon in which a sensation is felt at a site other than that where it was evoked. For example, auditory saltation is an illusion in which a train of clicks, the first half of which is presented at one location and the other half of which is presented from a second location, is perceived as originating not only from the anchor points but also from locations between them. [from Latin *saltatio*, "dance"]

SAM **1.** abbreviation for S-ADENOSYLMETHIONINE. **2.** abbreviation for SEARCH OF ASSOCIATIVE MEMORY.

same-sex marriage a long-term, intimate, stable, and in some jurisdictions legally recognized relationship between two people of the same sex. It is less frequently called **homosexual marriage**.

sample *n.* a subset of a POPULATION of interest that is selected for study.

sample space the collection of all possible outcomes of an experiment of chance. For example, for a toss of a single coin the sample space is heads and tails, whereas for a toss of two coins the sample space is heads–heads, heads–tails, tails–tails, and tails–heads.

sampling *n.* the process of selecting a limited number of subjects or cases for participation in experiments, surveys, or other research. It is important to ensure that a sample is representative of the population as a whole.

sampling distribution the distribution of a statistic, such as the mean, over infinite repeated samples drawn from a population; that is, the theoretical distribution of a statistic.

sampling error the predictable margin of error that occurs in studies employing sampling, as reflected in the variation in the estimate of a parameter from its true value in the population. Sampling error is exacerbated by the use of samples that are not representative of the population from which they were drawn.

sampling frame a complete listing of all of the elements in a POPULATION from which a sample is to be drawn.

sampling theory the principles underlying the drawing of samples that accurately represent the population from which they are taken.

sampling unit any of the elements that make up a sample. For instance, if classrooms are selected at random, then it is the classroom that is the sampling unit and not the students in the class.

sampling with replacement a SAMPLING technique in which a selected unit is returned to

the pool and may subsequently be redrawn in another sample. In **sampling without replacement** the sampling unit is not returned to the pool.

Sanfilippo's syndrome see MUCOPOLYSACCHARIDOSIS. [described in 1963 by Sylvester Sanfilippo, U.S. pediatrician]

sangue dormido a CULTURE-BOUND SYNDROME found among inhabitants (indigenous and immigrant) of Cape Verde. Symptoms include pain, numbness, tremor, paralysis, convulsions, stroke, blindness, heart attack, infection, and miscarriage. [Portuguese, literally: "sleeping blood"]

sanity *n.* in law, the state of soundness of mind or judgment, involving the ability to understand or appreciate one's acts or to conform to the requirements of the law. —**sane** *adj.*

Sapir–Whorf hypothesis see LINGUISTIC DETERMINISM. [Edward **Sapir** (1884–1939) and Benjamin Lee **Whorf** (1897–1941), U.S. linguists]

sapphism *n.* an older name for LESBIANISM.

sarcoma *n.* see CANCER.

SAT acronym for SCHOLASTIC ASSESSMENT TEST.

satiation *n.* **1.** the satisfaction of a desire or need, such as hunger or thirst; another name for SATIETY. **2.** the temporary loss of effectiveness of a REINFORCER due to its repeated presentation. —**satiate** *vb.*

satiety *n.* the state of being fully satisfied to or beyond capacity, as, for example, when hunger or thirst have been fully assuaged, which inhibits any desire to eat or drink more.

satisfaction of instincts in psychoanalytic theory, the gratification of basic needs, such as hunger, thirst, sex, and aggression, which discharges tension, eliminates UNPLEASURE, and restores the organism to a balanced state. Satisfaction may occur on a conscious, preconscious, or unconscious level. Also called **gratification of instincts**. See also LIBIDO.

satisfice *vb.* to choose an option that meets the requirements of a particular situation but that may not be the optimal choice when considered in the abstract. Given the constraints of BOUNDED RATIONALITY, individuals seek solutions that they find satisfactory rather than optimal.

saturation *n.* the purity of a color and the degree to which it departs from white. Highly saturated colors are intense and brilliant, whereas colors of low saturation are diluted and dull.

savant *n.* a person with mental retardation or an AUTISTIC SPECTRUM DISORDER (**autistic savant**) who demonstrates exceptional, usually isolated, cognitive abilities, such as rapid calculation, identifying the day of the week for any given date, or musical talent. The term **idiot savant** initially was used to denote such a person but has been discarded because of its colloquial, pejorative connotation.

savings method see RELEARNING METHOD.

sawtooth waves bursts of small, sharp waves recorded on an electroencephalogram during REM SLEEP.

SB abbreviation for STANFORD–BINET INTELLIGENCE SCALE.

SBS abbreviation for SHAKEN BABY SYNDROME.

scaffolding *n.* a teaching style that supports and facilitates the student as he or she learns a new skill or concept, with the ultimate goal of the student becoming self-reliant. Derived from the theories of Russian psychologist Lev Vygotsky (1896–1934), in practice it involves teaching material just beyond the level at which the student could learn alone. Technology (e.g., computer software) that may be used to assist in this process is known as **scaffolded tools**.

scala media one of the three canals that run the length of the COCHLEA in the inner ear. Located between the scala vestibuli and scala tympani, it is filled with fluid (ENDOLYMPH) and is delimited by REISSNER'S MEMBRANE, the highly vascular **stria vascularis**, and the BASILAR MEMBRANE, which supports the ORGAN OF CORTI. Also called **cochlear duct**.

scala tympani one of the three canals within the COCHLEA in the inner ear. It is located below the scala media, from which it is separated by the BASILAR MEMBRANE, and contains PERILYMPH. At its basal end is the ROUND WINDOW.

scala vestibuli one of the three canals within the COCHLEA in the inner ear. It is located above the scala media, from which it is separated by REISSNER'S MEMBRANE, and contains PERILYMPH. At its basal end is the OVAL WINDOW.

scale *n.* a system for arranging items in a progressive series, for example, according to their magnitude or value. The characteristic of an item that allows it to fit into such a progression is called **scalability**.

scaling *n.* the process of constructing a SCALE to measure or assess some quantity or characteristic (e.g., height, weight, happiness, empathy).

scanning *n.* in medicine, the process of using radiological, magnetic, or other means (e.g., a BRAIN SCAN) to visualize and examine the body or a portion of it to diagnose a disease or disorder.

scanning hypothesis the hypothesis that RAPID EYE MOVEMENTS observed during dreaming sleep correspond to subjective gaze shifts of the dreamer looking around in the dream with fixations in specific locations.

scanning speech speech that is slow with variable intonations and involuntary interruptions between syllables. It results from cerebellar lesions or other neuromuscular damage.

scapegoat theory an analysis of PREJUDICE that assumes that intergroup conflict is caused, in part, by the tendency of individuals to blame their negative experiences on other groups. The theory is supported by studies suggesting that ra-

cial prejudice increases during periods of economic downturn and high unemployment.

scatologia *n.* preoccupation with obscenities, lewdness, and filth, mainly of an excremental nature. The term is derived from the Greek word for dung. In psychoanalytic theory, scatalogia is usually associated with anal eroticism. Also called **scatology**. —**scatological** *adj.*

scatter *n.* the tendency of data points to diverge from each other. An example is the variation in scores across a series of tests on the same individual.

scatterplot *n.* a graphical representation of the location of data points in a two-dimensional space whose axes are defined by the variables under consideration. Also called **scatter diagram**.

Schachter–Singer theory the theory that experiencing and identifying emotional states are functions of both physiological AROUSAL and cognitive interpretations of the physical state. Also called **two-factor theory of emotion**. [Stanley **Schachter** (1922–1997) and Jerome E. **Singer** (1924–), U.S. psychologists]

schadenfreude *n.* the gaining of pleasure or satisfaction from the misfortune of others. [from German *Schaden*, "harm," and *Freude*, "joy"]

scheduled drug any of various drugs whose prescription or use has been restricted by the U.S. Drug Enforcement Administration. They range from Schedule I drugs, those for which all nonresearch use is illegal (e.g., LSD, heroin), through Schedule V drugs, those with the lowest abuse potential (low doses of codeine and other opiates). The Schedule of Controlled Substances, originally designed to restrict the prescription of commonly abused drugs, is periodically updated as the popularity of new agents—generally drugs of abuse—reaches the attention of authorities.

schedule of reinforcement in conditioning, a rule that determines which instances of a response will be reinforced. There are numerous types of schedules of reinforcement, entries for which are provided elsewhere in the dictionary. Also called **reinforcement schedule**.

Scheffé test a post hoc statistical test that allows for the testing of all possible contrasts (weighted comparisons of any number of means) while controlling the probability of a TYPE I ERROR for the set of contrasts at a prespecified level. [Henry **Scheffé** (1907–1977), U.S. mathematician]

schema *n.* (*pl.* **schemata**) **1.** a collection of basic knowledge about a concept or entity that serves as a guide to perception, interpretation, imagination, or problem solving. For example, the schema "dorm room" suggests that a bed and a desk are probably part of the scene, that a microwave oven might be, and that expensive Persian rugs probably will not be. Also called **cognitive schema**. **2.** an outlook or assumption that an individual has of the self, others, or the world that endures despite objective reality. For example, "I am a damaged person" and "Anyone I trust will eventually hurt me" are negative schemas that may result from negative experiences in early childhood. A goal of treatment, particularly stressed in COGNITIVE THERAPY, is to help the client to develop more realistic, present-oriented schemas to replace those developed during childhood or through traumatic experiences. See also SELF-IMAGE. —**schematic** *adj.*

scheme *n.* a cognitive structure that contains an organized plan for an activity, thus representing generalized knowledge about an entity and serving to guide behavior. For example, there is a simple sucking scheme of infancy, applied first to a nipple or teat and later to a thumb, soft toy, and so forth. This term is often used as a synonym of SCHEMA.

schizoaffective disorder an uninterrupted illness featuring at some time a MAJOR DEPRESSIVE EPISODE, MANIC EPISODE, or MIXED EPISODE concurrently with characteristic symptoms of schizophrenia (e.g., delusions, hallucinations, disorganized speech, catatonic behavior).

schizoid *adj.* characterized by lack of affect, social passivity, and minimal introspection.

schizoid personality disorder a personality disorder characterized by long-term emotional coldness, indifference to praise or criticism and to the feelings of others, and inability to form close friendships with others. The eccentricities of speech, behavior, or thought that are characteristic of SCHIZOTYPAL PERSONALITY DISORDER are absent in those with schizoid personality disorder.

schizophrenia *n.* a psychotic disorder characterized by disturbances in thinking (cognition), emotional responsiveness, and behavior, although some have argued that disorganized thinking (see SCHIZOPHRENIC THINKING) is the single most important feature. Originally named DEMENTIA PRAECOX, schizophrenia includes POSITIVE SYMPTOMS, such as delusions, hallucinations, and disorganized speech, and NEGATIVE SYMPTOMS, such as lack of emotional responsiveness and extreme apathy. These signs and symptoms are associated with marked social or occupational dysfunction. Five distinct subtypes of schizophrenia are described in DSM–IV–TR: CATATONIC SCHIZOPHRENIA, DISORGANIZED SCHIZOPHRENIA, PARANOID SCHIZOPHRENIA, RESIDUAL SCHIZOPHRENIA, and UNDIFFERENTIATED SCHIZOPHRENIA. —**schizophrenic** *adj.*

schizophrenic thinking pervasive, marked impairment of thinking in terms of LOOSENING OF ASSOCIATIONS and slowness of associations, representing POSITIVE SYMPTOMS and NEGATIVE SYMPTOMS, respectively, of schizophrenia. Because thinking must be inferred rather than merely observed, and because no single definition or test or technique of inference has been universally accepted, evaluation is usually limited to examining samples of speech or writing. On certain psychological tests, schizophrenic thinking is identified in terms of **deviant verbalizations**, which are unusual, exaggerated, or otherwise abnormal responses to items presented during the test, for example, inventing a word (see NEOLOGISM) to describe a Rorschach inkblot.

schizophreniform disorder a disorder whose essential features are identical to those of SCHIZOPHRENIA except that the total duration is between 1 and 6 months (i.e., intermediate between BRIEF PSYCHOTIC DISORDER and schizophrenia) and social or occupational functioning need not be impaired.

schizophrenogenic *adj.* denoting a factor or influence viewed as causing or contributing to the onset or development of schizophrenia. For example, **schizophrenogenic parents** are those whose harmful influences are presumed to cause schizophrenia in their offspring; this concept—the subject of much debate in the 1940s especially—is now considered an oversimplification.

schizotypal personality disorder a personality disorder characterized by various oddities of thought, perception, speech, and behavior that are not severe enough to warrant a diagnosis of schizophrenia. Symptoms may include perceptual distortions, MAGICAL THINKING, social isolation, vague speech without incoherence, and inadequate rapport with others due to aloofness or lack of feeling.

schizotypy *n.* in research contexts, a type of personality organization defined by milder forms of POSITIVE SYMPTOMS of schizophrenia, such as COGNITIVE SLIPPAGE, and NEGATIVE SYMPTOMS, such as inability to experience pleasure (see ANHEDONIA). Schizotypy is studied in individuals and family members as a predictor of or liability for the later occurrence of schizophrenia.

Scholastic Assessment Test (SAT) a test used in selecting candidates for college admission, formerly called the **Scholastic Aptitude Test**. The critical reading section (formerly called the verbal section) tests ability to understand and analyze what is read and to recognize relationships between parts of a sentence. The mathematics section tests ability to solve problems involving arithmetic, algebra, and geometry. The writing section tests ability to organize thoughts, develop and express ideas, use language, and adhere to grammatical rules.

school-ability test an assessment designed to evaluate a student's educational achievements in order to obtain information that will enhance his or her learning. The assessment can include a variety of widely accepted tests and measurement techniques as the bases for judgment.

school counseling guidance, offered at or outside the school to students, parents, and other caregivers, that focuses on students' academic, personal, social, and career adjustment, development, and achievement. Counseling is offered by certified and licensed professionals at all educational levels, from elementary through college and professional school.

school psychology a field of psychology concerned with the healthy growth and development of children in primary and secondary schools. The responsibilities of the **school psychologist** include curriculum assessment and planning, counseling of teachers and students, and diagnosis and treatment of behavioral problems and learning disabilities.

school readiness any of a variety of programs designed to prepare children of below kindergarten age for attending formal school by helping them acquire certain skills, such as being able to pay attention to adult-directed tasks for short periods of time, to speak in five- to six-word sentences, and to identify letters of the alphabet. These programs are often referred to as **prekindergarten** or **nursery school.**

school refusal persistent reluctance to go to school, which usually occurs during the primary school years and is often a symptom of an educational, social, or emotional problem. School refusal may be a feature of SEPARATION ANXIETY DISORDER or it may be triggered by a stressor (e.g., loss of a pet or loved one, a change of school, loss of a friend due to a move). School refusal is often associated with physical symptoms (e.g., upset stomach, nausea, dizziness, headache) and anxiety at the start of the day along with complaints that the child is too sick to go to school. Also called **school avoidance**; **school phobia.**

Schwann cell a type of nonneuronal peripheral nervous system cell (GLIA) that forms the MYELIN SHEATH around axons. [Theodor **Schwann** (1810–1882), German histologist]

schwannoma *n.* a type of tumor that develops from SCHWANN CELLS. Although typically benign, schwannomas tend to displace and compress surrounding neurons as they grow. A schwannoma is very similar to a NEUROFIBROMA but is distinguished by its capsule.

sciatic nerve a large peripheral nerve that connects the receptor and effector cells in the leg to the spinal cord. Pain in the leg, which may extend over the entire length of this nerve, from the buttocks to the foot, is called **sciatica.** The cause is most commonly a slipped disk—a condition in which the gelatinous interior of an invertebral disk is pushed through a weakened portion of its fibrous coating—pressing on the nerve root emerging from the spinal cord.

scientific management generally, the application of scientific methods to achieve improved worker efficiency and work conditions. More specifically, the term refers to the school of management thought introduced by U.S. engineer Frederick W. Taylor (1856–1915). This approach, also known as **Taylorism** or the **Taylor system of scientific management,** involved studying the work to determine the most efficient way of performing tasks (see TIME AND MOTION STUDY) and

paying workers piece-rate incentives to adopt these methods.

scientific method a group of procedures, guidelines, assumptions, and attitudes required for the organized and systematic collection, interpretation, and verification of data and the discovery of reproducible evidence, enabling laws and principles to be stated or modified.

scientific psychology the body of psychological facts, theories, and techniques that have been developed and validated through the use of the SCIENTIFIC METHOD. They thus depend on objective measurement and the replication of results under controlled or known conditions. See EXPERIMENTAL PSYCHOLOGY.

scientism *n.* an uncritical commitment to a particular view of science and scientific methods that leads its adherents to dismiss all other approaches as intellectually invalid. The term is mainly used by those who criticize the assumptions of Western science as arrogant or flawed, who maintain that scientific methods are inappropriate in certain fields or incapable of apprehending certain kinds of truth, or who reject the implication that all philosophical questions will one day reduce to scientific questions. **—scientistic** *adj.*

scientist-practitioner model a concept for the university training of doctoral clinical (or other applied) psychologists in the United States that is intended to prepare individuals both to provide services and to conduct research on mental health problems, essentially integrating these two functions in their professional work by making a laboratory of their applied settings and studying their phenomena and the results of their administrations scientifically. The purpose of the model is to ensure that practitioners contribute to the scientific development of their field. The training emphasizes research techniques applicable to applied (therapeutic) settings. The model emerged from a conference held in Boulder, Colorado, in 1949, which was sponsored by the U.S. Veterans Administration and the National Institute of Mental Health. Also called **Boulder model.**

scieropia *n.* a visual anomaly in which objects appear to be in a shadow.

sclera *n.* the tough, white outer coat of the eyeball, which is continuous with the cornea at the front and the sheath of the optic nerve at the back of the eyeball. Also called **sclerotic coat.**

sclerosis *n.* hardening of tissues, usually as a consequence of disease or aging. It particularly affects the nervous system (see AMYOTROPHIC LATERAL SCLEROSIS; MULTIPLE SCLEROSIS) and the circulatory system (see ARTERIOSCLEROSIS; ATHEROSCLEROSIS). **—sclerotic** *adj.*

SCL-90-R abbreviation for SYMPTOM CHECKLIST-90-REVISED.

scoliosis *n.* a lateral (sideways) curvature of the spine. See also KYPHOSIS; LORDOSIS.

score *n.* a quantitative value assigned to test results or other measurable responses.

score equating the process of equilibrating test scores in such a way that the score distribution remains equivalent over versions or administrations of the test.

scotoma *n.* an area of partial or complete loss of vision either in the central visual field (**central scotoma**) or in the periphery (**paracentral scotoma**). Vision may be decreased (**relative scotoma**), altered (**scintillating scotoma**), or completely lost (**absolute scotoma**). See also VISUAL FIELD DEFECT.

scotomization *n.* in psychoanalytic theory, the tendency to ignore or be blind to impulses or memories that would threaten the individual's EGO. Scotomization is a defensive process and may also be a form of RESISTANCE. Also called **scotomatization**. See also BLIND SPOT.

scotopic vision vision that occurs in dim light by means of the RETINAL ROD system. As scotopic vision does not permit color discrimination, the visual scene appears in shades of gray. However, the closer the illumination of a target is to 510 nm in wavelength, the brighter it will appear relative to other targets with the same energy, since this is the peak wavelength sensitivity for the rod system. Also called **twilight vision**. Compare PHOTOPIC VISION.

screen defense in psychoanalytic theory, a defense in which a memory, fantasy, or dream image is unconsciously employed to conceal the real but disturbing object of one's feelings.

screening *n.* **1.** a procedure or program to detect early signs of a disease in an individual or population. Individuals at increased hereditary risk of developing a disease are advised to follow regular screening plans. **2.** the initial evaluation of a patient to determine his or her suitability for medical or psychological treatment generally, a specific treatment approach, or referral to a treatment facility. This evaluation is made on the basis of medical or psychological history, MENTAL STATUS EXAMINATION, diagnostic formulation, or some combination of these. **3.** the process of determining, through a preliminary test, whether an individual is suitable for some purpose or task.

screening test any testing procedure designed to separate people or objects according to a fixed characteristic or property. Screening tests are typically used to distinguish people who have a disease, disorder, or predisease condition from those who do not; they may be used, for example, in primary health care settings to identify people who are depressed. Screening tests are designed to be broadly sensitive, and subsequent highly specific or focused testing is often required to confirm the results.

screen memory in psychoanalytic theory, a memory of a childhood experience, usually trivial in nature, that unconsciously serves the purpose of concealing or screening out an associated experience of a more significant and perhaps traumatic nature. Also called **cover memory**; **replacement memory**.

scree plot in FACTOR ANALYSIS, a plot of the EIGENVALUES in descending order. Break points in this distribution are used to help determine the number of factors to be retained.

script *n.* a cognitive schematic structure—a mental road map—containing the basic actions (and their temporal and causal relations) that comprise a complex action. For example, the script for cooking pasta might be: Open pan cupboard, choose pan, fill pan with water, put pan on stove, get out pasta, weigh correct amount of pasta, add pasta to boiling water, decide when cooked, remove from heat, strain, place in bowl. Also called **script schema**.

script theory 1. in TRANSACTIONAL ANALYSIS, the theory that an individual's approach to social situations follows a sequence that was learned and established early in life. **2.** the proposition that discrete affects, such as joy and fear, are prime motivators of behavior and that personality structure and function can be understood in terms of self-defining affective scenes and scripts.

S data see Q DATA.

SDS abbreviation for ZUNG SELF-RATING DEPRESSION SCALE.

SDT abbreviation for SIGNAL DETECTION THEORY.

search *n.* **1.** a mental process in which a set of memories or other MENTAL REPRESENTATIONS is checked for the presence or absence of a particular target item. For example, one might search one's memory for the name of a former teacher. **2.** a task in which a person is asked to check an array of presented stimuli to determine whether any of a set of target stimuli is in the array. **3.** in problem solving, the process by which the solver attempts to find the correct answer or best solution from among a range of alternatives.

search asymmetry in studies of VISUAL SEARCH, the situation in which search for the presence of a feature produces one pattern of results but search for the absence of that feature produces another. For example, searching for a Q in a field of Os (i.e., searching for the "tail" segment in the Q) is relatively easy, but searching for an O in a field of Qs (i.e., searching for the absence of this segment) is difficult.

search of associative memory (**SAM**) a mathematical model used to explain recall and recognition memory in laboratory studies. Information may reside in SHORT-TERM MEMORY, from which it may be stored in LONG-TERM MEMORY or used to search long-term memory. Associations can be formed among items in memory and between items and the context in which they occur.

seasonal affective disorder (**SAD**) a MOOD DISORDER in which there is a predictable occurrence of MAJOR DEPRESSIVE EPISODES, MANIC EP-

ISODES, or both at particular times of the year. The typical pattern is the occurrence of major depressive episodes during the fall or winter months. Also called **seasonal mood disorder**.

secondary aging changes due to biological AGING, but accelerated by disabilities resulting from disease or produced by extrinsic factors, such as stress, trauma, lifestyle, and environment. Secondary aging is often distinguished from PRIMARY AGING, which is governed by inborn and age-related processes, but the distinction is not a precise one.

secondary appraisal in the COGNITIVE APPRAISAL THEORY of emotion, assessment of one's ability to cope with the consequences of an interaction with the environment, which follows a PRIMARY APPRAISAL.

secondary care health care services provided by medical specialists (e.g., cardiologists, urologists, dermatologists), to whom, typically, patients are referred by the PRIMARY CARE provider. Compare TERTIARY CARE.

secondary circular reaction in PIAGETIAN THEORY, a repetitive action emerging at around 4 to 5 months, such as rattling the crib, that has yielded results in the past but that the infant does not modify to meet the requirements of a new situation. Such COORDINATION OF SECONDARY CIRCULAR REACTIONS emerges several months later. See also PRIMARY CIRCULAR REACTION; TERTIARY CIRCULAR REACTION.

secondary coping a type of COPING STRATEGY that enhances one's ability to adapt to events and environmental conditions as they are, such as rethinking about the stressor or problem in such a way as to facilitate acceptance. Also called **secondary control coping**. Compare PRIMARY COPING.

secondary drive an acquired drive; that is, a drive that is developed through association with or generalization from a PRIMARY DRIVE. For example, in an AVOIDANCE CONDITIONING experiment in which a rat must go from one compartment into another to escape from an electric shock, the secondary drive is fear of the shock and the primary drive with which it is associated is avoidance of pain.

secondary elaboration in psychoanalysis, the process of altering the memory and description of a dream to make it more coherent and less fragmentary or distorted. See also DREAM-WORK.

secondary emotion an emotion that is not recognized or manifested universally across cultures or that requires social experience for its construction. For some theorists, PRIDE represents a secondary emotion, stemming from the conjunction of a PRIMARY EMOTION (JOY) and a favorable public reaction. Other secondary emotions include ENVY, LOVE, and JEALOUSY.

secondary gains in psychoanalytic theory, advantages derived from a NEUROSIS in addition to the PRIMARY GAINS of relief from anxiety or internal conflict. Examples are extra attention, sympathy, avoidance of work, and domination of others. Such gains are secondary in that they are derived from others' reactions to the illness instead of causal factors. They often prolong the neurosis and create resistance to therapy.

secondary group one of the larger, less intimate, more goal-focused groups typical of more complex societies, such as work groups, clubs, congregations, associations, and so on. These social groups influence members' attitudes, beliefs, and actions, but as a supplement to the influence of small, more interpersonally intensive PRIMARY GROUPS.

secondary identification in psychoanalytic theory, identification with admired figures other than the parents.

secondary memory (**SM**) memory that retains a large number of items relatively permanently, in contrast to PRIMARY MEMORY. The term was used in DUAL-STORE MODELS OF MEMORY before being replaced by LONG-TERM MEMORY.

secondary motor cortex see MOTOR CORTEX.

secondary prevention intervention for individuals or groups that demonstrate early psychological or physical symptoms, difficulties, or conditions (i.e., subclinical-level problems), which is intended to prevent the development of more serious dysfunction or illness. Compare PRIMARY PREVENTION; TERTIARY PREVENTION.

secondary process in psychoanalytic theory, conscious, rational mental activities under the control of the EGO and the REALITY PRINCIPLE. These thought processes, which include problem-solving, judgment, and systematic thinking, enable individuals to meet both the external demands of the environment and the internal demands of their instincts in rational, effective ways. Also called **secondary process thinking**. Compare PRIMARY PROCESS.

secondary quality in the philosophy of English empiricist philosopher John Locke (1632–1704), a sensible quality of an object that does not exist in the object itself but rather in the experience of the perceiver. Color, for example, is a secondary quality, since the sensation of a particular color can only be produced by an object under certain conditions of light. Compare PRIMARY QUALITY.

secondary repression see REPRESSION PROPER.

secondary sensory area any of the regions of the cerebral cortex that receive direct projections from the PRIMARY SENSORY AREA for any given sense modality. An example is the SECONDARY SOMATOSENSORY AREA.

secondary somatosensory area (**S2**) an area of the cerebral cortex, located in the PARIETAL LOBE on the upper bank of the LATERAL SULCUS, that receives direct projections from the PRIMARY SOMATOSENSORY AREA and other regions of the anterior parietal cortex and has outputs to other parts of the lateral parietal cortex and to motor and premotor areas.

secondary symptoms 1. according to Swiss psychiatrist Eugen Bleuler (1857–1939), those symptoms of schizophrenia, such as delusions and hallucinations, that are shared with other disorders and therefore not specifically diagnostic of schizophrenia. Bleuler theorized that these symptoms do not stem directly from the disease but rather begin to operate when the person reacts to some internal or external process. Also called **accessory symptoms**. Compare FUNDAMENTAL SYMPTOMS. **2.** symptoms that are not a direct result of a disorder but are associated with or incidental to those that are (e.g., social avoidance accompanying obsessive-compulsive disorder).

secondary task methodology an experimental design used in the study of attention in which participants perform a primary task as well as possible and a secondary task to the extent possible while maintaining performance on the primary task. Performance on the secondary task provides a profile of the attention required by the primary task at various phases.

secondary taste cortex the area of cerebral cortex, located in the ORBITOFRONTAL CORTEX, that is the second cortical relay for taste (see also PRIMARY TASTE CORTEX). It identifies gustatory stimuli as either pleasant and rewarding or unpleasant and undesirable. This information from the secondary taste cortex interacts with analyses from visual, touch, and olfactory cells to permit an integrated appreciation of flavor.

secondary visual system the visual pathway that lies outside the PRIMARY VISUAL SYSTEM and is phylogenetically older than it. Retinal input travels directly to the superior COLLICULUS, then to visual nuclei in the thalamus other than the lateral geniculate nucleus before terminating in the PRESTRIATE CORTEX. The vision supported by the secondary visual system is relatively poor for the detection of form, but allows localization and detection of movement.

second-generation antipsychotic see ANTIPSYCHOTIC.

second messenger an ion or molecule inside a cell whose concentration increases or decreases in response to stimulation of a cell RECEPTOR by a neurotransmitter, hormone, or drug. The second messenger acts to relay and amplify the signal from the receptor (the "first messenger") by triggering a range of cellular activities. For example, receptors for catecholamine neurotransmitters (epinephrine and norepinephrine) are coupled to G PROTEINS, whose activation in postsynaptic neurons affects levels of second messengers that act to open or close certain ION CHANNELS.

second-order conditioning in PAVLOVIAN CONDITIONING, the establishment of a conditioned response as a result of pairing a neutral stimulus with a conditioned stimulus that gained its effectiveness by being paired with an unconditioned stimulus. See HIGHER ORDER CONDITIONING.

second-order schedule a SCHEDULE OF REINFORCEMENT in which the units counted are not single responses but completions of a particular reinforcement schedule (the **unit schedule**). For example, in a second-order fixed-ratio 5 of fixed-interval 30-s schedule [FR 5 (FI 30 s)], reinforcement is delivered only after five successive FI 30-s schedules have been completed. Often, a brief stimulus of some sort is presented on completion of each unit schedule.

second sight an alleged paranormal faculty that enables some individuals to see events that are remote in time or space. See CLAIRVOYANCE; PRECOGNITION.

secretion *n.* **1.** the synthesis and discharge of specific substances from cells (which may be organized in glands) into other parts of the body. The substance produced may be released directly into the blood (ENDOCRINE secretion) or through a duct (see EXOCRINE GLAND). **2.** the substance discharged by this process. —**secretory** *adj.*

sect *n.* a group whose members adhere to a distinctive set of doctrines, beliefs, and rituals. The term is often applied to a dissenting faction that breaks away from a larger religious, political, or other social organization. —**sectarian** *adj.*

section *n.* **1.** a thin slice of tissue that can be examined microscopically. **2.** an image of a body part in any plane obtained by such techniques as COMPUTED TOMOGRAPHY or MAGNETIC RESONANCE IMAGING.

sector therapy a therapeutic procedure in which patterns of association that have produced emotional problems in the client are replaced by more realistic and constructive patterns. Unlike DEPTH THERAPY, this process, described as **goal-limited adjustment therapy**, focuses on specific areas (**sectors**) revealed by the client's own autobiographical account. The procedure enables the client to understand his or her faulty associations and gradually establish new ones with the aid of the therapist.

secular humanism a broad perspective, increasingly influential in Western countries since the mid-20th century, that can be characterized by some or all of the following: (a) a belief in seeking solutions to human problems through science and rational thought, rather than religion or traditional forms of morality; (b) a focus on this world rather than a putative afterlife; (c) an emphasis on an intrinsic human potential for growth, rather than on human limitation or sinfulness; (d) a search for new truth, and a belief in free thought, free speech, and free inquiry as the means to find it; (e) an acceptance of cultural and human diversity, including sexual diversity; and (f) an acceptance of some degree of RELATIVISM in ethics, usually accompanied by some type of UTILITARIANISM in practice. See also HUMAN-ISM.

secular trend the main trend or long-term direction of a TIME SERIES, as distinguished from temporary variations.

secure attachment 1. in the STRANGE SITUATION, the positive parent–child relationship, in which the child displays confidence when the parent is present, shows mild distress when the parent leaves, and quickly reestablishes contact when the parent returns. **2.** an adult attachment style that combines a positive INTERNAL WORKING MODEL OF ATTACHMENT of oneself, characterized by a view of oneself as worthy of love, and a positive internal working model of attachment of others, characterized by the view that others are generally accepting and responsive. Compare DISMISSIVE ATTACHMENT; FEARFUL ATTACHMENT; PREOCCUPIED ATTACHMENT.

secure base phenomenon the observation that infants use a place of safety, represented by an attachment figure (e.g., a parent), as a base from which to explore a novel environment. The infant often returns or looks back to the parent before continuing to explore.

secure treatment setting a locked residential setting providing safety and treatment services for adolescent or adult offenders, usually felons, with mental retardation or developmental disabilities.

security *n.* a sense of safety, confidence, and freedom from apprehension. It is believed to be engendered by numerous factors, including warm, accepting parents and friends. In the psychotherapeutic context (where it is most often referred to as **trust**) security is seen as a mediating goal that encourages open exploration of emotional and behavioral issues and is viewed to be part of a strong and healthy THERAPIST–PATIENT RELATIONSHIP.

sedative *n.* a drug that has a calming effect, and therefore relieves anxiety, agitation, or behavioral excitement, by depressing the central nervous system. The degree of sedation depends on the agent and the size of the dose: A drug that sedates in small doses may induce sleep in larger doses and may be used as a HYPNOTIC; such drugs are commonly known as **sedative-hypnotics**.

sedative, hypnotic, and anxiolytic drugs CNS DEPRESSANTS that have been developed for therapeutic use because of their calming effect (i.e., sedatives) and ability to induce sleep (i.e., hypnotics) and reduce anxiety (i.e., anxiolytics). They include the BARBITURATES and the BENZODIAZEPINES. At low doses these drugs are prescribed for daytime use to reduce anxiety; at higher doses many of the same drugs are prescribed as sleeping pills.

sedative, hypnotic, or anxiolytic abuse a pattern of use of sedative, hypnotic, or anxiolytic drugs manifested by recurrent significant adverse consequences related to the repeated ingestion of these substances. See also SUBSTANCE ABUSE.

sedative, hypnotic, or anxiolytic dependence a cluster of cognitive, behavioral, and physiological symptoms indicating continued use of sedative, hypnotic, or anxiolytic drugs despite significant problems related to these substances. See also SUBSTANCE DEPENDENCE.

sedative, hypnotic, or anxiolytic intoxication a reversible syndrome specific to the recent ingestion of sedative, hypnotic, or anxiolytic drugs. It includes clinically significant behavioral or psychological changes (e.g., inappropriate sexual or aggressive behavior, mood lability, impaired judgment, and impaired social or occupational functioning), as well as one or more signs of physiological involvement (e.g., slurred speech, an unsteady gait, involuntary eye movements, memory or attentional problems, incoordination, and stupor or coma).

sedative, hypnotic, or anxiolytic withdrawal a characteristic withdrawal syndrome, potentially life-threatening, that develops after cessation of (or reduction in) prolonged, heavy consumption of sedative, hypnotic, or anxiolytic drugs. Symptoms may include autonomic hyperactivity; increased hand tremor; insomnia; nausea or vomiting; transient visual, tactile, or auditory hallucinations or illusions; psychomotor agitation; anxiety; either a transient worsening (rebound) of the anxiety condition that prompted treatment or a recurrence of that condition; and tonic–clonic seizures. See also SUBSTANCE WITHDRAWAL.

segment *n.* in linguistics, a consonantal or vowel PHONEME occurring as part of a consecutive sequence of these. See SUPRASEGMENTAL. —**segmental** *adj.*

segmentation *n.* a technique of BEHAVIOR MODIFICATION in which a complex sequence of behaviors is divided into parts so that the client can more easily learn and master one or two at a time.

segregation *n.* **1.** the separation or isolation of people (e.g., ethnic groups) or other entities (e.g., mental processes) so that there is a minimum of interaction between them. **2.** in genetics, the separation of the paired ALLELES of any particular gene during the cell division (see MEIOSIS), leading to sex-cell formation.

seizure *n.* a discrete episode of uncontrolled, excessive electrical discharge of neurons in the brain. The resulting clinical symptoms vary based on the type and location of the seizure. See EPILEPSY.

selected group a SAMPLE explicitly selected with respect to specific criteria related to the purpose of the research. For example, a sample of citizens age 65 and over might be selected for a study of patterns in the attitudes of older adults.

selection *n.* in animal behavior, the differential survival of some individuals and their offspring compared with others, causing certain physical or behavioral traits to be favored in subsequent generations. The general process is known as NATURAL SELECTION.

selection bias a systematic and directional error in the choosing of participants or other units for research, such as selecting specially motivated participants. Selection bias is associated with nonrandom sampling and with nonrandom assignment to conditions.

selection pressure a measure of the intensity with which NATURAL SELECTION favors the survival of some genotypes over others and thus alters the genetic composition of a population over successive generations.

selection research the use of empirical investigation to determine the reliability, validity, utility, and fairness of procedures used in personnel selection and to maximize the effectiveness of these procedures.

selective adaptation the observation that perceptual adaptation can occur in response to certain stimulus qualities while being unaffected by others. For example, color adaptation can take place independently of motion adaptation.

selective amnesia the forgetting of particular issues, people, or events that is too extensive to be explained by normal forgetfulness and that is posited to be organized according to emotional, rather than temporal, parameters.

selective attention concentration on certain stimuli in the environment and not others, enabling important stimuli to be distinguished from peripheral or incidental ones. Selective attention is typically measured by instructing participants to attend to some sources of information while ignoring others and then determining their effectiveness in doing this.

selective inattention 1. unmindful absence or failure of attention to particular physical or emotional stimuli. **2.** a perceptual defense in which anxiety-provoking or threatening experiences are ignored or forgotten.

selective information processing the processing of attitude-relevant information in a biased manner. Although a number of potential biases are possible, it has traditionally been assumed that when this type of processing occurs, the bias will be toward confirming the attitude.

selective learning learning to make only one of several possible responses or learning about one stimulus when several stimuli are available. A particular response or stimulus could have a selective advantage due to biological PREPAREDNESS, previous experience, or salience in a given situation.

selective mutism a rare disorder, most commonly but not exclusively found in young children, characterized by a persistent failure to speak in certain social situations (e.g., at school) despite the ability to speak and to understand spoken language. Generally, these individuals function normally in other ways and most learn age-appropriate skills and academic subjects. Currently, selective mutism is thought to be related to severe anxiety and SOCIAL PHOBIA, but the exact cause is unknown.

selective optimization with compensation a process used in SUCCESSFUL AGING to adapt to biological and psychological deficits associated with aging. The process involves emphasizing and enhancing those capacities affected only minimally by aging (optimization) and developing new means of maintaining functioning in those areas that are significantly affected (compensation).

selective perception the process in which people choose from the myriad array of stimuli presented to the senses at any one time that one or those few stimuli that will be attended.

selective rearing an experimental paradigm in which an animal is raised from birth or from the time of eye opening under conditions that restrict its visual experience. This induces long-term changes in the structure and function of its visual system. For example, MONOCULAR REARING reduces the number of neurons in the STRIATE CORTEX that are sensitive to binocular stimulation and alters the structure of the OCULAR DOMINANCE COLUMNS; rearing with prism goggles that restrict the orientations that are visible can alter the orientation selectivity of neurons and the ORIENTATION COLUMNS in the striate cortex.

selective reminding test any memory test in which the participant is given the answer when it cannot be remembered so that he or she is more likely to answer correctly on subsequent trials. For instance, if the word "pencil" is presented on a list-learning task and the participant is unable to recall it, the word would then be presented along with other words not recalled.

selective serotonin reuptake inhibitor see SSRI.

selective silence in psychotherapy, a prolonged silence imposed by the therapist to generate tension that may encourage the client to speak, thus beginning or resuming communication in a session.

self *n.* the totality of the individual, consisting of all characteristic attributes, conscious and unconscious, mental and physical. Apart from its basic reference to personal identity, being, and experience, the term's use in psychology is extremely wide-ranging and lacks uniformity, including, for example, the following perspectives: the person as the target of self-appraisal or as the source of AGENCY; the person as he or she gradually develops by a process of INDIVIDUATION; the individual identified with a LIFESTYLE; and the essence of the individual, consisting of a gradually developing body sense, IDENTITY, self-estimate, and set of personal values, attitudes, and intentions.

self-abasement *n.* **1.** the act of degrading or

demeaning oneself. **2.** extreme submission to the will of another person. Also called **self-debasement**.

self-acceptance *n.* a relatively objective sense or recognition of one's abilities and achievements, together with acknowledgment and acceptance of one's limitations. Self-acceptance is often viewed as a major component of mental health.

self-actualization *n.* the realization of that of which one is capable. According to U.S. psychologist Abraham Maslow (1908–1970), it is the "full use and exploitation of talent, capacities, potentialities" such that the individual develops to maximum self-realization, ideally integrating physical, social, intellectual, and emotional needs. The process of striving toward full potential is fundamental according to Maslow; however, he posited that self-actualization can only be fully realized if the basic needs of physical survival, safety, love and belongingness, and esteem are fulfilled. Also called **self-realization**. See also HUMANISTIC PSYCHOLOGY; MASLOW'S MOTIVATIONAL HIERARCHY.

self-advocacy *n.* the process by which people make their own choices and exercise their rights in a self-determined manner. For people with developmental and other disabilities, for example, self-advocacy might entail promoting increased control of resources related to services and making informed decisions about what services to accept, reject, or insist be altered.

self-affirmation *n.* **1.** any behavior by which a person expresses a positive attitude toward his or her self, often by a positive assertion of his or her values, attributes, or group memberships. SELF-AFFIRMATION THEORY assumes that the desire for self-affirmation is basic and pervasive and that many different behaviors reflect this motive. **2.** in psychotherapy, a positive statement or set of such statements about the self that a person is required to repeat on a regular basis, often as part of a treatment for depression, negative thinking, or low self-esteem.

self-affirmation theory a theory postulating that people are motivated to maintain views of themselves as well adapted, moral, competent, stable, and able to control important outcomes. When some aspect of this self-view is challenged, people experience psychological discomfort. They may attempt to reduce this discomfort by directly resolving the inconsistency between the new information and the self, by affirming some other aspect of the self, or both. Self-affirmation theory has been used to provide an alternative explanation to COGNITIVE DISSONANCE THEORY for some phenomena. See also SELF-CONSISTENCY PERSPECTIVE OF COGNITIVE DISSONANCE THEORY.

self-alienation *n.* a state in which the individual feels a stranger to himself or herself, typically accompanied by significant emotional distancing. The self-alienated individual is frequently unaware of or largely unable to describe his or her own intrapsychic processes.

self-analysis *n.* **1.** generally, the investigation or exploration of the SELF for the purpose of better understanding of personal thoughts, emotions, and behavior. Self-analysis occurs consciously and unconsciously in many contexts of daily life. To some degree or other, and with the assistance and sometimes interpretation of the therapist, it is a particularly crucial process within most forms of psychotherapy. **2.** an attempt to apply the principles of PSYCHOANALYSIS to a study of one's own drives, feelings, and behavior. It was proposed by Austrian psychiatrist Sigmund Freud (1856–1939) early in his career as part of the preparation of an analyst but later dropped in favor of a TRAINING ANALYSIS. **—self-analytic** *adj.*

self-assertion *n.* the act of putting forward one's own opinions or taking actions that express one's needs, rights, or wishes. Self-assertion is often seen as a goal of treatment and in some cases is specifically targeted by structured group treatments. **—self-assertive** *adj.*

self-as-target effect the tendency to assume wrongly that, or to overestimate the degree to which, external events refer to the self. For example, a person may think that other people's conversations are directed at him or her. In its milder forms the self-as-target effect is common and normal, but extreme forms are associated with PARANOIA.

self-awareness *n.* self-focused attention or knowledge. There has been a continuing controversy over whether nonhuman animals have self-awareness. Evidence of this in animals most often is determined by whether an individual can use a mirror to groom an otherwise unseen spot on its own forehead. A few chimpanzees, gorillas, and orangutans have passed this test.

self-care *n.* activities required for personal care, such as eating, dressing, or grooming, that can be managed by an individual without the assistance of others.

self-censure *n.* an individual's conscious self-blame, condemnation, or guilt in judging his or her own behavior to be inconsistent with personal values or standards of moral conduct.

self-completion theory the theory that many behaviors are performed to claim desired identities, so that by behaving in a certain way one is symbolically "proving" oneself to be a certain kind of person. For example, a person who takes pride in being very fit and active may respond to the first signs of illness or exhaustion by increasing, rather than reducing, his or her activities.

self-complexity *n.* the degree to which different aspects of the SELF-CONCEPT are disconnected from one another. Low self-complexity entails considerable integration; high self-complexity results from COMPARTMENTALIZATION, so that what affects one part of the self may not affect other parts.

self-concept *n.* one's conception and evaluation of oneself, including psychological and physical characteristics, qualities, and skills. A self-concept contributes to the individual's sense of identity over time and is dependent in part on unconscious schematization of the self (see SCHEMA). See SELF-IMAGE; SELF-PERCEPTION.

self-concept test a type of personality assessment designed to determine how participants view their own attitudes, values, goals, body concept, personal worth, and abilities.

self-confidence *n.* self-assurance, or trust in one's own abilities, capacities, and judgment. Because it is most typically viewed as a positive personality trait, the encouragement or bolstering of self-confidence is often a mediate or end goal in psychotherapeutic treatment. —**self-confident** *adj.*

self-conscious emotion an emotion that celebrates or condemns the self and its actions, generated when the self is known to be the object of another person's evaluation. Self-conscious emotions include SHAME, PRIDE, GUILT, and EMBARRASSMENT. Recently, the term **other-conscious emotions** has been suggested as a better name for these emotions, to emphasize the importance of the appraisal of other human beings in generating them.

self-consciousness *n.* **1.** a personality trait associated with the tendency to reflect on or think about oneself. Some researchers have distinguished between two varieties of self-consciousness: (a) **private self-consciousness**, or the degree to which people think about private, internal aspects of themselves (e.g., their own thoughts, motives, and feelings) that are not directly open to observation by others; and (b) **public self-consciousness**, or the degree to which people think about public, external aspects of themselves (e.g., their physical appearance, mannerisms, and overt behavior) that can be observed by others. **2.** extreme sensitivity about one's own behavior, appearance, or other attributes and excessive concern about the impression one makes on others, which leads to embarrassment or awkwardness in the presence of others. —**self-conscious** *adj.*

self-consistency perspective of cognitive dissonance theory a variation of COGNITIVE DISSONANCE THEORY postulating that COGNITIVE DISSONANCE is particularly likely to occur when an inconsistency involves some aspect of the self. This perspective differs from SELF-AFFIRMATION THEORY in that it assumes that dissonance can only be reduced by resolving the specific inconsistency that gave rise to the discomfort; it does not allow for the possibility that dissonance can be reduced by affirming some other aspect of the self.

self-control *n.* the ability to be in command of one's behavior (overt, covert, emotional, or physical) and to restrain or inhibit one's impulses. In circumstances in which short-term gain is pitted against long-term loss or long-term greater gain, it is the ability to opt for the long-term outcome. —**self-controlled** *adj.*

self-control therapy a form of BEHAVIOR THERAPY that involves self-monitoring (e.g., diaries of behavior), self-evaluation, goal setting, BEHAVIORAL CONTRACTS, teaching, self-reinforcement, and relapse prevention. Also called **self-management therapy**.

self-criticism *n.* the examination and evaluation of one's behavior, with recognition of one's weaknesses, errors, and shortcomings. Self-criticism can have both positive and negative effects; for example, a tendency toward harsh self-criticism is thought by some to be a risk factor for depression. —**self-critical** *adj.*

self-defeating behavior behavior that blocks an individual's own goals and wishes. An example is the tendency to compete so aggressively that one cannot hold a job.

self-degradation *n.* negative imagery or negative self-talk that causes one to think less of oneself and one's ability.

self-desensitization *n.* a procedure used in BEHAVIOR THERAPY in which the individual, when confronted with objects or situations that arouse fear or anxiety, engages in coping strategies designed to reduce anxiety, for example, repeating positive self-statements, mentally rehearsing a potential confrontation, or employing muscle relaxation. See also DESENSITIZATION; SYSTEMATIC DESENSITIZATION.

self-destructiveness *n.* actions by an individual that are damaging and not in his or her best interests. The behavior may be repetitive and resistant to treatment, sometimes leading to suicide attempts. The individual may not be aware of the damaging influence of the actions or may on some level wish for the resulting damage. —**self-destructive** *adj.*

self-determination theory a theory that emphasizes the importance of AUTONOMY and INTRINSIC MOTIVATION for producing healthy adjustment. According to this theory, negative outcomes ensue when people are driven mainly by external forces and extrinsic rewards.

self-differentiation *n.* the tendency to seek recognition for one's individuality and uniqueness, particularly in contrast to the other members of one's social group.

self-discipline *n.* the control of one's own impulses and desires, forgoing immediate satisfaction in favor of long-term goals or of improvement generally. —**self-disciplined** *adj.*

self-disclosure *n.* the act of revealing information about one's self, especially one's PRIVATE SELF, to other people. In psychotherapy, the revelation and expression by the client of personal, innermost feelings, fantasies, experiences, and aspirations is believed by many to be a requisite for therapeutic change and personal growth.

self-discrepancy *n.* an incongruence between

S

different aspects of one's self-concept, particularly between one's actual self and either the IDEAL SELF or the OUGHT SELF.

self-efficacy *n.* an individual's capacity to act effectively to bring about desired results, especially as perceived by the individual (see PERCEIVED SELF-EFFICACY).

self-enhancement *n.* any strategic behavior designed to increase esteem, either SELF-ESTEEM or the esteem of others. Self-enhancement can take the form of pursuing success or merely distorting events to make them seem to reflect better on the self. Compare SELF-PROTECTION.

self-enhancement motive the desire to think well of oneself and to be well regarded by others. This motive causes people to prefer favorable, flattering feedback rather than accurate but possibly unfavorable information. Compare APPRAISAL MOTIVE; CONSISTENCY MOTIVE.

self-esteem *n.* the degree to which the qualities and characteristics contained in one's SELF-CONCEPT are perceived to be positive. It reflects a person's physical self-image, view of his or her accomplishments and capabilities, and values and perceived success in living up to them, as well as the ways in which others view and respond to that person. The more positive the cumulative perception of these qualities and characteristics, the higher one's self-esteem. A high or reasonable degree of self-esteem is considered an important ingredient of mental health, whereas low self-esteem and feelings of worthlessness are common depressive symptoms.

self-evaluation maintenance model a conceptual analysis of group affiliations that assumes that an individual maintains and enhances self-esteem by (a) associating with high-achieving individuals who excel in areas with low relevance to his or her sense of self-worth and (b) avoiding association with high-achieving individuals who excel in areas that are personally important to him or her.

self-fulfilling prophecy a belief or expectation that helps to bring about its own fulfillment, as, for example, when a person expects nervousness to impair his or her performance in a job interview or when a teacher's preconceptions about a student's ability influence the child's achievement for better or worse. See PYGMALION EFFECT; UPWARD PYGMALION EFFECT.

self-guide *n.* a specific image or goal of the SELF that can be used to direct SELF-REGULATION. In particular, self-guides include mental representations of valued or preferred attributes, that is, ideals and notions of how one ought to be; these may be chosen by the self or may come from others.

self-handicapping *n.* a strategy of creating obstacles to one's performance, so that future anticipated failure can be blamed on the obstacle rather than on one's own lack of ability. If one

succeeds despite the handicap, it brings extra credit or glory to the self. The theory originally was proposed to explain alcohol and drug abuse among seemingly successful individuals. —**self-handicap** *vb.*

self-help *n.* a focus on self-guided, in contrast to professionally guided, efforts to cope with life problems. This can involve self-reliance, drawing upon publicly available information and materials, or joining together with others similar to oneself, as is the case in SELF-HELP GROUPS.

self-help group a group composed of individuals who meet on a regular basis to help one another cope with a common life problem. Unlike therapy groups, self-help groups are not led by professionals, do not charge a fee for service, and do not place a limit on the number of members. They provide many benefits that professionals cannot provide, including friendship, emotional support, experiential knowledge, identity, meaningful roles, and a sense of belonging. Examples of self-help groups are Alcoholics Anonymous, Compassionate Friends, and Recovery, Inc. See also MUTUAL SUPPORT GROUP; SUPPORT GROUP.

self-hypnosis *n.* the process of putting oneself into a trance or trancelike state, sometimes spontaneously but typically through AUTOSUGGESTION. Also called **autohypnosis**.

self-ideal Q sort a technique designed to measure the discrepancy between an individual's existing and ideal SELF-CONCEPTS. The technique requires participants to sort descriptions of characteristics twice, once with regard to how they see themselves and then in terms of how they would like to be.

self-identification *n.* the act of construing one's identity in particular terms, usually as a member of a particular group or category (e.g., "I am Hispanic," "I am a lesbian," "I am a father") or as a person with particular traits or attributes (e.g., "I am intelligent," "I am unlucky," "I am fat").

self-image *n.* one's own view or concept of oneself. Self-image is a crucial aspect of an individual's personality that can determine the success of relationships and a sense of general well-being. A negative self-image is often a cause of dysfunctions and of self-abusive, self-defeating, or destructive behavior. See also SCHEMA.

self-image bias the tendency of people to judge others according to criteria on which they themselves score highly. The more favorably a person rates himself or herself on some trait, the more central and important that trait is likely to be in how the person perceives others.

self-instructional training a form of COGNITIVE BEHAVIOR THERAPY that aims to modify maladaptive beliefs and cognitions and develop new skills in an individual. In therapy, the therapist identifies the client's maladaptive thoughts (e.g., "Everybody hates me") and models appropriate behavior while giving spoken constructive self-instructions (or self-statements). The client then copies the behavior while repeating these instructions aloud. See also SELF-STATEMENT TRAINING.

selfish gene hypothesis the postulate that the sole purpose of genes is to replicate themselves and that genes are the overriding units of selection (i.e., the entities upon which NATURAL SELECTION operates). Hence any mutation enhancing gene replication (and transmission) would be selected for. Many contemporary evolutionary biologists hold this view to oversimplify the relationship between genes and organisms and to be extreme in its notion that genes consistently override selection on the organism or population level.

self-management n. 1. an individual's control of his or her own behavior. Self-management is usually considered a desirable aspect for the individual personally and within the social setting, but some forms of self-management may be detrimental to mental and physical health. Psychotherapy and counseling often seek to provide methods of identifying the latter and modifying them into the former. 2. a BEHAVIOR-THERAPY program in which clients are trained to apply techniques that will help them modify an undesirable behavior, such as smoking, excessive eating, or aggressive outbursts. Clients learn to pinpoint the problem, set realistic goals for changing it, use various CONTINGENCIES to establish and maintain the desired behavior, and monitor progress.

self-monitoring n. 1. a method used in behavioral management in which individuals keep a record of their behavior (e.g., time spent, place of occurrence, form of the behavior, feelings during performance), especially in connection with efforts to change or regulate the self (see SELF-REGULATION). 2. a personality trait reflecting an ability to modify one's behavior in response to situational pressures, opportunities, and norms. High self-monitors are typically more in tune with the demands of the situation, whereas low self-monitors tend to be more in tune with their internal feelings. 3. a therapeutic technique in which the therapist assigns homework to encourage the client to record behavior, because behavior sometimes changes when it is closely self-monitored.

self-perception n. a person's view of his or her self or of any of the mental or physical attributes that constitute the self. Such a view may involve genuine self-knowledge or varying degrees of distortion. Also called self-percept. See also PERCEIVED SELF; SELF-CONCEPT.

self-perception theory a theory postulating that people often have only limited access to their attitudes, beliefs, traits, or psychological states. In such cases, people must attempt to infer the nature of these internal cues in a manner similar to the inference processes they use when making judgments about other people

(i.e., by considering past behaviors). Self-perception theory has been offered as an alternative explanation for some phenomena traditionally interpreted in terms of COGNITIVE DISSONANCE THEORY. The theory has also been used to explain the success of the FOOT-IN-THE-DOOR TECHNIQUE.

self-presentation n. any behaviors designed to convey a particular image of, or particular information about, the self to other people. Self-presentational motives explain why an individual's behavior often changes as soon as anyone else is thought to be present or watching. Some common strategies of self-presentation include exemplification (inducing others to regard one as a highly moral, virtuous person), self-promotion (highlighting or exaggerating one's competence and abilities), and supplication (depicting oneself as weak, needy, or dependent). See also IMPRESSION MANAGEMENT. —self-presentational adj.

self-preservation instinct the fundamental tendency of humans and nonhuman animals to behave so as to avoid injury and maximize chances of survival (e.g., by fleeing from dangerous situations or predators). In his early formulations of classic psychoanalytic theory, Austrian psychiatrist Sigmund Freud (1856–1939) proposed that the instinct of self-preservation was one of two instincts that motivated human behavior, the other being the SEXUAL INSTINCT. In his later formulations he combined both instincts into the concept of EROS, or the LIFE INSTINCT, and opposed them to THANATOS, the DEATH INSTINCT. Also called self-preservative instinct; survival instinct.

self-protection n. any strategic behavior that is designed to avoid losing esteem, either SELF-ESTEEM or the esteem of others. Self-protection fosters a risk-avoidant orientation and is often contrasted with SELF-ENHANCEMENT.

self psychology any system of psychology focused on the SELF.

self-rating scale any questionnaire, inventory, or other instrument used by participants to assess their own characteristics (e.g., attitudes, interests, abilities, or performance).

self-referral n. the act of consulting a clinical service provider or health care practitioner without being directed to by a medically qualified professional or similar person or without being forced to seek such help by an employer, a spouse, or the courts.

self-reflection n. examination, contemplation, and analysis of one's thoughts and actions. The condition of or capacity for this is called self-reflexivity.

self-regulation n. the control of one's own behavior through the use of self-monitoring (keeping a record of behavior), self-evaluation (assessing the information obtained during self-monitoring), and self-reinforcement (rewarding oneself for appropriate behavior or for attaining a goal). Self-regulatory processes are stressed in BEHAVIOR THERAPY.

self-regulation model a five-stage model of the process of self-management of directed behavior without the presence of external constraints. The stages are problem identification, commitment, execution, environment management, and generalization.

self-regulatory resources theory a model stating that SELF-REGULATION depends on a global, but finite, pool of resources that can be temporarily depleted by situational demands. See EGO DEPLETION; VOLITION.

self-reinforcement n. the rewarding of oneself for appropriate behavior or the achievement of a desired goal. The self-reward may be, for example, buying a treat after studying for an exam. Also called **self-managed reinforcement**.

self-report bias a methodological problem that arises when researchers rely on asking people to describe their thoughts, feelings, or behaviors rather than measuring these directly and objectively. People may not give answers that are fully correct, either because they do not know the full answer or because they seek to make a good impression.

self-report inventory a type of questionnaire on which participants indicate the degree to which the descriptors listed apply to them.

self-schema n. a cognitive framework comprising organized information about the self in terms of roles and actions, often in relation to a specific realm of experience (e.g., a clear conception of oneself as parent or worker).

self-serving bias the tendency to interpret events in a way that assigns credit to the self for any success but denies the self's responsibility for any failure, which is blamed on external factors. The self-serving bias is regarded as a form of self-deception designed to maintain high SELF-ESTEEM. Compare GROUP-SERVING BIAS.

self-statement modification a technique designed to change maladaptive ideas about the self that are uncovered in COGNITIVE BEHAVIOR THERAPY. See also SELF-INSTRUCTIONAL TRAINING.

self-statement training (SST) a type of COGNITIVE REHEARSAL that involves periodically thinking or saying something positive, such as "I am a capable individual who is worthy of respect." It is used in SELF-INSTRUCTIONAL TRAINING.

self-suggestion n. see AUTOSUGGESTION.

self-talk n. an internal dialogue in which an individual utters phrases or sentences to himself or herself. The self-talk often confirms and reinforces negative beliefs and attitudes, such as fears and false aspirations, which have a correspondingly negative effect on the individual's feelings and reactions. In certain types of psychotherapy, one of the tasks of the therapist is to encourage the client to replace self-defeating, negative self-talk with more constructive, positive self-talk.

self-terminating search any SEARCH process in which the search is ended as soon as a given target is detected. Compare EXHAUSTIVE SEARCH.

self-transcendence n. the state in which an individual is able to look beyond him- or herself and adopt a larger perspective that includes concern for others. Some psychologists maintain that self-transcendence is a central feature of the healthy individual, promoting personal growth and development.

self-understanding n. the attainment of insight into one's attitudes, motives, reactions, defenses, strengths, and weaknesses. The achievement of self-understanding is one of the major goals of psychotherapy.

self-verbalization n. **1.** self-directed private speech or thinking aloud. Self-verbalization can be a cognitive strategy that fosters internal self-regulation by verbally controlling behavior. Often used as a learning tool, it can be used to teach new skills, enhance problem-solving abilities, or alter previously held beliefs. **2.** see SELF-TALK.

self-verification hypothesis the hypothesis that people seek information about themselves that confirms their existing SELF-CONCEPT, regardless of whether this is good or bad. According to this theory, the CONSISTENCY MOTIVE, which seeks self-verification, is often stronger than the SELF-ENHANCEMENT MOTIVE, which seeks favorable information about the self, or than the APPRAISAL MOTIVE, which seeks accurate information about the self.

self-worth n. an individual's evaluation of him- or herself as a valuable, capable human being deserving of respect and consideration. Positive feelings of self-worth tend to be associated with a high degree of SELF-ACCEPTANCE and SELF-ESTEEM.

SEM abbreviation for STRUCTURAL EQUATION MODELING.

semantic code the means by which the conceptual or abstract components of an object, idea, or impression are stored in memory. For example, the item "typewriter" could be remembered in terms of its functional meaning or properties. Compare IMAGERY CODE.

semantic dementia a selective, progressive impairment in SEMANTIC MEMORY, leading to difficulties in naming, comprehension of words, and appreciation and use of objects. Nonsemantic aspects of language, as well as perceptual and spatial skills, are preserved. The syndrome results from focal degeneration of the polar and inferolateral regions of the temporal lobes.

semantic differential a technique used to explore the connotative meaning that certain words or concepts have for the individuals being questioned. Participants are asked to rate the word or concept on a seven-point scale with reference to pairs of opposites, such as *good–bad*, *beautiful–ugly*, *hot–cold*, *big–small*, and so on. Responses are then averaged or summed to arrive at a final index of attitudes. This procedure is one of the most widely used methods of assessing attitudes.

semantic dissociation a distortion between words and their culturally accepted meanings that is characteristic of the THOUGHT DISORDER of individuals with schizophrenia. It includes **semantic dissolution**, marked by a complete loss of meaning and communication; **semantic dispersion**, in which meaning and syntax are lost or reduced; **semantic distortion**, in which meaning may be transferred to neologisms; or **semantic halo**, marked by coherent but vague and ambiguous language.

semantic encoding cognitive ENCODING of new information that focuses on the meaningful aspects of the material as opposed to its perceptual characteristics. This will usually involve some form of ELABORATION. See also DEEP PROCESSING.

semanticity *n.* the property of language that allows it to represent events, ideas, actions, and objects symbolically, thereby endowing it with the capacity to communicate meaning.

semantic knowledge general knowledge or information that one has acquired; that is, knowledge that is not tied to any specific object, event, domain, or application. It includes word knowledge (as in a dictionary) and general factual information about the world (as in an encyclopedia) and oneself. Also called **generic knowledge**.

semantic memory memory for general knowledge or meanings, of the kind that allows people to name and categorize the things they see. According to some theories, semantic memory is a form of DECLARATIVE MEMORY, that is, information that can be consciously recalled and related.

semantic network a data structure used to capture conceptual relationships. Created by the artificial intelligence research community, this system has been used in an attempt to model human information storage (particularly the means by which words are connected to meanings and associations in long-term memory), with latencies in retrieval times supposedly reflecting the length of the path of the network searched for the required response.

semantic priming an effect in which the processing of a stimulus is found to be more efficient after the earlier processing of a meaningfully related stimulus, as opposed to an unrelated or perceptually related stimulus. For example, responses to the word *nurse* would be faster following *doctor* than following *purse*. See PRIMING.

semantic primitive in SEMANTICS, one of the fundamental building blocks thought to be involved in the construction of meaning. Many refer to a basic physical property or simple sensation; for example, the concept *car* could be reduced to the semantic primitives *moves*, *fast*, *noisy*, *shiny*, and so on. Semantic primitives are thought to play an important role in language development in young children.

semantics *n.* **1.** in linguistics, the study of meaning in language, as opposed to the study of formal relationships (GRAMMAR) or sound systems (PHONOLOGY). **2.** aspects of language that have to do with meaning, as distinguished from SYNTACTICS. **3.** in logic and philosophy, the study of the relationships between words or phrases and the things or concepts to which they refer. Compare SEMIOTICS.

semantic therapy a form of psychotherapy in which the clients are trained to examine undesired word habits and distorted ideas so that they can think more clearly and critically about their aims, values, and relationships. This approach is based on an active search for the meaning of the key words the client uses and on practicing the formation of clear abstractions, as well as on uncovering hidden assumptions and increased awareness of the emotional tone behind the words the client has been using.

semen *n.* the fluid released during ejaculation (see ORGASM). It contains sperm and secretions of the prostate gland, bulbourethral glands, and seminal vesicles. Also called **seminal fluid**.

semicircular canals a set of three looped tubular channels in the inner ear that detect movements of the head and provide the sense of dynamic equilibrium that is essential for maintaining balance. They form part of the VESTIBULAR APPARATUS. The channels are filled with fluid (endolymph) and are oriented roughly at right angles to each other. Hence they can monitor movements in each of three different planes. Each canal has an enlarged portion, the **ampulla**, inside which is a sensory structure called a **crista**. This consists of HAIR CELLS whose processes are embedded in a gelatinous cap (the **cupula**). When the head moves in a certain plane, endolymph flows through the corresponding canal, displacing the cupula and causing the hairs to bend. This triggers the hair cells to fire nerve impulses, thus sending messages to the brain about the direction and rate of movement.

semiconscious *adj.* describing states of partial wakefulness, or alertness, such as drowsiness, stupor, or intermittent coma.

semiotics *n.* the study of verbal and nonverbal SIGNS and of the ways in which they communicate meaning within particular sign systems. Unlike SEMANTICS, which restricts itself to the meanings expressed in language, semiotics is concerned with human symbolic activity generally. As an academic discipline, semiotics developed within the general framework of 20th-century STRUCTURALISM, taking as its premise the view that signs can only generate meanings within a pattern of relationships to other signs. Also called **semiology**.

semitone *n.* a half-step on the musical scale. More precisely, it is the logarithm of a frequency ratio.

senescence *n.* **1.** the biological process of growing old, or the period during which this process occurs. **2.** the state or condition of being old. —**senescent** *adj.*

senile *adj.* associated with advanced age, particularly referring to dementia or any other cognitive or behavioral deterioration relating to old age.

senile dementia see DEMENTIA.

senile plaque a clump of BETA-AMYLOID protein surrounded by degenerated dendrites that is particularly associated with symptoms of Alzheimer's disease. Increased concentration of senile plaques in the cerebral cortex of the brain is correlated with the severity of dementia. Also called **amyloid plaque**; **neuritic plaque**.

sensate focus an approach to problems of sexual dysfunction in which people are trained to focus attention on their own natural, biological sensual cues and gradually achieve the freedom to enjoy sensory stimuli. The procedures involve prescribed body-massage exercises designed to give and receive pleasure, first not involving breasts and genitals, and then moving to these areas. This eliminates performance anxiety about arousal and allows the clients to relax and enjoy the sensual experience of body caressing without the need to achieve erection or orgasm.

sensation *n.* an irreducible unit of experience produced by stimulation of a sensory RECEPTOR and the resultant activation of a specific brain center, producing basic awareness of a sound, odor, color, shape, or taste or of temperature, pressure, pain, muscular tension, position of the body, or change in the internal organs associated with such processes as hunger, thirst, nausea, and sexual excitement. —**sensational** *adj.*

sensationalism *n.* in philosophy, the position that all knowledge originates in sensations and that even complex abstract ideas can be traced to elementary sense impressions. See ASSOCIATIONISM; EMPIRICISM. —**sensationalist** *adj.*

sensation seeking the tendency to search out and engage in thrilling activities as a method of increasing stimulation and arousal. Limited to human populations, it typically takes the form of engaging in highly stimulating activities accompanied by a perception of danger, such as skydiving or race-car driving.

sense 1. *n.* any of the media through which one gathers information about the external environment or about the state of one's body in relation to this. They include the five primary senses—vision, hearing, taste, touch, and smell—as well as the senses of pressure, pain, temperature, kinesthesis, and equilibrium. Each sense has its own receptors, responds to characteristic stimuli, and

has its own pathways to a specific part of the brain. Also called **sensory modality**. **2.** *n.* a particular awareness of a physical dimension or property (e.g., time, space) or of an abstract quality, usually one that is desirable (e.g., humor, justice). **3.** *vb.* to make an emotional or cognitive judgment about something, such as another person's mood.

sense of equilibrium the sense that enables the maintenance of balance while sitting, standing, walking, or otherwise maneuvering the body. A subset of PROPRIOCEPTION, it is in part controlled by the VESTIBULAR SYSTEM in the INNER EAR, which contains receptors (see VESTIBULAR RECEPTORS) that detect motions of the head. Also called **vestibular sense**.

sensible *adj.* **1.** capable of receiving sensory input (e.g., feeling pain). **2.** receptive to external influences.

sensitive dependence the tendency for complex, dynamic systems to be highly sensitive to initial conditions, so that two such systems with starting points that are almost identical may become extremely divergent over time. In other words, the future states of complex systems are very dependent on small differences in their initial states. One possible explanation for this phenomenon is that measurements in chaotic systems are imprecise, so that prediction becomes extremely difficult. See CHAOS THEORY.

sensitivity *n.* **1.** the capacity to detect and discriminate. In SIGNAL DETECTION THEORY, sensitivity is measured by D PRIME (d'). **2.** the probability that a test gives a positive diagnosis given that the individual actually has the condition for which he or she is being tested. Compare SPECIFICITY. **3.** in physiology, the ability of a cell, tissue, or organism to respond to changes in its external or internal environment: a fundamental property of all living organisms. **4.** awareness of and responsiveness to the feelings of others.

sensitivity training a group process focused on the development of self-awareness, productive interpersonal relations, and sensitivity to the feelings, attitudes, and needs of others. The primary method used in sensitivity training is free, unstructured discussion with a leader functioning as an observer and facilitator, although other techniques, such as ROLE PLAY, may be used. Sensitivity training is employed in human relations training in industry and general life, with various types of groups (e.g., workers, executives, married couples) meeting, for example, once a week or over a weekend. See also ACTION RESEARCH; T-GROUP.

sensitization *n.* **1.** the increased effectiveness of an eliciting stimulus as a function of its repeated presentation. Water torture, in which water is dripped incessantly onto a person's forehead, is a good example. **2.** see REVERSE TOLERANCE.

sensor *n.* a RECEPTOR cell or organ.

sensorimotor *adj.* **1.** describing activity, behavior, or brain processes that combine sensory (afferent) and motor (efferent) function. **2.** describing a mixed nerve that contains both afferent and efferent fibers.

sensorimotor memory 1. a memory, commonly of a traumatic experience, that is encoded in SENSORIMOTOR, rather than verbal, forms. Frequently these are memories of events that occurred during the period of INFANTILE AMNESIA, which commonly lasts up to the age of 3 years. See also BODY MEMORY. **2.** see PROCEDURAL MEMORY.

sensorimotor stage in PIAGETIAN THEORY, the first major stage of cognitive development, extending from birth through the first 2 years of life. The sensorimotor stage is characterized by the development of sensory and motor processes and by the infant's first knowledge of the world acquired by interacting with the environment.

sensorineural deafness see DEAFNESS.

sensorineural lesion any damage to structures of the auditory system along the nerve pathway from the inner ear to the associated brain centers. **Childhood sensorineural lesions** are congenital and due to a failure of such structures to develop normally in the fetal stage or to an infection, whereas **adult sensorineural lesions** are due to injury or disease, such as a tumor.

sensorium *n.* the human sensory apparatus and related mental faculties considered as a whole. The state of the sensorium is tested through the traditional MENTAL STATUS EXAMINATION; the sensorium may be **clear** (i.e., functioning normally) or **clouded** (lacking ability to concentrate and think clearly).

sensory *adj.* relating to the SENSES, to SENSATION, or to a part or all of the neural apparatus and its supporting structures that are involved in any of these. See SENSORY SYSTEM.

sensory acuity the extent to which one is able to detect stimuli of minimal size, intensity, or duration and to discriminate minimal differences between stimuli.

sensory adaptation see ADAPTATION.

sensory aphasia another name for WERNICKE'S APHASIA.

sensory area any area of the cerebral cortex that receives input from sensory neurons, usually via the thalamus. There are specific sensory areas for the different senses, and they are functionally differentiated into PRIMARY SENSORY AREAS and SECONDARY SENSORY AREAS. Also called **sensory cortex; sensory projection area**.

sensory awareness training 1. the methods used in SENSATE FOCUS and similar therapies to help an individual become more acutely aware of his or her own feelings and sensations and to accept new ways of experiencing them. **2.** in sport, training an athlete to become aware of the kinesthetic sensations experienced while performing and of the sensations related to AROUSAL level.

sensory consciousness consciousness of sensory stimuli, having visual, tactile, olfactory, auditory, and taste qualities. Compare HIGHER ORDER CONSCIOUSNESS.

sensory cortex see SENSORY AREA.

sensory deprivation the reduction of sensory stimulation to a minimum in the absence of normal contact with the environment. Sensory deprivation may be experimentally induced (e.g., via the use of a **sensory deprivation chamber**) for research purposes or it may occur in a real-life situation (e.g., in deep-sea diving). Although short periods of sensory deprivation can be beneficial, extended sensory deprivation has detrimental effects, causing (among other things) hallucinations, delusions, hypersuggestibility, or panic.

sensory discrimination the perceptual differentiation of stimuli, particularly closely related sensory stimuli (e.g., very similar shades of blue).

sensory disorder any disturbance in the optimum transmission of information from a sense organ to its appropriate reception point in the brain or spinal cord, particularly when related to an anatomical or physiological abnormality. An auditory disorder, for example, may be due to damage from injury or disease to the cochlear structures.

sensory evoked potential a type of EVOKED POTENTIAL recorded from electrodes placed on the scalp, overlying the cerebral cortex, in response to sensory stimulation. The stimuli may be visual, auditory, somatosensory, or olfactory, and the mapping of sensory evoked potentials in the cortex helps to locate the different SENSORY AREAS. Compare MOTOR EVOKED POTENTIAL.

sensory homunculus a figurative representation, in distorted human form, of the relative sizes of the sensory areas in the brain that correspond to particular sensory parts of the body. The homunculus is arranged upside down with the largest proportional areas representing the face and hands. Compare MOTOR HOMUNCULUS.

sensory integration dysfunction a condition characterized by difficulties in organizing, processing, and analyzing sensory input (touch, movement, body awareness, sight, sound, smell, and taste).

sensory memory brief storage of information from each of the senses in a relatively unprocessed form beyond the duration of a stimulus, for recoding into another memory (such as SHORT-TERM MEMORY) or for comprehension. For instance, sensory memory for visual stimuli, called ICONIC MEMORY, holds a visual image for less than a second, whereas that for auditory stimuli, called ECHOIC MEMORY, retains sounds for a little longer. Also called **sensory-information store (SIS); sensory register**.

sensory modality see SENSE.

sensory modulation dysfunction a condition characterized by difficulties in responding appropriately to sensory input (touch, movement, body awareness, sight, sound, smell, and taste). A person may be overresponsive or underresponsive to sensations or alternate rapidly between both response patterns.

sensory neglect inability to attend to sensory information, usually from one side of the body, as a result of brain injury.

sensory nerve any nerve that conveys impulses from a sense organ to the central nervous system.

sensory neuron a neuron that receives information from the environment, via specialized RECEPTOR cells, and transmits this—in the form of nerve impulses—through SYNAPSES with other neurons to the central nervous system.

sensory organization the neural process of structuring and integrating impulses from sensory receptors so as to enable meaningful perception.

sensory overload a state in which the senses are overwhelmed with stimuli, to the point that the person is unable to process or respond to all of them.

sensory paralysis a condition in which sensory function is impaired but movement is not necessarily lost.

sensory pathway any of the routes followed by nerve impulses traveling from sense organs toward sensory areas of the brain. See NEURAL PATHWAY.

sensory preconditioning a form of PAVLOVIAN CONDITIONING established by initially pairing two neutral stimuli (A and B) and subsequently pairing A with an unconditioned stimulus. If B comes to elicit a response, then sensory preconditioning has occurred. Also called **sensory conditioning**.

sensory psychophysiology the study of the relation between psychological and physiological functioning as it pertains to the senses and perception.

sensory substitution the perception of a stimulus normally analyzed by one sense through the activity of another sense. Tactile sensations can substitute for visual input, for example, when the visual world is transcribed into tactile sensations for a blind individual. Sensory substitution requires an active translation of stimulation between sensory systems, in contrast to SYNESTHESIA, which is an involuntary association of one sense with another or one sensory attribute with another.

sensory suppression the phenomenon occurring in any sensory modality when an individual is given two sensory inputs simultaneously (such as touching the hand and face) but perceives only one of the stimuli.

sensory system the total structure involved in SENSATION, including the sense organs and their RECEPTORS, afferent sensory neurons, and SENSORY AREAS in the cerebral cortex at which these

tracts terminate. There are separate systems for each of the senses. See AUDITORY SYSTEM; GUSTATORY SYSTEM; OLFACTORY SYSTEM; SOMATOSENSORY SYSTEM; VISUAL SYSTEM; VESTIBULAR SYSTEM.

sensual *adj.* **1.** referring to the senses, particularly gratification of or appeal to the senses. **2.** referring to physical or erotic sensation.

sentence-completion test a language ability test in which the participant must complete an unfinished sentence by filling in the specific missing word or phrase. However, the test is used more often to evaluate personality, in which case the participant is presented with an introductory phrase to which he or she may respond in any way. An example might be "Today I am in a __ mood." As a projective test, the sentence-completion test is an extension of the WORD-ASSOCIATION TEST in that responses are free and believed to contain psychologically meaningful material. Also called **incomplete-sentence test**.

sentient *adj.* capable of sensing and recognizing stimuli.

sentinel event in health administration, an unexpected occurrence or variation to service delivery involving death or serious physical or psychological injury. The event is called "sentinel" because it sends a signal or sounds a warning that requires immediate attention.

separation anxiety the normal apprehension experienced by a young child when away (or facing the prospect of being away) from the person or people to whom he or she is attached (particularly parents). Separation anxiety is most active between 6 and 10 months.

separation anxiety disorder an anxiety disorder occurring in childhood or adolescence that is characterized by developmentally inappropriate, persistent, and excessive anxiety about separation from the home or from major attachment figures. Other features may include worry about harm coming to attachment figures or about major events that might lead to separation from them (e.g., getting lost), SCHOOL REFUSAL, fear of being alone or going to sleep without major attachment figures present, separation-related nightmares, and repeated complaints of physical symptoms (e.g., vomiting, nausea, headaches, stomachaches) associated with anticipated separation.

separation–individuation *n.* the developmental phase in which the infant gradually differentiates himself or herself from the mother, develops awareness of his or her separate identity, and attains relatively autonomous status.

sept *n.* a subdivision of a CLAN or other large social unit, especially one based on (supposed) common ancestry. See also DESCENT GROUP.

septal area a region of the forebrain that contains the **septal nuclei** and the **septum pellucidum**, which separates the lateral ventricles. The septal nuclei, which include the NU-CLEUS ACCUMBENS, form an integral part of the LIMBIC SYSTEM; they contribute fibers to the MEDIAL FOREBRAIN BUNDLE and have interconnections with the amygdala, hippocampus, and regions of the hypothalamus. Functionality of this area includes pleasure and anger suppression.

sequela *n.* (*pl.* **sequelae**) a residual effect of an illness or injury, or of an unhealthy or unstable mental condition, often (but not necessarily) in the form of persistent or permanent impairment. Examples include paralysis, which may be the sequela of POLIOMYELITIS, and flashbacks, which may be the sequelae of traumatic stress.

sequence effect in WITHIN-SUBJECT DESIGNS, the effect of the treatments being administered in a particular sequence (e.g., the sequence ABC versus ACB, versus BCA, and so forth). This is often confused with the ORDER EFFECT.

sequential analysis a class of statistical procedures in which a decision as to whether to continue collecting data is made as the experiment progresses. This approach is contrasted with studies in which the sample size is determined in advance and data is not analyzed until the entire sample is collected.

sequential effect in choice-reaction tasks, the influence of an immediately preceding trial (or trials) on performance in the current trial.

serial behavior an integrated sequence of responses that elicit each other in fixed order (e.g., playing music). The individual responses that comprise, and occupy specific positions within, the sequence are referred to as **serial responses**.

serial exhaustive search a hypothesized process of searching for a particular target item in SHORT-TERM MEMORY that involves inspecting each item in turn for a match.

serial learning the learning of a sequence of items or responses in the precise order of their presentation. For example, actors must learn their lines in sequence. Also called **serial-order learning**.

serial position effect the effect of an item's position in a list of items to be learned on how well it is remembered. The classic serial position effect shows best recall of the first items from a list (see PRIMACY EFFECT) and good recall of the last items (see RECENCY EFFECT), while the middle items are less well recalled.

serial processing INFORMATION PROCESSING in which only one sequence of processing operations is carried on at a time. Those who hold that the human information-processing system operates in this way argue that the mind's apparent ability to carry on different cognitive functions simultaneously is explained by rapid shifts between different information sources. Compare PARALLEL PROCESSING. See also SINGLE-CHANNEL MODEL.

serial recall recalling items in the order in which they were presented. For instance, to remember a telephone number, the digits must be correctly sequenced.

serial search in a search task, the process of searching for one target at a time. Compare PARALLEL SEARCH.

serotonergic *adj.* responding to, releasing, or otherwise involving serotonin. For example, a **serotonergic neuron** is one that employs serotonin as a neurotransmitter. In the brain most serotonergic pathways originate in the RAPHE NUCLEUS and project diffusely to other sites in the brain and to the spinal cord.

serotonin *n.* a common monoamine neurotransmitter in the brain and other parts of the central nervous system, also found in the gastrointestinal tract, in smooth muscles of the cardiovascular and bronchial systems, and in blood platelets. It is synthesized from the dietary amino acid L-tryptophan, and in the pineal gland it is converted to MELATONIN. Serotonin has roles in numerous bioregulatory processes, including emotional processing, mood, appetite, and sleep as well as pain processing, hallucinations, and reflex regulation. It is implicated in many psychological conditions, including depressive disorders, anxiety disorders, sleep disorders, and psychosis. Also called **5-hydroxytryptamine** (**5-HT**).

serotonin and norepinephrine reuptake inhibitor see SNRI.

serotonin receptor any of various receptors that bind and respond to SEROTONIN (5-hydroxytryptamine; 5-HT). They occur in the brain and in peripheral areas and have different sensitivities that can be measured by susceptibility to ligands or blockers. At least 15 classes of serotonin receptors, affecting a variety of physiological and psychological processes, have been identified. They are designated by subscript numbers and letters (e.g., 5-HT_{1A}, 5-HT_{1B}, 5-HT_{1D}, 5-HT_{2A}, etc.).

serotonin reuptake inhibitor (**SRI**) see SSRI.

serotonin syndrome a collection of symptoms, including agitation, confusion, delirium, and increased heart rate, due to excess activity of the neurotransmitter serotonin. It may result from drug interactions that increase amounts of available serotonin to toxic levels.

sertraline *n.* an SSRI that is used for the treatment of depressive and anxiety disorders, including major depression, panic disorder, posttraumatic stress disorder, and obsessive-compulsive disorder. It has also been indicated for the treatment of premenstrual dysphoric disorder. U.S. trade name: **Zoloft**.

SES abbreviation for SOCIOECONOMIC STATUS.

set *n.* a temporary readiness to respond in a certain way to a specific situation or stimulus. For example, a sprinter gets set to run when the starting gun fires (a **motor set**); a parent is set to hear his or her baby cry from the next room (a PERCEPTUAL SET); a poker player is set to use a tactic that has been successful in other games (a MENTAL SET). See also PREPARATORY SET.

set point as applied to physiological and behavioral systems, the preferred level of functioning of an organism or of a system within an organism. When a set point is exceeded (i.e., when physiological responses become higher than the set point), compensatory events take place to reduce functioning; when a set point is not reached, compensatory processes take place to help the organism or system reach the set point.

seven plus or minus two the number of items that can be held in short-term memory at any given time and therefore accurately perceived and recalled after a brief exposure (see CHUNKING). The phrase originated in the title of an article (1956) by U.S. cognitive psychologist George Armitage Miller (1920–), "The magical number seven, plus or minus two: Some limitations on our capacity for processing information."

severe mental retardation a diagnostic category applying to those with IQs of 20 to 34, comprising about 7% of people with MENTAL RETARDATION. While able to manage basic self-care activities such as dressing and eating, these individuals typically do not acquire much more than rudimentary communication, social, educational, and vocational skills and generally require significant assistance and supervision. Additionally, sensory and motor deficits are common.

severity error a type of rating error in which the ratings are consistently overly negative, particularly with regard to the performance or ability of the participants. Also called **severity bias**. Compare LENIENCY ERROR.

sex *n.* **1.** the traits that distinguish between males and females. Sex refers especially to physical and biological traits, whereas GENDER refers especially to social or cultural traits, although the distinction between the two terms is not regularly observed. **2.** the physiological and psychological processes related to procreation and erotic pleasure.

sex change see SEX REASSIGNMENT.

sex characteristics the traits associated with sex identity. **Primary sex characteristics** (e.g., testes in males, ovaries in females) are directly involved in reproduction of the species. **Secondary sex characteristics** are features not directly concerned with reproduction, such as voice quality, facial hair, and breast size.

sex chromosome a chromosome that determines the sex of an individual. Humans and other mammals have two sex chromosomes: the X CHROMOSOME, which carries genes for certain sexual traits and occurs in both females and males; and the smaller Y CHROMOSOME, which is normally found only in males. Disease genes that are carried only on a sex chromosome (usually the X chromosome) are responsible for SEX-LINKED inherited conditions.

sex counseling guidance provided by therapists to sex partners in such matters as birth control, infertility, and general feelings of inadequate sexual performance. Working on specific SEXUAL DYSFUNCTION problems is usually considered to be SEX THERAPY rather than sex counseling.

sex differences 1. the differences in physical features between males and females. These include differences in brain structures as well as differences in primary and secondary SEX CHARACTERISTICS. **2.** the differences between males and females in the way they behave and think. Sex differences are often viewed as driven by actual biological gender disparity (nature), rather than by differing environmental factors (nurture), and affect both cognition and behavior.

sex discrimination differential treatment of individuals on the basis of their gender. Although such treatment may favor women relative to men, in contemporary society most sex discrimination favors men over women; its usual manifestations include unfair hiring and promotion practices, lower wages paid to women doing the same type of work as men, and a tendency to undervalue characteristics and interests associated with women rather than men. Although in many societies legislation prohibits sex discrimination, nevertheless it persists and contributes to a number of social problems, including inadequate support for working women, lower standards of health care for women, and violence against women. Also called **gender discrimination**; **sexual discrimination**. See also PREJUDICE; SEXISM.

sex drive an arousal state precipitating the desire for sexual gratification and, ultimately, for sexual reproduction. Although it is not necessary for an individual's survival, it is considered a PRIMARY DRIVE as it is essential for species survival. In many animals, sexual activity is cyclical (e.g., seasonal or dependent on cyclical hormone release), although a variety of factors (e.g., external stimulation) may arouse the drive.

sex hormone any of the hormones that stimulate various reproductive functions. Primary sources of sex hormones are the male and female gonads (i.e., testis and ovary), which are stimulated to produce sex hormones by the pituitary hormones FOLLICLE-STIMULATING HORMONE and LUTEINIZING HORMONE. The principal male sex hormones (ANDROGENS) include testosterone; female sex hormones include the ESTROGENS and PROGESTERONE.

sex identity 1. the purely biologically determined sexual condition or status of an individual. **2.** a person's sense of him- or herself as male or female, regardless of physical or biological considerations.

sexism *n.* discriminatory and prejudicial beliefs and practices directed against one of the two sexes, usually women. Sexism is associated with acceptance of SEX-ROLE STEROTYPES and can occur at multiple levels: individual, organizational, institutional, and cultural. It may be overt, involving the open endorsement of sexist beliefs or attitudes; covert, involving the tendency to hide sexist beliefs or attitudes and reveal them only when it is believed that one will not suffer publicly for them; or subtle, involving unequal treatment that may not be noticed because it is part of everyday behavior or perceived to be of low importance. See also PREJUDICE; SEX DISCRIMINATION. —**sexist** *adj.*

sex-linked *adj.* describing a gene that is located on one of the SEX CHROMOSOMES, usually the X CHROMOSOME (**X-linked**), or a trait determined by such a gene. Sex-linked diseases, such as hemophilia, generally affect only males, because the defective gene is usually a RECESSIVE ALLELE. In females, who have two X chromosomes, it would be masked by the normal, dominant allele on the other X chromosome. In males, with just a single X chromosome, any sex-linked defective allele is expressed.

sex offense a sex act that is prohibited by law. Some crimes are acts of violence involving sex, and others are violations of social taboos; there is much variation, by culture and jurisdiction, concerning which behaviors are considered crimes and how they may be punished. See also MOLESTATION.

sex reassignment a process, involving hormone treatment and surgery, in which a person's sex characteristics are changed to conform to that person's sense of his or her own GENDER IDENTITY, particularly in cases of TRANSSEXUALISM. Also called **gender reassignment**; **sex change**. See also GENDER IDENTITY DISORDER.

sex role the behavior and attitudinal patterns characteristically associated with being male or female as defined in a given society. Sex roles thus reflect the interaction between biological heritage and the pressures of socialization, and individuals differ greatly in the extent to which they manifest typical sex-role behavior.

sex-role stereotype a fixed, overly simplified concept of the social roles that are believed to be appropriate to each sex.

sex therapy a multimodal therapeutic approach designed to improve sexual functioning, based on the assumption that sexual performance problems are caused by a combination of lack of knowledge, misinformation, and faulty learning. Several different techniques commonly are used in sex therapy (e.g., SENSATE FOCUS, COGNITIVE RESTRUCTURING, COUPLES THERAPY), but they share the goals of providing education, reducing performance anxiety, improving communication, and teaching skills to improve sexual pleasuring for both partners. Sex therapy incorporates homework assignments, ideally rehearsed with the participation of a partner.

sex typing the process by which particular activ-ities are identified within particular cultures as appropriate expressions of maleness and femaleness.

sexual abuse violation or exploitation by sexual means. Although the term typically is used with reference to any sexual contact between adults and children, sexual abuse can also occur in other relationships of trust.

sexual addiction any of a group of conditions characterized by intrusive sexual thoughts combined with poorly controlled sexual behaviors.

sexual and gender identity disorders a category of disorders involving sexual or gender identity problems not attributable to another mental disorder. It includes SEXUAL DYSFUNCTIONS, PARAPHILIAS, and GENDER IDENTITY DISORDERS.

sexual arousal a state of PHYSIOLOGICAL AROUSAL elicited by sexual contact or by other erotic stimulation (e.g., fantasies, dreams, odors, or objects), triggering the release of sex hormones, dilation of the arteries supplying the genital areas, and inhibition of vasoconstrictor centers of the lumbar nerves. The effects of sexual arousal are mediated through the hypothalamus. See SEXUAL-RESPONSE CYCLE.

sexual arousal disorder a class of sexual disorders characterized by the inability to attain or maintain an adequate physiological response in the excitement (arousal) phase of the SEXUAL-RESPONSE CYCLE. See FEMALE SEXUAL AROUSAL DISORDER; IMPOTENCE.

sexual aversion disorder negative emotional reactions (e.g., anxiety, fear, or disgust) to sexual activity, leading to active avoidance of it and causing distress in the individual or his or her partner. This can be lifelong or acquired, and although it usually applies to all sexual activity (**generalized type**), it may be specific to only some activities or some partners (**situational type**).

sexual behavior actions related to reproduction or to stimulation of the sex organs for pleasurable satisfaction without conception. Sexual behavior may include some form of COURTSHIP BEHAVIOR, foreplay, and coitus itself. In some species, sexual behavior may occur only at certain seasons or at specific stages of the ESTROUS CYCLE. Nonconceptive sexual behavior occurs in many species, including human beings, and may function to maintain social relationships or PAIR BONDS or to confuse mates about CERTAINTY OF PATERNITY.

sexual conditioning the learning of cues that predict opportunities for mating so that these learned cues subsequently control sexual behavior. In both fish and birds, sexual conditioning that predicts when a mate will be present increases the REPRODUCTIVE SUCCESS of the conditioned males. See also SEXUAL IMPRINTING.

sexual desire disorder a class of sexual disorders, including HYPOACTIVE SEXUAL DESIRE DIS-

ORDER and SEXUAL AVERSION DISORDER, characterized by a chronic lack of interest in sexual activity that causes marked distress or interpersonal difficulty.

sexual deviance any sexual behavior that is regarded as significantly different from the standards established by a culture or subculture. The corresponding psychiatric classification is PARA-PHILIA.

sexual dimorphism the existence within a species of males and females that differ distinctly from each other in form. See SEX CHARACTERISTICS; SEX DIFFERENCES.

sexual disorder any impairment of sexual function or behavior. Sexual disorders include SEXUAL DYSFUNCTION and PARAPHILIAS. See also SEXUAL AND GENDER IDENTITY DISORDERS.

sexual dysfunction a category of sexual disorders characterized by problems in one or more phases of the SEXUAL-RESPONSE CYCLE. Sexual dysfunctions include HYPOACTIVE SEXUAL DESIRE DISORDER, SEXUAL AVERSION DISORDER, FEMALE SEXUAL AROUSAL DISORDER, male erectile disorder (see IMPOTENCE), PREMATURE EJACULATION, MALE ORGASMIC DISORDER, FEMALE ORGASMIC DISORDER, DYSPAREUNIA, and VAGINISMUS.

sexual harassment conduct of a sexual nature that is unwelcome or considered offensive, particularly in the workplace. According to the U.S. Equal Employment Opportunity Commission (EEOC), there are two forms of sexual harassment: QUID PRO QUO and behavior that makes for a hostile work environment.

sexual identification the gradual adoption of the attitudes and behavior patterns associated with being male or female. A clear concept of sexual identity gradually develops out of a perception of physical sex differences, starting during the first 3 or 4 years of life, and, somewhat later, awareness of psychological differences determined by the particular culture and particular family. Also called **sex identification**. See SEX ROLE.

sexual identity 1. the individual's internal identification with heterosexual, homosexual, or bisexual preference, that is, with his or her SEXUAL ORIENTATION. **2.** an occasional synonym for SEX IDENTITY or GENDER IDENTITY.

sexual imprinting the development of a preference for a sexual partner during a sensitive or CRITICAL PERIOD. For example, if zebra finches are cross-fostered to Bengalese finch parents for the first 40 days of life, they will prefer to mate with Bengalese finches as adults.

sexual instinct 1. the basic drive or urge to preserve the species through mating and the activities that precede it, or, by extension, simply to express the self and the self's physiological and psychological needs through sexual activity. **2.** in psychoanalytic theory, the instinct comprising all the erotic drives and sublimations of such

drives. It includes not only genital sex, but also anal and oral manifestations and the channeling of erotic energy into artistic, scientific, and other pursuits. In his later formulations, Austrian psychiatrist Sigmund Freud (1856–1939) saw the sexual instinct as part of a wider LIFE INSTINCT that also included the self-preservative impulses of hunger, thirst, and elimination. Also called **sex instinct**. See also EROS; LIBIDO; SELF-PRESERVATION INSTINCT.

sexuality *n.* **1.** all aspects of sexual behavior, including gender identity, orientation, attitudes, and activity as well as interest in and the capacity to derive pleasure from such behavior. **2.** in psychoanalytic theory, the "organ pleasure" derived from all EROGENOUS ZONES and processes of the body, including the mouth, anus, urethra, breasts, skin, muscles, and genital organs, as well as such functions as sucking, biting, eating, defecating, urinating, masturbation, and intercourse.

sexually dimorphic nucleus a nucleus (mass of cell bodies) of the central nervous system that differs in size between males and females. In humans, for example, a nucleus in the medial PREOPTIC AREA of the hypothalamus that synthesizes GONADOTROPIN-RELEASING HORMONE tends to be larger and more active in males than in females because gonadotropin release is continuous (it is cyclical in females).

sexually transmitted disease (**STD**) an infection transmitted by sexual activity. More than 20 STDs have been identified, including those caused by viruses (e.g., hepatitis B, herpes, and HIV) and those caused by bacteria (e.g., chlamydia, gonorrhea, and syphilis). STDs are also known as **venereal diseases**, the term used traditionally for syphilis and gonorrhea.

sexual masochism a PARAPHILIA in which sexual interest and arousal is repeatedly or exclusively achieved through being humiliated, bound, beaten, or otherwise made to suffer physical harm or threat to life.

sexual object 1. in general language, a person regarded only in terms of his or her sexual attractiveness. **2.** in psychoanalytic theory, a person, animal, or inanimate object external to the individual's own body or psyche toward whom or which the sexual energy of an individual is directed. Also called **sex object**.

sexual orientation one's enduring sexual attraction to male partners, female partners, or both. Sexual orientation may be heterosexual, same-sex (gay or lesbian), or bisexual.

sexual pain disorder a class of sexual disorders, including DYSPAREUNIA and VAGINISMUS, characterized by persistent or recurring pain during sexual activity.

sexual perversion any sexual practice that is regarded by a community or culture as an abnormal means of achieving orgasm or sexual arousal. Sexual perversion is an older term that is little used nowadays, largely having been replaced by SEXUAL DEVIANCE or, in a psychiatric context, PARAPHILIA.

sexual preference 1. loosely, SEXUAL ORIENTATION. **2.** any particular sexual interest and arousal pattern, which may range from the relatively common (e.g., particular patterns of foreplay, particular positions) to those associated with a PARAPHILIA.

sexual-response cycle a four-stage cycle of sexual response that is exhibited by both men and women, differing only in aspects determined by male or female anatomy. The stages include the **arousal** (or **excitement**) **phase**, which lasts several minutes to hours (see SEXUAL AROUSAL); the **plateau phase**, lasting 30 s to 3 min, marked by penile erection in men and vaginal lubrication in women; the **orgasmic phase**, lasting 15 s and marked by EJACULATION in men and ORGASM in women; and the **resolution phase**, lasting 15 min to 1 day.

sexual sadism a PARAPHILIA in which sexual excitement is achieved by intentional infliction of physical or psychological suffering on another person. When practiced with nonconsenting partners, sexual sadism may involve inflicting extensive, permanent, or possibly fatal bodily injury. This activity is likely to be repeated, with the severity of the sadistic acts increasing over time.

sexual selection a theoretical mechanism for the evolution of anatomical and behavioral differences between males and females, based on the selection of mates (see MATE SELECTION).

sexual trauma any disturbing experience associated with sexual activity, such as rape, incest, and other sexual offenses. It is one of the most common causes of POSTTRAUMATIC DISORDERS and DISSOCIATIVE DISORDERS.

shadow *n.* in ANALYTIC PSYCHOLOGY, an ARCHETYPE that represents the "darker side" of the human psyche, mainly the sexual and aggressive instincts that tend to be unacceptable to the conscious ego and that are more comfortably projected onto others.

shadowing *n.* in cognitive testing, a task in which a participant repeats aloud a message word for word at the same time that the message is being presented, often with other stimuli being presented in the background. It is mainly used in studies of ATTENTION.

shaken baby syndrome (**SBS**) the neurological consequences of a form of child abuse in which a small child or infant is repeatedly shaken. The shaking causes diffuse, widespread damage to the brain; in severe cases it may cause death.

shallow affect significant reduction in appropriate emotional responses to situations and events. See also FLAT AFFECT.

shallow processing cognitive processing of a stimulus that focuses on its superficial, perceptual characteristics rather than its meaning. It is

considered that processing at this shallow level produces weaker, shorter-lasting memories than DEEP PROCESSING. See also BOTTOM-UP PROCESSING.

shame *n.* a highly unpleasant SELF-CONSCIOUS EMOTION arising from the sense of there being something dishonorable, ridiculous, immodest, or indecorous in one's conduct or circumstances. It is typically characterized by withdrawal from social intercourse, for example by hiding or distracting the attention of another from one's shameful action, which can have a profound effect on psychological adjustment and interpersonal relationships. Shame may motivate not only avoidant behavior, but also defensive, retaliative anger. Psychological research consistently reports a relationship between proneness to shame and a whole host of psychological symptoms, including depression, anxiety, eating disorders, subclinical sociopathy, and low self-esteem. Shame is also theorized to play a more positive adaptive function by regulating experiences of excessive and inappropriate interest and excitement and by diffusing potentially threatening social behavior. —**shameful** *adj.*

shamelessness *n.* behavior marked by an apparent absence of feelings of shame. This may arise as the result of psychological problems or reflect a loss of judgment after brain injury. —**shameless** *adj.*

sham surgery in experiments using surgical interventions, surgery that functions as a CONTROL because it mimics the features of the experimental surgery but does not result in the alteration or removal of any bodily structures, that is, it does not have the systemic effects of the experimental procedure. Also called **sham operation**.

shape constancy a type of PERCEPTUAL CONSTANCY in which an object is perceived as having the same shape when viewed at different angles. For example, a plate is still perceived as circular despite changes in its appearance when viewed from above, below, the side, and so forth.

shaping *n.* the production of new forms of OPERANT BEHAVIOR by reinforcement of successive approximations to the behavior (see METHOD OF SUCCESSIVE APPROXIMATIONS). Also called **approximation conditioning**; **behavior shaping**.

Shapiro–Wilks test a statistical test of the hypothesis that a sample was drawn from a population with a NORMAL DISTRIBUTION. [Samuel S. **Shapiro** (1930–) and Samuel Stanley **Wilks** (1906–1964), U.S. statisticians]

shared environment in behavior genetic analyses, those aspects of an environment that individuals living together (e.g., biologically related individuals in a family household) share and that therefore cause them to become more similar to each other than would be expected on the basis of genetic influences alone. Examples of shared environmental factors include parental child-rearing style, divorce, or family income and related variables. Compare NONSHARED ENVIRONMENT.

shared psychotic disorder a rare disorder in which the essential feature is an identical or similar delusion that develops in an individual who is involved with another individual (sometimes called the **inducer** or the **primary case**) who already has a psychotic disorder with prominent delusions. Shared psychotic disorder can involve many people (e.g., an entire family), but is most commonly seen in relationships of only two, in which case it is known as **folie à deux**.

Sheldon's constitutional theory of personality the theory that every person possesses some degree of three primary temperamental components that relate to three basic body builds (SOMATOTYPES), measured on a seven-point scale. The three body types **ectomorph** (thin, long, fragile), **endomorph** (soft, round), and **mesomorph** (muscular, athletic) are correlated with the three components of temperament: **cerebrotonia** (a tendency toward inhibition, introversion, and sensitivity), **viscerotonia** (a tendency toward love of comfort and food, relaxation, and sociability), and **somatotonia** (a tendency toward energetic activity, courage, and love of power). [William H. **Sheldon** (1899–1970), U.S. psychologist]

shell shock the name used during World War I for COMBAT STRESS REACTIONS.

sheltered workshop a work-oriented rehabilitation facility for individuals with disabilities that provides a controlled, noncompetitive, supportive working environment and individually designed work settings, using work experience and related services to assist individuals with disabilities to achieve specific vocational goals. Sheltered workshops differ from SUPPORTED EMPLOYMENT in that the latter occurs in a competitive, noncontrolled working environment.

shen-k'uei (shenkui) *n.* a CULTURE-BOUND SYNDROME occurring in males of Chinese or Taiwanese cultures and characterized by symptoms of anxiety, panic, and SOMATIZATION, such as sexual dysfunction, insomnia, and dizziness. Symptoms cannot be linked to a physical cause and are typically ascribed to excessive loss of semen due to unrestrained sexual activity. See also DHAT; JIRYAN; SUKRA PRAMEHA.

shin-byung *n.* a CULTURE-BOUND SYNDROME found in Korea, characterized by anxiety and such physical complaints as general weakness, dizziness, loss of appetite, insomnia, and gastrointestinal problems, followed by dissociation and alleged possession by ancestral spirits (see DISSOCIATIVE TRANCE DISORDER). It is considered by those affected to be a "divine illness," in which the individual experiences hallucinations of becoming a shaman, and a cure occurs when this conversion takes place.

shinkeishitsu *n.* a CULTURE-BOUND SYNDROME prevalent in Japan, with symptoms that include obsessions, perfectionism, ambivalence, social withdrawal, physical and mental fatigue, hypersensitivity, and hypochondriasis. This disorder is also prevalent in China, where it is known as **shenjing shuairuo**. See also MORITA THERAPY.

shock *n.* **1.** the application of electric current, for example, as in ELECTROCONVULSIVE THERAPY. **2.** acute reduction of blood flow in the body due to failure of circulatory control or loss of blood or other bodily fluids, marked by hypotension, coldness of skin, and usually TACHYCARDIA.

shock phase see GENERAL ADAPTATION SYNDROME.

shock–shock interval see SIDMAN AVOIDANCE SCHEDULE.

shock therapy see ELECTROCONVULSIVE THERAPY.

short-term dynamic psychotherapy see BRIEF PSYCHODYNAMIC PSYCHOTHERAPY.

short-term memory (STM) a temporary information storage system, enabling one to retain, reproduce, recognize, or recall a limited amount of material after a period of about 10–30 s. STM is often theorized to be separate from LONG-TERM MEMORY, and the two are the components of the DUAL-STORE MODEL OF MEMORY.

short-term therapy psychotherapy aimed at treating intrapsychic conflict, maladaptive interpersonal patterns, or negative feelings about the self during a short period (generally 10–20 sessions). To be effective, short-term therapy relies on active techniques of inquiry, focus, and goal setting. Short-term approaches may be applied on a deeper level, as in DYNAMIC PSYCHOTHERAPY; on a level of emotional REEDUCATION; or on a more symptomatic level, as in reconditioning and other forms of BEHAVIOR THERAPY. Also called **brief psychotherapy**. See also DIRECTIVE COUNSELING; REALITY THERAPY; SECTOR THERAPY.

shunt *n.* a congenitally occurring or surgically created passage diverting the flow of bodily fluids such as blood or cerebrospinal fluid from one part of an organ or body to another. For example, a **ventriculoatrial shunt** is an artificially formed passage for draining cerebrospinal fluid from the brain to the external jugular vein to relieve symptoms of HYDROCEPHALUS.

shuttle box a two-compartment box used for avoidance-conditioning research with animals. By regularly moving from one compartment to the other (i.e., shuttling between them), the animal can avoid an electric shock or other aversive stimulus. There is sometimes a small barrier that the animal must jump over or push to get from one compartment to the other.

shyness *n.* anxiety and inhibition in social situations, typically involving three components: (a) global feelings of emotional arousal and specific physiological experiences (e.g., upset stomach, pounding heart, sweating, and blushing); (b) acute public self-consciousness, self-deprecation, and worries about being evaluated negatively by others; and (c) observable behavior such as cautiousness, quietness, gaze aversion, and social withdrawal. Also called **timidity**. See also SOCIAL ANXIETY. —**shy** *adj.*

sialorrhea *n.* see PTYALISM.

sibilant *adj.* denoting a FRICATIVE produced by forcing the air through an opening between the tongue and the roof of the mouth and creating a hissing sound, for example, [s], [z], or [sh].

sibling *n.* a sister or brother: one of two or more children born of the same two parents.

sibling rivalry competition among siblings for the attention, approval, or affection of one or both parents or for other recognition or rewards, for example, in sports or school grades.

sib-pair method a technique used in genetics, particularly in attempting to discover the extent of inherited psychiatric factors, in which the incidence of a disorder among blood relatives is compared with the distribution of the disorder in the general population.

sick role the behavior expected of a person who is physically ill, mentally ill, or injured. Such expectations can be the individual's own or those of the family, the community, or society in general. They influence both how the person behaves and how others will react to him or her. For instance, people with a sick role are expected to cooperate with caregivers and to want to get well but are also provided with an exemption from normal obligations. See also FACTITIOUS DISORDER.

side effect any reaction secondary to the intended therapeutic effect that may occur following administration of a drug or other treatment. Often these are undesirable but tolerable (e.g., headache or fatigue), although more serious effects (e.g., liver failure, seizures) may also occur. Occasionally, harmful side effects are unexpected, in which case they more properly are termed ADVERSE DRUG REACTIONS.

Sidman avoidance schedule a procedure in which brief, inescapable aversive stimuli are presented at fixed intervals (**shock–shock intervals**) in the absence of a specified response. If the response is made, the aversive stimulus is postponed by a fixed amount of time (the **response–shock interval**) from that response. [Murray Sidman (1923–), U.S. psychologist]

SIDS acronym for SUDDEN INFANT DEATH SYNDROME.

sight method see WHOLE-WORD METHOD.

sign 1. *n.* an objective, observable indication of a disorder or disease. See also SOFT SIGN. **2.** *n.* in linguistics and SEMIOTICS, anything that conveys meaning; a sign may be either verbal (e.g., a spoken or written word) or nonverbal (e.g., a hairstyle). The term is now mainly associated with approaches deriving from the theory of Swiss linguist Ferdinand de Saussure (1857–1913), who emphasized the arbitrary nature of linguistic signs (i.e., the lack of any necessary relationship between the material SIGNIFIER and the idea signified). The application of this idea to nonlinguistic sign systems provided the basic method of STRUCTURALISM in the social sciences. **3.** *vb.* to communicate using SIGN LANGUAGE.

signal *n.* **1.** an intelligible sign communicated from one individual to another. **2.** a presentation of information, usually one that evokes some action or response. **3.** as used in SIGNAL DETECTION THEORY, a stimulus.

signal anxiety in psychoanalytic theory, anxiety that arises in response to internal conflict or an emerging impulse, and functions as a sign to the EGO of impending threat, resulting in the use of a DEFENSE MECHANISM. Compare PRIMARY ANXIETY.

signal detection task a task in which the observer is required to discriminate between trials in which a target stimulus (the signal) is present and trials in which it is not (the noise). Signal detection tasks provide objective measures of perceptual sensitivity. Also called **detection task**.

signal detection theory (**SDT**) a body of concepts and techniques from communication theory, electrical engineering, and decision theory that were applied during World War II to the detection of radar signals in noise. These concepts were applied to auditory and visual psychophysics in the late 1950s and are now widely used in many areas of psychology. SDT has provided a valuable theoretical framework for describing perceptual and other aspects of cognition and for quantitatively relating psychophysical phenomena to findings from sensory physiology. A key notion of SDT is that human performance in many tasks is limited by variability in the internal representation of stimuli due to internal or external NOISE. Also called **detection theory**. See D PRIME; RECEIVER-OPERATING CHARACTERISTIC CURVE.

signal-to-noise ratio (**S/N**) the ratio of signal power (intensity) to noise power, usually expressed in DECIBELS. When the signal is speech, it is called the **speech-to-noise ratio**.

significance *n.* the degree or extent to which something is meaningful or of consequence. In mathematics and related fields, the term denotes STATISTICAL SIGNIFICANCE.

significance level in null hypothesis SIGNIFICANCE TESTING, the probability of rejecting the null hypothesis when it is in fact true (i.e., of making a Type I error). It is set at some criterion, α, usually .01 or .05, and the actual value for a particular test is denoted p. Thus when the p-value is less than α, the null hypothesis is rejected. Also called **alpha level**.

significance testing a set of procedures that are used to differentiate between two models. In the most common form of significance testing, one model (the NULL HYPOTHESIS) specifies a condition in which the treatment being studied has no effect and the other model (the ALTERNA-TIVE HYPOTHESIS) specifies that the treatment has some effect.

significant difference the situation in which a SIGNIFICANCE TESTING procedure indicates that the two models being compared are different.

significant other 1. a spouse or other person with whom one has a committed sexual relationship. **2.** any individual who has a profound influence on a person, particularly his or her self-image and SOCIALIZATION.

signifier *n.* **1.** in linguistics and SEMIOTICS, the material form of a SIGN as opposed to the idea or concept indicated (the **signified**). In language, therefore, the signifier is the spoken or written word or component of a word. The distinction between signifier and signified is of central importance in STRUCTURALISM and POSTSTRUCTURALISM. **2.** in the theory of French psychoanalyst Jacques Lacan (1901–1981), a symbol, such as a word or symptom, that stands for some aspect of the patient's unconscious. Lacan's use of the term reflects his central belief that the unconscious is structured as a language.

sign language any system of communication in which signs formed by hand configuration and movement are used instead of spoken language. The term refers particularly to the system used by people who are deaf or have severe hearing loss, which has its own syntax and methods of conveying nuances of feeling and emotion and is now accepted by most linguists as exhibiting the full set of defining characteristics of human oral–aural language. The particular system of hand signs and movements used primarily in the United States and Canada is called **American Sign Language (ASL)**. Also called **signing**. See FINGERSPELLING.

sign stimulus see RELEASER.

sign system an epithet for PSYCHOTHERAPY, which highlights the discipline's dependence on language as the major tool for exploring and understanding the hidden causes of cognitive, affective, and behavioral problems and disorders.

sign test a nonparametric test of a hypothesis concerning the median of a distribution. It is commonly used to test the hypothesis that the median difference in matched pairs is zero.

sign tracking in conditioning, elicited behavior directed toward a stimulus that is reliably paired with a primary reinforcer.

silok *n.* a CULTURE-BOUND SYNDROME found in the Philippines, with symptoms similar to those of LATAH.

similarity *n.* one of the GESTALT PRINCIPLES OF ORGANIZATION. It states that people tend to organize objects with similar qualities into a perceptual group and interpret them as a whole. Also called **law of similarity**; **principle of similarity**.

Simon effect in a two-choice task, the finding that the response to a stimulus is facilitated if the location of the stimulus corresponds to the location of the response, even though stimulus location is irrelevant to the task. For example, if a left (rather than a right) keypress is the required response to a blue stimulus, reaction time will be quicker if this stimulus is presented on the left-hand side than if it is presented on the right (and vice versa). [discovered in 1969 by J. Richard Simon (1929–), U.S. psychologist]

simple cell a neuron in the STRIATE CORTEX that has a receptive field consisting of an elongated center region and two elongated flanking regions. The response of a simple cell to stimulation in the center of the receptive field is the opposite of its response to stimulation in the flanking zones. This means that a simple cell responds best to an edge or a bar of a particular width and with a particular direction and location in the visual field. Compare COMPLEX CELL.

simple deteriorative disorder a disorder in which the essential feature is the progressive development of prominent NEGATIVE SYMPTOMS, which are severe enough to result in a significant deterioration in occupational or academic functioning. The individual gradually loses emotional responsivity, ambition, and interest in self-care and becomes socially withdrawn or isolated. Historically, and in other classifications, this disorder is known as SIMPLE SCHIZOPHRENIA.

simple effects in a FACTORIAL DESIGN, the comparison of group means of one factor at specific levels of the other factor or factors.

simple factorial design an experimental design in which the two or more levels of each INDEPENDENT VARIABLE or factor are observed in combination with the two or more levels of every other factor.

simple random sampling the most basic form of RANDOM SAMPLING, in which the participants are selected individually by the use of a table of random digits or a random number generator.

simple reaction time the REACTION TIME of a participant in a task that requires him or her to make an elementary response (e.g., pressing a key) whenever a stimulus (such as a light or tone) is presented. The individual makes just a single response whenever the only possible stimulus is presented. Compare CHOICE REACTION TIME; COMPLEX REACTION TIME.

simple schizophrenia one of the four major types of schizophrenia described by German psychiatrist Emil Kraepelin (1856–1926) and Swiss psychiatrist Eugen Bleuler (1857–1939), characterized primarily by gradual withdrawal from social contact, lack of initiative, and emotional apathy. The current psychiatric diagnosis is SIMPLE DETERIORATIVE DISORDER.

simplicity principle see LIKELIHOOD PRINCIPLE.

Simpson's paradox a phenomenon that can occur when the raw data of two or more studies are merged, giving results that differ from those of either study individually. For example, two studies, each showing a correlation of .00 between two variables, X and Y, may show a strong positive correlation between variables X and Y when the data are merged. [Edward H. **Simpson**, 20th-century U.S. statistician]

simulated family a technique used in training and therapy in which hypothetical family situations are enacted. In training, the enactment is by clinicians or other professionals. In FAMILY THERAPY, one or more members of the family may participate with others, who play the roles of other family members. See also ROLE PLAY.

simulation *n.* **1.** an experimental method used to investigate the behavior and psychological processes and functioning of individuals in social and other environments, often those to which investigators cannot easily gain access, by reproducing those environments in a realistic way. **2.** the artificial creation of experiment-like data through the use of a mathematical or computer model of behavior or data. **3.** resemblance or imitation, particularly the mimicking of symptoms of one disorder by another or the faking of an illness.

simulator–real model see REAL–SIMULATOR MODEL.

simultanagnosia *n.* see VISUAL AGNOSIA.

simultaneous conditioning a PAVLOVIAN CONDITIONING technique in which the conditioned stimulus and the unconditioned stimulus are presented at the same time. Compare DELAY CONDITIONING.

simultaneous contrast the enhanced perception of the difference between two stimuli when these are presented in close proximity to one another in space. Compare SUCCESSIVE CONTRAST.

simultaneous discrimination in conditioning, DISCRIMINATION between two concurrently available stimuli.

single alternation in experimental research, a pattern in which one kind of event alternates with another. For example, in an OPERANT CONDITIONING experiment, a reinforced trial (R) may alternate with a nonreinforced trial (N), yielding the pattern RNRNRN.... See also DOUBLE ALTERNATION.

single blind see BLIND.

single-capacity model see UNITARY-RESOURCE MODEL.

single-case experimental design a WITHIN-SUBJECTS DESIGN involving only a single participant, group, or other sampling unit. Individuals serve as their own controls, and typically a number of observations are obtained at different times over the course of treatment.

single-case methods and evaluation a type of PSYCHOTHERAPY RESEARCH based on sys-

tematic study of one client before, during, and after intervention.

single-channel model a model of human INFORMATION PROCESSING in which only SERIAL PROCESSING is possible. Cognition is held to consist of a series of discrete sequenced steps involving one information source and one processing channel at a time.

single photon emission computed tomography (**SPECT**) a functional imaging technique that uses gamma radiation from a radioactive dye to create a picture of blood flow in the body. In the brain it can be used to measure cerebral blood flow, which is a direct measure of cerebral metabolism and activity.

single-session therapy (**SST**) therapy that ends after one session, usually by choice of the client but also as indicated by the type of treatment (e.g., ERICKSONIAN PSYCHOTHERAPY, SOLUTION-FOCUSED BRIEF THERAPY). Some clients claim enough success with one hour of therapy to stop treatment, although some therapists believe that this claim represents a FLIGHT INTO HEALTH or temporary relief from symptoms. Preparation for the session (e.g., by telephone) increases the likelihood of the single-therapy session being successful.

sinusoid *n.* in audition, see PURE TONE.

SIS abbreviation for sensory-information store (see SENSORY MEMORY).

situated cognition cognition seen as inextricable from the context in which it is applied. From this it follows that intelligence also cannot be separated from its context of application (**situated intelligence**). See also STREET INTELLIGENCE.

situated identities theory the theory that individuals take on different roles in different social and cultural settings, so that a person's behavior pattern may shift radically according to the situation and the others with whom he or she is interacting.

situated knowledge knowledge that is embedded in, and thus affected by, the concrete historical, cultural, linguistic, and value context of the knowing person. The term is used most frequently in perspectives arising from SOCIAL CONSTRUCTIONISM and POSTMODERNISM to emphasize the view that absolute, universal knowledge is impossible. It sometimes carries the further implication that social, cultural, and historical factors will constrain the process of knowledge construction itself. To the extent that knowledge is situated, it is difficult to avoid some kind of epistemological RELATIVISM.

situational attribution the ascription of one's own or another's behavior, an event, or an outcome to causes outside the person concerned, such as luck, pressure from other people, or external circumstances. Also called **environmental attribution**; **external attribution**. Compare DISPOSITIONAL ATTRIBUTION.

situational conditions all the relevant external variables within a setting that influence individual behavior. Situational conditions in a classroom setting, for example, include the variables affecting student learning and achievement: physical environment, teaching methods, time factors, goals, organization of material, methods of testing, consequences of performance, type of reinforcement, and social relationships.

situational determinant an environmental condition that exists before and after an organism's response and influences the elicitation of this behavior.

situational homosexuality same-sex sexual behavior that develops in a situation or environment in which the opportunity for heterosexual activity is missing and where close contact with individuals of the same sex occurs, such as a prison, school, or military setting where individuals are living together, segregated according to their sex. Once away from this setting, the person typically returns to heterosexual activity.

situationalism *n.* the view that an organism's interaction with the environment and situational factors, rather than personal characteristics and other internal factors, are the primary determinants of behavior. Also called **situationism**.

situational leadership theory a contingency LEADERSHIP THEORY that recommends leaders use varying amounts of directive (task-motivated) and supportive (relationship-motivated) leadership, depending on the maturity of followers. Maturity in this context refers to both job maturity (e.g., experience, ability, knowledge) and psychological maturity (e.g., level of motivation, willingness to accept responsibility). When maturity is low, leaders should be directive, concentrating on structure and task orientation. With increasing follower maturity, leaders need to increase supportive actions.

situational semantics a branch of SEMANTICS holding that the meaning of utterances, particularly their truth value, must be understood by considering not only the correspondence of the utterance to what is the case in the world, but also the situation in which the utterance is made. A major implication of this notion is that truth is situational, and that language expresses primarily situations rather than transitutional facts. This view is related to SOCIAL CONSTRUCTIONISM, POSTMODERNISM, and some species of feminism.

situation awareness conscious knowledge of the immediate environment and the events that are occurring in it. Influenced by a number of factors, including stress, situation awareness involves perception of the elements in the environment, comprehension of what they mean and how they relate to one another, and projection of their future states.

situation ethics the view that the morality or immorality of an action must be evaluated within the context of a given situation as interpreted according to some ethical norms. Compare MORAL ABSOLUTISM; MORAL RELATIVISM.

situation test a test that places an individual in a natural setting, or in an experimental setting that approximates a natural one, to assess either the individual's ability to solve a problem that requires adaptive behavior under stressful conditions or the individual's reactions to what is believed to be a stressful experience. For example, a course of DESENSITIZATION therapy aimed at reducing phobic reactions might begin with a situation test in which the individual encounters the phobic object. The individual's reactions are then assessed and considered in relation to individual needs or a specific therapy program. Also called **situational test**.

Sixteen Personality Factor Questionnaire (**16PF**) a comprehensive self-report instrument assessing personality on 16 key scales: warmth, vigilance, reasoning, abstractedness, emotional stability, privateness, dominance, apprehension, liveliness, openness to change, rule-consciousness, self-reliance, social boldness, perfectionism, sensitivity, and tension. The 16 factors (called SOURCE TRAITS) are grouped into 5 "global factors": extraversion, independence, tough-mindedness, anxiety, and self-control.

sixth sense 1. an INTUITION or INSTINCT that enables a person to make a correct judgment or decision without conscious use of the five senses or normal cognitive processes. **2.** the ostensible sensory modality responsible for mediating the phenomena of EXTRASENSORY PERCEPTION. See PSI.

size constancy the ability to maintain an unchanging perception of an object despite the fact that the size of its retinal image changes depending on its distance from the observer. It is a type of PERCEPTUAL CONSTANCY.

size cue any of a variety of means used by the visual system to interpret the apparent size of a stimulus, such as the size of the image that falls on the retina and the relationship of the object to others within the field.

size–distance paradox an illusion that an object is bigger or smaller than is actually the case caused by a false perception of its distance from the viewer. For example, in the so-called **moon illusion** the moon appears to be larger on the horizon, where DEPTH CUES make it appear to be farther away, than at its zenith, where there are no depth cues.

size-invariant neuron see LOCATION-INVARIANT NEURON.

skeletal muscle a muscle that provides the force to move a part of the skeleton, typically under voluntary control of the central nervous system. Skeletal muscles are attached to the bones by tendons and usually span a joint, so that one end of the muscle is attached via a tendon to one bone and the other end is attached to another bone. Skeletal muscles work in reciprocal pairs so that a bone can be moved in opposite directions. Skeletal muscle is composed of numerous slender, tapering MUSCLE FIBERS, each of which is bounded by a membrane (sarcolemma) and contains cytoplasm (sarcoplasm). Within the sarcoplasm are the longitudinal contractile fibrils (myofibrils), organized into arrays (sarcomeres) that give a striped appearance when viewed microscopically. Also called **striated muscle**. Compare CARDIAC MUSCLE; SMOOTH MUSCLE.

skepticism *n.* **1.** an attitude of disbelief or doubt. **2.** in philosophy, the position that certain knowledge can never be found. British philosopher David Hume (1711–1776) made skepticism a cornerstone of his system and provoked much later discussion when he taught that sensory experience provides no sure basis for knowledge and that nothing can be proved by observation. CAUSATION, for example, is only an inference that relates two observed events, and one has no knowledge that this relationship will apply in similar cases: It is a generalization that could be proved wrong by a different result. In modern philosophy, POSTMODERNISM and POSTSTRUCTURALISM are essentially systems of skepticism. —**skeptic** *n.* —**skeptical** *adj.*

skewness *n.* a measure of the degree or extent to which a batch of scores lack symmetry in their distribution around their measure of CENTRAL TENDENCY.

skill *n.* an ability or proficiency acquired through training and practice. For example, motor skills are characterized by the ability to perform a complex movement or SERIAL BEHAVIOR quickly, smoothly, and precisely, whereas SOCIAL SKILLS enable a person to interact competently and appropriately in a given social context.

skill theory the proposition that cognitive development is the result of a dynamic interaction between the individual and the environment. According to this theory, a **skill** (or **dynamic skill**) is the capacity to act in an organized way in a specific context, and in order for a skill to be developed to its OPTIMAL LEVEL, it must be exercised in the most supportive of environments. Also called **dynamic skill theory**.

skin *n.* the external covering of the body, consisting of an outer layer (epidermis) and a deeper layer (dermis) resting on a layer of fatty subcutaneous tissue. The skin prevents injury to underlying tissues, prevents the entry of foreign substances and pathogens, reduces water loss from the body, and forms part of the body's temperature-regulation mechanism through the evaporation of sweat secreted from sweat glands. Human skin typically has only a sparse covering of hair, except on the head and genital regions. The root of each hair arises from a hair FOLLICLE, into which the ducts of sebaceous glands dis-

charge sebum, an oily secretion that lubricates and waterproofs the skin surface. Various types of sensory nerve ending provide touch and pressure sensitivity, as well as sensations of pain and temperature (see CUTANEOUS RECEPTOR).

skin conductance the degree of resistance of the skin to the passage of a small electric current between two electrodes, changes in which are typically used to measure a person's level of AROUSAL or energy mobilization (see GALVANIC SKIN RESPONSE). The mechanism of skin conductance is not fully known: It seems to be related to the electrical activity of sweat glands but not to sweating itself.

Skinner box see OPERANT CONDITIONING CHAMBER. [Burrhus Frederic **Skinner** (1904–1990), U.S. psychologist]

skin receptor see CUTANEOUS RECEPTOR.

SLD abbreviation for SPECIFIC LEARNING DISABILITY.

sleep *n.* a state of the brain characterized by partial or total suspension of consciousness, muscular relaxation and inactivity, reduced metabolism, and relative insensitivity to stimulation. Other mental and physical characteristics that distinguish sleep from wakefulness include amnesia for events occurring during the loss of consciousness and unique sleep-related electroencephalogram and brain-imaging patterns (see SLEEP STAGES). These characteristics also help distinguish normal sleep from a loss of consciousness due to injury, disease, or drugs. See also DREAM STATE; NREM SLEEP; REM SLEEP.

sleep apnea the temporary cessation of breathing while asleep, which occurs when the upper airway briefly becomes blocked (**obstructive sleep apnea**) or when the respiratory centers in the brain fail to stimulate respiration (**central sleep apnea**). It can cause severe daytime sleepiness, and evidence is building that untreated severe sleep apnea may be associated with high blood pressure and risk for stroke and heart attack.

sleep cycle a recurring pattern of SLEEP STAGES in which a period of SLOW-WAVE SLEEP is followed by a period of REM SLEEP. In humans, a sleep cycle lasts approximately 90 min.

sleep deprivation deliberate prevention of sleep, particularly for experimental purposes. Studies show that the loss of one night's sleep has a substantial effect on physical or mental functioning; participants score significantly lower on tests of judgment and SIMPLE REACTION TIME and show impairments in daytime alertness and memory. Sleep loss also may be detrimental to the immune and endocrine systems.

sleep disorder a persistent disturbance of typical sleep patterns, including the amount, quality, and timing of sleep, or the chronic occurrence of abnormal events or behavior during sleep. Sleep disorders are broadly classified according to apparent cause, which may be endogenous or conditioning factors (**primary sleep disorders**), another mental disorder, a medical condition, or substance use. Primary sleep disorders are subdivided into DYSSOMNIAS and PARASOMNIAS.

sleep drive the basic physiological urge to sleep, which varies throughout the day but typically is strongest (for adults) between 2–4 a.m. and between 1–3 p.m. It appears to be governed in part by the hypothalamus and the RETICULAR ACTIVATING SYSTEM.

sleep efficiency the ratio of total time asleep to total time in bed. Sleep efficiency can be reduced in various psychological conditions (e.g., depression, anxiety) as well as by the use of some pharmacological agents (e.g., certain antidepressants).

sleeper effect the finding that the impact of a persuasive message increases over time. This effect is most likely to occur when a person carefully scrutinizes a message with relatively strong arguments and then subsequently receives a discounting cue (i.e., some piece of information suggesting that the message should be disregarded). The discounting cue weakens the initial impact of the message, but if the cue and the arguments in the message are not well integrated in memory, the cue may gradually be forgotten. If this occurs, the impact of the arguments will be greater at a later point in time than they were at the time of their initial presentation.

sleepiness *n.* see SOMNOLENCE.

sleeping state see S-STATE.

sleep laboratory a research facility designed to monitor patterns of activity during sleep, such as eye movement, breathing abnormalities, heartbeat, brain waves, and muscle tone. Sleep laboratories are typically found in neurology departments in hospitals and universities or in sleep disorder clinics.

sleep latency the amount of time it takes for an individual to fall asleep once the attempt to do so is made. Sleep latency is measured in the diagnosis of SLEEP DISORDERS. Sleeping pills (e.g., benzodiazepines) are designed to decrease sleep latency so that the individual can fall asleep more quickly.

sleep learning the learning of material presented while one is asleep. The possibility of true sleep learning is still a controversial issue. Simple learning, such as PAVLOVIAN CONDITIONING, may occur during sleep; more complex learning, such as the acquisition of a foreign language, has not been reliably demonstrated.

sleep-onset insomnia a DYSSOMNIA characterized by persistent difficulty initiating sleep. Also called **onset insomnia**. See also INSOMNIA; PRIMARY INSOMNIA.

sleep paralysis brief inability to move or speak just before falling asleep or on awakening. It may occur in any individual but is seen especially in individuals with NARCOLEPSY and may be due to a temporary dysfunction of the RETICULAR ACTIVATING SYSTEM.

sleep spindles characteristic spindle-shaped patterns recorded on an electroencephalogram (EEG) during stage 2 sleep. They are short bursts of waves with a frequency of about 15 Hz that progressively increase then decrease in amplitude and they indicate a state of light sleep. Sleep spindles are often accompanied by K COMPLEXES.

sleep stages the four-cycle progression in electrical activity of the brain during a normal night's sleep, as recorded on an electroencephalogram (EEG). The regular pattern of ALPHA WAVES characteristic of the relaxed state of the individual just before sleep becomes intermittent and attenuated in **stage 1 sleep**, which is marked by drowsiness with rolling eyeball movements. This progresses to **stage 2 sleep** (light sleep), which is characterized by SLEEP SPINDLES and K COMPLEXES. In **stage 3** and **stage 4 sleep** (deep sleep), DELTA WAVES predominate (see SLOW-WAVE SLEEP). These stages comprise NREM SLEEP and are interspersed with periods of dreaming associated with REM SLEEP. After a period of deep sleep, the sleeper may return to either light sleep or REM sleep or to both, and the cycles can recur multiple times over the course of the sleep period.

sleep terror disorder a SLEEP DISORDER characterized by repeated episodes of abrupt awakening from NREM SLEEP accompanied by signs of disorientation, extreme panic, and intense anxiety. More intense than NIGHTMARES and occurring during the first few hours of sleep, these episodes typically last between 1 and 10 min and involve screaming and symptoms of autonomic arousal, such as profuse perspiration, dilated pupils, rapid breathing, and a rapidly beating heart. See also PARASOMNIA.

sleep–wake cycle the natural, brain-controlled bodily rhythm that results in alternate periods of sleep and wakefulness. The sleep–wake cycle may be disrupted by a number of factors, such as flight across time zones, shift work, drug use, or stress (see CIRCADIAN RHYTHM SLEEP DISORDER; DISORDERS OF THE SLEEP–WAKE CYCLE SCHEDULE).

sleep–wake schedule disorder see CIRCADIAN RHYTHM SLEEP DISORDER.

sleepwalking disorder a SLEEP DISORDER characterized by persistent incidents of complex motor activity during slow-wave NREM SLEEP. These episodes typically occur during the first hours of sleep and involve getting out of bed and walking, although the individual may also perform more complicated tasks, such as eating, talking, or operating machinery. While in this state, the individual stares blankly, is essentially unresponsive, and can be awakened only with great difficulty; he or she does not remember the episode upon waking. Also called **noctam-**

bulation; somnambulism. See also PARA-SOMNIA.

slip of the tongue a minor error in speech, such as a SPOONERISM, that is episodic and not related to a speech disorder or a stage of second-language acquisition. Psychoanalysts have long been interested in the significance of such slips, believing them to reveal unconscious associations, motivations, or wishes. See also FREUDIAN SLIP.

slippage n. see COGNITIVE SLIPPAGE.

slope n. in mathematics and statistics, the change in vertical distance on a graph divided by the horizontal distance. It is represented by the slant of a line. See also ACCELERATION.

slow muscle fiber a type of muscle fiber found in SKELETAL MUSCLE that contracts slowly and is resistant to fatigue. Compare FAST MUSCLE FIBER.

slow-release preparation a drug preparation that is formulated in such a way that the active ingredient is released over an extended period. For example, drugs may be administered in the form of extended-release capsules, which contain quantities of the active drug surrounded by separate coatings that dissolve at different rates in the stomach and intestines. Also called **extended-release preparation**; **sustained-release preparation**.

slow-wave sleep deep sleep that is characterized by DELTA WAVES on the electroencephalogram, corresponding to stages 3 and 4 of sleep. It is controlled by SEROTONIN-rich cells in the brainstem: Increased levels of serotonin stimulate slow-wave sleep, whereas abnormally low levels of serotonin result in insomnia. Slow-wave sleep has a restorative function that helps eliminate feelings of fatigue. See also SLEEP STAGES.

SM abbreviation for SECONDARY MEMORY.

SMA abbreviation for SPINAL MUSCULAR ATROPHY.

smell n. an ODOR, or the sense that enables an organism to detect the odors of volatile substances. Molecules of odorant chemicals carried by air currents are absorbed into nasal mucus and stimulate the OLFACTORY RECEPTORS, where they are converted to neural messages. See OLFACTION; OLFACTORY TRANSDUCTION.

smell compensation the perception of a combination of odorants (airborne volatile substances) as less intense than the component odorants.

smoking cessation treatment interventions to help people quit smoking that typically involve behavioral techniques (e.g., reinforcement), social support, environmental change, and healthy activity substitution (e.g., exercise), which may be used in conjunction with nicotine replacement therapy or other drugs. Group treatment is often offered in community settings.

smoothing n. a collection of techniques used to reduce the irregularities in a batch of data or in a plot (curve) of that data, particularly in TIME SE-RIES analyses. The use of a "moving average" is one example of smoothing such data.

smooth movement see RAMP MOVEMENT.

smooth muscle any muscle that is not striated and is under the control of the AUTONOMIC NERVOUS SYSTEM (i.e., it is not under voluntary control). Smooth muscles are able to remain in a contracted state for long periods of time or maintain a pattern of rhythmic contractions indefinitely without fatigue. Smooth muscle is found, for example, in the digestive organs, blood vessels, and the muscles of the eyes. Also called **involuntary muscle**. Compare CARDIAC MUSCLE; SKELETAL MUSCLE.

smooth-pursuit movement a slow, steady eye movement that is responsive to feedback provided by brain regions involved in processing visual information, thus enabling continuous fixation on an object as it moves. Compare SACCADE.

S/N abbreviation for SIGNAL-TO-NOISE RATIO.

snowball sampling a method of recruiting new participants for a study by asking existing participants to recommend additional potential participants.

SNRI serotonin and norepinephrine reuptake inhibitor: any of a class of antidepressants that exert their therapeutic effects by interfering with the reabsorption of both serotonin and norepinephrine by the neurons that released them. They include venlafaxine and duloxetine. Also called **mixed serotonin and norepinephrine reuptake inhibitor**.

social adj. **1.** relating to human society. **2.** relating to the interactions of individuals, particularly as members of a group or a community. In this sense, the term is not restricted to people but rather applies to all animals.

social action 1. individual or group activities directed to achieving benefits for the community or a segment of the population. **2.** in sociology, any human activity seen in terms of its social context. Thus defined, such activity is the characteristic subject matter of the discipline of sociology.

social-adjustive function of an attitude the role an attitude can play in facilitating social interaction and enhancing cohesion among members of a social group. For example, a teenager may adopt positive attitudes toward certain styles of dress and types of music as a means of gaining acceptance by a peer group.

social adjustment accommodation to the demands, restrictions, and mores of society, including the ability to live and work with others harmoniously and to engage in satisfying interactions and relationships.

social age (SA) an estimate of a person's social capacities in relation to normative standards, which in clinical situations with young children often is assigned by interviewing parents and other adults to produce scores on the VINELAND ADAPTIVE BEHAVIOR SCALES.

social agency a private or governmental organization that supervises or provides personal services, especially in the fields of health, welfare, and rehabilitation. The general objective of a social agency is to improve the quality of life of its clients.

social anchoring basing one's attitudes, values, actions, and so forth on the positions taken by others, often to an extreme degree. Whereas social comparison (see SOCIAL COMPARISON THEORY) involves comparing one's position to that held by others, anchoring implies an inability to make an independent judgment.

social anxiety fear of social situations (e.g., making conversation, meeting strangers, or dating) in which embarrassment may occur or there is a risk of being negatively evaluated by others (e.g., seen as stupid, weak, or anxious). Social anxiety involves apprehensiveness about one's social status, role, and behavior. When the anxiety causes an individual significant distress or impairment in functioning, a diagnosis of SOCIAL PHOBIA may be warranted.

social anxiety disorder see SOCIAL PHOBIA.

social assimilation 1. the process by which two or more cultures or cultural groups are gradually merged, although one is likely to remain dominant. **2.** the process by which individuals are absorbed into the culture or mores of the dominant group.

social behavior 1. any action performed by interdependent conspecifics (members of the same species). **2.** in humans, an action that is influenced, directly or indirectly, by others, who may be actually present, imagined, expected, or only implied.

social breakdown syndrome a symptom pattern observed primarily in institutionalized individuals with chronic mental illness but also in such populations as long-term prisoners and older people. Symptoms include withdrawal, apathy, submissiveness, and progressive social and vocational incompetence. This decline is attributed to internalized negative stereotypes, such as identification with the SICK ROLE and the impact of labeling (see LABELING THEORY), the absence of social support, and such institutional factors as a lack of stimulation, overcrowding, unchanging routine, and disinterest on the part of the staff. Also called **chronicity; institutionalism; institutional neurosis; social disability syndrome**.

social category a group of people defined by SOCIAL CLASS or other common attributes of a social nature, such as homelessness, unemployment, or retirement.

social class a major group or division of society that shares a common level of status, income, power, and prestige as well as many common values and, in some cases, similar religious and social patterns. See also SOCIOECONOMIC STATUS.

social cognition 1. cognition in which people perceive, think about, interpret, categorize, and judge their own social behaviors and those of others. The study of social cognition involves aspects of both cognitive psychology and social psychology. Major areas of interest include ATTRIBUTION THEORY, PERSON PERCEPTION, SOCIAL INFLUENCE, and the cognitive processes involved in moral judgments. **2.** in animal behavior, the knowledge that an individual has about other members of its social group and the ability to reason about the actions of others based on this knowledge. In vervet monkeys, for example, after an individual in matriline (matrilineal line of descent) A attacks an individual in matriline B, other members of B are more likely to attack other animals from A.

social-cognitive theory a theoretical framework in which the functioning of personality is explained in terms of cognitive contents and processes acquired through interaction with the sociocultural environment.

social comparison theory the proposition that people evaluate their abilities and attitudes in relation to those of others (i.e., through a process of comparison) when objective standards for the assessment of these abilities and attitudes are lacking. Some also hold that those chosen as the comparison group are generally those whose abilities or attitudes are relatively similar to the person's own abilities or views.

social competence skill in interpersonal relations, especially the ability to handle a variety of social situations effectively.

social constructionism the position, mainly associated with POSTMODERNISM, that any supposed knowledge of reality (as, for example, that claimed by science) is in fact a construct of language, culture, and society having no objective or universal validity. See also SITUATED KNOWLEDGE.

social constructivism the school of thought that an individual's motivations and emotions are shaped predominantly by cultural training in modes of acting, feeling, and thinking, rather than being largely determined by biological influences. See NATURE–NURTURE.

social contagion see CONTAGION.

social contract orientation see POSTCONVENTIONAL LEVEL.

social control the power of the institutions, organizations, and laws of society to influence or regulate the behavior of individuals and groups. The human tendency to conform increases the power of social institutions to shape behavior.

social death a pattern of group behavior that ignores the presence or existence of a person within the group. Social death occurs in situations in which verbal and nonverbal communication would be expected to include all participants but in which one or more individuals are excluded.

social-decision scheme a strategy or rule used in a group to select a single alternative from among the various alternatives proposed and discussed during the group's deliberations. These schemes or rules are sometimes explicitly acknowledged by the group, as when a formal tally of those favoring the alternative is taken and the proposal is accepted only when a certain proportion of those present favor it, but are sometimes implicit and informal, as when a group accepts the alternative that its most powerful members seem to favor.

social deprivation 1. limited access to society's resources due to poverty, discrimination, or other disadvantage. See CULTURAL DEPRIVATION. **2.** lack of adequate opportunity for social experience.

social desirability 1. the extent to which someone or something (a trait, attribute, or the like) is admired or considered valuable within a social group. **2.** a bias that prompts individuals to present themselves in ways that are likely to be seen as positive by the majority of other people. See IMPRESSION MANAGEMENT.

social desirability response set the tendency of a respondent or participant to give answers that elicit a favorable evaluation rather than answers that genuinely represent their views. This often reduces the validity of interviews, questionnaires, and other self-reports.

social determinism the theory or doctrine that historical events or individual behaviors are determined by social phenomena, such as economic forces. See also CULTURAL DETERMINISM; DETERMINISM.

social development the gradual acquisition of certain skills (e.g., language, interpersonal skills), attitudes, relationships, and behavior that enable the individual to interact with others and to function as a member of society.

social differentiation the process by which a hierarchy in social status develops within any society or social group. For example, in a care facility for older people, social differentiation might be based on age, level of mobility, or physical impairment.

social dilemma an interpersonal situation that tempts individuals to seek personal, selfish gain by putting at risk the interests of the larger collective to which they belong. Such mixed-motive situations have reward structures that favor individuals who act selfishly rather than in ways that benefit the larger social collective; however, if a substantial number of individuals seek maximum personal gain, their outcomes will be lower than if they had sought collective outcomes. Social dilemmas are simulated in MIXED-MOTIVE GAMES, such as the PRISONER'S DILEMMA. See also SOCIAL TRAP.

social distance the degree to which, psycholog-

ically speaking, a person or group wants to remain separate from members of different social groups. This reflects the extent to which individuals or groups accept others of a different ethnic, racial, national, or other social background.

social distance scale a measure of intergroup attitudes that asks respondents to indicate their willingness to accept members of other ethnic, national, or social groups in situations that range from relatively distant ("would allow to live in my country") to relatively close ("would admit to close kinship by marriage").

social dynamics an approach to sociology that focuses on the empirical study of specific societies and social systems in the process of historical change. Compare SOCIAL STATICS.

social ecology the study of human or nonhuman organisms in relation to their social environment.

social exchange theory a theory envisioning social interactions as an exchange in which the participants seek to maximize their benefits within the limits of what is regarded as fair or just. Intrinsic to this hypothesis is the RECIPROCITY NORM: People are expected to reciprocate for the benefits they have received. Social exchange theory is similar to EQUITY THEORY, which also maintains that people seek fairness in social relationships.

social facilitation the improvement in an individual's performance of a task that often occurs when others are present. This effect tends to occur with tasks that are uncomplicated or have been previously mastered through practice. There is some disagreement as to whether the improvement is due to a heightened state of arousal, a greater self-awareness, or a reduced attention to unimportant and distracting peripheral stimuli. By contrast, the presence of other people is frequently an impediment to effective performance when the task is complicated, particularly if it is not well learned. See also AUDIENCE EFFECT.

social gerontology the study of the social process of aging and the interaction of older adults with their environments, including such issues as the contributions of older adults to the community, services provided in the community for older adults, and the utilization of group residences and communities for older adults.

social heritage culturally learned social behaviors that are constant across generations. Examples include giving gifts on particular occasions, greeting others when one enters a room, and shaking hands. See CULTURAL HERITAGE; SOCIAL TRANSMISSION.

social identity the personal qualities that one claims and displays to others so consistently that they are considered to be part of one's essential, stable self. This public persona may be an accurate indicator of the private, personal self, but it may also be a deliberately contrived image.

social identity theory a conceptual perspective on group processes and intergroup relations that assumes that groups influence their members' self-concepts and self-esteem, particularly when individuals categorize themselves as group members and identify strongly with the group. According to this theory, people tend to favor their INGROUP over an OUTGROUP because the former is part of their self-identity. With its emphasis on the importance of group membership for the self, social identity theory contrasts with individualistic analyses of behavior that discount the importance of group belongingness.

social immobility a feature of a society with fixed social norms or a rigid class system such that movement from one social class to another is virtually impossible and occurs only in very rare and prescribed instances. The traditional Hindu CASTE system is an example of such a fixed class society. Compare SOCIAL MOBILITY.

social impact theory a theory of social influence postulating that the amount of influence exerted by a source on a target depends on (a) the strength of the source compared to that of the target (e.g., the social status of the source versus that of the target); (b) the immediacy of the source to the target (e.g., the physical or psychological distance between them); and (c) the number of sources and targets (e.g., several sources influencing a single target). See also DYNAMIC SOCIAL IMPACT THEORY.

social imperception disorder a condition characterized by a lack of awareness of common social interaction and interpersonal behaviors, difficulty in recognizing and understanding other people's feelings and emotions, and a very limited awareness of typical social interpersonal issues.

social indicator any variable by which the quality of life of a society can be assessed. Many social indicators have been suggested by different authorities—among them, per capita income, poverty, unemployment, labor conditions, education, mental health, general health, pollution, the cost of housing, opportunities for leisure and recreation, crime rates, nutrition, life expectancy, and the status of the elderly.

social influence 1. any change in an individual's thoughts, feelings, or behaviors caused by other people, who may be actually present, imagined, expected, or only implied. **2.** those interpersonal processes that can cause individuals to change their thoughts, feelings, or behaviors. See SOCIAL PRESSURE.

social information processing a type of human INFORMATION PROCESSING in which social information is encoded, compared with other pertinent information, and retrieved to influence one's interactions with others.

social inhibition the restraint placed on an individual's expression of her or his feelings, attitudes, motives, and so forth by the belief that others could learn of this behavior and disapprove of it.

social insects insects that live together in groups, exhibiting reproductive division of labor, cooperation in care of the young, and multiple generations working together. Social insects are haplodiploid (have only one set of chromosomes), with males developing from unfertilized eggs. This means that workers (sterile females) share 75% of their genes (whereas queen and worker share only 50%), so they have greater INCLUSIVE FITNESS by tending their siblings than they would by breeding on their own.

social instinct 1. the desire for social contact and a feeling of belonging, as manifested by the tendency to congregate, affiliate, and engage in group behaviors. **2.** an innate drive for cooperation that leads normal individuals to incorporate social interest and the common good into their efforts to achieve self-realization. See also GREGARIOUSNESS.

social integration 1. the process by which separate groups are combined into a unified society, especially when this is pursued as a deliberate policy. Whereas **desegregation** refers to the formal termination of practices that create a segregated society, integration implies a coming together based on individual acceptance of the members of other groups. **2.** the process by which an individual is assimilated into a group.

social intelligence the ability to understand people and effectively relate to them. It is often contrasted with ABSTRACT INTELLIGENCE and CONCRETE INTELLIGENCE.

social interaction any process that involves reciprocal stimulation or response between two or more individuals. Social interaction includes the development of cooperation and competition, the influence of status and social roles, and the dynamics of group behavior, leadership, and conformity. Persistent social interaction between specific individuals leads to the formation of SOCIAL RELATIONSHIPS.

social interest communal feeling based on a recognition that people live in a social context; are an integral part of their family, community, humanity, and the cosmos itself; and have a natural aptitude for acquiring the skills and understanding necessary to solve social problems and to take socially affirmative action.

socialization *n.* the process by which individuals acquire social skills, beliefs, values, and behaviors necessary to function effectively in society or in a particular group. It involves becoming aware of the social or group value-system behavior pattern and what is considered normal or desirable for the social environment in which they will be members. **—socialize** *vb.*

social judgment theory a theory of attitude change postulating that the magnitude of PERSUASION produced by a particular message depends on how much the position advocated in the message differs from a person's attitude. Persuasion is likely to be greatest when a message advocates a position that a person finds neither clearly acceptable nor clearly objectionable.

social justice norm the SOCIAL NORM stating that people should be helped by others only if they deserve to be helped. Compare RECIPROC-ITY NORM; SOCIAL RESPONSIBILITY NORM.

social learning learning that is facilitated through social interactions with other individuals. Several forms of social learning have been identified, including LOCAL ENHANCEMENT, SOCIAL FACILITATION, EMULATION, and IMITATION.

social learning theory the general view that learning is largely or wholly due to imitation, modeling, and other social interactions. Behavior is assumed to be developed and regulated (a) by external stimulus events, such as the influence of other individuals; (b) by external reinforcement, such as praise, blame, and reward; and (c) by the effects of cognitive processes, such as thinking and judgment, on the individual's behavior and on the environment that influences him or her.

social limitation restriction attributed to social policy or barriers (structural or attitudinal) that limit individuals' fulfillment of roles or deny individuals access to the services and opportunities associated with full participation in society.

social loafing the reduction of individual effort that occurs when people work in groups compared to when they work alone.

social marketing the use of marketing techniques to prompt socially desirable behaviors, such as eating health foods, driving safely, undergoing regular medical examinations, and the like.

social maturity a level of behavior in accordance with the social standards that are the norm for individuals of a particular age.

social maturity scale an instrument that assesses the degree to which an individual performs age-appropriate behaviors. These behaviors are primarily concerned with functioning in the family and community and are sometimes considered in conjunction with measures of intellectual impairment to establish the presence of retardation.

social mobility the extent to which a society permits or encourages change in social class, social status, or social roles. Societies differ in the degree to which they permit or facilitate movement or change in their social hierarchy. Compare SOCIAL IMMOBILITY. See DOWNWARD MOBILITY; HORIZONTAL MOBILITY; UPWARD MOBILITY; VERTICAL MOBILITY.

social motive any motive acquired as a result of interaction with others. It may be universal (e.g., NEED FOR AFFILIATION) or culture-specific (e.g., NEED FOR ACHIEVEMENT). See also PSYCHOLOGICAL NEED.

social network the structure of the relationships that an individual or group has with others. Sociologists and social psychologists have developed quantitative analytic methods for measuring social networks (**social-network analysis**).

social-network therapy a form of psychotherapy in which various people who maintain significant relationships with the patient or client in different aspects of life (e.g., relatives, friends, coworkers) are assembled with the client present in small or larger group sessions.

social neuroscience an emerging discipline that aims to integrate the social and biological approaches to human behavior that have often been seen as mutually exclusive. Social neuroscientists use a range of methodologies to elucidate the reciprocal interactions of the brain's biological mechanisms (especially the nervous, immune, and endocrine systems) with the social and cultural contexts in which human beings operate.

social norm any of the socially determined consensual standards that indicate (a) what behaviors are considered typical in a given context (**descriptive norms**) and (b) what behaviors are considered proper in the context (**injunctive norms**). Unlike statistical norms, social norms of both types include an evaluative quality such that those who do not comply and cannot provide an acceptable explanation for their violation are evaluated negatively. Social norms apply across groups and social settings, whereas **group norms** are specific to a particular group.

social organization the complete set of SOCIAL RELATIONSHIPS among members of a society or other group, which determines the structure of the group and the place of individuals within it. These relationships can be based on several variables: kinship, age, sex, area of residence, and—in human beings—religion, matrimony, or common interests as well. The social organization is usually implemented by rules of behavior produced by social interactions involving DOMINANCE, TERRITORIALITY, the MATING SYSTEM, and COOPERATION.

social penetration theory a model stating that close relationships grow closer with increasingly intimate SELF-DISCLOSURES.

social perception an individual's awareness of social phenomena, especially his or her ability to infer motives, attitudes, or values from the social behavior of other individuals or of groups.

social phobia an anxiety disorder that is characterized by extreme and persistent SOCIAL ANXIETY or PERFORMANCE ANXIETY that causes significant distress or prevents participation in everyday activities. The feared situation is most often avoided altogether or else it is endured with marked discomfort. Also called **social anxiety disorder**.

social play 1. play that involves interacting with others for fun or sport. Examples include ROUGH-AND-TUMBLE PLAY and sometimes

SOCIODRAMATIC PLAY. It is one of three basic types of play traditionally identified, the others being OBJECT PLAY and LOCOMOTOR PLAY. **2.** patterns of play identified by the 1932 classification system of U.S. child-development researcher Mildred Parten and used to characterize the level of social development and participation of preschool children. The lowest level of this system is **solitary play**, in which a child is near others but focused on his or her own activity; it progresses to **parallel play**, in which a child is next to others and using similar objects but still engaged in his or her own activity. The latter is succeeded by **associative play**, in which a child interacts with others but there is no common purpose or organization to the shared activity, and the series culminates in the highest level, **cooperative play**, in which a child interacts with others in coordinated, directed activities.

social pressure the exertion of influence on a person or group by another person or group. Like GROUP PRESSURE, social pressure includes rational argument and persuasion (**informational influence**), calls for conformity (**normative influence**), and direct forms of influence, such as demands, threats, or personal attacks on the one hand and promises of rewards or social approval on the other (**interpersonal influence**). See also SOCIAL INFLUENCE.

social psychology the study of how an individual's thoughts, feelings, and actions are affected by the actual, imagined, or symbolically represented presence of other people. **Psychological social psychology** differs from **sociological social psychology** in that the former tends to give greater emphasis to internal psychological processes, whereas the latter focuses on factors that affect social life, such as status, role, and class.

social quotient the ratio between SOCIAL AGE and CHRONOLOGICAL AGE. A social quotient is a parallel concept to an IQ, where a score of 100 indicates average performance for age and scores less than 100 indicate below-average functioning.

social rehabilitation 1. the achievement of a higher level of social functioning in individuals with mental disorders or disabilities through group activities and participation in clubs and other community organizations. **2.** the achievement of a higher level of independent functioning in individuals with physical impairments or disabilities through provision of assistance with ACTIVITIES OF DAILY LIVING as well as other more social aspects of living, such as employment and the need for transportation and appropriate housing, that often present barriers to participation for those with disabilities.

social relationship the sum of the SOCIAL INTERACTIONS between individuals over a period of time. Momentary social interactions can be described in terms of parental care, dominant–subordinate or aggressive–fearful interactions, and so on, but a social relationship is the emergent quality from repeated interactions. A DYAD (interacting pair) may have a generally positive or generally negative social relationship that is reciprocal or complementary. Dyads with long-term social relationships will adjust behavior with each other according to feedback received.

social responsibility norm the social standard or NORM that, when possible, one should assist those in need. Compare RECIPROCITY NORM; SOCIAL JUSTICE NORM.

social role the functional role played by an individual who holds a formal position in a social group, such as the role of squadron leader, teacher, or vice president of an organization. Positions of this kind are termed **role categories**, and the attitudes and behavior associated with each category are termed **role expectations**.

social role valorization a principle, developed in succession to the NORMALIZATION PRINCIPLE, that stresses the importance of creating or supporting socially valued roles for people with disabilities. According to this principle, fulfillment of valued social roles increases the likelihood that a person will be socially accepted by others and will more readily achieve a satisfactory quality of life.

social science 1. any of a number of disciplines concerned with the social interactions of individuals, studied from a scientific and research perspective. These disciplines traditionally have included anthropology, economics, geography, history, linguistics, political science, psychiatry, psychology, and sociology, as well as associated areas of mathematics and biology. Additional fields include related psychological studies in business administration, journalism, law, medicine, public health, and social work. The focus of analysis ranges from the individual to institutions and entire social systems. The general goal is to understand social interactions and to propose solutions to social problems. **2.** these disciplines collectively.

social self the aspects of the SELF that are important to or influenced by social relations. See also COLLECTIVE SELF; PUBLIC SELF; SOCIAL IDENTITY.

social services services provided by government and nongovernment agencies and organizations to improve social welfare for those in need, including people with low income, illness or disability, older adults, and children. Services might include health care, insurance, subsidized housing, food subsidies, and the like.

social skills a set of learned abilities that enable an individual to interact competently and appropriately in a given social context. The most commonly identified social skills include assertiveness, coping, communication and friendship-making skills, interpersonal problem-solving, and the ability to regulate one's cognitions, feelings, and behavior. See also SOCIAL COMPETENCE.

social skills training (SST) **1.** techniques for teaching effective social interaction in specific situations (e.g., job interviews, dating). **2.** a form of individual or group therapy for those who need to overcome social inhibition or ineffectiveness. It uses many techniques, including BEHAVIOR REHEARSAL, COGNITIVE REHEARSAL, and ASSERTIVENESS TRAINING.

social statics an approach to sociology that focuses on the distinctive nature of human societies and social systems considered in the abstract, rather than on the empirical study of any particular society. Compare SOCIAL DYNAMICS.

social status the relative prestige, authority, and privilege of an individual or group. Social status can be determined by any number of factors—including occupation, level of education, ethnicity, religion, age, rank, achievements, wealth, reputation, authority, and ancestry—with different groups and societies stressing some qualities more than others when allocating status to members.

social stimulus any agent, event, or situation with social significance, particularly an individual or group, that elicits a response relevant to interpersonal relationships.

social stratification the existence or emergence of separate socioeconomic levels in a society. See SOCIAL CLASS; SOCIOECONOMIC STATUS.

social structure the complex of processes, forms, and systems that organize and regulate interpersonal phenomena in a group or society. The social structure of a group includes the status, attraction, and communication relations that link one member to another as well as a system of norms and roles (see GROUP STRUCTURE). The social structure of a society includes the complex of relations among its constituent individuals, groups, institutions, customs, mores, and so on.

social support the provision of assistance or comfort to others, typically in order to help them cope with a variety of biological, psychological, and social stressors. Support may arise from any interpersonal relationship in an individual's social network, involving family members, friends, neighbors, religious institutions, colleagues, caregivers, or support groups. It may take the form of practical help with chores or money, informational assistance (e.g., advice or guidance), and, at the most basic level, emotional support that allows the individual to feel valued, accepted, and understood. Social support has generally been shown to have positive physical and psychological effects, particularly in protecting against the deleterious effects of stress. See also COPING; SOCIAL INTEGRATION.

social therapy therapeutic and rehabilitative approaches that use social structures and experiences to improve the interpersonal functioning of individuals, for example, MILIEU THERAPY and the THERAPEUTIC COMMUNITY.

social transmission the transfer from one generation to the next of customs, language, or other aspects of the CULTURAL HERITAGE of a group. See SOCIAL HERITAGE.

social trap a SOCIAL DILEMMA in which individuals can maximize their resources by seeking personal goals rather than collective goals, but if too many individuals act selfishly, all members of the collective will experience substantial long-term losses. Many social traps involve a dilemma over a public good. The "tragedy of the commons" is an example: A grazing area will be destroyed if too many of the farmers who share it increase the size of their herds. More broadly, a social trap is a situation in which human behavior is shaped by reinforcements that conflict with the consequences of that behavior. Immediate positive reinforcements can lead to behaviors that in the long run are bad for the individual (e.g., addiction) or for society (e.g., the tragedy of the commons). Immediate negative reinforcements can prevent behaviors that in the long run would be good for the individual (e.g., studying) or for society (e.g., using mass transportation). See also MIXED-MOTIVE GAME.

social tunneling a psychological state, usually associated with a demanding task or stressful environment, characterized by a tendency to ignore social cues that may be relevant to the task, such as spoken commands or alert signals from other people. Compare COGNITIVE TUNNELING.

social work a profession devoted to helping individuals, families, and other groups deal with personal and practical problems within the larger community context of which they are a part. **Social workers** address a variety of problems, including those related to mental or physical disorder, poverty, living arrangements, child care, occupational stress, and unemployment, especially through involvement in the provision of SOCIAL SERVICES.

society *n.* **1.** an enduring social group living in a particular place whose members are mutually interdependent and share political and other institutions, laws and mores, and a common culture. **2.** any well-established group of individuals (human or animal) that typically obtains new members at least in part through sexual reproduction and has relatively self-sufficient systems of action. —**societal** *adj.*

sociobiology *n.* the systematic study of the biological basis for social behavior, particularly in the context of the Darwinian principle of NATURAL SELECTION. —**sociobiological** *adj.*

sociocentrism *n.* **1.** the tendency to put the needs, concerns, and perspective of the social unit or group before one's individual, egocentric concerns. See also ALLOCENTRIC. **2.** the tendency to judge one's own group as superior to other groups across a variety of domains. Whereas ETHNOCENTRISM refers to the selective favoring of one's ethnic, religious, racial, or national groups, sociocentrism usually means the favoring of smaller groups characterized by face-to-face interaction among members. Compare EGOCENTRISM. —**sociocentric** *adj.*

sociocultural perspective any viewpoint or approach to health, mental health, history, politics, economics, or any other area of human experience that emphasizes the environmental factors of society, culture, and social interaction. In developmental psychology, for example, the term refers to the view that cognitive development is guided by adults interacting with children, with the cultural context determining to a large extent how, where, and when these interactions take place. See also GUIDED PARTICIPATION.

sociodrama *n.* a technique for enhancing human relations and social skills that uses dramatization and ROLE PLAY. See also PSYCHODRAMA.

sociodramatic play a form of play in which the child takes on a social role (e.g., mother, father, police officer, doctor), elaborates a theme in cooperation with at least one other role player, and interacts with at least one other child both actively and verbally.

socioeconomic status (SES) the position of an individual or group on the socioeconomic scale, which is determined by a combination or interaction of social and economic factors, such as income, amount and kind of education, type and prestige of occupation, place of residence, and (in some societies or parts of society) ethnic origin or religious background. See SOCIAL CLASS.

sociogenic *adj.* resulting from social factors. For example, a **sociogenic hypothesis** of schizophrenia posits that social conditions, such as living in impoverished circumstances, are major contributors to and causal agents of the disorder.

sociogram *n.* a graphic representation of the relations among members of a social unit or group. In most cases each member of the group is depicted by a symbol, such as a lettered circle or square, and the types of relations among members (e.g., communication links, friendship pairings) are depicted by arrows. SOCIOMETRY uses objective data collected by observers or the self-reports provided by members of the group to generate sociograms. In practice, sociograms are used mainly to emphasize the patterns of liking and disliking in a group.

sociolinguistics *n.* the study of the relationship between language and society and of the social circumstances of language usage, especially as related to such characteristics as gender, social class, and ethnicity. Using techniques and findings from linguistics and the social sciences, sociolinguistics is concerned with the individual's language use in the context of his or her social community or culture.

sociology *n.* the scientific study of the origin, development, organization, forms, and functioning of human society, including the analysis of the relationships between individuals and groups, institutions, and society itself. —**sociological** *adj.* —**sociologist** *n.*

sociometer theory a theory holding that SELF-ESTEEM is important to individuals mainly because it serves as a sociometer (measure of social appeal). Specifically, high self-esteem signifies that the self has traits, such as competence, likability, moral virtue, and physical attractiveness, that will promote acceptance by other people.

sociometric differentiation the gradual development of stronger and more positive interpersonal ties between some members of a group, accompanied by decreases in the quality of relations between other members of the group.

sociometric test a self-report measure of intermember relations in a group, as used in SOCIOMETRY to analyze and develop a graphic representation of the group's structure (see SOCIOGRAM).

sociometry *n.* a field of research in which various techniques are used to analyze the patterns of intermember relations within groups and to summarize these findings in mathematical and graphic form. In most cases researchers ask the group members one or more questions about their fellow members, such as "Whom do you most like in this group?" or "Whom in the group would you like to work with the most?" These choices can then be summarized in a SOCIOGRAM, which in most cases is organized into a meaningful pattern by placing those individuals who are most frequently chosen (**stars**) in the center of the diagram and the **isolates** about the periphery. —**sociometric** *adj.*

sociopathy *n.* a former name for ANTISOCIAL PERSONALITY DISORDER.

sociosexual assessment an assessment of an individual to identify or measure his or her awareness of cultural standards regarding social relationships and sexual activity, knowledge of facts about sexuality and the nature and consequences of sexual interaction, and engagement (type and nature) in sexual activities. It may also include an assessment of risks that the individual may engage in culturally sanctioned sexual activities.

sociotechnical systems approach an approach to the design and evaluation of WORK SYSTEMS based on the theory that tasks and roles, technology, and the social system constitute a single interrelated system, such that changes in one part require adjustments in the other parts. The introduction of new technologies, for example, may automate some job tasks and lead to decreased job satisfaction and group resistance to the changes.

sociotherapy *n.* a supportive therapeutic approach based on modification of an individual's environment with the aim of improving the individual's interpersonal adjustment. The approach may be used in a variety of contexts, including working with parents and prospective foster parents, family counseling, vocational re-training, and assistance in readjusting to community life following hospitalization for severe mental illness.

sociotropy *n.* the tendency to place an inordinate value on relationships over personal independence, thought to leave one vulnerable to depression in response to the loss of relationships or to conflict.

Socratic dialogue a process of structured inquiry and discussion between two or more people to explore the concepts and values that underlie their everyday activities and judgments. In some psychotherapies, it is a technique in which the therapist poses strategic questions designed to clarify the client's core beliefs and feelings and, in the case of COGNITIVE THERAPY, to enable the client to discover the distortions in his or her habitual interpretation of a given situation. In psychotherapy, it is also known as the **Socratic-therapeutic method**.

Socratic effect the finding that mere expression of beliefs tends to produce greater logical consistency among belief structures.

sodomy *n.* anal intercourse between human beings or sexual intercourse of any kind between a human being and an animal.

soft data subjective data or data considered to be flawed in some way, for example because of lack of experimental randomization, lack of formal random sampling in survey research, or being based only on anecdote.

soft determinism the position that all events, including human actions and choices, have causes, but that free will and responsibility are compatible with such DETERMINISM. Compare HARD DETERMINISM.

soft palate see PALATE.

soft sign a clinical, behavioral, or neurological sign that may reflect the presence of neurological impairment. Soft signs are subtle, nonspecific, and ambiguous (because they are also seen in individuals without neurological impairment). Examples include slight abnormalities of speech, gait, posture, or behavior; sleep disturbances; slow physical maturation; sensory or perceptual deficits; and short attention span. Also called **equivocal sign**; **soft neurological sign**.

solipsism *n.* the philosophical position that one can be sure of the existence of nothing outside the self, as other people and things may be mere figments of one's own consciousness. Although psychologically unacceptable, such a position is notoriously difficult to refute, either logically or empirically. The question posed by solipsism has been put in various ways, but all arise from the fact that one's experience of one's own consciousness and identity is direct and unique, such that one is cut off from the same kind of experience of other minds and the things of the

world. See EGOCENTRIC PREDICAMENT. —**solipsist** *n.* —**solipsistic** *adj.*

solitary nucleus a collection of neural cell bodies in the medulla oblongata of the brainstem that relays information from the intermediate nerve (see GREATER SUPERFICIAL PETROSAL NERVE), glossopharyngeal nerve, and vagus nerve. Gustatory (taste) neurons project to the anterior division of the nucleus, with touch and temperature afferents immediately lateral and visceral afferents medial and caudal. Gustatory neurons project from the solitary nucleus to control reflexes of acceptance or rejection, to anticipate digestive processes, and to activate higher levels of the taste system (see THALAMIC TASTE AREA). Also called **nucleus of the solitary tract** (**NST**).

solitary play see SOCIAL PLAY.

Solomon four-group design an experimental design that assesses the effect of having been pretested on the magnitude of the treatment effect. Participants are randomly divided into four groups and each group experiences a different combination of experimental manipulations: the first group receives the pretest, the treatment, and the posttest; the second group receives only the treatment and posttest; the third group receives the pretest, no treatment, and a posttest; and the fourth group receives only a posttest. [Richard L. **Solomon** (1919–1992), U.S. psychologist]

solution-focused brief therapy SHORT-TERM THERAPY that focuses on problems in the HERE AND NOW, with specific goals that the client views as important to achieve in a limited time.

soma *n.* **1.** the physical body (Greek, "body"), as distinguished from the mind or spirit (see SOUL). See MIND–BODY PROBLEM. **2.** in neuroscience, the CELL BODY of a neuron.

somatic *adj.* **1.** describing, relating to, or arising in the body as distinguished from the mind. For example, a **somatic disorder** is one involving a demonstrable abnormality in the structure or biochemistry of body tissues or organs. **2.** describing, relating to, or arising in cells of the body other than the sex cells or their precursors (i.e., germ-line cells). Hence, a **somatic mutation** cannot be transmitted to the offspring of the affected individual.

somatic delusion a false belief related to one or more bodily organs, such as that they are functioning improperly or are diseased, injured, or otherwise altered.

somatic hallucination the false perception of a physical occurrence within the body, such as feeling electric currents.

somatic nervous system the part of the nervous system comprising the sensory and motor neurons that innervate the sense organs and the skeletal muscles, as opposed to the AUTONOMIC NERVOUS SYSTEM.

somatic obsession preoccupation with one's body or any part of it. This concern may be associated with compulsive checking of the body part (e.g., in a mirror or by touch), comparison with others, and seeking reassurance. Somatic obsession is the central feature of BODY DYSMORPHIC DISORDER.

somatic receptor any of the sensory organs located in the skin, including the deeper kinesthetic sense organs (see KINESTHESIS). Types of somatic receptors include free nerve endings, MERKEL'S TACTILE DISKS, MEISSNER'S CORPUSCLES, KRAUSE END BULBS, GOLGI TENDON ORGANS, and BASKET ENDINGS.

somatic sensory area see SOMATOSENSORY AREA.

somatic sensory system see SOMATOSENSORY SYSTEM.

somatization *n.* the organic expression of psychological disturbance. The first use of the word has controversially been attributed to Austrian psychoanalyst Wilhelm Stekel (1868–1940) to describe what is now called CONVERSION.

somatization disorder a SOMATOFORM DISORDER involving a history of multiple physical symptoms of several years' duration, for which medical attention has been sought but which are apparently not due to any physical disorder or injury. The complaints often involve abdominal and other pain, nausea, diarrhea, sexual indifference and other difficulties, shortness of breath, palpitations, and apparent neurological symptoms (such as blurred vision).

somatoform disorder any of a group of disorders marked by physical symptoms suggesting a specific medical condition for which there is no demonstrable organic evidence and for which there is positive evidence or a strong probability that they are linked to psychological factors. The symptoms must cause marked distress or significantly impair normal social or occupational functioning. See BODY DYSMORPHIC DISORDER; CONVERSION DISORDER; HYPOCHONDRIASIS; PAIN DISORDER; SOMATIZATION DISORDER.

somatognosia *n.* awareness of one's own body or body parts. Denial of one's body parts is called **asomatognosia** and is commonly seen in individuals with NEGLECT.

somatometry *n.* measurement of the human body, particularly in order to correlate physique and psychological characteristics. —**somatometric** *adj.*

somatosense *n.* any of the senses related to touch and position, including KINESTHESIS, the visceral sense (see VISCERA), and the CUTANEOUS SENSES. Also called **somatic sense**.

somatosensory area either of two main areas of the CEREBRAL CORTEX that can be mapped with EVOKED POTENTIALS to reveal points that respond to stimulation of the various SOMATOSENSES. The somatosensory areas vary somewhat among different species: In humans the PRIMARY SOMATOSENSORY AREA is located in the POSTCENTRAL GYRUS of the anterior parietal lobe, and the SECONDARY SOMATOSENSORY AREA is on the lateral surface of the parietal lobe just dorsal to the LATERAL SULCUS. Also called **somatic sensory area**; **somatic area**; **somatosensory cortex**.

somatosensory system the parts of the nervous system that serve perception of touch, vibration, pain, temperature, and position (see SOMATOSENSE). Nerve fibers from receptors for these senses enter the dorsal roots of the spinal cord and ascend to the thalamus, from which they are relayed (directly or indirectly) to the SOMATOSENSORY AREAS of the parietal cortex. Also called **somatic sensory system**.

somatostatin *n.* a hormone that is secreted by the hypothalamus and inhibits the release of the GROWTH HORMONE (somatotropin) by the anterior pituitary gland. It is also secreted by cells in the ISLETS OF LANGERHANS in the pancreas, where it inhibits the secretion of insulin and glucagon. Analogues of somatostatin are used therapeutically in the control of ACROMEGALY. Also called **somatotropin-release inhibiting factor** (**SRIF**).

somatotopic organization the topographic distribution of areas of the MOTOR CORTEX relating to specific activities of skeletal muscles, as mapped by electrically stimulating a point in the cortex and observing associated movement of a skeletal muscle in the face, the trunk, or a limb. See also MOTOR HOMUNCULUS.

somatotropin *n.* see GROWTH HORMONE.

somatotype *n.* the body build or physique of a person, particularly as it relates to his or her temperament or behavioral characteristics (see CONSTITUTIONAL TYPE). Numerous categories of somatotypes have been proposed by various investigators since ancient times. The classification of individuals in this way is called **somatotypology**.

somesthetic disorder any dysfunction involving the SOMATOSENSES, such as difficulty in maintaining postural or positional awareness or lack of sensitivity to pain, touch, or temperature. Somesthetic disorders are usually related to PARIETAL LOBE damage.

somnambulism *n.* see SLEEPWALKING DISORDER.

somnambulistic state in hypnosis, a phase in which the individual in a deep TRANCE may appear to be awake and in control of his or her actions but is actually under the influence of the hypnotist.

somnolence *n.* excessive sleepiness or drowsiness, which is sometimes pathological. The condition may be due, for example, to medication, a sleep disorder, or a medical condition (e.g., HYPOTHYROIDISM). —**somnolent** *adj.*

somnology *n.* the study of sleep and sleep disorders. —**somnologist** *n.*

sone *n.* see LOUDNESS.

sonography *n.* see ULTRASOUND.

SORC *n.* an acronym for the four variables employed in behavioral analysis: stimuli (situational determinants), organismic variables, responses, and consequences (reinforcement contingencies). A functional analysis of behavior may seek to determine how the presentation of certain stimuli leads to specific responses (perhaps influenced by individual, or organismic, variables), which are followed by consequences that may then reinforce the elicited responses.

Sorge *n.* care (German). The term has gained currency in psychology and philosophy chiefly through its use by German philosopher Martin Heidegger (1889–1976) to denote the uniquely human activity of caring or worrying about things.

S–O–R psychology *s*timulus–*o*rganism–*r*esponse psychology: an extension of the S–R PSYCHOLOGY of behaviorists incorporating the notion that biological or psychological factors within the organism help determine what stimuli the organism is sensitive to and which responses may occur. S–O–R psychology has been extended beyond PAVLOVIAN CONDITIONING and INSTRUMENTAL CONDITIONING to encompass such disciplines as marketing and consumer behavior. For example, an individual's emotional state when shopping may influence how many products he or she purchases and the particular types or brands.

sorting test a technique for assessing the ability to conceptualize, often used in adult neuropsychological assessments or in determining a child's level of cognitive development. The participant is asked to arrange an assortment of common objects by category.

sort-recall task a task used in memory research in which participants, usually children, have the opportunity to sort items into groups before having to recall the items at a later time.

soul *n.* the nonphysical aspect of a human being, considered responsible for the functions of mind and individual personality and often thought to live on after the death of the physical body. The concept of the soul was present in early Greek thinking, and has been an important feature of many philosophical systems and most religions. Some traditional areas of debate have included whether the soul is material or immaterial, whether animals, plants, or seemingly inert natural objects have souls (see PANPSYCHISM), and whether the soul is individual, allowing the personality to persist after death, or whether it is a reflection of a universal "cosmic" soul. Because the existence of the soul has resisted empirical verification, science has generally ignored the concept, while those who adhere to MATERIALISM, POSITIVISM, or REDUCTIONISM reject it absolutely. Despite this, the term survives in the general language to mean the deepest center of a person's identity and the seat of his or her most important moral, emotional, and aesthetic experiences.

sound *n.* variations in pressure that occur over time in an elastic medium, such as air or water. Sound does not necessarily elicit an auditory sensation—infrasound and ultrasound are respectively below and above the audible range of humans—but in psychology sound usually denotes a stimulus capable of being heard by an organism.

sound intensity the rate of flow of sound energy through a given area, measured in watts per square meter. In practice, sound intensity is seldom directly measured; it is indirectly determined using pressure measurements and often is expressed in DECIBELS. Sound intensity is proportional to the square of sound pressure.

sound localization see AUDITORY LOCALIZATION.

sound pressure the force per unit area exerted by a sound wave. The pressure is expressed as changes in the ambient or static pressure (e.g., atmospheric pressure), usually as root-mean-square (rms) pressure changes. The unit of measurement of sound pressure is the **pascal** (Pa). See also DECIBEL.

sound spectrography the procedure of analyzing a sound source (typically human speech) in terms of its variations in frequency and intensity over time. The visual record so produced is a **sound spectrogram**, a quasi-three-dimensional representation of sound, often shortened to **spectrogram**. The SOUND SPECTRUM, measured over a relatively brief interval, is plotted by the sound spectrograph as a function of time on the *x*-axis, while frequency is plotted on the *y*-axis, and intensity is depicted by shading or color. A spectrogram provides an imperfect representation of the perceptually relevant aspects of sound.

sound spectrum the representation of sound in terms of its frequency composition. These representations are uniquely related by the Fourier transform or Fourier series (see FOURIER ANALYSIS). The spectrum consists of the **amplitude spectrum** (or **power spectrum**) and the **phase spectrum**. Both are necessary to describe the sound completely. For example, a sound played backward has the same amplitude spectrum but an altered phase spectrum, and usually the sounds are perceptually very different. Sound spectra are useful partly because the mammalian auditory system performs an imperfect Fourier analysis. Also called **acoustic spectrum; auditory spectrum**.

source amnesia impaired memory for how, when, or where information was learned despite good memory for the information itself. Source amnesia is often linked to frontal lobe pathology.

source confusion misattribution of the origins of a memory. For example, an eyewitness hearing from a police officer that the perpetrator carried a gun may later believe that he or she saw the gun at the crime scene. See also UNCONSCIOUS TRANSFER.

source memory remembering the origin of a memory or of knowledge, that is, memory of where or how one came to know what one now remembers.

source monitoring determining the origins of one's memories, knowledge, or beliefs, for example, whether an event was personally experienced, witnessed on television, or overheard. Also called **reality monitoring**.

source trait in CATTELL'S PERSONALITY TRAIT THEORY, any of 16 personality traits, determined by FACTOR ANALYSIS, that underlie and determine SURFACE TRAITS. Examples are social boldness, dominance, and openness to change.

spasm *n.* a sudden, involuntary muscle contraction. It may be continuous or sustained (TONIC) or it may alternate between contraction and relaxation (CLONIC). A spasm may be restricted to a particular body part; for example, a **vasospasm** involves a blood vessel, and a **bronchial spasm** involves the bronchi. —**spasmodic** *adj.*

spastic *adj.* **1.** relating to SPASM. **2.** relating to increased muscle tension (see SPASTICITY).

spasticity *n.* a state of increased tension of resting muscles resulting in resistance to passive stretching. It is caused by damage to upper MOTOR NEURONS and is marked by muscular stiffness or inflexibility and exaggerated TENDON REFLEXES.

spastic paralysis a condition resulting from damage to upper MOTOR NEURONS and marked by tonic muscle SPASMS and increased TENDON REFLEXES. Compare FLACCID PARALYSIS.

spatial ability the skill required to orient or perceive one's body in space or to detect or reason about the relationship of objects in space, which is required, for example, in map reading and assembling jigsaw puzzles.

spatial attention the manner in which an individual distributes attention over the visual scene. Spatial attention is usually directed at the part of the scene on which a person fixates (see VISUAL FIXATION).

spatial disorder a disorder of space perception, usually associated with a lesion of the PARIETAL LOBE of the brain. It includes impaired memory for locations, inability to copy or assemble objects, route-finding difficulties, and poor judgment of distances.

spatial frequency the number of repeating elements in a pattern per unit distance. In a simple pattern of alternating black and white vertical bars (an example of a square-wave grating), the spatial frequency is the number of pairs of black and white bars per degree of visual angle, usually expressed as cycles per degree (cpd). See also CONTRAST SENSITIVITY.

spatial intelligence the ability to mentally manipulate objects in space and to imagine them in different locations and positions. Spatial intelligence is a component of both the MULTIPLE-INTELLIGENCES THEORY and the theory of PRIMARY ABILITIES.

spatial memory the capacity to remember the position and location of objects or places, which may include orientation, direction, and distance. Spatial memory is essential for ROUTE LEARNING and navigation.

spatial neglect a disorder in which individuals are unaware of a portion of their surrounding physical, personal, or extrapersonal space, usually on the left side. For example, if approached on the left side, an individual with spatial neglect may not notice the approaching person but would respond normally when approached on the right side.

spatial orientation the ability to perceive and adjust one's location in space in relation to objects in the external environment. See SPATIAL ABILITY.

spatial summation a neural mechanism in which an impulse is propagated by two or more POSTSYNAPTIC POTENTIALS occurring simultaneously at different synapses on the same neuron, when the discharge of a single synapse would not be sufficient to activate the neuron. Compare TEMPORAL SUMMATION.

spatial vision the ability of the eye and brain to encode and represent spatial patterns of light. The mechanisms of spatial vision are critical for all behavior that involves the processing of visual information.

speaking in tongues see GLOSSOLALIA.

Spearman–Brown prophecy formula the mathematical formulation of a basic theory of CLASSICAL TEST THEORY concerning the length (number of items) of a test and its reliability, whereby increasing the number of items results in increased reliability for the test. [Charles Edward **Spearman** (1863–1945), British psychologist and psychometrician; W. **Brown**, 20th-century British psychologist]

Spearman rank correlation see RANK CORRELATION. [Charles **Spearman**]

special care unit a unit in a health care institution designed to provide specialized care for people with severe problems, such as dementia, head injuries, or spinal cord injuries.

special education specially designed programs, services, and instruction provided to children with learning, behavioral, or physical disabilities (e.g., visual impairment, hearing loss, or neurological disorders) to assist them in becoming independent, productive, and valued members of their communities.

special factor see SPECIFIC FACTOR.

special needs the requirements of individuals with physical, mental, or emotional disabilities or financial, community-related, or resource disadvantages. Special needs may include SPECIAL EDUCATION, training, or therapy.

species *n.* in BIOLOGICAL TAXONOMY, the basic unit of classification, consisting of a group of organisms that can interbreed to produce fertile offspring. It is the main subdivision of a GENUS.

species recognition the ability of an animal to determine whether another animal is from the same or a different species. Species recognition is important in MATE SELECTION to avoid breeding with another species.

species-specific behavior behavior that is common to most members of a particular species, appears to be unlearned (though expression may be modified by experience), and is manifested by all species members in essentially the same way. Also called **species-typical behavior**. See also INSTINCT.

specific-attitudes theory the viewpoint that certain psychosomatic disorders are associated with particular attitudes. An example is an association between the feeling of being mistreated and the occurrence of hives. See also SPECIFIC-REACTION THEORY.

specific factor (symbol: *s*) a specialized ability that is postulated to come into play in particular kinds of cognitive tasks. Specific factors, such as mathematical ability, are contrasted with the GENERAL FACTOR (*g*), which underlies every cognitive performance. Also called **special factor**.

specificity *n.* **1.** the quality of being unique, of a particular kind, or limited to a single phenomenon. For example, a stimulus that elicits a particular response or a symptom localized in a particular organ (e.g., the stomach) is said to have specificity. **2.** the probability that a test yields a negative diagnosis given that the individual does not have the condition for which he or she is being tested. Compare SENSITIVITY.

specificity theory a theory holding that the mechanism of pain is—like vision and hearing—a specific modality with its own central and peripheral apparatus. According to this theory, pain is produced by nerve impulses that are generated by an injury and are transmitted directly to a pain center in the brain. Compare GATE-CONTROL THEORY; PATTERN THEORY.

specific language disability see LANGUAGE DISABILITY.

specific learning disability (SLD) a substantial deficit in scholastic or academic skills that does not pervade all areas of learning but rather is limited to a particular aspect, for example, reading or arithmetic difficulty.

specific phobia an ANXIETY DISORDER, formerly called **simple phobia**, characterized by a marked and persistent fear of a specific object, activity, or situation (e.g., dogs, blood, flying, heights). The fear is excessive or unreasonable and is invariably triggered by the presence or anticipation of the feared object or situation; consequently, this is either avoided or endured with marked anxiety or distress.

specific-reaction theory a concept that an innate tendency of the autonomic nervous system to react in a particular way to a stressful situation accounts for psychosomatic symptoms. See also SPECIFIC-ATTITUDES THEORY.

specific-status characteristics behavioral and personal characteristics relevant to the setting that people intentionally and unintentionally take into account when making judgments of their own and others' competency, ability, and social value. Compare DIFFUSE-STATUS CHARACTERISTICS.

specific transfer transfer of skills and knowledge acquired in one task to a similar task in which they are directly relevant. Compare GENERAL TRANSFER.

SPECT acronym for SINGLE PHOTON EMISSION COMPUTED TOMOGRAPHY.

spectator effect the effect on performance when a task is carried out in the presence of others. When an individual is confident of being able to perform the task, that is, has high task confidence, spectators improve performance; when task confidence is low, they worsen it.

spectrally opponent cell a type of neuron in the visual system that is excited by light in certain regions of the visible SPECTRUM and inhibited by light in other regions.

spectral sensitivity the relative degree to which light of different wavelengths is absorbed by the photopigments of the retina. Each type of photoreceptor has its own characteristic spectral sensitivity.

spectrogram *n.* see SOUND SPECTROGRAPHY.

spectrum *n.* (*pl.* **spectra**) a distribution of electromagnetic energy displayed by decreasing wavelength. In the case of the **visible spectrum**, it is the series of visible colors (with wavelengths in the range 400–700 nm) produced when white light is refracted through a prism. —**spectral** *adj.*

spectrum level the spectral density of a sound, usually expressed in DECIBELS sound-pressure level (dB SPL). For a waveform with a continuous spectrum, the **power spectral density** is the power in a band Δf Hz wide centered at frequency f as Δf approaches zero. The spectrum level at frequency f is the power spectral density expressed in decibels sound-pressure level.

speech *n.* communication through conventional vocal and oral symbols.

speech act an instance of the use of speech considered as an action, especially with regard to the speaker's intentions and the effect on a listener. A single utterance usually involves several simultaneous speech acts (see ILLOCUTIONARY ACT). The study of speech acts is part of the general field of PRAGMATICS.

speech and language disorder any disorder that affects verbal or written communication. A **speech disorder** is one that affects the production of speech, potentially including such problems as poor audibility or intelligibility;

unpleasant tonal quality; unusual, distorted, or abnormally effortful sound production; lack of conventional rhythm and stress; and inappropriateness in terms of age or physical or mental development. A **language disorder** is one that affects the production or reception of written language, potentially including such problems as reduced vocabulary, omissions of articles and modifiers, understanding of nouns but not verbs, difficulties following oral instructions, and syntactical errors. While speech disorders and language disorders are two distinct entities, they often occur together and thus generally are referred to together.

speech and language pathology the clinical field that studies, evaluates, and treats speech, voice, and language disorders.

speech and language therapy the application of remedies, treatment, and counseling for the improvement of speech and language.

speech area any of the areas of the cerebral cortex that are associated with verbal (oral, rather than written) communication. The speech areas are located in the left hemisphere in most individuals; they include BROCA'S AREA in the third convolution of the frontal lobe and WERNICKE'S AREA in the temporal lobe.

speech discrimination test a phonetically balanced word list used to measure an individual's ability to understand speech.

speech intelligibility the degree to which speech sounds (whether conversational or communication-system output) can be correctly identified and understood by listeners in a particular environment. Background or other system noise is one of the most important factors influencing speech intelligibility.

speech perception the process in which a listener decodes, combines, and converts into a meaningful sequence and phonological representation an incoming stream of otherwise meaningless sound produced by the SPEECH PRODUCTION process.

speech production the psychophysical and neurophysiological processes by which a person uses his or her neural, articulatory, and respiratory capacities to produce spoken language.

speech rehabilitation training to restore a lost or impaired speech function.

speed–accuracy tradeoff the tendency, when performing a task, for either speed or accuracy to be sacrificed in order to prioritize the other. In experiments, by varying the speed–accuracy criterion through instructions, payoffs, and deadlines, a person can respond quickly with many errors, slowly with few errors, or anywhere in between. In the area of motor control, FITTS LAW is a specific example of a speed–accuracy tradeoff.

speed test a type of test intended to calculate the number of problems or tasks the participant can solve or perform in a predesignated block of time. The participant is often, but not always, made aware of the time limit. Compare POWER TEST.

spelling dyslexia see WORD-FORM DYSLEXIA.

spermatogenesis *n.* the process of production of spermatozoa in the seminiferous tubules of the TESTIS. Male germ cells (**spermatogonia**) lining the seminiferous tubules mature into **primary spermatocytes**, which undergo MEIOSIS eventually resulting in mature spermatozoa (four per spermatocyte). In the first meiotic division, each primary spermatocyte gives rise to two HAPLOID **secondary spermatocytes**, each of which then undergoes a further division to form two **spermatids**. The latter, attached to protective, nourishing **Sertoli cells**, mature into spermatozoa. Spermatogenesis is continuous in humans after the onset of puberty and seasonal in some other animal species. —**spermatogenetic** *adj.*

spermatozoon *n.* (*pl.* **spermatozoa**) the GAMETE produced by males, which fuses with a female gamete (see OVUM) in the process of fertilization. Also called **sperm**.

sperm competition competition between the sperm of different males to fertilize the eggs of females that mate with multiple males. Males have several strategies for dealing with sperm competition, including MATE GUARDING, leaving an ejaculatory plug in the female genitalia to prevent other males from mating, or removing sperm from previous males prior to mating.

spherical aberration the failure of light rays to converge at the same focal point because of the curvature of a lens. See also ASTIGMATISM.

sphericity *n.* an assumption encountered in the analysis of data obtained when individuals are measured on two or more occasions that requires the correlation among the time points to be constant for all time points. See WITHIN-SUBJECTS DESIGN.

sphincter *n.* a ring-shaped muscle that partly or wholly closes a body orifice, such as the anal sphincters or the IRIS of the eye.

spina bifida any developmental defect in which the vertebral canal fails to close normally around the spinal cord. Individuals with spina bifida have difficulty with sensation, ambulation, and bowel and bladder control; experience weakness or paralysis of the muscles of the legs or feet; and are susceptible to infection. MENINGOMYELOCELE is the most common form of spina bifida.

spinal column the backbone, consisting of a series of bones (vertebrae) connected by disks of cartilage (intervertebral disks) and held together by muscles and tendons. It extends from the cranium to the coccyx, encloses the spinal cord, and forms the main axis of the body. Also called **spine**; **vertebral column**.

spinal cord the part of the CENTRAL NERVOUS SYSTEM that extends from the lower end of the

MEDULLA OBLONGATA, at the base of the brain, through a canal in the center of the spine as far as the lumbar region. In transverse section, the cord consists of an H-shaped core of gray matter (see PERIAQUEDUCTAL GRAY; ANTERIOR HORN; DORSAL HORN) surrounded by white matter consisting of tracts of long ascending and descending nerve fibers on either side of the cord that are linked by the WHITE COMMISSURE. The spinal cord is enveloped by the MENINGES and is the origin of the 31 pairs of SPINAL NERVES. See also SPINAL ROOT.

spinal ganglion a collection of cell bodies of sensory neurons found in the DORSAL ROOT of each SPINAL NERVE.

spinal gate in the GATE-CONTROL THEORY, a mechanism in cells of the SUBSTANTIA GELATINOSA of the spinal cord that transmits the net effect of both excitatory and inhibitory signals to the brain. The mechanism can modify the pain signals in accordance with messages from higher centers that reflect previous experience and the influence of emotional and other factors on PAIN PERCEPTION.

spinal muscular atrophy (**SMA**) a hereditary (autosomal) MOTOR NEURON DISEASE characterized by wasting (atrophy) of skeletal muscles associated with degeneration of nerve cells in the ANTERIOR HORN of the spinal cord. There are three common types, based on age of onset and symptom severity. Type I (also called **Werdnig–Hoffmann disease**) is evident at birth and is the most severe, resulting in death usually prior to age 2. Type II has an onset of symptoms between 6 months and 2 years and results in delayed motor development, progressive loss of strength, and variable loss of ambulation. Type III (also called **Kugelberg–Welander disease**) is identified between ages 1 and 15 and is the least severe, associated with slower progression and lower incidence.

spinal nerve any of the 31 pairs of nerves that originate in the gray matter of the SPINAL CORD and emerge through openings between the vertebrae of the spine to extend into the body's dermatomes (skin areas) and skeletal muscles. The spinal nerves comprise 8 cervical nerves, 12 thoracic nerves, 5 lumbar nerves, 5 sacral nerves, and 1 coccygeal nerve. Each attaches to the spinal cord via two short branches, a DORSAL ROOT and a VENTRAL ROOT. See also SPINAL ROOT.

spinal reflex a REFLEX that only involves neural circuits in the spinal cord, often controlling posture or locomotion. They are sometimes classed as **segmental reflexes**, if the circuit involves only one segment of the spinal cord, or as **intersegmental reflexes**, if the impulses must travel through more than one spinal segment. Reflexes that require brain activity are **suprasegmental reflexes**.

spinal root the junction of a SPINAL NERVE and the SPINAL CORD. Near the cord, each spinal nerve divides into a DORSAL ROOT, carrying sensory fibers, and a VENTRAL ROOT, carrying motor fibers, as stated by the BELL–MAGENDIE LAW.

spinal tap see LUMBAR PUNCTURE.

spindle cell a type of small neuron whose CELL BODY is spindle-shaped, that is, wider in the middle and tapering at the two ends. It should not be confused with a MUSCLE SPINDLE.

spinocerebellar tract a major nerve tract that carries impulses from the muscles and other proprioceptors through the spinal cord to the CEREBELLUM.

spinothalamic tract either of two ascending pathways for somatosensory impulses that travel through the spinal cord to the thalamus. They are part of the ANTEROLATERAL SYSTEM. The **anterior spinothalamic tract** serves touch and pressure sensations; the **lateral spinothalamic tract** carries principally pain and temperature information.

spiral ganglion the mass of cell bodies of the auditory nerve. It is located in the inner wall of the COCHLEA near the organ of Corti.

spiral test a type of assessment in which the focused themes being tested are distributed throughout the test, instead of being grouped together, and become increasingly difficult as the test progresses. Each subsequent spiral of difficulty covers a different domain of intelligence.

spirit *n.* **1.** the nonphysical part of a person: the mental, moral, and emotional characteristics that make up the core of someone's identity (e.g., *a noble spirit*; *it broke her spirit*). **2.** a vital force seen as animating the bodies of living creatures, sometimes identified with the SOUL and seen as surviving death. **3.** an immaterial or supernatural being, such as a ghost or a deity. **4.** the mood, temper, or disposition that temporarily or permanently characterizes a person.

spiritual healing see FAITH HEALING.

spiritualism *n.* **1.** in metaphysics, the position that the fundamental reality of the universe is nonmaterial. **2.** the belief that the spirits of the dead survive in another world or dimension, and that it is possible for the living to receive communications from them. Spiritualism may be considered the philosophical and religious counterpart to PARAPSYCHOLOGY. Also called **spiritism**. **3.** the belief that all humans, animals, plants, and natural objects possess souls and are part of a larger, universal spirit. See PANPSYCHISM. —**spiritualist** *adj., n.* —**spiritualistic** *adj.*

spirituality *n.* **1.** a concern for or sensitivity to the things of the SPIRIT or SOUL, especially as opposed to material things. **2.** more specifically, a concern for God and a sensitivity to religious experience, which may include the practice of a particular RELIGION but may also exist without such practice. **3.** the fact or state of being incorporeal.

splanchnic nerve any of certain nerves that

serve the abdominal VISCERA. They originate in the ganglia of the SYMPATHETIC CHAIN.

spleen *n.* an organ that produces lymphocytes, filters and stores blood, and destroys old red blood cells. Although it is not necessary to maintain life, the absence of a spleen may predispose an individual to certain infections.

splenium *n.* (*pl.* **splenia**) a blunt enlargement at the posterior end of the CORPUS CALLOSUM.

split brain a brain in which the cerebral hemispheres have been separated by severence of the corpus callosum (see COMMISSUROTOMY). Surgical transection of the corpus callosum is used to create split-brain animals for experimental purposes and is also occasionally performed on humans to alleviate some forms of severe epilepsy.

split-half reliability a measure of the internal consistency of a test, obtained by correlating responses on one half of the test with responses on the other half.

split-litter design in animal research, the assignment of litter mates to different groups in an experiment (e.g., the experimental group and the control group). This is an attempt to minimize genetic differences between the members of the different groups. Also called **split-litter technique**.

split personality a lay term for an individual with DISSOCIATIVE IDENTITY DISORDER. It is sometimes confused with SCHIZOPHRENIA, which means literally "splitting of the mind" but does not involve the formation of a second personality.

split-span test a test in which brief auditory messages in the form of two different lists of digits or words are presented rapidly and simultaneously, one list to each ear. Participants are required to report as many digits or words as possible in any order. Typically, participants report first the stimuli presented to one ear, then those presented to the other.

splitting *n.* **1.** in KLEINIAN analysis, the most primitive of all DEFENSE MECHANISMS, in which OBJECTS that evoke ambivalence and therefore anxiety are dealt with by compartmentalizing positive and negative emotions (see PART-OBJECT), leading to images of the self and others that are not integrated. It results in polarized viewpoints that are projected onto different people. This mechanism is found not only in infants and young children but also in adults with dysfunctional patterns of dealing with ambivalence; it is often associated with BORDERLINE PERSONALITY DISORDER. Splitting plays a central role in FAIRBAIRNIAN THEORY. **2.** in COTHERAPY, an appeal by a client to one of the therapists when he or she feels that that therapist would be more sympathetic than the other. Also called **splitting situation**.

spongiform encephalopathy see PRION DISEASE.

spontaneous alternation the instinctive, successive alternation of responses between alternatives in a situation involving discrete choices or exploration. For example, in a learning and memory experiment, a rat in a T maze tends to choose the left arm on one trial, the right arm on the next, the left arm again, and so on.

spontaneous memorialization voluntary public response to unexpected and violent death. Examples include the placement of messages, flowers, and other objects at sites associated with terrorist attacks or personal tragedies (e.g., when a shopkeeper has been murdered or a child struck down by a hit-and-run driver). The hallmark of spontaneous memorialization is an immediate emotional response on the part of individuals and small groups of people, as distinguished from institutionalized patterns of response.

spontaneous recovery the reappearance of a conditioned response, after either operant or Pavlovian conditioning, after it has been experimentally extinguished (see EXTINCTION).

spontaneous regression a phenomenon in which a person suddenly relives an event from an earlier age (e.g., childhood) and may exhibit appropriate behavior for that age.

spontaneous remission a reduction or disappearance of symptoms without any therapeutic intervention, which may be temporary or permanent. It most commonly refers to medical, rather than psychological, conditions. See also WAITING-LIST PHENOMENON.

spontaneous trait inference a judgment about an individual's personality traits that is made automatically, based on observed behavior. More specifically, it is the phenomenon by which people who hear others describe negative or positive behaviors in individuals attribute the qualities implied by those behaviors to the speaker.

spoonerism *n.* a SLIP OF THE TONGUE in which two sound elements (usually initial consonants) are unintentionally transposed, resulting in an utterance with a different and often amusing sense, for example, *sons of toil* for *tons of soil*. [W. A. **Spooner** (1844–1930), British academic noted for slips of this kind]

sport and exercise psychology the application and development of psychological theory for the understanding and modification or enhancement of human behavior in the sport and physical exercise environment. This discipline evolved from an exclusive focus on sport performance and historically has been called **sport psychology**. However, health and well-being through regular participation in vigorous physical activity programs have become of increasing interest to consumers, researchers, and practitioners to such an extent that the field is progressively becoming two separate disciplines as **exercise psychology** merges with HEALTH PSYCHOLOGY.

sport personality debate a debate about the role that personality characteristics have in decisions to participate in sport and in the ability to perform in sport. Research evidence supports the position that personality is not a relevant factor.

sport science the application of biophysical and social-scientific methods to study sport behavior and improve performance. Sport science includes biological, mechanical, psychological, sociological, and managerial disciplines.

sport socialization the process of using sport as a medium for teaching and learning the skills and characteristics necessary to function effectively in a society. It includes learning respect for authority (e.g., a referee), fulfilling commitments (going to practice, not quitting the team), and so on.

spotlight model of attention a model of attention that likens the focus of attention to a spotlight. Information outside the spotlight is presumed not to receive processing that requires attention.

Spranger's typology a system of classification that sorts humans by six basic cultural values: theoretical, economic, aesthetic, social, political, and religious. [proposed by Eduard **Spranger** (1882–1963), German philosopher and psychologist]

spread *n*. see DISPERSION.

spreading activation 1. in neuroscience, a hypothetical process in which the activation of one neuron is presumed to spread to connected neurons, making it more likely that they will fire. **2.** in cognitive psychology, an analogous model for the association of ideas, memories, and the like, based on the notion that activation of one item stored in memory travels through associated links to activate another item. Spreading activation is a feature of some NETWORK-MEMORY MODELS.

spreading depression a propagating wave of silence in neuronal activity accompanied by a relatively large negative electric potential. Spreading depression occurs in regions of gray matter, including the cerebral cortex and hippocampus. It may occur spontaneously or be evoked by intense local electrical, chemical, or mechanical stimuli.

spurious correlation a situation in which variables are correlated through their common relationship with one or more other variables but not through a causal mechanism. See THIRD-VARIABLE PROBLEM.

S–R abbreviation for stimulus–response.

SRI abbreviation for serotonin reuptake inhibitor. See SSRI.

S–R learning model the hypothesis that learning leads to the formation of stimulus–response connections. In PAVLOVIAN CONDITIONING, this connection is between the conditioned stimulus and the unconditioned response (e.g., between a tone and salivation); in INSTRUMENTAL CONDITIONING, the connection is between the discriminative stimulus and the response (e.g., between a tone and bar pressing).

S–R–O learning model stimulus–response–outcome learning model: in INSTRUMENTAL CONDITIONING, the hypothesis that associations are acquired between a discriminative stimulus, the instrumental response, and the outcome of reinforcement or punishment.

S–R psychology an approach to psychology that conceptualizes behavior in terms of stimulus and response. The fundamental goal is therefore describing functional relationships between stimulus and response, that is, manipulating a stimulus and observing the response. **S–R theories** tend to be behavioral rather than cognitive. Examples include reinforcement theory (see HULL'S MATHEMATICO-DEDUCTIVE THEORY OF LEARNING) and CONTIGUITY LEARNING THEORY. S–R theories are sometimes contrasted with cognitive theories of learning (see S–S LEARNING MODEL).

S–S learning model stimulus–stimulus learning model: any learning theory that is cognitive and emphasizes the formation of associations between stimuli, in contrast to theories based on stimulus–response connections (see S–R PSYCHOLOGY). Examples include PURPOSIVE BEHAVIORISM and Gestalt learning theory. In PAVLOVIAN CONDITIONING, the S–S learning model postulates associations between conditioned and unconditioned stimuli; in INSTRUMENTAL CONDITIONING, the association is between the discriminative stimulus and the reinforcing stimulus.

SSRI selective serotonin reuptake inhibitor: any of a class of antidepressants that are thought to act by blocking the reuptake of serotonin into serotonin-containing presynaptic neurons in the central nervous system. SSRIs also block the activity of certain subtypes of serotonin AUTORECEPTORS, and this may also be associated with their therapeutic effects. SSRIs have less adverse side effects than the TRICYCLIC ANTIDEPRESSANTS and the MONOAMINE OXIDASE INHIBITORS; common side effects include nausea, headache, anxiety, and tremor, and some patients may experience sexual dysfunction. SSRIs include FLUOXETINE, PAROXETINE, SERTRALINE, citalopram, and fluvoxamine. Also called **SRI** (serotonin reuptake inhibitor).

SST 1. abbreviation for SELF-STATEMENT TRAINING. **2.** abbreviation for SINGLE-SESSION THERAPY. **3.** abbreviation for SOCIAL SKILLS TRAINING. **4.** abbreviation for STIMULUS SAMPLING THEORY.

S-state *n*. the sleeping (or sleep) state, as opposed to the D-state (see DREAM STATE) and the W-state (waking state).

stability *n*. the absence of variation or motion, as applied, for example, to genetics (invariance in characteristics), personality (few emotional or mood changes), or body position (absence of body sway).

S

stabilized image an image on the retina that does not move when the eye is moved. A stabilized image will fade rapidly since neurons in the visual system are sensitive to change rather than to maintained stimulation. Even during VISUAL FIXATION images are normally not truly stabilized, because very small eye movements (**microsaccades**) continually refresh the stimulation of the retina by moving the eyes relative to a target.

stage n. a relatively discrete period of time in which functioning is qualitatively different from functioning at other periods.

stages of change the five steps involved in changing health behavior proposed in the TRANSTHEORETICAL MODEL: (a) precontemplation (not thinking about changing behavior), (b) contemplation (considering changing behavior), (c) preparation (occasionally changing behavior), (d) action (participating in the healthful behavior on a regular basis, resulting in major benefits), and (e) maintenance (continuing the behavior after 6 months of regular use).

stages of grief a hypothetical model, originally described in 1969 by Swiss-born U.S. psychiatrist Elisabeth Kübler-Ross (1926–2004), depicting psychological states, moods, or coping strategies that occur during the dying process or during periods of BEREAVEMENT, great loss, or TRAUMA. These begin with the DENIAL STAGE, followed by the ANGER STAGE, BARGAINING STAGE, DEPRESSION STAGE, and ACCEPTANCE STAGE. The model is nonlinear in that the stages do not necessarily occur in the given sequence or for a set period of time; moreover, they can recur and overlap before some degree of psychological and emotional resolution occurs. Also called **grief cycle model**.

STAI abbreviation for STATE–TRAIT ANXIETY INVENTORY.

staircase illusion a three-dimensional impossible figure in which a set of stairs appears to continue rising or descending endlessly. Also called **Penrose staircase**.

staircase method a variation of the METHOD OF LIMITS in which stimuli are presented in ascending and descending order. When the observer's response changes, the direction of the stimulus sequence is reversed. This method is efficient because it does not present stimuli that are well above or below threshold.

staleness n. in sport, the physical and psychological result of overtraining, which persists over time (e.g., 2 weeks or more) and causes a deterioration in performance.

stalking n. **1.** a repeated pattern of following or observing a person in an obsessional, intrusive, or harassing manner. Often associated with a failed relationship with the one pursued, stalking may involve direct threats, the intent to cause distress or bodily harm, and interpersonal violence. It may alternatively be associated with an erotic delusion about the person pursued. See

also DOMESTIC VIOLENCE. **2.** in animal behavior, see PREDATION.

stammering n. see STUTTERING. —**stammer** vb., n.

standard n. any positive idea about how things might be, such as an ideal, norm, value, expectation, or previous performance, that is used to measure and judge the way things are. Evaluation of the self is often based on comparing the current reality (or perceptions of the current reality) against one or more standards.

standard deviation (symbol: SD) a measure of the dispersion of a set of scores, indicating how narrowly or broadly they are distributed around the MEAN. It is equal to the square root of the VARIANCE.

standard error the standard deviation of a sampling distribution. For example, the **standard error of the mean** is the standard deviation of the sampling distribution of the mean, equal to $\sigma/\sqrt{n}$, where σ is the standard deviation of the original distribution and n is the sample size.

standard error of estimate a measure of the degree to which a regression line (a geometric representation of the REGRESSION EQUATION) fits a set of data. If y' is an estimated value from a regression line and y is the actual value, then the standard error of estimate is

$$\sqrt{[\Sigma(y - y')^2/n]},$$

where n is the number of points.

standard error of measurement (symbol: SEM) in measurement theory, the error in estimating true scores from observed scores.

standardization n. the process of establishing NORMS or uniform procedures for a test.

standardized test a test whose VALIDITY and RELIABILITY have been established by thorough empirical investigation and analysis and which has clearly defined norms.

standard language the generally accepted version of a language that is associated with formal and official contexts and with high-status users. Generally speaking, it will be the version used in the mainstream media and taught to schoolchildren and second-language learners. Most languages have a number of nonstandard varieties that differ from the standard language in pronunciation, vocabulary, and grammar.

standard observer in sensation and perception research, the hypothetical ideal observer.

standard score a score obtained from an original score by subtracting the mean value of all scores in the batch and dividing by the standard deviation of the batch. This conversion from raw scores to standard scores allows comparisons to be made between measurements on different scales. A standard score is often given the symbol z and is sometimes referred to as a **z score**.

standards of practice a set of guidelines that delineate the expected techniques and procedures, and the order in which to use them, for interventions with individuals experiencing a range of psychological, medical, or educational conditions. Standards of practice have been developed by the American Psychological Association and other professional associations to ensure that practitioners use the most researched and validated treatment plans.

standard stimulus a stimulus used as the basis of comparison for other stimuli in an experiment, for example, in comparing loud sounds to a sound of a given intensity.

Stanford–Binet Intelligence Scale (SB) a standardized assessment of intelligence and cognitive abilities. It currently includes five verbal subtests and five nonverbal subtests that yield Verbal, Nonverbal, and Full Scale IQs (with a mean of 100 and a standard deviation of 15) as well as Fluid Reasoning, Knowledge, Quantitative Reasoning, Visual-Spatial Processing, and Working Memory index scores. The Stanford–Binet test was so named because it was brought to the United States by U.S. psychologist Lewis M. Terman (1877–1956), a professor at Stanford University, in 1916, as a revision and extension of the original **Binet–Simon Scale** (the first modern intelligence test) developed in 1905 by French psychologist Alfred Binet (1857–1911) and French physician Théodore Simon (1873–1961) to assess the intellectual ability of French children.

stanine *n.* a division of a range of scores into nine parts, the scores having a NORMAL DISTRIBUTION. The stanine scale has a mean of 5 (i.e., stanine 5 is the average) and a standard deviation of 2. In a given set of scores, the lowest 4% fall in stanine 1, the next 7% in 2, the next 12% in 3, 17% in 4, 20% in 5, 17% in 6, 12% in 7, 7% in 8, and 4% in 9 (the highest scoring range).

stapedius muscle a middle ear muscle that controls the movement of the stapes, one of the ear OSSICLES. Its activation (the **stapedius reflex**) is part of the ACOUSTIC REFLEX.

stapes *n.* (*pl.* **stapedes**) see OSSICLES.

star compass see SUN COMPASS.

startle response an unlearned, rapid, reflexlike response to sudden, unexpected, intense stimuli (loud noises, flashing lights, etc.). This response includes behaviors that serve a protective function, such as closing the eyes, frowning by drawing the eyebrows together, compressing the lips, lowering the head, hunching the shoulders, and bending the trunk and knee. The reaction can be neutralized by context, inhibition, and habituation. Also called **startle reaction**.

stasis *n.* a condition of stability, equilibrium, or inactivity, as opposed to a state of flux or change. —**static** *adj.*

state *n.* the condition or status of an entity or system at a particular time that is characterized by relative stability of its basic components or elements.

state anxiety anxiety in response to a specific situation that is perceived as threatening or dangerous. State anxiety varies in intensity and fluctuates over time. Compare TRAIT ANXIETY.

state-dependent learning learning that occurs in a particular biological or psychological state and is better recalled when the individual is subsequently in the same state. For example, an animal trained to run a maze while under the influence of a psychoactive drug (e.g., pentobarbital) may not run it successfully without the drug. See also CONTEXT-SPECIFIC LEARNING.

state-dependent memory a condition in which memory for a past event is improved when the person is in the same biological or psychological state as when the memory was initially formed. Thus, alcohol may improve recall of events experienced when previously under the influence of alcohol. See also MOOD-DEPENDENT MEMORY.

statement validity analysis a collection of techniques used to assess the truth of statements given during investigations, such as the truth of allegations made by children during interviews concerning sexual abuse. The focus is on the words themselves, independent of case facts. These provide various criteria enabling interviewers to distinguish between plausible and implausible accounts. See also CRITERION-BASED CONTENT ANALYSIS.

state space a graphical representation used to characterize game playing and other search-based problem solving. A state space has four components: (a) a set of nodes or states, (b) a set of arcs linking subsets of the states or nodes, (c) a nonempty set of nodes indicated as the start nodes of the space, and (d) a nonempty set of goal nodes of the space. An architecture such as a PRODUCTION SYSTEM or CLASSIFIER SYSTEM can generate a state space search.

states versus transformations in PIAGETIAN THEORY, the extent to which a child's attention is focused on states (e.g., the appearance of an object) rather than transformations (i.e., what is done to the object), and vice versa, at different stages of cognitive development. At the PREOPERATIONAL STAGE children center their attention on specific states and ignore the transformations between states, whereas the reverse is true for children at the CONCRETE OPERATIONAL STAGE.

state theories of hypnosis theories positing that HYPNOTIC INDUCTION evokes a unique altered state of consciousness in the participant. Compare NONSTATE THEORIES OF HYPNOSIS.

State–Trait Anxiety Inventory (STAI) a self-report assessment device that includes separate measures of STATE ANXIETY and TRAIT ANXIETY. The state anxiety items measure the intensity of anxiety experienced by participants in specific situations; the trait anxiety items assess the frequency with which respondents experience anxiety in the face of perceived threats in the environment.

statistic *n.* any function of the observations in a

set of data. Statistics may be used to describe a batch of data, to estimate parameters in optimal ways, or to test hypotheses.

statistical analysis examination of data through the use of probabilistic models in order to make inferences and draw conclusions.

statistical control the use of statistical methods to reduce the effect of factors that could not be eliminated or controlled during an experiment.

statistical error any error of sampling, measurement, or analysis that interferes with drawing a valid conclusion from the data so obtained, for example, in the context of experimental results.

statistical learning theory a theoretical approach that uses mathematical models to describe processes of learning. The term is often specifically applied to STIMULUS SAMPLING THEORY but can be more generally applied to other theories.

statistical psychology the branch of psychology that uses statistical models and methods to derive descriptions and explanations of phenomena.

statistical significance the degree to which a result cannot reasonably be attributed to the operation of chance or random factors alone.

statistics *n.* the branch of mathematics that uses data descriptively or inferentially to find or support answers for scientific and other quantifiable questions. —**statistical** *adj.* —**statistician** *n.*

status *n.* **1.** the state or position of an individual or group, for example, an individual's standing in a social group. See SOCIAL STATUS. **2.** a persistent condition, as in STATUS EPILEPTICUS.

status epilepticus a continuous series of seizures. It is a life-threatening condition that requires immediate medical treatment, usually by intravenous medication.

status generalization the tendency for individuals who are known to have achieved or been ascribed authority, respect, and prestige in one context to enjoy relatively higher status in other, unrelated, contexts. Well-known athletes or wealthy individuals, for example, may rise rapidly to positions of authority in groups even when these DIFFUSE-STATUS CHARACTERISTICS (athleticism, wealth) are not relevant in the current group context. See also EXPECTATION-STATES THEORY.

status relations patterns of relative prestige and respect that determine deference and authority within a group or organization, that is, the "chain of command," DOMINANCE HIERARCHY, or pecking order.

STD abbreviation for SEXUALLY TRANSMITTED DISEASE.

steady state a condition of stability or equilibrium. For example, in behavioral studies it is a state in which behavior is practically the same over repeated observations in a particular context. In pharmacology, it refers to a state in the body in which the amount of drug administered is equal to that excreted.

Steele–Richardson–Olszewski syndrome see PROGRESSIVE SUPRANUCLEAR PALSY. [John C. **Steele** and John Clifford **Richardson**, 20th-century Canadian neurologists; Jerzy **Olszewski** (1913–1964), Polish-born Canadian neuropathologist]

stem-and-leaf plot a graphical method for the display of data that resembles a HISTOGRAM but carries more detailed information about the values of the data points.

stem cell a cell that is itself undifferentiated but can divide to produce one or more types of specialized tissue cells (e.g., blood cells, nerve cells). Stem cells are found in embryos (**embryonic stem cells**) but also occur in adults as **tissue stem cells**. Adult and embryonic stem cell research have the potential for changing treatment of disease through use of the cells to repair specific tissues and, even, to grow organs (see REGENERATIVE MEDICINE). Although the ethics of the more recent embryonic stem cell research are the subject of debate, stem cell research and treatments using adult cells has occurred since the 1960s (e.g., the use of bone marrow stem cells in the treatment of leukemia and lymphoma).

stem-completion task a task in which people are asked to provide complete words when given the first few letters. For example, given *ele*— a participant might say *elevate* or *elephant*.

stenosis *n.* the abnormal narrowing of a body conduit or passage. For example, **carotid stenosis** is narrowing of a CAROTID ARTERY (e.g., by atherosclerosis), which limits blood flow to the brain, and **aortic stenosis** is narrowing of the aortic valve leading from the left ventricle, thereby restricting blood flow from the heart to the general circulation. —**stenotic** *adj.*

step-down test a memory test used in studies of shock-avoidance learning in rats and mice. When the animal first steps down from an elevated platform in the test chamber, it is given an electric shock. On subsequent test trials, the time taken to step down is measured as an indication of memory for the shock experience.

stepfamily *n.* a family unit formed by the union of parents one or both of whom brings a child or children from a previous union (or unions) into the new household. Also called **blended family**; **reconstituted family**.

stepwise regression a group of regression techniques that enter predictor (independent) variables into (or delete them from) the REGRESSION EQUATION one variable (or block of variables) at a time according to some predefined criterion. It is contrasted with ordinary **least squares regression**, which enters all variables simultaneously.

stereoacuity *n.* see STEREOSCOPIC ACUITY.

stereoblindness *n.* the inability to see depth using the cue of BINOCULAR DISPARITY, causing impaired depth perception. Stereoblindness is thought to affect 5–10% of the general population. It is associated with STRABISMUS during early childhood, but may also be caused by occipitotemporal brain injury.

stereochemical smell theory the concept that certain odors are perceived because they are produced by odorants (airborne volatile substances) whose stereochemical properties have certain shapes. Seven classes of odorants are postulated: camphoraceous, ethereal, floral, minty, musty, pungent, and putrid. The odorant molecules are thought to fit receptors in a lock-and-key manner that causes the neural membrane to become depolarized or hyperpolarized, which in turn is the cue that produces an odor experience. Since many odorants that share a similar molecular structure produce different odor experiences, it has been hypothesized that the lock-and-key principle may be modified by the orientation of the molecules at the receptor surfaces. Also called **lock-and-key theory**; **steric theory of odor**.

stereocilia *pl. n.* see HAIR CELL.

stereognosis *n.* the ability to identify the form and nature of an object by touch.

stereogram *n.* a picture perceived to have depth because it is produced by the binocular summation of two separate images of the same scene, each image slightly offset from the other in the horizontal plane. Although a **stereoscope** is commonly used to view the images, some observers can fuse the two images by simply crossing or uncrossing their eyes.

stereopsis *n.* DEPTH PERCEPTION provided by means of the BINOCULAR DISPARITY of the images in the two eyes. Also called **stereoscopic vision**.

stereoscopic acuity visual acuity for the perception of depth. Also called **stereoacuity**.

stereotaxy *n.* determination of the exact location of a specific area within the body (e.g., the exact location of a nerve center in the brain) by means of three-dimensional measurements. Stereotaxy is used for positioning MICROELECTRODES, CANNULAS, or other devices in the brain for diagnostic, experimental, or therapeutic purposes and for locating an area of the brain prior to surgery. It involves the coordinated use of a **stereotactic atlas**, a map of the brain featuring a coordinate system and consisting of images and schematic representations of nerve fibers and other structures and serial sections of the brain, and a **stereotactic instrument**, a device that prohibits damage to neighboring tissues by holding the individual's head absolutely still in the appropriate position. **—stereotactic** or **stereotaxic** *adj.*

stereotype *n.* a set of cognitive generalizations (e.g., beliefs, expectations) about the qualities and characteristics of the members of a particular group or social category. Stereotypes simplify and expedite perceptions and judgments, but they are often exaggerated, negative rather than positive, and resistant to revision even when perceivers encounter individuals with qualities that are not congruent with the stereotype (see PREJUDICE). Unlike individually held expectations about others based on their category memberships, stereotypes are widely shared by group members. See NEGATIVE STEREOTYPE; POSITIVE STEREOTYPE. See also GENDER STEREOTYPE; INSTANCE THEORY; KERNEL-OF-TRUTH HYPOTHESIS. **—stereotypic** *adj.*

stereotype accuracy the ability to determine accurately in what way and to what extent a person's traits correspond to a STEREOTYPE associated with his or her age group, ethnic group, professional group, or other relevant group. Compare DIFFERENTIAL ACCURACY.

stereotypic movement disorder a disorder characterized by repetitive, nonfunctional, and often self-injurious behaviors, such as head banging, biting or hitting parts of the body, rocking, or hand waving. It may be associated with mental retardation and is distinguished from other disorders marked by stereotyped movements, such as TIC DISORDERS and PERVASIVE DEVELOPMENTAL DISORDERS.

stereotypy *n.* **1.** persistent pathological repetition of the same words, phrases, sounds, or movements. It is a common symptom in children with autism and in individuals with obsessive-compulsive disorder or catatonic schizophrenia. Stereotypy is also seen in nonhuman animals under conditions of social isolation, early social deprivation, or neglect. Also called **stereotyped behavior**. See STEREOTYPIC MOVEMENT DISORDER. **2.** repetitive behavior or gestures that are within the normal spectrum.

sterility *n.* the condition of being incapable of producing offspring, either because of INFERTILITY or surgical or medical intervention (see STERILIZATION). **—sterile** *adj.*

sterilization *n.* the process of rendering an organism incapable of sexual reproduction. This may be accomplished surgically or it may result from injury or from exposure to radiation, heat, or chemicals.

steroid *n.* any organic molecule that is based on four interconnected hydrocarbon rings. The male and female SEX HORMONES are steroids, as are the CORTICOSTEROIDS and other natural substances, such as vitamin D and cholesterol.

steroid hormone any of a class of hormones whose molecular structure is based on the steroid nucleus of four interconnected rings of carbon atoms. Examples include the SEX HORMONES and CORTICOSTEROIDS.

Stevens law a psychophysical relationship stating that the psychological magnitude of a sensation is proportional to a power of the stimulus producing it. This can be expressed as $\psi = ks^n$, where ψ is the sensation, k is a constant of proportionality, s is the stimulus magnitude, and n

is a function of the particular stimulus. Also called **Stevens power law**. See also FECHNER'S LAW; WEBER'S LAW. [Stanley Smith **Stevens** (1906–1973), U.S. psychophysicist]

stigma *n.* the negative social attitude attached to a characteristic of an individual that may be regarded as a mental, physical, or social deficiency. A stigma implies social disapproval and can lead unfairly to discrimination against and exclusion of the individual.

stimulant *n.* any of various agents that excite functional activity in an organism or in a part of an organism. Stimulants are usually classified according to the body system or function excited (e.g., cardiac stimulants, respiratory stimulants). In psychology, the term usually refers to the CNS STIMULANTS (or psychostimulants).

stimulation *n.* the act or process of increasing the level of activity of an organism, particularly that of evoking heightened activity in (eliciting a response from) a sensory receptor, neuron, or other bodily tissue. See also ELECTRICAL STIMULATION.

stimulus *n.* (*pl.* **stimuli**) **1.** any agent, event, or situation—internal or external—that elicits a response from an organism. See CONDITIONED STIMULUS; UNCONDITIONED STIMULUS. **2.** any change in physical energy that activates a sensory RECEPTOR. See DISTAL STIMULUS; PROXIMAL STIMULUS.

stimulus-bound *adj.* **1.** relating to a perception that is largely dependent on the qualities of the stimulation and thus involves little or no interpretation. **2.** describing relatively inflexible behavior that involves little if any deliberation or reflection and is determined primarily by the nature of the stimulus (e.g., a monkey issuing a particular alarm call when a leopard approaches).

stimulus control the extent to which behavior is influenced by different stimulus conditions. It can refer to different responses occurring in the presence of different stimuli or to differences in the rate, temporal organization, or physical characteristics of a single response in the presence of different stimuli.

stimulus differentiation 1. a process whereby an organism learns to discriminate between two stimuli by responding differently to them, for example, by responding in the presence of one stimulus but not the other. See also DISCRIMINATION LEARNING. **2.** in Gestalt psychology, the process of distinguishing different parts or patterns in a visual field.

stimulus discrimination 1. the ability to distinguish among different stimuli (e.g., to distinguish a circle from an ellipse). **2.** differential responding in the presence of different stimuli.

stimulus equivalence the condition in which two or more related stimuli elicit the same response.

stimulus evaluation checks assessments made on several dimensions when an individual

evaluates the impact of an event and hence its emotional intensity and quality. Examples of stimulus evaluation checks include checks for novelty, goal relevance, and congruity–incongruity of actions or events with social expectations.

stimulus filtering the specialization of the nervous system so that only critical stimuli reach the brain and irrelevant stimuli do not. For example, moths have ears with only two neurons: The neurons respond only to sounds in the frequency range of bat ultrasound, and successive filters in the moth's central nervous system ensure that only bat-produced sounds reach the brain.

stimulus generalization the spread of effects of conditioning (either operant or Pavlovian) to stimuli that differ in certain aspects from the stimulus present during original conditioning. For example, a dog conditioned to bark when a particular bell sounds tends to bark to bells of any pitch.

stimulus onset asynchrony the time between the onset of one stimulus and the onset of the following stimulus. The term is used mainly in experiments with MASKING.

stimulus overload the condition in which the environment presents too many stimuli to be comfortably processed, resulting in stress and behavior designed to restore equilibrium.

stimulus–response (**S–R**) see S–R PSYCHOLOGY.

stimulus–response compatibility the extent to which the relationship between stimulus and response facilitates response. Speed and accuracy are affected by this relationship; for example, a left keypress in response to a stimulus on the left will be quicker and more accurate than a right keypress for a stimulus on the left.

stimulus sampling a procedure for increasing the generalizability of research results by using multiple stimuli within a category as representative of an experimental condition, as opposed to selecting a single stimulus whose unique characteristics may distort results. For example, a study investigating the effects of gender on monetary generosity would demonstrate stimulus sampling if it employed a variety of different males and females to elicit donations from participants, instead of using a single male and a single female.

stimulus sampling theory (**SST**) a MATHEMATICAL LEARNING THEORY stating that stimuli are composed of hypothetical elements and that on any given learning trial a sample of those elements becomes associated with the desired response.

stimulus set in reaction-time experiments, the expectancy or readiness associated with concentration on the stimulus.

stimulus situation all the components of an occurrence or experience that, taken as a whole, comprise a stimulus to which an organism responds. The term is used to highlight the complexity of behavior-arousing events and contrasts with the approach of traditional behavior analysts, who tend to break down stimuli into smaller, separate elements.

stimulus–stimulus learning model see S–S LEARNING MODEL.

stimulus value 1. the strength of a given stimulus, measured in standard units (e.g., a shock of 40 volts). **2.** a theoretical characteristic of a stimulus said to index its effectiveness as a REINFORCER.

stirrup *n.* see OSSICLES.

STM abbreviation for SHORT-TERM MEMORY.

stochastic *adj.* **1.** random, or arising from chance or conjecture. **2.** describing a system or process that follows a random probability pattern, such that events may be analyzed according to their statistical probability but not accurately predicted. See PROBABILISM.

Stockholm syndrome a mental and emotional response in which a captive (e.g., a hostage) displays seeming loyalty to—even affection for—the captor. The name derives from the case of a woman who in 1973 was held hostage at a bank in Stockholm, Sweden, and became romantically involved with one of the robbers.

stop *n.* see PLOSIVE.

stop-signal task a procedure used in choice-reaction tasks in which a signal instructing the participant to withhold the response is presented on some trials at varying intervals after presentation of the stimulus. This is done to determine at what point in processing a response can no longer be inhibited.

storage *n.* the state of an item that is retained in memory, after ENCODING and before RETRIEVAL. See also RETENTION.

storytelling *n.* **1.** the recounting by a client of the events, concerns, and problems that led him or her to seek treatment. Therapists can learn much about the motives and origins of conflicts by attending carefully (see ACTIVE LISTENING) to the stories that clients bring to the session. **2.** the use of symbolic talk and allegorical stories by the therapist to aid the client's understanding of issues. Also called **therapeutic storytelling**.

stotting *n.* a stiff-legged jumping display, given by many species of ungulates, in which all four legs are off the ground at the same time. Stotting appears to communicate to predators that the individual has enough vigor to make capture difficult.

strabismus *n.* any chronic abnormal alignment of the eyes. Because strabismic eyes look in different directions, they give the brain conflicting messages, which may result in DOUBLE VISION or the suppression by the brain of one eye's view altogether. The most common form of strabismus occurs horizontally: One or both eyes deviate inward (**convergent strabismus**) or outward (**diver-**

gent strabismus). However, the deviation may be upward (**hypertropia**), downward (**hypotropia**), or, in rare cases, twisted clockwise or counterclockwise (**cyclotropia**). Also called **heterotropia**; **squint**. **—strabismic** *adj.*

straight *adj.* a colloquial term for heterosexual.

strain *n.* **1.** the state of a system on which excessive demands are made. Examples include muscular strain (excessive tension in a muscle usually due to an activity overload) and psychological strain, usually due to an emotional overload. **2.** a specific group within a species whose members possess a common distinguishing characteristic.

straitjacket *n.* an article of clothing that was formerly used to restrain patients in mental hospitals from injuring themselves or others and, in some cases, for punishment. It consisted of a canvas shirt with long sleeves that could be fastened behind the patient's back after folding his or her arms in front of the body.

stranger anxiety the distress and apprehension experienced by young children when they are around individuals who are unfamiliar to them. Stranger anxiety is a normal part of cognitive development: Babies differentiate caregivers from other people and display a strong preference for familiar faces. Stranger anxiety usually begins around 8 or 9 months of age and typically lasts into the 2nd year.

Strange Situation an experimental technique used to assess quality of ATTACHMENT in infants and young children (up to the age of 2). The procedure subjects the child to increasing amounts of stress induced by a strange setting, the entrance of an unfamiliar person, and two brief separations from the parent. The reaction of the child to each of these situations is used to evaluate the security or insecurity of his or her attachment to the parent.

strategic family therapy a group of approaches to FAMILY THERAPY in which the focus is on identifying and applying novel interventions to produce behavioral change rather than on helping the family gain insight into the sources of their problems. Also called **strategic intervention therapy**.

strategy *n.* a program of action designed to achieve a goal or accomplish a task. The term is used in a variety of contexts. For example, in artificial intelligence it denotes a specific approach used for designing SEARCHES of a problem or game space. Strategies in this sense are used to determine which state in the search is to be considered next and are often called HEURISTICS. In biology, however, the term refers to an approach for ensuring REPRODUCTIVE SUCCESS, as in a K-STRATEGY or an R-STRATEGY.

stratification *n.* arrangement into a layered configuration, as for example in SOCIAL STRATIFICATION. **—stratify** *vb.*

stratified random sampling RANDOM SAM-

PLING conducted within strata or subdivisions of a population, so that the sample obtained (called a **stratified sample**) includes individuals representing each stratum (e.g., young and old or men and women). The proportion of the sample to be collected from each stratum is determined before sampling begins.

stratum *n. (pl.* **strata**) a layer (typically one of a number of parallel layers) in a structure, such as a level or class within society (see SOCIAL STRATIFICATION) or any of the subpopulations in survey SAMPLING.

streaming *n.* **1.** in audition, the perception of a sequence of sounds as a unitary object. Under certain conditions several streams may be perceived nearly simultaneously, as in musical counterpoint. **2.** in education, the separation of students into different categories (streams) of academic ability based on, for example, test results or prior achievements, with each stream having a unique curriculum designed for the needs and capabilities of those within it.

stream of consciousness the concept of consciousness as a continuous, dynamic flow of ideas and images rather than a static series of discrete components. It emphasizes the subjective quality of conscious experience as a never-ending and never-repeating stream.

street intelligence the skills people apply in their everyday lives. The term evolved from research conducted in the 1990s, which found that children in Brazil did very poorly in paper-and-pencil tests of the skills that they showed themselves well able to use in street contexts. The street intelligence of these children can be viewed as situated intelligence (see SITUATED COGNITION) that failed to transfer to a specific testing environment.

strength of an attitude the extent to which an attitude persists over time, resists change, influences information processing, and guides behavior. Strong attitudes possess all four of these defining features, whereas weak attitudes lack these features.

strength of association in statistics, the degree of relationship between two or more variables. Common measures are OMEGA SQUARED and COEFFICIENT OF MULTIPLE DETERMINATION.

stress *n.* **1.** a state of physiological or psychological response to internal or external forces or events, involving changes affecting nearly every system of the body. For example, it may be manifested by palpitations, sweating, dry mouth, shortness of breath, fidgeting, faster speech, augmentation of negative emotions (if already being experienced), and longer duration of fatigue. Severe stress is manifested by the GENERAL ADAPTATION SYNDROME. By causing these mind–body changes, stress contributes directly to psychological and physiological disorder and disease and affects mental and physical health, reducing the quality of life. **2.** in linguistics, emphasis placed on a word or syllable in speech, generally by pronouncing it more loudly and deliberately than its neighboring units and slightly prolonging its duration. See also ACCENT.

stress-decompensation model a concept of the development of abnormal behavior as a result of high levels of stress that lead to the gradual but progressive deterioration of normal behavior to a level that is highly disorganized and dysfunctional.

stress immunization the concept that mild stress early in life makes an individual better able to handle stress later in life.

stress-induced analgesia a reduced sensitivity to pain that an organism may experience when exposed to extreme physical trauma. The precise mechanism is uncertain but may be related to the production of large quantities of ENDORPHINS.

stress-inoculation training a four-phase training program for stress-management often used in COGNITIVE BEHAVIOR THERAPY. Phase 1 entails the identification of reactions to stress and their effects on functioning and psychological well-being; phase 2 involves learning relaxation and self-regulation techniques; phase 3 consists of learning coping self-statements (see SELF-STATEMENT TRAINING); phase 4 involves assisted progression through a series of increasingly stressful situations using imagery, video, role playing, and real-life situations until the individual is eventually able to cope with the original stress-inducing situation or event.

stress interview an interview in which the person being questioned is deliberately subjected to confrontational, hostile, emotionally unsettling, or otherwise stressful conditions, such as a combination of aggressive questioning and environmental influences (e.g., harsh lighting). Such techniques are mainly associated with police or military interrogations; in personnel selection they have sometimes been used to test an individual's ability to manage pressure and handle stress but are generally considered of questionable validity.

stress management the use of specific techniques, strategies, or programs—such as relaxation training, anticipation of stress reactions, and breathing techniques—for dealing with stress-inducing situations and the state of being stressed.

stressor *n.* any event, force, or condition that results in physical or emotional stress. Stressors may be internal or external forces that require adjustment or COPING STRATEGIES on the part of the affected individual.

stress test 1. an examination or evaluation designed to ascertain an individual's capacity to perform a relatively complex task under purposefully stressful conditions. **2.** a medical evaluation designed to assess the effects of stress, typically induced by physical exercise, on cardiac function. The most common of such procedures is a test in which the patient walks or runs on a treadmill while cardiac, respiratory, or other physiological processes are monitored.

stress training activities designed to help individuals understand the causes of stress and learn strategies for managing and preventing it. Realistic training and simulation (e.g., water survival, escape training, firefighting) are seen as necessary instructional strategies to prepare personnel in certain types of work to operate in stressful environments.

stress–vulnerability model in schizophrenia and mood disorders, the theory that a genetic or biological predisposition to these illnesses exists and that psychological and social factors can increase the likelihood of symptomatic episodes. See also DIATHESIS–STRESS MODEL.

stretch receptor a RECEPTOR cell that responds primarily to stretching of muscles. Stretch receptors include the MUSCLE SPINDLES of skeletal muscle.

stretch reflex the contraction of a muscle in response to stretching of that muscle. Stretch reflexes support the body against the pull of gravity. Also called **myotatic reflex**.

striate cortex the first region of the cerebral cortex that receives visual input from the thalamus, particularly from the lateral GENICULATE NUCLEUS. The striate cortex is located in the occipital lobe and contains a dense band of myelinated fibers that appears as a white stripe (stripe of Gennari). Neurons in the striate cortex project to visual areas in the PRESTRIATE CORTEX and to subcortical visual nuclei. Also called **Brodmann's area 17**; **primary visual cortex**.

striated muscle see SKELETAL MUSCLE.

striatum *n.* see BASAL GANGLIA.

stridulation *n.* see VOCAL COMMUNICATION.

stroke *n.* disruption of blood flow to the brain, which deprives the tissue of oxygen and nutrients, causing tissue damage and loss of normal function and, potentially, tissue death. A stroke may result from massive bleeding into brain tissue (**hemorrhagic stroke**); an embolism (obstructing material) or thrombus (blood clot) blocking an artery in the brain (**embolic stroke** or **thrombotic stroke**); or multiple small areas of brain tissue death from occlusion of small branches of the cerebral arteries (**lacunar stroke**). This term is often used interchangeably with CEREBROVASCULAR ACCIDENT. See also TRANSIENT ISCHEMIC ATTACK.

Stroop Color–Word Interference Test a three-part test in which (a) color names are read as fast as possible; (b) the colors of bars or other shapes are rapidly named; and, most importantly, (c) color hues are named quickly when used to print the names of other colors (such as the word *green* printed in the color red). The degree to which the participants are subject to interference by the printed words is a measure of their cognitive flexibility and selective attention. Also called **Stroop test**. See also RESPONSE COM-

PETITION. [John Ridley **Stroop** (1897–1973), U.S. psychologist]

Stroop effect the finding that the time it takes a participant to name the color of ink in which a word is printed is longer for words that denote incongruent color names than for neutral words or for words that denote a congruent color. For example, if the word *blue* is written in red ink (incongruent), participants take longer to say "red" than if the word *glue* is written in red ink (neutral) or if the word *red* is written in red ink (congruent). See STROOP COLOR–WORD INTERFERENCE TEST. [John **Stroop**]

structural analysis 1. in psychology, any theory of the organization of mind or personality that attempts to differentiate between component parts and to define the relationship of part to part and part to whole. Such an analysis can be contrasted with one based on function, dynamics, or behavior. **2.** in linguistics, an analysis of a word, phrase, sentence, or longer unit in terms of its formal constituents. See PHRASE-STRUCTURE GRAMMAR.

structural disorder a disorder related to a defect in or damage to the structure of an organ or tissue, such as the nervous system.

structural equation modeling (**SEM**) a statistical modeling technique that includes LATENT VARIABLES as causal elements. SEM is an advanced statistical method for testing causal models involving constructs that cannot be directly measured but are, rather, approximated through several measures presumed to assess part of the given construct.

structural family therapy a type of FAMILY THERAPY that provides a method for the rational solution of problems, based on the theory that these problems are the result of poorly structured family relationships. For example, a father may behave more like a teenage son, whereas an elder daughter may behave more like a parent, a situation that eventually causes problems for one or both. To improve this structure, the entire family system and the part each person plays in that system must be modified.

structural group a therapeutic group made up of individuals selected for those characteristics that would make them most likely to be successful in achieving the goals sought in the therapy. People of different types, temperaments, personalities, and educational levels are combined in a group, based on the concept that their interaction will maximize each other's benefits in the therapeutic process. Also called **structured group**.

structuralism 1. a movement considered to be the first school of psychology as a science, independent of philosophy. Usually attributed to German psychologist and physiologist Wilhelm Wundt (1832–1920), but probably more directly influenced by British-born U.S. psychologist Edward Bradford Titchener (1867–1927), structuralism defined psychology as the study of mental experience and sought to investigate the structure of such experience through a systematic program of experiments based on trained INTROSPECTION. Also called **structural psychology**. **2.** a movement in various disciplines that study human behavior and culture that enjoyed particular currency in the 1960s and 1970s. The movement took its impetus from the radically new approach to linguistic analysis pioneered by Swiss linguist Ferdinand de Saussure (1857–1913). Against the prevailing approaches, Saussure maintained that a language is a closed system that must be approached through the detail of its internal structure; linguistic SIGNS (written or spoken words) acquire meaning not through their relationships to external referents but through their structural relationships to other signs in the same system (see ARBITRARY SYMBOL). The meaning of any particular use of language is therefore grounded in the total abstract system of that language, which is largely defined by a pattern of functional contrasts between elements (see BINARY FEATURE). The structuralist model of language was extended to cover essentially all social and cultural phenomena, including human thought and action, in the work of French anthropologist Claude Lévi-Strauss (1908–   ). For structuralists in anthropology and the other social sciences, there is a connection between the events of the lived world and a deeper structure of abstract relationships and ideas that provides meaning to the events. Structuralist explanations play down individual autonomy and agency, positivistic science, and linear-time causation in favor of explanations in terms of structural and systemic influences operating in the present to produce rule-governed behavior, the true nature of which can be revealed as the underlying structures are revealed. From the 1970s structuralism increasingly gave way to POSTSTRUCTURALISM.

structural model in psychoanalytic theory, the view that the total personality comprises three divisions or functions: (a) the ID, which represents instinctual drives; (b) the EGO, which controls id drives and mediates between them and external reality; and (c) the SUPEREGO, which comprises moral precepts and ideals. Austrian psychiatrist Sigmund Freud (1856–1939) proposed this model in 1923 to replace his earlier TOPOGRAPHIC MODEL, in which the mind was divided into three regions: the UNCONSCIOUS, PRECONSCIOUS, and CONSCIOUS. Also called **structural approach**. See also DYNAMIC MODEL; ECONOMIC MODEL.

structural psychology see STRUCTURALISM.

structural therapy a system of treatment for children with AUTISTIC DISORDER, which provides a structured environment emphasizing physical and verbal stimulation in a gamelike setting. The purpose is to increase the amount and variety of stimuli received by the children, thereby helping them to relate to their environment in a more realistic manner.

structure *n.* a relatively stable arrangement of elements or components organized so as to form an integrated whole. Structure is often contrasted with FUNCTION to emphasize how something is organized or patterned rather than what it does. —**structural** *adj.*

structured interview an interview consisting of a predetermined set of questions or topics. Structured interviews are popular in marketing research, personnel selection, and other fields. Compare PATTERNED INTERVIEW; UNSTRUCTURED INTERVIEW.

structured learning a complex system of psychotherapy based on the idea of teaching individuals the skills and behaviors associated with leading healthy and satisfying lives and then helping them gain the ability to consistently and reliably apply these skills outside therapy. This approach involves four essential components: MODELING, ROLE PLAY, performance feedback, and TRANSFER OF TRAINING. The individual is provided with examples of specific behavior to be imitated, is allowed to practice that behavior, is given feedback regarding the performance of the behavior, and completes HOMEWORK assignments that encourage the use of the behavior in real-world situations.

structured observational measures methods for measuring overt behaviors and interpersonal processes that require that each observed unit of action be classified into an objectively defined category. INTERACTION-PROCESS ANALYSIS and SYMLOG are examples of such classification systems.

structured play organized play that is governed by rules and controlled or directed by an adult. A teacher-initiated classroom activity is an example. Compare FREE PLAY.

structure of intellect model a model of intelligence that postulates five operations (cognition, memory, divergent production, convergent production, evaluation), six products (units, classes, relations, systems, transformations, implications), and five contents (symbolic, semantic, behavioral, auditory, visual), for a total of 150 separate factors of intelligence (120 in an earlier version of the theory). See also GUILFORD DIMENSIONS OF INTELLIGENCE.

structuring *n.* the explanation by a counselor or therapist, usually during the first session of a course of treatment, of the specific procedures and conditions of the process. This includes the intended results of treatment, time restrictions, fees, and the function and responsibilities of both client and counselor or therapist. See also CONTRACT.

student counseling see EDUCATIONAL COUNSELING.

Student's t distribution see T DISTRIBUTION. [**Student**, pseudonym of William S. Gosset (1876–1937), British statistician]

study *n.* **1.** any research investigation, but particularly a project, such as a survey or systematic observation, that is less rigorously controlled than a true EXPERIMENT. **2.** any attempt to acquire and remember information.

stupor *n.* a mental state in which an individual is unresponsive and immobile and experiences DISORIENTATION.

stuttering *n.* a disturbance in the normal fluency and time patterning of speech. It is characterized by frequent repetition or prolongation of sounds, syllables, or words, with hesitations and pauses that disrupt speech, particularly in situations where communication is important or stressful. Also called **stammering**. —**stutter** *vb., n.*

subacute spongiform encephalopathy (**SSE**) see CREUTZFELDT–JAKOB DISEASE.

subarachnoid space a space beneath the delicate arachnoid mater (the middle of the three MENINGES that surround the brain and spinal cord) occupied by cerebrospinal fluid. Bleeding into this space, typically as the result of trauma or a ruptured ANEURYSM, is a condition called a **subarachnoid hemorrhage** that initially manifests as a severe headache but rapidly may progress to loss of consciousness, coma, and death.

subception *n.* a reaction to an emotion-provoking stimulus that is not clearly enough perceived to be reportable, although its effects may be observed indirectly by the electrodermal response or by a longer than expected reaction time.

subconscious 1. *adj.* denoting mental processes that occur outside consciousness. **2.** *n.* in the STRUCTURAL MODEL of Austrian psychiatrist Sigmund Freud (1856–1939), the concept of the mind beneath the level of consciousness, comprising the PRECONSCIOUS and the UNCONSCIOUS.

subcortical *adj.* relating to structures or processes of the nervous system that are located or take place below the level of the cerebral cortex. For example, a **subcortical center** is any region of the brain at a level below the cerebral cortex that has a particular function or functions (e.g., the THALAMUS, HYPOTHALAMUS, and BASAL GANGLIA). Within each subcortical structure may be several special centers, such as nuclei of the hypothalamus that regulate sleep, water balance, protein metabolism, and sexual activity.

subculture *n.* a group that maintains a characteristic set of religious, social, ethnic, or other customs or beliefs that serve to distinguish it from the larger culture in which the members live. See also COUNTERCULTURE. —**subcultural** *adj.*

subiculum *n.* (*pl.* **subicula**) a region of the forebrain adjacent to the HIPPOCAMPUS that has reciprocal connections with the hippocampus and the DENTATE GYRUS. It forms part of the HIPPOCAMPAL FORMATION.

subitize *vb.* to perceive at a glance how many objects are presented, without counting. [from Latin *subito*, "at once"]

subject *n.* **1.** the individual human or nonhuman animal that takes part in an experiment or research study and whose responses or performance are reported or evaluated. PARTICIPANT is now often the preferred term for human subjects, because the word "subject" is depersonalizing and implies passivity and submissiveness on the part of the experimentee. **2.** an area or branch of knowledge or a course of study.

subjective *adj.* **1.** taking place or existing only within the mind. **2.** particular to a specific person and thus intrinsically inaccessible to the experience or observation of others. **3.** based on or influenced by personal feelings, interpretations, or prejudices. Compare OBJECTIVE.

subjective contour an edge or border perceived in an image as a result of the inference of the observer. A common form of a KANIZSA FIGURE contains a triangle with sides that consist of subjective contours. Also called **illusory contour**.

subjective–expected utility a hypothetical value that people are presumed to compute (nearly always unconsciously) in making a rational choice between alternatives. It combines the personal (or subjective) value (utility) placed by an individual on a specific act or outcome with the perceived probability (expectation) that the given alternative will lead to that outcome. Many analyses assume that the alternative selected is the one for which the product of the expectation and the subjective value is the highest.

subjective norm a perception that a person has regarding whether people important to that person believe that he or she should or should not perform a particular behavior. See also THEORY OF PLANNED BEHAVIOR; THEORY OF REASONED ACTION.

subjective organization the creation of one's own idiosyncratic set of associations or groupings among items to be learned in order to facilitate memory.

subjective responsibility in the moral reasoning typical of children over the age of 10, the idea that an individual's motives should be taken into account when judging an act. Compare OBJECTIVE RESPONSIBILITY.

subjective test an assessment tool that is scored according to personal judgment or to standards that are less systematic than those used in OBJECTIVE TESTS, as in an essay examination.

subjective well-being a judgment that people make about the overall quality of their lives by summing emotional ups and downs to determine how well their actual life circumstances match their wishes or expectations concerning how they should or might feel.

subjectivism *n.* **1.** in ethics, the proposition that the ideals, such as "the good," to which ethical propositions refer are reflections of personal judgment rather than independent realities. Subjectivism holds that ethical prescriptions reduce to mere statements of personal or cultural preference. **2.** in general, any position holding that judgments of fact or value reflect individual states of mind rather than states of affairs that can be said to be true or false independently of individuals. Compare OBJECTIVISM. —**subjectivist** *n., adj.*

subjectivity *n.* **1.** in general, the tendency to interpret data or make judgments in the light of personal feelings, beliefs, or experiences. **2.** in empirical research, the failure to attain proper standards of OBJECTIVITY.

subject variable a variable of individual differences in a study (e.g., the participant's sex or occupation). A variable of this type is neither manipulated by the experimenter, as an INDEPENDENT VARIABLE might be, nor is it usually changed in the course of the experiment, as a DEPENDENT VARIABLE might be.

sublimation *n.* in psychoanalytic theory, a DEFENSE MECHANISM in which unacceptable sexual or aggressive drives are unconsciously channeled into socially acceptable modes of expression. Thus, the unacceptable drives and energies are redirected into new, learned behaviors, which indirectly provide some satisfaction for the original instincts. For example, an exhibitionistic impulse may gain a new outlet in choreography; a voyeuristic urge may lead to scientific research; and a dangerously aggressive drive may be expressed with impunity on the football field. As well as allowing for substitute satisfactions, such outlets are posited to protect individuals from the anxiety induced by the original drive. —**sublimate** *vb.*

subliminal *adj.* denoting or relating to stimuli that are below the threshold of perception or awareness. —**subliminally** *adv.*

subliminal learning information, habits, or attitudes acquired from exposure to stimuli that were presented below the threshold for conscious awareness (i.e., subliminally).

subliminal perception the registration of stimuli below the level of awareness, particularly stimuli that are too weak (or too rapid) to affect the individual on a conscious level. It is questionable whether responses to subliminal stimuli actually occur and whether it is possible for subliminal commands or advertising messages to influence behavior. Evidence indicates that subliminal commands do not directly affect behavior but may influence responses via SUBLIMINAL PRIMING.

subliminal priming unconscious (below the threshold of awareness) stimulation that increases the probability of the later occurrence of related cognitive tasks. See PRIMING.

submissiveness *n.* a tendency to comply with the wishes or obey the orders of others. —**submissive** *adj.*

subnormal *adj.* denoting something that is below (often significantly below) the normal or

expected level. The use of this term with reference to intelligence is now largely obsolete, and the term BELOW AVERAGE is generally used.

suboccipital puncture an alternative procedure to LUMBAR PUNCTURE for obtaining access to the SUBARACHNOID SPACE for diagnostic or therapeutic purposes. It involves the insertion of a needle into the cisterna magna (a space between the CEREBELLUM and MEDULLA OBLONGATA) through an area near the base of the skull to collect cerebrospinal fluid. Also called **cisternal puncture; cistern puncture**.

subordinate category a subdivision of a BASIC-LEVEL CATEGORY formed at a more specific level of categorization. For example, "Siamese cat" is a subordinate category of the basic-level category "cat." A subordinate category is usually characterized by (a) high levels of resemblance among its members and (b) a relatively low level of difference between its members and those of neighboring categories.

subordination *n.* the placing of something into a lower ranking category or group. More specifically, it is the state of being subservient to and considered less important than others.

subspecies *n.* see BREED.

substance *n.* **1.** in psychopathology, a drug or a toxin that is capable of producing harmful effects when ingested or otherwise taken into the body. **2.** in philosophy, that which has an independent, self-sufficient existence and remains unalterably itself even though its attributes or properties may change. Philosophers have differed over what qualifies as a substance and whether reality consists of a single substance (see MONISM) or more (see DUALISM).

substance abuse a pattern of compulsive substance use manifested by recurrent significant social, occupational, legal, or interpersonal adverse consequences, such as repeated absences from work or school, arrests, and marital difficulties. DSM–IV–TR identifies nine drug classes associated with abuse: alcohol, amphetamines, cannabis, cocaine, hallucinogens, inhalants, opioids, phencyclidines, and sedatives, hypnotics, or anxiolytics. This diagnosis is preempted by the diagnosis of SUBSTANCE DEPENDENCE: If the criteria for substance abuse and substance dependence are both met, only the latter diagnosis is given.

substance abuse treatment inpatient and outpatient programs for individuals diagnosed with substance dependence (i.e., dependence on alcohol or any other drug) to achieve abstinence. These include but are not limited to short- and long-term residential programs (colloquially known as "rehab"), clinic- and hospital-based outpatient programs, METHADONE MAINTENANCE THERAPY, and TWELVE-STEP PROGRAMS. Also called **drug abuse treatment**.

substance dependence a cluster of cognitive, behavioral, and physiological symptoms indicating continued use of a substance despite significant substance-related problems. There is a pattern of repeated substance ingestion resulting in tolerance, withdrawal symptoms if use is suspended, and an uncontrollable drive to continue use. DSM–IV–TR identifies 10 drug classes associated with dependence: alcohol, amphetamines, cannabis, cocaine, hallucinogens, inhalants, nicotine, opioids, phencyclidines, and sedatives, hypnotics, or anxiolytics. This term currently is preferred over the equivalent ADDICTION. See also SUBSTANCE ABUSE.

substance intoxication a reversible syndrome due to the recent ingestion of a specific substance, including clinically significant behavioral or psychological changes, as well as one or more signs of physiological involvement. Although symptoms vary by substance there are some common manifestations, for example, perceptual disturbances; mood changes; impairments of judgment, attention and memory; alterations of heartbeat and vision; and speech and coordination difficulties. DSM–IV–TR identifies 10 drug classes associated with intoxication: alcohol, amphetamines, caffeine, cannabis, cocaine, hallucinogens, inhalants, opioids, phencyclidines, and sedatives, hypnotics, or anxiolytics.

substance intoxication delirium a reversible substance-specific syndrome that develops over a short period of time (usually hours to days) following heavy consumption of the substance. It includes disturbance of consciousness (e.g., reduced ability to focus, sustain, or shift attention), accompanied by changes in cognition (e.g., memory deficit, disorientation, or language disturbance) in excess of those usually associated with intoxication with that substance.

substance P a NEUROPEPTIDE that functions as a neurotransmitter in both peripheral and central nervous systems. High concentrations of neurons containing substance P are localized in the DORSAL HORN of the spinal cord, where they play a role in the modulation of pain. In peripheral tissues, substance P acts as a vasodilator. It also has a role in sexual behavior and has been implicated in the regulation of mood.

substance withdrawal a syndrome that develops after cessation of prolonged, heavy consumption of a substance. Symptoms vary by substance but generally include physiological, behavioral, and cognitive manifestations, such as nausea and vomiting, insomnia, mood alterations, and anxiety. DSM–IV–TR identifies six drug classes associated with withdrawal: alcohol, amphetamines, cocaine, nicotine, opioids, and sedatives, hypnotics, or anxiolytics.

substantia gelatinosa a gelatinous-appearing mass of extensively interconnected small neurons at the tip of the DORSAL HORN of the spinal cord. Some cells in the substantia gelatinosa contain ENDORPHINS and are involved in regulation of pain. Neurons of the substantia gelatinosa extend into the MEDULLA OBLONGATA, where they form the spinal TRIGEMINAL NUCLEUS.

substantia nigra a region of gray matter in the midbrain, named for its dark pigmentation, that sends DOPAMINERGIC neurons to the BASAL GANGLIA. Depletion of dopaminergic neurons in this region is implicated in PARKINSON'S DISEASE.

substitute formation see SYMPTOM FORMATION.

substitutes for leadership theory a contingency LEADERSHIP THEORY proposing that leadership is not important to effective group performance in some work situations. For instance, a highly structured task (see TASK STRUCTURE) may substitute for a structuring or directive leader and a highly cohesive work group may substitute for a supportive leader. See SITUATIONAL LEADERSHIP THEORY.

substitution n. the replacement of one thing with another. More specifically, particularly in psychoanalytic theory, it denotes the replacement of unacceptable emotions or unattainable goals with alternative satisfactions or feelings. Substitution may be viewed as a positive adaptation or solution (e.g., adoption when one cannot have a child of one's own) or as a negative, maladaptive response (e.g., emotional eating after a frustrating day at the office). See also DEFENSE MECHANISM.

substitution test any test in which the examinee substitutes one set of symbols for another. An example is a CODE TEST in which symbols or letters are substituted for numbers.

substrate n. a chemical compound that is acted on by an enzyme. The substrate binds specifically to the enzyme's active site, thereby lowering the energy required for the reaction, which therefore can proceed much faster.

subtest n. a separate division of a test or test battery, usually with an identifiable content (e.g., the multiplication subtest of a mathematics test).

subthalamic nucleus a part of the subthalamus that receives fibers from the GLOBUS PALLIDUS as a part of the descending pathway from the BASAL GANGLIA. It forms part of the EXTRAPYRAMIDAL TRACT.

subthalamus n. a part of the DIENCEPHALON of the brain, wedged between the THALAMUS and the HYPOTHALAMUS. It contains the subthalamic nucleus and functions in the regulation of movements controlled by skeletal muscles, together with the BASAL GANGLIA and the SUBSTANTIA NIGRA. —**subthalamic** adj.

subtherapeutic dose a dose of a drug that does not achieve a particular therapeutic effect. Although this is generally not desired, drugs intended for one purpose may be administered in subtherapeutic doses to achieve a different effect. For example, the TRICYCLIC ANTIDEPRESSANTS are rarely used in current practice in doses sufficient to alleviate depression; however, they are often used in low (subtherapeutic) doses to promote sleep or alleviate pain.

subthreshold potential a type of GRADED POTENTIAL resulting from a stimulus that is not of sufficient intensity to elicit an ACTION POTENTIAL and does not travel far beyond the immediate region of stimulation.

subtraction method see DONDERS'S METHOD.

subtractive bilingualism see ADDITIVE BILINGUALISM.

successful aging avoidance of disease and disability, maintenance of cognitive capacity, continued active engagement in life, and adaptation to the aging process through such strategies as SELECTIVE OPTIMIZATION WITH COMPENSATION.

successful intelligence in the TRIARCHIC THEORY OF INTELLIGENCE, the ability to succeed in life according to one's own definition of success, via adaptation to, shaping of, and selection of environments. Successful intelligence involves capitalizing on strengths and compensating for or correcting weaknesses.

successive-approximations method see METHOD OF SUCCESSIVE APPROXIMATIONS.

successive contrast the enhanced perception of the difference between two stimuli when these are presented in close temporal proximity to one another. Compare SIMULTANEOUS CONTRAST.

successive discrimination in conditioning, a DISCRIMINATION between stimuli that are presented in succession.

successive reproduction a method used to study the way in which information in LONG-TERM MEMORY is altered by RECONSTRUCTION. Participants are asked to reproduce or recall the same material several times in succession, and the variations in their reproductions are recorded.

succinimide n. any of a group of chemically related drugs that are effective in the treatment of absence seizures. **Ethosuximide** is an example of a succinimide and is sold in the United States under the trade name **Zarontin**.

succorance need in the PERSONOLOGY of U.S. psychologist Henry Alexander Murray (1893–1988), the need for protection, aid, and support.

sucker effect an effect in which individuals reduce their personal investment in a group endeavor because of their expectation that others will think negatively of someone who works too hard or contributes too much (regarding them as a sucker). Compare COMPENSATION EFFECT.

sudden infant death syndrome (SIDS) the sudden and unexpected death of a seemingly healthy infant during sleep for no apparent reason. The risk of SIDS is greatest between 2 and 6 months of age and is a common cause of death in babies less than 1 year old. Also called **cot death**; **crib death**.

suffering n. the experience of pain or acute distress, either psychological or physical, in response to a significant event, particularly one that is threatening or involves loss (e.g., the death of a loved one) or a physical trauma.

sufficient statistic a statistic that uses all the information in a sample for estimating a parameter of interest.

suffix effect impaired memory of the last items of an auditorily presented list when the list is followed by an item that does not need to be recalled.

suicidal ideation suicidal thoughts or a preoccupation with suicide, often as a symptom of a MAJOR DEPRESSIVE EPISODE. Most instances of suicidal ideation do not progress to attempted suicide.

suicide n. the act of killing oneself. Frequently, suicide occurs in the context of a MAJOR DEPRESSIVE EPISODE, but it may also occur as a result of a substance-use or other disorder. It sometimes occurs in the absence of any psychiatric disorder, especially in untenable situations, such as bereavement or declining health. —**suicidal** adj.

suicide-prevention center a CRISIS-INTERVENTION facility dealing primarily with individuals who have suicidal thoughts or who have threatened or attempted suicide. Suicide-prevention centers additionally provide community education and outreach, and staff may provide bereavement support for the relatives and loved ones of an individual who has killed himself or herself.

suicidology n. a multiprofessional discipline devoted to the study of suicidal phenomena and their prevention.

sui juris having the ability to make legal decisions and possessing full civil rights (Latin, literally: "of his own right"). A person who is *sui juris* must have reached the age of maturity (typically 18 years old), be fully mentally competent, and not be under the guidance or protection of another.

sukra prameha a CULTURE-BOUND SYNDROME found in Sri Lanka, with symptoms similar to those of SHEN-K'UEI.

sulcus n. (pl. **sulci**) a groove, especially one on the surface of the cerebral cortex. The term is often used synonymously with FISSURE. —**sulcal** adj.

Sullivan's interpersonal theory a theory that emphasizes social influences on development, focusing on key relationships and how they develop and change over time. It proposes that an individual's concept of selfhood is a reflection of others' attitudes toward that person (i.e., arising out of interpersonal relationships and situations). Sullivan hypothesized that threats to self-respect are experienced as anxiety and that assaults on self-esteem emanate from sources outside the person, particularly those most intimately related to the individual across early and adolescent development. [Harry Stack **Sullivan** (1892–1949), U.S. psychiatrist]

S

summated ratings method a method of constructing a scale to measure an attitude that uses ITEM ANALYSIS to select the best items.

summation *n.* **1.** the process in which a neural impulse is propagated by the cumulative effects of two or more stimuli that alone would not be sufficient to activate the neuron. See SPATIAL SUMMATION; TEMPORAL SUMMATION. **2.** (symbol: Σ) a mathematical operation involving the addition of numbers, quantities, or the like.

summation effect a feature of BINOCULAR CELLS in the visual cortex in which the activity of the cell is greater when stimulation occurs through both eyes than when stimulation occurs through one eye. A similar phenomenon occurs in the auditory system; when both ears are stimulated there is a **binaural summation effect** of enhanced loudness.

summation time 1. the longest interval over which the perceived intensity of a stimulus is determined by the total amount of energy during the interval. **2.** the longest interval between two successive stimuli such that they are perceived as a single, continuous stimulus.

sum of squares the total obtained by adding together the squares of each deviation score in a sample (i.e., each score minus the sample mean squared, and then added together).

sun compass the use of the sun as a directional stimulus in orientation and navigation. Because the sun appears to move across the sky during the day and has different trajectories in different seasons, a sun compass must be coupled with some form of TIME ESTIMATION. Studies of several species, ranging from bees to fish and birds, have demonstrated a time-compensated sun compass. For nocturnal species, there is evidence of a **star compass**.

sundown syndrome the tendency, particularly among older adults with dementia or individuals in institutional care, to experience reduced levels of psychological functioning late in the day. Also called **sundowning**.

superego *n.* in psychoanalytic theory, the moral component of the personality that represents society's standards and determines personal standards of right and wrong, or conscience, as well as aims and aspirations (see EGO-IDEAL). In the classic Freudian tripartite structure of the psyche, the EGO, which controls personal impulses and directs actions, operates by the rules and principles of the superego, which basically stem from parental demands and prohibitions. The formation of the superego occurs on an unconscious level, beginning in the first 5 years of life and continuing throughout childhood and adolescence and into adulthood, largely through identification with the parents and later with admired models of behavior.

superego anxiety in psychoanalytic theory, anxiety caused by unconscious superego activity that produces feelings of guilt and demands for atonement. Compare EGO ANXIETY; ID ANXIETY.

superego resistance in psychoanalytic theory, a type of RESISTANCE to the psychoanalytic process created by the superego. It generates a sense of guilt and gives rise to the need for punishment in the form of persistent symptoms. Compare REPRESSION-RESISTANCE; ID RESISTANCE.

superficial *adj.* **1.** in anatomy, located close to or at the surface of the body or of an organ. **2.** having no deep significance or real substance.

superior *adj.* in anatomy, higher, above, or toward the head. Compare INFERIOR.

superior colliculus see COLLICULUS.

superiority complex in the INDIVIDUAL PSYCHOLOGY of Austrian psychiatrist Alfred Adler (1870–1937), an exaggerated opinion of one's abilities and accomplishments that derives from an overcompensation for feelings of inferiority. See COMPENSATION. Compare INFERIORITY COMPLEX.

superior olivary complex a collection of brain nuclei located in the PONS. The cells receive excitatory input from the contralateral COCHLEAR NUCLEI in the brainstem and inhibitory input from the ipsilateral cochlear nuclei. The contralateral input comes through the TRAPEZOID BODY, a concentration of transverse nerve fibers in the pons. Also called **superior olive**.

superior temporal gyrus a ridge (gyrus) that extends along the upper surface of the TEMPORAL LOBE of the brain, bounded above by the LATERAL SULCUS and laterally by the superior temporal sulcus.

supernormal stimulus a stimulus that by virtue of being larger or more intense than those normally encountered has a greater behavioral effect than the natural stimulus. For example, a gull presented with its own egg and a much larger, artificial egg will attempt to incubate the larger egg.

superordinate category a high-level category that subsumes a number of BASIC-LEVEL CATEGORIES and reflects a more abstract level of categorization. For example, "animal" is a superordinate category including the basic-level categories "cat," "fish," "elephant," and so on. A superordinate category is usually characterized by (a) low levels of resemblance between members and (b) fundamental differences between its members and those of other categories.

supersensitivity *n.* heightened responsiveness to a particular neurotransmitter. For example, prolonged blockade of DOPAMINE RECEPTORS by some antipsychotic drugs leads to an increase in the number of dopamine receptors; discontinuation of the drug may then result in a marked increase of psychotic symptoms, a condition called **supersensitivity psychosis**.

superstition *n.* a belief or practice founded upon the operation of supernatural or magical forces, such as charms or omens. More specifically, a superstition is the illusion that one can influence events and their outcomes through various practices, including following specific behavior patterns (**superstitious rituals**).

supertaster *n.* a person with uncommonly low gustatory thresholds and strong responses to moderate concentrations of taste stimuli. Supertasters have unusually high numbers of TASTE BUDS.

supervised analysis see CONTROL ANALYSIS.

supervision *n.* in psychotherapy and counseling, clinical guidance and direction (i.e., critical evaluation) that is provided by a qualified and experienced therapist or counselor—the **supervisor**—to a trainee. Supervision is required while the trainee learns therapeutic techniques. A prescribed number of hours of supervision is required by state licensing boards as part of the requirements for obtaining a license in a mental health field. Also called **therapy supervision**.

supervisory attentional system a theoretical higher level cognitive mechanism active in nonroutine or novel situations, responsible for troubleshooting and decision making when habitual responses or automatic processes are ineffective or otherwise unsatisfactory. Thought to be involved in carrying out a variety of other EXECUTIVE FUNCTIONS as well, it is considered a network for the coordination and control of cognitive activity and intentional behavior.

supplementary motor area an area of the MOTOR CORTEX with SOMATOTOPIC ORGANIZATION involved in planning and learning new movements that have coordinated sequences. In contrast to the PREMOTOR AREA, neuronal input to the supplementary motor area is triggered more by internal representations than by external events.

supported employment a VOCATIONAL REHABILITATION program that places individuals with disabilities directly into the paid, competitive working environment. It emphasizes matching a person with an appropriate employer and work environment and providing ongoing support, training, and assessment that integrate vocational and personal needs. Supported employment differs from a SHELTERED WORKSHOP in that the latter occurs in a controlled, noncompetitive working environment. See also TRANSITIONAL EMPLOYMENT.

supported living a situation in which people with mental retardation live singly or in small groups in apartments or houses where drop-in assistance in performing activities of daily living and learning independent living skills is available.

supported retirement a daily or regular program or schedule of activity for an aging or aged person with mental retardation that emphasizes socialization and recreational engagement, rather than the habilitation activities and vocational involvement typical of adult mental retardation day services.

support group a group similar in some ways to a SELF-HELP GROUP, in that members who share a problem come together to provide help, comfort, and guidance. A primary distinguishing feature of support groups is in their leadership: a professional or agency-based facilitator who often does not share the problem of members. In addition, support groups often last for only a limited predetermined number of sessions, and a fee for attendance is sometimes charged.

supportive-expressive psychotherapy a form of brief DYNAMIC PSYCHOTHERAPY that focuses on the therapist–client relationship and on relationships outside of therapy to define a central relationship pattern that is the focus of treatment.

supportiveness *n.* in psychotherapy and counseling, an attitude or response of acceptance, encouragement, or reassurance displayed by the therapist or counselor.

supportive psychotherapy a form of therapy that aims to relieve emotional distress and symptoms without probing into the sources of conflicts or attempting to alter basic personality structure. Specific methods used include reassurance, reeducation, persuasion, environmental changes, advice, pastoral counseling, bereavement therapy, bibliotherapy, remotivation, and encouragement of desirable behavior. Such measures are frequently applied to individuals with relatively minor or limited problems, as well as to fragile or hospitalized patients, as a means of maintaining morale and preventing deterioration.

supportive services 1. programs ancillary to the treatment or rehabilitation of people with illnesses or disabilities. **2.** social service programs (e.g., child care or transportation) that are necessary to enable an individual to participate in the workforce or function more independently.

suppression *n.* a conscious effort to put disturbing thoughts and experiences out of mind, or to control and inhibit the expression of unacceptable impulses and feelings. It is distinct from the unconscious DEFENSE MECHANISM of REPRESSION in psychoanalytic theory. —**suppress** *vb.*

suppressor variable a variable that reduces (suppresses) the apparent relationship between two other variables. See THIRD-VARIABLE PROBLEM.

suprachiasmatic nucleus a small region of the HYPOTHALAMUS in the brain, above the OPTIC CHIASM, that is the location of the CIRCADIAN OSCILLATOR, which controls circadian rhythms. It receives direct input from the retina. See also BIOLOGICAL CLOCK.

supraliminal *adj.* describing stimulation that is above the threshold of awareness.

supraliminal perception the processing of sensory data that are above the threshold of perception. More specifically, it is the processing of information that can be detected by the senses but that is not consciously interpreted by the perceiver, such as the hum of conversation in a crowded room.

supranuclear palsy see PROGRESSIVE SUPRA-NUCLEAR PALSY.

supraoptic nucleus a nucleus of the HYPO-THALAMUS that lies above the OPTIC CHIASM. Neurons in this nucleus secrete the hormones OXYTOCIN and VASOPRESSIN.

suprasegmental *adj.* in linguistics, denoting those phonological features of speech that extend over a series of SEGMENTS rather than forming individual PHONEMES. In English the principal suprasegmental features are TONE (pitch) and STRESS. See also PARALANGUAGE; PROSODY.

surface dyslexia a form of acquired dyslexia in which a person is overly reliant on spelling-to-sound correspondence and therefore has difficulty reading irregularly spelled words.

surface structure (s-structure) in the TRANSFORMATIONAL GENERATIVE GRAMMAR of U.S. linguist Noam Chomsky (1928–), the structure of a grammatical sentence as it actually occurs in speech or writing, as opposed to its underlying DEEP STRUCTURE or abstract logical form. In Chomsky's theory, the surface structure of a sentence is generated from the deep structure by a series of transformational rules involving the addition, deletion, or reordering of sentence elements. Psycholinguists have investigated whether and to what extent this may serve as a model for the cognitive processes involved in forming and interpreting sentences.

surface therapy psychotherapy directed toward relieving the client's symptoms and emotional stress through such measures as reassurance, suggestion, and direct attempts to modify attitudes and behavior patterns, rather than through exploration and analysis of unconscious motivation and underlying dynamics. Compare DEPTH THERAPY.

surface trait in CATTELL'S PERSONALITY TRAIT THEORY, a characteristic manifested as a group of interrelated observable behaviors. For example, arriving early for appointments and leaving the office only after one's work is complete are visible verifications of the characteristic of conscientiousness. Surface traits appear consistently and are thought to cluster and form SOURCE TRAITS, which are regarded as the underlying building blocks of personality.

surgency *n.* in trait psychology, a personality trait marked by cheerfulness, responsiveness, spontaneity, and sociability, but at a level below that of EXTRAVERSION or MANIA. **—surgent** *adj.*

surprise *n.* an emotion typically resulting from the violation of an expectation or the detection of novelty in the environment. According to various theories, it is considered to be one of the emotions that have a universal pattern of facial expression. The physiological response includes raising or arching the eyebrows, opening the eyes wide, opening the mouth wide in an oval shape, and gasping.

surrogate *n.* a person or object that substitutes for the role of an individual who has a significant position in a family or group. For example, young children may use stuffed toys as surrogate companions.

surrogate decision making a provision in law or a regulation permitting the appointment of a surrogate for a person, frequently a person with mental retardation, dementia, or a mental disorder, who is not competent to make specific decisions regarding consent to medical, surgical, or other health care procedures. The surrogate makes these determinations on behalf of the person.

survey *n.* a study in which a group of participants is selected from a population and some selected characteristics or opinions of those participants are collected, measured, and analyzed. See also SURVEY RESEARCH.

survey knowledge a mental representation of a spatial environment that resembles a map, as if one has a bird's-eye view of the environment, as contrasted with route knowledge (see ROUTE LEARNING).

survey research a research method in which the investigator attempts to determine the current state of a population with regard to one or more attributes. Survey research does not involve any intervention imposed by the investigator.

survival analysis a set of statistical procedures used to build models calculating the time until some event occurs (e.g., the death of a patient, the failure of a piece of equipment). Also called **event history analysis**.

survival instinct see SELF-PRESERVATION INSTINCT.

survival of the fittest the tendency of individuals that are better adapted to a particular environment to be more successful at surviving and producing offspring. This concept is inherent in the theory of evolution by NATURAL SELECTION.

survivor guilt remorse or guilt for having survived a catastrophic situation when others did not. It is a common reaction stemming in part from a feeling of having failed to do enough to prevent the tragedy or to save those who did not survive.

survivorship *n.* the state of having a typical life and life span after overcoming severe diseases (e.g., cancer), traumatic life events (e.g., child abuse), or environmental disaster (e.g., earthquake).

susceptibility *n.* **1.** vulnerability to, or the increased likelihood of being affected by, a physical or mental disease or disorder. **2.** capacity for deep feeling or emotional arousal.

suspiciousness *n.* an attitude of mistrust toward the motives or sincerity of others. Although a degree of suspiciousness in certain situations can be natural and likely serves the purposes of self-preservation or survival, extreme, pervasive suspiciousness is a common characteristic of individuals with PARANOID PERSONALITY DISORDER.

sustained-release preparation see SLOW-RELEASE PREPARATION.

susto *n.* a CULTURE-BOUND SYNDROME occurring among Latinos in the United States and populations in Mexico, Central America, and South America. After experiencing a frightening event, individuals fear that their soul has left their body. Symptoms include muscle pains, headache, diarrhea, unhappiness, troubled sleep, lack of motivation, and low self-esteem.

switching *n.* **1.** in psychotherapy, changing the course of the discussion during a session. This may be done by the client, either purposefully or unconsciously, when the discussion is too close to sensitive issues. Switching may also be done by the therapist to change the discussion to more relevant therapeutic issues. **2.** in multiple personality disorders, the often rapid movement between one personality and another.

Sylvian aqueduct see CEREBRAL AQUEDUCT.

Sylvian fissure see LATERAL SULCUS.

symbiosis *n.* **1.** any relationship in which two species live together in close association, especially one in which both species benefit. For example, in tropical Amazonia, a species of ant lives on a particular tree species that it uses for food and shelter, at the same time removing lichen and other parasites that might harm the tree. **2.** any mutually reinforcing, interdependent relationship between individuals (e.g., between a mother and infant), but particularly one in which one person is overdependent on another to satisfy needs. The latter type of relationship hampers the development or independence of both individuals. —**symbiotic** *adj.*

symbol *n.* **1.** any object, figure, or image that represents something else, such as a flag, a logo, a pictogram, or a religious symbol (e.g., a cross). A written or spoken word can be regarded as a particular kind of symbol (see ARBITRARY SYMBOL; SIGNIFIER). In literature and art, symbols are generally suggestive rather than explicit in their meaning: For example, a rose may suggest ideas of beauty, love, femininity, and transience without being limited to any of these meanings in particular. **2.** in psychoanalytic theory, a disguised representation of a repressed idea, impulse, or wish. See SYMBOLISM. —**symbolic** *adj.*

symbol–digit test a task in which a person is given a list of symbols, each with a corresponding digit, and then a long list of symbols without the digits, each of which the participant has to fill in. The test measures the number of symbol–digit pairs completed in a fixed time or the time taken to complete a fixed number of pairs. See also CODE TEST.

symbol grounding the process of establishing and maintaining the correspondence between symbolic representations of objects and the actual physical objects in the real-world environment. For example, if a child is instructed to retrieve the green box from the shelf, he or she cannot do so properly unless able to associate the internal representation of the item conveyed by the concepts of "green" and "box" with the appropriate sensory experience actually associated with the physical object itself. Also called **perceptual anchoring**.

Symbolic *n.* the realm of symbols or SIGNIFIERS: one of three aspects of the psychoanalytic field defined by French psychoanalyst Jacques Lacan (1901–1981). The achievement of symbolization marks the beginning of ego differentiation and is associated with the infant's entrance into the world of language, culture, law, and morality. The other two realms are the IMAGINARY and the REAL. See also MIRROR PHASE.

symbolic function in PIAGETIAN THEORY, the cognitive ability to mentally represent objects that are not in sight. For example, a child playing with a toy can mentally picture and experience the toy even after it has been taken away and he or she can no longer see it. Symbolic function emerges early in the PREOPERATIONAL STAGE and is expressed through DEFERRED IMITATION, language, SYMBOLIC PLAY, and mental IMAGERY. Also called **semiotic function**.

symbolic interactionism a sociological theory that assumes that self-concept is created through interpretation of symbolic gestures, words, actions, and appearances exhibited by others during social interaction. In contrast to Freudian and other approaches that postulate extensive inner dispositions and regard social interaction as resulting from them, symbolic interactionists believe that inner structures result from social interactions. See GENERALIZED OTHER; LOOKING-GLASS SELF; REFLECTED APPRAISALS.

symbolic learning theory a theory that attempts to explain how IMAGERY works in performance enhancement. It suggests that imagery develops and enhances a coding system that creates a mental blueprint of what has to be done to complete an action.

symbolic logic the systematic use of symbols in logical analysis. In modern symbolic logic, the symbols used are those of mathematics, particularly those of set theory. The language of mathematics is well suited to the investigation of the precise conditions of validity in arguments because it is an ARTIFICIAL LANGUAGE, lacking the connotations and subjective meanings present in a NATURAL LANGUAGE, and because relations between mathematical entities are simple and precisely defined. See LOGIC.

symbolic mode see ENACTIVE MODE.

symbolic play a form of play in which the child uses objects as representations of other things. For example, a child may put a leash on a stuffed

S

animal, take it for a walk, and make it eat from a bowl. Symbolic play may or may not be social. See also IMAGINARY COMPANION.

symbolic process any cognitive activity in which ideas, images, or other MENTAL REPRESEN-TATIONS serve as mediators of thought. The term is often used to distinguish the HIGHER MENTAL PROCESSES from either (a) lower cognitive functions, such as perception, or (b) those neurophysiological processes that underlie processing at the symbolic level.

symbolic thinking the ability to think about objects and events that are not within the immediate environment. It involves the use of signs, symbols, concepts, and abstract relations, as evidenced by language, numeracy, and artistic or ritual expression.

symbolism *n.* **1.** in psychoanalytic theory, the substitution of a SYMBOL for a repressed impulse or threatening object in order to avoid censorship by the superego (e.g., dreaming of a steeple or other phallic symbol instead of a penis). Also called **symbolization**. **2.** the use of symbols in literature and the visual arts or in human culture generally (see SEMIOTICS).

symbolization *n.* **1.** see SYMBOLISM. **2.** in the SOCIAL-COGNITIVE THEORY of Canadian-born U.S. psychologist Albert Bandura (1925–), the ability to think about one's social behavior in terms of words and images. —**symbolize** *vb.*

symbol-substitution test see CODE TEST.

SYMLOG *n.* *s*ystematic *m*ultiple *l*evel *o*bservation of *g*roups: a theory and observational system for studying group behavior. The model assumes that group activities and group members can be classified along three dimensions (dominance–submissiveness, friendliness–unfriendliness, and acceptance–nonacceptance of authority). See also STRUCTURED OBSERVATIONAL MEASURES.

symmetry *n.* **1.** the mirrorlike correspondence of parts on opposite sides of a center, providing balance and harmony in the proportions of objects. **2.** one of the GESTALT PRINCIPLES OF ORGA-NIZATION. It states that people tend to perceive objects as coherent wholes organized around a center point; this is particularly evident when the objects involve unconnected regions bounded by borders. Also called **law of symmetry**; **principle of symmetry**. **3.** in mathematics and statistics, equality relative to some axis. —**symmetrical** *adj.*

sympathectomy *n.* a surgical procedure in which portions of the SYMPATHETIC NERVOUS SYSTEM are excised, severed, or otherwise disrupted. In **chemical sympathectomy**, this is accomplished by the administration of specific drugs.

sympathetic chain either of two beadlike chains of GANGLIA of the SYMPATHETIC NER-VOUS SYSTEM, one chain lying on each side of the spinal column.

sympathetic nervous system one of the two divisions of the AUTONOMIC NERVOUS SYSTEM (ANS, which controls smooth muscle and gland functions), the other being the PARASYMPA-THETIC NERVOUS SYSTEM. Anatomically it consists of **preganglionic autonomic neurons** whose fibers run from the thoracic and lumbar regions of the spinal cord to the chains of sympathetic ganglia. From these arise the fibers of **post-ganglionic autonomic neurons**, which innervate organs ranging from the eye to the reproductive organs. It is defined functionally in terms of its ability to act as an integrated whole in affecting a large number of smooth muscle systems simultaneously, usually in the service of enhancing "fight or flight" (see FIGHT-OR-FLIGHT RESPONSE). Typical sympathetic changes include dilation of the pupils to facilitate vision, constriction of the peripheral arteries to supply more blood to the muscles and the brain, secretion of epinephrine to raise the blood-sugar level and increase metabolism, and reduction of stomach and intestinal activities so that energy can be directed elsewhere. Also called **sympathetic division**.

sympathomimetic drug any pharmacological agent that stimulates activity in the sympathetic nervous system because it potentiates the activity of norepinephrine or epinephrine or has effects similar to these neurotransmitters (hence they are also known as **adrenergic drugs**). Sympathomimetic drugs include the amphetamines and ephedrine.

sympathy *n.* **1.** feelings of concern or compassion resulting from an awareness of the suffering or sorrow of another. **2.** more generally, a capacity to share in and respond to the concerns or feelings of others. —**sympathetic** *adj.* —**sympathize** *vb.*

sympatric *adj.* describing species that occupy the same habitat or overlapping habitats. Species that do not occur together or occupy the same habitat are described as **allopatric**.

symptom *n.* any deviation from normal functioning that is considered indicative of physical or mental disorder. A recognized pattern of symptoms constitutes a SYNDROME. —**symptomatic** *adj.*

symptomatic act an action that appears to be intended for one purpose (or to have no particular purpose) but that betrays a hidden intention or meaning. In psychoanalytic theory, such acts are thought to represent repressed impulses. See also FREUDIAN SLIP; PARAPRAXIS; SYMPTOM FOR-MATION.

symptomatic treatment treatment directed toward the relief of distressing symptoms, as opposed to treatment focused on underlying causes and conditions. Symptomatic treatment of chronic migraines, for example, would involve the use of analgesics to relieve pain without attempting to discover why they are occurring.

symptomatology *n.* **1.** the combined signs, markers, or indications of a disease or disorder.

2. the scientific study of the markers and indications of a disease or disorder.

Symptom Checklist-90-Revised (**SCL-90-R**) a 90-item self-report inventory that measures the psychological symptoms and distress of community, medical, and psychiatric respondents along nine primary symptom dimensions and three global indices. The SCL-90-R adds four dimensions to the five assessed in the HOPKINS SYMPTOM CHECKLIST, of which it is a direct outgrowth: hostility, phobic anxiety, paranoid ideation, and psychoticism.

symptom-context method a system of gathering data as symptoms arise in vivo in the psychotherapy session as an aid to psychotherapy research, case formulation, and treatment. It is similar to the CORE CONFLICTUAL RELATIONSHIP THEME method.

symptom formation 1. in psychoanalytic theory, the development of a somatic or behavioral manifestation of an unconscious impulse or conflict that provokes anxiety. Also called **substitute formation. 2.** the process by which the indications of physical or psychological illness or disease develop.

synapse *n.* the specialized junction through which neural signals are transmitted from one neuron (the presynaptic neuron) to another (the postsynaptic neuron). In most synapses the knoblike ending (terminal button) of the axon of a presynaptic neuron faces the dendrite or cell body of the postsynaptic neuron across a narrow gap, the synaptic cleft. The arrival of a neural signal triggers the release of NEUROTRANSMITTER from SYNAPTIC VESICLES in the terminal button into the synaptic cleft. Here the molecules of neurotransmitter activate receptors in the postsynaptic membrane and cause the opening of ION CHANNELS in the postsynaptic cell. This may lead to excitation or inhibition of the postsynaptic cell, depending on which ion channels are affected. See also ELECTRICAL SYNAPSE. —**synaptic** *adj.*

synapse rearrangement the loss of some synapses and the establishment of others that occurs as a refinement of synaptic connections often seen in development or that follows loss of or damage to some neurons.

synaptic bouton see AXON.

synaptic cleft the gap within a synapse between the knoblike ending of the axon of one neuron and the dendrite or cell body of a neighboring neuron. The synaptic cleft is typically 20–30 nm wide.

synaptic pruning a neurodevelopmental process, ocurring both before birth and up to the second decade of life, in which the weakest synapses between neurons are eliminated. In schizophrenia research, it is hypothesized that premature or excessive pruning may account for some forms of the disease.

synaptic vesicle any of numerous small spheri-

cal sacs in the cytoplasm of the knoblike ending of the axon of a presynaptic neuron that contain molecules of NEUROTRANSMITTER. The transmitter is released into the SYNAPTIC CLEFT when a nerve impulse arrives at the axon ending.

synaptogenesis *n.* the formation of synapses between neurons as axons and dendrites grow. See also EXPERIENCE-DEPENDENT SYNAPTOGENESIS; EXPERIENCE-EXPECTANT SYNAPTOGENESIS.

syncheiria (**synchiria**) *n.* a disorder of sensation in which a person experiences pain or touch sensations on both sides of the body when only one side is actually stimulated. It is considered a DYSCHEIRIA.

synchronicity *n.* in ANALYTIC PSYCHOLOGY, the simultaneous occurrence of events that appear to have a meaningful connection when there is no explicable causal relationship between these events, as in extraordinary coincidences or purported examples of telepathy. Jung suggested that some simultaneous occurrences possess significance through their very coincidence in time.

synchronization *n.* in ELECTROENCEPHALOGRAPHY, a pattern of brain-wave activity that appears to be coordinated, so that one set of neurons may oscillate in phase with another set.

synchronized sleep DELTA-WAVE sleep, when electroencephalogram recordings show slow, synchronous waves. See also SLEEP STAGES.

synchronous correlation in LONGITUDINAL DESIGNS, a correlation that represents the degree of relationship between variables at a specific moment in time.

syncope *n.* fainting: a transient loss of consciousness resulting from sudden reduction in the blood supply to the brain. —**syncopal** *adj.*

syndrome *n.* a set of symptoms and signs that are usually due to a single cause (or set of related causes) and together indicate a particular physical or mental disease or disorder. Also called **symptom complex.**

synecdoche *n.* see METONYMY.

synectics model an educational approach that emphasizes creative problem solving and the development of teaching methods that enhance student creativity, such as encouraging metaphorical thinking.

synergism *n.* the joint action of different elements such that their combined effect is greater than the sum of their individual effects, as in DRUG SYNERGISM. —**synergistic** *adj.*

synergogy *n.* cooperative learning that focuses on problem solving, learning within group activities, and joint projects.

synergy *n.* the coordination of forces or efforts to achieve a goal, as when a group of muscles work together in order to move a limb. —**synergic** *adj.*

synesthesia *n.* a condition in which stimulation of one sensory system arouses sensations in another. For example, sounds may be experienced as colors while they are being heard, and specific sounds (e.g., different musical notes) may yield specific colors. Research suggests that about one in 2,000 people regularly experience synesthesia. See also CHROMESTHESIA.

syntactic aphasia see AGRAMMATISM.

syntactics *n.* the structural and grammatical aspects of language, as distinguished from SEMANTICS.

syntax *n.* the set of rules that describes how words and phrases in a language are arranged into grammatical sentences, or the branch of linguistics that studies such rules. With MORPHOLOGY, syntax is one of the two traditional subdivisions of grammar. —**syntactic** or **syntactical** *adj.*

syntaxis *n.* a way of thinking and communicating that is logical and based on reality. —**syntaxic** *adj.*

synthesis *n.* **1.** the bringing together of disparate parts or elements—whether they be physical or conceptual—into a whole. For example, BIOSYNTHESIS is the process by which chemical or biochemical compounds are formed from their constituents, and MENTAL SYNTHESIS involves combining ideas and images into meaningful objects of thought. **2.** in philosophy, the final stage of a dialectical process: a third proposition that resolves the opposition between THESIS and ANTITHESIS. The synthesis then serves as the thesis in the next phase of the ongoing dialectic. —**synthetic** *adj.*

synthetic validity in industrial and organizational settings, a technique for inferring the validity of a selection test or other predictor of job performance from a JOB ANALYSIS. It involves systematically analyzing a job into its elements, estimating the validity of the test or predictor in predicting performance on each of these elements, and then combining the validities for each element to form an estimate of the validity of the test or predictor for the job as a whole.

system *n.* **1.** any collective entity consisting of a set of interrelated or interacting elements that have been organized together to perform a function. For example, a living organism or one of its major bodily structures constitutes a system. **2.** a structured set of facts, concepts, and hypotheses that provide a framework of thought or belief, as in a philosophical system. —**systematic** *adj.*

systematic desensitization a form of BEHAVIOR THERAPY in which COUNTERCONDITIONING is used to reduce anxiety associated with a particular stimulus. It involves the following stages: (a) The client is trained in deep-muscle relaxation; (b) various anxiety-provoking situations related to a particular problem, such as fear of death or a specific phobia, are listed in order from weakest to strongest; and (c) each of these situations is presented in imagination or in reality, beginning with the weakest, while the client practices muscle relaxation. Since the muscle relaxation is incompatible with the anxiety, the client gradually responds less to the anxiety-provoking situations. See also COVERT DESENSITIZATION; IN VIVO DESENSITIZATION; RECIPROCAL INHIBITION.

systematic error an error in data or in a conclusion drawn from the data that is regular and repeatable as a result of improper collection methods or statistical treatment of the data.

systematic multiple level observation of groups see SYMLOG.

systematic observation an objective, well-ordered method for close examination of some phenomenon or aspect of behavior so as to obtain reliable data unbiased by observer interpretation. Systematic observation typically involves specification of the exact actions, attributes, or other variables that are to be recorded and precisely how they are to be recorded.

systematics *n.* see BIOLOGICAL TAXONOMY.

systematic sampling a type of SAMPLING in which all the members of a population are listed and then some objective, orderly procedure is applied to select specific cases. For example, the population might be listed alphabetically and every seventh case selected.

systematized delusion a false, irrational belief that is highly developed and organized, with multiple elaborations that are coherent, consistent, and logically related. Compare FRAGMENTARY DELUSION.

systemic 1. *adj.* concerning or having impact on an entire system. For example, a systemic disorder affects an entire organ system or the body as a whole. **2.** *n.* the interplay of reciprocal processes between interactional partners, as in a family.

systemic thinking a combination of analytical and synthetic thinking that takes account of the impact of a system (or organization) and all its components together. Analytical thinking is concerned with breaking down a concept into its component parts, whereas synthetic thinking is the process of combining components to make a complete whole.

systems engineering a discipline that adopts an integrated, multidisciplinary approach to the design and analysis of WORK SYSTEMS in order to account for the complex interdependencies of system components, people, and processes. Its goal is to enhance efficiency and safety.

systems of support a framework for identifying the nature and profile of services and supports required by a person with mental retardation. This is based on considerations of intellectual functioning and adaptive skills, psychological and emotional factors, physical health and etiological factors, and environmental or situational factors.

systems theory see GENERAL SYSTEMS THEORY.

S

Tt

TA abbreviation for TRANSACTIONAL ANALYSIS.

tabanka (tabanca) *n.* a CULTURE-BOUND SYNDROME found in Trinidad, with symptoms that include depression associated with a high rate of suicide. It is seen in men who have been abandoned by their wives.

taboo (tabu) 1. *n.* a religious, moral, or social convention prohibiting a particular behavior, object, or person. The word derives from *tabu*, the Polynesian term for "sacred," which was used specifically in reference to objects, rites, and individuals consecrated to sacred use or service and, therefore, seen as forbidden, unclean, or untouchable in secular contexts. **2.** *adj.* prohibited or strongly disapproved.

tachycardia *n.* see ARRHYTHMIA.

tachyphylaxis *n.* a rapidly decreasing response to repeated administration of a drug. For example, the blood pressure of a patient might continue to rise despite repeated injections of a drug that normally would lower the blood pressure. —**tachyphylactic** *adj.*

tacit knowledge knowledge that is informally acquired rather than explicitly taught (e.g., knowledge of social rules) and allows a person to succeed in certain environments and pursuits. It is stored without self-reflective awareness and therefore not easily articulated. PRACTICAL INTELLIGENCE requires a facility for acquiring tacit knowledge. Also called **implicit knowledge**; **unconscious knowledge**. See TRIARCHIC THEORY OF INTELLIGENCE.

tactile agnosia loss or impairment of the ability to recognize and understand the nature of objects through touch. Several distinct subtypes have been identified, including **amorphagnosia**, impaired recognition of the size and shape of objects; **ahylognosia**, impaired recognition of such object qualities as weight and texture; and **finger agnosia**, impaired recognition of one's own or another person's fingers.

tactile communication the use of touch as a means of communication. In dogs and wolves, the placing of one individual's head and neck on the back of another is a signal of dominance. In many primates allogrooming (mutual grooming) is important in maintaining social relationships and may release hormones that serve to provide a physiological calming or reward effect.

tactile extinction see DOUBLE-SIMULTANEOUS TACTILE SENSATION.

tactile form recognition any test of the ability to recognize an object by touch alone. Such tests usually involve blindfolding the participants and asking them to name objects placed in their hands.

tactile hallucination a false perception involving the sense of touch. These sensations may include itching, feeling electric shocks, and feeling insects biting or crawling under the skin. Also called **haptic hallucination**.

tactile illusion an illusion involving the touch sense. Tactile illusions may occur when patterns are pressed on the skin rather than when patterns are experienced through voluntary movement to gain information about the object or surface. Compare HAPTIC ILLUSION.

tactile perception the ability to perceive objects or judge sensations through the sense of touch. The term often refers to judgments of spatial stimulation of the skin and patterns imposed on the skin. Tactile perception may also involve judging sensory events involving stimulation of the skin, for example, the thermal properties of a liquid. Some researchers restrict this term to PASSIVE TOUCH.

tactile perceptual disorder a condition, due to brain damage, that is characterized by difficulty in discriminating sensations that involve touch receptors. Individuals may be unable to determine the shape, size, texture, or other physical aspects of an object merely by touching it.

tactile receptor any of the CUTANEOUS RECEPTORS or other receptors involved in the SOMATOSENSES.

tactual display a device for transmitting information that is to be read or otherwise processed through the use of touch. Tactual displays may provide BRAILLE output from a computer or information in letter shapes. They may use simple vibrators, raised pins, or electrocutaneous stimulation of the skin. Tactual displays are useful for people with visual impairment, and some are used for assisting people with hearing loss.

tactual localization see POINT LOCALIZATION.

Tadoma method a technique of communicating with people having both hearing and visual impairment. People with these disabilities learn to place their fingers on the cheek and neck and their thumb on the mouth of the person speaking and translate the vibrations and muscle movements into words.

taijin kyofusho a phobia, similar to SOCIAL PHOBIA and unique to Japan, that is characterized by an intense fear that one's body parts, bodily functions, or facial expressions are embarrassing or offensive to others (e.g., in appearance, odor, or movement).

talent *n.* an innate skill or ability, or an aptitude to excel in one or more specific activities or subject areas. Talent cannot be accounted for by normal development patterns and is often not maximized, as this requires time, energy, sacrifice, dedication, and money. Ideal circumstances for the development of a talent include enjoyment of the talent for its own sake and a clear perception of how it can be exploited to fulfill the individual's long-term aspirations. —**talented** *adj.*

talented and gifted (**TAG**) describing children who display a level of intelligence significantly above average, special abilities, or both, as measured by appropriate standard assessment procedures. **Talented and Gifted** is an organization that promotes education advocacy, research, and the sharing of ideas between educators and parents of such children.

talking cure a synonym for psychotherapy, sometimes used dismissively. The term is apt in that the essence of certain psychotherapeutic approaches is for the client to "talk out" his or her problems with the therapist. First used in the context of psychoanalysis, the term was coined by the landmark patient ANNA O.

tandem reinforcement a SCHEDULE OF REINFORCEMENT for a single response in which two or more schedule requirements must be completed in sequence before reinforcement occurs and no stimulus change accompanies completion of each requirement. For example, in a tandem, fixed-interval 1-min, fixed-ratio 10 schedule, the first response after 1 min (see FIXED-INTERVAL SCHEDULE) would initiate the FIXED-RATIO SCHEDULE, and the 10th response would result in reinforcement. Compare CHAINED SCHEDULE.

tandem therapy in marriage therapy (see COUPLES THERAPY), a practice in which the therapist meets individually with each partner.

tangentiality *n.* a thought disturbance that is marked by oblique speech in which the person constantly digresses to irrelevant topics and fails to arrive at the main point. In extreme form it is a manifestation of LOOSENING OF ASSOCIATIONS, a symptom most frequently found in schizophrenia. Compare CIRCUMSTANTIALITY.

tantrum *n.* see TEMPER TANTRUM.

tapering *n.* a gradual reduction in the dose of a drug in order to avoid undesirable effects that may occur with rapid cessation. Such effects may be extreme (e.g., convulsions) or relatively mild (e.g., head pain, mild gastrointestinal distress). Drugs that produce physiological dependence (e.g., opiates, benzodiazepines) must be tapered to prevent a withdrawal syndrome; seizures can result from sudden cessation of benzodiazepines (see SEDATIVE, HYPNOTIC, OR ANXIOLYTIC WITHDRAWAL).

Tarasoff decision the 1976 California Supreme Court decision in *Tarasoff v. Regents of the University of California*, which placed limits on a client's right to confidentiality by ruling that mental health practitioners who know or reasonably believe that a client poses a threat to another person are obligated to protect the potential victim from danger. Depending on the circumstances, that protection may involve such actions as warning the potential victim, notifying the police of the potential threat posed by the client, or both. See also DUTY TO PROTECT; DUTY TO WARN.

tardive *adj.* denoting delayed or late-arriving symptoms or disease characteristics, as in TARDIVE DYSKINESIA.

tardive dyskinesia a movement disorder associated with the use of ANTIPSYCHOTICS, particularly conventional antipsychotics that act primarily as DOPAMINE-RECEPTOR antagonists. It is more common with prolonged use, and older patients, females, and patients with mood disorders are thought to be more susceptible. Symptoms include tremor and spasticity of muscle groups. Onset is insidious and may be masked by continued use of the antipsychotic, only appearing when the drug is discontinued or the dose lowered. Its incidence is estimated at up to 40% of long-term users of conventional antipsychotics; the incidence is lower with atypical antipsychotics. No effective treatment is known.

tardive dysmentia a behavioral disorder associated with long-term use of antipsychotic drugs and characterized by changes in affect, social behavior, and level of activity. Symptoms may include an inappropriately loud voice and loquaciousness, euphoria, intrusive behavior, and thought disorder. In addition, the individual may exhibit episodes of social withdrawal interspersed with episodes of hyperactivity, as well as excessive emotional reactivity and explosive hostility. Also called **iatrogenic schizophrenia**; **tardive psychosis**.

target *n.* **1.** an area, object, or person that is the focus of a process, inquiry, or activity. **2.** the goal object in a task. For example, the target in a VISUAL SEARCH might be to find a letter *S* in a randomly arranged array of letters. **3.** a tissue, organ, or type of cell that is selectively affected by a particular hormone, neurochemical, drug, or microorganism. **4.** a NEURON that attracts the growth of the DENDRITES or AXONS of other neurons toward it. **5.** in parapsychology, the object or event that the participant attempts to identify in tests of CLAIRVOYANCE, the message that he or she attempts to respond to in tests of TELEPATHY, or the object that he or she attempts to influence in tests of PSYCHOKINESIS.

target population the population that a study is intended to research and to which generalizations from samples are to be made.

task *n.* any goal-oriented activity undertaken by

an individual or a group. When such an activity is the subject of observation in an experimental setting (e.g., in problem-solving and decision-making studies or in studies of perception and cognition), the researcher may set particular objectives and control and manipulate those objectives, stimuli, or possible responses, thus changing task parameters to observe behavioral adjustments. See also SEARCH.

task analysis 1. the breakdown of a complex task into component tasks to identify the different skills needed to correctly complete the task. For example, in organizational settings, a job may be broken down into the skills, knowledge, and specific operations required. See also JOB ANALYSIS. **2.** in ergonomics, a method of evaluating a product or system in which researchers interview actual users to find out (a) what tasks are performed; (b) which of these are most frequently performed and which are most important; (c) how and in what sequence the tasks are performed; (d) what standards of performance apply; and (e) how different categories of user vary in their answers to the above. Although some scripted questions are asked, the interviews are otherwise unstructured, the better to reflect users' actual experience. Compare HEURISTIC.

task cohesion the degree to which members of a team or group are attracted to a task and work together through the integration of their skills to complete the task successfully.

task demands the impact of a task's characteristics, including its divisibility and difficulty, on the procedures that an individual or group can use to complete the task.

task identity a motivating characteristic of tasks specified in the JOB-CHARACTERISTICS MODEL. A job is high in task identity if it entails responsibility for a complete and identifiable piece of work, as in writing a book or planning and executing an action program from start to finish. Compare TASK SIGNIFICANCE.

task role one of several identifiable ROLES adopted by group members who perform particular behaviors that promote completion of tasks and activities. Some commonly cited task roles include the **initiator**, who sets goals and suggests ways of attaining them; the **opinion giver** (or information giver); the **opinion seeker** (or information seeker); the **summarizer**, who clarifies what others have said and pulls ideas together; and the **recorder**, who writes down suggestions and decisions. Compare RELATIONSHIP ROLE. See also GROUP ROLE.

task significance a motivating characteristic of tasks specified in the JOB-CHARACTERISTICS MODEL. Jobs high in task significance are those that are perceived to be important to the organization or to have high impact on the lives of others. Compare TASK IDENTITY.

task specificity of language the theory, mainly associated with U.S. linguist Noam Chomsky (1928–), that language use differs from other cognitive tasks in qualitative ways and makes use of components that are specific to this purpose. The theory accords with Chomsky's ideas of AUTONOMOUS SYNTAX and intuited GRAMMATICALITY but is incompatible with the approaches taken in FUNCTIONAL GRAMMAR, COGNITIVE GRAMMAR, or behaviorist accounts of language.

task structure the extent to which there is a clear relationship of means to ends in the performance of a task. In a highly structured task the procedures required to perform the task successfully are known, whereas in an unstructured task there is uncertainty about how to proceed.

tastant *n.* a substance that can be tasted.

taste *n.* the sense devoted to the detection of molecules dissolved in liquids (also called **gustation**), or the sensory experience resulting from perception of gustatory qualities (e.g., sweetness, saltiness, sourness, bitterness). Dissolved molecules are delivered to the taste receptors—TASTE CELLS—on the tongue, soft palate, larynx, and pharynx. Taste combines with smell, texture, and appearance to generate a sense of FLAVOR. See also PRIMARY TASTE.

taste adaptation a decrease in sensitivity to a stimulus that has been presented continuously to the GUSTATORY SYSTEM. Adaptation can be complete, and the perception lost, after minutes of stimulation. Adaptation is used to determine whether two stimuli share the same receptor population by inducing adaptation to the first stimulus and then evaluating the degree to which the perception of the second stimulus is diminished.

taste-aversion learning see CONDITIONED TASTE AVERSION.

taste blindness reduced sensitivity to the bitter taste of phenylthiocarbamide (PTC) or propylthiouracil (PROP). Originally thought to be a simple Mendelian recessive trait, taste blindness is now known to extend to other bitter tastes, as well as to salty and sweet tastes, and is associated with having fewer TASTE BUDS.

taste bud a goblet-shaped structure, 30×50 μm, about 6,000 of which occur in the human mouth. Each bud is a collection of about 50 TASTE CELLS arranged like sections of an orange. At its apex is a taste pore through which each taste cell sends a MICROVILLUS studded with receptor proteins to sample the environment.

taste cell a receptor cell for gustatory stimuli. Each has a hairlike extension (see MICROVILLUS) that protrudes from the opening in the TASTE BUD. Humans have about 300,000 taste cells, though the number can vary across individuals, and there are about 50 cells per taste bud. Taste cells can be divided into four anatomical types: TYPE I CELLS comprise 60% of the total, TYPE II CELLS 20%, TYPE III CELLS 15%, and TYPE IV CELLS 5%. All but Type IV cells may be involved in TASTE TRANSDUCTION. See also GUSTATORY NEURON TYPES.

taste pore a 6-μm opening at the top of each taste bud through which the MICROVILLI of its 50 taste cells project to sample the chemical environment.

taste system see GUSTATORY SYSTEM.

taste transduction the sequence of events involved in converting the detection of chemical molecules into taste signals. Taste stimuli interact with the MICROVILLUS of a taste cell, which results in changes in activity in the ion channels within taste receptors. The subsequent DEPOLARIZATION within these receptors triggers the release of neurotransmitters that stimulate sensory neurons in the peripheral nervous system. The mechanisms of transduction vary with the type of gustatory stimulus, although each taste cell is capable of transducing different stimuli. Also called **gustatory transduction**.

TAT abbreviation for THEMATIC APPERCEPTION TEST.

tau effect 1. the effect of the timing of stimuli on their perceived spatial location. For example, if three equidistant lights are flashed in succession, but the time interval between the first two is shorter than that between the second and third, then the first two lights are perceived to be closer together than the second and third. **2.** the invariant that the time to contact between an object and an observer moving at a constant speed toward each other is inversely proportional to the rate of expansion of the observer's retinal image of the object, regardless of the size of the object or the speed at which it travels. Research suggests that the tau effect is used in a variety of situations involving the control of movements, for example, by a ballplayer when preparing to catch a ball and by a diving gull in retracting its wings before hitting the surface of the water to catch a fish.

taxis *n.* (*pl.* **taxes**) active movement of motile organisms in response to a stimulus. Taxis can be a negative response, marked by movement away from the stimulus, or positive, in which case the organism moves toward the stimulus. Taxis differs from TROPISM, which refers to a simple orientation to or from a natural force (e.g., light or gravity) without changing place, as in plants. Compare KINESIS. —**taxic** or **tactic** *adj.*

taxonomy *n.* the science of classification, for example, BIOLOGICAL TAXONOMY, or any scheme of classification itself. —**taxonomic** *adj.* —**taxonomist** *n.*

Tay–Sachs disease an autosomal recessive disorder (see RECESSIVE ALLELE) due to a deficiency of the enzyme hexosaminidase A, resulting in the accumulation of G_{M2} gangliosides in all tissues. This process gradually destroys the brain and nerve cells by altering the shape of neurons. Development is normal until the 6th month of infancy, after which there is a deterioration of motor, visual, and cognitive abilities. Death usually occurs between 3 and 5 years of age. Also called G_{M2} **gangliosidosis**.

TBI abbreviation for TRAUMATIC BRAIN INJURY.

TCAs abbreviation for TRICYCLIC ANTIDEPRESSANTS.

T data *test data*: information about an individual gathered from formal scientific measurement and objective testing. See also L DATA; O DATA; Q DATA.

t distribution a theoretical PROBABILITY DISTRIBUTION that plays a central role in testing hypotheses about population means among other parameters. It is the sampling distribution of the statistic $(M - \mu_0)/s$, where μ_0 is the population mean of the population from which the sample is drawn, M is the data estimate of the mean of the population, and s is the standard deviation of the batch of scores. Also called **Student's t distribution**.

team *n.* an organized task-focused group. Members of such groups combine their individual inputs in a deliberate way in the pursuit of a common goal and are typically cohesive and united.

team building a structured intervention designed to increase the extent to which a group functions as a team. Such interventions often involve assessing the current level of GROUP DEVELOPMENT, clarifying and prioritizing goals, and increasing group cohesiveness.

technical eclecticism in INTEGRATIVE PSYCHOTHERAPY, the use of techniques from various theoretical frameworks to deal with the complex issues of a client. Technical eclecticism uses a systematic and carefully thought out approach that balances theoretical perspectives and treatment processes.

tectorial membrane part of the ORGAN OF CORTI in the cochlea. It consists of a semigelatinous membrane in which the stereocilia of the outer HAIR CELLS are embedded.

tectospinal tract see VENTROMEDIAL PATHWAYS.

tectum *n.* (*pl.* **tecta**) the roof of the MIDBRAIN, dorsal to the CEREBRAL AQUEDUCT. The tectum contains the superior COLLICULI, which act as relay and reflex centers for the visual system, and the inferior colliculi, which are sensory centers for the auditory system. —**tectal** *adj.*

tegmentum *n.* (*pl.* **tegmenta**) the central core of the MIDBRAIN and PONS. It contains sensory and motor tracts passing through the midbrain and also several nuclei, including the oculomotor nucleus (associated with the OCULOMOTOR NERVE) and the SUBTHALAMIC NUCLEUS. —**tegmental** *adj.*

Tegretol *n.* a trade name for CARBAMAZEPINE.

telegnosis *n.* in parapsychology, alleged knowledge of distant events without direct communication, as by CLAIRVOYANCE or TELEPATHY. See EXTRASENSORY PERCEPTION.

telegraphic speech 1. condensed or abbreviated speech in which only the most central words, carrying the highest level of information, are spoken. Nouns and verbs are typically featured, while adjectives, adverbs, articles, and connective parts of speech are omitted. **2.** the speech of children roughly between the ages of 18 and 30 months, which is usually in the form of two-word expressions up to the age of about 24 months (see TWO-WORD STAGE) and characterized by short but multiword expressions (e.g., *dog eat bone*) thereafter.

telehealth *n.* the use of telecommunications and information technology to provide access to health assessment, diagnosis, intervention, and information across a distance, rather than face to face. Also called **telemedicine**.

telekinesis *n.* see PSYCHOKINESIS.

telemetry *n.* the process of measuring and transmitting quantitative information to a remote location, where it can be recorded and interpreted. For example, a small radio transmitter may be implanted inside an animal to measure general activity level as well as a variety of physiological variables, including body temperature, heart rate, and blood pressure. This transmitter sends signals to a receiver located outside the animal. —**telemetric** *adj.*

telencephalon *n.* see CEREBRUM.

teleology *n.* **1.** the position that certain phenomena are best understood and explained in terms of their purposes rather than their causes. In psychology, its proponents hold that mental processes are purposive, that is, directed toward a goal. The view that behavior is to be explained in terms of ends and purposes is frequently contrasted with explanations in terms of causes, such as INSTINCTS and CONDITIONED RESPONSES. See also PURPOSIVE PSYCHOLOGY. **2.** the doctrine that the universe or human history or both have purpose and direction and are moving toward a particular goal. This position is often a religious one. —**teleologic** or **teleological** *adj.*

teleonomy *n.* **1.** the property of being goal-directed in terms of structures, functions, and behaviors, which is a fundamental characteristic of living organisms. **2.** the apparently directional or "purposeful" character of evolutionary adaptation. The term is used in this context in order to avoid the metaphysical implications of TELEOLOGY. —**teleonomic** *adj.*

teleopsia *n.* a VISUAL ILLUSION in which an object appears to be more distant than it is in reality. In some cases, this is caused by lesions in the parietal temporal area of the brain. See also METAMORPHOPSIA.

telepathy *n.* the alleged direct communication of information from one mind to another, in the absence of any known means of transmission. It is a form of EXTRASENSORY PERCEPTION. See also MIND READING; THOUGHT TRANSFERENCE. —**telepath** *n.* —**telepathic** *adj.*

telephone counseling 1. a method of treating and dealing with the problems of clients by tele-

phone. The skills for telephone counseling include (a) careful selection of problems that lend themselves to the medium, (b) ACTIVE LISTENING for cues to issues and ramifications of the problems, (c) good verbal skills that guide the client appropriately, and (d) ability to respond quickly to avoid gaps and awkward silences. **2.** free HOTLINE telephone services that provide listening and referral services rather than formal counseling. Hotline volunteers are trained to provide emotional support in serious situations, especially those involving suicidal thoughts, but not to give formal advice. See also DISTANCE THERAPY.

telepsychotherapy *n.* see DISTANCE THERAPY.

telic *adj.* purposeful or goal-directed in nature, as in **telic behavior**. See also TELEOLOGY.

telic continuum a typically J-shaped curve that describes purposeful behavior, plotting the degree of conformity to an established rule or principle. Also called **conformity curve**.

temper *n.* **1.** a display of irritation or anger, or a tendency to be quick to anger. See also TEMPER TANTRUM. **2.** a personality characteristic, disposition, or mood.

temperament *n.* the basic foundation of personality, usually assumed to be biologically determined and present early in life, including such characteristics as energy level, emotional responsiveness, demeanor, mood, response tempo, and willingness to explore. In animal behavior, temperament is defined as an individual's constitutional pattern of reactions, with a similar range of characteristics.

temperament trait a biologically based, inherited personality characteristic that involves emotional qualities and affective styles of behavior.

temperance *n.* any form of auspicious self-restraint, manifested as self-regulation in monitoring and managing one's emotions, motivation, and behavior and as self-control in the attainment of adaptive goals.

temperature sense a part of the SOMATOSENSORY SYSTEM concerned with the perception of hotness and coldness, with receptors at various depths in the skin and other body surfaces (e.g., the tongue) that may be exposed to the environment. Also called **thermoesthesia; thermesthesia**.

temper tantrum a violent outburst of anger commonly occurring between the ages of 2 and 4 and involving such behavior as screaming, kicking, biting, hitting, and head banging. The episodes are usually out of proportion to immediate provocation and sometimes regarded as an expression of accumulated tensions and frustrations. Also called **tantrum**. See also OPPOSITIONAL DEFIANT DISORDER.

template-matching theory the hypothesis that PATTERN RECOGNITION proceeds by comparing an incoming sensory stimulation pattern to mental images or representations of patterns (templates) until a match is found. This theory is largely considered too simplistic, since the same stimulus can be viewed from multiple perspectives, thereby altering the input pattern, and since a particular stimulus can have many different variations (e.g., a letter of the alphabet can be printed in numerous styles, sizes, orientations, etc.); it is impossible to store a template for each specific perspective or variation.

temporal *adj.* **1.** of or pertaining to time or its role in some process. **2.** relating or proximal to the temple, as in TEMPORAL LOBE. —**temporally** *adv.*

temporal appraisal theory a model stating that people's evaluations of themselves in the past tend to be more negative than their current evaluations of themselves.

temporal conditioning a procedure in PAVLOVIAN CONDITIONING in which the unconditioned stimulus is presented at regular intervals but in the absence of an accompanying conditioned stimulus. Compare TRACE CONDITIONING.

temporal construal theory a model stating that people rely on largely abstract representations (high-level construals) of future situations when making decisions for the distant future but on more concrete representations (low-level construals) when making decisions for the near future.

temporal gradient a pattern of retrograde AMNESIA characterized by greater loss of memory for events from the recent past (i.e., close to the onset of the amnesia) than for events from the remote past.

temporal lobe one of the four main lobes of each CEREBRAL HEMISPHERE in the brain, lying immediately below the LATERAL SULCUS on the lower lateral surface of each hemisphere. It contains the auditory projection and auditory association areas and also areas for higher order visual processing. The **medial temporal lobe** contains regions important for memory formation.

temporal lobe amnesia a memory disorder, secondary to injury of the temporal lobe (particularly medial structures, such as the hippocampus), that prevents the formation of new memories.

temporal lobectomy the surgical excision of a temporal lobe or a portion of the lobe. It may be performed in the treatment of temporal lobe epilepsy, the location and size of the lesion determining which tissues and related functions may be affected.

temporal lobe epilepsy a type of epilepsy characterized by recurrent COMPLEX PARTIAL SEIZURES of temporal lobe origin.

temporal lobe illusions distorted perceptions that may be associated with COMPLEX PARTIAL SEIZURES arising from abnormal discharge

of neurons in the temporal lobe. They often include distortions of the sizes or shapes of objects, recurring dreamlike thoughts, or sensations of déjà vu. Hallucinations, such as the sound of threatening voices, may also be experienced. Also called **temporal hallucinations**; **temporal lobe hallucinations**.

temporal perceptual disorder a condition, observed in some individuals with lesions in the left hemisphere of the brain, that is characterized by difficulty in temporal perception of visual and auditory stimuli. For example, individuals may be unable to identify the sequences of vowels repeated at measured time intervals.

temporal summation a neural mechanism in which an impulse is propagated by two successive POSTSYNAPTIC POTENTIALS (PSPs), neither of which alone is of sufficient intensity to cause a response. The partial DEPOLARIZATION caused by the first PSP continues for a few milliseconds and is able, with the additive effect of the second PSP, to produce an above-threshold depolarization sufficient to elicit an ACTION POTENTIAL. Compare SPATIAL SUMMATION.

temporary threshold shift a temporary condition in which the normal level of hearing is altered or disrupted. For example, after relatively prolonged exposure to very loud noise, the absolute threshold may shift so that minimal sound intensities one could normally detect are temporarily inaudible. A similar shift can occur in vision.

tendon *n.* a strong band of tissue that connects a muscle to a bone.

tendon reflex the reflex contraction of a muscle elicited by stretching a tendon. A well-known example is the PATELLAR REFLEX.

TENS *transcutaneous electrical nerve stimulation:* a procedure in which mild electrical pulses are delivered through small electrodes attached to the skin. TENS is most commonly used to relieve or reduce chronic pain: The pulses stimulate nerves that supply the region in which the pain is felt and thus inhibit transmission of pain signals.

tension *n.* **1.** a feeling of physical and psychological strain accompanied by discomfort, uneasiness, and pressure to seek relief through talk or action. **2.** the force resulting from contraction or stretching of a muscle or tendon.

tension law a concept that any deviation from an organism's optimal level of external conditions (e.g., temperature, atmospheric pressure) produces a state of tension. Compare HOMEOSTASIS.

tensor tympani a middle ear muscle that controls the movement of the TYMPANIC MEMBRANE (eardrum). Its activation (the **tympanic reflex**) is part of the ACOUSTIC REFLEX.

teratogenic *adj.* inducing developmental abnormalities in a fetus. A **teratogen** is an agent or

T

process that causes such abnormal developments, a process called **teratogenesis**; a **teratomorph** is a fetus or offspring with developmental abnormalities.

teratology *n.* the study of developmental abnormalities and their causes. **—teratological** *adj.*

terminal behavior 1. relatively unvaried behavior that is predominant in the period shortly before reinforcement occurs during operant or instrumental conditioning. Compare ADJUNCTIVE BEHAVIOR. **2.** a response that either falls outside an organism's current behavioral repertoire or is not occurring at a desired rate, strength, or magnitude. Increasing terminal behavior is the aim of specific behavioral interventions.

terminal button see AXON.

terminal care services for people with terminal illness, now usually provided by HOSPICES, which may be either freestanding units or associated with a hospital, nursing home, or extended care facility. The emphasis is on PALLIATIVE CARE, pain control, supportive psychological services, and involvement in family and social activities, with the goal of enabling patients to live out their lives in comfort, peace, and dignity.

terminal drop a rapid decline in cognitive abilities immediately before death. The cognitive abilities that appear to be most prone to terminal drop are those least affected by normal aging (see HOLD FUNCTIONS). Also called **terminal drop-decline**.

terminal insomnia a form of INSOMNIA in which the individual habitually awakens very early, feels unrefreshed, and cannot go back to sleep. It is a common symptom of a MAJOR DEPRESSIVE EPISODE. Compare INITIAL INSOMNIA; MIDDLE INSOMNIA.

terminal link the schedule in a CHAINED SCHEDULE that ends in primary reinforcement.

termination *n.* in therapy, the conclusion of treatment. Termination may be suggested by the client or therapist or may be by mutual agreement. Termination can be immediate or prolonged; in the latter case, a date for the final session is established and sessions are sometimes scheduled less frequently over a period. In **premature termination**, treatment is ended before either the therapist or client considers the therapy complete. This may result, for example, from difficulties in the relationship between the therapist and client, misunderstanding of the required length of treatment, a change in the client's financial circumstances, or departure of the client to another location.

territoriality *n.* **1.** the defense by an animal of a specific geographic area (its **territory**) against intrusion from other members of the same species. Territoriality is observed in a wide range of animals and is found most often where there are specific defensible resources, such as a concen-

tration of food or shelter. Territoriality is maintained through singing in birds and through scent marking in many mammals (e.g., antelope and dogs), as well as by active patrolling of territory boundaries. A resident is more likely to attack an intruder than vice versa, but attack probability decreases rapidly when the territory holder leaves its own territory. **2.** in humans, behavior associated with the need or ability to control and regulate access to a space, which reflects feelings of identity derived from use of and attachment to a familiar place.

terror management theory a theory proposing that control of death-related anxiety is the primary function of society and the main motivation in human behavior. Individual SELF-ESTEEM and a sense of being integrated into a powerful human culture are regarded as the most effective ways for human beings to defend themselves against the frightening recognition of their own mortality (see DEATH ANXIETY). The need for such defense may be heightened not only by any keen or sudden recognition of personal limitation, but also by any weakening of social institutions (see also DEATH SYSTEM).

tertiary care highly specialized care given to patients who are in danger of disability or death. Tertiary care often requires sophisticated technologies provided by highly specialized practitioners and facilities, for example, neurologists, neurosurgeons, thoracic surgeons, and intensive care units. Compare PRIMARY CARE; SECONDARY CARE.

tertiary circular reaction in the PIAGETIAN THEORY of cognitive development, an infant's action that creatively alters former SCHEMES to fit the requirements of new situations. Tertiary circular reactions emerge toward the end of the SENSORIMOTOR STAGE, at about the beginning of the 2nd year; they differ from earlier behaviors in that the child can, for the first time, develop new schemes to achieve a desired goal. See also PRIMARY CIRCULAR REACTION; SECONDARY CIRCULAR REACTION.

tertiary prevention intervention and treatment for individuals or groups with already established psychological or physical conditions, disorders, or diseases. Tertiary interventions include attempts to minimize negative effects, prevent further disease or disorder related to complications, prevent relapse, and restore the highest physical or psychological functioning possible. Compare PRIMARY PREVENTION; SECONDARY PREVENTION.

test 1. *n.* any procedure or method to examine or determine the presence of some factor or phenomenon. **2.** *n.* a standardized set of questions or other items designed to assess knowledge, skills, interests, or other characteristics of an examinee. See PSYCHOLOGICAL TEST. **3.** *n.* a set of operations, usually statistical in nature, designed to determine the VALIDITY of a hypothesis. **4.** *vb.* to administer a test.

testability *n.* the degree to which a hypothesis or theory is capable of being evaluated empirically.

test age see AGE EQUIVALENT.

test battery a group or series of related tests administered at one time, with scores recorded separately or combined to yield a single score.

test bias the tendency of a test to systematically over- or underestimate the true scores of individuals to whom that test is administered, for example because they are members of particular groups (e.g., ethnic minorities, sexes, etc.). See also CULTURAL TEST BIAS.

test construction the creation of a test, usually with a clear intent to meet the usual criteria of VALIDITY, RELIABILITY, NORMS, and other elements of test standardization.

test cutoff 1. the prearranged ending point or limit for an assessment. The limit may be in terms of time, number of answers given incorrectly, or number of questions administered. **2.** a predetermined score performance standard for a given test. Those who perform at or above this score will be considered, for example, for certain programs or colleges; those who perform below this score will not.

testicle *n.* a TESTIS and its surrounding structures, including the system of ducts within the scrotum. —**testicular** *adj.*

testing the limits 1. a method used to study adult age differences in cognition in which research participants are required to perform a task to the best of their ability and are then tested after extensive practice on the task. See also RESERVE CAPACITY. **2.** in psychological testing, allowing a participant to proceed beyond time limits (or waiving other standardized requirements) to see if he or she can complete an item or do better under alternate conditions. **3.** in general psychology, attempts by an individual to see how far he or she can test rules before the rules are enforced. An example would be seeing how much talking one can get away with in a class before being reprimanded by the teacher.

testis *n.* (*pl.* **testes**) the principal reproductive organ in males, a pair of which is normally located in the scrotum. The testes produce sperm in the SEMINIFEROUS TUBULES (see SPERMATOGENESIS) and male sex hormones (ANDROGENS) in INTERSTITIAL CELLS. Also called **orchis**. See TESTICLE.

test of significance any of a set of procedures used to assess the probability that a set of empirical results could have been obtained if the NULL HYPOTHESIS were true.

test of simple effects a statistical test of differences between levels of one factor (INDEPENDENT VARIABLE) in a FACTORIAL DESIGN at a single level of the other factors in the design.

testosterone *n.* a male sex hormone and the most potent of the ANDROGENS produced by the testes. It stimulates the development of male re-productive organs, including the prostate gland, and secondary SEX CHARACTERISTICS, such as beard, bone, and muscle growth. Women normally secrete small amounts of testosterone from the adrenal cortex and ovary.

test–retest correlation a CORRELATION that represents the stability of a variable over time.

test–retest reliability see RETEST RELIABILITY.

test selection the process of choosing the most useful or appropriate test or set of assessment instruments in order to provide accurate diagnostic or other psychological information. Test selection is made on the basis of psychological history (often in conjunction with medical history), interviews, other pretest knowledge of the individual or group to be tested, or some combination of these.

test theory see CLASSICAL TEST THEORY.

tetrahydrocannabinol (**THC**) *n.* one of a number of CANNABINOIDS occurring in the CANNABIS plant that is the agent principally responsible for the psychoactive properties of cannabis. THC is available in a synthetic pharmaceutical preparation known as **dronabinol** (U.S. trade name: **Marinol**) for use in the treatment of chemotherapy-induced nausea and vomiting and as an appetite stimulant for the treatment of HIV-related anorexia. Research suggests it may also be effective in reducing intraocular pressure and as an analgesic.

textons *pl. n.* elemental features of visual stimuli that provide the basis for preattentive segmentation of a visual scene, prior to the direction of focused attention on any one object within the scene (see FEATURE-INTEGRATION THEORY). There are three categories of textons: elongated blobs (with their attendant color, orientation, and width); terminators, which convey the end of a line segment; and crossings of line segments.

T-group *n.* training group: a type of experiential group, usually of up to a dozen or so people, concerned with fostering the development of "basic skills," such as effective leadership and communication, and attitude change. Although the term is sometimes used synonymously with ENCOUNTER GROUP, in a T-group less emphasis is placed on personal growth and more on SENSITIVITY TRAINING and practical interpersonal skills. One of the goals of T-groups is to foster greater understanding of group dynamics and of the individual members' roles within the group or organization.

thalamic taste area the area of the thalamus that relays taste information from the SOLITARY NUCLEUS to the PRIMARY TASTE CORTEX. About one third of its neurons respond to taste; others are activated by touch or temperature stimulation of the mouth or even the anticipation of an approaching taste stimulus.

thalamocortical system the THALAMUS and CEREBRAL CORTEX: parts of the brain that—especially in mammals—are so closely and reciprocally interconnected that they are often treated as a single system. Normal functioning of this system appears to be necessary for normal conscious experience and action.

thalamus *n.* (*pl.* **thalami**) a mass of gray matter, forming part of the DIENCEPHALON of the brain, whose two lobes form the walls of the THIRD VENTRICLE. It consists of a collection of sensory, motor, autonomic, and associational nuclei, serving as a relay for nerve impulses traveling between the spinal cord and brainstem and the cerebral cortex. Specific areas of the body surface and cerebral cortex are related to specific parts of the thalamus. —**thalamic** *adj.*

thanatology *n.* the study of death and death-related behaviors, thoughts, feelings, and phenomena. Death was mostly the province of theology until the 1960s, when existential thinkers and a broad spectrum of care providers, educators, and social and behavioral scientists became interested in death-related issues. —**thanatologist** *n.*

thanatophobia *n.* a persistent and irrational fear of death or dying. This fear may focus on the death of oneself or of loved ones and is often associated with HYPOCHONDRIASIS. —**thanatophobic** *adj.*

Thanatos *n.* the personification of death and the brother of Hypnos (sleep) in Greek mythology, whose name was chosen by Austrian psychiatrist Sigmund Freud (1856–1939) to designate a theoretical set of strivings oriented toward the reduction of tension and life activity (see DEATH INSTINCT). In Freud's DUAL INSTINCT THEORY, Thanatos is seen as involved in a dialectic process with EROS (love), the striving toward sexuality, continued development, and heightened experience (see LIFE INSTINCT). See also DESTRUDO.

that's-not-all technique a two-step procedure for enhancing compliance that consists of presenting an initial, large request and then, before the person can respond, immediately reducing it to a more modest target request. The target request is sometimes made more attractive by offering some additional benefit. Compliance with the target request is greater following the initial request than would have been the case if the target request had been presented on its own. See also DOOR-IN-THE-FACE TECHNIQUE; FOOT-IN-THE-DOOR TECHNIQUE; LOW-BALL TECHNIQUE.

THC abbreviation for TETRAHYDROCANNABINOL.

theater of consciousness a metaphor for, or conceptualization of, consciousness in which conscious events are compared to a play on a stage, while unconscious psychological functions are represented by the audience and the backstage crew.

Thematic Apperception Test (**TAT**) a projective test in which participants are held to reveal their attitudes, feelings, conflicts, and personality characteristics in the oral or written stories they make up about a series of relatively ambiguous black-and-white pictures. The examiner assures the participant that there are no right or wrong answers and indicates that the narratives should have a beginning, middle, and ending. At the end, the stories are discussed for diagnostic purposes. Systematic coding schemes, with demonstrated reliability and validity, have been developed to assess different aspects of personality functioning derived from TAT stories, including motivation for achievement, power, affiliation, and intimacy; gender identity; DEFENSE MECHANISMS; and mental processes influencing interpersonal relations. The TAT is one of the most frequently used and researched tests in psychology, particularly in clinical settings for diagnosis, personality description, and assessment of strengths and weakness in personality functioning.

theoretical integration the integration of theoretical concepts from different approaches to produce meaningful frames of reference that may help explain the dynamics or causes of problems or the functioning of an individual when any single traditional theoretical approach individually fails to explain the behavior adequately.

theory *n.* **1.** a principle or body of interrelated principles that purports to explain or predict a number of interrelated phenomena. See CONSTRUCT; MODEL. **2.** in the philosophy of science, a set of logically related explanatory hypotheses that are consistent with a body of empirical facts and that may suggest more empirical relationships. **3.** in general usage, abstract or speculative thought as opposed to practice or reality. —**theoretical** *adj.*

theory of mental self-government a model of COGNITIVE STYLES that proposes several dimensions to describe the preferred ways in which individuals think or express their cognitive abilities. The dimensions include (a) governmental—preferences in the legislative, executive, and judicial functions of cognition (i.e., in planning, implementing, and evaluating); (b) problem solving—styles labeled monarchic (a tendency to pursue one goal at a time), hierarchic (multiple goals with different priorities), oligarchic (multiple, equally important goals), and anarchic (unstructured, random problem solving); (c) global versus local thinking—preferring to think about large, abstract issues on the one hand or concrete details on the other; (d) internal versus external thinking—related to introversion–extraversion, social skills, and cooperativeness; and (e) conservative or progressive—rule-based leanings versus those that are creative and change-oriented.

theory of mind the ability to imagine or make deductions about the mental states of other individuals: What does the other individual know? What actions is that individual likely to take? Theory of mind is an essential component of attributing beliefs, intentions, and desires to others, specifically in order to predict their behavior. See also BELIEF–DESIRE REASONING; FALSE-BELIEF TASK.

theory of personal investment a motivational theory stating that the degree to which an individual will invest personal resources of time and effort in an activity, in anticipation of benefits, is a function of personal incentives (mastery orientation, competitive orientation, affiliation, status), beliefs about oneself (sense of competence, self-reliance, goal directedness, identity), and perceived options (behavioral options perceived to be available in the specific situation).

theory of planned behavior a theory that resembles the THEORY OF REASONED ACTION but also incorporates the construct of PERCEIVED BEHAVIORAL CONTROL. That is, the extent to which a person believes behavior is under his or her active control is added to attitude toward behavior and SUBJECTIVE NORMS as the antecedents influencing both the intention to perform a behavior and the performance of the behavior itself.

theory of reasoned action the theory that attitudes toward a behavior and SUBJECTIVE NORMS (perceived expectations) regarding a behavior determine a person's intention to perform that behavior. Intentions are in turn assumed to cause the actual behavior. Also called **reasoned action model**. See also THEORY OF PLANNED BEHAVIOR.

theory theory any model of cognitive development that combines NEONATIVISM and CONSTRUCTIVISM, proposing that cognitive development progresses by children generating, testing, and changing theories about the physical and social world.

therapeutic 1. *adj.* pertaining to **therapeutics**, the branch of medical science concerned with the treatment of diseases and disorders and the discovery and application of remedial agents or methods. **2.** *adj.* having beneficial or curative effects. **3.** *n.* a compound that is used to treat specific diseases or medical conditions.

therapeutic agent any means of advancing the treatment process, such as a drug, occupational therapy, a therapist, or a THERAPEUTIC COMMUNITY. The therapeutic agent is presumed to be the causative agent in patient change.

therapeutic alliance a cooperative working relationship between client and therapist, considered by many to be an essential aspect of successful therapy. Derived from the concept of the psychoanalytic working alliance, the therapeutic alliance comprises bonds, goals, and tasks. Bonds are constituted by the core conditions of therapy, the client's attitude toward the therapist, and the therapist's style of relating to the client; goals are the mutually negotiated, understood, agreed upon, and regularly reviewed aims of the therapy; and tasks are the activities carried out by both client and therapist. See THERAPIST–PATIENT RELATIONSHIP.

therapeutic community a setting for individuals requiring therapy for a range of psycho-

social problems and disorders that is based on an interpersonal, socially interactive approach to treatment, both among residents and among residents and staff (i.e., "community as method or therapy"). The term covers a variety of short- and long-term residential programs as well as day treatment and ambulatory programs. The staff is typically multidisciplinary and may consist of human services professionals and clinicians providing mental health, medical, vocational, educational, fiscal, and legal services, among others. See MILIEU THERAPY.

therapeutic factors curative factors that operate across models and techniques in GROUP PSYCHOTHERAPY. Factors identified include altruism, catharsis, cohesion, family reenactment, feedback, hope, identification, interpersonal learning, reality testing, role flexibility, universality, and vicarious learning. Therapeutic factors are often confused with COMMON FACTORS because both delineate effective change factors across theoretical models and techniques of therapy; however, common factors refer to individual psychotherapy, whereas therapeutic factors refer to group psychotherapy.

therapeutic index any of several indices relating the clinical effectiveness of a drug to its safety factor, the most common being the THERAPEUTIC RATIO. Other therapeutic indices include the ratio of the minimum toxic dose to the minimum EFFECTIVE DOSE and the difference between the minimum effective dose and the minimum toxic dose.

therapeutic process see PSYCHOTHERAPEUTIC PROCESS.

therapeutic ratio an index relating the clinical effectiveness of a drug to its safety factor, calculated by dividing the median LETHAL DOSE (LD_{50}) by the median EFFECTIVE DOSE (ED_{50}). A drug is often considered safe only if its therapeutic ratio is at least 10.

therapeutic role the functions of the therapist or other THERAPEUTIC AGENT in treating psychological disorders, alleviating painful responses or symptoms resulting from a distressing condition, or altering maladaptive thinking or behavior.

therapeutic touch see TOUCH THERAPY.

therapeutic window the range of plasma levels of a drug within which optimal therapeutic effects occur. Suboptimal effects may occur both below and above the therapeutic window. Evidence for true therapeutic windows was never well established; perhaps the best evidence existed for the tricyclic antidepressant nortriptyline. Few modern psychotropic drugs require therapeutic monitoring, although LITHIUM is a notable exception. Therapeutic windows are increasingly becoming less significant in modern clinical psychopharmacology.

therapist *n.* an individual who has been trained in and practices one or more types of therapy to treat mental or physical disorders or diseases:

often used synonymously with psychotherapist (see PSYCHOTHERAPY).

therapist–patient relationship the relationship formed in therapy between a psychotherapist and the patient (client) receiving therapy. There has been much theory and research concerning this interaction: how it varies and changes over time and the significant implications that the dynamic has for the way in which treatment is offered and its outcomes. The relationship has ethical dimensions that are often specified in PRACTICE GUIDELINES. See also THERAPEUTIC ALLIANCE.

therapy *n.* **1.** remediation of physical, mental, or behavioral disorders or disease. **2.** see PSYCHOTHERAPY.

therapy puppet a puppet used for ROLE PLAY in therapy with children. The use of a therapy puppet is sometimes more conducive to the child's revelation of thoughts and feelings than direct communication by the child with the therapist.

therblig *n.* a unit of movement sometimes used to describe and record industrial operations for the purposes of TIME AND MOTION STUDIES. It represents any one of the 18 fundamental, standardized activities involved in such operations: search, find, select, grasp, hold, position, assemble, use, disassemble, inspect, transport loaded, transport unloaded, pre-position for next operation, release load, unavoidable delay, avoidable delay, plan, and rest to overcome fatigue.

thermalgesia *n.* an abnormal reaction to heat in which a warm stimulus produces pain.

thermalgia *n.* a condition characterized by intense, burning pain.

thermoanesthesia *n.* **1.** loss or absence of the ability to distinguish between heat and cold by touch. **2.** insensitivity to heat. Also called **thermanesthesia**.

thermoreceptor *n.* **1.** a receptor or sense organ that is activated by temperature stimuli (e.g., cold or warm stimuli). **2.** a part of the central nervous system that monitors and maintains the temperature of the body core and its vital organs. There is evidence for separate thermoregulatory regions in the spinal cord, brainstem, and hypothalamus.

thermoregulation *n.* the behavioral and physiological processes, collectively, that maintain normal body temperature. These processes include sweating and shivering. See also HOMEOSTASIS.

thesis *n.* (*pl.* **theses**) **1.** in logic, a proposition to be subjected to logical analysis in the interest of proof or disproof. **2.** more generally, any idea or proposition put forward in argument. **3.** in philosophy, the first stage of a dialectical process: a proposition that is opposed by an ANTITHESIS, thereby generating a new proposition referred to as a SYNTHESIS. The synthesis serves as thesis for the next phase of the ongoing process.

theta wave in electroencephalography, a type of BRAIN WAVE with a frequency of 4–7 Hz. Theta waves are observed in the REM SLEEP of animals, stage 2 sleep in humans, and in the drowsiness state of newborn infants, adolescents, and young adults. Theta waves are also recorded in TRANCES, HYPNOSIS, and deep DAYDREAMS. Neurologically, the hippocampus is one well-known source of theta activity. Also called **theta rhythm**.

thigmesthesia *n.* sensitivity to pressure. See TOUCH SENSE.

think-aloud protocol a transcript of ongoing mental activity, as reported by a participant engaged in some task. The participant thinks aloud while performing the task, thus creating a record of his or her cognitive processing for later analysis.

thinking *n.* cognitive behavior in which ideas, images, MENTAL REPRESENTATIONS, or other hypothetical elements of thought are experienced or manipulated. In this sense thinking includes imagining, remembering, problem solving, daydreaming, FREE ASSOCIATION, concept formation, and many other processes. Thinking may be said to have two defining characteristics: (a) It is covert, that is, it is not directly observable but must be inferred from behavior or self-reports; and (b) it is symbolic, that is, it seems to involve operations on mental symbols or representations, the nature of which remains obscure and controversial (see SYMBOLIC PROCESS).

thinking through a typically multistage, multilayered thought process in which the individual attempts to understand and achieve insight into his or her own reactions, thought processes, or behavior, for example through consideration and analysis of cause and effect.

thioridazine *n.* a low-potency antipsychotic of the piperidine PHENOTHIAZINE class that, like others of its class, causes sedation and significant anticholinergic effects. Adverse effects unique to thioridazine include the potential to cause retinal changes possibly leading to blindness (retinitis pigmentosum) at doses exceeding 800 mg/day. It can also cause severe disturbances in heart rhythm: Its ability to prolong the Q-T interval may cause fatal arrhythmias (see ELECTROCARDIOGRAPHIC EFFECT). It should not be taken by patients who have cardiac arrhythmias or who are taking other drugs that may prolong the Q-T interval. U.S. trade name: **Mellaril**.

third-party administrator in health insurance, a fiscal intermediary organization that provides administrative services, including claims processing and underwriting, for other parties (e.g., insurance companies or employers) but does not carry any insurance risk.

third-party payer an organization, usually an insurance company, prepayment plan, or government agency, that pays for the health expenses incurred by the insured. The third party (to the agreement) is distinguished from the first party, the individual receiving the services, and the second party, the individual or institution providing the services.

third-variable problem the fact that an observed correlation between two variables may be due to the common correlation between each of the variables and a third variable rather than because the two variables have any underlying relationship (in a causal sense) with each other.

third ventricle a cavity of the brain, filled with CEREBROSPINAL FLUID, that forms a cleft between the two lobes of the THALAMUS beneath the cerebral hemispheres (see VENTRICLE). It communicates with the lateral ventricles and caudally with the fourth ventricle through the CEREBRAL AQUEDUCT.

thirst *n.* the sensation caused by a need for increased fluid intake in order to maintain an optimum balance of water and electrolytes in the body tissues. Water is lost from the body mainly in urine, sweat, and via the lungs. Dehydration causes reduced production of saliva and the feeling of a "dry mouth." In addition, a specialized area of the hypothalamus in the brain detects and responds to the changes in OSMOTIC PRESSURE that result from increased concentration of electrolytes in extracellular fluid subsequent to water loss (see OSMORECEPTOR).

Thomistic psychology the psychological principles found in the writings of Italian philosopher and theologian St. Thomas Aquinas (1225–1274) and revived in the early 20th century by a number of Roman Catholic thinkers. Aquinas emphasized ARISTOTELIAN logic, the compatibility of reason with faith, human free will, and the knowledge of God as ultimate happiness.

thoracic *adj.* pertaining to the **thorax**—the portion of the mammalian body cavity bounded by the ribs, shoulders, and diaphragm—or to a structure contained within this region, such as the thoracic vertebrae or the thoracic segments of the SPINAL CORD.

thoracic nerve see SPINAL NERVE.

Thorazine *n.* a trade name for CHLORPROMAZINE.

Thorndike–Lorge list an early and influential list of word frequencies in the English language, compiled in 1944 by U.S. psychologists Edward Thorndike (1874–1949) and Irving D. Lorge (1905–1961). There have been many subsequent updated lists, but this term is still sometimes used generically to mean an empirical list of word frequencies in a language.

thought *n.* **1.** the process of THINKING. **2.** an idea, image, opinion, or other product of thinking. **3.** attention or consideration given to something or someone.

thought avoidance the ability to evade or not consider unpleasant or dissonant mental events. It is a kind of psychological DEFENSE MECHANISM as well as a means of therapeutic change.

thought derailment disorganized, disconnected thought processes, as manifested by a tendency to shift from one topic to another that is indirectly related or completely unrelated to the first. Thought derailment is a symptom of schizophrenia; the term is essentially equivalent to COGNITIVE DERAILMENT. See DERAILMENT.

thought disorder a disturbance in the cognitive processes that affects communication, language, or thought content, including NEOLOGISMS, PARALOGIA, WORD SALAD, and DELUSIONS. A thought disorder is considered by some to be the most important mark of schizophrenia (see also SCHIZOPHRENIC THINKING), but thought disorders are also associated with mood disorders, dementia, mania, and neurological diseases (among others). Also called **thought disturbance**. See CONTENT-THOUGHT DISORDER; FORMAL THOUGHT DISORDER.

thought process any of the COGNITIVE PROCESSES involved in mental activities that are beyond perception, such as reasoning, remembering, imagining, problem solving, and making judgments. See THINKING. See also HIGHER MENTAL PROCESS; MEDIATION PROCESS; SYMBOLIC PROCESS.

thought sampling the process of noting the contents of the STREAM OF CONSCIOUSNESS, for therapeutic or empirical purposes.

thought suppression the attempt to control the content of one's mental processes and specifically to rid oneself of undesired thoughts or images.

thought transference a supposed phenomenon in which the mental activities of one person are transmitted without physical means to the mind of another person. With MIND READING it is one of the two main forms of TELEPATHY.

threat *n.* **1.** a condition that is appraised as a danger to one's self or well-being or to a group. **2.** an indication of unpleasant consequences for failure to comply with a given request or demand, used as a means of coercion. **—threaten** *vb.* **—threatening** *adj.*

threat display any of various ritualized animal communication signals used to indicate that attack or aggression might follow. Examples are fluffed-out fur or feathers, certain facial expressions or body postures, and low-frequency vocalizations (e.g., growls). Animals that are responsive to a threat display can submit or flee before an attack begins. The use of ritualized threat displays can minimize direct physical aggression to the benefit of both individuals.

three-stage theory the view that skill acquisition proceeds through three stages—cognitive, associative, and autonomous—that progressively require less attention and become more automatic.

three-stratum model of intelligence a psychometric model of intelligence based on a factorial reanalysis of several hundred data sets available in the literature. It is considered by some researchers to be the most thoroughly supported of the various PSYCHOMETRIC THEORIES OF INTELLIGENCE. The three strata correspond to (a) minor group factors at the first (lowest) level, (b) major group factors at the second level (fluid intelligence, crystallized intelligence, general memory and learning, broad visual perception, broad auditory perception, broad retrieval ability, broad cognitive speediness, and processing speed), and (c) the general factor at the third (highest) level.

threshold *n.* **1.** in psychophysics, the magnitude of a stimulus that will lead to its detection 50% of the time. **2.** the minimum intensity of a stimulus that is necessary to evoke a response. For example, an AUDITORY THRESHOLD is the slightest perceptible sound and an excitatory threshold is the minimum stimulus that triggers an ACTION POTENTIAL in a neuron. Also called **limen**; **response threshold**. See also ABSOLUTE THRESHOLD; DIFFERENCE THRESHOLD.

threshold of consciousness the psychological level at which stimuli enter awareness, characterized in terms of stimulus intensity, duration, and relevance. It applies to sensory stimuli (visual, auditory, olfactory, tactile, and gustatory) as well as memories and mood.

threshold theory a hypothesis in GROUP DYNAMICS positing that conflict is beneficial and useful provided it does not exceed the tolerance threshold of the group members for too long.

thrombosis *n.* the presence or formation of a blood clot (thrombus) in a blood vessel, including blood vessels in the heart (**coronary thrombosis**). Formation of a blood clot in a vein is called **venous thrombosis**. Thrombosis is likely to develop where blood flow is impeded by disease, injury, or a foreign substance. A thrombosis in the brain (**cerebral thrombosis**) can cause a thrombotic STROKE or CEREBROVASCULAR ACCIDENT. —**thrombotic** *adj.*

thrombotic stroke see STROKE.

Thurstone attitude scales a DIRECT ATTITUDE MEASURE that involves generating a large set of statements designed to reflect varying levels of negativity or positivity toward an ATTITUDE OBJECT. A group of judges are then asked to rate how positive or negative each statement is, usually on a 9- or 11-point scale. The central tendency and dispersion of the judges' ratings for each statement are computed, and a set of statements with low dispersions is selected. This set contains two statements reflecting each of the scale points on the rating scale (i.e., two statements having an average rating of 1, two statements having an average rating of 2, and so on) and makes up the final attitude scale. When the scale is administered, respondents are instructed to indicate which statements they endorse, and their attitude score is the median of the scale values for these statements. See also LIKERT SCALE; SEMANTIC DIFFERENTIAL. [Louis **Thurstone** (1887–1955), U.S. psychologist]

thymine (symbol: T) *n.* a pyrimidine compound in the nucleotides of living organisms. It is one of the four bases found in DNA that constitute the GENETIC CODE, the others being adenine, cytosine, and guanine. In RNA, uracil replaces thymine.

thymus *n.* an organ, located in the lower neck region, that is part of the IMMUNE SYSTEM. The thymus reaches maximum size at puberty, then shrinks. During infancy it is the site of formation of T LYMPHOCYTES.

thyroid gland an endocrine gland forming a shieldlike structure on the front and sides of the throat, just below the thyroid cartilage. It produces the iodine-containing THYROID HORMONES (thyroxine and triiodothyronine) in response to thyroid-stimulating hormone from the anterior pituitary gland. C cells (parafollicular cells) in the thyroid produce the hormone calcitonin, which controls levels of calcium and phosphate in the blood.

thyroid hormones any of the hormones synthesized and released by the THYROID GLAND. The primary thyroid hormone, thyroxine (T_4), is metabolized to the iodine-containing hormone triiodothyronine (T_3) within target tissues. Plasma levels of T_4 are much higher than those of T_3, but T_3 has the more potent physiological activity. Both hormones play a central role in regulating basic metabolic processes and the early development and differentiation of the brain. Extremes in secretion of these hormones have major effects on metabolism and cognitive function.

thyroplasty *n.* any surgical procedure to the cartilages of the larynx to alter the length or position of the VOCAL CORDS in order to improve voice and sound production. Also called **laryngeal framework surgery**.

thyrotoxicosis *n.* a condition caused by an excess of THYROID HORMONES, which may be produced by an overactive thyroid gland or administered therapeutically. **Endogenous thyrotoxicosis** may be familial and can involve an autoimmune reaction in which the patient's antibodies stimulate rather than destroy the cells producing thyroid hormone. Thyrotoxicosis is characterized by nervousness, tremor, palpitation, weakness, heat sensitivity with sweating, and increased appetite with weight loss. There may be abnormal protrusion of the eyeball associated with goiter. Thyrotoxicosis is frequently associated with enlargement of the thyroid gland, as in **Graves' disease**, or the development of thyroid nodules (**Plummer's disease**), which occurs in older people. See also HYPERTHYROIDISM.

TIA abbreviation for TRANSIENT ISCHEMIC ATTACK.

tic *n.* a sudden, involuntary contraction of a small group of muscles (motor tic) or vocalization (vocal tic) that is recurrent, nonrhythmic, and stereotyped. Tics may be simple (e.g., eye blinking, shoulder shrugging, grimacing, throat clearing, grunting, yelping), or complex (e.g., hand gestures, touching, jumping, ECHOLALIA, COPROLALIA). Tics may be psychogenic in origin; alternatively, they may occur as an adverse effect of a medication or other substance or result from a head injury, neurological disorder, or general medical condition.

tic disorder any disorder characterized by the occurrence many times a day of motor tics, vocal tics, or both that is not due to a general medical condition or the effects of a medication. The group includes TOURETTE'S DISORDER, CHRONIC MOTOR OR VOCAL TIC DISORDER, and TRANSIENT TIC DISORDER.

tight culture a homogeneous social group whose members share the same cultural attributes (e.g., language, social customs, religion) and tend toward a rigid adherence to the collective norms of their group. Compare LOOSE CULTURE.

tilt aftereffect see AFTEREFFECT.

timbre *n.* the perceptual attribute relating to the quality of a sound. Two perceptually different sounds with the same pitch and loudness differ in their timbre. Timbre is determined primarily by the SOUND SPECTRUM but also is affected by temporal and intensive characteristics. Also called **tone color. —timbral** *adj.*

time *n.* a concept by which events are ordered into past, present, and future and duration is measured. Time is used to mark the ubiquitous phenomenon of change. Through the observation of recurrent phenomena, such as the rotation of the earth, time is divided into periods and used to measure the duration of events and rates of change. It is a matter of debate whether time is an abstract construct arising from humanity's marking of change, or whether it is some sort of medium through which change occurs. Although classical mechanics regarded time as absolute, the special theory of relativity maintains that time is relative to motion.

time agnosia an inability to perceive the passage of time, usually due to a disorder involving the temporal area of the brain. Awareness of the existence of time is retained. Causes may include a stroke, alcoholic coma, or a head injury; soldiers have experienced time agnosia after a combat trauma. Individuals are unable to estimate short time intervals and believe long periods of time to be much shorter than they actually are.

time and motion study an analysis of industrial operations or other complex tasks into their component steps, observing the time required for each. Such studies may serve a number of different purposes, enabling an employer to set performance targets, increase productivity, rationalize pay rates and pricing policy, reduce employee fatigue, and prevent accidents. Also called **motion and time study**. See also THERBLIG.

time and rhythm disorders speech and language problems related to the timing of sounds and syllables, including repetitions, prolongations, and stuttering. The disorders are often functional and may be complicated by feelings of guilt. The condition may be treated with a combination of psychotherapy and speech therapy, using such techniques as cancellation (interrupted stuttering), voluntary stuttering, or rewarding or reinforcing fluent speech.

time discounting the preference of attaining a goal immediately, even with the knowledge that delay would result in attaining something more valuable.

time distortion a type of perceptual distortion, sometimes experienced in altered states of consciousness, in which time appears to pass either with great rapidity or with extreme slowness. Perception of past and future may also be transformed.

time error in psychophysics, a misjudgment due to the relative position of stimuli in time. For example, the first of two identical tones sounded consecutively tends to be judged as louder than the second.

time estimation the ability to monitor elapsed time. In operant-conditioning studies using FIXED-INTERVAL SCHEDULES, animals can estimate the time between one reward and the occurrence of the next reward. In nature, time estimation is important for finding prey that emerge at a fixed time of day or season and is essential for navigation when sun or star cues are used (see SUN COMPASS).

time-lag effect age differences seen in cross-sectional studies that are due to differences between COHORTS. This effect can be measured by testing people of the same age at different times and comparing the results (e.g., comparing 2002 results for people born in 1948 with 2007 results for people born in 1953).

time-lagged correlation the correlation of a measure at one point in time with the value of that same measure at a different point in time; for example, the correlation of IQ scores of individuals at 5 years of age with their IQ scores when they are 10 years of age.

timeless moment 1. the infinitely small dimension of the present instant as conceptualized by traditional linear time. **2.** an experience in which one's normal awareness of time dissolves and one feels a sense of holistic involvement with another person or thing or with the universe as a whole. Such PEAK EXPERIENCES are of particular interest in HUMANISTIC PSYCHOLOGY. See BEING COGNITION.

time-limited psychotherapy (TLP) therapy that is limited to a predetermined and agreed-upon number of sessions over a specified period of time. Also called **limited-term psychotherapy**. See also SHORT-TERM THERAPY.

time-of-measurement effect an effect that is due to the social and historical influences present at the time a measurement is made. These effects are difficult to separate from age effects in longitudinal designs.

time out 1. a technique, originating in BEHAVIOR THERAPY, in which undesirable behavior is weakened and its occurrence decreased by moving the individual away from the area that is reinforcing the behavior. For example, a child may be temporarily removed from an area when misbehaving. The technique is used in schools and by parents to decrease the undesirable behavior by isolating the misbehaver for a period. **2.** in OPERANT CONDITIONING, a time interval during which a behavior does not occur. A time-out procedure may be used to eliminate stimulus effects of earlier behaviors or as a marker in a series of events.

time sampling a strategy commonly used in direct observation that involves noting and recording the occurrence of a target behavior whenever it is seen during a stated time interval. The process may involve fixed time periods (e.g., every 5 min) or random time intervals. For example, a researcher may observe a group of children for 10 s every 5 min for a specific 30 min period each day, noting the occurrence or nonoccurrence of particular behaviors. Observations taken during these periods are known as **time samples.**

time sense the ability to estimate time intervals or the time of day without information from clocks. Numerous external and internal cues and stimuli contribute to a sense of time, including the position of the sun in the sky, regular daily events (e.g., mealtimes, school classes), and internal body rhythms (see BIOLOGICAL CLOCK). However, one's estimation of the passage of time can be influenced and distorted by many factors (see PSYCHOLOGICAL TIME).

time series a set of measures on a single attribute measured repeatedly over time.

time-series design an experimental design that involves the observation of units (e.g., people or countries) over a defined time period.

time sharing the process of rapidly switching attention from one task to another when two or more tasks are performed together. An individual's time-sharing ability can be used to predict his or her performance in complex tasks.

timidity *n.* **1.** the tendency to take great caution in approaching a perceived risk or to avoid the risk altogether. **2.** see SHYNESS. —**timid** *adj.*

tinnitus *n.* noises in one or both ears, including ringing, buzzing, or clicking sounds due to acute ear problems, such as MÉNIÈRE'S DISEASE, disturbances in the receptor mechanism, side effects of drugs (especially tricyclic antidepressants), or epileptic aura. Occasionally tinnitus is due to psychogenic factors.

tip-of-the-tongue phenomenon the experience of attempting to retrieve from memory a specific name or word but not being able to do so: The fact is ordinarily accessible and seems to hover tantalizingly on the rim of consciousness. See also RETRIEVAL BLOCK.

tissue *n.* a structure composed of identical or similar cells with the same or similar function, as in ADIPOSE TISSUE, erectile tissue (of the penis), or muscle tissue.

titration *n.* a technique used in determining the optimum dose of a drug needed to produce a desired effect in a particular individual. The dosage may be either gradually increased until a noticeable improvement is observed in the patient or adjusted downward from a level that is obviously excessive because of unwanted adverse effects or toxicity. To avoid unpleasant side effects when starting pharmacotherapy, some drugs must be slowly titrated upward to a therapeutic dose. Likewise, many drugs should be slowly titrated downward upon cessation of therapy both to avoid discontinuation side effects as well as to monitor for the recurrence of symptoms. See TAPERING.

TLP abbreviation for TIME-LIMITED PSYCHOTHERAPY.

TM abbreviation for TRANSCENDENTAL MEDITATION.

TMS abbreviation for TRANSCRANIAL MAGNETIC STIMULATION.

tobacco *n.* the dried leaves of the plant *Nicotiana tabacum* and other *Nicotiana* species, which are smoked, chewed, or sniffed for their stimulant effects. The main active ingredient is NICOTINE. The leaves also contain volatile oils, which give tobacco its characteristic odor and flavor. Tobacco has no therapeutic value but is of great commercial and medical importance because of its widespread use and associated detrimental cardiovascular, pulmonary, and carcinogenic effects.

Tofranil *n.* a trade name for IMIPRAMINE.

token economy in BEHAVIOR THERAPY, a program, sometimes conducted in an institutional setting (e.g., a hospital or classroom), in which desired behavior is reinforced by offering tokens that can be exchanged for special foods, television time, passes, or other rewards. See also BEHAVIOR MODIFICATION; OPERANT CONDITIONING THERAPY.

token reinforcer an object that has no inherent reinforcing value in itself but that can be exchanged for a REINFORCER. The best known example is money. Also called **token reward.** See CONDITIONED REINFORCER.

tolerance *n.* **1.** a condition, resulting from persistent use of a drug, characterized by a markedly diminished effect with regular use of the same dose of the drug or by a need to increase the dose markedly over time to achieve the same desired effect. Tolerance is one of the two prime indications of physical dependence on a drug, the other being a characteristic withdrawal syndrome. See SUBSTANCE DEPENDENCE. **2.** acceptance of others whose actions, beliefs, physical capabilities, religion, customs, ethnicity, nationality, and so on differ from one's own. **3.** a fair and objective attitude toward points of view different from one's own. **—tolerant** *adj.*

tomography *n.* a technique for revealing the detailed structure of a tissue or organ through a particular plane. Examples include COMPUTED TOMOGRAPHY and POSITRON EMISSION TOMOGRAPHY. **—tomographic** *adj.*

tonal attribute a perceptual characteristic of a sound. The primary tonal attributes are PITCH, LOUDNESS, and TIMBRE.

tonal gap a range of pitches to which a person may be partially or totally insensitive (**island deafness**), although able to perceive tones on either side of the gap.

tonal island a region of normal pitch acuity surrounded by TONAL GAPS.

tone *n.* **1.** a PURE TONE. **2.** a sound that has PITCH. **3.** in linguistics, a phonetic variable along the dimension of pitch. In a **tonal language**, such as Mandarin or Thai, tone has a phonemic function (see PHONEME), in that differences in tone are sufficient to mark a distinction between words that are otherwise pronounced identically. In English, tone is an important SUPRASEGMENTAL feature of speech, with different patterns of **intonation** serving to distinguish between different types of utterance, such as statements and questions. **—tonal** *adj.*

tone deafness see ASONIA.

tonic *adj.* of or relating to muscle tone, especially a state of continuous muscle tension or contraction, which may be normal (see TONUS) or abnormal. For example, a tonic phase of facial muscles prevents the lower jaw from falling open, a normal function. Abnormally, in the tonic phase of a TONIC–CLONIC SEIZURE, the muscles controlling respiration may undergo tonic SPASM, resulting in a temporary suspension of breathing.

tonic activation a form of AROUSAL mediated by the RETICULAR FORMATION and identified as tonic because of its persistent effect.

tonic–clonic seizure a seizure characterized by both TONIC and CLONIC motor movements (it was formerly known as a **grand mal seizure**). In the tonic phase the muscles go into spasm and the individual falls to the ground unconscious; breathing may be suspended. This is followed by the clonic phase, marked by rapidly alternating contraction and relaxation of the muscles, resulting in jaw movements (the tongue may be bitten) and urinary incontinence. See also EPILEPSY.

tonic receptor a receptor in which the frequency of discharge of nerve impulses declines slowly or not at all as stimulation is maintained. Compare PHASIC RECEPTOR.

tonic reflex 1. any reflex involving a significant delay between muscle contraction and relaxation. **2.** any reflex that enables a muscle or group of muscles to maintain a certain level of tension, or tonus. Signals from stretch receptors in muscles and tendons are integrated within the spinal cord, and the signals in the efferent motor neurons are adjusted accordingly. Such reflexes are crucial for maintaining posture and for movement.

tonometer *n.* **1.** a device that can produce a tone of a given pitch or can measure the pitch of other tones. **2.** see TONOMETRY.

tonometry *n.* a method of measuring INTRA-OCULAR PRESSURE in the diagnosis of GLAUCOMA and ocular hypertension. Tonometry is usually performed with a device (called a **tonometer**) that blows a puff of air against the eyeball and automatically measures the amount of indentation (resistance of the surface of the eye), which indicates the intraocular pressure.

tonotopic organization the fundamental principle that different frequencies stimulate different places within structures of the mammalian auditory system. This organization begins in the COCHLEA, where different frequencies tend to cause maximal vibration at different places along the BASILAR MEMBRANE and thus stimulate different HAIR CELLS. The hair cells are discretely innervated, and thus different auditory nerve fibers respond to a relatively limited range of frequencies, with the maximal response at the **best frequency** of the fiber. This frequency-to-place mapping is preserved in the AUDITORY CORTEX.

tonus *n.* a continuous, slight stretching, tension, or contraction in muscles when they are at rest. For example, the jaw muscles exhibit tonus when not used for eating or talking. Tonus serves to keep the muscles ready for action. See also TONIC.

topagnosis *n.* **1.** loss of the ability to localize touch. Individuals can feel tactile stimuli but cannot recognize the site of stimulation. **2.** loss of the ability to recognize familiar surroundings.

topalgia *n.* pain that is localized in one spot or small area without any lesion or trauma to account for it. Topalgia often is a symptom of a SOMATOFORM DISORDER, particularly in cases in which the pain seems to occur in unlikely segments of nerve or circulatory patterns.

top-down design see BOTTOM-UP DESIGN.

top-down processing information processing that proceeds from a hypothesis about what a stimulus might be: a person's higher level knowledge, concepts, or expectations influence the processing of lower level information. Typically, perceptual or cognitive mechanisms use top-down processing when information is familiar and not especially complex. Also called **conceptually driven processing; top-down analysis**. Compare BOTTOM-UP PROCESSING. See also DEEP PROCESSING.

topographagnosia *n.* a disturbance of topographical orientation resulting from damage to the PARIETAL LOBE in either hemisphere of the

T

brain. Individuals have difficulty navigating through their environments and may get lost in the streets, be unable to find their way about their homes, or be unable to draw or locate significant features on a map. Topographagnosia is most commonly attributed to an AGNOSIA for landmarks.

topographic *adj.* pertaining to a detailed description of a structural entity, including its surface features and the spatial relations among its parts. Also called **topographical**. See also TOPOGRAPHIC ORGANIZATION. —**topographically** *adv.* —**topography** *n.*

topographical disorientation a disorder of spatial visualization resulting from lesions in the cerebral cortex. It is exemplified by difficulty or inability to recall the arrangement of rooms in a house or the furniture in a room of a house in which the individual lives. Individuals with topographical disorientation also may be unable to recall or describe the location of landmarks or other objects in their neighborhoods.

topographical memory memory for the arrangement and relationships of objects in a spatial environment.

topographic model the original division of the psyche into three regions or systems as proposed by Austrian psychiatrist Sigmund Freud (1856–1939) in 1913. The divisions are: (a) the system UNCONSCIOUS (Ucs), made up of unconscious impulses clustering around specific drives or instincts, such as hunger, thirst, and sex, as well as repressed childhood memories associated with them; (b) the system CONSCIOUS (Cs), which enables the individual to adapt to society, distinguish between inner and outer reality, delay gratification, and anticipate the future; and (c) the system PRECONSCIOUS (Pcs), which stands between the conscious and unconscious systems and is made up of logical, realistic ideas intermingled with irrational images and fantasies. Also called **descriptive approach**; **systematic approach**; **topographic hypothesis**. Compare DYNAMIC MODEL; ECONOMIC MODEL. See also STRUCTURAL MODEL.

topographic organization the arrangement of components in a structure, for example, the orderly spatial relationship between the distribution of neural receptors in an area of the body and a related distribution of neurons representing the same functions in cortical sensory regions of the brain. Thus, the motor cortex shows SOMATOTOPIC ORGANIZATION, the primary visual cortex shows a topographic mapping of the retina (see RETINOTOPIC MAP), and the auditory system shows TONOTOPIC ORGANIZATION.

torsades de pointes see ELECTROCARDIOGRAPHIC EFFECT.

torticollis *n.* a continuous or spasmodic contraction of the neck muscles, resulting in rotation of the chin and twisting of the head to one side. This form of DYSTONIA may be neurological or congenital and may respond to drug treatment or BIOFEEDBACK training. However, it may also be psychogenic. Torticollis is sometimes classed as a complex (dystonic) TIC. —**torticollar** *adj.*

torture *n.* the subjection of individuals to severe, painful physical abuse and violence, which often includes treatment that simulates death or near-death experiences. Torture may also involve mental or psychological abuse.

total processing space the sum of storage and operating space (i.e., the total mental space) in WORKING MEMORY that is available to a person for the execution of a task.

total quality management in industrial and organizational theory, a comprehensive approach to management that involves a commitment to continuous improvements in quality and productivity. It usually entails improved training and communications in the workplace, greater participation of employees in making decisions, redesign of the work process, and the use of statistical techniques to monitor quality.

totem *n.* **1.** a revered animal, plant, natural force, or inanimate object that is conceived as the ancestor, symbol, protector, or tutelary spirit of a people, CLAN, or community. It is usually made the focus of certain ritual activities and TABOOS, typically against killing or eating it. **2.** as interpreted by Austrian psychiatrist Sigmund Freud (1856–1939) in *Totem and Taboo* (1912–1913), any symbol or representation of the primal father. —**totemic** *adj.* —**totemism** *n.*

touch *n.* the sensation produced by contact of an object with the surface of the skin. Sensitivity to touch varies in different parts of the body; for example, the lips and fingers are far more sensitive than the trunk or back. See also TOUCH SENSE.

touch sense the ability to perceive a stimulus (e.g., an object, surface, material) that comes into contact with the surface of the skin (e.g., by pressure, stroking). Also called **tactile sense**. See TACTILE PERCEPTION. See also CUTANEOUS SENSE.

touch therapy treatment that involves touching or manipulating parts of an individual's body to ease physical pain or to promote relaxation and a general sense of well-being. Touch therapy has been shown to have numerous benefits for children (among others), improving, for example, the physical and psychological development of preterm infants and bringing about a greater tolerance of touch by children with autism, which has resulted in improved bonding and communication with their parents. Also called **therapeutic touch**. See also COMPLEMENTARY AND ALTERNATIVE MEDICINE; MASSAGE.

tough love the fostering of individuals' well-being by requiring them to act responsibly and to seek professional assistance when they find it difficult to act in their own best interests. Often, strict oversight and restrictions of personal freedom and privileges must be willingly accepted by the target individual. Tough love is sometimes seen as a stance taken by a therapist or counselor or in interventions by family and friends of individuals with problem behaviors (e.g. substance abuse, violent behavior).

Tourette's disorder a TIC DISORDER characterized by many motor tics and one or more vocal tics, such as grunts, yelps, barks, sniffs, and in a few cases an irresistible urge to utter obscenities (see COPROLALIA). The tics occur many times a day for more than a year, during which time any period free of tics is never longer than 3 months. The age of onset for the disorder is before 18 years; in most cases it starts during childhood or early adolescence.

toxicity n. the capacity of a substance to produce toxic (poisonous) effects in an organism. The toxicity of a substance—whether a drug, an industrial or household chemical, or other agent—generally is related to the size of the dose per body weight of the individual, expressed in terms of milligrams of chemical per kilogram of body weight. Toxicity also may be expressed in terms of the median LETHAL DOSE (LD_{50}).

toxicosis n. (pl. **toxicoses**) see CONDITIONED TASTE AVERSION.

toxin n. a poisonous substance, especially one produced by a living organism.

trace conditioning a procedure in PAVLOVIAN CONDITIONING in which a conditioned stimulus and an unconditioned stimulus are separated by a constant interval, with the conditioned stimulus presented first. Compare TEMPORAL CONDITIONING.

trace-decay theory see DECAY THEORY.

tracking n. 1. the process of following a moving object with the eyes or using eye movements to follow a path of some kind. 2. a type of continuous movement task in which the goal is to make movements that follow a constantly moving target. 3. monitoring the progress of a student by means of recording test and homework scores, observing behavior within the classroom, eliciting a self-report, or a combination of these. —**track** vb.

tract n. 1. a bundle or group of nerve fibers within the central nervous system. The name of a tract typically indicates its site of origin followed by its site of termination; for example, the RETICULOSPINAL TRACT runs from the reticular formation of the brainstem to the spinal cord. Compare NERVE. 2. a series of organs that as a whole accomplishes a specific function (e.g., the digestive tract). 3. a region, passage, or pathway.

tractotomy n. the surgical interruption of a nerve tract in the brainstem or spinal cord. One form of tractotomy is of benefit in bipolar disorder that is resistant to other forms of treatment.

tradition n. a set of social customs or other ethnic or family practices handed down from generation to generation. —**traditional** adj.

traditionalism n. 1. a set of social practices and conditions considered typical of societies that are economically and technologically undeveloped, relatively static in their structures and customs, rural rather than urban, religious rather than secular, and which tend to emphasize family or collective responsibilities rather than individual rights and aspirations. The adequacy of this description, and of the dichotomy between traditional and modern societies that it implies, is by no means universally accepted. See MODERNIZATION. See also PRIMITIVE. 2. more generally, adherence to any set of political, religious, or cultural traditions. —**traditionalist** n. —**traditionalistic** adj.

traditional marriage 1. a marriage according to the traditional norms of a given society, usually for the primary purpose of establishing a family. Although prenuptial customs vary in different cultures, a traditional marriage generally follows a period of courtship, public announcement of wedding plans, and a wedding ceremony. Compare NONTRADITIONAL MARRIAGE. **2.** a marriage of husband and wife, wherein the former is the primary or sole breadwinner and the latter holds primary or sole responsibility for maintaining the home and managing child care.

trainer n. **1.** in mental health, a professional leader or facilitator of a sensitivity-training group (see T-GROUP). **2.** a teacher or supervisor of individuals learning to practice psychotherapy.

training analysis PSYCHOANALYSIS of a trainee analyst. Its purpose is not only to provide training in the concepts and techniques of psychoanalysis, but also to increase insight into personal sensitivities or other emotional reactions that might interfere with the process of analyzing patients in the form of a COUNTERTRANSFERENCE. Also called **didactic analysis**.

training group see T-GROUP.

training study a study in which a participant's task performance is assessed after he or she has been instructed in the use of a strategy. In cognitive developmental research, training studies are used to assess MEDIATIONAL DEFICIENCY and PRODUCTION DEFICIENCY.

training validity the success of a training program as judged by the performance of trainees on criteria that form part of the program. For example, the success of a program focusing on truck-driving skills might be evaluated on the basis of how well the trainees perform in driving a simulator used for instruction. This is to be distinguished from **transfer validity**, in which the program is evaluated on how well the trainees perform in the workplace after training (i.e., how well the trainee performs in driving real trucks on the job).

trait n. **1.** an enduring personality characteristic that describes or determines an individual's behavior across a range of situations. **2.** in genetics, an attribute resulting from a hereditary predisposition (e.g., hair color or facial features).

trait anxiety proneness to experience anxiety. People with high trait anxiety tend to view the world as more dangerous or threatening than those with low trait anxiety and to respond with STATE ANXIETY to situations that would not elicit this response in people with low trait anxiety.

trait-negativity bias the tendency for negative personality traits to play a greater role than positive personality traits in determining overall impressions and to be more often cited in attributions of motive. Also called **negativity bias**.

trait theory approaches that explain personality in terms of TRAITS, that is, internal characteristics that are presumed to determine behavior. An example is the FIVE-FACTOR PERSONALITY MODEL.

trance *n.* **1.** a state characterized by markedly narrowed consciousness and responsiveness to stimuli. **2.** a state induced by HYPNOSIS or AUTO-SUGGESTION and characterized by openness, or availability, to suggestion (see HYPNOTIC SUS-CEPTIBILITY). A deep trance might be characterized by such effects as an inability to open the eyes without affecting the trance, complete somnambulism, positive and negative posthypnotic hallucinations, and hyperesthesia (excessive sensibility). Also called **hypnotic trance**.

trance and possession disorder (TPD) see DISSOCIATIVE TRANCE DISORDER.

trance logic the presumed tendency of hypnotized individuals to engage simultaneously in logically contradictory or paradoxical trains of thought. It has been suggested that trance logic represents evidence of PARALLEL PROCESSING in that there appears to be simultaneous registration of information at different levels of awareness. See DIVIDED CONSCIOUSNESS; NEO-DISSOCIATIVE THEORY.

tranquilizer *n.* a drug that is used to reduce physiological and subjective symptoms of anxiety. In the past, distinctions were made between so-called **major tranquilizers** (ANTIPSYCHOTICS) and **minor tranquilizers** (ANXIOLYTICS, e.g., benzodiazepines).

transaction *n.* **1.** any interaction between the individual and the social or physical environment, especially during encounters between two or more people. **2.** in some psychotherapies, the interplay between the therapist and the patient and ultimately between the patient and other individuals in his or her environment.

transactional analysis (TA) a theory of personality and a form of dynamic group or individual psychotherapy focusing on characteristic interactions that reveal internal "ego states" and the games people play in social situations. Specifically, the approach involves: (a) a study of three primary ego states (parent, child, adult) and determination of which one is dominant in the transaction in question; (b) identification of the tricks and expedients, or games, habitually used in the client's transactions; and (c) analysis of the total SCRIPT, or unconscious plan, of the

client's life, in order to uncover the sources of his or her emotional problems.

transactionalism *n.* **1.** an approach to ENVI-RONMENTAL PSYCHOLOGY that emphasizes the continuing process of interaction between a person and his or her physical and social environment. This process is characterized as an ongoing series of "transactions" in which the person's behaviors are modified by environmental factors and vice versa. **2.** an approach to perception that emphasizes the interaction of people and their environment. Rather than being mere passive observers, people draw on past experiences in order to form perceptions of present situations and even of novel stimuli. —**transactionalist** *adj., n.*

transactional leadership a style of leadership in which the emphasis is on ensuring followers accomplish tasks. Transactional leaders influence others through exchange relationships in which benefits are promised in return for compliance. Compare TRANSFORMATIONAL LEAD-ERSHIP.

transactional model of development a framework that views development as the continuous and bidirectional interchange between an active organism, with a unique biological constitution, and its changing environment. See also DEVELOPMENTAL SYSTEMS APPROACH.

transactional psychotherapy psychotherapy that emphasizes the daily interactions between the client and others in his or her life. TRANSACTIONAL ANALYSIS is a specific type of therapy that is based on types of transactions that are considered dysfunctional.

transactive memory system a system in which information to be remembered is distributed among various members of a group, who can then each be relied on to provide that information when it is needed.

transcendence *n.* in metaphysics and in the study of CONSCIOUSNESS, a state of existence or perception that exceeds—and is not definable in terms of—normal understanding or experience. The term implies states that go beyond the physical world and the nature of material existence. —**transcendent** *adj.*

transcendence need in the psychoanalysis of German-born U.S. psychoanalyst Erich Fromm (1900–1980), the human need to create so as to rise above passivity and attain a sense of meaning and purpose in an impermanent and seemingly random or accidental universe. Both creativity and destructiveness are considered by Fromm to be manifestations of the transcendence need.

transcendence therapy a form of therapy that is spiritually oriented and intended to help people achieve an inner sense of peace by first understanding their role in the larger picture of life and then using that understanding to overcome disappointments, difficulties, and other hardships. It is based on the concept of **forma-**

tive spirituality, which postulates that humans are not passive givers or receivers of information or experience but, rather, active interpreters of reality, engaging in an inner dialogue to recognize, relate to, and modify individual construals of existence.

transcendentalism *n.* any philosophical position holding that ultimate reality lies beyond the level of sensory appearances or empirical investigation, such as the "theory of forms" of Greek philosopher Plato (c. 429–347 BCE). The philosophies of German thinkers Immanuel Kant (1724–1804), Georg Wilhelm Friedrich Hegel (1770–1831), and Johann Gottlieb Fichte (1762–1814) are later examples of transcendentalism. The philosophical ideas of U.S. essayist and poet Ralph Waldo Emerson (1803–1882) and some of his New England contemporaries, which are based upon a search for reality through intuition, are also described as transcendentalist. See also IDEALISM; MYSTICISM. —**transcendental** *adj.* —**transcendentalist** *adj.*

transcendental meditation (**TM**) a technique of CONCENTRATIVE MEDITATION for achieving a **transcendental state** of consciousness. TM consists of six steps that culminate in sitting with one's eyes closed, while repeating a mantra, for two 20-minute periods a day. Repetition of the mantra serves to block distracting thoughts and to induce a state of relaxation and tranquillity in which images and ideas can arise from deeper levels of the mind and from the cosmic source of all thought and being. The result is said to be not only a greater sense of well-being but also more harmonious interpersonal relations and the achievement of a state of ultimate self-awareness and restful alertness.

transcortical aphasia a type of APHASIA caused by a lesion between BROCA'S AREA and WERNICKE'S AREA that results in these areas being isolated from the rest of the brain. As a result, the individual will be able to repeat spoken words but will have difficulty producing independent speech or understanding speech.

transcortical motor aphasia see MIXED TRANSCORTICAL APHASIA.

transcortical sensory aphasia see MIXED TRANSCORTICAL APHASIA.

transcranial magnetic stimulation (**TMS**) localized electrical stimulation of the brain through the skull caused by changes in the magnetic field in coils of wire placed around the head. Depending on the parameters, TMS may elicit a response or disrupt functioning in the region for a brief time. The technique was originally devised and is primarily used as an investigatory tool to assess the effects of electrical stimulation of the motor cortex. It is also being investigated as a possible therapy for some types of movement disorders and psychological conditions, such as depression, obsessive-compulsive disorder, and Tourette's disorder.

Repetitive transcranial magnetic stimulation (rTMS) consists of a series of TMS pulses.

transcultural psychotherapy forms of PSYCHODYNAMIC PSYCHOTHERAPY that emphasize cultural sensitivity and awareness, including culturally defined concepts of emotion, psychodynamics, and behavior. In the psychiatric community the term is used somewhat more often in a sense similar to MULTICULTURAL COUNSELING in clinical psychology.

transcutaneous electrical nerve stimulation see TENS.

transduction *n.* the process by which one form of energy is converted into another, especially **sensory transduction**: the transformation of the energy of a stimulus into a change in the electric potential across the membrane of a RECEPTOR cell. See OLFACTORY TRANSDUCTION; TASTE TRANSDUCTION; VISUAL TRANSDUCTION.

transductive reasoning the tendency of a child in the PREOPERATIONAL STAGE of cognitive development to see a connection between unrelated instances, using neither deductive nor inductive means to do so. For example, the child might say, *I haven't had my nap, so it isn't afternoon.*

transection *n.* the severing or cutting of something transversely, such as a nerve tract or fiber or the spinal cord. —**transect** *vb.*

transfer 1. *vb.* to shift or change from one location to another, one form to another, or one situation or condition to another. **2.** *n.* the shift or change thus produced, as in TRANSFER OF TRAINING. **3.** *n.* in GESTALT PSYCHOLOGY, the use of the solution to one problem in solving a second problem that has elements in common with the first.

transfer-appropriate processing a concept of mental processing based on the idea that memory performance is better when a person processes material during study in the same way as the material will be processed during testing. For example, test performance should be relatively good if both study and test conditions emphasize either semantic processing on the one hand or perceptual processing on the other; but test performance will not be as good if study conditions emphasize one (e.g., semantic) and test conditions emphasize another (e.g., perceptual).

transferase *n.* any of a class of enzymes that catalyze the transfer of atoms or groups from one molecule to another; for example, the aminotransferases.

transference *n.* in psychoanalysis, the DISPLACEMENT or PROJECTION onto the analyst of unconscious feelings and wishes originally directed toward important individuals, such as parents, in the patient's childhood. This process, which is at the core of the psychoanalytic method, brings repressed material to the surface where it can be reexperienced, studied, and worked through. In the course of this process, it

T

is posited that the sources of neurotic difficulties are frequently discovered and their harmful effects alleviated. Although quite specific to psychoanalysis, the term's meaning has had an impact far beyond its narrow confines, and transference—as unconscious repetition of earlier behaviors and projection onto new subjects—is acknowledged as ubiquitous in human interactions. The role of transference in counseling and short-term dynamic psychotherapy is well recognized, and ongoing attempts to study its role in a range of therapeutic encounters promise to expand and elucidate its meanings. See also COUNTERTRANSFERENCE.

transference neurosis in psychoanalysis, neurotic reactions released by the TRANSFERENCE process that result from the revival and reliving of the patient's early conflicts and traumas. These reactions are posited to replace the original neurosis and help the patient become aware that his or her attitudes and behavior are actually repetitions of infantile drives. It is believed that the transference neurosis must be resolved if the patient is to free himself or herself from the harmful effects of past experiences and adopt more appropriate attitudes and responses.

transference resistance in psychoanalysis, a form of RESISTANCE to the disclosure of unconscious material, in which the patient maintains silence or attempts to act out feelings of love or hate transferred from past relationships to the analyst.

transfer of training the influence of prior learning on new learning, either to enhance it (see POSITIVE TRANSFER) or to hamper it (see NEGATIVE TRANSFER). Solving a new problem is usually easier if previously learned principles or components can be applied, but in some cases these may confuse or mislead. The general principles of mathematics, for example, transfer to computer programming, but a knowledge of Spanish may have both positive and negative effects in learning Italian. See also GENERAL TRANSFER; SPECIFIC TRANSFER.

transfer validity see TRAINING VALIDITY.

transformation *n.* **1.** any change in appearance, form, function, or structure. See also METAMORPHOSIS. **2.** the conversion of data to a different form through a rule-based, usually mathematical process. **3.** in psychoanalytic theory, the process by which unconscious wishes or impulses are disguised in order that they can gain admittance to CONSCIOUSNESS. —**transform** *vb.* —**transformational** *adj.*

transformational generative grammar in linguistics, a type of GENERATIVE GRAMMAR based on the idea that sentences have an underlying DEEP STRUCTURE as well as the SURFACE STRUCTURE observable in speech or writing, and that the former gives rise to the latter through the operation of a small number of **transformational rules** involving the movement, addition, and deletion of constituents. This approach to syntactic structures was pioneered by U.S. linguist Noam Chomsky (1928–) in the late 1950s as a means of supplementing the more limited analysis made possible by PHRASE-STRUCTURE GRAMMAR. Also called **transformational grammar**.

transformational leadership a charismatic, inspiring style of leading others that usually involves heightening followers' motivation, confidence, and satisfaction, uniting them in the pursuit of shared, challenging goals, and changing their beliefs, values, and needs. Compare TRANSACTIONAL LEADERSHIP.

transgender *adj.* having or relating to gender identities that differ from culturally determined gender roles and biological sex. Transgender states include transsexualism, some forms of transvestism, and intersexuality. These states should not be confused with same-sex sexual orientation. Also called **transgendered**. See also GENDER IDENTITY DISORDER. —**transgenderism** *n.*

transgenerational design see UNIVERSAL DESIGN.

transgenic *adj.* describing an organism in which a foreign or altered gene has been deliberately introduced into the GENOME.

transient global amnesia a sudden GLOBAL AMNESIA that typically resolves within 24 hours and occurs in the absence of any other neurological abnormalities. Individuals appear confused and disoriented and ask frequent repetitive questions to try and make sense of their experience. They are unable to acquire new memories (anterograde AMNESIA); they also exhibit retrograde amnesia for recently experienced events. As the episode clears, new learning gradually returns to normal and retrograde amnesia shrinks, but individuals are left with a dense memory gap. Transient global amnesia may be triggered by precipitating events, such as physical exertion. The mechanism responsible for its occurrence is poorly understood.

transient ischemic attack (**TIA**) an episode during which an area of the brain is suddenly deprived of oxygen because its blood supply is temporarily interrupted, for example by thrombosis, embolism, or vascular spasm. Symptoms are the same as those of STROKE but disappear completely, typically within 24 hours.

transient tic disorder a TIC DISORDER involving the presence of single or multiple tics occurring many times a day for a period of between 4 weeks and 1 year. The tics may be simple (e.g., eye blinking, facial grimacing, throat clearing, or sniffing) or more complex (e.g., hand gestures, stomping, ECHOLALIA, or meaningless change in vocal pitch or volume).

transitional employment a VOCATIONAL REHABILITATION program that places individuals with disabilities or those who are economically, socially, or otherwise disadvantaged (e.g., those who are homeless or dependent on long-term welfare) in paid entry-level positions in a competitive working environment to gain the skills and experience needed to eventually obtain a permanent job in the community workforce. Positions are often provided by participating companies, and each placement typically lasts 6–9 months. See also SUPPORTED EMPLOYMENT.

transitional living a supervised living situation that allows psychiatric or neurological patients to make the transition from the dependence of a hospital setting to greater independence before returning to fully independent living.

transitional object 1. a thing (e.g., a doll or a blanket) used by a child to ease the anxiety of separation from his or her first external OBJECT, the mother, until the child has established a secure internal object, or mental representation of her, that provides a sense of security and comfort. **2.** by extension, any person or thing that provides comfort, security, and emotional well-being.

transitive inference task a type of task used to assess children's ability to make transitive inferences, that is, to infer the relationship between two concepts or objects based on earlier acquired information. In one example a series of sticks is arranged in increasing length (e.g., A, B, C, D, E); if children know that D > C and C > B, they will make a correct transitive inference if they state that D > B, even though they have never seen these two sticks together.

transitivity *n.* the quality of a relationship among elements such that the relationship transfers across elements. For example, a transitive relationship would be: Given that a > b, and b > c, it must be the case that a > c. Compare INTRANSITIVITY. —**transitive** *adj.*

translation and back-translation a method of ensuring that the translation of an assessment instrument into another language is adequate, used primarily in cross-cultural research. A bilingual person translates items from the source language to the target language, and a different bilingual person then independently translates the items back into the source language. The researcher can then compare the original with the back-translated version to see if anything important was changed in the translation.

transmission *n.* **1.** the act or process of causing something (e.g., a disease) to pass from one place or person to another. **2.** in neurology, see NEUROTRANSMISSION. **3.** the inheritance of traits through successive generations. **4.** the handing down of customs and mores from generation to generation. See SOCIAL TRANSMISSION. See also CULTURAL HERITAGE. —**transmissible** *adj.* —**transmit** *vb.*

transorbital lobotomy see LOBOTOMY.

transpersonal psychology an area in HUMANISTIC PSYCHOLOGY concerned with the exploration of the nature, varieties, causes, and effects of "higher" states of consciousness and transcendental experiences. "Transpersonal" refers to the concern with ends that transcend personal identity and individual, immediate desires. See also BEING COGNITION; PEAK EXPERIENCE.

transplantation *n.* **1.** the surgical implantation of a tissue or organ from one part of the body to another or from one person (the donor) to another (the recipient). Such procedures often induce pre- and postoperative anxieties, resistance, and other behavioral manifestations that may have ramifications for psychological health and intervention. **2.** the removal of a person from a permanent home to a temporary residence or nursing home, which may result in anxiety, depression, and other disturbances.

transporter *n.* a protein complex that spans a cell membrane and conveys ions, neurotransmitters, or other substances between the exterior and interior of the cell. For example, at SYNAPSES between neurons, transporters in the PRESYNAPTIC membrane recognize and bind to neurotransmitter molecules and return them to the presynaptic neuron for reuse (see REUPTAKE). Transporters may utilize passive transport, in which a substance is transported into or out of a cell according to its concentration gradient across the cell membrane; or active transport, which is an energy-dependent process often relying on the hydrolysis of ATP to provide energy to facilitate movement of a substance from one side of the cell membrane to the other.

transposition *n.* the process of learning a relationship between stimuli rather than learning the absolute characteristics of the stimuli. For example, if an organism is trained to select a 10-cm diameter disk over a 7-cm disk, and then in a transfer test chooses a 13-cm disk over a 10-cm disk (even though reinforcement has been obtained only for choosing a 10-cm disk), transposition has been observed. —**transpositional** *adj.*

transposition of affect the transfer of the affective component associated with a particular idea or object to an unrelated idea or object, as frequently occurs in OBSESSIVE-COMPULSIVE DISORDER. Also called **displacement**; **displacement of affect**.

transsexualism *n.* a GENDER IDENTITY DISORDER consisting of a persistent sense of discomfort and inappropriateness relating to one's anatomical sex, with a persistent wish to be rid of one's genitals and to live as a member of the other sex. Many transsexuals feel that they belong to the opposite sex and are somehow trapped in the wrong body. They therefore seek to change their sex through surgical and hormonal means (see SEX REASSIGNMENT). —**transsexual** *adj., n.*

transtentorial herniation HERNIATION that occurs when increased INTRACRANIAL PRESSURE (resulting, for example, from a tumor or head injury) displaces the medial TEMPORAL LOBE or the deep hemisphere structures of the brain medially and downward through the tentorial notch (an opening in the fold of dura mater that separates the cerebellum from the cerebrum). This causes displacement of the midbrain laterally and downward, which in turn may cause death. Also called **tentorial herniation**; **uncal herniation**.

transtheoretical model a five-stage theory to explain changes in people's health behavior (see STAGES OF CHANGE). It suggests that change takes time, that different interventions are effective at different stages, and that there are multiple outcomes occurring across the stages (e.g., belief structure, self-efficacy).

transverse plane see HORIZONTAL PLANE.

transvestic fetishism a PARAPHILIA consisting of the persistent wearing by a heterosexual male of female clothes with the purpose of achieving sexual excitement and arousal. It typically begins in childhood or adolescence and should not be confused with transvestism, the nonpathological CROSS-DRESSING by men or women of any sexual preference.

transvestism n. the process or habit of wearing the clothes of the opposite sex. Transvestism, or CROSS-DRESSING, is distinct from TRANSVESTIC FETISHISM. Also called **transvestitism**. —**transvestic** adj. —**transvestite** n.

trapezoid body a bundle of transverse nerve fibers in the PONS carrying afferent fibers from the COCHLEAR NUCLEI to the SUPERIOR OLIVARY COMPLEX and the nuclei of the LATERAL LEMNISCUS, and efferent fibers from the inferior COLLICULI and lateral lemnisci to the cochlear nuclei.

trauma n. **1.** an event in which a person witnesses or experiences a threat to his or her own life or physical safety or that of others and experiences fear, terror, or helplessness. The event may also cause DISSOCIATION, confusion, and a loss of a sense of safety. Traumatic events challenge an individual's view of the world as a just, safe, and predictable place. Traumas that are caused by human behavior (e.g., rape, assault, toxic accidents) commonly have more psychological impact than those caused by nature (e.g., earthquakes). **2.** a physical injury. Such traumas include head injuries, such as blows to the head; brain injuries, such as hemorrhages and CEREBROVASCULAR ACCIDENTS; and injuries to other parts of the body, such as burns or amputations. —**traumatic** adj.

traumatic brain injury (**TBI**) damage to brain tissue caused by external mechanical forces, as evidenced by objective neurological findings, posttraumatic amnesia, skull fracture, or loss of consciousness because of brain trauma. A frequent form of TBI is DIFFUSE AXONAL INJURY.

traumatic grief a severe form of separation distress that usually occurs following the sudden and unexpected death of a loved one. Numbness and shock are frequently accompanied by a sense of futility and purposelessness. A defining characteristic of traumatic grief is a sense of the meaninglessness of life, although the total syndrome includes many other painful and dysfunctional responses.

traveling wave see BASILAR MEMBRANE.

trazodone n. a chemically unique antidepressant that was introduced as a safer alternative to the tricyclic agents. However, it was of limited use as an antidepressant due to its pronounced sedative effects and its association with prolonged, painful, and unwanted erections (priapism) in a very small number of men who took the drug. Its mechanism of antidepressant action is unclear; it is not a potent inhibitor of either serotonin or norepinephrine reuptake and it is an antagonist at the 5-HT$_2$ serotonin receptor. Although of little use as an antidepressant, trazodone is commonly used in low doses for bedtime sedation or in controlling agitation and hostility in geriatric patients. A related agent, nefazodone, which is less sedating and less associated with priapism, is now available. U.S. trade name: **Desyrel**.

treatment n. **1.** the administration of appropriate measures (e.g., drugs, surgery, therapy) that are designed to relieve a pathological condition. **2.** the level of an INDEPENDENT VARIABLE in an experiment, or the independent variable itself. See TREATMENT LEVEL.

treatment audit a procedure that measures quality assurance in health care. Audit activities include assessment of the structure, process, and outcome of the services provided. Audits occur in a cyclical process, thus enabling the results of the assessment to be fed back to improve or maintain the services assessed. See also PROGRAM MONITORING.

treatment combination **1.** the particular combination of treatments administered to a participant in a study. **2.** the combination of levels of different factors in a FACTORIAL DESIGN.

treatment effect the magnitude of the effect of a treatment (i.e., the INDEPENDENT VARIABLE) upon the response variable (i.e., the DEPENDENT VARIABLE) in a study. It is usually measured as the difference between the level of response under a control condition and the level of response under the treatment condition in standardized units.

treatment level the specific condition to which a group or participant is exposed in a study or experiment. For example, in a design employing four groups, each of which is exposed to a different dosage of a particular drug, each dosage amount represents a level of the treatment factor.

treatment plan the recommended steps for intervening that the therapist or counselor devises after an assessment of the client has been completed. Many MANAGED CARE plans require submission of formal, written treatment plans prior to approving mental health treatment. Compare TREATMENT PROTOCOL.

treatment protocol the formal procedures used in a system of psychotherapy. In some systems, such as EXPERIENTIAL PSYCHOTHERAPY, few explicit "rules" apply, whereas in others, such as BEHAVIOR THERAPY, strict adherence to a treatment protocol is often used to guide the work of the therapist. Compare TREATMENT PLAN.

treatment resistance 1. refusal or reluctance on the part of an individual to accept psychological or medical treatment or unwillingness to comply with the therapist's or physician's instructions or prescribed regimens. In psychotherapy it is the lack of a positive response by a client to the techniques being used or to what the client feels is a rupture in the THERAPEUTIC ALLIANCE, which requires the use of other strategies or efforts to repair the alliance by the therapist. Examples of treatment resistance is noncompliance with assignments, extended silences, talking about tangential issues, and seemingly pointless debates about the therapist's approach, suggestions, and interpretations. See also NONADHERENCE. **2.** failure of a disease or disorder to respond positively or significantly to a particular treatment method.

treatment withholding discontinuing medical treatment that has no benefit to the patient in terms of an eventual cure or short-term alleviation of symptoms.

tremor *n.* any involuntary trembling of the body or a part of the body (e.g., the hands) due to neurological or psychological causes. **Psychological** (or **psychogenic**) **tremor** may be mild, due to tension, or violent and uncontrolled in severe disturbances. Toxic effects of drugs or heavy metals may produce a **transient tremor**. A **coarse tremor** involves a large muscle group in slow movements, whereas a **fine tremor** is caused by a small bundle of muscle fibers that move rapidly. Some tremors occur only during voluntary movements (**action tremor**); others occur in the absence of voluntary movement (**resting tremor**). See also ESSENTIAL TREMOR.

trend analysis any of several analytic techniques designed to uncover systematic changes (trends) in a set of variables, such as linear growth over time or quadratic increases in response with increased dosage levels.

trephination *n.* a surgical procedure in which a disk of bone is removed, usually from the skull, with a circular instrument (a **trephine**) having a sawlike edge. On the basis of evidence found in skulls of prehistoric humans, **skull trephining** is believed to be one of the oldest types of surgery. Among the numerous conjectural reasons given for the practice is the possibility that it was a treatment for headaches, infections, skull fractures, convulsions, mental disorders, or sup-

posed demonic possession. Also called **trepanation**. —**trephine** *vb.*

triad training model an approach to training therapists and counselors that fosters greater understanding of clients of other cultures and develops greater multicultural counseling competencies. The didactic simulation matches a trainee therapist or counselor from a particular culture with a three-person team: (a) a "procounselor," representing the trainee therapist's or counselor's own culture; (b) a coached "client," who is hostile or resistant to the trainee, the therapy, or the trainee's culture; and (c) a catalyst "anticounselor," who represents the client's ethnic group, religion, or other affiliation. The catalyst serves as a bridge of communication and support for the client, and the dynamic among all parties reveals issues, content, and effective approaches to the trainee. See also MULTICULTURAL COUNSELING.

trial *n.* **1.** in tests or experiments, one practice session or performance of a given task (e.g., one run through a maze). **2.** see CLINICAL TRIAL. **3.** in parapsychology research, any single attempt by a participant to identify a TARGET by CLAIRVOYANCE or TELEPATHY or to influence a target by PSYCHOKINESIS. In experiments using ZENER CARDS, each turn of a card is therefore a separate trial.

trial-and-error learning a type of learning in which the organism successively tries various responses in a situation, seemingly at random, until one is successful in producing the goal. In successive trials, the successful response appears earlier and earlier. Maze learning, with its eventual elimination of blind-alley entrances, is an example of trial-and-error learning.

trial therapy a planned process of temporary treatment, either in the early sessions of therapy or as a set of sessions prior to the initiation of long-term therapy, to test whether the client is suitable or ready for a commitment to the therapeutic process. Trial therapy is also used to assess whether the therapist believes that his or her treatment approach is compatible with the client and is able to resolve the problem.

triangular theory of love the proposition that the various kinds of love can be characterized in terms of the degree to which they possess the three basic components of love relationships: passion, intimacy, and commitment. See COMPANIONATE LOVE; EROTIC LOVE; PASSIONATE LOVE; ROMANTIC LOVE.

triangulation *n.* **1.** the process of confirming a hypothesis by collecting evidence from multiple sources or experiments or using multiple procedures. The data from each source, experiment, or procedure supports the hypothesis from a somewhat different perspective. **2.** in FAMILY THERAPY, a situation in which two members of a family in conflict each attempt to draw another member onto their side. Triangulation can occur, for example, when two parents are in conflict and their child is caught in the middle. —**triangulate** *vb.*

triarchic theory of intelligence a theory of intelligence proposing three key abilities—analytical, creative, and practical—which are viewed as largely although not entirely distinct. According to the theory, intelligence comprises a number of information-processing components, which are applied to experience (especially novel experiences) in order to adapt to, shape, and select environments. The theory contains three subtheories: one specifying the components of intelligence (**componential subtheory**), another specifying the kinds of experience to which the components are applied (**experiential subtheory**), and a third specifying how the components are applied to experience to be used in various kinds of environmental contexts (**contextual subtheory**).

triazolam *n.* a short-acting BENZODIAZEPINE used primarily as a HYPNOTIC and also to manage anxiety associated with dental procedures. Following reports of severe psychological disturbances associated with its use, including behavioral disinhibition, aggression, agitation, and short-term memory impairment (anterograde amnesia), its sale was prohibited in the United Kingdom in 1991. U.S. trade name: **Halcion**.

trichotillomania *n.* an impulse-control disorder characterized by persistent hair pulling at any part of one's body on which hair grows, often with conspicuous hair loss. Feelings of increasing tension before the act and feelings of release or satisfaction on completion are common.

trichromatic theory one of several concepts of the physiological basis of color vision based on evidence from experiments on color mixture in which all hues were able to be matched by a mixture of three primary colors. The YOUNG–HELMHOLTZ THEORY OF COLOR VISION is the best known trichromatic theory. Subsequent studies determined that there are three different retinal cone photopigments (see IODOPSIN) with peak sensitivities roughly corresponding to the three primary colors of trichromatic theory: blue, green, and red. Also called **three-component theory**. See also OPPONENT PROCESS THEORY OF COLOR VISION.

trichromatism *n.* normal color vision: the capacity to distinguish the three primary color systems of light–dark, red–green, and blue–yellow, attributable to the presence of all three types of PHOTOPIGMENT. Also called **trichromatopsia**. See also ACHROMATISM; DICHROMATISM; MONOCHROMATISM.

tricyclic antidepressants (**TCAs**) a group of drugs, developed in the 1950s, that were the original FIRST-LINE MEDICATIONS for treatment of depression. They are presumed to act by blocking the reuptake of monoamine neurotransmitters (serotonin, dopamine, and norepinephrine) into the presynaptic neuron, thereby increasing the amount of neurotransmitter

available for binding to postsynaptic receptors. Side effects of TCAs include significant anticholinergic effects (e.g., dry mouth, blurred vision, constipation, urinary retention), drowsiness or insomnia, confusion, anxiety, nausea, weight gain, and impotence. They can also cause cardiovascular complications (particularly disturbances in heart rhythm). The tricyclics represented the mainstay of antidepressant treatment from the introduction of imipramine in 1957 until fluoxetine (Prozac)—the first SSRI—was introduced in 1987. Although they are effective as antidepressants, their adverse side effects and their lethality in overdose have led to a profound decline in their use. They remain, however, the standard against which other antidepressants are compared; no other class of antidepressants has demonstrated more clinical efficacy.

tridimensional theory of feeling the theory that feelings can vary along three dimensions: pleasantness–unpleasantness (hedonic quality), excitement–calmness, and arousal–relaxation. The tridimensional theory is used to define different emotions as characterized by different combinations and successions of feelings and by the specific course of change of the feelings along each of the three dimensions.

trigeminal chemoreception the stimulation of free nerve endings of the trigeminal nerve in the nasal cavity by odorous chemicals, leading to sensations of tickling, stinging, warming, or cooling. The trigeminal nerve is also sensitive to the airflow changes that occur during breathing.

trigeminal nerve the fifth and largest CRANIAL NERVE, which carries both sensory and motor fibers. The motor fibers are primarily involved with the muscles used in chewing, tongue movements, and swallowing. The sensory fibers innervate the same areas, including the teeth and most of the tongue in addition to the jaws. Some fibers of the trigeminal nerve innervate the cornea, face, scalp, and the dura mater membrane of the brain.

trigeminal neuralgia a form of unilateral facial NEURALGIA involving the trigeminal nerve, characterized by paroxysms of excruciating pain. Also called **tic douloureux**.

trigeminal nucleus either of two nuclei associated with the three main roots of each trigeminal nerve. The **spinal trigeminal nucleus** extends downward in the medulla oblongata to the upper region of the spinal cord and receives fibers from pain and temperature receptors. The **principal sensory trigeminal nucleus** receives large myelinated fibers from pressure receptors in the skin and relays impulses upward to the thalamus.

tri-mean *n.* a measure of CENTRAL TENDENCY computed as the average of the MEDIAN, the upper HINGE, and the lower hinge of the distribution of cases.

trimming *n.* the exclusion of a fixed percentage of cases at each end of a distribution before calculating a statistic on the batch of data. This is done to eliminate the influence of extreme scores on the estimate.

tripartite model of attitudes a theory of attitude structure proposing that an attitude is based on or consists of affective, cognitive, and behavioral components. The affective component refers to feelings associated with the attitude object, the cognitive component to beliefs about attributes associated with the attitude object, and the behavioral component to past behaviors and future intentions associated with the attitude object.

triple blind see BLIND.

triptans *pl. n.* a class of vasoconstrictor drugs (see VASOCONSTRICTION) used in the treatment of migraine headache, the prototype of which is **sumatriptan**. Triptans exert their therapeutic effect by acting as AGONISTS at 5-HT$_{1B}$ and 5-HT$_{1D}$ SEROTONIN RECEPTORS, causing the constriction of cerebral blood vessels. Triptans should not be administered concurrently with MONOAMINE OXIDASE INHIBITORS and should be used cautiously with SSRIs to avoid the risk of precipitating a SEROTONIN SYNDROME.

trisomy *n.* see AUTOSOME. —**trisomic** *adj.*

triune brain the view, now outmoded, that the brain consists of three layers reflecting its evolutionary development. The first and oldest is the archipallium, or R-complex (meaning reptilian complex and including the BRAINSTEM and CEREBELLUM); the second is the paleomammalian system, or LIMBIC SYSTEM; and the most recently evolved is the neopallium, or NEOCORTEX.

trochlear nerve the fourth CRANIAL NERVE, which contains motor fibers supplying the superior oblique muscle of the eyeball.

trophic *adj.* **1.** describing or relating to activities associated with nourishment, or the ingestion of food and metabolism of nutrients. **2.** describing or relating to the nourishing and supportive functions of the CELL BODY of a neuron, as distinct from the activity of impulse reception and transmission. See also NEUROTROPHIC FACTOR.

tropia *n.* the relative deviation of the visual axes during binocular viewing of a single target, resulting in abnormal alignment of the eyes that convergence cannot correct (see STRABISMUS). The term is most commonly used in compound words, such as **exotropia** (outward deviation) and **esotropia** (inward deviation).

tropic hormone (**trophic hormone**) any of a class of anterior pituitary hormones that affect the secretion of other endocrine glands. The tropic hormones include thyroid-stimulating hormone, CORTICOTROPIN, follicle-stimulating hormone, and LUTEINIZING HORMONE.

tropism *n.* a form of orientation observed in both plants and animals toward or away from a stimulus, such as sunlight or gravity. The flower of a plant may turn gradually to face the sun as it moves across the sky (**heliotropism**), while its roots follow magnetic lines of force and the pull of gravity. Tropism contrasts with TAXIS, which is a directed movement toward or away from a stimulus. Compare KINESIS. —**tropic** *adj.*

troposmia *n.* a distorted odor perception in the presence of an odor. Typically, pleasant or neutral stimuli are perceived as unpleasant. See also DYSOSMIA; PAROSMIA.

truancy *n.* absence from school without permission. Persistent truancy before the age of 13 is an example of a serious violation of major rules, one of the symptoms of CONDUCT DISORDER. Also called **school truancy**. —**truant** *adj.*

true score in CLASSICAL TEST THEORY, that part of a measurement or score that reflects the actual amount of the attribute possessed by the individual being measured.

true variance naturally occurring variability within or among research participants. This variance is inherent in the nature of the participant and is not due to measurement error, imprecision of the model used to describe the variable of interest in the research (e.g., a particular behavior), or other extrinsic factors.

trust 1. *n.* reliance on or confidence in the worth, truth, or value of someone or something. Trust is considered by most psychological researchers to be a primary component in mature relationships with others, whether intimate, social, or therapeutic. See BASIC TRUST; INTERPERSONAL TRUST; SECURITY; TRUST VERSUS MISTRUST. **2.** *vb.* to have trust in someone or something.

trust versus mistrust the first of ERIKSON'S EIGHT STAGES OF DEVELOPMENT. It covers the first year of life and corresponds roughly to the ORAL STAGE posited by Austrian psychiatrist Sigmund Freud (1856–1939). During this stage, the infant's attitudes of trust or mistrust toward other people and himself or herself is influenced by the kind of care received. See also BASIC MISTRUST; BASIC TRUST.

truth serum a colloquial name for drugs, especially the barbiturates amobarbital, pentobarbital, or thiopental, that are injected intravenously in mild doses to help elicit information by inducing a relaxed, semihypnotic state in which an individual is less inhibited and more communicative. The term is derived from the reported use of such drugs by police to extract confessions from suspects.

tryptamine derivatives a group of drugs that are chemically related to SEROTONIN (5-hydroxytryptamine). They include a number of agents with hallucinogenic effects similar to those of LSD, including DMT (dimethyltryptamine), DET (diethyltryptamine), bufotenin, and PSILOCIN. Tryptamine derivatives may also be classified as substituted indolealkylamines.

tryptophan *n.* one of the essential amino acids of the human diet. It is a precursor of the neurotransmitter SEROTONIN and plays a role in general physiological processes. In plants and many

T

animals it is also a precursor of the B vitamin nicotinic acid. Tryptophan depletion—loss of tryptophan in the brain—may be induced for research purposes.

T score any of a set of scores scaled so that they have a MEAN equal to 50 and STANDARD DEVIATION equal to 10.

t test any of a class of statistical tests based on the fact that the test statistic follows the T DISTRIBUTION when the null hypothesis is true. Most *t* tests deal with hypotheses about the mean of a population or about differences between means of different populations.

tubal ligation a surgical procedure for female STERILIZATION by cutting, cauterizing, tying, or blocking the FALLOPIAN TUBES. Tubal ligation does not affect sex drive, ability for coitus, or menstrual cycles. Although the effects of the procedure may sometimes be reversed and the ability to conceive restored, tubal ligation is usually considered permanent.

tubectomy *n.* see SALPINGECTOMY.

tuberoinfundibular tract one of three major neural pathways in the brain that use dopamine as their principal neurotransmitter (i.e., is DOPAMINERGIC). The cell bodies of this tract, which is a local circuit in the hypothalamus, project short axons to the pituitary gland. The tuberoinfundibular tract is associated with regulation of hypothalamic function and specific hormones (e.g., prolactin). Alterations in hormone function involving this tract are often seen in patients taking phenothiazine ANTIPSYCHOTICS.

tuberomammillary nucleus a nucleus in the HYPOTHALAMUS that contains neurons responsive to HISTAMINE and is involved in maintaining wakefulness and arousal.

tufted cell one of the specialized types of cells involved in the sense of smell. The tufted cells are efferent neurons located in the OLFACTORY BULB. They synapse with receptor neurons in the glomerular layer and exit the bulb in the lateral OLFACTORY TRACT.

Tukey's Honestly Significant Difference Test (**Tukey's HSD Test**) a post hoc testing procedure that allows for the comparison of all pairs of groups while maintaining the overall SIGNIFICANCE LEVEL of the set of tests at a prescribed level. [John Wilder **Tukey** (1915–2000), U.S. statistician]

Tukey Test of Additivity a statistical test of the assumption that there are no interactions in experimental designs in which there is only one individual per CELL. It is used as a preliminary step to utilizing the interaction SUM OF SQUARES to estimate the within-cell error. [John **Tukey**]

tumescence *n.* a state of swelling or being swollen, as in swelling of the penis or clitoris as a result of sexual stimulation. Compare DETUMESCENCE. —**tumescent** *adj.*

tumor *n.* **1.** see NEOPLASM. **2.** swelling, one of the cardinal signs of inflammation.

tuning curve a graph of neuronal response (usually measured in action potentials or spikes per unit time) as a function of a continuous stimulus attribute, such as orientation, wavelength, or frequency. A neuron is said to be "tuned" for the stimulus that evokes the greatest response, and the width of the curve from the half-maximum response on either side of the peak indicates how broadly or narrowly tuned a neuron is for a particular stimulus attribute. In the auditory system it is a measure of FREQUENCY SELECTIVITY. See TONOTOPIC ORGANIZATION.

tunnel vision a VISUAL FIELD DEFECT producing the effect of perceiving the world through a long tunnel or tube. Peripheral vision may be entirely lost. Tunnel vision can occur in one or both eyes in uncontrolled GLAUCOMA and RETINITIS PIGMENTOSA and in both eyes after bilateral injury to visual processing areas beyond the optic chiasm. It may also be a conversion symptom. Also called **tubular vision**.

turbinate *n.* any of three bony shelves in the nasal cavity. The turbinates produce turbulence in the airflow passing from the nostrils to the OLFACTORY MUCOSA, and this turbulence distributes air across the OLFACTORY RECEPTORS in the mucosa.

Turing test a test proposed in 1950 (originally called the **imitation game**) to determine in what situations a computer program might be said to be intelligent. The test isolates in a room an individual who is connected to either a computer or another person. If the person in the room cannot tell, by asking questions, whether he or she is talking to the computer or to the other person, then the program on the machine must be seen as intelligent. [Alan Mathison **Turing** (1912–1954), British mathematician]

twelve-step program a distinctive approach to overcoming addictive, compulsive, or behavioral problems that was developed initially in ALCOHOLICS ANONYMOUS (AA) to guide recovery from alcoholism and is now used, often in an adapted form, by a number of other SELF-HELP GROUPS. In the context of alcoholism, for instance, the twelve-step program in AA asks each member to (a) admit that he or she cannot control his or her drinking; (b) recognize a supreme spiritual power, which can give the member strength; (c) examine past errors, a process that is carried out with another member who serves as sponsor; (d) make amends for these errors; (e) develop a new code and style of life; and (f) help other alcoholics who are in need of support. Variations of this model also exist for drug abuse and addiction, gambling addiction, and other problems.

twilight state a state of clouded consciousness in which the individual is temporarily unaware of his or her surroundings, experiences fleeting auditory or visual hallucinations, and responds to them by performing irrational acts, such as undressing in public, running away, or committing violence. The disturbance occurs primarily in temporal lobe epilepsy, dissociative reactions, and alcoholic intoxication. On regaining normal consciousness, individuals usually report that they felt they were dreaming and have little or no recollection of their behavior. See also DREAM STATE.

twin control in a TWIN STUDY, a method in which the target twin—that is, the one who has had certain experiences or training or has been exposed to the experimental conditions—is compared against the twin who has not had the experiences, training, or treatment and therefore serves as a CONTROL. Also called **cotwin control**.

twins *pl. n.* see DIZYGOTIC TWINS; MONOZYGOTIC TWINS.

twin study any research design utilizing twins. The purpose of such research is usually to assess the relative contributions of heredity and environment to some attribute (e.g., intelligence). Specifically, twin studies often involve comparing the characteristics of identical and fraternal twins and comparing twins of both types who have been reared together or reared apart. The assumptions made in these studies are, however, never completely fulfilled. For example, the identical twins reared apart have had some common environment, if only their intrauterine experiences. Moreover, identical twins reared together usually have more similar environments than fraternal twins raised together. These differences can make the estimations of heritability of any attribute open to some doubts.

two-by-two factorial design an experimental design in which there are two INDEPENDENT VARIABLES each having two levels. When this design is depicted as a matrix, two rows represent one of the independent variables and two columns represent the other independent variable. See FACTORIAL DESIGN.

two-factor design a FACTORIAL DESIGN in which two INDEPENDENT VARIABLES are manipulated. Also called **two-way factorial design**.

two-factor theory 1. a theory of avoidance learning holding that avoidance behavior is the result of two kinds of conditioning. Initially, stimuli that precede the presentation of the stimulus to be avoided (e.g., an electric shock) are established by PAVLOVIAN CONDITIONING (Factor 1) as aversive. Next, the subject escapes (Factor 2) from the conditioned aversive stimulus (see ESCAPE CONDITIONING). **2.** a theory that intelligence comprises two kinds of factors: a GENERAL FACTOR, whose influence pervades all tests of intelligence; and specific factors of intelligence, each of whose influence extends only to a single test in a test battery (see SPECIFIC FACTOR).

two-factor theory of emotion see SCHACHTER–SINGER THEORY.

two-factor theory of work motivation see HYGIENE FACTORS; MOTIVATORS.

two-point discrimination the ability to sense the contact of a touch stimulus at two different points on the hand at the same time. The **two-point discrimination test** is used in studies of the effects of parietal lesions of the brain, particularly in patients with open head injuries.

two-point threshold the point of stimulus separation, that is, the smallest distance between two points of stimulation on the skin at which the two stimuli are perceived as two stimuli rather than as a single stimulus. Also called **spatial threshold**.

two-process model of recall the hypothesis that RECALL of a memory can involve two stages: a search that locates material in memory followed by a decision regarding whether this is the information sought. This model was proposed to explain the occurrence of higher rates of accurate memory in the RECOGNITION METHOD than in the RECALL METHOD. Also called **generate–recognize model**; **two-process model of retrieval**.

two-spirit *n.* in some Native American cultures, a person, typically male, who takes on the gender identity of the opposite sex with the approval of the society. The culture often views such individuals as having a special spiritual or guidance role in the community. In the Navajo culture such a person is termed a **nadle**, in the Lakota culture the term **winkte** is used, and in other cultures a literal translation of "man-woman" might be used. The traditional scholarly term **berdache** is now used less frequently because of its negative implications of male prostitution or of a "kept" status.

two-stage memory theory a concept that information acquired by learning is stored first in an IMMEDIATE MEMORY from which items are transferred into a permanent memory (see LONG-TERM MEMORY). For example, a new telephone number might be retained in immediate memory at first, but with repetition eventually transfers to permanent memory. This transfer is described sometimes in psychological terms, as due to REHEARSAL, and sometimes in biological terms, as in memory CONSOLIDATION. See DUAL-STORE MODEL OF MEMORY.

two-tailed test a statistical test of an experimental hypothesis that does not specify the expected direction of an effect or a relationship. Also called **nondirectional test**. Compare ONE-TAILED TEST.

two-way analysis of variance a statistical test analyzing the joint and separate influences of two INDEPENDENT VARIABLES on a DEPENDENT VARIABLE.

two-way factorial design see TWO-FACTOR DESIGN.

two-word stage the developmental period, between approximately 18 and 24 months of age, when children use two words at a time when speaking (e.g., *dog bone, mama cup*). See PIVOT GRAMMAR; TELEGRAPHIC SPEECH.

tympanic membrane a conically shaped membrane that separates the external ear from the middle ear and serves to transform the pressure waves of sounds into mechanical vibration of the OSSICLES. The first ossicle (malleus) is attached to the inner surface of the tympanic membrane. Also called **eardrum**.

tympanic reflex see TENSOR TYMPANI.

Type A personality a personality pattern characterized by chronic competitiveness, high levels of ACHIEVEMENT MOTIVATION, and hostility. The lifestyles of Type A individuals are said to predispose them to coronary heart disease. Compare TYPE B PERSONALITY.

Type B personality a personality pattern characterized by low levels of competitiveness and frustration and a relaxed, easy-going approach. Type B individuals typically do not feel the need to prove their superiority or abilities. Compare TYPE A PERSONALITY.

Type I cell a type of TASTE CELL that is electron-dense, that is, it appears dark when viewed by electron microscopy. Type I cells comprise about 60% of the cells in a TASTE BUD. Located peripherally in the bud, they may help hold its goblet shape. Each cell sends a spray of 30–40 MICROVILLI through the TASTE PORE to sample the chemical environment. Also called **dark cell**.

Type II cell a type of TASTE CELL that is electron-lucent, that is, it appears light when viewed by electron microscopy. Type II cells comprise 20% of the cells in a TASTE BUD. They are larger than TYPE I CELLS, though their volume comes from girth rather than length. They send short, blunt MICROVILLI through the TASTE PORE to sample the chemical environment. Also called **light cell**.

Type III cell a type of TASTE CELL that, when viewed by electron microscopy, is similar to a TYPE II CELL but has dense-cored vesicles in its basal region. Type III cells comprise 15% of the cells in a TASTE BUD; they contain acetylcholine and serotonin for activation of peripheral nerve fibers. Also called **intermediate cell**.

Type IV cell a type of cell assumed to be a STEM CELL for the creation of TASTE CELLS. Type IV cells comprise 5% of the cells in a TASTE BUD and are confined to its basal lamina. These cells have no receptor function, possessing neither access to the TASTE PORE nor synapses with peripheral nerve fibers. Also called **basal cell**.

Type I error the error of rejecting the NULL HYPOTHESIS when it is in fact true. Investigators make this error when they believe they have detected an effect or a relationship that does not actually exist. Also called **alpha error**.

Type II error the error of failing to reject the NULL HYPOTHESIS when it is in fact not true. Investigators make this error if they conclude that a particular effect or relationship does not exist when in fact it does. Also called **beta error**.

type–token distinction in semantics and semiotics, the distinction between a general category of items having certain defining features (type) and a particular exemplar of that category (token). A token is taken to possess the essential properties of the type to which it belongs and will thus have a representative function. According to some theories, the type–token distinction plays an important role in semantic memory.

Type-T personality a predisposition of an individual to seek situations that cause or increase arousal, stimulation, thrills, and an adrenaline rush. See SENSATION SEEKING.

typical antipsychotic see ANTIPSYCHOTIC.

typicality effect the finding that people are quicker to make category judgments about typical members of a category than they are to make such judgments about atypical members. For example, people are able to judge that a dog is a mammal faster than they are able to judge that a whale is a mammal.

typing *n*. **1.** identifying as a type, as in sex typing and gender typing. **2.** representing something in terms of its common or typical characteristics. See CLASSIFICATION.

typology *n*. any analysis of a particular category of phenomena (e.g., individuals, things) into classes based on common characteristics, for example, a typology of personality. —**typological** *adj*.

tyrosine *n*. a nonessential AMINO ACID present in most proteins. It is a precursor of the CATECHOLAMINE neurotransmitters dopamine, norepinephrine, and epinephrine, which differ structurally only in the group at one position of the molecule. Tyrosine is derived from the essential amino acid phenylalanine.

Uu

UCR abbreviation for UNCONDITIONED RESPONSE.

Ucs abbreviation for UNCONSCIOUS.

UCS abbreviation for UNCONDITIONED STIMULUS.

ulcer *n.* an erosion of a tissue surface, such as the mucosal lining of the digestive tract. **Peptic ulcers**, which affect the stomach and duodenum, are associated with increased secretion of hydrochloric acid and pepsin, a digestive enzyme, or increased susceptibility of the lining of the stomach and duodenum to the effects of these substances.

ulnar nerve the sensory and motor nerve that innervates the lateral (outer) side of the forearm and hand. Its fibers are derived from the eighth cervical and first thoracic SPINAL ROOTS, and they pass through the medial section of the BRACHIAL PLEXUS.

ultimate attribution error see GROUP-SERVING BIAS.

ultimate explanation an account or explanation for a particular behavior in terms of its adaptive value. Compare PROXIMATE EXPLANATION.

ultradian rhythm any periodic variation in physiological or psychological function (see BIOLOGICAL RHYTHM) recurring in a cycle of more than 24 hours, such as the human menstrual cycle. Compare INFRADIAN RHYTHM.

ultrasonic communication the use of sound frequencies above the range of human hearing (i.e., above 20 kHz) for animal communication. Ultrasonic communication is commonly used by bats and dolphins, in which ECHOLOCATION is important for navigation or finding prey. High-frequency signals do not travel very far but, because of their short wavelength, they can provide excellent spatial resolution of prey and other objects in the environment. Compare INFRASONIC COMMUNICATION.

ultrasound *n.* the use of sound whose frequency exceeds the human AUDIBILITY RANGE in order to measure and record structures and structural change within the body in the imaging technique called **ultrasonography** (or **sonography**). Echoes from ultrasound waves reflected from tissue surfaces are recorded to form structural images for diagnostic purposes, for example, to examine a growing fetus during pregnancy or to examine internal organs, such as the heart, liver, kidneys, and gallbladder, for signs of health or disease.

Umwelt *n.* in the thought of German philosopher Martin Heidegger (1889–1976), that aspect of DASEIN (being-in-the-world) that is constituted by a person's engagement with the world immediately around him or her. The term was introduced into the vocabulary of psychology chiefly through the work of Swiss existential psychologist Ludwig Binswanger (1881–1966). Compare EIGENWELT; MITWELT. [German, literally: "around world"]

unattended input any stimulus that is not a focus of attention. In dual-task performance tests, it is the flow of information that participants do not intend to monitor and of which they are not aware. See also DUAL-TASK COMPETITION.

unbiased *adj.* without BIAS or net error. In unbiased procedures, studies, and the like any errors that do occur are random and therefore self-cancelling in the long run.

unbiased estimator a statistic whose expected value is the value of the parameter being estimated. Thus if *G* is used to estimate the parameter Θ, *G* is said to be unbiased if and only if $E(G) = \Theta$.

unbiased sampling a survey design in which the values produced by the samples coincide in the long run with the true values in the population.

uncertainty *n.* **1.** the state or condition in which something (e.g., the probability of a particular outcome) is not accurately or precisely known. **2.** lack of confidence or clarity in one's ideas, decisions, or intentions. —**uncertain** *adj.*

uncertainty reduction theory a social theory of relationship development proposing that there is a need to gain information about other people through communication (reducing uncertainty) in order to be better able to predict and explain the behavior of those individuals.

uncinate fasciculus a bundle of nerve fibers that connects the anterior and inferior portions of the FRONTAL LOBE of each cerebral hemisphere in the brain. It forms a compact bundle as the fasciculus bends around the LATERAL SULCUS and spreads into a fan shape at either end.

unconditional positive regard 1. an attitude of caring, acceptance, and prizing on the part of the therapist, which is considered conducive to self-awareness and personality growth on the part of the client. This attitude is emphasized in CLIENT-CENTERED THERAPY. **2.** a parent or caregiver's spontaneous love and affection given without conditions, a universal need in infancy and a prerequisite for healthy development. It is internalized by the child and contributes to the development of an enduring sense of self-worth. Compare CONDITIONAL POSITIVE REGARD.

unconditioned reflex a response to a stimulus that is innate, reflexive, and occurs without prior conditioning (learning). See UNCONDITIONED RESPONSE.

unconditioned reinforcement see PRIMARY REINFORCEMENT.

unconditioned response (**UCR**; **UR**) the unlearned response to a stimulus: any original response that occurs naturally and in the absence of conditioning (e.g., salivation in response to the presentation of food). The unconditioned response serves as the basis for establishment of the conditioned response; it is frequently reflexive in nature. See PAVLOVIAN CONDITIONING. Compare CONDITIONED RESPONSE.

unconditioned stimulus (**UCS**; **US**) a stimulus that elicits an UNCONDITIONED RESPONSE, as in withdrawal from a hot radiator, contraction of the pupil on exposure to light, or salivation when food is in the mouth. Also called **unconditional stimulus**. Compare CONDITIONED STIMULUS.

unconscious 1. (**Ucs**) *n.* in psychoanalytic theory, the region of the psyche that contains memories, emotional conflicts, wishes, and repressed impulses that are not directly accessible to awareness but that have dynamic effects on thought and behavior. Austrian psychiatrist Sigmund Freud (1856–1939) sometimes used the term **dynamic unconscious** to distinguish this concept from that which is merely descriptively unconscious but "static" and with little psychological significance. Compare CONSCIOUS; PRECONSCIOUS. See also COGNITIVE UNCONSCIOUS; COLLECTIVE UNCONSCIOUS; PERSONAL UNCONSCIOUS. **2.** *adj.* relating to or marked by absence of awareness or lack of consciousness.

unconscious inference theory the hypothesis that perception is indirectly influenced by inferences about current sensory input that make use of the perceiver's knowledge of the world and prior experience with similar input. For example, consider two trees of the same height but different distances from the perceiver. The images of the trees that appear on the retina are of different sizes, but the knowledge that one tree is farther away than the other leads the perceiver to infer, without conscious effort, that in actuality the two trees are the same size.

unconscious knowledge see TACIT KNOWLEDGE.

unconscious learning the acquisition of TACIT KNOWLEDGE. See IMPLICIT LEARNING.

unconscious perception a phenomenon, the existence of which is controversial, in which a stimulus that is not consciously perceived nonetheless influences behavior. See PREATTENTIVE PROCESSING.

unconscious processing see PREATTENTIVE PROCESSING.

unconscious transfer a memory distortion that results from confusing the source of the information recalled (see SOURCE CONFUSION). In legal contexts, for example, a witness may mistakenly recognize an individual in the lineup as the perpetrator, when in fact the individual's face is familiar because it was earlier presented in a photograph. Also called **unconscious transference**.

uncontrolled variable a variable that is not regulated or measured by the investigator during an experiment or study.

uncovering *n.* in psychotherapy, the process of peeling away an individual's defenses and passing beyond a focus on symptoms to get to the underlying roots of a problem. **Uncovering techniques** may include psychoanalysis and other psychodynamic or depth therapies, deep exploration of issues, and the use of trust to encourage truthfulness on the part of the client.

uncriticalness *n.* a nonjudgmental attitude on the part of the therapist, which is considered essential in the nondirective approach of client-centered therapy, as well as in other forms of psychotherapy. Criticism is held to inhibit clients' efforts to recognize and revise their self-defeating patterns of thought and behavior.

uncued panic attack a PANIC ATTACK that occurs unexpectedly rather than being brought on by a specific situation or trigger. It is therefore perceived to have occurred spontaneously. Also called **unexpected panic attack**. Compare CUED PANIC ATTACK.

uncus *n.* a hook-shaped part of the rhinal sulcus (cleft) of the hippocampal formation in the RHINENCEPHALON. The lateral OLFACTORY TRACT makes connections with the uncus.

underclass *n.* **1.** a SOCIAL CLASS existing beneath the usual socioeconomic scale, often concentrated in the inner cities and usually characterized by poverty, inadequate educational or vocational opportunities, high unemployment or chronic underemployment, violent crime, substance abuse, poor social services, and few community-supporting institutions. **2.** broadly, any group without equal or direct access to the economic, educational, legal, medical, or other provisions of a society.

underextension *n.* the incorrect restriction of the use of a word, which is a mistake commonly made by young children acquiring language. For example, a child may believe that the label *dog* applies only to Fido, the family pet.

underload *n.* the situation in which a low level of task demand creates distress in such forms as boredom and fatigue. Compare OVERLOAD.

understanding *n.* **1.** the process of gaining insight about oneself or others or of comprehending the meaning or significance of something, such as a word, concept, argument, or event. See also APPREHENSION; COMPREHENSION. **2.** in counseling and psychotherapy, the process of

U

discerning the network of relationships between a client's behavior and his or her environment, history, aptitudes, motivation, ideas, feelings, relationships, and modes of expression. **—understand** *vb*.

undifferentiated schizophrenia a subtype of SCHIZOPHRENIA in which the individual exhibits prominent psychotic features, such as delusions, hallucinations, disorganized thinking, or grossly disorganized behavior, but does not meet the criteria for any of the other subtypes of the disorder.

undifferentiated somatoform disorder a SOMATOFORM DISORDER in which one or more physical complaints persist for 6 months or longer and cannot be explained by a known medical condition. Unlike FACTITIOUS DISORDER or MALINGERING, these symptoms are not intentionally feigned or produced.

unfinished business in therapy and counseling, the personal experiences that have been blocked or tasks that have been avoided because of feared emotional or interpersonal effects. Many therapists believe that people have an urge to complete unfinished business in order to achieve satisfaction and peace. Those working with the dying and their families believe that dealing with unfinished business is an important aspect of the dying and grieving processes.

unfolding *n*. a scaling procedure in which respondents' evaluations of a set of choices are used to form a continuum along which each respondent is placed in such a way as to reflect that respondent's relative evaluations of the set of choices.

unidimensional *adj*. having a single dimension or composed of a single or a pure factor. Compare MULTIDIMENSIONAL.

unified positivism an approach to the problem of the fragmentation of psychology that seeks to unify the field by emphasizing scientific work that integrates disparate findings and thus draws theories and models together. It derives its inspiration from one of the basic assumptions of LOGICAL POSITIVISM: that all science could be united, on the model of physics, through a strict empiricist approach.

unified theory of cognition any theory that attempts to provide a single architecture for explaining all cognitive activity, whether in humans, animals, or artificial intelligence. An example is the SOAR model, proposed by U.S. cognitive psychologist and computer scientist Allen Newell (1927–1992).

unilateral *adj*. denoting or relating to one side of the body or an organ or to one of two or more parties. For example, a unilateral cerebral lesion involves one cerebral hemisphere, left or right, with effects that may vary according to the dominance of the hemisphere and the function affected, and **unilateral couple counseling** is the counseling of one partner on his or her relationship with the other. **—unilaterally** *adv*.

unilateral neglect a disorder resulting from damage to the PARIETAL LOBE of the brain and characterized by a loss of conscious perception of objects in the half of the visual field (usually the left half) that is opposite the location of the lesion, ALIEN LIMB SYNDROME, and other striking neuropsychological features. Also called **hemineglect**.

unimodal distribution a set of scores that has one mode (represented by one peak in their graphical distribution), reflecting a tendency for scores to cluster around a specific value. See also BIMODAL DISTRIBUTION.

unipolar depression any DEPRESSIVE DISORDER, that is, any mood disorder marked by one or more MAJOR DEPRESSIVE EPISODES or a prolonged period of depressive symptoms with no history of manic or hypomanic symptoms or MIXED EPISODES.

unipolar neuron a neuron that has only a single extension of the CELL BODY. This extension divides into two branches, oriented in opposite directions and representing the axon. One end is the receptive pole, and the other is the output zone. Unipolar neurons transmit touch information from the body surface to the spinal cord. Also called **monopolar neuron**. Compare BIPOLAR NEURON; MULTIPOLAR NEURON.

unipolar rating scale see BIPOLAR RATING SCALE.

unitary-resource model a model that views attention as a single pool of undifferentiated resources that can be devoted to a variety of processes. Tasks place demands on the general pool, rather than on particular resources. The extent to which the total resources are taxed by a primary task will determine the performance decrement on other tasks carried out at the same time; when the demand on resources exceeds the supply, allocation strategies become important. Also called **single-capacity model**. Compare MULTIPLE-RESOURCE MODEL.

United Nations Declaration on the Rights of Mentally Retarded Persons a 1971 declaration by the United Nations affirming the human rights of people with mental retardation. These issues were largely subsumed under the 1993 Standard Rules on the Equalization of Opportunities for Persons with Disabilities.

unit schedule see SECOND-ORDER SCHEDULE.

unity of consciousness the concept that the contents of awareness are coherent, internally consistent, or shaped by a common goal. From this it follows that mutually inconsistent events cannot simultaneously appear in awareness.

univariate *adj*. characterized by a single variable.

universal *n*. see PSYCHOLOGICAL UNIVERSAL.

universal design a quality of a product or built environment so conceived as to make it optimally usable and comfortable for people of all ages and abilities. Universal design as a concept goes beyond mere accessibility and removal of barriers, in accordance with the mandates of such laws as the Americans With Disabilities Act, by emphasizing the inclusiveness of design to accommodate a wide range of physical and cognitive abilities. Also called **transgenerational design**. See also BARRIER-FREE ENVIRONMENT.

universal grammar a theoretical linguistic construct positing the existence of a set of rules or grammatical principles that are innate in human beings and underlie most natural languages. The concept is of considerable interest to psycholinguists who study LANGUAGE ACQUISITION and the formation of valid sentences. Research shows that BROCA'S AREA in the brain is selectively activated by languages that meet the criteria for universal grammar.

universalism n. the position that certain aspects of the human mind, human behavior, and human morality are universal and essential and are therefore to be found in all cultures and historical periods. Universalism is thus a form of ESSENTIALISM and is opposed to RELATIVISM. —**universalist** adj.

universality n. **1.** the tendency to assume that one's personal qualities and characteristics, including attitudes and values, are common in the general social group or culture. See also FALSE-CONSENSUS EFFECT. **2.** in mob and crowd settings, the tendency for individuals to assume that atypical, unusual behaviors are allowable because many others in the situation are performing such actions ("everybody's doing it"). See CONTAGION; EMERGENT-NORM THEORY. **3.** in self-help and psychotherapy groups, a curative factor fostered by members' recognition that their problems and difficulties are not unique to them, but instead are experienced by many of the group members. See also CURATIVE FACTORS MODEL.

universalizability n. in ethics, the principle that particular moral judgments always carry an implied universal judgment. So, for example, to say *Daphne shouldn't have lied to him* implies the universal judgment that anybody in the identical situation to Daphne should not have lied. The principle of universalizability is related to that of the CATEGORICAL IMPERATIVE. —**universalizable** adj.

universe of discourse 1. the total system of ideas, concepts, terms, and expressions within which a given topic can be analyzed and understood. The universe of discourse defines both what can be said about a subject and how it can be said. Statements that are meaningful within a particular universe of discourse may well be nonsensical within another; to say *The sad skies are weeping*, for example, might be permissible in poetry but would not be so in meteorology. **2.** in the field of artificial intelligence, any set of objects that can be represented within a given domain.

unobtrusive measure a measure obtained without disturbing the participant or alerting him or her that a measurement is being made. The behavior or responses of such participants are thus assumed to be unaffected by the investigative process or the surrounding environment. See also REACTIVE MEASURE. Compare OBTRUSIVE MEASURE.

unpleasantness n. an emotional state that is experienced when an event is incongruent with one's goals or is associated with pain. See also DIMENSIONAL THEORY OF EMOTION. —**unpleasant** adj.

unpleasure n. in psychoanalytic theory, the psychic pain, tension, and EGO suffering that is consciously felt when instinctual needs and wishes, such as hunger and sex, are blocked by the ego and denied gratification. [translation of German *Unlust*, "reluctance" or "listlessness"]

unresolved adj. **1.** in psychotherapy, denoting emotional or psychic conflicts not yet sufficiently dealt with and assimilated or understood. See also UNFINISHED BUSINESS. **2.** describing any stimulus whose characteristics cannot be determined by the perceiver.

unshared environment see NONSHARED ENVIRONMENT.

unspecified mental retardation the diagnosis made when an individual is presumed to have mental retardation but is too severely impaired or uncooperative to be evaluated through the use of standard intelligence tests and adaptive behavior measures.

unstructured adj. denoting an object, situation, or set of ideas that does not have a definite pattern or organization.

unstructured interview an interview that imposes minimal structure by asking open-ended (rather than set) questions and allowing the interviewee to steer the discussion into areas of his or her choosing. In personnel selection, the idea is that such an approach will reveal more of the applicant's traits, interests, priorities, and interpersonal and verbal skills than a STRUCTURED INTERVIEW. See also PATTERNED INTERVIEW.

unvoiced adj. denoting speech sounds that are articulated through breath, without vibration of the vocal cords. The unvoiced (or voiceless) sounds comprise some consonants (e.g., [p], [t], and [f]). Compare VOICED. See BINARY FEATURE.

upper motor neuron see MOTOR NEURON.

upper threshold 1. for a DIFFERENCE THRESHOLD, the threshold at which the stimulus is judged to be greater than the standard. **2.** the maximum intensity of a stimulus that can be perceived without pain.

upward communication written and oral messages that originate with individuals lower in the hierarchy of an organization and that flow upward to those occupying positions higher in the hierarchy. Upward communication is subject to distortions such as the **mum effect**, in which subordinates are unwilling to convey bad news to their superiors. The more levels in the hierarchy through which a message must pass, the more subject it is to distortion as the result of filtering at each level. Compare DOWNWARD COMMUNICATION; HORIZONTAL COMMUNICATION.

upward mobility the movement of a person or group to a higher social class. Upward mobility tends to be a feature of relatively relaxed class systems operating within expanding economies. Also called **social ascendancy**. See also SOCIAL MOBILITY. Compare DOWNWARD MOBILITY.

upward Pygmalion effect an effect in which the expectations of followers or subordinates lead to behavior on the part of the leader or superior that is consistent with these expectations. The behavior of the leader does not reflect his or her true abilities or personality traits, but rather the perception of the leader by subordinates. Compare PYGMALION EFFECT. See SELF-FULFILLING PROPHECY.

UR abbreviation for UNCONDITIONED RESPONSE.

urban behavior the behavior of people living in cities, who appear to be less attentive to the needs of strangers, walk faster, make less eye contact, and are exposed to more violence and aggressive behavior than their rural or suburban counterparts. The prevailing features of the urban environment—its size, density, and pace—led to the theory that urban behavior is characterized by adaptation to the INFORMATION OVERLOAD of city life, resulting in anonymity, powerlessness, aggression, and narrow self-interest among city dwellers.

urban ecology the study of the dynamics and organization of city life, particularly in relation to population density and the nature of the city environment. Urban ecology is based on principles derived from biology, sociology, psychology, and environmental science. See also URBANIZATION.

urbanization n. **1.** the trend toward living in cities, which are defined by the United States Bureau of the Census as having populations of 50,000 or more. **2.** the process of becoming a community with urban characteristics. Early psychological research on urbanization focused on the impact of urban life on mental health, purporting to find a link between inner-city residence and increased rates of mental illness; this position was later qualified (see DRIFT HYPOTHESIS). Inquiry has since expanded to investigate the psychological, physical, and behavioral consequences of the urban environment (e.g., population density, crowding, noise, and pollution) and the social, economic, and cultural dimensions of city life. See also URBAN ECOLOGY. **—urbanize** vb.

urban legend an incredible or lurid story, often involving a mixture of horror and humor, that is widely repeated as if true (often as the experience of a "friend of a friend") but can never be firmly documented. Urban legends differ from myths and folktales in that they nearly always have a contemporary setting and often involve modern technology (e.g., the many such tales about microwave ovens).

urethra n. a membrane-lined duct that carries urine from the urinary bladder to the exterior. In males it also serves as a channel for semen at ejaculation. In females the urethra is less than 4 cm long and runs almost directly to an opening anterior to the vaginal orifice. **—urethral** adj.

urination n. the discharge of urine from the bladder, which is effected by voluntary relaxation of the SPHINCTER at the junction of the bladder and urethra and reflex contraction of the bladder wall. Also called **micturition**.

urogenital adj. referring to organs concerned with both excretion and reproduction. Also called **urinogenital**.

US abbreviation for UNCONDITIONED STIMULUS.

usability engineering a specialty that applies knowledge of human capabilities and limitations to the design of systems (typically human–computer systems) with the goal of ensuring ease of use. This can be achieved by enhancing such attributes as design intuitiveness, learnability, and comprehensibility. See also HUMAN FACTORS PSYCHOLOGY; USER-CENTERED DESIGN.

user-centered design in ergonomics, design practice with a central focus on understanding the characteristics of the target group in order to produce usable products or systems. See also HUMAN FACTORS PSYCHOLOGY; USABILITY ENGINEERING.

usual, customary and reasonable fees see CUSTOMARY, PREVAILING, AND REASONABLE FEES.

uterus n. the hollow muscular organ in female mammals in which the embryo develops from the time of implantation until birth. It is connected to the ovaries via the FALLOPIAN TUBES and to the exterior via the vagina, into which the cervix (neck) of the uterus projects. The ENDOMETRIUM (lining) of the uterus undergoes changes during the MENSTRUAL CYCLE. Also called **womb**. **—uterine** adj.

utilitarian function of an attitude the role an attitude can play in obtaining rewards, avoiding punishments, or both. For example, a person might adopt a positive attitude toward a particular product because it is effective and a negative attitude toward its chief competitor because it is ineffective. See also FUNCTIONAL APPROACH TO ATTITUDES.

utilitarianism n. an ethical theory based on the premise that the good is to be defined as that which brings the greatest amount or degree of happiness; thus, an act is considered moral if, compared to possible alternatives, it provides the greatest good for the greatest number of people. The doctrine is often reduced to the single maxim: The greatest good for the greatest number. Utilitarianism is heavily influenced by HE-DONISM and EUDEMONISM; it also shares with BEHAVIORISM the notion that the fundamental motive for action is pleasure or benefit. Because it rejects the idea that actions may be intrinsically good or bad, irrespective of their consequences, and can provide no objective means of calculating the amount of happiness that derives from particular actions, utilitarianism is in practice a species of ethical RELATIVISM. Compare NATURAL LAW THEORY. —**utilitarian** *adj.*

utility *n.* **1.** the subjective value of some outcome to the individual. **2.** the value of an intervention or program judged on the basis of its monetary worth to the organization. For example, there are methodologies for assessing the monetary gains achieved from using particular tests to select employees or particular training programs. **3.** the usefulness of a characteristic in preserving the life of an organism or continuing the species. Both ARTIFICIAL SELECTION and NATURAL SELECTION operate to increase utility. **4.** in UTILITARIANISM, the "goodness" of an act as determined by the amount or degree of happiness derived from it.

utilization deficiency the inability of individuals to improve task performance by using strategies that they have already acquired and demonstrated the ability to use because they are not spurred to do so by memory. Although historically most frequently studied in children, current research suggests that such deficiencies are not developmental per se but may occur at any age as a by-product of diminished WORKING MEMORY capacity. Compare MEDIATIONAL DEFICIENCY; PRODUCTION DEFICIENCY.

utilization review a formal review of the necessity and quality of services provided in a hospital or clinic or by an individual provider. Conducted by a specially appointed committee, a utilization review often addresses whether the level of service provided is the most appropriate to the severity of the presenting problem. See also CONTINUED-STAY REVIEW; EXTENDED-STAY REVIEW.

utricle *n.* the larger of the two VESTIBULAR SACS in the inner ear, the other being the SACCULE. Like the saccule, the utricle senses not only the position of the head with respect to gravity but also acceleration and deceleration. This is achieved by a special patch of epithelium—the MACULA—inside both the utricle and saccule. —**utricular** *adj.*

utterance *n.* a unit of spoken language, which may be of any length but can usually be identified by conversational turn taking or by clear breaks in the stream of speech. MEAN LENGTH OF UTTERANCE is considered an important index of language development in young children.

uvula *n.* **1.** a fleshy appendage that hangs from the soft PALATE. It plays an important role as part of the apparatus for sound production of the human voice. **2.** any similarly shaped structure, such as those located in the urinary bladder and the cerebellum.

U

Vv

VABS abbreviation for VINELAND ADAPTIVE BE-HAVIOR SCALES.

vacuum activity in classical ethology, the occurrence of a FIXED ACTION PATTERN in the absence of the usual external stimulus (the RELEASER) that triggers the pattern. This is believed to be caused by a build-up of action-specific or motivational energy that overrides the INNATE RELEASING MECHANISM. Also called **vacuum response**.

vagina *n.* a tubelike structure in female mammals that leads from the cervix (neck) of the uterus to the exterior. The muscular walls of the vagina are lined with mucous membrane, and two pairs of vestibular glands around the vaginal opening secrete a fluid that facilitates penetration by the penis during coitus. —**vaginal** *adj.*

vaginismus *n.* a sexual dysfunction in which spasmic contractions of the muscles around the vagina occur during or immediately preceding sexual intercourse, causing the latter to be painful or impossible. Vaginismus is not diagnosed if the dysfunction is due solely to the effects of a medical condition, although medical conditions may be involved as a factor in the problem.

vagus nerve the tenth CRANIAL NERVE, a mixed nerve with both sensory and motor fibers that serves many functions. The sensory fibers innervate the external ear, vocal organs, and thoracic and abdominal VISCERA. The motor nerves innervate the tongue, vocal organs, and—through many ganglia of the PARASYMPATHETIC NERVOUS SYSTEM—the thoracic and abdominal viscera.

valence *n.* **1.** in the FIELD THEORY of German-born U.S. psychologist Kurt Lewin (1890–1947), the subjective value of an event, object, person, or other entity in the LIFE SPACE of the individual. An entity that attracts the individual has **positive valence**, while one that repels has **negative valence**. **2.** in certain theories of motivation, the anticipated satisfaction of attaining a particular goal or outcome.

valence–instrumentality–expectancy theory a theory of WORK MOTIVATION holding that the level of effort exerted by employees will depend on a combination of three variables: (a) the EXPECTANCY of employees that effort will lead to success in the job, (b) the belief of employees that success will lead to particular outcomes (see INSTRUMENTALITY THEORY), and (c) the value of these outcomes (see VALENCE). A numerical value can be obtained for variable (a) using the subjective probability estimates of employees,

for variable (b) by measuring the correlation of performance to rewards, and for variable (c) by asking employees to rate the desirability of the rewards. The motivational force, or the amount of effort employees will exert, can then be calculated. See also PATH–GOAL THEORY OF LEADERSHIP; PORTER–LAWLER MODEL OF MOTIVATION.

validation *n.* the process of establishing the truth or logical cogency of something, as in determining the accuracy of an instrument in measuring what it is designed to measure. In some forms of psychotherapy, this may take the form of MIRRORING of the client's judgment or experience by the therapist. —**validate** *vb.*

validity *n.* **1.** the characteristic of being founded on truth, accuracy, fact, or law. **2.** the degree to which a test or measurement accurately measures or reflects what it purports to measure. There are various types of validity, including CONCURRENT VALIDITY, CONSTRUCT VALIDITY, and ECOLOGICAL VALIDITY. —**valid** *adj.*

Valium *n.* a trade name for DIAZEPAM.

valproic acid a carboxylic acid (also formulated as **valproate sodium**; U.S. trade name: **Depacon**) used as an ANTICONVULSANT and MOOD STABILIZER. Although exact mechanisms of action remain unclear, valproic acid may exert its effects by reducing membrane sodium-channel activity (see ION CHANNEL), thereby slowing neuronal activity. It may also stimulate the synthesis of the inhibitory neurotransmitter gamma-aminobutyric acid (GABA). Valproic acid and valproate sodium are officially approved by the U.S. Food and Drug Administration for the management of seizures and of manic episodes associated with bipolar disorders. These drugs have been associated with fatalities due to liver failure, particularly in children under 2 years of age, as well as pancreatitis; serum monitoring of drug levels and liver function is therefore required, particularly on starting treatment. U.S. trade name: **Depakene**.

value *n.* **1.** the mathematical magnitude or quantity of a variable. **2.** a moral, social, or aesthetic principle accepted by an individual or society as a guide to what is good, desirable, or important. **3.** the worth, usefulness, or importance attached to something.

value-expressive function of an attitude the role an attitude can play in the expression of core values. For example, a person might adopt a positive attitude toward a religious symbol because that symbol is associated with important religious values. See also FUNCTIONAL APPROACH TO ATTITUDES.

value judgment an assessment of individuals, objects, or events in terms of the values held by the observer rather than in terms of their intrinsic characteristics objectively considered. In some areas, such as aesthetics or morality, value judgments are common, but in hard and social sciences they are frequently considered undesirable.

values clarification any process intended to promote an individual's awareness and understanding of his or her moral principles and ethical priorities and their relationships to behavior and place in daily life. Individuals may be asked to carry out a series of exercises to this effect in some forms of psychotherapy.

variability n. **1.** the quality of being subject to change or variation in behavior or emotion. **2.** in statistics and experimental design, the degree to which members of a group or population differ from each other.

variable n. a quantity in an experiment or test that varies, that is, takes on different values (such as test scores, ratings assigned by judges, and other personal, social, or physiological indicators) that can be quantified (measured).

variable-interval schedule (VI schedule) in free-operant conditioning, a type of INTERVAL REINFORCEMENT in which the reinforcement or reward is presented for the first response after a variable period has elapsed since the previous reinforcement. Reinforcement does not depend on the number of responses during the intervals. The value of the schedule is given by the average interval length; for example, "VI 3" indicates that the average length of the intervals between potential reinforcements is 3 min. This type of schedule generally produces a relatively constant rate of responding. It was formerly known as an **aperiodic reinforcement schedule.**

variable-ratio schedule (VR schedule) in free-operant conditioning, a type of INTERMITTENT REINFORCEMENT in which a response is reinforced after a variable number of responses. The value of the schedule is given by the average number of responses per reinforcer; for example, "VR 10" indicates that the average number of responses before reinforcement is 10.

variable stimulus any one of a set of experimental stimuli that are to be systematically compared to a constant stimulus.

variable-time schedule (VT schedule) a schedule of stimulus presentation in which stimuli are presented, independently of any behavior, at variable time intervals. The value of the schedule is given as the mean of the intervals. See also NONCONTINGENT REINFORCEMENT.

variance (symbol: σ^2) n. a measure of the spread, or DISPERSION, of scores within a sample, whereby a small variance indicates highly similar scores, all close to the sample mean, and a large variance indicates more scores at a greater distance from the mean and possibly spread over a larger range. Also called **index of variability**.

variate n. a specific value of a particular VARIABLE.

variation n. the existence of qualitative differences in form, structure, behavior, and physiology among the individuals of a population, whether due to heredity or to environment. Both ARTIFICIAL SELECTION and NATURAL SELECTION operate on variations among organisms, but only GENETIC VARIATION is transmitted to the offspring.

varied mapping in a SEARCH task, a condition in which target and distractor stimuli change roles randomly over the course of an experiment, so that a stimulus may be a target in one trial and a distractor in the next. Compare CONSISTENT MAPPING.

variety n. **1.** in BIOLOGICAL TAXONOMY, a subdivision of a species comprising those members of the species that are distinct with reference to particular minor characteristics that do not affect their ability to interbreed to produce fertile offspring. The various BREEDS of domestic animals are examples of varieties. **2.** in linguistics, a version of a language that is phonologically or grammatically distinct from the STANDARD LANGUAGE and may be associated with such categories as region, ethnicity, or social class. See also DIALECT; REGISTER.

vascular dementia severe loss of cognitive functioning as a result of cerebrovascular disease. It is often due to repeated strokes. Also called **multi-infarct dementia**.

vascular depression a MAJOR DEPRESSIVE EPISODE that occurs shortly after the onset or treatment of cardiovascular disease or that is assumed to be caused by cardiovascular disease. Often, this episode is characterized by ANHEDONIA rather than depressed mood.

vascular insufficiency failure of the cardiovascular system to deliver an adequate supply of blood to the body tissues. This may involve large regions of the body or a particular organ or area of an organ. ATHEROSCLEROSIS, for example, can reduce the blood supply to the leg muscles, causing cramplike pains and limping; the heart, resulting in angina pectoris; or the brain, causing symptoms of stroke.

vas deferens (pl. **vasa deferentia**) a duct that conveys spermatozoa from the epididymis (a convoluted tubule in which sperm from the testis mature and are stored) and unites with the duct of the SEMINAL VESICLE to form the ejaculatory duct, which leads to the urethra. Also called **seminal duct**.

vasectomy n. a surgical procedure for male STERILIZATION in which the vas deferens, which carries sperm from the testes to the urethra, is removed, segmented, or cut and the resulting openings blocked.

vasoconstriction *n.* narrowing of blood vessels, which is controlled by VASOMOTOR nerves of the sympathetic nervous system or by such agents as VASOPRESSIN or SYMPATHOMIMETIC DRUGS. It has the effect of increasing blood pressure.

vasodilation *n.* widening of blood vessels, as by the action of a VASOMOTOR nerve or a drug, which has the effect of lowering blood pressure.

vasomotor *adj.* describing or relating to nerve fibers, drugs, or other agents that can affect the diameter of blood vessels, especially small arteries, by causing contraction or relaxation of the smooth muscle of their walls. Fibers of the sympathetic and parasympathetic divisions of the AUTONOMIC NERVOUS SYSTEM have a vasomotor effect.

vasopressin *n.* a peptide hormone synthesized in the hypothalamus and released by the posterior pituitary gland. It plays an important role in the retention of water in the body (by signaling the kidneys to reabsorb water instead of excreting it in urine) and in regulation of blood pressure (by constricting small blood vessels, which raises blood pressure). Vasopressin secretion may also activate the HYPOTHALAMIC–PITUITARY–ADRENOCORTICAL SYSTEM and may be associated with mechanisms of learning and memory. Also called **antidiuretic hormone** (**ADH**).

vector *n.* **1.** in MULTIVARIATE ANALYSIS, a one-dimensional array in which the scores of *n* individuals on a particular measure are arrayed. **2.** a mathematical entity with magnitude and direction. **3.** an animal or other organism that carries and spreads disease.

vegetative *adj.* **1.** pertaining to basic physiological functions, such as those involved in growth, respiration, sleep, digestion, excretion, and homeostasis, which are governed primarily by the AUTONOMIC NERVOUS SYSTEM. **2.** living without apparent cognitive neurological function or responsiveness, as in PERSISTENT VEGETATIVE STATE. **3.** denoting ASEXUAL reproduction, especially in plants.

vegetative state a condition in which an individual is immobile and noncommunicative, unaware of self or the environment, and unresponsive to stimuli. The condition occurs primarily in individuals with serious brain injury and is characterized by a nonfunctioning cerebral cortex. See PERSISTENT VEGETATIVE STATE.

velar 1. *adj.* of or relating to the soft PALATE. **2.** *adj.* denoting a speech sound articulated by the soft palate, for example, the [hl] in Welsh *Llandovery* or the [kh] in Scottish *loch* or German *Bach*. **3.** *n.* a speech sound made in this way.

velum *n.* (*pl.* **vela**) **1.** an anatomical structure resembling a veil, such as the **velum medullare superior**, a thin layer of white matter that forms

the roof of the superior part of the fourth VENTRICLE of the brain. **2.** the soft PALATE.

venesection *n.* see PHLEBOTOMY.

ventral *adj.* pertaining to the front (anterior side) of the body or the lower (inferior) surface of the brain. Compare DORSAL. —**ventrally** *adv.*

ventral horn either of the bottom regions of the H-shaped pattern formed by the PERIAQUEDUCTAL GRAY in the spinal cord. The ventral horns contain large motor neurons whose axons form the ventral roots. Also called **anterior horn**. Compare DORSAL HORN.

ventral root any of the SPINAL ROOTS that carry motor nerve fibers and arise from the spinal cord ventrally on each side. Also called **anterior root**; **motor root**. Compare DORSAL ROOT. See also BELL–MAGENDIE LAW.

ventral stream a series of specialized visual regions in the cerebral cortex of the brain that originate in the STRIATE CORTEX (primary visual cortex) of the occipital lobe and project forward and downward into the lower temporal lobe. It is known informally as the "what" pathway of perception. Compare DORSAL STREAM.

ventral tegmental area an area in the midbrain ventral to the PERIAQUEDUCTAL GRAY and dorsal to the SUBSTANTIA NIGRA. It forms part of the LIMBIC SYSTEM, sending DOPAMINERGIC neurons to the MESOCORTICAL SYSTEM and MESOLIMBIC SYSTEM.

ventricle *n.* **1.** an anatomical cavity in the body, such as any of the ventricles of the heart. **2.** any of the four interconnected cavities inside the brain, which serve as reservoirs of CEREBROSPINAL FLUID. Each of the two **lateral ventricles** communicates with the THIRD VENTRICLE via an opening called the interventricular foramen; the third and fourth ventricles communicate with each other, via the CEREBRAL AQUEDUCT, and with the central canal of the spinal cord and the SUBARACHNOID SPACE. Also called **cerebral ventricle**. —**ventricular** *adj.*

ventricular puncture a surgical procedure in which an opening from the outside is made to the lateral ventricle areas of the brain. The procedure may be performed in order to reduce INTRACRANIAL PRESSURE, to inject medications (e.g., antibiotics) directly into the brain, or to obtain cerebrospinal fluid.

ventricular system the network of VENTRICLES and passageways in the brain, spinal cord, and subarachnoid space through which the CEREBROSPINAL FLUID circulates as a source of nutrients for tissues of the central nervous system.

ventricular zone a region of actively dividing tissue cells lining the cerebral VENTRICLES that provides neurons mainly early in development and glial cells (see NEUROGLIA) throughout life.

ventromedial hypothalamic syndrome a set of symptoms caused by experimental lesions in the VENTROMEDIAL NUCLEUS of the hypothal-

V

amus in the brain. The syndrome consists of two stages. The first (or **dynamic**) stage is characterized by HYPERPHAGIA (overeating) and subsequent weight gain, resulting in obesity. The second (or **static**) stage includes stabilization of body weight, resistance to food-getting behavior, and finickiness, such that the animal is willing to eat only easily obtainable and palatable foods. Also called **hypothalamic hyperphagia**. Compare LATERAL HYPOTHALAMIC SYNDROME.

ventromedial nucleus an area of the hypothalamus in the brain that receives input from the AMYGDALA and is associated particularly with eating and sexual behavior. The ventromedial nucleus traditionally has been referred to as the **satiety center** because of its presumed dominance over the cessation of eating, but it is now known that other neural areas are involved in this function as well. See also VENTROMEDIAL HYPOTHALAMIC SYNDROME.

ventromedial pathways some of the major descending pathways of the MOTOR SYSTEM, conveying information from diffuse areas of the cerebral cortex, midbrain, and cerebellum. These pathways include the anterior **corticospinal tract**, which descends directly from motor cortex to the anterior horn of the spinal cord; the **vestibulospinal tract**, which carries information from the VESTIBULAR NUCLEI for control of equilibratory responses; the **tectospinal tract**, for control of head and eye movements; and the **reticulospinal tract**, for maintaining posture.

VEP abbreviation for VISUAL EVOKED POTENTIAL.

verbal ability demonstrated skill to comprehend and communicate effectively with words. Sometimes a distinction is made between receptive abilities (comprehension) and productive abilities (fluency). Brain areas necessary for normal speech appear to be distributed over a broad region of the cerebral cortex and can be mapped by electrical stimulation. See also PRIMARY ABILITIES.

verbal behavior therapy a form of BEHAVIOR THERAPY that is based on the principles of OBSERVATIONAL LEARNING and CONDITIONING and incorporates the notion of RECIPROCAL DETERMINISM. The process involves a thorough inventory of symptoms and behavioral problems, the identification of those problems that will be the focus of the therapy, a careful FUNCTIONAL ANALYSIS of these target problems, development of specific reasonable goals for behavior change for each target problem, and the selection of appropriate therapeutic techniques to achieve the specific goal for each target problem.

verbal intelligence the ability to use words and combinations of words effectively in communication and problem solving.

verbal IQ see IQ.

verbalization *n.* **1.** the expression of thoughts, feelings, and fantasies in words. Verbalization is a common feature of most forms of psychother-

apy, which has led to the use of the terms SIGN SYSTEM and TALKING CURE to refer to the discipline and practice. **2.** in psychiatry, a symptom involving excessive or uncontrolled speech, as in CIRCUMSTANTIALITY or PRESSURED SPEECH. **—verbalize** *vb.*

verbal learning the process of learning about verbal stimuli and responses, such as letters, digits, nonsense syllables, or words. The methods used include PAIRED-ASSOCIATES LEARNING and SERIAL LEARNING.

verbal memory the capacity to remember something written or spoken that was previously learned (e.g., a poem).

verbal overshadowing the tendency for the verbal description of a stimulus to impair later accurate memory of the stimulus. For instance, verbally describing a face that has just been seen may reduce later recognition or identification of that face in a picture lineup.

verbal thought a reasoning process that requires language and thus represents the merging of language and thought. Children first use language to guide thought by speaking out loud; only later does speech go underground to become covert verbal thought. See EGOCENTRIC SPEECH.

verbatim trace see FUZZY TRACE THEORY.

vergence *n.* a turning movement of the eyes. If they turn inward, the movement is CONVERGENCE; if outward, it is DIVERGENCE.

veridical *adj.* **1.** truthful. **2.** of mental phenomena, such as memories or beliefs, corresponding to external reality.

verification *n.* the process of establishing the truth or accuracy of something, especially the use of objective, empirical data to test or support the truth of a statement, conclusion, or hypothesis.

verification time in studies of cognition, a measure of the time taken by a participant to indicate whether a statement is true or not, or to verify that a particular stimulus meets some prespecified condition.

vernacular *n.* the indigenous or characteristic language or DIALECT spoken routinely by a particular group of people: everyday language. It usually coexists with an official formal language used in schools and government. See DIGLOSSIA.

vertex potential a brain potential recorded by electrodes placed at the vertex of the skull. The vertex potential seems to be evoked by a variety of stimuli but is closely associated with attention.

vertical décalage in PIAGETIAN THEORY, the invariable sequence in which the different stages of development (sensorimotor, preoperational, concrete operational, formal operational) are attained. Compare HORIZONTAL DÉCALAGE.

vertical mobility the movement or displacement of individuals or groups from one social class to another. This may take the form of

UPWARD MOBILITY or DOWNWARD MOBILITY. Compare HORIZONTAL MOBILITY. See SOCIAL MOBILITY.

vertigo *n.* an unpleasant, illusory sensation of movement or spinning of oneself or one's surroundings due to neurological disorders, psychological stress (e.g., anxiety), or activities that disturb the labyrinth (which contains the organs of balance) in the inner ear (as in a roller-coaster ride).

vesicle *n.* a fluid-filled saclike structure, such as any of the SYNAPTIC VESICLES in axon terminals that contain neurotransmitter molecules. —**vesicular** *adj.*

vestibular apparatus the organ of balance and equilibrium, which is situated in the inner ear and contains receptors that detect the position and changes in the position of the head in space. It consists of the SEMICIRCULAR CANALS and VESTIBULAR SACS. See also VESTIBULAR SYSTEM.

vestibular nerve a division of the VESTIBULOCOCHLEAR NERVE that carries nerve fibers from the VESTIBULAR SYSTEM in the inner ear; it is associated with the sense of balance and orientation in space. Fibers of the vestibular nerve terminate in the VESTIBULAR NUCLEI of the brainstem.

vestibular nuclei NUCLEI in the dorsolateral part of the PONS and the MEDULLA OBLONGATA in the brain that receive fibers from the VESTIBULAR NERVE and serve the sense of balance and orientation in space. They send fibers to the cerebellum, reticular formation, thalamus, and the vestibulospinal tract (see VENTROMEDIAL PATHWAYS).

vestibular receptors nerve cells associated with the sense of balance, located in the cristae of the SEMICIRCULAR CANALS and in the MACULAE of the UTRICLE and SACCULE. They occur in two similar forms: a HAIR CELL enclosed in a chalicelike nerve ending and a cylindrical hair cell that synapses at its base with a nerve ending.

vestibular sacs two sacs in the inner ear—the UTRICLE and SACCULE—that, together with the SEMICIRCULAR CANALS, comprise the VESTIBULAR APPARATUS (see also VESTIBULAR SYSTEM). The vestibular sacs respond to gravity and encode information about the head's orientation. Low-frequency stimulation of the vestibular sacs can produce dizziness and rhythmic eye movements called NYSTAGMUS.

vestibular sense see SENSE OF EQUILIBRIUM.

vestibular system a system in the body that is responsible for maintaining balance, posture, and the body's orientation in space and plays an important role in regulating locomotion and other movements. It consists of the VESTIBULAR APPARATUS in the inner ear, the VESTIBULAR NERVE, and the various cortical regions associated with the processing of vestibular (balance) information.

vestibule *n.* a chamber that leads to a body cavity or that connects one cavity to another. The **vestibule of the inner ear** is the cavity of the bony LABYRINTH that contains the utricle and saccule (the VESTIBULAR SACS) and is connected to the semicircular canals and cochlea. —**vestibular** *adj.*

vestibulocochlear nerve the eighth cranial nerve: a sensory nerve containing tracts that innervate both the sense of hearing and the sense of balance. It has two divisions, the VESTIBULAR NERVE, originating in the vestibule and semicircular canals, and the AUDITORY NERVE (acoustic or cochlear nerve), originating in the cochlea. The vestibulocochlear nerve transmits impulses from the inner ear to the medulla oblongata and pons and has fibers that continue into the cerebrum and cerebellum.

vestibulo-ocular reflex the involuntary compensatory movement of the eyes that occurs to maintain fixation on a visual target during small, brief head movements. It is triggered by vestibular signals. Compare OPTOKINETIC REFLEX.

vestibulospinal tract see VENTROMEDIAL PATHWAYS.

VI abbreviation for variable interval. See VARIABLE-INTERVAL SCHEDULE.

vibration receptor a nerve ending that responds to various ranges of vibration frequencies. Vibration receptors have been located at depths ranging from the skin surface to the connective tissue covering the surface of a bone. Some vibration receptors seem most sensitive to vibrations between 100 and 500 Hz, whereas others are most sensitive to those below 100 Hz.

vibrotactile masking the interference of one vibrotactile stimulus pattern with another that may occur if the two patterns are presented in close temporal proximity. MASKING may be forward or backward.

vicarious *adj.* **1.** substitutive or second-hand: applied, for example, to the satisfaction obtained by viewing the experiences of others in television programs. It is widely believed that human conditioning of fear responses can occur through vicarious means, and that gratification of needs can be partially accomplished through watching the actions of others. **2.** occurring when one organ performs part of the functions normally performed by another.

vicarious function a theory to explain the ability to recover from the effects of brain damage. It is based on evidence that many functions are not strictly localized in the brain, and that many brain areas can assume a function previously performed by a brain area that has been damaged. Also called **vicarious brain process**.

vicarious traumatization the impact on a

therapist of repeated emotionally intimate contact with trauma survivors. More than COUNTERTRANSFERENCE, vicarious traumatization affects the therapist across clients and situations. It results in a change in the therapist's own worldview and sense of the justness and safety of the world. Therapist isolation and overinvolvement in trauma work can increase the risk of vicarious traumatization.

vicious circle a situation or behavioral pattern in which an individual's or group's problems become increasingly difficult because of a tendency to "address" or ignore them repetitively through unhealthy defensive reactions that, in fact, compound them.

Vierordt's law the principle that the TWO-POINT THRESHOLD for a stimulus is lower in mobile body parts than in those that are less mobile. [Karl von **Vierordt** (1817–1884), German physiologist]

vigilance *n.* a state of extreme awareness and watchfulness directed by one or more members of a group toward the environment, often toward potential threats (e.g., predators, intruders, enemy forces in combat). In animal behavior, vigilance increases in females after the birth of their young and in response to ALARM CALLS. In large groups there can be a division of labor, with individuals taking turns in vigilance. In a military context, vigilance tasks demand maximum physiological and psychological attention and readiness to react, characterized by an ability to attend and respond to stimulus changes for uninterrupted periods of time. This level of vigilance can produce significant cognitive stress and occasional physiological stress reactions. —**vigilant** *adj.*

vigilance decrement in a vigilance task, a decrease in the number of targets detected that occurs after a short period on the task. In many situations the decrement is due to a shift in the response criterion, although in some cases it reflects a decrease in sensitivity for detecting the target.

Vineland Adaptive Behavior Scales (**VABS**) an assessment of an individual's personal and social functioning in four domains: communication, daily living skills, socialization, and motor skills. The VABS currently contains items covering the age range from birth to 90 years. Data are gathered through a rating form or semistructured interview with the person's parents or caregivers. The scales are used not only to diagnose and evaluate individuals with various disabilities—dementia, brain injuries, mental retardation, autism, or other developmental problems—but also to formulate educational and treatment (habilitative or rehabilitative) programs. Originally published in 1984, the most recent version is the **VABS–II**, published in 2005.

violation-of-expectation method a technique, based on habituation and dishabituation procedures, in which increases in an infant's looking time are interpreted as evidence that the outcome expected by the infant has not occurred.

violence *n.* **1.** the expression of hostility and rage with the intent to injure or damage people or property through physical force. See also DOMESTIC VIOLENCE. **2.** passion or intensity of emotions or declarations. —**violent** *adj.*

viral hypothesis of schizophrenia the theory, first suggested in the early 20th century, that psychoses resembling schizophrenia are associated with influenza epidemics. It was later observed that several types of viral ENCEPHALITIS may include schizophrenia-like symptoms, and many studies have investigated the effect of exposure to viral agents, especially in utero, on subsequent development of schizophrenia. More recently, however, it has been suggested that virus exposure is a risk factor for—rather than a key causative event in—the development of schizophrenia.

virilism *n.* the presence in a female of secondary sexual characteristics that are peculiar to men, such as muscle bulk and hirsutism. The condition is due to overactivity of the adrenal cortex, with excessive secretion of androgen, which can be corrected in some cases. Also called **masculinization**.

virility *n.* the state of possessing the qualities of an adult male, especially capacity for coitus. See also MALENESS; MASCULINITY. —**virile** *adj.*

virtual pitch the low pitch of a complex sound. For a complex periodic sound, the virtual pitch generally corresponds to that of the fundamental FREQUENCY even when the fundamental is not present in the sound (the phenomenon of the **missing fundamental**). The terms **periodicity pitch** and **residue pitch** are now used synonymously with virtual pitch, although they have different historical antecedents.

virtual reality therapy a form of IN VIVO EXPOSURE THERAPY in which clients are active participants immersed in a three-dimensional computer-generated interactive environment that allows them a sense of actual presence in scenarios related to their presenting problems. This treatment is currently used primarily for anxiety-related disorders, such as fear of flying.

viscera *pl. n.* (*sing.* **viscus**) the organs in any major body cavity, especially the abdominal organs (stomach, intestines, kidneys, etc.). —**visceral** *adj.*

visceral brain in MACLEAN'S THEORY OF EMOTION, the area of the brain that is involved in the neurophysiological control of emotional behavior and experience (including motivated behavior). Its major structures are the AMYGDALA, HIPPOCAMPAL FORMATION, and SEPTAL AREA. These structures are considered to regulate responses organized, in principle, by the hypothalamus and basal ganglia and to provide them with much of the necessary information. It integrates cognitive aspects with commands for action.

visceral learning the use of INSTRUMENTAL CONDITIONING procedures, particularly BIO-FEEDBACK techniques, to enable an individual to deliberately modify physiological processes ordinarily and unconsciously regulated by the autonomic nervous system, such as heart rate and blood pressure.

viscerogenic need in the PERSONOLOGY of U.S. psychologist Henry Alexander Murray (1893–1988), one of the primary, physiological needs that arise from organic processes and lead to physical gratification. They include the needs for air, water, food, sex, urination, and defecation. Compare PSYCHOGENIC NEED.

visible spectrum see SPECTRUM.

vision *n.* **1.** the sense of sight, in which the eye is the receptor and the stimulus is radiant energy in the visible SPECTRUM. See also VISUAL SYSTEM. **2.** a visual hallucination often involving a religious or mystical experience. **3.** a mental image of something or someone produced by the imagination. —**visual** *adj.*

vision rehabilitation the REHABILITATION of individuals with visual impairment ranging from blindness to low vision. Services provided include functional assessments of a person's visual abilities, if any; ORIENTATION AND MOBILITY TRAINING; rehabilitation teaching (e.g., adaptive skills training in managing one's ACTIVITIES OF DAILY LIVING); instruction in the use of optical devices and ASSISTIVE TECHNOLOGY; career services and training; and psychological counseling.

visual acuity the degree of clarity, or sharpness, of visual perception. It may be measured in several ways, for example, by testing one's ability to detect very small gaps between two parts of a figure (the minimum separable method) or to discern a fine dark line on a light background or a fine light line on a dark background.

visual adaptation the changes that occur in the visual system itself or in visual perception as a result of continuous stimulation. For example, the range of light intensities over which photoreceptors are responsive changes with prolonged exposure to dark, and many visual AFTER-EFFECTS are caused by adaptation of neurons within the visual system. See also DARK ADAPTATION; LIGHT ADAPTATION.

visual agnosia loss or impairment of the ability to recognize and understand the nature of visual stimuli. Classically, a distinction between **apperceptive** and **associative** forms of visual agnosia has been made. Individuals with the former are said to have deficits in the early stages of perceptual processing, whereas those with the latter either do not display such problems or do so to a degree not sufficient to impair substantially the ability to perform perceptual operations. Subtypes of each form exist, based on the type of visual stimulus the person has difficulty recognizing, such as objects (**visual object agnosia** or **visual form agnosia**), multiple objects or pictures (**simultanagnosia**), faces (**prosopagnosia**), or colors (**color agnosia**).

visual apperception test a PROJECTIVE TECHNIQUE in which participants are presented with a visually oriented task, for example, to draw a person, object, or situation; to finish an incomplete drawing; or to create a narrative from a single or multiple visual stimuli.

visual area any of many regions of the cerebral cortex in which the neurons are primarily sensitive to visual stimulation. Together, all the visual areas comprise the VISUAL CORTEX. Most visual areas can be distinguished from one another on the basis of their anatomical connections (i.e., their CYTOARCHITECTURE) and their specific visual sensitivities. Individual areas are designated by "V" and a number (e.g., V1, V2...V5), which indicates roughly how distant the area is from STRIATE CORTEX.

visual association cortex any of the VISUAL AREAS in the cerebral cortex that lie outside the striate cortex, including V2, V4, and V5. See also PRESTRIATE CORTEX.

visual attention disorder any disturbance of a person's ability to detect and attend to visual stimuli. Examples include BÁLINT'S SYNDROME and VISUAL NEGLECT. See also PERCEPTUAL EXTINCTION.

visual blurring the sensation resulting from impairment of the ability to perceive form in the central field region, which is typically associated with poor visual acuity and reduced spatial CONTRAST SENSITIVITY. Visual blurring can occur as a result of retinal disease (e.g., MACULAR DEGENERATION) or damage to the optic nerve (e.g., associated with multiple sclerosis) or visual cortex; it has also been reported as a side effect of anticholinergic drugs.

visual cliff an apparatus to investigate the development of DEPTH PERCEPTION in nonverbal human infants and animals, in particular, whether depth perception is an innate ability or learned through visuomotor experience. The apparatus consists of a table with a checkerboard pattern, dropping steeply down a "cliff" to a surface with the same pattern some distance below the tabletop. The apparatus is covered with a transparent surface, and the participant is positioned on this at the border between the tabletop and the cliff. Reluctance to crawl onto the surface covering the cliff is taken as an indication that the participant can discriminate the apparent difference in depth between the two sides of the apparatus. Most infants as young as 6 months of age will not cross over to the side over the cliff.

visual communication the use of distinctive colors, shapes, or movements that are detected by the visual system as a means of communication between individuals. For example, animals may have distinctive colors in the breeding season to indicate reproductive state, fluff out fur to appear larger in a threat context, or gesture with limbs or head in a variety of other contexts.

visual constructional impairment see VISUOCONSTRUCTIONAL IMPAIRMENT.

visual-construction test see VISUOCONSTRUCTIVE TEST.

visual cortex the cerebral cortex of the occipital lobe, specifically the STRIATE CORTEX (primary visual cortex). In humans this occupies a small region on the lateral surface of the occipital pole of the brain, but most is buried in the banks of the calcarine fissure on the medial surface of the brain. The visual cortex receives input directly from the lateral GENICULATE NUCLEUS via the OPTIC TRACT and sends output to the multiple visual areas that make up the VISUAL ASSOCIATION CORTEX.

visual cycle the biophysical and biochemical sequence of events that includes the release of all-*trans* retinal from RHODOPSIN during light stimulation, followed by its conversion to 11-*cis* retinal in the retinal PIGMENT EPITHELIUM, and then the return of the 11-*cis* retinal to the photoreceptor for the reconstitution of rhodopsin.

visual discrimination the ability to distinguish shapes, patterns, hidden figures, or other images from similar objects that differ in subtle ways.

visual evoked potential (VEP) an electric potential recorded from the scalp overlying the visual cortex in response to visual stimulation.

visual extinction a form of VISUAL NEGLECT in which a previously visible stimulus in one half of the visual field disappears when a stimulus appears simultaneously in the other half of the visual field. Visual extinction occurs as a result of brain damage, usually to the parieto-occipital cortex contralateral to the visual field in which the extinction occurs.

visual fatigue the fading of visual images, particularly in bright light. Visual fatigue is often experienced by patients with optic neuritis; it can also occur after head injuries, especially after prolonged visual testing or when reading, as a result of reduced visual attention.

visual field the extent of visual space over which vision is possible with the eyes held in a fixed position. The outer limit of vision for each eye extends approximately 60° nasally, 90° temporally, 50° superiorly, and 70° inferiorly. The extent varies with age: Very young children and older people have a smaller visual field. Objects nearest to the fixation point are seen with greatest clarity because visual acuity, spatial contrast sensitivity, and color vision are best in the foveal region.

visual field defect a reduction in the normal extent of the visual field, characterized by partial or total blindness. This is caused by an interruption in the flow of visual impulses between the retina and the visual cortex, which may be caused by a lesion before, after, or in the OPTIC CHIASM or in all or a part of the OPTIC RADIATIONS; it can involve tracts of one or both eyes. Each possible lesion produces a different defect.

visual field sparing the extent to which normal vision is preserved in a visually impaired or deprived half of a visual field, expressed in degrees of visual angle measured from the fovea. **Foveal sparing** means that the foveal region (1°) is spared; **macular sparing** refers to the preservation of the macular region (5°); **macular splitting** denotes sparing ranging from 1° to 5°.

visual fixation the orientation of the eyes so that the image of a viewed object falls on the foveas, in the central part of the retinas.

visual form agnosia see VISUAL AGNOSIA.

visual hallucination visual perception in the absence of any external stimulus. Visual hallucinations may be unformed (e.g., shapes, colors) or complex (e.g., figures, faces, scenes). In hallucination associated with psychoses (e.g., paranoid schizophrenia, alcohol- or hallucinogen-induced psychotic disorder), the individual is unaware of the unreality of the perception, whereas insight is retained in other conditions (e.g., pathological states of the visual system). Visual hallucinations may arise in association with lesions of the peripheral or central visual pathway or visual cortical areas; they are often present in temporal-lobe epilepsy and may appear during prolonged isolation. See also PEDUNCULAR HALLUCINOSIS.

visual illusion a misperception of external visual stimuli that occurs as a result of either a pathological condition or a misinterpretation of the stimuli (see ILLUSION). Typical pathological visual illusions are persistence or recurrence of a visual image after the external stimulus is no longer in view (see PALINOPSIA), seeing multiple images on viewing one object (see POLYOPIA), transposition of visual images from one position to an opposite one (visual ALLESTHESIA), and distortion in color perception. Compare VISUAL HALLUCINATION.

visual imagery mental imagery that involves the sense of having "pictures" in the mind. Such images may be memories of earlier visual experiences or syntheses produced by the imagination (as, for example, in visualizing a pink kangaroo). Visual imagery can be used for such purposes as dealing with traumatic events, establishing DESENSITIZATION hierarchies, or improving physical performance. See VISUALIZATION.

visual impairment partial or total inability to see, or to see normally, due to partial or complete loss or absence of vision or to visual dysfunction. Visual impairment encompasses the continuum from BLINDNESS to LOW VISION. It can result from disease or degenerative disorder (e.g., cataract, glaucoma, diabetic retinopathy, or macular degeneration), injury, or congenital defects (e.g., refractive errors, astigmatism). The degree of visual impairment is assessed in terms of disability in everyday life. Also called **vision impairment**.

visualization *n.* **1.** the process of creating a visual image in one's mind (see VISUAL IMAGERY) or mentally rehearsing a planned movement in order to learn skills or enhance performance. **2.** in psychotherapy, the intentional formation by a client of mental visual images of a scene or historical incident that may be inhibited or the source of anxiety. The purpose is to bring the visualized scene into the present therapeutic situation where it can be discussed and worked out to reduce its negative implications. See also GUIDED AFFECTIVE IMAGERY. **3.** a hypnotic method used to induce or increase relaxation in which the individual is asked to imagine, for example, sitting comfortably at home and then to use all senses in perceiving the scene (e.g., the curtains blowing in the windows, the texture of the armchair). The more fully the individual concentrates on these features, the more deeply relaxed he or she becomes. **4.** in consumer psychology, a motivation-research technique using imaginary or fictitious situations or conditions in order to induce consumers to reveal the true reasons for their choice of products. For example, instead of being asked why they like or dislike a product, consumers may be asked to characterize the type of individual they would expect to buy the product. —**visualize** *vb.*

visual learning training or CONDITIONING that depends upon visual cues. The brain center for visual learning is believed to be in the INFEROTEMPORAL CORTEX, where cortical cells have been demonstrated to be highly active in analyzing visual inputs.

visual masking see MASKING.

visual memory the capacity to remember in the form of visual images what has previously been seen.

visual neglect a form of SENSORY NEGLECT in which the individual is unaware of half the visual field. This occurs most often in the left visual field following right parietal damage or dysfunction. See NEGLECT.

visual object agnosia see VISUAL AGNOSIA.

visual perception the awareness of visual sensations that arises from the interplay between the physiology of the VISUAL SYSTEM and the internal and external environments of the observer.

visual pigment see PHOTOPIGMENT.

visual preference paradigm a research technique for studying visual discrimination in infants in which the amount of time spent looking at different visual stimuli is measured to determine which stimulus the infants prefer. It is assumed that the stimulus looked at more often is the one that is preferred and that such preferences indicate an ability to discriminate between stimuli.

visual receptive field that region of visual space in which stimulation will evoke a response from a neuron in the retina. Also called **retinal receptive field**.

visual receptor see PHOTORECEPTOR.

visual search the process of detecting a target visual stimulus among distractor stimuli. In experimental studies, the characteristics of the target and distractors are manipulated to explore the mental operations that underlie visual attention. See also FEATURE-INTEGRATION THEORY.

visual-search perceptual disorder a disorder exemplified by difficulty in locating a specific number in a random array on a board as a result of a lesion in one cerebral hemisphere. Normally, participants perform better when the number sought is to the left of the midline. Participants with left-hemisphere damage also do better when the number is to the left of the midline, whereas those with right-hemisphere damage perform better when the number is to the right of the midline.

visual sensory memory see ICONIC MEMORY.

visual–spatial ability the ability to comprehend and conceptualize visual representations and spatial relationships in learning and in the performance of such tasks as reading maps, navigating mazes, conceptualizing objects in space from different perspectives, and doing various geometric operations.

visual system the components of the nervous system and the nonneural apparatus of the eye that contribute to the perception of visual stimulation. The anterior structures of the eye, such as the CORNEA and LENS, focus light on the RETINA, which transduces photons into neural signals. These are transmitted via the OPTIC NERVE and OPTIC TRACT to nuclei in the thalamus and brainstem. These in turn transmit the signals either to the VISUAL AREAS of the cerebral cortex for conscious analysis or directly to motor centers in the brainstem and spinal cord to produce eye movements.

visual threshold 1. the minimum level of stimulation that can be detected visually. **2.** any of the thresholds for detecting various aspects of visual stimulation, including intensity, resolution, contrast sensitivity, movement acuities, position acuities, and so on.

visual transduction the biochemical and biophysical process in which light energy is converted to a neural signal in a retinal PHOTORECEPTOR. See also VISUAL CYCLE.

visuoconstructional impairment an impairment characterized by difficulty in construction tasks, such as drawing or assembling the various parts of an object into a complete structure. Also called **visual constructional impairment**.

visuoconstructive test any of a wide range of tests that require a combination of visual and motor skills in the construction of an end product as an evaluation of these nonverbal skills.

The most common examples of these tests are drawing tests, BLOCK-DESIGN TESTS, and jigsaw-puzzle tests. Also called **visual-construction test**.

visuospatial agnosia a disorder of spatial orientation, which may be tested by asking the individual to point to objects or other stimuli located in different parts of his or her visual field. Individuals can report objects in their visual fields, but not the spatial relationships of the objects to one another.

visuospatial scratchpad see WORKING MEMORY.

visuotopic map see RETINOTOPIC MAP.

vital functions functions of the body (e.g., respiration, the circulation of the blood) that sustain life. Many vital functions are controlled by the brainstem.

vitalism *n.* **1.** the theory that the functions of living organisms are determined, at least in part, by a life force or principle. German biologist Hans Driesch (1867–1941) was the chief exponent of this view, holding that life processes are autonomous and purposive within the potentialities for growth, development, and self-fulfillment. French philosopher Henri Bergson (1859–1941) named this creative, vital force the *élan vital.* **2.** more generally, any theory that opposes NATURALISM and the reduction of psychological life to biological structures and processes. —**vitalist** *adj., n.*

vitality *n.* physical or intellectual vigor or energy: the state of being full of zest and enthusiastic about ongoing activities. See also FITNESS.

vitamin *n.* an organic substance that in minute quantities is essential for normal growth and health. Many vitamins function as coenzymes, aiding in the metabolism of carbohydrates, fats, and proteins. A few vitamins can be synthesized in the human body, but most must be supplied in the diet. The most important are vitamin A, the vitamin B complex, vitamin C (ascorbic acid), vitamin E, and vitamin K.

vitamin and mineral therapy the treatment of mental or physical conditions through a daily intake of diagnostic-specific vitamins or mineral supplements (or both) in specific dosages. These are typically prescribed in conjunction with some psychopharmacological agent, and effectiveness is still a matter of debate and research. See also MEGAVITAMIN THERAPY.

vitreous humor see EYE.

vivid data data that are salient or important to an individual (compared to so-called **pallid data**). Such data comprise observations (or, more generally, information), collected either by direct sensory experience or indirectly (e.g., by reading about something), that may then be used by the person to make deductions and generally reason about the world. A datum's vividness is a function of individual interests, the concreteness of the datum, its power, or its prox-

imity. Vivid data are more likely to be recognized, attended to, and recalled, generating a greater cognitive influence.

vivisection *n.* dissection performed on a living animal for research or experimental purposes. Many scientists and researchers oppose the practice, questioning its scientific validity and necessity, and numerous others criticize it as inhumane and unethical. See also ANIMAL CARE AND USE; ANIMAL RIGHTS.

VNO abbreviation for vomeronasal organ (see VOMERONASAL SYSTEM).

vocal communication communication by means of auditory signals usually produced by a vibrating organ, such as the larynx in the throats of mammals or the two **syringes** located in the bronchial branches in birds. Vibrations produced by these organs are altered by changing configurations of the tongue, lips, and shape of the oral and nasal cavities. Other sound-producing mechanisms in animals include **stridulation**, the rubbing of body parts together, as in crickets.

vocal cords a pair of tissue folds that project from the walls of the larynx. They vibrate, producing sounds, when expired air passes through the narrow space (**glottis**) between them. Also called **vocal folds**.

vocalization *n.* the production of sounds by means of vibrations of the vocal cords, as in speaking, babbling, singing, screaming, and so forth. —**vocalize** *vb.*

vocal tract the structures, collectively, that are involved in vocalization, including the VOCAL CORDS and glottis of the larynx together with the pharynx, nasal cavity, mouth, and ARTICULATORS.

vocation *n.* an occupation or profession to which one is particularly suited, especially one involving a sense of mission or calling. —**vocational** *adj.*

vocational adjustment the degree to which an individual succeeds in choosing the kind of work or career best suited to his or her interests, traits, and talents. The term differs from OCCUPATIONAL ADJUSTMENT in emphasizing the match of career to personal goals and aptitudes, rather than the match of the individual to objective work conditions.

vocational counseling 1. a counseling service provided to employees who seek guidance on such matters as adjusting to new jobs or roles, developing their careers within organizations, or any personal or other problems affecting job satisfaction or job performance. See also OUTPLACEMENT COUNSELING. **2.** see VOCATIONAL GUIDANCE.

vocational guidance the process of helping an individual to choose an appropriate vocation through such means as (a) in-depth interviews; (b) administration of aptitude, interest, and personality tests; and (c) discussion of the nature

V

and requirements of specific types of work in which the individual expresses an interest. Also called **vocational counseling**.

vocational rehabilitation the REHABILITA-TION of individuals with mental or physical disabilities or those who have been injured or ill in order to develop or restore PRODUCTIVITY. A vocational rehabilitation program includes assessment, VOCATIONAL GUIDANCE, and training and involves helping the individual to develop skills that have been lost or neglected and to find or return to employment in the competitive job market or another setting (see SHELTERED WORK-SHOP; TRANSITIONAL EMPLOYMENT). Also called **occupational rehabilitation**.

voice *n.* **1.** the sound produced by the larynx and modified by other elements of the vocal tract (e.g., lips, tongue) before it issues from the mouth. **2.** in phonetics, the quality of a VOICED, as opposed to an UNVOICED, speech sound.

voiced *adj.* denoting speech sounds that are articulated with accompanying vibration of the vocal cords. Voiced sounds include all the vowels, semivowels, and diphthongs, and a number of consonants. The dichotomy voiced–UNVOICED is an important BINARY FEATURE in English and many other languages.

voice disorder any disorder that affects the pitch, loudness, tone, or resonance of the voice.

voice-onset time in phonetics, the brief instant that elapses between the initial movement of the speech organs as one begins to articulate a VOICED speech sound and the vibration of the vocal cord. Voice-onset time has been the subject of intense research in adult and infant speech perception because of evidence that this continuous acoustic dimension is perceived categorically (see CATEGORICAL PERCEPTION).

voice therapy the diagnosis and remediation of voice disorders by a specialist in the physiology and pathology of voice production. See also SPEECH AND LANGUAGE THERAPY.

volition *n.* **1.** the faculty by which an individual decides upon and commits to a particular course of action, especially when this occurs without direct external influence. The term encompasses a crucial set of activities involving the self, including choice and decision, self-control, intentional action, and an active rather than passive response to events. **2.** the act of exercising this faculty. See also FREE WILL; WILL. **—volitional** *adj.*

volume of distribution (symbol: V_d) the amount of a drug in the body in relation to its concentration in various body fluids (e.g., blood, plasma, extracellular fluid). It is expressed by the equation V_d = dose (amount of drug in body)/concentration in body fluid.

voluntarism *n.* **1.** in psychology, the view that human behaviors are, at least in part, the result of the exercise of volition. See also FREE WILL. **2.** the general position that willing and choice are important factors in all human activities. For ex-

ample, in ethics, voluntarism emphasizes that commitment to any moral principle is, in large part, a "will to believe," over which the person has some control. In epistemology, the same is held to be true of knowledge. **3.** in metaphysics, the position that will, rather than mind, spirit, or some other substance, is the basis of reality. The best-known philosophy of this kind is that of German thinker Arthur Schopenhauer (1788–1866).

voluntary *adj.* describing activity, movement, behavior, or other processes produced by choice or intention and under cortical control, in contrast to automatic movements (e.g., reflexes) or action that is not intended (see IDEOMOTOR ACTIVITY).

voluntary admission admission of a patient to a mental hospital or other inpatient unit at his or her own request, without coercion. Such hospitalization can end whenever the patient sees fit, unlike INVOLUNTARY HOSPITALIZATION, the length of which is determined by a court or the hospital. Also called **voluntary commitment**; **voluntary hospitalization**.

volunteer bias any systematic difference between participants who volunteer to be in a study versus those who do not.

vomeronasal system a set of specialized receptor cells that in nonhuman mammals is sensitive to PHEROMONES and thus plays an important role in the sexual behavior and reproductive physiology of these animals. In humans this system responds physiologically to chemical stimulation and, in turn, excites brain centers, but its role in human olfaction is not known. Also called **Jacobson's organ**; **vomeronasal organ** (**VNO**).

von Restorff effect a memory-process theory stating that an item that is distinctive from others in a series will be remembered better than the nondistinctive items. For instance, if most of the words in a list are printed in blue ink, one word printed in red will be better remembered than the blue words. Also called **distinctiveness effect**; **isolation effect**; **Restorff phenomenon**. [proposed in 1933 by Hedwig **von Restorff** (1906–1962), German psychologist]

voodoo death a CULTURE-BOUND SYNDROME observed in Haiti, Africa, Australia, and islands of the Pacific and the Caribbean. An individual who has disobeyed a ritual or taboo is hexed or cursed by a medicine man or sorcerer and dies within a few days. The individual's strong belief in the curse is posited to be the cause of physiological reactions in the body resulting in death.

voyeurism *n.* a PARAPHILIA in which preferred or exclusive sexual interest and arousal is focused on observing unsuspecting people who are nude or in the act of undressing or engaging in sexual activity. Although the **voyeur** seeks no sexual activity with the person observed, orgasm is usually produced through masturbation during the act of "peeping" or later, while visualizing and remembering the event. —**voyeuristic** *adj.*

VR abbreviation for variable ratio. See VARIABLE-RATIO SCHEDULE.

Vroom–Yetton–Jago leadership model a model that can be used by leaders in judging how much they should allow followers to participate in decision making in different situations. The model consists of a set of decision rules and a decision tree in which the leader assesses several key situational attributes, such as the nature of the task, the degree of conflict expected among followers over preferred solutions, the degree of confidence that followers will accept decisions they do not agree with, and the extent to which such acceptance is important. On the basis of this assessment, the leader chooses from among several degrees of employee participation ranging from autocratic decision making by the leader, through consultative approaches, to full participation and delegation. [Victor H. **Vroom** (1932–), Canadian organizational psychologist; Philip W. **Yetton**, 21st-century Australian management expert; Arthur G. **Jago** (1949–), U.S. organizational psychologist]

VT abbreviation for variable time. See VARIABLE-TIME SCHEDULE.

vulnerability *n.* susceptibility to developing a condition, disorder, or disease when exposed to specific agents or conditions. —**vulnerable** *adj.*

vulva *n.* (*pl.* **vulvae**) the external female genitalia, including the clitoris, the labia, and the vestibule of the vagina. Also called **pudendum**. —**vulval** *adj.*

vulvectomy *n.* the surgical excision of all or part of the vulva. a vulvectomy is performed as a form of treatment for cancer of the vulva. It is also traditionally performed for cultural reasons (see FEMALE GENITAL MUTILATION).

Vygotskian theory of intelligence the theory that intelligence develops largely as a result of INTERNALIZATION, that is, by children absorbing what they observe in the environment and making it a part of themselves. Development occurs in part through a zone of proximal development, which distinguishes what children can do on their own from what they can do with the assistance of an adult mediator. [Lev **Vygotsky** (1896–1934), Russian psychologist]

Ww

WAIS abbreviation for WECHSLER ADULT INTELLIGENCE SCALE.

waiting-list control group a CONTROL GROUP, usually randomized, that will receive the same intervention given to the EXPERIMENTAL GROUPS but at a later time.

waiting-list phenomenon in psychotherapy and counseling, the unusual occurrence of a "cure" in a person who is on a waiting list for treatment. Such occurrences suggest that the anticipation of treatment, in and of itself, has profound psychological effects, which are similar to the PLACEBO EFFECT.

wakefulness *n.* a condition of awareness of one's surroundings, generally coupled with an ability to communicate with others or to signal understanding of what is being communicated by others. It is characterized by low-amplitude, random, fast-wave electrical activity in the brain, as recorded on an electroencephalogram.

waking hypnosis a technique—or the state produced by such a technique—in which hypnotic effects (see HYPNOTIC SUSCEPTIBILITY) are achieved in a participant's normal state of consciousness without reference to sleep or a relaxed state. It is induced through an apparently natural, but carefully considered, choice of simple words, gestures, and directives upon which to focus. There are almost as many definitional variations as there are practitioners, but the criteria of participants being in a normal state of awareness and there being no reference to sleep or trance are common to most.

waking state see W-STATE.

walk-in clinic a clinic in which diagnostic or therapeutic service is available without an appointment. See also DROP-IN CENTER.

Wallerian degeneration see ANTEROGRADE DEGENERATION. [Augustus **Waller** (1816–1870), British physiologist]

wanderlust *n.* a tendency or compulsion to travel or roam.

warehousing *n.* the practice of confining patients with mental disorders to large institutions for long-term, often lifetime, custodial care. This colloquial term implies lack of treatment beyond housing and feeding.

warmth *n.* **1.** the sensation experienced on the skin and some internal parts when the stimulus exceeds the normal skin temperature of about 33 °C (91 °F). However, a degree of adaptation may occur, which may cause variations in this temperature. For example, after putting a foot in a hot bath, a bowl of warm water will feel cool. **2.** colloquially, human interest and affection.

warning coloration the bright colors or patterns indicating that an organism is dangerous or unpalatable. Predators can learn quickly from a single encounter to avoid other organisms with similar markings. Examples include the black and white coloration of skunks; the yellow and black markings of many stinging insects; and the red, yellow, and black bands of a coral snake. Also called **aposematic coloration**. See BATESIAN MIMICRY.

war psychology the application of psychological principles and methods to military settings and operations during wartime. It covers individual and group human functioning in a variety of stressful environments, especially during times of crisis. See MILITARY PSYCHOLOGY.

Wason selection task a reasoning task involving four cards, each with a letter on one side and a number on the other, and a rule supposedly governing their correlation (e.g., if the letter is a vowel, then the number is even). One side of each card is shown (e.g., the cards might show E D 3 8), and the solver is asked which cards must be turned over to determine if the rule has been followed. Most participants demonstrate a CONFIRMATION BIAS, failing to check those instances in which the rule could have been breached (e.g., by turning over E and 3). Also called **four-card problem**. [developed in 1966 by Peter Cathcart **Wason** (1924–2003), British psychologist]

waterfall illusion see MOTION AFTEREFFECT.

watershed zone a zone that lies between the vascular distribution areas (vascular beds) of two arteries. Although the cerebral cortex is well supplied by arteries with collateral branches, there are areas at the junction of the parietal and occipital lobes and between the parietal and temporal lobes that are watershed zones. Such areas are particularly sensitive to decreased vascular perfusion or reduced oxygen content in the blood.

wavelength *n.* the distance between successive peaks in a wave motion of a given FREQUENCY, such as a sound wave or a wave of electromagnetic radiation. The wavelength is equal to the speed of propagation of the wave motion divided by its frequency.

way finding see ROUTE LEARNING.

WCST abbreviation for WISCONSIN CARD SORTING TEST.

weaning *n.* the process of acclimating a young child or animal to obtaining all nutriments from sources other than milk. It usually refers to the cessation of breast feeding.

weapons effect increased hostility or a heightened inclination to aggression produced by the mere sight of a weapon. If provoked, individuals who have previously been exposed to the sight of a weapon will behave more aggressively than those who have not. Subsequent research has shown that this aggressive behavior is primed by the sight of weapons (see PRIMING) and that any other object associated with aggression can have the same effect.

wear-and-tear theory of aging a theory of biological aging suggesting that aging results from an accumulation of damage to cells, tissues, and organs in the body caused by toxins in our diet and by environmental agents. This leads to the weakening and eventual death of the cells, tissues, and organs.

Weber–Fechner law the law stating that to increase the intensity of a sensation in arithmetical progression, it is necessary to increase the intensity of the stimulus in geometric progression. The law is usually given in the form $s = k \log i$, where s is sensory magnitude, k is a constant, and i is the physical intensity of the stimulus. Also called **Bouguer–Weber law**. [Ernst **Weber** (1795–1878), German physiologist and psychophysicist; Gustav Theodor **Fechner** (1801–1887), German physician and philosopher]

Weber's law a mathematical model of the DIFFERENCE THRESHOLD, stating that the magnitude needed to detect physical change in a stimulus is proportional to the absolute magnitude of that stimulus. Thus the more intense the stimulus, the greater the change that must be made in it to be noticed. This can be expressed as $\Delta I/I = k$, where ΔI is the difference threshold, I is the original stimulus magnitude, and k is a constant called **Weber's fraction**. See also FECHNER'S LAW. [proposed in 1834 by Ernst **Weber**]

Wechsler Adult Intelligence Scale (**WAIS**) an intelligence test, originally published in 1955. A modification and replacement of the Wechsler–Bellevue Intelligence Scale, the WAIS currently includes seven verbal subtests (Information, Comprehension, Arithmetic, Similarities, Digit Span, Vocabulary, Letter–Number Sequencing) and seven performance subtests (Digit Symbol, Picture Completion, Block Design, Picture Arrangement, Object Assembly, Matrix Reasoning, Symbol Search). The most recent version is the **WAIS–III**, published in 1997. [David **Wechsler** (1896–1981), Romanian-born U.S. psychologist]

Wechsler Intelligence Scale for Children (**WISC**) a children's intelligence test developed initially in 1949. It currently includes 10 core subtests (Similarities, Vocabulary, Comprehension, Block Design, Picture Concepts, Matrix Reasoning, Digit Span, Letter–Number Sequencing, Coding, Symbol Search) and 5 supplemental subtests (Word Reasoning, Information, Picture Completion, Arithmetic, Cancellation) that measure verbal comprehension, perceptual reasoning, processing speed, and working memory capabilities. The most recent version of the test is the **WISC–IV**, published in 2003. [David **Wechsler**]

Wechsler Memory Scale (**WMS**) a collection of memory tests, originally published in 1945, that assesses verbal (auditory) and nonverbal (visual) memory in older adolescents and adults by means of recall and recognition measures. The most recent version of the test (**WMS–III**, published in 1997) contains 11 subtests, several of which measure memory both immediately and following a delay. [David **Wechsler**]

Wechsler Preschool and Primary Scale of Intelligence (**WPPSI**) an intelligence test for young children that currently includes seven verbal subtests (Information, Vocabulary, Receptive Vocabulary, Word Reasoning, Similarities, Comprehension, Picture Naming) and seven performance subtests (Picture Completion, Picture Concepts, Block Design, Object Assembly, Matrix Reasoning, Symbol Search, Coding). The WPPSI was originally published in 1967; the most recent version is the **WPPSI–III**, published in 2002. [David **Wechsler**]

weekend hospitalization a form of PARTIAL HOSPITALIZATION in which psychiatric patients function in the community during the week but spend the weekend in the hospital.

weight *n.* a coefficient or multiplier used in an equation or statistical investigation and applied to a particular variable to reflect the contribution to the data. The process of doing this is called **weighting**.

well-being *n.* a state of happiness, contentment, low levels of distress, overall good physical and mental health and outlook, or good quality of life.

Wellbutrin *n.* a trade name for BUPROPION.

wellness concept the idea that health care programs should be actively involved in the promotion of **wellness**, seen as a dynamic state of physical, mental, and social well-being, rather than merely being concerned with the treatment and prevention of illness. Wellness is viewed as the result of four key factors over which an individual has some control: human biology, environment, health care organization, and lifestyle.

Weltanschauung *n.* any fundamental understanding of the universe, and of humankind's place within it, held by a person, a culture, or a subculture (German, "worldview"). Such a worldview will be influential in the material development of a culture, as well as in those theories and philosophies that a culture may produce. It establishes the UNIVERSE OF DISCOURSE that prevails among its adherents, affecting their practical attitudes and behaviors as well as their theoretical commitments.

Wernicke–Korsakoff syndrome a syndrome resulting from chronic alcoholism or nutritional insufficiency, associated with deficiency of vitamin B_1 (thiamine). The syndrome is characterized by an acute confusional stage, ATAXIA, and oculomotor problems (see WERNICKE'S ENCEPHALOPATHY), followed by chronic changes in mental status and memory (see KORSAKOFF'S SYNDROME). Lesions are centered in the midbrain, cerebellum, and DIENCEPHALON. [Karl **Wernicke** (1848–1904), German neurologist; Sergei S. **Korsakoff** (1854–1900), Russian psychiatrist]

Wernicke's aphasia a loss of the ability to comprehend sounds or speech (auditory amnesia), and in particular to understand or repeat spoken language and to name objects or qualities (see ANOMIA). The condition is a result of brain damage and may be associated with other disorders of communication, including ALEXIA, ACALCULIA, or AGRAPHIA. Also called **auditory aphasia**; **cortical sensory aphasia**. [Karl **Wernicke**]

Wernicke's area a region in the posterior temporal gyrus of the left hemisphere of the cerebrum in the brain, containing nerve tissue associated with the interpretation of sounds. Also called **Wernicke's speech area**. See also SPEECH AREA. [Karl **Wernicke**, who reported, in 1874, a lack of comprehension of speech in patients who had suffered a brain lesion in that area]

Wernicke's encephalopathy a neurological disorder caused by a deficiency of vitamin B_1 (thiamine). The principal symptoms are confusion, oculomotor abnormalities (GAZE PALSY and NYSTAGMUS), and ataxia. The disorder is most frequently associated with chronic alcoholism but is also found in cases of pernicious anemia, gastric cancer, and malnutrition. These symptoms are likely to resolve with thiamine treatment, although most individuals then develop severe retrograde and anterograde amnesia as well as impairment in other areas of cognitive functioning, including executive functions (see KORSAKOFF'S SYNDROME). [first described in 1881 by Karl **Wernicke**]

white blood cell see LEUKOCYTE.

white commissure a bundle of myelinated fibers (see MYELIN), both sensory and motor, that crosses from one side of the spinal cord to the other, linking the ascending and descending columns of WHITE MATTER fibers on either side. It arches about the ventral median fissure of the spinal cord. Also called **anterior white commissure**; **ventral white commissure**.

white matter parts of the nervous system composed of nerve fibers that are enclosed in a MYELIN SHEATH, which gives a white coloration to otherwise grayish neural structures. The sheaths cover only the fibers, so regions containing mainly CELL BODIES are gray. Compare GRAY MATTER.

WHO abbreviation for WORLD HEALTH ORGANIZATION.

whole-language approach a top-down approach to teaching reading that emphasizes the reader's active construction of meaning and often excludes the use of phonics.

whole method of learning a learning technique in which the entire block of material is memorized, as opposed to learning the material in parts. Compare PART METHOD OF LEARNING.

whole report a method used in studies of ICONIC MEMORY in which the participant attempts to recall all of the presented information. Compare PARTIAL REPORT.

whole-word method a widely used method of language and reading instruction based on the idea that students should grasp the meaning of entire words at a time and use complete words when they talk, without focusing on the individual sounds that make up those words. This method is based on learning strategies originally used to teach deaf children to read, although current findings show that deaf children actually use phonetics for learning and practicing sign language. Also called **look-say**; **sight method**. Compare PHONICS.

Whorfian hypothesis see LINGUISTIC DETERMINISM. [Benjamin Lee **Whorf** (1897–1941), U.S. linguist]

Wilcoxon test a nonparametric test of the difference in distribution for matched sets of research participants or for repeatedly observed participants. [Frank **Wilcoxon** (1892–1965), Irish mathematician and statistician]

Wilks's lambda (symbol: Λ) a statistic based on the difference in mean VECTORS among k samples used to test hypotheses about group mean vector differences in multivariate testing procedures, such as MULTIVARIATE ANALYSIS OF VARIANCE. [Samuel Stanley **Wilks** (1906–1964), U.S. mathematician]

will *n.* **1.** the capacity or faculty by which a human being is able to make choices and determine his or her own behaviors in spite of influences external to the person. See FREE WILL; VOLITION. **2.** a determined and persistent purpose or intent.

will disturbance a deficiency or lack of willpower identified by Swiss psychiatrist Eugen Bleuler (1857–1939) as a basic symptom of schizophrenia. The person may appear apathetic and lacking in objectives and motivation. Another form of will disturbance is characterized by a high degree of activity that is trivial, inappropriate, or purposeless.

Williams syndrome (**Williams–Barratt syndrome**; **Williams–Beuren syndrome**) see HYPERCALCEMIA. [described in the 1960s by J. C. P. **Williams**, 20th-century New Zealand cardiologist; Brian Gerald **Barratt–Boyes** (1924–   ),

W

British cardiologist; and Alois J. **Beuren** (1919–1984), German cardiologist]

will psychology see ACTION THEORY.

will therapy a form of psychotherapy based on the theory that neuroses can be avoided or overcome by asserting the will (or "counterwill") and by achieving independence. According to this theory, will is central to personality formation and life is a long struggle to separate oneself from the mother psychologically, just as one is physically separated from the mother during birth. Also called **Rankian therapy**. See also BIRTH TRAUMA.

will to meaning the need to find a suitable meaning and purpose for one's life. Will to meaning is the basis and fundamental motivation of LOGOTHERAPY, a technique for addressing problems related to the experience of MEANINGLESSNESS. See EXISTENTIAL VACUUM.

will to power 1. in the individual psychology of Austrian psychiatrist Alfred Adler (1870–1937), the determination to strive for superiority and domination, which he believed to be particularly strong in men who feel a need to escape the feelings of insecurity and inferiority that they associate with femininity. **2.** in the thought of German philosopher Friedrich Nietzsche (1844–1900), the determination to affirm oneself through courage, strength, and pride, which necessitates casting off the "slave morality" of Christianity, democracy, and false compassion. Also called **Wille zur Macht**.

will to survive the determination to live in spite of an adverse situation (e.g., a severe illness or disabling disorder) or extreme conditions (e.g., lack of food and water or long-term or harsh imprisonment). Also called **will to live**.

windigo *n.* a severe CULTURE-BOUND SYNDROME occurring among northern Algonquin Indians living in Canada and the northeastern United States. The syndrome is characterized by delusions of becoming possessed by a flesh-eating monster (the windigo) and is manifested in symptoms including depression, violence, a compulsive desire for human flesh, and sometimes actual cannibalism. Also called **whitiko**; **wihtigo**; **wihtiko**; **witigo**; **witiko**; **wittigo**.

winner effect in many species, the increased likelihood that an individual will win aggressive encounters as a result of having won previous encounters. The winner effect may be associated with increased levels of testosterone. Compare LOSER EFFECT.

win–stay, lose–shift strategy in discrimination learning, a mental or behavioral strategy in which an organism continues to give the same response as long as it is being rewarded for doing so but changes the response once it is no longer being rewarded. The opposite **win–shift, lose–stay strategy** may also be seen: An organism changes responses when rewarded and maintains the response when not rewarded.

WISC abbreviation for WECHSLER INTELLIGENCE SCALE FOR CHILDREN.

Wisconsin Card Sorting Test (**WCST**) a test that requires participants to deduce from feedback (right vs. wrong) how to sort a series of cards depicting different geometric shapes in various colors and quantities. Once the participant has identified the underlying sorting principle (e.g., by color) and correctly sorts 10 consecutive cards, the principle is changed without notification. Although the task involves many aspects of brain function, it is primarily considered a test of EXECUTIVE FUNCTIONS.

wisdom *n.* the ability of an individual to make sound decisions, to find the right—or at least good—answers to difficult and important life questions, and to give advice about the complex problems of everyday life and interpersonal relationships. The role of knowledge and life experience and the importance of applying knowledge toward a common good through balancing of one's own, others', and institutional interests are two perspectives that have received significant psychological study.

wish-fulfillment *n.* in psychoanalytic theory, the gratification, in fantasy or in a dream, of a wish associated with a biological INSTINCT.

withdrawal *n.* see SUBSTANCE WITHDRAWAL.

withdrawal reflex a reflex that may be elicited by any painful stimulus or unexpected threat to the well-being of the individual. It is characterized by sudden movement away from the potentially damaging stimulus, which requires rapid coordination of neuromuscular units.

within-group variance variation in experimental scores among identically treated individuals within the same group who experienced the same experimental conditions. It is determined through an ANALYSIS OF VARIANCE and compared with BETWEEN-GROUPS VARIANCE to obtain an F RATIO.

within-subjects design an experimental design in which the effects of treatments are seen through the comparison of scores of the same participant observed under all the treatment conditions. Also called **repeated measures design**; **within-group design**. Compare BETWEEN-SUBJECTS DESIGN.

WMS abbreviation for WECHSLER MEMORY SCALE.

Wolffian duct a rudimentary duct system in the embryo that develops into structures of the male reproductive system (the epididymis, vas deferens, and seminal vesicles). In the female, the Wolffian duct does not develop. Compare MÜLLERIAN DUCTS. [Kaspar F. **Wolff** (1734–1794), German embryologist]

Wolf Man a landmark case reported by Austrian psychiatrist Sigmund Freud (1856–1939) in 1918. It involved a conversion symptom (constipation), a phobia (for wolves and other animals), a religious obsession (piety alternating with blasphemous thoughts), and an appetite disturbance (anorexia), all of which proved to be reactions to early experiences. Freud saw this case as confirmation for his theory of infantile sexuality.

woman-centered psychology an approach to psychology that emphasizes the physical, psychological, and social experiences that are particularly characteristic of women. See FEMINIST PSYCHOLOGY.

womb envy in psychoanalytic theory, the envy felt by some men for the reproductive capacity of women, regarded as an unconscious motive that leads them to denigrate women.

word-association test a projective test in which the participant responds to a stimulus word with the first word that comes to mind.

word fluency the ability to list words rapidly in certain designated categories, such as words that begin with a particular letter of the alphabet. The ability is associated with a part of the brain anterior to BROCA'S AREA in the dominant frontal lobe. Individuals with lesions in that part of the brain are likely to experience word-fluency deficits in verbal tests and tasks. See also PRIMARY ABILITIES.

word-form dyslexia a type of acquired DYSLEXIA characterized by the inability to recognize and read whole words, which can be read only by spelling them out letter by letter. Also called **spelling dyslexia**.

word-fragment completion task an indirect way of detecting memory for a word presented previously. A word fragment consists of some of the letters of the word with blank spaces for deleted letters; the participant's task is to fill in the blanks. Word fragments are frequently used in tests of IMPLICIT MEMORY.

word-frequency study a study in which the frequency of to-be-remembered words is manipulated to investigate the effect of this variable on later memory. Typically, in studies of FREE RECALL, higher frequency words are better remembered, but in studies of RECOGNITION memory, lower frequency words are better remembered. See also FREQUENCY JUDGMENT.

word salad an extreme form of thought disorder, manifest in severely disorganized and virtually incomprehensible speech or writing. It is marked by severe LOOSENING OF ASSOCIATIONS strongly suggestive of schizophrenia. The person's associations appear to have little or no logical connection. Also called **paraphrasia**; **word hash**. See also SCHIZOPHRENIC THINKING.

word-superiority effect the finding that, when presented briefly, individual letters are more easily identified in the context of a word than when presented alone. A similar but weaker effect is obtained when letters are presented as part of a pronounceable but meaningless vowel-consonant combination, such as *deet* or *pling*. Also called **Reicher–Wheeler effect**. See CONFIGURAL SUPERIORITY EFFECT; OBJECT-SUPERIORITY EFFECT.

workaholic *n.* a colloquial name for an individual who has a compulsive need to work, works to an excessive degree, and has trouble refraining from work. This type of driven overinvolvement in work is often a source of significant stress, interpersonal difficulties, and health problems. See also ERGOMANIA.

work ethic an emphasis (frequently an overemphasis) on the importance of work or other forms of effortful activity as a social, moral, and psychological good. Associated attitudes include individualism, competitiveness, high personal expectations, and an emphasis on self-discipline, self-improvement, and deferred gratification. The term was introduced by German sociologist Max Weber (1864–1920), who drew a celebrated correlation between the emergence of such an ethic in 16th-century Protestant thought and the origins of European capitalism. Also called **Protestant work ethic**.

working memory a multicomponent model of SHORT-TERM MEMORY that has a **phonological** (or **articulatory**) **loop** to retain verbal information, a **visuospatial scratchpad** to retain visual information, and a **central executive** to deploy attention between them.

working through 1. in psychotherapy, the process by which clients identify, explore, and deal with psychological issues, on both an intellectual and emotional level, through the presentation of such material to, and in discussion with, the therapist. **2.** in psychoanalysis, the process by which patients gradually overcome their RESISTANCE to the disclosure of unconscious material and are repeatedly brought face to face with the repressed feelings, threatening impulses, and internal conflicts at the root of their difficulties.

working vocabulary see PRODUCTIVE VOCABULARY.

work motivation the desire or willingness to make an effort in one's work. Motivating factors may include salary and other benefits, desire for status and recognition, a sense of achievement, relationships with colleagues, and a feeling that one's work is useful or important. A variety of theories of work motivation exist, including the EXISTENCE, RELATEDNESS, AND GROWTH THEORY, the JOB-CHARACTERISTICS MODEL, the PORTER–LAWLER MODEL OF MOTIVATION, the VALENCE–INSTRUMENTALITY–EXPECTANCY THEORY, and the two-factor theory of work motivation (see HYGIENE FACTORS; MOTIVATORS). See also MOTIVATION.

work psychology see INDUSTRIAL AND ORGANIZATIONAL PSYCHOLOGY.

work system 1. from a traditional time and motion perspective (see TIME AND MOTION STUDY), the structures, operations, and schedules required to meet the demands of a production or process system. **2.** from a more holistic, ergo-

work therapy

nomic perspective, the totality of the technological and environmental factors (physical and social) that are relevant to the human achievement of an organizational objective. See MACROERGONOMICS; SOCIOTECHNICAL SYSTEMS APPROACH; SYSTEMS ENGINEERING.

work therapy the use of compensated or uncompensated work activities as a therapeutic agent for individuals with mental or physical disorders. For example, self-esteem or interpersonal or cognitive skills may be enhanced when these individuals function in a safe, controlled environment, where they may either acquire fundamental training for new skills or receive retraining in skills that have been lost or diminished.

world design in EXISTENTIAL PSYCHOLOGY, a person's worldview or fundamental orientation toward life: his or her essential mode of BEING-IN-THE-WORLD. The term and concept come from the work of Swiss psychiatrist Ludwig Binswanger (1881–1966). A person's world design includes the way in which that person integrates the totality of his or her personality with the world as he or she experiences it. In this approach, understanding a person's world design is essential in understanding the person.

World Health Organization (WHO) a specialized agency of the United Nations that promotes technical medical cooperation among nations, carries out programs to control and eradicate disease, and strives to improve the quality of human life. Founded in 1948, the WHO has four main functions: (a) to give worldwide guidance in the field of health; (b) to set global standards for health; (c) to cooperate with governments in strengthening national health programs; and (d) to develop and transfer appropriate health technology, information, and standards. The WHO defines health as "a state of complete physical, mental and social well-being and not merely the absence of disease or infirmity." Its headquarters are in Geneva, Switzerland.

world regions in the thought of German philosopher Martin Heidegger (1889–1976), three different aspects of a person's lived experience characterized as three worlds simultaneously inhabited by DASEIN: the EIGENWELT, or private and subjective world; the MITWELT, or social world; and the UMWELT, or immediate physical environment.

worry n. a state of mental distress or agitation due to concern about an impending or anticipated event, threat, or danger.

worship n. **1.** reverence or adoration for a divine or supernatural being, a person, or a principle. **2.** the formal expression of religious faith in ritual, prayer, and other prescribed practices. See RELIGION; SPIRITUALITY.

WPPSI abbreviation for WECHSLER PRESCHOOL AND PRIMARY SCALE OF INTELLIGENCE.

wraparound services a philosophy of care and related services that includes a planning process involving a focal person, concerned family members, and providers of services. It results in a highly individualized set of closely coordinated community services and natural supports for the person and his or her family, which achieves a variety of intervention outcomes. Wraparound services have been developed in several service sectors, including mental health, child welfare, and developmental disabilities, and have been proven effective as an alternative to residential services for multiproblem individuals and their families.

writer's block inhibited ability to start or continue working on a piece of writing. Such difficulty is attributed primarily to psychological factors (e.g., fear of failure) but may also result from fatigue or BURNOUT. Suggested remedies often include writing spontaneously about an unrelated topic, doing more reading, and changing something about the physical environment.

writing disorder any motor, sensory, or language disorder that interferes with the ability to write.

W-state n. the waking state (see WAKEFULNESS), as opposed to the D-state (see DREAM STATE) and the S-state (sleeping state).

Würzburg school a school of psychology developed at the end of the 19th century by German psychologist Oswald Külpe (1862–1915) and his associates in Würzburg, Germany. It arose largely as a reaction to the structuralist approach of British-born U.S. psychologist Edward B. Titchener (1867–1927), who insisted that conscious experience consisted of images that could be analyzed into basic elements (sensations, feelings). For the Würzburg school, the focus was on intangible mental activities, such as judgments and meanings, which were conscious but had no image quality associated with them (so-called imageless thought). See also AUFGABE.

W

Xanax *n.* a trade name for ALPRAZOLAM.

xanthines *pl. n.* see METHYLXANTHINES.

xanthocyanopsia *n.* a form of color blindness in which red and green are not perceived and, therefore, objects are seen in shades of yellow or blue.

xanthopsia *n.* see CHROMATOPSIA.

X chromosome the SEX CHROMOSOME that is responsible for determining femaleness in humans and other mammals. The body cells of normal females possess two X chromosomes (XX), whereas males have one X chromosome and one Y CHROMOSOME (XY). In humans, various authorities estimate that the X chromosome carries between 1,000 and about 2,000 genes, including many responsible for hereditary diseases (see SEX-LINKED). Abnormal numbers of X chromosomes lead to genetic imbalance and a range of disorders and syndromes.

xenophobia *n.* **1.** a strong and irrational, sometimes pathological, fear of strangers. **2.** hostile attitudes or aggressive behavior toward people of other nationalities, ethnic groups, or even different regions or neighborhoods. In animals xenophobia is manifested by territorial behavior (see TERRITORIALITY) and is also seen in social groups where intruders are typically attacked and repelled. —**xenophobic** *adj.*

X-linked *adj.* see SEX-LINKED.

X-ray *n.* an electromagnetic emission of short wavelength produced by bombarding a heavy metal target, such as tungsten, with high-energy electrons in a vacuum tube. X-rays are used for diagnostic purposes to visualize internal body structures: The radiation can penetrate most substances and produce images of objects on photographic film (see RADIOGRAPHY) or can cause certain chemicals to fluoresce. Prolonged or unnecessary exposure can be extremely damaging; therefore, when X-rays are used therapeutically for diagnosis or to destroy malignant cells (see RADIATION), great precautions are taken to limit and target exposure.

XXY syndrome see KLINEFELTER'S SYNDROME.

XYY syndrome a chromosomal anomaly discovered in 1961 and associated with males who were aggressive or violent in institutions for criminals. It was originally assumed that the extra Y chromosome predisposes males to such behavior, but the theory was modified when XYY anomalies were later found among normal males. Also called **double-Y condition**.

XYZ grouping a program in which school administrators assign students in the same grade to classes by virtue of their test scores and school records. Students with similar abilities are placed in the same classes, which are known as "high," "middle," and "low" groups; each group follows the same basic curriculum.

Yy

yawning *n.* the act of drawing in through the mouth a volume of air that is much larger than that inhaled in normal respiration, serving to improve oxygen supplies to the brain. Some research indicates that yawning is mediated by the same NEUROTRANSMITTERS in the brain that affect emotions, mood, appetite, and so forth (i.e., serotonin, dopamine, glutamic acid, and nitric oxide). The more of these compounds that are activated in the brain, the greater the frequency of yawns. Yawns can be a form of NONVERBAL COMMUNICATION in that they are contagious and can indicate boredom or disagreement as well as sleepiness.

Y chromosome the SEX CHROMOSOME that is responsible for determining maleness in humans and other mammals. The body cells of normal males possess one Y chromosome and one X CHROMOSOME (XY). The Y chromosome is much smaller than the X chromosome and is thought to carry just a handful of functioning genes. Hence, males are far more susceptible to SEX-LINKED diseases than females, because the Y chromosome cannot counteract any defective genes carried on the X chromosome.

yea-saying *n.* answering questions positively regardless of their content, which can distort the results of surveys, questionnaires, and similar instruments. Also called **response acquiescence**. Compare NAY-SAYING.

Yerkes–Dodson law a law stating that the relation between motivation (AROUSAL) and performance can be represented by an inverted U-curve (see INVERTED-U HYPOTHESIS). [Robert M. **Yerkes** (1876–1956) and John Dillingham **Dodson** (1879–1955), U.S. psychologists]

yes–no judgment task in psychophysics, a signal detection task in which participants undergo a series of trials in which they must judge the presence ("yes") or absence ("no") of a signal.

Y-linked inheritance a form of SEX-LINKED inheritance in which a recessive trait is inherited by way of a single gene on the Y CHROMOSOME. Because typically only males have a Y chromosome, Y-linked genes are only transmitted from father to son.

yoked control a procedure to ensure experimental control (e.g., baseline measures) in OPERANT CONDITIONING in which the rate of responding of an experimental subject is yoked—and, thus, compared—with that of a control subject. The subject and the control receive reinforcers or punishers on the same schedule, but the subject's receipt is dependent on behavior, whereas the control's is independent of behavior. For example, in one condition a nonhuman animal might press a lever so as to avoid electric shocks. In a yoked-control condition, the same temporal pattern of shocks received in the first case would be presented to the control animal independently of its behavior.

Young–Helmholtz theory of color vision a theory to explain color vision in terms of components or processes sensitive to three different parts of the spectrum corresponding to the colors red, green, and blue. According to this theory, other colors are perceived by stimulation of two of the three processes, while light that stimulates all three processes equally is perceived as white. The components are now thought to be RETINAL CONES, although the original theory was not tied to a particular (or indeed to any) cell type. See TRICHROMATIC THEORY. Compare HERING THEORY OF COLOR VISION; OPPONENT PROCESS THEORY OF COLOR VISION. [Thomas **Young** (1773–1829), British physician and physicist; Hermann Ludwig Ferdinand von **Helmholtz** (1821–1894), German physiologist and physicist]

young-old *adj.* see ADULTHOOD.

you statement see I STATEMENT.

youth counseling consultation that provides advice, information, and support to young people, usually in adolescence or slightly younger. Youth counseling may focus on any issue that raises concerns or conflicts related to studying, family involvement, sexuality and gender identity, or peer relationships. It may be used to counter low self-image and feelings of inadequacy that are often experienced by young people.

youth culture 1. a society that places a high premium on youth; physical health and beauty; and the values, tastes, and needs of young people. Such a society tends to derogate the values, experience, and needs of middle-aged and older people and may produce subtle psychological pressures for older adults to adapt to the culture of youth. **2.** the distinctive culture of teenagers and young adults, which often involves forms of dress, speech, music, and behavior that are deliberately at variance with those of the dominant culture. See also COUNTERCULTURE.

Zz

zaleplon *n.* a nonbenzodiazepine HYPNOTIC used for short-term treatment of insomnia. It has a rapid onset but short duration of action. Side effects are less frequent compared to other classes of hypnotics but commonly include headache, dizziness, abdominal pain, nausea, and amnesia. Although chemically unrelated to the benzodiazepines, zaleplon acts at the same GABA$_A$ RECEPTOR and carries a similar potential for abuse. U.S. trade name: **Sonata**.

zar (**zaar**) *n.* a CULTURE-BOUND SYNDROME, occurring in North African and Middle Eastern cultures, that is attributed to spirit possession. Occurring most frequently in women, zar often involves dissociative, somatic, and affective symptoms, such as shouting, laughing, apathy, and refusal to perform daily tasks.

Zeigarnik effect the tendency for interrupted, uncompleted tasks to be better remembered than completed tasks. Some theorists relate this phenomenon to certain GESTALT PRINCIPLES OF ORGANIZATION but at the level of higher mental processing (e.g., memory), rather than at the level of pure perception. [described in 1927 by Bluma **Zeigarnik** (1900–1988), Russian psychologist]

Zeitgeber *n.* a cue, such as day length, used to activate or time a BIOLOGICAL RHYTHM. See ENTRAINMENT. [German, "time giver"]

Zeitgeist *n.* the spirit of the times (German, "time spirit"). The term was used by German philosopher Georg Wilhelm Friedrich Hegel (1770–1831) to refer to a type of supraindividual mind at work in the world and manifest in the cultural worldview (see WELTANSCHAUUNG) that pervades the ideas, attitudes, and feelings of a particular society in a specific historical period. Used in this way, the term has a distinctly deterministic flavor. A Zeitgeist theory of history stresses the role of such situational factors as economics, technology, and social influences.

Zener cards a standardized set of stimulus materials, similar to a deck of playing cards, designed for use in experiments on EXTRASENSORY PERCEPTION and other parapsychological phenomena. The set consists of 25 cards, each of which bears one of 5 printed symbols (star, wavy lines, cross, circle, or square), with 5 cards in each category. In a typical test of TELEPATHY, the cards are shuffled and a designated "sender" turns the cards over one at a time to inspect the symbol, while a "receiver" attempts to guess the symbol by reading the thoughts of the sender. In an experiment on CLAIRVOYANCE, the receiver might attempt to identify the order of the shuffled deck without any inspection of cards by the sender. Also called **Rhine cards**. [named in honor of Karl E. **Zener** (1903–1964), U.S. perceptual psychologist who designed the symbols, by his colleague U.S. psychologist Joseph B. **Rhine** (1895–1980), who devised the deck]

Zen therapy psychotherapy that is informed by and incorporates the philosophy and practices of Zen Buddhism and that, like EXISTENTIALISM, is concerned with the unique meaning of the client's life within the universal context, rather than with simple adjustment to or removal of symptoms. Contemplation, through meditation and intuition, of human nature and human existence are believed to lead to a therapeutic alignment of the client with a sense of the oneness of the universe and to spiritual (and, thus, cognitive, affective, and behavioral) transformation.

zero-sum game in GAME THEORY, a type of game in which the players' gains and losses add up to zero. The total amount of resources available to the participants is fixed, and therefore one player's gain necessarily entails the others' loss. The term is used particularly in analyses of bargaining and economic behavior but is sometimes also used in other sociocultural contexts (e.g., politics).

Zöllner illusion a visual illusion in which parallel lines appear to diverge when one of the lines is intersected by short diagonal lines slanting in one direction, and the other by lines slanting in the other direction. [Johann Karl Friedrich **Zöllner** (1834–1882), German astrophysicist]

Zoloft *n.* a trade name for SERTRALINE.

zolpidem *n.* a nonbenzodiazepine HYPNOTIC for short-term management of insomnia. Although structurally different from the benzodiazepines, it acts similarly by binding to a specific site on the GABA$_A$ RECEPTOR. Though infrequent compared to other agents, side effects typically include dizziness, headache, nausea and vomiting, and amnesia. U.S. trade name: **Ambien**.

zone of optimal functioning the range of physiological AROUSAL within which an individual can perform at the peak of physical, mental, and skillful ability. Also called **zone of individual optimal functioning**.

zone of proximal development in the sociocultural theory of Russian psychologist Lev Vygotsky (1896–1934), the difference between a child's actual level of ability and the level of ability that he or she can achieve when working under the guidance of an instructor. See SOCIOCULTURAL PERSPECTIVE.

zonules *pl. n.* the delicate elastic fibers that connect the capsule of the LENS of the eye to the ciliary processes (extensions of the CILIARY BODY). Also called **suspensory ligament**. See also CILIARY MUSCLE.

zoomorphism *n.* **1.** the attribution of animal traits to human beings, deities, or inanimate objects. **2.** the use of animal psychology or physiology to explain human behavior. Compare ANTHROPOMORPHISM.

zoophilia *n.* a PARAPHILIA in which animals are repeatedly preferred or exclusively used to achieve sexual excitement and gratification. The animal, which is usually a household pet or farm animal, is either used as the object of intercourse or is trained to lick or rub the human partner, referred to as a **zoophile**. The most commonly used animals are pigs and sheep, in rural settings. Also called **zoophilism**.

zopiclone *n.* a nonbenzodiazepine HYPNOTIC used for the short-term treatment of insomnia. Like the related drug ZALEPLON, it is relatively selective for a specific subunit on the GABA$_A$ RECEPTOR complex. Side effects include excessive sedation or confusion, dry mouth, and a bitter taste. U.S. trade name: **Lunesta**.

z score see STANDARD SCORE.

Zung Self-Rating Depression Scale (SDS) a widely used adult self-report depression-screening instrument designed to measure the intensity of depressive or mood-related symptoms. It is also a tool for tracking a client's response to depression treatment over time. The SDS consists of 20 statements to which participants must respond using a 4-point LIKERT SCALE, ranging from "none or little of the time" to "most or all of the time." Half of the questions are worded positively (e.g., "I have trouble sleeping") and half are worded negatively (e.g., "I do not feel hopeful"). [originally developed in 1965 by William W. K. **Zung**, U.S. psychiatrist]

Zwaardemaker smell system a system for classifying odor qualities based on a scheme originally developed by Swedish botanist Carolus Linnaeus (1707–1778). According to this system, there are nine PRIMARY ODOR qualities: ethereal, aromatic, fragrant, ambrosiac, alliaceous, empyreumatic, hircine, foul, and nauseous. These qualities combine to produce the perceptions of smells. [Hendrik **Zwaardemaker** (1857–1930), Dutch physiologist]

zygomaticus *n.* the set of muscles, innervated by the FACIAL NERVE, that activates the movement of the upper lip outward, upward, and backward. Its activity is recorded in studies of emotion.

zygote *n.* a fertilized egg, or ovum, with a DIPLOID set of chromosomes, half contributed by the mother and half by the father. The zygote divides to become an EMBRYO, which continues to divide as it develops and differentiates—in humans eventually forming a FETUS. —**zygotic** *adj.*

zygote intrafallopian transfer a form of IN VITRO FERTILIZATION in which ova and sperm are combined in a laboratory container and the fertilized eggs (zygotes) are implanted into the fallopian tubes. Compare GAMETE INTRAFALLOPIAN TRANSFER.

Z

Appendixes

Significant Historical Figures in Psychology

Adler, Alfred (1870–1937) Austrian psychiatrist: the first disciple of Sigmund Freud to break away to found his own school, INDIVIDUAL PSYCHOLOGY, which evolved such concepts as the INFERIORITY COMPLEX and COMPENSATION.

Ainsworth, Mary Dinsmore Salter (1913–1999) U.S. developmental psychologist: assisted John Bowlby in formulating the highly influential ATTACHMENT THEORY; later devised the STRANGE SITUATION.

Allport, Floyd Henry (1890–1971) U.S. psychologist: a founder of experimental social psychology; his approach emphasized individuals over the group, established a behaviorist framework, and advanced experimental methodology; brother of Gordon W. Allport.

Allport, Gordon Willard (1897–1967) U.S. psychologist: a major figure in social psychology; originator of Allport's personality trait theory and coauthor of two personality inventories—the **Allport–Vernon–Lindzey Study of Values** and the **Allport AS Reaction Study**; brother of Floyd H. Allport.

Anastasi, Anne (1908–2001) U.S. psychologist: an important contributor to the discussion of the NATURE–NURTURE controversy and, especially, to psychological testing.

Angell, James Rowland (1869–1949) U.S. psychologist: a major spokesperson for the development of psychology as a science in the United States and a leading exponent of FUNCTIONALISM.

Asch, Solomon E. (1907–1996) Polish-born U.S. psychologist: best known for his contributions to social psychology, especially in showing how social context influences fundamental processes, such as perception (his studies of CONFORMITY influenced the research of Stanley Milgram).

Baldwin, James Mark (1861–1934) U.S. psychologist: an influential figure in the early development of experimental and professional psychology in the United States; a proponent of FUNCTIONALISM and early contributor in developmental psychology.

Bandura, Albert (1925–) Canadian-born U.S. psychologist: best known for his work on SOCIAL LEARNING THEORY; especially influential were his studies of OBSERVATIONAL LEARNING and, in the field of SOCIAL-COGNITIVE THEORY, of self-regulatory processes and their role in motivation and behavior.

Baltes, Paul (1939–2006) German developmental psychologist: helped to define the LIFE-SPAN PERSPECTIVE; with his wife, psychologist Margaret Baltes, described SELECTIVE OPTIMIZATION WITH COMPENSATION and introduced the TESTING THE LIMITS method to study adult age differences in cognition.

Bayley, Nancy (1899–1994) U.S. developmental psychologist: best known as the developer of the BAYLEY SCALES OF INFANT AND TODDLER DEVELOPMENT.

Beach, Frank A. (1911–1988) U.S. psychologist: a founder of BEHAVIORAL ENDOCRINOLOGY and an important comparative psychologist, known especially for research on patterns of sexual behavior.

Beers, Clifford (1876–1943) U.S. philanthropist: founder of the MENTAL HYGIENE movement, which helped establish psychology as a discipline in the United States through encouraging the use of mental tests and contributing to the rise of clinical and industrial and organizational psychology.

Békésy, Georg von (1899–1972) Hungarian-born U.S. physicist: groundbreaking researcher in auditory science, especially his studies of mammalian hearing and on the pattern of movement in the basilar membrane of the inner ear known as the TRAVELING WAVE.

Bekhterev, Vladimir Mikhailovich (1857–1927) Russian neuropathologist: founder of Russia's first psychophysiological laboratory and first institute for brain research on mental diseases; now credited with playing a greater role than Ivan Pavlov in the introduction of CONDITIONING to psychology.

Benussi, Vittorio (1878–1927) Italian psychologist: His research on optical illusions and time perception contributed to GESTALT PSYCHOLOGY; later research on posthypnotic states (e.g., POSTHYPNOTIC SUGGESTION) sought to provide evidence for Freud's concept of REPRESSION.

Binet, Alfred (1857–1911) French psychologist: often considered as the initiator of the modern approach to intelligence testing, especially as the developer of the Binet–Simon Scale (see STANFORD–BINET INTELLIGENCE SCALE).

Bingham, Walter Van Dyke (1880–1952) U.S. psychologist: the founder of industrial and organizational psychology and a key figure in the development of the U.S. Army mental testing program in World War I.

Bleuler, Eugen (1857–1939) Swiss psychiatrist: best known for naming SCHIZOPHRENIA and for his theory of its basic underlying symptomatology; advocated psychosocial treatments for people with severe mental illness and introduced OCCUPATIONAL THERAPY.

Boring, Edwin Garrigues (1886–1968) U.S. psychologist: perhaps the most influential definer of the field of experimental psychology from the 1930s through the 1960s.

Bowlby, Edward John Mostyn (1907–1990) British psychiatrist and psychoanalyst: best known as the developer of ATTACHMENT THEORY; his most important early work centered on the deleterious effects of maternal deprivation.

Brentano, Franz (1838–1917) German philosopher and psychologist: His research on the INTENTIONALITY of mental acts later developed as ACT PSYCHOLOGY and contributed to the debate in artificial intelligence about whether mechanical processes can assume the intentionality of genuine mental acts.

Breuer, Josef (1842–1925) Austrian physician and physiologist: called by Freud the "father of psychoanalysis," best remembered for his treatment of ANNA O.; Freud's technique of FREE ASSOCIATION evolved from the concepts behind Breuer's methods.

Broadbent, Donald E. (1926–1993) British psychologist: best known for his application of communications engineering and mathematical DECISION THEORY to psychology.

Broca, Paul (1824–1880) French physician and anthropologist: proved that motor aphasia (later known as BROCA'S APHASIA) was associated with the third frontal convolution of the cerebral cortex (now called BROCA'S AREA) and that fluent speech depends on this area; among the first to recognize the phenomenon of CEREBRAL DOMINANCE.

Bronfenbrenner, Urie (1917–2005) Russian-born U.S. developmental psychologist: originator of the watershed ECOLOGICAL SYSTEMS THEORY; later developed this approach into the BIOECOLOGICAL MODEL.

Brown, Roger (1925–1997) U.S. social psychologist: a classic contributor in the field of PSYCHOLINGUISTICS (particularly to the first stages of LANGUAGE ACQUISITION); coined the term FLASHBULB MEMORY.

Brunswik, Egon (1903–1955) Austrian-born U.S. psychologist: recognized for his research on VISUAL DISCRIMINATION and categorization and for the **Brunswik ratio**, a mathematical expression of PERCEPTUAL CONSTANCY.

Calkins, Mary Whiton (1863–1930) U.S. psychologist: known for her theoretical contributions to SELF PSYCHOLOGY; the first woman president of the American Psychological Association.

Campbell, Donald Thomas (1916–1996) U.S. social psychologist: known for developing methods for determining the CONSTRUCT VALIDITY of psychological measures and contributions to the philosophy of science.

Cannon, Walter Bradford (1871–1945) U.S. physician and physiologist: known particularly for his investigations of emotion, in which he identified the biological mechanisms associated with the FIGHT-OR-FLIGHT RESPONSE and proposed the CANNON–BARD THEORY.

Carr, Harvey A. (1873–1954) U.S. psychologist: a member of the CHICAGO SCHOOL; his contributions focused on adaptive human behavior as a manifestation of mental processes, on MAZE learning in rats, and on visual and spatial perception.

Cattell, James McKeen (1860–1944) U.S. psychologist: a founder of psychology in the United States and an influential journal editor; devised the first battery of psychological tests of special abilities; cofounded the Psychological Corporation.

Cattell, Raymond Bernard (1905–1998) British psychologist: developed, with colleagues, the SIXTEEN PERSONALITY FACTOR QUESTIONNAIRE, one of the most frequently used self-report personality inventories.

Charcot, Jean-Martin (1825–1893) French neurologist: sometimes called the "father of neurology" for his pioneering research on such disorders as locomotor ataxia, multiple sclerosis, and Parkinson's disease; his research on hysteria had great influence on the early careers of his students Sigmund Freud and Alfred Binet.

Chomsky, Noam (1928–) U.S. linguist: known for his revolutionary TRANSFORMATIONAL GENERATIVE GRAMMAR, which had major and controversial influence in the field of PSYCHOLINGUISTICS.

Claparède, Edouard (1873–1940) Swiss psychologist: a key figure in the child study and PROGRESSIVE EDUCATION movements; demonstrated the importance of intelligence testing in the educational context; also contributed significant research on the biology of sleep.

Clark, Kenneth Bancroft (1914–2005) U.S. psychologist: the first African American president of the American Psychological Association; his work was influential in the U.S. Supreme Court's 1954 ruling *Brown v. the Board of Education,* which banned racial segregation in U.S. public schools.

Cronbach, Lee J. (1916–2001) U.S. psychologist: an influential contributor to the topic of test VALIDITY and the developer of CRONBACH'S ALPHA.

Darwin, Charles R. (1809–1882) British naturalist: His theory of NATURAL SELECTION has had significant and ongoing influence in various approaches to psychology, including EVOLUTIONARY PSYCHOLOGY and SOCIOBIOLOGY.

Dewey, John (1859–1952) U.S. philosopher, educator, and psychologist: a founder of FUNCTIONALISM, who strongly influenced the field of education.

Doll, Edgar Arnold (1889–1968) U.S. psychologist: best known for the development of the Vineland Social Maturity Scale, the antecedent of the now widely used VINELAND ADAPTIVE BEHAVIOR SCALES.

Dollard, John (1900–1980) U.S. social scientist: developer of the FRUSTRATION–AGGRESSION HYPOTHESIS; also known for his work (with Neal E. Miller) on the importance of IMITATION in social behavior and learning.

Durkheim, Emile (1858–1917) French sociologist: known especially for his theories of suicide and schematic categorization encompassing four types—egoistic (resulting from abject loneliness), altruistic (self-sacrifice to save others), anomic (resulting from social adversity), and fatalistic (resulting from excessive social regulation).

Ebbinghaus, Hermann (1850–1909) German psychologist: a pioneer in the application of quantitative methods of psychophysics to the study of higher mental processes and in establishing experimental psychology as a scientific discipline.

Erickson, Milton Hyland (1901–1980) U.S. psychiatrist: developed the system known as ERICKSONIAN PSYCHOTHERAPY; devised a "strategic therapy," in which the therapist directly influences clients by initiating what happens during sessions.

Erikson, Erik H. (1902–1994) German-born U.S. psychologist: preeminent personality theorist and contributor to the field of EGO PSYCHOLOGY; known for his theory of life stages— ERIKSON'S EIGHT STAGES OF DEVELOPMENT—and as coiner of the term IDENTITY CRISIS.

Estes, William Kaye (1919–) U.S. psychologist: a founding figure of MATHEMATICAL PSYCHOLOGY and a pioneer (with B. F. Skinner) in the use of the CONDITIONED EMOTIONAL RESPONSE.

Eysenck, Hans Jurgen (1916–1997) German-born British psychologist: founder of the Institute of Psychiatry at the Maudsley Hospital at the University of London; popularized the terms "introvert" and "extravert" and developed the EYSENCK PERSONALITY INVENTORY.

Fechner, Gustav Theodor (1801–1887) German physician and philosopher: developer of still-used methods to study sensations—METHOD OF ADJUSTMENT, METHOD OF CONSTANT STIMULI, and METHOD OF JUST NOTICEABLE DIFFERENCES; developed the mathematical formula called FECHNER'S LAW.

Ferenczi, Sandor (1873–1933) Hungarian psychoanalyst: an early associate of Sigmund Freud who articulated an ACTIVE THERAPY as an alternative to Freud's psychoanalytic approach; later (with Otto Rank) advanced the concept of BRIEF PSYCHODYNAMIC PSYCHOTHERAPY.

Festinger, Leon (1919–1989) U.S. social psychologist: best known for his theory of COGNITIVE DISSONANCE and for his investigations into such group dynamics as COHESION, CONFORMITY, and SOCIAL COMPARISON THEORY.

Frankel, Viktor Emil (1905–1997) Austrian psychiatrist: a chief exponent of EXISTENTIAL PSYCHOLOGY; his approach, LOGOTHERAPY, is often referred to as the "third Viennese school of psychotherapy" (after Freud's psychoanalysis and Adler's individual psychology).

Freud, Anna (1895–1982) Austrian-born British psychoanalyst: Her studies on DEFENSE

MECHANISMS and pioneering work in CHILD ANALYSIS were original contributions to theory and practice in psychoanalysis; youngest daughter of Sigmund Freud.

Freud, Sigmund (1856–1939) Austrian neurologist and psychiatrist: inventor of the technique of PSYCHOANALYSIS and developer of many of its central theoretical concepts (e.g., DEFENSE MECHANISMS, PSYCHOSEXUAL DEVELOPMENT, TRANSFERENCE, etc.) and methods of practice, such as FREE ASSOCIATION and DREAM ANALYSIS.

Fromm, Erich (1900–1980) German-born U.S. psychoanalyst: developer of a broad cultural, yet personal, approach in analysis that focused on the search for meaning and the development of socially productive relationships, individuality, and the need to belong.

Galton, Francis (1822–1911) British scientist: developed theories about the HERITABILITY and selective breeding of human intelligence, from which emerged the idea of intelligence tests and the movement he later called EUGENICS; also introduced techniques of statistical CORRELATION; cousin of Charles Darwin.

Gemelli, Agostino (1878–1959) Italian psychologist: promoter of practical, applied psychology; cofounded an influential European academic journal on psychology, neurology, and psychiatry.

Gesell, Arnold L. (1880–1961) U.S. psychologist and physician: the first school psychologist in the United States; established SPECIAL EDUCATION classrooms, pioneered the co-twin technique to study the impact of learning and heredity, and advanced the concept of SCHOOL READINESS.

Gibson, Eleanor Jack (1910–2002) U.S. experimental psychologist: best known for her research on PERCEPTUAL LEARNING, especially on the VISUAL CLIFF; married to James J. Gibson.

Gibson, James Jerome (1904–1979) U.S. experimental psychologist: a highly influential researcher in the area of visual (and other sense) perception, known especially for developing the theory of ECOLOGICAL PERCEPTION; married to Eleanor J. Gibson.

Gilbreth, Lillian (1878–1972) U.S. psychologist: best known, with her husband Frank (an engineer), for developing TIME AND MOTION STUDIES.

Goddard, Henry Herbert (1866–1957) U.S. psychologist: a founder of intelligence testing in the United States; produced influential research in the fields of SPECIAL EDUCATION, mental retardation, and army testing.

Goldstein, Kurt (1875–1965) German neurologist: his investigations of neurological impairments resulted in an influential proposal that manifestations of brain damage (e.g., regression to concrete thinking) are often an individual's adaptive response to an impaired ability to form a whole perception of the outside world.

Goodenough, Florence (1886–1959) U.S. psychologist: developer of widely used tests of intelligence and verbal intelligence in children and adapter of the Stanford–Binet scale for use with preschoolers (called the Minnesota Preschool Scale); formulated the method now known as TIME SAMPLING.

Griffith, Coleman Roberts (1893–1960) U.S. psychologist: known as the "father of sport psychology"; established the first laboratory in the United States to investigate psychological and physiological problems associated with sports and athletic performance.

Guilford, Joy Paul (1897–1987) U.S. psychologist: best known for his contributions to psychometrics and his use of FACTOR ANALYSIS in personality and intelligence research.

Gulliksen, Harold (1903–1996) U.S. psychologist: a founder of the Psychometric Society; known for his applications of mathematical methods to psychophysics, MATHEMATICAL LEARNING THEORY, and attitude measurement, which contributed advancements in paired comparison scaling and MULTIDIMENSIONAL SCALING.

Guthrie, Edwin Ray (1886–1959) U.S. psychologist: best known for developing a variation in behaviorist theory termed stimulus–response CONTIGUITY LEARNING THEORY and for pioneering use of teaching evaluations for college faculties.

Hall, Granville Stanley (1844–1924) U.S. psychologist: chief founder and organizer of psychology in the United States and first president of the American Psychological Association.

Harlow, Harry Frederick (1905–1981) U.S. psychologist: best known for investigations on LEARNING SETS and on mothering, which disproved the idea that nonhuman animals were incapable of higher levels of information processing or METACOGNITION; also known for studying social development in rhesus monkeys.

Hathaway, Starke Rosencrans (1903–1984) U.S. psychologist: developer, in collaboration with psychiatrist John C. McKinley, of the MINNESOTA MULTIPHASIC PERSONALITY INVENTORY;

launched a doctoral training program in MEDICAL PSYCHOLOGY that became a model for programs nationwide in clinical psychology.

Head, Henry (1861–1940) British neurologist: remembered chiefly for his taxonomy of APHASIA and for his theory characterizing all types of aphasia as cognitive disturbances of symbolic formation and expression; coined the term "semantic aphasia."

Hebb, Donald Olding (1904–1985) Canadian psychobiologist: an important contributor to the understanding of the brain–behavior relationship; his proposal of CELL ASSEMBLIES remains influential in biological theories of memory.

Heider, Fritz (1896–1988) Austrian-born U.S. psychologist: a preeminent theorist on interpersonal relations (e.g., as formulated in his NAIVE ANALYSIS OF ACTION); established the conceptual foundations for much of social psychology research (e.g., ATTRIBUTION THEORY, COGNITIVE CONSISTENCY THEORY).

Helmholtz, Herman von (1821–1894) German physiologist and physicist: a founder of psychosensory physiology, whose research laid the foundations of modern visual and auditory science (see YOUNG–HELMHOLTZ THEORY OF COLOR VISION; HELMHOLTZ THEORY; UNCONSCIOUS INFERENCE THEORY).

Helson, Harold (1898–1977) U.S. psychologist: developed ADAPTATION-LEVEL theory to describe the effects of context on subjective judgment; studied the TAU EFFECT of time on spatial perception.

Hering, Evald (1834–1918) German physiologist: His sensory perception research (see HERING ILLUSION; HERING THEORY OF COLOR VISION) influenced the development of German psychology and the school of PHENOMENOLOGY.

Hilgard, Ernest R. (1904–2001) U.S. psychologist: an influential researcher and synthesizer in the fields of CONDITIONING, LEARNING THEORY, and HYPNOTHERAPY.

Hollingworth, Harry L. (1880–1956) U.S. psychologist: a pioneer in applied psychology and coauthor of the first textbook in that field; particularly known for his work in advertising psychology; married to Leta S. Hollingworth.

Hollingworth, Leta Stetter (1886–1939) U.S. psychologist: a major contributor in educational psychology, clinical psychology, and the psychology of women; her work in education focused on both children with mental retardation and gifted children; married to Harry L. Hollingworth.

Hooker, Evelyn (1907–1996) U.S. psychologist: performed the first major controlled study in which groups of gay and heterosexual men were compared on psychological measures of adjustment; her findings influenced the American Psychiatric Association to remove homosexuality from the *Diagnostic and Statistical Manual of Mental Disorders*.

Horney, Karen D. (1885–1952) German-born U.S. psychoanalyst: the first great psychoanalytic feminist and a member of the NEO-FREUDIAN school; stressed culture and disturbed interpersonal relationships as the causes of neuroses and emphasized the importance of current defenses and inner conflicts over early experience; recognized as one of the founders of HUMANISTIC PSYCHOLOGY.

Hovland, Carl Ivor (1912–1961) U.S. psychologist: contributor to the development of NEOBEHAVIORISM—through his research on the generalization of conditioning—and a pioneer in computer studies simulating human concept formation and thinking; studied the processes by which persuasive messages change attitudes (see MESSAGE-LEARNING APPROACH).

Hull, Clark Leonard (1884–1952) U.S. psychologist: originator of the influential DRIVE-REDUCTION THEORY and one of the founders of NEOBEHAVIORISM.

Hunt, Joseph McVicker (1906–1991) U.S. psychologist: known for his "feeding frustration" studies on rats, demonstrating a link between early food deprivation and adult HOARDING behavior, and for his A/S ratio (the ratio of association to sensory areas in the brain), highlighting the importance of INTRINSIC MOTIVATION; laid the conceptual foundations for programs (e.g., Project Head Start) emphasizing the value of early childhood education in cognitive development.

Hunter, Walter S. (1889–1954) U.S. psychologist: known especially for his studies of ANIMAL COGNITION, particularly the DELAYED-RESPONSE phenomenon; later contributed to the study of MAZE learning in animals.

James, William (1842–1910) U.S. psychologist and philosopher: one of the principal founders of psychology in the United States and, arguably, the most influential of the first generation of American psychologists; his promotion of FUNCTIONALISM in psychology and his pioneering contributions to the PSYCHOLOGY OF RELIGION had enduring effects.

Janet, Pierre (1859–1947) French psychologist and neurologist: His analysis emphasizing observable behavior and the continuity of subconscious and conscious events, largely dismissed by psychoanalysts of his day, has since been seen as a forerunner in the study of traumatic stress and DISSOCIATION and a precursor of INTEGRATIVE PSYCHOTHERAPY.

Janis, Irving Lester (1918–1990) U.S. social and health psychologist: noted for introducing the concept of GROUPTHINK; researched stress and decision making, especially in the contexts of individual personal health and group dynamics.

Jastrow, Joseph (1863–1944). U.S. psychologist: early U.S. contributor in psychophysics, particularly on how subliminal factors influence psychophysical judgments; influential in introducing the new scientific psychology to the American public.

Jones, Mary Cover (1896–1987) U.S. developmental psychologist: best known for her observational study of the development of infant behavior patterns, such as smiling, eye coordination, visual pursuit, and reaching.

Jung, Carl Gustav (1875–1961) Swiss psychiatrist and psychoanalyst: originator of ANALYTIC PSYCHOLOGY, which laid emphasis on personality dynamics, such as conscious versus unconscious, introversive versus extroversive tendencies, and rational versus irrational processes; originated such theoretical constructs as ARCHETYPES, the COLLECTIVE UNCONSCIOUS, and SYNCHRONICITY.

Kelley, Harold Harding (1921–2003) U.S. social psychologist: known for his formulation of ATTRIBUTION THEORY; conducted pioneering research on communication, persuasion, the social psychology of groups, and interpersonal relations.

Kinsey, Alfred (1894–1956) U.S. zoologist and sex researcher: an influential researcher on human sexual behavior; presented the first statistical data on a large range of sexual behaviors in both sexes; his **Kinsey (Six) Scale** offered an index on a continuum from "pure homosexual" to "pure heterosexual" orientation.

Klein, Melanie (1882–1960) Austrian-born British psychoanalyst: a pioneer in CHILD ANALYSIS and the first to use PLAY THERAPY as an analytic and treatment tool; her approach emphasized primal conflicts and the primary object relationship with the mother (see OBJECT RELATIONS THEORY).

Klineberg, Otto (1899–1992) Canadian-born U.S. social psychologist: a seminal figure through his research on race, which challenged racial superiority theories and contributed to the U.S. Supreme Court's 1954 ruling *Brown v. the Board of Education*; focused on cross-cultural studies and international affairs.

Koch, Sigmund (1917–1996) U.S. psychologist: author of a six-volume comprehensive survey outlining the parameters of psychology in the mid-20th century; promoted empirically grounded, rationally defensible investigation in a field he claimed could never become a single, coherent discipline.

Koffka, Kurt (1886–1941) German experimental psychologist: one of the founders of and chief spokesperson for GESTALT PSYCHOLOGY; contributed significantly to the study of visual perception (e.g., the study of APPARENT MOVEMENT).

Kohlberg, Lawrence (1927–1987) U.S. psychologist: originator of the groundbreaking KOHLBERG'S THEORY OF MORAL DEVELOPMENT; his use of INTERVIEW format was also influential.

Köhler, Wolfgang (1887–1967) German experimental psychologist: one of the founders of GESTALT PSYCHOLOGY; his contributions in primate learning (see INSIGHTFUL LEARNING) and to the concept of goodness of configuration (the significance of simplicity, regularity, or symmetry in a shape or form) remain influential.

Kraepelin, Emil (1856–1926) German psychiatrist: a founding father of modern psychiatry and pioneer theorist and researcher on serious mental disease; his development of the concept of DEMENTIA PRAECOX was the forerunner of the modern concept of schizophrenia (see KRAEPELIN'S THEORY).

Krech, David (1909–1977) Belarus-born U.S. psychologist: a major contributor in physiological psychology (e.g., on the brain–behavior relationship) and social psychology (e.g., on racial prejudice, international conflict).

Ladd-Franklin, Christine (1847–1930) U.S. psychologist and mathematician: an early authority on vision and color theory (see LADD-FRANKLIN THEORY).

Lashley, Karl Spencer (1890–1958) U.S. psychologist: an influential contributor in animal learning, comparative psychology, and neurophysiology; asserted that the brain could recover some disrupted functions in specific damaged areas (see EQUIPOTENTIALITY; MASS ACTION).

Lewin, Kurt (1890–1947) German-born U.S. social psychologist: developer of FIELD THEORY; particularly known for experiments on styles of LEADERSHIP, group COHESION, and GROUP DYNAMICS (a term he coined); promoted ACTION RESEARCH.

Lorenz, Konrad (1903–1989) Austrian zoologist: Nobel Prize-winning cofounder of ETHOLOGY; discovered several major concepts still useful for behavior study, including the FIXED ACTION PATTERN, the RELEASER, and IMPRINTING.

Luria, Alexander R. (1902–1977) Russian neuropsychologist: a major contributor to research on brain function and brain trauma; collaborated early in his career with Lev Vygotsky on a sociocultural theory of language.

Maslow, Abraham Harold (1908–1970) U.S. psychologist: a founder of HUMANISTIC PSYCHOLOGY and originator of MASLOW'S MOTIVATIONAL HIERARCHY; also a leader in the HUMAN-POTENTIAL MOVEMENT.

May, Rollo (1909–1994) U.S. psychologist and psychoanalyst: a central proponent and spokesperson for HUMANISTIC PSYCHOLOGY and EXISTENTIAL PSYCHOLOGY; emphasized the adaptive and curative qualities of positive human values, such as love, free will, and self-awareness.

McClelland, David (1917–1998) U.S. psychologist: best known for theoretical and empirical contributions to the study of personality and motivation; developed the highly popular THEMATIC APPERCEPTION TEST to assess ACHIEVEMENT MOTIVATION.

Meehl, Paul Everett (1920–2003) U.S. psychologist: a significant contributor to research in clinical psychology and clinicometrics (the use of mathematical statistics to analyze client historical data); his work on diagnosis and classification of mental disorders was revolutionary in its development of computerized scoring of psychology tests.

Michotte, Albert Edouard (1881–1965) Belgian psychologist: remembered for experimental-phenomenological studies of mechanical causality (see MECHANISTIC THEORY) that clarify commonly experienced adaptive situations.

Milgram, Stanley (1933–1984) U.S. social psychologist: best known for his BEHAVIORAL STUDY OF OBEDIENCE; pioneered the field of urban psychology, working on STIMULUS OVERLOAD and INFORMATION OVERLOAD.

Miller, Neal Elgar (1909–2002) U.S. psychologist: considered the founder of BEHAVIORAL MEDICINE; his work significantly affected the fields of learning, motivation, and clinical psychology.

Maria Montessori (1870–1952) Italian educator: one of the first women to attend medical school in Italy; developed a psychologically based educational system (see MONTESSORI METHOD).

Mowrer, O. Hobart (1907–1982) U.S. psychologist: best known for his contributions to the fields of learning (see TWO-FACTOR THEORY) and LANGUAGE ACQUISITION, which he explained using elementary principles of conditioning.

Münsterberg, Hugo (1863–1916) German-born U.S. psychologist: a founder in the field of industrial and organizational psychology; made early contributions in the fields of educational, abnormal, and FORENSIC PSYCHOLOGY (e.g., his studies of EYEWITNESS TESTIMONY and lie detection).

Murphy, Gardner (1895–1979) U.S. psychologist: encouraged psychological research on and the use of BIOFEEDBACK; greatly influenced the field through his texts, particularly that on experimental social psychology; recognized for his guidance of U.S. psychologist Rensis Likert (1903–1981) in the development of the LIKERT SCALE.

Murray, Henry Alexander (1893–1988) U.S. psychologist: His work ushered in a new era of personality psychology in the United States; noteworthy for establishing numerous professional opportunities for women in psychology and for collaborating in the creation of the THEMATIC APPERCEPTION TEST.

Neugarten, Bernice Levin (1916–2001) U.S. developmental psychologist: known for significantly advancing the study of adult development and aging; saw later adulthood as a period of increased activity and self-enhancement and proposed the distinctions of young-old and old-old (see ADULTHOOD).

Newcomb, Theodore Mead (1903–1984) U.S. social psychologist: a major contributor in the field, emphasizing its interdisciplinary nature (e.g., the integration of behavioral concepts from psychology, anthropology, and sociology); his attitudes and value research focused on real-setting social relations and placed attitude change in the context of norms, group membership, leadership, and friendship.

Nissen, Henry Wieghorst (1901–1958) U.S. comparative psychologist: a leading expert on the biology and behavior of chimpanzees (e.g., in the acquisition of resources, emotional expression, and social interaction); viewed behavioral sequences as clusters of independent acts, each with its own motivation.

Orne, Martin Theodore (1927–2000) Austrian-born U.S. psychiatrist: originator of the concept of TRANCE LOGIC and creator of the SIMULATOR–REAL MODEL in hypnosis research; applied the notion of DEMAND CHARACTERISTICS in his research.

Osgood, Charles Egerton (1916–1991) U.S. psychologist: a significant theorist and researcher in PSYCHOLINGUISTICS and CROSS-CULTURAL PSYCHOLOGY; developed the SEMANTIC DIFFERENTIAL model of determining word meanings.

Pavlov, Ivan Petrovich (1849–1936) Russian physiologist: best known for experimentation on the physiology of the digestive system and its control by the nervous system, which yielded the concepts of the UNCONDITIONED RESPONSE, the CONDITIONED STIMULUS, DISCRIMINATION of stimuli, and EXTINCTION of response.

Payton, Carolyn R. (1925–2001) U.S. psychologist: a powerful advocate of the mental health needs of African Americans; her highly successful Counseling Services program at Howard University was one of the few programs at any African American institution to offer accredited training for Black therapists and counselors.

Piaget, Jean (1896–1980) Swiss child psychologist and epistemologist: His theoretical and research work on the stages of cognitive development in children was enormously influential (see PIAGETIAN THEORY); a central proponent of the theoretical perspective known as CONSTRUCTIVISM.

Rhine, Joseph Banks (1895–1980) U.S. parapsychologist: coiner of the term EXTRASENSORY PERCEPTION and the first researcher to investigate a psychical topic scientifically—using ZENER CARDS (also called **Rhine cards**).

Ribot, Théodule Armand (1839–1916) French philosopher and psychologist: a founder of experimental psychology in France; proposed what is now called **Ribot's law**, the principle that the most recently acquired memories are the most vulnerable to disruption from brain damage.

Rogers, Carl (1902–1987) U.S. psychologist: originator of CLIENT-CENTERED THERAPY and the NONDIRECTIVE APPROACH; created such concepts as UNCONDITIONAL POSITIVE REGARD and UNCRITICALNESS as central to the psychotherapeutic endeavor.

Rorschach, Hermann (1884–1922) Swiss psychiatrist: originator of the RORSCHACH INKBLOT TEST of personality, which, although still widely used, has not demonstrated robust or consistent validity.

Sanford, Edmund Clark (1859–1924) U.S. experimental psychologist: author of the first English-language laboratory manual in experimental psychology; the first psychologist to promote the subsequently common study of MAZE learning in rats.

Schachter, Stanley (1922–1997) U.S. psychologist: an influential theorist and researcher in social and health psychology, focusing on such issues as SOCIAL PRESSURE, ATTRIBUTION THEORY, and addiction (see also SCHACHTER–SINGER THEORY).

Schneirla, Theodore Christian (1902–1968) U.S. comparative psychologist: one of the foremost 20th-century animal psychologists; elaborated the APPROACH–AVOIDANCE CONFLICT into **biphasic A–W theory**, which viewed approach and withdrawal as essential in all behavior—mainly governed by stimulus intensity yet subject to the organism's internal conditions as well as to environmental conditions.

Scott, Walter Dill (1869–1955) U.S. psychologist: a key figure in the development of applied psychology and, especially, advertising psychology and personnel selection.

Scripture, Edward Wheeler (1864–1945) U.S. psychologist and speech therapist: known for his research on localization of sound and other perceptual phenomena; studied speech and language pathology and conducted innovative speech therapy, combining psychoanalytic techniques (to address underlying emotional origins) with exercises (to correct faulty speech patterns).

Sears, Pauline Kirkpatrick (1908–1993) U.S. psychologist: known for rigorous and creative use of quantitative research methods, such as systematic TIME SAMPLING, to study socialization, family processes, and child rearing; her research focused on schoolchildren and the psychological factors affecting academic achievement and performance; married to Robert R. Sears.

Sears, Robert Richardson (1908–1989) U.S. psychologist: best known for research on the influence of parental discipline and other child-rearing practices on children's behavior, especially their levels of aggression and dependency; widely recognized for research on empirical evidence for psychoanalytic theory; married to Pauline K. Sears.

Seashore, Carl Emil (1866–1949) Swedish-born U.S. psychologist: a prolific designer and builder of research equipment, including the **Seashore audiometer** (which generated standardized stimulus tones to measure threshold sound intensity) and the **Seashore Measures of Musical Talent** (phonographically recorded tests of tonal memory, of time, rhythm, and timbre awareness, and of pitch and loudness discrimination).

Sechenov, Ivan Mikhailovich (1829–1905) Russian physiologist: He saw psychology as the physiological study of brain reflexes; described reflexes as tripartite units consisting of a sensory nerve, a central connection, and a motor nerve and proposed that they are modifiable by association from infancy.

Shakow, David (1901–1981) U.S. psychologist: best known for helping the American Psychological Association professionalize the field of clinical psychology and for helping develop the SCIENTIST-PRACTITIONER MODEL for training clinical psychologists.

Sherif, Muzafer (1906–1988) Turkish social psychologist: known particularly for his work on group norms (see SOCIAL NORM); articulated the notion that perception and behavior are determined in bipolar fashion by external and internal factors, the combined totality of which he termed FRAME OF REFERENCE; this view inspired the development of such novel theories as ADAPTATION LEVEL.

Sherrington, Charles Scott (1857–1952) British physiologist: His research on the mechanics of muscular activation revolutionized neurophysiology; introduced many basic terms and concepts in neuroscience, among them PROPRIOCEPTION, NOCICEPTION, NEURON, SYNAPSE, SPATIAL SUMMATION, and TEMPORAL SUMMATION.

Simon, Herbert Alexander (1916–2001) U.S. economist, political scientist, and psychologist: generally regarded as the founder of artificial intelligence and cognitive science; one of the first to use computers to model human decision making and problem solving.

Skinner, Burrhus Frederic (1904–1990) U.S. psychologist: originator of OPERANT CONDITIONING, a form of RADICAL BEHAVIORISM; also initiated the field of APPLIED BEHAVIORAL ANALYSIS.

Spearman, Charles Edward (1863–1945) British psychologist and psychometrician: formulator of the TWO-FACTOR THEORY of intelligence; renowned for his mathematical work, including the development of the SPEARMAN RANK CORRELATION and of the technique of FACTOR ANALYSIS.

Spence, Kenneth Wartenbee (1907–1967) U.S. experimental psychologist: developer, with Clark L. Hull, of an influential version of NEOBEHAVIORISM—the **Hull–Spence model**—which offered a theoretical system to explain animal learning and motivation on the basis of Pavlovian conditioning.

Sperry, Roger Wolcott (1913–1994) U.S. psychologist: best known for his nerve-regeneration theory and his research into the functions of the two hemispheres of the brain using the split-brain technique (see COMMISSUROTOMY).

Stern, Louis William (1871–1938) German psychologist: best known for developing the concept of the intelligence quotient (see IQ); also a pioneer in developmental psychology, applied psychology, and DIFFERENTIAL PSYCHOLOGY.

Stone, Calvin Perry (1892–1954) U.S. psychologist: the first comparative psychologist in the United States to focus on the scientific investigation of sexual behavior; particularly studied neural and hormonal influences and discovered evidence for the importance of SUBCORTICAL brain regions.

Strong, Edward Kellogg, Jr. (1884–1963) U.S. psychologist: a founder of applied psychology—especially in the areas of personnel selection and occupational analysis—and best known as a co-creator of the **Strong Interest Inventory**, a widely used INTEREST TEST.

Stumpf, Carl (1848–1936) German experimental psychologist: best known for investigating the psychological factors involved in acoustic perception; his institute produced many famous psychologists, including Koffka, Köhler, Lewin, and Wertheimer; his pioneering research on emotions proposed a cognitively based theory in which judgments are crucial.

Sullivan, Harry Stack (1892–1949) U.S. psychiatrist: a major contributor to personality theory through his INTERPERSONAL THEORY, which eventually gave rise to INTERPERSONAL PSYCHOTHERAPY; his approach derived from Freud's psychoanalysis but emphasized social elements over biological instincts and focused on how key relationships develop and change over time.

Sumner, Francis Cecil (1895–1954) U.S. psychologist: the first African American to receive a doctorate in psychology in the United States; became head of the psychology department at Howard University and had great influence in creating programs to train Black psychologists in the era of desegregation; his own department trained more Black psychologists than all other U.S. colleges and universities at this time.

Terman, Lewis Madison (1877–1956) U.S. psychologist: responsible for the validation of the Binet scales (see STANFORD–BINET INTELLIGENCE SCALE) and for the construction of the Army intelligence tests of World War I; also known for initiating (in the 1920s) a longitudinal study of some 1,500 gifted children.

Thibaut, John W. (1917–1986) U.S. social psychologist: developer of SOCIAL EXCHANGE THEORY (later known as INTERDEPENDENCE THEORY); proposed that the benefits derived from taking account of the broader context of behavior underlie the existence of such values as altruism, competitiveness, and fairness.

Thorndike, Edward Lee (1874–1949) U.S. psychologist: an important early contributor to the field of animal intelligence; developed the concept of TRIAL-AND-ERROR LEARNING and the theory of CONNECTIONISM.

Thurstone, Louis Leon (1887–1955) U.S. psychologist: a pioneer in psychometrics; developed and maintained the examination that was the forerunner of the SCHOLASTIC ASSESSMENT TEST; developed the statistical technique of FACTOR ANALYSIS to tease out PRIMARY ABILITIES.

Tinbergen, Nikolaas (1907–1988) Dutch-born British behavioral biologist: Nobel Prize-winning cofounder of ETHOLOGY; advanced the practice of FIELD RESEARCH in the study of nonhuman animals.

Titchener, Edward Bradford (1867–1927) British-born U.S. psychologist: a chief exponent of STRUCTURALISM, which emphasized the use of systematic introspection in laboratory settings to uncover the elements of experience (sensations, images, and feelings).

Tolman, Edward Chace (1886–1959) U.S. psychologist: a founder of NEOBEHAVIORISM and proposer of the theory of PURPOSIVE BEHAVIORISM; emphasized such mentalist concepts as purpose and COGNITIVE MAPS.

Troland, Leonard T. (1889–1932) U.S. scientist and psychologist: a significant contributor to visual science; the **troland** (a unit of retinal illumination) was named in his honor; his promotion of a comprehensive motivational psychology that accommodated feelings as a causal element in behavior anticipated later emphases on the cognitive–emotional factors in behavior regulation.

Tryon, Robert Choate (1901–1967) U.S. psychologist: widely known for his investigations of INDIVIDUAL DIFFERENCES in learning; his breeding of generations of rats based on performance in a standardized MAZE problem demonstrated the genetic substrate of learning ability; also developed computerized CLUSTER ANALYSIS.

Tversky, Amos (1937–1996) Israeli-born U.S. psychologist: known for his studies with Israeli-born U.S. psychologist Daniel Kahneman of similarity, judgment under uncertainty, and decision making.

Tyler, Leona Elizabeth (1906–1993) U.S. counseling psychologist: author of one of the first and seminally influential textbooks on INDIVIDUAL DIFFERENCES and of the leading textbook in the mid-20th century on counseling psychology.

Underwood, Benton J. (1915–1994) U.S. psychologist and methodologist: an inheritor of the traditions of ASSOCIATIONISM and FUNCTIONALISM, and author of the textbook that played the leading role in defining experimental psychology throughout the mid-20th century.

Upham, Thomas Cogswell (1799–1872) U.S. mental philosopher: author of the first U.S. textbook in psychology, which appeared in 1827 and remained in use through much of the 19th century.

Vygotsky, Lev Semenovich (or **Vigotsky**; 1896–1934) Russian psychologist: known for his sociocultural theory of cognitive development emphasizing the interaction of children's natural abilities with the cultural mediators of written and oral language; held that developmental stages were partially driven by education and that education should take place in the ZONE OF PROXIMAL DEVELOPMENT.

Washburn, Margaret Floy (1871–1939) U.S. psychologist: author of the first U.S. textbook of comparative psychology; served as the second woman president of the American

Psychological Association and only the second woman scientist to be elected to the National Academy of Sciences.

Watson, John Broadus (1878–1958) U.S. psychologist: an important figure in the early history of comparative psychology, best known as the founder of BEHAVIORISM; introduced PAVLOVIAN CONDITIONING in the United States.

Weber, Ernst Heinrich (1795–1878) German physiologist: a founder of psychophysics and formulator of WEBER'S LAW; later elaborated on this concept to propose the WEBER–FECHNER LAW; also known for his work on TWO-POINT DISCRIMINATION, which led to the formulation of the concept of the DIFFERENCE THRESHOLD.

Wechsler, David (1896–1981) Romanian-born U.S. psychologist: developer of the **Wechsler–Bellevue Intelligence Scale,** which eventually was standardized as the WECHSLER ADULT INTELLIGENCE SCALE; this latter and the WECHSLER INTELLIGENCE SCALE FOR CHILDREN remain the dominant psychological tests for measuring cognitive abilities.

Wertheimer, Max (1880–1943) German-born U.S. psychologist: a founder of GESTALT PSYCHOLOGY, whose research added greatly to theories of perception (see PHI PHENOMENON); also known for his GESTALT PRINCIPLES OF ORGANIZATION.

White, Robert W. (1904–2001) U.S. psychologist: best known for his holistic approach to the study of personality; argued the case of INTRINSIC MOTIVATION at a time dominated by DRIVE-REDUCTION THEORY; also advocated the CASE STUDY method rather than the statistical method of analyzing aggregated data.

Witmer, Lightner (1867–1956) U.S. psychologist: founder of clinical psychology in the United States; also considered a primary pioneer of school psychology and a major figure in the development of SPECIAL EDUCATION.

Wolpe, Joseph (1915–1997) South African-born U.S. psychiatrist: father of BEHAVIOR THERAPY, best known for his development of SYSTEMATIC DESENSITIZATION.

Woodworth, Robert Sessions (1869–1962) U.S. psychologist: best known for textbooks that shaped the field of experimental psychology; also known for his research on motivation, which led to his most important conceptual contribution, S–O–R PSYCHOLOGY.

Woolley, Helen Bradford Thompson (1874–1947) U.S. psychologist: a powerful advocate of child welfare, whose studies of young employed children were instrumental in reforming child labor and compulsory education laws in the United States; among the first to study psychological likenesses and differences of the sexes.

Wundt, Wilhelm Maximilian (1832–1920) German psychologist and physiologist: the founder of experimental psychology, establishing the first official psychology laboratory in 1879; his application of introspective and psychophysical methods to such subjects as reaction time, attention, judgment, and emotions had international influence.

Yerkes, Robert Mearns (1876–1956) U.S. psychobiologist: recognized as a preeminent comparative psychologist of his time through his research in animal behavior; also instrumental in the development of Army intelligence tests during World War I.

Psychotherapy and Psychotherapeutic Approaches Entries

acceptance and commitment therapy
action-oriented therapy
active therapy
adjunctive therapy
adjuvant therapy
affirmative therapy
analytical psychotherapy
anger control therapy
animal-assisted therapy
art therapy
Beck therapy
behavioral couples therapy
behavioral family therapy
behavioral group therapy
behavioral relaxation training
behavioral sex therapy
behavior modification
behavior therapy
bereavement therapy
bibliotherapy
biological therapy
brief intensive group cognitive behavior therapy
brief psychodynamic psychotherapy
brief stimulus therapy
cerebral electrotherapy
child analysis
child psychotherapy
client-centered therapy
cognitive-analytic therapy
cognitive behavioral couples therapy
cognitive behavioral group therapy
cognitive behavior therapy
cognitive processing therapy
cognitive therapy
collaborative therapy
combination therapy
combined therapy
computerized therapy
concurrent therapy
conjoint therapy
constructivist psychotherapy
contact desensitization
convulsive therapy
coping-skills training
core conflictual relationship theme
cotherapy
couples therapy
covert desensitization
dance therapy

depth therapy
developmental therapy
dialectical behavior therapy
directive group psychotherapy
distance therapy
drama therapy
dynamic psychotherapy
eclectic psychotherapy
ecosystemic approach
educational therapy
ego analysis
electroconvulsive therapy
electroshock therapy
electrotherapy
emergency psychotherapy
emetic therapy
emotional reeducation
emotion-focused couples therapy
emotion-focused therapy
Ericksonian psychotherapy
e-therapy
ethnotherapy
exercise therapy
existential–humanistic therapy
existential psychotherapy
experiential psychotherapy
exposure therapy
expressive therapy
eye-movement desensitization therapy
family group psychotherapy
family therapy
feminist family therapy
feminist therapy
focal psychotherapy
frontal lobotomy
functional family therapy
gestalt therapy
group-analytic psychotherapy
group psychotherapy
holistic education
humanistic therapy
hydrotherapy
hypnotherapy
imaginal flooding
imago therapy
implosive therapy
individual therapy
insight therapy
integrative behavioral couples therapy
integrative psychotherapy

integrity group psychotherapy
intensive psychotherapy
interpersonal group psychotherapy
interpersonal psychotherapy
interpersonal reconstructive psychotherapy
in vivo exposure therapy
leaderless group therapy
leukotomy
light therapy
logotherapy
long-term therapy
LSD psychotherapy
maintenance therapy
manualized therapy
marital therapy
medical family therapy
megadose pharmacotherapy
megavitamin therapy
metaphor therapy
methadone maintenance therapy
milieu therapy
Morita therapy
motivational enhancement therapy
movement therapy
multicultural therapy
multimodal therapy
multiple family therapy
multiple marital therapy
music therapy
narrative psychotherapy
network analysis
nondirective play therapy
nondirective therapy
operant conditioning therapy
panic control treatment
paraverbal therapy
parent effectiveness training
parent management training
pastoral counseling
personal construct therapy
persuasion therapy
phenomenological therapy
phototherapy
play-group psychotherapy
play therapy
poetry therapy
polypharmacy
process experiential psychotherapy
projective psychotherapy
psychedelic therapy
psychoanalysis
psychoanalytic group psychotherapy
psychoanalytic play technique
psychoanalytic psychotherapy

psychodynamic psychotherapy
psychopharmacotherapy
psychosocial therapy
psychosurgery
quadrangular therapy
rational emotive behavior therapy
reality therapy
reconstructive psychotherapy
recreational therapy
reeducation
reinforcement therapy
relationship therapy
release therapy
reminiscence therapy
reparative therapy
response prevention
restoration therapy
role therapy
sector therapy
self-control therapy
self-instructional training
self-management
semantic therapy
sex therapy
shock therapy
short-term therapy
single-session therapy
social-network therapy
social skills training
social therapy
sociotherapy
solution-focused brief therapy
strategic family therapy
stress-inoculation training
structural family therapy
structural therapy
structured learning
supportive-expressive psychotherapy
supportive psychotherapy
surface therapy
systematic desensitization
tandem therapy
time-limited psychotherapy
tractotomy
transactional psychotherapy
transcendence therapy
transcultural psychotherapy
transorbital lobotomy
trial therapy
verbal behavior therapy
virtual reality therapy
vitamin and mineral therapy
will therapy
work therapy
Zen therapy